Professional Series

GROUP INSURANCE
SEVENTH EDITION

Daniel D. Skwire
Principal Editor

Associate Editors
Kristi M. Bohn
Margaret D. Cormier
Stephen J. Kaczmarek
Sara C. Teppema

William F. Bluhm
Founding Editor

ACTEX Publications
New Hartford, CT

Copyright © 2016 ACTEX Publications.

All rights reserved. No portion of this book may be reproduced in any form or by any means without the prior written permission of the copyright owner.

Request for permission should be addressed to:
ACTEX Publications
PO Box 715
New Hartford CT 06057

Manufactured in the United States of America

10 9 8 7 6 5 4 3 2 1

Cover Design by Jeff Melaragno

Library of Congress Cataloging-in-Publication Data

Names: Skwire, Daniel D., editor.
Title: Group insurance / principal editor, Daniel D. Skwire ; associate
  editors, Kristi M. Bohn, Margaret D. Cormier, Stephen J. Kaczmarek, Sara
  C. Teppema ; founding editor, William F. Bluhm.
Description: Seventh edition. | New Hartford, CT : ACTEX Publications, 2016.
  | Includes bibliographical references and index.
Identifiers: LCCN 2016013734 | ISBN 9781625426826 (alk. paper)
Subjects: LCSH: Group insurance--United States. | Group insurance--Law and
  legislation--United States.
Classification: LCC HG8058 .G748 2016 | DDC 368.300973--dc23 LC record available at
https://lccn.loc.gov/2016013734

ISBN: 978-1-62542-682-6

TABLE OF CONTENTS

Preface vii

◄SECTION ONE►
INTRODUCTION

Chapter 1	The Group Insurance Marketplace *Kara L. Clark*	3
Chapter 2	Overview of Sales and Marketing *John Elliott and William A. Raab, Updated by Brian Marsella*	15
Chapter 3	Product Development *Andrea Sheldon*	27
Chapter 4	Health Care Policy and Group Insurance *Sara C. Teppema*	39

◄SECTION TWO►
GROUP INSURANCE BENEFITS

Chapter 5	Medical Benefits in the United States *Darrell D. Knapp*	53
Chapter 6	Dental Benefits in the United States *Joanne Fontana and Herschel Reich*	71
Chapter 7	Pharmacy Benefits in the United States *David M. Liner and Michelle N. Angeloni*	91
Chapter 8	Retiree Group Benefits *Dale H. Yamamoto*	113
Chapter 9	Government Health Plans in the United States *Jack Burke, John W. Bauerlein, and Bruce D. Schobel*	131
Chapter 10	Health Benefits in Canada *Stella-Ann Ménard*	151
Chapter 11	Group Life Insurance Benefits *Frank Cassandra and Michael J. Thompson*	171

Chapter 12	Group Disability Income Benefits *Daniel D. Skwire and Paul L. Correia*	189
Chapter 13	Group Long-Term Care Insurance *Malcolm Cheung*	199
Chapter 14	Miscellaneous Benefits *William J. Thompson*	217

◄SECTION THREE►
LEGAL AND REGULATORY ENVIRONMENT

Chapter 15	Principles of Health Insurance Regulation *Julia T. Philips and Leigh M. Wachenheim, Updated by Kristi M. Bohn*	229
Chapter 16	Regulation in the United States *Keith M. Andrews, Robert B. Davis,* *Stephen LaGarde, and Edward P. Potanka*	237
Chapter 17	Regulation in Canada *Nicola Parker-Smith*	275
Chapter 18	The Affordable Care Act *Elaine T. Corrough and Sara C. Teppema*	291
Chapter 19	Health Benefit Exchanges *Christopher S. Girod*	307

◄SECTION FOUR►
FUNDING AND RATING

Chapter 20	Pricing of Group Insurance *Kristi M. Bohn, Jay Ripps, and Richard S. Wolf*	325
Chapter 21	Estimating Medical Claim Costs *Gerald R. Bernstein, Shelly S. Brandel, David Cusick,* *and James T. O'Connor, Updated by Margaret A. Chance*	337
Chapter 22	Estimating Dental Claim Costs *Courtney Morin, Leigh M. Wachenheim, and Laurence Weissbrot*	367
Chapter 23	Estimating Pharmacy Claim Costs *Tracy Margiott and Eric Patel*	387

Chapter 24	Estimating Life Claim Costs *Stephen T. Carter and Daniel D. Skwire, Updated by Paul L. Correia*	403
Chapter 25	Estimating Disability Claim Costs *Daniel D. Skwire, Updated by Paul L. Correia*	419
Chapter 26	Pricing Group Long-Term Care Insurance *Amy Pahl*	435
Chapter 27	Experience Rating and Funding Methods *William F. Bluhm, Updated by Dorina A. Paritsky*	455
Chapter 28	Group Insurance Rate Filings and Certifications *Kristi M. Bohn, Margaret A. Chance, and James T. O'Connor*	485
Chapter 29	Medicare-Related Rate Filings and Certifications *Patrick J. Dunks and Eric P. Goetsch, updated by Bradley J. Piper*	501

◄SECTION FIVE►
UNDERWRITING AND MANAGING RISK

Chapter 30	Group Insurance Underwriting *James T. Lundberg, Ann Marie Wood, Gregory Fann, and James Juillerat*	513
Chapter 31	Managing Selection in a Multiple-Choice Environment *Catherine L. Knuth and Clark E. Slipher*	541
Chapter 32	Claim Administration and Management *Jeffrey L. Smith and Sheila K. Shapiro*	555
Chapter 33	Health Risk Adjustment *Robert B. Cumming, P. Anthony Hammond, Syed M. Mehmud, and Ross Winkleman*	571
Chapter 34	Medical Claim Cost Trend Analysis *Joan Barrett*	595

◄SECTION SIX►
GROUP INSURANCE FINANCIAL REPORTING

Chapter 35	Group Insurance Financial Reporting *Tim Harris and Sherri Daniel*	613
Chapter 36	Group Insurance Reserves *Daniel D. Skwire*	635
Chapter 37	Claim Reserves for Short-Term Benefits *Doug Fearrington, Mark E. Litow, Hans K. Leida, and Doug Norris*	643
Chapter 38	Claim Reserves for Long-Term Benefits *Daniel D. Skwire*	661
Chapter 39	Risk-Based Capital Formulas *Rowen B. Bell, Robert B. Cumming, and Constance Peterson*	677

◄SECTION SEVEN►
FINANCIAL AND ACTUARIAL ANALYSIS

Chapter 40	Applied Statistics *Robert B. Cumming, Stuart A. Klugman, Hans K. Leida, and Doug Norris*	699
Chapter 41	Analysis of Financial and Operational Performance *Douglas B. Sherlock*	727
Chapter 42	Enterprise Risk Management for Group Health Insurers *Thomas Nightingale*	751
Chapter 43	Management of Provider Networks *Robert B. Cumming*	775
Chapter 44	Medical Care Management *Alison Johnson*	793

About the Editors	813
About the Authors	817
Index	837

PREFACE

Like so many others, I initially encountered Bill Bluhm's *Group Insurance* text when studying for actuarial exams. Then in its first edition, the book was a model of breadth and clarity, covering an immense range of subjects in a straightforward manner that was both technically precise and easy to understand. I never imagined at the time that this book would become such an important part of my own career.

Some 15 years ago, Bill invited me to write a chapter on claim reserves for this text. That chapter originally appeared in the fourth edition, published in 2003. With each passing edition, Bill encouraged me to take on a little greater responsibility, from revising and updating several other chapters in the fifth edition to serving as an associate editor for the sixth edition.

Now that Bill has retired from Milliman and moved on to run the Dancing Dragonfly winery, I find myself serving as Principal Editor for this seventh edition of *Group Insurance*. It is an honor to serve in this capacity, and I am deeply grateful to Bill for providing me with both the encouragement and the opportunity to succeed him in this role. The success of this text is an extraordinary legacy Bill has left to our profession. I hope that this edition will live up to the high standard he has set over the past 25 years.

I am very thankful for the dedication of the four hard-working associate editors who have done much of the heavy lifting to create this book: Kristi Bohn, Maggie Cormier, Steve Kaczmarek and Sara Teppema. Their combination of technical knowledge and editorial talent has been instrumental in planning the changes and enhancements for this edition and in working with our long list of authors to make the vision a reality. Without their labors over the past 18 months, I would probably still be making notes on a legal pad about ideas for new chapters!

Thank you also to the many authors who devoted their time and effort in order to share their knowledge with our readers. Their willingness to invest their personal time to inform and educate the next generation of actuaries is a tremendous service to our profession, and all of the other editors and I appreciate and acknowledge their commitment.

The editorial staff at Actex Publications has been a pleasure to work with. I would particularly like to acknowledge Gail Hall, who has been so helpful in leading this first-time editor through all of the steps involved in producing a volume of this scope. Best wishes in your retirement, Gail—we will miss you!

I am fortunate to have a family that is very supportive of my professional efforts, not only on this textbook, but in all aspects of my career. I do my best to balance my commitments to work and family, but there are inevitably times when projects like this temporarily pull me away from those I love. Denise, Adam and Luke—thank you for your understanding!

One of my earliest memories is walking to the local library with my parents and two sisters, pulling a red wagon behind us. Each member of the family was permitted to check out five books each week, and the wagon was the only way to carry them back and forth. Books and reading have always been part of my life.

The same is true of writing. My father is a professor of English, now retired, and from my first school days through my most recent writing endeavors, he has been my one indispensable teacher, editor, and critic. His own textbooks on English composition helped support our family and my education, and to this day there is nowhere I would rather be than in his study, trading thoughts on favorite books and writers while soliciting advice on whatever project I have underway.

This book is lovingly dedicated to my father, in happy anticipation of many more hours together, only some of which will be spent discussing the comma splices I failed to catch in this manuscript.

Portland, Maine
April, 2016

Daniel D. Skwire, FSA, MAAA
Principal Editor

SECTION ONE

INTRODUCTION

THE GROUP INSURANCE MARKETPLACE
Kara L. Clark

OVERVIEW OF GROUP INSURANCE

Group insurance is an effective and efficient means of providing protection from the adverse financial impact of unforeseen events to individuals who share a common bond. Group insurance, as used throughout this text, means a benefit program where coverage is provided to a group of individuals. These programs include not only traditional coverage provided under insurance policies, but also include self-insured benefit programs provided by employers, associations, labor unions, government programs, and health care service corporations such as health maintenance organizations.

Group insurance is provided to a group of individuals who are connected to one another through some common characteristic. Typical groups include employees of a single employer or group of employers, debtors to a common creditor, members of professional or trade associations, labor unions, or individuals eligible under a government plan.

A fundamental principle underlying all insurance is the pooling of risk. The risks covered by insurance policies are typically infrequent and potentially costly events, although in the case of health insurance, even relatively small and frequent risks can be included under the policy. The policyholder pays a relatively small, predetermined amount in the form of the insurance premium to the provider of the insurance coverage. In return, the provider of the coverage pays for the cost of the insured's covered event, or provides services directly, should the event occur. In this way, the participants in any particular insurance program share in the financial risk of the covered events.

Another key principle underlying insurance programs is the concept of insurable interest. That is, the policyholder and beneficiaries of a program must experience loss or hardship if the covered event should occur, and therefore have a vested interest in mitigating the risk. Insurable interest on behalf of the policyholder and beneficiaries is required for an insurance program to be financially, and often legally, viable.

Group insurance shares these basic principles with other types of insurance. Group insurance differs from individual insurance in that the provider of the insurance coverage considers the entire group of eligible individuals as a whole in evaluating the risk, in deciding whether or not to insure the risk, and in setting the price for the risk. In this determination, emphasis is placed on the characteristics of the group (for example, is the sponsoring entity viable with a good history of financial performance?). Individual members of the group often have to meet requirements that proxy individual underwriting requirements, such as enrolling at the first opportunity and being actively at work on the day that coverage begins. Often a key factor in underwriting groups is participation, since low participation among eligible lives often implies the possibility of antiselection on the part of those that enroll. Antiselection is to be avoided, since the presence of a disproportionate percentage of high claimants in a group leads to the need to raise rates, which in turn causes healthier lives to seek cheaper alternatives outside the group, in turn leading to the need for further rate increases for those still covered under the group plan. An external subsidy, such as a payment by an employer, is often sufficient to ensure good participation, while the structure of benefits and underwriting provisions for self-supporting groups can be complex.

Group plans also provide a more efficient means of marketing and delivering insurance programs. The primary level of marketing is to the plan sponsor, which can be an employer, an association or other entity. A secondary level of marketing is to eligible individuals, and is typically accomplished in a common setting, either in the workplace or through other regular communications to the group, such as association newsletters. Group plans are marketed through a variety of distribution networks, including agents, brokers, consultants, and by direct sales. However, instead of needing to make the sale with every potential insured, the primary sales effort can be focused toward the sponsor decision-makers. Therefore, the cost of the marketing effort is typically lower on a per-participant basis than for individual insurance. Likewise, administrative expenses are typically lower on a per-participant basis for group insurance, because individual premium billing is not required, and plan sponsors often provide low-cost access to participants for communication and information distribution.

The group insurance market includes a diversity of product lines. Medical coverage represents a large portion of group coverage in the United States, and may include medical indemnity insurance, preferred provider organization (PPO) plans, point of service (POS) plans, and health maintenance organization (HMO) plans, as well as products to supplement or replace the government-sponsored Medicare and Medicaid programs, which are available only to certain disabled, needy and older Americans. In Canada, where nearly all residents are covered by the provincially sponsored health care system known as Medicare, private group medical plans cover only those benefits not generally available under the public system. Therefore, while group medical coverage is widespread in Canada, it is not as large a part of the total group insurance market as it is in the United States. In both the United States and Canada, a variety of other coverages are also sold on a group basis, including indemnity and managed dental plans, short and long term disability income coverage, life insurance, vision and hearing coverage, long term care insurance, pre-paid legal, group property and casualty, and other special risk coverages such as accidental death and dismemberment and travel accident.

HISTORY OF GROUP INSURANCE

Group insurance has its roots in ancient times, as far back as the Romans. For example, medieval craft guilds used insurance concepts in their operations, and membership groups such as "Friendly Societies" in the U.K. operated much like mutual insurance programs, providing a source of financial protection for sickness or old age. Large numbers of people participated in these societies prior to the establishment of social insurance programs toward the end of the nineteenth and into the early twentieth century.

In the early 1900s, academics began to identify the economic security needs of individuals related to accident, illness, old age, and death, and interest in socially based solutions to these issues began to grow. A sickness insurance program as well as the first social insurance program for old age was established in the late 1800s in Germany. The National Insurance Act of 1911 in the U.K. established sickness and unemployment benefits, and the U.S. passed Social Security legislation in 1935, providing benefits for old age and unemployment.

The industrial revolution also contributed to the growth of group insurance concepts late in the nineteenth century. As transition occurred from an agricultural to an industrial economy, many workers moved from self-employment to larger employers. Employer liability law began to develop, and employee benefit programs began to emerge.

The first group plans offered in the late 1800s were typically cash accident and sickness (disability) plans. These were followed by group prepaid medical services plans; Baylor University Hospital's prepaid hospital services plan in the 1929 was the first of its kind and a precursor to the early Blue Cross programs. A number of group insurance plans were already in place by the 1940's, when United States governmental price-wage controls limited employers' opportunities to increase wage scales to attract and retain employee talent. In order to differentiate themselves in the marketplace, employers looked to other benefits, including group insurance coverages that could be provided to employees without violating the wage control regulations. The 1950s brought additional governmental price-wage controls, further spurring the growth in group insurance coverages. Additional support for group insurance growth was provided through a landmark court decision in 1949 (the *Inland Steel* decision), which allowed for pension and other employee benefits to be included in the scope of collective bargaining.[1] Tax policy has also often favored benefits provided through group insurance coverages, further contributing to their proliferation. For all these reasons, insurance coverages became an integral part of many employee compensation packages.

By the mid-20th century, major medical plans emerged as a melding of the prepaid medical services approach used by early Blue Cross/Blue Shield carriers ("the Blues") and the indemnity (fixed dollar) reimbursement approach used by traditional insurance carriers. Self-insurance became popular in the 1970s among larger employers, who viewed the concept as a way of saving some group insurance costs, through the elimination of premium taxes and the opportunity for control of invested assets. The Employee Retirement Income Security Act of 1974 (ERISA), while primarily addressing pension issues, also had an impact in the group insurance market by preempting state regulation of self-insured health plans (although what is considered "self-insured" under ERISA has at times been subject to legal interpretation).

In the United States, Internal Revenue Code Section 125 was established by the Revenue Act of 1978, which stipulated that otherwise nontaxable benefits provided under Section 125 plans would not be subject to the doctrine of constructive receipt (and therefore taxed), even if the plan participants could have elected to receive cash instead.[2] In the 1980s, medium and large-sized employers began offering their employees flexible benefit plans under Section 125, as a means to limit employer cost while providing employees the appeal of choice. Under flexible benefit plans, employers provided employees with some predetermined amount of funds or credits, which the employee could then use to purchase coverage from among a range of benefit offerings to best suit the employee's particular financial needs.

The Health Maintenance Organization (HMO) Act of 1973 provided funds to stimulate the growth of HMOs and required certain employers to offer HMOs (later legislation altered the impact of this Act). Rapid increases in health insurance costs instigated the move toward more

---

[1] Jerry S. Rosenbloom and G. Victor Hallman, *Employee Benefit Planning*, 3rd Edition.
[2] Ibid.

managed health plan offerings in the 1980s and 1990s, including Health Maintenance Organization (HMO), Preferred Provider Organization (PPO), and Point of Service (POS) plans. Plan sponsors gave up some freedom of choice in provider selection and agreed to care guidelines, in return for much lower premiums than available under traditional indemnity plans. The 1990s also saw the emergence of laws and regulations designed to increase access to health care insurance coverage, including the extension of coverage to individuals for whom the period of coverage would have typically terminated, as well as limitations on health status underwriting. Late in the 1990s, the public's dissatisfaction with restrictive managed care increased. This dissatisfaction, in conjunction with less willingness from provider groups to accept managed care payment discounts, and the concern of employers over potential liability, led to a move toward less restrictive managed care plans, such as PPO plans.

Around the year 2000, Health Savings Accounts and Health Reimbursement Accounts began to gain industry, government, and media attention. While there are many variations, these arrangements often involve an employer-provided amount of funds (the "account") for each employee, combined with a high-deductible health plan. Funds in the account can then be used by the employee to cover their out-of-pocket costs (for example, the deductible, coinsurance amounts, or possibly care not covered by the insurance plan at all). These plans are intended to involve the employee more closely in health care purchasing decisions, and they often include access to consumer education and other support tools specific to these decisions.

In 2014, 52% of U.S. employees with health coverage were enrolled in a PPO plan, compared to 14% in HMOs, 24% in a high deductible health plan with savings option (HDHP/HRA or HSA-qualified HDHP), 10% in POS plans, and 1% in conventional plans.[3]

In March 2010, the Affordable Care Act ("ACA"), was signed into law. This act represented the most significant set of reforms to the U.S. health care system since the establishment of Medicare and Medicaid through the Social Security Act in 1965 and was intended to address all aspect of the "Triple Aim": to expand access, lower costs, and increase quality. Key provisions of the ACA include (but are not limited to): a requirement that individuals not covered by Medicare, Medicaid, or other government programs carry health insurance or face financial penalties (there are some exceptions to the requirement); a requirement that employers with more than 50 employees offer a health insurance option or face "shared responsibility" payments; changes in provider payment mechanisms to focus more on outcomes rather than volume; limitations on health plan underwriting and pricing practices; requirements with respect to health plan benefit designs; the establishment of health insurance exchanges in each state; and the opportunity to expand Medicaid eligibility. The ACA has had a significant impact on the health care marketplace. It has expanded coverage and standardized benefit levels to facilitate sound cost comparisons. It has also contributed to a wave of consolidation for both providers and health plans.

In Canada, the public health care system was initiated with the passage of the Hospital Insurance and Diagnostic Services Act of 1957 and the Medical Care Act of 1966. These two acts established the health insurance programs that covered medically necessary services for nearly all Canadian residents. The Canada Health Act of 1984 replaced the two prior acts, although it

---

[3] *Employer Health Benefits, 2014 Annual Survey*, Kaiser Family Foundation and Health Research and Educational Trust.

maintained their basic premises. In addition, the 1984 Act included provisions to discourage user fees and extra billings as related to insured health care services.[4]

Flexible benefit programs in Canada received increased attention in the 1980s for many of the same reasons these programs became popular in the United States. These reasons included the change in workforce demographics since the origin of employee benefit programs, as well as government rulings that enhanced the ability of employers to offer choice to meet different employee needs and manage benefit costs.[5]

Regulation of group insurance occurs at both the state and federal level in the United States. Federal regulations apply to employer benefit plans, which include those plans provided on a self-insured basis. State law generally applies to the business of insurance. Therefore, insured benefits provided by an employer must comply with state laws, since the state regulations will apply to the insurance company providing the insurance program. On the other hand, self-insured benefits provided by an employer are not considered "the business of insurance" and are therefore not subject to state regulations. However, the lines of distinction can be blurry, as the federal government has implemented legislation which impacts health insurance, especially with regard to the availability and continuation of coverage.

Insurance companies in Canada may also be subject to both federal and provincial regulations. Companies that elect to be federally registered because they operate in more than one province are subject to federal law. Companies must also have a license from each province in which they do business, no matter where they are registered.

BUYERS OF GROUP INSURANCE PRODUCTS AND SERVICES

State or provincial laws and regulations may define valid groups eligible for group insurance. The National Association of Insurance Commissioners' (NAIC) model law provides a typical list. In general, the individual members of a group share some common characteristic or trait, independent of being covered by the same insurance policy. That is, the group should already have a purpose and should not be formed solely for the purpose of obtaining insurance coverage. The NAIC model law has been adopted by all states.

There are many different categories of group insurance purchasers:

SINGLE EMPLOYERS

Group insurance plans issued to a single employer cover the employees and their dependents. The employer is usually the policyholder, although in some cases a trust may be established and becomes the policyholder. Single employers may choose to purchase coverage from an insurer or managed care organization in return for a fixed premium, or in the case of larger employers, may elect to self-insure some or all of the risk. In fully insured plans the employer pays premiums, but employees are often required to contribute to the cost. In self-insured plans, the employer may similarly require the employees to contribute to the cost of the coverage. Self-insured employers may administer their own insurance plans, but more commonly purchase administrative services only (ASO) contracts from an insurance company or third-party

---

[4] The History of Health Care in Canada, 1914-2007; http://www.hc-sc.gc.ca/hcs-sss/medi-assur/index-eng.php
[5] Robert J. McKay. *Canadian Handbook of Flexible Benefits*, Third Ed.

administrator. Under such arrangements, the employer bears the risk of claims exceeding projected levels while the plan administrator (often an insurance company) provides services associated with building provider networks, processing claims and providing customer service to employees covered by the plan.

MULTIPLE EMPLOYER TRUSTS

Two or more employers may join together to form a multiple employer trust for the purpose of buying and funding group insurance for their employees. In this case, the trust is the policyholder, and the employers are known as participating employers. As with single employers, coverage may either be purchased on a fully insured basis, or be self-insured. Employees may be required to contribute toward the cost of coverage, whether the plan is fully insured or self-insured. Participating employers usually elect to join the trust because they anticipate greater purchasing power or spreading of risk if they combine their covered workforce with that of other employers. In some cases, the participating employers may have found it difficult to be accepted as an individual employer by an insurer, given their particular risk status. Joining a multiple employer trust allows for a greater pooling of risk that an insurer may then be willing to accept. Some multiple employer trusts are formed by insurance companies or third party administrators in order to make coverage available to smaller employers more efficiently. In addition, participating employers might also have unique administration requirements (such as an employee hours bank), and a multiple employer trust may provide a more efficient means of providing for those needs.

ASSOCIATIONS

An association may also offer group insurance coverage to its individual members. Associations are defined as groups of individuals or institutions that share common professions, interests, activities, or goals. Associations include, among others, professional organizations, trade organizations, and alumni organizations. Other groups, often known as affinity groups, also may be purchasers of group insurance. These groups are formed because members have a common interest. Examples are the American Automobile Association (AAA) and the American Association of Retired Persons (AARP). The association or a trust formed by the association is the policyholder.

Most often, the full cost of coverage is borne in some manner by the association member. The association member may remit the premium directly to the association for payment to the insurance provider, to a third party administrator working on behalf of the association, or directly to the provider of the insurance coverage.

Associations may automatically provide their members with some types of group insurance coverage, such as group accident or term life, and the premiums may be included as part of the membership dues. This is an important underwriting provision because it avoids the antiselection inherent in the purchase decision on the part of a non-subsidized insured. Associations may be in the market for group insurance coverage simply to provide an additional benefit to their membership for the dues that members pay.

LABOR UNIONS

A labor union may be the policyholder of a group insurance plan. A union may also negotiate benefits with employers participating in a Taft-Hartley multiple employer trust (named after the

U.S. federal law which authorized such trusts), in which case the trustees are the policyholders. Coverage may be fully insured or self-insured. Benefits and employee contributions, if any, are generally provided for in a collective bargaining agreement. Premiums may be required of the union, the employers, or the union members. Benefits are paid directly to the union members or their dependents, or may be assigned to a provider of medical services.

GOVERNMENT EMPLOYEE GROUPS

Collectively, the United States government is the largest employer in the country and the largest purchaser of group insurance for employees and their dependents. Some of the most prominent plans are the Federal Employees' Group Life Insurance (FEGLI) and Federal Employees' Health Benefits (FEHB) plans, in addition to numerous smaller agency plans and state and local government sponsored plans.

TRICARE provides health benefits to the retired members of the United States military and their dependents, as well as dependents of active service personnel. The program covers services rendered outside of military treatment facilities, and includes medical, dental and other services.

At the federal level, employees often have a choice of plans. At the state level, plans are often established for state employees and local governments are given the option to join. The governmental sponsor is the policyholder, and the plans may be insured or self-insured, and trusts are often used.

GOVERNMENT SOCIAL INSURANCE PROGRAMS

In the United States, the government also sponsors group insurance coverage in the form of many social insurance programs, including Medicare (health care for the aged and disabled), Medicaid (health care for those with limited income and financial resources), and Social Security disabled-worker and survivor benefits (disability and life benefits for disabled workers and their dependents).

In Canada, the vast majority of the general population is covered by provincial government sponsored health coverage, also known as Medicare.
The costs of these social insurance programs are paid through a combination of general revenues, payroll taxes, and insured premiums. These programs are discussed in detail in later chapters.

CREDITOR GROUPS

Creditor organizations, including banks and other lenders, may purchase group insurance coverage on those to whom they have lent funds. Coverages purchased typically include life and/or disability income coverage. The creditor organization is usually the policyholder, and charges the premium to the debtor. Should the insured become disabled or die, the insurance company would pay the benefits to the creditor organization to reduce the amount of the insured's outstanding debt.

Discretionary Groups

Groups are sometimes established primarily for the purpose of providing insurance or self-insured group benefits. The group may have to apply to the state insurance department for approval to be considered a discretionary group for this purpose. These plans may be either insured or self-insured and are generally issued to trusts. Discretionary groups are much more common in the United States than in Canada.

Sellers of Group Insurance Products

Group insurance products are sold by a variety of entities. Some of the products are sold on a self-insured basis, by (1) insurance companies under ASO contracts, (2) third party administrators, or (3) health care service organizations.

Insurance Companies

In both the United States and in Canada, group insurance products may be sold by life, health, or property and casualty companies. Insurance companies may offer the full range of group insurance products, including indemnity medical plans, PPO plans, POS plans, capitated or subcapitated medical plans, dental, disability, life, and long term care. As the management of health insurance has required more clinical expertise, many insurance companies no longer offer medical coverages, and the trend in the United States has been to withdraw from the medical market, leaving the market to a smaller number of companies who specialize in this coverage. The passing of the ACA has also led to some health insurers withdrawing from the market rather than accept the increased administrative burdens. Insurers also provide ASO contracts or provide services that offer some blend of insurance and administration to self-insured employers or multiple employer trusts. ASO is generally limited to medical and dental coverages, although some ASO disability plans may be found as well.

Insurance company ownership may be structured in stock or mutual form. Stock companies, the majority, are owned by stockholders. These companies are typically in the group insurance market to make a reasonable return on investment for their shareholders, and have some advantages over mutual companies and not-for-profit organizations in accessing capital in the financial markets. Mutual companies are owned by their policyholders, and allow for any positive financial experience to be returned to the participating policyholders. They are limited in their ability to raise capital and must rely on surplus and earnings to finance growth opportunities.

In the United States, insurers may have some advantages over other group sellers to the employer market, since they often have a national presence, are licensed in multiple states, and can offer policyholders a range of benefits from a single source.

Health Care Service Organizations

Health care service organizations are not-for-profit entities, and are often exempt from state premium or income tax. The majority are Blue Cross / Blue Shield or Delta Dental plans, although not all Blue Cross / Blue Shield plans are health care service organizations.

Health care service organizations generally sell only medical and dental products, including indemnity, PPO, POS, or capitated plans, but many offer other coverages through affiliated companies. They also typically offer ASO and other alternative funding contracts. They often have a strong local presence, and may only be licensed in a single state.

Health care service organizations sell to employers, union trusts, associations, and other groups. To the extent the buyer also provides other group products to its membership, such as disability or life, those products need to be purchased from another carrier.

A Note about Blue Cross/Blue Shield Organizations

Blue Cross / Blue Shield plans are all independent organizations operating under a common trademark, but not a common organizational structure. While the origin of these plans was as health care service organizations, over the years many Blues organizations have explored alternative corporate arrangements. Some Blues organizations are now structured as stock or mutual companies, and they may be involved in other arrangements such as joint ventures as well.

Health Maintenance Organizations

Health maintenance organizations (HMOs) are typically licensed as different entities from insurance companies or health care service organizations. They have a variety of types of owners, including the public, insurance companies, Blue Cross/Blue Shield organizations, and provider groups. They may be organized as for-profit or not-for-profit, although for-profit is more common.

HMOs contract with providers of care, such as hospitals and physicians or physician groups, to form networks. HMOs are also directly involved in the management of health care. HMOs tend to be local. They typically provide only medical benefits, although some dental and vision benefits may also be provided. Benefits provided to participants are generally comprehensive, but the participants are often limited to receiving care from only the providers with whom the HMO has contracted, except in the case of emergencies. In the late 1990s, the public's level of satisfaction with HMOs received considerable media attention. Concerns about cost savings at the expense of quality of care, choice of provider, and selection of treatment plans, led to the movement away from restrictive HMO plans to those providing more choice.

Provider Owned Organizations

In the 1990s, provider owned organizations such as physician hospital organizations (PHOs), provider-sponsored organizations (PSOs), and provider-sponsored networks (PSNs) began to form. These organizations often emerged due to providers' increased interest in more control of their own delivery of medical care and in the reimbursement of provided services. These organizations consist of provider groups, usually a hospital or hospital system and the associated group of physicians with admitting privileges. The group accepts a scheduled payment, known as global capitation, in return for accepting the risk of providing specified health care services. They may contract directly with employers, government, insurance companies or managed care organizations.

The local focus of these organizations, as well as their direct affiliation with providers, may offer marketing advantages relative to other types of organizations. However, historically these groups did not appear to be as well prepared to accept risk (in terms of both capital and management expertise) or perform administrative services as well as other types of organizations. For many of these reasons, the number of these organizations has declined significantly, with a few exceptions. The successful ones, such as the Kaiser Foundation Health Plan, Intermountain Healthcare and the Geisinger system in Danville PA, attracted considerable attention during the discussions leading to the 2010 health care reform legislation. Following the passage of the ACA, there is a renewed interest in these and other related organizational structures (such as Accountable Care Organizations, or ACOs). As the ACA puts an emphasis on paying providers based on value instead of volume, many provider groups are looking for ways in which they can share in the savings or otherwise benefit from the investments they are making in population health and other forms of value-based care.

SELF-INSURED EMPLOYERS

Self-insured employers do not provide group insurance coverage in the same way as insurance companies or Blue Cross/Blue Shield organizations, but they do accept risk. Self-insured benefits most often include medical, dental, and short-term disability. Due to the lower frequency and higher severity of life and long-term disability coverage, and also because of income tax considerations, these benefits are often insured. Employers may elect to self-insure for a variety of reasons. Self-insured plans are not generally subject to state premium tax or state mandated benefit provisions. Also, since the self-insured plan pays claims as they are submitted, the sponsor retains the use of the funds until they are paid and the benefit of the investment return. Finally and most importantly, the promises made by the employer are backed by the general assets of the employer or the trust, and (unlike insured benefits) self-insured plans are not subject to regulatory capital requirements (risk-based capital, or RBC). The combination of the exemptions from RBC, state premium taxes and mandated benefits can make a self-insured plan 5% - 6% less costly than an insured plan. Self-insured employers often contract with an insurance company or third-party administrator to provide for the administrative aspects of the plan.

In Canada, group insurance products and services are offered by insurance companies and Blue Cross plans, which tend to operate more like insurance companies than Blue Cross/Blue Shield plans found in the United States. Canadian Blue Cross plans may offer other group insurance products, such as disability plans, besides group medical coverages. Because the mix of public and private care is different than in the United States, managed care organizations such as HMOs and other provider owned organizations are rare in Canada. Self-insured employer plans are common in Canada as in the United States.

GOVERNMENT INSURANCE PROGRAMS

UNITED STATES MEDICARE

Established in 1965, Medicare provides health coverage to the eligible aged and disabled in the United States. Part A coverage provides for inpatient hospital, skilled nursing facility, and home health benefits. Providers of Part A services must accept the government's payment as payment in full, that is, cannot balance bill. Part B coverage provides for outpatient hospital benefits, physician services, durable medical equipment, ambulance, and other non-physician providers. There is generally a premium required to participate in Part B (some financial support may be available for those that qualify). In addition to the premium, beneficiaries are also subject to some cost-sharing provisions for Part B services (there can be some limited cost sharing in Part A as well). Physicians are not required to accept the government's payment as payment in full, although many do, and there are limits to the amount they can charge in excess of the government's payment. Medicare Part D, providing prescription drug coverage, was added to Medicare in 2006. Participation in Part D is voluntary, although eligibles who do not enroll within certain timeframes may be subject to late enrollment penalties. Medicare Part D may be offered through a stand-alone prescription drug plan ("PDP") or a Medicare Advantage ("MA") plan (discussed below). The benefits and premiums vary by plan and plan sponsor. Eligible beneficiaries may have many options of stand-alone PDPs or MA plans from which to choose. Funding for Medicare is provided through payroll taxes, general revenues, and beneficiary premiums.

Many Medicare eligible beneficiaries also have the opportunity to forego traditional Medicare coverage and participate in a Medicare Advantage ("MA") plan (sometimes called Medicare Part C). The majority of MA plans are managed care plans, such as HMOs or PPOs. The government provides a payment to the MA plan for each enrolled beneficiary, risk-adjusted to recognize the relative condition-related risk of different enrollees. The MA plan then assumes the risk of providing services for the covered insured. Some MA plans may offer additional benefits beyond those normally provided by Medicare Parts A, B, and D. Insureds covered by an MA plan pay Part B premiums to Medicare, and may pay additional monthly premiums to the MA plan.

The significant cost-sharing and gaps in coverage that exist in Parts A and B of Medicare led to the growth of a large market in Medicare Supplemental or "Medigap" insurance which is sometimes purchased by traditional Medicare beneficiaries to cover large and unplanned out-of-pocket expenses associated with some services. Retirees are sometimes provided with group Medicare supplement plan coverage by their former employer, though this has become less common over time because of the rising cost.

UNITED STATES MEDICAID

Medicaid provides health coverage for certain individuals with limited income and financial resources in the United States. Prior to the ACA, eligibility criteria generally included children; parents or caregivers of children; disabled children or adults; and aged adults. The ACA established an expansion of Medicaid eligibility to nearly all Americans under age 65 with income up to 138% of the federal poverty level. However, a Supreme Court ruling in 2012 effectively made the expansion of Medicaid eligibility optional for the states. Implementation by state varies and by the end of 2015, 30 states had adopted the higher income threshold for coverage and expanded the program. Medicaid coverage is comprehensive, with many benefits covered at 100%. Medicaid provides broad coverage, including benefits such as dental, vision, and custodial nursing care, in addition to traditional health benefits. Cost-sharing levels for beneficiaries are very low. Medicaid reimburses providers at rates that often represent deep discounts from standard charges, which must be accepted as payment in full. Physicians are not required to participate in Medicaid, although hospitals frequently must participate. Medicaid programs are administered by state governments and are funded by state revenues with matching Federal funds. States may pay providers on a fee-for-service basis, or may provide for services through prepaid programs such as HMOs (called "MCOs" in state Medicaid). The number of

Medicaid beneficiaries in managed care plans has grown from 14% of enrollees in 1993 to 59% in 2003 to 74% in 2011.[6]

CANADIAN MEDICARE

Provincial government sponsored health care programs known as Medicare cover the majority of the population of Canada. Medicare provides coverage for a variety of medical services, such as hospital services, inpatient and outpatient physician services, as well as extended health care services, which include long-term residential care. Benefits are on a service basis, meaning that patients do not need to pay first and then submit a claim. Federal standards for provincial programs discourage user fees. Although they are not required to do so, a vast majority of physicians participate in the Medicare program. Under Medicare, physicians are generally compensated on a fee-for-service basis. Medicare is funded by the provinces through general revenues, and in some provinces, payroll taxes and premiums. Provincially sponsored Medicare plans that meet federally established criteria for portability, universality, comprehensiveness, accessibility, and public non-profit management are eligible for a federal funds transfer to offset some of the costs of the provincial program. Private health insurance plans are also available as supplements to the public program, and many Canadians have this additional coverage through their employers.

---

[6] http://www.medicaid.gov/Medicaid-CHIP-Program-Information/By-Topics/Data-and-Systems/Downloads/2011-Medicaid-MC-Enrollment-Report.pdf

2 OVERVIEW OF SALES AND MARKETING

John Elliott
William A. Raab
Updated by Brian Marsella

INTRODUCTION

A textbook on group insurance would not be complete without a description of how sales and marketing fits with the other group functions. A company can have state-of-the-art systems and efficient administration, and actuaries can develop competitive rates and funding alternatives, but nothing will happen until products have been properly developed, marketed, and sold.

The American Marketing Association defines marketing as "the process of planning and executing the conception, pricing, promotion, and distribution of ideas, goods, and services to create exchanges that satisfy individual and organizational objectives."[1] This is a broad description of the process that begins with the original product or service concept and concludes with an exchange of something of value for the product or service – the "sale" to the customer.

It is more common in practice to separate the marketing and sales functions. The separation occurs not because there is a dichotomy between marketing and sales, but rather because there is a close relationship that can be explained with the analogy, "marketing is to sales as strategy is to tactics." This frame of reference shows marketing as an overall process, with distribution and sales as the implementing component.

In the context of group insurance, the relationship between marketing and sales will vary depending on the insurance product, employer size, and intermediaries.

MARKETING

This chapter on marketing and sales includes an overview of some basic marketing concepts. When necessary, it also includes explanations relating these concepts to group insurance.

MARKETING FUNCTIONS

Marketing is the process of preparing the way for sales. The following sections consider some of the marketing functions and how they fit into the overall strategic planning process.

Strategy is conventionally viewed as the overall game plan or blueprint that guides the company toward achieving its stated goals and objectives. The marketing area plays a key

---

[1] E.N. Berkowitz, *Essentials of Health Care Marketing,* (Gaithersburg, Md., Aspen Publications, 1996) p. 4.

role in this strategic plan by providing important information about the company's current position in the market as well as possible future opportunities. The marketing area can also participate in the overall planning process by developing strategies and tactics for specific products, customers, and distribution channels.[2]

Market research is an important part of this overall planning process. The role of research is, quite simply, to focus on understanding customers. Who are the potential customers for our products, what features do they wish to purchase, where are they located, how much are they willing to pay, and from what types of distribution arrangements do they wish to buy? Who are our competitors and what are they doing?[3] Scientific survey techniques and sophisticated statistical analysis are employed. In fact, market research is a profession in itself, with its own trade organization. It is not unusual for a company to supplement the efforts of its own research department by using an outside specialty firm.[4]

Market research is commonplace in the consumer product industry and is gaining ground in financial services. The traditional group insurance companies may have lagged behind durable goods companies in implementing a research-based approach. This is probably due, at least in part, to their focus on product and distribution. In today's environment that has changed. Insurers and managed care organizations recognize the role research plays in the marketplace, particularly as insurers work to try and change the behaviors of the consumers.

The development of competitive products is one of the processes identified in the marketing planning process. Common sense tells us that companies need products and services to sell to make a profit. How are new products developed? Although there is a general pattern to the process, the specifics are different at every company. Two different approaches are summarized below. The first might be called a traditional product-driven process; the second is market-driven.

The Traditional Product Development Process:[5]

The product development process under a traditional, product-driven approach can be conceptualized into seven steps:

- Idea Generation: Ideas can come from a number of sources, such as product managers, a product committee, customers, competitors, or employees.
- Idea Screening: The product ideas are screened to determine which are compatible with the company's strategy, resources, and skills.
- Concept Development and Testing: A team refines the concept into a product, and questions such as "What are the benefits?" and "Who will buy this?" are answered.
- Business Analysis: Costs are projected, and a return on investment (or return on equity) analysis is done.
- Product Development: The actual product is given concrete form.

---

[2] A. Hiam and C.D. Schewe, *The Portable MBA in Marketing*, (New York, NY, John Wiley and Sons, Inc., 1992) p. 24.
[3] Ibid, pp. 103-108.
[4] Ibid, pp. 108-110.
[5] Ibid, pp. 244-253.

- Test Marketing: The product is tested in limited real-world markets.
- Commercialization: Full-scale manufacture and distribution.

The Market-Driven Product Process:[6]

The market-driven process can be thought of as having three major steps:

- Assessment of Target Market Needs: A target market is chosen, and market research is done to assess the needs of that market. Competitive analysis is a critical part of this research.
- Identification of Differential Advantage: Since the needs of the buyer and the competition's approach are known, a determination is made of how to differentiate one's own product or service from the competition, to better serve the customer's need.
- Strategy Formulation: A strategy is developed to build and deliver the product, based upon the differential advantage. This is then followed by either a pre-test (a limited market test), or full implementation.

Marketing in the Group Insurance Marketplace

Although there may be subtle differences from industry to industry, this overall marketing process applies to a broad range of products and services, from laundry detergent, to mutual funds, to group insurance. The application of the marketing process for the group insurance industry has its own particular considerations.

As described previously, organizations can employ many methods and strategies for marketing products, and group insurance is no different. One issue that group insurance marketing professionals must decide on is the audience for their campaign. The need for multiple marketing campaigns is due to the complexity of the distribution model for group insurance. Insurers create marketing strategies targeted to intermediaries that advise their clients, to group policyholders (most often employers), and to individual consumers. In general, most insurance companies will have marketing plans for all three of these consumers of their products and services. The level of focus on these different consumers will change by company and by insurance product.

Another consideration for the marketing process in the group insurance environment is state and federal regulation. Group insurance is primarily regulated at the state level, meaning insurers' marketing efforts and new product offerings must be compliant on a state-by-state basis (even if a single strategy across states.) In March 2010, President Obama signed into law the Affordable Care Act (ACA), which defined public exchanges, intended to assist the uninsured to purchase individual health. Since the ACA has taken effect, employers are looking for new ways to be compliant with the law and avoid future taxes. There are also new options such as private exchanges that are causing health insurers to reexamine their marketing strategies for brokers, employers and consumers. The ACA has also added federal regulations that require compliance.

---

[6] Berkowitz, pp. 17-19.

At this point, the company has developed its strategy and done necessary planning, researched the market, developed products to meet the demands of that market, and implemented an advertising and promotional campaign to build awareness of its products and services. Let's now turn our attention to sales.

SALES

In a sense, sales can be seen as the culmination of the marketing process, although this is a somewhat oversimplified view. Ongoing customer service after the sale completes the marketing and sales process. Organizations cannot survive if they must focus their sales efforts on replacing dissatisfied customers who have terminated their relationship. In the context of market-driven organizations, marketing, sales, and ongoing service are all one continuous process.

Group insurance often has two levels of sale. The initial sale is made to the plan sponsor. This entails selection of plans to be offered and their cost, and includes a discussion of financial management, administration, and services offered to the sponsor. Later, a "second sale" is often made to the participants. This can include selection of a particular plan from among those offered by the sponsor, and for certain products, such as group universal life and long-term care, may be similar to the sale of an individual insurance product. The second sale is discussed in more detail later in the chapter.

Historically, group insurers have organized their sales efforts to targeted market segments. For a given market segment, the distribution model is dependent on plan sponsors' size and industry, as well as the sophistication of their employee benefit plans. This section examines the most common market segmentations and distribution models along with the role of the intermediaries in the sales process. It also discusses emerging strategies in the group distribution process.

MARKETING SEGMENTATION

Group insurers often look at sales (and, more generally, distribution) from the perspective of target market segments. Segmentation analysis is not designed to replace emphasis on distribution channels. Rather, it enables the company to understand its potential customers and focus its distribution efforts appropriately. As a result of the analysis, management can make specific decisions as to which market segments to pursue, with which products, and through which distribution channels.

For example, an insurer could segment employers by industry, manner in which they purchase benefits (i.e. paternalistic, procurement driven etc.) or geographic area. An insurer might focus on public sector employees and dedicate its resources to the specific needs of that market. Certain group long-term disability insurers, for example, have focused on educators as a sub-segment of the public sector market. Meanwhile, another insurer might choose to limit distribution to certain geographic areas where it has greater physical presence or brand recognition. Additionally, with the advent of private exchanges, some groups may focus on whether an employer may be more prone to looking at a defined contribution approach or staying the course of the standard market.

One common way for group insurers to segment business is by employer size. This is a convenient way for insurers to look at market segments and focus its distribution channels. Certain size segments tend to be serviced by specific distribution models, described later in this chapter.

SIZE SEGMENTS

Smallest Groups (2 to 100 Employees)

In the U.S., the small group segment is heavily regulated by the ACA. Insurers are required to comply with benefit coverage, plan design actuarial value and premium rating restrictions. Insurers offering products in this size segment often use the brokerage or general agency distribution methods, with little or no group field force involvement. Agents and brokers who operate in this market usually specialize in small groups. The clientele tends to be less sophisticated regarding group insurance and does not have the resources to maintain full-time benefit managers or human resource departments and so relies on brokers for advice on benefit plan management. Small group coverage is also offered on state exchanges and the definition of small group expands to cover 2-100 employees in 2016.

Mid-Market Groups (100 to 1,000 Employees)

In this size segment, a group's own claim experience is usually available for a variety of insurance products, which has a major impact on product pricing. Flexibility of plan design is necessary because employers in this size category are relatively sophisticated and have benefit managers who closely monitor their benefit offerings. They require benefits customized to the needs of their business and the type of employees they hire. For certain benefits, self-insurance is a major consideration. These customers typically use specialized brokers and large local or regional brokerage firms. The process of obtaining and analyzing information needed to prepare a proposal requires a highly skilled group benefit specialist, both on the broker and the insurer side of the negotiation. Consequently, a group field force model is usually favored by insurers in this size segment. In addition, insurers often have account managers who focus on servicing and renewing these groups. The account management team can be key to the overall success of retention and will be discussed later.

Large Groups (1,000 Employees and Up)

The large group segment has the greatest variety of solutions and distribution models to match the complexity and geography of these employers. Very large groups are usually multi-site and multi-state and have full-time benefit and risk management departments that manage a complex array of benefit plans. Employees typically have a number of plan options – and possibly multiple insurers – from which to choose. These customers usually deal only with large employee benefits consulting firms or highly skilled local brokers. Many insurers have "national account" or "special account" field forces dedicated to this size segment. The larger the group and the more geographically dispersed, the less likely local or regional health insurers are able to provide adequate coverage or services.

ROLE OF INTERMEDIARIES

Employers tend to rely on third-party advisors to assist them with their employee benefit plans. This assistance includes advice on issues such as plan design, pricing, and comparative analysis of competing insurers' products and services. The advisor usually gets involved in ongoing customer service and often acts as the employer's representative in resolving disputed billing and claims issues. At renewal, the advisor surveys the marketplace to see if the client would be better served by renewing the plan with the current insurer or by changing insurers. This analysis includes a discussion of plan design alternatives, either with the current insurer or a competitor.

These advisors fall into three general categories: brokers, agents, and consultants.

A "broker" is a somewhat generic term for an individual who represents more than one insurers. The broker's compensation is usually based on sales commissions for products sold. The commissions are a percentage of premium paid or a fee per covered employee. In either case, the commission is built into the price of the product.

"Agents" are similar to brokers, except that they are typically associated with a single insurer. Their compensation is also based on commissions.

"Consultants" work primarily with large employers. Compensation is typically based on a fee for services rendered, as opposed to commissions, and is paid by the employer rather than by the insurer. The consultant could be paid an annual retainer, and/or could be paid an hourly fee for consulting services. There could also be fees negotiated for specific projects, such as a vendor selection project or creating customized communication materials explaining the various benefit packages available at open enrollment. In many cases, products are usually quoted net of commissions. Some brokerage firms operate as consultants in certain instances and as brokers in others.

In late 2004, the Attorney General of the State of New York announced an investigation into the business practices of several large property and casualty insurance brokerage firms. Among the allegations was bid-rigging, in order to place business with preferred insurers, thus earning higher contingent commissions (which are additional commissions granted to brokers who meet a new or continuing enrollment goal with a insurer). The National Association of Insurance Commissioners (NAIC) got involved as did several other state insurance departments and attorney generals. Even though the original allegations involved property and casualty coverage, the inquiries were expanded to include other lines, including group insurance. There were numerous civil actions, and the NAIC strengthened commission disclosure requirements in its Producer Licensing Model Act.[7]

It is also important to point out that with the advent of consultant-driven private exchanges, some employers are beginning to question the ability for such consultants to be unbiased as they have been in the past with regard to an employers' options. It remains to be seen as to how this will change the landscape moving forward, but there is an expectation that some

---

[7] The NAIC website (www.naic.org) provides archival material on this subject, as does the website of the New York Attorney General (www.oag.state.ny.us).

boutique vendors will enter the arena to help employers choose between multiple consultant-led exchanges.

DISTRIBUTION MODELS

BROKERAGE

Under the brokerage distribution model, the insurer relies on independent brokers to distribute products. These brokers are self-employed entrepreneurs, who are responsible for maintaining their own office space and clerical staff. This method can be used for wholesale distribution (such brokers are often called general agents), retailing, or a combination of both. This model is attractive to some companies, especially those with limited resources, because it does not require the large commitment of capital and staff resources necessary to house, train, supervise, and maintain a branch-office field force. A portion of these savings may be given back in the form of higher commission rates, overrides, and expense allowances to the brokers.

This model is characterized by a single, narrow distribution channel. The broker does not have the sale of the company's products as his or her sole responsibility. Other companies' products are also sold. This makes the insurer vulnerable to price competition, since the business will often flow to the insurer with the lowest rate.

As an independent, the broker may choose to specialize in other product lines, such as property and casualty or financial planning. Even if the broker is specializing in the desired product, distribution can be limited to a local area or a specific client base. In order to maintain sufficient revenue flow, the insurer must support a broad variety of products for many market niches.

This method is most frequently used to distribute individual and small group insurance products, including various types of life insurance, annuities, Medicare supplement coverage, critical illness coverage, and long-term care policies, where the agent relationship is an important element of the sale. Group products tend to be sold based on price and value, and this model has not been widely used by group insurers.

GROUP FIELD FORCE

The group field force model is the traditional model used for years by most large group insurers. Under this distribution system, the insurer employs a full-time salaried field force of captive group representatives. The group representatives are usually paid an incentive for sales in addition to a base salary. This distribution method is typically a wholesale model, where the insurer representatives call on and sell through brokers and consultants, and in certain situations directly to the employer.

This distribution channel is wider than in the pure brokerage model. The sales force is totally dedicated to the sale of the insurer's products. There is no specialization in outside product lines, no distribution of other companies' products, and distribution is not limited to a small local area. Rather, the group sales force tends to operate in as many market niches as possible. Relationships are developed with a large variety of brokers, thereby gaining access to a large, diverse base of prospects. This enables the insurer to generate sufficient sales volume while serving a narrower market with a more focused portfolio of products.

Overhead expenses are higher than in the brokerage model. However, this may be partially compensated for by the loyalty of the field force, which will sell value instead of low price. This permits pricing at levels sufficient to cover expenses while maintaining profit margins. Company growth can be managed by increasing the size of the sales force. Although overhead increases as sales representatives are added, economies of scale are possible. Revenue increases as a result of expansion are more predictable because the sales people are employees, not independent brokers.

Within this model, there are often separate teams that work to manage employers once they become customers. The account management team is responsible for making sure the service to the employees and the employers is sound as well as working in a consultative capacity to determine what other products or services might be useful to the employer. The team is also involved in cross-selling to gain additional work from the employer, which should have a positive impact on retention.

MULTIPLE LEVEL

The multiple level distribution model is the most advanced model currently in use for distribution of group insurance and is more complex than the others. Under this model, the insurer uses different types of distribution, layered one on top of the other, to sell its products. The layers include a mix of wholesalers, retailers, brokers, life agents, general agents, salaried representatives, telemarketers, and direct sellers.

The distribution channels are extremely broad and enable the insurer to focus specific products into different channels. There is a mixture of low-expense models (like brokers) with higher expense models (like salaried representatives compensated on a sales incentive plan). This permits the insurer to have the advantages of a dedicated field force without the severe impact on pricing. The expense loads of the field force are blended with the lower expense methods. Because of the complexity of this system, sophisticated sales management and marketing support are critical to success. This model is widely employed by insurers with a national presence. It gives the insurer the flexibility to exploit whichever channel or channels work in specific marketing areas.

SALES TO PARTICIPANTS

Some group sponsors offer multiple choices of plans and insurers that require the insurer to sell their product to individual employees, after the initial sale has been made to the employer (this is the "second sale" mentioned above.) These sales are usually made by specialized enrollment staff (who may be paid through commissions), or by salaried enrollment specialists. The employees may meet with these specialists in the workplace, or respond to printed or website information at their own convenience. This second sale is often needed where plan sponsors offer multiple different models such as HMO, PPO or consumer-driven plans. In situations like these, the person doing the enrollment is attempting to "sell" his or her product.

Second-sale events are typically called "benefit fairs" and organized by the employer. At a benefit fair, representatives from all of the insurers whose products the employer is sponsoring, including group life, disability, dental, medical, and pharmacy, are available in a conference room or near the cafeteria. The insurers use tabletop displays and give away inexpensive promotional items. Employees visit the insurers they choose, asking questions, and obtaining marketing materials, plan information, and enrollment forms. The enrollment forms are usually completed and submitted at a later date.

In recent years, technology has played a larger role in helping employees make a decision on their benefits with the advent of interactive programs, particularly among larger employers. Technology helps the employee think through a number of decisions they need to make and helps to frame those choices about the tradeoff between premium rates and benefit levels. The ultimate approach to such technology would be the private exchange programs that some employers are implementing that help employees make choices from a large number of products.

LICENSING REQUIREMENTS

With the exception of second-sale activities, brokers, general agents, and field sales require licensing to sell insurance products. Each state, through its Department of Insurance, has its own state licensing and continuing education requirements. For sales professionals operating in multiple states, non-resident licenses are available and the National Insurance Producer Registry is dedicated to making licensing cost-effective and streamlined for the industry across all states.

ADDITIONAL DISTRIBUTION METHODS

Thus far, the discussion of distribution methods has focused on traditional models. However, there are other methods of distributing group insurance, often referred to as "alternative distribution." Alternative distribution methods involve mass-marketing techniques, such as television, radio, newspaper advertising, direct mail solicitation, internet website sales, and worksite marketing.

With the exception of internet and worksite marketing, the products distributed through these alternative methods are generally not the same as the employee benefits that have been the focus of this chapter. Among the products sold this way are critical illness coverage (such as cancer-only coverage), hospital confinement benefits, accidental death benefits, and term life insurance. Television, radio, and newspaper advertising often include a celebrity endorsement or an entertaining theme or mascot to gain attention. Direct mail solicitations are usually linked to a credit card or to membership in an association. Since the insurer is marketing the coverage directly to the consumer, there is no broker or group field force compensation. However, there are significant marketing expenses involved, and insurers often retain specialty marketing firms.

WORKSITE MARKETING

Worksite marketing of voluntary programs is more closely related to traditional distribution methods. There is usually a broker involved, and sometimes the group field force is involved as well. Employees are solicited at the jobsite in group meetings, which are often followed by individual one-on-one meetings where the final sale is made and the application taken. In addition to traditional enrollment materials, the enrollment specialist often uses a laptop computer that includes an electronic application for coverage, policy illustrations, and other marketing material.

The coverage is typically 100% paid by the employee through payroll deductions. Sales commissions are higher than under the employer's base plan due to the expense of an enrollment team. Products distributed in this manner often include dental, vision, short and long-term disability, supplemental term life insurance, accidental death, and critical illness coverage. Another product that may be solicited at the worksite is "Gap" insurance, designed to reimburse the deductible and coinsurance under the employer-provided health plan.

Certain products that accumulate benefits over an extended period of time, such as group universal life and long-term care, are also effectively marketed through these enrollment specialists.

INTERNET MARKETING

Another alternative distribution method is internet marketing, often referred to as e-commerce. E-commerce goes beyond simple product distribution. Companies are using this non-traditional tool for some of the traditional marketing functions that pave the way for sales, including advertising, public relations, product promotion, image building, and brand management. For example, most major insurers have websites where individuals can obtain information about the company, its products and services, local sales offices, charitable and community activities, the current stock price, employment opportunities, and so on. Recent research (primarily focusing on insurers marketing individual products) indicates that insurers specifically view the Internet as a strategic vehicle for effective communications and for enhancing service to agents, brokers, and customers.[8] It is reasonable to conclude that results would be similar for group products.

Many insurers are using the Internet for transaction management by giving their customers access to secure websites for plan administration purposes. Plan sponsors can do additions and deletions to their group bill, and participants can obtain information on policy and account values, find primary care physicians, download important forms, and check on the status of claims. The insurer is in effect using the Internet as a tool to manage the ongoing customer relationship. The cost per transaction using the Internet can be significantly lower than toll-free telephone lines and email.[9]

In addition to communication and transaction management, insurers also use e-commerce for product sales. Through the insurer website, consumers can obtain quotes for various forms of insurance coverage. Unless the insurer is a direct writer, the consumer is usually referred to a

---

[8] MarketTrends, *LIMRA's Factbook: 2005 Trends in the United States*; p. 64; LIMRA International, Windsor, CT, 2005.
[9] Ibid, p. 62.

local sales office for assistance, generating leads for the insurer's agents and brokers. This is particularly true for group insurance coverage.

A recent innovation is group internet enrollment. The employee enrolls for benefits directly through the Internet, making paper communication and forms unnecessary.

Internet enrollment can be done through the employer's website, through a third-party vendor, or through a link to the insurer website. This creates yet another opportunity to sell voluntary products such as accidental death benefits, supplemental group term life, and universal life. Because of the additional expenses involved, Internet enrollment is more practical for large employers.

Insurers are not the only ones using the internet for product sales. There are websites operated by insurance brokerage firms where consumers can obtain proposals for various insurance products, including group insurance. This is a variation of the brokerage and general agency distribution methods described above. The consumer would have access to the products of several insurers, and could obtain comparative pricing and benefit information. The brokerage firm would be required to maintain appropriate licensure for the various states where proposals would be delivered. This channel is usually viewed as a supplement to, but not a replacement for, the traditional broker intermediary favored by employers for purchasing group insurance. However, brokers who do not adapt to this new environment risk losing a portion of their customer base.

CONCLUSION

The group insurance landscape is dynamic, as employers continuously strive to manage the cost of a competitive benefits program. The passage of ACA has caused all employers to re-evaluate their benefit strategy with the social contract they have with their employees. They need to weigh the additional taxes and benefits against their ability to deliver such benefits in a cost-effective manner. The ACA has also given many employers the platform to have a dialogue with their employees about these costs that they previously felt they could not have in a constructive manner. In particular, this conversation has begun with unions and could cause some major changes in the union benefit world. Economic performance, evolving regulation, competition for labor, and demographic changes will all play a role in the evolution of the insurance industry.

As the group insurance landscape evolves, each organization will define its future by developing and executing its marketing strategies. Regardless of the size, scope or scale of the organization, all group companies will identify their primary markets, develop products, strive for sales targets, and work to satisfy their customers. The thrill and the challenge are in the execution of the marketing and sales process and the corresponding account management.

3   Product Development

Andrea Sheldon

Introduction

What is Product Development?

Product development is the process by which new products are created and existing products evolve. All products used on a daily basis are at some phase in their life cycle. At one point, each product was a mere concept. Eventually that concept evolved into a fully developed product that was brought to market. That product will evolve to adapt to a changing market, or it will risk being removed from the market and replaced with a better or less expensive new product.

The same general product development processes used for consumer goods are also used in the insurance market. While every industry, and every company within each industry, takes a slightly different approach to product development, this chapter explores the overriding principles that can be found in the typical product development cycle: innovating an idea, designing the idea, building the idea into a product, selling the product, and continually assessing and revising the product throughout its life cycle. In the context of this chapter, product development is not limited to the development of a new idea—it takes place throughout the entire life cycle of a product.

The Product Development Cycle

Innovate

The first step of the product development cycle is the innovation of a new product or the next evolutionary stage of an existing product. The process of innovating is made up of (1) understanding the company's strategic perspective, (2) idea generation, (3) idea screening, and (4) market assessments.

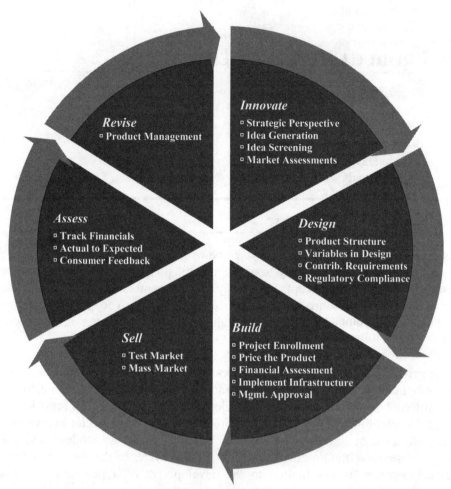

Understanding Company's Strategic Perspective

The innovation of a new product begins with an idea. However, it is important to understand the company's strategic perspective before discussing and evaluating ideas. This goes beyond understanding the strategic goals of the company and includes understanding why the goals were developed. Understanding why a company has adopted a particular strategic goal will help the product development department better align its work with the goals of the broader organization.

For example, if a company's strategic goals include growing membership in the senior segment, it may be that this is a strategic goal because of projected growth in the senior population in the United States. The product development team would naturally be led to evaluate product needs in markets where the population segment is projected to grow. There is an ongoing shift in various population segments across different states driven by climate, state tax policies, and other factors that make some states more desirable than others for retirees. Understanding the strategic goals will lead a product development team to incorporate geography into its analysis of market needs, and thus into the product development process.

Understanding strategic goals will also help reduce unnecessary work and focus the product development department on ideas that are aligned with company goals. If a company's overall strategy is to exit or reduce emphasis on a given market, then it may not make sense to spend time creating and vetting ideas that would lead the company to grow in that particular market. If management within a company is considering a particular product, understanding why they are thinking about that product will enable the product development team to create ideas that fit in with corporate strategic goals.

Understanding whether the insurer would consider entering a particular product market, whether defined by geography or product type, will provide direction for the product development team. This level of understanding will help define the parameters that are needed to narrow the potential scope of ideas and give guidance to the team members responsible for creating product ideas. Overall, it is critical that the product development team is informed of strategic corporate goals so it can efficiently generate new ideas.

Idea Generation

Product evolution depends on the development of new ideas. Each of the following describes a common driver of product ideas:

Innovator or Follower: There are companies that successfully innovate, and there are companies that successfully follow the market. There are advantages and disadvantages to both positions. The company that innovates must invest in the development of concepts, while the company that follows can learn from their competitors by observing what works and does not work for the products that their competitors bring to the market. There are costs incurred by innovators that followers do not pay. On the other hand, the innovator will have access to a larger initial market since they will be the only company with a particular product (albeit for a limited amount of time), while the follower may lag behind the market and will not have the advantage of the initial surge from members attracted to a particular new product.

Changing Laws and Regulations: Compared to other markets, the insurance industry is highly regulated. For example, there are oversight bodies that regulate the pricing of insurance products, and there are laws and regulations that dictate the benefits that can be sold. While these rules can limit some product development, since products must operate within this tightly regulated market, this can also be the genesis of new ideas. When new laws or regulations are created, or existing laws or regulations are changed, products are developed to operate within these new sets of rules.

Consumer Demand: It is very important that companies remain attentive to the needs and desires of consumers. Companies interested in remaining competitive must constantly seek consumer feedback and market intelligence. If there is an element of a particular product where consumers are consistently providing negative feedback, this may induce a change in the product. If consumers are particularly happy with a component of a product, this may encourage growth in that area. There is an entire market of companies that are paid by the industry to seek consumer feedback through surveys and other outreach. The results of this research are used to shape future product development.

Marketing and Sales Demand: Marketing and sales teams have direct access to the market, and are often aware of the demand from the market. They can spot gaps in the product spectrum where consumer demand is not being fully met. This insight may lead to new ideas.

Incorporating sales feedback into the product development process is essential to gaining a comprehensive understanding of market needs.

Leveraging Insurer's Capabilities: While insurers are looking for ideas to develop new products and even acquire other companies to grow in new areas, product development does not necessarily need to encourage growth into new product areas. There are efficiencies gained by leveraging the insurer's existing capabilities. Product development teams will be more successful if they fully understand what the insurer does well and find ways of growing in those areas. For example, a dental insurer may benefit more from adding a new type of dental product than from adding a vision product to its portfolio. Consideration of the organization's strategic goals, and the prioritization of the opportunities that each idea presents, is necessary to determine which product better leverages existing capabilities and fits with the company's goals.

Social Need: Products are developed to address specific social needs. For example, the Affordable Care Act created subsidies making health care insurance more affordable for lower income citizens of the United States. Many companies have developed products to sell to this market through state exchanges. Medicare Part D is another example of product development originated by new legislation that was intended to serve social needs. Prescription drug costs grew from approximately 1% of health care costs in 1965 (when Medicare was started) to more than 15% by the early 2000s. Some seniors on limited budgets had to choose between food and the cost of their expensive medications. The social need for this coverage emerged from high pharmacy cost inflation and expensive new drug innovations.

Changing Demographics: With the aging baby boomers and people generally living longer, the demographics in the insurance markets are changing. Changing demographics means a shift in the types of products that will be marketable and saleable. Changing demographics can lead product development teams to generate ideas that address the shifting market needs.

Changing Economy and Financial Markets: Shifts in the economy and financial markets change purchasers' views of their need for insurance. Insurance products that do not appear critical to the market may lose members during downward swings in the economy and financial markets. However, insurance products that purchasers believe will increase their financial stability may gain members. The attractiveness of a new product is influenced by the economy and financial markets; therefore, the genesis of ideas should be influenced by the economy and financial markets.

Competitive Advantage: Insurers often have a competitive advantage in one or more areas. The competitive advantage may be in a particular geographic area due to name recognition or within a particular demographic due to affinity relationships (for example, with retiree associations or military associations). Any competitive advantage should be utilized to its fullest extent, and thus should influence product development ideas.

Idea Screening

Product development teams create many varied ideas. For the initial idea generation phase, teams may take the approach that no idea is a bad idea, which generates as many ideas as possible. One idea, perhaps not a great one, may influence the creation of a different, great idea.

After the initial surge of ideas, it is critical to begin screening these ideas for consistency with corporate goals, and for feasibility within the corporation's abilities while still meeting financial targets. A variety of processes can be used for screening, such as size and scope appropriateness, fit with corporate goals, resources and cost, or other filters that will help assess the feasibility of the product idea. A repository for discarded ideas is often a good idea, since the ideas that may not fit well today may be better suited for the future.

Market Assessment

Once the large list of ideas is screened down to a few that are worth pursuing further, it is important to determine if a market exists for the potential products. This is often referred to as a "market assessment" or "opportunity analysis." The market assessment commonly answers the following questions:

What exists in the market today? An analysis of the products sold both by competitors and the insurer in the target market will help the team to determine how the product fits in the market and identify the product's competitive advantage.

What is the product objective for the consumer? This analysis helps to determine if the product is meeting the needs of the consumer. If there is a demand for a particular product, the team should ensure that the product it is developing meets that need.

What is the regulatory environment for this product? This analysis will help the team understand whether the product features it is developing would be allowed in the market. It will also help the team understand whether the regulations that govern this product are expected to change in the near future in such a way that the product will not be feasible.

Financial value and other benefits for the consumer: Market assessments can help the product development team to better understand the financial value consumers place on the type of product being sold. This financial value will influence the price targets for the product.

Price Targets: Based on the market assessment, pricing for the new product may be an input to, or an output from, the product development process. There is a balance, or interplay, between price and product features. More specifically, a market assessment may indicate that a certain range of prices are acceptable in the market. The team may then use that range to back into a plan design (and product provisions) that meet profit targets at the given price. Alternatively, the market may be more sensitive to the product features. In this case, the team develops the desired product features, and then determines the price expected to make such a plan profitable.

Competitors' likely reaction: The market assessment will help the product development team understand how competitors will likely react to the proposed product. For example, if competitors are expected to follow up with a similar product, this may create a very price competitive environment that will impact the financial projections for the product, and thus the product's feasibility.

Sales reaction: This stage of the market assessment determines whether the sales team thinks that such a product is saleable at the price targets. If the product would be priced out of the market, then it may not be worth pursuing further.

Each of these steps helps to sort out and revise ideas, until the decision-maker (perhaps the group as a whole) decides that one or more ideas are worth pursuing further.

DESIGN THE PRODUCT

Once the team decides that they are going to pursue a particular idea further, it moves to the design phase of the product development cycle. This phase consists of determining (1) product structure, (2) variables in plan design, (3) contribution requirements, and (4) regulatory compliance.

Product Structure

When a new insurance product is designed, the product team must consider how the product will work. It must decide on the features to be included with the product. In group medical coverage, issues like network size, network structure, and medical management will typically define whether a product will be a health maintenance organization, preferred provider organization, or some other type of product. In addition to the product type, a very important component to the structure is the inclusion of risk mitigation features. This can be especially challenging for certain types of group insurance products that have the potential for antiselection, such as voluntary dental coverage or products that offer coverage that is relatively rich compared to other insurance coverage.

Variables in Design

The team needs to analyze plan design options, such as coverage duration (very often annual) as well as member cost share. Cost share for group medical insurance could include deductibles, coinsurance, copays, and other cost sharing requirements. Defining the scope of coverage (whether and how to limit coverage in any way) is also considered in the design phase of the product's development. These variables help to refine the idea into a product that can be both marketable and profitable.

Contribution Requirements

The product development team must consider how the product will be marketed and sold. If it is marketed to employer groups, the team should decide if it can be a voluntary benefit that is 100% paid by the employee (which comes with antiselection risk), or if the employer will be required to contribute to the premium (to reduce the risk). Also, there will be antiselection risk if this product will be one of various options available for the employee (for example, dual choice or multi-choice products). The team can create marketing and underwriting requirements around these options in order to manage the risk.

Regulatory compliance

The new or revised product will not go far if it does not comply with insurance regulations. It is critical that the proposed plan and plan features be reviewed by someone well versed in the applicable regulations to verify that the product will comply. For example, guaranteed renewability of a plan is a feature that will make the plan riskier for the insurer, but it may be required for regulators to approve the plan. Also, the development team needs to be aware of minimum loss ratio requirements or benefit mandates that may modify the plans for the product. Early discussions with regulators can often help the product team understand the requirements that must be met and prevent rework later in the process.

BUILDING THE PRODUCT

After the new product or the revision to the existing product has been designed, it is time to begin building the product. To build the product, the company must project enrollment, price the product, perform financial assessments, implement necessary infrastructure, and receive approval from senior management.

Project Enrollment

Now that the product is designed, the team will estimate how many members will purchase this new or modified product. Projection of enrollment is critical to helping senior management decide whether the product is worth pursuing. It is also essential to estimate the volume of claims, as this will likely help determine staffing, reporting, and information technology (IT) requirements associated with the product. Primary market research, as well as surveying the market for similar products, may be used to assess the demand for the product.

Price the Product

There are many challenges associated with pricing a new product. Finding appropriate sources of data is generally a good place to start (for example, finding products with similar structure and design). Determining the necessary assumptions needed to translate the source data into a claim projection, and selecting those assumptions are both important in this step of the process. A consulting firm may also have appropriate data that can be used to price the product. Once initial pricing is completed, the marketing team should reassess its enrollment projection to see if a revision is needed. This is an iterative process, since the projected membership will impact pricing, which will in turn impact projected membership. Part of this step includes an assessment of the market price sensitivity for the type of product being designed.

The projected enrollment will impact the pricing, mainly because of the spreading of fixed costs across members. (Higher projected enrollment will result in a lower required price to achieve the same profit, since fixed costs are spread across more members). In addition, changes to the projected enrollment might imply risk selection, so antiselection must also be reconsidered. The product team must work closely with the pricing team to ensure that pricing and enrollment projections are in sync with each other.

Financial Assessment of Product

Once the projected premium and projected enrollment have been developed, there are a few critical financial measures that a new product will be expected to meet or exceed in order for it to be implemented. Each company has different targets that must be met for a new or revised product to be pursued. A few common measures include return on investment (ROI- the projected profit from the sale of the product over the investment required to build and sell the product), and the return on equity (ROE- the projected profit from the sale of the product over the amount of equity that will be allocated to the product). The finance department is typically charged with performing this analysis and providing the results to senior management for discussion and decisions. If the corporate financial objectives are not met by the projections, then the team must consider what would have to change to meet the objectives. The product must be revised, and these steps must be repeated with the revised product.

Implement Necessary Infrastructure

Before a product can be sold, the company must build the infrastructure necessary to administer the product. This includes the abilities to process claims, bill and collect premium, and service member inquiries. Unique marketing materials, website development, and revisions to existing websites must also be planned. Development of this necessary support may take time, and coordination is needed to ensure that the product release goes smoothly. The product team often oversees the efforts of a cross functional group that includes finance, pricing, information technology, sales, marketing, compliance, actuarial, and other areas. Having their involvement throughout the entire product design process will often prevent unnecessary rework. Also, it is important that the company fully understands what needs to be built and the costs associated with this build, so that it can determine if it is worth the investment. That analysis is part of the ROI assessment mentioned above.

Senior Management Approval

Once all analyses are completed, senior management will decide if they want to proceed with the product. There are typically check points throughout the process, allowing for continuation if the results of each step of the process are positive, and discontinuation if not. If ultimately continued through to full approval, then the company can begin building infrastructure, training sales staff, and preparing marketing material.

SELL THE PRODUCT

Once a product has been fully designed and built, it is time to begin selling the product to the market. However, in many cases before the product is offered in all markets, companies will test market. Test marketing is selling the product to a subset of the market. This is done to ensure that the infrastructure is functional, incorporate consumer feedback, refine pricing assumptions, and to improve the product so that it will be more successful when the product is offered to the full market. Once the necessary revisions are complete and the company is satisfied with the product, the product will be mass marketed.

ASSESS THE PRODUCT

One of the most critical phases of the product development process is assessing the product after it has been sold. The insurer should track the financial results of a new product very closely. As soon as actual experience becomes available, the insurer can begin "actual to expected" studies. These studies compare how the emerging experience compares to what was expected to happen. These studies can indicate that a product was overpriced or underpriced. If the product was underpriced, a reserve may be needed to cover the unfunded liabilities. This is known as a premium deficiency reserve. Additionally, the sooner the actuaries realize that there is a pricing problem, the sooner they can adjust their pricing assumptions, so that ongoing sales are not bringing in additional unprofitable business. If the experience is emerging as better than expected, this may lead to a decrease in the price and an increase in the sales projections.

In addition to assessing the financial results, it is critical to assess the ongoing consumer and market feedback to determine if revisions may enhance the performance and sales of the product. Consumer focus groups and surveys may be used to gather feedback along with discussions with the organization's sales force.

REVISE THE PRODUCT

Based on the ongoing assessments of the product, the teams involved in the product may determine that a revision is necessary. This is part of the ongoing revision and evolution of the product. This may include changes to the product features, plan design, or pricing.

Secular forces will impact a product and require periodic updates to its structure and design, as well as how it gets marketed and sold. Regulatory requirements must be monitored, and changes will often force a new version of the product. Consumer demand also impacts the success of a product, and often dictates which elements of the product that must be changed. During the early 2000s, consumers became dissatisfied with certain medical management features. As a result, preferred provider organizations and other "open access" plans (plans not requiring a primary care physician as a "gatekeeper" to specialty and referral services) increased in popularity.

The ongoing assessment and revisions to a product are often considered product management. Product management is a part of the product development cycle.

TEAMS INVOLVED IN PRODUCT DEVELOPMENT

Product development teams are often responsible for the generation of new product ideas. The product development team will spend a significant amount of time studying the market, including the behaviors of consumers and competitors. However, the product development process takes place during the entire life cycle of a product. Therefore, there are several key players at an insurance company that are involved in product development in addition to the product development team:

Senior Management: Senior management plays a critical role in the product development process. Senior management includes corporate senior management (the Board of Directors, CEO, CFO) as well as the line of business management and segment management. Each of these levels of management set the tone and general direction for new and revised products. In addition, they set the goals that determine if a product meets the minimum requirements to be worth pursuing or continuing. Lastly, senior management is ultimately responsible for making the decision to pursue a proposed idea based on input from the other teams involved in the development of the idea.

Marketing: The marketing teams are focused on the types of advertisements that will attract and retain customers. They build name recognition and branding for companies. When the product development team is vetting an idea, they will often include insights from the marketing team on the types of products that are marketable in the current environment.

Sales: The sales teams work directly with customers and brokers to sell products. Unlike marketing, which is focused on general advertisements, the sales teams are focused on a particular customer and a particular sale. The sales teams often have insights into the price sensitivity of customers as well as the types of products customers may favor.

Underwriters: The underwriting team can help to quantify the risk associated with certain plan features. The databases and research that underwriters use to underwrite business can help shape the product as it is developed.

Information Technology (IT): IT teams can help the product development team understand the feasibility of the infrastructure needed to properly administer a product. In addition, they can help the product development team better understand the risks associated with the launch of the new product. For example, if the product attracts more membership than expected, there could be infrastructure problems that may result in aggravated customers and a tarnished brand name. The IT team can also estimate the costs associated with building up the required infrastructure, or modifying the existing infrastructure to accommodate the new business. These costs are used to determine whether the new product is worth the investment as well as to develop the pricing of the product.

Operations: Operational teams work with the IT teams to create fully operational claim processing, billing and collection, and policyholder administration functions.

Compliance: The compliance team keeps the rest of the teams informed about laws and regulations that govern the product. It is responsible for ensuring that the product is fully compliant with these laws and regulations.

Actuarial: The actuarial teams work on the projections and feasibility studies that help senior management determine if they should proceed with the product. The actuarial teams also perform the pricing and reserving operations that are necessary to keep the product both profitable and fairly priced for the consumer.

Finance: The finance team reviews the projected enrollment, pricing, and the projected capital stream to determine whether the projections meet corporate targets. To advise senior management, the finance team stress tests the assumptions to assess the impact on the company's financial results.

PRODUCT DEVELOPMENT CONSIDERATIONS FOR VARIOUS INSURANCE LINES

While the general process of product development is similar across industries, each line of group insurance benefits will require unique considerations.

Group Medical, Prescription, Dental, Vision: Products under this category are often marketed both to the plan sponsor (who usually pays for much of the cost of the benefits), and the consumer (who might have a choice of products from two or more insurance companies). The Affordable Care Act is dramatically affecting these product lines, and product development will play an essential role in sustaining and growing membership for insurers that offer these products.

Group Disability: Group disability products must be integrated with the plan sponsor's absence management policy. For example, if an absence plan changes from a standard number of sick days per employee to a paid time off (PTO) approach, where vacation and sick days are combined, then adjustments to the disability policies will be necessary.

Group Life: Employer-paid group life insurance benefits can generate imputed (taxable) income for some individuals in the group, and this must be considered when deciding how much life insurance to choose as standard design parameters. Many group life plans involve a combination of employer-paid and employee-paid coverage.

Group Long Term Care (LTC): LTC policies are purchased for events that may not happen for decades. Educational materials that explain the policies and provide some basis for helping the consumer decide how much coverage to purchase are essential.

Retiree Health Care Benefits: Plan sponsors that offer retiree health care benefits must comply with accounting standards that require that they measure and report their other post-employment benefit (OPEB) obligations. These standards include FAS 106, GASB 43 and 45 (soon to be replaced by GASB 74 and 75), and SOP 93-6 for Taft Hartley plans. There can be certain advantages to the plan sponsor's liability by structuring benefits in certain ways, and plan sponsors should be made aware of them.

CONCLUSION

Product development is a critical component to the growth and ongoing success of insurance companies. It is a continuing, cyclical process that allows for the evolution of existing products, and the generation of new products. At each phase of the process, revisions are made based on the insights gained from that step of the process. Along the way, senior management will be involved to determine if the product is worth pursuing further or if development of the product should be stopped for the time being.

4. Health Care Policy and Group Insurance

Sara C. Teppema

Introduction

Health policy can be defined as a field of study and practice in which the priorities and values underlying health resource allocation are determined.[1] Such actions are generally undertaken by governments (national, state/provincial, and local) in order to advance the public's health. However, prioritization and resource allocation is also performed by health insurers, health care providers, employers, and families.

When studying group insurance, health policy is important because of its far-reaching direct and indirect impacts. Governmental health policy can be a model for other types of health policy, such as an insurance company's philosophy on allocation of resources, or an employer's health care strategy. For example, local governmental health policy in the form of public health infrastructure (such as smoking bans in restaurants, construction of bike paths, or subsidies for fresh produce in low-income neighborhoods) can be a model for an employer's health strategy (such as smoking bans on company property, construction of walking paths on a corporate campus, or pricing incentives for healthy choices in the employee cafeteria).

The study of policy also helps illuminate the context within which current health care systems have evolved and will continue to develop. To be effective, public policy initiatives must be founded on careful, objective analysis of economic principles, health care dynamics, and the behavior of individuals and organizations. Debates on public policy take place amid a flurry of often contradictory information, undefined health care needs, financial constraints, and unknown program dynamics. Actuaries add value to the health policy process by applying objective analysis to health policy issues. This analysis may involve developing and testing financial theories relating to the health care system, and projecting reasonable scenarios that show how the health care system would work under alternative circumstances.

This chapter outlines basic principles of health policy, which are the building blocks for the formulation of priorities and resource allocation in any health care system. The chapter briefly discusses health financing in a few other countries, but most of the details and examples focus on the United States health care system.

Three basic principles – better care for individuals, better health for populations, and lower cost – are the building blocks of health policy. In a time of rapidly increasing costs and limited resources, it is also important to understand how these building blocks are financed in various health systems, and thus financing of health care is also discussed in this chapter.

---

[1] http://medical-dictionary.thefreedictionary.com/health+policy, accessed 14 Aug. 2015.

Health Policy Principles

Background

Health policy is grounded in questions of philosophy, politics, and ethics. Is a basic level of quality health care a right or a privilege? What level of expense is justified for medical treatment? Should health insurance be mandatory? Who should finance health care? What role should the government play? How should individuals be held personally accountable for their own health?

Much of the traditional health policy literature has attempted to address these questions by viewing three, often conflicting, elements of health care: high quality, wide access, and low cost. It may be possible for a health care system to achieve two out of the three elements, but it is rare to achieve all three at once. For example, high quality care may not be accessible to all, or if it is accessible, may be expensive.

With the recent implementation of the Affordable Care Act (ACA) in the U.S., the dialogue has shifted from this traditional view of quality, access, and cost, toward a modified paradigm, commonly called "the triple aim"[2] of health policy. This triple aim, adopted by former Centers for Medicare & Medicaid Services (CMS) Administrator Dr. Donald Berwick, consists of the following elements:

1. Better care for individuals
2. Better health for populations
3. Lower per-capita costs

This chapter does not attempt to address the inherent barriers to implementing the triple aim, nor does it explore the improved outcomes that could result from its implementation; rather, this chapter uses the triple aim as a platform to discuss three key policy elements.

Medicare and Medicaid are the two main publicly-funded health care programs in the U.S. and are projected to constitute over one third of national health expenditures in 2015. That share is projected to grow in the future,[3] as will be discussed later in this section. It is significant that Berwick, as the Administrator of these programs, chose to expand his policy focus from looking only at health *care*, which comprises the former paradigm of cost, quality, and access, to add the important element of population health. In other words, health policy must begin to address upstream causes of poor health that lead to a greater need for health care. The remainder of this chapter will go into more detail on each of the elements of the triple aim.

The discussion of the third aim (lower costs) naturally leads into the final section of this chapter on how health care is financed. The financing of health care is separate and distinct from health care costs. This fact may be obvious to some, but the concept of health care *financing*, or how health care is paid for (for example, through insurance premiums or the

---

[2] Donald M. Berwick, Thomas W. Nolan, and John Whittington. "The Triple Aim: Care, Health, and Cost." *Health Affairs*, 27, no.3 (2008): 759-769.
[3] Sean P. Keehan, Gigi A. Cuckler, Andrea M. Sisko, Andrew J. Madison, Sheila D. Smith, Devin A. Stone, John A. Poisal, Christian J. Wolfe, and Joseph M. Lizonitz. National Health Expenditure Projections, 2014-24: Spending Growth Faster than Recent Trends, *Health Affairs*, July 2015.

Medicare program) is frequently interchanged with the concept of the *cost* of health care (the amounts that providers are compensated for providing that care).

Health policy principles may not seem to have a clear intersection with group insurance, but these principles are in fact very important in that they frame the overall view of the health care marketplace and the public health infrastructure. In addition, these principles can be applied when planning a group insurance program for an insurer or employer.

BETTER CARE FOR INDIVIDUALS

Improving care for individual patients must begin with a focus on health care quality. The quality of health care is widely discussed, yet a concrete and consistent definition remains elusive. Many organizations focus on health care quality, including measurement and reporting of quality. The Society of Actuaries' report on quality and efficiency[4] includes an extensive inventory of quality programs, including the following:

- The Agency for Healthcare Research and Quality (AHRQ), an agency of the Department of Health and Human Services (HHS). AHRQ's mission is to improve the quality, safety, efficiency, and effectiveness of health care for all Americans.
- National Quality Forum (NQF), a nonprofit organization that builds consensus among health care stakeholders regarding national priorities and goals.
- National Committee for Quality Assurance (NCQA), a nonprofit organization that assesses and measures health care organizations through accreditation and recognition programs. NCQA also administers the Healthcare Effectiveness Data and Information Set (HEDIS), a tool to measure health plan performance on important dimensions of care and service.

Many other quality programs also exist within health plans, provider organizations, and other outside organizations.

In order to frame the discussion of health care quality, we look to the Institute of Medicine's (IOM's) 2001 often cited report "Crossing the Quality Chasm."[5] IOM's report lists six required dimensions that are characteristics of health care performance. Health care must be safe, effective, patient-centered, timely, efficient, and equitable.

Safety

Health care must avoid injuries to patients from the care that is intended to help them. Adverse events at hospitals may occur in one-third of all hospital admissions.[6] Based on a

---

[4] Greger Vigen, Sheryl Coughlin, and Ian Duncan. *Measurement of Healthcare Quality and Efficiency: Resources for Healthcare Professionals, From Measurement to Improved Performance, Third Update.* Society of Actuaries, 2013, https://soa.org/research/research-projects/health/research-quality-report.aspx, accessed 14 Aug. 2015.
[5] Institute of Medicine, *Crossing the Quality Chasm: A New Health System for the 21st Century.*(Washington: National Academies Press, 2001).
[6] David C. Classen, Roger Resar, Frances Griffin, Frank Federico, Terri Frankel, Nancy Kimmel, John C. Whittington, Allan Frankel, Andrew Seger, and Brent C. James, Global Trigger Tool Shows That Adverse Events In Hospitals May Be Ten Times Greater Than Previously Measured, Health Affairs, 30, no.4 (2011): 581-589.

2010 Society of Actuaries study conducted by Milliman, approximately 6.3 million medical injuries occurred in the U.S. in 2008. Of these, 1.5 million are estimated to be associated with a medical errors, at a total cost of $19.5 billion in cost for medical errors.[7] Note that medical injury is not necessarily the same as medical error; an error is a special case of an injury. Injuries can nonetheless frequently be avoided.

In 2006, NQF published a list of "Never Events", adverse events that are unambiguous (clearly identifiable and measurable), serious (resulting in death or significant disability), and usually preventable.[8] Medicare has adopted the policy to not pay providers for eight of these events (and providers are not allowed to bill patients for these events either). Medicare's list of Never Events includes wrong-site surgeries, transfusion with the wrong blood type, pressure ulcers (bedsores), falls or trauma, and nosocomial infections (hospital-acquired infections) associated with surgeries or catheters.

Effectiveness

Health care must provide services based on scientific knowledge to all who could benefit, and refrain from providing services to those not likely to benefit (avoiding underuse and overuse, respectively).

Considerable attention has lately been paid to the concept of comparative effectiveness and comparative effectiveness research (CER). According to the IOM,[9]

> CER is the generation and synthesis of evidence that compares the benefits and harms of alternative methods to prevent, diagnose, treat, and monitor a clinical condition or to improve the delivery of care. The purpose of CER is to assist consumers, clinicians, purchasers, and policy makers to make informed decisions that will improve health care at both the individual and population levels.

An interesting case in comparative effectiveness played out in late 2009 and early 2010, when the U.S. Preventive Services Task Force (USPSTF) changed its recommendations on routine mammography. The revised recommendation stated that most women should not receive routine mammography scans until age 50, rather than at age 40 as had been previously recommended. The revised recommendation also reduced the recommended frequency of scans to every two years, from once a year. This change caused considerable controversy between several parties: researchers, who weighed several factors in the revised recommendation; health care providers, who saw both the pros and cons of less frequent screenings; and patients, who were concerned that insurers may reduce benefits for screenings.[10] Some insurers have followed the USPSTF guidelines in providing coverage of screenings, but may others decided to continue to cover screenings more liberally than the USPSTF guidelines. This demonstrates that comparative effectiveness research is one

---

[7] Jonathan L. Shreve, Jill Van Den Bos, Travis Gray, Michael Halford, Karan Rustagi, Eva Ziemkiewica, *The Economic Measurement of Medical Errors*, (Society of Actuaries, 2010).
[8] http://psnet.ahrq.gov/primer.aspx?primerID=3, accessed 15 Aug. 2015.
[9] Institute of Medicine, *Initial National Priorities for Comparative Effectiveness Research*, (Washington: National Academies Press, 2009).
[10] At the time of this writing, the USPSTF had issued updated draft guidelines, which reaffirmed its 2009 guidelines, but added that screenings in the 40-49 age range should be individualized. A summary of these draft recommendations by the AAFP can be found at this link: http://www.aafp.org/news/health-of-the-public/20150424mammograms.html, accessed 15 Aug., 2015.

consideration in health policy, weighed with other considerations such as provider and patient backlash, public relations, and cost.

Patient Centeredness

Health care should be respectful of and responsive to individual patient preferences, needs, and values, and should ensure that patient values guide all clinical decisions.

Patient centeredness includes the concept of the patient experience. The patient experience is not defined as patient *satisfaction*, such as how much a patient likes his or her physician or how nicely decorated the waiting room is. Rather, patient *experience* focuses on whether care was provided as it should have been, whether the patient understands the diagnosis and treatment, and whether the patient's values were accounted for in medical decision making.

A common manifestation of patient-centeredness is the concept of a Patient Centered Medical Home (PCMH), a model of primary care that delivers care that is patient-centered, comprehensive, coordinated, accessible, and continuously improved through a systems-based approach to quality and safety. Health Information Technology, workforce development, and payment reform are critical to achieving the potential of the PCMH.[11] The ACA included several pilot programs for PCMHs in Medicare and Medicaid, and this model is beginning to grow in the commercially insured market.

Timeliness

Health care should strive to reduce wait times and delays that can be harmful for both those who receive care and those who give care. Health care quality is improved by making the best use of the patient's and the provider's time.

Related to timeliness is the concept of health care access, or the ability for an individual to seek and receive health care services when they are needed. Many factors can impact an individual's ability to seek and receive health care, including geographic location, technology challenges, available transportation, cultural barriers, and ability to pay. These factors should not provide a barrier to timely care.

Efficiency

Health care should avoid waste, including waste of equipment, supplies, ideas, and energy. In addition to avoidance of waste, efficiency includes avoidance of unnecessary care. Structuring incentives to avoid waste and unnecessary care is viewed by many as the crucial next policy focus in the U.S., now that implementation of the ACA has greatly increased system access. The U.S. may spend as much as one third of its health care dollars on care that does nothing to improve health.[12]

Currently the U.S. health care system has many structural incentives that encourage, rather than discourage, waste and unnecessary care. These incentives include (but are not limited to) the following:

---

[11] http://www.pcmh.ahrq.gov/portal/server.pt/community/pcmh__home/1483/what_is_pcmh_
[12] Shannon Brownlee, *Overtreated: Why Too Much Medicine Is Making Us Sicker and Poorer*. (Bloomsbury USA, New York, 2007).

- Fee-for-service payment systems, which pay providers for each service they perform, rather than paying providers for outcomes. Alternative payment systems that pay higher amounts for better outcomes, or that pay a "bundled" amount for an episode of care, may help reduce waste and unnecessary care. New models of care, such as the Accountable Care Organizations and PCMHs, may also help shift payment incentives by having providers take on more financial risk based to an increasing degree on patient outcomes.

- Third-party payment, such as from an insurance company or Medicare, shields the ultimate consumer (the patient) from the cost of the service, and can discourage efficient use of funds.

- Fear of litigation can encourage health care providers to perform unnecessary services.

Equity

Health care should not vary in quality because of personal characteristics such as gender, ethnicity, geographic location, and socioeconomic status. Yet, wide disparities in the delivery of health care among varying populations continue to exist.

Equity in health care also relates to access to care, such that health policy should seek to ensure that all populations have similar access to needed health care services, regardless of key population factors:

- Payer – individuals with public health care assistance such as Medicaid should not be restricted to lower quality providers, or providers who place such patients as a lower priority for appointment times, etc.

- Geographic location – not all neighborhoods or regions have an appropriate balance of health care providers or facilities.

- Race and culture – Race and cultural heritage should never be factors in an individual's ability to receive needed care.

BETTER HEALTH FOR POPULATIONS

According to the World Health Organization, "Health is a state of complete physical, mental, and social well-being and not merely the absence of disease or infirmity."[13] In other words, the concept of health is much broader than whether an individual receives appropriate medical care.

Because of this broad definition of good health, health policy can reach beyond the individual and address health at the level of larger populations. Populations can be defined in many ways, such as by geography, age, health insurance coverage, or race. Such definitions can be as narrowly defined as "early retirees of XYZ corporation" for, say, a wellness program; or as broad as "Citizens of Sweden in 2011" for, say, a public health anti-smoking campaign.

At the broadest and most public level, health policy should address the upstream causes of ill health through public health initiatives that enable healthier populations and enable individuals

---

[13] http://www.who.int/about/definition/en/print.html, accessed 15 Aug., 2015.

to make better choices about their own health. Some of these upstream causes are discussed below.

Environmental Factors

A significant contributor to good or poor health at the population level is the population's physical environment. The discipline of public health has studied environmental factors at length and has identified several key areas that must be addressed before a population can achieve good health. These include (but are not limited to) the following:

- Lack of sanitized water;
- Pollution, in the air and water;
- Violence - including domestic, street, and gun violence;
- Unhealthy living environment, such as housing that is unsafe or infested with mold, insects, or rodents;
- Food-borne illnesses; and
- Lack of access to fresh, healthy foods that often occur in inner city neighborhoods or rural areas (dubbed "food deserts").

Community Disease Prevention

Another significant population and public health factor is a community's level of commitment to prevent disease. Like environmental factors, this covers a broad category of activities, but includes activities and programs such as childhood immunization requirements, free or reduced flu shots, free or reduced preventive screenings, hand washing programs in schools, and other public awareness campaigns.

Lifestyle

The U.S. is in the midst of an obesity epidemic: in 2011-2012 about 35% of the U.S. adult population had Body Mass Index (BMI) greater than or equal to 30.[14] In addition, 17% of children aged 2 to 19 were obese in 2011-2012. Although the rate of childhood obesity has declined recently, general obesity is a major public health concern, because it can lead to chronic conditions such as diabetes, heart disease, musculoskeletal conditions, some cancers, and other illnesses. Obesity is not solely a U.S. phenomenon. Worldwide obesity has more than doubled since 1980, and obesity is a leading risk for global deaths.[15]

Health policy can enable healthier lifestyle choices with policies and funding for programs such as healthy school lunches, safe pedestrian walkways, bicycle paths, fresh produce to areas difficult to reach, and taxes on unhealthy foods such as sugary beverages.

Smoking and Substance Abuse

Tobacco use can be classified as a lifestyle issue, but it is also a substance abuse issue, since tobacco's addictive nature makes it difficult to quit. Smoking rates have declined over many

---

[14] www.cdc.gov/obesity/data/trends.html, accessed 15 Aug. 2015.
[15] www.who.int/mediacentre/factsheets/fs311/en/, accessed 15 Aug. 2015.

years, and have recently leveled off at about 19% of the U.S. population. According to the Centers for Disease Control and Prevention (CDC), rates of smoking are highest among the most vulnerable populations, especially the poor and less educated.[16]

Smoking contributes to a host of health problems, including heart disease, lung disease, and various cancers. In addition, secondhand smoke can be especially harmful to children.

Anti-smoking laws can be effective. For example, since California adopted a long-running tobacco control program, its smoking rate has dropped nearly 50%.[17]

Other forms of substance use, including alcoholism and drug addiction, also contribute to poor health.

Socioeconomic Factors

The fact that income is directly related to poor health has been widely discussed but is difficult to address. Social insurance programs such as Medicaid provide health care coverage for low-income people. However, access to quality providers can be challenging for people on Medicaid, since reimbursements to providers for Medicaid patients are typically lower than commercial or Medicare reimbursements. In addition, poverty can place great stress on an individual or family in many ways, and many studies have shown that high stress contributes to poor health.

Wellness and Disease Management Solutions

At a more granular level, public health concepts can be applied to smaller populations, such as employer-sponsored health plan participants or insured populations. Disease management and wellness programs have become common among employers and insurers. These programs range from targeted disease management programs, in which a nurse or coach keeps in touch with identified patients who have opted into the program, to employer strategies around wellness, disease prevention, and disease management that permeate the entire corporate structure and environment. Such programs might include mandatory or highly incentivized participation in health risk assessments that can identify risk factors in employees and their families before the disease manifests itself. They may also include strategies and programs around smoking, diet, fitness, or weight loss. Some employers reward employees for their participation, some penalize for non-participation, and some just make programs available for anyone interested.

LOWER PER CAPITA COSTS

The third element of the triple aim is lower per capita costs. Health care is an expensive part of every economy, especially in the U.S. The significance of health care within an economy is frequently measured by the percentage of the Gross Domestic Product (GDP) of a country that is represented by health expenditures. The health expenditures-to-GDP portion is nearly one-and-one-half times higher in the U.S. than in all other countries that are part of the

---

[16] www.cdc.gov/vitalsigns/AdultSmoking/index.html#Risk, accessed 15 Aug. 2015.
[17] http://www.tobaccofreeca.com/successes/highlights/, accessed 15 Aug. 2015.

Organization for Economic Cooperation and Development (OECD).[18] Furthermore, health expenditures have grown faster than the rest of the economy and consume a greater and greater portion of the GDP in almost every country over the past several years.

Health care growth historically outpaces economic growth in the OECD countries, as evidenced by the growth in health care's share of GDP in almost all periods for almost all countries. Representative OECD countries are shown in Figure 3.1.

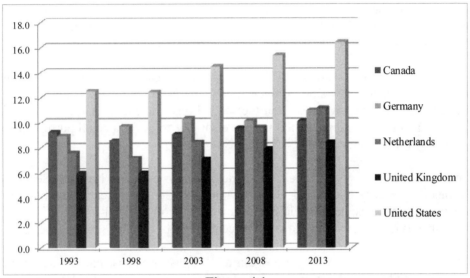

Figure 4.1

The U.S. stands out among other countries in terms of the substantially higher portion of GDP taken up by health. These high costs have rendered health care unaffordable for many, either because health insurance premiums are too high, or because they cannot afford the out-of-pocket costs of care. Yet, for the cost of health care, outcomes are not measurably better in the U.S. and could even be deemed worse: the U.S. lags most other OECD countries in indicators such as life expectancy and infant mortality.

U.S. employers are struggling to continue to provide health insurance to their employees as health insurance costs take up a larger and larger portion of their budget, and many find it hard to compete globally because of health insurance costs for active and retired employees.

---

[18] Source: Organization for Economic Co-operation and Development (OECD), OECD Health Data Frequently Requested Data File, http://www.oecd.org/health/health-systems/oecd-health-statistics-2014-frequently-requested-data.htm, accessed 15 Aug. 2015.

Financing of Health Care

The last section looked at health care spending as a percent of GDP in the U.S. and other countries. It is instructive to note the various mechanisms of financing the health economies of the U.S. and other countries.

Financing in Other Systems

In most countries, health care is financed by a combination of public and private sources. These combinations can range from primarily public funding, such as in Canada or England, where most health care is paid for by tax revenues; to primarily private funding, such as in Germany, where most health care is paid by employer and employee-funded non-government (albeit highly regulated) health insurance pools.[19]

In Canada's health care system, all Canadians have access to provincial health care. Canada's provinces are the single payers and administrators of care, and they receive funding from general tax revenues from the federal government. In addition, roughly two-thirds of Canadians have supplemental private insurance to cover a small portion of services not covered by the provincial plans.

The English health care system is also a single-payer system. The National Health Service (NHS), funded primarily by general taxes, pays private General Practitioners, hospital-based specialists, and public hospitals. In addition, a mix of for-profit and not-for-profit insurers cover supplemental services, amounting to a small percentage of the country's total spending.

In contrast to the publicly-financed Canadian and English systems, the German health care system is financed by private Statutory Health Insurance (SHI) funds (called "sickness funds"), which are non-governmental, non-profit bodies regulated by law. There are about 180 SHI funds nationally, and they are funded by compulsory wage-based contributions from employers and employees, with a complex risk adjustment system.[20] About 10% of Germans are exempt from SHI and are required to purchase insurance from private health insurers.

In the Netherlands, health insurance coverage is mandatory and provided by private health insurers. The statutory health insurance system is financed by a mixture of income-related contributions and premiums paid by the insured, and employers must reimburse their employees for this contribution. The Dutch system, like the German system, has a sophisticated risk adjustment system for private insurance premiums.[21] This employer-funded system is supplemented significantly by general tax revenues contributed by the

---

[19] D. Squires, International Profiles of Health Care Systems, The Commonwealth Fund, June 2010. www.commonwealthfund.org/Publications/Fund-Reports/2010/Jun/International-Profiles-of-Health-Care-Systems.aspx#citation, accessed 15 Aug. 2015.
[20] P. Fleischacker, A. McLure, S. Mateja, J. Meidlinger, Health Care Reform: Learning from Others: Germany, *Contingencies,* January/February 2010, American Academy of Actuaries. www.contingenciesonline.com/contingenciesonline/20100102?sub_id=qxyLfphSqUiJ#pg42, accessed 15 Aug. 2015
[21] Ian Duncan, Health Care Reform: Learning from Others: Netherlands, *Contingencies,* November/December 2009, American Academy of Actuaries. www.contingenciesonline.com/contingenciesonline/20091112?sub_id=qxyLfphSqUiJ#pg54, accessed 15 Aug. 2015

Dutch government, including coverage for all children under age 18. The Dutch system bears the closest resemblance to the system that is blueprinted by the Affordable Care Act.

Financing in the U.S.

As discussed, the U.S. system is a mix of public and private funding. In the U.S., public health financing is made up primarily of Medicare (federal funding) and Medicaid (federal and state funding). Medicare covers elderly and disabled, and Medicaid covers lower income children and adults.

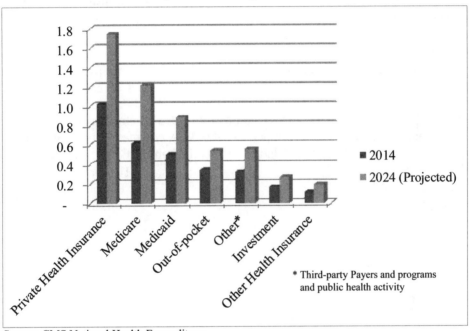

Figure 4.2

Figure 3.2, based on CMS' National Health Expenditure Projections,[22] shows the sources of funding of health care in the U.S. Spending in all categories is projected to increase substantially from 2014 to 2024. Also, the portion of the total that is paid for by public sources Medicare and Medicaid is projected to grow from 36% in 2014 to 39% in 2024. Taking into account the state and federal sponsorship of health care as employers, over 50% of the U.S. health care system will be financed by public funds within a few years.

Private health insurance accounts for about one third of U.S. National Health Expenditures, just over $1 trillion in 2014. Most health insurance is sponsored by employers on behalf of their employees, with a portion of the premiums paid by the employer and the remaining portion paid by the employee.

---

[22] Sean P. Keehan, Gigi A. Cuckler, Andrea M. Sisko, Andrew J. Madison, Sheila D. Smith, Devin A. Stone, John A. Poisal, Christian J. Wolfe and Joseph M. Lizonitz, National Health Expenditure Projections, 2014–24: Spending Growth Faster than Recent Trends, *Health Affairs*, July 2015.

CONCLUSION: GROUP INSURANCE IN A NEW POLICY ENVIRONMENT

The passage and implementation of the ACA in the U.S. has introduced many new challenges to all major stakeholders in the U.S.: patients/consumers, insurers, providers, and policymakers. The law has changed the way insurance is priced, approved, administered, purchased, sold, and regulated.

Several provisions in the new law are particularly relevant and will be challenging for group insurers and raise many questions: How effective will the employer and individual mandates be in reducing the uninsured? How will shifts in public funding impact the private market, and vice versa? What is the future of employer-sponsored health insurance? How will the health insurance market change in terms of corporate competition and consolidation? Will new models of provider payment improve quality and bend the cost curve? How will wellness, disease management, and lifestyle incentives impact the health of the population and its costs? How can benefit designs be structured to make health insurance appropriate yet affordable?

All of these questions will have complicated answers that will emerge over the next several years as the many direct and indirect impacts of the ACA emerge. More details on the ACA are supplied throughout this text in relation to specific topics; Chapter 18 summarizes the entire law.

SECTION TWO

GROUP INSURANCE BENEFITS

5   Medical Benefits in the United States

Darrell D. Knapp

Group medical benefits have grown to be the predominant group insurance coverage in the United States, both in terms of premium dollars and covered lives. In 2013, more than 169 million people received employment-based health insurance, representing 54% of the population.[1] Although this is down some from prior periods due to economic conditions and citizens aging into Medicare, it still is the primary source of health care coverage in the U.S. Medical benefit plans include all coverages that facilitate the provision of medical services to individuals. Some plans that provide medical services directly (service benefits) and others pay for expenses incurred related to medical care (indemnity benefits).

Service benefits typically involve some restrictions of provider selection and assure no additional cost to the insured beyond the designated deductible, copay, or coinsurance.[2] Blue Cross originated as a service benefit provider, providing for hospital care at designated hospitals in return for a periodic prepayment. Modern day health maintenance organizations (HMOs) are another example of service benefit plans.

In contrast, *indemnity benefit plans* typically involve limited or no provider restrictions and were designed to indemnify (or insure) members for expenses that they incur when using health care facilities and providers. The expenses are reviewed to determine if they qualify for coverage under the indemnity policy, and the claim is adjudicated for payment.

Benefit plans involving the provision of services or reimbursement for services related to dental care, vision care, hearing care, and prescription drugs not covered under the main medical care program (often called stand-alone prescription drug programs) will be covered in later chapters in the book.

The growth of medical benefit plans has been largely aided by favorable federal income tax treatment of benefits. Under the U.S. Internal Revenue Code, employer payments for medical insurance or benefits generally do not generate taxable income to the employee, meaning that the dollars the employer pays for a group medical plan are of greater value to the employee than dollars paid directly to the employee, which would then be taxable.

This tax advantage has become a double-edged sword. Many employee benefit plans now provide benefits for services that go beyond the theoretical definition of an *insurable event*.

---

[1] U.S. Census Bureau, *Health Insurance Coverage in the United States: 2013*.
[2] The term "coinsurance" refers to a percentage of cost split between the payer and the member. It may refer to either the payer's share or the member's share of the costs. Where specificity is required and the context is otherwise unclear, this text uses terms such as "payer coinsurance" or "member coinsurance" to identify which party is responsibility for paying a given coinsurance amount.

Theoretically, an insurance system will only be effective if benefits are provided for events that are random, catastrophic in nature to the beneficiary, and outside the control of the insured. If these conditions are not present, there is no insurable event and the system is subject to a level of antiselection that may cause the system to fail. Logically, this requirement would lead the health insurance industry to provide coverage only for non-routine, non-budgetable services that result in the incurral of significant expense. However, the impact of tax policy has led the industry down an entirely different path where benefits are often provided on a first-dollar basis for routine events such as annual physicals and immunizations. Recent legislative actions, including a requirement that certain preventive services be covered with no cost-sharing, have further removed health insurance in the U.S. from the true concept of insurance. Preventive services fail all of the conditions of an insurable event, in that they are not random, are not catastrophic, and are entirely within the control of the insured.

One recent detour from that path is the tax treatment for Health Savings Accounts (HSA) and Health Reimbursement Arrangements (HRA). Under those programs, a high deductible health plan (HDHP) is typically[3] coupled with a spending account that can carry over from year to year. Tax benefits accrue to both the insurance program and the spending accounts, placing this combination of programs on a similar tax footing as a traditional medical program. The primary theory behind these programs is that by returning some of the financial consequences for utilization of health care to the individual, wiser consumption of resources will occur. This could take the form of consumers looking for more cost-effective (or lower cost) providers, or consumers choosing to forego discretionary medical services. A side benefit is that the insured portion of the program more clearly has an element of requiring an insurable event.

DIMENSIONS OF A MEDICAL PLAN

Compared to many years ago, when all medical benefit plans were somewhat similar, there is currently a wide variety of the types and structures of medical benefit plans available in the marketplace. However, in an effort to describe broadly all medical benefit plans, it is possible to define any given medical benefit plan by its position on each of three dimensions or continuums. The first dimension is the definition of covered services and the conditions under which those services will be covered. The second dimension is the degree to which the insured individual participates in the cost of covered expenses or services received, commonly referred to as cost sharing. The third dimension relates to relationships with the providers, including the breadth of the network and the degree to which the provider of services participates in the risk related to the cost of services.

THE FIRST DIMENSION

The definition of services covered and conditions under which they are covered include the following elements:

- Definition of incurral date
- Covered services, limitations and exclusions

---

[3] HSAs must be accompanied with an HDHP. HRAs are typically paired with an HDHP, but could be used with other types of medical coverage that have high cost sharing provisions (for example, a $1,000 inpatient copay).

- Covered facilities
- Covered professional services
- Other covered services.

Incurral Date

In order to receive medical benefits, coverage must generally be in effect on the date on which contractual liability to pay for that service occurs. That date is referred to as the incurral date of the benefits. Medical benefit plans have a variety of definitions of incurral date. The most common definition is the *date of service* (for professional services) and the *date of admission* (for inpatient hospital services). A more limiting definition of incurral date is date of service for all covered services. This definition could result in denying a portion of a hospital charge, if coverage lapsed while a covered individual was actually in the hospital.

A less limiting definition would have contractual liability attached at the *date of onset of a disability*. This definition would result in all claims related to a given disability or illness to be said to be incurred at the first date of that disability. Under this type of provision, the definition of disability can vary widely, from being unable to perform the normal functions of a similarly situated person such as returning to work, to requiring continued institutionalization. This type of definition of incurral date is commonly used for plans that provide disability type benefits, such as disability income policies or long-term care policies, but it is not common in medical benefits, though the same timing concept can be used in applying exclusions of medical benefit coverage.

Another alternative definition has contractual liability attached at the *date a claim was paid*. Excess risk or stop-loss policies commonly attach liability on either a "paid" basis or a "paid and service date" basis. For example, many stop-loss contracts accumulate claims on a basis such as incurred in 12, paid in 15. This definition requires that a valid claim be both incurred during a 12-month period (generally the policy year), and paid or submitted for payment in a coinciding 15-month period (that is, within three months from the end of the policy year).

In addition to the definition of when liability attaches on an ongoing basis, many contracts include a provision that extends benefits in the event that an individual is disabled at contract termination. This type of provision is usually stated either in terms of a number of days from the date of termination, provided an individual remains disabled under a normal activities definition of disability, or until the end of an institutional stay beginning prior to coverage termination. The benefits covered under an *extended benefit provision* are normally limited to medical services related specifically to that disability and subject to the availability of other insurance. For example, if an individual receiving benefits under this provision due to a disability from a heart condition were to be injured in an accident, the charges stemming from that injury would not be covered. Likewise, if an individual has new coverage that replaces the terminated coverage, the extended benefits provision may not be applicable.

Covered Services, Limitations, and Exclusions

In addition to determining whether coverage exists as of the date the claim is incurred, it must also be determined if a given medical service is covered. Many *covered services*, and limitations or exclusions to those covered services, are subject to regulatory requirements that can differ broadly, depending on the regulatory entity that has jurisdiction over a given medical benefit plan:

- Insured medical plans are regulated by the state Departments of Insurance, which have varying mandated benefits in spite of efforts by the National Association of Insurance Commissioners (NAIC) to encourage similar legislation from state to state.

- Self-funded plans are broadly regulated by the Department of Labor under the Employee Retirement Income Security Act (ERISA) that has very few specific references to covered services and limitations. Some states regulate certain aspects of self-funded plans that are not pre-empted by federal ERISA regulation.

- The regulatory bodies for HMOs vary from state to state, sometimes being the Insurance Department, and sometimes being another entity. This creates a potentially varying set of benefit requirements for an HMO plan than for an indemnity plan. On a benefit-by-benefit basis, HMO benefit requirements may be either more restrictive or more liberal than those of insured plans.

- The federal government has begun adding an additional level of regulation, through legislation specifying certain benefit provisions and operational practices, such as mental health parity and minimum stay requirements for maternity.

- As the Affordable Care Act (ACA) has been implemented, the level of federal regulation regarding covered benefits has significantly increased. Changes due to the ACA include coverage of a standardized set of preventive services at 100%, prohibition of lifetime and annual limits, and plan design limits on the maximum annual out-of-pocket cost when using in-network providers. In addition, the ACA defined a set of *essential health benefits* that must be included in any plan sold in the individual and small group markets.[4] Although the specifics of the essential health benefits vary by state, the ACA requires coverage of the following broad categories of medical services in every state:
  o Ambulatory patient services
  o Emergency services
  o Hospitalization
  o Maternity and newborn care
  o Mental health and substance abuse disorder services, including behavioral health treatment
  o Prescription drugs
  o Rehabilitative and habilitative services and devices
  o Laboratory services
  o Preventive and wellness services and chronic disease management
  o Pediatric dental and vision care.

Covered Facilities

Covered facilities can include acute care inpatient hospital facilities, emergency rooms, outpatient hospital and surgery facilities, inpatient or outpatient psychiatric facilities, inpatient or outpatient alcohol and drug treatment programs, skilled nursing facilities or nursing homes, and home health care.

---

[4] Excepting plans that have been designated as, and maintained, grandfathered status since 2010.

Hospital inpatient services include all services by a hospital related to inpatient medical, surgical, and maternity admissions. Benefits are typically limited to the cost of average semi-private room and board charges, and related ancillary charges. Reimbursement for intensive care units and recovery rooms are often limited to a multiple of the average semi-private cost. Treatment must occur in an appropriately licensed and certified facility.

Inpatient facility services may require some sort of *pre-certification* or *concurrent review* by the benefit plan administrator in order to be covered. Pre-certification generally requires that the covered member or their physician contact the plan administrator to obtain pre-approval of the number of days of the hospital stay; approval is based on the medical appropriateness of the admission and the requested length of stay. Failure to comply with pre-certification requirements may result in a cutback of benefits payable, ranging from a fixed dollar amount (such as $500) to a percent of the total charges (such as 50%).

Emergency room services often have some limitations to avoid excess utilization. Limitations frequently involve defining emergency as requiring a treatment event such as the administration of an intravenous needle, life-threatening illness, treatment due to accidental injury, or a condition that requires admission to the hospital.

Facility charges for outpatient surgery may be covered in full or may require deductibles, coinsurance, or copays. Outpatient surgery is often mandatory for a defined list of procedures in an effort to discourage unnecessary hospital admissions, and may be subject to pre-certification requirements. Another method to encourage the use of outpatient surgery is to design the health plan with decreased member cost sharing relative to inpatient benefits.

Charges related to psychiatric admissions and alcohol and drug treatment are typically required to be performed in a facility or by a provider licensed for that particular service. In 1996, the federal government passed legislation restricting the types of limits allowed on many benefit plans. This legislation prohibits fixed dollar benefit maximums. However, that legislation still allowed programs to limit the level of reimbursement available or the number of services provided. Subsequent federal mental health parity legislation has required that internal coverage maximums, visit limits, and member cost sharing for mental health conditions be comparable to those for other medical services. The ACA extended federal mental health parity requirements to the small employer and individual marketplaces.

Skilled nursing facility charges are generally covered if performed by a licensed facility providing skilled nursing care, as opposed to custodial care. Limitations include that the admission is in lieu of hospitalization and that the patient is showing improvement. This is in contrast to long-term care insurance, which often provides coverage based on a deficiency in the ability to perform specified activities of daily living or on the medical necessity of custodial (non-acute) care. These requirements severely limit the breadth of available coverage for long-term care services included in traditional medical benefit plans.

Coverage for home health care services is also limited to those services performed in lieu of other required treatment. Home health care services beyond those covered by the medical benefit plan are often approved by a case manager working on behalf of the plan administrator, if the services are deemed to be more cost-effective than other covered services.

Certain programs attempt to direct the insured to a specific facility through either varying the level of available benefit (such as in a preferred-provider organization or PPO), or through limiting coverage only to specified providers (such as in a closed-panel HMO). This direction is generally coupled with provider contracts favorable to the insurer, which creates a less expensive product for the consumer. Some carriers are currently experimenting with tiered benefit plans that charge the insured lower cost sharing for preferred hospitals.

Covered Professional Services

Coverage for professional services is generally limited to licensed or board-certified providers. Covered providers are explicitly defined in the benefit plan and may exclude certain provider types, such as dentists, chiropractors, naturopaths, or podiatrists. These exclusions are often limited by state mandates requiring coverage for certain providers.

Coverage for professional services related to surgery includes surgeries performed on an inpatient, outpatient, and office basis. Coverage for outpatient or office surgery frequently will include a list of procedures for which surgery is required to be performed on that basis. Other typical limits include a provision reducing the provider's payment for multiple procedures and limits on the charges from an assistant surgeon, such as paying at a reduced percentage fee schedule or refusing to pay at teaching hospitals where interns are readily available as assistant surgeons. Charges related to anesthesia are typically covered with similar limits.

Covered services provided by physicians may include office visits, home visits, hospital visits, emergency room visits, and preventive care. Hospital visits are generally limited to one visit per day and are usually assumed to be included in surgical fees if the visit is a follow-up to a surgical procedure. Physicians' charges in the emergency room are often subject to the same restrictions as emergency room facility charges. Visits related to preventive care were not historically covered by many insurance plans, but were generally covered by HMOs. The ACA now requires preventive services without cost to the member. The rationale for not covering preventive benefits historically had been that a preventive office visit is a small expenditure in which utilization is controlled by the individual obtaining the service, and thus does not meet the definition of an insurable event. This results in coverage for preventive physician visits being somewhat inappropriate for a true insurance contract, but entirely appropriate for an employee benefit plan. Conversely, managed care plans assert that these preventive services, which the insurer may forgo if not covered, ultimately reduce the cost of medical care through prevention and early detection and interdiction of medical conditions.

Services for an obstetrician or a gynecologist are generally covered as any other provider. Physician services related to a pregnancy are covered comparably to facility charges.

Additional professional services include consultations (which may require referral), outpatient psychiatric treatment, outpatient alcohol and drug treatment, physical therapy (which may include a requirement to establish improvement or anticipated improvement in a defined period), and immunizations and injections.

Certain benefit plans attempt to direct the insured to a given set of providers, in a fashion similar to that discussed earlier. In addition, some plans require that certain conditions be met before coverage is available. The most common example of this is referred to as a *gatekeeper requirement.* This is where an insured designates a primary care physician. Then all access to other covered services requires a referral from that designated physician.

The selection of providers to be included in an insurer's "preferred" list involves contracting with those providers and a process called *credentialing.* The credentialing process includes assuring the provider meets the licensing, quality, and efficiency standards of the insuring organization. After the initial contracting stage, providers periodically go through a similar process of *recredentialing* to assure the standards continue to be met. Some carriers use stronger recredentialing requirements to replace or loosen gatekeeper referral requirements.

Other Covered Services

Other covered services under medical contracts typically include diagnostic, X-ray and lab, prescription drugs, appliances and durable medical equipment, ambulance services, private duty nursing, and wellness benefits.

Plans covering just prescription drugs have become their own industry. Prescription drug benefits are often part of a freestanding drug program that includes a separate deductible or a schedule of copayments for each prescription. Other common provisions include requiring use of mail order services for maintenance drugs, and incentives or requirements to use generic drugs when available. Another facet of prescription drug coverage is the inclusion or the exclusion of oral contraceptives. This expense is typically felt to be an uninsurable event, yet is considered a valuable benefit in an employee benefit plan. Oral contraceptives are required to be provided in a number of states, and the ACA has now included oral contraceptives as part of the preventive services category.

Coverage related to appliances and durable medical equipment is usually centered around a decision whether it would be more economical to rent or purchase a given apparatus. Durable medical equipment purchases frequently require the approval of a case manager acting on behalf of the plan administrator to assure benefit dollars are spent judiciously.

Coverage related to ambulance services normally contains a provision providing transportation to the nearest facility and may have special conditions on the use of an air ambulance.

Private duty nursing coverage is generally provided only in the event that such service is in lieu of other more expensive services. This coverage is often approved in conjunction with the case manager.

In addition to providing reimbursement for medical services, many employee benefit plans also provide *wellness benefits*, which can include training classes and encouragement for healthy life styles, such as smoking cessation, weight loss, and dietary training. In addition, wellness benefits often include profiling of, and recommendations regarding, each covered individual's health status and lifestyle. This profiling may include analysis of questionnaires completed by the covered individuals and medical analysis such as blood work.

Nurse help lines are another benefit growing in popularity. This dial-in service provides the insured contact with a nurse to perform triage for virtually any medical condition. This service includes the dual benefits of providing an additional service to the insured, while helping assure the medical care is high quality and cost-efficient.

Disease management benefits are typically non-contractual benefits provided to specifically identify individuals at increased health risk due to the presence of chronic diseases. Some carriers have found that targeting specific additional benefits to individuals with chronic conditions, such as diabetes or heart disease, will result in both better health for these individuals and lower long term costs if conditions are promptly treated before complications or co-morbidities occur.

THE SECOND DIMENSION

The second dimension in defining a medical benefit plan is the degree to which the insured shares in the cost of medical services.

Purposes

Generally, requiring cost sharing of the insured serves the following purposes:

- *Control of Utilization.* It is widely believed that requiring a covered individual to share in the cost of medical services significantly controls utilization. Several studies have shown drastic reductions in utilization when an insurance plan is subject to deductibles, copays, or coinsurance.[5] Proponents of this philosophy argue that it is desirable to place cost concerns in the hands of the ultimate purchaser of health care services—the covered individual. Opponents are concerned that the reduced utilization will result in either decreased general health status or increased health care expenditures at a slightly delayed time, as untreated medical conditions fester and worsen.

- *Control of Costs.* Requiring the covered individual to share in the cost lowers the premium and thus provide more affordable coverage. A counterargument is that federal tax policy, which currently provides for full deductibility of employer-provided insurance premiums and only limited deductibility of medical care costs, actually encourages maximizing premiums and minimizing the amount of cost sharing at point of claim.

- *Control of Risk to the Insurer.* As discussed earlier, many covered benefits, although valuable, do not truly meet the definition of an insurable risk. Increased cost sharing results in a benefit program that more truly represents an insurable risk.

Provisions for Cost Sharing

Individuals share in the cost of the benefit program through contributions (premiums) or through participating in the cost of medical care services. Sharing in contributions primarily addresses the objective of controlling the employer's cost and essentially results in all employees sharing equally (or sometimes proportionally to income level), regardless of the level of health care resources consumed. However, as contributions grow, the number of people dropping out likely increases, because some individuals will no longer consider participation as either a reasonable purchase or affordable. As a group, those dropping out will tend to be healthier and generally will consume fewer health care services, because the sicker individuals find the coverage more valuable. This leaves the remaining participating pool to have a higher average cost.

---

[2] The first of these studies was a study by the Rand Corporation entitled "Does Free Care Improve Adults' Health?" published in The New England Journal of Medicine on December 8, 1983. In addition to published studies, many experienced actuaries have observed the phenomenon. A number of organizations that offer high deductible programs or "medical savings accounts" are also noting this phenomenon.

There are a number of plan provisions that result in the covered individual sharing in the cost of medical care. These include deductibles, coinsurance, copays, UCR (usual, customary, and reasonable) charge levels, paying at a fee schedule or per diem (per inpatient day), daily limits on specified services (also called internal limits), and limits on the number of days covered.[6]

A *deductible* is a dollar amount of covered health care services that must be paid by the individual before any services are paid for by the plan. Most plans exempt certain services from the deductible, such as preventive care services. Other plans define deductibles to apply to very specific services, such as hospital admissions. These narrowly defined deductibles are similar to copays, discussed below.

Family contracts can define deductibles in several ways. Some contracts define a family deductible as a dollar amount of covered health care services that must be paid in total by the family before any services are paid for by the plan. Other contracts define a deductible for each individual, but have family limits, such as a family paying a total deductible of no more than two times the individual deductible.

Another provision relating to deductibles is a *carryover provision* whereby any claims applied to the deductible in the last quarter of a deductible accumulation period (often a calendar year) are also carried over and applied to meet the deductible in the subsequent period. This attempts to correct a perceived inequity that may arise if, for example, an individual has no charges until the end of December in a calendar year deductible plan, and then meets the deductible only to have it reapplied on January 1. This provision is often difficult to administer and has become less common.

For commercial health insurance plans, *coinsurance* usually refers to the percentage of covered services paid for by the insurer after the insured meets the deductible. The most common coinsurance level for these plans is 80% up to a given amount. For example, a plan with a $100 deductible and 80% coinsurance of the next $5,000 of charges would require a covered individual to pay the first $100 of covered expenses and 20% of the next $5,000 of charges to a maximum limit of $100 + (.20)(5,000) = \$1,100$. The contract should specify whether the deductible and dollar copays are considered as out-of-pocket expenses in relation to the maximum limit.

The coinsurance level can vary for different services to control or encourage specific behavior. For example, an insurer might provide 100% benefit payment for outpatient surgery but 80% for inpatient surgery. In addition, a lower payer coinsurance level is often used to control behavior and control the insurer's risk when medical necessity is not clearly definable for a covered service. This more severe coinsurance, often as low as 50%, has the double impact of reducing risk to the medical benefit plan as well as creating a significant utilization control on behalf of the covered individual who is personally funding a higher portion of the cost.

Another common method of cost-sharing is the use of *copays*. Copays are typically a fixed dollar amount paid at the time of each covered service. Copays can vary significantly by service type to create incentives that influence utilization. For example, a plan might include a higher copay for emergency room use than for office visits. Copays are most frequently

---

[6] Grandfathered plans may also have lifetime or annual dollar limits.

used in service benefits contracts such as in HMOs, where the concepts of deductibles and coinsurance do not readily apply because no reimbursement actually takes place. Copays have also become common in PPO plans for specific services such as physician office visits.

Limiting reimbursement to UCR charges may result in increased cost sharing on behalf of the insured. *UCR maximums* are set by a plan administrator and generally attempt to represent a reimbursement level that reflects the lowest of thee items: a given provider's usual charges (U), the charges that are customary in that given geographic region for similar procedures (C), and a charge level that is reasonable in relationship to the specific services provided (R). These limits are generally not applicable to plans providing service benefits. The provisions are a tool to limit cost. However, some reduction in utilization of specified high cost providers may result from the insured being required to make up the difference between a provider's bill and the UCR reimbursement provided by the insurer. For many network plans, UCR reimbursement must be accepted by participating providers as payment in full as a requirement for participation in the network. There are other industry terms which refer to the same concept, including usual and customary (U&C), and reasonable and customary (R&C).

Varying deductibles and coinsurance are often used to encourage the insured to comply with certain requirements or use certain providers. For example, a *PPO* plan will often waive the deductible and/or reduce the payer coinsurance if the insured seeks care from a predefined list of providers. Occasionally, use of a network provider is a requirement for any benefit. This is a standard provision for HMOs, but is also increasing in use in insurance contracts through both *Exclusive Provider Organizations* (EPOs) and *Centers of Excellence*. EPOs are similar to standard HMOs in that no benefits other than emergency services are provided if care is obtained from a non-network provider. Centers of Excellence have been established by many carriers to provide a high quality cost efficient mechanism of arranging for high intensity services such as transplants. Coverage for those services is often limited to services provided by the Centers of Excellence. Another example of varying deductibles and coinsurance is an open panel HMO or *Point of Service* (POS) program. Similar to a PPO, this program will provide a much higher level of benefits if the insured follows all of the protocols and restrictions of the HMO, and a lower level of benefits if the insured receives care otherwise. A *tiered network* is a variation of this concept where a carrier can define multiple networks inside a given benefit plan with varying copays dependent on which provider is used. With this variation, the insured retains greater choice of providers, but has additional cost sharing if they choose providers deemed to be expensive or inefficient.

A classic example of attempting to modify insured behavior using copays can be found in prescription drug programs. These programs have evolved from simple fixed dollar copays per prescription to multiple tiers of copays and coinsurance levels depending on whether a drug is brand or generic, on or off a carrier's formulary, and whether or not a therapeutically equivalent is available. Although quite complicated, these multi-tier copay prescription drug programs appear to be very effective at modifying consumer behavior.

Annual maximums and *lifetime maximums* are provisions that attempt to provide bounds on the risk undertaken by the insurer. Most often annual maximums are used on covered services where either medical necessity is difficult to define or the course of treatment is vague. In addition, annual maximums can be used on catastrophic or somewhat experimental items, such as certain organ transplants. However, the ACA has eliminated most plans' annual and lifetime maximums.[7]

Limits on the benefit payable per day of covered services are an effort to control costs, to encourage the insured's awareness of costs and to encourage wise consumption of health care resources. A limit on the number of days for which services will be covered is an attempt to control utilization. Both *daily limit maximums* and *number of day limits* are most commonly used on benefits such as skilled nursing facilities, home health care, and private duty nursing.

In some plans, all of the above provisions may be waived, or coverage increased, depending on which provider is used or on completion of certain requirements such as pre-certification. Such provisions again reflect an attempt to influence the behavior of the insured.

Different combinations of the above limits have historically been given specific labels. For example, a *base plan* generally provides for first dollar coverage, without deductible or coinsurance, for hospital coverages. Provisions may include a number of days limit, and a limit to either room and board charges and/or ancillary charges for each day of hospitalization. A *supplementary major medical plan* typically excludes services provided under a base plan and provides coverage for all other services subject to a corridor deductible and coinsurance. In contrast, a *comprehensive major medical program* has all covered services in one program, subject to a deductible and coinsurance.

In an effort to allow consumers to compare the value of various health plans, the ACA requires health plans in the individual and small employer markets to be assigned a "metal level", based on the overall expected plan's share of the average cost. The assignment is based on a standardized tool; the actual coverage percentage is dependent on the specific utilization pattern of the individual. The assigned metal levels are platinum (90%), gold (80%), silver (70%), and bronze (60%) of the essential health benefits.[8]

THE THIRD DIMENSION

The third dimension in defining a medical benefit plan involves the relationship between providers and the health plan, including the breadth of the provider network and the degree to which the provider participates in the cost. This may include not only discounts or other modifications to provider payments, but also conditional payments based on some element of plan utilization. Having providers participate in benefit plan costs is intended to both reduce the costs of the underlying plan of benefits through provider reimbursement rate concessions, as well as to provide incentives for the providers to control utilization, particularly in the areas of referrals to expensive specialists and hospital admissions.

---

[7] Exceptions where annual and lifetime maximums may continue to exist include (1) grandfathered plans, and (2) specific coverages within non-grandfathered plans that are not specifically included as essential health benefits by the state (examples might include chiropractic visits or infertility benefits). Interestingly, while the ACA's essential health benefits coverage requirements apply to the individual and small employer markets, this particular annual and lifetime maximum provision also applies to large employer and even self-insured health plans.

[8] A +/- 2 % corridor around the metal level targets is allowed.

Providers gain anticipated increases in patient volume by being on a plan's preferred provider list.

In an effort to provide lower cost health insurance products, many health insurers offer very narrow provider networks, which exclude a large percentage of the providers in a given service area. Providers retained in these narrow networks usually are either low cost providers or have agreed to very favorable contract terms in exchange for being included in the narrow network.

The algorithm establishing provider cost sharing can take on many forms, each of which has their own subtle impacts on underlying costs and behavioral incentives. These forms include the following:

- Discounts from billed charges
- Fee schedules and maximums
- Per diem reimbursements
- Hospital Diagnostic Related Grouping (DRG) reimbursement, ambulatory payment classifications, or global payments
- Bonus pools based on utilization
- Capitation
- Integrated delivery system

Straight *discounts for billed charges* are the simplest form of establishing provider cost sharing. However, this form only acts to reduce costs of the underlying benefit plan and provides no incentives for utilization modifications. In addition, reimbursement based on a predefined percentage of billed charges may have little impact to control health care costs if used extensively, since a provider may increase billed charges.

Reimbursement based on *fee schedules* or *fee maximums,* although simple to implement, also acts only to reduce costs and fails to affect utilization patterns. This reimbursement method has some cost-saving advantage to the insurer over a straight discount from billed charges in that the provider is unable to adjust billed charges to affect the overall level of claims. Under both discounts from billed charges and fee schedules and maximums, the provider remains able to increase utilization, either through changes in how procedures are coded on bills, or in an actual increase in the number of services.

Per diem contracts are most commonly used for hospitalization benefits. An amount per day of hospital stay is negotiated. This per diem often varies based on the level of care, such as normal care, intensive care unit, cardiac care unit, and maternity ward. A hospital accepting a per diem contract is undertaking some risk of the intensity of services provided per bed day. Per diem contracts can act both to reduce costs and to have some basic controls on the provision of services ancillary to hospital room and board. However, per diem contracts generally provide no incentive to encourage either outpatient use in lieu of inpatient use, or reduced lengths of stay. Many per diem contracts also include some outlier provisions where the longest hospital stays revert to payment of a percentage of billed charges for either charges in excess of the threshold or for total charges. These provisions further complicate any incentives from the payment system, especially if exceeding the threshold results in a modification on the amounts below the threshold.

Reimbursement based on *DRG* provides a set reimbursement to a hospital for a stay regarding a given diagnosis, regardless of the length of stay or the level of services provided. Some adjustment may be made under these contracts for cases involving inordinately short or long stays as compared to the norm for a diagnosis. This is the reimbursement mechanism used by individuals covered under the Medicare fee-for-service program. The impact of this reimbursement mechanism is that the hospital accepts risk for the length of a given admission as well as the amount of ancillary services provided during the admission. This reimbursement mechanism provides effective utilization incentives during a hospital admission, but limited incentives for influencing the number of admissions. In addition, DRG payments are highly sensitive to the coding of the diagnosis. Some observers believe that any significant reductions in costs may be offset through aggressive coding.

A similar reimbursement mechanism for hospital outpatient charges is reimbursement based on *Ambulatory Payment Classifications (APCs)*. Another similar mechanism is *case rate payments* or *global payments*, where a single reimbursement is negotiated to cover all services associated with a given condition (the case payment can include both facility and professional fees). The most common uses of global payments include maternity cases and transplant cases.

Bonus pools based on utilization refer to a contractual provision whereby a provider would receive an additional bonus if personal or overall utilization of medical services was below a pre-defined target, or if other quality criteria are met. This bonus pool is generally funded out of a percentage of provider payments withheld from initial payment. Conceptually, this reimbursement mechanism appears to provide excellent incentives for a provider to have heightened awareness of utilization. However, effective implementation is much more difficult. If the bonus is not a significant proportion of a provider's income, a provider can do more to maximize income by increasing utilization than by controlling utilization and receiving the bonus. In fact, many physicians have stated they view such a withhold program as a benefit which they do not expect to receive, and thus it has little influence on their behavior. If the bonus is developed to be a significant portion of income, it may be difficult to enroll a broad base of providers willing to accept the risk of adverse experience deviations, which may be perceived as beyond their control. Furthermore, this type of bonus pool creates difficult ethical questions when a provider is given a strong financial incentive not to provide medical care to a patient. In addition to providing utilization incentives, bonus pools are probably most popular in their ability to provide an acceptable risk for the insurer. For example, if all reimbursement for medical services is subject to a 25% withhold, the insuring organization has effectively established a 25% cushion for excess utilization above the targets, in which its charges paid to providers will not increase.

A *capitation* model is one in which the insurer subcontracts with a provider to perform a defined range of services in return for a set amount per month per enrollee. This represents the far end of the spectrum in terms of minimizing risk to the insurer, in that virtually all risk is passed along to the provider. Essentially the only risk remaining with the insurer is the solvency of the provider and the ability of the provider to deliver services. Capitation agreements may also effectively reduce costs and provide utilization incentives in that a provider's income will be maximized to the extent they can provide fewer services. This utilization incentive raises the same ethical questions as mentioned above in the discussion on bonus pools.

Capitation contracts have extended beyond the services performed by a single provider, to capitating a provider group for most or all health care services. This type of arrangement is called *global capitation*. Under this arrangement, the provider group essentially replaces the insurer as the primary risk taker. The regulatory status for this type of arrangement is unclear. Some jurisdictions are requiring providers to obtain an HMO license in order to accept global capitation, while some jurisdictions are requiring no regulatory oversight if the entity offering the capitation is regulated.

Another capitation alternative is *specialty capitation*. Under this arrangement a fixed payment is made for all of the medical expenses associated with the treatment of a given condition or for all of the services provided by a given physician specialty. These capitations are often woven into disease management programs by providing a fixed capitation for treatment of chronic conditions, such as diabetes or heart disease.

An *integrated delivery system* model is one where the insurer actually owns or employs the providers of care. This is most frequently seen in a staff model HMO, but also exists when hospital or physician organizations develop managed care plans that accept insurance risk.

The underlying theme of all of the mechanisms in which providers participate in the insurance risk is to increase the providers' awareness of costs and utilization. It is important to the long-term viability of a plan that such mechanisms be constructed to be beneficial for both the provider and the insurer. If either party is significantly disadvantaged in the contractual arrangement, the forces of economics will eventually dismantle that entire program.

One end of the provider spectrum (narrow provider network with significant provider risk sharing) offers a lower cost product but limits the insured's freedom to see any provider and acquire any service. The other end of the spectrum provides greater freedom to the insured around provider selection and services but has a higher price tag. Variation in the provider dimension is a significant reason why two plans with comparable metal benefit levels (e.g. two silver plans) may have very different premium rate levels.

OTHER MEDICAL PLAN PROVISIONS

In addition to the three basic dimensions that define a medical benefit plan described in the previous section, there are a number of other provisions that are standard in any benefit plan. These include the following:

- Overall exclusions,
- Mandated benefits,
- Coordination of benefits,
- Subrogation, and
- COBRA continuation.

Most medical benefit plans exclude charges for or services related to the following:

- Services deemed not to be *medically necessary* in order to treat a specific condition. There are several exceptions to this exclusion, the most common of which is preventive care.
- Services that are deemed experimental by some accepted medical authority. These services are generally excluded either because the usefulness of the treatment has not been clinically established, or because, as an experimental treatment, alternative funds may be available to provide the treatment.
- Services related to cosmetic surgery. Although possibly excluded under the medical necessity clause, most contracts also have a specific exclusion that limits services related to cosmetic surgery. Reconstructive surgery resulting from accidents or mastectomies is often exempted from this exclusion.
- Other specified services including hearing services, vision services, care of the feet, and spinal manipulation. These services are often delineated because medical necessity for these types of services is somewhat difficult to establish.
- For plans that are grandfathered from ACA requirements, transplants could have an inside limit, such as a $100,000 maximum for a transplant. In addition, specific plan provisions may cover or exclude costs associated with acquiring a transplanted organ from a donor. Contractual provisions specifically addressing transplants are increasing in popularity, and some court rulings have indicated that transplants can no longer effectively be excluded as experimental procedures.
- Services for which payment is not otherwise required. This exclusion covers a host of situations including free care provided through governmental programs, care provided as part of a controlled group for an experimental program in which no payment is required, and care provided as part of a school or employer-related facility.
- Services required due to an act of war.
- Services provided because of a work-related injury. These services are generally excluded from group medical benefit plans because expenses would be reimbursable under a workers' compensation program.
- Services provided by, or charges from, a provider related to the patient.

Medical benefit plans also include provisions for specific benefits mandated by the appropriate regulating bodies. As mentioned previously, these *mandated benefits* vary significantly from state to state, creating administrative difficulty for multi-state insurers. There are also extra-territoriality issues raised when an insurance contract is written in one state and covers individuals in other states. Some states mandate provisions for individuals covered in that state, whereas some states mandate provisions based on the situs of the contract. An additional issue regarding mandated benefits is the pre-emption claimed by self-funded benefit plans regulated under ERISA. ERISA provides exemption from state laws for self-funded employee benefit plans.

Most employee benefit plans also contain a provision discussing *coordination of benefits* procedures. Coordination of benefits refers to the process used to adjudicate claims when a service is covered under multiple benefit plans. Such a clause will designate one carrier as primary and responsible for coverage as if they were the only insurer. The alternative carrier is designated as secondary and is responsible for any additional benefits that their plan may provide. The secondary carrier can coordinate based on either total charges or total benefits. The most common approach is coordination based on total charges in which the secondary carrier will pay the total benefits it would have normally paid, less any benefits covered by the primary carrier, up to a maximum of the total charges incurred. When coordinating based on benefits, the secondary carrier will first calculate the normal level of benefits it would have provided had it been primary, and then reduce those benefits for any benefits provided by the primary carrier.

The current NAIC model bill on coordination of benefits specifies the primary carrier based on the following hierarchy:

1. The benefit plan not containing a coordination of benefit clause in the event one of the plans does not contain such a clause.
2. The carrier covering the covered individual as an employee.
3. If both carriers cover the individual as a dependent, the benefit plan for which the covered employee (not the dependent) has the birthday that falls earliest in the calendar year.
4. If both benefit plans cover an individual as an employee, or if both employees covering a dependent have the same birthday, the plan that has had coverage in effect the longest.

Benefit plans covering individuals as employees, or as dependents of active employees are primary with respect to Medicare for employers with more than 20 employees. Benefit plans covering individuals as retirees or as dependents of retirees are secondary if Medicare can be a primary carrier.

Medical benefit plans generally contain a *subrogation clause* that assigns the right of recovery from any injuring party to a carrier that has provided services or reimbursed charges for medical services. In addition, this clause generally gives the carrier the full right to act on behalf of the covered individual in seeking such damages, and is often referred to as *third party liability*. Subrogation clauses most commonly come into play when addressing workers' compensation claims or automobile accidents.

The *Consolidated Omnibus Budget Reconciliation Act* (COBRA) requires employers with 20 or more employees to offer continued coverage beyond a person's termination date. This can arise when a dependent loses eligibility due to either divorce or death of the employee, when an employee or a dependent loses eligibility due to termination of employment, or when a dependent no longer meets the definition of a dependent child. Continued coverage is required to be offered for a period between 18 and 36 months. The length of the continuation period varies dependent on the terminating event. The employer may charge the individual insured up to 102% of cost for the coverage.

SPECIAL SITUATIONS

The three dimensions of a medical benefit plan described earlier in this chapter broadly categorize any medical benefit plan. However, specific combinations of these descriptions have been referred to as a given type of program. As the group medical benefit market has matured over the past decade, there has been considerable lack of strict definition of what is an HMO, what is a PPO, and what is a traditional indemnity plan.

MANAGED CARE PLANS

A *Health Maintenance Organization (HMO)* is a service benefit plan that broadly involves significant provider sharing in costs and minimal insured sharing in costs. The general philosophy of the HMO is that providers control the utilization of health care and the end consumers have little input into the purchasing decisions. Therefore, to manage costs the provider component must be controlled. A common benefit plan would require a $10 or $20 copay for an office visit, varying copays for prescription drugs (depending on the type of drug), and a $50 copay for emergency room utilization. However in order to receive coverage, an insured may have to follow specific guidelines including having all care managed by a primary care physician, who would provide referrals to specialists, as necessary, except in the event of an emergency. HMOs typically have restrictive provider networks involving a small proportion of physicians and hospitals in a given community. In return, the physicians and hospitals agree both to conform to the HMO's utilization protocols and to provide care at a reduced fee level.

An *Exclusive Provider Organization* (EPO) generally has a similar design to an HMO. The primary distinction is that an EPO is regulated as an insurance contract or self-funded plan while an HMO may be subject to different regulatory requirements.

A *Point-of-Service* (POS) program is similar to an HMO in that the insured selects a primary care physician and has low copayment benefits similar to that described above if guidelines are followed. However, under this program the insured also has the alternative of seeking care outside of the network with additional cost-sharing requirements.

A *Preferred Provider Organization* (PPO) is a plan that offers an insured the freedom to use either a designated panel of providers or their provider of choice. To encourage the insured to use the preferred provider panel, a lower level of payer coinsurance is often used and deductibles are lower if participating providers are used. PPOs typically involve significant provider sharing in the cost, although generally less than HMOs. A typical PPO plan would feature a more generous deductible and coinsurance (such as $500 and 90%) if the preferred provider panel were used, and a less generous deductible and coinsurance (such as $1,000 and 70%) if the panel were not used. The provider cost sharing in a PPO is generally more focused on reducing the overall costs to the benefit plan than on attempting to impact provider utilization.

Flexible Spending Accounts

Another example of a medical benefit plan is a *Flexible Spending Account* (*FSA*). An FSA is a benefit plan whereby an employee contributes pre-tax dollars on an annual basis that are then used to provide reimbursements for their own medical expenditures. The amount of reimbursement is limited to the amount contributed by the employee. There are virtually no limitations in a flexible spending account regarding benefits or providers. There would be no insured cost sharing beyond their initial funding of the account, and there is no provider cost sharing. The FSA is basically an opportunity for an insured individual to use pre-tax dollars to pay what would otherwise be after-tax reimbursements for medical care. The ACA created an annual limit of $2,500 for 2013 (indexed for inflation).

6 DENTAL BENEFITS IN THE UNITED STATES

Joanne Fontana
Herschel Reich

INTRODUCTION

Dental coverage is one of the most popular employee benefits in the United States. According to the National Association of Dental Plans, more than 187 million people, or 60% of the population, were estimated to have dental benefits as of December 31, 2012.[1] The vast majority of people with dental insurance are covered via the private commercial market under employer-sponsored group plans, with the remainder covered by individual policies, Medicaid, or other social insurance programs.

The Affordable Care Act (ACA), passed in 2010, instituted important changes in how people access dental benefits. Pediatric oral care, listed as one of the required benefits in the ACA's "essential health benefit package", is now required to be offered in the individual and small group markets. In addition, the ACA provided for the expansion of the Medicaid program. All states cover pediatric dental services under Medicaid or Children's Health Insurance Program (CHIP); some states also include at least some dental coverage for adults. Thus, in the states that expanded Medicaid eligibility, additional adults as well as children gained dental coverage as a result.

This chapter will focus largely on group dental benefits, the largest component of the private commercial market. The individual dental market has historically been quite small; however, the advent of the ACA's state health insurance exchanges presents new opportunities for individuals to purchase dental policies. Thus, at the end of this chapter, emerging changes in the dental coverage landscape are discussed.

OVERVIEW OF THE GROUP DENTAL INSURANCE INDUSTRY

HOW GROUP DENTAL INSURANCE IS SOLD

The vast majority of large employers offer dental benefits to their full-time employees. According the National Association of Dental Plans, 91% of employers with 101 or more employees, and 87% of employers with 51 to 100 employees offer the benefit. As with health insurance, smaller employers are less likely to offer dental coverage, with 57% of employers with 50 or fewer employees offering the benefit.[2] Plans generally cover both employees and their dependents.

---

[1] NADP 2013 State of the Dental Benefits Market.
[2] Ibid.

Group dental policies are largely sold as separate polices from medical coverage. Originally, most employers in the U.S. offered dental benefits under a comprehensive medical plan in which dental expenses were combined with major medical benefits. Over time, product designs have shifted away from that approach toward standalone dental plans, with almost all dental policies today being offered in standalone form. Today, only 0.4% of all dental policies are integrated into medical plans.[3] Separating dental and medical insurance plans, whether the plans are purchased from the same insurer or separate insurers, allows employers to best meet their insurance goals.

Group dental coverage is similar in most fundamental characteristics to other forms of group benefits. Coverage is provided through a master policy or contract issued to the group policyholder or sponsor, and employees receive individual booklets or certificates of coverage. Both documents outline the details of the group-specific plan design and the eligibility rules to receive coverage.

Dental insurance is marketed by a wide variety of organizations, including multiline and dental-only insurance companies, dental service corporations such as Delta Dental, Blue Cross and Blue Shield plans, Dental Health Maintenance Organizations (dental HMOs), dental referral plans, and third party administrators. The primary distribution vehicle is independent brokers and consultants working in conjunction with insurer sales representatives. Some plans are sold directly to larger employers without the use of a broker. Increasingly, the internet is being used to help distribute product, either directly as an electronic intermediary, or in support of traditional intermediaries and brokers. In addition, dental products are being sold via benefits exchanges. The ACA has introduced public health insurance exchanges as a distribution mechanism for small group and individual dental benefits, and the recent proliferation of privately operated benefits exchanges presents potential new sales avenues for large group, small group, and individual business.

WHY GROUP DENTAL INSURANCE IS PURCHASED

Employers generally consider dental insurance to be an important employee benefit and offering a plan can help to attract and retain employee talent. Although the cost of dental care is much more limited than medical care, employer-sponsored dental insurance may still provide significant value to the employee.

First, employee contributions to employer-sponsored benefits are often purchased with pre-tax dollars, giving the employee a financial advantage over independently purchasing an individual dental policy or paying for care out-of-pocket.

Second, while the cost of a dental procedure may be small relative to many medical procedures, dental insurance provides a budgeting mechanism whereby, rather than paying for services as they occur, consumers pay a steady monthly premium with lower out-of-pocket costs at the point of service. This budgeting feature makes dental insurance attractive to consumers with moderate incomes. In fact, 47.9% of people with dental insurance in 2012 had annual household incomes under $50,000 and 36.3% have incomes between $50,000 and $100,000.[4]

---

[3] NADP/DDPA 2013 Dental Benefits Joint Report: Enrollment.
[4] NADP Consumer Survey 2012.

Third, for most dental HMO and dental Preferred Provider Organization (PPO) products, the consumer has access to a contracted network of dental providers who have agreed to provide services at a discounted cost. These providers are generally subject to a credentialing process by the insurer, helping to ensure quality of care.

Dental insurance also provides broad value in the form of better oral, and potentially physical, health. People with dental insurance are more likely to receive dental care. According to the National Association of Dental Plans 2012 Consumer Survey, 78% of insured consumers report having had a dental checkup in the past year, while only 46% of those without insurance report a checkup during the same period. Oral health has increasingly been linked to overall health in clinical studies. For example, gum disease has been shown to be correlated with medical conditions such as Type II diabetes, vascular disease, arthritis, and adverse pregnancy outcomes. Prevention of gum disease, starting with access to dental care in childhood and progressing to treatment of oral health issues in adults, could lead to improvements in other health outcomes.

THE BASIC COMPONENTS OF DENTAL PLAN DESIGN

Dental benefits, like medical benefits, are designed to provide coverage for the prevention, diagnosis, and treatment of disease or injury. The benefit structure of dental plans, however, differs from that of medical plans to better fit the unique utilization and cost patterns of dental services.

Dental claims are typically smaller in size than medical claims. According to Centers for Medicare and Medicaid Services (CMS), per capita consumer expenditures for dental services were roughly $354 in 2012, compared to $8,404 for all national health care expenditures.[5] While medical bills can reach hundreds of thousands or even millions of dollars over a short time period, dental costs are usually limited in even the most extreme circumstances to several thousand dollars, making dental claim costs relatively more predictable than medical claim costs.

On the other hand, dental services are often more elective than medical services, increasing the difficulty in underwriting and pricing a dental benefit plan. Insureds may have more control over both the timing and the type of treatments for dental care than for medical care. Compounding this higher degree of insured control of dental costs is that group dental insurance is often offered to the employee on a voluntary basis, with the employee responsible for contributing some or all of the cost of the dental premium. In fact, 23.8% of group dental plans require the employee to bear the full cost of the dental premium.[6] Thus, a decision to purchase dental insurance may be based on whether the employee expects to have dental expenses during the policy period; employees may forego dental insurance if they do not think they will need it. Another difficulty in underwriting and pricing dental benefit plans occurs when an employer group is offering dental insurance for the first time. Employees may have existing, previously untreated dental problems, resulting in higher than average utilization of services for new plans.

---

[5] Centers for Medicare and Medicaid Services, Office of the Actuary, National Health Statistics Group.
[6] NADP/DDPA 2013 Dental Benefits Joint Report: Enrollment.

Dental benefit plan designs encourage routine preventive care through comprehensive coverage of cleanings, examinations, and diagnostic services such as x-rays. Maintaining good oral health via preventive procedures and treating dental disease in its earliest stages are less expensive than treating problems after they worsen.

Dental benefit plan designs have been structured to include cost sharing by the insured to help ensure that insureds use services appropriately while still receiving a meaningful benefit. To reduce antiselection, benefit plans generally differentiate the level of coverage by the type of service; for example, routine preventive services, such as cleanings, are often covered at little to no cost to the insured, while more advanced services require more insured cost sharing.

Dental benefits are generally divided into four classes by type of service. While different dental insurers and dental benefit plans may not use exactly the same classification of dental services, the general classifications are consistent:

Preventive and Diagnostic (Class I) procedures: These procedures aim to maintain oral health, prevent disease, and diagnose disease at its earliest stages. Oral exams, cleanings, fluoride treatments, sealants for children, x-rays, diagnostic tests and laboratory exams generally fall into this category.

Basic (Class II) procedures: These procedures correct dental problems and treat dental disease. Various types of restorations (fillings), extractions, endodontics (root canal procedures), periodontics (treatment of gum disease), and oral surgery are generally included in this category. Some dental plans consider emergency dental treatment as a Class II procedure while others classify it under Class I.

Major (Class III) procedures: Inlays, onlays, and crowns and prosthodontics, including bridges and dentures are generally included in this category.

Orthodontic (Class IV) procedures: Orthodontic care is not always covered by dental plans.

Each class of dental service is governed under the plan by a cost-sharing structure that splits the cost of the procedure between the insurer and the insured. Plans are generally designed to encourage prevention and require more significant cost sharing on more expensive or elective procedures. A typical plan design might use a coinsurance structure by which the plan will reimburse 100% for Class I services, 80% for Class II, and 50% for Class III. Such a plan is often described as a 100/80/50 plan. A copay-based structure may also be used, and is commonly used in dental HMO plans, in which copays are minimal or $0 for Class I procedures, and higher for Class II and III procedures. Copays vary by procedure, with the copay designed to represent a particular proportion of the service's total cost.

Group dental plans commonly have a deductible, which is often waived for Class I services to encourage insureds to seek routine preventive and diagnostic visits. The typical deductible is $50 to $100 per year.[7] Similar to medical insurance, family deductibles are often set as a particular multiple of the individual deductible (for example, a family deductible may be set at three times the individual deductible). Deductible carryover provisions, which generally allow for expenses applied to the deductible during the last three months of a policy year to

---

[7] NADP Dental Benefits Report: Premium and Utilization Benefit Trends. December 2013.

be counted toward the following policy year, are much less common in dental plans than in medical plans due to the small size of dental deductibles.

As the cost of dental insurance has increased, insurers have increasingly begun to adjust the class in which services are categorized. Some common examples include shifting certain types of x-rays from Class I to Class II, moving space maintainer coverage to Class II, and shifting certain kinds of surgical treatments such as surgical periodontal procedures from Class II to Class III. Shifting services to a higher class generally increases the proportion of the cost borne by the insured.

While medical plans typically have very high or unlimited benefit maximums, dental plans commonly have annual plan maximums, generally in the range of $1,000 to $2,500 per person.[8] Within the policy year, dental benefits will be paid by the plan on behalf of an individual up to the annual maximum benefit amount. Once the maximum has been exceeded, the insured is responsible for any additional dental costs incurred during the year. Dental HMOs do not commonly use an annual maximum. Some dental plans have a maximum carryover provision by which some portion of unused benefit amounts from the prior policy period may be carried over to the current period.

Conversely, annual out-of-pocket maximums, standard in medical plans, are generally not a benefit feature of dental plans. Due to the more elective nature of dental procedures and the increased ability of a dental patient to control timing of claims as compared to medical, this plan design element could be problematic for dental plans and is rarely used. One notable exception is for ACA-compliant pediatric dental coverage offered in the individual and small group markets. The ACA mandates an out-of-pocket maximum for these plans to ensure that covered children with severe dental issues do not incur excessive out-of-pocket costs.

Orthodontic services, when covered by a dental plan, are considered separately as Class IV services. Orthodontic services are generally subject to their own lifetime maximum benefit per person, separate from the dental annual maximum. This lifetime maximum is designed to ensure that the insured shares significantly in the cost of orthodontic treatment. Orthodontic procedures are meant to correct tooth positioning and irregular bite via braces or other devices. They can improve oral health but are also often performed for cosmetic reasons. Sometimes dental plans that cover orthodontic services do so only for children under a certain age and do not offer coverage for adults.

Some dental services may overlap with those provided under medical insurance plans, including treatment required due to accidental injury to natural teeth, removal of impacted teeth, and coverage for surgical treatment for jaw disorders. Coordination-of-benefit provisions are used to avoid duplication of coverage.

In addition to cost-sharing structures and benefit maximums designed to limit plan cost and antiselection, dental plans often use other provisions to further limit risk. These provisions include:

---

[8] Ibid.

- *Frequency limitations*: Benefit plans may limit the number of services that will be covered during the policy period, so that dental providers are not encouraged to offer more services than are necessary for dental health. For example, two cleanings per year and one set of x-rays per year are common provisions. These limitations are usually set based on clinical guidelines.

- *Pre-existing conditions limitations*: Most plans will not cover any charges incurred by a covered person before the beginning of the policy period. Coverage for treatments started before the policy effective date may be excluded as well as coverage for conditions existing before the effective date. The most common example is a missing tooth exclusion in which a plan would not pay for a prosthetic device replacing a tooth that was missing before the person became insured, unless other teeth lost or extracted during the policy period were also being replaced. The missing tooth exclusion, which is fairly standard in the industry, has recently begun to become less universal, because insurers recognize that it may be more cost effective to replace the tooth than to allow it to remain missing which could lead to other oral health issues.

- *Least expensive alternative treatment*: A particular dental condition may be resolved via several different treatment plans with similar clinical outcomes but different costs. Under a Least Expensive Alternative Treatment (LEAT) provision, sometimes called LEPAAT (Least Expensive Professionally Acceptable Alternative Treatment), the insurer would reimburse based on the least expensive clinically acceptable treatment plan. For example, a cavity may be filled using a variety of materials ranging from basic metal fillings to relatively more expensive tooth-colored enamel. A LEAT provision would reimburse only for the least expensive acceptable treatment regardless of which material the provider actually used.

- *Waiting periods*: To reduce antiselection, dental benefit plans often use waiting periods that must be satisfied before coverage begins. Waiting periods, if used, are generally applied to Class III and Class IV procedures, and sometimes to Class II. Waiting period lengths generally range from three to twelve months, but they can extend to 24 months for some procedures. The risk profile of the group is assessed when deciding on whether to use a waiting period. Longer waiting periods will be used for groups with higher risks of antiselection. Group risk characteristics include group size, employer contribution level, and whether the group is new to dental insurance. Waiting periods are less common in large group coverage than in small group, and they are uncommon in dental HMO plans except for orthodontic services.

- *Exclusions*: Dental plans often exclude coverage for services that are purely elective, not essential for good oral health, or covered by other plans. The most common exclusions are for cosmetic procedures, experimental treatments, and items such as ambulance or hospital services that would typically be covered under a medical plan.

- *Benefits after insurance ends*: Dental plans contain a very limited set of extended benefits after termination. The typical plan provision will pay for work started before the termination date and finished within 31 days of termination.

UNDERWRITING AND RATING PARAMETERS

Underwriting, or the assessment of insurance risks to be covered, is extremely important for dental plans due to the sometimes elective nature of dental procedures and the prevalence of voluntary coverage. Group dental plans employ group underwriting processes that serve to mitigate risk and control antiselection. The premium rate charged to a particular group should reflect the plan provisions and group characteristics. This section will describe these underwriting controls and key rating variables. More detail on the determination of expected claims is discussed in Chapter 22, "Estimating Dental Claim Costs."

GROUP SIZE

Dental plans generally have a minimum group size to which coverage can be offered. The limit is typically five, although some plans are offered to groups as small as two. Often, group size requirements are determined in conjunction with other underwriting requirements. For example, the minimum group size may be larger for voluntary coverage than employer-paid coverage. Groups that fall below the minimum required size may be terminated according to the terms of the group contract. Since dental services are highly elective and subject to antiselection, group size provisions should be strictly enforced.

In general, all else being equal, the larger the group the lower the price, because of both economies of scale in administrative costs and decreased risk variability. Once groups reach a certain size level, their experience is considered credible, and premium rates may be developed based on the group's experience data. Groups of smaller size with non-credible experience are charged manual rates developed based on the cumulative experience of the insurer's entire manually rated block of business. Partially credible groups are rated using a combination of the manual rate and the experience rate.

ELIGIBLE INDIVIDUALS AND GROUPS

Generally, dental plans will cover employees and their dependents. Dependents can include spouses and legally dependent children, including foster children and stepchildren. While dental plans are not required to expand the definition of dependent children to meet the ACA mandate for medical plans, many dental insurers have liberalized their dependent definition to be consistent with the ACA requirement.

Group plans may be sold to active employees only or may include retirees. In general, employees are covered until the earlier of the termination of their employment or the group's cancelation date. Dependents are similarly covered until the earlier of the end of the employee's eligibility or the cessation of dependency status. For example, a spouse's coverage will usually cease on divorce. COBRA continuation provisions are applicable to dental plans as with medical plans, although fewer people elect to continue dental coverage.

Some dental insurers exclude coverage for groups from certain industries, most often for voluntary dental coverage or for very small group sizes where significant antiselection may occur. Alternatively, premium rates may be significantly increased for these industries. Occupations with high levels of utilization include actors, teachers, and sports teams. Also, employer groups with strong union affiliations are usually more aware of their dental benefits than other employees, and tend to have higher than average utilization.

PARTICIPATION

Dental plan underwriting generally uses minimum participation requirements; that is, a minimum percentage of eligible employees must elect to participate in the dental plan. The higher the participation in the dental plan, the better spread of risk for the insurer. Groups with participation significantly below 100% may have their premium rates loaded or benefits reduced to adjust for the increased antiselection inherent in the group's low enrollment.

Many voluntary (100% employee-paid) and contributory (partially employee-paid) dental plans may allow for participation as low as 25% of eligible employees, and they often combine the participation requirement with a minimum required number of enrollees. Premium rates sometimes may be adjusted for the actual participation once the open enrollment process is complete. Benefits also can be adjusted downward to avoid a price adjustment.

Most non-voluntary plans require a minimum level of employer contribution, usually 50% of the single employee premium, which helps to ensure a high employee participation rate in the plan. Plans that are non-contributory, that is when the employer pays the entire premium, may be quoted at lower premium rates than contributory plans, due to the reduction in potential antiselection when 100% of employees participate in the plan. Fully employer-paid plans have declined in recent years, with contributory and voluntary dental coverage becoming more prevalent.

OTHER COVERAGES

Bundling dental coverage with other coverages, such as medical insurance, is favorable from an underwriting perspective. The opportunity for an individual to select against a dental plan is reduced significantly if dental coverage is packaged with medical.

NEW BUSINESS

Dental utilization levels during the first few years of dental coverage may be much higher than in later years, due to the pent up demand for dental services. Dental plans may apply a pricing load to rates for groups who are offering dental coverage to employees for the first time. The necessity and magnitude of this load depends on the other characteristics of the plan, including whether it is being offered on a voluntary basis, whether waiting periods for certain services are being employed, and whether coverage of pre-existing missing teeth is included.

GEOGRAPHIC LOCATION

Geographic location is also considered in dental underwriting and pricing, because prevailing costs for dental services as well as dental utilization patterns may vary significantly by area. Area rating factors may vary by state, service area, zip code, or other constructs. A single geographic factor may be developed for each area, or separate pricing factors for utilization and cost may be used.

DEMOGRAPHICS

Age and gender are important pricing variables for dental insurance. In general, groups with more females have higher dental claim costs. Claim costs generally increase with age, although not nearly as steeply as with medical claims. Pricing models often incorporate age/gender rating factors, sometimes even differentiating age/gender utilization and cost factors by class of dental service.

Premium rates are usually presented in a tiered rate structure such that families with different compositions will be charged different rates. Two tier (Employee, Employee plus Family), three tier (Employee, Employee plus One Dependent, Employee plus Two or More Dependents) and four tier (Employee, Employee plus Spouse, Employee plus Child(ren), Employee plus Spouse and Child(ren)), are all common tier structures.

WAITING AND DEFERRAL PERIODS

Dental plans often impose a waiting period before a new employee is eligible to join the plan. Closely aligned with the waiting period is a provision that contains a limit on certain Class II and Class III services. These limits can apply to both new entrants and to late entrants, which are those who join a plan more than 31 days after first becoming eligible. Some plans will limit benefits in the first year for late entrants to coverage for preventive services and other services due to accidental injury only. For some groups, especially those without prior dental coverage or voluntary plans, some service types, most often Class III services, may be deferred for the entire group for a period of one year or more. These provisions are extremely important, because many dental services are highly elective and can be postponed.

INCENTIVE COINSURANCE

Another approach to guard against poor experience in the first few years of a dental plan, especially on plans with no prior coverage, is an incentive coinsurance approach. Under incentive coinsurance, benefits are initially provided at a lower coinsurance level for Class II and III services, and increase each year, as long as an individual uses preventive services each year. For example, benefits may start out with employer coinsurance levels of 100% for Class I, 70% for Class II, and 35% for Class III in the first year and go up 10 percentage points for Class II services and five percentage points for Class III services each year that a specified series of preventive procedures has been performed, until an ultimate benefit level of 100%/100%/50% is reached. If in any year, an individual fails to see a dentist, then his or her benefits are reset to the year one level.

TRANSFERRED BUSINESS

Dental plans will generally pay for certain charges incurred before the plan's effective date, as long as the plan is a replacement of another plan without any break in coverage. Payment is usually limited to the lesser of the old plan benefit and the new plan benefit, less any benefits paid under the old plan's extension provision.

In the first year of a plan, it is common to reduce the deductible by the amount of covered charges applied against the old plan's deductible. Also, in the first benefit year, the new plan generally will charge benefit payments by the old plan against its payment limits.

REIMBURSEMENT MODELS AND DELIVERY SYSTEMS

MAJOR TYPES OF DENTAL PLANS

The three main types of provider reimbursement systems for dental benefit plans mirror those for medical plans: dental indemnity plans, dental PPO plans, and dental HMO plans. Dental PPOs are by far the most prevalent type of dental plan in today's marketplace. According to the National Association of Dental Plans, 78% of individuals were covered by dental PPO plans, 7% by indemnity plans, and 8% by dental HMO plans in 2012, with the remainder of the market largely belonging to discount dental plans.[9] Over the past decade, the popularity of the dental PPO has increased while dental indemnity business has waned. Dental HMO market share increased in the 1990s, but has decreased since then, declining from 15% in 2002 to 8% in 2012.[10] Dental HMOs are more prevalent in particular geographic regions such as California.

Dental Indemnity Plans
Dental indemnity plans use traditional fee-for-service reimbursement for dental providers, and plan members may see any dental provider of their choosing.

Scheduled indemnity plans cover services up to a dollar maximum per procedure set by the plan. All dentists are eligible to provide care, and those that charge above the maximum reimbursement may bill the patient for the balance. The schedule is often fairly low. These plans were quite popular in the past and are still used in the voluntary market, but have generally been replaced by Usual, Customary and Reasonable (UCR) plans. However, with the rise in employee-pay-all-plans in recent years, the low cost of a scheduled plan design is once again appealing.

UCR plans are the typical traditional fee-for-service indemnity plans that are common in today's market. Services are covered up to the UCR limit, subject to the plan's deductibles, coinsurance, and benefit maximums. The UCR limit is determined by the insurer based on the prevailing charge level for a given dental procedure in a particular geographic area. As with the scheduled indemnity plan, dentists who charge more than the UCR limit may bill the patient for the difference between their charge and the amount covered by the plan.

Dental Preferred Provider Organizations
Dental preferred provider organizations, or dental PPOs, offer a contracted network of dental providers who agree to discounted fee-for-service reimbursement arrangements with the insurer. Plan members may obtain services inside or outside that contracted network but reap the benefit of discounted costs inside the network. Provider contracts may be developed as a discounted fee-for-service arrangement, in which providers agree to a specified percentage discount off their standard charges, or as a fee schedule, in which a dollar fee for each dental

---

[9] 2013 NADP/DDPA Joint Dental Benefits Report.
[10] Ibid.

procedure representing a discount off the provider's standard fee is agreed upon. In-network providers generally must accept the discounted fee-for-service reimbursement or the fee schedule amount as their full reimbursement and may not bill the patient for the balance.

Some dental PPO plans provide for the same level of benefits in and out of network; these plans are commonly referred to as "passive PPOs" or "managed indemnity plans". Members are encouraged to use the provider network, because the cost of services will be reduced by the contracted provider reimbursement arrangements. However, many plans offer richer benefits in network to provide additional incentive for plan members to use the contracted providers. For example, in-network dental PPO plan coinsurance may be 100%/80%/50% for Class I / Class II / Class III while out-of-network coinsurance might be 90%/70%/40%.

Dental exclusive provider organization plans, or dental EPOs, are dental PPO plans in which only in-network services are covered. Because these plans allow for greater steerage to the contracted provider network, greater discounts may be negotiated in the provider contracts.

Dental HMOs
Dental HMOs generally reimburse dentists via prepaid or capitated arrangements, paying a predetermined amount per member per month (PMPM) to dental providers regardless of whether a member seeks care or not. Dental HMOs require use of the contracted network; out-of-network services are generally not covered by the plan. Like medical HMOs, dental HMO care is usually overseen by a primary care dentist.

There are two types of dental HMOs. Independent provider association dental HMO plans construct their provider panels from independent dentists who agree to a capitation style of reimbursement. The amount that the dentist is paid is not directly tied to the frequency or the value of services performed. In essence, the dentist assumes the majority of the financial risk involved in treating a group of patients. However, specialists, who are available on referral, are typically compensated on a discounted fee-for-service basis. Primary care and specialty dentists are chosen from a limited panel of participating providers. For capitation to work from a provider's standpoint, the provider needs to have a minimum number of patients over which to spread his or her risk.

Staff model dental HMO plans employ their own dentists and offer dental insurers the greatest control over the cost of care.

Point of Service (POS) plans are a hybrid of the indemnity, PPO and dental HMO concepts. The insured can pick, via choice of dentist, among receiving benefits from an in-network HMO provider, a PPO provider, or any other provider, at different levels of benefit. This choice is most commonly made once a year, but in some plans members may choose once a month or, in rare instances, at the point of service.

Discount Dental Plans
In recent years, discount-only dental plans have become more prevalent. These plans simply give the patient access to contracted provider discounts. The patient is responsible for the full cost of services, but may save money by accessing network providers at reduced rates. Because no dental benefit is provided, discount-only dental plans do not constitute dental

insurance; however, the product competes with dental insurance products. Discount dental plans represented 6% of the market in 2012.[11]

COMPARING THE MAJOR PLAN TYPES

Premium

Dental HMO premiums are typically lower than dental PPO or dental indemnity premiums, largely due to the capitation mechanism as well as utilization management protocols and care coordination by a primary care dentist. Dental indemnity plans are generally more expensive than dental PPO plans with similar benefits, because indemnity plans lack a discounted provider network and generally do not employ any significant utilization or cost controls.

Patient Access

In an indemnity plan, a patient may receive covered care from any dentist. Dental PPO plans also allow patients to receive coverage regardless of which dentist provides the care, but in-network discounts and often richer in-network benefits make visiting an in-network dentist more appealing to the patient. Dental HMO plans generally restrict access to the contracted provider network, allowing out-of-network coverage only for specified situations such as emergencies.

Access to covered care depends not only on the type of dental plan but also the breadth of the plan's contracted provider network. Some plans may contract with a large proportion of area dentists, allowing patients greater provider choice, while other plans may choose to contract with a narrower set of providers, potentially allowing greater discounts to be achieved but limiting the number of in-network providers from which the patient may choose. Also, in some areas of the country, the number of dental providers is insufficient to serve its population, requiring people to drive long distances to receive dental care. Dental plans must consider this issue when developing their network of contracted providers.

Benefit Richness

Dental PPOs use the same basic plan design construct – deductible, coinsurance by class of service, and annual maximum – as indemnity plans. As described previously, dental PPOs often offer different benefit levels for in-network and out-of-network services to incentivize use of the network. Some examples of dental PPO plan designs compared with a standard indemnity plan are as follows:

- A 100/100/60 in-network, 100/80/50 out-of-network dental PPO would reward the patient for going in-network, relative to a standard 100/80/50 indemnity design.

- A 100/80/50 in-network, 80/70/40 out-of-network dental PPO would penalize the patient for not going in-network when compared to standard 100/80/50 indemnity design.

- A 100/80/50 in and out-of-network passive dental PPO plan would be similar to a standard 100/80/50 indemnity plan, with only the risk of balance billing on out-of-network services to encourage patients to use in-network dentists.

---

[11] 2013 NADP/DDPA Joint Dental Benefits Report.

Large coinsurance differentials between in- and out-of-network benefits in dental PPO plan benefits are rare and may be prohibited by state PPO laws.

As dental costs have increased, employers have mitigated premium rate increases by instituting changes in their dental benefit plan that require patients to pay more out-of-pocket when they seek dental care. According to the National Association of Dental Plans, annual benefit maximums have decreased and plan deductibles on average have increased from 2011 to 2013.[12]

The typical dental HMO plan will include coverage for the same dental services provided for under indemnity and dental PPO models, but often with a lower out-of-pocket expense to the insured, usually in the form of copays for each service. The typical dental HMO plan also has no deductible, and no annual or lifetime maximum. Most dental HMO plans do not pay benefits for out-of-network services, other than a small emergency services benefit. This is changing, however, as the dental HMO industry mirrors the increasing popularity of medical point-of-service (POS) plans.

Cost Management

Indemnity programs manage cost through UCR limits, LEAT (least expensive alternative treatment, discussed previously), clinical logic, and predetermination of dental necessity for certain procedures. Dental PPOs generally use the same techniques, and additionally reap the benefits of the credentialing programs that are set up to contract with cost-effective, quality dentists. Dental HMO plans, in addition to the above techniques, control utilization and costs via the primary care dentist gatekeeper and the referral process for specialty dental care.

Utilization

Fee-for-service reimbursement in both medical and dental insurance plans may encourage overutilization of services. Dentists may be motivated to perform extra services to offset the income given up via contracted discounts with insurers. When compared with medical providers, dentists service a higher proportion of patients that do not carry insurance and are willing to pay undiscounted standard billed rates for dental procedures; thus, dentists may view contracted discounts as a giveaway that may be partially offset by performing additional services on the insured population. An effective utilization management program employing predetermination for benefits and claim review may limit these potential manipulations. Meanwhile, the capitation-based contracting of a dental HMO may produce the opposite incentive, for dentists to perform only the minimum level of care to maximize per-patient revenue. Quality assurance programs, provider profiling, and patient satisfaction measures can help to ensure that appropriate yet cost-effective levels of care are being provided.

Quality Assurance

Dental indemnity plans allow for patients to receive covered care from any provider, and thus do not offer any significant assurances regarding care quality. A major value proposition of dental PPOs and dental HMOs is the provider credentialing process, which screens and reviews the practices of contracted providers to help assure quality care. Most

---

[12] National Association of Dental Plans. 2013 State of the Dental Benefits Market.

managed care dental plans – 69% of dental PPOs and 88% of dental HMOs – re-credential providers every three or more years, with the remainder performing re-credentialing even more frequently.[13]

Fraud Potential

Dental insurance is extremely susceptible to fraud. Insurers may employ methods of tracking provider claim submissions and comparing to industry norms to identify outliers in terms of the number of procedures billed per patient or per visit, an unusually large number of a particular type of procedure, or other suspect practices. While the effectiveness of combating fraud is really a function of the insurer's utilization management efforts, and not of the particular plan type sold, dental HMOs and their capitation approach minimize many of the incentives to commit fraud from either the dentist or insured.

Provider Contracting

Both PPOs and dental HMOs use contracts with dental providers to arrange for services to be provided at agreed-upon rates. Most contracts are for a one-year term and are automatically renewable. In the contract, the dentist agrees to abide by the plan's quality assurance and utilization management programs, and to discounted charges, a fee schedule, or capitation arrangement. In return, the insurer promises to encourage patients to use network providers. The contract also spells out the grievance, review, and provider relationship functions. Dental HMO contracts will also spell out specialty referral guidelines.

Contracts are generally offered to providers who have undergone an extensive credentialing process. In addition to collecting biographical and practice information, dentists are asked to divulge criminal offenses and past malpractice complaints. Dental HMOs often conduct on-site reviews of a dentist's practice, checking the office for OSHA compliance and reviewing sample patient records. The credentialing process is generally more extensive in dental HMO plans.

Managed care plans are becoming more popular with dentists. According to the National Association of Dental Plan estimates, approximately 64% of dentists participate in dental PPO plans and 15% in dental HMO plans.[14] Dentists are becoming more selective in joining dental HMO plans as the capacity equation – the ratio of private dental practitioners to the number of U.S. residents – has moved in their favor. Also, the number of yearly dental school graduates has declined 20% since 1980.[15] With the number of dentists per U.S. resident declining, dentists may have more power in contracting. Contracting trends also vary between general and specialist dentists.

While medical PPO programs may expect a high proportion of claims – 80 to 90% or more – to be incurred in-network, dental PPOs generally experience a substantial proportion of claims out-of-network. This may be due to the lower relative cost of dental services, making choosing an out-of-network provider less financially taxing than for medical care, or the smaller size of some dental networks relative to the total universe of dental providers in the area.

---

[13] NADP/LIMRA 2011 U.S. Group Dental Administrative Metrics, October 2013.
[14] NADP / DDPA 2011 Joint Dental Benefits Report: Network Statistics.
[15] U.S. Census Bureau, Health and Nutrition, *Statistical Abstract of the United States: 2000, No. 188.*

FUNDING MECHANISMS

In 2012, about half of commercial dental plans were fully insured, with the insurance company bearing the risk, while the other half were self-insured by employer groups.[16] All of the funding mechanisms common to group medical insurance are available to dental, although individual stop loss is generally not seen in the dental realm due to relatively low claim costs and the annual maximum benefit provision which limits plan liability even for high-cost cases. As with medical insurance, larger employer groups are more likely to self-insure than smaller-sized groups.

One of the provisions of the ACA imposes an industry tax on fully-insured health insurance plans, including standalone dental plans. It is still too early to tell whether this tax will cause a shift in the industry toward more self-insurance of dental benefits.

Direct reimbursement, which is a concept endorsed by the American Dental Association (ADA), encourages employers to administer their own dental programs, potentially reducing overall plan cost. Even if the insurance risk is manageable to the employer, the insurer's claim paying capabilities and cost control procedures argue strongly for administration provided by a third party. Direct contracting or reimbursement plans have not materially gained in popularity, despite the ADA endorsement; in 2012 they represented just 0.6% of the market.[17]

CLAIM PRACTICES

Dental costs are relatively modest when compared with medical benefits, but the elective nature of many services can cause claim costs to vary significantly. Acceptable treatment plans can vary widely, and proper coding of procedures is important. To control the cost of dental plans, claim administration procedures unique to dental plans are necessary. The chapter on Claim Administration and Management that follows later in this text gives details for many of the claim practices common to all health plans. Here, the claim practices that are important for dental claims are discussed.

PREDETERMINATION OF BENEFITS

Most plans suggest that patients who are about to undergo a treatment plan with expected costs more than a specified dollar limit, or a specified procedure such as a dental implant, submit their treatment plan for pre-treatment review to verify coverage under the plan. While mainly intended as a protection for the insured to ensure the procedure is covered before undergoing treatment, this policy also serves as a deterrent against overutilization of services. Predetermination often requires that x-rays and diagnostic models be submitted to provide evidence on the necessity of treatment and the services rendered.

---

[16] NADP 2013 State of the Dental Benefits Market.
[17] 2013 NADP/DDPA Joint Dental Benefits Report.

LEAST EXPENSIVE ALTERNATE TREATMENT (LEAT)

Predetermination is crucial to plan success, because dental problems can often be treated with differing procedures that vary widely in cost. Plans are generally cover the cost of the least expensive alternate treatment, so long as it meets clinically and professionally accepted standards of practice. The principal area where the alternate benefit provision is cost-effective is with Class III services, especially crowns and fixed partial dentures.

Each of the services under the plan is governed by an extensive series of age and frequency limitations. Oral exams, cleanings, fluoride treatments, and x-rays are commonly limited to a specified number of services per year. Services such as sealant treatments may be covered only for children under a certain age. The purpose of these limitations is to lower overall plan costs within the framework of clinically accepted standards of dental practice.

COORDINATION OF BENEFITS

Plans will not pay for charges to the extent that they are also paid by another health or dental plan sponsored by the plan holder or by Medicare. If a covered person also received benefits from another plan (other than the ones mentioned above), the plans will generally coordinate benefits to ensure that the patient will not receive benefits greater than the charges incurred. Benefits from other plans cannot be used to meet the plan's deductible. Dual coverage for dental coverage can be relatively more valuable than for medical coverage, because reimbursement can be much higher if the patient has two separate plans with separate annual maximums.

Since dental is such a high frequency insurance coverage, speedy and accurate claim administration is a vital aspect of good customer service. Claims are generally processed much more quickly than medical claims: well over 90% of dental claims are processed in ten days or fewer.[18] Advances in claim paying ability through higher levels of electronic claim filing and more sophisticated automated claim adjudication can help dental claim payers achieve a competitive advantage in the marketplace.

DENTAL REVIEW

Administration of a dental plan requires a sophisticated claim payment system to properly adjudicate claims. The system must automatically check eligibility, age and frequency limitations. ADA service codes can also be manipulated in some situations by unbundling certain charges to the dentist's advantage. Comprehensive systems will re-bundle these procedures. Most dental plans also employ dental professionals serving in a consultant capacity to review difficult claims, ensure dental necessity, and evaluate and approve prescribed treatment plans.

MAXIMUM ALLOWABLE CHARGE

Maximum Allowable Charge (MAC) or UCR provisions limit covered expenses for a particular service to the lesser of:

- The dentist's usual fee for the procedure;

---

[18] NADP/LIMRA 2011 U.S. Group Dental Claims Processing Metrics, September 2013.

- The fee level set by the plan administrator based on charges submitted in the same geographical area; and

- The reasonable fee charged for a service, even when unusual circumstances or complications exist.

Most payers use a percentile approach, typically covering expenses in the range of the 80th to 90th percentile, to assure that they are establishing a reasonable level of MAC. This means that charges will be 100% covered for 80% to 90% of dentists in the area.

THE FUTURE OF DENTAL BENEFITS

The group dental coverage landscape continues to evolve due to changing employer and employee needs, the economy, the declining number of dental providers, new distribution channels, and the impact of the ACA.

With employers continuing to face large medical plan cost increases, dental insurers are increasingly developing lower-cost products to meet employer needs. It is likely that voluntary plans will continue to grow in popularity and that, among non-voluntary plans, the employee's contribution percentage will continue to grow. On the other hand, dental plans may try to differentiate themselves with unique added benefit components that are appealing to the employee such as teeth whitening or oral cancer screenings. Balancing the marketing value of these added benefits against their clinical appropriateness and added cost is an important component of plan design analysis.

The consumer-driven health care phenomenon is spreading to dental insurance, with greater access to information and benefit choice becoming important to plan participants. For example, some plans are adding treatment cost estimators to websites so patients can assess their costs and compare fees of in-network and out-of-network providers in advance of treatment.

Shortages in dentist capacity and supply are expected to continue. This may put pressure on the ability of dental plans to build and maintain sufficient dental networks in particular geographies. Dental providers may have the opportunity to be more be more selective in the networks they join and more power in the contract negotiation process.

Private health benefit exchanges have recently proliferated and are a potential new distribution mechanism for both individual and group dental products. These private exchanges serve a wide variety of purchasers – some focus on large groups while others may focus on retirees, small groups, or individuals. Many dental insurers are assessing whether these private exchanges fit into their distribution strategy, determining which exchanges might be most advantageous to join, and developing products specifically tailored to the private exchange customers.

THE AFFORDABLE CARE ACT

The ACA introduced major changes to the dental insurance industry when it was passed in 2010, particularly in the individual and small group segments. A comprehensive review of the impact of the ACA on dental plans is beyond the scope of this chapter; however, the following section reviews some of the major tenets of the law that affect the group dental insurance market.

The ACA defined a set of minimum "essential health benefits" required to be offered in the individual and small group markets both on each state's public exchange as well as outside the exchanges. Pediatric oral care was included as an essential health benefit, requiring dental insurers to contend with the ramifications of the ACA on their business model. As discussed previously, almost all dental plans are purchased as standalone dental policies separate from medical, via employer groups, with coverage for employees and their dependents. The ACA also required dental insurers to reconsider several aspects of their product and distribution strategy.

With pediatric dental a required benefit offering but adult dental not considered an essential health benefit, child-only policies are being developed, and the additional antiselection potential associated with adults being able to purchase insurance for themselves separately from their child dependents (or to forego coverage on themselves completely) has to be considered.

Prior to the ACA, medical plans generally excluded dental services. Under the ACA some medical plans have chosen to embed the pediatric dental care within the medical policy so that all the essential health benefit could be made available under a single policy rather than having to combine a medical and a dental plan. Dental insurers in the individual and small group market now not only must contend with other dental insurers as competitors, but also medical insurers who were embedding pediatric dental benefits. On the other hand, dental plans are presented with a new opportunity to partner with medical plans to subcontract the pediatric dental component of the medical policy.

The required construct of the pediatric dental essential health benefit is quite different from standard dental plan design. No annual or lifetime dollar limits on the benefit are permitted, and an annual out-of-pocket maximum, set for 2016 at $350 per child and $700 for multiple covered children within a family, is required. As previously discussed, standard dental plan designs rely on benefit limits to control utilization and cost, and out-of-pocket maximums are generally not seen in the dental industry. Dental insurers must determine the financial impact of this new and different benefit design, and also develop the functionality to administer an out-of-pocket maximum to participate in this marketplace. In addition, almost all states require the pediatric dental essential health benefit to include medically necessary orthodontia coverage. Most standard orthodontia benefits have little to no medical necessity criteria; utilization and cost are instead controlled via a lifetime maximum benefit. Under the essential health benefit design, insurers must consider how to administer medical necessity rules and contemplate the impact on plan cost of the application of the out-of-pocket maximum on expensive orthodontia treatments.

The ACA also provided for the expansion of Medicaid eligibility. In the states that have elected to expand their Medicaid programs, additional children may gain dental coverage, as well as adults to the extent that a particular state incorporates adult dental coverage in their Medicaid benefits. The additional funds that states receive for Medicaid expansion may cause some states to consider instituting or improving their adult dental Medicaid benefit. However, Medicaid dental provider shortages in some areas may limit the ability of patients to receive care even if benefits are available.

Health care reform, private exchanges, economic uncertainty, and changing employer and employee needs all point to an era of change in the dental benefit industry over the upcoming several years.

7 Pharmacy Benefits in the United States

David M. Liner
Michelle N. Angeloni

Introduction

The cost and complexity of pharmacy benefit coverage continues to increase due to new drug treatment innovations and evolving market dynamics. New drugs, including high-cost specialty medications, are regularly introduced and may improve the health and quality of life for many individuals. Physicians are increasingly able to treat medical conditions through the use of drug therapies before they require acute care. Prescription drugs are vastly changing the face of health care in the twenty-first century.

There are a variety of factors that influence prescription drug costs and benefit offerings:

- *Prescription drug pipeline*: Research and development (R&D) brings powerful new drugs to market, providing new solutions for patients. Some of these new drugs represent completely new therapies, offering hope to patients with diseases that were previously untreatable. Others provide increased convenience in dosage, or fewer side effects than existing drugs. Pharmaceutical manufacturers often have a significant investment in research and development of new drugs, and attempt to recover these costs through the sale of new drug therapies.

- *Brand patent protection*: New drugs are covered by patents that protect the original manufacturer from competition for a period of time. This helps the manufacturers to recoup research costs for the drug and creates an incentive for further investment in new drug therapies. Upon patent expiration, competitor drug manufacturers are allowed to produce generic equivalents of the existing brand drug, usually selling at a fraction of the original brand drug cost. In recent years, manufacturers have been able to extend the profitable life of popular brand drugs, through litigation against generic competitors, and by creating modified versions of the original brand product that help them to retain patents for several years after the original molecular patent has expired.

- *Specialty drugs:* These drugs have relatively high cost and often have lower utilization than other brand name drugs. The only broadly accepted formal definition of specialty drugs comes from the Centers from Medicare and Medicaid Services (CMS) which defines specialty drugs as those that cost $600 per month or more. It is not uncommon for specialty drugs to cost more than ten times the cost of a traditional drug that is used to treat the same medical condition. The high revenue potential helps to attract interest and investment from pharmaceutical manufacturers. Biologics are a subset of specialty drug medications.

- *Biologics*: These drugs are particularly expensive, often costing $2,000 to $500,000 per patient per month. Biologics are produced by complex manufacturing processes that are not easily replicated. For this reason, many biologics may not be genericized in a manner similar to traditional branded drugs. The U.S. Food and Drug Administration (FDA) is currently developing a process for approval of biologic drugs that are functionally equivalent to the previously existing brand, but made by a different manufacturer. These products are currently called biosimilars, and are analogous to the generic version of traditional brand drugs. Due to the complexity of their manufacturing, it is unlikely that biosimilars will ever reach the current generic price relativity for traditional drugs. Current expectations place biosimilar costs at about 75% of the original brand drug cost while traditional generics typically fall to 25% or less of the original brand drug cost within a year of patent expiration.

- *Direct-to-consumer advertising*: Marketing to consumers through television, radio, print, internet, and other media has increased consumer awareness of new, high cost drugs. Many of these advertisements encourage patients to ask their doctors about the benefits of a certain drug or to ask for free trial samples. Prescribing health care providers are now feeling pressure to use certain drugs from both the drug manufacturer's sales force and their patients. Studies have shown that this pressure is effective,[1] and that physicians and the public are divided as to whether they believe the net effect is beneficial.[2]

- *Member cost sharing offsets:* Along with direct-to-consumer advertising, many drug manufacturers are now offering to pay for most or all of the out-of-pocket cost of their expensive brand prescriptions. This undermines the effect of the benefit plan's tiered copays, which are often intended to steer utilization toward preferred brand products and generics. As an example of this effect, consider a member with a $60 copay for an expensive brand product and a $10 copay on a therapeutically-equivalent, but lower-cost, generic product. The drug manufacturer could offer a copay card that pays $50 of the member's out-of-pocket cost. With this card, the member pays exactly the same price at the pharmacy counter for the brand ($60 - $50 = $10) as they would have paid for the generic alternative ($10). Copay cards make it increasingly difficult to influence member behavior and manage the cost of pharmacy benefits.

- *Faster approval process:* The process through which the FDA approves drugs for use in the market has been streamlined. This increase in the speed of approval for drugs increases the number of high-cost drugs coming to the market, adding additional upward pressure on the trend in both average cost of drugs and utilization of the new drugs. Recent concerns about the safety of several FDA-approved drugs may reduce this effect. Manufacturers of biologics are increasingly targeting diseases for which there is no current effective treatment. This will often convince the FDA to grant a fast-track approval, which takes approximately half the time to process.

---

[1] Kravitz RL, Epstein RM, Feldman MD, et al. Influence of patients' requests for direct-to-consumer advertised antidepressants: a randomized controlled trial. *JAMA*. 2005 Apr 27;293(16):1995-2002.
JAMA. 2005 Apr 27;293(16):1995-2002.
Free Full Text Influence of patients' requests for direct-to-consumer advertised antidepressants: a randomized controlled trial.
JAMA. 2005 Apr 27;293(16):1995-2002.
[2] Robinson AR, Hohmann KB, Rifkin JI, et al. Direct-to-consumer pharmaceutical advertising: physician and public opinion and potential effects on the physician-patient relationship. *Arch Intern Med*. 2004 Feb 23;164(4):427-32.

- *Aging population*: An older population tends to use more drugs than younger populations since older people typically have more medical conditions. As the proportion of the population at older ages increases, the demand for drug therapy increases.

- *Increase in awareness of, and testing for, disease*: When a manufacturer launches a new drug for a previously untreatable disease, it often deploys an extensive physician education campaign to raise awareness of the condition. Recent years have shown a greater awareness of, and a propensity to test for, medical conditions. Once diagnosed, individuals often receive drug therapy to treat the condition. Bone density tests and cholesterol screenings are examples of such tests which often result in drug therapies to avoid acute illness and complications.

- *Personalized medicine*: Genomic testing is still in its infancy, but public awareness is growing rapidly. Many genetic tests are available to consumers without a prescription. Sometimes it is difficult to know how to interpret the results, and untargeted genetic screening can lead to overestimating or underestimating an individual's lifetime risk of a particular disease. Overestimating can lead to unnecessary medication use, and underestimating may cause an individual to adopt unhealthy lifestyles. For example, if people believe that they are at low risk of heart disease, they may be less diligent in exercising and eating healthy foods, thus raising their risk. In the future, personalized medicine may help doctors choose the right drug for a patient, eliminating often costly and dangerous trial and error. Unfortunately, except for a few treatment protocols, this advancement is still years away from realization.

The Medicare Prescription Drug, Improvement, and Modernization Act (MMA) introduced the Medicare Part D program in 2006, which provides federally-funded prescription drug benefits to Medicare eligible beneficiaries. The Medicare Part D plan design is complex, and includes a variety of dynamics that influence how prescription drugs are covered and paid for, including federally-sponsored reinsurance, increased member cost sharing at a certain phase through a "coverage gap", and varying cost sharing based on income status. The MMA also created a Retiree Drug Subsidy (RDS) and an Employer Group Waiver Plan (EGWP) as a means of monitoring and subsidizing employers that offer retiree drug coverage and meet certain criteria.

This chapter introduces a framework to conceptualize the pharmacy benefit system in the United States. The framework describes major entities and their relationships within the current prescription drug benefits system. The framework is a simplification of the practices actually in place, and does not include all dynamics of the complex industry. Following the introduction of this simplified framework, this chapter will present several important concepts required to understand the current United States pharmacy benefit system. Using the concepts discussed, the chapter will conclude with a description of the relationships between the entities involved in the system.

THE PHARMACY BENEFITS SYSTEM FRAMEWORK

Figure 7.1 presents a framework for the current prescription drug benefits system in the United States.

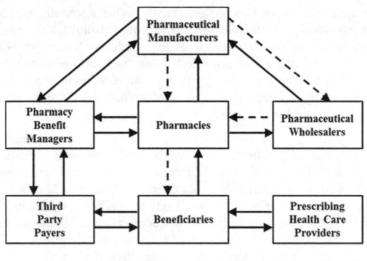

Figure 7.1

There are seven entities in the prescription drug benefits system framework:

1. **Pharmaceutical Manufacturers** research, obtain approval for, produce, and distribute pharmaceutical products and prescription drugs.
2. **Pharmaceutical Wholesalers** purchase prescription drugs from manufacturers and distribute drugs to pharmacies.
3. **Pharmacies** dispense prescription drugs directly to beneficiaries, and purchase prescription drugs either from pharmaceutical wholesalers or directly from pharmaceutical manufacturers.
4. **Pharmacy Benefit Managers (PBMs)** administer prescription drug benefit programs. PBMs are either affiliated with an insurance company or operate independently.
5. **Third Party Payers** are insurance companies, employers, or government programs that fund the prescription drug benefit. In some instances, third party payers may assume the risk associated with fluctuations in pharmacy claims.
6. **Beneficiaries** are consumers of prescription drugs.
7. **Prescribing Health Care Providers** diagnose and prescribe drugs for beneficiaries.

The lines in Figure 7.1 represent the relationships between entities in the prescription drug benefits system. Dashed lines represent the flow of prescription drugs within the system. Solid lines represent the flow of non-drug items, such as prescriptions and payments.

Pharmaceutical Manufacturers

Pharmaceutical manufacturers research, obtain approval for, produce, and distribute pharmaceutical products and prescription drugs. Table 7.1 summarizes some of the largest pharmaceutical manufacturers by revenue.[3]

Table 7.1

Manufacturer	2013 Revenue (billions)	Notable Drug Products[4]
Pfizer	$47.9	Lyrica, Prevnar family
Novartis	$47.5	Glivec, Gleevec, Gilenya
Roche	$39.2	Rituxan, Avastin, Herceptin
Merck and Co.	$37.4	Januvia, Zetia, Nasonex
Sanofi	$37.1	Lantus Solostar, Lantus
GlaxoSmithKline	$33.3	Advair Diskus, Flovent HFA, Lovaza
AstraZeneca	$25.7	Nexium, Crestor, Symbicort
Lily	$21.0	Humalog, Humulin, Cialis
AbbVie	$18.8	Humira, AndroGel, Synthroid

Manufacturers interact with wholesalers, pharmacies, and pharmacy benefit managers in the prescription drug benefits system. These interactions involve the transfer and distribution of the drugs produced, as well as the actions taken to increase the distribution and sale of the drug.

Manufacturers provide drugs to wholesalers and also directly to pharmacies, in exchange for payment. Payment is typically a function of a reference price, such as Wholesale Acquisition Cost (WAC) or Average Wholesale Price (AWP). Manufacturers may also pay wholesalers a chargeback as a reward for meeting certain sales or volume distribution goals to pharmacies. Larger pharmacy chains typically purchase drugs directly from the drug manufacturer, while smaller, independent pharmacies generally purchase drugs through a wholesaler. Figure 7.2 shows the relationship between manufacturers, wholesalers, and pharmacies.

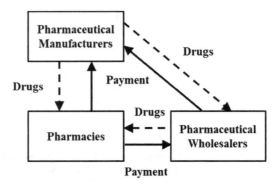

Figure 7.2

---

[3] "Top 25 Pharma Companies by Global Sales." *PMLiVE Site*. Web. 18 Mar. 2015. http://www.pmlive.com/top_pharma_list/global_revenues.

[4] Notable drug products found from product search in official company websites and other sources.

In addition to selling pharmaceutical drugs to wholesales and pharmacies, drug manufacturers also negotiate with PBMs to encourage individuals to purchase their product. Drug manufacturers offer rebates to PBMs in exchange for favorable formulary placement of certain drugs. Favorable formulary placement is often associated with member incentives to take certain drugs through lower beneficiary cost sharing and fewer utilization management requirements. Figure 7.3 shows the relationship between manufacturers and PBMs.

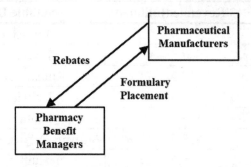

Figure 7.3

Other financially important relationships that some drug manufacturers are involved in are related to the 340B drug pricing program. This program enables health care organizations that provide care for underserved populations to procure pharmaceutical drugs at a significant discount. Only certain organizations, members, and drugs are eligible for this pricing program, because the program's purpose is to assist with the funding of drugs provided to those in financial need.

In addition to the relationships described above, manufacturers also interact with beneficiaries and prescribing health care providers in an effort to maximize the distribution of their drugs. They often employ a sales force that meets with medical professionals to increase awareness of their drug's benefits. Manufacturers may also interact directly with beneficiaries using copay cards or coupons to further encourage the use of certain drugs.

Pharmaceutical Wholesalers
Pharmaceutical wholesalers purchase prescription drugs from manufacturers and distribute drugs to pharmacies. This creates a drug acquisition channel for pharmacies in addition to pharmacies purchasing drugs directly from the drug manufacturers. Pharmaceutical wholesalers may be able to purchase drugs from manufacturers at a lower cost than smaller pharmacies because of their size and buying power. This depends on the negotiating leverage of both purchasing entities. Table 7.2 summarizes some of the largest wholesalers by revenue.[5]

Table 7.2

Rank	Wholesaler	2013 Revenue (billions)
1	McKesson Corporation	$111.0
2	AmerisourceBergen Corp.	$94.1
3	Cardinal Health, Inc.	$83.8

---

[5] "Drug Distribution and Related Revenues at Big Three Wholesalers, Calendar Year 2013." Web. 18 Mar. 2015. http://www.mdm.com/2014_pharmaceuticals_mdm-market-leaders.

Pharmacies

Pharmacies dispense prescription drugs directly to beneficiaries and health care providers that administer drugs. There are approximately 65,000 retail pharmacies in the United States according to information published by the National Council for Prescription Drug Programs. Some of the largest pharmacy chains currently in the United States include CVS Health, Walgreens, Rite Aid, and Walmart.

There are also many community, independent, and franchise pharmacies in addition to the large retail pharmacy chains. The most common type of pharmacy is a retail pharmacy. Other pharmacy types include mail order and specialty pharmacies. Specialty pharmacies focus on high-cost drugs or drugs with particular complexity in handling or administration.

PBMs negotiate discounted drug pricing from pharmacies in exchange for inclusion in the PBM's pharmacy network. Inclusion in the PBM's pharmacy network generates more customers for the pharmacy and allows for coverage of drugs dispensed at a pharmacy through the beneficiary's plan. These negotiated discounts decrease the cost of the drug covered by the benefit plan.

Pharmacies dispense drugs to beneficiaries in exchange for cost sharing,[6] which is generally in the form of a copay or coinsurance.[7] Other forms of cost sharing are possible, including a deductible or coverage gap in certain Medicare Part D plans. Pharmacies also perform other functions, such as checking plan eligibility, performing generic drug substitutions in certain states, checking for adverse drug interactions, providing guidance and answers to beneficiary questions, and in some cases member outreach to improve drug adherence.

Figure 7.4 shows the relationship of pharmacies with PBMs and beneficiaries.

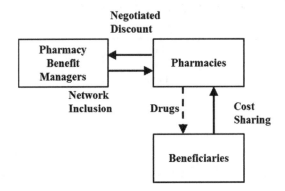

Figure 7.4

---

[6] Pharmacies are also paid the balance of the drug's cost by the PBM which is then reimbursed by third party payers.
[7] The term "coinsurance" refers to a percentage of cost split between the payer and the member. It may refer to either the payer's share or the member's share of the costs. Where specificity is required and the context is otherwise unclear, this text uses terms such as "payer coinsurance" or "member coinsurance" to identify which party is responsibility for paying a given coinsurance amount.

Pharmacy Benefit Managers

PBMs administer prescription drug benefit programs to its customers. When a PBM operates independently, its customers are insurance companies, employer groups, or other third party payers that require assistance with pharmacy benefit administration. Some of the largest PBMs currently include Express Scripts Inc., CVS Health, OptumRx, and Prime Therapeutics.

PBM administrative duties often include managing claim payment and adjudication systems as well as other member services. Member services may include managing a call center, or issuing insurance cards. In addition to administration, PBMs negotiate rebates with manufacturers, negotiate discounts with pharmacies, and manage relationships with third-party payers. PBMs manage drug benefits by establishing a formulary of drug therapies, building a network of pharmacies that offer access to discounted drugs, and providing claims data and other information to third party payers that can be analyzed to determine cost drivers and create interventions to manage cost increases.

Additional features offered by PBMs include utilization management controls, benefit feature incentives, adherence programs, and medical benefit integration. Third-party payers pay PBMs an administrative fee, either directly or indirectly, for its services. A direct retention fee includes per claim or per member per month administration fee. An indirect retention fee may be in the form of a differential (spread) on discounts or in the form of retention of a portion of rebates negotiated by the PBM, or on other bases. Figure 7.5 shows the relationship between PBMs and third-party payers.

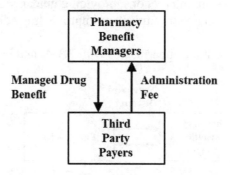

Figure 7.5

Third-Party Payers

Third-party payers are insurance companies, employers, or government programs that fund the prescription drug benefit. Third-party payers interact directly with PBMs and beneficiaries.

An employer's beneficiaries are often its employees and covered dependents. Employees provide labor in exchange for a total compensation package, which may include a prescription drug benefit. The employer may be the risk-bearing entity, which contracts with PBMs to administer prescription drug benefits.

Alternatively, the employer may pass the risk of prescription drug claim fluctuations to an insurance company in exchange for a fixed premium. An insurance company's beneficiaries are the members of the group that are purchasing prescription drug coverage. A premium is paid to the insurance company in exchange for insurance coverage. Figure 7.6 shows the relationship between third-party payers and beneficiaries.

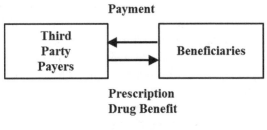

Figure 7.6

Beneficiaries

Beneficiaries are the consumers of prescription drugs. Beneficiaries may receive a prescription from a prescribing health care provider as a result of a medical encounter. Encounters include office visits, outpatient procedures, and inpatient stays. Figure 7.7 shows the relationship between beneficiaries and prescribing health care providers.

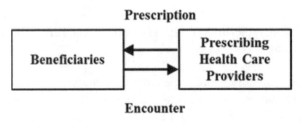

Figure 7.7

Prescribing Health Care Providers

Prescribing health care providers diagnose, treat medical conditions, and prescribe drugs to beneficiaries. Medical doctors, physician assistants (PAs), advanced practice registered nurses (APRNs), and other health care professionals may write prescriptions to patients. Prescribing laws may vary by state and certain specialists may have limited prescribing power for a specific disease state, therapeutic class, or set of drugs.

Other Relationships

This framework is a simplification of a complex prescription drug benefits system. As a result, there are other relationships and interdependencies that exist in practice, but are not depicted in the framework.

Third-party payers, in addition to PBMs, may sometimes contract directly with pharmacies to build a broad, preferred, or narrow network of pharmacies. PBMs are typically able to negotiate lower drug prices from network pharmacies in narrow or preferred network arrangements.

Preferred networks are common within the Medicare Part D market and with some employer plans. Through these arrangements, third-party payers are able to offer reduced out-of-pocket beneficiary cost sharing when members obtain drugs from preferred pharmacies. This approach can be used to encourage members to use preferred network pharmacies.

There are many interrelationships and strategic partnerships within the prescription drug benefits system. CVS Health currently operates a PBM, mail order pharmacy, specialty pharmacy, clinic services, and a retail pharmacy chain. Many PBMs either own or have exclusive relationships with mail order and specialty pharmacies, which create cost saving and quality improvement opportunities and in some cases result in increases in utilization. Pharmacies may also have strategic partnerships and ownership of wholesalers. Insurance companies may own a PBM (e.g., UnitedHealth Group currently owns OptumRx, which is a large PBM). These complex interrelationships are not directly reflected in the simplified pharmacy benefits structure framework, but are important aspects of the pharmacy system in the United States. Interrelationships may evolve over time, creating new opportunities and new risks for entities within the prescription drug benefit system.

TYPES OF PRESCRIPTION DRUGS

There are over 180,000 distinct prescription drugs by National Drug Code (NDC). The NDC system categorizes prescription drugs by manufacturer, chemical compound, dosage, and packaging.

Generic drugs are typically the lowest cost and most commonly dispensed drugs for most prescription drug benefit plans.

Brand name drugs are generally more expensive than the generic equivalent version of the drug, if the generic version exists. A generic equivalent drug is a generic version of a brand drug. These drugs are often created once a brand drug's patent expires, allowing competing manufacturers to produce and distribute a similar drug. Single-Source Brand (SSB) drugs are brand drugs that do not have a generic equivalent. Multi-Source Brand (MSB) drugs are brand name drugs that have a generic equivalent.

Specialty drugs are typically associated with high cost and low utilization. For a commercial population, it is not uncommon for specialty drugs to account for approximately 2% of total pharmacy benefit[8] prescription drug utilization and 20-30% of total pharmacy benefit prescription drug cost. Many specialty drugs require special treatment and delivery (e.g. temperature controlled, administered by a health care provider). There is no uniform definition of specialty drugs in the pharmaceutical industry but the CMS definition is used for Medicare Part D coverage.

Biologic drugs are derived from living organisms and are usually very expensive. Biosimilars, or follow-on biologics, are subsequent versions of biologic drugs developed by different manufacturers. The relationship of biosimilars to biologic drugs may be compared to the relationship of generics to brand drugs for traditional medications. However, the cost and efficacy of biosimilars relative to biologics may not be as effective as that for generics relative to traditional brand medications. For traditional medications, generic drugs are usually sold at a fraction of the brand drug cost and are often therapeutically interchangeable

---

[8] The term "pharmacy benefit" is used here to explicitly exclude prescription drugs that are covered as part of the medical benefit including drugs administered during inpatient stays and as part of outpatient treatment (including chemotherapy).

with brand drugs. Conversely, biosimilars may not be as cost-effective or therapeutically-equivalent relative to biologics.

Biologics are generally considered to be specialty drugs due to their high costs. Table 7.3 summarizes some of the top biologic drugs by revenue.[9]

Table 7.3

2013 Top Biologic Drugs by Revenue			
Rank	Biologic	Class[10]	2013 Revenue (billions)
1	Humira	TNF-blocker	$10.7
2	Remicade	TNF-blocker	$8.9
3	Rituxan	Monoclonal Antibody	$8.9
4	Enbrel	TNF-blocker	$8.3
5	Lantus	Insulin	$7.8
6	Avastin	VEGF inhibitor	$7.0
7	Herceptin	Monoclonal Antibody	$6.8
8	Neulasta	Granulocyte colony-stimulating factor	$4.4

Compound drugs are drugs mixed by a pharmacist. Compound drugs may be high-cost drugs but can deliver a customized strength and dosage to meet a beneficiary's specific needs. Some compound drug combinations are not FDA-approved.

Over-the-Counter (OTC) drugs do not require a prescription to purchase. Examples of OTC drugs include Advil, Prilosec OTC, Kaopectate, NyQuil, and Tylenol.

A prescription drug benefit plan may cover certain supplies, including diabetic test strips and alcohol pads. Supplies are generally low cost, representing a small portion of total prescription drug costs.

THE PRESCRIPTION DRUG LIFECYCLE

The prescription drug lifecycle spans decades, from initial drug discovery to widespread generic availability. The lifecycle includes:

1. Research and development
2. Brand patent protection period
3. Generic exclusivity period
4. Generic drug lifespan

The prescription drug lifecycle starts with *research and development* (R&D) performed by pharmaceutical manufacturers. R&D includes initial drug discovery, preclinical testing,

---

[9] "Biologics Still on Top in Best Selling Drugs of 2013." *Cell Culture Dish*. 13 Mar. 2014. Web. 18 Mar. 2015. http://cellculturedish.com/2014/03/top-ten-biologics-2013-us-pharmaceutical-sales-2/
[10] "PDR Search." *PDR.Net*. Web. 18 Mar. 2015. http://www.pdr.net/

clinical trials, and review by the FDA. A successful R&D effort results in FDA approval and large scale production of the drug to consumers.

There are typically 5,000 to 10,000 potential compounds considered in the initial drug discovery period. During preclinical testing, the number of compounds is reduced to approximately five. The remaining compounds are further narrowed to one compound in three phases of clinical trials, each with an increasing sample size of human subjects. The FDA reviews one compound that emerges from clinical trials and approves the compound for large scale production upon a successful review.

The R&D process typically lasts fifteen years, from initial drug discovery to FDA approval. Once a drug is approved for large scale production, pharmaceutical manufacturers are awarded the exclusive right to manufacturer the approved drug during the *brand patent protection period*. The brand patent period typically lasts 12 years and is intended to give manufacturers the opportunity to offset R&D costs.

The *generic exclusivity period* typically lasts six months and often immediately follows the brand patent period. During the generic exclusivity period, only the brand name manufacturer and one additional manufacturer are allowed to manufacture the generic equivalent. The intent of the generic exclusivity period is to reward the generic manufacturer that incurs significant legal costs to end the brand patent period.

After the conclusion of the generic exclusivity period, all pharmaceutical manufacturers may produce and sell the drug. During the *generic drug lifespan*, the lack of additional R&D costs and new competitive market forces contribute to lower generic prices relative to equivalent brand name drugs.

METHODS OF PRESCRIPTION DRUG DISTRIBUTION

There are a variety of methods by which drugs are distributed to beneficiaries, including:

1. Retail pharmacies
2. Mail order pharmacies
3. Specialty pharmacies

Retail pharmacies have brick and mortar locations that beneficiaries can visit to fill and pick up prescription drugs. Retail pharmacies typically dispense a one-month supply of prescription drugs. Extended supplies of up to three months are occasionally dispensed by retail pharmacies. Shorter supplies are dispensed for certain acute conditions. For example, a one-week supply of an antibiotic prescription drug may be dispensed to treat a bacterial infection.

Mail order pharmacies send prescriptions to beneficiaries through the mail. Mail order pharmacies are often owned and operated by PBMs. Mail order pharmacies typically dispense up to a three-month supply of prescription drugs and are often used to dispense maintenance medications to beneficiaries. Maintenance medications often treat chronic conditions. Unlike acute conditions, which are sometimes sudden and severe, chronic conditions are often persistent and are effectively treated with routine mail order refills. Some plans include a mandatory mail order provision on certain maintenance medications to reduce costs.

Beneficiary cost sharing for mail-order prescriptions may be reduced to encourage mail-order utilization. Mail-order cost sharing for a three-month supply may be 2 or 2.5 times that of one-month supply dispensed at a retail pharmacy. This creates an out-of-pocket cost-saving incentive for the beneficiary because members pay less than 3 times the one-month retail copay for a three-month supply at mail. For example, a three-tier formulary may have a retail copay structure of $10/$20/$40, with a mail-order copay structure of $20/$40/$80 or $25/$50/$100. This provides lower cost to participants on a one-month supply equivalent basis and encourages the use of the mail order program.

Specialty pharmacies focus on the delivery of specialty drugs. Specialty drugs often require special treatment in terms of storage and administration. Specialty pharmacies identify the most effective method of administration for each drug. There are other methods of prescription drug distribution, including drugs dispensed at a health provider's facility. Certain long-term care facilities, hospice facilities, and home health professionals may dispense prescription drugs.

BENEFIT DESIGN

Benefit designs are structured to control costs by encouraging the efficient use of available drugs. Current drug program benefit designs include the use of copays, coinsurance, and formularies. Benefit contracts may limit or exclude certain drugs, such as over-the-counter items and lifestyle drugs. In the last several years, the ability to exclude certain types of drugs has been increasingly limited by federal and state statutes and regulations that mandate coverage of specific drugs.

COST SHARING

Cost-sharing options include copayments, coinsurance, deductibles, and combinations.

Copay plans, often seen with health maintenance organization (HMO) style medical plans, are also available with Preferred Provider Organization (PPO), Point of Service (POS), and indemnity plans. Copay plans typically have different copay amounts for the various formulary tiers. Coinsurance plans may have a deductible for drugs subject to the coinsurance in the plan design. With a tier-based formulary design, the member coinsurance may increase with the tier of the formulary. If the coinsurance plan is part of a major medical integrated plan, the plan's integrated medical and pharmacy deductible must be met before the coinsurance takes effect.

If the coinsurance plan is not integrated with a major medical plan, a separate prescription drug deductible may apply. If there is a prescription drug deductible, only drug claims are counted when determining if the drug deductible has been met. Once the deductible is met, coinsurance is then applied to the drug claims. Coinsurance plans are also available with HMO, PPO, POS, and indemnity plans.

Some combination cost-sharing designs use the larger of a copay value or the percentage coinsurance as cost sharing. For example, a plan might have member cost sharing of the greater of $10 or 10% of the drug cost. A drug that costs $75 would require a cost sharing payment of $10 (the copayment is larger than the resultant member coinsurance), and a drug that costs $170 would require a cost sharing payment of $17 (the resultant member coinsurance is larger than the copayment).

Cost-sharing maximums can occur as well, such as percentage coinsurance with a dollar-value maximum, which protects the participant from the high cost of certain drugs, such as AIDS drugs. Here, a participant might pay 10% of the cost, subject to a maximum of $75. A drug that costs $50 would require a $5 cost sharing payment, and a drug that costs $1,000 would require a $75 cost-sharing payment (the resultant coinsurance would be higher than the maximum and is thus capped). Plan design combinations that include copays with coinsurance on excess costs also exist. For example, a drug that costs $100 may be subject to a $10 copay, with 10% member coinsurance on the excess cost above $10, for a total cost sharing amount of $19, derived as $10 + ($100 - $10) x 10%.

A coverage gap is a common feature of Medicare Part D plans. The Affordable Care Act (ACA) phased out the coverage gap, which previously required 100% cost sharing in a certain spending phase. According to current plans, the coverage gap will be completely eliminated by 2020.

Many commercial plans also include an out-of-pocket maximum to limit beneficiary cost sharing over the plan year. Qualified Health Plans, as defined by the ACA, have mandatory out-of-pocket limits on combined medical and pharmacy spending. The ACA created other mandates, with exceptions, for the coverage of prescription drugs, including mandating 0% member cost sharing on preventative drugs, as well as on contraceptives. Prescription drug coverage is additionally listed as an Essential Health Benefit (EHB) under the ACA, making it part of the set of health care service categories that must be covered by certain plans.

As pharmacy claims trend upward, member cost sharing is also increasing, especially in the private employer-funded sector. Offsetting otherwise increasing beneficiary premiums with higher member cost sharing helps to control rising premium costs, shifting claim payment responsibility to the members in the form of out-of-pocket cost sharing. To the opposite effect, failing to increase member cost sharing when pharmacy costs themselves are rising implicitly (and perhaps unintentionally) creates a richer benefit offering for the member. These are important concepts for employers that are covering all or a portion of the beneficiary premium as part of the total compensation package.

Studies have shown that members will indeed use less medication as the out-of-pocket cost increases, but the unintended consequence of members sometimes choosing not to purchase and receive necessary drugs may adversely affect health outcomes.[11] As employers shift costs to employees through increased out-of-pocket costs, they should consider the impact on the total compensation package, and in turn, their ability to recruit and retain talent based on the totals compensation offerings of their competitors.

---

[11] Gibson TB; Ozminkowski RJ and Goetzel RZ. "The Effects of Prescription Drug Cost Sharing: A Review of the Evidence." *Am J Manag Care*. 2005;11:730-740.

FORMULARIES

Formularies are lists of preferred drugs, selected by a health system, health plan or PBM. A formulary is developed by a Pharmacy and Therapeutics (P&T) committee which is typically comprised of actively practicing physicians, pharmacists, and other clinicians. If a drug is listed on the formulary, it is said to be a *formulary* or *preferred drug*. If not listed, it is *non-formulary* or *non-preferred*. Whether a drug is on the list may affect member cost sharing and access to the drug. Formulary benefit design and how drugs are selected for a formulary are discussed in other sections of this chapter.

Three types of formulary-related benefit designs currently exist in the prescription drug coverage market:

- *Closed*: Closed formularies only cover drugs that are listed on the formulary. Closed formulary plans must have a process to allow for coverage of non-formulary medications for individual patients, based on medical necessity. The prescriber must justify the exception based on the medical condition of that particular patient. Closed formularies are commonly found in Medicaid plans, where cost sharing is very small or nothing. In a commercial plan, cost sharing may depend on whether the drug is generic or brand name. Some commercial designs have a fixed percent coinsurance for all covered drugs.

- *Open*: Open formularies do not restrict whether or not a drug is covered, but do usually affect the cost sharing. Some open formulary products have fixed percent coinsurance, while other have tiered cost sharing. Tiers are described below.

- *Tiered (Incentive)*: Tiered formularies have more than one cost sharing tier. The individual tiers may be assigned fixed-dollar amounts (copays), percentages of prescription cost (coinsurance) or a combination of the two. For example, a fixed copay might be $30 per prescription, regardless of the drug cost. The same drug in a coinsurance design might have a member cost sharing provision of 30% of the drug cost. A combination of coinsurance with a fixed minimum or maximum amount may also be used. This is discussed further in the section on cost sharing.

FORMULARY TIERS

Formulary benefits may sometimes group drugs into categories referred to as *tiers,* and differentiate in level of payments or cost sharing by tier. An incentive formulary benefit may have two or more tiers. The following are the most common designs, but as third-party payers and PBMs seek creative solutions, it is likely that others may emerge:

- *Two-tier:* These designs have two tiers of drugs, usually tier 1 (generics) and tier 2 (brand name drugs). Tier 1 drugs generally have a low cost-sharing amount, and tier 2 drugs will have a higher cost sharing. For example, the formulary benefit design might have a $10 copay for generics, and $30 copay for brand-name drugs. Or, it might have 10% member coinsurance for generics, and 20% for brands.

- *Three-tier*: Three-tier designs became popular in the late 1990s. The tiers can be defined in various ways, but most commonly tier 1 is generic drugs, tier 2 is preferred brands, and tier 3 is non-preferred drugs. In this design, non-preferred drugs are still covered, although at the highest cost sharing. Cost-sharing increase as the tier level increases. For example, tier 1 (generics) may have a $10 copay, tier 2 (preferred) may have a $30 copay, and tier 3 (non-preferred) may have a $50 copay. Copay and coinsurance tiers can be mixed in the same design. For example, tier 1 might have a fixed copay of $10, while tiers 2 and 3 have member coinsurance of 20% and 50% respectively. This design is intended to help manage costs, by encouraging patients and their physicians to use the preferred tier of drugs, through higher cost sharing for the non-preferred drugs. The introduction of the preferred brand tier creates an opportunity for PBMs to negotiate rebates with drug manufacturers in exchange for preferred-brand tier placement. Preferred-brand tier placement offers lower out-of-pocket cost sharing, and in turn an incentive for beneficiaries to use that drug manufacturer's preferred brand drugs.

- *Four-tier*: Most four-tier designs are variations of the three-tier designs, with a particular group of drugs assigned to a fourth tier. One such plan identifies a separate tier for chronic use, maintenance drugs. This tier of drugs may have a cost sharing between the generic drug tier and the preferred drug tier. Another four tier design may put lifestyle drugs (drugs that are not medically necessary but add value to someone's lifestyle, such as Viagra) at 100% member cost sharing. Formulary placement, albeit at 100% cost sharing, is still beneficial to the beneficiary, as they will be able to benefit from the discounts negotiated by the PBM with pharmacies. The most common fourth tier is defined by taking specialty pharmaceuticals (biologics and other very high cost, targeted drugs that are usually dispensed by specialty pharmacies) out of the standard three-tier benefit and placing them in a fourth tier with cost sharing that is commensurate with their high cost. Other four-tier formulary designs also exist.

- *Five-tier*: Five-tier designs have become fairly common in Medicare Part D and can be created by taking a four-tier design (with the fourth tier being specialty drugs), and dividing the generic tier into two tiers, creating a preferred generic and non-preferred generic tier. The resulting tier structure includes two generic tiers, two brand tiers, and one specialty tier. Another possible five-tier formulary design splits the specialty tier into a preferred and non-preferred tier.

- *Six-tier*: Six-tier designs are beginning to appear within the prescription drug benefits system. These can be structured in a number of ways, including dividing specialty drugs into three tiers, tier 4 being biosimilars, tier 5 preferred specialty drugs and tier 6 non-preferred specialty drugs. An alternate six-tier formulary design includes two generic tiers, two brand tiers, and two specialty tiers. In this alternate configuration, each drug class (generic, brand, and specialty) has preferred and non-preferred tiers.

VALUE-BASED INSURANCE DESIGN

Increasing out-of-pocket costs can effectively limit access to or discourage utilization of certain drugs that might be important in controlling or preventing chronic diseases or other medical illnesses. Not taking these drugs may cause the underlying condition to get worse. For this reason, these drugs are often called *high-value drugs*.

The extent to which a patient takes a prescription drug exactly as directed is called *medication adherence*. Affordability is only one of several factors patients consider in terms of medication adherence. Others include forgetfulness, side effects, and believing they do not really need to take the drug. As out-of-pocket cost sharing rises, affordability increasingly becomes an issue.

One solution to the problem of affordability of high-value drugs is value-based benefits or value-based insurance design (VBID).[12]

Value-based benefits selectively reduce cost sharing on drugs and other medical treatments that are identified as being high value. This commonly focuses on drugs for chronic diseases, such as diabetes, high blood pressure, and high cholesterol. This can reduce overall drug cost in the long run by avoiding the unnecessary cost of treating these conditions as they worsen without proper drug therapy.

LIMITATIONS ON USAGE

Limitations will often exist with respect to the amount dispensed and frequency of refills. For example, a typical prescription dispensed at a pharmacy will provide a 30 to 32 day supply of a drug. With this quantity limit (QL), refills can only be made close to the expected time when the previous prescription will have been used up. In the example above, a participant may only be allowed to get a refill after 23, 25, or 28 days. Permission for early refills or larger quantities may be obtained for valid reasons, such as travel.

Other types of drug management controls include prior authorization (PA) and step therapy (ST) "edits". These edits are used by plans to manage the beneficiaries' drug usage based on cost, availability of a generic alternative, safety, possibility for adverse drug interactions, effectiveness, likelihood of fraud and abuse, or medical necessity. When a PA edit is in place, members are required to obtain prior authorization from the plan prior to gaining coverage of a certain drug that is prescribed by a physician. When a ST edit is in place, members are required to try and document failure of a certain preferred drug or set of drugs prior to gaining coverage for the drug with the ST edit in place.

MANDATORY GENERICS AND "DISPENSE AS WRITTEN" BENEFIT ISSUES

Another benefit plan option for reducing or managing drug cost is to mandate generic dispensing when a generic product is available. Most states' generic substitution laws permit a physician to mark the prescription "dispense as written" or "DAW," which requires the pharmacy to dispense the brand name drug rather than the generic substitute, even when a mandatory generic provision is in place. In the event that a DAW order is allowed, the plan may choose to impose a DAW penalty. The DAW penalty can be structured a number of ways. One such way would make the third-party payer cost neutral, where the member pays the brand cost, excluding the amount the plan would have paid for the corresponding generic. Many plans will make temporary exceptions when the generic equivalent is unavailable to pharmacies due to manufacturing shortages.

When there is no generic equivalent, a plan may still reduce drug cost by encouraging substitution of a therapeutically interchangeable drug. Therapeutically interchangeable drugs are those drugs that have the same therapeutic effect to treat a condition, despite the fact that their chemical structure differs.

---

[12] VBID is a rapidly developing concept. For current information, see the University of Michigan Center for Value-Based Insurance Design Web site, www.sph.umich.edu/vbidcenter/

Formulary Design

Assignment to Tiers

Formulary design can vary widely between prescription drug plans and may be based on drug cost, drug manufacturer rebate offerings, clinical safety and effectiveness, or availability. PBMs and third-party payers often work together to make decisions on which drugs to cover and formulary tier placement, with the intention of using cost-sharing differentials to steer members to certain drugs.

Consider the following sample three-tier formulary:
- Tier 1: Generics, subject to $5 copay
- Tier 2: Preferred brands (all of which are single-source brand), subject to $25 copay
- Tier 3: Multi-source brands and non-preferred single-source brands, subject to $45 copay

This sample formulary may have been structured to encourage members to use lower-cost generics whenever available. When no generic equivalent is available, members are able to purchase the drugs they need at a more moderate cost-sharing level. The PBM may divide single-source brand drugs into preferred and non-preferred groupings based on safety, effectiveness, cost, or other considerations. Creating preferred and non-preferred drug tiers allows the PBM to leverage cost sharing differentials to negotiate better rebates from drug manufacturers

Because single-source brand drugs are typically higher cost than multi-source brand drugs, the average cost of drugs on tier 2 may exceed that on tier 3. This will not always be the case, and in many instances, PBMs and third-party payers will structure cost-sharing differences to consistently steer members toward the lower cost drugs. Formulary tier assignment can vary widely across pharmacy plans, based on the intentions and goals of the plan sponsor.

A formulary designed with participants in mind should generally include the majority of their drug needs. This might result in a formulary covering 90-95% of the medication needs of the participants. Depending on the pharmacy product, state, and current legal environment, protected classes of drugs and coverage requirements exist to ensure adequate drug coverage for beneficiaries.

Many hospitals, and some medical provider groups and integrated health systems, have their own formularies as well. Physicians do not always have information on health benefit plan formularies when they prescribe a medication for a patient. Thus, confusion can occur when a participant goes to the pharmacy and is expecting certain coverage of a prescribed drug. This can be rectified if computerized physician order entry is available to the physician at the point of prescribing the drug. Prescribing tools such as Epocrates, an app-based drug information system available on web- and mobile-based platforms, may contain formulary information. Some PBMs are making this type of information available through such tools on their own websites.

Pharmacy and Therapeutics (P&T) Committees

The choice of which drugs to put on the formulary is primarily based on clinical criteria but financial considerations are evident. The clinical considerations include safety, efficacy, and adequate coverage within a therapeutic class of drugs and are determined by the PBM's Pharmacy and Therapeutics (P&T) Committee. The P&T Committee typically consists of actively practicing physicians, pharmacists and other clinicians who work together to determine whether a drug should be added to the formulary.

It is considered desirable that the voting members not be employees of the PBM in order to ensure independent, objective, and unbiased formulary coverage decisions. One way to accomplish this is to have the voting members consist of a group of respected physicians and pharmacists who represent the geographical area served by pharmacy plans, and have an interest in the well-being of the beneficiaries served by the formularies being managed. The PBM's staff still attends the meetings as non-voting members, establishes the committee charter, selects voting members, and plans the agenda, but does not control the meetings or the resulting decisions.

The P&T committee typically comes to one of three decisions as they evaluate drugs for formulary coverage:

- Don't cover the drug.
- Cover the drug.
- Interchangeable/May cover.

The P&T committee first must deem the product to be safe, effective, and a worthwhile formulary coverage option given the existing alternatives. Once these conditions are met, the PBM then proceeds to determine the financial impact of this formulary change, as well as the process for implementation. The PBM may use the information regarding drugs deemed interchangeable to negotiate the best possible financial position between itself, its customers, and the drug manufacturers, leveraging formulary coverage to increase the rebate compensation received from the manufacturers. Consider two drugs that are deemed interchangeable by the P&T committee. The PBM and third-party payer could choose to cover one of these options, but not the other, with the covered drug selected based on the drug manufacturer that offers the most rebates. The extent to which third-party payers are involved in formulary design and pharmacy management may vary by third-party payer, and the PBM may choose to develop customized options for its various customers.

There are numerous examples of drug pairs that are typically considered interchangeable, and thus offer opportunity for formulary coverage leveraging to increase negotiated rebates with drug manufacturers. One such example relates to two expensive drugs used to treat the Hepatitis C virus: Harvoni and Viekira Pak. Harvoni is manufactured by Gilead Sciences and Viekira Pak is manufactured by AbbVie. Some PBMs have decided to cover one or the other, using that selectivity to negotiate rebates from the drug manufacturers.

PBMs and Pharmacy Networks

The contract between the PBM and the third-party payer will typically state the discount and dispensing fee levels that the third-party payer's claims will be subject to when using the PBM network of pharmacies. In some cases, the third-party payer may negotiate contracts directly with pharmacies and establish its own network. In these cases, the third-party payer performs the contracting functions described in this section. Discounts off of AWP will vary between mail and retail, with mail discounts often being higher than retail. Discounts off of

AWP will also vary between generic and brand name drugs with generic discounts typically being significantly higher than brand discounts.

Generic discounts may be based on the use of a MAC (Maximum Allowable Cost) list, which implicitly creates a discounted price by capping the maximum allowable cost. The Center for Medicare and Medicaid Services (CMS) has its own defined MAC list. Most PBMs also have their own defined MAC list(s). It is important to identify which MAC list is being used when contracting with a PBM. Specific identification in the PBM contract will help avoid confusion when determining the amount the third-party payer will pay for drugs and the amount the pharmacies will receive in exchange for dispensing drugs.

MAC discounts for generics can range from approximately a 50% discount off of AWP to over an 80% discount off of AWP, depending on the drug under consideration. Brand name discounts can range from a 10% discount off of AWP to over 20% off of AWP, depending on the drug, region (rural versus urban area), and any applicable supplemental pharmacy rebate arrangement with the PBM.

Dispensing fees will also vary between mail and retail, with mail being close to $0 per script, and retail ranging from below $1.00 to over $3.00 per script. Dispensing fees could vary between brand name and generic drugs.

The PBM may have more than one pharmacy network and may have more than one set of contracted rates. The PBM contracts discounts and dispensing fees separately with each pharmacy and may use network placement leverage as a negotiating tactic for better rates.

A PBM may have a single set of discounts and dispensing fees with a third-party payer. The PBM/pharmacy contracts may differ from the PBM's contract with the third-party payer. Thus, there is the possibility that the amount the PBM pays the pharmacies for drugs may be different from what the third-party payer pays the PBM for drugs, due to the fact that two separate sets of contracts are being used.

There are two primary models by which PBMs contract with third-party payers: a transparent model and a traditional model. A transparent model is often referred to as a *pass-through* model and a traditional model is referred to as a model that offers *lock-in* pricing.

In a transparent model, pharmacy discounts negotiated by the PBM are used to determine the claim liability for the third-party payer. In a traditional model, pharmacy discounts are not passed directly to the third-party payer. The third-party payer (and its beneficiaries) receives the rates that they contract with the PBM at each pharmacy. In this situation, the PBM reimburses the pharmacies based on its own contracts, which may be different from what the third-party payer reimburses the PBM.

REBATES

Drug manufacturer rebates are payments from manufacturers to PBMs in exchange for preferred placement of the manufacturer's drugs on the PBM's formulary. Rebates may be a fixed amount times the number of units (e.g., pills) sold or could be variable based on the market share or volume.

When third-party payers contract directly with a manufacturer without the use of a PBM, it is often thought that the volume of a particular third-party payer is probably not large enough to get a favorable arrangement. For this reason, PBMs may be able to get better rebate arrangements than individual third-party payers, although this is not always the case. Three key factors that determine negotiating leverage with manufacturers are (1) number of lives represented, (2) control of market share, or ability to move market share to preferred products in a drug class, and (3) consistency of behavior, meaning the degree of predictability of the plan's response to a manufacturer's actions. In general, successful contracting requires at least 500,000 lives over which the plan can exert a reasonable degree of formulary control. If the plan is smaller, they will usually be able to obtain better rates through the PBM's contracts.

A PBM is an intermediary which often has various sources of revenue. These include administrative fees explicitly charged to the third-party payer, retention of a portion of the rebates negotiated with manufacturers, spread on drugs dispensed, price protection that limits purchase price increases, and other sources.

When contracting with a PBM for multi-year contracts, a third-party payer should consider an inflation factor on the minimum rebate guarantee if it is on a per script basis, if it is expected that the cost per script will be increasing over time. Without an inflation factor, the minimum rebate guarantee per script will actually decrease as a percentage of the script cost.

Transparency of prescription drug contracts, including discounts and rebates, is often required by large employer group clients or government programs. From a third-party payer perspective, this might affect how a plan contracts with a PBM or with pharmacies and manufacturers. Or, the plan may develop a communication and pricing plan that provides transparency as to how the contracts affect the group's claim costs.

LEGAL ISSUES ARISING WITH RESPECT TO PBMS

There have been legal concerns with PBMs that are owned by manufacturers, to the point where no PBMs are currently owned by manufacturers. At the time when PBMs were owned by manufacturers, they were sometimes seen as using anti-competitive pressures, in that they might have pushed third-party payers to add drugs from the owner manufacturer as preferred drugs on the third-party payer's formulary.

Merck was the first pharmaceutical company to purchase a PBM, acquiring Medco in 1993. Other manufacturers quickly followed suit, thinking this would be a smart way to market their products. Most of these ventures were short-lived, due to regulatory scrutiny and adverse publicity. With the exception of Merck, the drug companies that purchased PBMs sold them within less than five years at a considerable loss.

A more recent trend is the consolidation and strategic partnerships between PBMs and pharmacies. It is not clear to what extent these new relationships will be scrutinized by the industry and by regulators.

No matter the ownership of the PBM, it is recommended that, when contracting with a PBM, the third-party payer be aware of the formulary management process and the decisions surrounding formulary design, and that the third-party payer develop a well-documented process for formulary design that shows no undue conflict of interest pressure from the perspective of the PBM, manufacturer, or pharmacy.

8. Retiree Group Benefits

Dale H. Yamamoto

Overview of Retiree Group Benefits

Retiree life and medical benefits were generally introduced to U.S. employee benefit programs in the late 1960s. Those medical plans were first designed to supplement the Medicare program and were viewed as a no-cost benefit. At the time, the benefits were very low cost, because medical costs were relatively low and there were few retirees. Life insurance benefits for retirees were often added as a natural expansion of retiree benefits.

In recent years, some employers have expanded their post-employment offerings to include long-term care insurance and continuing-care retirement communities. These benefits are usually offered to employees at their own cost (employee-pay-all). Other benefits offered to employees after employment include severance, dental, vision, and hearing benefits.

In some respects, these benefits are similar to pension benefits. They are provided to employees after they have contributed their services to their employer. Many times, the benefits are continued for the retirees' lifetime. Like pension plans, some plan designs even vary the benefits based on service. But, unlike pension benefits, these retiree group benefits are generally not extensively prefunded.

Retiree group benefits gained attention in the early 1990s primarily because of the Financial Accounting Standards Board's (FASB) accounting changes that applied to most companies in 1993. These rules (FAS No. 106 and since then recodified under Accounting Standards Codification 715-60)[1] require employers to account for retiree group benefits while employees work, rather than waiting until they are retired and benefits are paid. A similar rule issued by the Governmental Accounting Standards Board (GASB) under GASB 43 and 45 impacted most U.S. states and municipalities starting in 2006 or shortly thereafter.

Cost has also forced attention on retiree group benefit plans. In 1960, when many employers were adopting retiree health care plans, the U.S. spent $28 billion on health care-related costs, which was 5.2 percent of the gross domestic product (GDP). Spending continued to grow every year, reaching $2.9 trillion or 17.4 percent of GDP in 2013, and projected to reach 19.3 percent of GDP by 2023.[2] Most executives are very aware of how their companies' medical plan costs have increased over the same period. Add to that challenge the increasing number

---

[1] Financial Statement of Accounting No. 106, *Employers' Accounting for Postretirement Benefits Other Than Pensions*, Financial Accounting Standards Board, December 1990 as recodified by the Board to *Accounting Standards Codification 715 Compensation – Retirement Benefits: 60 Defined Benefit Plans – Other Postretirement (ASC 715-60)*.
[2] Centers for Medicare & Medicaid Services, Office of the Actuary, National Health Expenditure Data. December 2014.

of retirees due to the aging population, layoffs, early retirement incentive plans, and greater overall financial pressures, the conclusion that retiree medical plans are very expensive comes very fast!

This chapter discusses the key issues of retiree group benefits. In this discussion, it is important to recognize how concepts of pensions and health care interact with each other, as well as differences in the delivery of the benefits for active employees and retirees.

Many retiree surveys show fewer employers offering retiree health care benefits. Figure 8.1 shows the typical decline in retiree group benefit. The largest decline took place in the early 1990s, when the then-new accounting standard, FAS 106, became effective. However, many believe that the Affordable Care Act (ACA) will further hasten the decline of retiree benefits, given that employers no longer need to be concerned over whether early retirees have access to health insurance.

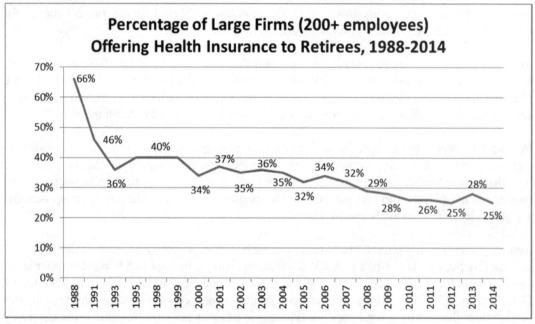

Source: Kaiser/HRET Survey of Employer-Sponsored Health Benefits, 1999-2014: KPMG Survey of Employer-Sponsored Health Benefits, 1991, 1993, 1995, 1998. The Health Insurance of America (HIAA), 1988

Figure 8.1

The public sector's offering of retiree health benefits may begin to trend downward also, given the accounting standards[3] that went into effect from 2006-2009, as well as the ACA's effect of guarantee issue in the individual market that went into effect in 2014. The accounting standards require public sector employers to include the value of retiree health plan obligations on their financial statements on an accrual basis, similar to the FAS 106 rules for private sector employers. FAS 106 is commonly blamed as the reason for the decline in employer-sponsored retiree health care benefits. However, many view the accounting standards as an eye-opener to the real current value of the benefits that were often considered a nominal benefit prior to the new accounting

---

[3] Statement No. 43, *Financial Reporting for Postemployment Benefit Plans Other Than Pension Plans*, Government Accounting Standards Board, April 2004 and Statement No. 45, *Accounting and Financial Reporting by Employers for Postemployment Benefits Other Than Pension Plans*, Government Accounting Standards Board, June 2004.

standard. The fact that no dramatic drop-off in coverage has occurred yet in the public sector may be due to differences between public and private sector employment relationships, including greater union involvement as well as constitutional requirements to continue coverage for public-sector retirees.

MEDICARE

Employer-sponsored retiree group benefits continue to be an important source of coverage for Medicare-eligible retirees, with 30% to 35% of Medicare beneficiaries covered under employer plans.[4]

The Medicare program in the U.S. is usually the primary health insurance source for citizens and permanent legal residents age 65 and over. Unlike many other countries, the U.S. does not have a socialized health care system for the majority of its population. For persons covered under employer-provided health plans, employees and family members (usually) are provided care in a private system that is reimbursed by the health plans.

The Medicare system is similar to a fee-for-service plan, though other options are available. Most Medicare beneficiaries are over age 65, though some disabled persons are covered. Medicare is the primary payer of health for the aged, as long as the person is not covered as an active employee in an employer-provided health plan. Thus, there is a very large decrease in the employer's plan cost as retirees turn age 65. The 18th annual Towers Watson/National Business Group on Health Employer Survey on Purchasing Value in Health Care estimated that the average cost in 2013 was $9,064 for pre-65 retirees and $4,583 for post-65 retirees. While a welcome cost decrease, Medicare coordination creates challenges for employers both in terms of plan design and valuation.

The introduction of prescription drugs to the Medicare program in 2006 created a new set of delivery models under the program, as well as opportunities for employers to coordinate their programs around the new benefit.

Other governmental systems have distinctions by age. For example, some of Canada's provincial plans do not cover certain prescription drugs after a person becomes age 65.

MEDICARE HEALTH PLANS

The Medicare program offers several alternative health plans. Beneficiaries have the option to elect either the "Original Plan" or one of the "Medicare Advantage" (MA) options. In addition, they can voluntarily enroll in a prescription drug plan either separately (a private prescription drug plan option) or through a MA plan that includes prescription drugs (MA-PD). Many experts have been concerned that the availability of these multiple choices has created confusion among the beneficiary population.

Original Medicare Plan

The original Medicare plan is the original fee-for-service plan that has been offered under the

---

[4] Kaiser Family Foundation analysis of the Medicare Current Beneficiary Survey 2010 Cost and Use file.

Medicare program from inception. The two parts of Medicare—Part A and Part B—were originally the plan design separation between hospital and medical services. A description of the original Medicare program, including the services provided, is included in Chapter 9, "Government Health Plans in the United States." That chapter also includes further detail on a number of Medicare related topics.

Coordinated Care Plans (Part C)

"Coordinated care" or managed care plans have their genesis in the "risk contract" programs first offered in 1982. The program paid managed care organizations (primarily risk-bearing health maintenance organizations known as risk HMOs) to provide at least the same coverage as the fee-for-service Medicare plan under their managed network systems. In return, the organizations were paid a fixed amount per covered beneficiary (capitation). The fixed amount was originally intended to pay about 95 percent of what Medicare was paying. Medicare beneficiaries began to enroll in the risk HMOs because of the lower copay requirements and richer benefits. Many HMOs provided added services, such as preventive care and prescription drugs, that were not provided under the Medicare fee-for-service plan at that time. By 1997, 70 percent of Medicare beneficiaries lived in areas where a risk plan was available to them, and 5.2 million beneficiaries (13.5 percent of Medicare population) had enrolled in one of the plans. MA enrollment has grown to cover 12 million beneficiaries (20 percent of Medicare population) in 2015. Medicare Advantage medical plans (discussed briefly in this chapter, as well as in Chapter 9) technically fall under Part C.

Prescription Drug Plans (Part D)

The Medicare Modernization Act of 2003 (MMA) was the most expansive set of changes to the Medicare program since its inception. Most significantly, the legislation added a prescription drug benefit beginning in 2006. The plans may be stand-alone prescription drug plans (PDPs) or plans added on to a managed care plan under Medicare Advantage (MA-PD). The prescription drug benefit is a voluntary benefit under the Medicare program and is provided by private insurance companies. Details of the Part D plan design can be found in Chapter 9.

FINANCING

The Centers for Medicare & Medicaid Services (CMS) is the agency under the Department of Health and Human Services (HHS) responsible for the administration of the Medicare program. The program is financed through two trust funds—the Hospital Insurance (HI) Trust Fund covering Medicare Part A, and the Supplementary Medical Insurance (SMI) Trust Fund covering Parts B and D.

Medicare Advantage Plans

Medicare payments to Medicare Advantage plans are based on a blend of local and national capitated rates. Actual payments to plans are risk adjusted, based on demographics and health status of individual beneficiaries. The method for determining the capitated rates has changed over time, with the latest modification made by the ACA, which linked rates more closely to the cost of the fee-for-service Medicare plans.

Prescription Drug Plans (PDPs)

Payments to PDPs are based on a combination of direct subsidy payments, catastrophic benefit reinsurance, and risk sharing payments. On average, the federal government subsidizes approximately 74.5% of the total plan costs. In addition, Medicare pays for the premium and cost-sharing assistance provided to low-income beneficiaries.

Employer Retiree Drug Subsidies

Starting in 2006, employers who directly offer retirees and dependents prescription drug coverage (rather than offering a PDP) may receive a subsidy from CMS. Employers are required to demonstrate in advance that their drug plan is at least actuarially equivalent to the standard PDP, both in terms of total benefits delivered as well as in terms of the level of employer premium subsidy to retirees relative to the government subsidy to the standard PDP.

Additional details on the financing of each these programs can be found in Chapter 9.

PROVIDER PAYMENTS

Medicare payments for most inpatient hospital services are made under a reimbursement method called the prospective payment system (PPS). Under the PPS, a specific predetermined amount is paid to the provider for each inpatient hospital stay, based on a diagnosis-related group (DRG) classification. In some cases, the payment that the hospital receives under this system is less than the hospital's actual cost of providing the services, and, in other cases, it is more. The hospital absorbs any of the loss or makes a profit. There are some payment adjustments for very high-cost inpatient hospital stays. Payments for other Part A covered care (skilled nursing care, home health care, inpatient rehabilitation and psychiatric care) are made under separate prospective payment systems.

Physicians are paid on the basis of allowed charges that are defined as the lesser of: (1) the submitted charges, or (2) the amount determined by a fee schedule that is based on a resource-based relative value scale (RBRVS). Payments for durable medical equipment and clinical laboratory services are also based on a fee schedule. Most hospital outpatient services and home health care are reimbursed using the PPS method.

If a Part B provider agrees to accept the Medicare-approved rate (that is, accepts assignment of benefits), then the Medicare payment provided to them (both the Medicare benefit payment and the beneficiaries' coinsurance payment) are considered as payment in full for that service. The provider may not request any additional payments from the beneficiary or insurer. If the provider does not take assignment, the beneficiary may be charged for the excess (a practice referred to as "balance billing"). Physicians are "participating physicians" if they agree before the year to accept assignment for all Medicare services they furnish during the year. Since Medicare beneficiaries may select their doctors, they have the option to choose those who participate. Non-participating physicians receive a lower payment from Medicare but can bill up to 15% more than the Medicare approved payment in total.

RETIREE BENEFIT DESIGN

When retiree group benefits were first introduced in employer programs, they tended to be an extension of the active benefit design. Retirees were offered a full range of benefits including medical, dental, vision, hearing, and life insurance benefits.

As employers began to understand the cost of continuing retiree benefits, many reviewed the programs from the perspective of the needs of retirees. For example, most retirees have a reduced need for life insurance because they have accumulated sufficient savings, at least from the perspective of their unexpected early death.

Today, the typical health plan for pre-65 retirees is a continuation of the same program available while they were working; generally, a preferred provider option arrangement (PPO). The post-65 retirees convert to an indemnity plan, using Medicare payment rates as the approved charge level. Generally, dental coverage is terminated at retirement and life insurance benefits are reduced.

Given the implications of the ACA in terms of providing guarantee-issue protections through the individual market starting in 2014, along with its comprehensive major medical coverage and prohibitions on exclusions for preexisting conditions, many employer retiree health plans are moving towards defined contribution approaches. That is, many employers are considering simply providing financial benefits to retirees expressly for the purchase of health benefits. This gives retirees myriad plan choices, and leaves the complications of benefit administration to the individual market insurers for pre-65 retirees, and the Medicare Advantage and Medicare Supplement insurers for post-65 retirees.

The reasons often cited for offering retiree group benefits include the following:

- Retiree group benefits are a tax-effective means of providing retirement financial security;
- It is a valuable benefit for those currently receiving the coverage or who are soon to retire;
- The benefits can support workforce planning and growth opportunities for employees;
- Providing ongoing health care coverage is a social responsibility of the employer;
- Providing retiree health care benefits helps provide a competitive package of total compensation;
- The current cash costs are nominal relative to the total spending on benefits; and
- Retiree benefits are often at the top of the list of union demands.

MEDICARE INTEGRATION

Most retirees in the U.S. are covered under the Medicare program when they turn age 65. In the U.S. as well as most other countries, the government plan is the primary payer. That is, it pays first, and the secondary insurer (in this case, the employer plan) pays next. In general, most plans that directly coordinate benefits with government programs use one of three methods – standard coordination of benefits (COB), exclusion, or carve-out. These coordination methods typically apply to Medicare Parts A and B. The coordinated care plans under Medicare Part C (also known as Medicare Advantage) are paid directly by Medicare, so no explicit coordination is necessary. There are several alternative strategies to coordinate employer plans with Part D drug plans. In the following examples, Medicare is the primary plan, and the employer plan is the secondary plan.

Standard Coordination of Benefits (COB)

Standard COB usually results in full payment of the covered medical expense when the benefits of both the primary and secondary coverages are combined. Technically, the plan pays the lesser of the regular plan benefit (assuming it was the only plan) and the difference between covered expenses and the primary plan benefit payment. If:

- C = covered expense (the medical charge that is covered by the plan),
- M = the Medicare payment, and
- % represents the application of the employer's benefit provisions (accounting for any copays, deductibles, and member coinsurance),

then the following formula represents the resulting standard COB payment:

$$\text{The lesser of } (C \times \%) \text{ or } (C - M)$$

Most times, the latter part of the formula is the result. Note that if $C - M$ is the resulting benefit, combining the above plan benefit and the Medicare benefit yields C, or the covered expense. The retiree has had his or her entire cost paid (assuming the entire service was a covered expense).

Exclusion

The exclusion method of integration first excludes any benefits paid from the primary plan and then applies the benefit formula of the secondary plan. Under this method, there is usually a benefit paid, because Medicare will pay less than the covered expense. The following formula describes this method.

$$(C - M) \times \%$$

Carve-out

The carve-out method produces the smallest benefit under the employer plan. Under this method, the benefit is first determined assuming that Medicare did not exist, and then Medicare is subtracted from the result.

$$(C \times \%) - M$$

Supplement

Another form of integration is to "supplement" the primary plan. A supplement plan pays expenses for which the primary plan does not pay (additional services, copays, deductibles, and member coinsurance).[5] This approach is possible only when the secondary plan has advance knowledge of the primary plan design, which is easy if the primary plan is a government plan. In non-U.S. countries with a national health plan, employer-based plans generally use this approach to coordinate benefits.

An example of a supplement plan to Medicare is one that pays for the Part A deductible ($1,260 in 2015), and 50% of any member coinsurance that Medicare does not pay. These

---

[5] The term "coinsurance" refers to a percentage of cost split between the payer and the member. It may refer to either the payer's share or the member's share of the costs. Where specificity is required and the context is otherwise unclear, this text uses terms such as "payer coinsurance" or "member coinsurance" to identify which party is responsibility for paying a given coinsurance amount.

designs are commonly referred to as "Medigap" plans in the U.S., because they fill in the "gaps" that Medicare does not pay.

Individually-sold Medigap plans are regulated in the U.S. by state insurance laws. Ten specific plan designs are promulgated by federal law; no other type of plan may be sold. The following table summarizes the design requirements of the ten plans offered in most states for calendar year 2015.[6]

Standard Medigap Plan Designs

Design Feature	A	B	C	D	F*	G	K	L	M	N
Part A member coinsurance	✓	✓	✓	✓	✓	✓	✓	✓	✓	✓
Part B member coinsurance	✓	✓	✓	✓	✓	✓	50%	75%	✓	✓*
First 3 pints of blood	✓	✓	✓	✓	✓	✓	50%	75%	✓	✓
Part A hospice coinsurance	✓	✓	✓	✓	✓	✓	50%	75%	✓	✓
Skilled nursing facility			✓	✓	✓	✓	50%	75%	✓	✓
Part A deductible		✓	✓	✓	✓	✓	50%	75%	50%	✓
Part B deductible			✓		✓					
Part B excess charges					✓	✓				
Foreign travel emergency care			✓	✓	✓	✓			✓	✓
Out-of-pocket limit	NA	NA	NA	NA	NA	NA	*	*	NA	NA

* Plan F may also offer a high deductible plan up to $2,180 (2015). Out-of-pocket limit for Plan K is $4,940 (2015) and for Plan L is $2,470 (2015). Plan N pays 100% of the Part B member coinsurance except for a copayment up to $20 for some office visits and up to a $50 copayment for emergency room visits that do not result in admission to the hospital.

MEDICARE PRESCRIPTION DRUG COORDINATION

The Medicare Modernization Act of 2003 (MMA) was signed into law in December, 2003, and CMS released final regulations in January, 2005. Included in both the MMA and regulations was a variety of alternatives that employers could take advantage of, including the following:

- Maintain their current employer-sponsored plan and receive the Retiree Drug Subsidy from Medicare, based on actual drug spending;

- Contract with a PDP or Medicare Advantage prescription drug (MA-PD) plan to provide pharmacy benefits to their Medicare-covered retirees (an individual must be enrolled in Medicare Parts A or B to be eligible for Part D);

- Contract with CMS directly to become a PDP or MA-PD for its own retirees; or

- Provide a separate prescription drug plan that coordinates or supplements a PDP.

---

[6] Massachusetts, Minnesota and Wisconsin offer designs that are slightly different. There have been changes to these plan designs over time.

In 2006, most employers initially elected to continue their prescription drug plan and accept the Retiree Drug Subsidy. This was partially due to the lack of time to adequately study the alternatives, but also because the alternatives had too many unknowns. Effective in 2013, the ACA eliminated the tax advantage of the Retiree Drug Subsidy that originally allowed plan sponsors to not include these subsidies in gross income. The ACA also provided pre-65 retirees with guarantee issue protections through the individual market starting in 2014, along with comprehensive major medical coverage options. Many employer retiree drug plans are being reevaluated given these massive environmental changes.

RETIREE PLAN CHANGES

Plan changes to significantly reduce employers' future obligations started in the early 1980s and continue. These changes focused on who pays what share of the premium cost – the employer or the retiree. This was followed by a period where changes were focused on the control of health care spending.

Most of the changes made in the early 1980s, when the FASB first started to review the accounting of the benefits, were modest:

- Introducing or slightly increasing the level of retiree contributions;
- Adopting policies of setting retiree contributions as a fixed percentage of plan cost; and
- Changing the method of coordinating benefits with Medicare.

This was followed by a period where features similar to pension plans were introduced to many retiree medical programs:

- Redefining eligibility requirements to be more stringent, such as requiring a person to be at least age 60 with 15 years of service, rather than age 55 with five or ten years of service;
- Introducing service-related benefits; that is, the employer portion of plan cost varies depending on the employee's years of service at retirement;
- Adjusting retiree contributions based on the employee's age at retirement; that is, introducing early retirement reductions;
- Stating the employer subsidy as a fixed dollar amount, rather than a percentage; and
- Providing an account-based employer subsidy; for example, the employee earns a $1,500 subsidy for each year of service, so an employee with 20 years of service at retirement has $30,000. Retiree plans differ in how the funds can be used, with some employers allowing for only the purchase of employer-designated options, while other employers allow for a broad choice of products available to the retiree through the individual and the Medicare Advantage/Medicare Supplement markets (markets which vary based on each retiree's residence), and other employers allow the notional accounts to be used to defray direct medical expenses. New private exchanges provide the administratively capabilities for employers to offer a number of plan options for those deciding to use this "defined contribution" approach.

Due to the ACA, more and more employers are considering simply providing financial benefits to retirees expressly for the purchase of health benefits. This gives retirees myriad plan choices, and leaves the complications of benefit administration to insurers.

Most early plan design changes shifted costs from the employer to retirees. It is likely that future changes will continue this trend. However, if retiree health plans are to remain an employer-provided benefit, future changes will need to find ways to reduce total costs to make the plans affordable. The basic framework for these changes will likely be similar to that used to reduce costs for active employees. These recent changes were seldom applied to retiree plans, because of the thought that retirees are different. This is especially true for those eligible for Medicare.

Retirees are different from active employees in many ways. It is harder to communicate with them, because they do not come to work. Many have family physicians that they have been seeing for a long time, making it uncomfortable and difficult to change providers. Some move away from where they worked, and it is difficult to physically meet for a company-sponsored event. Despite these obstacles, many health care management strategies used for active employee plans can work for retiree plans. However, they may have to be designed with a different emphasis for retirees.

Future efforts will be to change the value proposition of retiree health care, including:

- Providing an account-based employer subsidy (generally non-funded accounts);
- Consumerism initiatives to encourage efficient care;
- Overall total cost management; and
- Other methods to effectively coordinate the employer plan with Medicare.

Most of the plan design changes outlined above do not have the same dramatic accounting cost reductions seen by some of the active employee, fixed-dollar benefit designs introduced in the early 1990s. However, they will help control overall retiree health care costs. And, if a fixed-dollar benefit design has not been adopted, these changes will reduce future cost increases, justifying a lower accounting cost.

Some employers are making the hard decision that they can no longer afford to subsidize retiree group benefit coverage. It is common that these retiree benefits are no longer available to many actively working employees at their future retirement dates, though many employers continue to allow existing retirees and a subset of older or longer service workers to be eligible for retiree group coverage.

OTHER BENEFITS

In addition to medical benefits, many employers offer other benefits to retirees, including:

- Dental,
- Vision,
- Hearing,
- Death Benefits, and
- Medicare Part B premium reimbursement.

Dental, Vision, and Hearing

Dental, vision, and hearing benefits are sometimes continued for retirees. Many employers provide these benefits only up until age 65. Plans that are continued for retirees generally have the same benefits that the active employee programs provide. Eligibility for the plans is usually tied to the same requirements as used for the medical plan.

Death Benefits

Few employers currently offer some level of life insurance coverage for retirees. Death benefit coverage has declined significantly in the last decade from 62% offering some level of coverage in 1998, to 15% in 2013, according to the Aon Hewitt SpecSummary survey. When offered, the face amount of the life insurance is commonly $5,000 or $10,000 (theoretically related to funeral costs), $50,000 (fitting with tax-exemption rules), or a gradually reducing percentage of the life insurance available when the person had stopped actively working.

Medicare Part B Premium Reimbursement

Most retiree medical plans require that the retiree enroll in both Medicare Parts A and B. Part A is mostly paid for through payroll taxes. For Part B coverage, the federal government pays about 75% of the cost, and beneficiaries pay the other 25%. Some employers pay for all or a portion of this premium. However, the prevalence of employers reimbursing retirees for the Part B premium has declined rapidly. Part B reimbursement policies are often included in union demands during benefit negotiations. Salaried employees generally have not had their premiums reimbursed.

PREFUNDING IN THE UNITED STATES

Although not often a popular notion for controlling retiree group benefit costs, many very large employers have some assets set aside for a portion of their obligations. Most employers do not prefund the obligation because they believe that their internal rate of return far outweighs the returns that they could achieve by prefunding retiree group benefit plans. The key impetus for prefunding is generally more philosophical than financial.

Due to the rules on selecting a discount rate under the Governmental Accounting Standards Board (GASB) Statement No. 45, which permit the use of higher discount rates for partially or fully funded liabilities than for unfunded liabilities, governmental entities may conclude that prefunding makes sense from a financial statement perspective.

An ideal funding vehicle would provide the following:

- A current company tax deduction for contributions that adequately fund retiree health benefits;
- A tax-free or tax-deferred savings mechanism for employees;
- Investment earnings that accumulate in a tax-sheltered environment;
- Tax-free benefits paid to retirees;
- No implications or constraints to plan design;

- Assets that are recognized in applicable accounting standards; and
- Assets that are revocable without penalty if the obligation decreased.

Traditionally, two types of investment vehicles have been used to prefund retiree benefits:

- Welfare benefit funds (a very general term, but commonly either: (1) Internal Revenue Code (IRC) Section 501(c)(9) trusts, often referred to as Voluntary Employees' Beneficiary Associations (VEBAs), or (2) continuance funds held by insurance companies); or
- IRC Section 401(h) funding in a qualified pension trust.

Recently, a few companies have begun to fund in less traditional vehicles, such as:

- Incidental accounts under a profit sharing plan;
- Employee-purchased group annuities;
- Employee Stock Ownership Plans with a money purchase plan account; and
- Qualified retirement trust funds (pension plans or §401(k) profit sharing plans).

Only in limited situations do any of the above currently meet all of the requirements to be an ideal funding vehicle. Two exceptions are VEBAs that are exempt from funding limitations due to collective bargaining, and tax-exempt sponsor exemptions under IRC.

The Deficit Reduction Act of 1984 (DEFRA) severely limits the use of welfare benefits funds (§501(c)(9) trusts/VEBAs) and insurance company reserves (continuance funds) to fund retiree life and health benefits. It places limits on deductible contributions, and it taxes some or all of the investment income earned by the trust. It also places limits on coverage amounts allowed to be funded for retiree life insurance benefits:

- Retiree health benefits funded in a pension plan (§401(h) fund) have limits on the amount that may be funded from both plan qualification and tax deductibility perspectives.
- Typical profit-sharing/savings plan arrangements can accumulate funds tax-effectively, but, in general, retirees are taxed on benefits when they receive them. Profit-sharing/savings plans also have limits placed on the amount that can be contributed on a pre-tax basis.
- Employee contributions to purchase group annuity contracts are made with after-tax money. The IRS has not specifically addressed the taxability of benefits from these annuities, but there is an argument that they may be delivered tax-free.

LEGAL ISSUES IN THE UNITED STATES

Retiree group benefits have been the subject of several court cases. These cases have primarily dealt with a plan sponsor either terminating a plan or making modifications to the program. Many involve collectively bargained contracts, although there have been some involving salaried employees. Early court cases tended to favor the plaintiffs, and employer plans were required to continue or maintain the provisions in their plans indefinitely. After several of these cases were decided, employers began to include language in their communication of retiree group benefit plans that they have the right to amend or terminate the plans in the future. Since that time, courts have tended to favor employers, because this type of language was provided in legal documents and summary plan descriptions provided to employees and retirees.

Congress amended the Bankruptcy Code in 1988 to prohibit a debtor (the employer) in reorganization from terminating their health and life insurance programs for retirees and their dependents without first negotiating the proposed modifications with representatives of the retirees, and seeking and receiving court approval to make the changes. This generally requires that the debtor must continue retiree health and life insurance coverage while undergoing Chapter 11 reorganization. It may be possible to lower benefit levels, and even terminate the plans, if they negotiate it with the retirees' representatives or receive permission from the bankruptcy court. Payments that are made under reorganization are given high priority administrative expense status. However, if an employer ends up liquidating, retiree claims become unsecured claims – the same as any other unsecured creditor.

Under the Age Discrimination in Employment Act of 1967 (ADEA), it was understood in the benefits community that retiree medical benefit design could differ between retirees under age 65 versus those age 65 and over due to Medicare coordination. However in 2000, a U.S. District Court in Pennsylvania ruled that Erie County, Pennsylvania violated the ADEA when it provided its post-65 retirees with medical benefits that were "inferior" to those provided to its pre-65 retirees.[7] This decision raised many concerns among plan sponsors of retiree medical benefits, because virtually all plans could now be considered in violation of the ADEA. After reversing its own initial ruling on the case, there were several attempts by the Equal Employment Opportunity Commission (EEOC) to remedy the situation administratively by stating the prevalent practice was appropriate. The EEOC's rulings were challenged by several groups. The final EEOC rule went into effect on December 26, 2007, and allows employers to coordinate with Medicare without violating the ADEA.[8] The resulting rule ensures that the Erie County decision does not induce unions, state and local governments, and employers to eliminate retiree health benefit programs altogether.

Another key legal topic has been the prefunding of retiree group benefits. Two cases in particular are rich with actuarial testimony and worth reading. The *General Signal* case found that the employer should not have taken tax deductions for prefunding their retiree medical plan, because the money was subsequently used to pay for other benefits.[9] In the *Wells Fargo* case, the tax court allowed the employer to take the position that the present value of benefits for currently retired employees may be tax deductible in the year of funding. The rationale is that the Internal Revenue Code states that funding must be over the working lifetimes of the participants, and retirees have no remaining working lives and thus can be funded immediately.[10]

---

[7] *Erie County Retirees Association v. The County of Erie Pennsylvania*, 220 F.3d. 193 (3rd Cir. 2000).
[8] A copy of the rule is available on the EEOC's web site at www.eeoc.gov/policy/regs/index.html
[9] *General Signal Corp. & Subs v. Commissioner*, 103 T.C. 216, 232 (1994)
[10] *Wells Fargo & Company (f.k.a. Norwest Corporation) and Subs v. Commissioner*, 120 T.C. 5 (2003).

RECENT HEALTH CARE REFORM IN THE UNITED STATES

The ACA contains many provisions that affect retiree group benefits:

- The reduction in Medicare Advantage plan payments over time that could result in higher premium rate increases, lower benefit levels for these plans, or both.

- The loss of tax deductibility of the Retiree Drug Subsidy; this change caused plan sponsors to reconsider whether to seek the subsidy as opposed to other alternatives, such as offer PDPs.

- The excise tax on high-cost plans becomes effective in 2018 and is a non-deductible tax of 40 percent of the excess of the value of health coverage over specified dollar thresholds. For a pre-65 retiree plan, it is effectively $11,850 for single coverage and $30,950 for family coverage. For post-65 retiree plan, it is $10,200 and $27,500, respectively. It is likely that most retiree plans will be subject to this tax shortly after its effective date.

- The Early Retiree Reinsurance Program (also known as "ERRP") provided $5 billion in federal subsidies for the continuation of employer-based retiree medical coverage for pre-65 retirees.

- Additional funding of Medicare Part D standard benefits that gradually closes the coverage gap by 2020. The funding for this change comes through a required 50% discount for brand named drugs by the pharmaceutical industry that started in 2011. In addition, both generic and brand-name drugs costs will be paid, so that the total benefit is 75% (for brand named drugs, the federal subsidy will pay for 25% of the costs, and for generic drugs, it will pay 75%). The federal subsidy is phased in from 2011 to 2020. These changes encourage plan sponsors to revisit the need and format for providing prescription benefits to Medicare-eligible retirees, since the standard Medicare Part D design will not only be gradually more generous for their retirees, but offer a more logical plan design, and possibly become even more affordable.

- The introduction of health insurance exchanges and the individual coverage mandate in 2014 has changed the landscape of available insurance for pre-65 retirees. For plan sponsors who have been concerned about the insurability of these retirees, the worry goes away. For individuals concerned about health insurance coverage, it opens up new opportunities for them.

Employers have and will continue to react to the above changes differently. Further, retirees may react differently because their choice of insurance plans has now changed. This will require actuaries to rethink assumptions used in their work for these programs.

ACCOUNTING

The change in accounting treatment of retiree group benefits in the early 1990s had a dramatic impact on the designs of these programs. The Financial Accounting Standards Board's introduction of Statement of Financial Accounting No. 106 (FAS 106) in 1992 increased many employers' current costs of retiree group benefits by factors of five to ten times their previously recognized costs.[11] Although not changing the true nature or cost of retiree group benefit plans,

---

[11] Note that the Financial Accounting Standards Board reorganized all of their accounting standards and moved all of the retiree group benefit accounting rules under Accounting Standards Codification 715-60.

the requirement to accrue for the cost of benefits similar to pension plan accounting generally accelerated the accounting recognition of the cost of the plans from "someday" to "today." The accounting treatment is very similar to pension plan accounting concepts, including estimating the current year claim costs as well as future costs. There are also some special additional assumptions, such as: (1) the probability of future participation in the plans, and (2) assumptions to anticipate the future costs of the program.

The GASB issued Statements 43 and 45 in 2004, which provided standards of accounting for public-sector retiree group benefit plans (and their trust funds), and for state and local governmental employers' financial statements, respectively. Patterned after FAS 106, the accounting statements are expected to have a similar impact on the delivery of retiree group benefits to these governmental entities.[12]

Other accounting bodies have rules set out in their respective organizations, including the Canadian Institute of Chartered Accountants in Section 3461 of their Handbook, the Federal Accounting Standards Advisory Board (FASAB) under FASAB No. 5 to report accrual costs using a specific actuarial method (the aggregate entry age level cost method) for U.S. federal agencies, and the Cost Accounting Standards Board (CASB) rules on how U.S. government contractors must report retiree group benefit costs in their contract costs.

International standards are similar in their focus on accrual accounting; that is, the focus on the accounting for benefits during working lifetimes, rather than based upon the later timing of cash flows during the retirement phase. The primary difference is that the international standard (IAS 19) offers much less ability for employers to smooth unexpected plan experience and plan design changes. Efforts to align U.S. standards and international standards have been in progress and may result in changes to either the U.S. standard or international standards.

ACTUARIAL METHODS AND ASSUMPTIONS

The projection of retiree group benefit payments blends the actuarial expertise of pension and health actuaries. Pension actuaries have the background and knowledge to project long-term costs, and health actuaries have the expertise to estimate the current costs of health care and their likely costs in the short-term.

Pension plan benefits are generally paid over a period that may extend 40 to 60 years in the future. As a result, assumptions must be chosen that reflect what the actuary expects to happen during the entire time period. Pension actuaries have been making these assumptions for many years. These assumptions are usually divided between two basic sets: (1) economic, and (2) demographic, or personnel-related, assumptions.

Economic assumptions may include predictions of the following future values: inflation, discount rate (or environmental interest rate), asset returns, salary increases, and Social Security increases.

---

[12] Statement No. 43, *Financial Reporting for Postemployment Benefit Plans Other Than Pension Plans*, Governmental Accounting Standards Board, April 2004; and Statement No. 45, *Accounting and Financial Reporting by Employers for Postemployment Benefits Other Than Pensions*, Governmental Accounting Standards Board, June 2004. Actual first effective for financial statements beginning after December 15, 2005 for GASB 43 and after December 15, 2006 for GASB 45.

Demographic assumptions about employees include the following future estimates: termination or turnover of employment, mortality, disability, and retirement incidence.

In addition to the typical pension plan assumption, a retiree group benefit valuation requires additional assumptions including the following economic assumptions: current retiree plan costs, current retiree contributions, health care cost trend rate, Medicare Part B premium increases, and retiree contribution increases.

Additional demographic assumptions are: plan participation, spouse age, marital status, spouse plan continuation after death of retiree, dependent children plan termination, and choice of health plan options (if not considered in plan costs above).

Any of the commonly used pension actuarial methods may be used, but the projected unit credit is the most common because it is the method prescribed under ASC 715-60 (aka, FAS 106).

AN INSURER'S PERSPECTIVE ON RETIREE PLANS

This chapter focused on long-term retiree plan considerations from the perspective of the employer. However, insurers also need to estimate the upcoming year's claim and administrative cost of the retiree plan, a function that is particularly important for insured products.

It is customary that an insurer's underwriting tools are developed assuming a more typical, broad age distribution of risks. These assumptions break down when a retiree plan is evaluated.

First, pre-65 retirees cost much more than actives and their dependents. The deductible and out-of-pocket maximums are much more likely to be exceeded, thus the benefit relativities should be specifically examined if benefit design changes are contemplated, often without reference to the usual underwriting tools. High cost claimants are much more likely, and there are often different geographic compositions of retired plan members. There are also fewer dependents covered per retiree, but those that are covered tend to be very high cost as well.

Ironically, since post-65 retirees normally have Medicare, they may cost less than active employees. However, since Medicare is generally primary, the composition of what is covered by the employer is completely different than what it is for active employees. Again, standard underwriting tools should reflect these differences.

Below is a list of other common underwriting considerations for retiree plans:

- Post-65 retiree claims can be more difficult to process because of coordination of benefits. Proportionally, many more claims must be manually adjudicated, driving up administrative costs.
- Retirees have a higher number of claims, and thus use proportionally more claims and customer service resources.
- The choice of coordination type, while not financially material for active plans, has an enormous financial impact on retiree plans.

- While pharmacy costs may be 15% to 20% of total health costs for active employees, the pharmacy proportion is high for retirees, typically 40% to 60% of benefits paid.
- Selection issues could be significant for retiree plans; it is not uncommon that a retiree plan, where premiums are generously subsidized, may cost half that of retiree plans that are unsubsidized. Thus, employer subsidization is a very important underwriting consideration.
- The existence of the individual insurance exchange starting in 2014 expands retirees' options to obtain affordable health insurance options. The added ability for retirees to select between choices will have a significant effect on the cost of both exchange products as well as employers' retiree plans.

9. GOVERNMENT HEALTH PLANS IN THE UNITED STATES

Jack Burke
John W. Bauerlein
Bruce D. Schobel

The U.S. government provides a variety of entitlement and other benefits, many of which are under the authority of the Social Security Act. The most familiar such benefits are retired-worker benefits payable by the Old-Age, Survivors, and Disability Insurance (OASDI) program, (what the public ordinarily calls "Social Security"). In addition, OASDI provides cash benefits similar to group insurance benefits—Social Security disabled-worker benefits and survivor benefits. Other benefits authorized by the Social Security Act include medical benefits—Medicare and Medicaid. This chapter provides an overview of Medicare, Medicaid and the Social Security disabled-worker and survivor benefits. It also provides a brief overview of state disability insurance programs.

MEDICARE AND MEDICAID

From the 1930s through the early 1960s, government health insurance was proposed periodically, but never fully established, other than limited federal funding of state payments to cover medical services to the poor. Private health insurance, mostly through group insurance offered as an employee benefit, grew to be the predominant form of health care coverage. Over time, Congress perceived an increasing need to improve access to medical care for the elderly, the disabled, and individuals on public assistance. Legislation passed in 1965 – Title XVIII and Title XIX of the Social Security Act – created the Medicare and Medicaid programs, providing health care for the elderly and the poor, respectively.

Medicare is a federal program, while Medicaid is a joint federal and state program. Currently, the programs are administered at the federal level by the Centers for Medicare & Medicaid Services (CMS), a unit of the Department of Health and Human Services (HHS). Individual states have some control over the management, design, and administration of their state Medicaid programs.

A large percentage of the U.S. population receives health care coverage through these programs. Medicaid covered 17.5% of the U.S. population in 2013. At that time, Medicare covered about 15.6% of the U.S. population and over 93% of the population age 65 years and older. The following table shows recent population and enrollment figures:

2013 Medicare and Medicaid Enrollment Relative to U.S. Population[1]		
	Enrollment (000s)	% of Population
Total U.S. Population	313,401	100%
Medicare Beneficiaries	49,020	15.6%
Medicaid Beneficiaries	54,919	17.5%

Note: Some beneficiaries participate in both Medicare and Medicaid.

Medicare and Medicaid have achieved their goals of expanding access to health insurance coverage and protecting those who cannot afford the cost of catastrophic events. Both programs have helped increase life expectancy and reduce the poverty rate for the elderly. However, these programs face funding and cost challenges that will only grow worse in the future. Health care cost trend, rapid increases in the number of beneficiaries, Medicaid expansion under the Affordable Care Act (ACA) starting in 2014, and longer life expectancies will require substantial changes to keep these programs solvent.

Costs for Medicare and Medicaid have grown much more than anticipated at the time they were established, putting a significant strain on federal and state budgets. Total expenditures for the fiscal year ending September, 2013 were $585.7 billion under Medicare and $449.4 billion under Medicaid.[2]

Total Medicare cost, about 3.5% of 2013 GDP, is projected to increase to about 8.3% of GDP over the next 75 years under the intermediate Board of Trustees assumptions if the program is kept in its current form. Medicare enrollment, which has already increased from 19 million beneficiaries in 1966 to about 54 million in 2013, has begun to rise rapidly as the baby boom generation reaches eligibility age.[3]

MEDICARE

Medicare covers most persons over 65 years of age, some disabled individuals under 65, and most individuals with end-stage renal disease (ESRD). Eligibility for coverage is available to the following:

- Persons at least age 65 and eligible for Social Security or Railroad Retirement benefits.
- Individuals entitled to Social Security or Railroad Retirement disability benefits for a period of at least two years.
- Insured workers with ESRD for a period of two years, including spouses and children with ESRD.
- Some other aged and disabled individuals who pay mandatory premiums.

Medicare is not scheduled to change the eligibility age of 65 as the Social Security normal retirement age increases from 65 to 67.

---

[1] U.S. Census Bureau, Current Population Survey, Annual Social and Economic Supplement, Table HI01, https://www.census.gov/hhes/www/cpstables/032014/health/h01R_000.htm
[2] National Health Expenditures 2013 Highlights.
[3] CMS Financial Report fiscal year 2014, pages 3, 85-86, though results are highly sensitive to assumptions; the sensitivity analysis begins on page 87.

Medicare consists of four "Parts." Part A provides Hospital Insurance (HI), Part B provides Supplementary Medical Insurance (SMI), and Part D provides outpatient prescription drug insurance. Part C is called Medicare Advantage, and is an alternative to Parts A and B, available to beneficiaries through a program whereby Medicare enters into contracts with voluntary private sector managed health plans. Medicare Advantage is discussed more below.

Part A

Eligible persons receive HI coverage automatically at no premium charge. HI services include:

- Inpatient hospital benefits cover semi-private room and ancillary services and supplies.
- Skilled nursing facility benefits cover semi-private room, meals, skilled nursing and rehabilitative services, and other services and supplies after a related three-day inpatient hospital stay.
- Home health agency benefits generally cover services following discharge from a hospital or skilled nursing facility.
- Hospice care is provided to terminally ill patients with life expectancies less than six months.

HI does not cover custodial services in a nursing homes or long-term care.

Unlike most private sector health plan designs, HI coverage is tied to a "benefit period" starting at admission date and ending sixty days after discharge from the hospital or skilled nursing facility. There are no HI beneficiary premiums, but there are cost sharing provisions and limits on coverage when care is provided. The cost-sharing amounts change each calendar year, and the amounts for 2015 are shown in the table below:

2015 HI Cost Sharing and Coverage Limits		
Type of Service	**Cost-Sharing**	**Coverage Limits**
Inpatient Hospital	• $1,260 deductible per benefit period • $315 per day for 61st – 90th day each benefit period • $630 per day for the 91st – 150th day each lifetime reserve day	• Maximum coverage of 150 days per benefit period • 60 nonrenewable lifetime reserve days, no coverage beyond lifetime reserve
Skilled Nursing Facility	Up to $157.50 per day for 21st – 100th day of each benefit period	• No coverage beyond 100 days each benefit period
Home Health Agency	None	100 visits/illness
Hospice Care	None	None
Blood	Beneficiary pays first three non-replaced pints of blood	None

Part B

SMI coverage (Part B) requires a monthly premium subject to change each calendar year and is designed to cover 25% of the Part B program cost each year. The standard 2015 monthly premium is $104.90, which is automatically deducted from the beneficiary's Social Security payment. In 2015, higher income individuals will be subject to an additional premium ranging from 35% to 80% of the total cost, depending on income. A beneficiary can decline SMI coverage. However, if a beneficiary elects SMI coverage at a later date, the monthly premium increases 10% for each 12-month period that available coverage was declined. Nearly all beneficiaries receiving HI coverage also elect SMI coverage.

SMI covers most medically necessary services not covered by HI insurance. SMI also covers certain preventive care services. The following list describes specific SMI covered services:

- Outpatient hospital (includes services such as emergency room and outpatient surgery);
- Medical care (covers services provided by physicians and other qualified health practitioners. Also covers cost of diagnostic tests, supplies, durable medical equipment, prosthetic devices, and ambulatory surgical center fees);
- An initial preventive visit within 12 months of enrolling in Part B and yearly wellness visits thereafter;
- Ambulance services;
- Clinical laboratory and radiology services;
- Physical and occupational therapy services;
- Speech pathology services;
- Outpatient rehabilitation, including partial hospitalization services;
- Radiation therapy services;
- Transplants;
- Dialysis;
- Home health care beyond that covered by Part A;
- Certain drugs and biologicals (SMI only covers those that cannot be self-administered, except certain cancer drugs);
- Certain preventive services (largely with no cost sharing), including an annual flu shot, bone mass measurement, colorectal cancer screening, diabetes services, mammogram screening, Pap test, pelvic exam, prostate cancer screening, and certain vaccinations.

Similar to HI coverage, SMI does not cover services that are custodial or deemed medically unnecessary (except as noted above). SMI also does not cover dental care, routine foot and eye care, eyeglasses, hearing aids, cosmetic surgery, and most retail pharmacy prescription drugs.

Beneficiaries pay a $147 deductible (in 2015) once per calendar year. After the deductible, beneficiaries pay, with some exceptions, coinsurance of 20% of the Medicare-approved amount. The beneficiary coinsurance varies for certain outpatient hospital services, and it does not apply for clinical lab and certain preventive care services. Unlike most private sector health plan, there is no annual limit on the amount of out-of-pocket costs incurred by beneficiaries.

Beneficiaries often purchase private Medicare Supplement or "Medigap" insurance to fill in out-of-pocket costs and provide benefits not covered by Medicare. This coverage is usually purchased on an individual policy basis and is only available to beneficiaries enrolled in Medicare. Ten standardized plans, lettered "A" through "N", are available in most states, though some are now available only for renewing policyholders and not for new purchasers. Medigap carriers are prohibited from selling a Medigap policy to beneficiaries enrolled in a Medicare Advantage plan.

Part C

Medicare Advantage plans (also known as MA plans or Part C plans) are also available as an option that substitutes for HI and SMI coverage in many locations. MA plans typically offer lower out-of-pocket costs, including a limit on out-of-pocket expenses, increased coverage limits, and coverage for some services and items that would not be covered under traditional Medicare, such as eyeglasses, hearing aids, dental care, and non-emergency transportation. The MA program is described in detail later in this chapter.

Part D

Coverage for outpatient prescription drugs became available starting on January 1, 2006, as a result of the Medicare Prescription Drug, Improvement, and Modernization Act (MMA), passed in 2003. Coverage was substantially modified by the Affordable Care Act (ACA), passed in 2010. Part D provides coverage for most prescription drugs used by Medicare enrollees. Medicare provides this coverage through contracts with private sector insurers. Most contracts are made with two types of carriers: (1) Prescription Drug Plans (PDP), which provide prescription drug coverage on a standalone basis, and (2) Medicare Advantage-Prescription Drug plans (MA-PD) which provide prescription drug coverage alongside Part C medical benefits.

MMA also provided for ongoing annual subsidies to employers and other plan sponsors who offer prescription drug coverage through retiree health care plans for Medicare eligible members who do not separately enroll in a PDP or MA-PD plan. This is called the Retiree Drug Subsidy (RDS) and is also administered by CMS.

Each year, CMS determines the monthly rate that Medicare will pay contractors to provide "standard" coverage. The member premium amount is set to be 25.5% of the total cost of the standard benefit based on the national average bid and average reinsurance. CMS pays the remaining 74.5%. To the extent a particular Part D carrier bids more or less than the national average bid, its member premium likewise differs from the national average member premium. Premium rates vary significantly by carrier and plan. Premium subsidies are available for low income beneficiaries. Though the program is voluntary, members who do not sign up when they are initially eligible pay a penalty for late enrollment, if they subsequently enroll.

The law defines standard Part D coverage in terms of Medicare versus beneficiary liabilities relative to annual drug costs. The table below summarizes the standard Part D coverage in 2015. In 2015, beneficiaries were subject to a $320 annual deductible and then were responsible for 25% of costs up to an "initial coverage limit" of $2,960. Beneficiaries were then responsible for a higher percent of costs, until reaching the "true out-of-pocket" threshold of $4,700. The ACA dictates that this percentage differ for generic versus brand name drugs, and it is scheduled to decrease gradually from 65% for generic and 45% for brand drugs in 2015, to 25% for both brand and generic drugs in calendar year 2020. For brand name drugs, about one half of the ingredient cost is covered by a rebate from the brand manufacturer. Each year, the deductible, coverage limit, and out-of-pocket threshold are subject to inflationary adjustments. Member cost sharing is subsidized for low income beneficiaries.

2015 Part D Standard Cost Sharing and Coverage Gap		
Annual Drug Cost	**Medicare Pays...**	**Enrollee Pays...**
$ 0 to $320 (Deductible)	0%	100%
$320 to $2,960	75%	25%
Until member true out-of-pocket costs (TrOOP) reach $4,700	35% generic 55% brand[1]	65% generic 45% brand
After $4,700 member TrOOP	About 95%	About 5%[2]

[1] Includes brand pharmaceutical manufacturer's rebate of 50% described above.
[2] or, if more, a $2.65 copay for generics and preferred multiple source drugs and $6.60 for other drugs, subject to inflationary adjustments after 2015.

Some drugs are specifically excluded from standard Part D coverage, including drugs covered by Part A or B; drugs used to treat anorexia and weight loss; fertility drugs; drugs used for cosmetic conditions including hair loss; drugs used to relieve cough and cold symptoms; vitamins and minerals (except for prenatal vitamins and fluoride); and over-the-counter drugs. Participating carriers are permitted to define their own formularies within certain parameters.

Each plan offered by an insurance carrier must provide at least the Standard Part D coverage outlined above. However, contractors may enhance their plans to include coverage for drugs not covered by Part D, or to reduce or eliminate cost sharing or fill in the coverage gap, and they may charge a member additional premium for the additional coverage.

PROGRAM FINANCING

Medicare is designed to be funded on a pay-as-you-go basis. There is no prefunding of premiums, set aside as reserves, to fund future benefit payments. The HI program is financed primarily through payroll taxes paid through employment. These taxes paid by current employees bear no direct relationship to those employees' future Medicare costs, and employees have no ownership of their past contributions. The SMI program is financed through a combination of contributions from the general fund of the Treasury (75%) and beneficiary premiums (25%). Part D is financed through a separate account within the SMI trust fund. Like Part B, Part D is funded through appropriations from general revenues (74.5%), so that appropriations plus premiums (25.5%) equal expenditures. These monies are deposited to the individual HI and SMI trust funds. Benefit costs and administrative expenses are charged against the funds.

The HI payroll tax rate is 1.45% of earnings, with a matching amount paid by the employer (self-employed individuals pay the full 2.9%). Unlike payroll taxes that fund Social Security income benefits, there are no earnings caps on application of the HI tax. To the contrary, the ACA added an additional 0.9% payroll tax on high incomes starting in 2013. The tax rate can only be changed by an act of Congress, which has occurred periodically to ensure solvency, at least in the short term.

The ACA additionally added a 3.8% tax on investment income for single taxpayers with income over $200,000 and married couples with income over $250,000. These thresholds are not indexed for inflation. Investment income includes interest, dividends, capital gains, rents, royalties, and passive business income.

Similar to Social Security, the HI program was originally intended to be self-supporting. However, Medicare cost increases have consistently exceeded original projections, and the 2015 funding levels are projected to be inadequate to support current law benefits over time. A board of trustees manages the HI and SMI funds. The board must report to Congress on the financial status of the trust funds by April 1 of each year. The CMS chief actuary issues an annual opinion certifying that the assumptions and cost estimates used in determining the financial status are reasonable. As of the 2015 trustees' report, the HI fund is projected to be exhausted by 2030 under the intermediate assumptions. The Part B and Part D expenses are funded by general revenues and premiums that are reset annually and thus are not projected to be exhausted; but instead are projected to grow as a percent of GDP. The changing demographics, high medical cost trend, and pay-as-you-go financing approach will make it difficult to achieve intergenerational equity.

Aside from higher taxes, other approaches to improving Medicare solvency include the following:

- Reduce or eliminate some covered services;
- Increase Medicare cost sharing through higher deductibles and copays;
- Raise the eligibility age for benefits, for example to age 66 or 67;
- Adjust reimbursement to providers of care; and
- Encourage new initiatives and expand existing initiatives that lower trend.

MEDICARE PROVIDER REIMBURSEMENT

Medicare uses a complex system of reimbursement to pay hospitals, physicians, and ancillary providers. Medicare has implemented numerous reimbursement methods designed to encourage appropriate utilization and lower Medicare cost trends.

Inpatient Hospital Services

Currently, most hospitals are reimbursed on a prospective payment system (PPS) basis. Hospitals are paid a set amount for each admission based on the diagnosis-related grouping (DRG) methodology, which classifies each admission based on the patient's condition and the services performed by the hospital. The DRG approach encourages hospitals to provide services efficiently (once a patient is admitted), as reimbursement generally does not increase with each additional day in the hospital or additional services. Hospitals can also receive additional reimbursement for some outlier hospital stays, graduate medical education costs, and disproportionate share (DSH) adjustments. Hospitals qualify for DSH adjustments depending on the portion of overall hospital services delivered to uninsured and low-income patients. Under the ACA, DSH adjustments were significantly reduced starting in 2014, since more patients are insured as a direct result of the core goals of the ACA.

Professional Services

A complex fee schedule defines physician services reimbursement. The fee schedule uses a resource-based relative value scale (RBRVS) to assign relative values to medical services. The fee reimbursed for a particular service is based on the following elements:

- *Nationwide Conversion Factor.* This factor is updated annually. The nationwide conversion factor is based on certain budget and growth rate targets for Medicare expenditures. This factor applies to all services except anesthesia, which has a different conversion factor and unit values set by the American Society of Anesthesiologists.

- *Units for the procedure.* Medicare has assigned a unit value to each physician procedure. Separate unit values apply to the components representing the resources needed to deliver a service. Unit values are adjusted annually and are based on three practice components:
  - Work value, measuring the physician's time and skill needed to perform the service;
  - Practice expense, reflecting the cost of rent, staff, supplies, equipment, and other overhead requirements; and
  - Malpractice value, measuring the professional liability costs associated with the service.

- *Geographic Area.* Each of the three components have area adjustments applied to them, producing area-adjusted unit values.

Reimbursement for a particular service is equal to the sum of area-adjusted unit values, multiplied by the nationwide conversion factor. Most physicians accept Medicare reimbursement as full payment for services. Physicians that are not "participating" may bill patients an additional amount, subject to about a 10% limit above the Medicare reimbursement amount.

Additional bonus payments are available that reflect the goals of CMS, such as quality incentive payments or payments to doctors that staff underserved areas.

Outpatient Hospital Services

Hospital outpatient services are reimbursed based on an outpatient prospective payment system (OPPS). This system, also called ambulatory payment classification (APC), covers facility charges only. The APC system works in many ways like a fee schedule, but with packaging of some services to control overall reimbursement to the hospital for delivering care to a patient.

Medicare is consistently revising its payment methodologies to attempt to control costs and incent desired behavior. For example, hospital value-based purchasing is an effort to link Medicare payments to quality, efficient care in the inpatient hospital setting. Some initiatives may be proposed as demonstration projects, such as the Medicare Shared Savings Program (MSSP) for accountable care organizations.

MEDICARE ADVANTAGE

The Tax Equity and Fiscal Responsibility Act of 1984 (TEFRA) introduced risk contracting between Medicare and private health plans. In exchange for a defined capitation payment, private health plans, (HMOs, point-of-service plans, and PPOs) were obligated to offer benefits at least as generous as basic Medicare, but could use excess payments to provide additional benefits. HMO payment rates for aged and disabled beneficiaries were initially set at 95% of the projected Medicare fee-for-service program costs for the average beneficiary. Payment rates were established on a county-specific basis, and adjusted to a beneficiary's demographic, Medicaid eligibility, working aged, and institutional status.

Enrollment in Medicare HMOs grew rapidly, particularly during the 1990s, such that by 1998, there were 346 risk contracts with enrollment at about 6 million Medicare beneficiaries. In 1998, 74% of Medicare beneficiaries resided in an area with at least one HMO option, and in many counties, the majority of Medicare beneficiaries had opted for an HMO instead of original fee-for-service Medicare coverage.[4] HMO plans were attractive to beneficiaries because of richer benefits and lower out of pocket costs at little to no additional premium. In many areas, HMO plans often included prescription drug coverage, a benefit then not available through Medicare, but highly valued by the elderly.

The Balanced Budget Act (BBA) and the Medicare Modernization Act (MMA)

The Balanced Budget Act of 1997 (BBA) created the Medicare+Choice program, which significantly altered how these private health plans were paid. The Act attempted to address the belief that HMOs had been overpaid due to favorable selection by healthier-than-average beneficiaries. Legislators also saw cutbacks in HMO payments as a source of savings as they worked towards a balanced budget. HMO payments were reduced to less than 95% of the average Medicare beneficiary cost. The net effect for HMOs was that annual increases in payment rates were curtailed to levels much lower than the underlying cost trends. HMOs responded by reducing benefits, increasing out-of-pocket amounts, and requiring supplemental premium payments from beneficiaries. The results of the BBA payment rate adjustments were not surprising. After the 1998 peak, Medicare+Choice enrollment declined substantially. Most HMOs withdrew from counties with low payment rates or exited the Medicare+Choice line of business entirely. As of September 2002, there were only 155 Medicare+Choice plans, and enrollment was at about 5 million.[5]

The Medicare Prescription Drug, Improvement and Modernization Act of 2003 (MMA) reversed this trend. MMA triggered monumental changes to the Medicare program. Perhaps most significantly, the legislation created the Part D outpatient prescription drug benefit described earlier. The legislation, which renamed the Medicare+Choice (Part C) program as Medicare Advantage, also revitalized the interest of the insurance industry in this line of business. Payment rates in some areas of the country were increased significantly. Moreover, trends in payment rates are required to keep pace with fee-for-service Medicare cost trends going forward. The legislation also introduced new market opportunities, including regional PPOs and Special Needs Plans (SNPs). Regional PPOs must offer PPO coverage across an entire region, with the goal of increasing managed care offerings in rural areas. SNPs are plans designed to meet the needs of specific groups, such as institutionalized beneficiaries, dual eligibles (those covered by both Medicaid and Medicare), and beneficiaries with severe chronic conditions. Finally, the legislation introduced a bidding approach to the contracting process between Medicare and private Medicare Advantage contractors. In this process, contractors prepare a bid for each of their plans. The bid is compared to a benchmark rate developed by

---

[4] CMS Fact Sheet, 8/29/01.
[5] CMS Fact Sheet, 9/02.

CMS. If the bid is under the benchmark, the plan keeps a percentage of the difference (the "rebate"), which it must use to increase benefits, reduce cost sharing, or reduce Part B or Part D premiums.[6] The government keeps the remaining amount as savings. A bid over the benchmark results in a premium to the member. A similar bidding process is used for Part D coverage, except that the Medicare payment amount is based on an average of all bids instead of a benchmark amount.

Risk Adjusted Payments

Another change to payment rates introduced by the BBA was risk adjustment. MMA mandated risk adjustment by January, 2000, but gave the Secretary broad discretion to develop a methodology whereby capitation payments would recognize the health status of HMO enrollees. CMS's original methodology, called the Principal Inpatient Diagnostic Cost Group Model (PIP-DCG), relied on inpatient hospital diagnoses to assign Medicare beneficiaries to risk categories. Inpatient hospital data, rather than all inpatient and outpatient diagnoses, was used initially to ease the administrative burden on HMOs and moderate the immediate impact of risk adjustment. Under risk adjustment, HMOs were paid a base amount (varying by age and gender) with potential add-ons for dual eligibles, those originally eligible for Medicare due to disability, and health status (defined using PIP-DCG groups).

A new methodology, the Centers for Medicare & Medicaid Services Hierarchical Condition Categories (CMS-HCC) model, was implemented in 2004 and is updated periodically. This model uses both inpatient and outpatient diagnostic data and includes 70 diagnostic categories (HCCs). In addition to health conditions, the payment model takes into account age and gender, Medicaid eligibility, originally disabled status, working-aged status, and institutionalized status. The CMS-HCC model is additive in that it will recognize and incrementally increase payment for multiple conditions that are not closely related in the same beneficiary. By contrast, the PIP-DCG model recognized only the principal diagnosis for each beneficiary. Conditions that are closely related are placed in hierarchies, and only the most costly condition within each related category is recognized. The transition from the prior demographic method to risk-adjusted payments was phased in over several years to 100% by 2007.

A separate risk adjustment model was developed for Part D prescription drug coverage. This model is similar to the CMS-HCC model, but designed to reflect Part D costs instead of costs for Part A and B services.

The Affordable Care Act

The ACA significantly modified the Medicare Advantage payment methodology in a variety of ways intended to reduce overall funding and introduce payments based on quality measures.

Each Medicare Advantage plan is now assigned an aggregate star rating from one to five stars based on multiple quality measures. Bonus payments are made for higher rated Medicare Advantage plans, as well as other financial and enrollment advantages. Funding is cut for lower-rated plans.

---

[6] ACA lowered the rebate percentage and made it a function of the MA plan's "star rating," based on quality measures.

A minimum loss ratio of 85%, measured retroactively, was introduced by the ACA beginning in 2014. To the extent a Medicare Advantage plan experiences favorable variation and the loss ratio is less than 85%, the difference must be returned to CMS.

The other payment reductions are being phased in over a period that stretches out to 2017. Over that time, Medicare Advantage plans will likely experience payment reductions, increasing premiums, and industry consolidation, much as they did under the BBA.

MEDICAID

Medicaid provides medical assistance for individuals and families with low income and resources. The federal and state governments finance the program jointly. Most low-income people in the U.S. receive medical coverage through Medicaid.

The federal government sets national guidelines. Within these guidelines, states determine provider reimbursement rates, eligibility criteria, and the level and scope of covered services. Unlike the federally administered Medicare program, states administer Medicaid. There is substantial variation in Medicaid program provisions from state to state, leading to 56 distinct Medicaid programs – one for each state, territory, and the District of Columbia. Although states have broad discretion over many aspects of the program, they must follow federal requirements to receive matching funds.

ELIGIBILITY

Individuals can qualify for Medicaid under many categories of eligibility. The federal government sets the minimum criteria and states are free to expand eligibility. The "categorically eligible" groups include children, parents or other caretakers with dependent children, pregnant women, individuals with disabilities, and seniors. In addition to categorical requirements, certain income and asset requirements must be met. Income requirements are defined as a percentage of the federal poverty level (FPL). For example, states must cover all pregnant women and children under age 6 with incomes below 133% of the FPL. The annual FPL in 2015 for a family of one was $11,770 in most states (used for determining 2016 eligibility). Minimum eligibility criteria for all categories are set by the federal government, with states having the option to set income and asset limits at a higher level. Flexibility in eligibility rules has helped states substantially in their coverage and reform efforts.

The above requirements refer to the *categorically* needy. States also often extend coverage to the *medically* needy. These individuals can qualify for Medicaid when their medical expenses reduce income below defined limits. Such coverage may have less extensive eligibility and benefit provisions. However, to receive federal matching funds, certain groups and medical services must be covered. Most states have programs for medically needy individuals.

As of 2013, the total Medicaid population was around 55 million; non-disabled children make up over 50% of that amount.[7]

Title XXI of the Social Security Act, known as the State Children's Health Insurance Program (SCHIP), was initiated by the Balanced Budget Act of 1997. SCHIP allows states to expand coverage, with support from federal funding, to substantial numbers of uninsured low-income children not eligible for Medicaid. The upper income limit for eligibility is typically 200% of the FPL. As of 2006, each state had an approved SCHIP plan in place. CHIPRA (the Children's Health Insurance Reauthorization Act of 2009) expanded support to low-income children, and the program is now referred to as CHIP instead of SCHIP.

A major component of the ACA was the expansion of Medicaid eligibility beginning in 2014. Under the ACA, nearly everyone under age 65 with income up to 133% of FPL is eligible for Medicaid. Thus, this expansion extended coverage to many low income adults who have no dependent children. However, due to a key 2012 Supreme Court decision[8], states were given the *option* to expand Medicaid Some states have chosen to not expand the Medicaid eligibility, but even those states have experienced a material upswing in Medicaid enrollment, as those who would have qualified under preexisting categories have newly sought coverage during the ACA exchange open enrollment period. Overall, between October 2013 and June 2015, CMS estimates that an additional 13.1 million people are now covered by Medicaid and CHIP.[9]

FINANCING

Each state finances its own Medicaid program, with substantial support from the federal government. The source of federal funding is general revenues; there are no earmarked payroll taxes or beneficiary premiums, as there are for Medicare. Since Medicaid is an entitlement program, total financing requirements are driven by the number of recipients and the cost of services provided.

By fiscal year 2014, the federal government financed between 50% and 73% of each state's Medicaid program costs.[10] The level of federal support to each state depends on the state's average per capita income. The lower a state's average per capita income, the higher the federal support percentage. By law, the federal government funds a minimum of 50% of the state's cost to administer the program, but not more than 83%. The average federal match percentage was approximately 59% in fiscal year 2014 for Medicaid and 71% for CHIP.[11] In spite of the federal match, Medicaid program costs are a significant portion of overall state budgets. In fiscal 2013, Medicaid costs were 24.5% of state general funds; the fiscal 2014 burden is expected to be 25.8%.[12]

---

[7] U.S. Census Bureau, Current Population Survey, Annual Social and Economic Supplement, Table HI01, https://www.census.gov/hhes/www/cpstables/032014/health/h01R_000.htm
[8] http://www.supremecourt.gov/opinions/11pdf/11-393c3a2.pdf
[9] Monthly state enrollment reporting can be found at http://www.medicaid.gov/medicaid-chip-program-information/program-information/medicaid-and-chip-enrollment-data/medicaid-and-chip-enrollment-data.html
[10] CMS Office of the Actuary *Brief Summary of Medicare & Medicaid,* November 1, 2014, page 28.
[11] Ibid.
[12] National Association of State Budget Officers, 2014 State Expenditure Report.

Under the ACA, the federal government will cover 100% of the cost for the new Medicaid eligibles between 2014 and 2016. Thereafter, the federal share phases down until it is 90% by year 2020.

COVERED SERVICES

States must offer a broad range of basic medical services to categorically needy individuals, including inpatient and outpatient hospital, physician, lab and x-ray, skilled nursing facility, home health care, preventive care, prenatal care, screening, vaccines for children, family planning, services at federally qualified health centers and rural health clinics, and transportation. Other optional services, which nearly all states offer, are dental, outpatient prescription drugs, prosthetic devices and hearing aids, optometric services and eyeglasses, and rehabilitation and physical therapy.

States are required to pay Medicare Part B premiums and cost sharing for low-income Medicare beneficiaries. States can require that some individuals share in the cost through premiums and copayments. However, significant cost sharing is prohibited by federal regulations. Most Medicaid beneficiaries pay little to no cost when they access medical care.

PROVIDER PARTICIPATION AND REIMBURSEMENT

Participating providers must accept the state's defined reimbursement as payment in full. Providers may not bill Medicaid patients additional amounts, and they are forbidden from withholding services if the patient is unable to pay the requisite cost-sharing amounts. State provider reimbursement rates must be sufficient to enlist enough providers such that access and availability is comparable to that received by the general population. Due to low reimbursement and other restrictions, Medicaid programs often do not achieve this objective, as providers are not required to accept Medicaid patients. Medicaid reimbursement is generally lower (often substantially lower) than Medicare or private health plan reimbursement. State budget limitations often restrict their ability to reimburse providers at higher rates.

Hospital Payments: States reimburse hospitals in a variety of ways. Many states use a prospective payment approach similar to that used by Medicare. Others reimburse based on the cost to deliver services. Some hospitals with a high proportion of Medicaid, low income, and uninsured patients receive additional reimbursement known as the disproportionate share hospital (DSH) adjustment.

Physician Payments: States typically reimburse physicians according to a fee schedule. Medicaid physician reimbursement is often much lower than reimbursement for private payers and Medicare, and as a result, many physicians limit their participation in the Medicaid program. Physicians have also expressed concern over continuity of coverage and litigation issues with Medicaid patients.

In addition to covering medically necessary treatments, Medicaid pays for the long-term care needs of qualifying individuals, both in the home and at facilities. Long-term care costs represented 34% of Medicaid costs in fiscal years 2012 through 2014, but are expected to be a lower proportion starting in 2014 due to the ACA's Medicaid expansion discussed earlier.[13]

MEDICAID COSTS AND MANAGED CARE

Both utilization and total costs of services under Medicaid, particularly for aged, blind, and disabled recipients, are higher than for the commercial population. The following table shows fiscal year 2013 average Medicaid payments per person served[14]:

Eligibility Category	FY 2013 Annual Cost
Adults	$4,391
Children Under 21	$2,807
Blind and Disabled	$17,352
Age 65 and Older	$15,483
Total	$6,897

Rising Medicaid costs and state budget limitations have encouraged states to pursue alternatives to the traditional fee-for-service delivery system. Federal government waivers allow states to contract with managed care organizations, which include HMOs, prepaid health plans, and primary care case management programs. States contract with HMOs and prepaid health plans to provide medical services for a fixed payment rate per member (often varying by category of eligibility, location, and demographics). As required by the waiver, payment rates in aggregate are less than expected Medicaid program costs, and the participating health plans are responsible for providing, delivering, and administering services to Medicaid recipients.

Since the 1990s, states have aggressively introduced new programs to enroll recipients in managed care. The types of programs and managed care penetration vary significantly by state. Managed care penetration is lower in those states that have retained the traditional fee-for-service program, where managed care enrollment is voluntary. The percentage of Medicaid recipients enrolled in some form of managed care program nationally was 71.7% in 2013.[15]

THE FUTURE OF MEDICARE AND MEDICAID

Medicare and Medicaid continue to be challenged with increasing enrollment, excess health cost growth relative to GDP, and severely challenged state and federal budgets. Like private health plans, these government plans are (and are likely to continue) experimenting with alternative financing methods, such as accountable care organizations, bundled payments for packages of services, payments based on quality, and competitive bidding. Government leaders will be challenged to adopt changes to improve the programs while making difficult and unpopular moves to address financial solvency.

Despite the dire outlook for the long-term financial status of Medicare and Medicaid, these programs enjoy broad public support. Program costs will undoubtedly take up an increasing

---

[13] *Medicaid Expenditures for Long-Term Services and Supports (LTSS) in FY 2013*, CMS with subcontractor Truven Health Analytics, June 30, 2015.
[14] CMS Office of the Actuary *Brief Summary of Medicare & Medicaid,* November 1, 2014, page 29, preliminary.
[15] CMS 2013 Medicaid Managed Care Enrollment Report.

share of government expenditures, and may require higher payroll and other taxes, which are always an unpopular step politically. Other methods that will be considered to address the funding shortfall are provider fee reductions, limiting or delaying eligibility, rationing of care, reducing coverages, and enrollees' premiums or cost sharing. The public expects that Medicare will be there for them during their retirement years and believes that Medicaid fulfills its mission to provide needed health care to the poor and disabled. To continue to fulfill that mission, moderate changes to many of the above cost levers are needed to avoid more drastic cuts later.

SOCIAL SECURITY CASH BENEFITS (OASDI)

In addition to retired-worker benefits payable by the OASDI program, The Social Security Act provided for certain cash benefits--Social Security disabled-worker benefits and survivor benefits. These additional insured cash benefits are described below.

COVERED POPULATION

Today, most workers in the U.S., both employees and the self-employed, are covered by Social Security. As an illustration of this, about 97% of Americans age 60-89 either receive benefits today or will receive benefits in the future.[16] The only notable exceptions are federal employees hired before 1984 (a closed group); about one fourth of state and local government employees (those covered by retirement plans that are comparable to Social Security are not compulsorily covered); a very small number of people who object to receiving governmental benefits on religious grounds (such as many Amish); certain agricultural and domestic workers; and railroad employees, who have a separate government-run retirement system that is financially integrated with, and in many ways equivalent to, Social Security.

Workers in covered employment pay Social Security taxes under the Federal Insurance Contributions Act (FICA) in the case of employees, or under the Self-Employment Contributions Act (SECA) in the case of the self-employed, on their earnings up to an annual maximum. They receive coverage credits on the basis of their covered (and taxable) earnings.

In 2014, workers receive one coverage credit for each $1,200 of covered earnings in the year, up to a maximum of four credits for $4,800 or more in covered earnings, regardless of when those earnings occurred during the year.[17] The amount of earnings required to earn coverage credits has changed annually since 1978 and will continue to do so in the future, based on changes in the national average wage.[18] Workers with sufficient coverage credits establish insured status for various types of Social Security benefits.

---

[16] Whitehouse.gov, *9 Facts About Social Security*, August 14, 2015.
[17] Social Security Administration (SSA) *Fast Facts & Figures About Social Security, 2014*.
[18] Section 213 of the Social Security Act (42 U.S.C. 413).

Insured Status

Disability-Insured Status

To become eligible to receive disabled-worker benefits in the event of qualifying disability, a worker must have disability-insured status. The number of coverage credits required for this status varies, depending on the worker's age at disability onset, from six coverage credits at ages in the early 20s, to 40 coverage credits at ages 62 or older (since 1991). In addition, some or all of the coverage credits must have been earned recently (the "recent-attachment" test). For those required to have 20 or more coverage credits, at least 20 of them must have been earned in the 40 calendar quarters ending with the quarter of disability onset. For those required to have fewer than 20 but more than 6 coverage credits, at least half must have been earned after age 21. For those required to have only 6 coverage credits, they must have been earned in the 12 calendar quarters ending with the quarter of disability onset.

Fully-Insured or Currently-Insured Status

Eligible family members of a deceased worker may receive survivor benefits if the worker was either fully insured or currently insured at the time of death. Fully-insured status, which provides eligibility for the full range of survivor benefits, requires that the deceased worker have earned coverage credits generally equal to the calendar age at death less 22, with a minimum of 6 and a maximum of 40 coverage credits. These need not have been earned at any particular time. Currently insured status, which provides eligibility for young-survivor benefits only, requires just 6 coverage credits in the 13 calendar quarters ending with the quarter of death.

Other Eligibility Conditions

Disabled-Worker Benefits

A worker with disability-insured status can receive disabled-worker benefits if he or she becomes unable to engage in any "substantial gainful activity" (SGA) because of a physical or mental impairment that has lasted or is expected to last for 12 months or to result in prior death. The level of earnings that represents SGA has varied over the years, and is currently subject to automatic adjustment. The level for 2014 is $1,070 per month for non-blind individuals.[19] To be disabled, a worker must be judged unable to engage in SGA (that is, consistently earn the threshold amount) in any job that exists in the national economy, regardless of whether he or she would be hired for such a job, if it exists. In many but not all cases, the disability determination is required to take into account the worker's age, education and work experience.

Initial disability determinations are made by state agencies on behalf of the Social Security Administration (SSA), under agreements authorized by federal law. A large percentage of initial claims are denied (approximately 65%),[20] for a variety of reasons. Many claims are appealed and result in hearings before administrative law judges employed by SSA. Unfavorable decisions can ultimately be appealed to the federal courts, and many are. A few even reach the U.S. Supreme Court.

Disabled-worker benefits are paid after a waiting period of five full calendar months. For example, a worker who becomes disabled on March 15 cannot count March toward that

---

[19] Social Security Administration (SSA) *Fast Facts & Figures About Social Security, 2014*.
[20] http://www.ssa.gov/oact/STATS/table6c7.html

waiting period because he or she was not disabled for the full month. The five relevant months would be April through August. Benefits would be payable for the month of September, and the payment would ordinarily be made on the designated payment date in October. Of course, because of the time needed to collect medical evidence and to handle appeals, many disabled-worker claims are not processed quickly enough to permit benefits to begin so soon after disability onset. In those cases, retroactive benefits are paid in a lump sum.

The Social Security Act requires[21] that disabled workers be periodically reviewed to see whether they remain disabled according to the definition in the law. Typically, these reviews are required every three years, but they can be done more or less frequently, depending on the medical condition. In general, the SSA must establish that a disabled beneficiary's condition has improved before he or she can be removed from the benefit rolls. In other words, the SSA is bound by its previous determination, absent some change in circumstance.

Disabled-worker benefits are automatically converted to retired-worker benefits when disabled workers attain normal retirement age (NRA, which is age 65 for 1938 and before birth years, grading to age 67 for 1959 and beyond birth years).

Survivor Benefits

Eligible family members of a deceased worker can receive survivor benefits if the worker met the insured-status requirements described above at the time of death. Surviving spouses and surviving ex-spouses must establish that the marriage relationship existed or was deemed to exist for the required length of time. Social Security has no dependency test for spouses. Children must establish dependency, which is deemed to exist for most natural and adopted children under age 18 (or age 18 and still a full-time high-school student). Disabled adult children can receive survivor benefits for life, provided that disability began before the child attained age 22 and continued uninterrupted since then. In very rare cases, parents age 62 or older of a deceased worker can receive survivor benefits, if the parents were financially dependent on the deceased worker and not receiving larger benefits in their own right.

BENEFIT AMOUNTS

Disabled-Worker Benefits

Disabled-worker benefit amounts are computed using essentially the same procedures as are used to compute Social Security retired-worker benefit amounts. The worker is treated as if he or she had already attained age 62, the earliest eligibility age for retired-worker benefits, but no early-retirement reduction factor is applied to disabled-worker benefits (except in unusual cases where the disabled worker had previously received retired-worker benefits before becoming disabled). Cost-of-living benefit increases are generally effective every December, starting with the year of entitlement (even if retroactively entitled). In years when inflation is zero or negative, as measured by the third-quarter-over-third-quarter CPI-W, then no cost-of-living adjustment (COLA) is made.

---

[21] Section 221(i) of the Social Security Act (42 U.S.C. 421(i)).

Under certain circumstances, the spouse and each child (under age 18, generally, or themselves disabled) of the disabled worker can receive additional monthly benefits. The amount payable to a family member is nominally 50% of the worker's primary insurance amount (PIA); however, the total benefits payable to the family, including the disabled worker, are limited by a maximum family benefit that in disability cases never exceeds 150% of the worker's own benefit.

Social Security disability benefits are integrated with workers' compensation and certain other public disability benefits. In general, the total benefits from all such programs cannot exceed 80% of "average current earnings" (as defined in the law), with triennial redeterminations to reflect inflation. In 37 states and the District of Columbia, the disabled-worker benefit is reduced to bring the total within the limit, and in 12 states, usually the reverse occurs. Nevada is a special case.

Survivor Benefits

The deceased worker's PIA is computed using the standard procedures, but treating young deceased workers as if they were age 62 at the time of death and not applying any actuarial reduction. In addition, earnings in the year of death are used in the computation before the year is over (which is not allowed in the computation of retired- or disabled-worker benefits). Survivors receive a percentage of the deceased worker's PIA, ranging from 75% for eligible children (under age 18, generally, or disabled) to 100% for a widow(er) first claiming benefits at or above his or her own NRA. The widow(er) cannot generally receive more than the worker was receiving, if the worker was already receiving a benefit. A widow(er) claiming benefits before his or her NRA has an actuarial reduction. This reduction causes the benefit percentage to grade linearly from 71.5% of the deceased worker's PIA at age 60 to 100% at the widow(er)'s NRA. A widow(er) can "inherit" delayed-retirement credits from a deceased worker who had earned such credits at the time of death. A *disabled* widow(er) at ages 50-59 can receive 71.5% of the deceased worker's PIA if disability occurs within seven years of the worker's death. An eligible surviving parent receives 82.5% of the PIA, and 75% each if both parents receive benefits.

A maximum family benefit applies to survivor benefits. It ranges from 150% to 188% of the PIA, with most families being limited to 175%. Surviving ex-spouses of the deceased worker are excluded from the family for this purpose.

STATE DISABILITY INSURANCE

There are several states that provide disability wage replacement insurance to workers, funded by mandatory employee contributions and optional employer contributions: California, Hawaii, New Jersey, New York, and Rhode Island.[22]

California's disability insurance plan provides income replacement of 55%, up to a maximum weekly benefit, for up to 52 weeks after the eighth consecutive day of disability. Paid family leave is also available.[23] It is the most generous of the state disability insurance plans.

---

[22] The U.S. commonwealth of Puerto Rico also offers a state disability program.
[23] http://www.edd.ca.gov/Disability/State_Disability_Insurance_(SDI)_Eligibility.htm

The Hawaii Temporary Disability Insurance program provides income replacement of 58%, up to a maximum weekly benefit, for up to 26 weeks after the eighth day of disability.[24] Employers can self-insure this benefit or participate in collective bargaining arrangements that provide sick leave benefits at least as rich.

The New Jersey Temporary Disability Insurance program provides income replacement of 67%, up to a maximum weekly benefit, for up to 26 weeks, but also limited to an overall maximum benefit amount of one-third of New Jersey base year total wages.[25]

New York disability benefits insurance program provides income replacement of 50%, up to a statutory minimum or an enriched maximum weekly benefit, for up to 26 weeks.[26]

The Rhode Island Temporary Disability Insurance program provides income replacement of about 60%, up to a maximum weekly benefit, for up to 30 weeks. Rhode Island's program also provides a dependent children allowance and provides temporary caregiver insurance.[27]

---

[24] http://labor.hawaii.gov/dcd/home/about-tdi/
[25] http://lwd.dol.state.nj.us/labor/tdi/tdiindex.html
[26] http://ww3.nysif.com/DisabilityBenefits.aspx
[27] http://www.dlt.ri.gov/tdi/

10 HEALTH BENEFITS IN CANADA

Stella-Ann Ménard

THE CANADIAN MEDICARE SYSTEM

Nearly every person who lives in Canada is covered by the Medicare program of his or her province of residence. The program is similar from one province to another. It provides service benefits mainly for physician care, surgery, and hospitalization in a public ward in Canada.

Since the most expensive services (physician care and surgery) are already covered by Medicare, there are no comprehensive managed care organizations such as health maintenance organizations (HMOs) or large-scale preferred provider organizations (PPOs) in Canada. As a result, nearly all private plans are underwritten or administered by insurers (whether on an insured or self-insured basis).

THE CANADA HEALTH ACT

Under the Canadian constitution, matters related to health, including regulation of hospitals and licensing of physicians, fall under provincial jurisdiction. However, the federal government can initiate social security measures in areas that fall under provincial jurisdiction by setting national standards and subsidizing provinces that set up programs that conform to these standards.

The Canada Health Act (CHA)[1] is the Canadian federal legislation for publicly funded health care insurance. It sets out the primary objective of Canadian health care policy, which is "to protect, promote and restore the physical and mental well-being of residents of Canada and to facilitate reasonable access to health services without financial or other barriers." The CHA establishes criteria and conditions related to insured health services and extended health care services that the provinces and territories must fulfill to receive the full federal cash contribution under the Canada Health Transfer (CHT). It also aims to ensure that all eligible residents of Canada have reasonable access to insured health services on a prepaid basis, without direct charges at the point of service for such services.

While the federal government is responsible for the subsidies, the provincial and territorial governments are responsible for the management, organization, and delivery of health services for their residents.

The federal government initiated Medicare in 1958 for hospital insurance, with all provinces and territories having their plans in effect by 1961, and for medical insurance in 1967, with

---

[1] http://www.hc-sc.gc.ca, *Canada Health Act.*

all provinces and territories having their plans by the beginning of 1972. The initial federal subsidy was approximately 50% of the cost of these plans.

To be eligible for the federal subsidy, provincial Medicare plans have to comply with the following five principles of the Canada Health Act.

- Comprehensiveness: All medically required hospital and physician services must be covered under the plan.

- Universality: All legal residents of a province or territory must be entitled to the insured health services provided for by the plan on uniform terms and conditions.

- Accessibility: Reasonable access by residents to hospital and physician services must not be impeded by charges made to them.

- Portability: The plan may not impose a waiting period in excess of three months for new residents and coverage must be maintained when a resident moves or travels within Canada or is temporarily out of the country.

- Public Administration: The plan must be administered and operated on a non-profit basis by a public authority.

Extra-billing and user charges are discouraged by provisions of the Canada Health Act; if any province allows these charges to be covered in its Medicare plan, the federal grants to that province are reduced by dollar for dollar by amounts collected by physicians through extra-billing or user charges.

Several provinces prohibit private insurance of hospital and medical services obtained outside their provincial Medicare program, if these services are available under the provincial program. The other provinces allow private insurance to cover these services. The prohibition of private insurance for these services is based on an interpretation of the Canada Health Act that private insurance would undermine its objectives, especially accessibility, by diverting resources from the public sector.

This prohibition was challenged in *Chaoulli v. Quebec* in 2005, where the Supreme Court of Canada ruled that, because of long waiting lists, the anti-insurance prohibition in the Quebec law infringed the rights to life and personal inviolability guaranteed by the Quebec Charter of Rights and Freedoms. The consensus has been that private coverage of medical services covered by a provincial Medicare program is legal only if the waiting list for these services is recognized as too long.

Since the Supreme Court did not define the concept of "too long," it is up to the Minister of Health of a province to specify, in the law or in regulations, which services are eligible for private coverage. After many years following the Chaoulli decision, only hip replacement, knee reconstruction, and cataract surgery can be privately insured in Quebec. As these medical conditions are prone to antiselection and concern mostly retirees, there has been no significant pressure from the public, or willingness from insurers, to sell insurance covering them.

Private Health Care

There are two different areas where private health care can exist in Canada. The first area consists of services that are available free of charge under Medicare but are rendered by physicians who practice outside Medicare. Even after the Chaoulli case, these services are not covered by group insurance plans, because private insurance for the vast majority of these services is illegal in most provinces. Further, covering these services in provinces where it is legal may make a plan more difficult to administer, and might raise questions about equity between employees living in different provinces. The other area of private health care in Canada includes all services that are not available under Medicare. These services are the main focus of group health insurance plans.

Provincial Medicare Plans

Officially, there are two different plans: hospital insurance and medical insurance. However, provinces tend to centralize the administration of both plans, so they can be considered as the two main features of a single plan. Coverage is provided on a service basis (except for out-of-Canada coverage, which is on a reimbursement basis).

Any resident of any province can choose to be treated by any physician who practices in his or her province of residence, as long as the physician practices within the system. Most of these physicians charge their fees directly to the provincial plan. Other physicians (in rare instances) may collect their fees (as long as these fees are those agreed between the provincial plan and the physicians' association) directly from the patient who, in turn, will be reimbursed by the provincial plan. Services provided by physicians practicing outside the system are not reimbursed.

Due to the lack of the most modern technology in some parts of the country, some specialized services are not available in every province. In this case, the provincial board usually pays the cost of those services if they are obtained in another province.

Eligibility and Coverage

All permanent residents of a province or territory are eligible for coverage. Coverage for services other than prescription drugs is available without charge, except in British Columbia where a small premium is charged.

Reciprocity agreements among provinces allow a person who moves from one province to another to become eligible in his or her new province of residence as soon as coverage terminates under the Medicare plan of his or her former province of residence. Coverage may be continued for up to 12 months when a resident is temporarily absent from his or her province subject to the applicable conditions of the jurisdiction. These conditions may include the requirement for a resident to be physically present in the province for a minimum number of consecutive months.

BENEFITS

Benefits are similar in all jurisdictions, with only minor differences. The following services are generally covered in most jurisdictions:

- Hospital services:
  - Room and board in a public ward;
  - Physicians' services administered in the hospital, diagnostics, anesthesia, nursing care, drugs, supplies and therapy, laboratory and diagnostic services in a hospital, operating facilities, and emergency services. (These services are available on either an inpatient or an outpatient basis);
  - Room and board in a nursing home or long term care hospital (partial coverage in most provinces);
- Physicians' services administered in an office or clinic, including services of a general practitioner, specialist, psychiatrist, surgeon, anesthetist, or obstetrician;
- Services of other professionals such as chiropractors, osteopaths, podiatrists or chiropodists, and naturopaths (coverage is often for lower-income families but could also be for all other residents depending on the jurisdiction);
- Services of physiotherapist are usually covered if in hospital facilities;
- Prescription drugs for social assistance recipients and residents over age 65 in most provinces (British Columbia, Saskatchewan, Manitoba, Newfoundland, Nova Scotia, and Ontario also have high-deductible prescription drug plans for other residents. The enrollment in these plans is voluntary. Quebec has a compulsory plan for everyone not covered under a group insurance plan);
- Prostheses and therapeutic equipment;
- Other diagnostic services, such as laboratory tests and X-rays performed outside a hospital;
- Dental care:
  - Medically necessary oral and dental surgery performed in hospital;
  - Diagnostic, preventive, and minor restorative services performed out of hospital are covered for young children (the maximum age differs by each jurisdiction) and youth of families with low incomes; fillings are usually not covered except for medical complications;
  - Some jurisdictions may cover social assistance recipients (adults and their dependents);
- Out-of-province coverage:
  - Expenses related to medically necessary services;
  - Hospital and medical expenses incurred in Canada:
    Reciprocal agreements exist between all jurisdictions (provinces or territories). Expenses are covered provided they are covered under the jurisdiction where services are provided. Expenses are usually paid according to the amount payable in the province where the person is treated, except for professional services for Quebec residents which are reimbursed according to the Quebec fee schedule;
  - Hospital expenses incurred out of Canada:
    Expenses are reimbursed partially only and are expressed on a per diem limits

published by each jurisdiction; medical expenses out of Canada may be reimbursed up to the amount that would have been paid for the same treatments in the province of residence (physician's services) or on per diem basis. The actual cost incurred by the resident may largely exceed the covered expenses.

FINANCING

In 2012, health expenses in Canada amounted to approximately $205 billion, or 11.3% of the GDP (up from 9.1% in 2000).[2]

Most provincial Medicare plans are financed through the following sources:
- general tax revenues in all provinces;
- employer specific payroll taxes in Quebec, Ontario, Manitoba and Newfoundland, and Labrador;
- residents' premiums either directly (British Columbia) or through the income tax report (Quebec and Ontario); and
- transfer payments from the federal government. The Federal transfer payments take two forms: cash transfers and tax point transfers. Tax point transfers occur when the federal government agrees to lower its tax rate so that the provinces and territories can raise theirs by the same amount.[3]

During the 1980s and early 1990s, the huge size of the Canadian federal debt (70% of GDP) and repeated budget deficits prompted the federal government to restrain its expenses. The federal cash transfer payments to the provinces for maintaining their Medicare plans did not keep pace with inflation on health costs. As a result, the federal cash subsidy proportionally decreased until it represented only 24% of the cost of provincial Medicare plans in 1995 and was expected to continue decreasing even faster.

This could have led to a situation where the federal cash subsidy would have become a marginal component of funding. Consequentially, a province might have been able to collect much more money through user fees and extra-billing than the amount of the federal subsidy that would have been forfeited as a result of the provisions of the Canada Health Act. In 1996, to avoid such a situation and make sure that the provinces would still conform to the requirements of the Canada Health Act, federal grants for Medicare were combined with all other social transfer payments (for services such as education) into the Canada Health & Social Transfer. As a result, a province that would allow user fees or extra-billing could be penalized up to the full amount of the Canada Health & Social Transfer.

It is noteworthy that in 2002, federal funding (i.e., the Health component of total Federal Transfers and Health component of federal tax points transfers) represented approximately 44% of the cost of physicians and hospitals. The federal transfers represented only 27.5% of the total provincial health expenses in 2002, compared with 37.5% in the early 1970s, prompting the provinces to ask for more federal health care funding.[4]

---

[2] Canadian Institute for Health Information: National *Health Expenditure Trends 1975 to 2013*.
[3] Canadian Department of Finance; www.budget.gc.ca/transfers/taxpoint/taxpoint
[4] Commission on the Future of Health Care in Canada: *Building on Values: Final Report*, November 2002, p. 312.

In 2004, the Canada Health & Social Transfer was replaced by two new transfers, the Canada Health Transfer and the Canada Social Transfer. Having a federal transfer specifically devoted to health was a recommendation of the Romanow Commission.[5]

CHALLENGES FOR THE CANADIAN MEDICARE SYSTEM

In recent years, the provinces were caught in a situation where they had less money to spend on their Medicare plans, while at the same time they were prevented from sharing the cost of these plans with patients through user fees or extra-billing. Raising taxes was not an option due to the already very high level of taxes and major increases to the Canada/Quebec Pension Plans contribution rate, so the provinces had to cut their spending on health care.

This prompted provincial boards to cut or reduce benefits not required under the Canada Health Act, such as out-of-Canada coverage, dental services, optometric services, and prescription drugs. At the same time, various rationing schemes were put in place, such as reducing the number of physicians and nurses providing services within the provincial plans, limiting their compensation, reducing or limiting the number of services that they can perform, or reducing the number of hospital beds. This resulted in queuing and longer delays, mostly for non-emergency care.

At the turn of the millennium, the Medicare system had continued deteriorating. The following concerns were raised in reports[6,7] published in early 2002:

- Waiting for months to see a specialist is common, because of a shortage of some specialists, poor scheduling practices, and inappropriate assessments of need;
- Shortages of equipment, specialists, and technicians cause waiting for diagnostic procedures such as MRI;
- Waiting for elective and non-emergency surgery is common, due to a lack of operating room time and a shortage of hospital beds;
- Emergency rooms are overcrowded, due to the unavailability of after-hours clinics, the non-emergency use of emergency rooms, the inability to transfer patients to regular wards, and poor distribution of caseloads with neighboring facilities;
- People who need long-term care tend to wait in hospitals because of a shortage of beds in long-term care, insufficient community care and housing alternatives, and non-standardized admission criteria;
- Technology-intensive services are not available everywhere;
- The demand for services exceeds the supply, resulting in rationing; and
- Some services that are essential to the treatment of a medical condition, such as prescription drugs for chronic illnesses, are not covered by Medicare.

When Medicare was implemented, hospital and physician services were the two major components of health care. Now, these services account for less than half of the total cost of

---

[5] Federal Commission on the Future of Health Care in Canada, *Romanow Report, November 2002.*
[6] Commission on the Future of Health Care in Canada: *Shape the Future of Health Care: Interim Report, February 2002*, p. 30.
[7] Commission on the Future of Health Care in Canada: *Canadians' Thoughts on Their Health Care System: Preserving the Canadian Model through Innovation,* pages 5-6 & Figure 32.

the system. In 2014, hospital expenditures have decreased but remain the major component of the health expenditures with an approximate share of 30% and the pharmacy component slowly increasing to 16%, slightly higher than the physicians' expenditures at 15.5%.

RESPONSE TO THESE CHALLENGES

The 10-year period between 1995 and 2005 was characterized by an unprecedented number of committees, commissions, and reports on how to fix the problems of Medicare. These include the National Forum on Health[8] (F), the Federal Commission on the Future of Health Care in Canada[9] (R), the Alberta Premier's Advisory Council on Health[10] (MZ), the Standing Senate Committee on Social Affairs, Science and Technology[11] (K), and the Quebec Working Committee on the Permanence of the Health and Social Services System[12] (ME). The most important recommendations formulated in these reports are shown below, using letters above to indicate the reports in which the recommendation appears.

Scope

- Keeping the requirements of the Canada Health Act unchanged or expanding them (F, K, R);
- Maintaining a single-payer universal health care model for the provincial public health care programs (F);
- Expanding the scope of publicly funded provincial public health care programs to include home care and prescription drugs (F, R);
- Expanding Medicare to cover the portion of the cost prescription drugs that exceeds 3% of total family income (K);
- Expanding Medicare to cover post-acute and palliative home care (K, R);
- Establishing a partially pre-funded national long-term care insurance program (ME);
- Redefining comprehensiveness under the Canada Health Act to avoid putting Medicare under the obligation to cover the full range of health services, treatments, or technologies available today or in the future (MZ).

Philosophy

- Reforming primary care to focus on patients instead of services (F; MZ)
- Emphasizing prevention of illness and injury and promotion of good health (R);
- Promoting health by changing the compensation of physicians from a fee-for-service basis to a more appropriate basis, such as capitation (F, K, MZ, R)
- Providing incentives to attract, retain, and best utilize health providers (MZ, K);
- Basing health care spending on Canadian values (R).

---

[8] National Forum on Health, *Final Report, 1997.*
[9] Federal Commission on the Future of Health Care in Canada, *Romanow Report, November 2002.*
[10] Alberta Premier's Advisory Council on Health, *Mazankowski Report, December 2001.*
[11] Standing Senate Committee on Social Affairs, Science and Technology, *Kirby Report, October 2002.*
[12] Quebec Working Committee on the Permanence of the Health and Social Services System, *Menard Report, July 2005.*

Delivery

- Creating multi-disciplinary primary health care groups, providing a wide range of services 24 hours a day, 7 days a week (K);
- Re-configuring the health system to encourage more choice, competition, and accountability (MZ);
- Making quality a top priority (MZ);
- Using the private sector to deliver health services, within the framework of the public Medicare system (ME);
- Removing barriers to expansion of care initiatives (R);
- Expanding use of nurse practitioners (R);
- Delivering more health services in communities or at home (R).

Administration

- Using information technology and computerized databases, including electronic health records, for making health-related decisions, while guaranteeing privacy (F, MZ, K, R);
- Giving more powers and responsibilities to regional health authorities (MZ, K);
- Providing residents with a guarantee of access to selected health services within a reasonable time frame (R, MZ, K);
- Appointing a National Health Care Commissioner who would report annually on Canada's health care system (K).

Research and Analysis

- Appointing a National Health Council to measure the performance of the health care system, collect information, report publicly on efforts to improve quality, access and outcomes in the health care system, and coordinate activities in health technology assessment (R);
- Developing indicators to measure performance of the system and health outcomes (R);
- Determining what the community can afford to spend on health care (ME).

Treatment

- Implementing new and more effective diagnostic tests (R);
- Developing evidence-based decision-making, including clinical guidelines (R).

Funding

- Shifting from lump sum funding of hospitals to service-based funding (K);
- Increasing or finding other sources of revenues for the health care system (MZ, K, ME, R);
- Establishing a new dedicated cash-only federal transfer as part of the Canada Health Act, with increased federal funding and an escalator provision set in advance for five years (R);
- Implementing stable, predictable, long-term funding arrangements with clearly defined rules (R).

Some of these recommendations are clearly in direct conflict with others, and illustrate the diversity of views on the future of Medicare in Canada.

So far, little has been done to implement these suggestions. The most notable progress is on the prescription drug front, where public plans have gradually been expanded to cover low-income residents, with deductibles or coinsurance[13] based on the patient's net income. Some progress is also being made on the use of information technology and computerized databases, including electronic health records.

THE QUEBEC PRESCRIPTION DRUG ACT

In January 1997, Quebec implemented mandatory coverage of prescription drugs for all residents of the province. Any resident who is eligible for coverage, either as a worker or as a dependent, under a private group insurance plan set up by an employer or trade association, must be covered by such plan. All other residents must enroll in a prescription drug plan managed by the province. The only exception is for persons aged 65 or older, who may choose to be covered under the plan of their employer or former employer, if they are eligible for such plan, the provincial plan, or under both, with the provincial plan being primary. All private plans must at least cover the drugs covered by the provincial plan.

Since the plan was implemented, premiums for non-senior working adults have more than tripled (from $175/year in 1997 to $611/year in mid-2014) despite a deductible increase (from $8.33/month in 1997 to $16.65/month in 2014) and an out-of-pocket maximum increase (from $750/year in 1997 to $83.83/month in 2014). Over the same period, the coinsurance paid by the plan decreased from 75% to 67.5%.

THE CANADIAN DRUG INSURANCE POOLING CORPORATION (CDIPC)

Effective January 1, 2013, the Canadian Drug Pooling mechanism was implemented. The purpose of the pooling is for the industry to collectively protect the small- to medium-sized plan sponsors from the financial hardship of catastrophic costs drugs, hence providing their employees the continued access to drug treatments they require.

This self-regulated pooling mechanism is the result of a joint effort between the Canadian Life and Health Insurance Association (CLHIA), a non-profit organization which represents nearly 100% of the insurers, and the CLHIA members in good standing. As part of its mission, the CLHIA is committed to ensuring that the views and interests of its members and of the public are addressed in an equitable fashion.

CDIPC covers the plans sold on fully insured arrangements on the basis that the plans sold on a retention or administrative services only (ASO) arrangements have the financial stability to absorb the loss of catastrophic drug claims. The pooling has six underlying principles[14]:

- Availability: All fully insured groups in Canada should be able to continue to purchase group extended healthcare coverage from an insurer designed to meet their specific needs.

---

[13] The term "coinsurance" refers to a percentage of cost split between the payer and the member. It may refer to either the payer's share or the member's share of the costs. Where specificity is required and the context is otherwise unclear, this text uses terms such as "payer coinsurance" or "member coinsurance" to identify which party is responsibility for paying a given coinsurance amount.

[14] http://cdipc-scmam.ca/KeyPrinciples.html#navep3

- Affordability: All fully insured groups should be able to purchase group extended healthcare coverage at a reasonable price. A plan sponsor should not see unaffordable rate increases due to the incidence of a large recurring drug claim from one of its members or their dependents.
- Transferability: All fully insured groups should be able to select the participating insurer of their choice and not be tied to their current participating insurer in the presence of a large recurring drug claim.
- Viability: No solution should unduly undermine the ability of a participating insurer to continue. Both large and small participating insurers should be able to abide by these principles and continue to offer health insurance products.
- Participative: Any sustainable solution should be available to all interested eligible insurance companies.
- Competitive: Any solution must be pro-competitive and continue to encourage an active and vigorous competition in the market

The pooling limits, at inception, were as follows:
- Any certificate (i.e., policy coverage of an employee and dependents) with claims equal or exceeding at least $50,000 for two consecutive years is eligible for pooling.
- When eligible, any certificate with claims exceeding $25,000 will be pooled up to a maximum pooled amount of $400,000 per certificate per year.

The above limits are set to increase annually.

An industry claims reconciliation is performed every year and determines the portion that each insurer is due to receive or needs to pay.

PRIVATE MEDICAL PLANS

Extended health care plans usually include six types of benefits: hospital expenses, prescription drugs, health professional practitioners, miscellaneous expenses, vision care, and out-of-Canada emergency care.

In recent years, prescription drugs and out-of-country medical have evolved toward becoming more separate from the remainder of health insurance, with their own cost containment features (deductible, co-payment and/or coinsurance and maximums). Hospital benefits were already treated somewhat differently from the other health benefits.

Hospital and prescription drug benefits are usually provided on a direct-pay basis where the private plan pays the provider directly; other benefits are generally provided on an indemnity basis, with coverage for reasonable and customary charges, except for health professional practitioners who may be covered for a scheduled amount per treatment. Out-of-country benefits are typically provided at 100%, and may include a limit on the number of days covered per trip.

Coverage is based on the date of incurral, which is the date when services are provided. Benefits are paid according to the coinsurance level, after satisfying the deductible and subject to the maximum benefits payable.

DEDUCTIBLE

Deductibles for extended health care plans in Canada are much lower than in the United States. Typical deductibles vary from $25 to $100 per person or per family, and usually apply to all covered expenses except hospitalization, out-of-country, and often prescription drug. Flexible plans tend to offer options with higher deductibles such as $100, $250, or $500.

Deductibles in most extended heath care plans have not been increased for the last thirty years, despite sustained inflation on covered expenses. As a result, many deductibles are now lower than the average cost of a single claim. Such deductibles have lost much of their efficiency as a cost containment feature, since they no longer cause insureds to self-pay small claims. With the wide popularity of pay-direct drug cards, several plans have replaced their deductibles with co-payments on prescription drugs.

Some employers have increased or indexed the deductible under their extended health care plan. In addition, some employers have implemented high deductibles, along with the introduction of health care spending accounts to be used to pay for the smaller claims. This approach requires extra care, because high deductibles tend to be more vulnerable to inflation leverage than smaller ones.

COINSURANCE

Coinsurance levels paid by the plans vary from 80% to 100% and are not necessarily the same for the six types of coverage. Hospital charges are usually paid in full, with no deductible. Prescription drugs are evolving into a separate coverage, with both deductible and coinsurance often being replaced with flat co-payments. Plan sponsors and insurers have been reluctant to provide plans that pay the full cost of prescription drugs with no deductible. Some plans (typically flexible benefits plans) have recently implemented progressive coinsurance (such as 70% of the first $1,000 and 100% of the remainder). As an attempt to control the ever-increasing cost of prescription drug coverage, some plans have implemented a two-tier coinsurance, where generic drugs are reimbursed at 100% while other drugs are reimbursed with a lower coinsurance. Health professional practitioners' services and other eligible expenses are generally reimbursed at 80% or 90%, with or without a deductible. Out-of-Canada emergency expenses are generally covered at 100% without any deductible.

OVERALL LIMITS

There is generally no overall limit to insured benefits payable for expenses incurred in Canada by an active employee. The extended health care plans are not exposed to catastrophic claims because the most expensive treatments are covered by the provincial Medicare plan. As drug therapy treatments are being developed and may replace some treatments previously covered in the provincial Medicare plans, the extended health care plans costs are increasing. Although no overall limit applies to extended health care plans, internal limits exist as a cost control measure. However, for the out-of-Canada emergency care a maximum (typically $1,000,000) applies for active employees. For retirees, there is frequently an overall maximum, which is expressed either on a one-year, three-year, or five-year basis, or as a lifetime limit (generally no more than $10,000 to $50,000).

Eligible Expenses

Eligible expenses are expenses related to services, care, and supplies that meet the following requirements:
- They are incurred in Canada;
- They are not payable or reimbursable under a provincial medical and hospitalization plan, even if the insured person is not eligible or insured under the provincial plan;
- They are medically required; and
- If for emergency out-of-Canada, they are due to an accident or a sudden and unexpected illness that started during a trip outside of Canada.

Hospital Charges

Extended health care plans usually pay charges for room and board, up to a maximum per diem which is expressed either as a flat dollar amount or, more frequently, as the difference between the cost of a semi-private or private room and the cost of public ward. The cost of the public ward is paid by the provincial Medicare plan. The hospital charges must be incurred in Canada for the treatment of an acute condition or for pregnancy. There is no maximum benefit, either in dollars or as a total number of days of hospital confinement. Chronic care is usually not covered. The out-of-Canada hospital charges incurred under emergency care are often covered within the out-of-Canada medical expenses.

Prescription Drugs

In Canada, prescription drugs represent approximately 70% to 75% of the cost of extended health care plans. This area of coverage has therefore been the focus of much attention from both insurers and plan sponsors over the years. As a result, various definitions of eligible drugs have been designed, such as the following:

- All drugs prescribed by a physician.

- All drugs for which coverage is mandated by law.

- All drugs that require a prescription from a physician.

- All drugs prescribed by a physician, up to the cost of the lower-priced generic drug that is an acceptable substitute (found only in direct-pay drug plans), unless the physician specifically requests that the drug may not be substituted.

- All drugs prescribed by a physician, up to the cost of the lower-priced generic drug that is an acceptable substitute (found only in direct-pay drug plans), also called mandatory generic.

The following substances are generally not considered to be prescription drugs, and thus are excluded from most plans: any substitute of food or household products (salt, sugar or milk, dietary products, vitamins, proteins, minerals, hormones, cosmetics, soaps, shampoos, antacids, and laxatives), and vaccines. Natural products are normally excluded unless registered in the Licensed Natural Health Products Database and subject to a specific set of criteria; an example would be insulin which is covered. Contraceptives other than oral contraceptives are not covered; however, intrauterine devices are often included with prescription drugs.

Prior authorization programs exist whereby specific drugs must be pre-approved by the insurer. These programs mainly target very expensive drugs or drugs with a high potential for misuse.

Provincial governments have implemented Specialty Drug Programs for specific drugs whereby the Medicare plan provides for full or partial reimbursement of the costs given a set of conditions. Insurers coordinate with provincial programs to cover the amounts not reimbursed under the Medicare plans.

Generic drugs have been given a fair amount of attention in recent years as the provincial governments have reduced the generic drug price reimbursements to anywhere from 25% to 45% of the brand name drug price.

Direct-pay drug plans have become prevalent in recent years, because most providers are now able to provide real-time claims adjudication. This feature is quite attractive since it allows the plan sponsor to set up its own list of covered drugs. With online claims adjudication, the pharmacist can tell the patient whether a drug is covered or not, and whether a substitute is covered or not. Hence, generic and therapeutic substitutions are encouraged. This also allows the plan sponsor to decide which new products (nicotine patches, for example) should be covered and to what extent.

A variant is deferred-pay drug plans, where adjudication is online and the insurer makes payment to the insured afterwards (within ten days for large claims and three months for very small claims). The main advantage of these plans is that they typically cost approximately 10% less than direct-pay plans for a similar coverage. This difference has been linked to utilization, but the exact reasons why utilization is lower with a deferred-pay plan are not clear. It is thought that, for a patient with a particular medical condition, physicians may prescribe several drugs, one of which is aimed at curing the conditions and others that are aimed at enhancing the patient's comfort. With direct payment, it is felt that the patient will buy all prescribed drugs while with deferred payment, the patient would first buy the main drug, and then buy the other drugs only if they are really needed.

Mail-order drugs are now available in most provinces, and generate some savings, mostly occurring on maintenance drugs such as contraceptives, and drugs such as insulin that are used for chronic conditions.

Health Professional Practitioners
Practitioners can be classified in two categories: those whose services are covered only if prescribed by a physician (physiotherapist, audiologist, speech therapist, and dietitian), and those whose services do not require a prescription (optometrist, psychologist, psychoanalyst, chiropractor, naturopath, osteopath, podiatrist, and acupuncturist).

Eligible expenses for health professional practitioners are usually subject to inside limits. For all practitioners, there is a limit of one treatment per day, and a maximum number of treatments per year or an annual dollar maximum. Also, for practitioners whose services are eligible without a prescription, there often is a maximum dollar amount per treatment, which typically represents approximately 50% to 75% of the average cost of a treatment. Such a limitation is necessary because of the elective nature of the treatments.

Limits usually apply separately to each type of practitioner. However, as a cost containment measure, some plan sponsors have begun grouping several practitioners (such as chiropractors, osteopaths, and physiotherapists who all work on the musculoskeletal system) under a single inside limit of, say, $500 per year.

Miscellaneous Expenses
While prescription drug expenses and health professional practitioners' fees are frequently claimed for the treatment of minor conditions, miscellaneous expenses are much less frequent, and generally incurred for serious illnesses. These expenses are usually eligible only if prescribed by a physician and include almost any insurable medical expense that is not otherwise covered in the plan or by the provincial Medicare plan, such as the following:

- Ambulance transportation (including air travel where ground transportation is either unavailable or inappropriate);
- Laboratory tests, X-rays, electrocardiograms;
- Radiotherapy;
- Oxygen;
- Blood and blood products;
- Serums injected by a physician;
- Needles, syringes and glucometers, including reagent strips, for control of diabetes;
- Ostomy supplies;
- Rental or purchase of medical equipment such as wheelchairs, hospital-type beds, and respiratory devices;
- Purchase of artificial limbs and eyes;
- Prostheses (including breast prostheses) up to a maximum dollar per year;
- Casts, splints, trusses, braces and crutches;
- Other orthopedic apparatus;
- Therapeutic apparatus;
- Elastic support stockings;
- Hearing aids up to a maximum dollar amount;
- Orthopedic shoes (only part of the cost is normally eligible, up to a maximum dollar amount per year); and
- Confinement in a convalescent home

Miscellaneous expenses also include the following items:
- private duty nursing out of hospital, up to an annual limit such as 20 shifts or $4,000 to $25,000;
- dentist's fees for treatments required because of an accidental injury to the mouth for services incurred within 12 months of the injury.
- confinement in a convalescent home, subject to a maximum number of days (typically 120) per confinement or per calendar year.

No maximum or inside limits generally apply to miscellaneous expenses other than those already mentioned.

Vision Care

Eye examinations by an optometrist are generally included in the extended health care portion of the plan. Prescription glasses or contact lenses may either be included in the medical plan, using the same deductible and coinsurance percentage, or be provided on a stand-alone basis, generally with no deductible and with a high level of coinsurance. Laser eye surgery, being elective, is generally covered with the same limits as prescription glasses.

Out-of-Canada Coverage

Out-of-Canada coverage has been the focus of much attention in recent years, due to cutbacks and limits in many provinces of reimbursement for out-of-Canada medical expenses under the provincial Medicare plan as well as the increase in frequency of traveling outside of Canada. Eligible expenses typically are the expenses beyond what is reimbursed by the provincial plan, and they may be subject to inside limits.

There are two main areas of out-of-Canada coverage: emergency coverage and referrals.

Emergency coverage cover expenses are for emergency care only, during a short (usually less than three months) trip outside Canada, and include hospitalization and medical care provided by a physician or a surgeon. The coverage includes repatriation expenses for return to Canada and travel assistance services provided, such as arrangement of hospital admission, negotiations of hospital and physicians bills. The travel assistance services aim at reducing the cost of claims by directing the patient to the most cost-efficient resources available.

The deductible is waived on out-of-Canada emergency coverage, because it would have no impact on the cost or utilization of the plan. out-of-Canada claims tend to be of low frequency, high severity nature. Because of the usually large size of claims, it is felt that the application of a coinsurance percentage would cause undue hardship to the insured. Thus, the plan's coinsurance amount is generally 100%. There is usually a very high maximum benefit, such as $1,000,000 per trip or per calendar year, often set by a stop-loss insurance carrier.

The insured employee must be covered by their provincial Medicare plan, otherwise the private extended health care plan will pay only the expenses over what the provincial plan would have paid if the insured had been covered under this plan.

Referrals for services not available in the province of residence of the insured person are rarely covered by private plans, since most referrals are already covered by the provincial Medicare plan. Referral must be in writing, and obtained from a doctor located in the province of residence. Services must be rendered in Canada, or out of Canada only if they are not available in Canada. In the latter case, the provincial Medicare plan must approve the treatment and pay its part of the cost. The plan's coinsurance amount on referrals may be lower than for emergency treatments.

EXCLUSIONS

All services covered by the provincial Medicare plan generally are excluded, except to the extent that the law allows private plans to pay for expenses in excess of those paid by provincial Medicare plan.

Other exclusions are similar to those in the United States for services or expenses:
- in excess of usual, customary, and reasonable charges;
- resulting from a treatment considered in excess if the current therapeutic treatment practice at the time the services are rendered;
- considered non-medically necessary;
- related to experimental drugs or treatments;
- resulting from self-inflicted injuries;
- resulting from insurrection, war, or service in the armed forces; and
- resulting from cosmetic surgery or treatment (except for accidental injuries).

OTHER PROVISIONS

The Canadian Life and Health Insurance Association (CLHIA) has adopted guidelines for coordination of benefits between insurers. These guidelines recommend that the "Total Allowable Expenses" approach be used whenever possible. This approach ensures that total benefits payable to an individual cannot exceed total allowed charges and specifies the order in which carriers pay. Theoretically, the secondary carrier should pay the minimum between what it would pay if it were primary carrier and the amount of eligible expenses not reimbursed by the primary carrier.

Some plans provide for an extension of benefits to dependents for up to two years after an employee dies. Benefits may also be paid for a number of months (usually three months) after insurance terminates, if the employee or dependent is disabled at the time of termination. These provisions are becoming less common, being replaced by a restricted waiver-of-premium provision.

Premiums are frequently waived after a three-month to six-month elimination period (usually the same period as for long-term disability income benefits and waiver of premium for life insurance), if the insured employee is totally disabled. This continues for as long as the insured employee remains totally disabled, provided that the group insurance policy remains in effect. Provisions relating to termination of coverage due to retirement or attainment of a specified age continue to apply.

FUNDING

Due to the comprehensive coverage already provided by provincial Medicare plans, extended health care plans typically cost from 2.5% to 4.0% of employer payroll (before tax), depending on their richness.

Funding arrangements available in Canada for extended health care and dental benefits vary from fully insured to retention[15] and self-insurance arrangements. Fully insured arrangements are mostly seen in the smaller size plan sponsors, for example, employers with less than 100 employees. Larger employers tend to use retention or self-insured arrangements (administrative services only, or ASO) as their experience tends to be more stable. In nearly all group sizes, the premiums are experience-rated. The introduction of new and more expensive drugs over the years has led to large drug amount pooling coverage by

---

[15] The term "retention" refers to a type of coverage where a specified amount must be paid by the insured before the insurer pays (similar to stop loss coverage in the U.S.).

the insurers; it is also common to see a portion or all of the out-of-Canada claims in the pooling arrangement. The pooling thresholds vary and usually increase by group size. It is worthwhile to note that in comparison with the United States, large health care claims that would be most subject to large fluctuations are covered by the provincial Medicare plan in Canada, so the large claims are mostly related to drugs and out-of-Canada claims.

Flexible plan offerings are gaining popularity with larger employers, because the group benefits are part of the employees' compensation package. Most flexible benefits plans in Canada use a modular, or a "core-plus" approach, rather than a pure cafeteria approach, mostly because employers believe that they ought to provide a minimum safety net to their employees in most types of benefits. Also, the workforce of most large Canadian employers is too small to justify the higher administrative expenses under a pure cafeteria plan.

DENTAL PLANS

The only dental benefits provided under the provincial Medicare plans are medically required oral and dental surgery performed in hospital and, in some provinces, preventive and minor restorative services for young children. Thus, dental coverage remains mostly a private matter. As a result, dental care coverage has evolved with the same pattern as the fee-for-service approach in the United States.

Virtually all plans use a type of scheduled approach, under which the eligible expenses are based on the current fee guide published by the Dentists' Association of the employee's (or employer's) province of residence leading to the use of consistent schedules between insurers. An exception exists in the province of Alberta where the Dentists' Association no longer publishes a fee guide; this may mean that the insurers may no longer use consistent schedules. In a minority of cases, to contain costs, eligible expenses are based on the fee guide from the previous year or even from an earlier year.

The fee guide assigns a code to each dental procedure. These codes are defined by the Canadian Dental Association Procedure Coding System, except in Quebec where a different coding system is used. The fee guides also include a description of the procedure and the suggested fee. Some guides also show the relative value units assigned to a procedure. Plans define their eligible expenses either as a list of dental procedures or as a specific list of codes from the fee guide.

There are five main areas of dental coverage in Canada:

- Basic Care
  o Diagnostic and preventive care (oral exams, X-rays, fluoride application)
- Minor restorative care and surgery (fillings, extractions, repairs to dental prostheses)
- Periodontal and endodontal treatments (such as root canal therapy)
- Major Care
  o Prostheses (bridgeworks, dentures)
  o Major restorative treatments (crowns, inlays)
- Orthodontia

Most dental plans cover the first four areas of coverage, while a much lower proportion of the plans cover orthodontia; when covered, orthodontic services are generally covered for children only.

EXCLUSIONS

All services covered by the provincial Medicare plan generally are excluded, except to the extent that the law allows private plans to pay for expenses in excess of those paid by provincial Medicare plan.

Other exclusions are similar to those in the United States for services or expenses:
- dental implants or all treatments related to implants;
- relating to any appliance worn in the practice of a sport;
- rendered free of charge, or which would be free of charge were it not for insurance coverage, or which are not chargeable to the insured person;
- resulting from self-inflicted injuries;
- resulting from insurrection, war, or service in the armed forces; and
- resulting from cosmetic surgery or treatment or which exceed ordinary services given in accordance with current therapeutic practice.

DEDUCTIBLE

The deductible on a dental plan is quite similar to that applicable to the extended health care plan. A typical deductible is $25 to $50 per person, or $100 for the whole family. It usually applies to all covered expenses except orthodontia and, frequently, diagnosis and preventive care. Combined deductibles for extended health care and dental plans are rare.

As for accident and sickness insurance, deductibles in most dental plans have remained stable for a long time, despite moderate inflation on covered expenses. The average deductible is now lower than the cost of the minimum claim that can be incurred. As a result, it is now seen more as a user's fee than as a utilization disincentive.

OTHER COST-SHARING AND LIMITS

Coinsurance varies among the five main areas of coverage. Diagnostic and preventive care is usually paid in full, with no deductible. The rationale is that by encouraging prevention, the plan sponsor will avoid being faced with more expensive claims for extensive restoration later. Minor surgery and restorative care is reimbursed at 80% to 100%, generally after satisfying a deductible. Prostheses and major restorative treatments are reimbursed at 50% to 80% after the deductible. The reimbursement on periodontal and endodontal treatments varies depending on their classification, from 80% to 100%, if they are included in routine care or, from 50% to 80%, if included in major care. Orthodontia is typically reimbursed at 50%, with no deductible.

There is usually a $1,000 to $2,500 annual maximum reimbursement for all eligible expenses except orthodontia, which is subject to a separate, lifetime maximum (generally $1,500 to $3,000). Internal maximums for diagnostic and preventive care, periodontal, and endodontal care as well as major treatments care are also available services.

Due to the higher level of antiselection of the dental benefits, other internal limits exist and include:
- Limit on the frequency of diagnosis and preventive services, with some services such as X-rays and scaling being eligible only after a number of months have elapsed since a prior, similar, treatment. A six-month delay was the standard practice until recently, when several major plan sponsors implemented a nine-month delay. This longer delay has met some opposition from the dentists, who consider it too long.
- The replacement of a prosthesis is usually eligible expense only if at least five years have elapsed since the prosthesis has been installed.
- Lower annual maximums exist when dental coverage is a new benefit to the group or in the cases where employees became insured beyond the normal eligibility period.

COST CONTROLS

Some cost control features are typical of dental plans, such as the alternative treatment clause, the pre-certification and the missing-tooth exclusion.

The alternative treatment clause is found in nearly all dental plans. It allows the insurer to pay only the cost of the least expensive appropriate treatment. To avoid resentment from the claimant, this clause is usually associated with a pre-certification clause that requires advance approval by the insurer of the treatment if it is expected to cost more than a specified sum of money (usually $300 to $500). After receiving the treatment plan, the insurer informs the claimant of the amount of reimbursement to which he or she is entitled, and may eventually propose an alternative, less expensive, treatment.

The missing-tooth exclusion is intended to exclude the cost of a dental prosthesis that replaces a tooth that has been extracted before the claimant became insured under the plan. The rationale behind this clause is that the plan does not have to indemnify the insured for an event (the loss of the tooth) that occurred before coverage began. This rationale has been somewhat contested on the ground that a problem which is left untreated (due to this exclusion) may lead to another problem which would be covered, but might be more expensive to solve.

FUNDING

Dental plans in Canada typically cost from 1.0% to 1.5% of payroll (before tax), which is less than the cost of a medical plan. Insurers write smaller plans, either on a fully pooled basis (for very small plans) or on a retention basis. Large employers usually self-insure their dental plans, along with their medical plan. They retain the services of an insurer on an ASO basis, rarely with an aggregate stop-loss policy. Large amount pooling is very rare since the largest possible claim for a dental treatment is limited to the annual maximum that is much lower than the cost of a large medical claim.

Capitation

In the end of the 1980s, insurers and insurer-sponsored organizations tried to take advantage of the rapidly increasing number of dentists competing for a limited number of insured patients, by introducing capitated plans. These plans were patterned after American plans, and were not necessarily adapted to the Canadian market. In particular, the choice usually given to employees was either to join the capitated plan or to remain with a less generous traditional plan. This forced employers to maintain two concurrent dental plans. This was not very practical for the average Canadian employer.

Several dental associations were strongly opposed to capitation, and exerted pressure on their patients not to join capitated plans and on insurers not to offer such plans. After a few years most insurers ceased to offer capitated plans, and very few such plans remain in effect.

Direct-Pay Dental Plans

While capitated plans floundered, direct-pay dental plans have become increasingly popular. Under this type of plan, the insured person is given an identification card that includes information relative to the dental plan, along with an expiration date.

When the insured has dental treatments, the dentist uses the card to submit a claim to the insurer. The claim is adjudicated by a computer that informs the dentist of the amount payable by the plan. This amount is paid directly by the insurer to the dentist. The insured person only has to pay the difference between the total cost of the dental treatment and the amount payable by the plan.

TAX ENVIRONMENT

A premium tax is charged on the net premiums (premiums less experience rating refunds) of insured plans in all provinces. The tax rate varies from 2% to 4%. This tax must be considered when setting the gross premium. This tax is also charged on benefits paid by self-insured plans (also called ASO plans) in Quebec, Ontario, and Newfoundland.

In addition, Quebec and Ontario apply a special sales tax on group insurance premiums or their equivalent in self-insured plans. Manitoba applies its retail sales tax on group life, AD&D, critical illness, and disability income, but it does not apply to health and dental or to self-insured plans.

The 5% federal Goods and Services Tax (GST), and its counterpart, the Harmonized Sales Tax (HST) in provinces where the federal and provincial sales taxes have been combined, does not apply to insurance premiums but is charged on administrative expenses billed by an insurer or a third-party administrator on ASO contracts which are not supplemented by stop-loss. The GST/HST also applies to the supplies (computers, paper, and so on) used by insurers and by providers of health care. Hence, even though the GST/HST does not apply directly to insurance premiums, it does slightly increase the cost of group insurance.

Quebec applies income tax to employer contributions for health and dental plans, whether such plans are insured or not. All other provinces have their income tax collected by the federal government and do not tax employer contributions to health and dental plans. The federal government and all provinces charge their income tax on employers' contributions to group life insurance coverage.

11 GROUP LIFE INSURANCE BENEFITS

Frank Cassandra
Michael J. Thompson

Group life insurance benefits were first introduced in 1911. The initial focus was on basic group term life insurance on the lives of employees. Coverage was intended to provide for final expenses in the event of an employee's premature death. Benefits were typically defined as simple flat amounts: a simple function of earnings, or a flat amount based on the employee's position in the firm. There was no selection of amounts by individual insureds. Premiums were charged to the employer using a composite rate for the group, mainly to keep administration of the plan simple.

Group life insurance benefits have gradually expanded over time to meet the more varied needs of employees and their dependents. While traditional basic group term life insurance is still the most common form of group term life insurance today, more specialized and tailored coverage has gradually been developed. The most common types of other benefits now offered include:

- Supplemental or Optional Group Term Life Insurance
- Dependent Group Term Life Insurance
- Accidental Death and Dismemberment Insurance
- Survivor Income Benefits
- Group Permanent Insurance
- Group Universal Life Insurance
- Group Variable Universal Life Insurance

This chapter provides a description of the types of group life insurance plans, plan provisions, and related tax and statutory considerations associated with each of these benefits. There is also a brief description of group credit life insurance.

BASIC GROUP TERM LIFE INSURANCE

TYPES OF PLANS

Basic group term life insurance plans are designed to provide a common level of basic insurance protection for the covered group of employees. Typical plan designs include the following:

- Flat dollar plans, such as a flat $10,000 for all employees.
- Multiple of earnings plans, such as one or two times earnings. This is the most common type of plan design.

- Salary bracket plans, such as the plan described in the following table:

Salary	Life Insurance Amount
Up to $20,000	$ 20,000
$20,001 - $40,000	$ 40,000
$40,001 - $60,000	$ 60,000
$60,001 - $80,000	$ 80,000
$80,001 and over	$100,000

- Position plans, such as the plan shown in the following table.

Position	Life Insurance Amount
Hourly Employees	$ 25,000
Non-officer Management	$ 50,000
Officers	$100,000

Such plans are designed to preclude individual selection of amounts and hence minimize antiselection risk.

Many basic group term life insurance plans include age-related or retirement-related reductions in specified face amounts of insurance. Such reduction formulas are designed primarily to reflect the generally reduced need for life insurance at ages greater than 65 and in retirement. Additionally, such reductions help to control the overall cost of the plan to the employer by mitigating the substantial increase in term insurance costs at higher ages.

A typical basic group term life insurance plan may contain the following type of reduction formula:

For Active Employees	
Ages less than 65	100% of Basic Annual Earnings
Ages 65 through 69	70% of Basic Annual Earnings
Ages 70 and above	50% of Basic Annual Earnings
For Retired Employees	50% of Final Year's Basic Annual Earnings

In the United States, age related reductions must be actuarially cost justified under the Age Discrimination in Employment Act (ADEA).

PLAN PROVISIONS

Basic group term life insurance includes plan provisions relating to eligibility, continuity of coverage, disability provisions, and benefit payment. The following discussion describes the provisions found in most plans.

Eligibility Provisions

Under most basic group term life insurance plans, the eligible class of employees is usually defined as all full-time employees working more than a minimum number of hours (typically 20 hours).

Most policies also include an actively-at-work requirement. This provision requires that an employee be actively at work, performing all the usual duties of his or her job at the normal place of employment, before the life insurance becomes effective.

Basic group term life insurance may be non-contributory (no employee contributions toward the cost of coverage are required) or contributory (employees contribute toward the cost of coverage). Non-contributory plans typically require 100% participation. Contributory plans typically require 75% minimum participation. The participation requirement may be a function of underwriting constraints, the size of the group, and regulatory considerations.

Basic group term insurance plans may contain a "medical evidence of insurability" provision. Such a provision typically requires an employee to provide medical evidence of insurability (most often by means of a medical questionnaire) for amounts in excess of a defined threshold. The threshold is typically a function of the size of the group and the underwriting standards of the insurer. Such provisions are designed to avoid a disproportionate amount of coverage on substandard lives within a group.

Most plans also contain a specified plan maximum amount of insurance. This provision is generally necessary to avoid disproportionate amounts of coverage on a single life or on a handful of highly paid individuals within a single group.

Continuity of Coverage Provisions and Conversion Rights

The insurance laws of virtually every state and province require basic group term life insurance plans to contain a conversion provision. The conversion provision describes the insured's right to convert his or her group term insurance coverage to an individual life insurance policy upon termination of employment or membership in the eligible class. The individual life insurance policy may have a face amount less than or equal to the amount of the lost group insurance coverage. Premiums are based on rates for a standard individual policy based on the insured's age at time of conversion. The individual policy must be of a form generally made available by the insurer. A more limited conversion right is available if the group insurance for an insured's class ends due to termination or amendment of the group policy. The insured generally has a specified period (usually 31 days) after group coverage ends to elect a conversion policy. If the insured dies within the conversion period, the amount that was eligible for conversion is payable on death.

Disability Provisions

Most basic group term life insurance plans contain one of the following three disability provisions.

- Waiver of Premium: Group term life insurance is continued without premium payment when an employee becomes totally disabled, provided the insured is less than a certain age, usually 60 or 65, when the disability begins, and remains continuously disabled until death. The precise parameters of waiver of premium benefits, include the duration of waiver coverage and the age by which disability must begin, vary from plan to plan.

- Total and Permanent Disability: When an insured becomes totally and permanently disabled, this provision typically provides a benefit on a monthly installment basis, equal to all or a portion of the life insurance benefit. On death, the original death benefit would be reduced by any disability installments made.

- Extended Death Benefit: Under this provision, a death benefit is payable if an insured's insurance terminates prior to age 60 and he or she dies within a year of the termination date, while being continuously and totally disabled from the termination date to the date of death.

Benefit Payment Provisions

Group life insurance benefits are payable to the beneficiary who is designated by the insured. If a beneficiary has not been designated, the insurance is paid to the insured's estate. In general, the employer may not be named as beneficiary. A "facility of payments" provision allows for payment of the life benefit to specified persons related to the insured, or in some instances to a funeral home, in lieu of payments to the estate.

On death, several settlement options may be available to the beneficiary, including a lump sum, a monthly installment, or a money market-like account that typically includes check-writing privileges.

Many plans now contain an Accelerated Benefits Provision, which allows a limited payout of the death benefit prior to death if the insured becomes terminally ill. The insured must typically have a limited number of months (usually 24 or less) to live. Typical plans provide for a payout of 25% or 50% of the face amount, with an overall maximum of $25,000 or $50,000. The trend over time has been for group policies to contain less restrictive limits on accelerated payment amounts. The insurer may pay an actuarially determined, discounted value to cover lost interest and administrative expenses.

Some insurers allow viatical assignment of group term life benefits. In a viatical assignment, the certificate holder "sells" (assigns) all of his or her incidents of ownership in the group coverage to a third party (viatical settlement provider). The viatical settlement provider pays the certificate holder a lump sum determined as an actuarially discounted value of the specified face amount. Viatical settlement providers are not regulated by state insurance departments, and cases of abuse of terminally ill individuals (by taking inappropriate discounts) and investors (by promising specified rates of return by investing in viatical settlements) have been reported.

FEDERAL INCOME TAX IMPLICATIONS

Deductibility of Premiums

Premiums paid by an employer to provide group life insurance on the lives of its employees are generally deductible on the employer's income tax return in both the United States and Canada. This applies to most basic life, supplemental life, survivor's benefits, dependent life, accidental death, and group universal life plans that are described in the following sections.

Taxability of Proceeds

Death benefits payable under basic group term life insurance plans are excludable from a beneficiary's gross income in both the United States and Canada. This also applies to most basic life, supplemental life, survivor's benefits, dependent life, accidental death, and group universal life plans. Payments made to a terminally ill insured under an accelerated benefit option are excludable from the insured's gross income, provided that the insured has been certified by a physician to have an illness that can reasonably be expected to result in death within 24 months from the date of the certification.

Taxable Income to Employees

In the United States, under Section 79 of the Internal Revenue Code, employees are taxed on the value of employer-provided group term life insurance to the extent that such insurance exceeds $50,000. The first $50,000 of employer-provided group life insurance is received tax-free by employees. IRC Section 79 defines the value of group term life insurance in excess of the first $50,000 using a schedule of uniform premium rates known as Table I. Table I is promulgated by the Internal Revenue Service and is updated periodically to reflect changes in the level and slope of insured mortality in the United States. The most recent version of Table I was published in 1999 and applies to insurance provided after June 30, 1999. It is presented in the following table:

Table I U.S. IRS Uniform Premium Rates	
5 Year Age Bracket	**Monthly Cost per $1,000 of Coverage**
Under 25	$0.05
25 to 29	0.06
30 to 34	0.08
35 to 39	0.09
40 to 44	0.10
45 to 49	0.15
50 to 54	0.23
55 to 59	0.43
60 to 64	0.66
65 to 69	1.27
70+	2.06

Income is imputed to an employee based on the economic value of the coverage in excess of $50,000. The imputed income is determined as follows:

- The Table I rate for the insured's attained age on the last day of his or her taxable year is multiplied by the total amount of group term life insurance in excess of $50,000 divided by $1,000.
- Any required employee contributions are then subtracted from the calculated amount.

To illustrate the calculation, suppose an employee age 50 on December 31st of a particular tax year, is covered for $125,000 of group term life insurance, and contributes $0.10 monthly for each $1,000 of coverage. The calculation of imputed income for that employee is then:

- Table I monthly rate per $1,000 for an insured age 50: $0.23
- Table I cost of group term life insurance over $50,000:

$$[(\$125{,}000 - \$50{,}000) / \$1{,}000] \times 0.23 \times 12 = \$207$$

- Employee contributions: ($125,000 / $1,000) x 0.10 x 12 = $150
- Imputed income: $207 − $150 = $57

All of an employee's contribution, even contributions on the first $50,000, can be used to offset the value that would otherwise be taxable.

The favorable tax treatment specified under IRC Section 79 only applies to group term life insurance plans that do not discriminate in favor of "key employees." The term "key employee" has the specific meaning in IRC Section 79. If a plan is found to be discriminatory in favor of key employees, the $50,000 exclusion does not apply to them, and imputed income for key employees is determined using the greater of the Table I rates and the actual cost of the insurance.

In Canada, employer payments for group life premiums, including the applicable provincial sales taxes, are considered to be taxable to the employee. This applies to all types of plans except accidental death and dismemberment coverage, which is taxed only in Quebec.

REGULATORY CONSIDERATIONS

Federal Regulation

On the federal level in the U.S., the Employee Retirement Income Security Act (ERISA) provides significant protections to participants in employee welfare benefit plans. In general, it imposes standards of conduct for plan sponsors and imposes certain reporting and disclosure requirements. Group term life insurance plans are subject to many provisions of ERISA. The Age Discrimination in Employment Act (ADEA) prohibits discrimination in the workplace based on age. Particularly for group life insurance, it requires that any applicable age-related reductions in group life insurance coverage be actuarially cost justified.

State and Provincial Regulation

In addition to federal requirements, any group term life insurance plan design must consider applicable state or provincial insurance law. Some common state laws govern the contents of group term life insurance policies and certificates. The provisions that may be regulated and some common requirements include (but are not limited to) the following:

- Requirements which preclude plans that permit individual selection of the face amount of insurance,
- Maximum employee contribution requirements, and
- Minimum participation requirements.

Various other state and provincial statutes or regulations may apply. These are discussed further in the chapters on regulation in the United States and Canada.

GROUP SUPPLEMENTAL LIFE PLANS

TYPES OF PLANS

Supplemental or optional life plans provide additional insurance beyond basic group term life, and are typically provided on an employee-pay-all basis. Generally, employee-pay-all optional life plans are written with a unisex, step-rated premium structure. Rates vary by five-year age brackets. The amounts of insurance available are usually a choice of flat amounts (such as $25,000, $50,000, or $100,000), or a choice of a multiple of earnings (such as one to four times basic annual earnings). As many as three to five options may be available to employees in a typical plan.

PLAN PROVISIONS

Plan provisions for supplemental or optional life insurance are generally the same as basic group term life insurance; however, there are a number of potential differences.
bIf a disability provision is included, it is usually limited to a waiver of premium provision.
If a disability provision is included, it is usually limited to a waiver of premium provision.

Minimum participation requirements tend to be more liberal (lower) than for basic group term life, such as 25% rather than 75%. Also, due to the selective nature of supplemental group term life insurance, evidence of insurability requirements are generally more stringent than for the basic coverage. Medical evidence of insurability is typically provided by means of a medical questionnaire, commonly referred to as a Statement of Good Health. Some plans offer no coverage or very modest amounts of coverage without at least limited medical evidence of insurability via a short-form questionnaire of four or five medical questions.

Also, due to the voluntary nature of the coverage, a suicide exclusion is common in supplemental group life insurance plans. Such provisions typically exclude deaths caused by suicide within the first two years of coverage and within two years of any employee-initiated increase in coverage election.

It is now common for employee-pay-all group supplemental life insurance plans to include a portability option. Portability provisions allow plan participants who terminate employment to continue their group coverage by paying premiums directly to the insurer. Under some portability arrangements, the premium rates paid by portable lives remain the same as those paid by similarly situated individuals under the active group. Under these arrangements, experience on portable lives is combined with the experience of the active group for experience rating purposes. More commonly, however, the rates applicable to portable lives are based on a separate schedule of rates applicable to the insurer's "portability pool" and include a monthly administration charge to defray the cost of direct billing. Under these arrangements, the experience on portable lives is usually not included with the experience of the active group for experience rating purposes.

Mortality experience emerging thus far on portable lives has proven to be significantly worse than mortality experience on similarly situated active lives, reflecting the antiselective nature of the portability decision.

FEDERAL INCOME TAX IMPLICATIONS

Taxable Income to Employees

Generally, supplemental group life insurance plans are made available on a fully contributory (employee-pay-all) basis. In the U.S., IRC Section 79 allows for such employee-pay-all supplemental life insurance plans to be considered outside of IRC Section 79 (thereby avoiding imputed income consequences) provided two conditions are met:

(1) The plan is employee-pay-all with no direct or indirect employer subsidies; and

(2) The optional life premium step-rates are all at or below the Table I premium step-rates; or alternatively, are all at or above Table I premium step-rates. (This comparison of a particular plan's rates to the officially published Table I rates is commonly referred to as the "Straddle Test." If a particular plan's rates do not "straddle" Table I, it is generally held that the plan does not contain any overt subsidy by age).

When a particular supplemental plan's premium rates are all at or below the Table I rates, it is generally advantageous for the basic and supplemental group life programs to be treated as separate plans for the purposes of IRC Section 79. This is because income based on the supplemental plan would otherwise be imputed at the Table I level, offset by (relatively lower) employee contributions. Any supplemental plan provided outside of IRC Section 79 is not considered an employer-provided group term life insurance plan and therefore, does not generate imputed income.

The most recent update to Table I, in 1999, decreased rates by up to 50% for some age bands. The premium rates for many existing supplemental group term life insurance plans may now, as a result of the decrease, be higher than the Table I rates. Plan sponsors may now want to consider this fact in determining whether or not to treat their current basic and supplemental plans as separate plans for the purposes of IRC Section 79.

An alternative approach to keeping an optional life plan outside Section 79 (supported by some IRS private letter rulings) may be to provide the optional life plan through a Voluntary Employees' Beneficiary Association (VEBA). Under this approach, the employer's involvement in the program becomes much more restricted.

REGULATORY CONSIDERATIONS

While the same state and provincial laws governing basic group term life insurance apply to supplemental or optional life insurance, it is worthwhile pointing out how these laws have generally been interpreted.

- Laws "precluding individual selection of amount" have generally been interpreted as not precluding offering an employee a limited number of selections under each of which an employee is entitled to a specific dollar or multiple of earnings amount of insurance.

- Maximum employee contribution requirements have been viewed in the aggregate where step rate contributions have applied.

- Minimum participation requirements apply to all group term life insurance provided through an employer. Consequently, if the basic group term plan meets a regulatory

75% minimum participation requirement, then all the group term life insurance provided through that employer meets the minimum participation requirements (even if less than 75% participate in the supplemental or optional life insurance plan).

GROUP ACCIDENTAL DEATH AND DISMEMBERMENT (AD&D) INSURANCE

Group AD&D insurance is typically offered as companion coverage to group term life insurance. The AD&D benefit is payable if an employee dies as the result of a covered accident. A percentage of the benefit (commonly 50%) may also be payable if the employee loses a member (defined as a hand, a foot, or the sight of an eye). If more than one member is lost in a covered accident then the full AD&D benefit is typically payable. Most policies provide that no more than 100% of the specified face amount is payable for all losses due to a single covered accident.

Many employers provide a basic AD&D plan where the AD&D face amount is defined as 100% of the basic group life insurance face amount. Supplemental or voluntary AD&D plans may also be offered providing supplemental accident coverage on an employee-pay-all basis. The coverage may be either non-occupational (only covering accidents not related to employment) or 24-hour (covering both on-job and off-job accidents). Typically a covered loss must occur within a specified period (usually one year) after the accident. Voluntary AD&D plans may also provide coverage to other family members such as spouses and children.

Business Travel Accident Coverage is a common specialized form of AD&D coverage that provides benefits if an employee dies as a result of a covered accident while traveling on company business. The coverage amount is usually a function of salary (such as two times basic annual earnings) and is always 100% employer paid.

This coverage is described in greater detail in Chapter 14, "Miscellaneous Benefits."

DEPENDENT GROUP LIFE INSURANCE

TYPES OF PLANS

Dependent group life insurance is designed to provide a lump sum benefit to the employee in the event of death of a covered dependent. This coverage is generally only available when employee group life insurance is in force.

The definition of a dependent was historically limited to an employee's legally married spouse and the natural and legally adopted children of the employee. Societal trends have resulted in employers and insurers increasingly expanding the definition of a dependent to include same-sex married spouses, civil union partners, same-sex domestic partners, and the children of the domestic partners. Employees seeking coverage on domestic partners are usually required to demonstrate that insurable interest exists on the life of the domestic partner (such insurable interest is assumed to exist automatically in the case of blood relationships and legal marriage). The demonstration typically involves certifying economic interdependence by means of an affidavit and/or providing documentary evidence of the interdependence. Generally, insurers accept valid domestic partnership registrations provided by certain local, provincial, and state jurisdictions.

Originally, dependent group life insurance was designed as non-contributory or partially contributory coverage that provided very modest benefits to cover burial and other final expenses. The plan typically provided flat amounts of insurance on the lives of spouses and children. A typical schedule of benefits might have been as follows:

Coverage On	Specified Face Amount
Spouse	$5,000
Each Child age 6 months or older	$2,000
Each Child less than 6 months	$500

Where these limited amounts of insurance were provided, premiums were generally based on a composite rate developed from the age and gender distribution of the employee group. Any required employee contributions were also generally on a flat-rate basis for ease of administration.

Reflecting the greater prevalence of households with two working parents, and the desire of employers to provide expanded access to benefits with limited cost to the employer, dependent group life insurance benefits have evolved into predominantly employee-pay-all programs with much more liberal benefit amounts. In many plans, multiple coverage choices (either as flat dollar amounts or as a percentage of the employees base annual earnings) are provided to employees. Maximum benefit amounts up to, and in some limited cases, exceeding $100,000 on spouses and $10,000 on children are common. To avoid severe antiselection, amounts on the spouse may be limited to some percentage (most commonly 50%) of the employee coverage amount. A typical schedule of benefits might be as follows:

Coverage On	Specified Face Amount
Spouse	Option 1: No coverage Option 2: $ 10,000 Option 3: $ 25,000 Option 4: $ 50,000 Option 5: $100,000
Each Child	Option 1: No coverage Option 2: $ 5,000 Option 3: $ 10,000

Where higher amounts of spousal coverage are permitted, it is common to see premium rates based on age-related step rates. To simplify administration, such rates may be based on the age of the employee rather than the age of the spouse, assuming an age distribution of employees and spouses. Such structures are more risky for plans with multiple-choice options and where there are higher maximum amounts.

Coverage on children normally ends when the child attains age 19. Coverage may be extended to some later age, such has 21 or 23, if the child is attending college full time. As a result of the passage of health care reform in the United States, many plan sponsors have extended coverage to age 26 for children to maintain consistency with required coverage under medical plans. There is a continued trend to extend coverage even beyond the otherwise applicable limiting age in the case of totally and permanently disabled dependent children.

PLAN PROVISIONS

Eligibility Provisions

The eligibility rules for dependents are usually the same as for health coverage, except that newborn children may not be eligible until they reach a specified age such as 14 days.

A deferred effective date provision may apply that provides that the effective date of coverage on a dependent who is currently confined for medical treatment in an institution or at home is deferred until the dependent is medically released from that confinement.

In addition, where higher amounts of spousal coverage are offered, they may be subject to medical evidence of insurability requirements, typically in the form of a medical questionnaire.

Continuity of Coverage Provisions

Coverage generally continues only while the employee's group term life coverage continues. Dependent coverage usually ends when the employee retires, even if the group term life insurance is continued on the life of the former employee into retirement. Conversion rights, consistent with those required on employee coverage, are generally included for spouse and child coverage. Conversion rights typically also apply when group coverage ends due to divorce or due to a child reaching the limiting age. Disability provisions are generally not available on dependent coverage.

Benefit Payment Provisions

The beneficiary for dependent group life insurance is usually the employee, and benefits are typically payable in a lump sum.

FEDERAL INCOME TAX IMPLICATIONS

Taxable Income to Employees

In the United States, if the amounts of dependent group life insurance available on the lives of spouses, domestic partners, and children are less than $2,000, the benefits are considered an excludable *de minimus* fringe benefit under IRC Section 132 and result in no imputed income to employees.

Where the amounts of dependent group life insurance exceed $2,000, income may be imputed to employees under IRS Notice 89-110. Imputed income is based on the IRS Table I premium rates less any applicable required employee contributions.

In Canada, premiums paid by the employer, including any applicable provincial sales taxes, are considered taxable income to the employee.

REGULATORY CONSIDERATIONS

Some jurisdictions establish a maximum amount of insurance that may be provided on the lives of dependent spouses and children, or place restrictions on children's eligibility. Such laws were adopted out of concern for the welfare of spouses and children. The trend has been for states to liberalize or repeal such restrictions, particularly on spouses, over time.

SURVIVOR INCOME BENEFITS

TYPES OF PLANS

Survivor income benefit plans provide a monthly payment to the employee's spouse and children on the employee's death in lieu of a lump sum death benefit. The benefit is typically expressed as a percentage of the employee's monthly earnings, and is intended to more closely meet the needs of the employee's surviving dependents. An example of such a benefit plan would be (a) a spouse benefit of 25% of the employee's monthly earnings, and (b) a children's benefit of 15% of those earnings.

The duration of the monthly benefit varies by plan. A typical spouse benefit is payable to the earliest of remarriage, attainment of a limiting age such as 62, or death. A typical children's benefit is payable to age 19, or age 23 if still a full-time student.

Survivor benefit plans were developed mainly out of concern for the welfare of financially unsophisticated spouses and were once very common. Such plans have grown much less common in the last 30 years, but remain relatively popular with employers in blue-collar industries and with some union sponsored plans.

PLAN PROVISIONS

Survivor income benefit plan provisions for eligibility and continuity of coverage are similar to group basic term life insurance, with two potential differences: (1) the conversion privilege applies to the commuted value (the present value) of the monthly survivor benefit, and (2) the disability provision is limited to a waiver of premium provision.

Benefit payment provisions are established by the plan and may include the following:

- *Guaranteed Benefit Period:* A period for which the benefit is payable, regardless of the surviving spouse's death or remarriage.
- *Maximum Benefit Period:* Benefits are not paid beyond a maximum number of years, such as ten, or not beyond a limiting age, such as 62.
- *Remarriage Provision:* Benefits may or may not cease on remarriage.
- *Dowry Provision:* A lump sum benefit may be payable on the remarriage of the spouse, to reduce the incentive not to remarry.

- *Social Security Offset:* Some plans may provide for an offset of Social Security survivor benefits.
- *Last Survivor Provision:* Benefits may be defined by the composition of the remaining eligible survivors. A level last survivor benefit would pay the same amount regardless of how many survivors are eligible. A joint and 2/3 last survivor would provide a benefit to a spouse alone or child(ren) alone that is 2/3 of the benefit while both are eligible.

Survivor income benefits are usually paid to the employee's spouse if eligible, otherwise in equal shares to the children.

FEDERAL INCOME TAX IMPLICATIONS

Taxability of Proceeds

With survivor benefit plans, the death benefit is received by the beneficiary in the form of an annuity. Each monthly payment is considered to be composed of a non-taxable portion and a taxable interest portion. In the United States, the portion of each monthly payment that is excluded from taxable income is calculated as the ratio of the commuted value (actuarial present value) of the expected survivor annuity (using the interest basis of the insurer) to the commuted value of the expected survivor annuity using a 0% interest rate for discounting. The mortality tables found in IRC Section 72 are used as the mortality basis for discounting.

Taxable Income to Employees

Survivor income benefits in the United States and Canada are considered group term life insurance. In the United States, they may give rise to imputed income for benefits in excess of the $50,000 IRC Section 79 exclusion. Since benefits under survivor income benefit plans are received in the form of an annuity, imputed income calculations are based on the commuted value of the expected payments the insurer is obligated to make to the beneficiary. In the United States, the present value calculation uses a mortality table specified in IRC Section 72 and the interest rate used by the insurer to calculate the amount of insurance held by the insurer.

GROUP PERMANENT LIFE INSURANCE

TYPES OF PLANS

Although once more popular, group permanent life insurance is rarely provided today, largely because of the tax limitations discussed below. The following outlines the types of plans that may be available.

Single-Premium Group Paid-Up Life Insurance

A level death benefit is provided for a fixed premium, based on attained age. This product may be used by an employer to buy out a retiree life insurance benefit, thus avoiding the need for future premium payments. It generally includes a level face amount and growing cash value.

Group Ordinary Life Insurance

This is the group counterpart to individual whole life insurance generally with a fixed life insurance amount, level premiums, and a growing cash value.

Group Term and Paid-Up Plans

This coverage provides level insurance similar to group ordinary coverage. This coverage, however, splits the coverage into a combination of group paid-up life insurance paid by the employee and corresponding decreasing group term life insurance paid by the employer. The total face amount (term plus paid-up) is maintained according to the employer's prescribed plan.

PLAN PROVISIONS

Plan provisions for group permanent life insurance are similar to group term life insurance with the following potential differences:

- No continuity-of-coverage provisions are necessary for group paid-up insurance.
- The disability provision is usually limited to waiver of premium on the term portion of group term and paid-up insurance.
- The conversion privilege is limited to the face amount less cash value for group ordinary life insurance.

TAX CONSIDERATIONS

In the United States, employer-provided group permanent life insurance benefits are subject to onerous tax treatment under Section 79. Essentially, since Section 79 imputes income to an employee based on a formula using conservative interest and mortality assumptions (1958 CSO and 4% interest), the imputed taxable income for group permanent life insurance can be substantially *greater* than the economic value provided to the employee using the cash values defined in the policy. Employee-pay-all group permanent life insurance may be excludable from Section 79 and may not generate any imputed income under the following conditions:

- The insurer sells the insurance directly to the employee, who pays the full cost.
- The employer's participation is limited to such functions as selection of insurer and type of insurance, providing the insurer with lists of employees and use of premises, and collecting premiums.
- The insurer or employer does not condition the sale on the purchase of other obligations.

GROUP UNIVERSAL LIFE INSURANCE

TYPES OF PLANS

Group universal life (GUL) insurance plans were developed in the mid-1980s as the group insurance counterpart to individual universal life plans started in the late 1970s. In general, they consist of two components, namely term life insurance and a side fund that accumulates with interest, to provide tax-favored savings and long-term life insurance protection. Coverage on dependent spouses and children may also be included under GUL policies.

The death benefit under GUL plans is defined as the sum of the term life insurance component plus the side fund component. The term life insurance component can be designed similarly to an optional life plan (a multiple of salary or a flat amount) with the side fund being added on. This results in an increasing death benefit. Alternatively, the overall GUL death benefit (term plus side fund) can be a level benefit, with the term amount (net amount at risk) decreasing as the side fund grows.

The GUL premium may be credited to the fund net of premium tax and expense charges. The term costs can then be charged to the fund, with the balance accumulating with interest. The GUL premium may be determined flexibly, with the minimum amount allowable being enough to satisfy the cost of the term insurance element, and the maximum amount being defined by the GUL policy. A target premium may be defined as the periodic premium necessary to fund a given level death benefit by a certain age, assuming the current interest crediting rate. The cost of term insurance, or term cost, is typically based on either one-year or five-year step rates, and are subject to change annually. In addition, a schedule of maximum term costs may be included in the GUL policy.

The credited interest rate for the side fund is set by the insurer, generally based on prevailing market conditions and investment performance in the general account segment supporting the GUL product. Rates are most commonly reset annually. There may also be a guaranteed minimum credited interest rate included in the GUL policy, typically 3% or 4%.

PLAN PROVISIONS

Eligibility provisions for GUL are similar to group supplemental or optional life plans. GUL may provide for continuity of coverage through some combination of the following approaches:

- A waiver of premium disability provision may apply to the term portion of the premium.
- A portability provision, similar to that described earlier for supplemental life plans, may apply where employees can continue coverage at termination or retirement, on a premium-paying basis.
- The accumulation fund may be used by the certificate holder to purchase paid-up insurance on retirement or termination. The paid-up insurance would generally include a cash value of its own.
- Coverage may continue on a non-premium paying basis, with monthly term costs being withdrawn from the accumulation fund until exhausted.
- A conversion privilege may be provided. The amount convertible may be limited to the total GUL death benefit (term plus fund) prior to termination, less any paid-up insurance purchasable by the fund.

The death benefit payment provisions in GUL certificates are similar to group term life insurance. In addition, all or a portion of the fund may be paid out as a surrender or a policy loan. As a surrender, the amount is directly deducted from the fund. A reinstatement provision is typically also included. As a policy loan, the amount continues to be considered part of the fund earning interest, but an offsetting policy loan interest charge is assessed. The policy loan interest charge is typically 1% to 2% higher than the crediting rate. On death, any outstanding loans and interest charges are deducted from the death benefit otherwise payable.

REGULATORY CONSIDERATIONS

Generally, most provincial and state insurance laws and regulations that apply to group term life insurance are also applicable to GUL policies. In addition, many jurisdictions, in the absence of specific laws related to GUL, have extended certain individual insurance regulations to GUL coverage such as non-forfeiture provisions that afford protection to insureds with regard to cash value insurance.

To address past abuses of policy cash value illustrations in the sale and marketing of insurance in the United States, the National Association of Insurance Commissioners (NAIC) promulgated the NAIC Model Illustration Regulation (1997). In general, the model regulation regulates the form and content of any illustration (defined as any presentation or depiction that includes non-guaranteed elements of a policy of life insurance over a period of years used in the sale of cash value life insurance.) The goal of the regulation is to ensure that illustrations do not mislead purchasers of life insurance, and to make illustrations more understandable. Insurers must specify which policy forms they wish to market with an illustration. To the extent that an insurer designates any GUL policy as a form to be marketed with an illustration, the GUL illustration must meet the form and content requirements of the regulation.

FEDERAL INCOME TAX IMPLICATIONS

Taxable Income of Employees

The tax implications of group universal life insurance are very favorable, provided the plan is maintained outside of Section 79 (in the United States). They include the following features:

- The interest on the fund accumulates on a tax-deferred basis.
- Cash surrender of the accumulation fund is taxable on the gain on surrender. Gain on surrender is defined as the excess of the cash surrender over the certificate holder's basis in the contract. Basis in the GUL contract is defined as the total deductions from the accumulation fund that were used to pay cost of insurance charges, premium tax expense charges, and any applicable administrative expense charges. Consequently, interest accumulations are only taxable to the degree they exceed the term costs plus premium tax and expense charges.
- The total death benefit (term plus fund) is payable tax-free to the beneficiary.

A GUL plan may be maintained outside of Section 79 similarly to group permanent life plans. A GUL plan that is maintained outside of IRC Section 79 does not generate imputed income. A GUL plan provided under Section 79 (if employer contributions are involved) is subject to the onerous group permanent life insurance tax provisions discussed earlier.

Also in the United States, Section 7702 of the Internal Revenue Code contains certain requirements that assure that an insurance contract contains sufficient protection elements such that the savings elements of the program do not inappropriately dominate.

In order to satisfy the definition of life insurance under IRC Section 7702, the GUL certificate must satisfy either: (1) the cash value accumulation test, or (2) both the guideline level premium test and the cash value corridor test, both specified in that section of the code. If a contract fails to meet the requirements, it is not considered life insurance with the following serious consequences:

- All income in the contract becomes immediately taxable; and
- The contract loses the advantage of tax-free buildup of cash value; and
- Only death benefits in excess of the net surrender value are excludable from the beneficiary's gross income.

To the extent that the cash value of the accumulation fund in a particular GUL certificate exceeds a defined limit in relation to the specified face amount, the certificate may become a Modified Endowment Contract (MEC). A contract may become a MEC if it meets the definition of life insurance specified in IRC Section 7702, but fails to meet the seven-pay test defined in Section 7702A of the Internal Revenue Code. If a certificate becomes a MEC, it is subject to less favorable tax treatment. Specifically, policy distributions from the certificate, such as withdrawals and policy loans, are treated as taxable interest first rather than non-taxable basis first and are subject to an IRS penalty of 10%.

GROUP VARIABLE UNIVERSAL LIFE INSURANCE

TYPES OF PLANS

Group Variable Life Insurance (GVUL) plans were developed in the 1990s in response to the generally superior performance of equity versus fixed income investments during the 1980s and 1990s. GVUL plans are very similar to GUL plans; however, under GVUL plans, there are several investment options available to the certificate holder to invest the cash accumulation fund. The options most commonly include various equity investment fund choices. In addition, most GVUL plans also include a money market or fixed interest rate option in addition to the equity options.

PLAN PROVISIONS

All plan provisions commonly found in GUL plans are found in GVUL plans as well. In addition, certain provisions specific to GVUL are included. Mainly these involve limitations on the amounts and timing of allowable withdrawals and movement of funds among and between the various available investment options and the fixed interest fund option.

REGULATORY CONSIDERATIONS

As is the case with GUL, most state and provincial insurance laws and regulations that apply to group term life insurance, are also applicable to GVUL policies. Similarly, many jurisdictions, in the absence of specific laws related to GVUL, have extended certain individual insurance regulations to GVUL coverage such as non-forfeiture provisions that afford protection to insureds with regard to cash value insurance.

The NAIC Model Illustration Regulation explicitly exempts variable insurance policies, and GVUL illustrations are not required to meet the form and content requirements of the NAIC Model Illustration Regulation.

Unlike GUL or Group Term Life Insurance products, GVUL is considered an investment product as well as an insurance product and is therefore subject to Securities and Exchange Commission (SEC) and Financial Industry Regulatory Authority (FINRA) regulation. Most notably, for example, a prospectus describing the elements of the insurance program and the underlying investment options must be delivered to each prospective insured before an application for insurance is taken.

12 GROUP DISABILITY INCOME BENEFITS

Daniel D. Skwire
Paul L. Correia

Disability insurance is an excellent example of a coverage for which the insurance mechanism was created. While it has a relatively low likelihood of occurrence compared to other employee benefit coverages, an extended period of disability can be financially and psychologically devastating.

Disability insurance is designed to replace lost income resulting from a serious accident or sickness. The purpose of the coverage is generally to enable insureds to meet their basic financial obligations rather than to assure a continuing lifestyle. The proportion of lost income replaced by disability insurance is usually less than 100% of the insured's earnings prior to disability. Unlike other employee benefits where the occurrence of a claim can easily be determined, determining whether someone is disabled can sometimes be quite challenging. Setting the proportion of lost income to something less than 100% of the earnings prior to disability encourages disabled employees to return to work as soon as they are capable of doing so.

There are two basic forms of group disability income protection that have been marketed in the United States. Group short-term disability (STD) typically protects income for periods of disability lasting up to one year. Group long-term disability (LTD) protects against loss of income for longer periods of disability lasting up to normal retirement age. Both STD and LTD provide valuable protection against catastrophic income loss and are critical elements in a well-designed employee benefits package.

LONG-TERM DISABILITY

DEFINITION OF DISABILITY

The definition of disability is the key element of any group LTD insurance contract because it is used to determine who is eligible to receive disability benefits. A typical definition of disability in an LTD policy might contain the following language:

- During the first 24 months after the elimination period, disability means that the employee, as the result of sickness or accidental injury, is unable to perform some or all of the material and substantial duties of the employee's own occupation and has a loss of 20% or more of pre-disability earnings.

- Following the first 24 months after the elimination period, disability means that the employee, as the result of sickness or accidental injury, is unable to perform some or all of the material and substantial duties of any gainful occupation for which the employee is reasonably suited by education, training, and experience and has a loss of 40% or more of pre-disability earnings.

There are several important elements of this definition. First, disability depends not on medical symptoms, but on the insured's inability to perform material and substantial occupation duties as the result of sickness or accident. Thus, a condition such as a bad back might prove disabling for an occupation that requires heavy lifting, but not for one that requires only office work. Because it can be difficult to make an objective assessment of a claimant's ability to work, the definition of disability is inherently subjective. It is not uncommon to find two claimants with similar medical conditions and similar occupations, one of whom is disabled and one of whom continues to work.

Second, the definition refers to the employee's "own occupation" in the first 24 months following the elimination period (the time period after the date of disability before benefits are payable), and to "any gainful occupation" thereafter. It also has a higher loss of earnings requirement after 24 months. The own occupation definition used in the first 24 months is more generous, because it refers to a more specific set of duties and, therefore, may make it easier to qualify for disability benefits. Once an employee has been disabled for some period of time such as 24 months, it is common to use the stricter "any gainful occupation" definition to qualify for continued benefits. The stricter definition may encourage some employees to return to work in occupations other than their own. The length of the own occupation period varies for different disability policies. While 24 months is the most common provision, some policies use an own occupation definition for only 12 months, and some keep the own occupation definition for the entire benefit period.

Finally, the sample definition may allow someone who is working part-time to qualify for disability benefits (although, as described below, those benefits may be reduced by their work earnings while disabled), as long as the person's income is reduced by 20% or more of pre-disability earnings. This definition of disability is known as a "partial," "residual," or "loss of earnings". Some policies, known as "total disability" policies, require the insured to be unable to perform any of their material and substantial occupational duties in order to qualify for LTD benefits.

Some LTD contracts require that the insured receive Social Security disability benefits after some period of time of disability, such as two or three years, to continue receiving LTD benefits. This type of definition attempts to limit the cost of LTD coverage by ensuring that benefits are paid for only the most severe disabilities. Although it sounds simple to administer, it can be challenging in practice, because it relies on disability determinations made by the Social Security Administration, rather than by the insurer's own claim staff, and because it can take a prolonged period of time for Social Security applications to be reviewed, evaluated, appealed, and resolved.

ELIMINATION PERIOD

A second key feature of an LTD contract is the elimination period. The elimination period is the period of time that covered employees must be disabled before they are eligible to collect disability income benefits. A longer elimination period eliminates the costs associated with paying many short-duration claims and reduces the cost of the disability insurance program. Elimination periods vary from 1 month to 2 years, but the most common elimination periods are 3 months and 6 months. These two elimination periods are popular because they avoid gaps and overlaps in coverage when coordinating with 13-week and 26-week sick leave or STD programs typically offered by today's employers.

LTD insurers may offer various enhancements to the elimination period requirement. For example, some contracts allow a disabled employee to satisfy the elimination period with a period of partial disability. Similarly, some contracts allow the insured to return to work for a number of days or months without having to satisfy a new elimination period. This prevents a disabled employee from being penalized as a result of an unsuccessful attempt at returning to work.

BENEFIT PERIOD

Once an insured has met the definition of disability requirements and satisfied the elimination period, monthly benefit payments begin. The most common benefit periods are expressed as a number of years—typically two or five years—or to age 65. The "to age 65" concept arose from historical traditions of retirement at age 65. Since Social Security retirement benefits and company pension benefits commenced at this age, the disabled insured would no longer be in need of the income provided by LTD benefits. However, this paradigm no longer holds true. U.S. citizens are living longer, and choosing to work longer, than ever before. In the United States, the normal retirement age for collecting full Social Security retirement benefits has been gradually increasing from 65 to 67. As a result, the "to age 65" benefit period is evolving into a "Social Security Normal Retirement Age" ("SSNRA") benefit period.

The Age Discrimination in Employment Act (ADEA) requires that the cost of benefits provided to employees must not decline with advancing age of the employees. Currently, the federal government has provided employers with a "safe harbor" for meeting this requirement if they provide a benefit period equal to the longer of "to age 65" or five years. The ADEA also allows for other benefit periods if the employer can demonstrate that the costs of benefits provided to older employees are actuarially equivalent to those provided to younger employees. Most companies offer a Reducing Benefit Duration (RBD), which provides for benefits to be paid until age 65 for disability prior to age 60, and then grading down between ages 60 and 70, with a minimum benefit period of 1 year. The key issue for any employer using the RBD benefit period is to demonstrate that the shorter benefit period at older ages is offset by higher claim rates, so that the total expected cost for a particular age is not lower than that for a younger age.

BENEFIT AMOUNTS

Monthly benefits payable are typically equal to a defined percentage of pre-disability earnings (such as 60%), not to exceed a predetermined dollar amount or maximum benefit amount. Since group insurance is provided by the employer, the earnings that are used for pre-disability earnings are those from the employer providing the coverage. Depending on the needs of the employer, earnings may include base salary, along with various sources of additional income such as deferred compensation, commissions, or bonuses.

The benefit percentage elected by the employer has a direct impact on the cost of the coverage beyond the difference in the percentages. Industry claim studies show that claim costs per dollar of benefit increase as the percentage of income insured increases.[1,2] Additionally, employer-paid premiums generally result in taxable benefits to the employee, and employee-paid premiums result in tax-free disability benefits. Therefore, the same benefit percentage will result in a higher percentage of after-tax income being replaced when employees pay all or a portion of the premiums. This tax impact must be considered when determining the expected level of income replacement when pricing and underwriting voluntary and payroll-deduction programs.

The maximum benefit amount helps to prevent concentration of risks with one or a few insured individuals. These maximums may vary by industry to reflect the risks of certain occupations, group sizes, and the average salaries within groups.

BENEFIT OFFSETS

The LTD benefit is almost always offset by income from certain other sources. This ensures that the sum of disability income benefits plus income received by the disabled employee from other sources does not exceed pre-disability earnings. If not for benefit offsets, the combination of Social Security benefits, retirement benefits, workers compensation, part-time work earnings, and LTD benefits could exceed pre-disability earnings for many insureds. In that case, the employee's disability would result in an increase in net income creating little incentive to return to their pre-disability status as an active and contributing employee.

Integration with Social Security benefits is treated in a variety of ways as selected by the employer: (a) only the primary Social Security benefit may be deducted, (b) any family Social Security benefits received may be deducted as well, or (c) the primary and family Social Security benefits may be deducted only if the combination of the benefit otherwise payable and the Social Security benefit would exceed some higher income percentage such as 70%. This last method is commonly referred to as "all sources" integration.

There are many advantages arising from a disabled individual receiving Social Security benefits for the employer and disabled employee:

- It reduces the cost of the insurance program for the employer.
- The employee may receive higher replacement of income since Social Security benefits aren't fully taxed.
- It allows continued Social Security credits for the disabled individual.
- It qualifies the disabled person for Medicare benefits.

For these reasons, LTD insurers often provide assistance to their claimants in applying for Social Security disability benefits.

Another common offset to the basic LTD benefit consists of any income earned by the claimant from working while disabled. There are various methods in use to reduce LTD benefits by a disabled employee's earnings:

---

[1] Society of Actuaries TSA Reports 1982 & 1984, Committee on Group Life and Health Insurance, Group Long Term Disability Insurance.
[2] Milliman & Robertson, Disability Newsletter, June 1993, "The Impact of Replacement Ratios."

1. The proportionate loss formula looks at the percentage of lost work earnings due to disability and applies this percentage to the benefit otherwise payable. This is a version of partial or residual benefits, as described earlier.
2. The 50% offset method reduces the benefit by $1.00 for every $2.00 of work earnings received by the disabled employee.
3. The work incentive benefit ignores all earnings during an initial period of disability (such as 12 months) unless the sum of work earnings plus benefits otherwise payable exceeds 100% of pre-disability earnings. At that point, the benefit payable is reduced dollar for dollar by the excess amount. After the work incentive period, either the proportionate or 50% offset is used. This method provides a large incentive to return to work at the end of the work incentive period, and encourages a gradual transition back to work.

As an example, suppose an individual has pre-disability earnings of $10,000 per month, and an LTD policy that provides a basic ("gross") benefit of $6,000 per month. Further suppose the individual is working part-time and earning $2,500 per month. The final ("net") LTD benefit under the proportionate loss, 50% offset, and work incentive formulas is determined as follows;

- Proportionate Loss: The loss of income percentage is 75%, since the insured formerly earned $10,000 and now earns $2,500 per month. Therefore the net LTD benefit is 75% of the gross benefit, or $4,500 per month.

- 50% Offset: The gross LTD benefit is reduced by 50% of the $2,500 of work earnings. Therefore the net LTD benefit is $6,000 – 50% * $2,500, or $4,750.

- Work Incentive: The insured is earning $2,500 and eligible for a gross LTD benefit of $6,000. Since these amounts total $8,500, which is less than the $10,000 pre-disability earnings, the net LTD benefit is the full $6,000. If the insured had been earning $4,500, then the gross LTD benefit would have been reduced to $5,500, so that the net LTD benefit plus the work earnings would total $10,000.

LIMITATIONS AND EXCLUSIONS

LTD contracts typically contain certain limitations and exclusions. These are used to manage the risk of antiselection by an employer or employee and to avoid the potentially costly administration of subjective claims. As an example, it is common in the United States to limit benefits for mental illness or substance abuse to the first two years of disability. The two-year limit is effective in managing the cost for certain types of disabilities that are particularly challenging to evaluate. As a result, some companies have expanded its use to include other disabling conditions, like chronic fatigue syndrome, as a way to manage the cost of certain high-risk industries or occupations. This exclusion is typically referred to as the Special Conditions Limitation clause.

For smaller size groups, where antiselection by the policy owner (who is typically also an employee of the company) is common, preexisting condition exclusions may be used. A typical exclusion would not pay benefits for disabilities occurring during the first 12 months of the policy for conditions which manifested themselves within 3 to 12 months prior to issuance of the policy.

Other common exclusions are for disabilities resulting from an act of war, those caused by an intentionally self-inflicted injury, and those occurring during the commission of a felony.

OPTIONAL BENEFITS

The above paragraphs describe the basic benefits provided by LTD policies. However, there are a number of options that may be added to disability contracts, depending upon the needs and desires of the employer and its employees. Examples of these options are as follows:

- COLA: A cost-of-living adjustment linked to an inflation index and used to provide inflation protection for benefits received during disability.
- Survivor Benefit: A lump sum benefit payable to the insured's survivors upon the death of the insured.
- Expense Reimbursement: Reimbursement for day care expenses.
- Pension Benefit: An additional benefit payment in lieu of employer or employee contributions to retirement plans that would otherwise be lost due to lost earnings caused by a period of disability.
- Portability: The ability for an insured who leaves the group to continue group coverage by paying premiums directly to the insurer.
- Conversion Option: The ability for insureds who lose coverage under the LTD plan to convert to either group or individual disability coverage.
- Spousal Benefits: Disability protection for spouses of insured employees.
- Catastrophic Benefits: An additional amount paid for a more serious type of disability, such as one resulting in total paralysis, or in the loss of two or more activities of daily living.

Election of these options varies dramatically by market segments in which the LTD product is sold. LTD insurers must have a full complement of these features available to meet the needs of employers in the market segments in which they compete.

SELF-INSURED LTD PLANS

Many larger employers choose to self-insure all or a portion of their LTD benefits. For LTD, some employers may choose to insure claims after an extremely long elimination period (during which benefits are self-insured) or to purchase some type of stop-loss coverage, in which they are reimbursed by an insurer for claims that exceed a specified cost. When offering a self-insured plan or relying on stop-loss coverage, an employer must be confident that it has enough funds on hand to handle the volatility that can occur with LTD claim costs. LTD has a low rate of claims but a high cost amount per claim. Tax reform legislation enacted in 1993 and GAAP accounting guidelines, such as ASC 712 (the codification of the standard known as FAS 112, applicable to private employers) and GASB 43 and GASB 45 (for public sector benefit plans and employers, and soon to be replaced by GASB 74 and 75), have made self-insurance less attractive because limits on deductions, coupled with specific rules regarding recognition of liabilities, may adversely impact an employer's balance sheet.

Voluntary LTD Plans

The majority of LTD coverage sold in the United States today is non-contributory, meaning it is entirely paid for by the employer. However, there are a number of trends that have contributed to a rise in recent sales of contributory and voluntary LTD coverage, in which some or all of the premium, respectively, is paid by employees:

- Rising medical costs, leading employers to pass some of the costs of employee benefits on to the employees;
- Expansion into new markets where employers have not typically provided LTD benefits for their employees; and
- Greater recognition of the need for disability coverage.

As was discussed earlier, one consideration for contributory or voluntary LTD plan design is the taxability of benefits. Under current tax regulations, generally if premiums are paid with employee after-tax dollars, then the LTD benefit is non-taxable. This results in higher after-tax income-replacement ratios when compared to a non-contributory plan utilizing an identical benefit design.

The emergence of private health insurance exchanges in recent years provides insurers with a new distribution channel for their voluntary products. To purchase LTD insurance through private exchanges, employers generally establish pretax payroll deduction defined-contribution plans, such as Section 125 cafeteria plans, from which contribution funds can be used by employees to purchase insurance. The insurance plans made available to employees are selected in advance by the employer, and employees then choose whether or not to participate in the plan within the exchange.

Short-Term Disability

Short-term disability is another commonly available group disability insurance coverage. The primary differences between STD and LTD are:

- STD benefits are paid weekly vs. monthly under LTD contracts;
- The benefit period for STD is considerably shorter than under LTD, typically 13 or 26 weeks; and
- Much of the claim cost for STD plans comes from normal maternity claims and accident claims, while much of the claim cost for LTD plans comes from illness.

Definition of Disability

To be considered disabled, the insured typically needs to be unable to perform all the duties of the insured's own occupation. Also, the disability may be focused only on accidents or sicknesses occurring outside of the workplace (known as "non-occupational" coverage). This avoids overlap with workers' compensation coverage, which covers on-job disabilities.

Partial disability benefits can be found on STD contracts. Historically, disability insurers avoided partial benefits on STD contracts in order to ensure a simplified contract, to limit potential benefit abuse, and to keep administrative costs low. However, STD and LTD are increasingly sold together and this joint sale has forced disability insurers to look differently at some of these plan provisions in order to better coordinate the STD and LTD programs.

ELIMINATION PERIOD

The elimination period for STD is very short. Eight days is fairly common, but the elimination period can be as short as zero days. It is common to have a shorter elimination period for accidents than for sicknesses. Accident claims tend to be less challenging to administer. It is usually easier to verify that a disability was caused by an accident than it is to show that a disability was caused by a sickness.

Due to the short elimination period, STD has a much higher frequency of claim than LTD. It is not uncommon to see incidence rates for STD that are at least ten times the incidence rates for LTD. Conversely, STD has much shorter claim durations. Overall STD costs tend to be much less volatile than LTD, and the historical experience on STD plans becomes statistically credible more quickly at small case sizes than is the case for LTD plans. This results in a greater proportion of STD programs being self-insured by the employer than is common with LTD programs.

In order for STD plans to align properly with LTD plans, it is common for insurers to design STD programs such that the sum of the STD elimination period and maximum benefit period equals the most common LTD elimination periods of 90 days (13 weeks) or 180 days (26 weeks). For example, an STD plan may offer a one-week elimination period matched with a 12 week or 25 week benefit period.

BENEFITS

Relative to LTD, STD maximum benefit amounts are typically smaller for two reasons. First, most employees have other sources of funds which they can tap into to meet their basic needs for the short term. Second, an employer sick leave program often supplements the STD plan.

STD benefit payments are usually not integrated with Social Security disability benefits or part-time earnings since the SSDI program has a long elimination period, and part-time work typically disqualifies an insured from eligibility for STD payments. STD benefits will occasionally be integrated with employer sick leave benefits, however.

Again due to the short-term nature of the benefits, exclusions for STD are few. They typically involve excluding certain causes of disability, such as acts of war and intentionally self-inflicted injuries. Pre-existing condition exclusions may be used, but they are less common than for LTD plans, since there is less time to investigate such conditions before benefits become payable, and since the maximum benefit duration is so short.

OPTIONAL BENEFITS

Several types of optional benefits are commonly available on STD plans:

- 24-Hour Coverage: Basic STD benefits are payable for on-job, as well as off-job, injury and sickness. In this case, STD benefits are typically offset for worker's compensation payments received by the claimant.
- First Day Hospital Coverage: The elimination period is waived, and benefits begin immediately, if the insured is confined in the hospital due to the disabling condition.
- Survivor Benefit – As with LTD plans, a lump sum benefit is payable to the insured's survivors upon the death of the insured.

Other, less common benefits, include portability (the right to continue coverage after leaving the group), and work incentive benefits.

MANDATED STATE DISABILITY INSURANCE PROGRAMS

Five states and the territory of Puerto Rico have mandated state disability insurance (SDI) programs. California, New Jersey, New York, Rhode Island, and Hawaii have short-term disability programs for workers in their state. To avoid over-insurance, insurers either offer longer elimination periods for LTD to avoid double payments, or reduce the amount of the STD benefit amount so that the sum of the STD and SDI programs match the benefit desired by the employer. SDI programs require continual monitoring, because they vary by state and change frequently, requiring insurers to update their STD plan design and rating formulas accordingly. As a result, some carriers offer longer LTD elimination periods and let the SDI program serve as the short-term disability program for employees in a state with mandated benefits. For all states except Rhode Island, the employer can elect to cover the mandated benefits under a private program. This can often be done at a lower cost than under the state run plan.

FAMILY AND MEDICAL LEAVE ACT

The Family and Medical Leave Act (FMLA) permits eligible employees to take extended leaves of unpaid absence from work for personal or family medical reasons, with continued group insurance coverage from their employer during the leave period. Employees on FMLA leave may be absent from work for up to 12 weeks over a 12 month period, unless the leave is to care for a family member who was injured while serving in the military, for which the leave may last up to 26 weeks. FMLA programs have proven to be difficult for some employers to administer. The systems requirements can be expensive to develop and maintain on a daily basis. Also, the criteria for determining leave eligibility may be somewhat subjective, and an employer may not want to take a position that could be perceived unfavorably by employees, union groups, or other affiliates. Recognizing the complexities of administering FMLA and other leave programs, STD insurers have begun to offer full leave administration services to their customers, which include STD insurance coverage along with administrative support for FMLA, sick leave, vacation, and other leave programs.

TRENDS

During the 1980s group disability carriers enjoyed a period of solid growth and high profits. As a result, many insurers offering group disability products increased their commitment to disability. Additionally, many insurers that had not previously sold disability products decided to enter the market. In an effort to maintain and increase market share, disability insurers began playing "product leapfrog" with a constant progression of benefit liberalizations: maximum benefits spiraled upwards; own-occupation periods lengthened; "specialty own occupation" and "own job" definitions of disability were introduced to provide greater protection for insureds in occupations with highly specific and technical duties; and other product features were liberalized in order to respond to marketplace needs. Additionally, because profit margins were high, many of these liberal plan features were introduced without rate increases, or at rates that did not adequately reflect the true cost of these benefits.

In the early 1990s, there was a major push by U.S. business to become more competitive in the global market. As a result, many corporations experienced management cutbacks, financial restructurings, downsizing, re-engineering, and other productivity improvement programs. At the same time, increasing medical costs in the U.S. forced health insurers to look at alternative ways to manage the utilization of health care expenditures. The result was a period of tremendous economic stress on many professional occupations – the primary markets for disability insurers at the time.

The convergence of these marketplace forces caused many employees to use their disability coverages as never before, increasing claim costs and severely eroding group disability profits. As a result, disability insurers took many actions designed to increase the profitability of their disability lines of business. Rate increases, product changes, underwriting guidelines changes, and investments in more sophisticated claims adjudication systems and methods were all designed to better manage the risk of disability products and increase profits.

Fortunately for group disability carriers, rate guarantees on group disability coverages average about two years. Thus, group disability carriers were able to take needed rating actions, and LTD profits during 1996 and 1997 rebounded from their low point in 1995. Profits have generally remained in the 6% to 8% since that time.

As of 2013, the group disability market totals approximately $14.1 billion, consisting of $10.2 billion of LTD inforce premiums and $3.9 billion of STD premiums. The recent economic recession and the continued low interest rate environment has caused a decline in group disability growth rates. In the past three years, STD premium in force has grown by about 3-5% per year and LTD premium in force has grown by only 0-3% per year. Prior to the recession, the average annual growth rate was approximately 6% for both STD and LTD products.[3]

Many insurers once theorized that packaging STD and LTD benefits would result in lower LTD claim costs due to the opportunity for companies to begin managing complex claims at an earlier date. As a result, they offered discounts to LTD customers who also purchased STD policies. More recently, however, it appears that this type of packaging has not justified the discounts being offered, perhaps because the presence of STD benefits makes it easier for employees to remain out of work during the LTD elimination period, therefore increasing the number of LTD claims. This phenomenon is difficult to measure, but group disability insurers remain focused on balancing the demands of growth and profitability however they can.

---

[3] 2013 Gen Re Group Disability Market Survey.

13 GROUP LONG-TERM CARE INSURANCE

Malcolm Cheung

GROUP MARKETPLACE OVERVIEW

HISTORY AND OUTLOOK FOR THE FUTURE

Group long-term care (LTC) insurance is a group coverage that has been marketed to employers and associations since 1987. Although the group LTC insurance market experienced rapid growth until 2004, inforce growth since then has been very modest, with 2013 being the first year the industry saw total inforce decline from the prior year.[1] The forces driving the recent decline in LTC insurance sales (both individual and group) include the effects of the 2008-2009 financial crisis, insurer withdrawals from the market, and consumer and employer concerns about the large inforce rate increases that have become common in the LTC insurance industry.

The market for LTC insurance is more advanced in the United States than in Canada. This is because Canadian Medicare covers certain LTC expenses, and there is less perceived need. However, Canadian insurers have begun to show interest in LTC insurance on a group basis, and that interest is expected to increase in the future as the Canadian population ages and its public long-term care system is stretched to provide adequate care. The discussion that follows is based on LTC insurance in the United States.

LTC insurance addresses an individual's need for protection against the high costs of long-term care services, services that are generally custodial in nature and are needed by individuals so that they can perform the basic activities of daily living (ADLs). The need for LTC services may be the result of an accident or an illness, or may simply be due to the effects of aging.

Increasing life expectancies have resulted in a larger proportion of Americans reaching ages where chronic illnesses and disabilities and hence the need for LTC services are much more likely. The aging of 75 million baby boomers, many of whom are currently approaching retirement age, will increase the demand for LTC services. Combined with Americans' concern about outliving their retirement savings and assets, interest in LTC insurance, as well as in other ways to fund future care needs, is likely to continue to increase.

Most of the cost of LTC services in the United States is paid for by those needing the care or by their families. Although the government also pays a significant share of long-term care costs, primarily through Medicaid, governmental entities at both the federal and state levels recognize that public funding will not be able to keep pace with the future anticipated

---

[1] "U.S. Group LTC Insurance - Annual Review 2013," LIMRA 2014.

increased demand for LTC services. Consequently, Congress enacted tax incentives for the purchase of private LTC insurance in 1996, as have a number of states.

One development that sparked additional interest in group LTC insurance was the introduction in the fall of 2002 of a voluntary group LTC insurance plan for all federal employees, retirees, and their eligible family members. As of the end of 2013, more than 270,000 individuals have enrolled in the plan, making it the largest single employer group LTC plan in the nation.

MARKET SIZE

As of the end of 2013, roughly 11,500 employers and associations have sponsored group LTC insurance plans for their employees or members, as well as for their qualified family members. These plans have almost 2.5 million participants and generate approximately $2.3 billion in annualized premium. In-force employer-sponsored group LTC insurance premiums have grown at an average annual rate of 4% between 2008 and 2013.[2] The group LTC insurance market is relatively small when compared to the market for individual LTC insurance, for which there are 4.9 million in-force policies and $9.8 billion of annualized premium as of the end of 2013.[3]

GROUP LTC INSURANCE REGULATION

Regulation of LTC products is covered in Chapter 26.

THE SALES AND MARKETING PROCESS

Like many other voluntary group insurance products, the group LTC insurance sales and marketing process has two distinct components – the selection of the LTC insurer or administrator by the plan sponsor (the first sale), and then the execution of an education and marketing campaign to convince the sponsor's employees or members to enroll for coverage (the second sale). This section covers aspects of sales and marketing that are unique to group LTC insurance.

EMPLOYER SPONSORSHIP

Although most employer-sponsored group LTC insurance plans are employee-pay-all, some employers may subsidize the cost of group LTC insurance coverage for their employees. This is usually done in one of three ways:
- the employer buys a basic, or "core" level of coverage for all of its employees and gives employees the option to voluntarily buy up to a richer level of coverage;
- the employer makes a contribution to the cost of coverage if the employee elects to enroll. This contribution can be either a percentage of the premium cost or a flat dollar amount; or
- the employer buys comprehensive coverage for a subset of its employees, which is typically the management group only. This is called an executive carve-out.

---

[2] LIMRA U.S. Group Long-Term Care Insurance – 2013 Sales and In-Force Survey.
[3] LIMRA Individual Long-Term Care Insurance – 2013 Sales and In-Force Survey.

The plan sponsor selects a carrier based on competing proposals, including consideration of each insurer's claim paying ability and credit rating. By choosing to offer a group LTC insurance plan, the plan sponsor has taken on a fiduciary duty to choose an insurer that will best meet the needs of enrollees; thus, documentation of their reasoning for their insurer of choice may help reduce their own liability risks should the insurer have trouble paying claims at a later date.

PLAN PARTICIPATION

Since group LTC insurance is usually offered as a voluntary benefit, the success of the enrollment campaign in generating high plan participation is critical to the financial viability of the plan. This is due to the need to recover up front marketing and acquisition costs, as well as the need to control antiselection if coverage is made available on a guaranteed-issue basis. Currently, typical plan participation rates are relatively low, averaging less than 5% of eligible employees and retirees. Participation rates do, however, vary significantly from group to group and are driven by a number of factors, including employee demographics (age, income, gender, marital status), the level of employer sponsor support and advocacy for the plan, the simplicity and affordability of the offered plans, and the effectiveness of the educational and marketing campaign during the initial enrollment. A good participation rate would be 10% or higher.

PLAN ELIGIBILITY

Employer sponsors usually make group LTC insurance coverage available not only to employees and retirees, but also to their spouses, parents, grandparents, and in some cases to adult children (and their spouses) and to domestic partners (where permitted by law). The individual underwriting applicable to the various members of the eligible class varies, and will be discussed in detail in the section on underwriting. Coverage provided on a guaranteed-issue basis is typically restricted to full-time, actively-at-work employees.

INSURED DEMOGRAPHICS

Individuals who purchase group LTC insurance coverage are typically in their early forties to mid-fifties in age. The typical buyer is a married college graduate who earns at least $50,000 per year and who has significant assets to protect. Women are somewhat more likely to purchase group LTC insurance than men, because women typically outlive their spouses and consequently may have a greater need for this coverage. Married people are also more likely to purchase group LTC insurance than those who are single, and it is very common for both spouses to enroll for coverage at the same time.

Types of Group LTC Insurance Plans

There are several types of group LTC insurance plans that are distinguished by the manner in which plan benefits are paid to the insured. These variations are described below.

Service Reimbursement Model

Currently, the most popular type of group LTC insurance plan is the service reimbursement model. Under this model, the insurer reimburses the cost of LTC services for the insured after the benefit trigger and the waiting period are satisfied. This reimbursement is subject to fixed limits that are specified in the group certificate and that vary by type of service received. These limits can be applied on a daily, weekly, monthly, annual, or lifetime basis, depending on the particular plan purchased. For example, a typical plan might reimburse up to $150 per day for nursing home care, $90 per day for care provided in an assisted living facility or in the insured's home, and up to $1,000 per year for informal care, all subject to a total lifetime maximum reimbursement of $275,000. Bills and receipts from qualified LTC providers, as defined in the group certificate, are submitted for review by the insurer before reimbursement is authorized. Payment can be made directly to the provider, or to the insured. As mandated by the Health Insurance Portability and Accountability Act (HIPAA) for a tax-qualified plan, most insurers require that every claimant have a formal plan of care developed by a qualified health care practitioner, and only LTC services consistent with that care plan are eligible for reimbursement.

Service Indemnity Model

Under the service indemnity model, once the benefit trigger and the waiting period have been satisfied, a fixed benefit payment is made for any day or week that formal LTC services are received, regardless of the actual charges incurred for those services. For example, if a plan has a $90 per day home health care benefit, the insured would receive $90 for each day he or she received home health care services, even if the cost of those services was less than $90 per day.

Disability or Cash Model

Under a disability or cash model plan, a predetermined benefit is paid for each day an insured is eligible for benefits, having met the benefit trigger and satisfied the waiting period, whether or not the insured is actually using formal LTC services. This model provides the insured with maximum flexibility in how plan benefits can be utilized and is the simplest to explain. Although there should be administrative savings associated with this model because bills and receipts do not need to be reviewed and processed, the additional benefit utilization and faster benefit payout make the premiums for this model significantly higher than those for the other models. Cash models are also more susceptible to antiselection and claim fraud, because cash benefits can exceed the actual cost of LTC services received, and can come to be viewed by the claimant and the claimant's family as an additional source of income. Industry claims experience under cash model plans has emerged significantly worse than expected. Consequently, cash model plans are generally not available for sale in the market today and where cash benefits are available, they are significantly limited in amount and/or duration.

UNDERWRITING GROUP LTC INSURANCE

Most group LTC insurance plans offer coverage to actively-at-work, full-time employees on a guaranteed-issue basis if they enroll during the open enrollment period.

Members of the eligible group other than full-time, actively-at-work employees are usually required to complete a fairly lengthy health questionnaire (also known as a long form) to qualify for coverage. This form includes information related to the applicant's height and weight, prior health history, medications, and primary and specialty care physicians. Telephone interviews and pharmacy database searches are often used to verify the information provided in the long form. The medical underwriting process for group LTC is typically more intensive than for group life and disability insurance.

When indicated by the applicant's responses to the questionnaire, the insurer will request health-related information directly from the applicant's physician on an attending physician's statement before completing the underwriting review. Commonly, applicants over the age of 70 are also interviewed either by telephone or in person to screen out those who may already be cognitively impaired. Insurers have begun to use new tests to identify individuals who are mildly cognitively impaired. These new tests include A Quick Test of Cognitive Speed (AQT), the Minnesota Cognitive Acuity Screen (MCAS), and the Enhanced Mental Skills Test (EMST), among others. Since the most common reason for an LTC insurance claim is severe cognitive impairment, many insurers are now requiring these tests even when underwriting applicants younger than age 70.

Some group LTC insurance plans allow spouses of active employees to enroll for coverage with simplified underwriting. This usually means that spouses fill out a short-form questionnaire with typically three to five questions that screen out those who have medical conditions or current care needs that would make them uninsurable. The Federal LTC Insurance Plan actually uses a short-form questionnaire for both active employees as well as their spouses.

Group LTC insurance coverage is usually issued on an accept or decline basis, with little or no use of substandard or rated coverage. This is in contrast to the individual LTC insurance market, where preferred and substandard risk or premium classes are common, as are modified, reduced coverage offers to substandard risks. Underwriting group LTC insurance is discussed further in Chapter 26.

GROUP LTC INSURANCE PREMIUMS

Unlike premiums for other group health benefits, which are usually group-rated or based on the insured's attained age, premiums for group LTC insurance coverage are based on the age of the applicant at issue. They are intended to remain the same over the lifetime of the insured. The older an individual is at issue, the higher the premium. The combination of level premiums and a morbidity risk that increases significantly with age requires the insurer to hold significant policy reserves to pre-fund anticipated future claims.

LTC insurance coverage is guaranteed renewable, and insurers reserve the right to adjust rates prospectively on a class basis if plan experience warrants, and if the appropriate regulatory authorities approve. Group LTC insurance premiums are typically guaranteed for a limited period of time after the effective date of a group contract. Guarantees usually last at least three years, but no more than 10 years. Since 2010, most of the leading group LTC insurers have announced the suspension of group LTC insurance sales, as well as their intention to file regulatory requests for significant rate increases (40% or more) on business inforce. These actions have been driven, in part, by emerging product experience that has not been consistent with early pricing assumptions, especially relative to coverage lapse rates and morbidity. The recent, persistent low interest rate environment has also posed challenges to insurers' ability to effectively manage LTC insurance. Premiums for group LTC insurance coverage currently average approximately $900 per enrollee per year. Policy premiums are usually waived if the insured is eligible to receive plan benefits.

PLAN PROVISIONS

BENEFIT TRIGGERS

To become eligible to receive benefits under a LTC insurance plan, the insured individual must satisfy the plan's benefit trigger. Benefit triggers have evolved considerably over the years that LTC insurance has been marketed.

Many policies issued in the 1980s required that an insured be confined in a hospital for at least three days and that the need for LTC services commence within two days of the hospital stay in order for plan benefits to be payable. Other early plans included a medical necessity trigger, which required that a physician certify that LTC services are needed. Plans sold in the late 1980s and the early 1990s typically included benefit triggers based on the inability to perform Activities of Daily Living (ADLs) or the presence of a significant cognitive impairment.

ACTIVITIES OF DAILY LIVING

In 1996, HIPAA established minimum standards that an LTC insurance plan must meet in order to receive the same income tax treatment under the Internal Revenue Code as medical insurance policies. This preferential tax treatment is discussed in Chapter 16. Under HIPAA, the benefit trigger of a tax-qualified LTC insurance policy must be the inability to perform (without substantial assistance from another individual) at least two activities of daily living, or a cognitive impairment that requires substantial supervision to protect the health and safety of the insured. Since the passage of HIPAA, LTC insurance benefit triggers on new group LTC insurance policies have basically conformed to the HIPAA standard, as almost all group LTC insurance plan sponsors require a tax-qualified plan design.

The ADLs allowed by HIPAA and most commonly used in group LTC insurance benefit triggers are bathing, dressing, eating, toileting, maintaining continence, and transferring from bed to chair. The definition of what an insured needs to be able to do to be considered independent in any particular ADL can vary from plan to plan.

COGNITIVE IMPAIRMENT

Federally tax-qualified LTC insurance plans are also required to trigger benefits if there is a severe cognitive impairment that requires substantial supervision to protect the insured from threats to health and safety. Examples of behaviors that can be used to qualify insureds for benefits include wandering and getting lost, combativeness, inability to dress appropriately for the weather, and poor judgment in emergency situations. Common tools that are used by insurers to assess degrees of moderate to severe cognitive impairment include the Short Portable Mental Status Questionnaire developed at Duke University in 1978, and the Folstein Mini-Mental State Examination.

ELIMINATION OR WAITING PERIOD

Once benefit eligibility has been triggered, most group LTC insurance plans have an elimination period or waiting period, during which the insured needs to remain disabled and benefit eligible, before benefits are paid.

This waiting period is usually expressed in days and varies from zero to 365 days. The purpose of this waiting period is to ensure that benefit payments are only for long-term chronic disabilities, and thereby to moderate the premium cost of the plan. Most group LTC insurance plans are marketed with a single waiting period option, the most common of which is 90 days.

How the waiting period is satisfied varies from plan to plan. Some plans simply count the calendar days that an insured has been benefit eligible. In other plans, only days in which formal LTC services are actually received count toward satisfying the waiting period. One variation of this approach is to count a full week towards the satisfaction of the waiting period if formal services were received during any single day of that week. There are also different ways for plans to handle those situations in which the waiting period starts but is not totally satisfied before an insured recovers, or in which there are multiple periods of disability. Some plans will require that a full waiting period be satisfied again if two periods of disability are separated by more than 180 days, while others will require that the waiting period be satisfied only once in a lifetime, even over multiple periods of disability.

It is common for the waiting period to be waived for certain types of benefits, such as respite care, care management services, hospice care, and caregiver training benefits. These benefits will be described fully later in this chapter.

COVERED SERVICES

LTC insurance plans utilizing the service reimbursement or service indemnity models can provide coverage for a relatively narrow set of covered services, or for a broader and more comprehensive range of services. In the early years of LTC insurance, many, if not most, LTC insurance plans only provided benefits for care provided in a nursing home. As other types of LTC services emerged, and as consumer interest in these care alternatives increased, LTC insurers in the late 1980s and early 1990s started to develop LTC insurance products that also provided benefits for home and community-based care, assisted living facility care, and informal care provided by an unlicensed or uncertified provider. Plans that cover a full range of LTC services are called comprehensive plans and are the most commonly sold LTC insurance plans. There are even some plans that provide coverage only for home and community-based care.

Although the definition of the types of covered services can vary from plan to plan, generally speaking, the following types of LTC services are covered:

Nursing Home Care – care provided in a facility that provides skilled, intermediate, or custodial care, and is either Medicare-approved as a provider of skilled nursing care services, or is state-licensed as a skilled nursing home, intermediate care facility, or a custodial care facility.

Assisted Living Facility Care – care provided in a facility that is state-licensed or certified as an Assisted Living Facility (ALF). For states that do not license or certify such facilities, an ALF is a facility that meets the following minimum criteria:

- is a group residence that maintains records for services to each resident;
- provides services and oversight on a 24 hour a day basis; and
- provides a combination of housing, supportive services, and personal assistance with the Activities of Daily Living.

Care in an ALF is becoming increasingly popular as ALFs provide a more pleasant, homelike environment than do nursing homes for those whose needs for skilled care are not significant.

Home and Community-Based Care – medical and non-medical services provided to ill, disabled, or infirm persons in their residences or in a community-based facility, like an adult day care center. Such services may include assistance with ADLs, homemaker services, and respite care services, and are typically provided by a home health care agency, a licensed nurse registry, or by an informal care provider.

Hospice Care – services and supplies provided through a state-licensed or certified facility or community-based program designed to provide services to the terminally ill.

Caregiver Training – training and educational programs designed to help informal caregivers obtain state licensure or certification as a home health care provider.

Respite Care – formal, paid care provided to relieve an informal care provider.

Independence Support Services – services designed to allow an individual to remain at home rather than be institutionalized. Such services would include personal emergency alert systems and home modifications such as the installation of wheelchair ramps or grab bars in the bathroom, and the widening of doorways.

Care Management Services – services provided by a geriatric case manager or a nurse to develop an insured's plan of care, identify local provider resources, and coordinate all necessary LTC, medical care, personal care, and social services.

ALTERNATE PLAN OF CARE

Many group LTC insurance plans have a provision that allows the insurer to pay benefits for services that may not be explicitly defined or covered by the group contract and certificate. This provision is typically called an alternate plan of care provision, and allows the plan to continue to provide meaningful benefits even as new ways to provide LTC emerge over time. Determination of eligibility for this benefit is usually at the sole discretion of the insurer.

BENEFIT LIMITS

Almost all group LTC insurance plans impose limits on the amount of benefits that will be paid for any given day, week, month, or year, as well as over the entire lifetime of the insured. These limits usually vary by the type of LTC service received.

Almost all plans have daily limits for institutional care (nursing home and ALF care). Although home and community-based care limits are also usually applied on a daily basis, it is not uncommon to see these applied on weekly or monthly basis. When group LTC insurance plans are marketed to the eligible population, the enrollee selects the level of institutional care daily maximum benefit that he or she would like in the plan. A choice of three or four alternative institutional daily maximums is typically offered (such as $100/day, $150/day, $200/day, and $250/day). The daily maximum benefit for home and community-based care is expressed as a percentage of the institutional daily maximum. In group plans, that percentage is typically 60% or 75%, but higher percentages are not uncommon.

Limits for other covered services, such as caregiver training and independence support, are usually expressed as a flat dollar amount or as a fixed multiple of the institutional daily maximum benefit amount, and are applied on either an annual or a lifetime basis.

Most group plans have a lifetime maximum benefit limit that is applied to all benefits that are paid to an insured. Although it is common to refer to the lifetime maximum in terms of the number of years of institutional benefit available, most of these limits are administered as a "pot of dollars" that is drained as benefits are used. For example, consider a plan that pays up to $150 per day in a nursing home, $90 per day for home and community-based care, and that has a five year lifetime benefit maximum. Expressed in dollars, the lifetime maximum would be five years multiplied by 365 days per year multiplied by $150 per day, or $273,750. This lifetime maximum benefit would last significantly longer than five years (more than 15 years, in fact) if the insured only uses home health care every other day and received a reimbursement of $90 per day.

INFLATION PROTECTION

In light of the limits that are usually imposed on the level of benefits provided by group LTC insurance plans, most plans have an inflation protection feature that would increase these limits as LTC costs increase over time. There are two major ways that this inflation protection can be provided, as follows:

1. **Periodic Increase Offers**

    Under this approach to inflation protection, the insured is periodically given the opportunity to voluntarily purchase additional amounts of coverage on a guaranteed-issue basis. The most common period between offers is three years. For protection against antiselection, some insurers either cease making these offers or require full underwriting if an insured declines two or three consecutive offers. The amount of each inflation offer is typically equal to the difference between the existing policy benefit (institutional daily maximum benefit) and the benefit equal to the original benefit purchased at issue compounded annually at a rate of 5% for the period beginning with policy issue and ending in the year in which the inflation offer is made. Some insurers also make simple inflation riders available at a lower premium than their compound inflation counterparts.

    Some insurers will only offer adjustments that reflect the impact of inflation since the last offer, so if an insured declines an offer, there is no opportunity to "recover" that adjustment in the future without providing evidence of insurability.

    An insured is usually given 30 days to accept an inflation offer on a guaranteed-issue basis. If an offer is accepted, the premium for the policy will increase by an amount equal to the premium, based on the insured's age at the time the offer is accepted, for the increase in coverage. On acceptance of the offer, all benefit limits that are linked to the institutional daily maximum benefit would increase proportionally.

    Although this approach to inflation protection keeps the premium cost of initial coverage low, premiums will increase significantly over time as inflation adjustments are added and as the insured ages.

2. **Automatic Inflation Protection**

    Under a policy with automatic inflation protection, all benefit limits increase automatically each year by a preset percentage on either a compound or a simple basis. Although 5% has been the most common annual inflation percentage offered, group LTC insurers are beginning to offer alternatives such as 3%, 4%, or indexed to the Consumer Price Index to moderate the high premium cost of automatic inflation protection. The premium for this increasing coverage, however, is level over time and is based on the insured's age at issue. As a result, the premiums for a policy with automatic inflation protection are significantly higher than the initial premiums for a policy with periodic increase offers, although that relationship will reverse over time if the periodic inflation offers are consistently accepted.

NONFORFEITURE BENEFITS

Group LTC insurance plans are often sold with a nonforfeiture benefit available as an option, or included in the base coverage. A nonforfeiture benefit allows an insured who voluntarily terminates or lapses coverage to receive a reduced, paid-up benefit without having to continue to pay premiums. This option is particularly appealing in the group LTC insurance market, since the average issue age is relatively young, and there may be many years before claims are expected to occur.

The most common nonforfeiture benefit in current group LTC insurance plans is the "Shortened Benefit Period" (SBP). The SBP nonforfeiture benefit is the minimum standard for a tax-qualified LTC insurance plan as established by HIPAA, and it pays the same benefits in both amount and frequency as are in effect at the time of lapse. However, the lifetime maximum benefit is reduced to an amount equal to the sum of all premiums paid prior to lapse, less plan benefits paid to date. This benefit is usually not available until a policy has been in effect for at least three years. A minimum SBP benefit of 30 times the institutional daily maximum is usually provided. When offered as an enrollee-level option, there is an additional premium if this option is selected.

Some older group LTC insurance plans provide nonforfeiture benefits on a reduced paid-up benefit basis or on an extended-term benefit basis. Under a reduced paid-up benefit, both the daily and lifetime benefit maximums are reduced, and coverage is extended for the life of the insured. Extended-term nonforfeiture benefits do not reduce the inside benefit limits of the coverage, but only cover disabilities that commence within a limited period of time after lapse.

Increasingly, plans now include a contingent nonforfeiture benefit if an optional nonforfeiture benefit is not selected by the insured. This contingent nonforfeiture benefit is only provided to an insured if he or she lapses coverage due to a "substantial" premium increase. The National Association of Insurance Commissioners (NAIC) Model LTC Insurance Regulation specifies the triggers for a "substantial" premium increase. The nonforfeiture benefit provided is the same as the SBP benefit described above. Due to the large inforce rate increases that are common in the LTC insurance market today, some regulators have required carriers to offer a contingent nonforfeiture option to insureds impacted by a rate increase even if their contract does not include such a benefit. Some regulators also require that the carrier waive the "substantial" premium increase trigger for the contingent nonforfeiture benefit to be offered.

OTHER PLAN FEATURES

DEATH BENEFIT

Many group LTC insurance plans include a death benefit. Typically, this provision would pay the spouse of an insured (or, if the insured does not have a spouse, the estate of the insured) an amount equal to a percentage of the cumulative plan premiums paid prior to the insured's death, less any plan benefits paid. The percentage paid is usually a function of the age of the insured at the time of death and decreases to 0% if death occurs after age 70 or 75. A typical death benefit would pay 100% of cumulative premiums paid, less benefits, for death occurring prior to age 65, decreasing in 10% increments for each year of increasing age at death until no benefit is paid for death occurring at age 75 or older.

Like the nonforfeiture benefit, this feature is particular appealing to younger insureds who may have many years until they are likely to receive benefits and may value the ability to recoup their premiums should they die prematurely before utilizing the plan.

Cash Alternative Benefit

To increase plan flexibility, some group LTC insurance plans give the insured the option of receiving claim payments for home and community based care as a cash benefit, rather than as a reimbursement benefit. Typically, the amount of the cash payment is restricted to 30% to 50% of the daily reimbursement benefit maximum.

Bed Reservation Benefit

Most group LTC insurance plans have a bed reservation benefit that will continue to reimburse insureds for institutional care even if they need to temporarily transfer out of the LTC facility to an acute care facility due to a medical condition. The purpose of this benefit is to help ensure that the LTC facility bed will be available to the insured on return from the acute medical facility, because many LTC facilities have long waiting lists and will not hold a bed for a patient temporarily without payment. Most plans limit the bed reservation benefit to 21 days per calendar year or per hospital stay.

Spousal Riders and Discounts

Most employer plan sponsors prefer not to offer voluntary group LTC insurance coverage to married employees on a more preferential basis than to unmarried employees. However, group plans are available with a premium discount for individuals who are married. This marital discount can be as large as 40%, and is quite common in the individual LTC insurance and individual LTC insurance multi-life markets. It can be actuarially justified by the fact that married people would have a natural live-in informal care provider, and that married people tend to be healthier than those who are not married.

Some group plans also include a spousal waiver of premium benefit or a survivor waiver of premium benefit. Under a spousal waiver of premium provision, if both spouses are insured under the group plan, the premiums for both policies would be waived if one of the spouses becomes benefit eligible. Under a survivor waiver of premium provision, if both spouses are insured and one spouse dies, then the premiums for the surviving spouse would be waived for life. The survivor benefit is usually only paid if both policies have been inforce at least 10 years and neither policy has paid any benefits.

Restoration Of Benefits

Many currently offered plans include a restoration of benefits provision. This plan feature restores the lifetime maximum benefit limit if an insured who is on claim recovers before exhausting the plan's benefits. Most plans require that the insured not satisfy the benefit trigger for a specified period of time (typically 90 days to up to a year) before benefits are restored. Some plans will also limit the number of times the lifetime maximum benefit limit can be restored in an insured's lifetime. This feature would be of greatest value to younger insureds, who may initially use plan benefits as a result of an accident and still be able to access the full lifetime maximum benefit to cover a chronic condition later in life.

International Coverage

Some group plans will only pay benefits if the care is provided within the United States. Others, however, will also provide benefits if care is received abroad. There are some special considerations that insurers need to address if they are to effectively manage claims abroad. These would include how to determine whether an insured located in another country has satisfied the benefit trigger, and whether a foreign care provider has the qualifications required by the policy. Claim administration would also be complicated by language and currency differences. Given these issues, insurers typically limit the amount or duration of benefits payable for care received abroad.

SHARED LIFETIME MAXIMUM BENEFIT POOLS

The shared lifetime maximum benefit pool was first introduced in the individual LTC insurance market, but has found its way into some group LTC insurance plans. Shared lifetime maximum benefit pools allow an insured who uses up all of his or her benefits to tap into any remaining lifetime benefits of a spouse's policy, or to leave any unutilized benefits at death to a surviving spouse.

INDEPENDENCE SUPPORT BENEFITS

Independence support benefits are paid for home modifications and personal emergency alert systems that would enable an insured to remain in the home for a longer period of time. Qualifying home modifications would include the installation of entrance ramps, the widening of doorways, and the installation of grab bars in the bathroom. Often, independence support benefits will also pay for the training of informal caregivers to enhance the quality of the care that they are able provide.

POLICY EXCLUSIONS

Group LTC insurance policies do not pay benefits in certain situations. The most common policy exclusions are those that are allowed to be included in a tax-qualified plan, as defined by HIPAA and the NAIC LTC Insurance Model Regulation. These are:

- pre-existing conditions or diseases;
- mental illness (other than Alzheimer's Disease);
- alcoholism and drug addiction;
- illness, treatment, or medical condition arising out of:
  - war or an act of war;
  - participation in a felony, riot, or insurrection;
  - service in the armed forces;
  - suicide, attempted suicide, or intentionally self-inflicted injury; or
  - aviation (as a non-fare-paying passenger).
- treatment provided in a government facility or services for which benefits are available under Medicare or other governmental program (except Medicaid);
- services provided by a member of the insured's immediate family or for which no charge is normally made in the absence of insurance;
- expenses for services paid under another LTC or health insurance policy; and
- expenses for services or items that are reimbursable under Title XVIII of the Social Security Act (Medicare), or would be so reimbursable but for the application of a deductible or coinsurance amount. This applies to tax-qualified LTC insurance policies only.

TERMINATION PROVISIONS

INDIVIDUAL PORTABILITY

Group LTC insurance coverage is usually portable, which means that if an insured's relationship with the sponsoring organization terminates, coverage can be continued.

Many group contracts allow such insureds to continue coverage under the same group plan with the same premium rates. Other group contracts move these ported lives to a pooled group conversion plan or offer an individual LTC insurance conversion policy. In these latter situations, the conversion coverage needs to be as good as the insured's existing coverage, but the conversion premiums may not necessarily be the same as the current premiums.

GROUP CONTRACT TERMINATION

If a group LTC insurance contract is terminated, and the plan sponsor is replacing the initial insurer with a successor insurer's plan, contracts (especially those involving the larger group plan sponsors) will often allow existing insureds to be transferred to the new insurer's plan with an associated transfer of plan reserves or assets. This would allow these transferred insureds to pay premiums under the successor insurer's plan on an original issue age or close to an original issue age basis. The amount of assets transferred in such a situation is typically defined in the initial insurer's master group contract or administrative agreement with the plan sponsor. Not all group contracts, however, include such a transfer of reserve or assets provision.

If a group contract is terminated and the plan sponsor does not choose a successor insurer, then some states require that the insureds be given the right to convert their coverage to a comparable individual LTC insurance policy. In other states, certificate coverage can remain in effect even if a group contract has been terminated.

CLAIM ADMINISTRATION

An LTC insurer or administrator needs to be consistently fair and objective in the administration of LTC claims without creating an unnecessary burden on the insured or the insured's family. The two major components of the claim administration process are benefit eligibility assessment and care management.

BENEFIT ELIGIBILITY ASSESSMENT

The benefit eligibility assessment process typically begins with the insured or the insured's family contacting the insurer, either by submitting a claim form or by telephone. In those situations where there is clear written documentation of the insured's condition from the insured's attending physician or LTC service providers, the process can generally be completed without an on-site assessment. Otherwise, the insurer, at its own expense, will arrange for an assessor (typically a geriatric nurse or social worker) to conduct an on-site assessment and interview at the insured's home. This interview is particularly important in determining whether significant cognitive impairment exists. The information gathered by the assessor, who is usually an external contractor to the insurer, is then reviewed by the insurer to determine whether the benefit trigger has been satisfied.

Benefit eligibility reassessments are conducted periodically, but no less frequently than once a year, as required by HIPAA for tax qualification.

CARE MANAGEMENT

Once deemed eligible, the insurer will usually require that a licensed health care provider develop a plan of care. The insurer will confirm that the plan is appropriate and will monitor future claim activity to ensure that the care being received by the insured is consistent with the established plan of care.

Care management in the LTC insurance environment is quite different than care management in the medical insurance environment. Medical care management is focused on cost and utilization containment. In the medical insurance world, care management involves the imposition of restrictions as to which health care providers an insured can use, as well as to the types of medical procedures and medications that an insured can receive. LTC management, however, is not focused on cost containment, but rather on helping the insured find and coordinate the LTC services that will allow him or her as much independence as possible.

Although LTC care case managers can make recommendations with respect to available care providers that the insured can use, the insured typically has complete freedom to choose any appropriately licensed or certified provider and receive full plan benefits.

TAX ISSUES

THE HEALTH INSURANCE PORTABILITY AND ACCOUNTABILITY ACT

HIPAA provided tax incentives to individuals who take financial responsibility for their own LTC needs by purchasing qualified LTC insurance policies. There are several tax benefits associated with a qualified LTC insurance policy. Generally, these include deductibility of premiums paid by employers and employees (subject to general medical expense rules), employer contributions not being treated as taxable to the employee, and benefits not being considered taxable income to the beneficiary. LTC insurance premiums are an acceptable expenditure for Medical Savings Accounts (MSA) that are available to the self-employed as well as to employees of small businesses, for Health Savings Accounts (HASs) that are available to employees enrolled in high-deductible medical plans, and for Medical Reimbursement Accounts (MRAs). However, LTC insurance is not permitted in a Section 125 Cafeteria or Flexible Spending Account Plan.

Qualified LTC insurance policies that provide benefits on a "per diem" basis, such as under a service indemnity or a disability model, are treated differently for tax purposes than reimbursement policies. The tax-free receipt of per diem benefits is limited, so that policyholders are taxed on the amount of benefits exceeding the greater of a daily dollar limit that is indexed for inflation and published annually by the IRS, and the amount of qualified LTC expenses incurred by the insured. If the periodic payments exceed this cap, the benefit amounts in excess of the cap are included in gross income.

More detail on the requirements for qualified LTC insurance plans is found in Chapter 16.

STATE TAX INCENTIVES

An increasing number of states have also enacted state income tax incentives for the purchase of LTC insurance. States are increasingly interested in promoting the purchase of private LTC insurance because state Medicaid budgets are straining under the burden of rapidly increasing LTC costs. These state tax incentives can take the form of either a tax deduction or a tax credit for qualified plan premiums. As of the end of 2014, 29 states had enacted an LTC insurance tax incentive.

PUBLIC-PRIVATE LONG-TERM CARE PARTNERSHIP

The Deficit Reduction Act of 2005 (DRA) included provisions that tightened Medicaid eligibility rules, and allow for an expansion of the Partnership LTC insurance concept to all 50 states. Partnership LTC insurance policies allow individuals who apply for Medicaid LTC benefits to protect an amount of personal assets that is greater than the amount normally permitted by state Medicaid programs. The additional asset protection is equal to the dollar amount of benefits received from the Partnership LTC insurance policy. Medicaid programs can also extend reciprocal asset protection to those who currently reside in a state that is different from the state in which a Partnership policy was issued. The DRA also established a National Clearinghouse for LTC Information, which will help consumers make educated choices regarding their LTC insurance coverage. This legislation has heightened public interest in LTC insurance as a means to help achieve retirement security.

DIFFERENCES BETWEEN GROUP AND INDIVIDUAL LTC PRODUCT DESIGN

In addition to currently being a significantly larger market than that for group LTC insurance, the individual LTC insurance market is characterized by a more consultative one-on-one marketing and sales process, as well as significantly higher initial commissions. First year commissions for individual LTC insurance are typically in the range of 50% of premium for the writing agent or broker, with another 25% to 35% of first year premium paid as a management override. Individual LTC insurance policies are usually fully underwritten with long form questionnaires, although simplified short form underwriting is sometimes used for employer groups. The target market for individual LTC insurance has been somewhat older (55 years and higher) than for group LTC insurance, but that difference is shrinking as individual LTC insurance producers are now marketing to pre-retirement baby boomers.

The traditional differences between the group and individual LTC insurance are summarized in the table below.

	Group LTC Insurance	**Individual LTC Insurance**
Sales Compensation	Broker 　15% First and Renewal Years 　No override 　Not Vested Insurer funds marketing Group Sales Representative	Agent/Broker 　45-55% First Year 　25-35% First Year Override 　5-15% Renewal Year 　Vested Producer funds marketing
Application Forms	Single state situs with extra-territorial variations	State specific forms
Rating	Field/Home Office Enrollment Kit/Website Single risk class Some spousal discounts Payroll deduction	Producer Web quote generator Multiple risk classes Spousal/Group discounts Direct billed
Underwriting	Guaranteed issue for active employees Short form for active spouses Long form for others Accept or decline	Long form health questionnaire for all applicants Modified offers made
Benefit Features	Limited benefit choices 　2-4 Daily benefit levels 　Inflation protection 　Non-forfeiture Home Health at 50-75% Lifetime max: 3 years to 5 years Periodic inflation protection most common Death Benefit No spousal riders	Full design flexibility Home Health at 100% Lifetime max: 3 years to unlimited Automatic inflation protection most common No Death Benefit Spousal waiver/death benefit riders available

Despite these differences, there are similarities. Both are rated on a level premium basis where the premium is a function of the insured's age at issue. Furthermore group LTC insurance coverage is typically fully portable, so if an insured's relationship with the sponsoring organization terminates, coverage can continue as long as premiums continue to be paid, often with no change in benefits or rates. If coverage is not continued under the original group contract, coverage can be extended through an individual conversion policy.

As the group LTC insurance market has shrunk significantly due to the withdrawal of most of the true group LTC insurers and as the individual LTC insurance market shifts its focus to the baby boomers, many of whom are still working, employer-sponsored LTC insurance plans using individual policy forms have increased in popularity, especially in the small- to mid-size group (fewer than 500 employees) marketplace. Under an individual multi-life arrangement, individual policies are issued to each plan participant, and there is no need for a contract between the plan_sponsor and the insurer. Compared to true group plans, individual multi-life plans generally offer greater flexibility in available plan designs and options. The solicitation and enrollment process is typically driven by the agent or broker, targets key segments of the eligible population, and is more consultative in nature than a true group enrollment campaign, often including onsite one-on-one meetings. In addition, available plan options are often limited, which is a common practice in group LTC insurance plans.

Individual multi-life underwriting of active employees is often abbreviated and less rigorous than individual product underwriting, as the employer sponsor can verify an employee's actively-at-work status. Individual product premium rates are used, but a multi-life or group discount is usually applied, to reflect administrative and marketing efficiencies or reduced sales compensation.

SUMMARY

The group LTC insurance market has seen much disruption over the past five years, with most of the leading insurers discontinuing sales to new groups and some also discontinuing enrollment activity with existing clients. The very long tail of the group LTC insurance risk as well as the uncertainty relative to future experience and the ability to secure approval of rate increases needed to maintain product profitability have all contributed to these insurer decisions. However, increasing life expectancies, the maturing of 75 million Baby Boomers, heightened concerns about outliving one's assets, and constraints on the continued public funding of long-term care services will all contribute to the continued need for long-term care financing solutions. As LTC insurance evolves so that it becomes more affordable for consumers and presents a more acceptable risk profile to insurers, it is likely that the group market will ultimately play a significant role in its future.

14 MISCELLANEOUS BENEFITS

William J. Thompson

INTRODUCTION

In addition to the most visible employee benefits, namely life insurance, medical care, dental benefits, and disability coverages, there are a variety of additional benefit programs that are typically written as group insurance plans. Some of them, such as vision and hearing benefits, critical illness, group legal, and group property and casualty, may be offered as part of an employer's employee benefits program. With the use of flexible benefit dollars that many employers provide in a "cafeteria program," several of these types of benefits have appeal as optional coverages.

Miscellaneous benefits written as group coverages may be offered through other distribution channels, such as banks or credit card companies, associations or clubs (such as motor clubs, alumni associations, and schools), or as supplemental products to group health insurance plans to meet specific needs, such as short-term medical coverage.

While this chapter provides an overview of miscellaneous coverages, many of the benefits summarized in this chapter are also discussed in more detail in other chapters within this book.

VOLUNTARY COVERAGES

Because medical coverage consumes such a large and growing share of the employer's budget for benefits, employers have at times cut back on the funding for other benefits, such as life insurance and disability plans. Cutting back on the funding of medical insurance is also becoming more common. This takes the form of less rich benefit plans, potentially including higher employee premium sharing. It is becoming increasingly common for employers to allow employees to "top up" their benefits – benefits that may not be as rich as the employer once provided – by purchasing additional coverage on a voluntary basis through payroll deduction.

CRITICAL ILLNESS BENEFITS

Historically known as "dread disease insurance," critical illness (CI) policies have become mainstays in many countries that have national health insurance programs, where the CI coverage can be used to supplement the national program. In addition, CI may be used to cover services not provided by the insurance program, such as providing a lump sum benefit in the event of a qualifying condition, travel expenses for family members who travel to a center of care with the patient, or possibly some income replacement coverage.

Critical illness insurance is a popular benefit in Canada, Europe and other countries. Over the past several years, it has become more common in the United States, with several insurers offering this coverage, most often on a voluntary basis.

BENEFIT DESIGN

Most CI policies provide a lump sum benefit upon the diagnosis of certain specified conditions, such as cancer, heart attack, or stroke. With benefits that average close to $100,000, they are most commonly sold as stand-alone coverage rather than as riders on other policies. In Canada, this coverage is typically sold as noncancelable insurance and usually as an individual policy.

In the United States, there are examples of both group and individual CI policies. Individual programs are commonly offered through an affinity arrangement. Group programs are commonly voluntary programs, under which each employee can decide whether to purchase the coverage through payroll deduction. Benefits range from lump sum payments upon the diagnosis of specified conditions, similar to the Canadian approach, to indemnity benefits to cover deductibles or services not covered by the employer's group medical program.

SELECTION AND PRICING ISSUES

Since CI programs are either sold to individuals or on a voluntary basis in a group or association setting, the opportunity for individuals to select against the insurer is obvious. It is common to require a short form medical application for group coverage and sometimes a more thorough medical application for individual coverage. Policy language commonly employs a strong pre-existing condition limitation clause. In a group setting, some insurers require a minimum participation rate of at least 10% to as much as 20% before putting the coverage in place.

Other product design approaches to protect against antiselection include graded benefit provisions and attained age benefit limits. Graded benefit provisions provide only a very limited benefit if the specified condition is diagnosed during the first two years after coverage commences. Attained age benefit limitations reduce the amount of benefit when the specified illness is diagnosed after a certain age. For example, the policy may pay only 50% of the face amount if the diagnosis occurs after age 70.

CI products are most commonly designed with a level premium based on the participant's issue age. Therefore, pricing requires projections of assumptions far into the future. Morbidity and mortality data that directly relates to CI insurance is not readily available. Therefore, it is common to rely on government publications and population data to obtain baseline information. The actuary must make adjustments for antiselection, with the adjustment based on the questions contained in the application, the marketing approach, and policy provisions such as pre-existing condition limitations.

Because of their level premium structure, CI policies can produce substantial policy reserves (also called active life reserves or contract reserves), making investment income an important assumption. Persistency assumptions are also important, since the release of active life reserves on terminating policies contributes to the stream of earnings. High persistency can have an adverse effect on profitability, since the expected reserve release into earnings may not occur as anticipated.

Some Canadian policies are issued as noncancelable, so substantial margins on top of expected claims are necessary to protect against the pricing risk. Because rates can not be changed on noncancelable business, the insurer has no ability to increase rates if experience emerges at a worse level than anticipated. The actuary needs to test this business regularly to determine if a premium deficiency reserve is needed.

Most CI policies provide either fixed amount lump sum or indemnity benefits upon the occurrence of the prescribed insurable event. Medical inflation is not a factor in the pricing of these plans, but changing patterns in utilization of healthcare services is a risk that should be addressed in pricing. During the 1990s, when HMOs in the United States were practicing aggressive care management, inpatient utilization trends were negative. CI plans that provided indemnity benefits for each day of hospitalization saw favorable results, since this negative trend in inpatient days translated into fewer and shorter claims. Such favorable results may return if the more efficient care management arrangements being implemented now are successful.

VISION AND HEARING BENEFITS

Though some coverage for routine vision and hearing exams is required under the Affordable Care Act (ACA), it is becoming more common to find separate riders that provide for hardware and supplies, along with coverage for examinations. Some states mandate coverage for hearing or vision exams for children up to a certain age. In those instances, hearing and vision exams are covered as part of an insured medical program. When hearing benefits are not mandated, vision benefit riders tend to be more popular.

BENEFIT DESIGN

The most common benefit designs provide for periodic examinations to detect any problems with vision or hearing. One exam per year is a common limitation. The benefit may have a prescribed dollar maximum, or the patient may be required to receive care from a participating vision or hearing provider who has agreed to a negotiated reimbursement schedule. Should the examination detect a serious medical problem, the regular medical plan covers the follow-up care for the treatment of that problem.

Corrective devices are also typically covered. A vision plan will normally provide for one set of lenses each year or two, and for frames every two years. A hearing plan will typically provide for new devices about every five years, and adjustments more frequently. Normally, benefits are subject to scheduled dollar amounts.

Occasionally, employers will offer an affinity vision program that looks like an insurance benefit; however, it is actually just a discount arrangement with certain optical providers, normally offering a discounted eye examination and discounts on glasses and contact lenses. These arrangements are not insurance plans.

Though most insurers and HMOs offer hearing and vision programs, there is a rapidly growing number of independent companies that contract with insurers, and sometimes directly with large employers, to provide vision or hearing benefits. With the growth of high deductible health plans, and resulting individual antiselection, it is likely there will be further growth in these specialized companies.

SELECTION AND PRICING ISSUES

The most significant issues that need to be addressed in the pricing of hearing and vision benefits are antiselection and demographics. Both coverages show rapid increases with age, in both cost and incidence. Because of this, it is important to recognize the demographic characteristics of the covered population. For example, the expected utilization of both vision and hearing services roughly doubles between age 35 and 55.

Individual antiselection greatly contributes to the cost of the program. Smaller groups, separate employee premium payments, and cafeteria plan election of the benefit all contribute to higher utilization and higher than average costs. There may also be a first year spike in cost for a group that did not have the coverage before. This is the "pent up demand" phenomenon that is also often seen in new dental programs.

TRENDS

These benefits are commonly offered. With the aging of the population and the workforce, employee demand for vision and hearing services may increase, adding further to the availability of these benefits. On the other hand, when health care costs are rising rapidly, employers may look for ways to cut back on services. When hearing and vision benefits are viewed as optional riders, they are more vulnerable to being eliminated, except to the extent that coverage is required under the ACA.

Because of the predictable nature of hearing and vision services, these benefits lend themselves to coverage through flexible spending accounts and health reimbursement arrangements.

GROUP LEGAL

Group legal coverage began with collectively bargained plans, such as those for the major automakers, and through plans sponsored by local bar associations. It is not a commonly offered benefit.

BENEFIT DESIGN

Benefit designs vary from limited to comprehensive. A very limited benefit design offers a certain number of hours of telephone consultation per year for a narrow range of services, such as a preparation of a will. A more comprehensive plan covers a wider array of common legal services, such as real estate transactions for primary residence, and preparation of wills, leases, and adoptions. Some plans may cover divorce and legal separations. More extensive services, including business and investment matters and criminal law, are normally excluded.

The structure is often similar to a preferred provider organization plan, under which certain attorneys agree to accept negotiated fees. Out of network benefits may be payable, with the employee responsible for costs in excess of the negotiated rates.

SELECTION AND PRICING ISSUES

As indicated above, group legal has traditionally had a relatively small market, primarily through large organizations. In collectively bargained arrangements, the employer often pays premiums. As a result, individual antiselection is relatively small. However, if the employee has an option to purchase the benefit with employee dollars, or if the plan is offered through smaller groups, individual antiselection issues must be addressed.

GROUP PROPERTY AND CASUALTY

Some large employers make arrangements with a property and casualty insurer to offer auto or homeowner's coverage to their employees. Homeowner's protection normally extends to condominium or rental coverage. The property and casualty insurer may issue a group policy through the employer with certificates to the employee; another alternative is to issue individual policies.

Employees normally pay 100% of the premium via payroll deduction. Premiums may be lower than individually purchased insurance, due to savings in commissions and some administrative cost savings to the insurer. Payroll deduction also makes premium payments more convenient. Risks are individually underwritten and priced accordingly. Due to the group nature of the offerings, some marginal risks may be accepted that would otherwise be declined.

Employers value the benefit because it provides a valuable benefit to employee with limited expenses, generally tied to the cost of setting up payroll deduction plans. This can serve as an employee recruitment and retention advantage over other employers.

SPECIAL RISK COVERAGES

Certain limited risk benefits are offered to employers, educational institutions, or affinity groups (such as motor clubs) to provide specific limited coverage to eligible persons. The most common of these are travel accident insurance, student medical plans, and hospital indemnity plans (HIP).

TRAVEL ACCIDENT INSURANCE

As its name implies, travel accident insurance provides coverage only for accidental death (and sometimes injury) while traveling according to the terms of the policy. This coverage is inexpensive. Employers may purchase such coverage for employees while on business travel, with amounts tied to salary or job title. Benefit amounts may be several hundred thousand dollars. In some instances, an accidental medical benefit of several thousand dollars may be added to the coverage, normally applying after a deductible of several hundred dollars to eliminate incidental claims. The employer typically pays premiums, although employee-paid coverage is possible.

Credit card companies sometimes offer similar coverage that applies if airline tickets are purchased using the credit card. Motor clubs also provide their members with similar coverage, which is paid for as part of the annual membership fees. These organizations sometimes provide a base amount and invite participants to enroll for higher optional amounts.

STUDENT MEDICAL PLANS

Student medical plans can take a variety of forms. At one extreme is a limited student accident program, typically offered to elementary, middle school, and high school students. A school district makes this coverage available at the parent's cost. Benefits are limited to certain accidental medical claims that occur at school, or on the way to or from school. Scheduled benefits are common with relatively low limits, sometimes with a deductible. Parents complete a simple application at the beginning of the school year, and submit a single premium with the application for coverage during the year.

The other common form of student medical plans is a more comprehensive program, typically offered by colleges and universities. Protection is more comprehensive, covering both accidents and illnesses that occur during the semester. Coverage is normally paid secondary to any other medical insurance the student may have. In some instances, the insurance makes payments to the student health clinic on campus for visits there. Premium bills normally come with each semester's tuition bill. Coverage is usually mandatory, unless the student or parent can provide evidence of other comprehensive healthcare coverage. Since group medical plans must extend eligibility to dependent children to age 26, the majority of students opt out of this program, though it is common for foreign students to take advantage of this coverage.

Usually, a licensed insurance company underwrites student coverage on a group platform. For enrollment purposes, the educational institution identifies the covered persons to the insurer, who then issues certificates to the covered students. Claims are administered by the insurer.

HOSPITAL INDEMNITY PROTECTION (HIP)

HIP is commonly offered through affinity groups to supplement traditional medical coverage. These programs offer a limited daily benefit while the participant is confined in an acute care hospital. The benefit period is often limited, with 30 days being typical. Some policies offer an additional benefit when confinement is in an intensive care unit, with the regular benefit being increased by 50% to 100% for those intensive care days. The benefits provided by these policies are paid in addition to any benefits paid under the participant's regular group medical program.

Typical affinity groups that offer hospital indemnity protection include travel clubs, credit card companies, and the American Association of Retired Persons (AARP). The plans are written as a group contract, with certificates of coverage for participating members. Participation is voluntary, with monthly or quarterly premium payments being required. Coverage continues as long as premiums are paid and the participant remains a member of the sponsoring affinity group. Coverage can also terminate if the affinity group ceases to sponsor the program.

Pre-existing condition limitations are commonly used as the principal underwriting tool for this benefit.

Benefit amounts are usually under $100 per day of inpatient care. Therefore, in pricing HIP, there is no need to recognize trends in the unit cost of the benefit provided. Over the past decade, hospital utilization has been declining due to the effects of medical management programs under managed care plans. As a result, there have been negative total utilization trends for HIP programs. However, hospital inpatient utilization has crept upwards again in recent years, with admission rates growing around 1% per year, and length of stay growing by 2% to 3%. This has produced a total utilization trend increase of as much as 3% to 4%. These utilization trends must be monitored and managed to ensure that the pricing of the HIP program recognizes those changes in utilization of inpatient services. Tighter care management programs and coordination of care are becoming more common and may slow or even reduce this trend over time.

CREDIT INSURANCE

Credit insurance pays benefits, upon occurrence of an insured event, which help pay off debt of the insured. The most common form of credit insurance is life insurance. Somewhat less common is credit disability protection. Credit insurance is made available when a consumer takes out a loan (such as a mortgage, home equity loan or line of credit, or a new or used car loan), or when opening a new credit card.

The creditor (often a bank) is both the group policyholder and the beneficiary. Premiums are normally paid by the debtor, either as a single premium when money is borrowed, or as a monthly charge that is added to the cost of the debt. Though the debtor pays the premiums, experience refunds or dividends (as well as commissions) are paid to the policyholder, which is the bank or other creditor. Consequently, low premium rates are not important to the policyholder. In fact, the higher the rates, the greater the experience refund. To manage this situation, credit insurance is tightly regulated. Many jurisdictions have established maximum rates in order to avoid excess premium charges, and by limiting the amount of dividend that the creditor may receive and retain.

CREDIT LIFE INSURANCE

Credit life insurance pays a lump sum benefit to the creditor on the death of the debtor. The benefit amount is directly tied to the debtor's outstanding account balance. The purpose of credit life insurance is to pay any remaining debt on the death of the debtor.

Credit life is priced as a decreasing term benefit. The length of the term is the number of years for which the loan has been taken out. The rate of decrease is tied to the loan's rate of interest. As indicated above, the debtor pays a fixed rate for this insurance, while the group policyholder (the creditor) has either a guaranteed rate with a commission payment or an experience-rated policy with experience refunds or dividends. In either case, the pricing is typically set at or very close to the statutory maximum rates that are allowed to be charged for credit life insurance.

CREDIT DISABILITY

Though less common than credit life insurance, credit disability is regularly available through consumer lending institutions, such as banks, credit card companies, and credit unions. Unlike credit life insurance, the loan is not paid off in the event of a covered disability. Instead, credit disability makes a monthly payment equal to the minimum payment required to keep the debtor's account current.

When it is issued on an account with a revolving line of credit, such as a credit card, both credit life and credit disability premiums are charged monthly based on the balance on the account that month.

CAFETERIA PLANS

As its name suggests, a cafeteria plan is an arrangement under which an employee is allowed to select from a menu of various benefit plan offerings. Cafeteria plans are regulated under Section 125 of the Internal Revenue Code. That code allows employees to either receive cash, which is taxable income, or to receive non-taxable fringe benefits of equal value on a before-tax basis. Other than Section 125 plans, the choice between taxable and non-taxable income is generally not allowed under the "constructive receipt" principles of the U.S. tax code.

There are two primary benefits that arise through the use of a cafeteria plan. First, both the employer and the employee can achieve tax savings through the use of pre-tax purchasing of benefits. Second, employees have more options among benefits, thereby receiving a program of benefits that matches their personal needs.

Tax savings are achieved in the following way: the value of the benefits provided is not included in the employee's gross income before taxes, thereby reducing the employee's taxable wages. The employee's federal income taxes and, in most states, state income taxes are reduced because the wage base has been lowered. Similarly, the employer's basis for certain payroll taxes is also lowered as a result of the salary reduction.

More detail on the legal requirements for a cafeteria plan is included in Chapter 16.

The types of benefits that may be offered to an employee in a cafeteria plan include:

- Group term life insurance (though the cost of benefits in excess of $50,000 are added to the employee's income),
- Medical coverage,
- Dental coverage,
- Prescription drug coverage,
- Vision benefits,
- AD&D,
- Disability income benefits,
- Travel accident coverage,
- Dependent care assistance plans (offered under Section 129),

- Flexible Spending Accounts,
- Participation in a qualified cash or deferred 401(k) plan, and
- Paid vacation days, under certain circumstances.

Typically, each year the employer establishes a certain dollar amount or credit that the employee can use to purchase benefits from the cafeteria plan. Historically, those credits have been sufficient to cover the employer's expected contribution to the group life and health insurance benefits, though, with the recent shift toward more employee cost-sharing, those credits may start dropping. Employees select the benefits that are most appropriate for their personal circumstances. If the employee's selections cost less than the employer contribution, the balance can be taken in cash, which is treated as additional taxable income. If the cost of the selections exceeds the employer's contributions, the excess is treated as a salary reduction from the employee's gross income. As indicated above, this salary reduction results in an income tax saving for the employee.

Because employees are allowed to choose the benefits that are most appropriate for their own situations, the pricing of benefits in a cafeteria plan requires anticipation of a degree of antiselection that would not otherwise exist. More detailed discussion on this topic is contained in Chapter 31, "Managing Selection in a Multiple-Choice Environment."

SECTION THREE

LEGAL AND REGULATORY ENVIRONMENT

15 PRINCIPLES OF HEALTH INSURANCE REGULATION

Julia T. Philips
Leigh M. Wachenheim
Updated by Kristi M. Bohn

INTRODUCTION

This chapter presents some of the principles underlying insurance regulation, particularly of health insurance and group life insurance. It begins by describing the problems that can occur in an unregulated market, the goals of regulation, and the means used to regulate. The rest of the chapter presents examples mostly drawn from real situations in the United States. The examples were chosen to illustrate broad principles, and therefore should be useful in aiding the understanding of any system of insurance regulation.

PROBLEMS IN AN UNREGULATED MARKET

It is possible to envision an insurance marketplace that does not need any kind of government regulation. Insurers have managers, actuaries, customer service representatives, and agents who act together in the best interests of policyholders and potential policyholders. They voluntarily make sure that their customers have the most complete information possible in order to purchase the most suitable policies at a fair and adequate price, and they hold sufficient reserves to be certain to have enough assets to pay any future claims or other obligations.

In fact, this vision is not too far from the truth. Most people working for insurance companies and other insuring organizations, such as HMOs, are honest people interested in the welfare of their customers. However, an unregulated market would be a very unstable one, because one dishonest company could gain a competitive advantage. If just one company enters a market with misleading marketing materials, an unfair price, and inadequate reserves, it would be sure to attract a substantial number of customers away from the other companies. Those customers do not have the time or expertise to investigate companies and establish which ones are operating in a fair and safe manner.

In an unregulated market, a customer may purchase a policy that is based on fraudulent claims and misleading presentations by a company. Or, a company may become insolvent with no warning, leaving the policyholder without the promised insurance protection. Or, the customer could purchase a policy that only appears to be a good value, but in fact returns more profit to the company than protection to the policyholder.

Almost all of the specific insurance laws that are on the books of any jurisdiction were originally written in response to a problem that consumers encountered with their insurance policies.

Goals of Insurance Regulation

The primary goal of insurance regulation is to prevent serious problems for the consumer such as those described earlier. However, regulation is often used to accomplish four other goals: (1) to prevent less serious problems for the consumer, (2) to maintain fairness among competing companies, (3) to raise tax money, and (4) to advance social goals. This chapter will focus on the primary goal: how regulation is designed to address consumer protection.

Serious consumer problems can be divided into two main categories: (1) insolvency or financial problems of the insurer, and (2) the purchase of policies that are a poor value or that do not provide the benefits that the consumer expected.

One of the most serious problems an insurance policyholder can face is the loss of benefits due to the insolvency of the insurer. Sometimes, even monetary compensation would not fix the resulting problem, such as a delay in urgently needed medical treatment. In addition to the actual loss of benefits, the worry about possible insolvency and the long aftermath of insolvency can be frightening and stressful to consumers.

Another serious problem faced by consumers is the purchase of a policy that is not a good value. This may be the result of such problems as a bad match between the consumer's needs and the policy benefits, or an unreasonably high premium rate. Sometimes the consumer realizes soon after purchasing the policy that it is not a good value, and sometimes the consumer realizes this many years later, or never. It is the rare consumer that has enough knowledge of the marketplace to identify an overpriced or unsuitable policy.

Unfortunately, even the best regulation cannot prevent all insolvencies and problems. Insurance regulation is aimed at accomplishing as much as possible, given existing constraints, such as budget and social acceptance.

Preventing consumer problems is important, but there are other necessary characteristics of regulation. Regulations should also be fair, honest, and cost-efficient.

Legal Basis

One philosophical decision that must be made in any regulatory system is its level of complexity. Both simplicity and complexity have advantages and disadvantages in different situations.

Simplicity may be effective where regulation can rely on other standards. For example, in the United States, a state may require that an insurer's reserves be certified by a Member of the American Academy of Actuaries. This simple requirement rests on the complex qualifications to be a member of the Academy and the potential for professional discipline if the actuary does not follow prescribed actuarial standards. Therefore, the complex details are elsewhere. Simplicity may also be effective where there is general understanding and agreement on the standards. For example, it may be sufficient to state that a company's advertising may not be misleading. It is unnecessary to list the possible misleading statements if a consumer and a regulator can identify what is misleading based on a common understanding.

Complexity may be necessary in cases where the markets themselves are complex, or where simple requirements have not been effective in preventing problems. Some complexity in regulation accumulates over time, as more and more requirements are added to the body of regulation. Although it seems possible to go back and rewrite such laws to be simpler, in practice that does not usually happen. First, there is no compelling reason to invest the effort, and second, many laws are controversial and cannot be simplified without raising arguments over their meaning.

A typical regulatory body of law may have different categories of requirements in order to give some form to the complexity. For example, a government may have a constitution, laws, regulations, and administrative directives or bulletins. The constitution is simple, stating broad principles. The laws are still simple, but there are many of them, addressing specific issues. The regulations may be detailed and complex. The administrative directives address very specific and timely issues. Each of these levels of regulation generally gain their authority from prior levels. For example, the legislature gets its authority to pass laws from the state's constitution. A state's Insurance Department gets its authority to enforce the state's laws from the legislature.

In the United States, generally insurance *laws* are enacted by elected governments, written to set forth general standards of protection that are intended to be implemented or administered by the state's executive department. Such laws are likely to stand without change for many years. Accompanying *regulations* are promulgated by agencies to implement those laws, and give specific standards that may change from time to time.

REGULATORY ENFORCEMENT OF LEGAL FRAMEWORK

The means, or steps, of regulation can be divided into five categories: (1) licensing, (2) information gathering, (3) prior approval, (4) enforcement, and (5) receivership.

LICENSING

The first and most fundamental step in regulation is licensing. This establishes which companies are subject to regulation. If a company does not agree with regulatory authorities that its business subjects it to insurance regulation, the issue must be decided in the judicial system. Licensing involves giving a unique legal name to each company. Licensing can be as simple as providing the company's name for a list, or as complicated as submitting detailed business plans, financial projections and product information for scrutiny before a license is issued. Aside from reviewing the initial application of companies to become established as an insurer, state regulators have authority over the expansion of licensed non-domicile insurance companies entering into their state, as well as authority over insurers' expansion into new product lines.

Any company that wishes to be licensed must demonstrate that it is not likely to become insolvent. It must also agree to follow the rules of the jurisdiction in which it wishes to be licensed. Generally the company must have a minimum level of capital available. In addition, it must have a reasonable business plan that projects financial success.

Generally, if an insurer is denied a license, it must first exhaust any administrative remedies laid out by regulation (such as a hearing by the Insurance Department) before instituting judicial proceedings.

In addition to licensing companies, regulators often license agents in order to monitor sales practices more closely as well as ensure that each agent has met a minimum threshold of basic and continuing education requirements.

INFORMATION GATHERING

After licensing, information gathering is the next step. The type of information gathered varies widely among regulatory bodies and for different types of coverage. In some cases, no information is gathered until an apparent violation is found.

However, often much time and effort is devoted by regulators to gathering information (either on a preset schedule or on an ad hoc basis) for purposes such as the following:

- Monitoring financial soundness of companies,
- Confirming compliance with regulatory requirements,
- Providing information to consumers, and
- Designing new regulatory requirements.

PRIOR APPROVAL

A third step in regulation is prior approval for business activities, such as issuing policies or changing premium rates. This step is useful in cases where prevention is more effective than hindsight enforcement. For example, if an unfair insurance policy has been issued, it can be too late for the consumer to acquire a different policy. Therefore, legislation may require that the exact policy language be scrutinized for compliance with statutory requirements, before the policy can be issued to consumers. Prior approval is required in some jurisdictions for certain types of insurance, and often includes oversight over policy form language, sales collateral, provider network access, premium rate levels, variables used in underwriting policies, expected loss ratios, reinsurance arrangements, dividend payments, mergers, assumptions and novations of insurance blocks between insurers, investments, and other actions of companies.

ENFORCEMENT

The fourth step in regulation is enforcement. This is a critical step, since regulation without enforcement ultimately can be ignored by the regulated. In order to protect the vast majority of insurers who operate with integrity, a regulatory structure must include penalties for those who violate the law. Enforcement by state regulators may occur through regular financial and market conduct examinations, as well as through required filings and disclosures. Often, however, enforcement relies on consumer complaints to discover violations, and then requires the company to make the consumer whole. Sometimes the regulator imposes fines or other penalties on the company. If the company disputes the violation, an investigation must take place. Sometimes the dispute must be settled in the judicial system. Ultimately, the most extreme penalty is to withdraw the company's license to sell insurance in the jurisdiction.

Another circumstance leading to a complaint can occur when the company is complying with the law, but the policyholder does not understand the legal requirements. Thus, a major task of enforcement is determining whether a violation has taken place, and if it has not, educating the policyholder. Some regulation puts the burden on the company to make sure the customer understands the policy and its provisions before buying it.

RECEIVERSHIP

The last step involves regulating companies that are financially impaired. This can range from receiving and reviewing special reports on financial condition, to regulators taking over an insolvent company and running it until it is liquidated.

SOLVENCY REGULATION

A primary focus of insurance regulation is to safeguard the solvency of all types of insurers. This section discusses actions commonly prescribed by state law and regulations to help prevent insolvency and to protect the interests of policyholders, insureds, and beneficiaries when an insurer impairment or insolvency occurs. Regulators charged with enforcing such laws include a variety of governmental entities, including Departments of Insurance, Departments of Health, Departments of Corporations, and other agencies.

CAPITAL REQUIREMENTS

All insurers need capital to protect against adverse deviations in experience. "Capital" for this purpose refers to the difference between an insurer's assets and liabilities. It is equivalent, depending on the nature of the insurer, to "net worth" or "surplus," or "free reserves." Insurers are generally required to meet minimum capital requirements before beginning operations in a particular regulatory jurisdiction.

Insurers that are going concerns may have differing risk characteristics, and therefore have differing needed levels of capital. Those risk characteristics are a function of the lines of business they insure and the types of assets they hold. Regulators review their actual capital in relation to those considerations. For example, in the United States, state regulators use "risk based capital" formulas to estimate needed capital. These formulas have been adopted by the National Association of Insurance Commissioners (NAIC) as part of the instructions for insurers' annual statements. The formulas vary for life insurance companies, property/casualty insurance companies, and various types of managed care organizations. The formulas are discussed in more detail elsewhere in this book.

Once the company has used a risk based capital formula to determine the ratio of total adjusted capital (TAC) to risk-based capital (RBC), the regulatory response is based on state law. The formula is used as a simple, uniform, objective, standardized way to identify those carriers who may have financial problems. As the ratio reaches below certain thresholds, more corrective actions are called for and the regulatory role at the carrier will become more direct and frequent. Once the formula indicates potential problems, the state uses expert financial examiners to analyze many aspects of the company and the situation. That analysis could find that the problems are not as severe as indicated by the formula, or that capital relief is coming or has already been infused to improve the financial outlook. There are different actions that a company or regulator can take to alleviate a capital problem, such as placing the business into "runoff" mode where no new business can be sold until the capital position returns to adequate levels. Placing an insurer into runoff can often gradually remedy the situation in itself, since new business growth stresses capital resources and other alternatives, such as liquidation of a company, is quite costly and thus not often in the best interest of policyholders.

GUARANTY FUNDS

In the United States, one method of protecting insureds from insurer insolvency is the use of "guaranty funds," after an insolvency takes place. In this situation, the fund makes a monetary assessment of all similar insurers in order to cover some of the financial consequences of the insolvency. In order to help establish uniformity among states, the NAIC has adopted the *Life and Health Insurance Guaranty Association Model Act* as a guide to states. Most states have enacted legislation based on the model act. The purpose of this model act is to protect against loss of two general categories of benefits: (1) payment of current claims and cash values and (2) continuation of coverage.

The model act establishes separate accounts for two types of insurance: (1) life insurance and annuities and (2) health insurance. An association is established and is empowered to make two types of assessments, one for the purpose of covering administrative, legal, and other such expenses and the other for the purpose of paying claims and providing continued coverage.

Certain types of insurers, such as hospital and medical service organizations and health maintenance organizations, may be exempted from participation in these funds. Also, certain insurance arrangements may not be covered by the fund, such as employer self-funded plans that are exempt from state regulation.

RESERVES

Another important regulatory method to protect solvency is requiring adequate levels of reserves for future payment of current liabilities. A detailed source of information about regulatory requirements for health insurance reserves in the United States is the *Health Reserves Guidance Manual,* developed by the Accident and Health Working Group of the NAIC with the assistance of the American Academy of Actuaries. The manual provides a summary of statutory guidance regarding the following types of health insurance reserves, along with explanatory material:

- *Claim reserves and liabilities,* which are a measurement as of the valuation date of an insurer's contractual obligation to pay future benefits (including capitation payments);
- *Contract reserves,* which are a measurement of the portion of premium payments in early policy years that is needed to pay for higher claim costs in later years;
- *Provider liabilities,* which are a measurement of an insurer's obligation to make future payments to providers under a risk-sharing arrangement; and
- *Premium deficiency reserves,* which are a measurement of the extent to which future premiums and current reserves are not expected to be sufficient to cover future contractual claim payments and expenses.

Consumer Protection Regulation

The large body of consumer protection law in the United States grew over time in response to specific actual or perceived problems. Typically, a state legislature will choose to investigate a particular consumer problem, and have witnesses testify about the issue. Therefore, some areas have little regulation and other areas have considerable regulation. Consumer protection regulation generally varies significantly by type of coverage. For coverage such as dental insurance, medical stop loss sold to employers, and many types of group insurance, regulation is minimal. For other coverage, such as comprehensive medical, Medicare Supplement, and long-term care insurance, regulation is extensive and complex, dealing with marketing, rating, policy forms, and consumer education.

Consumer protection regulation can be divided into categories of disclosure, reasonableness, and fairness. There is much disagreement on the appropriate type and level of consumer protection regulation. In the fifty states, five territories, and one district whose insurance commissioners are members of the NAIC, there is wide variation in consumer protection regulation. Provider network adequacy and accurate provider directory disclosure has been a major consumer protection focus of the NAIC in recent years, as attractive pricing has made limited network plans more popular in the initial years of the individual exchange. These limited network plans have not been without consumer and health care provider complaints.

Disclosure

Many state laws require disclosure to the potential customer of key features of the insurance policy. The insurance company may be required to provide a standardized "shopper's guide," an outline of coverage, a summary of the benefits, and/or an illustration of the results of the policy under different future scenarios. Sometimes the wording of these disclosures is specified by regulation, or is subject to prior approval.

The actual policy language is also regulated in the interest of disclosure. The policy must include certain information in a prominent place in typographic fonts of at least a certain size. The policy may be required to have the application form attached, and may have to contain tables of future guaranteed costs or benefits under the policy.

Reasonableness

Many states require that some types of policies include certain benefits or do not include certain exclusions. These requirements are usually considered part of a general requirement that benefits be "reasonable," or that they aren't unfair, unjust, inequitable, or discriminatory. For example, well before the federal legislature enacted Mental Healthy Parity, many states required medical policies to provide mental health treatment with deductibles or co-payments by the insured that are no greater than those required for any other medical service. As another example, a Medicare supplement policy may be prohibited from excluding coverage for emergency medical treatment provided in foreign countries.

Many states also require that health benefits be reasonable, usually "in relation to premiums," at least for small groups. The loss ratio is nearly the universal method of measuring premium reasonableness. The loss ratio is the ratio of claims to premiums. The typical state-required minimum loss ratio for small groups is 65-72%. The Affordable Care Act (ACA) imposes a minimum loss ratio of 80% for individual and small employer coverage, which does not preempt the state's minimum loss ratio where different.

The loss ratio definitions and application between state and ACA law is often different, depending on the state. The ACA loss ratio has adjustments to both the numerator and denominator in order to recognize certain taxes, assessments, risk mitigation program cash flows, and quality improvement investments. Also, the ACA loss ratio is applied as a hindsight protection, meaning rebates will need to be paid out to policyholders if the loss ratio is not met in actuality. However, some states further require that the ACA loss ratio also be anticipated to be met prospectively, based on the actuary's stated assumptions. The ACA's loss ratio is based on three years of past experience, and has credibility adjustments to assist carriers with small enrollment. State loss ratios tend to be simple comparisons of claims and premiums, and are typically prospective in nature, simply relying upon the carriers' actuarial estimates. For states that have not adjusted regulations to repeal former loss ratio standards, both loss ratio standards must be met by the carrier, which is a more restrictive definition that provides consumers with additional protections.

Large group rates are generally not as big a concern to regulators, since the competitive nature of this marketplace, as well as the savvy nature of group purchasers, has not led to consumer protection concerns. That said, the ACA minimum loss ratio is 85% for the large group market in hindsight application, and states often have additional prospective, actuarial minimum loss ratio requirements in place as well.

FAIRNESS

Some regulations are designed to prohibit discrimination among classes of policyholders. For example, the ACA now prohibits different premium rates by gender, even though statistical analysis shows a meaningful correlation between gender and claim cost for many types of insurance.

Insurers generally try to use techniques such as underwriting and risk classification as much as possible, setting their rates differently for many different classes of policyholders, or refusing to issue coverage to some applicants. They do this for three reasons. First, the insurer who uses more risk classification has a competitive advantage over the insurer who uses less. For example, an insurer who gives a discount for nonsmokers will attract more of them, and fewer smokers. A competitor who does not have a nonsmoker discount may find that claim costs are higher than expected, due to the higher proportion of smokers purchasing its policies relative to the proportion of smokers in the general population.

Second, failing to use such techniques can actually destroy a market in certain circumstances. As an extreme example, if an insurer issues cancer indemnity insurance, which pays a fixed benefit upon diagnosis of cancer, without screening out those applicants who already know they have cancer, it is impossible to set a correct rate. Paying claims on those who have cancer at the time they purchase coverage will drive the rates up so high that the *only* purchasers will be those who know they have cancer. Then the rate will have to be higher than the benefit in order to cover administrative costs, and no one will buy the policy.

Third, some feel it is fairer to charge insureds premiums based on the risk they are at issue, rather than intentionally subsidizing higher cost risks. Others feel that social fairness requires such subsidies.

However, there is a clear public opinion that everyone should be able to purchase insurance at an affordable price. Therefore, regulation must strike a balance between prohibiting discrimination and preserving the private market for insurance.

16 REGULATION IN THE UNITED STATES

Keith M. Andrews
Robert B. Davis
Stephen LaGarde
Edward P. Potanka

Insurance is a regulated business. Historically, the business of insurance has been regulated by the states. In 1944, the pre-eminent role of the states in regulating insurance was cast in doubt. In *U.S. v. South-Eastern Underwriters Ass'n.*, the U.S. Supreme Court ruled that insurance transactions crossing state lines were regulated by the federal government under the commerce clause of the Constitution. Congress quickly responded in 1945 by enacting the McCarran-Ferguson Act that confirmed the pre-eminent role of the states in regulating insurance:

> *The business of insurance, and every person engaged therein, shall be subject to the laws of the several States which relate to the regulation and taxation of such business... No Act of Congress shall be construed to invalidate, impair, or supersede any law enacted by any State for the purpose of regulating the business of insurance... 15 U.S.C.A. 1012(a) and (b)*

Until recently, the McCarran-Ferguson Act left the regulation of insurance, insurance companies, and the group insurance business almost exclusively to the states. While a few federal regulations affected group insurance benefits prior to 2010, the group insurance business has been profoundly affected by federal regulation ever since the passage of the Affordable Care Act (ACA) in 2010.

This chapter outlines the salient features of state and federal regulation of group insurance, including HMOs. State regulation is discussed in Part 1, while federal regulation is discussed in Part 2.

♦ PART ONE ♦

STATE REGULATION

Every state has enacted comprehensive laws regulating virtually all aspects of the business of insurance. Few businesses are as heavily regulated as the business of insurance. Part One of this chapter summarizes the salient features of state regulation of group insurance and HMOs. While all lines of group health insurance are regulated by the states, the regulatory requirements relating to group health insurance and HMOs are far more extensive than those relating to the other major group insurance lines (life, accidental death & dismemberment, disability, and long term care). This disproportionate regulatory attention to group health insurance is reflected in this summary.

STATE REGULATION OF GROUP INSURANCE GENERALLY

ORGANIZATION OF STATE INSURANCE DEPARTMENTS

All state insurance laws provide for the creation of an Insurance Department or Bureau in the executive branch to administer the laws regulating insurers and the business of insurance. State insurance laws typically establish a single Commissioner or Superintendent as the head of the Insurance Department (in a few cases there is an Insurance Board). In addition to overseeing the operation of the Insurance Department, the Commissioner is empowered by statute to interpret the insurance laws, make regulations implementing the insurance laws, and to license insurance companies, authorized reinsurers, third-party administrators, insurance agents, brokers, and consultants. The Commissioner is also empowered to conduct examinations of the operations of licensed insurers, and to assess penalties (including termination of licensure) for violations of insurance laws and regulations.

ORGANIZATION AND LICENSING OF INSURANCE COMPANIES

In order to engage in the insurance business in a state, a company must obtain an insurance license from that state's insurance commissioner. The license pertains to specific lines of business, and must be renewed annually. The requirements for a license vary, depending on whether the insurer is a domestic insurer (domiciled in that state), a foreign insurer (a U.S. company domiciled in another state), or an alien insurer (domiciled outside the U.S.). The licensing requirements for foreign and alien insurers are more stringent than for domestic insurers, encouraging insurers to domicile in the state and providing policyholders and consumers greater protection from abuses by foreign and alien companies (over which the Insurance Commissioner has less regulatory control).

POLICY/CERTIFICATE FORM AND RATE FILING REGULATIONS

Either by law or regulation, virtually all states require the filing of group life and health policy and certificate forms used in the state. "Prior approval" states require that the Commissioner approve the policy and certificate forms prior to use, while "file and use" states require only that the forms be filed prior to use. A few states have "extraterritorial" insurance policy form filing requirements that in some situations (for example, policies issued to multiple-employer trusts) require prior approval on group insurance certificate forms issued to individuals residing in the state, even though the group insurance policy is issued in another state.

Many states also require the filing of group health premium rates or rating methodologies. State insurance laws typically require that premium rates not be excessive, inadequate, nor unfairly discriminatory. In response to concern that state rate regulation was ineffective, the ACA established a federal review process designed to supplement state rate regulation specifically for the individual and small group marketplaces. The ACA requires the Secretary of Health and Human Services (HHS) to collaborate with state insurance commissioners to conduct an annual review of "unreasonable increases in premiums." The determination of "unreasonable" is left to HHS or states designated as having an effective rate review process, though insurers and HMOs must submit justifications for any rate increase over 10 percent. HHS makes those justifications publicly available on its website.[1]

---

[1] https://ratereview.healthcare.gov/

The ACA also provided states with a pool of $250 million in federal grants to support enhanced rate review.

LICENSING PRODUCERS

Most states require that producers (insurance agents, brokers, and other insurance intermediaries) be licensed in order to conduct business in the state. Many states require that agents pass tests as a condition of granting licensure. In addition, there are state laws that require agents to take continuing education classes in order to maintain their licenses. The Commissioner may revoke or suspend a license, or impose financial penalties, for violations of regulatory requirements.

As a result of perceived abuses, in recent years many states have enacted laws or promulgated regulations imposing disclosure requirements on producers. Such requirements oblige disclosure to clients of the compensation producers are entitled to receive from the insurer or HMO whose products are being recommended. As a result of the intensified regulatory scrutiny, insurers and HMOs have similarly imposed additional client disclosure requirements in their producer agreements or compensation policies.

As discussed in Part Two of this chapter, the ACA requires that insurance companies and HMOs pay a rebate to their group policyholders if their block's medical loss ratio (the percentage of premium spent on clinical services, plus activities to improve health care quality) is less than a minimum amount. That minimum is 85% in the large employer market and 80% in the small employer market. To reduce their rebate exposure under the new law, some group insurers are either reducing or eliminating commissions, or carving benefit advisor compensation out of the group insurance premium and billing it separately to group policyholders.

ADVERTISING REGULATION

Most states have adopted, by statute or regulation, the National Association of Insurance Commissioners ("NAIC") model regulations relating to advertisements for life and health insurance products. These laws and regulations are intended to protect consumers from unfair, inaccurate, deceptive, and misleading advertisements, and to prevent disparaging, unfair, or incomplete comparisons with other insurance companies or their products.

REGULATION OF BUSINESS PRACTICES

Virtually all states have adopted, in some form, the NAIC Unfair Trade Practices and Unfair Claim Settlement Practices Model Acts. These regulations govern the conduct of insurance companies by prohibiting specified unfair practices relating to policy issuance, renewal, or termination, and their underwriting, advertising, rebating, and claim practices. Repeated violations indicating a pattern or practice that is in violation of the prohibitions can subject the insurer to a cease and desist order from the insurance regulator, as well as fines or license revocation.

PROMPT PAY LEGISLATION

Health care providers have successfully lobbied state legislators to enact laws requiring that insurers and HMOs pay "clean" claims (that is, claims for which all of the information required to process the claim has been provided) within a specified period of time (typically 30-45 days). Interest charges, at relatively high annual rates, are required for claims not paid within the required timeframe. Insurance regulators in some states have embraced enforcement of these laws against health insurers and HMOs more aggressively, and in some instances, imposed seven figure fines for violation of prompt pay laws.

REGULATION OF INSURER SOLVENCY

One of the most important duties of the Insurance Commissioner in any state is to assure the financial soundness of the licensed insurers and HMOs doing business in the state. The financial soundness of the company is assessed initially during the licensing process. Once licensed, insurers and HMOs must maintain adequate reserves, specified minimum levels of capital and surplus, and in some cases, deposits for the protection of policyholders. To facilitate monitoring of the financial condition of insurers, financial report filing is required both annually and quarterly.

The financial statements prepared by insurers were first designed by the NAIC in 1871 and have undergone many revisions over time. The last major revision was in the 1950s. Each year, minor revisions are made. These statements are commonly referred to as the "NAIC Blank." The information submitted in the financial statement is subject to periodic on-site financial audit review by the insurance department. These audits are directed by the insurance department, but are at the expense of the insurer or HMO subject to the audit.

Investments

In keeping with the purpose of assuring the solvency of licensed insurers, even the types of investments that an insurer may make are regulated. The regulatory restrictions depend on the type of investment. Capital may be invested in conservative and secure investments, such as government bonds and mortgages. Capital investments are required for funds that are equal to the legal minimum surplus for the particular line of insurance. Reserve investments may be made with all of the other funds available to insurers. In addition to the conservative investments allowed for capital investments, other investments are allowed for reserve investments. Regulatory restrictions pertaining to investments do vary by state, with some states requiring more conservative investment strategies than others. State laws or regulations typically require that any investments be approved by the board of directors or another committee charged with the insurer's investment operations. Persons charged with approval are permitted no interest in the investments or their sale to the insurer. The Insurance Commissioner sets the asset valuation standards at a level that is consistent with NAIC rules.

Reserves

Adequate reserves must be established by insurers to deal with prospective claim liabilities. Life insurers must establish a minimum life insurance reserve by law. The NAIC has developed model requirements for this purpose. Although reserves are required, determination of their adequacy is usually left to the insurer. Most states require that reserve levels be certified as being adequate at the end of each calendar year by an actuary that is a member of the American Academy of Actuaries and is considered as the appointed actuary for the insurer.

Surplus and Dividends

Mutual insurers are limited by law in many cases as to how much surplus can be accumulated. The purpose of this is two-fold. First, it limits the amount that is available for use as excess funds. Second, it allows for the payment of reasonable dividends. State insurance laws also require that the dividends be paid annually and not be deferred. Similarly, some not-for-profit organizations have their respective levels of surplus (called "free reserves") limited by state statute, regulation, or regulatory practice.

Liquidation and Rehabilitation

If a licensed insurer is in jeopardy of becoming insolvent, state insurance laws authorize the Commissioner to apply to a state court for an order allowing the Commissioner to assume the insurer's assets. An insurer's impending insolvency may initially come to the attention of the regulator in a variety of ways, and is usually confirmed by means of an on-site financial examination of the insurer. There must be actual evidence of financial insufficiency or wrong-doing to support the application for an order assuming an insurer's assets. The grounds for assuming the assets of an insurer include non-cooperation with examiners, refusing to remove questionable officers, charter violations, state law violations, endangered capital or surplus, and technical insolvency. The insurer may apply for a court hearing to appeal the takeover; however, during this process the Commissioner will have control of the company's assets.

The NAIC has developed a Model Insurers Supervision, Rehabilitation, and Liquidation Act. By the terms of this act, the Commissioner may seek reorganization of the insurer to preserve its tangible assets. In this instance, the name is usually changed and the company is returned to the hands of private management. If the Commissioner determines that rehabilitation is impossible, then liquidation is proposed. However, liquidation is a very expensive alternative (generally due to legal fees), so regulators often place troubled insurers into "runoff mode," where new business cannot be sold but existing business continues as usual. Runoff mode is a form of rehabilitation which typically improves the insurer's financial condition over time. If liquidation is sought, the Commissioner obtains another court order asking for liquidation of the insurer's assets. The Commissioner is named as the liquidator, collects all assets and pays all obligations that are due. An attempt is often made to have a reinsurer assume some or all of the obligations of the company. Notices advising of the liquidation are sent to other commissioners, guarantee funds, insurance agents, providers, and any others with claims against the insurer.

Guaranty Associations

States have enacted laws creating guaranty associations to protect insureds when life and health insurers fail to perform their contractual obligations due to financial impairment or insolvency. To provide this protection, an association of insurers licensed in the particular line of business is created to pay the claims and continue the coverages of the impaired or insolvent insurer up to specified limits. To fund these continuing obligations, association members (usually all insurers licensed in the particular line) are required to pay a periodic assessment. Generally, HMOs are not subject to guaranty fund laws nor do their policyholders receive the guaranty fund's financial protections.

Insurance Regulatory Information System (IRIS)

The NAIC has developed an early warning testing system designed to reveal indications of financial problems and insolvency. It is called the Insurance Regulatory Information System (IRIS). The NAIC conducts an IRIS test series for insurers that voluntarily submit their annual statements for the tests and pay the required fee, as well as for those insurers with a history of financial problems. Under IRIS, an annual statement is subjected to tests where certain ratios are developed. These ratios are meant to indicate future financial problems that could potentially result in insolvency. When these results are combined with other factors, such as the results of previous examinations, the insurance department (who has access to IRIS) and the insurer are better able to assess the company's financial future.

GROUP LIFE AND HEALTH DEFINITIONS

The vast majority of states have laws that define what constitutes a group for the purposes of issuing a group life or health insurance policy. These "group definition" laws typically permit an insurer to issue a group insurance policy to the following groups:

- Single-employer groups covering their employees and their dependents,
- Labor union groups covering their members,
- Association groups covering their members,
- Multiple-employer trust groups (METs) made up of employers, unions or a combination of the two, covering employees of the employer or members of the union, and
- Creditors of financial institutions.

There is often a "catch-all" category referred to as "discretionary groups." This is a group that is not delineated in the insurance law definition of permissible groups, but to whom an insurer can issue a group policy, if approved to do so at the discretion of the insurance commissioner. Not all states allow these groups, and the laws are by no means uniform or consistent from state to state.

STANDARD CONTRACT PROVISIONS

State insurance laws often require that group insurance policies contain specified standard provisions, or similar provisions which (in the opinion of the Commissioner) are more favorable to the persons insured than the standard language. Examples include the following:

- *Grace Period.* There must be a 31-day grace period provision for the payment of premium during which time the policy will remain in force. The policyholder is liable for payment of premium for any period the group policy is in effect.

- *Incontestability.* There must be a provision that provides that the validity of the policy shall not be contested after it has been in force for two years, except for nonpayment of premium. The provision must also state that no statement made by any insured relating to his or her insurability shall be used to contest the validity of the person's insurance after it has been in force prior to the contest for two years.

- *Application and Statements.* A provision is required to the effect that the application for the policy has to be made a part of the policy, and the insured's statements in the application are to be considered representations and not warranties.

- *Evidence of Insurability.* There must be a provision indicating when evidence of insurability, if any, is required.

- *Misstatement of Age Provision.* If premiums or benefits vary by age, there must be a provision stating how premiums or benefits will be adjusted due to a misstatement of age.

- *Certificates.* A provision must be included in the group policy stating that the insurer will issue certificates to the policyholder for delivery to each insured. These statutory provisions do not themselves require the insurer to provide certificates to enrollees; rather, once the provision is included in the group insurance policy, provision of the certificates to the group policyholder becomes a contractual obligation of the insurer.

- *Benefits/Eligibility.* Policy provisions must set forth the benefits, identify to whom they are payable and include specific terms of eligibility for coverage.

POLICY PROVISIONS FOR GROUP HEALTH PLANS ONLY

- *Pre-existing Conditions.* When not banned, state law typically requires that a provision must be included in the policy describing any exclusions or limitations that apply to medical conditions that existed prior to the person's coverage under the policy. Any such provision must be limited to conditions for which advice or treatment was received within 6 months of the person's coverage effective date, and cannot generally apply for longer than 12 months after the coverage effective date. Details on the federal HIPAA law and the ban on pre-existing condition limitations under the ACA are provided in Part Two of this chapter.

- *Notice and Proof of Claims.* A group health insurance policy must include a provision that specifies the periods of time following the occurrence of a loss in which a notice of claim and proof of loss must be provided to the insurance company. This is waived if it is not reasonably possible to give it. The insurer must furnish the appropriate claim forms to the insured.

- *Legal Actions.* A provision specifying the periods of time when a legal action may not be brought on a claim must be included in the policy. For example, a legal action may not be brought any earlier than 60 days nor later than 2 years following a claim submission.

POLICY PROVISIONS FOR GROUP LIFE PLANS ONLY

- *Beneficiaries.* There must be a provision identifying the designated beneficiary.

- *Conversion Rights.* The group policy must give the insured the right to convert his or her group life insurance to an individual life insurance policy, if his or her group life coverage ceases due to termination of employment or termination of membership in an insured class. The amount that can be converted cannot exceed the amount in effect immediately prior to termination. Conversion must be offered without evidence of insurability, and at the insurer's customary rate for the person's class of risk and attained age. The person must make application and pay the first premium within a specified time following termination of group coverage. The conversion privilege is also available to insured dependents whose group life insurance ceases due to the employee's death or because they no longer qualify as a dependent. If termination of group life insurance is due to termination of the group policy or the covered person's class, the person may also convert to an individual policy if he or she was covered under the group policy for at least five years prior to termination. However, the amount that can be converted is limited to the lesser of the amount in effect immediately prior to conversion or $10,000.

- *Death During the Conversion Period.* A provision must be included which states that if a person dies within the 31-day conversion period, the amount which could have been converted will be paid as a claim under the group policy, regardless of whether he/she has applied to convert.

- *Disability Continuance.* There must be a provision stating that if an active employee becomes totally disabled while insured, he or she may continue coverage under the group policy by payment of the premium for up to six months. Coverage will cease, in any case, when either the person is approved for coverage under a premium waiver provision of the policy, or the policy terminates.

MANDATED BENEFITS

Statutes that mandate that group insurance policies must include certain benefits ("mandated benefits") focus principally on health insurance. States mandate benefits primarily to meet the perceived needs of their citizens, or to satisfy the demands of interest groups such as health care providers. Mandated benefits have been viewed by state legislatures as politically attractive since they allow legislators to demonstrate a benefit to specific constituents. As a result, mandated benefit laws have proliferated and there is little in common from state to state, except that most states require minimum levels of coverage for alcohol and drug treatment. Even where states mandate a particular benefit, there is little consistency between states as to the specifics of the coverage required. The list of coverage mandates is extensive. More common mandated benefits include coverage for mental health/behavioral disorders, alcoholism and drug dependency, handicapped children beyond their normal termination age, recognition of a variety of health care practitioners (such as chiropractors and podiatrists) to provide services that are within the scope of their respective licenses and would be payable under a policy to other licensed medical providers, coverage of children under policies covering non-custodial parents, and applied behavior therapy for children with autism.

Some mandates apply only to policies issued or delivered in the state. Others apply "extraterritorially" to the citizens of a state even if covered under a group policy that is issued in another state. As a result, insurers covering people in multiple states under a group insurance policy must include the mandated benefits of the state where the contract is issued and offer people living in other states any applicable extra-territorial benefits. Consequently, employees covered under the same employer-sponsored insured group health plan may be entitled to different benefits depending on where they live.

Although mandated benefit laws were politically attractive to state legislators because they came at no cost to the state, they did have a cost for consumers. Increased awareness of the cost of mandated benefits has in some instances resulted in state legislatures imposing a moratorium on additional mandates. In an effort to thwart further state mandates, the ACA requires that new mandates in the individual and small group markets be paid for by the state. This has slowed the enactment of further mandates considerably.

COORDINATION OF BENEFITS

It is not uncommon for an individual covered under a group health plan to have other insurance coverage for health care expenses. For example, a person may be covered under his/her employer's group plan and covered under his/her spouse's plan as a dependent. With more than one group plan in effect, there is the possibility of duplication of benefit payment and of the covered person profiting from an injury or sickness. This leads to unnecessary increases in the cost of group insurance coverage.

During the 1960s, group insurers attempted to develop rules for coordinating their coverages to avoid duplication of claim payments. In 1970, the NAIC adopted a Group Coordination of Benefits Model regulation to establish rules for insurers to use in determining which insurer would be primary and which would be secondary in duplicate coverage situations. The model act has been continually updated and adopted by all but a handful of states. Even where not adopted, it provides a useful model for determining the order of benefit determination in duplicate coverage situations, and is followed by most insurers and HMOs.

The coordination of benefit (COB) rules apply to group and group-type plans only. Individual plans (other than automobile no-fault plans) would not be included in the list of plans with which a group plan could coordinate its benefits. The COB rules establish a precise order of benefit payment determination. The COB rules are typically included in the group insurance policy or HMO service agreement. In application, the COB administration rules can be very complex, but they do serve the intended purposes of prescribing a hierarchy to determine which plan pays what in duplicate group coverage situations.

DISCONTINUANCE AND REPLACEMENT OF COVERAGE

Employers sometimes discontinue coverage under one group insurance policy and replace it with coverage issued by another company, which can pose problems. Because many group policies exclude from eligibility the replacement coverage for persons with pre-existing conditions or not actively at work, some people would be left without coverage as a result of the change.[2] To address these issues, the NAIC developed a Group Coverage Discontinuance and Replacement Model Regulation, which has been implemented in some form in half the states. The model regulation addresses these issues by defining the responsibilities of both the prior carrier and the succeeding carrier. Under the model, the prior carrier must provide an extension of benefits to the following extent:

- For life insurance, if a disability extension is included, it will not be terminated by the policy's discontinuance.

---

[2] The ACA largely took care of this problem in the major medical arena, with its widely applicable prohibition on preexisting condition exclusions.

- For long-term and short-term disability, termination of the plan during an existing disability will not affect benefit payments for the disability.

These rules help assure a smooth transition to the succeeding carrier's plan in a transfer of coverage situation. The prior carrier is only responsible to the extent of its contractual extension of benefits provisions and any accrued liabilities. The succeeding carrier's responsibilities with regard to persons eligible under its plan (who were also covered under the prior carrier's plan on its termination date) are also specified in the model.

SMALL GROUP REFORM

During the late 1980s and early 1990s, national attention was focused on the plight of the working uninsured and the perceived abuses occurring in the small employer health insurance market. To promote the availability of health insurance coverage to small employers, and to prevent abusive underwriting and rating practices, most states enacted so-called "small group" legislation during the decade of the 1990s. Small group laws typically require insurers and HMOs to issue coverage to small employers on a guaranteed issue basis. Small group carriers are required to renew small groups except in limited situations, such as non-payment of premium and fraud. The ACA greatly standardized and expanded small group reforms effective in 2014, including (1) pooling risk at the statewide level through a permanent risk adjustment mechanism, (2) greatly limiting the rating factors that a carrier can use (only area, standardized age factors, benefit design, network and tobacco use factors can be used), (3) expanding the definition of small group to 100 (effective in 2016), and (4) extending guarantee issue through a one month open window where participation and contribution standards cannot constrain eligibility. More information on these and the many other reforms applicable to small groups can be found in Chapter 18, "The Affordable Care Act."

REGULATION OF MEDICARE SUPPLEMENT INSURANCE

Medicare Supplement insurance is coverage that is designed and marketed as a supplement to reimbursement under Medicare by filling in the deductible and co-insurance amounts not paid by Medicare. The NAIC Medicare Supplement Insurance Minimum Standards Model Act outlines uniform standards for Medicare supplement insurance benefits, and for its advertising, marketing, and disclosure. The coverage may be issued on an individual or group basis. Virtually all states have enacted some form of the NAIC Model Act.

REGULATION OF LONG-TERM CARE INSURANCE

The NAIC Long-Term Care Insurance Model Act and the Long-Term Care Insurance Model Regulation have been adopted in some form in the vast majority of states. Common elements of all long-term care laws and regulations applicable to group plans include:

- benefit "triggers" (the physical or mental failures that cause benefits to start)
- continuation or conversion options on termination of group coverage
- protection against unintentional lapse of coverage
- offer of automatic increase in benefits to offset the impact of inflation
- standards for advertising, marketing and the applicant's suitability for coverage
- limits on pre-existing conditions and other restrictions to benefits

- type used in printed material, and
- form and rate filing requirements.

Long-term care insurance is defined in the NAIC Long-Term Care Model Act as insurance designed and marketed to provide at least 12 months of coverage for necessary diagnostic, preventive, therapeutic, rehabilitative, maintenance or personal care services, not provided in an acute care unit of a hospital. The most striking difference between long-term care and medical care is that long-term care is driven by the insured's need for maintenance or custodial care, while medical care is designed to cover the costs incurred for treatment of illnesses and injuries.

HIPAA includes a provision that makes premiums for "qualified" LTC plans deductible for federal and state income tax purposes. Prior to HIPAA, deductibility of LTC coverage premium was not addressed in the law. The law applies to contracts issued after December 31, 1996, and "grandfathers" many contracts issued prior to 1997.

More detail on regulation applicable to LTC plans can be found in Chapters 13 and 26.

STATE REGULATION OF PREFERRED PROVIDER ARRANGEMENTS

Insurers and others have sought to emulate HMOs by developing arrangements that include the quintessential feature of HMOs – a relationship with providers. This has led to the development of preferred provider arrangements. These are more often, but less accurately, called preferred provider organizations (PPOs). A preferred provider arrangement involves a group of health care providers that have contracted directly or indirectly with an insurer. These providers become "preferred" by virtue of the insurer providing a meaningful financial incentive for plan participants to use the providers in its provider network. Typically, insurers encourage the use of their panel of preferred providers by means of lower co-insurance requirements when preferred providers are used. However, even health insurance plans with no coinsurance differential between preferred and non-preferred providers can still afford a meaningful economic incentive for insureds to use preferred providers, since their coinsurance is calculated on the provider's discounted charge.

Preferred provider arrangements take many forms. To achieve its objectives, a preferred provider arrangement should have both a carefully selected network of efficient providers and negotiated compensation arrangements with those providers. It is no accident that these elements of successful PPOs are also the building blocks that are critical to the success of an HMO. An HMO gatekeeper feature can easily be added to the basic PPO, making it look even more like an HMO.

The resemblance to an HMO is closer yet with an exclusive provider arrangement (EPA or EPO), in which coverage is limited to services provided by the panel of preferred providers (except in emergencies). Adding paperless claim processing and capitated compensation arrangements with providers makes this structure, for all practical purposes, indistinguishable from the coverage offered by an HMO. The feature that distinguishes this arrangement from an HMO is that it is indemnity-based. That is, insurers *reimburse* or *indemnify* an insured for covered expenses. HMOs, by statutory definition, *provide* or arrange for the provision of covered services.

To implement PPOs, the insurer can either contract with providers directly or with third party vendors with established networks (often referred to as rented networks). An insurer may even secure the necessary building blocks by contracting directly with an HMO that can sell its network services to an insurer.

As the preceding discussion suggests, PPOs are really hybrids that combine traditional features of indemnity insurance products and the managed care features typically associated with HMOs. As a result of insurance products mimicking HMOs, the once clear distinctions between HMOs and insured plans have become blurred. Indeed, by emulating HMOs, insurers have switched from a passive to an active management of health care, with a direct contractual relationship with providers.

All of these changes take place in a heavily regulated environment. While the alternatives for PPOs are virtually limitless, in the real world the form that these alternatives take is shaped by the preferences of plan sponsors and the restrictions imposed by laws, regulations, and regulatory attitude. Determining what will work requires an understanding of the interplay of a spectrum of laws and regulations, which are discussed in the following section.

To date, approximately 30 states have enacted specific PPO laws or promulgated some form of PPO regulation. Even in states with no PPO law or regulations (New York, for example), insurance regulators have developed informal policies regarding permissible PPO activities. Most state PPO laws and regulations are based on the NAIC Preferred Provider Arrangements Model Act.[3] PPO laws clarify doubt as to the applicability of existing freedom-of-choice or anti-discrimination laws (discussed subsequently) that never contemplated PPOs. In the absence of any express prohibitions, insurers have the right to contract with providers and alter policy provisions to provide benefit incentives for their insureds to use preferred providers. In many states, PPO arrangements operate in the absence of enabling laws and regulations. PPO laws and regulations generally serve to affirm insurers' rights to engage in particular activities, rather than create such rights. The salient feature of most PPO enabling measures is that they regulate and restrict the activities of insurers, generally to afford protection to providers and consumers.

PROVIDER PROTECTIONS

Some state statutes reflect successful efforts of physicians and other health care providers to prevent insurers from excluding from their panel of preferred providers any providers willing to meet the insurer's terms for participation in the panel. For good reason, any-willing-provider laws are not favored by insurers offering PPOs. Restrictions on an insurer's ability to selectively limit its preferred provider panel can pose a serious threat to the effective operation of a PPO. For example, they can undermine the insurer's ability to negotiate volume-based discounts with providers, and impair the insurer's ability to control utilization and assure quality. In addition, if any willing provider is permitted to participate in the preferred provider network, the management of the larger panel can result in increased administrative costs. The majority of states have enacted some form of any-willing-provider law, although in many instances their scope is limited to pharmacies or other provider categories.

---

[3] Note that this Model Act is now archived and no longer actively supported by the NAIC. Still, many existing statutes are based on this Model Act.

Another significant provider protection feature commonly found in PPO laws and regulations is a restriction on differences in benefit levels (usually measured in terms of coinsurance levels) applicable to covered charges of preferred versus non-preferred providers. More than a dozen states have imposed limitations on benefit differentials between preferred and non-preferred providers, generally in the range of twenty to thirty percent, and some reflect successful lobbying efforts by providers to *require* that preferred provider plans reimburse non-preferred providers. By requiring coverage of non-preferred providers, these provisions effectively preclude an insurer from offering an EPA. Some states expressly forbid EPAs. Benefit differentials are, by design, behavior modification devices. Regulatory restrictions on benefit differentials obviously impair an insurer's ability to create incentives for insureds to seek care from preferred providers.

Other provider protection provisions that infrequently show up in laws and regulations include requirements that allied medical practitioners (such as chiropractors, dentists, optometrists) be included in preferred provider arrangements.

CONSUMER PROTECTIONS

Provisions designed to protect participants in preferred provider plans are also reflected in numerous state statutes and regulations. These statutes seek to assure that PPO mechanisms that seek to limit provider choice will, at the same time, assure the availability and access to all appropriate care. Most state statutes require an insurer to assure reasonable access to covered services available under the preferred provider arrangement and an adequate number of preferred providers to render those services. The ACA requires emergency care to be covered at the same benefit level regardless of provider participation. The freedom of insureds to go to any provider is preserved by restrictions on benefit differentials, and largely assures the accessibility and availability of health care services to participants in insured PPOs. EPAs are a different matter. Like an HMO, an EPA severely limits the participant's provider choice. Assuring the availability of, and access to, a full range of health care providers and services is far more important in the EPA context. Not surprisingly, therefore, the few states that expressly recognize EPAs have extensive requirements or review processes (similar to requirements imposed on HMOs) to assure the adequacy and accessibility of health care services available through the EPA. In 2014 and 2015, the NAIC engaged in an extensive overhaul of network considerations, resulting in the Health Benefit Plan Network Access and Adequacy Model Act. While this model act is not prescriptive in terms of methods and metrics due to the great variation in health care delivery throughout the country, it is expected that states will revisit network statutes, since the delegation of the effort to the NAIC from federal regulators was contingent upon success.

A related concern is quality, which is a difficult issue to deal with through regulation. It is relatively easy to assure availability and accessibility by reviewing the number, type, and location of providers. But how do you measure quality? Because it is difficult to measure, legislators and regulators have attempted to deal with it only in general terms in terms of legislation. The ACA requires many[4] of the individual and small group carriers to obtain accreditation from a nationally recognized organization, and to create improvement plans when a low quality score is earned.

---

[4] Exceptions exist for low volume carriers.

OTHER INSURANCE LAWS

Existing anti-discrimination and freedom-of-choice laws have frequently been cited as possible impediments to PPO development, but rarely have they actually impeded PPO development.

Two-thirds of the states have enacted statutes that prohibit insurance policy provisions requiring that a medical service be rendered by a particular doctor or hospital.

"Freedom-of-choice" laws are patterned after an old NAIC model act that did not contemplate PPOs. It was adopted decades ago to address a concern that workers' compensation policies might limit reimbursement to certain physicians and hospitals. The greater the benefit differential, the greater the risk that an insurance regulator may attempt to apply a freedom-of- choice statute. A group insurance policy incorporating an exclusive provider arrangement is vulnerable to freedom-of-choice statutes.

CORPORATE PRACTICE OF MEDICINE

To date, the common law prohibition against the corporate practice of medicine has not been an important consideration for insurers and others in developing PPOs. In part, this may be attributable to the fact that most insurers, and certainly most insurance regulators, are not even aware of the doctrine or because the doctrine has lost its persuasive value. The doctrine evolved because of the public policy concern that corporations may influence the decisions of medical care professionals in their employ. It seems possible that a regulator might invoke the doctrine where, for example, the utilization review or incentive compensation mechanisms in a PPO were seen to influence the decisions of health care professionals. Unlike HMO laws, no state's PPO law contains an exemption from the prohibitions on corporate practice of medicine.

ANTITRUST LAWS

The application of state and federal antitrust laws to various health care delivery alternatives is a complicated subject. Whenever selective contracting arrangements exist involving competitors (in this case, health care providers) and payers, and those contracts deal with issues related to price, the basic ingredients for anti-competitive behavior exist.

While any alternative health care delivery systems like PPOs must be structured with due consideration of the antitrust laws, the fact is that they have not, to date, been a significant impediment to their development. This may be attributable to the care with which various arrangements have been structured. In addition, the courts have been cautious to condemn arrangements that appear to offer lower prices to consumers. Similarly, the Department of Justice and the Federal Trade Commission have, on several occasions in the past, indicated their view that PPOs have a potentially beneficial pro-competitive effect and should, therefore, not be discouraged. However, in 2015, antitrust lawsuits against Blue Cross and Blue Shield insurers were advancing through the federal court system. The suit contends that these insurers avoid competing against one another, driving up customers' prices and pushing down the amounts paid to providers.

Many insurers have attempted to include provisions in their agreements with health care providers guaranteeing that the provider will not afford any more favorable financial terms to any other payer. The so-called "most favored nation" clauses can have a pro-competitive or anti-competitive effect, depending upon the insurer's market share. In the past, federal anti-trust regulators have successfully challenged the use of "most favored nation" clauses by some Blue Cross plans with very high market shares because of their anti-competitive effect. They have the effect of raising cost of all payers. The use of most favored nation clauses became a focus of the Antitrust Division of the Department of Justice in 2011, when it sued one insurer in Michigan and began an investigation of insurers using such clauses in a number of other states.

STATE REGULATION OF HEALTH MAINTENANCE ORGANIZATIONS

Like insurers, HMOs are heavily regulated. Currently, all jurisdictions have laws which regulate aspects of HMO operations. Even in the absence of specific HMO laws, HMOs could be established. However, the absence of specific HMO-enabling laws leaves HMOs subject to general corporation law, insurance or health service corporation laws, malpractice laws, and common law prohibitions on corporate practice of medicine. These laws do not specifically contemplate HMOs and can impair their operation. Thus, the enactment of comprehensive HMO laws has generally promoted the formation and operation of HMOs.

HMO laws vary considerably from state to state. However, nearly 30 states have based their HMO laws on the NAIC Health Maintenance Organization Model Act (originally adopted in 1973). Reviewing this model act serves as a useful framework for examining state regulation.

Only entities meeting the definition of a health maintenance organization are subject to HMO regulation and can derive the benefits of HMO legislation. Most state HMO laws define an HMO along the lines of the NAIC Model:

> *"Health Maintenance Organization" means any person that undertakes to provide or arrange for the delivery of basic health services to enrollees on a prepaid basis, except for enrollee responsibility for co-payments and/or deductibles.*

This definition reflects the fact that an HMO is predicated on three basic principles:

1. It is an organized system that *provides or arranges for the provision of health care services* to enrollees. Unlike insurers, which simply reimburse health care expenses incurred by insureds, HMOs combine the delivery and financing of health care. HMOs accomplish this by establishing relationships with providers. The relationships may either be direct (employing or owning providers) or indirect (independent contractor arrangements).

2. It makes available all basic health services that the enrollee might reasonably require. An entity providing less than all "basic health care services" on a prepaid basis typically will not qualify as an HMO. Moreover, as the name health *maintenance* organization suggests, an HMO emphasizes the promotion of health and the prevention of illness.

3. The payments for coverage are only on a *prepayment* basis, whether made by individual enrollees, employer groups, Medicare or Medicaid.

Most state laws include in the definition of basic health care services preventive care, emergency care, in-patient and out-patient hospital and physician care, diagnostic lab and diagnostic and therapeutic radiological services. At a minimum, an HMO must provide these basic health care services. State laws typically exclude dental services, vision services, mental health or alcohol/substance abuse services, and long-term rehabilitation services from the definition. HMOs are, however, free to supplement their basic mandated coverage with these additional services. Because the definition of basic health care services is so broad to begin with, most HMO laws do not include many of the state mandated benefits commonly applied to insured plans.

REGULATORY OVERSIGHT OF HMOS

The definition of an HMO evidences the fact that the HMO arrangement combines the provision and financing of health care services to enrollees. Thus, HMOs exhibit both provider and insurer characteristics. States have had to grapple with the issue of where HMO regulatory oversight should properly reside. Logically, state health departments are more capable of overseeing the provider aspects of HMO operations and insurance departments are more capable of overseeing the insurer aspects of HMO operations. While the majority of states have resolved this problem by assigning all regulatory responsibility to the insurance regulator, in some cases it is shared by the insurance and health regulators (although the primary responsibility is usually assigned to the insurance regulator).

REQUIREMENTS FOR CERTIFICATE OF AUTHORITY

In order to operate as an HMO, state HMO laws require the HMO entity to secure a certificate of authority. To obtain and maintain a certificate of authority, the HMO must generally submit a detailed filing including the following eight major categories of information that demonstrate initial and ongoing compliance with various ongoing regulatory requirements:

- *A Description of the HMO's organization, governance, and management.*
- *Contracts with Providers.* This includes copies of standard forms of contracts between providers, third-party administrators, and other third-party vendors.
- *Coverage Agreements*
- *Financial Information.* Financial statements and a detailed financial feasibility plan (business plan) demonstrating the viability of the organization are required.
- *Provider Information.* This includes a map or description of the HMO's geographic service area and a list, with addresses, of all providers having employment or contractual arrangements with the HMO. HMOs are also required to give this information to enrollees.
- *Grievance Procedure*
- *Quality Assurance Program*
- *Insolvency Protection Measures*

An area of heightened concern is the potential insolvency of insurers and HMOs. HMOs must satisfy minimum net worth requirements identified in the HMO law, and thereafter continually maintain that minimum net worth. A deposit of cash or securities is usually required. This deposit is made with the regulator or a trustee acceptable to the regulator, and it is required as a reserve against unfunded claims. Additional protections against the risk of insolvency (such as reinsurance or corporate guarantees) are typically required. Many state laws require HMOs to cover the enrollees of other HMOs that become insolvent. Very few states have guaranty funds applicable to HMOs.

HMO Rate Regulation

While some states do not regulate the rates that an HMO may charge, most do. Generally, no rate may be used until a schedule of premium rates or a methodology for determining premium rates has been filed with and approved by the designated regulatory agency. Most state laws regulating rates require simply that premium rates be actuarially sound and that they not be "excessive, inadequate, or unfairly discriminatory." This is the same general requirement imposed on insurance company rates. The ACA established a federal rate review process to determine whether proposed rate increases in the small group market are unreasonable (this will be discussed in more detail in Section Two).

To compete with insured plans, HMOs have desired to experience rate. Following the 1988 amendments to the federal HMO Act, which for the first time allowed federally qualified HMOs to prospectively experience rate specific groups, states began to take a more flexible attitude toward HMO experience rating. The vast majority of state HMO regulators allow HMOs to prospectively experience rate specific groups. Many permit retrospective experience rating, although this seems inconsistent with the basic definition of an HMO as a prepaid arrangement. A minority of states do impose more stringent requirements on rates. New York, for example, generally requires that HMOs community rate.

Financial Regulation

All state HMO laws require the filing of financial statements annually (more frequently in some states). In addition, the majority of states require that annual reports include identification of any material changes in information submitted with the original application for a certificate of authority, as well as information regarding the enrollee population. A number of states also require that the annual report include information regarding grievances, utilization patterns, and other matters. HMOs are subject to periodic examination of their operations by their regulator(s). Most states require that HMOs be examined at least every three years. Approximately one-third of the states subject HMOs to premium taxes or a similar assessment.

Powers

State HMO laws enumerate the powers of HMOs, which typically include the following:

- The purchase, lease, construction or operation of hospitals, other medical facilities and other property necessary for the conduct of the business;
- Transactions with affiliates, such as loans or transfer of responsibility;
- Furnishing health care services through providers, provider associations, or agents or providers which are under contract with, or employed by, the HMO;

- Contracting with third parties for the performance of functions such as marketing, enrollment, and administration;
- Contracting with licensed insurance companies or hospital or medical service corporations for insurance, indemnity, or reimbursement against the cost of health care services provided by the HMO;
- The offering of health care services in addition to basic health care services on a prepaid basis, either alone or as a supplement to basic health care services; and
- The joint marketing of products with a licensed insurer or hospital or medical service corporation.

Most state HMO laws make clear that the powers of an authorized HMO are not limited to those specifically enumerated in the statute. Thus, HMOs can engage in non-HMO activities such as preferred provider arrangements in conjunction with insurers, third party administrators, or plan sponsors. Moreover, most HMOs are corporations or partnerships having a legal existence quite apart from their licensure as HMOs. An entity that is licensed as an HMO, if it is also incorporated, will generally have the power to engage in any business transaction that any other business corporation can under applicable state law. The powers conferred by the HMO law are in addition to those that the HMO entity may have as a general business corporation or partnership. These powers may, however, be limited in the HMO's organizational documents (such as articles of incorporation, charter, partnerships agreement or articles of association).

REGULATION OF PRODUCERS

HMO producers are generally subject to similar or identical licensing requirements as those applicable to insurance agents.

POINT-OF-SERVICE PRODUCT RESTRICTIONS

Following the 1988 amendments to the federal HMO Act, a number of states, by statute, regulation, or regulatory discretion, began to permit HMOs to offer reimbursement for care received outside the HMO's network of providers. These "point-of-service" or "open-HMO" products offer HMOs the ability to compete with insurers and others that offer open access products, such as PPOs. However, some states have questioned whether offering non-emergency care outside the HMO network to indemnity subscribers constitutes engaging in the business of insurance, which would require licensure of the HMO as an insurance company. A growing number of states by regulation, statute, or administrative discretion, have authorized HMOs to begin offering open-HMO products.

CORPORATE PRACTICE OF MEDICINE

State laws restrict the practice of medicine to persons who satisfy various professional licensing requirements that typically include graduation from an accredited medical school, successful completion of residency requirements, and passing a state examination. Because a corporation is incapable of meeting these licensing requirements, the courts have uniformly held that corporations or other non-human legal "persons" are precluded from engaging in the practice of medicine. The corporate practice prohibition evolved because of the public policy concern that corporations may influence the decisions of medical care professionals in their employ. As a provider of medical care services, it is critical for an HMO to be free of the common law prohibitions against the corporate practice of medicine. Thus, Section 27.C. of the Model Law states the following:

> *Any health maintenance organization authorized under this Act shall not be deemed to be practicing medicine and shall be exempt from the provisions of [citation] relating to practice of medicine.*

Many HMO laws incorporate a similar provision. It is important to note that this exemption from the prohibitions on corporate practice of medicine applies to the entity authorized as an HMO, and arguably frees the entity from these strictures even when the entity engages in non-HMO activities. This is important in the development of alternative delivery systems when the HMO provider network is used in a preferred provider arrangement.

ANY-WILLING-PROVIDER LAWS

Health care providers, faced with the threat of being excluded from HMO provider networks, have succeeded in persuading some legislatures to enact various forms of any-willing-provider laws which impair the ability of HMOs to selectively contract with providers. As applied to HMOs, any-willing-provider laws have often been challenged as preempted by ERISA with respect to ERISA-governed group plans. However, in 2003, the Supreme Court indicated that such laws were not pre-empted by ERISA.

STATE REGULATORY FOCUS

While state HMO laws regulate most aspects of HMO operation, most HMO regulators would probably view their chief roles as (a) protecting consumers in those areas where marketplace forces do not offer adequate protection, and (b) establishing and maintaining ground rules for competition among rival entities. The marketplace does not offer consumers protection against the risk of insolvency. Thus, assuring the fiscal solvency of HMOs is a critical focus of HMO regulators. Similarly, the closed delivery systems of HMOs create unique risks for consumers, including a limited choice of providers, gatekeeper mechanisms, and financial incentives for providers that may result in under-treatment or poor quality care. Accordingly, quality assurance and accessibility of care are also major concerns of regulators.

UTILIZATION REVIEW REGULATION

Beginning as early as the mid-1970s, state legislators and regulators began to consider the merits of various forms of utilization review (UR). Until very recently, most legislation and regulation has either been permissive or actually sought to promote UR activities by insurers. Several states were apparently so taken with the promise of various forms of UR services that they actually required insurers to abandon their role as passive indemnitors and include UR provisions in their policies. Florida, for example, enacted a statute that required a health insurance policy to include procedures or provisions to contain health insurance costs, such as UR, and required second opinions for surgery. Nevada enacted the following requirement:

> *The commissioner shall not approve any proposed policy of health insurance unless he determines that the insurer has adopted and is using three or more practices in administering benefits that control or reduce the cost of health care.*

As early as 1976, New York required insurers to cover second opinions for surgery, and other states have enacted measures promoting various forms of cost containment activity. The PPO laws in some states require that the insurer offering preferred provider arrangements have in place standards for assuring appropriate utilization.

By the end of the 1980s, the regulatory environment had begun to change dramatically. By then, virtually all health insurers had incorporated some form of UR into some of their policies, and many had developed the capacity to provide UR services to third parties. In addition, numerous independent companies providing utilization management services had sprung up. Even HMOs began to sell UR services. Utilization management programs proliferated to the point where surveys indicated that, by 1989, half of all large employers included utilization management provisions in their health benefit programs, up from just 5% in 1984.

Utilization management firms had clearly complicated life for hospitals and for physicians, who responded by pushing for regulation of utilization management firms. This provider backlash was first manifested in 1988, when Maryland enacted the first comprehensive law regulating utilization management firms. The Maryland law became a model advanced by hospital associations in other states. By 1998, approximately 35 states had enacted comprehensive UR laws and/or regulations. It is evident that the pendulum has swung away from regulation that promotes utilization management activities. In addition to requiring licensure of firms engaged in providing utilization management services, these new laws have imposed requirements including the following:

- Restrictions on the use of UR procedures and criteria used by firms;
- Restrictions on the type or qualifications of personnel to qualify for licensure to carry out UR;
- Payments to providers for the cost of responding to requests for information;
- Mandates on the hours of operation;
- Restrictions on access to medical information;
- Restrictions on the location at which UR must be performed;
- Burdensome regulatory filings of UR data;
- Requirements that medical necessity denials be made by a physician in the same or similar specialty as the attending physician; and
- Requirements that the physician making the UR determination be licensed in the state where the member resides.

PHARMACY LAWS

Another example of provider backlash to managed care is the enactment of open pharmacy laws backed by state pharmacy associations, typically taking one or more of these forms:

- Any-willing-provider laws, which require the inclusion of any pharmacy willing to meet the HMO's or PPO's terms and conditions.
- Laws directly or indirectly limiting the use of mail order drug firms.

- Requirements that out-of-state pharmaceutical vendors to become licensed in order to do business.
- Laws requiring coverage of certain classes of drugs (or options within a class) be available at favorable coinsurance levels, such as oral chemotherapy, HIV drugs, and other specialty drugs.

Because of their ability to steer members to particular drugs through the use of formularies (restricted lists of drugs that are covered), drug manufacturers have been willing to extend discounts on drugs to hospitals, HMOs and other organizations. Pharmacies do not "steer" business in this way and have been unable to secure similar discounts. They have fought back by lobbying state legislatures to enact "unitary pricing" laws which require manufacturers to offer the same discounts to every purchaser on the same terms. To date, few states have enacted such laws.

RECENT STATE LAW CHANGES

Managed Care "Backlash"

In the late 1990s and early 2000s, state legislatures considerably broadened the scope of regulatory oversight over HMOs, PPOs, and other managed health care plans. One clear trend at the state level was to impose regulation on all facets of HMO operations. Not surprisingly, these reforms focused chiefly on assuring consumer rights and protections, as perceived abuses gained notoriety. The following consumer oriented reforms are illustrative:

- Most states enacted patient protection laws that, among other things, create an external appeal process for appealing plan benefit decisions to an independent third party.
- Several states (including Virginia, Tennessee, and Maryland) enacted laws requiring HMOs to offer point-of-service plans, to assure access to non-network providers.
- Texas and Missouri stripped away the malpractice protection of corporate practice of medicine laws that are enjoyed by HMOs in most states. The Texas legislation has gone further than any other state, in creating a statutory cause of action for failing to use "ordinary care" in denying or delaying payment for care recommended by a physician. Interestingly, other states have gone just as far in court decisions.

Risk Shifting

The various reimbursement arrangements that shift risk away from regulated entities like HMOs and insurers toward unregulated provider entities are a source of concern for state regulators. Such arrangements raise issues regarding sufficiency of capitalization, reserve adequacy, adequate information systems, and sufficiency of administrative capacity. The concern of regulators is that the inability of these unregulated entities to assume risk or added administrative responsibilities can result in the denial of access to medical care and/or disruption in the continuity of medical care for patients.

Existing laws may already deal with some risk shifting arrangements. For example, if a provider group, hospital, or vendor enters into a capitated arrangement with an HMO or insurer for services rendered by it or by other providers, it would seem that it is acting as an insurer or reinsurer, and that it should be regulated as such. Similarly, a provider organization that agrees to provide health care services on a capitated basis may fall within the ambit of the HMO definition in those states where an HMO is defined in terms of providing less than all basic health care services, such as in California and Texas.

A handful of insurance commissioners have issued bulletins reflecting their position on this issue. A minority of the states have regulations or laws that apply to these "downstream" risk arrangements. Typically, they require that financial solvency standards be met by the risk-assuming entity, and that their contracts with group insurers and HMOs be filed. The fact that increasing numbers of risk-assuming provider entities have failed to meet their obligations to pay providers assures that this will be an area of legislative focus in the future. California has advanced this issue furthest, creating new solvency metrics that their provider organizations must at least annually report on, and monitoring the financial position of hundreds of provider organizations who take on risk.

Collective Provider Activities

Physicians complain that they are at a disadvantage when negotiating with large HMOs and insurers over reimbursement and other terms. In response to intense lobbying by the American Medical Association and state medical societies, Texas and New Jersey have enacted laws granting physicians an exemption from state anti-trust laws in order to negotiate on a collective basis with HMOs and insurers.

♦ PART TWO ♦

THE ROLE OF FEDERAL REGULATION

In the McCarran-Ferguson Act, Congress clearly expressed its intent to leave the regulation of the business of insurance to states. In keeping with this intent, until recently, most federal laws did not attempt to directly regulate the activities of insurers and HMOs. Instead, federal laws regulated the activities of employers sponsoring group health plans and the group health plans themselves. That all changed with the enactment of the ACA in 2010, which included health insurance reforms that apply directly to "health insurance issuers" (licensed insurance companies and HMOs) as well as to insured and self-insured group health plans. These federal laws have a profound impact on insurers and HMOs, and are the subject of this section.

THE FEDERAL HMO ACT OF 1973

In 1973, Congress enacted the federal HMO Act to promote the development of the then fledgling HMOs. To accomplish this, the federal HMO Act conferred a number of distinct advantages on those HMOs that met the requirements of the act and, thereby, became "federally qualified." However, HMOs are not required to become federally qualified. In order to obtain the advantages of federal qualification, HMOs must voluntarily comply with the requirements of the Act, but there is no requirement that they do so. In this sense, the federal HMO Act does not really regulate HMOs in the way that state laws do.

ADVANTAGES OF FEDERAL QUALIFICATION

Many of the original advantages of federal qualification under the federal HMO Act were stripped away by 1988 amendments. Congress concluded that HMOs became a viable alternative to insurance and no longer needed the advantages originally conferred. One of the last remaining vestiges of the original act is the "equal contribution requirement." Employers that happen to offer a federally qualified HMO as a benefit option may not financially discriminate against persons enrolling in a qualified HMO. The regulations give five illustrative examples of employer contributions that would be considered non-discriminatory:

- Equal dollar contributions for HMO and non-HMO plans;
- Equal contributions for demographic classes of employees;
- Contributions of an equal percentage of premium for all plans;
- Contributions of a negotiated amount mutually acceptable to the employer and the HMO; or
- If the employer requires employees to contribute to all health plans, it may require employees to make a contribution to a qualified HMO that does not exceed 50% of the employee contribution to the principal non-HMO alternative. This alternative is useful in cases where the HMO would otherwise be available to employees at little or no cost.

Employers must be careful to examine their contribution strategy if they offer coverage through a federally qualified HMO. Any federally qualified HMO can challenge the employer's contribution strategy if it feels that the employer financially discriminates against it. The penalties for non-compliance can be severe – a civil fine of up to $10,000 for the initial violation, and a like amount for each additional month of non-compliance. Enforcement is the responsibility of CMS.

Federal qualification can be an advantage to HMOs desiring to contract with government plans. Federal qualification or qualification as a certified medical plan (as defined in 42 CFR 417) is required in order for an HMO to contract as a Medicare or Medicaid carrier.

The federal HMO Act contains a provision that preempts all state laws which prevent the federally qualified entity from operating as an HMO in accordance with the terms of the federal HMO Act. This preemption may be useful in thwarting state anti-managed care legislation.

Most HMO business involving employer groups is subject to the Employee Retirement Income Security Act (ERISA). ERISA requires that employee benefit plans implement procedures for appealing denied claims for plan benefits. A federally qualified HMO that satisfies the claim appeal requirements in the federal HMO Act is automatically deemed to comply with the somewhat less stringent claim procedures required by ERISA.

DISADVANTAGES OF FEDERAL QUALIFICATION

Becoming federally qualified and maintaining federal qualification means subjecting the HMO to additional regulatory requirements, which may, in some cases, outweigh the advantages derived from being federally qualified. These disadvantages include:

- The necessity of establishing a separate line of business for any non-qualified HMO business (such as insurance, PPO, or third party administration);
- The requirement that specified minimum coverage be offered. This has the effect of a benefit mandate for qualified HMOs. The federal minimum may exceed the state law requirements;
- Restrictions on the use of anything more than "nominal" co-payments, which limits benefit design; and
- Restrictions on rating that may be more restrictive than state requirements.

The once powerful allure of federal qualification has greatly diminished. As a result, some HMOs that were once federally qualified have voluntarily relinquished their federal qualification.

THE EMPLOYEE RETIREMENT INCOME SECURITY ACT OF 1974 (ERISA)

ERISA imposes broad reporting and disclosure requirements on parties (generally employers) sponsoring employee welfare benefit plans.

APPLICABILITY OF ERISA

There is a misconception that ERISA applies only to self-insured plans. In reality, ERISA governs any employee benefit plan established or maintained by an employer or by an employee organization, or by both, to the extent that such plan was established for the purpose of providing the following benefits for its participants or its beneficiaries:

- Medical, surgical, or hospital care or benefits in the event of sickness, accident, disability, death, or unemployment,
- Vacation benefits,
- Apprenticeship or other training programs,
- Day care centers,
- Scholarship funds,
- Prepaid legal services, or
- Any benefit (other than pensions at retirement or death, and insurance to provide such pensions) described in Section 302(C) of the Labor Management Relations Act of 1947.

ERISA applies to these types of plans regardless of whether the group plan is funded by means of a group insurance policy, a group service agreement from an HMO, or is self-insured. Only the following types of benefit plans are exempt from ERISA's requirements:

- Government plans maintained by the federal, state, or local governments or agencies for their employees
- Church plans maintained by a tax-exempt church for its employees
- Plans required by state law, such as worker compensation, unemployment compensation, and (in a few states) mandatory short-term disability insurance

- Plans maintained mainly outside of the U.S., substantially covering nonresident aliens
- Plans covering self-employed persons such as sole proprietors and partnerships.

In view of the fact that ERISA applies to the vast majority of group benefit plans, insurers and HMOs administer such plans to ensure compliance on behalf of their customers.

PLAN OPERATION

The party establishing and maintaining an employee benefit plan (typically an employer or union) is called the plan sponsor. The plan sponsor is responsible for designating a plan administrator that is identified to plan participants as the party responsible for the administration of the plan. Normally, the plan sponsor serves as the plan administrator.

ERISA establishes standards of conduct for plan "fiduciaries." A fiduciary is a party that:

- Exercises any discretionary authority or control respecting management of the plan or disposition of its assets;
- Renders investment advice for a fee or other compensation, direct or indirect, with respect to any moneys or other property of the plan, or has any authority or responsibility to do so; or
- Has any discretionary authority or responsibility in the administration of the plan.

Each plan must designate one individual to act as the "named fiduciary" of the plan, usually the plan sponsor or the plan administrator. However, any party meeting the definition of "fiduciary" is considered a fiduciary, and subject to the rules governing fiduciary conduct. ERISA requires that a fiduciary:

- Act in the sole interest of the plan and for the exclusive purpose of providing benefits to participants and their beneficiaries and defraying reasonable administrative expenses;
- Act with prudence and care in carrying out his or her duties;
- Diversify the investments of the plan to minimize risk and loss, unless circumstances show that this is not prudent; and
- Adhere to the plan documents in discharging its duties.

PLAN DOCUMENTS

The most basic requirement reflected throughout ERISA's various provisions is disclosure. Among other things, ERISA requires that every employee benefit plan maintain written plan documents including a Summary Plan Description (SPD) which must be provided to plan participants. The SPD must be written in a manner that is understandable by the average plan participant, and must disclose to participants the benefits under the plan, the appeal process when a claim for plan benefits is denied, and other information regarding the parties responsible for the administration of the plan. The SPD need not be a single document. Typically, employers treat the insurer's group policy or HMO's group service agreement as the benefit description component of its SPD.

Effective for plan years beginning on and after September 23, 2012, the ACA added to ERISA, and to the Public Health Service Act, a requirement that insurers and HMOs (as well as the employer sponsoring the group plan) provide a summary of benefits and coverage (SBC) to individuals using HHS' uniform template and glossary. The summary must be provided at the time of application for coverage and at re-enrollment. The SBC includes uniform definitions of insurance terms, overall cost sharing (deductible, coinsurance, copayments, and out of pocket maximums) for the plan as well as each essential health benefit category, exceptions, limitations of coverage, examples of common benefits scenarios, contact information for the beneficiary to ask questions, and an Internet address for the beneficiary where a certificate of insurance, provider network, and pharmacy formulary can be viewed.

PREEMPTION OF STATE LAW

ERISA's requirements apply to employee benefit plans, not directly to insurers or HMOs (except to the extent that they are considered plan fiduciaries, in which case the fiduciary standards apply). Nonetheless, because insurance companies and HMOs provide the funding vehicle and administrative services for group plans, there are many opportunities for conflict between the ERISA requirements and the laws regulating insurance companies and HMOs. Congress contemplated these conflicts between ERISA and state law, and included in ERISA a provision (Section 514) stating that ERISA preempts any state law that "relates to" an employee benefit plan. In so doing, Congress recognized that many people were covered by benefit plans of larger employers covering people in multiple states. To ensure the uniform application of these benefit plans for all participants in these plans, the preemption provision was added to insulate plans from inconsistent state laws affecting plan administration. However, mindful of the fact that the McCarran-Ferguson Act left the regulation of insurance to the states, the preemption provision excluded from preemption "any law of any State that regulates insurance." This is known as the insurance "savings" clause. ERISA also makes clear that employee benefit plans shall not be deemed to be insurance companies for purposes of the "savings clause."

As a result of the preemption provision, no state insurance law that regulates the business of insurance may apply *directly* to an employee benefit plan. However, state insurance law can apply *indirectly*, as a result of the plan being funded and administered by an insurance company or HMO that is subject to state regulation. Self-funded plans are not subject to state insurance laws, and the states are prohibited from considering these plans to be insurance companies for the purposes of making state laws apply to them. The fact that stated mandated benefits had to be included if an employer chose to fund its employee benefit plan through an insurance policy or group service agreement created an incentive for employers to self-insure their benefit plans, to escape the additional costs of these mandated benefits.

Smaller employers, too small to self-insure their employee benefit plans, also sought to avoid state mandated benefits by participating in self-funded multiple employer welfare arrangements (MEWAs). States challenged the right of MEWAs to escape insurance regulation under the "deemer" clause, especially after several MEWAs failed. In an attempt to clarify the situation, in 1983 Congress passed the Erlenborn-Burton Act, which defined a MEWA for the first time in ERISA. It allows self-funded MEWAs that obtain an exemption from the Department of Labor (DOL), and are subject to state laws that relate to reserves and contribution levels, to avoid state insurance regulation. MEWAs that do not obtain the DOL exemption are subject to all state laws. As a result of this clarification, state insurance regulators have been more aggressive in requiring self-funded MEWAs to become licensed as insurance companies.

Insurers and HMOs have also attempted to take advantage of ERISA's preemption provision. Attempts by insurers and HMOs to avoid various state laws by application of ERISA's preemption provision have been the source of considerable litigation and an inordinate number of these cases have been decided by the U.S. Supreme Court. For example, state laws imposing punitive damages on group insurers for "bad faith" denials of employee benefit plan claims have been held preempted, meaning insurers are generally exempt from liability for punitive damages for bad faith claim administration of ERISA plans. On the other hand, the Supreme Court has held that state external review laws and any-willing-provider laws are not preempted by ERISA, since these laws directly relate to the state's authority to regulate the insurance business. These laws therefore take precedence over ERISA rules.

CLAIM REVIEW PROCEDURES

ERISA requires that an employee benefit plan establish a reasonable procedure for plan participants to appeal a decision to deny, in whole or in part, a claim for plan benefits. A claim procedure is deemed "reasonable" if it meets the minimum standards for review of a denied claim set forth in the law and regulations promulgated by the DOL. In 2000, the DOL published final regulations that set comprehensive standards for processing claims under ERISA covered plans, establishing timeframes for claim and appeal determinations (which vary depending on whether an urgent, pre-service, concurrent care, or post-service claim is involved) and setting standards for the content of denial letters.

In 2010, the ACA expanded the applicability of ERISA's claim appeal procedures. The procedures apply not only to the group health plan, but also to health insurers (insurers and HMOs). The ACA also added a number of additional requirements:

- An external review process must be implemented to allow claimants to have their claim denial reviewed by an independent review organization, following the final level of internal appeal;
- Appeal notices must be provided in a culturally and linguistically appropriate manner in certain situations;
- Diagnosis and treatment codes must be provided upon request; and
- The definition of adverse benefit determination has been expanded to embrace rescissions of coverage.

COBRA

The Consolidated Omnibus Budget Reconciliation Act of 1985 (COBRA) gives certain persons the right to continue their group health benefits beyond the date that their coverage would otherwise terminate. The entire cost (plus an additional administration fee of 2%) must be paid by the COBRA continuant. Generally, COBRA applies to employers with 20 or more full or part-time employees, though some states extend COBRA provisions to include smaller employers and continue for longer periods. Federal workers have their own continuation law similar to COBRA. State and municipal workers are usually subject to COBRA. Only church plans are exempt from COBRA or COBRA-type coverage extensions. Group life insurance, accidental death and dismemberment, and short or long-term disability coverage are not subject to COBRA requirements.

Under COBRA, coverage may be continued up to 18 months for an employee and covered dependents when coverage terminates due to reduction of hours worked or termination of employment for reasons other than gross misconduct. An individual who is disabled at the time of termination may have COBRA coverage extended to 29 months provided he/she is considered disabled for Social Security purposes, and he/she notifies the plan administrator within 60 days of the Social Security Administration's determination of disability. Coverage is available for up to 36 months for a child who ceases to be a covered dependent, a covered dependent of a deceased employee, a former covered spouse whose coverage ceases due to divorce or legal separation, or a covered dependent when the employee's coverage ceases due to eligibility for Medicare. There are special rules for continuing retired employees and their dependents when the employer declares Title 11 bankruptcy. Coverage may cease before the maximum period is reached, for example in cases where the employer ceases to provide a group health plan, or when the qualified beneficiary first becomes covered under another group health plan or becomes entitled to Medicare, or when the qualified beneficiary fails to pay the COBRA premium on time.

Complete instructions on how to elect continuation must be provided by the plan administrator within 14 days of receiving notice of the qualifying event. Qualified beneficiaries then have 60 days in which to elect continuation. The 60-day period is measured from the later of the date coverage terminates or the date the person receives notice of the right to continue. If continuation is not elected in that 60-day period, the right to elect continuation ceases.

An excise tax of $100 per day for each qualified beneficiary is imposed when the employer fails to comply with COBRA. The tax can be fully or partially waived if the failure to comply is due to reasonable cause and not willful neglect. If the failure was inadvertent, the start of the tax period can be delayed. Also, it will not usually apply if corrected within 30 days and due to a reasonable cause. The maximum tax liability for a plan during a year due to reasonable cause and not willful neglect is the lesser of (1) $500,000, or (2) 10% of the amount paid or incurred by the employer (or trust in the case of multi-employer plans) during the preceding tax year for the employer's group health plan.

CIVIL RIGHTS ACT OF 1964

Both gender and pregnancy discrimination in the workplace are generally prohibited by the Civil Rights Act of 1964, Title VII. This law applies to employers that are engaged in an industry affecting interstate commerce, and employ at least 15 employees for each working day in each of 20 or more calendar weeks in the current or preceding calendar year. The Civil Rights Act was subsequently amended to include the Pregnancy Discrimination Act. This act provides that employers must treat disabilities and medical claims that arise from pregnancy to the same extent as they are treated for any other disability.

AMERICANS WITH DISABILITIES ACT (ADA)

The ADA prohibits employers of more than 15 employees from discriminating based on disability in employment. Employers and labor organizations cannot discriminate against qualified disabled persons regarding the terms, conditions, and privileges of employment, including (among other things) fringe benefit plans, whether or not employer-administered. Insurance plans may continue to underwrite, classify, or administer risks based on state law. Also, an organization's bona fide benefit plan may use these practices whether or not based on state law. However, when the plan is not based on state law, it cannot use the practices as a subterfuge to avoid ADA. Coverage limits are permissible under health care plans, but the plan may not discriminate against disabled participants.

MEDICARE AS SECONDARY PAYER LAWS

When Medicare was enacted, there was a question as to how its benefits would be paid in relation to hospital and medical expense benefit plans. Initially, there was no federal guidance and Medicare was considered the primary payer. After Medicare had paid its benefits, other benefit plans would consider their obligation as secondary payer. Changes in the law over the years have resulted in Medicare being treated as the secondary payer in nearly all situations, other than for retired covered individuals.

THE HEALTH INSURANCE PORTABILITY AND ACCOUNTABILITY ACT OF 1996

The Health Insurance Portability and Accountability Act of 1996 (HIPAA) made reforms in three general areas: insurance portability and availability, health care fraud and abuse prevention, and administrative simplification.

PORTABILITY AND AVAILABILITY REFORMS

To facilitate access to health insurance coverage for individuals who lose group coverage because they change jobs or their employer changes insurers, HIPAA prohibits group health plans, and health insurance issuers providing coverage to groups, from imposing pre-existing condition exclusions in most situations. The ACA now bans pre-existing condition exclusions for nearly every plan and made the individual market available to everyone on a guarantee issue basis, which makes the requirement in HIPAA for providing certification of prior creditable coverage unnecessary, but the ACA did not change HIPAA.

Due to HIPAA, a group health plan, group insurer, or group HMO may not establish eligibility rules or premium levels based on health status-related factors; thus, requiring evidence of insurability is prohibited.

HIPAA requires health insurers and HMOs to accept nearly every small employer group in that state that applies for coverage, and every eligible individual that applies for coverage in the initial enrollment period. Insurers can, however, establish employer contribution and participation rules as conditions of coverage, though the ACA created a one month window

(November 15 through December 15) when all small groups must be accepted, even those that fail to meet the insurer's contribution and participation rules.

HIPAA requires that with certain limited exceptions, group insurers and HMOs that offer coverage in the small or large group market must renew or continue in force such coverage for all groups at the option of the plan sponsor. Under HIPAA, coverage may only be terminated by the insurer or HMO for nonpayment of premiums, fraud or misrepresentation, uniform modification or withdrawal of a particular product from the market, or discontinuance of all health insurance coverage (provided specified notice is given to policyholders). The ACA expanded these consumer protections by requiring guarantee issue in the large group market, reducing the representations that insurers can require (such as financial strength demonstrations and having workers compensation coverage) and reducing the ability for carriers to rescind coverage.

PREVENTING HEALTH CARE FRAUD AND ABUSE

HIPAA established a Health Care Fraud and Abuse Control Program designed to coordinate federal, state and local law enforcement activities to control fraud with respect to *all* "health plans," not just Medicare and Medicaid.

ADMINISTRATIVE SIMPLIFICATION AND PRIVACY

In order to encourage more widespread adoption of electronic data interchange technologies and uniform standards for financial and administrative data, HIPAA directed the Secretary of HHS to adopt standards for electronic information transactions and data elements for such transactions, as well as security standards relating to the transfer of individually identifiable health information; standards relating to electronic signatures and standards necessary for transferring coordination of benefit information. Compliance with these regulations required extensive changes by insurers and HMOs. The objective was to reduce cost in the health care system through the use of uniform data sets and through the increased use of electronic transfers of information.

Final privacy regulations became effective in 2001. These regulations cover all aspects of the health care delivery system, and address the use and disclosure of individually identifiable health care information in any form, whether communicated orally, electronically or in writing. The regulation affords a patient the right to education about privacy safeguards, access to their medical records, and a process for correction of records. It also requires the patient's permission for disclosure of personal information for purposes unrelated to health care. Compliance with the regulations was required by April of 2003. The regulation does not preempt state laws that afford more stringent privacy protections.

NEWBORNS' AND MOTHERS' HEALTH PROTECTION ACT

The Newborns' and Mothers' Health Protection Act of 1996 requires group health plans to extend coverage for hospitalization for childbirth. Health plans must provide coverage for at least 48 hours of hospitalization following a normal delivery, and for 96 hours following a cesarean delivery.

MENTAL HEALTH PARITY

The Mental Health Parity Act of 1996 mandated parity in annual and lifetime dollar limits for mental health benefits and medical-surgical benefits; however, the ACA largely removed lifetime and annual dollar limits from nearly all health plans (mental health and medical/surgical). The act does not specifically require health plans to provide mental health benefits. The law applies to employers with over 50 employees. The law raised debate over whether it encouraged or discouraged plans to include parity between mental health benefits and other health benefits. Proponents claimed it made much-needed coverage more widely available at modest cost. Others believed it increased claim costs substantially and resulted in plans eliminating mental health benefits.

The Paul Wellstone and Pete Domenici Mental Health Parity and Addiction Equity Act of 2008 expanded consumer protections by preventing insured and self-insured group health plans from providing mental health benefits with less favorable cost sharing requirements and visit limits than those used for substantially all medical/surgical benefits. Substance abuse coverage was afforded these parity protects. Standards for medical necessity determinations, and reasons for denial of benefits relating to mental health and substance abuse benefits must be disclosed upon request. The ACA extended parity protections to the small group and individual marketplaces.

THE FAMILY MEDICAL LEAVE ACT (FMLA)

FMLA allows eligible employees to take unpaid leave for specific family and personal situations and applies to employers who employ 50 or more employees, including public agencies and schools. Eligible employees are those who have worked 12 months or more for the employer. An employee may take up to a total of 12 weeks of family medical leave time during a 12-month period.

WOMENS' HEALTH AND CANCER RIGHTS ACT OF 1998

This law requires group health plans to cover post-mastectomy reconstructive surgery.

MICHELLE'S LAW

For group health plans that condition eligibility for employees' dependents on full-time student status,[5] this law generally prohibits the plan from terminating coverage when an enrolled dependent leaves school to take a medically necessary leave of absence.

---

[5] As noted, the ACA now requires group health plans to allow employees' dependent children to remain eligible until age 26 regardless of whether they are full-time students. As a result, Michelle's Law – which was enacted before the ACA – will apply only in rare cases where group health plans allow employees' dependent children to remain covered after they turn 26 so long as they are full-time students.

Genetic Information Nondiscrimination Act (GINA) of 2008

In addition to the HIPAA ban on group health plans discriminating against any *individual* with respect to eligibility or contributions based on genetic information, GINA prohibits group health plans from setting *group* premium or contribution amounts based on genetic information. Additionally, GINA prohibits group health plans from requesting or requiring an individual or family member to undergo a genetic test, and from requesting, requiring, or purchasing genetic information for underwriting purposes.

The Affordable Care Act

In 2010, the ACA ushered in federal regulation of group insurance that is unprecedented in scope and depth. Prior to the ACA, federal regulation of group insurance was indirect. ERISA, COBRA, HIPAA and other federal laws applied to group health plans, rather than directly to insurance companies and HMOs offering group coverage. The ACA applies many of its health insurance reform provisions directly to both group health plans and to the "health insurance issuers" whose group insurance policies and group service agreements fund the group health plans. However, in keeping with the principle underlying the McCarran-Ferguson Act, the ACA allows the states to be the primary enforcers of the private health insurance reform provisions that were added by the ACA. The Department of Health and Human Services is required to enforce those provisions only if a state has substantially failed to do so. The major provisions of the ACA are summarized in chapter 18.

Summary of Federal Regulation

Prior to enactment of the ACA in 2010, federal regulation of group health insurance reflected attempts by Congress to reform the health care system incrementally following the demise of President Clinton's proposal for a national health insurance program in the 1990s. These incremental reforms reflected two trends that presaged the reforms in the ACA. First, Congress began to mandate substantive coverage requirements, a role historically eschewed by Congress since the enactment of the McCarran-Ferguson Act. Second, the federal regulation did not attempt to preempt state regulation but instead attempted to establish a floor on which states could impose additional requirements.

The regulation of group insurance by the federal government has fundamentally changed. The federal government, which previously regulated group health plans but not group health insurers, has now stepped into the role of direct regulation of group insurers and HMOs in collaboration with the states. This will make the job of compliance for group insurers and HMOs more difficult.

TAXATION OF GROUP INSURANCE BENEFITS IN THE UNITED STATES

EMPLOYER-SPONSORED BENEFITS

It is commonly known that favorable tax treatment is available in the U.S. for most employer-provided insurance coverage. One of the themes of U.S. tax law, however, is that favorable tax treatment is only available when detailed requirements are satisfied. Therefore, this chapter will explore not only the favorable tax treatment, but also some of the more important requirements for obtaining it. Tax law in the U.S. comes from a variety of sources and changes frequently. Therefore, this overview is, by necessity, filled with generalities that may not apply to every particular situation.

Employer-provided insurance coverage is a form of compensation. In the U.S., compensation is generally subject to income and employment taxes at both the state and federal levels. The general rule is that the form compensation takes (cash, property, or anything else of value) does not affect how it is taxed. Therefore, unless a special rule or exemption applies, the fair market value of all forms of compensation is subject to state and federal income and employment taxes on an annual basis. All of the types of insurance coverage we will explore here are subject to special rules or exemptions, providing for more favorable tax treatment than the general rule. Because the favorable tax treatment is only available if the related requirements are satisfied, it is important to know the default rule that applies in the case of noncompliance. An understanding of the general rule is also necessary to appreciate the value of the special rule or exemption.

Health Coverage

No form of compensation is more tax-favored than health benefits. In most cases, the employer is entitled to a current tax deduction for the expenses as they are incurred, but the value of the benefits (both the coverage and the proceeds) is forever free from income and employment taxes. This makes health benefits not only more tax-favored than cash (generally deductible and subject to income and employment taxes as it is paid), but also more tax-favored than retirement benefits (which is generally deductible as contributions are made and sometimes exempt from employment taxes, but subject to income taxes as amounts are distributed). Moreover, whereas there are strict limits on the amount of tax-favored retirement benefits that may be provided, currently there are no comparable limits on the value of an employee's tax-favored health benefits.[6]

To appreciate the significance of the tax advantages of employer-provided health coverage, it is not enough to compare health benefits to other forms of compensation. It is also necessary to compare employer-provided health benefits to health coverage obtained outside the employment context. Suppose, for example, that an employer does not offer health benefits. If the employees obtain health insurance on their own, they likely will receive no tax benefit. For many years, only expenses in excess of 7.5% of adjusted gross income have been deductible for U.S. federal income tax purposes. Beginning in 2013, that percentage generally became 10%, but this increase does not take effect until 2017 for individuals age 65 and older. Therefore, if an individual under age 65 with adjusted gross income of $100,000 pays $10,000 for health

---

[6] Under ACA, an excise tax on annual health plan costs that exceeds $10,200 for single coverage ($27,500 for family coverage) is scheduled to begin in 2018. For this purpose, cost is based on averages (or insurance premiums, if the plan is insured), as opposed to the health costs incurred or expected for any particular person.

insurance premiums, copayments, and other medical expenses in 2013, he or she likely will receive no tax deduction. Moreover, even if he or she were to pay $12,000 (thereby giving a $2,000 deduction), that deduction would likely only be available for income tax purposes; no matter how much was spent, the employment tax liability probably would not be affected. The tax rules are more favorable for self-employed individuals without access to an employer health plan (such as from an employed spouse's employer), but they are still significantly less favorable than for employees with employer-based coverage. Self-employed individuals generally may deduct all of their health insurance premiums, without having to apply the 7.5% or 10% limits. However, deductions for any additional expenses they incur, such as copayments and coinsurance, would be subject to those limits. And, once again, this deduction generally would not be available for employment taxes.

The favorable tax treatment of employer-provided health coverage generally applies to insured as well as self-insured plans, so long as they satisfy the applicable requirements. In general, the requirements for insured and self-insured plans are the same. Perhaps the most important requirement is that insurance cover only "medical expenses." A detailed definition of that term is beyond the scope of this chapter. For our purposes, suffice it to say that major medical, dental, vision, and prescription drug expenses are all included. Some examples of expenses that generally do not qualify are vacations and gym memberships.

An important difference between the requirements for insured and self-insured plans is the extent to which highly compensated employees may receive more generous benefits than other employees. If a self-insured plan impermissibly discriminates in favor of highly compensated employees (HCEs), then some or all of the benefits provided to the HCEs may lose their tax-favored status. The tax-favored status of other employees' benefits would not change. Historically, there has been no such requirement for insured plans. As a result, it became very common for employers with self-insured health plans to offer more generous insured plans to their most senior employees. As part of the ACA, Congress extended the self-insured plan nondiscrimination rules to cover insured plans, but the consequences of HCE discrimination are different. There is no tax consequence to any employee; instead, the employer must pay an excise tax. In light of the numerous uncertainties surrounding this new rule, the IRS and the Treasury Department have issued guidance providing that the insured plan nondiscrimination rules will not apply until further notice and that employers will be given time to comply once detailed rules are released. As of September, 2015, the delay was still in effect and guidance still had not been released.

It is not only the employee's own personal medical expenses that may be provided on a tax-favored basis. An employee's spouse and dependents (as defined in the rules) also may receive these benefits. Under the ACA, children of an employee may receive tax-favored benefits through the end of the year in which they turn 26, regardless of their tax dependency status. In some cases, either state law or the employer's independent business judgment will cause an employer to provide coverage to someone whose benefits are not eligible for tax-favored status. Two common examples are adult children and domestic partners. In those cases, the employer must determine the value of the benefits provided and treat them as taxable wages to the employee (not the individual receiving the benefits).

Some health insurance plans are designed with an account associated to the coverage, in an effort to encourage the patient to seek cost effective treatments. Customarily, this account is associated with a high deductible plan, and helps the employee pay for claims falling below the deductible (or coinsurance and copayments). A Health Reimbursement Account (HRA) is notional in that it is not an actual account with money in it, but rather a recordkeeping device. While the account seems separate from the insurance, it is generally the insurance policy that is covering the claims. The value of the HRA is part of the overall insurance policy and is treated for tax purposes in the same favorable way.

Health Savings Accounts (HSAs) are another common type of account. Unlike HRAs, HSAs are a separate entity from the insurance policy. HSAs can accept contributions from the employee or the employer, and the account is portable from year to year, as well as when the employee terminates employment. HSAs receive optimal tax treatment, as the employee contributions reduce taxable earnings when contributed, employer contributions are not recognized as earnings, and if the withdrawals are used to defray medical expenses, the withdrawals also escape taxation and penalties. Many HSAs provide investment choices after a certain minimum account value is reached; capital gains also escape taxation and penalties if used for approved medical expenses. There are annual contribution limits that apply to the overall amount from both the employee and employer (for 2016, the annual contribution limit was $3,350 for individuals and $6,750 for families). Annual contributions are allowed only in years when covered by an eligible high deductible plan. Rollovers of unused account values are unlimited, and are not forfeited upon termination of employment, nor if the person chooses an ineligible insurance plan in the future.

The ACA created many tax implications, assessments, penalties, and tax incentives for employers. An overview of the major provisions of the ACA is provided in chapter 18, though employer financial implications are briefly summarized below:

- Employer Mandate: Employer responsibility in the ACA includes penalties for not offering coverage, particularly to those employees who enroll in the individual market and receive premium tax credits. Effective January 1, 2015, employers with 50 or more full-time employees must offer coverage or pay a fee of $2,000 per full-time employee (excluding the first 30 employees from the assessment). The penalty is adjusted based on the number of employees who receive a premium tax credit. Employers with less than 50 full-time employees are exempt from this penalty.

- Small Business Tax Credits: Employers with 25 employees or fewer, and average annual wages of less than $50,000, can receive a tax credit if they purchase health insurance for employees through the SHOP exchange. Beginning in 2014, employers are required to contribute at least 50% of the total premium cost. The maximum credit is 35% of the employer's contribution, available to employers with 10 or fewer employees and average annual wages of less than $25,000. The credit phases out as firm size and average wages increase.

- Excise Tax for High-Cost Health Plans: Effective January 1, 2018, employer-sponsored health plans with aggregate values that exceed $10,200 ($27,500 for family coverage), are subject to a tax of 40% of the excess cost over the threshold. This excise tax is commonly referred to as the "Cadillac" tax. The tax is imposed on the issuer of the policy (the plan administrator or employer). The thresholds will be indexed in the future.

- Transitional Reinsurance: The ACA established a temporary reinsurance program to operate on behalf of the 2014 through 2016 benefit years to reimburse insurers for claims related to the costs of "high risk individuals" in the individual market. The program is funded through fees paid by health insurers and self-funded employer plans.

- Retiree Drug Subsidy: An employer alternative to offering group Part D plans is called the Retiree Drug Subsidy (RDS), where groups receive a partial rebate based upon their retirees' actual drug costs in the employer's own pharmacy plan. The ACA removed the income tax exemption of RDS starting in 2013, such that many taxable employers discontinued RDS in favor of the Part D alternative.

- Patient-Centered Outcomes Research Institute (PCORI): PCORI was established to identify research priorities and conduct research that compares the clinical effectiveness of medical treatments. The institute is funded through a temporary annual assessment paid by health insurers and employers with policy years ending after September 30, 2012, and before October 1, 2019.

Group Term Life Insurance

The tax treatment of group term life insurance is very similar to that of health insurance. The employer is generally entitled to a current deduction for the expenses it incurs to provide the benefit, and both the coverage and the insurance proceeds are generally free from income and employment taxes. Unlike health benefits, however, the amount that may be provided tax-free is limited for most tax purposes. The longstanding limit is the cost of $50,000 of death benefit. Employer-paid premiums for coverage in excess of that amount are taxable to employees in the form of imputed income.

As with health benefits, there are nondiscrimination requirements. Thus, impermissibly discriminatory benefits provided to a key employee may lose their tax-favored status. Unlike health benefits, only an employee may receive tax-favored group-term life insurance; coverage for spouses and dependents would be taxed as compensation to the employee.

Disability Insurance

The tax treatment of employer-provided disability insurance is very different from other types of insurance. In effect, a choice is available. To the extent the value of the coverage (in the case of an insured plan, this is basically the premium) is treated as taxable compensation, the proceeds paid to disabled individuals would not be taxable. To the extent the value of the coverage is not treated as taxable, the proceeds would be taxable. It is common for employers to allow employees to make this choice individually. Regardless of the choice made, the employer's expenses generally are deductible as they are paid.

To qualify as disability insurance, benefits must be payable only for personal injury or sickness. For tax purposes, there is no distinction between short- and long-term disability.

Long-Term Care Insurance

For many years, the tax treatment of long-term care insurance was uncertain. In particular, there was disagreement concerning the extent to which proceeds could be viewed as paying for medical expenses, and therefore should obtain the same tax-favored status as health insurance. Congress clarified the rules in the 1990s; coverage under a "qualified long-term care insurance contract" is deemed to be health insurance and eligible for the same tax-favored treatment. Recognizing that long-term care expenses include the costs of housing and other personal expenses that generally are not deductible, Congress imposed numerous requirements on "qualified long-term care insurance contracts." Among other requirements, proceeds may only be used to pay for services that are required by a chronically ill individual (an annual certification is required by a licensed health care practitioner), and they must be provided pursuant to a plan of care prescribed by a licensed health care practitioner.

Cafeteria Plans

In the context of employee benefits, the word "cafeteria" is meant to evoke the idea of choice. A cafeteria plan offers employees a choice between taxable and nontaxable forms of compensation. Perhaps the simplest example of a cafeteria plan would be one providing employees a choice between cash (a taxable benefit) or health insurance (a nontaxable benefit). But a cafeteria plan could be far more extensive, allowing employees to choose among a variety of taxable and nontaxable benefits. Without a cafeteria plan, employees offered this choice would be taxed as if they chose the most valuable taxable benefit, even if they actually chose nontaxable benefits. A cafeteria plan does not create tax-favored status for any particular benefit; it merely prevents the tax-favored status of a benefit from being lost because a taxable benefit was available as an alternative. In effect, cafeteria plans are what allow employees to contribute toward the costs of coverage on a pre-tax basis: employees choose to receive nontaxable benefits in lieu of cash, and the cash that they could have received but did not is not taxable.

Not surprisingly, cafeteria plans must comply with detailed requirements. The plan must be in writing, and there are separate nondiscrimination rules for highly compensated and key employees. If the nondiscrimination rules are violated, then the individuals receiving the impermissibly discriminatory benefits must pay tax on the most valuable taxable benefit available under the plan, even if they chose tax-favored benefits. Employees are generally permitted to make their elections only once per year, but in some cases (such as marriage or the birth of a child) a mid-year change may be allowed. Only certain nontaxable benefits may be available. These include health, group-term life, dependent care, and disability benefits. Some benefits, however, may not be offered even if they are treated as taxable benefits. One example is long-term care insurance.

Flexible spending arrangements (FSAs) are a popular feature in cafeteria plans. They allow employees to elect (before the beginning of a year) to reduce their taxable compensation by an amount. That amount is then available for them that year, to pay for a particular nontaxable benefit. There are three types of FSA: health, dependent care, and adoption assistance. If an employer sponsors more than one type, employees must elect which FSA they are contributing to, and contributions from one type may not be used to pay any other benefits. For example, an employee may be given the opportunity to elect in November whether to contribute to a health FSA or a dependent care FSA (adoption assistance FSA's are uncommon) the following year. If the employee elects to contribute $1,300 to each, then $100 will be withheld from each biweekly paycheck the following year, but the maximum distribution for the year from the health FSA would be $1,300 and the maximum distribution from the dependent care FSA would be $1,300. Therefore, if the employee incurs $2,000 of dependent care expenses and only $600 of medical expenses the following year, then $700 cannot be paid from the health FSA.

All FSAs are subject to certain requirements, such as the requirement that employees substantiate the expenses they incur (by submitting receipts, for example). There are annual limits on how much can be contributed to FSAs (for 2015, $2,550 for health FSAs, $13,400 for adoption assistance FSAs, and $5,000 for dependent care FSAs). In an effort to help pay for federal costs of the ACA, a health FSA annual contribution limit was introduced in 2013.

Starting in 2011, the ACA also disallowed the use of health FSAs for over the counter medicines, unless specifically prescribed by a doctor. Historically, any amount that was not used each year was forfeited, rather than carried forward. In 2013, the IRS allowed employers to adopt either a 75 day grace period for using up the entire account, or allow up to a $500 rollover without a deadline. Health FSAs are also subject to a rule that allows employees to be reimbursed anytime during the year for the entire amount they have elected to contribute, even if the total amount that has been withheld from their pay is not enough to cover the expense.

Prefunding Benefits

In the early 1980s, Congress significantly decreased the amounts eligible for tax-favored treatment under qualified retirement plans. In response, some tax advisors suggested that taxpayers, especially small businesses, use welfare benefit plans instead. Congress quickly became aware of this strategy and enacted rules to limit employers' tax deductions for prefunded welfare benefits.

Because they were intended to be anti-abuse rules, the deduction limits for prefunded welfare benefits are very broad. Although it is common to think of these rules as applying to tax-exempt trusts known as VEBAs (Voluntary Employees' Beneficiary Associations), they apply to virtually any entity used to prefund welfare benefits. Therefore, the rules refer generically to "welfare benefit funds" rather than specifically to VEBAs. Likewise, the term "welfare benefit" is defined very broadly to include not only medical benefits, but also severance, disability, and life insurance. In fact, any benefit that is not restricted stock, or a U.S. or foreign retirement plan, generally is a "welfare benefit" under these rules.

Congress generally limited an employer's deduction for welfare benefits to the expenses actually incurred during the year. For most types of welfare benefits, the only additional deduction permitted is for claims that have been incurred during the year but have not yet been paid by the end of the year, plus the associated administrative claims. For other types of welfare benefits, however, Congress recognized that prefunding was appropriate. Retiree medical benefits, for example, may be funded on a tax-deductible basis over employees' working lives. Regardless of whether a VEBA or a taxable welfare benefit fund is used for this prefunding, tax may be generated by the assets held in the fund.

Over time, changes in the health insurance market and the tax rules have eroded the tax advantages of prefunding. In some cases, however, a VEBA or taxable welfare benefit fund may still be necessary or advisable.

17 REGULATION IN CANADA

Nicola Parker-Smith

In Canada, insurance companies are governed by various Insurance Acts at both the federal and provincial levels, as well as numerous provincial regulations, industry guidelines and codes of business standards. At the federal level, the 1992 Insurance Companies Act consolidated the Canadian and British Insurance Companies Act and the Foreign Insurance Companies Act. In addition, it included other matters previously covered in the Canadian Business Corporations Act relating to the governance of insurance companies. This chapter provides a brief overview of the Canadian regulatory infrastructure and major legislation applicable to insurers and group insurance.

FEDERAL REGULATION

Federal legislation applies to companies that choose to be licensed federally because they operate in more than one province and deals primarily with matters relating to financial soundness, solvency, investment limitations, and corporate powers. This legislation is subject to review every five years.

The Office of the Superintendent of Financial Institutions (OSFI) is responsible for supervising federally regulated life and health insurance companies, including assessing their safety and soundness, material risks, quality of risk management, and corporate governance policies. OSFI monitors the financial and economic environment for the potential impact on these institutions, and it provides input into developing legislation, regulations, and accounting and actuarial standards. OSFI issues guidelines pertaining to these regulations and standards, and it incorporates them into the regulatory framework.

The Financial Institutions Supervisory Committee including OSFI, the Bank of Canada, the Department of Finance, the Canada Deposit Insurance Corporation and Financial Consumer Agency of Canada refine regulatory requirements and promote sound risk practices.

In ensuring financial soundness, OSFI measures capital adequacy by applying the Minimum Continuing Capital & Surplus Requirements (MCCSR) guidelines. Insurance companies are expected to maintain a target capital level of 150% or more of their MCCSR requirement, with a minimum requirement of 120 % of MCCSR. Capital is comprised of Tier 1 (or Core Capital) and Tier 2 (or Supplemental Capital). OSFI expects each financial institution to maintain ongoing Tier 1 Core Capital at 105%.

The capital requirements are determined as the sum of five risk components: asset default risk, mortality/morbidity/lapse risk, changes in interest rate environment risk, segregated funds guarantee risk, and foreign exchange risk.

Insurance companies are required to provide corporate and financial information to OSFI on a regular basis. Certain rules apply to the valuation of assets as well as the basis for reserve liabilities. With the 1992 Insurance Companies Act, a shift took place toward reporting on generally accepted accounting principles basis. The Canadian Institute of Actuaries has developed standards of practice for the valuation of policy liabilities of life insurers, which provide guidelines in determining reserve liabilities.

OSFI developed a Supervisory Framework in 1991 and updated it in 2010. The framework outlines a process for assessing safety and soundness of regulated financial institutions. OSFI reports annually to the Minister of Finance on the safety and soundness of financial institutions and their compliance with legislation.

In September, 2012, OSFI released a regulatory framework which included upcoming initiatives affecting life insurance companies. These initiatives included enhancing guidance on governance, promoting Own Risk and Solvency Assessments (ORSA) and incorporating the use of internal models in the determination of regulatory capital requirements. OSFI also committed to an in depth review of regulatory capital requirements.

A provincially incorporated company comes under provincial authority for its powers as a corporation as well as its contracts and authority to transact business. For a federally incorporated company, its contracts and authority to transact business come from provincial law. An insurance company incorporated outside Canada must obtain a federal license to operate, but its contracts and authority to transact business are subject to provincial law. More than 90% of the premium income in Canada is sold through companies that are federally registered.

PROVINCIAL REGULATION

PROVINCIAL INSURANCE ACTS

Each province has enacted legislation affecting the operation of insurance companies and the activities of agents and brokers. This includes the licensing and marketing of insurance company products, standards of competence for insurance agents, and consumer protection. Provinces have attempted to keep their respective insurance legislation uniform to avoid inconsistencies. For example, Quebec has adopted reforms with the objective of greater harmonization and standardization with federal companies, to improve the stability of provincial companies and to assist such companies in their future growth. All provinces continue to pursue further harmonization.

The provincial Insurance Acts cover many aspects of group life and health insurance, including the following:

- Rights and obligations of insured and beneficiary,
- Designation of beneficiaries,
- Content of contracts and member certificates,
- Administration of contract including payment of premiums,
- Payment of claims,

- Requirements on termination, and
- Requirements on takeover or change of carrier.

In Quebec, legislation requires that employers extend a given level of prescription drug coverage to employees who are residents of Quebec if the employer is offering other health related benefits. The legislation requires employer sponsored prescription drug coverage to pay at least 67.5% of the cost of each prescription and 100% of the cost of prescriptions in a year which exceed $1,006 for each insured adult. The legislation includes a requirement for all insurers doing business in Quebec to share in the risk through a pooling mechanism. As a result, an industry pooling plan was created requiring the pooling of drug claims for employers with less than 3,000 employees.

GROUP INSURANCE GUIDELINES

Guidelines established by the Canadian Life and Health Insurance Association (CLHIA) provide the consistent standards and practices for group insurance. The guidelines apply to life and accidental death and sickness (including health and dental) insurance. Where provincial legislation covers matters dealt with in the guidelines, such legislation takes precedence over the guidelines. The guidelines include the following:

- *Group Insurance Plan Description for Members.* Requires an insurer to issue to each member a plan description which outlines the principal benefits and conditions under the contract, including exclusions and limitations, termination conditions and rights, and claims procedures.

- *Conversion/Continuation Privileges.* Describes the conditions under which an insurer must continue life insurance coverage on an individual. Every contract of group insurance must permit conversion to an individual policy without evidence of insurability prior to age 65, both in the case of employment termination as well as the termination of the plan up to $200,000 (for Quebec, $400,000). Conversion can be to a one-year term plan, term to 65, or to any individual contract of insurance under any regular plan then being issued by the insurer. The premium paid by the member would be the premium then in effect for individual insurance. In the event a plan that contains a disability provision is terminated, insurance for any person disabled at the time of termination is to be continued as if the plan was still in effect. Group health insurance contracts do not have to provide conversion privileges.

- *Change of Insurer.* Rules regarding replacement of a group contract are designed to ensure that no member loses coverage or has to re-qualify for certain coverages solely because of not being actively at work on the date the replacing coverage comes into effect. Outstanding benefits are paid either under the old contract or the replacing contract, depending on the financial arrangements that have been made.

- *Coordination of Cost-of-Living Adjustments in Government Plans.* The disability benefit payable to an insured under a contract of group insurance is not to be reduced because of a government sponsored plan's (or other support program's) cost-of-living adjustment occurring after the date on which the benefit becomes payable under the terms of the contract. In addition, there are guidelines pertaining to the hierarchy of coordination of benefits (such as which party pays primary versus secondary).

- *Creditor's Group Insurance.* The guidelines with respect to creditor's group insurance have been developed to assist insurers in protecting the interests of debtors insured under group insurance contracts and in response to concerns that have been expressed by consumers and regulators.

While the CLHIA guidelines are not enforceable by law and are still considered voluntary, CLHIA members are expected to follow the guidelines during their normal course of business.

OTHER GOVERNMENT LEGISLATION

HUMAN RIGHTS

Human Rights legislation has been in place in most provinces since 1970. Generally, any business or industry registered or incorporated in a province is governed by the Human Rights Code of that province. In Ontario, the Employment Standards Act applies as well as the Human Rights Code. The federal government has authority to regulate certain types of businesses, such as banking, transportation, communications, and radio and television broadcasting. Federally regulated industries are governed by the Canadian Human Rights Code. Human Rights legislation is considered "fundamental," so it will often take precedence over any other legislation that may conflict. Individuals may not make private contracts in which they agree to waive the rights accorded by Human Rights Statutes.

The intent of the legislation is to provide equal treatment without discrimination in several areas of daily life, including housing, employment, and the provision of goods and services to the public. Employee benefits, such as life and health plans, are considered to be "a term or condition of employment," and insurance contracts are characterized as "goods or services to the public."

Characteristics such as sex, age, marital and family status, mental and physical handicap, and criminal conviction are "prohibited grounds of discrimination" frequently found in the codes of many jurisdictions. Statutes, however, may contain explicit exceptions to the various prohibited acts and bases of discrimination. This permits, for example, employer contributions to a group insurance plan to vary by age or sex, in order to provide equal benefits. Regulations and guidelines for employee benefits passed in conjunction with Human Rights Acts also make further exceptions to the act's protection, defining with more precision which groups the act may not apply to and which activities do not come within the scope of the act.

The Ontario Human Rights Commission released a report that urges the insurance industry to avoid discrimination in its pricing and risk assessment on the basis of genetic testing. This could limit an insurer's ability to apply a preexisting condition clause.

Most Human Rights Acts are administered by locally appointed commissions, which investigate individual complaints and attempt to settle them by negotiation. If settlement fails, a Board of Inquiry may be appointed to hear both sides. The Board's decision may be appealed to the appropriate court.

Human rights codes reflect changing social conditions. As a result, they are frequently amended with new grounds of prohibited discrimination and new definitions coming into force, and existing grounds are tested before the courts.

EMPLOYMENT STANDARDS ACTS

The Labour or Employment Standards Acts set out the rights and responsibilities of both employees and employers, including minimum wage, hours of work, overtime pay, paid public holidays, vacation entitlement, leaves of absence, pay equity, and termination notice and severance pay.

Most jurisdictions have group termination provisions requiring the employer to give notice to the Minister of Labour in the event that particular numbers of employees are terminated at the same time or within a specified number of weeks. The length of notice period depends on the number of employees terminated, and ranges between 8 and 16 weeks.

Changes to the Employment Standards Act in Ontario eliminated the ability of employers to suspend disability benefits during maternity leave. Employers and insurers who provide benefit plans are required to deliver the same level of benefit to individuals who are experiencing a health related absence from work due to pregnancy as they do for other health related absences.

LABOR LEGISLATION — CHILD CARE LEAVE OF ABSENCE

All jurisdictions have labor legislation requiring employers to provide unpaid maternity leave to qualifying employees and to protect their jobs while away on leave. The legislation also prohibits an employer from terminating an employee solely because of pregnancy. The employee must have worked for that employer between 5 and 12 months in most provinces to qualify for leave ranging from 17 to 52 weeks.

The labor laws of several jurisdictions require employers to provide unpaid child care leave to fathers of newborns or to adopting parents.

PRIVACY LEGISLATION

The federal government passed privacy legislation in April of 2000. This legislation is intended to balance an individual's right to privacy of personal information with the need of organizations to collect, use, or disclose personal information for legitimate business purposes. Rules to ensure organizations advise individuals about their intent to collect and use personal information and to obtain consent are set out in the Personal Information Protection & Electronic Documents Act (PIPEDA). PIPEDA, which has been fully effective since 2004, applies to personal information collected, used, or disclosed by all organizations engaged in commercial activities. For organizations under federal jurisdiction, PIPEDA also applies to the personal information of employees. This legislation applies to all provinces without similar legislation. Quebec, Alberta, and British Columbia have introduced similar privacy legislation.

Ontario, Alberta, Saskatchewan, and Manitoba have passed specific privacy legislation for health care providers that protect the confidentiality of personal health information.

Demutualization

In 1999, the federal government passed legislation allowing mutual life and health insurance companies to demutualize. The legislation required that the insurance company remain widely held (no individual can hold more than 10% of the shares of a company) for two years following demutualization. This was known as the transition period. In 2001, legislation was passed which set December 31, 2001 as the end of the transition period for demutualized companies. After this date, companies with equity of less than $5 billion were eligible to be closely held, while those with more than $5 billion must continue to be widely held, but investors could now purchase up to 20% of voting shares. Large banks are not permitted to acquire or merge with large demutualized insurance companies, and vice versa.

The legislation also allowed life and health insurance companies access to the Canadian Payments System, enabling them to offer payment and other services to customers. The Financial Consumer Agency of Canada enforces consumer-related aspects of the legislation.

In March, 2015, the federal government announced plans to set up a regulatory framework for property and casualty mutual insurance companies to demutualize.

Government Programs

Employment Insurance

Canada's Employment Insurance is a federal benefit program governed by the Employment Insurance Act (EI) and administered by Service Canada. The Employment Insurance Act, which was fully implemented in January 1997, was a fundamental restructuring of the old Unemployment Insurance Act 1971. As federal legislation, EI is applied consistently throughout Canada, with special variations on eligibility and benefit durations due to regional levels of unemployment. In 2006, Quebec introduced the Quebec Parental Insurance Plan, which replaces the Federal Employment Insurance Plan for maternity, parental and adoption benefits.

The legislation requires employers and employees to contribute premiums. As of January 1, 2015, the weekly employee contribution is $1.88 per $100 of insurable earnings, subject to a maximum annual earnings of $49,500. The weekly contribution rate for employers is 1.4 times the employee premium or $2.632 per $100 of insurable earnings. In Quebec, the weekly contribution effective on January 1, 2015 is $1.54 for employees and $2.156 for employers per $100 of insurable earnings. Also effective on January 1, 2015, the weekly contribution to the Quebec Parental Insurance Plan is $0.559 for employees and $0.782 for employers per $100 of insurable earnings, to a maximum annual earnings of $70,000. EI compensates employees for interruptions of earnings caused by unemployment, illness, and the birth or adoption of a child. More than one type of special benefit (maternity, parental, or sickness) may be claimed within one benefit period, up to a maximum of 50 weeks.

- *Regular Benefit.* To be eligible for regular benefits, an individual must have worked between 420 and 700 hours within the qualifying period of the last 52 weeks, or since the start of their last claim, if shorter. The number of hours depends on the region's unemployment rate. Eligibility generally also requires at least 490 hours in the 52 week period prior to the qualifying period (attachment period). The basic benefit rate is 55%

of average insured earnings to a maximum, but may be adjusted if an individual has drawn regular benefits in the past. Regular benefits are paid from 14 to 45 weeks. The maximum EI benefit is $524 per week. Individuals can usually earn up to $50 per week or 25% of their weekly benefit (whichever is higher) without affecting their EI benefit. Over this amount, the EI benefit is adjusted dollar for dollar.

- *Sickness Benefit.* To be eligible for sickness benefits, an individual must have worked and paid EI premiums for at least 600 hours in the last 52 weeks, or since the start of the last EI claim. Also, regular weekly earnings must have decreased by more than 40%. The basic benefit rate is 55% of average insured earnings up to a maximum of $524 per week. If an individual is in a low-income family with children and receives the Child Tax Benefit, the benefit rate could be higher, but subject to the same maximum benefit. EI is second payer and the benefit is reduced by the amount of disability payments received from group insurance for sickness or loss of income. The benefit is paid for a maximum of 15 weeks after a two-week waiting period.

- *Maternity Benefit.* Pregnant women who have worked a minimum of 600 hours in the past 52 weeks, or since the start of their last claim, are eligible for benefits. The benefit amount is the same as for the Sickness Benefit. The 15 weeks of benefit can be taken up to eight weeks before birth is scheduled but cannot be received later than 17 weeks after the baby is due or born, unless the infant is confined to a hospital.

- *Parental Benefit.* Parental benefits can be collected for up to 35 weeks by either natural or adoptive parents while they are caring for a newborn or adopted child. Benefits are only available within the 52 weeks following the child's birth, or for adoptive parents, from the date the child arrives home. Eligibility requirements and benefit amounts are the same as the maternity benefits.

- *Compassionate Benefit.* Compassionate benefits are payable for up to six weeks to a person who has to be absent to care for a gravely ill family member at risk of dying within 26 weeks. Other eligibility requirements and the benefit amount are the same as those for the sickness benefits.

- *Special Benefits for Parents of Critically Ill Children.* Benefits are payable for up to 35 weeks to a parent who has to be absent from work to provide care for a critically ill or injured child. Other eligibility requirements and the benefit amount are the same as for the sickness benefits.

- *Supplemental Unemployment Benefit (SUB).* An employer may set up a SUB plan to add to EI's payments under the unemployment, sickness, pregnancy and/or adoption benefits. Services Canada must approve the SUB plan prior to its implementation and has established detailed requirements for a qualifying plan. Without approval, payments are considered earnings for EI purposes, and will be deducted from any benefits paid to employees.

Special eligibility requirements and benefit provisions apply to self-employed fishers.

WORKER'S COMPENSATION

Worker's compensation (WC) is a program regulated by each province's Worker's Compensation Act, providing benefits to an employee or the employee's family in the event of injury, illness, or death arising from or in the course of employment. Benefits include loss of income payments, survivor benefits, and health care benefits. WC acts apply to most businesses, and cover approximately 70% to 90% of the workforce. Boards or commissions in each province administer the act and determine a claimant's eligibility for benefit payment. Employers pay the entire cost of WC by their contributions to the compensation fund. Most classes of industry participate in collective liability, and are assessed contribution rates on the basis of all injuries related to that collective class of employers. Private insurers are not involved in insuring WC benefits.

WC legislation establishes mandatory coverage for most industries. All full-time or part-time employees of industries with coverage are eligible for benefits. Executive officers, partners, and sole proprietors in covered industries are not automatically covered, but may apply for coverage. Any individual covered by WC loses the right to sue an employer for injuries resulting from employment.

WC loss of income benefits are based on salary and are payable to compensate for earnings lost during the period the injured worker is unable to work. Most compensation schemes have a waiting period between the injury date and the commencement of eligibility of benefits. Once the waiting period has elapsed, benefits in many cases are backdated to the date of injury. Most short-term disability (STD) and long-term disability (LTD) benefits are reduced directly by WC benefits. Benefits continue until the injured is no longer impaired or reaches age 65. Loss of retirement income benefits may be available at age 65.

A benefit for non-economic loss may be available for claimants suffering a permanent impairment.

Survivor benefits generally include an immediate lump sum, funeral costs, transportation of the deceased when required, a monthly pension, and lump-sum payments on remarriage. The monthly pension payments in many provinces are earnings related. They are generally set at 80% to 90% of the deceased worker's net average earnings for a sole dependent spouse, and from 10% to 15% of earnings for a dependent child. There is a maximum on covered earnings, which varies by province.

All provinces pay the cost of medical care arising from a WC claim for as long as it is needed. For these cases, no benefits are payable under insured health plans.

CANADA/QUÉBEC PENSION PLANS

The Canada/Québec Pension Plans (C/QPP) are contributory, earnings-related Government programs providing retirement pensions and supplementary benefits. The supplementary benefits include surviving spouses' pensions, surviving children's benefit, allowance for survivors, disability pensions, benefits for the disabled contributor's children, as well as a death benefit. Almost all working Canadians are covered by the C/QPP, with few exceptions.

The employee and the employer make matching contributions. In 2015, this is 4.95% of the employee's salary and wages, up to the Year's Maximum Pensionable Earnings (YMPE) of $53,600 reduced by the Year's Basic Exemption (YBE), which has been frozen at $3,500. Self-employed people pay the combined contribution of 9.9%.

The standard age for CPP to begin is 65. However, a reduced pension is available beginning at age 60 or an increased pension is available for a delay in payments, up to age 70. A person between ages 60 and 70 who is working and contributing to CPP and receiving a pension from CPP or QPP may be eligible for a post retirement benefit. The benefit amount is dependent on age, earnings and the level of CPP contributions.

CPP contributors under age 65 are eligible for a disability pension if their mental or physical disabilities are "severe and prolonged," such that they cannot support themselves by regular employment at any job. QPP contributors under age 65 are eligible for the disability pension if their disabilities are severe and permanent.

Although practices vary, an insured LTD benefit is normally reduced by the basic disability benefit under the C/QPP. Generally, benefits for dependent children are not a direct offset to the LTD benefit but are included in the "all source" maximum. Cost-of-living increases in C/QPP are not taken into account for benefit payment purposes, as mentioned earlier.

Medical adjudicators determine eligibility for disability. To qualify for the CPP disability benefit, there must have been contributions in four of the last six years, or three of the last six years if the claimant contributed for at least 25 years. The disability benefit is made up of a flat monthly amount and a component related to earnings. Benefits are paid to recovery, death, or age 65, after which it is replaced by a retirement pension. The retirement benefit is based on the YMPE at the time disability occurs and then indexed to CPI until age 65. To qualify for the QPP disability benefit, there must have been contributions in two of the last three years in the contributory period, or in five of the last ten years in the contributory period, or in 50 % of the total years in the contributory period of not less than two years.

Survivor benefits are payable to survivors of contributors who have met the requirement of the minimum qualifying period. Survivors who are at least 35 years old, or less than 35 and either disabled or with dependent children, are entitled to the CPP benefit. The amount of the benefit is dependent on age, contributions of the deceased, and other CPP benefits received by the survivor. QPP survivors are entitled to a benefit which varies by age, contributions of the deceased, retirement pension of the deceased, whether or not the survivor supports dependent children, whether or not the survivor is disabled, and other QPP benefits received by the survivor.

The financial state of CPP is reviewed every three years. Recommendations are based partly on the results of an actuarial review by the Chief Actuary. Legislation requires that the Chief Actuary prepare an actuarial report whenever a bill is introduced that has a material impact on estimates in the actuarial review.

The most recent review, effective at December, 2012, confirmed that the CPP is financially sound.

AUTOMOBILE INSURANCE

In Canada, automobile insurance is governed by various provincial acts and regulations as well as by CLHIA Guidelines. Most auto insurance policies have a common structure and common provisions. Accident benefits, which include medical, funeral, rehabilitation, and loss of income compensation, must be included in auto insurance in most provinces. An auto insurer is required to compensate the accident victim first, before any finding of fault. Benefits are similar to those provided under employer sponsored group plans, so coordination of benefits is used to avoid duplication. Unfortunately, this practice does vary by province. In most cases, a group disability plan pays first, with the auto insurer paying only if the benefit does not meet the minimum statutory amount.

PROVINCIAL MEDICAL PLANS

All provinces have their own medical and hospital plans. Private insurance plans are designed to supplement these provincial plans. The services covered by private plans vary by province, and it is the provinces that decide what can be covered. Standard contracts exclude expenses for which benefits are payable under a government plan. When claims are paid, the assumption is made that a claimant is covered by a provincial plan. To the extent that the full cost of a service is not covered by a provincial plan, the balance can be insured where permitted.

There has been considerable cost shifting from provincial medical plans to private insurance health care plans, as health care costs have increased at rates that exceed rates of general inflation. As a result of rising health care costs, the federal government and many of the provincial governments are evaluating the health care system and continue to implement health care reforms.

TAXATION

INCOME TAXES

The Income Tax Act of Canada governs the taxation of employee benefits. Interpretation Bulletins published by Revenue Canada (Taxation) explain how the law will be administered. Section 6 of the Act outlines all the amounts that are included as income from employment for tax purposes. Paragraph 6(1)(a) provides for certain exclusions, including employer contributions to a deferred profit sharing plan, an employee life and health trust, a group sickness or accident insurance plan, private health services plan, supplementary unemployment benefit plan, or group term life insurance plan and benefits under a retirement compensation arrangement, an employee benefit plan or an employee trust.

All employer contributions for group life insurance premiums are considered taxable income to an employee. Death benefits paid under a group life insurance plan are not included in a person's income for tax purposes when settling their estate, nor are such benefits considered taxable income to the beneficiary.

Premiums paid by an employer on behalf of an employee for loss of income benefits (STD & LTD) are not taxable to the employee if the benefits are provided under a group sickness or accident plan, private health services plan, or supplementary unemployment plan. The tax status of any loss-of-income benefits depends on who has paid the premiums. In the case of an employee-pay-all plan, the benefits paid are not taxable to an employee. Where the employer has made a contribution, the benefits are taxable regardless of the amount of the employer contribution. When loss-of-income benefits are taxable, an employee is allowed to deduct contributions made to the plan by the employee before the end of the tax year.

Except in Québec, premiums paid by an employer on behalf of an employee to a supplementary health plan or a dental plan are not included in the employee's income for tax purposes. Premiums paid by the employee may be included in medical expenses to determine the amount that can be deducted for tax purposes. Any benefits received under a health or dental plan are not taxed.

Some social benefits must be repaid if net income for the year exceeds a certain level. This is done through the tax system and applies in the case of Employment Insurance benefits and the Old Age Security pension.

SALES TAX

Québec imposes a 9% sales tax on all insurance premiums. In the case of self-funding administrative-services-only (ASO) arrangements, the tax is applied to the claims paid. Expenses of operating the plan are taxed at a rate of 9.975%. The tax is applicable to employees who reside in Quebec.

Ontario assesses an 8% Retail Sales Tax on group insurance premiums and ASO equivalents, except for employer-funded ASO disability plans. Any person residing or conducting business in Ontario is required to pay tax on group life and health premiums. For plan sponsors, the tax is based on where the employee reports to work each day. In the case of self-funded arrangements, the tax base depends on whether the plan is considered as being funded. To be funded, contributions must be sufficient to cover benefits and expenses foreseeable and payable within the next 30 days. The sales tax is applied to the contributions for a funded plan, and to the claims plus expenses for an unfunded plan.

Manitoba assesses retail sales tax on group insurance premiums for group life, accidental death & dismemberment (AD&D), critical illness and disability insurance plans. The retail sales tax rate in 2015 is 8%. This tax is applicable to employees who reside in Manitoba.

PREMIUM TAXES

All provinces impose premium taxes on group life and accident and sickness insurance premiums. The tax is applied to the gross premiums paid, less any dividends that are declared. Premium tax rates in effect on March 1, 2015 are as follows:

Region	Premium Tax Percent
Newfoundland	4.00%
Prince Edward Island	3.50%
Québec	3.48%
Nova Scotia, Saskatchewan, North West Territories, Nunavut	3.00%
Other provinces	2.00%

In Ontario, ASO plans for life, medical and dental benefits and Health Care Spending Accounts are subject to premium taxes assessed on premium equivalents. ASO employee paid disability plans are subject to premium taxes assessed on benefits paid. In Quebec and

Newfoundland, all ASO plans and Health Care Spending Accounts are subject to premium taxes assessed on premium equivalents.

GOODS AND SERVICES TAX

Group insurance premiums are exempt from Canada's Goods and Services Tax (GST), as are most services provided for under a group insurance policy. Administrative fees paid under a self-insured plan are subject to GST. Where a self-insured plan has an insurance element, such as stop-loss coverage, the stop loss fees paid under the self-insured plan are exempt from GST. The GST rate in effect on January 1, 2015 is 5%.

In Ontario, Prince Edward Island, Newfoundland, New Brunswick, and Nova Scotia, the GST and the provincial sales tax have been harmonized and are referred to as the Harmonized Sales Tax (HST). Administrative fees paid under an ASO plan are subject to HST where services are rendered. HST rates in effect on January, 2015 are as follows:

Region	HST Percent
Ontario, New Brunswick, Newfoundland	13%
Prince Edward Island	14%
Nova Scotia	15%

ASSURIS

Assuris is a consumer protection plan established to protect both policyholders and group certificate holders against the loss of benefits due to the insolvency of an insurance company. It is administered by the CLHIA, and is funded by most of the insurance companies operating in Canada. In the event of an insolvency, the plan provides for coverage: (1) up to $200,000 or 85% of the promised death benefit, whichever is higher for life insurance, (2) up to $60,000 or 85% of promised health expenses, whichever is higher for health benefits, and (3) up to $2,000 per month or 85% of the monthly income benefit, whichever is higher for disability benefits. In order to deal with various issues that arise, Assuris, formerly known as CompCorp, incorporated its own insurance company.

GENERAL SUMMARY

The following tables provide a summary of government benefits, effective January 1, 2015 (unless otherwise stated). Note that some of the benefits are adjusted quarterly to reflect increases in the cost of living.

Summary of Government Benefits

I. Canada/Québec Pension Plan (2015)

	CPP	QPP
Year's Maximum Pensionable Earnings	$53,600.00	$53,600.00
Year's Basic Exemption	3,500.00	3,500.00
Maximum Contributory Earnings	50,100.00	50,100.00
Maximum Contributory Earnings	50,100.00	50,100.00
Maximum Employer/Employee Contribution (4.95% each of contributory earnings for CPP; 5.25% each of contributory earnings for QPP)	2,479.95	2,630.25
Death Benefit		
Maximum Death Benefit	2,500.00	2,500.00
Maximum Monthly Spouse's Pension		
(age less than 45)	581.13(1)	865.19(2)
(age 45 but less than 65)	581.13	865.19
(age 65 or older)	639.00	639.00
Monthly Orphan's Pension	234.87	234.87
Disability Benefit		
Maximum Monthly Contributor's Pension	1,264.59	1,264.56
Monthly Children's Pension	234.87	74.57
Maximum Monthly Retirement Benefit (age 65)	1065.00	1065.00
Maximum Monthly Post Retirement Benefit	26.63	n/a

1. Benefits are not payable to survivors under age 35 who are not disabled or who do not have dependent children
2. Maximum monthly pension for survivors under age 45 who are not disabled but have dependent children is $831.89; maximum monthly pension for survivors who are not disabled and have no dependent children is $518.68

II. Employment Insurance (2015)

All Provinces except Quebec

Maximum Insurable Earnings	
per week	$ 951.92
per annum	49,500.00
Maximum Annual Contribution	
Employee (1.88% of insurable earnings)	930.60
Employer (1.4 times employee contributions)	1302.84
Maximum Weekly Benefit	
Regular Claimants (55% Benefit)	524.00

Quebec

Maximum Insurable Earnings	
per week	$ 951.92
per annum	49,500.00
Maximum Annual Contribution	
Employee (1.54 % of insurable earnings)	762.30
Employer (1.4 times employee contributions)	1067.22
Maximum Weekly Benefit	
Regular Claimants (55% Benefit)	524.00

III. Worker's Compensation

Province	Maximum Earnings Covered *	Weekly Benefits for Temporary Disability	Maximum Monthly Benefits for Permanent Disability
B.C.	$78,600	90% average net earnings	90% average net earnings
Alberta	95,300	90% net earnings	90% net earnings
Sask.	65,130	90% net earnings	90% net earnings
Manitoba	121,000	90% net earnings	90% net earnings
Ontario	85,200	85% net average earnings	85% net average earnings
Québec	70,000	90% net income	90% net income
N.B.	60,900	85% net income	85% net average earnings
N.S.	56,800	75% net earnings for 26 weeks, 85% after	75% net earnings for 26 weeks, 85% after
P.E.I.	52,100	85% of net earnings	85% net average earnings
Newfoundland	61,615	80% net earnings	80% net earnings
N.W.T. & Nunavut	86,000	90% net earnings	90% net earnings
Yukon	84,837	75% gross earnings	75% gross earnings

* According to figures available as of June 2015.

IV. Old Age Security

(Effective July 1, 2015)   Maximum Monthly Benefit Level

Basic Benefit	$ 564.87
Allowance	1,072.74
Allowance for Survivor	1,200.98
Guaranteed Income Supplement (GIS)	
Single	765.93
Spouse – non pensioner	765.93
Spouse – pensioner of allowance recipient	507.87

OAS pensioners with annual income that exceeds $72,809 in 2015 must repay part or all of their OAS pension. Pensioners with annual income greater than $117,123 are required to repay their entire OAS pension. Allowance benefits cease when annual income exceeds $31,680. Similarly, GIS payments cease when annual income exceeds $41,088.

V. Taxation of Employee Benefits

Government Plan	Employee Contributions Tax Deductible?	Employer Costs Tax Deductible by Employer?	Employer Contributions Taxable to Employee?	Benefits Received Taxable to Recipient?
C/QPP	Yes	Yes	No (1)	Yes
Old Age Security				
Basic Benefit	N/A	N/A	N/A	Yes
Spouse's Allowance	N/A	N/A	N/A	No
GIS	N/A	N/A	N/A	No
Employment Insurance	Yes	Yes	No (1)	Yes
Worker's Compensation	N/A	Yes	No	No
Provincial "Medicare" Plans	No	Yes	Yes	No
Group Life				
Member	No	Yes	Yes	No
Dependent	No	Yes	Yes	No
Group AD&D	No	Yes	No (4)	No
Survivor Income Benefit (2)				
Combined Coverage	No	Yes	Yes	Interest element only
Group Health (Medical and Dental)	No (2)	Yes	No (4)	No
Group Income Replacement (STD and LTD)	No	Yes	No	Yes (3)
Salary Continuance (sick pay)	N/A	Yes	N/A	Yes

(1) Taxable benefit is conferred if employer pays employee's portion, but employee can claim the corresponding amount as a tax deduction.
(2) Employee contributions deductible only under allowable medical expense deduction.
(3) Benefit is not taxable (a) if employee-pay-all policy, or (b) until benefit payments exceed an employee's contributions.
(4) Employer contributions to Group AD&D and Group Medical and Dental plans are taxable to employees in Quebec.

VI. Provincial Health Care Programs

	Monthly Premium Rates		
Province	Adult	Adult plus one dependent	Adult plus two dependents
British Columbia (2014)	$69.25	$125.50	$138.50
Quebec, Ontario, Alberta	Premium is per adult, dependent on income and collected through income tax returns		
Other Provinces	No premiums are required		

18 THE AFFORDABLE CARE ACT

Elaine T. Corrough
Sara C. Teppema

In 2010, the health insurance landscape in the United States was permanently altered with the passage of the Affordable Care Act. The Patient Protection and Affordable Care Act (P.L. 111-148), enacted March 23, 2010, and the Health Care and Education Reconciliation Act of 2010 (P.L. 111-152), enacted March 30, 2010, are referred to in this text collectively as "The Affordable Care Act" or ACA. Most provisions of the law were upheld in a series of four rulings by the U.S. Supreme Court in 2012. Other challenges to the law have been raised, but as of this writing, the law is largely intact.

This chapter is intended to provide a summary of the ACA's major provisions of interest to practicing actuaries. Other chapters of this book provide more detailed technical examinations of specific provisions.

INTRODUCTION

The ACA was intended to improve access to affordable quality health care in the U.S. The law includes a wide array of initiatives to achieve that goal, including improving access to health care coverage (insurance), defining the role of public programs, and improving the quality and efficiency of health care. Several measures are written in the form of amendments to the Public Health Service Act (PHSA) or Internal Revenue Code (IRC). These initiatives vary in terms of timing, including effective dates, temporary versus permanent application, and transitional allowances. There are many variations between finalized rulings and the original law; actuaries practicing in this area should review recent rulings for any changes.

The implementation of ACA provisions since its enactment has been guided by regulations and guidance from the Department of Health and Human Services (HHS), and more specifically for actuaries, the Center for Medicare and Medicaid Services (CMS) and Center for Consumer Information and Insurance Oversight (CCIIO). Guidance is generally reflected in proposed and final rules issued by HHS, as well as frequent presentations, articles, and online seminars explaining those rules. On an annual basis, HHS releases the Notice of Benefit Payments and Parameters, which provides specific implementation rules and figures related to ACA provisions. Further, health insurance is generally regulated at the state level; state regulatory agencies and departments of insurance also issue guidance specific to plans offered in their respective states. Finally, certain entities, such as the Secretary of HHS and the National Association of Insurance Commissioners (NAIC), participate actively in the implementation of various provisions.

Individual and Group Market Reforms

Improving Coverage

The first part of the ACA targeted immediate improvements in health care coverage for all Americans, and was implemented by September 23, 2010, six months after the enactment of the ACA. Provisions in this portion included the following:

- Expanded Dependent Coverage: All individual and group plans must cover dependent children up to age 26.

- Limits on Rescissions: Insurers are prohibited from rescinding coverage except in cases of fraud.

- Restrictions on Lifetime and Annual Coverage Limits: No individual or group plans may impose lifetime coverage limits. Further, plans may impose annual limits only for non-essential health benefits, though this requirement was graded in through 2014. Grandfathered plans (see below) are exempt from this requirement.

- Preventive Care Coverage: Services rated A or B by the U.S. Preventive Services Task Force, including immunizations, must be covered at 100% (that is, without any patient cost sharing). Grandfathered plans (see below) are exempt from this requirement.

Medical Loss Ratio

Provisions related to an insurer's Medical Loss Ratio (MLR) are characterized in the act as "bringing down the cost of health care" (Title I, Subtitle A, Sec. 1003.) Starting in plan year 2010, health plans were required to report MLRs – the proportion of premium dollars spent on clinical services, quality, and other costs. Starting in 2011, plans must provide rebates to consumers if the MLR is below 85% for large group plans (101 employees or greater), or 80% for small group (100 or fewer employees) and individual plans. Beginning in 2014, the MLR is calculated based on each of the past three years of premiums and claims. Calculation of the MLR is guided by detailed formula requirements promulgated by HHS, including which specific items should be included in the numerator and denominator of the ratio.

Premium Rate Reviews

Provisions related to premium rate reviews are characterized in the act as "ensuring that consumers get value for their dollars." The ACA specifies that the HHS Secretary must establish a process for reviewing annual increases in health plan premiums and require plans to justify "unreasonable" premium increases. The ACA also requires states to report on trends in premium increases and recommend whether plans should be excluded from the exchanges based on unjustified premium increases.

The ACA directs HHS to assist with effective rate review and set forth grants to states to establish medical reimbursement data centers, to support developing fee schedules, and to provide consumer information. As of April, 2012, over $12 billion had been awarded across states through ACA programs since the law's passage in March, 2010. Approximately one third of the amount, or about $4 billion, was awarded to state and local governments; the remainder went to private entities.

EARLY RETIREE REINSURANCE PROGRAM (ERRP)

The first part of the ACA included immediate actions to preserve and expand coverage. Among these initiatives was the early retiree reinsurance program (ERRP). Starting in June, 2010, $5 billion was appropriated to finance a temporary reinsurance program for employers providing health insurance coverage to retirees over age 55 who were not yet eligible for Medicare in order to partially reimburse employers for high-cost claimants. (ACA Sec. 1102) CCIIO discontinued enrollment in the ERRP in early 2011, and suspended reimbursements to plan sponsors in September 2012, as the program approached the $5 billion appropriation limit.

NATIONAL HIGH-RISK POOL

Until 2014, when insurers were required to offer coverage to individuals with pre-existing conditions, previously uninsurable individuals who had been uninsured for at least six months could receive subsidized coverage through a temporary, national high-risk pool.

HEALTH INSURANCE MARKET REFORMS

This section outlines general market reforms. Among these are several rating requirements which went into effect on January 1, 2014. First, no health plan may impose a pre-existing condition exclusion to limit or deny coverage based on health status. Plans and wellness programs may not impose any rules for eligibility based on health status, medical condition, claim experience, receipt of health care, medical history, genetic information, evidence of insurability, disability, or other health status-related factors.

Second, under the ACA's provision for "fair health insurance premiums," rate variation is only allowed based on certain items:

- Age: limited to a 3:1 ratio of the highest rated age band (64 and older) to age 21;
- Geographic rating area: with area boundaries established by each state, while area factor relativities are determined actuarially by each health plan;
- Plan design and network relativities (referred to as "pricing actuarial value"); and
- Tobacco use: with smoker rates limited to 1.5 times the nonsmoker rates.

Premiums may also vary based on family composition.

Third, all health plans in the individual and small group market are required to provide policies on the basis of guaranteed issue and guaranteed renewability; that is, they must accept every employer and individual in the state that applies for coverage (except in certain limited cases).

Fourth, waiting periods for coverage must not exceed 90 days.

Finally, the concept of essential health benefits (EHBs) is introduced as a requirement for comprehensive health insurance coverage. This concept is covered next.

ESSENTIAL HEALTH BENEFITS

Starting January 1, 2014, all qualified health benefits plans offered inside or outside the exchanges, for individual and small group plans, are required to offer an essential health benefits package. Grandfathered plans, discussed in the following section, are exempt from this requirement. Essential health benefits must include at least the following general categories, and items and services covered within these categories:

1. Ambulatory patient services
2. Emergency services
3. Hospitalization
4. Maternity and newborn care
5. Mental health and substance use disorder services, including behavioral health treatment
6. Prescription drugs
7. Rehabilitative and habilitative services and devices
8. Laboratory services
9. Preventive and wellness services and chronic disease management
10. Pediatric services, including dental and vision care

As with many other provisions of the ACA, coverage details for these categories vary by state. The law does not prohibit insurers from providing coverage for other categories in addition to the EHBs. Some states have mandated benefits that extend beyond the EHBs.

GRANDFATHERED PLANS

Effective September 23, 2010, existing group and individual plans could be grandfathered with their current plan provisions unchanged. However, grandfathered plans were required to extend dependent coverage to adult children up to age 26, are prohibited from issuing rescissions of coverage, and are required to eliminate lifetime limits on coverage. Grandfathered plans were also required to eliminate pre-existing condition exclusions for children. Beginning January 1, 2014, in addition to the requirements above, grandfathered plans were required to eliminate annual limits on coverage, pre-existing condition exclusions for adults, and waiting periods for coverage of greater than 90 days. As of this writing, no date has been set for expiration of grandfathered status, though a plan can itself lose this status if material plan design or coverage changes are made.

In March, 2014, the federal government announced that non-grandfathered plans could continue through 2016, subject to state allowance, as "transitional plans" not yet subject to the design, coverage and rating allowance changes that took effect in 2014. Many states allowed transitional plans, though some of those states did not allow the full length of the span permitted by federal guidance.

QUALIFIED HEALTH PLANS AND EXCHANGES

One of the most visible components of the ACA is the creation of new marketplaces (exchanges) where individuals and small employers can purchase health insurance coverage. The ACA also established requirements for a health plan to be deemed a "qualified health plan" (QHP), which itself is a requirement for participating in the newly created exchange marketplaces.

Under the ACA, each state, via a governmental agency or separate nonprofit organization, was required to create an American Health Benefit Exchange for individuals and Small Business Health Options Program (SHOP) Exchanges for businesses with up to 100 employees (50 in 2014 and 2015). Exchange marketplaces were implemented beginning January 1, 2014. Insurers participating in the exchanges are subject to all the insurance market reforms listed in the above section.

States have had flexibility with respect to implementing the exchange marketplaces. The forms of marketplaces (and the number of states employing each form, as of this writing) are as follows:

- State-based marketplace: States running a state-based marketplace are responsible for performing all marketplace functions. Consumers in these states apply for and enroll in coverage through marketplace websites established and maintained by the states. (14 states)

- Federally-supported state-based marketplace: States with this type of marketplace are considered to have a state-based marketplace, and are responsible for performing all marketplace functions, except that the state will rely on the federally facilitated marketplace IT platform. Consumers in these states apply for and enroll in coverage through heatlhcare.gov. (3 states)

- State-partnership marketplace: States entering into a partnership marketplace may administer in-person consumer assistance functions and HHS will perform the remaining marketplace functions. Consumers in states with a partnership marketplace apply for and enroll in coverage through healthcare.gov. (7 states)

- Federally facilitated marketplace: In a federally facilitated marketplace, HHS performs all marketplace functions. Consumers in states with a federally facilitated marketplace apply for and enroll in coverage through healthcare.gov. (27 states)

To support the ongoing sustainability of these marketplaces, the ACA sets forth certain requirements that apply to all participants, as described below.

COST-SHARING REQUIREMENTS

Plans sold through the exchanges, and non-grandfathered plans in the individual and small group markets sold outside of the exchanges, must cover EHBs, must have an out-of-pocket limit at or below the Health Savings Account (HSA) limit, and must fall into one of the "metal" levels described below. In addition, insurers may offer through the exchanges a catastrophic plan, generally available to those under age 30. The ACA also defines cost-sharing as including all copayments, deductibles, and coinsurance paid by the insured individual, in contrast with the earlier common practice of excluding copayments from applying towards out-of-pocket maximums. All non-grandfathered plans sold inside and outside of the Exchanges must fall into one of the following benefit categories:

Plan type	Metal Target Actuarial Value
Platinum	90% of total allowed costs of benefits
Gold	80% of total allowed costs of benefits
Silver	70% of total allowed costs of benefits
Bronze	60% of total allowed costs of benefits

Plans must be within +/-2% of the target actuarial value in order to comply with the metal requirements. Grandfathered plans and large employer-sponsored plans do not have to meet the metallic standards. The tool used to determine actuarial value is produced by HHS, standardized and currently used consistently across the U.S.

SINGLE RISK POOL

For purposes of setting premiums, health insurers must consider all enrollees in all health plans (other than grandfathered plans) offered by the insurer in the individual market to be members of a single risk pool. This includes enrollees covered in plans outside the exchange. Similarly, insurers must consider all small group enrollees from all plans, including plans outside the exchange, in a single small group risk pool. Some states have chosen to merge the individual and small group markets into one single risk pool.

OTHER EXCHANGE PROVISIONS

Exchanges are subject to a number of requirements in terms of governance, reporting and consumer interfaces. Insurers participating in exchanges must meet qualification requirements with respect to networks, marketing, reporting, and consumer assistance. Quality is to be rewarded through market based incentives, such as payment structures that reward such activities as prevention of re-admissions, patient safety improvement, reduction of health care disparities, quality reporting, and other activities.

Exchanges may also offer Consumer Operated and Oriented Plans (CO-OPs) offered by nonprofit, member-run health insurance companies that were granted federal low interest rate loans to provide initial funding for expenses and required capital. Exchanges often offer Multi-State Plans (MSPs) managed by the Office of Personnel Management (OPM). MSPs were established by the ACA, which directed OPM to contract with private health insurers to offer qualified health plans to individuals and small businesses in more than one state. These plans are required to offer a benefit package that is uniform in each state, includes essential health benefits, meets the metal level requirements, and complies with market rating rules.

ALTERNATIVE PROGRAMS

States have the option to create a Basic Health Plan for uninsured individuals with incomes between 133-200% of the federal poverty level (FPL) who would otherwise be eligible to receive premium subsidies in the exchange. States offering a Basic Health Plan receive 95% of the funds that would have been paid as federal premium tax credits and cost-sharing reductions, subject to certain restrictions. Minnesota is the only state thus far offering a Basic Health Plan.

RISK MITIGATION FOR INSURERS IN THE EXCHANGE MARKETPLACES

Mechanisms known colloquially as the "Three Rs" were included in the ACA as a means of mitigating risk for health insurers entering the marketplaces. These are the transitional reinsurance program, the transitional risk corridors program, and the permanent risk adjustment program.

TRANSITIONAL REINSURANCE

The ACA established a transitional state-based reinsurance program to operate in benefit years 2014 through 2016. The reinsurance program provides reimbursement to insurers for claims related to the costs of "high risk individuals" in the individual market, and it is represented in the final rule as reimbursement of a certain percentage of individual claims costs above a given threshold and below a maximum cap. The program is funded through fees paid by health insurers and self-funded employer plans.

TRANSITIONAL RISK CORRIDORS

For the 2014 through 2016 benefit years, HHS maintains a risk corridor program for the individual and small group markets. The program compares a plan's actual costs to target costs, and the plan will either pay a portion of a gain or collect a portion of a loss, according to a defined schedule. Payments to those with losses are expected to be offset by collections from insurers with gains.

RISK ADJUSTMENT

Starting in 2014, a permanent risk adjustment mechanism assesses a charge to health plans whose actuarial risk is below average, and provides payments to health plans whose risk is above average in the individual and small group market (excluding grandfathered plans). States have the option to develop their own risk adjustment program (subject to HHS approval) or participate in the federal risk adjustment program. Thus far, only Massachusetts uses its own risk adjustment program. The ACA's risk adjustment program is described in more detail in Chapter 33.

PREMIUM AND COST-SHARING ASSISTANCE

PREMIUM SUBSIDIES FOR INDIVIDUALS

Effective January 1, 2014, premium credits and cost-sharing subsidies became available to certain individuals and families with income below certain limits. Employees are not eligible for premium credits if their employer offers coverage, unless that employer plan does not have an actuarial value of at least 60%, or if the employee share of the premium exceeds 9.5% of income. Premium credits are available to qualified individuals and families with incomes between 133-400% of the FPL for qualified coverage purchased through the Exchanges and are tied to the premium of the second lowest cost silver plan in the area, though on a sliding income scale.

COST-SHARING REDUCTIONS

Referred to as cost-sharing reduction (CSR) variations, these plan design subsidies are available to individuals and families for plans purchased through the exchanges, based on income relative to the FPL. Currently, CSR variations are available for individuals and families with incomes up to 250% of the FPL. CSR plans reflect lower cost-sharing amounts and limits, and are established as variations of silver plans. The targeted actuarial value for these plans are 94%, 87%, and 73%, within a +/-1% corridor.

SMALL BUSINESS TAX CREDITS

Employers with 25 employees or fewer, and average annual wages of less than $50,000, can receive a tax credit if they purchase health insurance for employees through the SHOP exchange. Beginning in 2014, employers are required to contribute at least 50% of the total premium cost. The maximum credit is 35% of the employer's contribution, available to employers with 10 or fewer employees and average annual wages of less than $25,000. The credit phases out as firm size and average wages increase.

OTHER PROVISIONS

INDIVIDUAL MANDATE

Beginning in 2014, U.S. citizens and legal residents are subject to a tax penalty for lack of coverage, which will be phased in from 2014 to 2016 and is ultimately equal to the greater of $695 (up to three times that amount for a family, indexed annually) or 2.5% of household taxable income. Certain exemptions apply, including exceptions for financial hardships. This penalty was upheld by the U.S. Supreme Court in 2012, stating that it falls within Congress' power under the Constitution to "lay and collect taxes" as long as the level is not coercive.

EMPLOYER MANDATE

Employer responsibility in the ACA is reflected by amending the Internal Revenue Code to include penalties for not offering coverage, particularly to those employees who enroll in the individual market and receive premium tax credits. Effective January 1, 2015, employers with 50 or more full-time employees must offer coverage or pay a fee of $2,000 per full-time employee (excluding the first 30 employees from the assessment). The penalty is adjusted based on the number of employees who receive a premium tax credit. Employers with less than 50 full-time employees are exempt from this penalty. Employers who have more than 200 full-time employees and who offer one or more health benefit plans are required to enroll new employees in a plan automatically, with an option for the employee to opt out. The ACA sets forth rules for determining employer size, exemptions, and other aspects of the mandate.

THE ACA AND PUBLIC PROGRAMS

The ACA establishes several initiatives applying to public programs (Medicaid and Medicare) which are directed toward the goal of improving access to quality health care coverage. Below is a brief description of some of these initiatives.

MEDICAID PROVISIONS

The ACA expanded Medicaid to all non-Medicare eligible individuals with incomes up to 133% of the Federal Poverty Level (FPL). States receive supplemental federal funding to support this expansion. The U.S. Supreme Court decision in 2012 limited the ACA's ability to require this eligibility expansion by limiting the federal financing at risk to the incremental funding, not the original population's financing, as initially enacted.

The ACA includes provisions for quality improvement in Medicaid. Medicaid payments for primary care services will increase to 100% of Medicare rates, and the increase will be federally financed.

The ACA also supports new Medicaid programs and demonstration projects, such as Health Homes for high risk enrollees, bundled payments, global capitation to safety net hospitals, pediatric ACOs, and payment for certain emergency mental health services.

Other Medicaid provisions include (but are not limited to) an increase in the federal match to the Children's Health Insurance Program (CHIP), an increase in Medicaid drug rebates from manufacturers, new programs for fraud and abuse screening, and prohibition of federal payments for Medicaid services for hospital-acquired conditions. Additional provisions relate to services such as free-standing birth centers, hospice care for children, family planning, long-term care services and supports, and skilled nursing facilities. Finally, the ACA creates a new federal coordinated health care office to improve coordination of care for dual eligibles (dual eligibles are those enrolled in both Medicare and Medicaid).

MEDICARE PROVISIONS

The ACA sets forth a wide range of initiatives to address health care quality and efficiency within the Medicare program and amended the Social Security Act to implement these initiatives.

Linking Payments to Quality Outcomes

ACA initiatives linking payments to quality outcomes include the following.

- Hospital Value-Based Purchasing Program: provides value-based incentive payments to hospitals that meet specific defined performance standards (other than readmissions). At a minimum, performance standards must include measures related to five specific conditions or procedures: acute myocardial infarction, heart failure, pneumonia, surgeries, and healthcare-associated infections.
- Requirements for the calculation of incentive payments and sources of funding
- Improvements to the physician quality reporting system
- Improvements to the physician feedback program
- Quality reporting for long-term care hospitals, rehabilitation hospitals, and hospice
- Quality reporting for PPS-exempt cancer hospitals
- Plans for value-based purchasing for skilled nursing facilities and home health agencies
- Value-based payment modifier under the physician fee schedule, and
- Payment adjustment for conditions acquired in hospitals.

National Strategy to Improve Health Care Quality

The ACA sets forth a range of initiatives designed to improve health care quality. First, the Secretary of HHS is directed to establish a national strategy to improve the delivery of health care services, patient health outcomes, and population health. The ACA requires the strategy plan to include, among other things, coordination among agencies within HHS, agency-specific strategic plans, establishment of annual benchmarks for each agency, and strategies to align public and private payers with regard to quality and patient safety. Second, the ACA directs the President to appoint a working group on health care quality to achieve collaboration, cooperation, and consultation among federal departments and agencies, and to avoid inefficient duplication of effort and resources. Finally, the ACA also sets forth provisions related to quality measure development, quality measurement, data collection, and public reporting.

Encouraging the Development of New Patient Care Models

The ACA includes several reforms addressing quality and efficiency, including payment reforms and new patient care models. First, the ACA establishes an Innovation Center within CMS to test, evaluate, and expand different payment structures and methodologies to reduce program expenditures to Medicare, Medicaid and CHIP, while maintaining or improving quality of care. Known as the Center for Medicare and Medicaid Innovation (CMMI), this entity supports pilot programs and similar initiatives through grants and other support. Next, CMMI oversees a voluntary Bundled Payments for Care Improvement Model Program, which groups payments to hospitals and physicians for episodes of care, including hospitalizations and post-acute care. CMS has also established the Medicare Shared Savings Program (MSSP), which allows providers to organize as Accountable Care Organizations (ACOs), and established the Independence at Home demonstration project.

Medicare Plan Improvements

In Medicare's Fee-for Service ("Traditional" Medicare Parts A and B) program, traditional Medicare has a number of changes due to the ACA, including adjustments to the annual market basket, a freeze on the threshold on income used to determine Medicare Part B premiums, and reductions in payments for Disproportionate Share Hospitals, preventable readmissions, and certain hospital-acquired conditions.

The ACA also included improvements to Medicare Advantage (Medicare Part C). Beginning in 2012, a new "blended benchmark" is used to determine payments for most MA plans, and plans may receive bonuses or re-allocations of rebates based on certain quality measures. Medicare Advantage plans also became subject to MLR requirements effective July 2013.

The beneficiary coinsurance in the Medicare Part D coverage gap (commonly called the "Donut Hole") will be phased down from 100% to 25%, from 2010 to 2020. Other Part D changes are in effect, including (but not limited to) certain reductions in cost sharing and inclusion of certain classes of drugs of "clinical concern" in all formularies.

Ensuring Medicare Sustainability

Specific ACA initiatives related to Medicare sustainability include: (1) incorporation of productivity improvements into market basket updates, with further reductions through 2019 for inpatient acute care, skilled nursing facilities, long-term care hospitals, inpatient rehabilitation facilities, and psychiatric hospitals; (2) implementation of similar initiatives related to ambulance services, ambulatory surgical centers, laboratory, and durable medical equipment; (3) submission of data on quality measures by psychiatric hospitals; and (4) temporary adjustment to the calculation of Part B premiums.

Health Care Quality Improvements

A variety of specific initiatives are set forth in the act as health care quality improvements. Topics addressed include the following items:

- Availability of grants, including funding, requirements, eligibility, and reporting
- Research activities and requirements
- Technical assistance and implementation issues
- Establishing community health teams to support patient-centered medical homes
- Medication management services in the treatment of chronic disease
- Regionalized systems for emergency care
- Trauma care centers and service availability
- Facilitating shared decision-making with patient decision aids and recognition of preference-sensitive care
- Presentation of prescription drug benefit and risk information
- Demonstration program to integrate quality improvement and patient safety training into the clinical education of health professionals
- Improving women's health
- Patient navigator program

Prevention and Wellness Provisions in Medicare

Effective January 1, 2011, cost sharing for preventive services has been eliminated. Effective in 2011 through 2015, Medicare provided a 10% bonus payment to primary care physicians and to surgeons in certain shortage areas.

Other Medicare Provisions

The ACA outlines several other provisions related to Medicare, including new demonstration programs, coordination of Medicare/Medicaid dual eligibles, and additional payments to and protections of certain hospitals.

The ACA also includes provisions to improve accuracy and refinement of Medicare payments in several areas including home health, hospice, skilled nursing, and certain drugs and devices. New restrictions, transparency rules and reporting rules now apply to physician-owned hospitals, relationships between manufacturers (of drugs, devices, etc.) and physicians, pharmacy benefit managers, and nursing homes. In addition, several provisions have been implemented related to provider screening, fraud, and abuse for Medicare and Medicaid.

REVENUE OFFSET PROVISIONS

HEALTH INSURER TAX

The ACA created a new tax, with total tax revenues collected starting from $8 billion in 2014 and increasing to $14.3 billion by 2018, and indexed thereafter. Only 50% of net premiums are taken into account in calculating the fee for nonprofit insurers, and certain plans are exempt from the tax.

EXCISE TAX FOR HIGH-COST HEALTH PLANS

As stated in the act, effective January 1, 2018, employer-sponsored health plans with aggregate values that exceed $10,200 ($27,500 for family coverage), are subject to a tax of 40% of the excess cost over the threshold. This excise tax is commonly referred to as the "Cadillac" tax. The tax is imposed on the issuer of the policy (the plan administrator or employer). The thresholds can vary for certain higher-cost plan enrollees and the thresholds will be indexed in the future.

OTHER TAX-RELATED CHANGES

Several other tax-related changes were effective in 2011 through 2013, including but not limited to (1) limits to the tax-deductibility of health care employee compensation, unreimbursed medical expenses, and Blue Cross Blue Shield organizations; (2) lower tax-favored allowances for flexible spending accounts; and (3) new taxes on certain medical devices such as stents, pacemakers and defibrillators, as well as indoor tanning services and the pharmaceutical manufacturing sector.

OTHER ACA PROVISIONS

It is beyond the scope of this chapter to address every initiative set forth by the ACA. This section provides broad descriptions of other significant provisions.

PREVENTION OF CHRONIC DISEASE AND IMPROVING PUBLIC HEALTH

A variety of initiatives were included in the ACA to address services in support of public health. These provisions focus on modernizing disease prevention and public health systems, increasing access to clinical preventive services, creating healthier communities, and supporting innovation. A few of the public health initiatives established by the ACA are as follows:

- A National Prevention, Health Promotion and Public Health Council, with the Surgeon General as chairperson, to coordinate and lead federal activities related to prevention, wellness and health promotion practices, the public health system, and integrative health care
- An independent Preventive Services Task Force to review scientific evidence related to the effectiveness, appropriateness, and cost-effectiveness of clinical preventive services
- A grant program in support of school-based health centers

- A national education campaign focused on oral healthcare prevention and education along with a grant program supporting research-based dental caries disease management effectiveness
- A vehicle for the Secretary of HHS to award grants to State or local health departments and Indian tribes to carry out pilot programs involving public health community interventions, screenings, and other services
- Funds for research in the area of public health services and systems
- Support for various research initiatives affecting public health

These provisions and programs are subject to review as part of the federal budget, and as a result, funding may vary from program to program. The ACA further instructs the Secretary of HHS to evaluate federal health and wellness initiatives and in particular, their impact on the health status of the American public and federal workforce, including absenteeism, productivity, workplace injuries, and medical costs.

HEALTH CARE WORKFORCE

The ACA is intended to improve access to and delivery of health care services for all individuals, and particularly those considered low income, underserved, uninsured, minority, health disparity, and rural populations. This can be accomplished by gathering and assessing comprehensive data in order for the workforce to meet the health care needs of individuals, including research on supply/demand, distribution, diversity, and skills needed; increasing the supply of qualified health care workers to improve access; enhancing health care workforce education and training; and providing support to the existing health care workforce. Among other things, the ACA establishes a National Health Care Workforce Commission to serve as a national resource and a National Center for Health Care Workforce Analysis to provide for information describing and analyzing the health care workforce and workforce-related issues.

TRANSPARENCY AND PROGRAM INTEGRITY

The ACA addresses transparency issues, including (1) physician ownership of hospital organizations, (2) nursing home ownership, enforcement, and staff training, (3) background checks on employees of long term care facilities, and (4) Medicare and Medicaid program integrity initiatives. The ACA also amends the Elder Justice Act and establishes associated programs to prevent elder abuse and fraud.

PATIENT-CENTERED OUTCOMES RESEARCH INSTITUTE (PCORI)

A new nonprofit institute has been established to identify research priorities and conduct research that compares the clinical effectiveness of medical treatments. The institute includes a Board of Governors and expert advisory panels and is funded through an annual assessment paid by health plans and employers.

IMPROVING ACCESS TO INNOVATIVE MEDICAL THERAPIES

As part of improving health care quality, the ACA establishes certain initiatives related to innovative medical therapies. The ACA establishes required information for licensure of biological products as biosimilar or interchangeable. In addition, the ACA expands entities receiving discounted prices to provide more affordable medicines for children and underserved communities.

RESOURCES

As noted at the beginning of this chapter, the implementation of ACA provisions has been driven primarily by federal and state-level rules and regulations.

Commonly used resources for practicing actuaries doing work under ACA include the following:

- Proposed and final rules released by HHS, implementing certain portions of the ACA. In most cases, these rules provide technical guidance and interpretation to ensure consistent application of ACA-related initiatives.
- Perhaps the most widely referenced HHS rule is the annually updated HHS Notice of Benefit and Payment Parameters. This rule sets forth important limits and dollar amounts for practicing actuaries to incorporate into their work. For example, while the ACA establishes a transitional reinsurance program, the rule sets forth the attachment point, coinsurance level, and required premium for the program.
- Because insurance is regulated at the state level, actuaries should also be familiar with state rules. Depending on the state, these rules can be accessed on state websites or by contacting the state department of insurance directly.
- Regulatory guidance from CCIIO should be referenced as well. For example, CCIIO manages and releases the annual Actuarial Value Calculator and Minimum Value Calculator with technical documentation, as well as instructions for preparing certain required forms. At a higher level, actuaries may also want to attend ongoing webinars hosted by CMS and CCIIO on a variety of ACA-related topics.
- The actuary should review all applicable Actuarial Standards of Practice (ASOPs) and Academy Practice Notes. Under the purview of the American Academy of Actuaries, ASOPs and Practice Notes have been developed regarding various aspects of ACA.
- Industry and professional research reports can be useful in understanding the impact of the ACA. For example, the Society of Actuaries' *Health Watch* provides many excellent articles relating to the ACA.

REFERENCES

Patient Protection and Affordable Act (P.L. 111-148) and Health Care and Education Reconciliation Act of 2010 (P.L. 111-152).

Public Health Service Act (PHSA).

CMS/CCIIO Regulations and Guidance: https://www.cms.gov/CCIIO/Resources/Regulations-and-Guidance/index.html, accessed Aug. 20, 2015.

Internal Revenue Code (IRC).

Kaiser Family Foundation State Health Facts: http://kff.org/health-reform/state-indicator/state-health-insurance-marketplace-types/, accessed Aug. 20, 2015.

GAO, Enrollment and Spending in the Early Retiree Reinsurance and Pre-existing Condition Insurance Plan Programs, April 2013.

19 HEALTH BENEFIT EXCHANGES

Christopher S. Girod

INTRODUCTION

One of the major market reforms of the Affordable Care Act (ACA) of 2010 was the requirement that consumers have the ability to purchase insurance through health benefit exchanges, starting in 2014. Exchanges are also referred to as health insurance marketplaces, or simply as marketplaces, particularly by the federal government. We use the term "exchanges" in this text.

The concept of an exchange is not new, and exchanges have existed in various forms since the 1990s. Nevertheless, throughout this chapter, except where noted otherwise, the term refers to exchanges as they are defined in the ACA.

This chapter provides an overview of exchanges. As of this writing, residents of all states have access to an exchange. However, most exchanges are still evolving rapidly. Their structures and capabilities are likely to continue to grow, although their missions will continue to be focused primarily on facilitating access to health insurance coverage, and in some states, on managing health insurance prices and product offerings. This chapter focuses on what is known at the time of writing, and strives to avoid speculation about future developments. A variety of government and private organizations provide excellent resources for tracking the implementation of health care reform, including exchanges.[1]

Further details about the ACA are provided in Chapter 18, "The Affordable Care Act."

WHAT IS AN EXCHANGE?

Defined most simply, an exchange is a market for health insurance products offered by multiple insurers. For consumers, it is potentially a one-stop shopping place for health insurance. Consumers can select from among a variety of benefit plans offered by a variety of insurers.

The ACA requires states to set up an exchange that offers individual insurance and an exchange that offers insurance to small employer groups. Alternatively, states can set up a single

---

[1] Sources of current information on exchanges include:
- US Department of Health and Human Services Center for Consumer Information & Insurance Oversight (CCIIO): www.cms.gov/cciio/
- The federal website which is a portal for all public exchanges: https://www.healthcare.gov/
- National Conference of State Legislatures (NCSL): www.ncsl.org
- National Association of Insurance Commissioners (NAIC): www.naic.org
- Kaiser Family Foundation: www.kff.org

exchange that serves both individuals and employers. The ACA refers to the employer exchange as a Small Business Health Options Program, or SHOP exchange.

States are the primary regulators of health insurance, both inside and outside of exchanges. However, if a state is not enforcing one or more provisions of the ACA, then the federal government will enforce them. States currently fall into one of three groups. Approximately one-third of states have established their own exchanges and are enforcing federal law. Nearly two-thirds of states have allowed the federal government to impose a federally facilitated exchange (FFE), but the states have assumed responsibility for enforcing the requirements around health plan certification and rate review. Five states, known as "direct enforcement states", have allowed the federal government to perform all exchange functions on their behalf.

The concept of an exchange is not new. Examples of exchanges that existed prior to the ACA include the Massachusetts Health Connector, the Utah Health Exchange, CaliforniaChoice, and the Health Insurance Plan of California (HIPC), now called Pacific Health Advantage (PacAdvantage). Brief overviews of the Massachusetts and Utah exchanges are presented near the end of this chapter, along with a section on private exchanges.

WHY DID THE UNITED STATES MANDATE IMPLEMENTATION OF EXCHANGES?

The challenges presented by America's health care system include high costs of care and insurance, uneven access to care and insurance, and less-than-perfect quality of care. Solutions are elusive, however. Prior to passage of the ACA, and even after its passage, the national debate over health care reform has been broad and enthusiastic, but without simple answers. The ACA ultimately requires a patchwork of changes, some of which are intended to improve access to and affordability of health insurance. Exchanges are just one element of that patchwork.

An exchange's primary function is to facilitate the purchasing of insurance by allowing consumers to find, compare, and purchase insurance from multiple companies. It can also serve as a financial clearing house for premiums, premium subsidies for lower income participants, and employer contributions, directing funds to the appropriate parties.

Proponents also believe that exchanges have the potential to facilitate improvements in cost and quality, primarily through the transparency and comparability of competing products, their prices, and their quality ratings. The degree of transparency, and consumers' ability to make comparisons efficiently, is likely much greater than in pre-exchange markets. However, degrees of success have varied widely among states, for a variety of reasons. In particular, the small group exchanges have struggled to overcome challenges around the complex interactions between employee choice among health insurance companies and benefit plans, employer desires to predict and control their health insurance expenses, and employer desires and requirements around the equitable treatment among employees.

EXCHANGES UNDER THE AFFORDABLE CARE ACT

WHO PURCHASES INSURANCE THROUGH AN EXCHANGE?

The exchanges required by the ACA sell individual and small group health insurance. The people most likely to seek individual coverage through an exchange are those who were previously uninsured, or who already had individual insurance but qualify for premium and cost sharing subsidies (discussed later) if they purchase in the exchange. Some consumers who currently have access to employer group insurance might also choose to purchase individual policies in the exchange if their employer's plan is non-qualified or unaffordable. The exchange has also been attractive to high-risk people who lost their insurance coverage when certain states' high risk pools closed in 2014.

Small employers may purchase through the exchange to take advantage of employer tax subsidies (discussed later) that will only be available on insurance purchased in the exchange. Depending on how the exchange is structured and the services it provides, an employer might also find the exchange to be an attractive, transparent and diverse, one-stop shop for their insurance needs.

In 2014 and 2015, each state had the option to define small employers who may participate in the exchange as those having 50 or fewer employees, or 100 or fewer employees. By 2016, all states must allow groups with 100 or fewer employees to participate in the exchange. Starting in 2017, states have the option to extend eligibility to larger employers.

Exchanges are also important marketplaces for Consumer Operated and Oriented Plans (commonly called co-ops). Co-ops are non-profit health insurance companies that received an initial government investment. They were a compromise between political factions wanting a "government public option" to be a part of health care reform, and those who opposed a public option. The ACA ultimately did not include a public option, but did include co-ops.

People who will generally not be served by exchanges include consumers who already have insurance through some other insurance plan such as a large employer plan, Medicare or Medicaid. The ACA included a major expansion of the Medicaid program, extending eligibility to adults up to 138% of the federal poverty level (FPL) starting in 2014. Previously, most states only covered adults up to 100% of FPL. In June, 2012, a U.S. Supreme Court decision on the ACA significantly restricted "one major portion of the law: the expansion of Medicaid, the government health-insurance program for low-income and sick people. The ruling gives states some flexibility not to expand their Medicaid programs, without paying the same financial penalties that the law called for."[2] Approximately 60% of states have adopted the ACA's Medicaid expansion, and other states have implemented or are exploring alternatives to Medicaid expansion that typically involve the involvement of the commercial insurance market.

The ACA also gave states the option to set up a Basic Health Plan (BHP), which would provide coverage to all people having incomes between 138% and 200% of FPL (federal poverty level). The BHP would not be part of the exchange, but would instead be administered somewhat like

---

[2] *The New York Times*, http://topics.nytimes.com/top/reference/timestopics/organizations/s/supreme_court/affordable_care_act/index.html

Medicaid. People eligible for a BHP, Medicaid, or Medicare, can choose to purchase insurance on the exchange, but they will not qualify for subsidies. When people apply for insurance in the exchange, they will be notified if they are eligible for one of those government insurance programs. States choosing to implement a BHP may do so starting in 2015.

BENEFIT PLANS OFFERED IN THE EXCHANGE

A benefit plan must be "qualified" to be sold in the exchange.[3] A qualified health plan (QHP) is one that provides the "essential benefits" and is offered by an insurer that meets certain requirements.

Essential benefits represent those offered by a typical comprehensive employer insurance plan. States have various options they can use to define this benchmark plan. Ten options are available, including the three largest (by enrollment) Federal Employee Health Benefit Program plans, the state's three largest State employee plans, the state's three largest small group products, and the state's largest HMO.[4] States are also free to have mandated benefit requirements in excess of the essential benefits. However, if they do so, the state must pay the cost of those benefits, for insurance provided through the exchange, for all exchange members.[5]

The ACA establishes five levels of benefit plans that may be offered in an exchange. Four of the levels are defined by the value of their benefits, as measured by actuarial value (AV), or the percentage of expected average allowed charges which are paid by the health plan as benefits. These four levels of coverage, sometimes called "metal plans," are bronze (60% AV), silver (70%), gold (80%), and platinum (90%). The fifth level of benefit plan allowed by the ACA is catastrophic, which is a high-deductible plan available only to people under age 30 or who meet certain affordability requirements. Catastrophic plans are only available in the individual market, and not in the small group market.

A qualified, participating health plan must offer at least one silver plan and one gold plan in the exchange and must agree to charge the same premium rates for each qualified health plan whether offered inside or outside of the exchange. Some states may impose additional requirements. For example, California requires insurers participating in the exchange to offer at least one product within each of the five levels of coverage.

For small groups, an employer may pick a level of coverage and allow all employees to pick a plan within that level. The exchange can then allow employees to choose other levels of coverage, in spite of the plan level the employer has chosen to fund. This flexibility will give more choices to employees, but may also introduce additional antiselection among the benefit tiers.

FINANCIAL PENALTIES FOR NOT PURCHASING INSURANCE

One of the most controversial elements of the ACA is the "individual mandate", which is a requirement that individuals either purchase insurance or pay a financial penalty.[6] Financial

---

[3] ACA Section 1301.
[4] "Essential Health Benefits Bulletin" published by the Center for Consumer Information and Insurance Oversight on December 16, 2011.
[5] ACA Section 1311(d)(3)(B)(ii)
[6] ACA Section 1501

penalties are imposed on individuals, and on employers who have 50 or more employees and do not provide qualifying coverage. Most health insurance industry experts recognize that the individual mandate is critical if exchanges are to succeed. Without it, exchanges would be subjected to antiselection as less healthy people choose to purchase insurance in the exchange and more healthy people may choose to not purchase coverage at all.

FINANCIAL INCENTIVES TO PURCHASE INSURANCE THROUGH AN EXCHANGE

Employers and individuals have financial incentives to purchase their insurance through an exchange. For small employers, the incentive is a tax credit on health insurance premiums. Only certain small employers qualify for the tax credit: those having fewer than 25 full-time equivalent employees and whose average employee earns less than $50,000 per year. The tax credit is as high as 50%, but it is only available on insurance purchased through an exchange. Starting in 2014, the credit is only allowed for an employer's first two years of exchange coverage.[7]

For individuals, the financial incentives can be even greater. The federal government will provide premium and cost-sharing subsidies to low income individuals, but only if they purchase individual coverage through the exchange. Subsidies are available in two ways.

The first subsidy is a premium subsidy.[8] Premium subsidies are limited to the lesser of (1) premiums actually paid, and (2) the excess of a benchmark premium over a percentage of household income. The subsidy grades down as income increases, until it reaches zero at 400% of FPL.[9] A person does not qualify for a subsidy if the employer offers coverage meeting the minimum value requirements and the employee contribution for single coverage is more than a defined percentage of the person's income.

The second subsidy is a cost-sharing subsidy. Cost-sharing subsidies help pay for a person's out-of-pocket expenses such as deductibles, copays, and coinsurance. The amounts of cost sharing subsidies are also based on household income, and are available to people having incomes of up to 250% of FPL. The subsidies are employed by requiring that every silver plan offered on an exchange also have subsidized plans with lower cost sharing amounts. Specifically, each silver QHP will be accompanied by three cost share reduction (CSR) plans having actuarial values of 94%, 87%, and 73%. Depending on applicants' income, they will be offered one of those CSR plan levels. Additionally, for all QHPs at all metal levels, two levels of subsidized plans must also be offered for qualifying Native American enrollees.

OTHER IMPORTANT ELEMENTS OF THE ACA THAT AFFECT EXCHANGES

The ACA includes many health care reforms that are not specific to exchanges, but which will influence them. These reforms include requirements for guaranteed issue and adjusted community rating, and premium rate restrictions, all effective in 2014.

---

[7] ACA Section 1421
[8] ACA Section 1401
[9] As of this writing, the US Supreme Court will hear a case challenging the IRS's ability to grant premium subsidies in the form of tax credits, in FFE states.

The individual and small group markets are now guaranteed issue, which means that any applicant who meets the eligibility criteria must be offered coverage. Before the ACA, most states already required guaranteed issue for small group insurance, as part of the small group reforms enacted before the ACA. For individual insurance, some states required guaranteed issue, while others allowed insurers to decline or underwrite applicants based on their health status.

Both individual and small group health plans must now be rated using adjusted community rating, as it is defined in the ACA. Premium rates must be defined on a per-person basis, as opposed to a per-employee, per-family, or some other basis. Rates are only allowed to reflect an enrollee's benefit plan, geographic area, age, family size, and tobacco usage. Gender rating is no longer allowed. Additional premium rate adjustments based on the health status of individuals or small group enrollees are not allowed. An insurer's premium rates for the individual market must be based on a combined risk pool that includes all of the insurer's individual policyholders, including plans sold in the exchange or out of the exchange. The same is true for small group coverages, for which premium rates must be based on the combined risk pool that includes all of an insurer's small group insureds. The state also has the option to require that insurers combine their individual and small group risk pools for purposes of setting premium rates, and a few states have elected this option.

Specific restrictions are imposed on variations within the adjusted community rates. The maximum difference in premium rates due to age is limited to a 3-to-1 ratio. Tobacco users may be charged higher premium rates than non-tobacco users, but only up to a 1.5-to-1 ratio. Finally, families are charged premiums for no more than three children.

HOW IS THE PURCHASING PROCESS AFFECTED BY EXCHANGES?

In an exchange, insurance is purchased by individuals and employers, who are often assisted by agents and brokers. An additional party, known as a navigator, may also play a role in the purchasing process. The ACA requires exchanges to establish a navigator program that provides grants to entities who educate and assist consumers with insurance purchasing. These navigators serve a crucial role by educating the public about subsidies and plans offered in the exchange. Many consumers are now purchasing insurance for the first time, and their education needs may be extensive. Navigators have a variety of defined duties, including educating consumers on plans available, availability of subsidies, and processes for filing grievances.[10]

Navigators must be qualified and licensed. They must be monitored to ensure that the information they provide is fair, accurate, and impartial. Navigators may not be insurance companies, and they may not receive any compensation from insurance companies for their services.

Many agents and brokers continue to serve their traditional roles in the purchasing process, although their roles may decline or evolve according to how much of the individual and small group markets are sold through the exchanges, the tools exchanges make available to consumers, and the extent to which agents and brokers also offer other products. For example, an individual purchaser may continue to use an insurance agent for health insurance if that

---

[10] ACA Section 1311(i)(3)

agent also provides other products to the individual (such as retirement products, property insurance, and life insurance).

EXCHANGE ADMINISTRATIVE FUNCTIONS

As defined in guidance provided by the Center for Consumer Information and Insurance Oversight (CCIIO), an exchange must provide at least a minimum set of administrative functions. Some of the most critical functions are certifying plans, assigning quality ratings to plans, presenting benefits information in a standardized format, providing consumers with eligibility determinations, and providing certifications for people who are determined to be exempt from the individual responsibility requirement. In addition, the exchange is responsible for ensuring that all participating health plans satisfy the exchange's requirements.

EXCHANGE INFLUENCE ON THE BROADER HEALTH CARE MARKET

An exchange has the opportunity to provide value to both exchange and non-exchange participants, by promoting improvements in quality of care and access to care, and increasing the transparency of costs and quality measures. The extent to which the exchange's activities benefit the non-exchange market will be a function of the exchange's market share, and a state's view of where the exchange should fall along the spectrum of potential market influence. This spectrum can range from a minimalist facilitator of insurance purchasing to an aggressive participant in the insurance and health care delivery markets.

The services that the exchange provides, and the requirements that it imposes, can drive changes in cost, quality, and access to care both in and out of the exchange. Specific administrative functions that may be most likely to drive change are the health plan certification process and standardized reporting of cost and quality information.

The exchange may help promote cost control via transparency, scrutiny of premium rates and health care service costs, and possibly even price comparisons among specific providers for specific services. In some exchanges, consumers are given access to tools that will help match their health care needs, financial resources, desired providers, and geographic location with a health insurance company and benefit plan.

It is possible that exchanges may help drive improvements in care quality. The ACA requires that a plan meet certain quality standards in order to be certified as a qualified health plan. Since the exchange must certify all plans participating in the exchange, it may choose to impose higher standards than those required by the ACA, such as by promoting use of disease management, case management, electronic medical records, and standardized measurements of quality, patient safety, and member satisfaction.

KEY ELEMENTS OF EXCHANGES THAT MAY VARY BY STATE

Although some aspects of exchanges are clearly prescribed by the ACA, many design and operational decisions are left up to the states. Some of the key variations involve decisions that states either have made or must make on an ongoing basis, and are explored in the following section.

State or Federal Exchange

The ACA required an exchange be operational in each state by 2014. However, states were not required to establish their own exchanges. If they chose to not establish an exchange, the federal government was required to establish and run one for them. Approximately one-third of states have established their own. This includes several states which have federally supported exchanges, meaning they have established their own exchanges, but use the federal (www.healthcare.gov) where consumers can shop and enroll. The other two-thirds of states have not built their own exchanges, and instead use the federal government's exchange. The federal exchange is commonly known as the federally facilitated exchange, or FFE. Some states which use the FFE have also chosen to provide certain consumer assistance functions and are known as state partnership exchanges.

Governance Structure

States that choose to establish an exchange have several options for structuring the exchange's administrative entity. Exchange administration can be established within an existing state agency such as the Department of Insurance, it can be established as a wholly independent non-profit organization, or the State can create an independent quasi-government entity to run the exchange.

In deciding which governance structure would be best, states considered that the exchange would need to work with multiple government agencies and the legislature (information needs to be transferred efficiently between the exchange and those other entities), respond reasonably quickly to changing market conditions and consumer demands for new products, possibly maintain some degree of freedom from political pressures, and maintain a positive public image.

Just over half of the state-based exchanges are new quasi-governmental entities, separate from other state agencies, which gives them more freedom to support their unique missions. For example, the Colorado exchange was established as a "nonprofit unincorporated public entity".[11] Several other states elected to establish their exchanges within existing state agencies, such as New York, whose exchange is contained within the Department of Health. A few states, such as Hawaii, chose to establish their exchanges as non-profit organizations.

Maximizing Exchange Participation

Some states, particularly those which established their own exchanges, have worked to maximize exchange participation among individuals and small employers. Maximizing participation should create a more robust exchange market, minimize antiselection, spread exchange administration expenses over more people, and possibly have greater influence over the total insurance market.

States wanting to maximize exchange enrollment have encouraged both insurer and consumer participation in their exchanges. At the extreme, both Vermont and the District of Columbia have encouraged insurer participation by requiring that individual and small group

---

[11] Colorado Senate Bill 11-200, which established the Colorado exchange.

coverage can only be purchased on exchange, effectively eliminating the off-exchange markets for those products.

Making the exchange attractive and available to more customers also increases insurer and consumer participation. Attractiveness can be maximized in a number of ways, including ensuring ease of use, providing value-added services, providing effective marketing, and supporting consumer education and outreach. However, regardless of the exchange's efforts, low income individuals have a strong incentive to enroll on exchange, since low income premium subsidies are not available on policies purchased off exchange.

Merging Individual and Small Group Rating Pools

The ACA requires that all of a insurer's individual insurance, both in and out of the exchange, be pooled for purposes of setting premium rates. A similar requirement applies to small group insurance. The ACA also gives states the option to require that individual and small group experience be combined into a single risk pool. Several states have chosen this option, including Massachusetts, Vermont, and the District of Columbia.

Due to possible differences in the health status of the average individual and small group populations, merging the markets can result in higher premium rates for one population and lower premium rates for the other population. When the markets are first merged, individuals and small groups that get the greatest premium rate increases are most likely to drop coverage.

The decision of whether to merge the markets also affects insurers, but the effects are different for each insurer, depending on their mix of members by market and the risk profiles of those members. For example, if the average individual market member is expected to have higher claims than the average small group member, a insurer having only small group business and no individual business might gain some premium rate advantage if the individual and small group risk pools were merged. That insurer's premium rates might be less unaffected by the merger, but competitors having both individual and small group business might have to increase their small group premium rates. The ACA's risk adjustment program, discussed later in this chapter, is intended to help eliminate any such morbidity-based premium differences among insurers.

Standardized Benefit Packages

Some states require that participating insurers offer a set of standardized benefit plans which the exchange defines. In addition, insurers may also offer plans of their own design.

The standardized benefit plans make it easier for consumers to compare plans and premium rates among insurers. Insurers compete on price and on other measures of value, including their provider networks, quality of care, customer service, and financial stability. Insurers can still compete via benefit design by offering non-standardized plans. With their non-standardized plans, insurers have the ability to innovate, respond to needs of employers and consumers, take advantage of unique market situations or provider arrangements, or otherwise differentiate themselves from other insurers.

At the extreme, exchanges could ultimately restrict insurers to offering only standardized plans. Although they would have the responsibility of defining those plans, exchange administration and plan regulation would be simplified significantly.

Establishing a Basic Health Plan

The ACA allows states to create a Basic Health Plan (BHP) for residents under 200% of FPL who are not eligible for Medicaid and lack affordable access to comprehensive employer based coverage. If a BHP is established, the eligible population must obtain coverage through the BHP and cannot purchase coverage through the exchange. If a state does not opt to implement the BHP, this population is still eligible for subsidized coverage under the exchange.

A state might want to implement a BHP if it can offer participants richer benefits or lower premiums than they could get through the exchange. However, the State would also take on additional administrative burden and financial risk, and would remove a significant population from the exchange thus possibly influencing the BHP's success.

At the time of this writing, Minnesota is the only state which has established a BHP, although several others have expressed interest.

The Exchange as an Active Purchaser or Open Market

A state can be more or less aggressive in its control over which insurers participate in the exchange. The spectrum of possibilities ranging from least to most restrictive includes allowing participation of all plans that meet the minimum ACA requirements (Open Market), setting additional standards for qualified health plans, selecting plans based on comparative value (Selective Contracting Agent), and negotiating health plan premiums with insurers (Active Purchaser).[12]

The Open Market approach is the least disruptive to the pre-ACA market, and imposes the least administrative burden on the State. At the other extreme, the Selective Contracting and Active Purchaser approaches may provide greater value to consumers, although they may ultimately result in fewer choices for consumers. Federally facilitated exchanges use the Open Market approach. Among the state-based exchanges, the Open Market and Selective Contracting approaches are the most common.

Administration Expense Funding

Exchanges have significant administrative expenses regardless of whether they are created by the state or federal government. The ACA requires that each exchange be self-sustaining. The administrative expenses could be funded through premium taxes, insurer assessments per covered life, provider assessments, or via other methods. Some combination of these mechanisms might produce an allocation of costs that is the most broadly accepted among stakeholders. There may also be pressure to apply some assessments to the self-insured population. However, it has historically been very difficult, due to ERISA regulations, for states to collect assessments on self-insured lives that are not covered under stop-loss insurance.

---

[12] Carey, Robert, Health Insurance Exchanges: Key issues for State Implementation, Academy Health, State Coverage Initiatives, September 2010

CONTROLLING ANTISELECTION

States must control antiselection between the exchange and non-exchange markets, and among insurers within the exchange. Allowing antiselection to take hold could quickly reduce the number of insurers and consumers that choose to participate in the exchange. Antiselection is an issue that underlies many of the design and operations decisions that a State makes in setting up and running an exchange. Specific provisions of the ACA itself, and many decisions that states will make, can help control antiselection.

FEDERAL REQUIREMENTS THAT HELP CONTROL ANTISELECTION AGAINST THE EXCHANGE

The ACA includes provisions that will automatically help protect exchanges against antiselection. One of the most important of these is encouragement of enrollment. It does this in several ways. First, the ACA mandates that all individuals be covered, bringing more people into the market, although they may still buy their coverage outside the exchange. Second, the ACA makes premium subsidies and cost sharing subsidies available to lower income individuals who enroll in exchange plans. Finally, the ACA makes tax credits available to small businesses that participate in the exchange.

The ACA also has plan design and pricing rules that help mitigate antiselection because they apply to plans both inside and outside the exchange. For example, all plans must cover at least the essential health benefits and cannot offer plans more lean than bronze or catastrophic inside or outside the exchange. Additionally, there are prohibitions on lifetime and annual benefit limits, and on pre-existing condition exclusions.

Rating rules also help prevent antiselection within the insured market. Those rules include the requirement to use adjusted community rating, and to offer the same premium rates in and out of the exchange. Depending on the strength of the individual mandate, however, considerable selection differences may still exist between the insured market and people who choose to remain uninsured.

FEDERAL REQUIREMENTS THAT HELP CONTROL ANTISELECTION AMONG INSURERS WITHIN THE EXCHANGE

The ACA also includes three risk management tools that can mitigate the effects of antiselection among insurers within the exchange. Two are transitional programs and the third is permanent. The first program is a transitional reinsurance program that operates from 2014 to 2016 and provides insurers with protection against very high cost members. The second is a risk corridor program, which also operates from 2014 to 2016. It gives insurers protection against total claims across all members being higher than expected. An insurer will receive payments if its cost-to-premium ratio is greater than 103%, and make payments if the cost-to-premium ratio is less than 97%. The third program is risk adjustment, which operates indefinitely. Under this program, plans with healthier participants subsidize plans with less healthy participants. Insurers set premium rates based on plan design and community rating, and risk adjustment transfer payments among health plans will compensate for health status differences not fully reflected in the premium rates.

STATE OPPORTUNITIES TO CONTROL ANTISELECTION AGAINST THE EXCHANGE

States can also help control antiselection against the exchange. Methods can be broadly grouped into those related to insurer participation, benefit offerings, and pricing rules.

Antiselection against the exchange will be minimized by maximizing the number of participating insurers and consumers. Methods for maximizing exchange participation were discussed earlier in this chapter. A state might also specify that if an insurer elects to leave the exchange, re-entry is prohibited for a period of time (perhaps five years). This might prevent insurers who enroll a disproportionately unhealthy mix of insureds from canceling the policies, leaving the market, and then quickly re-entering the market in the hopes of enrolling a healthier mix of people.

Benefit plan restrictions can also be used to minimize selection against the exchange. For example, the exchange could require that all participating insurers offer plans at all benefit tiers (platinum, gold, silver, bronze, and catastrophic). Without this requirement, an insurer could offer only its richer plans in the exchange, and only leaner plans outside of the exchange, thus likely enrolling the least healthy members in the exchange and the most healthy members out of the exchange. A state could also place additional restrictions on benefit plans offered outside the exchange. At one extreme, the state might stipulate that only those plans offered in the exchange may be offered outside the exchange. A more moderate approach would be to restrict the differences between plans offered in and out of the exchange in order to prevent insurers from offering non-exchange plans that are designed to attract lower risk individuals.

It is critical that states ensure consistency of pricing rules in and out of the exchange, and that their risk adjustment systems be effective and timely. To the extent that insurers believe the risk adjustment system protects them from antiselection, they may be more likely to participate in the exchange and may consider setting their premium rates with lower risk margins.

EXAMPLES OF EXCHANGES THAT EXISTED PRIOR TO THE ACA

As previously mentioned, exchanges are not new. This section provides an overview of two exchanges that preceded passage of the ACA.

THE MASSACHUSETTS HEALTH CONNECTOR

Immediately prior to passage of the ACA, the most well-known exchange was the Massachusetts Health Connector. Started in 2006 as part of the state's effort to have universal health insurance coverage, the Connector helped reduce the state's uninsured population to approximately 3%.

The Connector included some key provisions which the ACA ultimately mirrored to some degree. A key element of the Connector's success was Massachusetts' implementation of an individual mandate, meaning that people who could afford to purchase insurance were required to do so, or they had to pay a tax penalty. There were specific requirements for minimum "creditable coverage." The tax penalty equaled 50% of the least costly available creditable coverage, and it varied by age, family size, and income. There were no penalties for incomes below 150% of FPL.

Since implementation of the ACA, the Connector has conformed to the new federal requirements.

THE UTAH HEALTH EXCHANGE

Along the spectrum of possible services that an exchange could provide, the Utah Health Exchange tended toward the minimalist extreme. It was essentially an electronic portal through which employers and employees could purchase insurance. Insurance was only offered to small employer groups, having 2 to 50 employees. Individual insurance was not offered. The exchange opened to a pilot group of small employers in 2010, and then to all small groups in 2011.

Utah described its exchange as a defined contribution model. Employers could define a maximum contribution level, and then allow employees to choose from among all plans offered on the exchange. If the premium rate for a chosen plan exceeded the employer contribution, then the employee paid the difference using pre-tax contributions. At least 75% of employees had to participate in order for the employer to be eligible.

When the ACA's exchange requirements were implemented in 2014, Utah elected to continue running its own small group exchange to meet the federal requirements, but is using the federal exchange for individuals.

PRIVATE EXCHANGES

Although they have existed for many years, private exchanges have recently become much more popular. Like the public exchanges, they are essentially virtual marketplaces for purchasing insurance, but they were set up to meet the unique needs of employer groups, including large employers. One of the oldest and most successful private exchanges is CaliforniaChoice, which has been serving small employers since 1996.

The value proposition for CaliforniaChoice is that it provides small employers one-stop shopping for employer and employee choice among multiple health plans, access to supplemental benefits (e.g., dental, vision, life), and administrative simplicity. The value proposition is similar for the newer generation of private exchanges, although they cater primarily to large employers and their degrees of sophistication and flexibility are even greater.

A typical private exchange might be established by a large employee benefits firm, or by a collection of employers. Insurance companies are asked to participate, offering their benefit plans on the exchange. Products are not limited to health insurance, and may include life insurance, disability, long term care, dental, vision, or other products, including products for retirees, such as Medicare supplement and Medicare Advantage plans. COBRA administration is also provided.

Private exchanges tout their ability to facilitate a defined contribution approach for employers. In such an approach, an employer defines how much they want to contribute for insurance for specific categories of employees, and then employees have the freedom to choose from among the products available. Employees pay the premium difference between the costs of the products they have chosen and their employer's contribution. Using a private exchange can give employees more choice and help reduce an employer's administrative burden. An exchange may limit the number or types of benefit plan options which an employer may offer to their employees. That helps control administrative expenses and adverse selection among plans.

For large groups, private exchanges can underwrite groups and set their premium rates based on the group's own claims experience and other unique characteristics. An employer can also be declined coverage. Underwriting and premium rate development for large groups would be performed by the participating insurers.

Private exchanges can also serve self-funded employers and provide stop-loss insurance. All insurance risk is borne by the insurance companies, or by the employer if self-funded, and the exchange itself does not assume the insurance risk.

With regard to comprehensive health insurance, private exchanges that serve large employers have much more flexibility than public exchanges, or exchanges like CaliforniaChoice, that serve only small employers and whose health insurance plans must conform to the ACA's small group rules. When serving large employers, private exchanges can offer benefit plans which are customized for a specific employer, are fully insured or self-funded, have special coverages for different classes of employees, and have flexibility in defining employee versus employer contribution rates and tiers. Benefit plans can be adjusted at any time, and are not constrained by calendar year filing requirements used by public exchanges.

Because private exchanges tend to cater to large employers, they are more likely to provide those services which large employers expect, including: claims experience reporting; facilitation of employee education and communications; HRA/HSA administration; provision of stop-loss insurance; and quotes for unbundled fees such as network access fees, PBM fees, experience reporting fees.

Major forces currently driving the private exchange movement are likely to continue or become even more powerful. One force is the increasing popularity of defined contribution approaches to health insurance purchasing. The defined contribution movement has been fueled by high health care cost inflation rates and our country's continuing struggle to reduce trends to sustainable levels. When consumers are more financially engaged in purchasing health insurance and in purchasing specific health care services, they are expected to help slow health care spending growth. The need for that consumer engagement is unlikely to diminish.

A second major force behind the private exchange movement is the evolution of on-line purchasing technology. Amazon.com and other on-line businesses have fueled the development of technological innovations which make on-line purchasing efficient and preferable for many consumers. The federal government's vision of public exchanges being Amazon-like marketplaces is coming to fruition, although the process has not been perfectly smooth. With more flexibility and less bureaucracy, private exchange evolution should be characterized by quicker growth and more diversity than public exchanges.

The Future

Health reform, and the development of the ACA-defined exchanges, is still an evolving process, particularly for the employer group market. Over the next few years, as federal guidance is published and as states adjust their exchanges, and as experience data is accumulated, a clearer vision will emerge of how the exchanges influence health care cost, quality, and access for millions of Americans.

SECTION FOUR

FUNDING AND RATING

20 PRICING OF GROUP INSURANCE

Richard S. Wolf
Jay Ripps
Kristi M. Bohn

GROSS PREMIUM DEVELOPMENT

For any group coverage, the "gross premium" represents the cost of the coverage to the customer. It is composed of four main elements: estimated claim costs, expenses, taxes, and profit (or contribution to surplus for not-for-profit organizations). Some products might generate investment income, which is used to reduce the premium. Where the coverage is self-insured, through an administrative services only (ASO) arrangement, the term "gross premiums" is replaced by "contribution rate" or "premium equivalent."

The rating process begins with the development of claim costs. For purposes of this chapter, we assume that claim costs have already been determined, with appropriate reflection of pooled claims and pooling charges, since these topics are covered elsewhere in the text. This chapter will concentrate on the other elements of gross premiums, such as expenses. Then the specifics of manual rate development and subsequent adjustments for group specifics are presented.

PRICING ASSUMPTIONS

Gross premiums consist of the expected claim costs, loaded to reflect additional items:

- Expenses, including administrative expenses, commissions and other sales expenses
- Premium and other taxes
- Contributions to surplus, which typically reflect the level of risk and the expected profit for the assumption of that risk

Gross premiums also include a credit for investment income on assets and cash flow.

Some insurers explicitly build up claim costs into gross premiums by adding amounts for each cost element, while others use target loss ratios to develop gross premiums, which are calculated as projected claims divided by target loss ratios. In either method, each cost element must be considered and quantified.

ADMINISTRATIVE EXPENSES

To be viable in the long run, the premium structure for a group insurance product must make adequate provision to cover the expenses of designing, developing, selling, underwriting, and administering the product, including allocations of overhead expenses not directly attributable to the administration of the product (for example, salaries and benefits of executive or corporate staff, and maintenance of information technology infrastructure supporting multiple products). Design and development expenses are generally amortized over a number of years; it is important to quantify and consider such expenses explicitly in developing gross premiums. These expenses vary significantly by product, group size, and from insurer to insurer.

Expenses associated with the development and administration of provider networks for medical or dental coverages may be recovered with a network access charge. This type of charge may also be used to recover the expenses associated with utilization management. High network access charges may be worthwhile if they equate to fewer claim dollars, through aligning the choice of providers, achieving higher discounts, or through increased utilization management. Some insurers and administrators must pay for, and then recover, network access charges to pay a different company who actually formed the network, thus extending the geography in which they can compete for business (also known as "rented networks").

As part of the insurer's strategy and marketing plan, an insurer may choose to ignore overhead expenses for a new product or market segment, to offer introductory products at a lower price. This is called "pricing on the margin," where only expenses associated directly with the new product are included. Usually, the insurer intends to eventually cover an appropriate portion of overhead expenses, once the new product reaches a sufficient level of membership. Before that time, the overhead exists but must be borne by other products.

Expenses frequently vary between first year and renewal years. Administrative expenses are higher in the first year due to the time involved in setting up a new group on computer systems and issuing participant ID cards. Marketing expenses are also higher in the first year, with the expense of sales brochures, time spent on the sales activities, and possibly higher first-year commissions. As with design and development expenses, an insurer may choose to amortize first year expenses over a number of years, to promote the growth of a new product.

Amortization of design and development expenses, amortization of first year expenses, and pricing on the margin should be used with caution, because they can result in unrealistically low initial premiums that require unsellable rate increases in later years to maintain the financial viability of the product.

Considerations

In developing the administrative expense component, there are a number of considerations:

- How are expenses allocated to the product? A corporate strategy of equitable overhead allocation is needed, or one product or business segment can inadvertently subsidize the expenses of another, distorting the profitability of both. There are many allocation methods, most of which are combinations of the following:
    - *Activity Based Allocation.* This method allocates expenses according to some measure or estimate of use for the products or functions. For example, a transfer charge approach may be established for mailing expenses; one that charges the actual postage

expense back to a particular function or product. The transfer charge may be established at the beginning of the year, and may be updated during the year to keep the charges in line with actual expenses.

- *Functional Expense Allocation.* The functional expense allocation process involves determining how total expenses for an organization are split by major and minor activity categories, by line of business for new and renewal business. The process requires surveying each employee (or category of employees) to determine how time is allocated to the various tasks being performed. This can be done either by recording information about activities as tasks are performed, or by retrospectively estimating how time was spent.
- *Multiple Allocation Methods.* Both allocation methods described above may be used within the same financial report; for example, an activity-based allocation method may be used for mail, customer service, and claim staff, while a functional expense allocation could be used for all other departments.

• How should administrative expenses be allocated to groups? Expenses can be expressed in a variety of ways, but the primary objective is often to achieve equity among group customers without unduly complicating the process. Sometimes the equity objective is secondary to an overriding strategic objective of the insurer. Expenses are generally expressed on one or more of the following bases, differentiating between first year and renewal year expenses for each coverage:

- percent of premium
- percent of claims
- per policy
- per employee (certificate)
- per member (each person covered)
- per claim administered

Certain expenses might be charged separately to the group customers who use them, rather than being spread over all customers via the expense allocation formula. For example, some groups are particularly demanding concerning service and special reporting. If possible, it might be better for overall premium equity if the expenses of these special services were charged separately.

When justifying an allocation to a specific customer, it is helpful to consider what would change in expenses if the customer were to leave. This process may require assumptions or inquiries about how management would react to the loss of that customer.

It is generally preferable to charge administrative expenses (to groups and products) on a basis that best reflects the activities that generate the expense. For this reason, a basis that combines a number of factors is generally used, since some expenses vary by members or certificates, some by number of groups, some by number or amount of claims, or by other units. For example, high deductible health plans (HDHP) with accounts (health savings accounts or health reimbursement arrangements) may require higher levels of customer service per claim, since the coordination between the insurance portion of the plan and the account portion might confuse participants. However, because these participants are typically healthier than traditional health plan counterparts, these products often generate fewer claims per participant. As a further example, retiree health products experience more claims per participant than other major medical health products, and more customer service time per claim, and more manual claim work because of the coordination of benefits with Medicare.

- What does the competition include as expenses in its pricing? If the competition charges extra for special services or is subsidizing one block with the profits of another, an adjustment may be needed to accommodate the market place. Competitive considerations must be reflected in choosing the basis for charging expenses, since the choice may determine the relative competitiveness of rates. The example below is a simple illustration of this consideration.

Contract issuance total expense:	$1,000,000
Number of contracts issued:	1,000
Cost per contract issued:	$1,000 / contract
Premium collected:	$30,000,000
Cost as a percent of premium:	3.3%

If Company A charges $1,000 per contract for expenses, and Company B charges 3.3% of premium, there will be a tendency for company A to attract groups with larger premium, because the fixed $1,000 per contract, expressed as a percent of premium, diminishes as the size of the group grows. For example, the $1,000 charge represents five percent of premium for a group with $20,000 in premium, while it represents only one percent of premium for a group with $100,000 in premium. There is less financial risk if the insurer uses an approach that most accurately reflects the actual expense drivers. For example, the cost of issuing a policy might be expressed as a fixed dollar amount, since each group, whatever the size, gets only one policy. On the other hand, the cost for providing enrollment support might be a function of group size or total premium, since larger groups more employee meetings and communication materials.

Sources of Data

In general, the data for determining expense factors could come from either internal or external sources. Internal sources show what is needed to cover operating costs, and external sources show what the market demands.

Internally, the main data source is a functional cost study that systematically measures how many resources (such as employees or computer systems) are used to perform each function for various categories of group size, coverage, or line of business.

External sources include (1) studies by industry associations, (2) published expense data from annual statements, (3) competitive feedback (primarily based on competitive quotes or state rate filings), and (4) special surveys. External sources must be interpreted with caution, first because the data itself may not be accurate, and second because comparisons with other companies are subject to distortion from differences among companies in defining or accounting for expenses.

Internal sources are generally the insurer's accounting systems. These systems usually record all expenses by type of expense and by area or function. The types of expenses include expenses for salary, bonuses, benefits, rent, postage, travel, office and computer equipment, and a number of other types of expenses. The level of detail to be recorded is typically driven by expense distinctions required for the annual statement or tax calculations.

Expenses can be categorized as either direct or overhead expenses. The direct expenses can be attributed to products by a number of expense attributions or allocations.

Once the allocation method is determined, as described above, either the accounting system automatically allocates expenses as they accrue to product lines by using time accounting and account codes on payments or expenses, or these allocations will be performed at the end of each period. In some cases, expenses cannot be automatically allocated by the accounting system, and special surveys or reports of time spent must be used to allocate total costs at the end of the accounting period.

COMMISSIONS AND OTHER SALES EXPENSES

Group insurance products are generally marketed by agents or brokers who are compensated on a commission basis. Some insurers use only salaried representatives or use a combination of salaried representatives and brokers. Often there are commissions paid to general agents who are responsible for managing a number of agents. These are known as commission overrides.

Commissions should in some way reflect the value of the services being performed. This value is based on the volume and complexity of work being performed, general payment practices among other companies' brokers, and what customers are willing to pay for the services.

Insurers typically pay supplemental compensation as incentives to salaried representatives or brokers. Supplemental compensation can be based on persistency, volume, types of groups sold, or other measures that align with the insurer's marketing goals. Insurers must disclose supplemental compensation programs to their group customers.

In addition to commissions and salaries paid to sales personnel, other sales expenses may include advertising or promotional expenses, which can be significant. These expenses may include both expenses directly related to the product, as well as an allocation of expenses attributable to promotion in general, such as advertising to promote brand name recognition.

Commissions are generally expressed as a percent of premiums, with the percent decreasing with group size. Alternatively, commissions may be expressed on a sliding premium scale basis. Some insurers pay commissions as a flat dollar amount per member; in this way, commissions do not automatically increase in proportion to premiums.

Under either approach, commission rates for large groups will generally not vary between first and renewal years. In the small group area, there are sometimes higher first-year commissions in product lines such as vision and dental. However, small group major medical health insurance products generally can no longer have higher first-year commissions due to the Affordable Care Act (ACA). Commission structures are one of the reasons why gross premiums generally vary by group size.

Commission structures for certain retiree health products (Medicare Advantage and Part D drug plans) have many rules and much oversight by the Centers for Medicaid and Medicare Services (CMS). The commission structure rules were promulgated to ensure that brokers and agents cannot "churn" participants from product to product in order to continually earn high first-year commissions.

PREMIUM TAXES

Premium taxes are paid by insurers and are reflected within insurers' premium quotes. The tax level varies, and is typically set by states' statutes at 1% to 3% of premiums. Taxes are generally based on the state(s) from which the group contract(s) was issued, without respect to the state where the covered employees or dependents actually reside. Accordingly, premiums for large groups commonly reflect the premium tax level in the state where the large group is headquartered. Due to competitive concerns or regulatory rating oversight, insurers operating in multiple states often consider the state premium tax level in which the large group is headquartered when setting premiums, though others may simply set the premium tax assumption at the weighted average premium tax of the states where the insurer operates. For small-group major medical health insurance, each state's tax rate is generally specifically reflected, because the ACA requires state-based small-group risk pools for non-grandfathered products and effective regulatory rate oversight at the state level. Self-insured products and government program products, such as Medicare Advantage, do not pay premium taxes.

OTHER TAXES AND ASSESSMENTS

Insurers are subject to other taxes – notably federal and state income taxes. These taxes are generally levied on the insurer as a whole and must be allocated to its various products. Allocations may be a common percentage of premiums across all products, or the allocations may reflect the pre-tax operating results of each product or product segment.

The ACA introduced a new federal assessment on nearly all health insurance coverage (even self-insured groups) that began in 2014, planned at $8 billion across the health insurance industry, increasing to $14.3 billion by 2018. Thereafter, the assessment increases with the rate of premium growth. The ACA also introduced a seven-year comparative effectiveness research assessment on nearly all health insurance coverage (even self-insured groups). The fee started at $1 per member per year in late 2012, but stepped up one year later to $2, and is annually adjusted to reflect national health expenditure inflation. This fee supports the non-profit Patient-Centered Outcomes Research Institute, which uses the funds to sponsor research comparing the clinical effectiveness of medical treatments. ACA assessments must be allocated across products and customers. Insurers doing business in states that had formerly sponsored a high-risk pool (high-risk pools covered those who could not obtain health insurance prior to the ACA due to health), the elimination of high-risk pool assessments has partially offset newly introduced ACA fees.

RISK AND PROFIT CHARGES

The chosen level of risk and profit charges should, in theory, reflect the degree of risk involved, the amount of insurer capital allocated to support the coverage, and the return expected on the capital. The degree of risk varies by group size, depending on the benefits provided, the funding vehicle, and the degree of resources required to administer the account. In practice, risk and profit charges reflect not only the appropriate risk considerations, but also competitive market prices.

For the smallest groups, coverages are often pooled. The insurer's risk is largely one of underestimating claims in the pricing of the pool. This underpricing can be due to either statistical fluctuations, such as shock or catastrophic claims, or mis-estimation. Small group rate and benefit regulations introduce additional risks that premiums may not be sufficient. Risks resulting from new benefit mandates or from regulations that restrict underwriting flexibility must be considered. Also, rate regulation may restrict rate increases so that premiums cannot be increased sufficiently to cover costs.

For larger groups, which may involve financial arrangements other than the full assumption of insurance risk by the carrier, the risk is a combination of underestimating the claims of the large group and financial risk. If the insurer carries forward experience deficits for recovery in later years, there is less risk to the insurer than under a fully insured arrangement, but there is a risk of the customer terminating its contract while in a deficit position.

For self-insured accounts, where only administrative services are provided, there is a risk that administrative fees will not be adequate to cover costs. There is also a risk that certain claims will be incorrectly processed, or that the customer, although self-insuring, might be unable to meet its financial obligations under the plan. If this occurs, the customer, its employees, or regulators may look to the administrator for financial support.

For jumbo accounts, there is a risk that expenses will be unable to be reduced fast enough in response to a termination to avoid losses until its expenses are appropriately reduced.

The following table illustrates a sample return-on-surplus approach to setting risk and profit margins:

Coverage	Required Surplus	Required Return on Surplus	Target Risk/ Profit Margin
Small Groups	25% of annual premium	18% before tax	4.500%
Large Groups	12.5% of annual premium	15% before tax	1.875%
ASO	5% of annual premium equivalents	12% before tax	0.600%

These target profit margins could also be adjusted to reflect other risks like those associated with a new product launch including the risk that the initial expenses might not be recovered.

Risk or profit margin charges should reflect profit margins built into expense charges, investment income credits, and pooling charges. That is, to the extent that profits may be expected from those sources, additional explicit risk and profit charges may be reduced, such that the total of all expected profit sources equals target margins. Some insurers use risk-based capital (RBC) requirements to evaluate needed return on capital. These analyses typically involve allocations of capital in proportion to RBC requirements by line of business or by subsidiary. Returns are then measured against target returns on RBC requirements.

INVESTMENT EARNINGS

Investment earnings are typically thought of as being earned on assets related to medical claim reserves, other reserves (such as life insurance premium waivers or present value of amounts-not-yet-due on long-term disability insurance), and on cash flows.

An insurer may provide cash flow advantages to the customer under an insured arrangement by allowing the customer to hold its own medical claim reserves. In these cases, the amount of investment earnings available to the insurer will be substantially reduced. When this option exists, the administrative fees are often increased since there is no investment income being generated to reduce the insurer's administrative cost. The insurer's internal cost allocations should be sensitive to unusual reserve deals.

Unless the insurer uses the investment year method of calculating returns, or otherwise segregates assets by product line, the rate of return credited in the premium formula is generally based on the insurer's portfolio rate of return, which represents the composite return on the general portfolio of investments. The credited interest rate may also take into account the investment strategy, and the character of liabilities involved, especially the type and timing of the liabilities. If either presents significant risk, a margin may be retained by the insurer as a return for assuming that risk.

Investment earnings may be reflected in pricing (1) as an explicit rate component, (2) as an offset to expenses, or (3) as an offset to the provision for risk or profit. Some companies do not explicitly reflect investment earnings, but rather adjust target loss ratios or profit margins to reflect them.

Manual Premium Rates

For a particular coverage, manual premium rates for a whole block of business are often determined as part of the overall rating structure. These are the rates that would be charged in the absence of any credibility being given to past claim experience and with no health underwriting of the group. Often, manual rates are weighted in some way (as described in Chapter 27, "Experience Rating and Funding Methods") with a group's own experience to establish the gross premium for a particular group.

Rating Characteristics

The manual rate structure reflects all of the major variables affecting cost that the insurer intends to include in its rate structure. These variables could include plan characteristics, age, gender, geographic adjustments, industry adjustments, group size, period for which the rates are being set, and others.

The average gross premium rate for a product will then be adjusted to reflect various rating characteristics of the group. These rating adjustments are done using factors that may have been calculated many years earlier, but which are evaluated regularly to verify that they are still appropriate.

The U.S. federal government restricts the use of gender-based employee contribution rates for groups, other than very small groups. However, the rate charged to the group by an insurer can be based on a number of rating characteristics. Common rating characteristics include:

- age,
- gender (though this rating variable is also restricted in many states),

- health status (risk adjustment scores has become a common tool),
- rating tiers,
- geographic factors,
- industry codes,
- group size, and
- length of premium period.

As of January 1, 2014, insurers in the small-group non-grandfathered health insurance market must use the age curve applicable in the state, and can only rate on plan design factors, network factors, geographic factors, and tobacco use.

Age and gender are used as rating characteristics to reflect differences in morbidity. The gender-based elements of rates can be averaged out of the final rate quote provided to the group, so that even though the quoted rates *depend* on the gender mix, the rate structure quoted to the group does not reflect it.

Rates can be adjusted for specific substandard health conditions present in the group. This individual medical underwriting often occurs in setting premium rates for grandfathered small-group plans, but does not generally occur in larger groups, where the rates are more often based on the group's past claim experience. Risk adjustment scoring techniques, which are discussed in depth elsewhere in this text, are gradually being incorporated into insurers' rate adjustment calculations. These tools score each person based on age, gender, and diagnosis and/or episodes and/or pharmacy use, and can take the place of age, gender, and prior health status adjustments.

Another decision in setting rates includes choosing how the dependent rate will be expressed, and how many rating tiers there will be. The common rating tier choices are:

One Tier: Composite
Two Tier: Employee only, family
Three Tier: Employee only, employee and one dependent, family
Four Tier: Employee only, employee with one dependent, employee with children, family
Five Tier: Employee only, couple, employee with child, employee with children, family

Even more complicated rating tiers exist than the five tier structure shown above. Due to the ACA, nearly all groups that offer dependent coverage now must offer this coverage to age 26. This requirement has not changed the tier choices above, even though this new regulation has increased the number of dependents on family contracts, the number of elections of family contracts, and has further triggered some insurers and employers to increase their relative charges for family coverage and/or to move to a more complicated rating tier structure.

Geographic location is an important consideration, since claim costs can vary considerably by geographic location. Expenses charged, as a percentage of claim costs, may result in overstated expenses in high cost areas and understated expenses in low cost areas.

Regulatory factors and risks mentioned earlier vary by state, and may be built into geographic factors.

The group's industry type (commonly designated by Standard Industry Classification (SIC) code) can be an element of setting premium rates, since significant variation is found in medical costs between different industries. For example, high medical cost industries may include transportation, health care professionals, educators, attorneys, and government employees. However, before adjusting for industry, it is important to review whether the risk has already been accounted for by the other adjustment factors in the model (such as age or health status).

Since expenses and risk charges vary significantly by group size, group size is a common rating characteristic.

Most group premium rates are set on a one-year term basis, so that claim costs, expenses, taxes, commissions, investment income, and any other premium elements, must be projected for the next year only. Typically, this involves projections for 15 to 18 months beyond the period of the data on which they rely, since rates must be set well in advance of the date they become effective. Rates for some coverages, however, are established for more than one year – generally as a level premium over a number of years. This category includes long-term care insurance and some forms of group life insurance. Premium rates based on projections over a longer time period involve greater risk and require greater risk charges. Investment income assumptions and persistency assumptions are typically more important elements when setting multi-year rates than when setting one-year term rates.

MARKETING, COMPETITIVE, AND REGULATORY ISSUES

Typically, manual rates are ultimately adjusted for competitive and market strategy considerations. Manual rates are often determined separately for different group size categories and different products. There needs to be a rational relationship between these categories. For example if the small group division of an insurer rates groups from groups size 11-100, and the large group division rates groups from size 100+, the rates for comparable products for a group size 95 and for a group size 105 should not differ significantly.

Differences in premium rates between products should generally reflect differences in expected costs (their "actuarial value"), although for strategic, competitive or selection reasons, premium rates might deviate from strict actuarial equivalence. When a significant change to product relativities is implemented, the result may be shifts in enrollment within products, between products and competitors.

Management sometimes deviates from theoretically derived rates when setting final rates. It is important to understand the subsidies being created with such deviations, so it is critical that the profitability across rating categories be transparent.

Each insurer must match its financial plan and market strategy with competitive forces to determine where it wants its gross premiums to be relative to the competition.

State and provincial group insurance laws restrict how rates can vary due to differences in rating characteristics, as well as by how much rates can increase from year to year. Further, the ACA has introduced overarching federal rating restrictions and made state and federal oversight stricter for nearly all health insurance products sold to individuals and groups with less than 100 employees in the U.S.

GROUP SPECIFIC ADJUSTMENTS

Manual rates are often used as a reference point for a particular group. The premium rates for a group may be expressed as a percentage of the manual rates, such as "manual + 10%," or "manual − 5%." The determination of the appropriate percentage of manual rates involves determining the ratio of expected claim and other costs for the particular group to the comparable costs expected under manual rates.

Premium rates for larger groups are based entirely on each group's own experience. For smaller large groups, each group's past or estimated claim experience can be used in adjusting manual rates. The larger the group, the more consideration is given to the past claim history of the group. For groups whose rates are based on manual rates, adjustments might be made to manual rates for new business discounts and credible prior claim experience. New business discounts are sometimes used to encourage a group to change carriers. Discounts are often justified based on lower claim expectations due to the effect of group underwriting or other reasons. Such discounts should be supported by analysis of claim experience by duration. Caution must be used in the level of first-year discounts, since renewal rates will then have to be increased for trend plus the discount, which may result in upset customers and the loss of the group in later years. Further, recovery may be limited by group rating restrictions in some states. More information on the process and considerations for rating groups can be found in the chapters on experience rating and group insurance underwriting.

Expected claims for a group may represent a blend of actual claims, based on that group's prior claim experience combined with the claim component of manual premiums. The blending process may involve the use of pooling high claims, with the level of pooling being a function of the coverage and the spread of risk involved. This depends on the coverages, risks involved, and the insurer's overall risk strategy. This topic is discussed in more detail in the chapter on experience rating.

For jumbo groups, there may be pressure to reduce rates as much as possible to make a sale. Such groups may sometimes be perceived to offer a measure of prestige that provides a marketing advantage. Additionally, jumbo groups may increase am insurer's negotiating power with providers, which could lead to larger provider discounts. There may also be significant economies of scale with jumbo groups in enrollment, billing, and general administration. On the other hand, these groups often demand a lot of special attention. They often work through consultants who require special reporting, and may even suggest dedicated claim processors or other special services. It is important to quantify, as much as possible, the net effect of these considerations in setting premium rates.

For self-insured groups, similar issues are considered, but the size of adjustments are limited, given the cost of administrative services and stop-loss insurance.

MONITORING OF EXPERIENCE

As discussed in this chapter, gross premiums are based on a wide range of assumptions regarding claim costs, expenses, taxes, sales expenses, and investment income. Actual experience will never conform precisely to these assumptions; therefore, an essential element of pricing is to develop and implement systems and procedures to monitor actual experience in a manner that allows for ready comparison of actual experience to pricing assumptions, so that pricing assumptions can be appropriately modified in light of emerging experience.

21 ESTIMATING MEDICAL CLAIM COSTS

Gerald R. Bernstein
Shelly S. Brandel
James T. O'Connor
David Cusick
Updated by Margaret A. Chance

Medical claim costs, which represent the estimated cost of medical care, are the essential element in the pricing of medical benefit products. This chapter discusses the development of the estimated claim costs that are used in establishing the price of a medical care plan.

The wide range of available health insurance products means that various risk-bearing entities assume the cost of providing health insurance, from insurance companies to HMOs, employers, and provider groups. Over the past few decades, there has been a shift from pure indemnification for medical costs to the prepayment of services, and in many cases, back to pure indemnification. In addition, with the passage and implementation of the Affordable Care Act (ACA) in 2010, changes in the requirements regarding services covered, cost-sharing, and allowable risk-mitigation techniques transformed the landscape for estimating costs, particularly in an environment of health care provider consolidation, mergers of traditional payers, and the introduction of new insurers. These transformations continue to challenge risk takers' ability to accurately estimate the cost of care.

Insurers often produce a group rate manual that contains detailed claim cost information. This manual enables the actuary to make pricing adjustments for variations in plan design, demographic characteristics, level of utilization management, size of group, geographic area, underwriting practices, and other factors that are likely to impact future costs. The use of a group manual allows a company to adjust its own historical data to be more reflective of the specific population being rated. This manual can be developed from a company's own experience, but it is often supplemented by data from public sources or purchased from industry sources. Group manuals are also available from actuarial consulting firms.

The term "small group" historically refers to insurance offered and sold to employers with two to 50 employees in most states. However, the ACA expanded the definition of small group to employers with up to 100 employees starting in 2016. Under the ACA, estimated costs for an insurer's small group population must be calculated based on an insurer's entire book of small group business within a given state (that is, a "single-risk pool"), which is further pooled with risks of competing small group carriers in the state through risk adjustment. To the extent that the experience of a given book of business is not fully credible, other state data, public data, or purchased data can be considered in setting expected costs. The overall considerations for developing a small group rate manual are similar to those used for large group, though there are many regulations, as well as many rating and underwriting limitations, in small group under the ACA that affect expected costs and the ability of a carrier to differentiate costs among groups. Small group considerations are also discussed in Chapter 18, "The Affordable Care Act" and Chapter 28, "Group Insurance Rate Filings and Certifications."

This chapter describes the development of an insurer's expected medical costs, which serve as a key component for the development of large and small group rate manuals. These expected costs, in turn, are used in developing premium rates for benefit plans. The chapter discusses the entire process of developing expected claim costs, including the collection of experience period data, the adjustment or normalization of the data to a set of standard characteristics, the projection of the data to the rating period, and the adjustment of expected costs for specific situations. Considerations specific to small groups and the changes under ACA that affect cost projections are also addressed.

This chapter focuses only on the process of developing the medical cost portion of the manual rate. Other chapters in this text discuss the issues involved in adjusting the manual rate to include administration and other premium loadings, as well as other group-specific rating methodologies.

DATA CONSIDERATIONS

Summarizing medical claim data is a complex process due to the multitude of benefit plan designs, variations in provider claim coding conventions, and varying group characteristics. In the past, it has been difficult to capture all of the information necessary to adjust for all these variables. However, improvements in information systems and database technology now enable the actuary to manipulate complex data more efficiently.

Estimating medical claim costs is a process that involves projecting historical claim information to a future period, recognizing factors such as case characteristics, demographic data, and provider contracting details. This process begins with the selection of an appropriate data source. There are many factors to consider when selecting the appropriate data source, several of which are described below.

IS THE DATA APPROPRIATE FOR ESTIMATING CLAIM COSTS?

The source data should generally reflect the characteristics of the company's population and benefits. For example, commercial data should not be used to estimate claim costs for a population aged 65 and over. Any data will need to be adjusted, or normalized, for several factors, including the insurer's demographic mix, benefit levels, provider contracting details, and rating period.

WHAT LEVEL OF DETAIL IS NEEDED?

Aggregated data is usually sufficient to estimate medical claim costs. In other words, data is summarized into broad service categories and across all benefit plans and other group characteristics. For example, the process of renewal pricing for a large, stable group often starts with a comparison of actual to expected loss ratios, or a comparison of actual to expected claim costs per person (or per employee). For estimating costs across an entire line of business, data may be segmented into more refined categories, such as geographic areas or benefit type groupings (such as metallic tiers in small group), to the extent that these groupings are credible.

For development of large and small group expected costs, the insurer's data for the entire line of business is typically used. To the extent that the data for the entire line of business is not fully credible, an insurer will supplement it with available external data sources. In the case of developing an experience rate for a particular large group, data for that group is used, if credible. To the extent that the large group's data is not fully credible, it will typically be blended with the manual rate. Experience for specific small groups cannot be used for rating purposes under ACA regulations.

As the ability to handle large volumes of data has expanded, and the focus on controlling medical costs has grown, aggregate methods are often supplemented with more detailed analyses. Further, an increasing number of plans allow employee choice between multiple plan options, causing greater need for more detailed analysis. In the past, a group may have covered all employees through one medical program, and historical medical costs per employee may have been a reasonably stable predictor of future medical costs. Now, many groups offer multiple plan choices, including HMOs, PPOs, and high deductible health plans (HDHPs), and the age, gender, and health characteristics of those covered by the different plans may be constantly changing. Similarly, a multitude of plans are available across the small group market, so insurers need to consider the mix of benefit plans within the small group single risk pool and how that may be expected to change in the future.

In general, aggregate data is an appropriate option when the block of business being rated is stable, and few differences exist between the experience period and the rating period in terms of population and delivery system characteristics. Conversely, more detailed data will be needed when the block is less stable, and significant differences exist between the experience period and the rating period.

DATA SOURCES

The best source of data is usually a company's own experience, as long as there is sufficient volume for the data to be credible. This data will reflect the company's cost patterns as well as administration, risk selection, and other characteristics.

There are a variety of internal sources that may be available for analyzing a company's own claims experience. It is very likely that these sources come from different systems and in varying formats. As such, it should be carefully reviewed for reasonability, consistency, and recognition of data collection limitations, as well as definitional and timing variances. Actuarial Standards of Practice (ASOPs) address issues regarding the use of data. ASOP No. 23, "Data Quality," applies to all areas of practice and provides guidance regarding selecting, relying on, reviewing, using, and disclosing data. ASOP No. 5, "Incurred Health Claim Liabilities," requires that the actuary check the reasonability of data and "make appropriate efforts" to obtain accurate data from claim processing and accounting systems.

There are typically several sources of available internal information, described below.

Medical Claim Systems Data

The sophistication and complexity of claims systems continues to improve, making available a tremendous amount of potential data. For every claim that is processed, a claim adjudicator (or adjudication system) must review insured eligibility, benefit exclusions, presence of other health coverage (for coordination of payment with other benefits), prior authorization for medical care, provider contracting and payment rates, and benefit plan provisions. Claim records also include details from the claim form(s) (for example, UB-92 hospital forms and CMS 1500) such as incurred date, type of service, place of service, and procedure and diagnosis codes.

Claim systems typically capture billed claims, eligible claims, allowed amounts, and paid amounts. Each of these can be useful in the rate-setting process. Allowed amounts reflect the reductions from billed amounts negotiated between the payer and provider. Paid amounts are those that are the responsibility of the health plan to pay after deducting member payments (deductibles, copayments, and coinsurance).[1]

Pharmacy Benefit Manager (PBM) Data

A number of organizations use third-party PBMs for the management and payment of prescription drug claims. As a result, it is often necessary to collect PBM data as a distinct source from medical claims data.

Premium Billing and Eligibility Data

Premium billing and eligibility data contains various identifiers regarding the demographic and benefit plan information by member within an insurer's line of business. This data can be used to calculate historical claim costs on a per member or employee basis, as it provides the appropriate exposure information to use in conjunction with the claims data files for this calculation. In addition, this data can be used to assess the historical mix of business and consider what changes may be expected in the future.

Provider Contract System

Managed care medical products often pay providers according to fixed contractual rates. If contracting is done directly by the insurer, or if discounts are applied automatically through the claim system, a file must be maintained of the appropriate reimbursement rates. Also, special systems are often set up for processing capitations, financial settlements, withholds, bonus payments, and other forms of provider risk-sharing. Data from these systems should be reviewed to understand the payment arrangements underlying historical claim experience, as well as future anticipated changes in contracting arrangements and their impact on projected costs.

Sometimes internal data is not appropriate for projecting future costs, especially in situations where changes are occurring in benefit design, type of group, provider contracts, utilization management, underwriting practices, or claim administration. Movement to plan options that

---

[1] The term "coinsurance" refers to a percentage of cost split between the payer and the member. It may refer to either the payer's share or the member's share of the costs. Where specificity is required and the context is otherwise unclear, this text uses terms such as "payer coinsurance" or "member coinsurance" to identify which party is responsibility for paying a given coinsurance amount.

may attract a different type of consumer due to their innovative plan design features, underwriting, or care management provisions (for example, HDHPs) only compounds this issue. Additionally, insurers do not always track information at the detailed claim level, since individual claims are not always the basis for benefit payments (for example, when a policy has a family deductible only). In situations of significant change, or if the volume of a company's own claims data is not sufficient to be credible, it must be supplemented with other external data. In addition, an insurer may use external data as a check for reasonableness against internal company data.

When using external data, it is important to understand the characteristics of the population that may affect experience, as well as the time period from which experience is gathered. It is also important to consider any limitations which may be inherent in the data collection mechanism, such as over- or under-reporting, or simplified assumptions. External data source providers are typically not as adept as internal sources at understanding how population characteristics can affect accuracy. As such, it is essential for the actuary to analyze and understand the credibility and appropriateness of the data source used for any particular assignment.

External data can be from public sources such as the Centers for Medicare & Medicaid Services (CMS), the Center for Disease Control and Prevention (CDCP) and the Bureau of Labor Statistics (BLS), or purchased from industry sources or actuarial consulting firms. There is a more detailed listing of available data sources in the appendix at the end of this chapter.

COLLECTING DATA FOR MANUAL RATES

Data to develop medical claim costs should be collected in a level of detail that is consistent with the company's rating methodology. The variables discussed below should be considered, both in collecting data to use in the development of the manual rate, and in adjusting the manual rate for a group-specific rate development.

Companies will often only capture data that is needed to facilitate prompt claim processing, though as data entry techniques and the ability to handle data files continues to improve, the amount of information collected is also increasing. To the extent they can, insurers protect their data as proprietary information making it less available publicly. That being said, the availability of filed actuarial memoranda, and Supplemental Health Care Exhibits provided within statutory annual reports, has increased the public availability of competitive information. However, this information is summarized at a much less detailed level, which should be considered carefully when using this data as an alternate source of information. The following section describes variables that should be considered during the collection process.

FINANCIAL INFORMATION

When collecting financial data in order to estimate medical claim costs, there are a few important considerations. One is to define the type of claim dollars to be collected. If benefit plans or provider reimbursement arrangements are changing, it will be useful to collect not only paid claim amounts, but also billed and allowed claim dollars. The billed and allowed amounts, similar to the paid amounts, should reflect only services covered by the insured arrangement.

The difference between paid and allowed amounts normally reflects the value of any insured cost sharing (deductible, coinsurance, or copayments). The difference between allowed and billed amounts normally reflects the negotiated provider reimbursement arrangements.

Other items that must be clearly defined in the data include the treatment of reinsurance recoveries and coordination of benefit (COB) recoveries. The preferred situation is to have the claim information reflect 100% of the claims for covered services, before reductions for reinsurance and COB recoveries. It is also important, however, to be able to identify these recoveries and, potentially, adjust for them as part of the rating process.

EXPERIENCE PERIOD

If possible, data should be collected for an incurral period of at least twelve months. A twelve-month period ensures the data being studied includes a complete seasonal cycle of incurrals and payments. Capturing the complete seasonal cycle is important because claim levels vary over the year. One examples of seasonal variation is the fact that individuals may use fewer elective care services than average during the months of November and December since they will often postpone elective treatment during the year-end holidays. A second example of seasonal variation involves plans with deductibles, for which incurred claims in the earlier months of the year are often lower because the insurance benefits do not apply until after the deductible is paid. The seasonality of claims for HDHPs is particularly significant. HDHPs with non-calendar-year deductibles add another level of complexity, as their seasonal pattern may differ from that of plans with calendar year deductibles.

Collecting data for a two or three-year time period should be considered, since it allows for identification of variances that may have taken place between years. This is particularly important for risk taking entities that may have less credible data.

Claims may be analyzed on either an incurred basis or a paid basis. In either case, care should be taken to capture the corresponding exposure information (that is, the number of covered members or contracts during the experience period). Further, assuming claims are being analyzed on an incurred basis, the claims should be completed, or reflective of all claims incurred by the exposed lives over the designated experience period. This can be done by collecting data for a specified incurral period with payment dates extending far enough beyond the incurral period that most claims incurred during the service period will have been paid. Alternatively, the historical payment patterns can be analyzed to estimate completion factors to apply to the data in order to complete the claims to project ultimate incurred claim levels.

EXPOSURE BASIS

Exposure units, or employee and dependent units, are monthly counts of insureds summarized over the experience period. Exposure units have historically been defined as the number of employees, contracts, subscribers or covered persons (members).

Per-capita claim costs calculated on the first three bases are subject to mis-estimation when the covered family composition changes. The fourth basis requires exposure counts for spouses and each child, which often had not been available for many traditional large group plans. However, under the ACA, this information should be available for small groups since premiums are charged on a per-member basis.

In some cases, spouse and children exposure counts are estimated in order to calculate costs on a per-member-per-month (PMPM) basis, as is traditionally done in HMO and other managed care calculations. PMPM-based analyses have become much more prevalent in recent years, as carriers have integrated their managed care and traditional operations. In particular, it is important to perform a PMPM analysis of small group data, given the requirement that premium rates are charged on a PMPM basis. To the extent that large group data is being used as a source for manual rates on small group, this should be considered.

FREQUENCY OF DATA COLLECTION

If a company does a detailed study on an annual basis, the results can be used to study trend and the impact of items such as cost containment programs, plan design changes, or utilization management improvement efforts. When a detailed study cannot be performed annually due to timing, budget, or other constraints, a less detailed study can be performed to evaluate overall medical costs and trends.

NORMALIZING DATA FOR IMPORTANT RATING VARIABLES

In most cases, the historical data must be normalized for a number of factors, including demographic mix, geographic area, benefit plan, group characteristics, utilization management efforts, and provider reimbursement arrangements. Then, when calculating a rate for a specific large group, the manual rate must be adjusted to reflect the characteristics specific to that group, subject to any applicable rating restrictions. This section describes important rating variables to consider when normalizing historical data.

AGE AND GENDER

The variation in claim cost by age and gender can be substantial. For example, adult males under age 25 have roughly 20% of the claim costs of men and women ages 55-64. These age/gender cost relationships do not change significantly from year to year, so it is common to perform age/gender studies relatively infrequently, perhaps every three years.

In the development of a manual rate, the historical costs should reflect the demographics of the block of business being analyzed. The actuary may adjust the historical costs to a standard population using appropriate age/gender factors. Alternatively, the actuary may treat the historical experience as representative of a standard population. In other words, the population underlying the historical experience is defined, by default, as the standard population. The latter is the simpler approach.

Cost variances by age and gender typically vary by major service categories such as hospital, physician, or prescription drugs, particularly if such benefits are sold independently of other coverages (for example, an optional drug rider). Also, variances may occur for higher deductible plans compared to lower cost sharing plans since the incidence of low claim dollars can be different by age and gender than the incidence of high claim dollars. These variances should be considered when developing expected claim costs for large and small group business, to the extent credible. Given these potential variances, companies may develop separate age/gender cost factors by service category and/or benefit plan types in their large group rating manual. Typically these would be set in 5-year or 10-year age bands. For small groups, the insurer must develop average expected costs across the single risk pool based on the overall mix of business by age/gender, as well as the overall expected mix of service categories.

When developing a group-specific rate for a large group, a manual rate is developed to reflect the actual age/gender composition of the group being rated. For small groups, while the underlying expected costs are reflective of the age/gender mix within the single risk pool, the ACA eliminated gender-specific premium rates[2] and restricts the amount of allowable premium rate variation due to age factors. Also, age-based rating factors are defined by the government rather than by the insurer. These limitations need to be accounted for when developing the final small group manual premium rates.

GEOGRAPHIC AREA

In many cases, data may be collected from a broad geographic area where significant differences in claim costs by finer geographic area exist. The variation in claim costs by geographic area for a comprehensive benefit plan can vary widely, even as much as +/- 50%. As such, when collecting experience period data, it is important to normalize the raw data to reflect one specific geographic area.

As with age/gender factors, area factors can be studied at either a detailed level or in aggregate. Many companies lack sufficient volume to credibly study their own claim cost variations at the ZIP code, county, or metropolitan statistical area (MSA) level in all states where they do business. A company might use area factors from a competitor or from an actuarial consultant, and then monitor loss ratios by area as experience emerges. Higher variation between the actual versus expected loss ratio indicates areas that require adjustment.

Separate utilization and charge area factors at a detailed level are often difficult to establish because of limited amounts of data. For details on selected services, one might focus on a fine level of service, while keeping the area dimension broad, such as by state. For details at a fine level of geography, such as ZIP code, one might focus only on total claim costs. Computer statistical packages can be helpful in evaluating such data.

For small groups, the ACA allows insurers to vary costs by predefined geographic areas. Under the ACA, area factors are allowed to differ for provider contract differences, but area factors are not allowed to differ for better or worse *morbidity;* this impact is required to be spread across the entire single risk pool and cannot be included in area factors. For example, if Area A is expected to have 10% higher costs than Area B due to a company's negotiated payment arrangements, but then actually has 20% higher experience costs given a population with worse health status, only the 10% differential is allowed to be included in the area

---

[2] Many states had already disallowed gender as a rating variable before the ACA.

factor under ACA's small group rules. Similar to the age/gender rating limitations, a company would develop expected claim costs across the entire single risk pool based on the expected mix by geographic area, but would then consider any rating limitations that must be applied in developing final small group manual premium rates. The government defines the geographic rating areas within each state but, unlike the age factors, each insurer can determine which geographic factors to use.

BENEFIT PLAN

Different benefit plans can produce significantly different claim costs, even when all other variables are identical. Claim costs often must be adjusted to reflect a different benefit plan from the average plan included in the claim data.

Plan design variations in traditional plans often include deductibles, coinsurance, copayments, and out-of-pocket limits. Other variations can include wellness benefits, prescription drugs, inside limits on specified services (if allowed under the ACA), the definitions of family deductibles, and carry-over provisions. Managed care plans often have hybrid benefit designs that include combinations of copayments on some services and deductibles and coinsurance on other services.

Different benefit plans are likely to experience different utilization patterns depending on the degree of insured cost sharing. This is often referred to as "induced utilization" or "induced demand". For example, a group with a $5,000 deductible may have lower utilization than a group with a $100 deductible, simply because the higher deductible often acts as a deterrent to an individual seeking medical care. Further, data on a $5,000 deductible plan may not reflect all physician office visits, because relatively few office visit claims are paid on claims in excess of the deductible, and people are less likely to submit such claims if they know they fall under the deductible. That being said, the impact from underreporting has likely diminished as electronic filing of claims has increased. Similarly, a plan that does not cover chiropractors is not likely to have data on chiropractic charges. Other information or assumptions will be needed to assess the value of benefit changes in those instances.

Once again, it is important to normalize the experience period data to reflect a common benefit plan. In many cases, it is most practical to adjust all experience data to reflect the richest benefit plan. This process normally involves using allowed charge data and adjusting utilization to reflect the estimated impact on utilization if all insureds had the richest benefit plan. The adjustments can be quite detailed, depending on the cost structures underlying the benefit plans.

HDHPs can have an additional level of complexity, as utilization (and thus cost) of benefits under plans with identical benefits may vary based on how much money from an underlying account (either a Health Savings Account or a Health Reimbursement Account) is available to pay for benefits.

To some extent, the variance in utilization under different benefit plans is the result of induced utilization. However, costs will also be affected in that members who are more or less healthy will select benefit plans because they are aware of the services they will or will not need (also referred to as "plan selection"). This effect is more prevalent in the small group market, at least when options are offered, since small employers generally have a greater awareness of their employees' medical needs.

Under the ACA, insurers are not allowed to reflect plan selection in small group plan rates since that is related to morbidity variance, which is prohibited. Similar to geographic area, this impact is required to be spread across the entire risk pool and cannot be included in the benefit plan specific rating factors. As such, a company would develop expected claim costs in total based on the expected benefit plan mix across the single risk pool, and then consider any rating limitations that must be applied in developing final premium rates.

GROUP CHARACTERISTICS

The manual rate should represent the average group in terms of group characteristics, such as industry and group size. Therefore, historical experience must be adjusted to reflect average group characteristics.

Industries with above average costs typically involve physical labor, such as mining or construction, or those where employees tend to be highly aware of available benefits and services, such as educational institutions and health care providers. Additionally, certain industries are more attractive to people with lifestyles that may be healthier or less healthy.

Group size can also be a significant rating factor. As the size of a group decreases, the influence of individuals with serious conditions is magnified, and the cost per exposure unit can increase significantly, with even just one high cost individual. As the size of a group increases, the impact of individuals with serious conditions is dampened. The ACA restricts small group pricing from using rating variables based on group size, though it is important to understand the mix of group sizes within the single risk pool in evaluating experience and determining average costs.

There is some tendency for smaller employers to provide medical coverage in a way that selects against insurers, since these employers may be aware of specific health conditions of their employees, and may choose the plan most beneficial to covering a particular condition. With the removal of underwriting and coverage limitations for pre-existing conditions under the ACA, this is even more important to consider when looking at small group historical experience.

UTILIZATION MANAGEMENT PROGRAMS

Most managed care plans use a process known as utilization review or utilization management (UM) to assess the necessity of a given treatment or the appropriateness of the setting in which care is delivered. A well-designed UM program helps ensure timely delivery of appropriate care by qualified providers in an efficient setting.

Conceptually, UM can take place either before, during, or after care is delivered. The focus of prospective UM is typically on necessity of proposed treatment and appropriateness of setting. Prior to the delivery of care, UM involves preauthorization programs where certain proposed treatments must be approved before it is delivered. During the delivery of care, UM involves monitoring patient progress and planning for conclusion of care. Post-treatment, or retrospective, UM focuses on ensuring that all reported care was actually delivered, to see if charges for required care were appropriate, or to assess whether certain care was necessary. UM also includes disease management, which focuses on providing appropriate care to patients with chronic diseases, such as diabetes, that require ongoing care for an extended period. A more detailed discussion of UM programs can be found in Chapter 44, "Medical Care Management".

The source data should be adjusted for any significant changes in UM programs, either during the experience period or between the experience period and the rating period. In making such adjustments, it should be kept in mind that the impact of any given UM program can vary significantly from one health plan to another, depending on the size and active involvement of the plan's provider network in such care management.

PROVIDER REIMBURSEMENT ARRANGEMENTS

Compensation arrangements between insurers and health care providers take a wide variety of forms. For example, hospital reimbursement can be based on discounts from billed charges, per diems, case rates, Medicare payment levels, capitation, or other arrangements. More recently, providers have started entering into risk-sharing arrangements with insurers, whereby they share in the risk (and also reward) with insurers.

If any provider reimbursement arrangements changed during the experience period, it is important to adjust the experience to reflect a common reimbursement level. An obvious example would be if a managed care organization had a capitation arrangement with their primary care physicians that terminated during the experience period. There would most likely be little or no information on the capitated services prior to the change, but the services would appear in the data after the arrangement was terminated. In this case, an adjustment would be necessary to reflect the claim amounts on a non-capitated basis throughout the entire experience period.

Similar adjustments would be required if a physician fee schedule, per diem schedule, or even a discount arrangement changed during the experience period.

OTHER RISK ADJUSTERS

Age and gender factors are a form of risk adjustment used historically in the health insurance industry. However, more refined methods of risk adjustment have emerged and become more common, particularly with the risk adjustment program for small groups under the ACA. More refined risk adjusters, based primarily on claim, diagnosis, encounter data, and/or pharmacy claim information, may eventually replace age and gender adjustments, as well as potentially geographic and industry adjustments, as the primary method of risk adjustment in the future. The use of these factors for small groups is helpful in evaluating experience across the single risk pool, but would not be allowable as a rating variable for a specific employer group.

PROJECTING EXPERIENCE PERIOD COSTS TO RATING PERIOD

Claim costs are trended from the experience base time period over which data is collected, to the rating period (the period over which rates will be effective). This is done for developing expected manual costs for large and small group, as well as when looking at a particular large group's experience.

For purposes of estimating medical claim costs, measuring and projecting trend is a critical component of the process. When projecting experience from a base period to a rating period, it is usually necessary to estimate cost increases for a period of fifteen months or more. For this purpose, trend includes all elements that may influence average medical claim costs. These elements include not only changes in the average unit cost per service, but also changes in the utilization of services, as well as changes in medical practice patterns, in the mix of services, and in provider reimbursement arrangements. New technologies, drugs, and services also have an impact on trend. The implementation of the ACA had an influence on trend, particularly in the early years of its implementation. Finally, plan design can affect trends, due to deductible and copay leveraging.

In establishing appropriate trend adjustments to reflect all of these elements, the actuary should separate the elements between secular trends and other factors. Secular trends are defined as the percentage change in average claim costs resulting only from those factors that affect a static population with first dollar, 100% benefits. The two major components of secular trend are changes in the utilization of services and changes in the average unit cost per service.

Secular trends can be estimated by examining historical changes in both utilization and average unit costs, as well as by reviewing external information such as health care market studies, surveys, or econometric models. Historical changes in claim costs can be reviewed in various levels of detail, depending on the detail available in the experience data and the desired precision in the trend assumptions. Trends can be examined by comparing total medical costs for all services combined, or can be reviewed by individual types of service (hospital inpatient, hospital outpatient, physician, and prescription drugs), or even in more detailed categories. Within each of these categories, historical trends can be separated further between changes in utilization and changes in unit costs.

Whatever level of detail is used in the analysis of historical trends, it is useful to measure trends over three-month and twelve-month rolling periods. The pattern of twelve month trends indicates the magnitude of annual trends, while the three month pattern can be a leading indicator of trend direction. When reviewing historical trend patterns, it is important to keep in mind the historical changes in provider reimbursements, utilization management efforts, and average benefit levels. Changes in these factors over time could explain some of the historical trend patterns.

When looking at small group data, it will be important to consider the effect of the ACA on experience after the new rating and underwriting rules took place in 2014. During this transition period of the market from pre- to post-ACA, the variances in demographic mix and morbidity risk will likely have an impact on evolving trends. It is important to note that this transition period will last longer than expected due to regulatory changes that allowed small groups to keep their pre-ACA coverage in many states through the 2016 plan year (which for many, ends sometime in 2017). There may also be some effect on large group data, but on a lesser scale given fewer changes in underwriting and rating rules.

When negotiated arrangements include scheduled reimbursements, such as inpatient per diems, case rates, or physician fee schedules, the secular trend on unit costs can be estimated by examining the changes in these arrangements between the experience period and the rating period. However, negotiated arrangements based on discounts off billed charges are less useful in estimating trend, as the unit costs will also be heavily affected by changes in billed charges.

Managed care plans have historically been able to moderate health care trends to some extent, through a combination of UM efforts and negotiated reimbursement arrangements. However, managed care trends have gradually increased and become closer to traditional health care trends over the years, as UM efforts have softened and providers have become more aggressive in reimbursement negotiations.

Furthermore, cost shifting among payers has resulted in disproportionate provider cost increases to commercial plans. For example, as government programs such as Medicare and Medicaid limit payments to providers, providers raise charges for insured patients to ensure that their overall costs are covered by their reimbursements from all sources.

Finally, trends are influenced by plan design. Deductibles and copayments can create trend leveraging, which increases the impact a secular trend has on claim costs. Trend leveraging is becoming a more significant issue as deductibles are increasing and HDHP's have become more prevalent. Trend leveraging is discussed greater detail in Chapter 34, "Medical Claim Cost Trend Analysis".

METHODS OF ADJUSTING MANUAL BASE RATES

Once the data has been collected, properly normalized, and trended to the rating period, it represents a standardized set of claim costs. The insurer is then ready to calculate the manual rate for a specific large group or situation. The manual rate must be adjusted to reflect the characteristics of the specific group or situation to be rated. These characteristics include all the variables considered in the manual rate development (including demographics of the group, geographic area, group size, industry, tobacco use, and other rating factors not specifically discussed in this chapter). For small group business, the insurer will consider the mix of business across the entire risk pool, as well as the allowable rating variables and their limitations, to determine expected average costs and manual premium rates for small group members.

Once the characteristics of the group are recognized, the benefit plan must be reflected. The method chosen to calculate claim costs depends most importantly on the style of benefit plan. Benefit adjustments for traditional insurance products with deductibles and coinsurance are calculated very differently from benefit adjustments for traditional managed care products, which likely have first dollar coverage and fixed copayments on specified services.

CLAIM PROBABILITY DISTRIBUTIONS

Claim probability distributions (CPDs) are typically used to estimate the impact of deductibles, coinsurance, copayments, and out-of-pocket maximums. CPDs are sometimes called "continuance curves" if continuous, or "continuance tables" if discrete. They are most commonly used for plans whose reimbursement methodology and benefit design are primarily a deductible and coinsurance structure (such as PPOs and HDHPs).

In this method, the estimated medical claim costs are determined using a CPD from an established database. As discussed above, there are many factors that might change between the experience period and the rating period. Further, where data is obtained from sources other than the block for which claims are being estimated, there may be differences in these factors.

An example of a CPD is shown in Table 21.1, though this is only an excerpt from a full CPD table; an actual CPD table will display the full range of claims.

To construct a CPD, the annual claims are first summarized on a per member basis. The members are then grouped into cost ranges based on their annual claim payments. The data in columns (2) and (3) are calculated on a per member per year basis, and these two columns define the CPD. The remaining columns are calculated to help ease the use of the CPD, and are developed as follows:

- Column (4) is the product of Columns (2) and (3)
- Column (5) is the backsum of Column (2)
- Column (6) is the backsum of Column (4).

Table 21.1

(1)	(2)	(3)	(4)	(5)	(6)	(7)	(8)
Range of Claims (excerpts)	Frequency	Average Annual Claims	Annual Cost	Accumulated Frequency	Accumulated Annual Cost	Value of Claim Cost in excess of the high end of range	Value of Deductible equal to high end of range
$0	0.250000	$0	$0.00	1.000000	$3,000.00	$3,000.00	$0.00
$0.01-50.00	0.050000	40	2.00	0.750000	3,000.00	2,963.00	37.00
$50.01 - $150.00	0.100000	100	10.00	0.700000	2,998.00	2,898.00	102.00
$150.01-250.00	0.100000	200	20.00	0.600000	2,988.00		
....	....	....	....	....	....	....	....
$4,000.01-5,000.00	0.025000	4,500	112.50	0.150000	2,500.00	1,762.50	1,237.50
$5,000.01-6,000.00	0.020000	5,400	108.00	0.125000	2,387.50	1,649.50	1,350.50
$6,000.01-7,000.00	0.015000	6,900	103.50	0.105000	2,279.50	...	...
....	....	....	....	....	....	....	....
>$900,000.01	0.000005	1,050,000	5.25	0.000005	5.25	0.00	3,000.00

Column (7), the Value of Claim Cost in excess of the high end of range, is the difference between the following Accumulated Annual Cost, Column (6), and the product of the high end of the range and the following Accumulated Frequency, Column (5).

Examples:

Value of Claim Cost in excess of $50 deductible = $2963.00 = $2998.00 − $50 × 0.70
Value of Claim Cost in excess of $150 deductible = $2898.00 = $2988.00 − $150 × 0.60
Value of Claim Cost in excess of $5000 deductible = $1762.50 = $2387.50 − $5000 × 0.125

Column (8), the Value of Deductible equal to high end of range, is essentially the complement of Column (7), where for each point in the claim distribution, the entire total value of average claim cost (in this example, $3,000), is broken up between that above a specific point, and that below. Columns (7) and (8) always add to $3,000 in this example.

The values in Column (8) can be used to estimate the value of any deductible. If a deductible is not explicitly one of the breakpoints on the CPD table, the value of the plan's deductible is calculated by simply interpolating the *change in deductible values* higher and lower than the deductible being analyzed, and adding back the value of the lower deductible.

As seen in Table 33.1, the claim distribution is neither uniform nor steady. Still, most actuaries and underwriters use simple straight-line interpolation in calculating the value of the deductible in question. This does not introduce too much error, as long as the CPD claim ranges are not too broad.

The equation for this interpolation is as follows:

$$D_x = [(C_x - C_A)/(C_B - C_A) \cdot (D_B - D_A)] + D_A$$

where:

D_x = Unknown value of deductible

C_x = Deductible proposed for plan design in question

C_A = Deductible on table just lower than that being analyzed

D_A = Value of deductible just lower than that being analyzed

C_B = Deductible on table just higher than that being analyzed

D_B = Value of deductible just higher than that being analyzed

Example:

Consider a plan with a $100 deductible, 80%/20% coinsurance to an out-of-pocket limit of $900 (including the deductible). Thus, the plan covers 0% of the first $100 in claims, 80% of the next $4,000 in claims, and 100% of any charges above $4,100. From the CPD in Table 33.1, the values of the proposed plan design thresholds can be calculated, as illustrated in Table 21.2 below:

Table 21.2

Deductible	Value of Claims Over Deductible	Value of Deductible
$0	$3,000.00	$0.00
50	2,963.00	37.00
100 (interpolated)	2,930.50	69.50
150	2,898.00	102.00
4,000	1,737.50	1,262.50
4,100 (interpolated)	1,733.50	1,266.50
5,000	1,697.50	1,302.50

The estimated claim cost for this plan is calculated as follows:

$$
\begin{aligned}
&(\$69.50) &\times\ &0.00 \\
+\ &(\$1{,}266.50 - \$69.50) &\times\ &0.80 \\
+\ &(\$3{,}000.00 - \$1{,}266.50) &\times\ &1.00 \\
& &=\ &\$2{,}691.10
\end{aligned}
$$

This method is most useful for pricing comprehensive or major medical coverages, where there is a comprehensive deductible, coinsurance, and an out-of-pocket limit. When member cost-sharing varies by detailed type of service, an actuarial cost model is useful, as described in the next section.

ACTUARIAL COST MODELS

The actuarial cost model method builds an estimated total claim cost by developing a claim cost in detail by type of service category. This method is used to rate many HMO plans, and is also useful for PPO, POS, and other plans utilizing copayments. The actuarial cost model method is most useful where there are copayments and limits, which apply to specific services, rather than to all services combined.

The actuarial cost model method uses a per-member-per-month (PMPM) basis for a cost estimate for various medical service categories, which collectively reflect all the services covered under the benefit plan. This method projects the annual utilization (or frequency) of services provided and the average cost per service for each category.

The gross benefit cost is typically quoted in PMPM units, and is calculated as one-twelfth (for a monthly rate) of the product of: (1) the annual frequencies and (2) the average allowed charges per service. The gross benefit cost is then reduced by the value of any plan copayments to arrive at the net benefit cost (PMPM) for each type of service. A total net benefit cost (PMPM) is then derived.

In developing the estimated cost per service targets, applicable provider arrangements should be recognized. For example, if an HMO had a fully capitated arrangement with all network physicians, the net benefit cost would be known in advance, and actual utilization and cost per service would not affect the capitation rate. However, if a capitation rate had a risk-sharing element, an estimate of the results of the risk-sharing arrangement would have to be developed.

In practice, an HMO might have a fully capitated rate with one group of physicians, a risk sharing arrangement with another, and discount arrangements with others for the same set of services. In this case, the cost model would reflect a weighted average of such arrangements. Additionally, if the HMO had a per diem arrangement with network hospitals, the per diem rate would be used to develop the associated unit costs for inpatient hospital services.

Table 21.3 illustrates an application of the cost model method. In this example, the total net benefit cost is $432.97 PMPM, comprised of $208.83 for hospital services, $152.50 for physician services, and $71.64 for ancillary services. In this table, the net benefit cost is developed by major service category: hospital, physician, and ancillary services. When applying the cost model method, assumptions and methods must be chosen to be consistent with the plan provisions and contract arrangements, which may vary by service category. For example, a special form of utilization review may apply to a particular benefit. Further, contractual limitations and benefit restrictions may apply, each of which should be reflected in the calculations.

Table 21.3

Actuarial Cost Model Method – Illustrative Case

Services	(1) Annual Services per 1,000 Members		(2) Avg Cost per Service	(3) Gross PMPM Benefit Cost (1)/1000 × (2)/12	(4) Copay Amount	(5) Value of Copay (1)/1000 × (4)/12	(6) Net Benefit Cost PMPM [(3)-(5)]
I. Hospital Services							
A. Inpatient							
1. Medical	120	Days	$4,800	$48.00	$200	$2.00	$46.00
2. Surgical	85	Days	9,000	63.75	200	1.42	62.33
3. Maternity	30	Days	3,600	9.00	200	0.50	8.50
4. Mental Health	30	Days	1,010	2.53	200	0.50	2.03
5. Substance Abuse	15	Days	750	0.94	200	0.25	0.69
6. Skilled Nursing	20	Days	650	1.08			1.08
B. Outpatient							
1. ER	175	Cases	$1,300	$18.96	$100	1.46	$17.50
2. Radiology	310	Cases	700	18.08			18.08
3. Pathology	370	Cases	220	6.78			6.78
4. Surgery	125	Cases	3,400	35.42			35.42
5. Other Outpatient	500	Cases	250	10.42			10.42
Subtotal				$214.96		$6.13	$208.83

II. Physician Services						
A. Physician Encounters						
1. Office Visits	5,100 Visits	$115	$48.88	$15	$6.38	$42.50
2. Consultations	200 Visits	275	4.58			4.58
3. Immunizations	750 Procedures	50	3.13			3.13
B. Inpatient Visits	250 Visits	$225	$4.69			$4.69
C. Surgery						
1. Inpatient	50 Procedures	$2,700	$11.25			$11.25
2. Outpatient	600 Procedures	570	28.50			28.50
D. Emergency Room	170 Visits	$270	$3.83			$3.83
E. Lab/X-ray	4,500 Procedures	$105	$39.38			$39.38
F. Maternity	30 Procedures	$2,010	$5.03			$5.03
G. Outpatient Mental Health	600 Visits	$145	$7.25			$7.25
H. Outpatient Substance Abuse	20 Visits	$100	$0.17			$0.17
I. Other	75 Services	$350	$2.19			$2.19
Subtotal			**$158.88**		**$6.38**	**$152.50**
III. Ancillary Services						
A. Ambulance	20 Cases	$1,400	2.33			$2.33
B. Rx	10,200 Scripts	75	63.75	$10	$8.50	55.25
C. Home Health	40 Visits	400	1.33			1.33
D. DME	350 Procedures	200	5.83			5.38
E. PT	720 Visits	115	6.90			6.90
Subtotal			**$80.14**		**$8.50**	**$71.64**
Total			**$453.98**		**$21.01**	**$432.97**

USING COST MODELS TO ESTIMATE THE IMPACT OF BENEFIT PLAN CHANGES

Many changes in benefit design can be evaluated based on the actuarial cost model described above. For example, the impact of a proposed increase in an office visit or prescription drug copayment can be most precisely predicted in terms of average utilization and average cost per service.

Unless a change in benefit design actually influences the use of resources or the cost of care delivered, the total cost of care is not changed, but simply allocated differently between the insured and the health plan. One basic question that follows is whether costs should be measured with or without member cost-sharing. In setting rates, insurers will often measure cost changes net of copayments and other items for which they are not responsible. Unless utilization is affected, however, a change in copayment is really cost shifting, not cost savings. Providers will tend to measure the effect of any change in terms of their total compensation, including carrier payments, copayment revenue, and recoveries from other parties.

Table 21.4 shows the estimated cost impact of increasing prescription drug copayments from $10 to $15. All values shown are illustrative.

Table 21.4

(1)	(2) Annual Utilization per 1,000	(3) Gross Cost Per Script	(4) Copay	(5) Net Cost Per Script	(6) Gross PMPM (2) × (3) ÷ 12,000	(7) Net PMPM (2) × (5) ÷ 12,000
Before	10,200	$75.00	$10.00	$65.00	$63.75	$55.25
After	9,800	$75.00	$15.00	$60.00	$61.25	$49.00
Difference	(400)	$0.00	$5.00	($5.00)	($2.50)	($6.25)

As can be seen, the $5 increase in the per prescription copay is assumed to decrease gross costs (the total cost of the prescription) by $2.50 PMPM and net costs (the cost to the plan sponsor) by $6.25 PMPM. The change in gross costs is due entirely to assumed changes in utilization, while the net cost savings reflects both utilization changes and cost shifting.

This example includes several simplifying assumptions that are not likely to be precisely satisfied in practice. First, it is implicitly assumed that all prescriptions cost at least $15. Second, it is assumed that the average cost per script remains the same following the change in utilization. Depending on the time available and the degree of precision desired, the simplified pricing shown above could be expanded to reflect these factors.

Some expected utilization changes are fairly obvious, while others are more subtle. If the office visit copayment is increased, for instance, it is likely that overall office visit utilization will decrease somewhat, as the increased copayment provides a larger disincentive for members to seek care. What is less obvious is that the cost of prescription drugs might also decrease when the office visit copayment is increased, since the decrease in office visits is likely to lead to a decrease in the number of prescriptions written.

For POS and PPO plans, the net cost of care to an insurer or plan sponsor might seem intuitively lower when care is delivered out-of-network. That is, since members bear responsibility for a greater portion of total costs for out-of-network care, it seems probable that the carrier's or employer's cost would be lower. However, depending on the ability of in-network providers to deliver efficient care, and depending on reimbursement and benefit levels, the net cost to the plan sponsor of in-network services might actually be lower. These costs are also affected by which services are obtained out-of-network. Often an insured member may be willing to go out-of-network for treatment if the cost is relatively low, but would use in-network providers for higher cost treatments. Decisions to use out-of-network providers also are dependent on whether cost-sharing provisions are applied separately to in- and out-of-network, or whether some out-of-network cost-sharing applies toward fulfilling in-network cost-sharing limits, or vice versa.

The cost changes due to benefit design change might also be affected by the contractual arrangement in place. For example, if the cost of a certain benefit is covered under a capitation arrangement, a change in the copayment for that benefit will not have any rate impact unless the capitation payment can be adjusted accordingly.

SMALL GROUP CONSIDERATIONS

As discussed earlier in this chapter, there are a number of rules and restrictions applicable to small group rating under the ACA. The following provides additional details regarding small group rating requirements, as well as general background and perspective on the small group market to be considered when looking at historical small group experience and using it to project future expected costs and set premium rates.

GENERAL CONSIDERATIONS

The term "small employer group" was first defined with the enactment of the federal Health Insurance Portability and Accountability Act (HIPAA), effective in July 1997. HIPAA and all states define a small employer group as an employer group of 2-50 eligible employees for purposes of guaranteed availability and renewability, though some states also include employer groups of 1 (self-employed persons). Under the ACA, this definition was further changed to include up to 100 employees, including 1 employee, and also to consider part-time, temporary, and seasonal employees as part of the employee count. The prevailing state definitions for employee count were allowed to be used up until January 1, 2016, at which time the federal definition became effective.[3] However, the distinction of including part-time, temporary, and seasonal workers was effective immediately.

Small employer groups represent 79% of U.S. business establishments, but only 35% of employees, according to the U.S. Agency for Healthcare Research and Quality tabulation. The following table illustrates this fact and presents the distribution of firms by size.

Number of Employees	Distribution of Establishments	Distribution of Employees
< 10	59.6%	11.5%
10-24	11.5%	8.8%
25-99	8.0%	14.6%
100-999	6.5%	18.3%
1000+	14.4%	46.7%
Total	100.0%	100.0%

Source: 2014 Medical Expenditure Panel Survey (MEPS), Agency for Healthcare Research and Quality

Although small groups comprise a large potential market, many do not offer group medical plans to their employees (only 34% of groups with fewer than 100 employees offered a health plan, according to the 2014 MEPS survey). Those groups that offer a plan often include substantial cost-sharing for their employees (in both premiums and benefits), frequently without any employer contribution for dependents of employees. This is primarily due to basic cost considerations and to comparatively high rates of employee turnover.

A small business owner must carefully consider the purchase of group medical insurance in

---

[3] As of the drafting of this chapter, the change to up to 100 employees is still expected to be implemented, although there is bipartisan support in Congress to amend the ACA to give each state the decision as to whether to keep the definition of small group at 50 employees or extend it to 100.

terms of its impact on the success of the business. Since medical insurance is a relatively expensive item, a small employer may elect to cover only the owner and perhaps a few key employees through individual insurance. As with all insurance coverage, owners are much more likely to purchase medical coverage if they suspect their employees or dependents are more likely than average to incur medical expenses. Cost pressures on small business, often coupled with greater first-hand knowledge of the medical status of employees and dependents, create a market with substantial potential for adverse selection.

Under the ACA, small groups with 50 or more employees are required to offer coverage or pay a fee per employee. In addition, though not required by law, small groups with under 50 employees are offered temporary tax credits for providing coverage, with the smaller and lower average wage groups getting higher credits. These regulations and incentives may make the offering of coverage more prevalent in the small employer market. That being said, with many of the barriers to entry removed for the individual market under ACA, employees have more options for getting alternate coverage, and the employer may then be less compelled to provide benefits if, in spite of the fees and tax credits, it does not make business sense to do so.

EVOLUTION OF UNDERWRITING AND RATING

Under HIPAA, small group insurers were required to offer all of their major medical and comprehensive health insurance products on a guaranteed acceptance and renewal basis with very limited exceptions. However, insurers were allowed to consider rating characteristics such as a group's health status, size, and industry in setting premium rates, though many states had limitations around the range of allowable rating factors that could be used for these items (for example, plus or minus 25% for health status). With the group-specific rating variations allowed, insurers would use underwriting to assess a group's characteristics and specific risks and charge an appropriate rate, subject to state limitations. Underwriting of small groups traditionally took place on two levels: (1) evaluating the business entity, and (2) examining the health status and other characteristics of each individual to be covered. These processes were typically quite in depth and allowed the insurer to best understand the risks associated with each group.

With the implementation of the ACA, there were a number of changes effective in 2014 to the underwriting and rating process that have the potential to impact expected costs, including:

- Essential health benefit requirements and standardized benefit tiers ("metal levels") that provide various levels of coverage (for example, 80% for a Gold plan).
- The elimination of a number of allowable rating variables, such as gender, health status, industry, and group size. The removal of health status rating eliminated the need for medical underwriting.
- Further limitations on the range of allowable rating factors for various characteristics and cost considerations, as discussed in more detail below.

With the introduction of the underwriting and rating limitations, the result is a greater amount of subsidy among small groups. For example, those that are older or less healthy than other groups get better rates then they would have without the ACA reforms, while the younger, healthier groups subsidize their costs. As such, when the rules were effective as of January 1, 2014, those groups for which the new rating limitations were most advantageous were the first to adopt the new ACA plans, while those that would experience higher premium increases were more likely to wait. With the extension of the transition period in many states for groups with "pre-ACA" coverage through and including their pre-October 1, 2016 plan year renewals, this created potential disparity between the pre-ACA and ACA plan experience, with the ACA experience more likely comprised of groups adversely selecting against the pool.

Understanding these issues is critical to the evaluation of small group historical experience during this time period, and relative to pre-ACA experience. In addition, it should be considered that some small groups will exit the market due to the new requirements and higher cost to the employer, leaving a potential increased impact to average and thus overall expected costs for those that remain. To some extent, the adverse selection a specific insurer may experience will be offset through the federal risk adjustment program, designed to spread adverse selection across all carriers in the state's market. However, to the extent that adverse selection is a market-wide impact, then relief to insurers and small employers will be negligible.

EXPERIENCE CONSIDERATIONS

With the removal of health status rating and most other allowable underwriting criteria, an insurer may be open to a greater amount of adverse selection from its small groups. While an insurer cannot decline to offer coverage or rate groups for various characteristics, the factors below should be considered in evaluating small group experience to understand potential drivers of poor or favorable experience.

Financial viability

It is important to understand an employer's financial viability and the nature of its employees. Is this a legitimate commercial business? How many years have they been in operation? Is there a significant amount of employee turnover and/or seasonal or temporary workers?

Industry/Occupation

The type of business and the duties performed by its employees are also related to expected future claim costs as certain types of businesses are exposed to higher health risks. Some of these risks are clearly work-related, such as a job that requires handling hazardous chemicals. Other risks are related to lifestyle issues. For example, employees of a motorcycle dealership are more likely to ride motorcycles and present a greater average accident risk than employees of an accounting firm.

Group Size

Group size impacts both expected claims levels and per capita acquisition and maintenance expenses. The larger the group, the more lives over which the morbidity risk can be spread. An individual employee's health status in a larger group will be a smaller factor in the decision to purchase insurance and the level of benefits chosen. Also, the administrative expenses incurred in writing a group of 35 are lower on a per capita basis than those for a group of 10.

Workers Compensation

In states that do not require small employers to purchase workers compensation insurance, insurers will be more susceptible to increased risk since they can no longer deny groups for not having this coverage and will have to cover additional expenses that workers compensation would typically cover for these groups.

Participation

Historically, small groups typically had to meet certain participation requirements set by the insurer in order to qualify for medical coverage. This allowed some protection against adverse selection by prohibiting a significant number of employees (presumably the most healthy) from opting out of coverage. Under the ACA, these limitations are no longer allowed, unless a group is issued outside of its annual renewal date and the open enrollment period designated by the government (Nov. 15 through Dec. 15). However, there are some indirect protections against participation-driven adverse selection under the ACA, including the requirement that groups with over 50 full-time employees offer coverage, and the offering of tax credits to smaller small groups.

Employer Contributions

Groups with higher employer contribution rates are most likely to have the highest number of employees participating. Similar to participation requirements, small groups were historically able to apply reasonable requirements around employer contributions, but this is no longer allowed under the ACA (unless issued outside a renewal date and open enrollment period).

Prior Coverage

The motives of the group for changing carriers or offering insurance for the first time should be understood to the extent possible. Is the group increasing benefits or seeking more competitive premium rates? Is the group seeking to add employees who were not covered under the prior carrier and would have been considered late entrants? Are certain dependents being added who were not covered by the prior plan? There are other motives for antiselection that might also be detected by soliciting information about the prior coverage.

UNDERWRITING THE SMALL EMPLOYER

The insurer still has the ability to perform limited underwriting for small groups in an otherwise guaranteed-available environment. Allowable criteria include the following:

- Verification that the entity is a licensed employer in the state. This particularly impacts small groups with under five employees, usually family-owned businesses. Such checks include verifying that the employer has a tax ID, is making social security contributions for each employee, and other such typical payments required by law.
- Participation and contribution requirements for issues outside the open enrollment period.
- A requirement that a group's employees live, work, or reside within the service area of the plan's network.

- Employee eligibility requirements as to number of hours, being on the payroll, eligibility class, etc.
- Enforcement of employer restrictions on coverage for late entrants (such as waiting periods).

RATING PARAMETERS & STRUCTURES

Under the ACA, the allowable rating parameters for small groups have been greatly limited compared to those allowed historically. Rate adjustments for health status, group-specific experience, gender and other case characteristics are no longer allowed, leading to potential adverse selection by those groups for which it may be most advantageous to purchase coverage. This additional antiselection must then be spread across the entire single risk pool.

Allowable rating factors for small groups under the ACA are outlined below.

Age

Specified rating factors for each age are set by regulation and were determined based on a range limitation of 3:1 for adults. A separate rating factor is specified for children, which does not vary by child age. Most states use the federally defined set of age factors, though states are allowed to file their own age curve for approval by the federal government, which some have done. State alternatives must also be within the 3:1 range, though they may have a narrower range.

Geographic Area

Each state has a defined set of allowable rating zones set by the government for individual and small group insurance, typically defined by county, 3-digit ZIP code, or MSA. Insurers are allowed to vary rates for each of these geographic zones, and the rate variations typically address all or some of the following topics:

- Expected claim cost variation
- Provider payment arrangements
- Area variation in the impact of managed care programs
- Marketing or administrative expense differences by area
- Competitive posturing by area
- Variances in loss ratio minimums by state

Insurers may not vary rating factors by geographic zone based on morbidity variances within a given state. Any expected cost due to morbidity variances must be spread across the single risk pool.

Benefit Plan

Pricing for the specific plan of benefits is a critical component of rating. In the past, there was relatively little regulation in the small group market on how benefits were priced. Reliance on market forces generally produced reasonable rates relative to the benefits provided. Under the ACA, premium rates for benefit plans may differ only by the amounts attributable to plan design and may not vary due to the expected health status for groups selecting particular benefit plans (that is, healthier members selecting less rich benefits and vice versa).

Managed Care and Negotiated Discounts

Insurers are allowed to vary benefit plan premiums for expected cost variance due to different network arrangements and anticipated care management protocols. These variations must be included in the rate factor for the particular benefit plan to which the cost variations are expected. As with other rating factors, the adequacy and competitiveness of the plan's rates are dependent on accurate assumptions as to the impact of managed care, the provider discounts, and the relative use of network providers and out-of-network care.

Family Composition

Small group premiums under ACA are determined based on the insurance certificates to be issued and members to be covered on each certificate. The premium is calculated for each certificate based on the per-member premiums from the insurer's small group rate manual, and then the per-certificate premiums are totaled for the entire group. On a certificate covering children under 18, only the first three children are charged the per-child premium.

Under the ACA, carriers are allowed to charge premiums to the small group based on a composite premium methodology. A composite structure reflects a single premium to be charged based on the family composition of the certificate and the group's total premium rate and demographic mix. Composite premiums have historically been set by family structure (for example, Two Tier - Employee Only / Employee and Family, or Four Tier - Employee Only / Employee and Spouse / Employee and Children / Employee and Family). However, under the ACA, insurers must use the prescribed federal composite structure, unless their state has approved an alternative methodology. As of 2015, the federal methodology prescribes that the composite premium is calculated based on an average enrollee premium amount for covered individuals age 21 and older, and an average enrollee premium amount for covered individuals under age 21. The premium for a given family composition is determined by summing the average enrollee premium amounts applicable to each family member covered under the plan, taking into account no more than three covered children under age 21.

Tobacco Use

Under the ACA, small group premiums are allowed to use a tobacco use rating factor load of up to 50%. Some states may have more restrictive limitations. Small group employer plans that charge a tobacco use surcharge must offer a smoking cessation benefit to offset the surcharge (at least in part) for those who participate in the program.

RISK ADJUSTMENT PROGRAM

The federal government introduced a risk adjustment program applicable to all small group business on a state-by-state basis in an attempt to normalize the risk of guaranteed issue and new rating restrictions under the ACA. The formulas generally break the risk-sharing into two pieces: (1) demographic risk, and (2) health status risk. The federal risk adjustment program is set up to be a "zero-sum game," whereby those insurers with higher risk members will get payments and those with healthier risks will pay into the pool. The transfer payments are determined based on the market-wide pool of business within a given state. In setting premium rates, the impact of a company's risk adjustment transfer or payment should be considered.

Further discussion of risk adjustment formula programs is included in Chapter 33, "Health Risk Adjustment".

SUMMARY

This chapter has presented various methods, criteria, and considerations that insurers employ for evaluating claims experience and developing expected medical costs for use in setting premium rates for group business. Specific considerations are necessary for small groups given their general dynamics, as well as the underwriting and rating limitations that were introduced under the ACA.

APPENDIX: DATA SOURCES

FEDERAL GOVERNMENT PUBLICATIONS

There are many sources of data compiled by the federal government relating to causes of morbidity, mortality and disability as well as price trends and demographics. Most government studies are published on the Internet, while many others are available electronically from the national Technical Information Service, a division of the U.S. Department of Commerce.[4] Useful other sources include:

The National Ambulatory Medical Care Survey (NAMCS)

The Centers for Disease Control and Prevention[5] (CDC) sponsors this detailed annual survey of physicians on the ambulatory medical care rendered at non-federally employed physicians' offices. A number of detailed analyses are published from this survey, including encounter rates by physician specialty, outpatient department visits by geographic area, drug and lab test prescribing patterns, and reason for encounter. Since the survey has been performed over a number of years, historical information and trends are also available. Many results are presented by age and sex, which can facilitate the extrapolation of results to the insured population.

The National Hospital Discharge Survey (NHDS)

This is an annual CDC survey[6] which focuses on the experience among hospitalized individuals in the general population. Patient discharge records from a sample of non-Federal short stay hospitals are compiled. As with the NAMCS, a number of specific analyses are published from this survey, including hospitalization frequency by diagnosis and by region, and length of stay by diagnosis. This survey has also been performed over a number of years, which allows for analysis of trends. As with the NAMCS, the NHDS is a general population survey rather than a survey of the insured population, so some adjustments in results may be appropriate.

---

[4] www.ntis.gov
[5] www.cdc.gov/nchs/ahcd.htm
[6] www.cdc.gov/nchs/nhds.htm

The National Health Interview Survey (NHIS)

This is an annual survey of individuals which covers demographic characteristics, illnesses, impairments, chronic conditions and utilization of health care services. The survey can be found at Center for Disease Control website[7].

Consumer Price Index (CPI)

The Bureau of Labor and Statistics[8] publishes CPI information monthly. This index examines the cost of fixed "market baskets" of goods and services nationally and in specific localities. Medical, dental, prescription drugs, and other health care services are included in the analysis. Since this is a market basket analysis, it reflects inflationary trends only, not trends in utilization of services.

National Nursing Home Survey (NNHS)

This is a series of national surveys sponsored by the National Center for Health Statistics (NCHS). These surveys provide information regarding nursing homes, their services, staff and residents. They include metrics such as size, ownership, Medicare/Medicaid certification, services provided, programs offered and charges. The survey can be found at National Center for Health Statistics website.[9]

Health, United States Annual Report

This annual report on the health status of the Nation is compiled by the CDC. The report presents current trends in morbidity, health care utilization, health risk factors, prevention, health insurance, and personal health care expenditures. The report can be found at National Center for Health Statistics website.[10]

Public Health Service Sources

- Center for Disease Control and National Center for Health Statistics
  - National Vital Statistics Systems
  - National Survey of Family Growth
  - National Health Interview Survey
  - National Health and Nutrition Examination Survey
  - National Hospital Discharge Survey
  - National Nursing Home Survey
  - National Ambulatory Medical Care Survey
  - Seasonal Influenza Website

- Center for Infectious Diseases, AIDS surveillance
- Epidemiology Program Office, National Notifiable Diseases Surveillance System
- Center for Chronic Disease Prevention and Health promotion, Abortion Surveillance
- Center for Prevention Services, U.S. Vaccines and Immunization Survey

---

[7] www.cdc.gov
[8] www.bls.gov/cpi
[9] www.cdc.gov/nchs/nnhs.htm
[10] www.cdc.gov/nchs/hus.htm

Health Resources and Services Administration

- Bureau of Health Professions, Physician Supply Projections

Alcohol, Drug Abuse, and Mental Health Administration

- National Institute on Alcohol Abuse and Alcoholism, National Survey of Drinking
- National Institute on Drug Abuse
  - National Household Surveys on Drug Abuse
  - The Drug Abuse Warning Network
- National Institute of Mental Health, Survey of Mental Health Organizations

National Institutes of Health

- National Cancer Institute, Surveillance, Epidemiology, and End Results Program

Centers for Medicaid and Medicare Services

- Office of the Actuary
  - National Health Expenditures and Indicators
  - Monthly Trend Report for Medicare, Medicaid and SCHIP

Bureau of the Census

- U.S. Census of Population
- Current Population Survey
- Population Estimates
- Statistical Abstract of the United States

Bureau of Labor Statistics

- Consumer Price Index
- Employment and Earnings

ACTUARIAL PUBLICATIONS

A number of actuarial publications provide useful data for pricing or analyzing all group lines. These data usually reflect insured populations, which can be an advantage over the more general population data available through federal sources.

Even though data may reflect insured populations, it is still necessary to examine the underlying population from which data is derived, particularly underwriting source (medically underwritten, guaranteed issue, and so forth) and product (individual or group; PPO or HMO).

Some of the primary sources of actuarial data are briefly described below. More detailed descriptions can be found at the Society of Actuaries SOA website.[11]

---

[11] www.soa.org

Society of Actuaries Research Department

The Society of Actuaries sponsors research activities and projects in the area of health, as well as in Knowledge Extension Research, Finance, Life Insurance, and Retirement Systems. Questions regarding research projects can be directed to the SOA Research Management Coordinator, or the web site can be searched for specific projects.[12]

Research Reports

The Society of Actuaries sponsors reports on areas of special interest. Of particular interest to the group actuary are the reports on "Variation by Duration in Small Group Medical Insurance Claim Costs" and the AIDS and HIV reports.

Tables

Certain mortality and disability tables are available from the Society. Some programs and data are available electronically, including the data from the "Variation by Duration in Small Group Medical Insurance Claim Costs" report.

Serials

The Society of Actuaries sponsors a number of periodicals that can provide useful data. The *Transactions Reports* of Mortality and Morbidity Experience include studies of interest such as group long-term disability morbidity and group annuity mortality. The *Transactions* and the *Records* of the Society of Actuaries and the *Actuarial Research Clearing House* all contain many articles and useful studies.

OTHER EXTERNAL SOURCES

Depending upon the need, the group actuary may look to many other sources of data. As always, the actuary must carefully consider the population source of data and the applicability to the problem at hand. Some particularly useful data sources follow.

State Health Data Organizations

Most states sponsor health data organizations which capture and compile hospital discharge data and ambulatory care data. An excellent reference which describes the available state data can be obtained from the National Association of Health Data Organizations (NAHDO) in Washington, D.C.[13] These sources generally do not include exposures, therefore the actuary must look to other sources, such as census data and other demographic statistics, to develop claim cost estimates. The migration of patients from one area to another must be considered when this is done.

---

[12] www.soa.org/research
[13] www.nahdo.org

HMO and PPO Data Sources

Data on the usage of services in HMOs is available from several sources, including the America's Health Insurance Plans (AHIP),[14] HealthLeaders-InterStudy,[15] and the American Association of Preferred Provider Organizations (AAPPO).[16]

The National Committee for Quality Assurance

The National Committee for Quality Assurance (NCQA)[17] is an organization formed for assessing and reporting on the quality of Managed Care plans. NCQA has designed the Health Plan Employer Data and Information Set (HEDIS), a set of 75 standardized measures used to compare health plans' performance. HEDIS is updated annually to reflect advancements in the science of performance measurement, information systems technology, and changes in the managed care industry.

Hospital, Medical and Other Periodicals and Sources

The American Hospital Association (AHA) and the American Medical Association (AMA) publish directories of hospital and physician resources and other items of interest. There are numerous other medical publications which may be useful, including the *Journal of the American Medical Association*[18] and the *New England Journal of Medicine*.[19] In addition, useful statistics can be found at the American Association of Health Plans' website.[20]

Actuarial Consulting and Analytics Firms

A number of firms, such as Milliman, Inc.,[21] publish pricing manuals and guidelines that include extensive data on health care utilization and costs. Organizations such as Truven Health Analytics[22] provide detailed data sources that can be used for analysis.

Other Organizations

Organizations established by a charitable trust like the Kaiser Family Foundation,[23] The Robert Wood Johnson Foundation,[24] The Commonwealth Fund,[25] and The RAND Corporation[26] regularly publish health research and often provide additional sources of data for practitioners to consider.

---

[14] www.ahip.org
[15] hl-isy.com
[16] www.aappo.org
[17] www.ncqa.org
[18] www.ama-assn.org
[19] www.nejm.org
[20] www.ahipresearch.org
[21] www.milliman.com
[22] www.truvenhealth.com
[23] www.kff.org
[24] www.rwjf.org
[25] www.commonwealthfund.org
[26] www.RAND.org

22 ESTIMATING DENTAL CLAIM COSTS

Courtney Morin
Leigh M. Wachenheim
Laurence Weissbrot

The basic techniques and considerations involved in developing claim costs for dental insurance plans are very similar to those for medical plans. This chapter discusses the data sources commonly used as a basis for developing claim costs for dental plans, as well as the factors that affect claim costs, including characteristics of both the benefit plan and the insureds. Additional considerations related to voluntary plans, plans offered in a multiple option setting, networks, and experience rating are also discussed. This chapter includes numerical examples that are based on a typical comprehensive benefit plan, as outlined in Table 22.1.

Table 22.1

	A Typical Comprehensive Dental Plan		
Class	**I** Diagnostic and Preventive	**II** Basic	**III** Major
Payer Coinsurance	100%	80%	50%

Covered Benefits	Oral Evaluations
	Prophylaxis
	Fluoride Treatments
	X-Rays
	Laboratory and
	  Other Diagnostic
	  Tests
		Emergency
		  Treatment
		Space Maintainers
		Simple Extractions
		Surgical Extractions
		Oral Surgery
		Anesthesia Services
		Restorations
		Periodontics
		Endodontics
			Inlays/Onlays/Crowns
			Dentures and Other
			  Removable
			  Prosthetics
			Bridges and Other
			  Fixed Prosthetics
			Denture and Bridge
			  Repair
			Other Prosthetics
			Implants

Annual Deductible	$0	$100	
Annual Maximum	$1,500		

While the results discussed in this chapter could be expected to change somewhat with the plan, the general principles they illustrate still apply.

This chapter covers only the development of claim costs – the amounts paid to the dentists and ancillary providers who deliver dental care, less the portion of those amounts paid by the insured through cost sharing. In order to turn these claim costs into premiums, provision must be added for other costs, such as sales commissions, administration, network access fees, premium taxes, federal fees created under the Affordable Care Act (ACA), risk margins, and profit.

DATA SOURCES

Estimated claim costs for dental plans are typically developed by analyzing and adjusting experience from some recent past period. If available and credible, an insurer's own historic data may well be the best experience base. This data reflects not only the carrier's particular benefit plans, negotiated fee levels, and population demographics, but also its specific business practices in critical areas such as underwriting, claims adjudication, and utilization management. In addition, a carrier is likely to be aware of any problems or biases in its data.

Historic experience is not always available or may not be appropriate for developing expected claim costs. For example, a carrier may plan to enter a new geographical area or market segment, or may develop an unusual benefit plan, or simply may not believe that its own data is credible. In those cases, there are a number of other data sources that can be used as a supplemental or primary source.

Several databases of fee level information are available, including:

- Prevailing Health Care Charges System® (PHCS) and MDR Payment System®: These databases contain fee data by Current Dental Terminology (CDT) procedure code and geographic area. Both of these databases are now maintained by FAIR Health, Inc., a private, not-for-profit company that was created pursuant to a January, 2009 settlement agreement between the New York Attorney General and UnitedHealth Group.
- National Dental Advisory Service®: This database includes fee percentiles by CDT code and three digit zip code. It is based on surveys of practicing dentists.
- American Dental Association "Survey of Dental Fees": This survey includes mean, modal, and percentile fee levels for close to 200 CDT codes. Data is also provided separately by region.

Detailed utilization data is more difficult to obtain. Some consulting firms sell datasets that include utilization statistics by CDT code, as well as average charge data. They may also include adjustment factors for age and gender, industry, area, and other variables that affect dental claim cost.

Another source to consider is the actuarial memoranda and rate filings of other carriers, which are publicly available in some states. These filings can contain fairly detailed information regarding both covered benefits and the rating factors being used to reflect various risk characteristics, such as those discussed in this chapter. While the rates and factors included in these filings may not be appropriate for general use, they can provide a broad overview of how other insurers are reflecting these risk factors in their premium rates.

Finally, insurers may be able to get both charge level and utilization information from third party administrators or reinsurers, particularly where an existing or proposed business relationship exists.

As a general principle, it is important to consider the source and quality of information before using it to develop claim costs or premium rates. The American Academy of Actuaries has issued an Actuarial Standard of Practice on Data Quality (ASOP No. 23). Although it was written with actuaries in mind, this ASOP provides helpful guidance to anyone who is faced with selecting, analyzing, or relying on data for the purposes of developing claim costs. The ASOP recommends that data be selected with due consideration of the appropriateness of the data for its intended use, the reasonableness and comprehensiveness of the data, limitations of the data, modifications or assumptions needed to use the data, the cost and feasibility of alternatives, and the sampling methods used to collect the data.

CLAIM COST FACTORS

The factors that impact claim costs for dental plans can be divided broadly into three categories: (1) those that have to do with the plan, (2) those that have to do with the service providers (networks) and their reimbursement levels, and (3) those that have to do with the covered population (the insureds).

Some factors interact with others and may even overlap the above categories. For example, many insurers use rate manuals that include separate adjustments for group size and participation level, but both adjustments are intended to capture an aspect of antiselection. As another example, trend factors based on billed charge levels may not be appropriate for plans that include negotiated fees or scheduled payments. Therefore, when developing or using claim cost adjustment factors, it is necessary to document and understand how they have been adjusted to reflect these relationships.

THE PLAN

Plan characteristics that affect claim costs include covered benefits and cost sharing provisions, waiting periods, and the period of coverage.

COVERED BENEFITS AND COST SHARING PROVISIONS

It is essential to keep in mind the highly discretionary nature of dental services when designing and developing claim costs for these plans. There is often a wide range of options available for treating a specific dental disease, both in terms of cost and timing. For example, the cost of acceptable treatments for a one-surface posterior restoration could range from $100 for an amalgam filling to $1,400 for a titanium crown. Economic theory and evolving experience suggests that the utilization of discretionary services is very sensitive to the cost paid by the member. For this reason, the member cost sharing provisions of dental plans have a significant impact on the assumed utilization used in developing dental claim costs.

Insureds are usually required to share some of the cost of covered dental services with the insurer through deductibles, coinsurance[1] and co-pays, and annual and lifetime maximums.

---

[1] The term "coinsurance" refers to a percentage of cost split between the payer and the member. It may refer to either the payer's share or the member's share of the costs. Where specificity is required and the context is

Cost sharing provisions have a significant impact on claim cost for at least two reasons: (1) they reduce the cost to the insurer of the services that are provided and (2) they provide an incentive for the insured to choose less expensive services where possible. Many payers believe that encouraging preventive care is cost effective, because it reduces the need for more expensive restorative services. This reduces claim costs. For this reason, cost sharing is usually waived for Class I (diagnostic and preventive) services.

Deductibles

The typical comprehensive plan, outlined in Table 22.1, features a $100 deductible that is waived for Class I services. However, $0 and $50 deductibles are also common designs. These lower deductibles can easily increase claim costs by 5% and 2.5%, respectively, from that of a comprehensive plan with a $100 deductible. Most of this impact will come from an increase in the cost to the insurer of services that have been provided rather than from changes in utilization. Deductibles have a very different effect under voluntary dental plans, as described later in this chapter.

Coinsurance and Co-pays

The level of coverage for one class of dental services can significantly affect the utilization of other covered classes. In particular, richer benefits for basic restorative dental services are frequently tied to higher utilization of preventive and diagnostic services. For example, utilization of Class I services (diagnostic and preventive) under a 100/100/100 (Class I/II/III) coinsurance plan could easily be 25% to 30% higher than utilization of the same services under a 100/80/50 coinsurance plan, where the plan pays for less than 100% of some services. This is because patients would be much more likely to visit a dentist to take care of Class II and III work and, as long as they are at the dentist, much more likely to catch up on Class I services. Also, they are more likely to elect more costly restorative services when several alternatives exist.

"Scheduled" plans pay the provider a fixed, pre-defined amount for each procedure. The patient is responsible for paying the difference between the fee charged by the provider (which can sometimes be a discounted amount) and the coverage amount determined by the schedule. When pricing these plans, actuaries will estimate the total cost per service, and subtract the scheduled amount to determine the effective patient coinsurance for each service. This is important to determine, because utilization levels are so dependent on these amounts paid by the patient. When estimating these patient-paid amounts, it is important to take into account the proportion of providers who will "balance bill" patients for the difference between the pre-defined scheduled fee level and the provider's billed charges. This billing practice varies from provider to provider, and will increase in frequency and amount for lower fee schedules.

Maximum Limits

Like medical plans under the ACA, dental plans for children sold on the Marketplaces may no longer have annual maximum limits. However, unlike essential benefits in medical plans, non-ACA certified child dental plans sold outside of the Marketplaces and all adult plans are allowed to retain annual and lifetime maximums under the ACA. These are common features of dental plans, with annual maximums frequently applied to Class I, II, and III services, and lifetime maximums applied to orthodontic services. In some cases, annual maximum limits are applied only to Class II and III services. Annual maximum limits typically vary between

---

otherwise unclear, this text uses terms such as "payer coinsurance" or "member coinsurance" to identify which party is responsibility for paying a given coinsurance amount.

$1,000 and $2,500, which is the range where they have the most impact. For example, increasing the annual maximum on a comprehensive plan from $500 to $1,500 might easily increase expected claim cost by over 13%; however, increasing the maximum from $1,500 to $2,500 or more will have a relatively minor impact – increasing expected claims by just over 4%. In addition, some expensive dental procedures, such as implants, can be done in stages over a period of years to work around annual maximums, further dampening the impact of higher maximums.

ACA certified pediatric plans sold both on and off the Marketplace may not have an annual maximum, and do have a maximum-out-of-pocket (MOOP) limit. For 2015, the MOOP was set at $350 per child with a $700 per family limit.

Other Considerations

In the case of employer plans, it is important to take into account any interaction with an existing group medical plan, both in terms of cost sharing and covered services. For example, an integrated deductible, where both dental and medical costs can be used to satisfy the deductible, will lessen the value of the deductible in reducing claim costs (relative to a stand-alone deductible of the same amount).

As another example, if certain surgical services (such as the removal of impacted teeth) are also covered under a medical plan, a reduction in dental claim costs may be warranted. This is particularly significant in surgical cases, since patient cost sharing is generally less under the medical plan than it is under the dental plan. Further, coverage for specific benefits can have a material impact on costs. Examples include coverage of the replacement of teeth missing prior to the plan effective date (often excluded), the replacement of existing dentures (often limited to once every five to seven years), dental implants, orthodontic coverage, and radiographs.

WAITING PERIODS

Carriers use waiting (or elimination) periods to discourage prospects from enrolling with the intention of having significant dental problems treated in the first year, and then dropping coverage. The waiting period is the period between enrollment and eligibility to receive benefits. For example, a plan may include no waiting period for Class I services, a 3 or 6-month waiting period for Class II services, and a 12-month waiting period for Class III services. Orthodontia benefits, if they are offered, may be subject to a fairly long waiting period, such as 12-24 months. Not only does the insurer collect premium for a longer time, but the insured has an incentive to keep the coverage in order not to have to repeat the waiting periods the next time coverage is desired.

PERIOD OF COVERAGE

The estimation of claim costs usually involves projecting changes in cost and utilization levels from some base period into the future period of coverage. Therefore, both the rate of change and the length of time between the experience period and the projection period need to be recognized. Trends in dental costs have generally been lower than trends in medical costs in recent years. Dental cost trends have been in the range of 2% to 7% annually, while medical trends have been in the range of 6% to 8%.

Another important factor to consider is the number of effective (potential treatment) days within each period. In some regions, dentists work only four days each week. A "long" month can have as many as 30% more effective days, therefore higher incurral, than a "short" month. Similarly, depending on the calendar, twelve-month periods used for the base period and the projection period can vary by over 2% in the number of effective days. Snowstorms and floods can also affect the availability of dental services differently in different periods. If the number of these events in the base period was unusually high, an adjustment may be appropriate when projecting to a future period.

The rate of change of claim costs for any specific dental plan will also be a function of many other factors, including changes in negotiated reimbursement levels or the method or data used to determine reasonable and customary levels, covered benefits or other policy provisions (such as pre-authorization requirements), provider networks, and general dental practice. The economy can also play a large part in dental claim trend. For example, the poor economy in 2010 – 2012 resulted in increased utilization: increasing numbers of insureds elected major restorative services, presumably due to fear of job loss and resulting loss of dental coverage.

Dental trend is also affected by the leveraging impact of deductibles, a well-known phenomenon in the world of medical insurance pricing. In the case of dental insurance, it is also important to consider the related dampening impact of maximum benefit limits, which are common features that partially offset the leveraging impact of deductibles.

For example, consider a dental plan with the distribution of insureds by annual claims shown in Table 22.2.

Table 22.2

	Impact of Annual Maximums on Expected Claim Cost					
	No Maximum		$1,500 Maximum		$1,000 Maximum	
Percent Insureds	Before Trend	After Trend	Before Trend	After Trend	Before Trend	After Trend
(a)	(b)	(c)	(d)	(e)	(f)	(g)
35.0%	$0.00	$0.00	$0.00	$0.00	$0.00	$0.00
25.0%	150.00	159.75	150.00	159.75	150.00	159.75
20.0%	350.00	372.75	350.00	372.75	350.00	372.75
10.0%	550.00	585.75	550.00	585.75	550.00	585.75
6.0%	850.00	905.25	850.00	905.25	850.00	905.25
3.0%	1,400.00	1,491.00	1,400.00	1,491.00	1,000.00	1,000.00
0.7%	2,000.00	2,130.00	1,500.00	1,500.00	1,000.00	1,000.00
0.3%	3,500.00	3,727.50	1,500.00	1,500.00	1,000.00	1,000.00
Average Claim	$280.00	$298.20	$270.50	$287.11	$253.50	$267.38
Cost Increase		6.5%		6.1%		5.5%

Column (a) is the percentage of insureds in each claim cost grouping bucket. Columns (b) and (c) are annual claims for each bucket before and after applying a 6.5% annual trend factor, assuming no limit on benefits. Columns (d) and (e) and columns (f) and (g) show the same experience, with a $1,500 and $1,000 maximum on annual claims, respectively. The final row ("Cost Increase") shows that, as the annual maximum decreases, the influence of the annual trend factor on the plan's expected claim cost decreases.

NETWORK AND CARE MANAGEMENT

The level of reimbursement to service providers has a major impact on claim cost. Insurers have implemented care management practices to help keep this cost under control.

PROVIDER REIMBURSEMENT

The methods insurers use to reimburse dentists can be broadly separated into three categories: (1) fee-for-service, (2) Preferred Provider Organization (PPO) and (3) capitation. In some cases, a combination of these methods is used to reimburse dentists in a given plan. When analyzing the impact of reimbursement levels on provider incentives, it is important to keep in mind that, for dentists, patient payments for coinsurance and non-covered services is also a critical component of revenue. This is quite different from the medical market, where insurer reimbursement tends to be a significant majority of a provider's revenue among commercially insured patients.

Fee-for-Service

Fee-for-service was the traditional method of reimbursing dentists, but its use has dropped dramatically over the last decade from 35% of dental plans in 2002 to 7% in 2012. The fee-for-service method of reimbursement is appealing due to its simplicity: a dentist performs a service for a covered member and is paid for that service. When fee-for-service reimbursement is used, rather than a capitation payment, the dentist is compensated only when services are actually performed.

Dental insurers typically pay up to the provider's billed amount, but also set a maximum on what they will pay for a particular service. This maximum fee-for-service reimbursement level is normally set at the lower of (1) a high percentile (for example, 90th) of nationally charged fees (considered a "reasonable fee" filter), and (2) a high percentile (for example, 80th) of the locally charged fees (that is, a "customary fee"). This statistic provides a Reasonable and Customary (R&C) fee schedule that varies by geography, where the local and national fee statistics come from a nationally recognized claims database (such as the PHCS maintained by FAIR Health, Inc.) Customary fees are frequently defined as the 80th or 90th percentile (or something similar) of fees being charged locally. Occasionally, lower levels such as the 50th percentile are used.

Some insurers, most notably some of the Delta Dental plans, have their participating dentists pre-file their fees for approval. This then allows these carriers to develop Usual, Customary and Reasonable (UCR) fees. Although the definition of UCR can vary somewhat from plan to plan, it typically refers to a maximum fee schedule which is the lower of: (1) the provider's usual fee for the service, (2) the customary fee in that geographic area, and (3) the reasonable fee based on the circumstance.[2] This method is subject to high inflationary trends as providers have a strong financial incentive to make their usual fees equal to customary fees.

Plans based on UCR reimbursement may also permit the provider to balance bill the patient for any excess between his or her fee and UCR. This effectively increases the insured's coinsurance and should be considered when choosing utilization adjustments to expected claim costs based on cost-sharing levels.

---

[2] *Fundamentals of Employee Benefit Programs*, Sixth Edition. Employee Benefit Research Institute, (2009).

Preferred Provider Organization (PPO) Networks

The concept of prohibiting dentists from balance billing beyond an approved fee schedule led to the development of PPO networks. The insurer contracts with a limited number of dentists in each region and agrees to list the dentist in its network in exchange for a reduced fee schedule, above which the dentist may not bill. That is, while payment may be split between the insurer and the patient according to the cost sharing provisions of the plan, the dentist is not permitted to balance bill the patient for any difference between his or her usual charge and the amount in the fee schedule. Depending on the laws of the state, a dentist may or may not be able to bill above the fee schedule for services not covered by the insurer or the specific group contract, or when the plan maximum has been exceeded. Dental benefit carriers have been competing based on the strengths (size and discount) of their networks. PPO business has risen from 42% of the dental benefits market in 2002 to 78% in 2012. With a PPO, the fee inflation portion of trend can be tightly controlled by the insurer.

Plan design features are designed to encourage insureds to use contracted network providers. In plans that feature a provider network, cost sharing is frequently lower if a participating provider is used. The claim cost for these plans is usually calculated by estimating the claim costs separately for in- and out-of-network services (on a stand-alone basis), and weighting them together using expected usage for weights. Also, some plans will require more cost sharing if a specialist is used for certain services, although this is relatively uncommon, as it can be difficult to administer and may cause confusion among insureds.

PPO maximum fee schedules are typically set by insurers based on an analysis of the distribution of fee levels in the local community, similar to the analysis of R&C maximum schedules described earlier, but with lower percentiles and thus lower maximums. There are a number of data sources available that provide percentiles by CDT procedure code and zip code, including some of those mentioned above. Historically, large national insurers have used maximum fee schedules that are 15% to 25% lower than the 50th percentile or the community average.[3] Maximum fee schedules that are too deeply discounted will impair the insurer's ability to attract providers to the network, which makes it difficult for patients to locate participating dentists.

When analyzing the impact of maximum fee schedules on claim cost, there are several factors to take into account. First, providers may tend to use the insurer's maximum fee schedule to determine the *minimum* amount they will charge for a service, instead of the *maximum* amount they are allowed to charge, as intended by the insurer. Table 22.3 illustrates the impact this might have on claim costs for periodic oral evaluations, one of the most common dental procedures and frequently reimbursed by the insurer at 100%.

In this example, using the fee schedule as a minimum instead of a maximum increases the average fee paid for services by 13%. The potential impact of this practice on claim costs for a given procedure will depend on the range of fees and the fee level that is chosen for the schedule. In reality, providers are not likely to act uniformly in treating the fee schedule either as a minimum or a maximum and the impact would be somewhere in between. Also, there are insurers who, if they are in a position to do so, choose not to share the actual dollar amounts in their maximum fee schedule with the providers, in order to mitigate the tendency to charge the maximum.

---

[3] Mayes, Donald S., *Dental Benefits: A Guide to Dental PPOs, HMOs and Other Managed Plans.* International Foundation of Employee Benefit Plans, Inc. (2002)

Second, many insurers increase their maximum fee schedules only every two to four years. This may result in a few years of constrained charge level trends, followed by a spike when the schedule is modified.

Finally, while maximum fee schedules do control cost levels at the procedural levels, they do nothing to control utilization rates or the intensity of the services provided. To meet their own revenue needs, some dentists may attempt to offset the financial impact of maximum fee schedules by providing more services or by substituting a more expensive service for a less expensive service.

Table 22.3

Average Charges Under a Fee Schedule Procedure: Periodic Oral Evaluation (CDT 0120) Fee Schedule Amount: $44 (60th Percentile)			
Percentile	Average Charge	Dentist's Fee Using the Schedule as a	
		Maximum	Minimum
0 - 20	$29	$29	$44
20 - 30	34	34	44
30 - 40	37	37	44
40 - 50	40	40	44
50 - 60	42	42	44
60 - 70	44	44	44
70 - 80	47	44	44
80 - 100	60	44	44
Average	$43	$39	$44

A recent development in PPO networks is the concept of a tiered network, with more heavily discounted fees offered by dentists in the highest tier (with richer benefits), intermediate fees going to the next tier, and the highest reimbursements going to dentists who are willing to sign up but not willing to accept much of a discount. As mentioned previously, the insurer uses benefit variations (higher coinsurance levels/lower co-pays, lower deductibles, higher maximums) to reward the dentists in the most preferred tiers. Tiering may be done strictly on fee levels, or by an analysis of claims to determine which dentists are achieving the best outcomes at the lowest cost. New data analytics allow insurers or Accountable Care Organizations to measure the state of oral health of each patient and assign a score. Dentists achieving greatest score improvement at lowest cost get into the most preferred tier. Some plans will use a higher level of reimbursement to attract such providers, which would offset the savings associated with conservative practice patterns, to some degree.

Scheduled Plans

Scheduled plans were described earlier and use a table of allowances similar to a maximum fee schedule, but the allowances are part of the plan design, not part of the dentists' reimbursement contract. Many of the older union plans include a table of allowances that specifies exactly how much the plan will reimburse for each procedure code. Unless that fee is lower than the dentist's charge, the insured is required to pay the difference between the dentist's charge and the amount allowed by the plan. The allowed fee usually reflects the intended or target company payment at the time the table was created. Increases are at the request of the policyholder, often following union negotiations. The fee inflation component of trend is zero in years without increases, and exactly equal to the table increase otherwise.

Capitation

Capitation is commonly associated with dental HMO plans. When dentists are reimbursed on a fee-for-service basis, they are paid for services actually performed; however, a dentist reimbursed on a capitated basis is paid a fixed amount per member enrolled with that dentist, or a "per capita" amount, even if no services are performed. Dental HMOs have decreased dramatically since 2000, when they represented 17% of all dental plans sold. In 2012 they accounted for only 8% of the dental benefits marketplace.

The dental plan and the dentist negotiate the capitation payment made to the dentist on a periodic basis (usually monthly) before the coverage period. The calculation of the capitation payment, therefore, is of major importance. If the capitation is set too low, the dentist may lose money and become dissatisfied. If the capitation is set too high, the plan will lose money if it is able to market the plan at all.

The primary components making up the capitation rate per member are: (1) the assumed utilization of services by members (the number of times a member will use each service during the covered period), and (2) the allowed average payment per service when a procedure is performed.

Table 22.4 on the following page illustrates the calculation of a monthly capitation rate paid to a participating dentist by a hypothetical dental plan. This dentist is paid a capitation for diagnostic and preventive services as well as certain simple restorations. All other services are reimbursed according to a significantly discounted negotiated fee schedule.

Adjustments may be needed to historic fee-for-service claims experience before it is used to develop capitation rates, because capitated arrangements often lead to reductions in the utilization of certain services and increases in others. For example, the frequency of major restorations might be expected to decrease when dentists are reimbursed on a capitated rather than fee-for-service basis; however, the utilization of other less costly services may be expected to increase, as dentists have a financial incentive to use less expensive alternatives where possible.

Providers who accept capitation from insurers may ask for some downside protection, in case the services required by the members assigned to them turns out to be more expensive than was assumed in the capitation rate calculations. Sometimes this protection takes the form of a periodic alternative minimum revenue calculation, based on a significantly discounted fee schedule and the actual mix of services. This type of guarantee may lessen the inherent financial incentives to the provider to avoid more costly services which capitation might otherwise create. These guarantees need to be taken into account when estimating potential variance in claim costs.

Table 22.4

Development of a Per Member Per Month Capitation Rate					
Procedure	Assumed Annual Services per 1,000	Allowed Cost per Service	Gross PMPM Benefit Cost	Member Coinsurance	Net PMPM Benefit Cost
Diagnostic					
A. Oral Exams	700	$28	$1.63		$1.63
B. X-Rays	630	25	1.31		1.31
Preventive					
A. Prophylaxis	650	50	2.71		2.71
B. Fluoride	200	20	0.33		0.33
Restorations					
A. Amalgam	250	85	1.77	0.35	1.42
B. Resin	220	100	1.83	0.37	1.46
Capitation Per Member Per Month					$8.86

A risk margin may also be appropriate in this situation.

The key to making this reimbursement method feasible is assigning a sufficient number of members to the capitated provider (usually 200 or more where the provider is capitated for a comprehensive set of services).[4]

DISCOUNT CARDS

There are many products that exist on the open market for both individuals and employers that have no insurance aspect at all, but rather steer people to a network of dental providers because of discounted, pre-defined pricing on services. Often, these deals involve no meaningful administrative burden on the provider, intermediary, or the employer. These programs may require a membership fee in order to receive the discount. Providers may also pay a fee to be listed in the intermediary's website search tools. Discount programs are even offered through insurers, who likely already have more complicated reimbursement arrangements in place with providers, like those described earlier. Insurers offer discount programs in order to offer a wider range of solutions and price points, keep up with their competition, and strengthen their clout with dental service providers.

CARE MANAGEMENT

Care management, focused on ensuring that patients receive professionally appropriate treatment at a reasonable cost, has the potential to reduce claim costs. The care management program that will be most effective in any particular plan depends on the methods used to reimburse dentists. Dentists paid on a fee-for-service basis have a financial incentive to over-treat their patients – to provide more services or more expensive alternatives than may be strictly needed or reasonable – especially if they are in a PPO network with lower reimbursement levels for the most common procedures. Dentists paid on a capitated basis may have an incentive to under-treat their patients, since they are paid the same amount by the plan regardless of the number or type of services provided.

---

[4] Mayes, Donald S., *Dental Benefits: A Guide to Dental PPOs, HMOs and Other Managed Plans.* International Foundation of Employee Benefit Plans, Inc. (2002)

Preauthorization

The primary technique used to manage the utilization of dental services in traditional fee-for-service plans has been the "preauthorization" or "predetermination" provision. Preauthorization requires insureds to submit a treatment plan to the insurer for review and prior authorization before services are delivered, whenever costs are projected to exceed some specified level, such as $200 - $300.

The impact of preauthorization on claim costs depends heavily on how the insurance carrier administers the provision. Insurers who actively enforce the provision, and who limit payment for expensive procedures to the cost of less expensive alternatives, will realize the biggest reductions in claim costs. Claim costs for a plan with a preauthorization requirement which is vigorously enforced can be 10 - 20% lower than costs for a plan with no such provision, all other things being equal.

Self-Management Under Capitation

Experts have indicated that a well-designed and administered dental HMO can be expected to cost 15 - 40% less than a fee-for-service plan with comparable benefits.[5] In part, this is because capitated providers may be managing themselves differently than they would under a fee-for-service plan, due to the different financial incentives. Capitated dentists may have more incentive to recommend less expensive treatment where a range of alternatives exists (depending on patient cost-sharing), and they have little incentive to upcode or unbundle their charges. In addition, due to the rigor of the provider selection process, dental HMOs may tend to favor dentists who are better business managers, which may also lead to lower costs.

On the downside, capitated dentists may also have more incentive than fee-for-service dentists to undertreat their patients, since their reimbursement from the plan does not depend on the number or type of services performed (although this is not true of patient cost sharing payments). Many dental HMOs use quality assurance mechanisms to guard against this problem.

THE INSUREDS

Characteristics of insureds that affect claim costs include age and gender, geographic area, group size, prior coverage and pre-announcement, employee turnover, occupation or income, contribution levels, and participation.

AGE AND GENDER

Dental costs can vary significantly depending on the age and gender of the patient. For example, adults receive expensive major restorative services, such as bridges and dentures, much more frequently than do children. For that reason, premium rates are often adjusted at the policy level to reflect the age and gender composition of the covered insureds. For group plans, particularly large group plans, age and gender information for dependents may not be available, in which case rating factors based on general assumptions may be used.

---

[5] Mayes, Donald S., *Dental Benefits: A Guide to Dental PPOs, HMOs and Other Managed Plans*. International Foundation of Employee Benefit Plans, Inc. (2002)

Table 22.5 shows the relative cost at various ages for males and females, by major service category before cost sharing, for a standard commercial population. The relative cost is a ratio of the average claim costs for each category of people compared to the total insured population.

Table 22.5

Relative Dental Costs by Age and Gender				
Demographic Group	Class			Total I, II, and III
	I: Diagnostic/Preventive	II: Basic Dental	III: Major Dental	
Younger Male (under 40)	0.76	1.03	0.60	0.85
Older Male (over 40)	0.94	1.10	1.68	1.10
Younger Female (under 40)	1.00	1.11	0.79	1.02
Older Female (over 40)	1.11	1.04	1.94	1.20
Child	1.06	0.85	0.14	0.85
Member Average	1.00	1.00	1.00	1.00

Source: 2013 Milliman Health Cost Guidelines – Dental®

GEOGRAPHIC AREA

The cost of dental services can vary significantly by geographic area. For example, Table 22.6 shows relative charge levels in selected cities, based on typical billed charge levels, assuming a typical mix of dental services in a comprehensive plan.

Table 22.6

Average Billed Charge Levels as a Percent of National Average Charge Levels	
City	Billed Charge Levels as a Percentage of National Average
Fairbanks, AK	146%
Miami, FL	115%
Charlotte, NC	102%
Midland, TX	89%

Source: 2013 Milliman Health Cost Guidelines – Dental®

In addition, different area adjustments may be appropriate for different service categories. For example, a lack of oral surgeons in a particular area may make those services relatively more expensive than basic diagnostic and preventive services in that same area. Therefore, if Class III services (including surgery) are not covered by a plan, an adjustment to the numbers in Table 22.6 may be appropriate.

Finally, many dental plan services today are delivered by providers who have agreed to accept negotiated reimbursement levels. These might also vary dramatically from billed charge levels by area. In those cases, the development of expected claim cost levels should include an analysis of the impact of these agreements, as described above.

GROUP SIZE

As with medical insurance, smaller groups are more likely than larger groups to make benefit decisions based on detailed information regarding the specific needs of their employees. It would not be surprising to see claim costs for very small groups (and individuals) be 30% to 40% higher than claim costs for larger groups (100+ employees), for the same benefit plan. Claim cost variation by group size may also be caused by premium subsidization and bundling practices that are common with employers of similar size (see below).

PRIOR COVERAGE AND PRE-ANNOUNCEMENT

Because of the discretionary nature of most dental services, utilization rates within a group that has not had prior coverage can be expected to be high relative to a group that has had such coverage. The period of time between when notification is first given to employees that they will be enrolled in a dental plan and the start date of the plan is particularly important where there was not prior coverage, or where benefits are being upgraded. This is because employees who require dental work are more likely to postpone treatment until the plan becomes effective. It is not unreasonable to anticipate a 5% to 10% increase in claim cost in the first year for each month of pre-announcement. On the other hand, where there is no (or a short) pre-announcement period, claim costs in the second year may be slightly higher than they would be with a longer pre-announcement period, as treatment may be postponed.

EMPLOYEE TURNOVER

A corollary to the principle mentioned above is that claim costs among groups with higher turnover can also be expected to be higher than those with lower turnover – since some portion of new employees will not have had prior coverage. Some carriers make an explicit adjustment to premium rates to recognize this. When experience rating a dental benefits plan, it is important to determine whether there have been any changes in the group's turnover from prior years.

OCCUPATION OR INCOME

There is a positive correlation between the utilization of dental services and occupation. Entertainers and professionals (such as accountants, writers, doctors, and others) are, as a group, higher than average users of dental services. Semi- or unskilled workers tend to be lower than average users. Also, the kinds of services used will be different. Professionals and their dependents are more likely to use preventive services, while unskilled workers will avoid the dentist until a major restorative need can no longer be ignored. Another consideration is the benefit awareness level of the group. For example, some union groups may be better informed than other groups about their coverage and, consequently, more likely to use the plan. Claim costs between groups can easily vary by as much as 50%, depending on occupation, all other things being equal. Some carriers adjust expected claim cost based on income or education instead of (or along with) occupation.

CONTRIBUTION AND PARTICIPATION

Again due to the highly elective nature of dental work and the significant risk of antiselection, groups that do not have 100% participation are typically expected to generate higher per capita claim costs than those that do. Appropriate loading factors can vary significantly, depending on the level of participation and options from which the employee is allowed to choose. For example, if employees are required to choose dental coverage on the same contract basis (for example single or family) as their medical coverage, the risk of antiselection will be reduced. The level of participation is directly and inversely related to the required contribution level. In difficult economic times, employers require more contributions, and after layoffs, employees must pay the full cost to continue coverage under COBRA. The people who choose not to participate are the ones who intend not to use the plan. The ones who continue coverage are also the ones using the benefits. With fewer participants but the same level of claims, the cost per unit of exposure increases. Also, people who expect to lose their coverage will get expensive restorative work done while they still have benefits.

ADDITIONAL CONSIDERATIONS

THE AFFORDABLE CARE ACT

The Affordable Care Act (ACA) included pediatric oral services in the definition of essential benefits and allowed dental benefits to be offered through the federally facilitated and state-run exchanges. Since dental coverage tends to be separate from medical coverage, this seemingly simple inclusion created confusion and new financial risk for dental insurers. A summary of key considerations follows.

- The pediatric oral services benefit is not a required purchase under the ACA. Children that have coverage through a family member employed through a large employer are not required to have this essential health benefit (EHB).
- Coverage, benefit levels, and age limits for pediatric dental vary by state. Each state is responsible for setting its own guidelines for satisfying the EHB. Benchmark plans can be either the state's Children's Health Insurance Plan (CHIP) or the Federal Employees Dental and Vision Plan (FEDVIP). For more information about state benchmarks, visit the National Association of Dental Plans website at www.nadp.org.
- The inclusion of a maximum-out-of-pocket (MOOP) to pediatric dental coverage was a significant change in the design of dental benefits. From year one to year two of the exchanges, the MOOP was reduced from $700 per child/$1,400 per family to just $350/$700.
- Actuarial values (AV) for a stand-alone dental plan must be at either 70% (low plans) or 85% AV (high plans). The AV calculators created for medical plans are not able to separate out pediatric dental services from the medical categories, so stand-alone dental plans must develop their own AV calculator in accordance with generally accepted actuarial principles and methodologies, and it must be certified by a member of the American Academy of Actuaries.
- Typically, advanced premium tax credits, which offset the premiums of plans purchased on the exchanges for lower-income consumers, are depleted before the purchase of a stand-alone dental plan, so there will be little to no subsidy for consumers purchasing a stand-alone dental plan.

- For plans where the dental benefits are embedded within a medical plan, the MOOP must be combined for the medical and dental plans (there is no separate MOOP for dental in this case). Deductibles can either be separate for medical and dental, or combined.
- There remain more outstanding issues related to the ACA that may yet be resolved for dental offerings, including healthcare.gov allowing the purchase of a dental plan without the need to buy a medical plan first, which would benefit Medicare enrollees and other individuals who are only interested in purchasing a dental plan.

Individuals were able to purchase dental benefits on the federal exchange starting in 2014, and small businesses were able to do so in 2015. States determine how these exchanges will operate, and how dental benefits should be included. In 2017, employers with 100 employees or more also have the opportunity to purchase benefits from the exchanges. This dramatic market change poses antiselection risk and member loss risk for dental insurers' group business, a risk that will vary depending upon how each state approaches dental coverage. For more information on this topic, and to monitor future answers to these open questions, see the National Association of Dental Plans website at www.nadp.org.

VOLUNTARY PLANS

Employers use voluntary group products as a way to provide access to certain insurance benefits. While the employee usually pays the entire premium for these benefits, the group vehicle does offer certain advantages. These include the availability of group rate discounts, the use of group underwriting standards, and pre-tax payroll deduction of premiums. Sometimes, benefit design is used to control utilization, as described below.

Since coverage is voluntary and employee-paid, voluntary products are subject to significant antiselection, particularly in the first year or two of coverage. Carriers may use alternative benefit designs to control the impact of this selection. These include tiered coinsurance and maximum benefit structures, which vary by year of coverage as illustrated by example in Table 22.7, and lifetime, rather than annual, deductibles.

Table 22.7

	Tiered Dental Plan			
	Payer Coinsurance by Class			Maximum Benefit
Plan Year	I	II	III	(All Classes)
1	70%	50%	50%	$500
2	90%	65%	50%	$1,000
3	100%	90%	50%	$1,500

An annual deductible is a cost-sharing mechanism in any group insurance product. A higher deductible means the employee pays more of the cost and the employer's premium is lower. As voluntary insurance is generally not subsidized by the employer, the person purchasing the insurance is able to compare the difference in deductible amounts with the corresponding premium differences, while having superior knowledge of the likelihood of having a claim. Thus, as a cost-sharing device in voluntary products, an annual deductible is generally not useful. Instead, the product might have a "lifetime deductible" of $50 to $100 per individual family member. Once met, benefits are payable subject only to the coinsurance and annual maximums. If the insured drops coverage, he or she must satisfy the deductible again the next time coverage is purchased. This provides an incentive to keep the coverage in force. Insurers will also use waiting periods to discourage employees from enrolling with the intention of having significant dental problems treated in the first year and then dropping coverage.

Other techniques used to control selection in voluntary situations include participation requirements. Frequently, carriers require: (1) a minimum number of employees to be enrolled, typically five to ten, but sometimes fewer and (2) a minimum percentage participation level, frequently in the range of 20% - 25%. Additionally, the plans may include restrictive networks or capitation payment arrangements to control costs.

Sometimes, voluntary dental benefits are made available on a subsidized basis through an employer's "cafeteria plan." In this case, dental insurance may be offered, along with a number of other options including vision, disability, long-term care, legal assistance, life insurance, or taxable cash. While selection may be somewhat tempered in this case, since employer dollars are being used to reduce the overall cost to the employee, selection is still significant to the extent that dental coverage is being chosen instead of other attractive benefits. A well-designed cafeteria plan will require at least a basic level of dental benefits, either at a very low premium or paid fully by the employer, and the ability to buy up to richer dental benefits. While it is simplest to pass along the insurer's prices, a better design will provide some subsidy to the cost of the richer benefit to minimize antiselection. Further, eligibility rules may be used to keep people from enrolling in the richer plan only to get expensive work done, then dropping back to the low plan.

MULTIPLE OPTION SETTINGS

Sometimes employers will offer a choice of more than one dental plan, with differing levels of benefits or provider access. Insureds can be counted on to select the plan that is the most advantageous to them – those who are likely to use more dental services will tend to choose a richer plan, while those who are not aware of any exceptional dental needs will tend to choose the leaner plan, especially where there is a significant difference in required contributions.

Key drivers of selection in a multiple option environment that should be considered when projecting claim costs include:

- Differences in the actuarial value of the benefits. Cost sharing levels on Class II and III benefits and maximum limits are particularly important. Availability of orthodontic benefits in only one plan would also be a key driver;
- The relative cost to the employee of the various plan options; and
- Access to current providers.

Methods used to control selection might include minimum participation levels, sole carrier requirements and underwriting loads.

EXPERIENCE RATING

The experience rating process for dental plans is similar to the process used for medical plans, as described elsewhere in this book; however, there are a few important differences.

First, as a general rule, dental insurance experience tends to be much more credible than medical insurance experience at the same group size. (Credibility is a measure of the degree to which a group's own past experience can be relied on as a statistically valid basis for projecting future experience. For most insurers, credibility is primarily a function of group size – the larger the group, the higher the credibility, other things being equal.) This increased credibility is primarily due to the relatively narrow range between the lowest and highest annual claims that might be experienced by any insured under most dental plans.

A major element of credibility is the extent to which random statistical fluctuation causes deviations in experience. This is the element of credibility that is driven by group size. This is illustrated in Figure 22.1, which shows the expected distribution of aggregate claim costs for a group of 500 members around the expected level (set at 0.00) due to random fluctuations. Separate curves are shown for a comprehensive dental plan and a comprehensive medical plan, with the dental curve being much tighter than the medical curve.

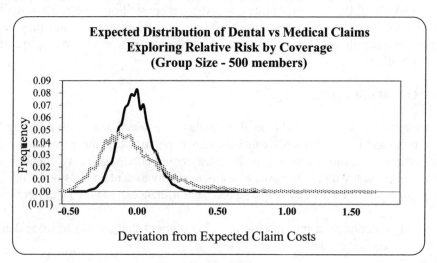

Figure 22.1

Another way of looking at these results is to measure the probability that claims will exceed a given percentage of the expected level, as shown in Table 22.8.

Table 22.8

Probability Aggregate Claims will Exceed Expected Level Comprehensive Coverage - 500 Members		
Aggregate Claims as a Percentage of Expected	Dental	Medical
110%	16%	25%
115%	6%	18%
120%	2%	13%

Despite this reliability of past experience, there may be reasons a dental carrier would choose not to rely completely on a group's own experience, even with a very large group. For example, due to the elective nature of most dental procedures, even a sizable group may apply some credibility to adjusted manual rates if they have high turnover, low participation, or a significant plan design change that makes past experience less reliable.

Second, an important part of experience rating in the medical arena is the removal of large claims and assignment of pooling charges. Because very large claims are unusual in dental insurance, large claims analysis and pooling is generally not a part of the experience rating process.

Many carriers have added various twists to their dental plans. One such is the "rollover maximum," in which if certain conditions are met, a portion of the unused maximum can be carried into the next contract period. When this is done, for the first few years benefits accrue without being reflected in the experience, so the next year's benefit has the potential to be higher than experience would show because, in effect, the plan's richness has been increased. It is necessary to consider this reduced patient obligation in the projected claim costs.

MEDICAL-DENTAL INTEGRATION

A significant body of knowledge is developing that demonstrates a strong correlation between certain systemic medical conditions and oral health. The most prominent is the link between diabetes mellitus and periodontal disease. There are also measurable correlations between periodontal disease and ischemic heart disease, as well as gestational periodontal disease with early births and low birth weights.

Based on this research, some dental carriers with a link to medical carriers are offering enhanced dental benefits to specific individuals, such as extra cleanings and periodontal maintenance procedures. While this generally represents an increase in the cost of the dental plan, it can lead to a decrease in the long-run cost of the medical plan for patients who receive the added benefits.

23 ESTIMATING PHARMACY CLAIM COSTS

Tracy Margiott
Eric Patel

INTRODUCTION

Prescription drugs are an increasingly important part of the United States health care system. Prescription drug spending totaled $271 billion in 2013 and represented 12% of total private health insurance spending. This is expected to grow to $483 billion in 2023.[1] Nearly half of all Americans reported taking at least one prescription drug in the past 30 days in 2010.[2] The widespread use of prescription drugs, coupled with the materiality of the associated costs, makes these products a critical component of the United States health care system.

The increasing cost and use of prescription drugs places additional emphasis on understanding and analyzing prescription drug data when pricing pharmacy benefits. There are also some unique considerations when pricing pharmacy benefits compared to pricing medical benefits. This chapter addresses some of the key concepts and considerations in prescription drug pricing and analytics as well as key components of prescription drug claim data.

DATA CONSIDERATIONS

Pharmacy data is typically collected electronically at the time a prescription is filled. Data is often validated at the point of service, so it is usually more complete and accurate than medical data. Many pharmacies and pharmacy benefit managers (PBMs) perform safety screening and drug utilization review (DUR) prior to the prescription being dispensed. These checks ensure that the prescription being dispensed will not have adverse interactions with other drugs that an individual is taking and that the drug being dispensed complies with prior authorization, step edit and quantity limits imposed by the formulary. For more information on pharmacy benefits, see Chapter 7, "Pharmacy Benefits in the United States."

Pharmacy claims are typically processed at the point of sale which is much faster than medical claims. Pharmacies generally submit claims for reimbursement to PBMs every two weeks, resulting in a shorter lag between the date a prescription is dispensed (incurred date) and the date that the plan pays the claim. As a result, the pharmacy claims data is readily available for data analytics.

---

[1] Centers for Medicare and Medicaid Services, Office of the Actuary, National Health Statistics Group. http://www.cms.gov/Research-Statistics-Data-and-Systems/Statistics-Trends-and-Reports/NationalHealthExpendData.

[2] Health, United States, 2013: With Special Feature of Prescription Drugs. U.S. Department of Health and Human Services, Centers for Disease Control and Prevention, National Center for Health Statistics. Page 289.

Some drugs are supplied in a hospital or clinical setting, rather than through a pharmacy. These drugs would appear on a medical claim form and would not be included as a prescription record in a pharmacy claim dataset.

DATA SOURCES

There are numerous sources available to obtain pharmacy claim data. An insured group's experience is often the best source to use for plan-specific pricing or analyses, if it is credible. Other potential sources that aggregate pharmacy claim experience include data vendors, the Centers for Medicare and Medicaid Services (CMS), and consulting firms.

Historical data has shown that there is variability when people fill their prescriptions throughout the year. People are most likely to get prescriptions filled on Mondays and are least likely to fill prescriptions on holidays. When projecting future pharmacy claims, at least 12 months of data should be used to avoid reflecting this type of seasonality in the projection. Alternatively, adjustments could be made to the data to account for these patterns.

KEY DATA FIELDS

Pharmacy data files include one row (record) per prescription. The standard format for pharmacy claim data is set by the National Counsel for Prescription Drug Programs (NCPDP). Each drug record generally contains information on the patient (age, gender, and date of birth), fill date, claim ID, prescribing provider ID, pharmacy provider ID, drug name (brand name and generic compound), tier, National Drug Code (NDC), days supply, units (quantity or dosage), allowed amount (ingredient cost, dispensing fee, vaccine fee, and sales tax), refill indicators, member cost, and plan cost.

Pharmacy records may also contain information on the therapeutic class, Generic Product Identifier (GPI), RxNorm Concept Unique Identifier (RxCUI), average wholesale price (AWP), and wholesale acquisition cost (WAC). When this information is not provided in the claim dataset, it can be added by using vendor data (e.g. Medi-Span®).

Age, Gender, and Date of Birth

These fields are important when performing demographic based analytics. Typically data summaries are grouped by gender and age bands.

Fill Date

The fill date for a prescription drug claim is the date that the claimant received the prescription. This is typically assumed to be the incurred date for the claim.

Claim ID

The claim ID is a unique identifier assigned to each prescription drug claim.

Prescribing Provider ID

The prescribing provider ID is a unique code that identifies the prescribing physician for the prescription drug claim.

Pharmacy Provider ID

The pharmacy provider ID is a unique code that identifies the pharmacy that dispensed the prescription drug associated with a given claim.

Drug Name

The drug name can either provide the brand drug name or the generic drug name, which is typically the name of the chemical compound associated with the drug. When working with drug names, it is critical that a consistent source is used to avoid errors resulting from using two different names for the same drug. The analyst should also be able to research drug names to be able to identify generic versus brand drugs in the data.

There are many different abbreviations that can be used when identifying a drug name. For example, one vendor may use the drug name Metformin Hydrochloride while another may use Metformin HCL.

Tier

The tier associated with a prescription drug claim is the numeric value corresponding to the member cost sharing amount described within the plan design documents. The tier included on a prescription drug claim record is typically the tier the claim was adjudicated on.

National Drug Codes

A National Drug Code (NDC) is an eleven-digit code used to identify a specific form of a drug. The first five digits indicate the manufacturer, the next four digits identify the drug name and dosage, and the last two digits indicate the packaging. The digits used to identify the drug name and packaging are not standardized and vary by manufacturer.

Since NDCs vary by dosage and quantity, there are multiple NDCs for the same drug name. For example, a 10 mg tablet would have different digits in spaces 6 through 9 than a 20 mg tablet of the same drug, and a bottle of 100 tablets would have different digits in spaces 10 through 11 than a bottle of 150 tablets. A mapping of NDCs to drug names can be obtained from data vendors.

Days Supply

Days supply refers to the number of days supply of a prescription drug that are dispensed for a given fill. Prescriptions (scripts) are generally grouped into 30-day, 60-day, or 90-day categories, because most prescriptions are supplied on a monthly basis for one to three months at a time. Sometimes, the 30-day category is further broken out into "partial fills," which includes less than one-month supplies. Scripts for different quantities of time are grouped with the most appropriate category. For example, any number of days less than 35 days may be categorized as a "30-day" supply.

Units

Units typically refer to the number of pills or a measurement of volume for liquid medications. Using units is often critical when accounting for varying dosage amounts by NDC.

Allowed Amount

The allowed amount is the amount that is charged for the prescription drug and typically includes up to four of the following components.

- *Discounted ingredient cost*: The cost of the prescription drug after any negotiated discounts. These discounts are typically negotiated by the PBM.
- *Dispensing fee:* The fee charged by the pharmacy for filling a prescription.
- *Vaccine fee:* The charge associated with administering vaccinations.
- *Sales tax*: The charge associated with sales tax for a given prescription. Only a few states require state tax collection for prescription drug sales.

Allowed amount may be referred to by the interchangeable terms "gross cost," "discounted cost," "allowed cost," or "discounted allowed amount."

Refill Indicators

A prescribing provider may allow a patient to refill a prescription multiple times without requiring a new prescription for a given drug. The refill indicator identifies which fill, under the refill guidelines set by the prescribing provider, the claim was dispensed.

Member and Plan Costs

The allowed amount that is charged for a drug is paid for by either the member or claimant; the third-party payer providing prescription drug coverage (e.g., insurer, employer); or some combination of the two. These two fields will contain the amount paid by each party. These fields are critical when evaluating the richness of a prescription drug benefit.

The amount paid by the plan is often referred to as the "plan liability." The plan liability typically does not reflect a reduction in cost due to pharmaceutical manufacturer rebates. The plan liability including the reduction due to rebates is typically referred to as the "net plan liability." Rebate information is not typically included in prescription drug claim datasets and must be attained from the PBM separately.

Therapeutic Classes

Therapeutic classes categorize drug products based on the conditions that the drugs are intended to treat. The American Hospital Formulary Service (AHFS) developed an eight-digit therapeutic classification system, where the first two digits represent the major classification grouping. However, therapeutic class definitions may differ between other published sources and internal company terminology. Therapeutic class groupings play a key role in pharmacy analytics, since there may be savings opportunities for the plan if members switch to a different drug within the same therapeutic class.

RxNorm Concept Unique Identifier (RxCUI)

Another type of drug code that may be used is the RxCUI. RxCUIs are typically 7-digit codes developed by the National Library of Medicine to create a standard nomenclature for clinical drugs based on the ingredients, strength, and form of the drug. RxCUIs were developed because different organizations use different names for the same drug (for example, "Acetaminophen 500 MG Tablet" versus "Acetaminophen Tab 500 MG"). There are multiple NDCs related to a given RxCUI. CMS has adopted use of RxCUIs for Medicare Part D.

Generic Product Identifiers

A Generic Product Identifier (GPI) is a fourteen-digit code assigned by Medi-Span® that classifies drugs hierarchically from drug group down to the specific strength. The code also includes identifiers for the drug class, sub-class, name, and dosage form. Note that the GPI therapeutic class differs from the AHFS therapeutic class categorization.

Pharmaceutical drugs can be identified by their name, RxCUI, NDC, or GPI. Table 23.1 contains the relevant information for one dosage of the drug Nexium®.

Table 23.1

\	Pharmaceutical Drug Identifier		
Drug Name	RxCUI	NDC	GPI
Nexium®	1297660	00186402501 00186402502	49270025103004

METHODS OF COUNTING UTILIZATION

Units of a drug may be expressed in terms of number of prescriptions, days supply, dosage (e.g. mg, mL), or number of pills. Script counts and days supply are most commonly used in analyses.

In a pharmacy data file, there is one record per prescription. The count of these records is equivalent to the total number of scripts in the data. In other words, each record represents one script that an individual received (either at a retail or mail pharmacy). Each script received, regardless of days supply, is counted as one "raw" script.

An alternate approach to counting scripts is to instead use "normalized" script counts. In this approach, scripts that are filled for multiple months at a time are normalized to a monthly basis. For example, a 90-day supply of medication would be counted as one raw script, but as three normalized scripts. The normalization converts the raw script to a one-month equivalent basis.

In some counting systems, both retail and mail scripts are normalized (so that either a 90-day retail or 90-day mail script would count as three normalized scripts). In other counting systems, only retail scripts are normalized (and a 90-day mail script would be counted as only one normalized script).

Script normalization is used to appropriately denominate various metrics on a per script basis. For example, assume a claim dataset contained data for two members taking the same prescription drug for three months. Member A has three claims for a 30-day supply at $120 per fill. Member B has one claim for a 90-day supply at $360. If the raw script basis were used to determine the cost per script for these two members, Member A's cost per script would be equal to $120 and Member B's cost per script would be $360. Since we did not normalize the script counts, it appears that Member B is taking prescription drugs that are much more expensive than Member A. However, this is not the case once script normalization is applied. Member B is taking the equivalent of three 30-day scripts. Therefore, the cost per normalized script for Member A and Member B is $120.

CALCULATING PREMIUM

The basic concepts for pharmacy pricing are similar to those for pricing medical benefits. Premium calculations require projecting expected claim costs, applying member cost sharing, and rebates to determine the expected net plan liability, and finally adding expenses and profit margin to develop a premium rate. Premium rates are typically developed at the group or market level. The following sections outline important pharmacy specific considerations related to each of these steps.

ALLOWED COST TREND DEVELOPMENT

The first step in premium development is to project base period claims experience data to the rating period. The analyst must account for all changes between the two periods. These changes can be grouped into allowed cost trend and other rating factors.

Allowed cost trend is impacted by changes in unit cost, utilization, and the mix of drugs.

- *Unit cost change*: Factors that impact unit cost include changes in average wholesale price (AWP) of drugs (inflation) and new drugs entering the market through the prescription drug pipeline.

- *Utilization change*: Factors that impact utilization include changes in formulary management (e.g. prior authorization, step therapy, quantity limits), access to prescription drugs, and new drugs entering the market.

- *Mix change*: Mix change refers to changes in the types of drugs used. For example, a shift from generic use to brand use is reflected as mix change. Table 23.2 illustrates how changes in drug mix affect average unit cost but not overall utilization.

Table 23.2

Mix Change Example			
	Unit Cost	Starting Utilization	Adjusted Utilization
Generic	$20.00	100	175
Brand	$80.00	200	125
Overall Utilization		300	300
Weighted Average Unit Cost		$60.00	$45.00

When selecting an allowed trend to use for projecting future pharmacy costs, the analyst should consider both historical trends and expected changes in unit cost and utilization, including mix change.

IMPORTANT RATING FACTORS

Many rating variables that impact pharmacy allowed cost may or may not be reflected in allowed cost trend. The derivation of trend and other rating factors will vary by group. When projecting experience period costs to the rating period, the analyst may also need to account for changes in the items listed below. Each of these factors may impact utilization, unit cost, or drug mix.

- *Demographics*: The types and quantities of drugs used vary by age and gender.
- *Area*: Drug costs and utilization vary by geographical region.
- *Benefit design*: Changes in benefits may affect the number of prescriptions filled by each member. For example, adding a deductible or increasing member coinsurance would likely result in decreased utilization. The impact of benefit design on drug use is referred to as induced utilization. Changes in cost sharing for medical office visits may also impact pharmacy utilization, since a change in the number of office visits is likely to result in a change in the number of prescriptions being written.
- *Formulary, including brand patent expirations*: The list of covered drugs, tier placement of drugs, formulary management programs, and brand patent expirations all impact a plan's expected cost and utilization. Formulary management programs may include prior authorization requirements, step therapy, or quantity limits.
    - *Prior Authorization*: Prior authorization requires approval from the PBM prior to filling a prescription. This is the most restrictive formulary management method and restricts the use of a particular drug.
    - *Step Therapy*: Step therapy requires a patient to try a different drug or a series of drugs before providing coverage for the drug in question. For example, patients newly diagnosed with hypertension may be required to try first-line drug therapies like diuretics or beta blockers prior to beginning treatment with newer, costlier and often riskier medications like calcium channel blockers or ACE inhibitors.
    - *Quantity Limit*: Quantity limits restrict the number of days supply or the number of units per day dispensed for a given prescription. This might be done as a safety measure, to avoid waste, or as a cost savings measure. For example, some pain medications have a limit on the number of pills per day that can be dispensed to avoid overuse.

    In recent years, brand patent expirations have been one of the most important rating factors to consider; as drugs come off patent, members often switch from using an expensive brand name drug to a less expensive generic equivalent. New drugs entering the market also affect pharmacy cost. For example, pharmacy costs increased due to the release of high cost drugs that cure Hepatitis C which initially cost $84,000 for a 12-week course of treatment.
- *Contracting (discounts and dispensing fees)*: Discounts (the reduction in cost that a pharmacy is willing to provide from a price reference like AWP) and dispensing fees are negotiated with pharmacies by PBMs. Discounts and dispensing fees may change due to changes in the pharmacy network or changes in negotiated contracting terms with existing pharmacies. Pharmacy discounts are calculated as follows:

$$Discount = 100\% - Ingredient\ Cost\ /\ AWP,\ where$$

$$Ingredient\ Cost = Allowed\ Amount - Dispensing\ Fee - Vaccine\ Fee - Sales\ Tax$$

EXAMPLE:

Tables 23.3 and 23.4 illustrate how to adjust the allowed amount for changes in dispensing fees and discounts. This adjustment is typically made using average allowed amounts per normalized script. The following example demonstrates this concept for a 30-day script with an allowed amount of $60. This example assumes that there is no vaccine fee or sales tax included in the allowed amount.

Table 23.3

Impact of Change in Dispensing Fee on Allowed Amount				
(1)	(2)	(3)	(4)	(5)
Allowed Amount	Current Dispensing Fee	New Dispensing Fee	Dispensing Fee Change (3) - (2)	Adjusted Allowed Amount (1) + (4)
$60.00	$2.00	$1.00	($1.00)	$59.00

Table 23.4

Additional Impact of Change in Discount on Allowed Amount					
(6)	(7)	(8)	(9)	(10)	(11)
Current Discount	New Discount	Ingredient Cost (5) - (3)	Discount Change Factor [1-(7)] / [1-(6)]	Adjusted Ingredient Cost (8) x (9)	Adjusted Allowed Amount (10) + (3)
75%	77%	$58.00	0.920	$53.36	$54.36

In addition to affecting the allowed amount, the change in discount and dispensing fee will affect member cost sharing and plan liability. The impact will vary depending on whether member cost sharing is structured as a coinsurance or copay. Table 23.5 illustrates the impact of the above discount change on member and plan liability. This example assumes a fixed dispensing fee of $2 per script.

Table 23.5

		(1) Starting AWP	(2) Discount	(3) Ingredient Cost (1) × [1 - (2)]	(4) Allowed Amount (3) + $2.00
Coinsurance Scenario	Baseline	$232.00	75%	$58.00	$60.00
	Change in Discount	$232.00	77%	$53.36	$55.36
Copay Scenario	Baseline	$232.00	75%	$58.00	$60.00
	Change in Discount	$232.00	77%	$53.36	$55.36

		(5) Member Coinsurance or Copay	(6) Effective Member Cost Sharing (4) × (5), or (5)	(7) Expected Plan Liability (4) - (6)
Coinsurance Scenario	Baseline	25%	$15.00	$45.00
	Change in Discount	25%	$13.84	$41.52
Copay Scenario	Baseline	$15.00	$15.00	$45.00
	Change in Discount	$15.00	$15.00	$40.36

A discount increase results in greater plan savings when copays are used compared to coinsurance. In both baseline scenarios in the above example, the effective member cost sharing is $15.00, and the member and plan would be indifferent between the coinsurance or copay scenario. After the discount is increased to 77%, the plan liability decreases to $40.36 under the copay scenario, but is reduced to only $41.52 under the coinsurance scenario. This is because, under the coinsurance scenario, a portion of the cost reduction due to the more favorable discount is shared with the member, while under the copay scenario, the plan realizes the entire discount savings.

- *Other Factors*: Other potential differences between the experience period and projection period that should be accounted for when projecting allowed costs include changes in mail order utilization, changes in the generic dispensing rate, and changes in utilization management or cost management programs. Expected rebates should also be accounted for when determining net plan liability, but changes in rebates will not impact the allowed cost projection.

In certain cases, some of the rating variables listed above may be included in pharmacy trend. For example, trend may include the impact of brand patent expirations. If any of these variables are already included in the trend being used, it is not appropriate to make additional adjustments for these changes. The analyst should understand what is included and excluded from the trend being used to ensure that factors are not missed or double-counted in analyses.

DETERMINING EXPECTED MEMBER COST SHARING

After projecting the expected allowed cost adjusted for important rating variables, we can apply the benefit design to calculate the implied average member cost sharing. That is, how much of the allowed cost is expected to be paid by the member.

Claim Probability Distributions

Claim probability distributions can be used to value the deductible and overall plan design. The process of using a claim probability distribution to estimate the impact of plan design on claim costs is discussed in more detail in Chapter 21, "Estimating Medical Claim Costs."

Cost per Prescription Tables

When applying pharmacy benefits to allowed cost, it is important to consider the impact of nominal versus effective copays. The nominal copay is the copay value stated in the plan design. For example, a member may have a $10 nominal copay on generic drugs. However, the member may pay less than the $10 copay if the cost of the drug is less than $10. The actual amount paid by the member is the effective copay. Cost per prescription tables are used to value nominal versus effective copays.

EXAMPLE:

Tables 23.6 and 23.7 illustrate one method of using a cost per prescription table to determine the corresponding effective copay for a $20 nominal copay.

Table 23.6

(1) Nominal Copay	$20
(2) Dispensing Fee	$1
(3) Discount	70%

Table 23.7

(4) Average Wholesale Price (AWP)	(5) Frequency	(6) Average AWP per Prescription	(7) Allowed Amount = (6) x [100% - (3)] + (2)	(8) Min[(7),(1)]
$0.00 - $20.00	0.20	$10.00	$4.00	$4.00
$20.01 - $50.00	0.25	$40.00	$13.00	$13.00
$50.01 - $100.00	0.25	$80.00	$25.00	$20.00
$100.01 - $200.00	0.20	$150.00	$46.00	$20.00
>$200.00	0.10	$500.00	$151.00	$20.00
Overall [1,2]			$34.60	$15.05

[1] Allowed Amount = Σ (5) x (7)
[2] Effective Copay = Σ (5) x (8)

The effective copay in the above example is $15.05.

Effective copays account for the portion of the nominal copay that is not realized when the nominal copay exceeds the cost of the drug. Valuing effective copays is important because if the full value of the nominal copay were deducted from the allowed cost, plan liability would be underestimated.

DETERMINING NET PLAN LIABILITY AND PREMIUM

After applying the benefit design to the projected allowed cost to determine the effective member cost sharing, we can compute the expected net plan liability as follows:

Expected Net Plan Liability = Projected Allowed Amount − Expected Member Cost Sharing − Expected Rebates

Rebates are generally estimated on a percent of gross cost or per script basis, based on the rebate contracts that will be in place during the projection period.

EXAMPLE:

Table 23.8 illustrates the calculation of net plan liability from a starting incurred allowed amount. If using paid claim data, the analyst must convert the data to an incurred basis. The "other adjustment factor" in step 3 accounts for all changes between the experience and projection periods other than trend (e.g. changes in demographics, formulary, or contracting).

Table 23.8

(1) Starting Incurred Allowed Amount PMPM	(2) Trend Factor	(3) Other Adjustment Factor	(4) Projected Allowed Amount PMPM (1) x (2) x (3)	(5) Effective Member Cost Sharing
$200.00	1.090	0.900	$196.20	20%

(6) Expected Member Cost Sharing PMPM (4) x (5)	(7) Rebates as % of Allowed Amount	(8) Expected Rebates PMPM (4) x (7)	(9) Expected Net Plan Liability PMPM (4) - (6) - (8)
$39.24	8%	$15.70	$141.26

The final step in calculating prescription drug plan premium is to add expenses and profit margin to the expected net plan liability.

Premium = Expected Net Plan Liability + Expenses + Profit Margin

ANALYTIC PRICING CONSIDERATIONS

The analyst should consider the following in developing prescription drug plan premiums.

Timing of Rebates

Plans often use PBMs to negotiate rebates on their behalf. Rebates are initially paid from the manufacturer to the PBM, and then from the PBM to the plan. Plans typically collect rebates from the PBM quarterly or semi-annually, which creates a lag between when rebates are earned and when the plan receives the rebate payment.

Credibility

Some plans may not have sufficient experience to use for projecting future claims. In these cases, the analyst may need to rely entirely or partially on a manual rate basis to develop the projected allowed amount. This is typically done by using a credibility factor to weight the plan's experience based projected allowed amount with the manual. The manual basis can be created by using a similar plan's experience or a combination of prescription drug claim data from multiple plans.

Integrated Plans

Many plans today integrate the pharmacy and medical benefit designs. For example, a plan may include a single deductible or out-of-pocket maximum that applies to both medical and pharmacy benefits. This can create challenges in pricing the medical and pharmacy benefits separately. If the pharmacy and medical benefits are being priced separately for these plans, the analyst should make sure to use an appropriate approach for valuing the pharmacy portion of the integrated plan.

Fixed Cost Leveraging

Fixed cost leveraging refers to the fact that the trend in plan liability will be greater than the trend in allowed costs whenever deductibles or copays are part of the plan design. Put another way, plan liability increases at a greater rate than allowed costs if the member pays the same fixed amount in cost sharing. For example, consider a plan with $1,000 in expected costs and a $200 deductible. The expected plan liability is $800 (= $1,000 - $200). If allowed costs increase by 10%, the new expected plan liability would be $900 (= $1,100 - $200). This represents a 12.5% increase in plan liability, which is higher than the 10% increase in allowed costs. The increase in plan liability would translate to a higher premium increase.

Coinsurance plans will not experience fixed cost leveraging because a change in allowed cost would result in a proportional increase in plan liability.

Note that fixed cost leveraging impacts the trend in plan liability but does not impact allowed cost trend.

OTHER TYPES OF PHARMACY ANALYTICS

VALUING FINANCIAL IMPACT OF FORMULARY DECISIONS

Health plans are tasked with creating formularies that accomplish several key goals. These goals include adequate coverage, marketability, and cost control. Each change that is made to a plan's formulary has associated financial considerations that must be valued.

The first component of formulary development is negotiating discounts with retail and mail order pharmacies. As previously described in this chapter, health plans negotiate discounts off of the AWP or price differential offsets from WAC. This form of cost control affects both the health plan and the member whenever a prescription drug plan design uses coinsurance percentages for member cost sharing.

Tier placement and the associated cost sharing is also an important formulary development decision with significant financial impact. Changing the tier placement of a covered drug affects the cost sharing the plan will receive from members taking that drug, but more importantly, it causes members to potentially change the drug they are taking if a cheaper alternative is available to them. Plans also use tier placement for leverage in rebate negotiations with pharmaceutical drug manufacturers. Putting a drug on a preferred tier with lower cost sharing would increase utilization of that drug, which may warrant an increase in the negotiated rebate offered to the plan. Removing drugs from a formulary also creates the same dynamic as tier placement changes. However, when removing drugs, the financial impact of exceptions must be valued. Exceptions are prescription drug claims that are processed for members who require a drug that is not covered by the formulary. The member submits an exception request to the plan to get coverage of the drug based on the prescribed necessity for that drug.

EXAMPLE:

A health plan has a 5 tier formulary with member cost share amounts listed in Table 23.9 below.

Table 23.9

Tier Placement and Plan Liability Example		
Tier	Tier Description	Member Cost Share Amount
1	Preferred Generics	$5.00
2	Non-Preferred Generics	$10.00
3	Preferred Brands	$25.00
4	Non-Preferred Brands	$50.00
5	Specialty	30%

The plan has decided to move a drug that was previously covered on tier 4 to tier 3. Moving the drug to the Preferred Brand tier has increased the rebates received for each prescription drug fill from $10.00 to $30.00. If the allowed amount for the drug is $80.00, the change in net plan liability after accounting for rebates is shown in Table 23.10.

Table 23.10

Tier Placement and Plan Liability Example			
Tier Placement	Discounted Allowed Amount	Member Cost Share Amount	Rebate	Net Plan Liability
4	$80.00	$50.00	$10.00	$20.00
3	$80.00	$25.00	$30.00	$25.00

The plan has a higher net plan liability moving the drug to tier 3 than it did when the drug was covered on tier 4 with a lower rebate. The plan might use this information to renegotiate with the pharmaceutical drug manufacturer to receive additional rebates to make the net plan liability the same as or lower than that when the drug was covered on tier 4. The rebate required for the plan to be indifferent to either scenario would be $35.00 when covered on tier 3. The plan would want this outcome, because placing the drug on tier 3 would make the formulary more attractive to members due to the lower member cost sharing.

When valuing tier changes for a formulary, the change to all drugs within a therapeutic class must be accounted for. Changing the tier of one drug in a class can affect utilization of all drugs within that therapeutic class, since the tier change may encourage members to switch to an alternate drug for the same condition. Projecting the market share utilization change is a key component to valuing the financial impact of formulary changes. Discussion of the details of a financial projection model for formulary decisions is beyond the scope of this chapter.

COVERING OVER-THE-COUNTER (OTC) DRUGS

Plans may choose to include OTC drugs in their formularies. For this to be beneficial to a plan, the savings from members who switch from prescription drugs to OTC drugs must be greater than the cost of covering new claimants. New claimants are those who did not previously take a prescription drug but would choose to take an OTC drug if it were covered. The results of this cost benefit analysis can help plans determine if covering OTC drugs would result in savings.

PRICE PROTECTION

Price protection is a negotiating strategy between pharmaceutical drug manufacturers and health plans to control increases in the price of prescription drugs. Health plans that offer pharmaceutical drug coverage can include price protection while negotiating discount and rebate contracts. Price protection is the agreement between a pharmaceutical drug manufacturer and a health plan where the price for a given drug will not exceed an agreed upon threshold. If the price of a prescription drug exceeds the threshold, the pharmaceutical drug company pays the health plan in the form of an additional rebate.

EXAMPLE:

The health plan has negotiated price protection for a drug that currently has an AWP of $80.25 as of January 1, 2015. The terms of the price protection set the maximum AWP to $82.00 in 2015. On June 1, 2015 the AWP for the drug increases to $84.50. Table 23.11

shows the impact of the price protection contract on the total net plan liability for this drug assuming a 15% negotiated discount and a $12.00 member copay:

Table 23.11

			Price Protection Example			
Date of Service	Price Protection	AWP	Discounted Cost	Member Cost Sharing	Price Protection Rebate	Net Plan Liability
5/3/2015	Yes	$80.25	$68.21	$12.00	$0.00	$56.21
6/3/2015	Yes	$84.50	$71.83	$12.00	$2.50	$57.33
6/3/2015	No	$84.50	$71.83	$12.00	$0.00	$59.83

In Table 23.11 the claim that occurs on 6/3/2015 that includes price protection saves the plan $2.50 in net plan liability as compared to the claim that does not have price protection.

24 ESTIMATING LIFE CLAIM COSTS

Stephen T. Carter
Daniel D. Skwire
Updated by Paul L. Correia

RISK SELECTION

The typical group covered for group life insurance consists of the employees of a single employer. However, other groups – such as multiple-employer trusts, negotiated welfare funds, union groups, and professional, public, and fraternal associations – can be provided group life insurance with appropriate underwriting and pricing safeguards. The important considerations are that insurance be incidental to the group's existence and to each insured's membership in the group.

Risk selection considerations for group life are very different from those for individual policies. Individual life insurance is sold to people who essentially have total freedom of choice regarding the timing of the purchase and the amount and type of coverage. Only the underwriting practices of the insurance company prevent those with terminal illnesses from buying new or additional insurance. As a result, the health of the applicant, insurable interest, and background investigations are all an integral part of the individual life underwriting and pricing processes.

By contrast, group life insurance is usually sold with features designed to minimize the effect of selection. These features include eligibility rules, benefit design, and rate structure. Group life insurance is generally sold under a single specified plan of insurance, which precludes individual selection of amounts. However, a growing number of plans allow an employee some freedom of choice by offering several benefit options. Typical plans provide for a flat amount of insurance, a multiple of earnings, or a schedule of amounts based on occupational titles. Minimum participation rates (the percentage of eligible employees in a group insured under the plan) are usually established to minimize antiselection.

Additionally, most plans require that an employee be actively at work on the date coverage is to become effective. If dependent coverage is offered, coverage for a dependent hospitalized on the effective date of the plan is not effective on that person until the day following the date of discharge. New employees are usually not eligible for the plan until after they have completed a waiting period, typically one month of employment.

By insuring a group of actively working individuals, there is a degree of risk selection in the very fact that daily employment requires a minimum state of physical health. Aged and impaired lives tend to drop out of the workforce. Also, some companies require prospective employees to pass a physical examination or undergo drug testing.

Standardized benefit amounts, participation minimums, waiting periods, and actively-at-work requirements all serve to minimize the effects of antiselection. Thus, group life insurance for medium and large groups is generally offered without evidence of insurability provided the amount of insurance is moderate and coverage is elected at the earliest opportunity. Some level of individual medical underwriting is usually required for high amounts of coverage, late entrants, small groups (less than 25 employees), some multiple-employer and association plans, and certain optional benefits.

Medical underwriting usually consists of an individual health statement – that is, a health questionnaire that requests information about the applicant's current health status and medical history. Depending on the information submitted, the insurer might require additional information, including a physical examination. A physical examination may be required for applicants who do not enroll at their earliest opportunity.

Because group life insurance is not normally individually underwritten, it does not exhibit the select and ultimate mortality patterns found in individual life insurance. The mortality rate among people insured under group policies covering non-hazardous industries is comparable to the rate of mortality among standard ordinary life insurance policyholders after the benefit of individual underwriting wears off.

PREMIUM STRUCTURE

The premium for a group life insurance product is composed of the expected claim cost, a margin for adverse claim fluctuations, the expenses attributed to the product and the specific group, and a risk and profit charge. There is an interrelationship among these elements, so they need to be considered in total as well as separately. Risk charges may not be included for completely pooled business, but groups that participate in their own experience through some form of cash refund require risk charges that vary by the size of the risk involved.

The most significant part of the pricing process is the development of the expected claim cost. In general, unisex treatment of employees is legally required for virtually all aspects of employment. This means that, while the recognition of gender in developing rates is necessary and appropriate (because gender is a proven indicator of expected claim experience), the final employee contributions must be the same for both males and females.

Typically, group life insurance rates are expressed as an average monthly premium rate per $1,000 of insurance, such as $0.14 per month per $1,000. This average premium rate depends on the age and gender composition of the group. Once calculated, however, it applies to each $1,000 of insurance regardless of the insured's age or gender.

Because of the volatility of group life insurance, where a single claim can often exceed the group's annual premium for small groups, companies generally use a manual table for pricing. There are two different approaches to this.

MANUAL PREMIUM TABLES

The first approach is to develop a manual premium table. For fully pooled business, the rate charged is usually established by first calculating the manual premium, then adjusting it for group size, and then reflecting the margin (if any), risk and profit, and expense elements appropriate for the size of the case, relative to the averages built into the table. For cases which participate in their own experience through alternate funding or some form of cash refund, the rate charged is usually established by calculating the manual rate, multiplying it by an average expected claim factor to get an expected claim rate, and then adding the appropriate expense, risk and profit, and margin elements.

For larger groups, the charged rate may be based on a combination of the manual rate (with appropriate adjustments) and the group's own experience. The more credible a group's own experience is, the more weight is given to its own experience in developing the rate. To better predict a group's experience, several prior experience years are often combined with the current experience year.

For the very largest groups, the rate charged is developed solely from its own past experience, adjusted for any benefit and demographic changes. These adjustments can be developed by comparing the relationship of manual rates for the old plan and old demographic basis to those for the new plan and new demographic basis.

MANUAL CLAIM TABLES

The second method used by some companies is to directly develop a manual claim table. Under this approach, for either fully pooled or cash refund business, the charged rate is established by calculating the manual claim rate and then explicitly adding the appropriate expense,[1] risk,[2] and profit, and margin elements (rather than relying on estimated amounts built into a premium rate as in the prior method). For larger groups, the claim rate may be based on a combination of the manual claim rate and the group's own experience.

Manual claim tables will typically show expected monthly claim costs for each age and sex. Table 24.1 is an example.

Table 24.1

Monthly Claim Rate per $1,000 of Coverage					
Age	Male	Female	Age	Male	Female
15	$0.09	$0.04	40	$0.16	$0.08
20	0.09	0.04	45	0.22	0.15
25	0.09	0.05	50	0.34	0.18
30	0.09	0.08	55	0.64	0.29
35	0.12	0.08	60	0.83	0.45

To calculate the expected claims for a group, the volume of group life insurance is split into amounts for each age-sex category, and then is multiplied by the corresponding claim rate, as shown in Table 24.2.

---

[1] Practices differ widely in the extent to which expenses are recognized as percentages of premiums, percentages of expected claims, amounts per group, amounts per life, or combinations of these variables. Because premiums are typically small, these assumptions significantly affect a company's competitiveness in different market segments and for groups with different characteristics.

[2] Company practices also vary widely in whether a risk margin is included in expected claims tables and whether the risk margin is expressed as a percentage of expected claims, a constant per $1,000 of insurance, or a combination of both.

Table 24.2

Employee	Sex	Age	Insured Amount	Monthly Rate	Expected Claims
A	M	25	$ 72,000	0.09	$6.48
B	M	35	90,000	0.12	10.80
C	F	30	130,000	0.08	10.40
D	F	50	180,000	0.18	32.40
E	M	40	270,000	0.16	43.20
		Total	$742,000		$103.28
Average Expected Claim Rate: $0.139 per Month per $1,000					

In this example, the average expected claim rate is $0.139 per month per $1,000.

To illustrate the combination of manual claim rate and a group's own experience, suppose the group had an actual experience claim rate of $0.10 per month that was considered 20% credible. An adjusted claim rate would then be developed by applying a 20% weighting to the experience rate of $0.10 and an 80% weighting to the manual rate of $0.139 for a final rate of $0.131. Expected monthly claims would be calculated by multiplying $742,000 by $0.131 per $1,000, or $97.20.

DEVELOPING A MANUAL CLAIM TABLE

Developing a manual claim table for group life depends on finding appropriate and current group mortality experience. For individual life insurance, the underwriting process that is used identifies many characteristics of the individual insureds that can be retained and used to analyze mortality experience. In group insurance, detailed information about individuals insured under larger group plans may not be recorded and tracked. In fact, group insurance for large groups may be self-administered for billing purposes. That is, the insurer relies on the employer to report aggregate insured volumes each month, and all the insurer may receive on the billing reports is the total volume of insurance, the average life rate, and the total premium. While the insurer may attempt to get individual census data annually or biennially, many larger groups are not able to submit information, and when they do, it may cover only a portion of the group.

As a result, it is difficult even for a large insurer to obtain substantial amounts of exposure data on its own group mortality experience. To develop a manual claim table, most carriers must rely on studies done by the Society of Actuaries and the Canadian Institute of Actuaries, together with studies of their own experience and the use of population statistics.

When using these studies, special attention must be paid to any inherent limitations in the studies being used. Typical limitations include treatment of disability claims, completeness of accidental death experience, combined male and female data, experience only on single employer groups, and improvements in mortality. In developing the manual claim tables, group mortality trends must be recognized, along with the costs of reinsurance and conversion policies.

INDUSTRY STUDIES

Society of Actuaries Studies

The principal sources of group life insurance mortality data are intercompany studies produced by the Group Life Insurance Experience Committee of the Society of Actuaries. The most recent study includes experience from 2007 through 2009 and was published by the Society of Actuaries in 2013 (referred to as the 2013 Study).[3] The prior study included experience from 1999 through 2001 and was published in 2006 (referred to as the 2006 Study).[4] The exposure base for the 2013 Study was 25.5 million life-years and $1.724 trillion of insurance submitted by 17 companies. Experience is analyzed by amounts of insurance as well as by lives.

While the exposure base may appear to be substantial, the 2014 *Life Insurance Fact Book*[5] reveals that the type of groups covered by the study had $8.2 trillion of group life insurance inforce in 2013. Although this total includes some types of policies excluded from the 2013 Study, the disparity indicates the difficulty insurers have in developing substantial amounts of exposure data.

The 2013 Study excluded the following types of business: group universal life, group variable universal life, groups for which all business was medically underwritten, conversions, waiver reserve buyouts, paid up coverage (including retirees), dependent coverage, mass-marketed business, and reinsurance assumed. The study included business with a variety of disability provisions. For credibility reasons, separate results were provided for only two types of disability provisions:

1. The insured becomes disabled prior to age 60, and benefits are provided to age 65.
2. Unknown provision or more than one definition applies.

An earlier mortality study sponsored by the Society of Actuaries and published in 1996 computed waiver incidence rates by using an adjustment factor of 75% to reflect the average present value of death benefits due to disabled lives. The 2013 Study, however, provides unadjusted waiver incidence rates, and permits users to assign their own claim costs to the waiver benefits. Other studies, including the Society of Actuaries 2005 Group Term Life Waiver Reserve Table Report, indicate that the 75% factor is high, especially when coverage cancels or reduces at a specified age.

The experience in the 2013 Study is available for a wide range of categories (age, sex, industry, disability provision, exposure type, coverage type, region, and group size) through a pivot table that can be downloaded from the Society of Actuaries website. Ratios of actual experience to expected experience, as well as crude claim rates, are presented.

Canadian Institute of Actuaries Studies

The Canadian Institute of Actuaries (CIA) also conducts studies of group life insurance experience. The last published report includes experience for 1989-91. The Canadian experience is published both on number of lives and amounts of insurance.

---

[3] Report of the Society of Actuaries Group Life Insurance Experience Committee, May 2013, Revised September 2014.
[4] Report of the Society of Actuaries Group Life Insurance Experience Committee, August 2006.
[5] *Life Insurance Fact Book*. Washington: American Council of Life Insurance, 2014.

Tabulations of experience are given for three different disability provisions: waiver of premium to age 60, waiver of premium to age 65, and total and permanent disability.

Ratios of actual to tabular are given, with tabular represented by the 1968-72 Canadian Basic Group Life Tables with waiver of premium adjustment. Tabulations of data are displayed by group size, sex, disability provision, and region. Disability and accident claims are shown separately.

Use of Actual to Expected or Tabular Ratios

Actual-to-expected ratios are very useful for coverages, like group term life, with low claim frequencies. For example, to see which size groups have better experience, Table 24.3 can be constructed from the 2013 SOA study.

Table 24.3

2013 SOA Group Life Study Annual A/E Mortality Rates by Group Size (Expected Basis is Overall Experience from 2013 Study)		
Group Size	A/E by Lives	A/E by Amount
< 10	118%	126%
10 - 24	97%	94%
25 - 49	97%	96%
50 - 99	99%	96%
100 - 249	103%	100%
250 - 499	83%	99%
500 - 999	88%	95%
1,000 - 4,999	115%	106%
5,000 +	121%	131%
All Groups	*100%*	*100%*

According to the 2013 Study, mortality experience is worse for the smallest and largest groups. Ratios of actual to expected claims must be used carefully, however, because expected claims may not reflect all of the variables known to influence claim rates.

Population Statistics

Population statistics are not entirely appropriate for generating expected claim levels, since mortality levels in the general population tend to be higher than the mortality levels of group plans, except for certain hazardous occupations. There are a number of reasons for this.

Generally, there is a flow of healthy individuals into a group, while aged and impaired lives tend to drop out. Prospective employees must pass a physical exam at many companies. Actively-at-work and waiting periods are required by most group plans, and individual medical underwriting is required for certain risks.

However, population statistics can be very useful in estimating annual improvements in mortality, in determining ratios of mortality by age bracket, in comparing male and female mortality, and in developing rates for the very young and the very old.

For example, the 2013 Study has limited data for ages 65 and over. In fact, the combined total of years exposed for all ages 65 and over is less than the years exposed for the 60-64 age-bracket alone. An extension of a claim table for ages 65 and over can be accomplished by using the 2013 SOA data. However, this approach may produce rates for the older ages that are not consistent with general population mortality data.

A scale of ratios for extending claim rates can be devised by comparing ratios of three sources that represent national data: the National Center for Health Statistics (NCHS), the Social Security Administration, and U.S. Decennial Life Tables.

COMPANY EXPERIENCE

Data can also be obtained from studies of a carrier's own business. Claim tables can be constructed from a carrier's experience by determining the number of claims per unit exposed in a study cell (age, sex, and other characteristics). Exposure units can be based on either lives or amounts of insurance. When available, these studies are the best source of mortality assumptions because they reflect the carrier's underwriting and marketing practices.

Since most results require graduation and interpolation (for rates at individual ages), a published table that has already been smoothed can be used as a basis for graduation, or the experience data itself can be graduated. The ratio of the total study results to a tabular base can be used to adjust the results into a smooth progression.

The relationship between a carrier's experience and intercompany experience is also useful for assessing current business practices. It can also be used to evaluate changes in marketing focus or benefit design. For example, if existing business is concentrated in small groups, but the company plans to increase emphasis on larger groups, the experience-to-expected relationships can be an indicator of future results for the company.

CHANGES IN MORTALITY

Changes in overall mortality levels since the experience data was developed need to be considered. If a carrier has used a study of its own experience to develop a manual claim table, it may be possible to recognize group mortality trends by studying its emerging experience. By doing ongoing studies of experience, a carrier could adjust its manual claim table every two to four years.

Another approach is to calculate average annual improvements in mortality between two known mortality tables for each age bracket, and use these as an estimate of future mortality improvements.

Table 24.4 shows the ratio of the monthly mortality rates in the Society of Actuaries 2006 Study (central year 2000) to the monthly mortality rates in the 1996 Study (central year 1987), along with a calculation of the average annual rate of improvement implied by those results:

Table 24.4

Central Age	Ratio of 2013 / 2006		Annual Improvement	
	Male	Female	Male	Female
27	84%	103%	2.14%	0.00%
32	76%	81%	3.32%	2.63%
37	78%	79%	3.08%	2.97%
42	76%	78%	3.32%	3.00%
47	80%	81%	2.76%	2.59%
52	78%	75%	3.10%	3.58%
57	76%	67%	3.37%	4.91%
62	84%	75%	2.20%	3.61%

Estimated Annual Improvement from SOA Studies

The estimated annual improvements shown above should be read with caution. For example, the 2006 Study contains the following comments related to mortality improvements:

> As in prior studies we continue to see mortality improvements of over 1% per year; however, the rate varies by age and gender. These results have not been adjusted for changes in the underlying mix of industries or any other factors. The ratio of the 2006 death rates by lives for males is relatively stable, but for females it is much more variable. The progression of female mortality rates is relatively smooth by age in the 2006 Study. The prior study contained some anomalous results for female mortality at certain ages that could not be resolved. (p. 5)

Another approach is to approximate group mortality trends by analyzing changes in general population mortality. It is reasonable to expect that changes in general population mortality will be comparable to changes in insured group mortality over a given period. Table 24.5 shows the average annual mortality improvement from 2000 to 2010 derived from data provided by the Social Security Administration 2014 Trustees Report.

Table 24.5

Average Annual Rates of Reduction in Death 2000 through 2010		
Age	Male	Female
< 15	1.57%	1.33%
15 - 49	1.22%	0.62%
50 - 64	1.16%	1.50%
65 - 84	2.40%	1.79%
85 +	1.57%	1.26%
Total	1.83%	1.48%

The impact of new developments on mortality also needs to be considered. While new treatments for illness and heroic measures are likely to increase longevity, in many instances they may replace death claims with disability claims.

REINSURANCE

Many small and medium-size group carriers limit the amount of coverage that they will retain on any one individual, and they usually reinsure a portion of their life risks.

Prior to the terrorist attacks of September 11, 2001, nearly all carriers purchased catastrophe reinsurance coverage to protect against the adverse financial effect of a catastrophic event causing multiple deaths among their insureds. Following those events, however, the availability of catastrophe reinsurance was greatly reduced, and deductibles and prices have increased by five to ten times. Now many carriers have chosen to self-insure that risk or to participate in various forms of pooling mechanisms in order to reduce the concentration of risk inherent in group life insurance.

The net cost of reinsurance should be factored into the claim table or into the expense charges used in the pricing of group life, and should reflect whatever reinsurance the company elects to use, including self-insurance for catastrophe risk.

CONVERSIONS TO INDIVIDUAL LIFE POLICIES

Under most group life policies, if group coverage terminates insureds can convert to an individual permanent life insurance policy (other than term insurance) at standard rates. Many companies do not provide disability benefits or accidental death benefits under the converted policy, allow conversion of reductions due to retirement or attainment of a specified age, or pay commissions on converted policies.

This benefit is subject to severe antiselection. Generally, unhealthy lives are more likely to convert than healthy lives and the standard rates for an individual policy are not enough to cover this antiselection. The excess cost needs to be recovered from the group policies, since the individual business line typically charges the group line for them. Additionally, many insurers permit a dual application system and issue regular individual coverage to those who qualify. This further exacerbates the situation since only the truly impaired lives will receive a conversion policy.

The manual claim table should be adjusted to include the anticipated excess cost of conversions, which may range as high as 1% to 1½% of total claims. When conversions occur, the present value of expected excess cost over the life of the conversion policy is usually charged to groups that are experience rated. A typical charge is in the neighborhood of $100 per $1,000 of coverage converted, although many carriers have introduced schedules of conversion charges that vary by age.

Some companies offer a portability provision along with the conversion option. This feature, which is gaining popularity, allows the employee to keep his or her group life coverage in force after termination of employment. There is the same antiselection concern as with conversions; however, because of the lower cost of term insurance versus a permanent policy, the portability feature should also attract some of the healthier terminating employees. There is currently little published information on the expected mortality level for this feature.

Manual Claim Table Adjustments

Once a manual claim table has been developed, the manual claim rates determined from that table are adjusted based on the characteristics of the group such as industry, geographic location, marketing considerations, employee contributions, plan options, effective dates, and disability provisions.

Disability Factors

The manual claim table usually assumes that group life insurance on totally disabled employees is subject to a standard waiver of premium disability benefit provision. Under the standard approach, once a disability claim has been approved, a disabled life reserve (essentially a net single premium for the future death benefit payable to the disabled individual) is established for that claim. The disabled life reserve may be established through a direct calculation using assumptions regarding future interest rates, recovery rates, and mortality rates, or it may be determined in simpler fashion by multiplying the amount of group life insurance by a reserve factor such as those in Table 24.6 (these are illustrative factors only):

Table 24.6

Coverage after Disability Continues	Illustrative Reserve Factor
Lifetime	60%
Lifetime but Reduces at Age 65	50%
Terminates at Age 65	35%

Recent experience pertaining to disability provisions on group life insurance is contained in the Society of Actuaries 2005 Group Term Life Waiver Reserve Table Report, including detailed mortality and morbidity studies on disabled lives.

If the group is experience rated, the reserve is charged against the plan's experience. If the employee recovers, the plan is credited with the reserve. If the employee dies, the reserve is released to pay part of the claim and the remaining amount (25%, 35%, 50%) is charged against the plan's experience. If the group terminates, the insurance carrier typically retains the liability for future benefits payable to disabled employees covered by a waiver of premium provision.

Where there is no waiver provision in the plan, but life insurance for disabled employees is provided by means of the employer continuing to pay premiums, the expected claims are initially lower than under the waiver of premium approach because no disabled life reserve is created when a disability occurs. However, as the case matures, the ultimate claim level will be the same as if reserves were funded at the time of disability.

Effective Date Adjustment

If employee ages are computed exactly when a case is rated, then no effective date adjustment is needed. In some situations, however, employee ages are determined in simplified fashion by subtracting the employee's year of birth from the current year. Thus, assuming a central birth date of July 1 in each year, the manual claim table is appropriate for rates effective on a July 1 central date, or for policy years that coincide with the calendar year. If the plan's rates are effective on another date, the rates should be adjusted by multiplying the manual claim rates by a factor. For example, if the plan began on April 1, then the central effective date is October 1, which is ¼ of a year later than the ages being measured. Therefore, the claim rates should be adjusted for ¼ year older mortality. One set of such factors is illustrated in Table 24.7:

Table 24.7

Central Date	Factor
January	0.97
February – March	0.98
April – May	0.99
June – July	1.00
August – September	1.01
October – November	1.02
December	1.03

INDUSTRY FACTORS

Different industries reflect varying mortality patterns, in part because of the hazards of the particular industry and its occupations, and in part because of the socio-economic status, leisure time activities, and general health of those employees.

The typical method of adjustment for industry mortality is to multiply the manual claim rates by a factor. Factors are usually assigned by Standard Industry Classification (SIC) Code, or North American Industry Classification System (NAICS) code, and may range from a 25% discount for groups such as banks and insurance companies, to a 50% load for mining companies. For extremely hazardous industries, such as mining, the characteristics of a particular group need to be carefully studied for a proper appraisal of the risk, and the group may be declined. Table 24.8 illustrates sample industry factors:

Table 24.8

SIC Code	Industry	Factor
1230-1239	Anthracite Mining	1.50
6011-6059	Banking	.75

Most industry adjustments are based on studies, such as the 2013 SOA study. However, white-collar workers tend to exhibit better mortality than blue-collar workers, even within a given industry. If only white-collar workers are to be covered, the factor for that industry should be adjusted. If a particular group has employees in several different industries, a single industry factor is usually determined by weighing the various industry factors by the volume of insurance in each industry.

REGIONAL FACTORS

United States and Canadian population statistics and comparisons show regional differences in mortality patterns. Differences at working ages are small, and most carriers assume they are covered by the differences implicit in industry adjustments. Some carriers make a specific adjustment to the manual claim rates based on the geographical location of the group's employees. Table 24.9 illustrates a regional factors table.

Table 24.9

State	Region	Factor
Massachusetts	Boston Area	0.95
Massachusetts	All Other Areas	1.05

LIFESTYLE FACTORS

A few companies have adopted a distinction between smokers and non-smokers. This distinction can only be applied on groups where information on smoking can be obtained, which may require that insureds sign a form indicating whether they smoke or not. Since a group with more smokers will generate higher mortality and disability claims, the method provides for a more favorable rate for groups with fewer smokers. A typical pricing pattern is to reduce each manual claim rate by about 5% for non-smokers, and to increase it by about 30% for smokers. Under those assumptions, a group with 15% or fewer smokers will have a lower manual claim cost than would have been produced without the smoker/ non-smoker distinction.

There has been some experimentation with lifestyle rating. A carrier will offer discounts for a group with healthy lifestyles with respect to smoking, drinking, and exercise habits. These experiments have met with limited success because of the difficulty in obtaining experience data for evaluating risk factors, and the extreme difficulty in obtaining data from employees to price a group. Additionally, part of the reason different industries have different mortality patterns is due to the lifestyles of their employees.

MARKETING CONSIDERATIONS

Experience is sometimes influenced by the source of business. Sometimes, business produced by captive agencies will have more favorable results than other business, provided that special underwriting concessions are not made. Welfare funds and union groups tend to have worse experience than single employer groups. For this reason, some carriers adjust manual claim rates to reflect the source of business.

Competition in the group life business has increased the frequency and duration of rate guarantees. Normally, rates are guaranteed for one year. If rates are guaranteed for a longer period, an additional charge should be made. A typical charge would be a 5% increase in the rate for a two-year guarantee.

CONTRIBUTION SCHEDULES

Where an employer pays the full cost of the group life insurance plan (the plan is non-contributory), antiselection is minimized because all employees, both healthy and unhealthy, participate. Consequently, the best experience usually emerges under a non-contributory plan. Some carriers apply a discount of up to 5% to the manual claim rates if the plan is non-contributory.

If contributions are required, either a flat contribution approach or an age-rated approach is used. Under a flat contribution approach, everyone pays the same rate per $1,000 of coverage. This discourages the younger, healthier employees from enrolling in the plan since they often can buy individual policies at a lower cost; older employees who are receiving a bargain tend to enroll and remain in the plan. Generally, these programs produce less favorable results than non-contributory plans. However, if the amount of insurance is modest, fewer employees waive coverage, and the experience should be similar to a non-contributory plan.

Under an age-rated approach, the rates that employees are required to contribute vary by age groupings, such as ages 20 to 24, 25 to 29, and so forth. This type of approach is more equitable to all employees. As a result, the experience under this type of plan tends to be closer to the experience of a non-contributory plan.

CASE SIZE FACTORS AND VOLUME ADJUSTMENTS

Many group life insurance plans contain adjustments for case size, premium volume, or both. Case size factors are generally based on the number of insured lives, and they are designed to reflect anticipated differences in underlying mortality based on the size of the case. Premium volume adjustments generally consist of discounts for cases with higher total premium amounts, and they are intended to reflect the lower expenses (particularly commissions) associated with larger cases.

PLAN OPTIONS

Plan options may also cause experience to vary from standard. For example, a plan might allow an employee to choose group life coverage of one, two, or three times earnings. Usually, these plans are completely paid for by employee contributions. To minimize antiselection, it is imperative that an age-rated approach be used. Employee participation of 25% or higher is generally required for these plans.

The number of options offered and the frequency with which elections are permitted will influence the experience results. If everyone has only a single option, the experience will tend to be more favorable than a plan that permits the election of different coverage levels.

Plans that permit frequent changes by an employee from one plan option to another without requiring evidence of insurability will tend to experience a higher claim level than plans which do not. If the elections are tied to modules in a flexible benefits program where, for example, an employee must choose between high life insurance amounts and a lower medical deductible, the results will tend to be better than under plans that allow an independent life election.

OTHER COVERAGES

DEPENDENT LIFE

Dependent group life coverage is often offered to groups with employee life coverage. Usually the amounts are modest, but there has been a recent trend toward substantial amounts on spouses. Child amounts are usually small, often with a reduced amount during the first year of life. A typical benefit might provide $5,000 or $10,000 on the spouse, and $1,000 or $2,000 of coverage on each child.

The expected claims level will generally not be as favorable as group employee experience, for a number of reasons. First, dependents need not be actively at work to obtain coverage. Second, dependent life coverage is virtually always employee-pay-all due to federal tax considerations, and is therefore subject to the antiselection factors of optional coverages. If significant amounts of insurance are provided, the contributions are generally age-rated. Most companies price dependent group life coverage rather conservatively.

SURVIVOR INCOME BENEFIT

Survivor income benefits provide for payment of a monthly benefit to an eligible survivor of an employee who dies while insured. It differs from group term life insurance principally in that a benefit is payable only if there is an eligible survivor, and continued payment of the benefit is contingent on the continued eligibility of the survivor.

A typical survivor benefit might provide a monthly benefit of 10% to 40% of the employee's monthly salary to a spouse until age 65, or re-marriage if earlier, and 5% to 15% to each dependent child, with a total spouse and children benefit limit of 50%. Determining the present value of this benefit requires assumptions about interest, number and ages of dependents, mortality, remarriage, and salary information. Manual claim rates are then applied to the present values as if they were regular group life insurance amounts.

The survivor benefit has not been widely accepted by either employees or employers. As a result, new business in this area is seldom written.

ACCIDENTAL DEATH AND DISMEMBERMENT BENEFIT

Accidental death and dismemberment is offered in conjunction with a group term life plan or on a stand-alone basis. Usually, both occupational and non-occupational accidents are covered, which is called 24-hour coverage. For some riskier industries, insurers may provide only non-occupational coverage.

The type of industry is the most significant rating factor for the more hazardous industries. While this is primarily because of on-the-job hazards, the experience still tends to reflect the lifestyles of the employees insured, even for non-occupational deaths.

Gender is also an important rating factor because female accidental death claim rates are less than half of the male claim rates for most ages. Accidental death claims also tend to vary with age – high at the younger ages, lower in the middle years and high again at the older ages. At the older ages, it is often difficult to determine whether a death was due to an accident, so coverage normally terminates when the employee retires.

Although most insurers do not vary AD&D rates by age, all carriers vary the AD&D rates by industry. Some also vary the rates by female content, as shown in Table 24.10.

Table 24.10

Percent of Volume on Females	Monthly Premium Rate per $1,000 of Coverage by Industry Classification				
	AA	A	B	C	D
0 - 14	0.05	0.06	0.09	0.11	0.15
15 - 29	0.04	0.05	0.08	0.10	0.14
30 - 44	0.03	0.05	0.07	0.09	0.12
45 - 69	0.03	0.04	0.06	0.08	0.11
70 - 100	0.02	0.03	0.04	0.06	0.08

AD&D is a popular coverage with group members because of its high benefits and relatively low cost. Because of the volatility of the experience, it is normally sold on a fully pooled basis.

Experience with respect to accidental death and dismemberment claims is available in the Society of Actuaries 2013 Study and may be used as a basis for developing manual claims.

GROUP UNIVERSAL LIFE (GUL)

In recent years, universal life insurance has been introduced as a group product on two different bases. The first product is term insurance with a side fund, where the employee has the option of electing term insurance alone or term insurance with a side fund. The side fund continues to grow with interest earnings and as additional contributions are made.

The second product is an individual universal life product based on group mortality and marketed on a group basis. The fund account is an integral part of this package, and the employee cannot elect to omit it. Under this approach, employees have less latitude in determining the amount of their contributions.

Both product types are portable; that is, an employee can choose to keep coverage inforce on termination of employment. These products are virtually always employee-pay-all because of federal tax considerations, and are generally offered in addition to the regular, employer-paid group life plan, either to employees only or to employees and their dependents.

To encourage good participation and thus better mortality experience under the GUL plan, the underlying employer-paid group life plan should ideally provide no more than one times earnings. At this level, it will be apparent to many employees that they need more insurance. The level of the underlying group life plan and other underwriting requirements, such as actively-at-work requirements, multiple of earnings options, level of guaranteed issue, and type of health statement, must all be considered in establishing appropriate mortality levels.

LIVING BENEFITS

The growth of HIV and AIDS marked the beginning of recognition that the terminally ill need to have early access to their life insurance proceeds, to pay for medical expenses and improve the quality of their remaining life. Companies were formed by entrepreneurs to buy the life policies of the terminally ill at a discount from the face amount. These events spurred both regulators and the insurance industry into action.

Now, living benefits (also called accelerated death benefits) coverage is being added to individual life products, group universal life, and group term life. Coverage generally falls into three basic models (and combinations of these), which primarily differ as to the event that triggers benefits: long-term care, catastrophic illness, or terminal illness.

Long-term care benefits typically provide for a monthly benefit of 2% of the face amount beginning with permanent confinement in a nursing home. Some plans also include additional services, such as permanent home health care, as benefit triggers. The monthly benefit is paid until a specified portion of the death benefit is paid, ranging from 50% to 100%. The remaining portion of the death benefit is paid to the beneficiary on the insured's death.

Critical illness benefits pay a single amount, typically 25% of the face amount, on the occurrence of a listed disease, such as heart attack, stroke, cancer, coronary artery surgery, or renal failure. Other conditions are often included. After a claim, the policy is typically rewritten to 75% of its previous amount.

It can be difficult to precisely define some of the diseases and to develop claim assumptions. For example, very limited forms of cancer are sometimes excluded from critical illness coverages.

Terminal illness benefits pay a single amount, from 25% to 50% of the face amount, when the insured has been diagnosed with a terminal illness by a physician who certifies the insured has less than 6 or 12 months to live. The remaining portion of the death benefit is paid to the beneficiary on the insured's death. The benefit cost is either factored into the manual claim rates or a separate premium charge is made.

In other terminal illness plans, carriers discount the advance payment for interest, and may also make an administrative charge of $100 to $300. There are no premium charges under this approach. The beneficiary and the insured pay the cost of this feature out of the death benefit. Regulations limit the level of the interest rate but not the discount period. Some carriers with a "less than six months to live" requirement will use a twelve-month discount period. It is argued that this is justified because of antiselection, errors in physicians' opinions, and fraud.

If living benefits coverage is added to a group's life plan, it should apply to all insureds, to avoid antiselection and administrative problems. To further avoid antiselection, a 30-day waiting period could be used before coverage becomes effective.

25 ESTIMATING DISABILITY CLAIM COSTS

Daniel D. Skwire
Updated by Paul L. Correia

This chapter describes how average expected claim costs can be determined for long and short-term disability income insurance offered on a group basis. This includes net manual premium rates for standard plans covering standard groups. It also includes manual rate adjustments for variations in benefit provisions and underwriting and variations in characteristics of covered groups. Chapter 12, "Group Disability Income Benefits," provides a detailed discussion of disability plan provisions.

Usually several data sources are researched, including an insurer's own claim experience. If the insurer's own experience data is unavailable or insufficiently reliable or credible, frequently used alternative sources include the following:

- Intercompany experience studies compiled by committees of the Society of Actuaries,
- Rate filings made by other insurers in various states, which are public information, and
- Basic research through governmental and business publications and discussions with experts in various fields.[1] An increasing amount of information is available on the Internet.

Reinsurers and consulting firms can also be helpful. When sources other than an insurer's own experience are used, appropriate adjustments should be considered to reflect the insurer's underwriting approach and benefit management.

LONG-TERM DISABILITY (LTD)

The determination of expected claim costs or net manual rates for LTD is more complicated than for other group insurance coverages, because it involves the present value of a disabled life annuity as well as a claim incidence rate. The present value of the disabled life annuity depends on factors such as the assumed interest rate, the claim termination rates reflecting claimants' deaths and recoveries, the maximum duration of benefits, and the likelihood and amount of benefit offsets such as Social Security and Workers Compensation benefits. Often the assumed interest rate and claim termination rates are the same as those used in calculating claim reserves, unless a risk or profit margin is built into these pricing assumptions, which differs from the conservatism in the reserving assumptions. The margin in the assumed interest rate and claim termination rates is in addition to any margin built into

---

[1] An example of a government publication relevant to long-term disability claim costs is the "Annual Statistical Report on the Social Security Disability Insurance Program" which is updated annually and available on the Social Security Administration website at www.ssa.gov.

the claim incidence rates assumed in calculating net premiums and any explicit margin built into the gross premium.

The pricing and reserving interest assumptions should reflect the insurer's investment strategy for assets used to back the reserves—generally investment grade bonds and mortgages with investment durations consistent with liability durations. Increasingly, claims adjudication practices have used negotiations to settle disputed claims and provide other claimants with alternative payment schemes. These practices may impact the expected duration of claims, the reserve assumptions, and possibly the reserving interest assumption.

SOURCES OF DATA

Insurer Studies

Studies of an insurer's own LTD claim experience can take the form of loss ratio studies, actual-to-expected (A/E) claim incidence studies, or A/E claim termination rate studies.

Loss ratio studies can be performed in two basic ways. A **calendar year loss ratio study** computes the ratio of incurred claims to earned premium for a given calendar year, where incurred claims are defined as paid claims plus the *increase* in claim reserves during the year for all claim incurral years combined. This type of loss ratio study bears the closest relation to a company's financial statements, but it may not provide the clearest picture of historical trends, because the results for each calendar year are affected by payments and changes in reserves pertaining to claims that may have been incurred long ago. Calendar year loss ratio studies may also overstate morbidity costs unless the change in reserves is adjusted to remove that portion of the increase attributable to the required interest on reserves.

An **incurral year loss ratio study** addresses these issues by using a different type of calculation. Incurral year loss ratios are computed as incurred claims divided by earned premium for a specific claim incurral year, where incurred claims are defined as the present value of claim payments made to date plus the present value of the current claim reserve, all discounted back to the year of incurral. The earned premium in the denominator is the earned premium for the year of incurral. Incurral year loss ratios, though they do not correspond directly to financial statements, do provide a better historical trend, by attributing the full cost of a claim to the year in which that claim is incurred. Because an incurral year loss ratio is computed using present values, no further interest adjustment is required.

When performing any type of loss ratio study, an insurer should include the reserves for incurred but not reported (IBNR) claims. In the case of an incurral year loss ratio study, it will be necessary to estimate what portion of the total IBNR reserve applies to each incurral year (the largest portion will apply to the most recent incurral year). Failure to include IBNR reserves in a loss ratio study will result in understated values for recent years in which claims have not been fully reported.

A/E claim incidence rate and claim termination rate studies measure a company's actual claim incidence rates or claim termination rates relative to expected rates. The results are often expressed as ratios, where 100% signifies actual experience equal to the expected basis. Expected values are often based on a published table such as the Society of Actuaries 2008 Group Long Term Disability Experience Table or the 1987 Commissioners Group

Disability Table (1987 CGDT). A company with a large block of business may rely on its own historical experience as an expected basis, rather than a published table.

Loss ratio studies and A/E studies can be segmented into many classifications, including age group, gender, elimination period, benefit percentage, type of social security offset, employee contribution percentage, size of group, industry, area, or others. This type of analysis is very useful in identifying experience trends that can be reflected in pricing.

1987 Commissioners Group Disability Table

In December 1987, the National Association of Insurance Commissioners adopted the 1987 Commissioners Group Disability Table (1987 CGDT), which was published in *TSA XXXIX* as the GLTD Valuation Table (Table E-1),[2] as the statutory minimum reserve basis for LTD. Although more recent intercompany data exists for claim termination rates, the 1987 CGDT remains the most recent intercompany incidence rate study for LTD.

The 1987 CGDT can be a useful starting point in pricing LTD insurance, but it should be used with caution due to the age of the underlying experience data. Many insurers have found, for example, that the claim termination rates they experience bear a closer resemblance to more recent industry studies, particularly in the first several years of disability. It also appears that the age slope of current LTD incidence rates is somewhat flatter than the pattern in the 1987 CGDT.

Appendix G of the report of the Committee to Recommend New Disability Tables for Valuation in *TSA XXXIX* offers suggestions on how to modify the termination rates of the GLTD Tables to recognize differences by occupation of claimant, industry of employer, income replacement ratio or other specific factors (such as union groups or members of other organizations).

SOA 2008 GLTD Experience Table

Several intercompany studies have been performed by the Society of Actuaries Group LTD Experience committee with the object of updating the 1987 CGDT. The committee has continued to gather intercompany data on LTD claim termination rates (though not on claim incidence rates) and to publish periodic studies of their findings. The most recent studies are available on the SOA's website.[3] One formal table that was released for review and testing was the 2008 GLTD Experience Table. It provided for a longer select period, based on elimination period, and broke total claim termination rates into separate rates for deaths and recoveries. It also incorporated an adjustment for the own occupation versus any occupation transition found in most LTD contracts, and provided considerable detail on the pattern of claim termination rates by diagnosis. It is clear, for example, that cancer claims have significantly higher mortality rates than other types of LTD claims. The 2008 GLTD Experience Table contains valuable information for pricing LTD insurance.

A modified table known as the 2012 GLTD Valuation Table was recommended to the NAIC as a replacement for the 1987 CGDT for use in developing minimum statutory reserves for

---

[2] Society of Actuaries Committee to Recommend New Disability Tables for Valuation, "Group Long-Term Disability (GLTD) Valuation Tables," *TSA* XXXIX (1987), 393.
[3] www.soa.org

LTD, and in 2014 the NAIC approved changes to the model regulation. As a result, the 2012 GLTD Valuation Table will be used for determining minimum standards for claims incurred on or after October 1, 2016. The 2012 GLTD Valuation Table originated from the 2008 GLTD Experience Table, from which claim termination rates were modified to include 15% margin and a provision for mortality improvement.

NET MANUAL PREMIUMS FOR STANDARD PLANS

Once a company has developed morbidity assumptions using the types of studies and reports described in the previous sections, with possible modifications for the company's underwriting and claim practices, it is then possible to compute net manual premium rates. The net monthly premium is calculated as

$$(IncidenceRate) \times \sum_{\substack{Benefit \\ Period}} Benefit_t \times Continuance_t \times InterestDiscount_t.$$

Depending on the sophistication desired and the amount of data available, the incidence rate and claim termination rates (which are used to develop the continuance factors) may be separated into different diagnosis groupings, such as mental disorder, maternity, cancer, and all other conditions, since the different diagnosis groups have different morbidity patterns.

Social Security Offsets

After the elimination period, LTD benefits are reduced by anticipated state disability benefits and workers compensation awards during the early months of disability. For later months of disability, Social Security offsets are also anticipated.

One precise approach to reflecting these offsets in premium calculations would be to calculate the expected Social Security award directly, according to a table of probabilities of Social Security disability awards (varying by age and gender), the formula for primary and family Social Security disability benefits, and the various features of the plan. Those features include the gross benefit percentage, plan minimums and maximums, and the type of Social Security offset (direct offset of family or primary benefits or indirect offset of family benefits via a "backdoor" or "all source" limit, such as 70%, which is higher than the gross benefit percentage).

The Social Security probabilities should represent the chance that an LTD claimant will receive a disability benefit, after exhausting all levels of appeal. The table below shows some illustrative probabilities. For a female, age 30-39, there is a 35% chance a Primary award will be made and a 15% chance a Family award will be made.

Table 25.1

Ages	Primary Benefit		Family Benefit	
	Male	Female	Male	Female
0-29	.35	.30	.15	.10
30-39	.40	.35	.20	.15
40-49	.50	.45	.20	.15
50-54	.60	.60	.20	.10
55-59	.65	.70	.20	.05
60-64	.70	.80	.20	.05
65+	.75	.85	.20	.05

When pricing Social Security offsets, many carriers also consider the timing of Social Security approvals. Many claimants are denied for Social Security on their first application, and the ultimate approval rates may not be achieved for several years after the claim is initially filed.

The amount of the primary Social Security Disability Insurance (SSDI) benefit depends on "bend points" which are adjusted for inflation each year. For example, the Primary Insurance Amount (PIA) in 2015 is 90% of first $826 of AIME, plus 32% of next $4,185 plus 15% of AIME in excess of $4,980 where AIME is the Average Indexed Monthly Earnings over the worker's entire career covered by Social Security. Family SSDI is 150% of the PIA for a claimant with a spouse or child (although the family benefit cannot exceed 85% of AIME).

One source of recent data on Social Security disability benefit approval rates and offset amounts is a research study published by the Society of Actuaries in 2012 and available on the SOA website.[4]

The gross benefit percentage and the type of Social Security offset (and other features of the plan that determine the income replacement ratio) will also affect claim incidence rates and claim termination rates. Such effects are discussed later in the chapter.

CANADIAN INTEGRATION

In Canada and Quebec, integration occurs with disability benefits from the Canadian Pension Plan (CPP) and Quebec Pension Plan (QPP). These benefits are generally available after five months of disability. Both CPP and QPP benefits vary somewhat from Social Security benefits, in amounts and likelihood of receipt. Generally, primary awards under CPP and QPP are less than Social Security, but dependent awards can be larger. Pricing and reserving based on U.S. models should be modified for earlier integration and level of likely awards.

Some insurers provide LTD benefits that are based on an after-tax replacement level. Hence, the level of integration with CPP and QPP benefits may depend on the claimant's expected income tax rate. This can be approximated, based on salary.

---

[4] Beal, Robert. *Group Long Term Disability Benefit Offset Study.* Society of Actuaries, 2012.

ADJUSTMENTS FOR PLAN VARIATIONS

Adjustments of manual rates will be needed for variations from standard plans in benefit provisions and underwriting.

Benefit Percentage

LTD claim incidence is generally lower for plans that provide a lower income replacement percentage, since claimants are less likely to file a claim if they stand to lose a larger proportion of their pre-disability income. Likewise, plans with lower income replacement amounts also often see higher recovery rates since claimants are highly motivated to return to work. These effects could be represented by an income replacement factor as a rating multiplier, such as the following:

Table 25.2

Gross Benefit	Rating Factor
50%	0.880
60%	1.000
66 2/3%	1.067
70%	1.100

In addition, the savings from Social Security and other offsets become proportionately smaller as benefit amounts increase (since the size of the savings remains unchanged while the gross benefit increases), resulting in higher rating factors for plans with higher benefit percentages.

Maximum Benefit

When the actual maximum benefit issued without evidence of insurability exceeds the underwriting guideline, it would be prudent to charge a higher rate for the excess, on the grounds that higher claim rates will result from the incentives implicit in large benefits, in spite of the favorable high income class of risk.

Minimum Benefit

Rating adjustments are needed for non-standard minimum benefits. Social Security 'freeze' regulations prevent offsetting with Social Security cost-of-living increases, hence the minimum benefit does not have to consider the leveraging of Social Security offsets.

Elimination Period

The claim incidence rates of 1987 CGDT and claim termination rates of the 2008 GLTD Experience Table provide a basis for varying manual premium rates among elimination periods. It is important to consider whether the elimination period may be satisfied with total or partial disability. A plan that permits the elimination period to be satisfied with partial disability is more generous and should have a higher cost.

Benefit Period

Variations in the benefit period from the traditional benefits to age 65 can be priced by doing routine net premium calculations on the basis of the 2008 GLTD Experience Table. This includes variations in the extension of benefits above 65 to satisfy the Age Discrimination in

Employment Act, or to replace age 65 with the Social Security normal retirement age for people born after 1937.

Definition of Disability

The majority of LTD plans have an own occupation period of 2 years from the start of benefit payments, after which benefits continue only if the insured is unable to perform the duties of any reasonable occupation. LTD rate manuals incorporate factors for longer and shorter own occupation periods, based on the anticipated impact on claim termination rates and incidence rates from the change in definition. Illustrative factors are shown below:

Table 25.3

Own Occupation Period	Factor
1 Year	0.95
2 Years	1.00
5 years	1.10
to age 65	1.15

Other Offsets

In addition to offsets for Social Security benefits, most LTD plan contain offsets for other sources of income, including state cash sickness plans (in five states and Puerto Rico), Workers' Compensation, pension benefits, sick pay, and part time work. These offsets are priced with varying degrees of sophistication.

The impact of sick pay and part time work earnings is generally included implicitly, by ensuring that premium rates are consistent with historical experience – unless a company's block of business has unusual characteristics, such as a high proportion of insureds with large amounts of accrued sick leave.

The percentage of LTD claimants receiving Workers' Compensation (WC) income replacement benefits has been increasing and ranges between 3% and 12% for different industries. State-specific rate credits are not generally necessary for WC offsets, because WC is provided for occupational disability in all states with considerable uniformity (such as two-thirds of covered wages or 80% of spendable wages, although there is substantial variation in the maximum benefit). Texas permits an employer to opt out of coverage so the actuary must consider loading the LTD rates when an employer does not have separate Worker's Compensation benefits. The effect on overall LTD claim costs is reflected in the insurer's loss ratio studies.

Specific rate credits are generally unnecessary for offsets of retirement benefits under employers' pension and profit sharing plans. When material, credits for disability benefits under retirement plans are determined on an ad hoc basis, recognizing the specifics of the group's case. These calculations can be extensive, but it is not practical to standardize them. Approximations are often warranted, although the credits are usually large, ranging from 20% to 60% of the LTD premium otherwise payable.

Specific LTD rate credits are desirable for offsets of the temporary disability benefits mandated by Hawaii, New Jersey, New York, Puerto Rico and Rhode Island if the elimination period is shorter than 6 months, and are necessary for similar benefits in California if the elimination period is shorter than 12 months. These benefits extend for up to 52 weeks in California, 30 weeks in Rhode Island and 26 weeks in the other three states and Puerto Rico.

Limits on Mental Illness and Substance Abuse

Many LTD plans impose a lifetime limit of 24 months on benefits for disabilities due to mental illness when not confined to an institution. Most LTD plans that do contain such a limit also impose a similar limit on substance abuse. Some plans subject all of these non-confined disabilities to a single, combined lifetime limit of 24 months.

Illustrative rating adjustments for variations regarding non-confined disabilities would be as shown in the table below. These factors assume an identical limit for mental illness and for substance abuse, although separate limits for these two categories of disabilities are sometimes used. All of these loadings and credits could be greater for certain industries where disabilities due to mental illness and substance abuse are more prevalent.

Table 25.4

Limitation	Percentage of Total LTD Cost
Conditions excluded	0.90
12 months	0.95
24 months	1.00
No limit	1.20

The purpose of the 1990 Americans with Disabilities Act (ADA) is "to provide a clear and comprehensive mandate for the elimination of discrimination against individuals with disabilities." It specifically addresses insurance and states that "this Act shall not be construed to prohibit or restrict an insurer...from underwriting risks, classifying risks, or administering such risks that are based on or not inconsistent with State law."

The Equal Employment Opportunity Council (EEOC) has brought numerous suits against insurers and employers, arguing that the two year limitation for mental illness benefits violates the ADA. Disability actuaries need to be aware of recent court decisions affecting the two-year mental illness limitation.

Optional Features

Optional LTD features are described below.

- Determining the extra premium for a *pension supplement* is simply a matter of evaluating the amount of additional disability benefit represented by the pension contributions. Each case must be analyzed according to its unique characteristics.
- *Survivor benefits* also must be evaluated to determine the equivalent LTD monthly benefit, which involves probabilities of LTD claimants dying and having eligible dependents.
- *Cost-of-living adjustment (COLA) riders* typically involve rather extensive tables of rate loadings which depend on the terms of the COLA, CPI-related or flat percentage adjustment; the annual limit on recognized changes in the CPI (such as 5%); the cumulative limit on recognized increases in the CPI; and the limit on the number of

years of adjustment after disablement. These loading percentages can be determined for various ages, elimination periods and benefit periods.

- *Catastrophic disability riders* that pay benefits if the insured suffers the loss of two or more activities of daily living or experiences a cognitive impairment may be priced using assumptions similar to those used for pricing long-term care insurance.

Underwriting Variations

Many variations in the details of actively-at-work requirements, evidence of insurability (EOI) requirements, and preexisting condition (pre-ex) limitations are possible, for various group size ranges. The discussion that follows considers the effect on LTD claim costs of variations in pre-ex rules. It is assumed that evidence of insurability (via short health questionnaires) is required for groups of fewer than 10 employees and for late entrants in all groups and that the employee is not eligible until actively-at-work for one day on or after the date of normal eligibility.

Preexisting condition limitations are typically described with three numbers, such as "6-6-24". The first "6" indicates that a condition is defined as preexisting if treated during the six months prior to the effective date of LTD coverage. The second "6" indicates that the exclusion expires after the employee goes six months without treatment for the preexisting condition (or a related condition). The final number, "24", indicates that the exclusion expires after the employee has been insured for 24 months, regardless of treatment.

The following table illustrates rate adjustments for changes in pre-ex limitations from 6-6-24 for 10 to 24 employees, 3-3-12 for 25 to 99 employees, and no limitation for 100 or more employees. Requests for liberalized limitations on a case basis should usually be refused, unless the underwriter is persuaded that adverse selection is not an important reason for the request.

If an insurer is considering the effect of a change in its standard pre-ex limitation, the first year adjustment can be divided by 4 and added to the all-years adjustment (which happens to also equal the all-years adjustment in this illustration).

Table 25.5

Number of Employees	6-6-24	3-3-12	No Limit
First-Year Adjustment re Original Entrants (non-transfer cases)			
10-24	0%	+12%	EOI
25-99	−8	0	+16%
100+	−8	−4	0
All-Years Adjustment re New Hires (percent of entire premium for all employees)			
10-24	0	+3	EOI
25-29	−2	0	+4
100+	−2	−1	0

EMPLOYEE CONTRIBUTION/PARTICIPATION

The level of pre-tax employee contribution affects the taxability of the LTD benefit. For plans paid with pre-tax dollars, disability benefits are taxable. For plans paid with after-tax dollars, which is often the case with employee-paid plans (called "contributory" or "voluntary" plans), disability benefits are non-taxable. For a plan that pays non-taxable benefits, a 60% benefit may effectively replace 70% or more on an after-tax basis. Likewise, a 66⅔% benefit may provide replacement of over 85% on an after-tax basis, which is why benefit ratios in excess of 60% are written less often and only on select groups. Hence, the rating factor for contributory plans should reflect the level of after-tax replacement: a 60% contributory plan may need to be rated using the loads discussed in the section on benefit percentages. Increased employee awareness is also an argument for loading contributory plans.

Finally, contributory plans should reflect the level of participation by employees in the plan. Presumably, the least healthy employees will be the most likely to participate, resulting in antiselection and requiring a rate load. This load increases as participation decreases. At participation levels below 25%, the load should be replaced by individual underwriting. Alternatively, a voluntary product should be offered, with strict pre-existing limitations and lower benefit levels.

The following table illustrates how the level of employer participation can be introduced into the rating of business.

Table 25.6

Employee Participation	Rate Factor
90-100%	1.00
80-89	1.07
70-79	1.17
60-69	1.29
50-59	1.44
40-49	1.67
25-39*	2.00

*If participation is lower than 25%, consider re-enrollment or cancellation (unless EOI was obtained from all enrollees). Alternatively, a voluntary product should be offered.

ADJUSTMENTS FOR GROUP CHARACTERISTICS

Age and Gender

The claim incidence rates from the 1987 CGDT and claim termination rates from the 2008 GLTD Experience Table, adjusted based on company experience, provide a basis for varying manual premium rates by age and gender. To the extent that maternity benefits are included on plans with elimination periods less than 90 days, however, adjustments to female claim costs may be necessary.

Occupation

Before considering variations in LTD claim costs by industry, it is desirable to establish rate adjustment factors for broad categories of occupation, such as (a) hourly and salaried employees, (b) blue collar, grey collar, and white collar occupations, (c) union and non-union employees, and (d) commissioned sales personnel.

The blue-grey-white-collar classification involves many subjective judgments, whereas the hourly-salaried classification is objective and simple in practice. The goal of occupational rating factors is to reflect differences in job duties and/or compensation structure that may occur among employees working within a single industry. For example, the expected level of claims among factory laborers, supervisors, and executives may vary significantly due to the manual duties involved in each position, even though all employees work in a single location in a single industry.

Industry

Some LTD insurers use occupational rating factors that depend on a detailed classification of occupations, similar to those found in rate manuals of individual disability income insurers. However, for group insurance it seems more appropriate to charge premiums according to the industry of the group, rather than the occupation of the individual, other than very broad categories of occupations suggested above. Often industry rating factors are based more on underwriting judgment than on credible experience.

Pure industry factors are discussed above with the hourly factor completely excluded (and the blue collar-union-commissioned factor also excluded). Likewise, if an earnings factor is used, this will have a theoretical impact on the industry factors. Care must be taken to avoid double-counting.

Average Earnings per Employee

There is a fairly widespread belief that disability incidence rates are lower for higher paid workers. Therefore, a sophisticated LTD manual rate structure might also incorporate an adjustment factor based on the average earnings of the group. For example, the following table provides illustrative earnings factors:

Table 25.7

Average Monthly Earnings per Employee	Earnings Factor
Less than $1,800	1.00
$1,800-2,199	0.98
2,200-2,599	0.96
2,600-2,999	0.94
3,000-3,499	0.92
3,500-3,999	0.90
4,000 or more	0.88

Not all industries experience more favorable claims with higher average earnings, however. For example, surgeons and stockbrokers (occupations in the medical and financial services industries), while enjoying high income, may have high rates of disability due to the physical requirements, economic uncertainty, or stress associated with their professions. Therefore, insurers should carefully consider how average earnings factors interact with occupation and industry factors.

Area

Credible experience by geographical area is not nearly so available for LTD as for medical coverage. However, the few insurers who have sufficient LTD experience for this purpose have apparently concluded that area variations in LTD claim costs are quite significant. Insurers who have introduced area factors in their LTD manual rates generally distinguish only between entire states, although there are a few exceptions, such as within California. An insurer who lacks meaningful data on LTD experience by state or region may get some idea of appropriate area adjustments by looking at the rate filings of a few of the leading carriers, which are available from several state insurance departments as a matter of public record.

Reasons for the very adverse experience of most insurers in California (or at least southern California) seem to include the entitlement culture, litigiousness, and the attitudes of lawyers and judges, including the threat of punitive damages against insurers or plan sponsors. Variations by state or by sales office territory can also be caused by varying quality of field underwriting.

Size of Group

Many carriers have observed claim cost patterns that vary by case size, with the highest claim costs occurring for the largest and smallest employers. Typical LTD rating factors for case size thus often follow a "U" shaped curve:

Table 25.8

Number of Employees	Factor
Less than 100	1.05
100-249	0.95
250-499	0.90
500-999	0.95
1,000 or more	1.10

Separately, insurers generally provide volume discounts based on the size of the group. The volume discount reflects the LTD commission scale (which itself varies by size) and the greater spreading of fixed expenses. This is a separate issue than the claim cost assumptions describe here, however.

MISCELLANEOUS FACTORS AFFECTING LTD CLAIM COSTS

Economic Cycle

Increasingly, LTD insurers are becoming aware of the significant impact the economy can have on LTD experience. For example, during the economic downturn that started in 2009, many carriers first observed lower claim termination rates as disabled employees found it harder to return to work due to high unemployment rates and a lack of available jobs. Subsequently, carriers observed increased claim incidence rates.

Most insurers have an overall rate adjustment factor used to change all LTD manual rates simultaneously, to reflect changes in overall profitability due to the economic cycle or for other reasons. On the other hand, many insurers recognize that LTD is a volatile risk and try to avoid over-reacting to cyclical swings. Surplus accumulated during favorable periods can be used to absorb some increase in claim costs during unfavorable periods. A tightening of underwriting posture in certain regions or industries may be a more flexible response than an increase in manual rates because it can be quickly relaxed when the external picture brightens.

Distribution System

A group insurer's distribution system will affect its LTD claim costs, although not as much as the quality of its home office underwriting and claim administration. Claim costs are usually higher on groups covered under association programs because adverse selection is greater than under single employer cases, unless the underwriting is tight enough to overcome this tendency.

Terrorism Risks

On September 11, 2001, the United States suffered an enormous loss from terrorist attacks on the World Trade Center and the Pentagon. Although property-casualty insurers and life insurers suffered massive losses as the result of these attacks, the impact on disability insurers was much smaller.

It is important, however, for disability insurers to consider the potential impact of catastrophic events in the pricing of their products. An event such as a chemical or biological terrorist attack could result in very significant morbidity with comparatively small mortality, for example. Since 2001, the cost of catastrophe reinsurance, which many companies use to protect themselves from catastrophe risk, has increased significantly and may need to be considered explicitly in the pricing of disability insurance.

It will be increasingly important for disability actuaries to consider concentrations of risk and exposure to potential terrorism in the pricing and reserving of disability costs in the future.

SHORT-TERM DISABILITY (STD)

Determination of net manual rates for short-term disability (STD) insurance is not much different from other group life and health insurance coverages, when based on an insurer's studies of its own experience. Unlike LTD, it is not necessary to separately determine rates of disablement (claim incidence rates) and disabled life annuities (claim reserves). An insurer's studies of its own short-term disability experience will generally be based on loss ratio studies. Manual rates can be adjusted periodically, using the incurred loss ratios multiplied by ratios of actual premium to manual premium.

Manual loss ratios may be available separately by STD plan, and perhaps by size of group and industry, but usually not by age or gender. The original determination of net manual rates according to all of these parameters must be based on data from other sources, either from special, detailed studies of the insurer's own experience (if sufficiently credible), or outside sources as discussed below.

SOURCES OF DATA

Due to the high frequency and low severity of STD claims relative to LTD claims, historical STD experience gains statistical credibility much faster than LTD business, and it is possible to make pricing decisions based on much smaller volumes of inforce business for STD than for LTD. Therefore, the best source of data for pricing STD is generally a company's own experience.

There has been little useful information published regarding historical STD experience. If a company has none of its own data available, however, or wishes to supplement its own data with industry statistics, the following sources may be helpful, though less than ideal.

TSA 1983 Reports

The 1983 *Reports* contain the thirty-sixth and final annual report of intercompany experience under group weekly indemnity insurance contracts.

Experience by Industry

The 1980 *Reports* contains exposure and A/T ratios for each of 83 industry classifications, according to the first two digits of the 1972 Standard Industrial Classification codes. This was the last quinquennial report on intercompany STD experience by industry. It combines policy years ending in 1975 through 1979 for all plans, with and without maternity, using 40% of the $3.42 tabular for the six-week maternity benefit. It does, however, separate experience on groups smaller and larger than 1,000 employees.

1985 Commissioners Individual Disability Table A (1985 CIDA)

The 1985 CIDA table was adopted by the NAIC to replace the 1964 Commissioners Disability Table as the basis of active life reserves and claim reserves for individual policies issued after 1986. The 1985 CIDA tables are published in *TSA XXXVII*.[5]

Despite the fact that individual experience will differ from group STD (and LTD) experience in frequency and duration, the 1985 CIDA tables can be of considerable value in developing rate adjustment factors for group STD (and LTD) – especially by age and occupation class – although not in establishing the overall level of claim costs. 1985 CIDA incidence and termination rates vary among four occupation classes.

In using data from 1985 CIDA for pricing STD, it is critical to note that normal maternity claims, which represent a very high proportion of total STD claim costs, are excluded from 1985 CIDA, while normal maternity benefits are nearly always included in group STD plans.

Individual Disability Experience Committee 1990-2006 Study

The Society of Actuaries Individual Disability Experience Committee recently published an intercompany study of individual disability experience from 1990 to 2006. Although there are many important differences between individual and group policies that affect the usefulness of this information in pricing STD benefits (including underwriting methods and offset formulas), the wealth of detailed experience on short benefit period and occupation

---

[5] "Report of the Committee to Recommend New Disability Tables for Valuation," *TSA XXXVII* (1985), 449.

groupings is of significant interest to STD insurers. As with the 1985 CIDA table, however, it is critical to note that this study excludes claims due to normal maternity.

ADJUSTMENTS TO EXPERIENCE STUDIES

The experience of a group insurer with short term disability (or any other coverage, for that matter) will depend on its marketing strategy, distribution system, field, and home office underwriting, and claim administration, as well as the accuracy of its pricing. The STD experience available from the sources described above can be used as guides in developing manual rates, but the overall level of claim costs or net manual rates must be adjusted to the insurer's own actual or anticipated experience.

Adjustments are usually required to graduate or smooth crude data, so that the final rates have reasonable internal relationships. Any significant trends should be recognized, whether unique to the particular insurer or applicable to all STD insurers. For example, many sources of published data have little detail on maternity claims, and companies must be sure that they have made appropriate allowance for maternity costs, which can be quite significant for STD.

STATE MANDATED CASH SICKNESS BENEFITS

The only available data on state mandated cash sickness benefits are certain statistical reports published by government agencies, such as a report produced on New York's Disability Benefits Law (DBL) by the New York State Insurance Department. However, unless there is a major exposure to these coverages, an insurer can probably use its regular STD manual rates for these plans, including adjustments for any unusual features. Some insurers already have accumulated significant data and may be open to requests for assistance.

CREDIT DISABILITY INSURANCE

Banks will often require smaller businesses to purchase credit disability insurance in order to protect their loans against the disablement of key staff within the business' leadership. Thus, credit disability insurance is purchased in conjunction with a consumer credit transaction and provides a monthly benefit equal to the required repayment of the debt while the insured is disabled during the term of coverage.

Credit disability premium calculations are typically much simpler than those for credit life insurance. They are usually single premiums specified in the prima facie rates specified by regulation or law in the state. Prima facie rates are the maximum rates an insurer may charge, unless the insurer can demonstrate a need for higher rates. They are usually promulgated by each state's insurance commissioner in credit insurance regulations. The prima facie rate is intended to produce a loss ratio at least equal to the benchmark loss ratio, which is 50% in most states. The practical result is that most insurers charge the prima facie rates of each state. Therefore, there is not much need for extensive experience data and actuarial judgment in devising more accurate pricing.

If creditors and their insurers were more able and willing to reduce their profit margins by competing on price, they would have a greater need for accurate pricing and their actuaries would need claim experience extensive enough to be statistically significant for creating pricing differentials for important influencing factors, such as type of lenders and borrowers. The large disability credit insurers may have sufficient data for this purpose.

26 PRICING GROUP LONG-TERM CARE INSURANCE

Amy Pahl

INTRODUCTION

Long-term care insurance is a unique group product for three major reasons. First, it is entry-age (or issue-age) rated and is the only group insurance product that is always provided on this basis. Entry-age rating is required by regulation for ages 65 and greater. Even though younger issue ages could be rated on attained age, there are virtually no products offered in the U.S. with attained age rating.

Second, the product is overwhelmingly offered as optional coverage, where employees pay 100% of premium. There are examples of employer-paid group long-term care insurance, typically with the employer providing the premium for a minimum benefit level with optional upgrades. While about 54% of large employers offer group long-term care insurance, however, only 4% of large employers partially or fully subsidize that coverage.[1]

Third, group long-term care insurance has a unique set of eligible insureds. It is offered to actively-at-work employees and their spouses, parents, grandparents (including in-laws), as well as to retirees. It is becoming more common to include adult children and siblings in the family member offering. The ability to offer the coverage to such a broad class of eligibles hinges on the different underwriting protocols used for each subset. In turn, this introduces unique pricing challenges.

These three characteristics make the actuarial issues faced in pricing and managing the product more akin to traditional individual health insurance than to group health insurance. However, there are special issues to consider in the group product line that do not occur in individual long-term care insurance, with the most significant being the decreased ability to predict the risk characteristics of the block of business at the time of pricing. Additional issues not present in individual insurance are experience rating, policyholder reporting, and handling reserves when the group changes carrier or the individual changes groups.

This chapter will discuss state and federal regulatory issues, policy design features from the point of view of the employer, employee, insurer, and broker, and the resulting pricing asset share model and assumptions. Background on policy types and plan features in group long-term care insurance policies is provided in the chapter titled "Group Long-Term Care Insurance."

---

[1] Towers Watson's Benefit Data Source information cited in testimony to the House of Representatives on March 17, 2011

STATE REGULATORY ISSUES

Employer groups do not typically self-fund long-term care (LTC) insurance benefits. LTC insurance is a classic insurance risk with low frequency and high claim amounts, and self-funding is typically not an attractive option. Even the Federal Employees' LTC plan, with over 20 million people eligible for coverage, is fully insured. Therefore, the majority of group LTC insurance is regulated by the states. For an overview of state regulation, see the "Regulation in the United States" chapter.

LTC insurance is tightly regulated and monitored at the state level, and all states have adopted statutes and regulations concerning LTC insurance. Many regulators view LTC insurance as having a high potential for abuse, since it is primarily a senior product. Like Medicare Supplement insurance regulation, LTC insurance regulation addresses product design, the way the product is sold, and what needs to be disclosed to the consumer in the sales process. LTC insurance regulation also has some additional features that are intended to protect consumers who purchase a product that has a long tail for claims. These regulations typically mandate a non-forfeiture benefit and inflation protection offers.

Similar to the group accident and health eligibility laws, the LTC insurance regulations usually define the types of groups to which LTC insurance can be sold, as well as any specific requirements concerning the type of group.

The most significant recent state regulatory issue is rate stabilization. Prior to 2000, most states used minimum loss ratios requirements to regulate the reasonableness of LTC insurance premiums. Today, state regulation focuses on ensuring that rate increases will not be necessary.

Subsequent to the rate stability regulation, most states modified their regulations to add more LTC insurance consumer protections. Producer training requirements were increased. Consumers were granted more options when new LTC services or provider types became available in the market, and they were given greater flexibility to reduce coverage to make premiums more affordable. Claim handling regulations were strengthened.

NAIC LONG-TERM CARE INSURANCE MODEL ACT AND REGULATION

The National Association of Insurance Commissioners (NAIC) has drafted and adopted both a LTC Insurance Model Act and a Model Regulation. The LTC Insurance Model Act and Regulation have been revised a number of times since their original adoption by the NAIC. State legislatures enact the LTC Insurance Model Act. Generally, state insurance departments promulgate the Model Regulation to implement the Model Act. Like most NAIC models, not all states enact the Model Act exactly as written nor do they promulgate the Model Regulation exactly as written.

The Model Act provides the definition of LTC insurance and applies to all health business sold by any organization. The Act and Regulation cover renewability, policy exclusions, unintentional lapses, minimum benefit standards, and standards for disclosure, reporting, advertising and marketing. They also require that the policyholder be offered compound inflation protection (which, in most states, may be offered to the group policyholder – the employer – as opposed to each certificate holder) and non-forfeiture benefits.

The LTC Insurance Model Regulation adopted by the NAIC in October, 2000 made significant changes to the required actuarial certification that is made by the LTC pricing actuary in state rate filings.

There are two sections in the Act and Regulation of particular interest when pricing group LTC insurance. First, the Model Regulation requires that group LTC insurance be issued with a basis for continuation and conversion that preserves the entry age of the individual, and does not require additional underwriting for similar benefits. The result is that once certificate holders are in an insurer's risk pool, they are expected to remain unless the group changes insurers. This is unlike group health insurance, where it is typical for individuals to frequently enter and leave a group.

Second, the Model Act also defines extraterritorial jurisdiction. In this context, "extraterritoriality" is a state's claim that the coverage of its residents must comply with its requirements, regardless of the requirements of the state in which the group policy is sitused. For those states that adopted the model act, group LTC insurance coverage may not be offered to a resident in a given state under a group policy issued in another state, unless the second state has LTC insurance regulations substantially similar to those adopted by the first. There are many state variations.

The major changes in the 2000 LTC Insurance Model Regulation apply to both individual and group LTC insurance, and these changes had a significant impact on pricing. The intent is to change the focus away from minimum loss ratio requirements towards rate stability. The Model Regulation requires disclosure of rating practices, requires an actuarial certification at the time of initial rating that rates will be adequate in the event of moderately adverse experience, and eliminates minimum loss ratio requirements in the initial rate filing. The Model Regulation also places limits on expense assumptions in the event of a rate increase, requires reimbursement of unnecessary rate increases, and provides policyholders the option to escape the effect of rising rate spirals by guaranteeing the right to switch to currently sold insurance without underwriting. The Model Regulation authorizes the insurance commissioner to ban companies that persist in filing inadequate initial premiums from the marketplace for five years.

The 2014 Model Regulation changes, although minor by comparison to the 2000 changes, further the concept of rate stability by requiring a minimum level for moderately adverse experience and by requiring an annual rate certification that the current premium rate schedule is sufficient and reasonable.

Disclosure of Rating Practices

Disclosure of rating practices must be made to the applicant at the time of application. The required elements to be disclosed are (1) a statement that the policy may be subject to rate increases in the future, (2) an explanation of potential future rate revisions, (3) the premium rates or rate schedules currently effective, (4) a general explanation for applying premium or rate schedule adjustments, and (5) information regarding each premium increase on the policy or similar policy forms over the past ten years. The insurer may add explanatory information and has the right to exclude from disclosure certain premium rate increases on business acquired from other insurers.

Actuarial Certification at Initial Rate Filing

At the time of the initial rate filing, older LTC insurance policies issued prior to the adoption of the 2000 Model Regulation required an actuarial certification that a minimum 60% loss ratio would be met over the life of the policy. The 2000 and later Model NAIC LTC Insurance Regulations are designed to minimize the need for future rate increases (although the insurance commissioner may ask for a demonstration that premiums are reasonable in relation to benefits). The actuary must include the following items in a certification:

- A statement that the initial premium rate schedule is sufficient to cover anticipated costs under moderately adverse experience;
- A statement that policy design and coverage have been reviewed and taken into consideration;
- A statement that the underwriting and claims adjudication processes have been reviewed and taken into consideration;
- A statement that the premium rate schedule is not less than that of existing, similar policy forms except for reasonable differences attributable to benefits;
- A comparison of the premium schedules for similar policy forms currently sold by the insurer, with an explanation of the differences; and
- A statement that reserve requirements have been reviewed with support including sufficient detail or a sample calculation, and a statement that the difference between the gross and net valuation premium for renewal years is sufficient to cover expected renewal expenses.

As of early 2015, 43 states and the District of Columbia have adopted the 2000 Model Regulation, or a substantially similar version of the Model Regulation. Therefore, the pricing actuary must certify to the minimum 60% loss ratio in only a few states, and for the other states, certify that the rates are sufficient under moderately adverse experience.

The pricing actuary must also consider the definition of "moderately adverse" experience. The American Academy of Actuaries completed a Practice Note in May of 2003, to provide guidance to a pricing actuary when completing an actuarial certification under moderately adverse experience.

The 2014 Model Regulation amendment requires the actuary to make a statement that the premiums contain at least the minimum margin for moderately adverse experience which, in most cases, is at least 10% of expected claims. The Model Regulation amendment also requires an annual rate certification to be submitted to the states which adopt the Model Regulation, stating that the premium rate schedule is sufficient to cover anticipated costs under moderately adverse experience, and that the premium rate schedule is reasonably expected to be sustainable over the life of the form, with no future premium increases anticipated. If the actuary cannot make this statement, a plan of action to re-establish the margin for moderately adverse experience must be submitted to the state.

Premium Rate Schedule Increases

The 2000 Model Regulation makes a distinction between exceptional rate increases and other increases. Exceptional rate increases are those required due to: (1) changes in laws or regulations applicable to LTC insurance coverage, or (2) increased and unexpected utilization that affects the majority of insurers of similar products. Examples of other reasons for rate increases that are not "exceptional" would be lower lapses than assumed in pricing, or lower investment income earnings than assumed in pricing.

The Model Regulation requires the following condition be met for rate increases: the sum of accumulated value of incurred claims and the present value of future incurred claims (without the inclusion of change in active life reserves) will not be less than the sum of:

(i) the accumulated value of initial earned premium times 58%;

(ii) 85% of the accumulated value for prior premium rate schedule increases on an earned basis;

(iii) the present value of future projected initial earned premiums times 58%; and

(iv) 85% of the present value of future projected premiums not included in (iii), on an earned basis.

In the case where both exceptional and other rate increases are present, the amounts in (ii) and (iv) will be 70% for the exceptional rate increase amounts. Accumulations and present values are calculated using valuation interest rates specified in the NAIC Health Reserves Model Regulation.

The 2014 Model Regulation amendment provides a revised basis by which states may approve premium rate schedule increases. For policies issued prior to the adoption of the 2014 Model Regulation amendment, the minimum loss ratio as described above continues to apply. For those policies issued after the adoption of the 2014 Model Regulation amendment, the greater of a 58% loss ratio and the original pricing loss ratio is used in place of the prior 58% loss ratio requirement of items (i) and (iii) above.

The requirement in the 2014 Model Regulation amendment for an annual rate certification encourages companies to file for needed rate increases sooner, which may allow for smaller, more frequent rate increases. The annual submission requirements include:

- An actuarial certification providing a statement of sufficiency of the current premium rate schedule based on calendar year data and submitted annually by May 1; and

- An actuarial memorandum in support of the certification that provides an explanation of the data and the review performed, a description of experience assumptions, a description of the credibility of experience, and an explanation of the analysis performed in determining the current margins, to be submitted at least once every three years.

The 2014 Model Regulation amendment allows for companies to request a lower rate increase than needed to certify to rate stability if the rate increase needed to certify to rate stability is disclosed and if the lower request, in the opinion of the insurance commissioner, is in the best interest of policyholders.

Unnecessary Rate Increases and Replacement of Coverage in Rate Spirals

The Model Regulation includes the requirement that, in the event of revised premium schedules being greater than 200% of the initial rates, lifetime projections must be submitted to the insurance commissioner of insurance every five years. In the event that actual experience does not match projected experience, or that minimum loss ratio requirements are not met following rate increases, the insurance commissioner may require premium rate schedule adjustments or other measures to reduce the difference between projected and actual experience.

In the event that antiselective lapsation is anticipated in a rate filing, or is evidenced by actual experience following rate increases, the insurance commissioner may determine that a rate spiral exists. The insurer may then be required to offer replacement coverage without underwriting.

Groups of 5,000 or more eligible employees where 250 or more are insured, or groups where the employer pays more than 20% of premium are exempted from the requirements of the refund or reduction of unnecessary rate increases, and from the requirement to offer replacement coverage in the event of rate spirals.

Extraterritorial Application of State Requirements

Most states require submissions of certificate forms and rates for out-of-state LTC insurance group contracts that are issued to discretionary groups, with supporting documentation that the benefits are reasonable in relation to the premiums charged. Some states have a section within the LTC law or regulation that specifically addresses out-of-state filing requirements, indicating the types of groups that are subject to the requirement.

Some states have extra-territorial authority stemming from their accident and health insurance code or regulations, or from their definition of conducting the business of insurance.

More and more states are expanding extra-territorial authority, especially for products like LTC insurance, which regulators think may be sold in an inappropriate manner. While the numbers are in transition and may depend on each insurer's own interpretation of a particular state's regulations, approximately 30 states extend extra-territorial authority over LTC insurance to association groups, and roughly 22 states extend that authority to employer/employee groups. Filing requirements vary, from informational copies of the certificates to prior approval of the forms and rates. Typically, there are additional filing requirements and assurances that must be made for affinity groups and associations. If the extra-territorial requirements of a particular state are at odds with the LTC insurance requirements of the situs state of a group LTC insurance plan, it may be necessary to offer a different plan to residents of the extra-territorial state than to those of the group plan's situs state. This can complicate the marketing and administration of the plan. The Interstate Insurance Product Regulation Commission (also known as the Interstate Compact) has improved the speed at which new LTC insurance products can be brought to market and has lowered product administration costs by eliminating or reducing product variations by state. The Interstate Compact has been enabled for individual LTC insurance filings and 33 states (including Puerto Rico) are considered to be fully participating. The group LTC insurance standards are expected to be developed following the development of group disability filing standards.[2]

---

[2] This section on extraterritoriality was largely written by Malcolm Cheung, author of the chapter titled "Group Long-Term Care Insurance."

NAIC Health Insurance Reserves Model Regulation

The NAIC Health Insurance Reserves Model Regulation provides the basis for LTC insurance reserves: claim reserves, premium reserves, and contract reserves. For group or individual LTC insurance, the mortality table is specified (the 1994 Group Annuity Mortality Table without projection), but morbidity tables are not.

The Reserves Model Regulation adopted in July, 1998, by the NAIC changed the total termination rates (voluntary lapse plus the mortality table) that may be included in the reserve basis for LTC insurance. The change in the Reserves Model Regulation explicitly recognized that mortality is a significant portion of total policy termination rates in LTC insurance, unlike other health coverages, and not being able to include 100% of the mortality assumption at the older ages resulted in reserve redundancy. In 2005, the Reserves Model Regulation was revised to limit voluntary lapse rates to a maximum of 6% in policy year one, 4% in policy years two through four, and 3% (2% for individual) in policy years five or later.

Another departure from other health lines is the requirement that the contract reserves be calculated on one-year preliminary term basis. LTC insurance policies issued prior to December 31, 1991, may use a two-year preliminary term method.

Professional Actuarial Issues

LTC pricing actuaries have been criticized in the past for aggressive rating practices that, while technically meeting the requirements of the LTC rate regulations and the applicable Actuarial Standard of Practices (ASOPs), do not meet the spirit of the requirements.

The following ASOPs are most relevant to group LTC insurance pricing:

- ASOP Number 5, Incurred Health and Disability Claims, which discusses the data, methods, assumptions, and other aspects of calculating or reviewing health and disability claims;
- ASOP Number 18, Long Term Care Insurance, which is a general standard discussing designing, pricing, funding, and calculating liabilities of LTC products; and
- ASOP Number 23, Data Quality, which discusses selecting and reviewing data to be used, and disclosures with respect to data limitations.

Federal Regulatory Issues

Both the Health Insurance Portability and Accountability Act of 1996 (HIPAA) and the Deficit Reduction Act of 2005 (DRA) have provisions that affect LTC insurance.

Health Insurance Portability and Accountability Act

The major impacts of HIPAA on LTC insurance are to define qualified plans, clarify taxation of premium and benefits, standardize benefit triggers (the insurable event that causes benefits to be paid), and allow tax reserves to be calculated on a one-year preliminary term basis.

The stated intention of HIPAA is to make health insurance coverage available, portable, and guaranteed renewable for individuals. However, portability and guaranteed renewability were already universal for group LTC insurance, because LTC insurance state regulation required guaranteed renewability, along with conversion or continuation of coverage. Even without regulation, market forces likely would have required group LTC insurance to be portable.

HIPAA did, however, have a major impact on the LTC insurance market with respect to availability of coverage. HIPAA included the codification of the taxability of benefits, and the benefit triggers required of a tax-qualified policy. HIPAA Section 321 settled a longstanding question on the taxability of premium and benefits, by stating that a qualified LTC insurance contract shall be treated as an accident and health insurance contract. Therefore, premium paid by an employer is not taxable income to the employee. Premium paid by individuals is a qualified medical expense, and is deductible from their income once the 7.5% of income threshold is met. Benefits provided by a qualified LTC policy, as with other medical insurance, are not taxable income.

HIPAA Section 321 also defines the benefit triggers of a tax-qualified policy. Prior to 1996, there was great variation in the benefit triggers in LTC insurance policies. HIPAA has had the effect of rapidly moving the LTC insurance industry to standardized triggers. Qualified LTC services are defined as the "necessary diagnostic, preventive, therapeutic, curing, treating, mitigating, and rehabilitative services, and maintenance or personal care services" of a "chronically ill individual" provided "pursuant to a plan of care prescribed by a licensed health care practitioner." A person must be certified by a licensed health care practitioner as:

(i) being unable to perform at least two activities of daily living (ADLs) for a period of at least 90 days; or
(ii) having a level of disability similar to that described in (i); or
(iii) requiring substantial supervision to protect such individual from threats to health and safety due to severe cognitive impairment.

Another change due to HIPAA that has pricing implications is the change of the tax reserve basis. One-year preliminary term tax reserves are now allowed for tax-qualified LTC insurance policies. Since many states previously required one-year preliminary term for contract reserves, this creates more consistent timing between statutory contract reserves and tax contract reserves and increases the return on investment for LTC insurance from prior levels.

THE DEFICIT REDUCTION ACT OF 2005

The Deficit Reduction Act of 2005 (DRA) encourages individuals to take personal responsibility for funding their LTC needs through private insurance. The DRA included provisions that tighten Medicaid eligibility rules by changing the qualification rules relating to allowable asset transfers prior to Medicaid benefit eligibility and excluding individuals with more than $500,000 in home equity from qualifying for Medicaid. The DRA provisions also allow for an expansion of the Partnership LTC insurance concept to all 50 states.

Partnership LTC insurance policies allow individuals who apply for Medicaid LTC benefits to protect an amount of personal assets that is greater than the amount normally permitted by state

Medicaid programs. The additional asset protection against Medicaid "spend-down" rules[3] is equal to the dollar amount of benefits received from the Partnership LTC insurance policy. Medicaid programs can also extend reciprocal asset protection to those who currently reside in a state that is different from the state in which a Partnership policy was issued. The DRA established a National Clearinghouse for LTC Information, which helps individuals make educated choices about LTC insurance coverage. This legislation has increased public interest in LTC insurance as a means to help achieve retirement security.

The most recent, though failed, federal regulatory initiative was the Community Living Assistance Services and Support (CLASS) Act, a provision in the Affordable Care Act (ACA) passed in March 2010. The CLASS Act would have created a national voluntary employee-pay LTC insurance program, which would provide a modest cash benefit to eligible beneficiaries for their LTC needs. Most working adults of participating employers would have been eligible to enroll, with premiums based on age at purchase and increasing with the consumer price index each year. Benefits adjusted for inflation would have been available following a five-year vesting period and continue as long as the covered individual qualified for benefits. The CLASS Act was not implemented, because the Department of Health and Human Services questioned the viability of the program, including the pricing of the product, likely low participation rates, and resulting antiselection.

PRICING CONSIDERATIONS

The policy provisions of a group LTC insurance offering obviously have major implications on pricing. There are four major stakeholders in the policy design process of group LTC insurance: the employer group (the policyholder), the insurer, the employees (certificate holders), and the insurance broker. The concerns and goals of each group should be understood by the pricing actuary.

THE EMPLOYER GROUP

A major pricing assumption is the choice of participation rates expected to be obtained by voluntary employer groups. Enrollment participation of 5-10% is considered good, but may be too low to overcome issues relating to high start-up costs and antiselection.

There are various ways to increase the participation rate, including: (1) underwriting for suitability, and (2) vigorous enrollment, including enrollment of eligible relatives of employees. Underwriting for suitability involves understanding the characteristics and demographic make-up of the group and designing a benefit package that will be desirable and affordable.

The offered benefits should be tied to the cost of services and availability of services in the geographic area. A typical offering has three or four prepackaged plans with varying levels of benefit period, daily benefit amount, and home health care percentage. Often only one elimination period is offered. Of special importance is the offer of inflation protection. The

---

[3] Medicaid spend-down rules require individuals to basically impoverish themselves, selling off nearly all assets, in order to be eligible for Medicaid.

NAIC Model Regulation requires that 5% annual compound inflation protection must be offered to the policyholder, but it is not necessary to make the offer to each individual certificate holder.

Another appeal to employers is that LTC insurance complements other products. It can be seen as an extension of the group's long-term disability coverage, 401(k) benefits, and life insurance. In contrast to major medical plans, which are perceived as very expensive and are subject to rate increases every year, employers may provide a minimal LTC benefit at low cost and with less frequent rate increases to employees.

The level of underwriting rigor applied to the actively-at-work requirement is a decision for the employer group and the insurer to make together. Employer groups are used to offering all benefits without underwriting, other than an actively-at-work requirement. However, many people with a diagnosis or condition that is predicted with high certainty to lead to a future LTC insurance claim may be actively-at-work. These high frequency claims must be accounted for in the premium rates, and this may require premium levels that are higher than what healthy employees could obtain in the individual market. Because of this problem, "modified guaranteed issue" is often used, meaning employees must (1) be actively at work, (2) not have been ADL[4] dependent in the past one to two years, and (3) not have received any LTC services in the past one to two years. In addition, other questions are often included about specific diagnoses, the use of assistive devices, and prescription drug use.

Modified guaranteed issue allows an affordable LTC insurance for the group but does exclude some employees, and this may be problematic for employers. This is a difficult issue that must be addressed by the employer group and insurer together. Not all employer groups are willing to give up the benefit of guarantee issue.

INSURERS

The concerns of group LTC insurers include the need to sell both to employers and employees, up-front marketing and distribution costs, and the risk of low enrollment. A major pricing problem is the level of participation to assume, and therefore the morbidity level to assume. Morbidity can vary significantly by the level of participation. Some insurers can distinguish claim cost patterns that differ by participation groupings, such as ≤ 3%, 3-10%, and ≥ 10%. Others report similar claim costs for all groups with less than 10% participation. The current practice is to price to the average expected participation rate, and to monitor experience to make sure this level is achieved.

The size of the group is also a consideration in the overall morbidity. The group LTC insurance market, like its counterparts of other group health lines of business, consists of many markets of varying group size, from association groups and small groups, to mid-size and large groups. The premium rate structure may include discounts for group size, but unless discounts are based on commission and expense savings, this is only appropriate to the extent that the premium structure reflects the level of antiselection anticipated or reflects the underwriting tools and procedures used with groups of different sizes.

---

[4] ADL stands for Activities of Daily Living; see Chapter 13, "Group Long-Term Care Insurance," for more information on ADLs, and the application of ADLs in relation to LTC insurance.

Another pricing strategy is to use an individual policy form and its premium rates with group discounts based on commission and expense savings, and expected relative morbidity. This means issuing an individual policy to each employee. This strategy has the advantage of a premium rate structure that allows the matching of appropriate rate levels to the risk. Parents and parents-in-law may be offered spousal discounts along with individual underwriting. This strategy is often not understood by employer groups, however, who may believe the group vehicle to be intrinsically better.

The insurer has a cash outlay to implement a group case. Costs include integration of the product into the employer's payroll deduction plan, and the enrollment and education of eligible prospects. The insurer must work closely with the employer group to ensure a level of participation that will recover these costs, as discussed above.

EMPLOYEES

For employees, the concerns are two-fold. First, a group insurance offering may be their first introduction to LTC insurance, and their first awareness of the risk that this insurance is designed to cover. Employees may have aged from providing for young families, where the desired ancillary benefits may be supplemental life insurance and dental, to planning retirement, where the desired benefits are retirement income and LTC insurance.

The second major concern is cost. Employees typically pay 100% of LTC insurance premiums, and the premiums may be expensive. Issue-age premiums for younger ages may be lower than for individual insurance, due to lower commission and underwriting costs. However, it is a pricing challenge to retain this differential at older ages, because individual products may be able to offer spousal discounts and preferred rating, and are basing their rates on full underwriting.

BROKERS

Brokers have found that group LTC insurance provides an opportunity to open the door to the competitive life and disability markets with a product that is less familiar. There is then an opportunity to extend the market to parents and grandparents.

EXPERIENCE RATING

As in other types of group health insurance, groups of a certain size may choose to experience rate. To have a high degree of confidence that claims are credible in LTC insurance, the number of participants necessary is much larger than with other coverages, due to both the low frequency and the variance in size of claims. One suggested threshold is 32,000 participants, which, with an expected participation rate of about 10%, implies about 300,000 eligible employees.

Prospective experience rating is fairly unusual in group LTC insurance, since these products are relatively new, and due to the regulatory pressures described earlier. Specifically, the fact that group LTC uses entry-age rates and a guaranteed renewable structure means that prospective rate changes on inforce business, based on a group's experience, are very challenging from a regulatory perspective.

A hallmark of retrospective experience rating is that the employer is taking some risk in the outcome of the group. An experience fund may be established to track emerging results.

The actual level of the fund may depend on emerging claims, expense, lapse, investment, and mortality experience, though pricing assumptions may be used for some of these elements. Experience that lowers the fund may necessitate the insurer earning less profit than expected. Should the fund fall significantly lower than expected levels, the program should be reviewed for possible corrective actions, either administrative (for example, tighter underwriting and care management) or rate increases. Likewise, better than expected experience allows the insurer to earn greater than expected profits. Some contracts require that a portion of favorable experience be returned to the group certificate holders, through improved benefits or lower premiums.

Additionally, many large group contracts include performance standards with respect to underwriting and claims adjudication, account servicing, and data reporting. If performance standards are not met, the experience fund may be assessed penalties, or there may be a one-time premium reduction. Poor experience and subpar performance compared to standards may cause the group to open the case to a rebidding process. Transfer of groups under such scenarios is discussed in the next section.

GROUP TRANSFER

The possibility of changing insurers is present for both small and large groups. Early group contracts often did not contain terms to cover what happened in the event that a group desired to change insurers. The industry quickly learned that transfer issues should be included in the request for proposal and the group contract. A group may wish to transfer from one insurer to another when performance levels are not met in areas such as claim experience, enrollment penetration, return on investment, administrative expenses, financial stability, and customer service.

Because of potential problems in changing insurers, this action is only taken if the group feels that performance measures can be improved by such a change.

Another reason that a group may change insurers is the current insurer is leaving the group LTC insurance market. If the group's current insurer has decided not to take additional new enrollees, an employer plan sponsor who wants to continue the program will need to move the insurance to an insurer willing to accept new enrollees.

The request for proposal should address which certificate holders will transfer in the case of insurer change. It may be elected to transfer only new issues, although the employer group may not wish to leave any part of the group behind if administrative or service issues are the reason for the change. The advantages of leaving existing insureds with the original insurer are that the administrative transfer difficulties are avoided, and the original insurer pays for any past mistakes. Most often, the individuals are given the choice of whether to stay or go, and this creates antiselection challenges for both the old and new insurer. The request for proposal should also consider the time of the transfer, and the asset segregation for the group.

On transfer, the active life reserves (that portion of past premium set aside for future claims) or the experience fund (if applicable) should be transferred to the assuming insurer. Problems that may occur with transfer include difficulties in determining the actual experience of the group, inadequacy of the statutory reserves held due to inappropriate assumptions or methods, inadequacy of the experience fund, and difficulties in data and record transmission.

An important consideration is that the reserves to be transferred are not necessarily the statutory active life reserves. If the group is large enough, the experience fund is probably the best measure of the amount to transfer. This fund measures premium, less claims incurred, less a provision for profits and expenses accumulated to date. Many contracts, especially those for smaller groups, use the statutory active life reserve as the amount to be transferred. The problem with transferring the statutory active life reserves is that these reserves reflect the requirements of the state of domicile of the current insurer, which may not be the requirement of the assuming insurer. In addition, statutory reserving methods vary from company to company, and may not reflect actual experience.

Finally, the request for proposal should consider how the amount to be transferred relates to the assets supporting the reserves. Should these actual assets or cash be transferred? Do assets need to be liquidated for a cash transfer? Are the assets for the particular group segregated, and if so, may actual securities be transferred, and at what market value?

The request for proposals for large groups should consider these issues at the time of initial bidding, to avoid later conflicts. Periodic rebidding may be built into the contract, but generally at not less than five to seven year intervals.

PRICING MODELS

LTC insurance pricing is typically based on lifetime asset share projection models. This section provides a general overview of such asset shares, and a discussion of assumption setting for pricing.

The general pricing problem in LTC insurance is to set premium rates that are appropriate for the life of the business. This is typically done through a multi-cell model, where each cell is a projection of future financial results for a representative policy with a given set of rating characteristics (options and demographics). These cell-based results are then composited and averaged, assuming a distribution of options and demographics. Compositing and averaging may result in subsidization of one option or demographic group by another, and if so, introduces a pricing risk if the assumed distribution is not achieved.

ASSET SHARES

An asset share model is used to project the financial income and outgo for a given cell. Assumptions are made in order to build the year-by-year projection, and premium rates are then determined that will result in the required profit criteria, given the income and outgo modeled over the lifetime of the policy. The asset share technique is an important pricing tool because of the steep increase of LTC claim cost by age, the level premium structure, and the extended length of time a certificate holder is expected to remain in the risk pool.

Because of the low lapse rates that occur with this line of business and the very steep slope of the claim costs over time, projections must be fairly long. For certificates issued to those in their fifties, projections should be longer than 30 years.

The first pricing step is choosing the model's cells. The asset share model is defined by cells that vary from cell to cell by risk characteristic. Premium is either taken directly from the model, or is interpolated. Enough cells should be modeled in order to capture the different possible relationships between claim costs and premium slopes. In addition to different cells for different benefit plans (such as different home health care benefits, inflationary options and other benefit options), this means creating cells by different gender, issue age, and underwriting method. The process of selecting model cells is extremely important. Pricing to averages can lead to inappropriate premiums, and subsequently to misleading expected results against which emerging results are measured.

MODEL ASSUMPTIONS

The major assumptions needed to define the pricing model include lapsation, mortality, morbidity, selection, expenses, interest, and the reserve basis for the asset share model.

Lapsation

Voluntary lapse rates are much lower in a block of LTC insurance than with other types of health insurance. This result is logical when the entry age and level premium structure is considered, but was misestimated by the LTC insurance industry when the product was first introduced. Group LTC insurance voluntary lapse rates in duration one may be as high as 10% to 14%, compared to a much lower initial duration rate of 6% to 7% for individual LTC insurance. The group LTC insurance ultimate voluntary lapse experience is slightly higher than individual, running 1.5% to 2.5%, compared to some companies' individual rates of 0.5% to 1.0%. Employer-paid groups experience higher lapse rates, as expected, due to employees dropping the coverage when they leave the employer and must begin to pay on their own.

Because of the steep claim cost slope and entry age rating, the premium rates are very sensitive to changes in lapse assumptions. This is especially true for products with inflation protection. Changing from a typical set of assumptions used in the early to mid-1990s (for illustration, 15% grading to 7.5%), to lapse experience seen in the late 1990s and into the early twenty-first century (6% grading to 3%) requires a significant change in premium, especially at younger ages. For example, the premium change due to the change in lapse assumptions required for issue age 62 might be about 10% for non-inflationary products, and about 19% for inflationary products; while for issue age 47, the required increases would be about 13% and 43%, respectively. The impact is quite dramatic and illustrates the importance of this assumption. Although many carriers were fortunately conservative in setting morbidity assumptions in the early generations of LTC insurance, they had difficulty predicting the lapse behavior of purchasers of LTC insurance. The greater impact on inflationary products has led to smaller profit margins on these options. Although an unpopular move, companies have begun to increase inflationary rider rates, reducing the subsidization of inflationary benefits by non-inflationary benefits.

Mortality

At this writing, the 1994 Group Annuitant Mortality table (94 GAM) is the mortality table required for statutory reserves by the NAIC's Health Insurance Reserves Model Regulation. Because of this, and because of state insurance department expectations, the 94 GAM is often used in pricing. However, this table was chosen because it was expected to be conservative, not because it was demonstrated to be the appropriate mortality model for those who purchase LTC insurance.

Some carriers have observed better than 94 GAM mortality on underwritten business in individual lines. For those segments where good individual underwriting is performed, use of selection factors or a table with lower mortality rates, such as the Annuity 2000 table, should be considered.

As is the case for lapsation, premium rates are sensitive to changes in the mortality assumption. A mortality assumption that is set too high, either because an inappropriate table is used or because the effect of selection is misestimated or ignored, leads to premiums that are too low. Similarly, inadequate consideration for mortality improvement will lead to understated premiums, particularly if mortality continues to improve as it has in the past. Mortality is a major source of overall policy terminations that are expected to occur prior to individuals making any LTC claims.

Other carriers have an easier time measuring total termination rates and set their voluntary lapse rates equal to the total termination rate with the 94 GAM, or the chosen pricing mortality basis, backed out. However, the risk with this latter method is that if mortality is set too high, the effect is leveraged at the tail, producing voluntary lapse rates that are negative.

Morbidity/Claim Costs

Developing appropriate claim costs is a major task for the pricing actuary. Claim costs are developed both from public data and insured data, whether the company's own or obtained through a consultant or reinsurer. The primary sources of public morbidity data are The National Long Term Care Survey (NLTCS) and the National Home and Hospice Care Survey (NHHCS). The only publicly available reports of experience on lives insured under private LTC insurance plans in the U.S. are those prepared by the Society of Actuaries LTC Experience Subcommittee. Data in the most recent report, published in two phases in January, 2015 and April, 2015, reflects claim experience from January 1, 2000 to December 31, 2011.

Claim costs can be thought of as (1) frequency of claim, times (2) length of stay, times (3) the daily benefit amount. The frequency of claim is (1) the probability of meeting the criteria for claim, times (2) the probability of satisfying the elimination period. The length of stay is a discounted annuity value of $1 of daily benefit, derived from claim termination probabilities.

Other assumptions needed for home health care claims are the percentage of claims made up of each type of service; the expected number of services used each month, and the expected cost of each service. The usual technique used to create claim cost tables is to measure prevalence of ADL deficiencies and cognitive impairment, measure the continuance and prevalence of care on various care paths, and back into claim frequency from the two. For plans with integrated benefits, that is with a single benefit period or maximum and a single elimination period applicable to multiple types of benefits, transfer from one type of care to another should be considered to avoid overstating claim costs.

Salvage adjustments, which are adjustments made to claim costs to account for when the actual expense incurred by claimants is less than the maximum daily benefit per day, are not usually made for nursing home services. It is assumed that most policyholders purchase the appropriate level of daily benefit, or even purchase a lesser amount as a form of coinsurance. It is also assumed that inflation takes care of any overinsurance before the time of claim. However, salvage should be considered in pricing the home health care and assisted living facility (ALF) portion of claims, and in order to price the relativity of daily limits to benefits, versus weekly or monthly limits.

Public data is very beneficial in a young industry where emerging experience is not credible in all model cells. This is particularly true at attained ages over 90 where fully credible insured experience is not yet available. In using such population data, it must be adjusted for the presence of the Medicaid population, benefit eligibility criteria, and the fact that some discharges are for short returns to home during a period of care that would be considered one claim on a policy. In general, population data includes higher frequencies and shorter stays than insured data. Population data must therefore be modified for expected insured utilization.

Claim costs may be expressed on the basis of total exposure, or non-institutional exposure, and the asset share model may be developed for either exposure basis. Care must be taken, however, when extrapolating claims for use with total exposure. It is tempting for the pricing actuary to use slopes developed to extrapolate claim costs at extreme ages where credible experience is not yet available. However, if the claim costs for use with a total exposure base are built by extending the available curve with no modification to slope, the claim costs could imply 100% institutionalization by insureds in their mid-nineties, which is obviously not a valid outcome.

Choosing claim costs for benefits that will not be used until well into the future is a pricing challenge. This challenge is helped by the continual morbidity improvement that has been observed, both in population and insured data. The difficulty lies in predicting the norm of the medical delivery system that will be providing benefits thirty years or more from when the policy is purchased. This problem is illustrated by the industry's experience with covering ALFs. ALFs, which provide supervision and assistance in an independent living setting, were introduced in the 1990s. For some policies, such as stand-alone nursing home, covering ALFs represented a significant increase in claim costs. Policy language may not have addressed ALFs, and, in some cases, companies determined either to cover ALFs extra contractually or that they had no basis to deny coverage. For other policies, such as comprehensive policies, the ALF represented a shift in claim costs, but not a significant increase in total.

There are many important variables that dictate the level of claim costs, or the choice of adjustments to make to claim costs.

Marital Status: LTC claim costs may be differentiated by marital status or by the presence of another potential caregiver (such as by two siblings living together). Marital discounts are common in individual LTC insurance for this reason, and discounts for unrelated persons living together are becoming popular. Marital discounts are not popular in group LTC insurance, but the effect of marital status should be considered when developing composite claim costs.

Gender: Claim costs vary significantly by gender, with females having a much steeper slope, and significantly higher ultimate costs than males. Some of this differential is due to the sociological phenomenon that females are usually younger than their partners, and are more inclined to be caregivers. Females tend to provide care for their older spouses, but do not have a caregiver available to them, due to their spouse's infirmity or death. Because of the large gender differential in claim costs, it is important to model males and females separately, and composite results to obtain unisex premiums. Virtually all group LTC insurance policies are offered with unisex premiums since gender-distinct rates are prohibited in the employer marketplace.

Benefit Trigger: Policies with different benefit triggers have different claim cost patterns. A trigger of medical necessity is more difficult to price because of its less objective nature. The standardization of benefit triggers by HIPAA has made the pricing actuary's job easier, as data will be more uniform going forward. Since HIPAA, over 90% of all group and individual LTC insurance policies are issued with the standard tax-qualified trigger.

Area: Utilization patterns of LTC services vary by geographic area. Of special note is the increased utilization of nursing homes in the upper Midwest, most likely due to the decreased availability of home health care services in more rural and remote areas. Also, there is increased utilization of home care services in Florida, most likely due to attitudinal differences regarding outside caregivers, and, in some cases, to fraudulent overutilization. Area rating is not common in the individual LTC insurance market, much less the group market. The problem for the group actuary is that it is harder to predict the area distribution of risks. A single large group with specific geographic concentration could skew results from pricing assumptions.

Case Management: LTC case management is a benefit included in many policies, and is provided by a professional care manager. This person coordinates paid care with informal and community based care, in order to maintain the highest level of independence possible for a patient with ADL deficiencies or cognitive impairment. Because the purpose of the case manager is to help the insured maintain independence, and also because it is very difficult for patients and their families to know and optimize the possible solutions to LTC needs, policyholders tend to be very receptive to the use of care planners and case managers. Companies that incorporate a case manager into the claim adjudication process usually experience lower claim costs. Partially offsetting these lower claim costs, however, is additional expense associated with ongoing case management.

Selection

Selection refers to the adjustments by policy duration made to claim costs tables, for input into the asset share model. Selection is a measurement of underwriting impact and the wear-off of initial selection. In LTC insurance, selection might also measure a comparable "marriage wear-off," as the effect of having a companion caregiver changes durationally. The durational changes in claim costs are much longer in LTC insurance than with other health insurance products, and part of this is due to the change in available caregiver status.

Appropriate selection factors can vary significantly due to the level of underwriting performed on the product. Some actuaries feel that there are permanent changes in the ultimate claim costs due to the degree of underwriting, but others feel that morbidity ultimately returns to an average level. It is important for the actuary to have a thorough understanding of the underwriting performed in order to model selection, and the new model regulation requires a certification that underwriting has been considered in determining the premium rates.

The group LTC insurance actuary has an especially difficult time modeling selection relative to the individual actuary. The group LTC insurance actuary may have three distinct underwriting styles used in the development of the risk pool: guaranteed issue or modified guaranteed issue for employees actively at work, short-form or simplified for spouses, and full individual underwriting used for other eligibles. The expected risk pool must be determined at each issue age from a composite of all three styles. While this is simpler at the extreme ages, at the very critical issue ages of about 50 to 65, the mix of applicants must be monitored frequently to make sure pricing assumptions match actual emerging experience.

Expenses

As with other coverages, the LTC insurance pricing actuary models the overall expense of issuing and administering the policy, and develops a method to allocate expenses to each pricing cell. Generally, expenses are modeled as the sum of expenses expressed as a percent of premium, per policy year exposed, percent of claims paid or incurred, and per application or policy issued.

A difficulty with LTC insurance is the high start-up expenses relative to other blocks of business. With individual LTC insurance, one component of the high initial expenses is heaped commissions. Group LTC insurance typically has lower and more level commissions, but it has higher initial enrollment expenses. The per enrollee cost of the significant fixed expense of enrollment is heavily dependent on the participation rate of the group, which is not known at the time of pricing.

Initial underwriting expenses are also part of the high start-up expenses relative to group health lines. The group LTC insurance actuary has the same difficulty with setting underwriting expense assumptions as he does with setting the appropriate selection factors: determining the mix of underwriting styles, and therefore the cost of underwriting, at each issue age.

Interest

Interest is used in three ways in the asset share model. First, it is used to model the investment income on the assets that support the reserves. Because of the large amount of reserves held on this line of business, this is a very important assumption. This assumption is usually set as the anticipated new money rate over the anticipated sales life of the policy.

Second, interest is used to choose a discount rate for the present value calculations. Usually the investment income earnings rate is chosen.

Third, an interest rate is used in the statutory reserve calculation, which is, by the current regulation, the interest rate use in the valuation of a whole life policy. During times of extreme interest rates, or in a rapidly changing interest environment, the pricing actuary may need to choose an average rate over the anticipated sales life of the policy.

Reserve Basis

As described earlier, premium rate filings must include a statement that reserve requirements have been reviewed with support including "sufficient detail or sample calculation provided so as to have a complete depiction of the reserve amounts to be held, and a statement that the difference between the gross and net valuation premium for renewal years is sufficient to cover expected renewal expenses."

Because a high level of policy reserves is generated at early durations, and the valuation interest rate is typically lower than the investment earnings rate, there are two important considerations. First, the level of margins to include in the reserve basis must be determined, and whether to provide this margin through changes in lapse assumptions, in morbidity (including the level of selection), or in interest rates. Second is the impact, on a present value basis, of the way these margins are included.

Other Assumptions

There are other pricing considerations in LTC insurance that could lead to significantly different rate structures. The average daily benefit chosen by the policyholder can vary greatly by individual and by group, depending on affordability, and the attitude towards purchasing a lower daily benefit amount as a form of coinsurance. This affects the amount of premium needed to cover fixed policy expenses.

Individual LTC insurance often has a significant proportion of insureds paying annually, and the modal load structure needs to be reviewed to avoid inconsistency and antiselection opportunities between the group and individual lines. Marital discounts and tiering by rate class is unusual in group insurance, but common in individual, and could also lead to material differences between the group and individual lines.

PROFIT CRITERIA

The asset share model is used to calculate the premium rates needed to achieve the pricing profit criteria. Typically, long-term care rating is based on lifetime goals of pre-tax profits, post-tax profits, or return on investments (ROI), or a criterion that examines all three measures. Some companies also consider GAAP return on equity (ROE) in conjunction with these statutory measures. Loss ratios are not typically used as criteria in pricing, even before the change in model regulation; however, resulting lifetime loss ratio expectations should be examined carefully to make sure regulatory restraints are met, and also as a measure of the degree of relative risk levels between pricing cells.

SUGGESTIONS FOR FURTHER READING

The reader is encouraged to refer to the following materials on LTC insurance.

NAIC Publications

- The NAIC Long-Term Care Insurance Model Act, October 2009
- The NAIC Long-Term Care Insurance Model Regulation, September 2014
- The NAIC Guidance Manual for Rating Aspects of the Long-Term Care Insurance Model

Actuarial Standards of Practice and Practice Note

- ASOP Number 5, Incurred Health and Disability Claims
- ASOP Number 18, Long Term Care Insurance
- ASOP Number 23, Data Quality
- Practice Note, May 2003, Long-Term Care Insurance Compliance with the NAIC LTCI Model Regulation Relating to Rate Stability

References on Asset Shares

- *Individual Health Insurance*, edited by Francis T. O'Grady, Society of Actuaries, 1988. This text provides a general overview of asset share calculations.
- *Life Insurance Products and Finance*, David B. Atkinson and James W. Dallas, Society of Actuaries, 2000. This text provides discussion on cash-flow projections for Life Insurance.
- *Actuarial Mathematics*, Bowers et al., Society of Actuaries, 1997. This text provides the foundation for setting premium and reserves.

Experience Reports

- *Long-Term Care Intercompany Experience Study – Policy Terminations Aggregate Database 2000-2011 Report*, Society of Actuaries, July 2015
- *2000-2011 Long-Term Care Experience Basic Table Development*, Society of Actuaries, April 2015
- *2000-2011 Long-Term Care Intercompany Experience Study – Aggregated Databases and Report*, Society of Actuaries, January 2015
- *1984 - 2007 Long-Term Care Experience Committee's Intercompany Study & Tables*, Society of Actuaries, 2011
- *2005 – 07 U.S. Long-Term Care Insurance Persistency Report*, LIMRA International and Society of Actuaries, 2011
- *Long Term Care Insurance Experience Reports*, NAIC, published yearly

27 EXPERIENCE RATING AND FUNDING METHODS

William F. Bluhm
Updated by Dorina A. Paritsky

Experience rating is the process whereby a policyholder is given the financial benefit of, or held financially accountable for, its past claim experience in insurance rating calculations. There are two broad categories of experience rating: prospective and retrospective.

Prospective rate calculations are the evaluation of past experience to predict the probable experience for a future rating period, leading to gross premium rates to be charged. The coverage period is often but not always the upcoming policy year. In the absence of experience rating, rates are based on "manual" rates (from a rating manual) or "community" rates (based on average rates over the insurer's portfolio), which are prospective rates based on the demographic or other underwriting characteristics of the group, but not on its specific claim experience. Community rates, often defined by law or regulation, limit the demographic factors being recognized. When manual rates are based on the combined experience of a pool of similar policies, they are often called "pooled" rates.

Retrospective rate calculations are the evaluation and measurement of financial experience for a past period of time, usually a contract year, determined in great part by the cost of providing insurance for that period to the policyholder. This is necessary because of special contractual rating arrangements where a policyholder is held financially responsible (at least in a limited way) for that cost after the fact.

In this chapter, the use of experience rating methods and formulas and their interrelationship with the rating of group policies will be addressed. The use of human judgment in setting a rate for a particular policy, more properly addressed under the subject of underwriting, is beyond the scope of this chapter.

This chapter has four major sections. This first section provides information on the context and background of experience rating; the second section describes prospective experience rating; the third section describes retrospective experience rating; and the last section describes alternative funding methods (usually intertwined with experience rating) in use today. These practices are often combined with one another, but often are not. The theoretical bases are similar—and often identical—for prospective experience rating, retrospective experience rating, and alternative funding methods. However, the reader should keep in mind that these different practices serve different purposes in group insurance, despite their frequent use of similar theory and techniques.

INTRODUCTION

REASONS FOR EXPERIENCE RATING

There are a number of reasons for the use of experience rating. Primarily, it is used because many group policyholders prefer to pay insurance premium based on the unique experience of their own group rather than having their experience pooled with other groups.

Pooling of experience is, in a sense, the opposite of experience rating; a number of groups' experience is averaged together for rating purposes into an experience pool. Some groups in a pool will have higher than average claims, so that if their premium rate were based solely on their own experience, they would have to pay a higher than average premium. By combining their experience with that of other groups, their premium will be closer to the average. This then means that groups with lower than average claims will have to pay premiums higher than that dictated by their own experience, which they may view as an unjustified subsidization of the groups with higher claims.

The insurer, on the other hand, would generally like to quote and charge premiums that are as competitive (low) as possible, while still meeting profit objectives. If a group requests a quote for insurance from the insurer, and if the insurer believes the group truly to have lower than average claim expectations, the insurer would prefer to base its quote on that group's characteristics rather than on an average claim expectation. Obviously, the insurer cannot charge the lower-than-average claim group a lower-than-average premium without offsetting this by charging the higher claim groups a higher premium.

The insurer may not want (for philosophical, political, or social reasons) to credit a group with its good experience where this is not theoretically justified, since this would require the parallel crediting of unjustified bad experience to other groups. However, competitive pressures may cause this to happen, despite the theoretical justification.

The insurer must then set a group size level at which past claim experience is considered statistically credible. Setting this level involves a balance between theoretical and practical considerations.

Theoretical: In developing theoretical models of group claims in the past, a common assumption was stochastic independence of the claims of each individual in the group from one year to the next. This assumption implies that the existence and size of a claim in a given period (such as an upcoming policy year) is independent of the claims that occurred in a prior period. This may be more or less true for some coverages, such as non-occupational accidental death. It is definitely not true with others, such as medical expense coverages. For this reason, many early models used to develop credibility levels understated the relevance of past experience. The correlation of certain coverages' experience over sequential time periods at least partially justifies the competitively-based experience rating formulas commonly in use.

The extent to which a group's experience in a year depends on its own experience in prior years can be measured by the statistical measure called *autocorrelation*. The assumption of temporal independence is equivalent to an assumption of zero autocorrelation. Rigorous development of credibility factors today requires recognition of non-zero auto correlation.[1]

Recent work in this area has included algorithms that not only recognize an individual's past claim experience (in the sense of dollars of past claims), but also take into account the actual conditions and procedures of that individual. Such models are generically called "risk adjusters," and are described in another chapter.

Practical: Consider the competitive pressures that an insurer might feel in setting the credibility levels that it will use in its experience rating formulas. If an insurer erroneously pools the experience of groups that actually have their own statistically valid experience, then groups with higher-than-average claim expectations will be subsidized by groups with lower-than-average claim expectations. If the insurer's competitors are not making the same error, they will be validly quoting lower premiums on the low-claim groups, inducing those groups to migrate away from the insurer's pool. The high-claim groups will be left behind in the pool, where they will no longer have the low-claim groups to subsidize them, causing the average claims in the pool to rise. This antiselection is an important reason why an insurer cannot afford to pool credible groups.

There have been instances where a policyholder will believe its experience to be credible where it is not, and will then move the coverage to a basis where its costs are based on actual claims, such as a self-insured plan. Unfortunately, when the occasional large claim does occur, the policyholder suddenly understands the value of pooling.

APPLICABILITY – COVERAGES AND GROUP SIZES

Experience rating can be applied to any coverage where there is reason to believe that future claim experience will be reliably altered from the otherwise expected level by knowledge of past claim experience. In group insurance, when the size of a group is larger than some chosen level, this is usually applied where the individuals belonging to a group are believed to have characteristics that make that group have reliable claim expectations that might differ from the average represented by manual rates. These characteristics might be demographic characteristics, lifestyle, employee turnover rates, average income, industry, or many others. However, since the question of why a group's experience is credible is usually fairly immaterial, what truly matters is whether it is credible, and how credible it is.

The minimum size chosen for experience rating is an expression of the minimum credibility that an insurer chooses to recognize, whether for theoretical or practical reasons.

Several theoretical considerations enter into the choice of credibility levels for experience rating. First, coverages and benefit designs with low frequency of claim are more volatile, and will require a larger exposure base for a given credibility level than coverages with a high frequency of claim. As well, coverages with widely varying claim sizes will tend to be more volatile.

Second, the insurer is choosing a Confidence Interval (CI), whether explicitly or implicitly, and whether knowingly or unknowingly. A CI can be thought of as the level of credibility

---

[1] Fuhrer, Charles S., "Some Applications of Credibility Theory to Group Insurance." *Transactions*, Society of Actuaries, Volume XL, 1988.

where you can be X% sure that the claim level will fall within Y% of the observed value. When explicitly set, X is often chosen to be 90 or 95. An insurer could choose a single CI, which then implies a curve of credibility values as group size varies. In practice, credibility formulas often don't follow this curve, implying different CIs by size of group.

Third, the portion of experience due to statistical fluctuation was, for many years, treated as varying inversely to the square root of the number of claims or exposed lives. In nontechnical terms, this could be interpreted as saying that it will take four times the exposure to double the credibility.

Fourth, the typical measure of credibility is the number of lives covered. Coverages with stochastically independent claims, however, can increase credibility by using longer experience periods, rather than simply more lives. The measure then becomes the number life-years, rather than lives. Even coverages with non-zero autocorrelation can get some increased credibility by adding longer periods of experience, but the increase in predictive value tends to be quite limited, as the experience gets older.

These theoretical considerations must be examined in the light of practical considerations, including the following:

- Regulatory restrictions on the use of experience rating for certain group sizes;
- Competitive pressures;
- Administrative and managerial units within the company, and their ability to accept the level of experience rating;
- The trade-off between the added cost of applying experience rating and the potential added gains in the volume and quality of new business;
- The effect on any existing business of a change in the credibility level;
- Management philosophy regarding experience rating; and
- The need for internal self-consistency between classes of business.

These factors must be synthesized by the group insurer into a unified approach to experience rating, possibly both prospective and retrospective – an approach which reflects an understanding of both theoretical and practical considerations.

PROSPECTIVE EXPERIENCE RATING

The setting of prospective premium rates for individual groups, based on each group's own experience, can be considered a part of the underwriting process – the process of evaluating and quantifying the risk associated with particular cases. The pricing actuary's most valuable tool for this purpose is the evaluation of past experience of the group. This evaluation of past experience for prospective rating will generally take place regardless of whether retrospective experience rating will apply, and regardless of the funding method.

The estimation of future claim costs based on the nature of specific past claims of individuals is more of an underwriting function than an experience rating one, and is beyond the scope of this chapter. Rather, this chapter is concerned with the analysis of group claims from a statistical and algebraic point of view. Underwriting plays a critical role in the rating process, however, and should be considered along with experience rating concerns in any company or plan sponsor's management decisions.

DEVELOPMENT OF CLAIM EXPERIENCE

The starting point for prospective experience rating is the past claim experience for the group, and, to the extent used in the algorithm, the past claim history or risk scores of individuals in the group. The use of individual-specific conditions is not common in the large group experience rating process, and the use of aggregate group experience is preferred. For the claim experience to be useful and appropriate, there are certain adjustments and calculations that must be made.

Most claim data starts with the dollar amount of claims paid over the experience year. As an example, consider the experience year for a sample group contract to be $1/1/Z$ through $12/31/Z$. The paid data would then be all claims paid in this period.

Since the purpose of the analysis is to evaluate the contractual claim liability during the experience period, it is necessary to derive claim figures that express that liability. Since some of the claims paid in year Z were actually incurred in Z minus 1 or earlier, and since some of the claims incurred in Z have not yet been paid as of $12/31/Z$ (or perhaps not even reported yet), it is necessary to make an adjustment in the paid claim figure to remove claims paid in Z but incurred prior to Z, and to include an estimate for claims incurred in Z but not yet paid. This process of adjustment results in "incurred claims," which represents (at least theoretically) all claim payments, regardless of when paid, which became contractual liabilities during the experience period.

Since premium rates must, as a practical matter, be known in advance of the policy anniversary, it follows that the experience of the immediately preceding policy year will not be available at the time of the rating process. The experience year used will thus usually end a few months in advance of the renewal date or the re-rating date.

The common formula for incurred claims is

Incurred Claims
= Paid Claims + Ending Reserve − Starting Reserve
= Paid Claims + Increase in Reserve (which might be negative).

For prospective rating, it is also fairly common to restate the reserve values to the level that we later believe *should* have been held, rather than what *was* held.

In most insured group cases, there are conversion policies or COBRA coverage offered to insureds leaving the group, who are thus losing their group coverage. Conversion policies tend not to be self-supporting, often because of law or regulation, thus creating an unfunded liability for the insurer arising out of the conversion. Antiselection under COBRA coverage tends not to be as extreme as conversion.

When there is an added liability because of unfunded antiselection, or when there are any other miscellaneous, recurring liabilities arising out of the insurance contract, such liabilities should be included in the incurred claims figure. An alternative approach is to make an explicit charge for these liabilities later in the rating process, outside the incurred claim calculation. The important point is that such charges need it be included somewhere in the rating calculations.

POOLING METHODS

At this point, the insurer will often apply techniques to dampen the random statistical fluctuations, which might cause a particular group's experience not to be representative of its true underlying risk. These techniques are called pooling methods, meaning algebraic methods whereby the group's experience is combined with that of other groups in an averaging process.

Keep in mind that the purpose of this procedure, in the context of *prospective* experience rating, is to develop premium rates to be charged in the future. The guiding principle for the insurer is to choose methods that will make the rates resulting from this exercise as attractive as possible to the policyholder, while still meeting the insurer's related corporate objectives. These procedures are not part of the contractual relationship between the insurer and the policyholder, but rather inform the insurer on the policyholder's expected claim level.

Regardless of the pooling method used, it is important to remember that, over time, the pooling charge included in the experience analysis of all groups must be large enough to equal the average cost of claims modifications made through the pooling process.

Catastrophic Claim Pooling

This method of pooling typically takes the form of forgiveness of exceptionally high claims on individuals within the group. This is accomplished by removing the portion of paid or incurred claims due to individual claims above a certain limit. Such claims are often called "catastrophic," "stop-loss," or "shock" claims. In return for this forgiveness, an average charge is made to all groups participating in this pool, regardless of whether a particular group actually had a catastrophic claim.

Theoretically, an analysis involves two expected claim distributions:

- A claim distribution for individuals, such as the comprehensive major medical claim distribution shown in Figure 27.1.
- A distribution of the total claims expected by a group whose individuals are each subject to the individual claim distribution. This is the random variable on which experience rating is based, and which is modified by the various pooling methods.

Figure 27.2 illustrates the results of a Monte Carlo simulation repeated 1,000 times for a group of 50 lives. If this procedure were continued, the results would gradually tend toward the limiting distribution of aggregate group claims. Figure 27.2 thus represents the probabilities of fluctuation of a group's claims, which can be expected to happen due to purely random fluctuation.

Figure 27.3 is similar to Figure 27.2, but shows a simulation of 1,000 groups of size 50,000. This illustrates how the group claim distribution changes with the size of the group. As the group size increases, the distribution has lower variance and is less skewed.

The effect of individual stop-loss pooling on the Figure 27.2 distribution is shown in Figure 27.4. The specific stop-loss curve demonstrates what would happen if individual claim amounts exceeding a particular catastrophic claim limit were removed from each group's total claims.

Loss Ratio/Rate Increase Limits

Another frequent pooling mechanism puts an upper limit on the loss ratio, which will be used in setting future rates. This is essentially equivalent to two other mechanisms that are used far more often: (a) setting an upper limit on the percentage rate increase that a group will be charged, and (b) setting an upper limit on the aggregate claim dollars a group will be charged (called aggregate stop-loss). The results of this technique on the hypothetical pool of 50 life groups are illustrated in Figure 27.5, where the limit is set at 125% of expected claims.

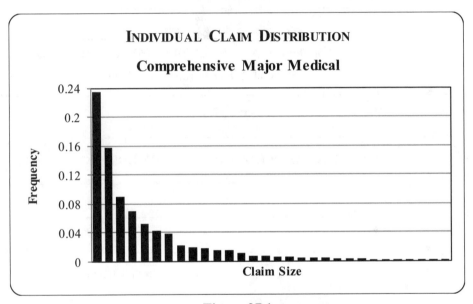

Figure 27.1

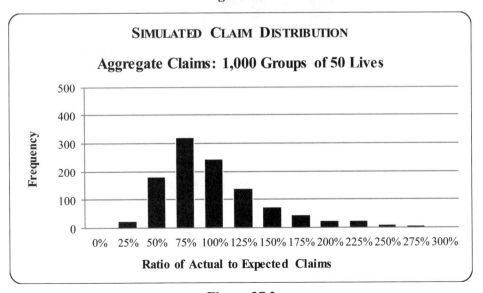

Figure 27.2

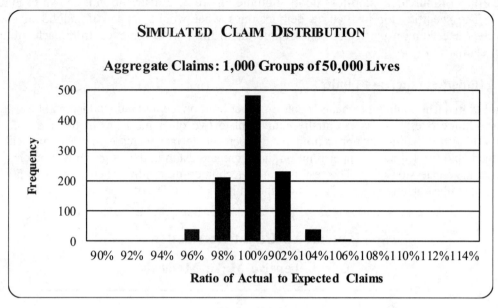

Figure 27.3

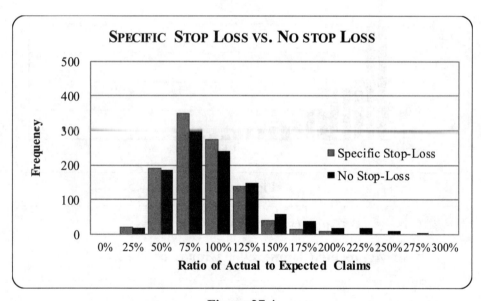

Figure 27.4

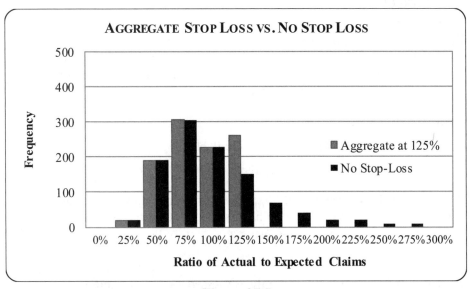

Figure 27.5

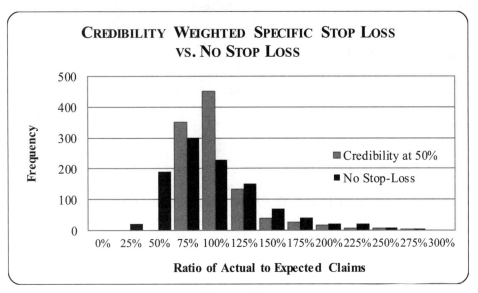

Figure 27.6

As was true in the catastrophic claim pooling case, and as is true for all pooling mechanisms, any lost income resulting from the pooling technique must be recouped through an average charge over all groups in the pool. Conceptually, this pool is not a collection of identical risks, but rather all risks participating in this particular pooling mechanism. It can be made up of a variety of different risks, each partly pooled, perhaps at differing pooling levels.

Credibility Weighting

Credibility weighting starts by attaching a credibility factor to groups in each of various size categories. This factor can be zero (equivalent to no credibility, meaning that the group's own experience is not to be considered at all), one (meaning the group's experience is fully credible, and therefore will not be pooled at all under this method), or some value in between. The standard formula used in this method is

Incurred Claims after Pooling
$$= (C) \text{(Incurred Claims before Pooling)}$$
$$+ (1 - C) \text{(Expected Incurred Claims)},$$

where C is the credibility factor, and "Expected Incurred Claims" is the amount of claims which would have occurred if the group had experienced claims at the average level of the pool. The effect of this pooling method using a credibility factor $C = .50$ is shown in Figure 27.6.

This pooling method is often equivalently expressed as the credibility weighting of loss ratios, rather than of incurred claims. This can be seen by dividing both sides of the above formula by the same earned premium figures. The formula then becomes

Loss Ratio after Pooling
$$= (C) \text{(Loss Ratio before Pooling)}$$
$$+ (1-C) \text{(Pooled Loss Ratio)}.$$

Multi-Year Averaging

One other pooling method, which can be used as a modification to other methods or by itself, is to combine several years of experience to smooth out the statistical fluctuations inherent in the experience of a single year. This will often take the form of a weighted average, such as the following formula that gives the greatest weighting to the most recent year:

Pooled Loss Ratio in Year Z
$$= \{(5 \times (Z\text{'s unpooled ratio})) + (3 \times (Z-1)\text{'s}) + (1 \times (Z-2)\text{'s})\}/9.$$

This method will be less useful when there is high turnover or any other dramatic population changes in the group (for example, expanding coverage to a broader employee population to comply with the Affordable Care Act's employer mandate in 2015). This method will also be less useful for accidental death insurance, or in any other case where older experience is of limited use. The weightings used often lack the rigorous statistical justification to support them.

When applying this method, it is important to adjust the loss ratios by year, to reflect a consistent treatment of the Affordable Care Act (ACA) taxes and fees, which may have a different impact on premiums across different experience periods.

Combination Methods

Most of the pooling methods described above are not mutually exclusive methods. They can be, and often are, used simultaneously. For example, specific stop-loss pooling might be applied to a group's claim experience to derive a needed rate increase. That increase might then be lowered because it exceeded a given limit, constituting aggregate stop-loss pooling.

AFTER POOLING

Since most insurers have group portfolios with renewal dates spread throughout the year, prospective experience rating is an ongoing process. It is very difficult to look at the aggregate experience of the whole pool at one time. Most insurers therefore assume the experience underlying their manual rates represents the aggregate experience of the pool, and rely on updates to the manual rates to keep them in line with the pooled experience.

If the pooled or manual level of claims (or equivalently, the loss ratio level) is correctly set at the average level for the whole pool, the aggregate result of applying a pooling formula to all groups will be that the total of all post-pooling incurred claims, including pooling charges, will be equal to the total pre-pooling incurred claims. With respect to credibility-weighting pooling, if the manual level is incorrectly set to a level not equal to the true average, the result of pooling will be pooled claims or loss ratios which average somewhere between the true average and the manual level. Similar results occur with the other pooling methods when the value of pooled claims is not correctly estimated.

Another important consideration is the calculation of the correct pool averages. Since only the non-credible portion of claims is pooled, it is important that only this portion is the pool that is averaged. The combination of (1) an insurer's experience that is biased to higher or lower claim levels by size of group, and (2) the credibility formula or table with credibility that varies by size of group, implies that the level of average non-credible claims will be different than the credible claims' average as well as the overall average.

The result of the pooling process produces an amount sometimes called "charged claims." As in most actuarial analyses of experience, it is necessary to look at the exposure base that corresponds to the charged claims. This can be the non-credible portion of either earned premium or a measure of the number of people covered. The terminology for the people covered has evolved from "employees" to "members," "contract holders," or "subscribers." These are not different names for the same thing – care should be taken to ensure that the measurement of exposure is consistent with the rate basis. For example, if rates are charged per contract holder, it would be inappropriate to apply those rates based on a per member exposure basis.

When claims and exposure have been derived on a consistent basis, their ratio provides a unit cost, the cost per unit of exposure. This historical unit cost forms the starting point for projected unit costs.

One word of caution is in order. Frequently, a block of business is analyzed in this way and may involve the commingling of claims and exposure for two populations that have different expected unit costs; for example, two medical plans with different deductibles, or disability coverage for two different classes of employees within a single group. Care should be taken to be sure the mix of business in the historical period is representative of the business in the projected rating period, or at a minimum, is adjusted to represent the expected rating period mix. Additional analysis is needed in the blending of populations that have very different underlying characteristics This is an especially important consideration in the current post-ACA environment, because of several new changes, including mandated changes to medical plan design parameters, expanded coverage to newly eligible populations and the impact on population demographics of the exchanges .

The next step in the experience rating process is the translation of historical experience to expected future experience. This involves the trending of the experience to account for changes in claim cost due to time. Some of the factors influencing future expected costs are group-specific, while some are environmental and apply to all groups. Both are important.

The factors that might have an impact on the expected costs in the prospective rating period include the following:

- Changes in government programs affecting the cost of benefits intended to supplement them (for example, the impact of the ACA on the covered population and the plan designs);
- Secular or cyclic trends in rates of disablement or length of disability;
- Mortality trends;
- Utilization or cost trends in medical care, including the effects of new technologies and changes in negotiated provider agreements and the impact of benefit design on those trends;
- Changes in the demographic characteristics of the group be analyzed;
- Changes in benefits in the specific group's plan design itself;
- Antiselection opportunities by insureds, whether on going, due to changes in benefits or premiums, or due to changes in the insured environment, such as increased competition in a multi-option environment;
- Other changes in the demographics of insureds, the economy, or the financial environment; and
- Any other factors which could be expected to have an effect on the expected costs of the group.

Extreme care should be used in the application of trends. One specific area needing special concern is the choice of appropriate endpoints for the trend period. Although the endpoints are typically the midpoints of the experience period and the future rating period, there may be reasons, such as the following, why this choice is not appropriate.

- If a group grew rapidly during the experience period, the average exposure date may be well beyond the midpoint of the experience period.
- If the group is a multiple employer trust where rates change on an employer's anniversary, the average effective date of the rates may extend beyond the midpoint of the rating period.

Many such examples are possible, and the analyst should always examine possible reasons for adjusting the trend period. Another point to keep in mind is that some trends are one-time events, such as benefit design changes or governmental coverage mandates, while others are continuous, such as inflation or changes in practice patterns.

The result of this trending process is the expected claim cost in the rating period for the group per unit of exposure. It represents the expected cost of the claims themselves in the rating period, excluding expenses. One further note is in order. Many times, insurers will perform the described calculations on an aggregate level, without dividing by exposure. This simplifies some of the calculations and makes others more difficult. If done correctly, however, the calculation is equivalent and should result in the same level of aggregate "needed income," a term sometimes used to describe the product of expected claim cost (perhaps increased for retention) and expected exposure. One consideration in choosing which method to use is the relative usefulness of the methods in marketing situations. For example, exhibits given to policyholders are generally better understood if stated in aggregate terms, rather than in unit costs.

CALCULATING GROSS RATES FROM NET RATES

Gross premiums, or the premiums actually charged, must account for expected claims as well as a number of other items. Such items are generally referred to as "loadings" on the net premium. The generic term for such items is the "retention" of the insurer, although the term is not well defined and will be discussed in more detail later in this chapter. Some of the most common retention items follow.

- *Expense Loadings.* Expenses are usually the largest part of retention, and are generally included as a number of separate charges. Each company generally allocates expenses by line of business, and then each line develops unit expenses that would theoretically reproduce overall expenses for the line when applied to all business.

- *ACA fees.* The ACA includes a number of fees that generally must be included in premium rates. These include the Insurer Fee, Transitional Reinsurance Fee, and Patient-Centered Outcomes Research Trust Fund Fee.

- *Deficit Recovery Charge.* If a policyholder has caused incurred losses by the insurer in prior years, and those losses have not yet been recovered, the insurer may build in a deficit recovery charge intended to recoup past losses within a reasonable period of time. Of course, such charges will increase premiums, and thus increase the chance that the rates will become noncompetitive. It is not necessary that the policyholder is subject to retrospective experience rating to have such a charge built into the prospective rates; it is only necessary that the insurer is keeping a policyholder account and wishes to recover deficits.

- *Termination Risk Charge.* Occasionally, a policyholder in a deficit position will terminate its contract, leaving the insurer who has chosen a deficit recovery charge philosophy without means to recover the losses from that policyholder. For this reason, a risk charge is made in advance on all policyholders to finance this business risk. The size of this charge will depend not only on the policyholder's accumulated surplus position, but also on any other policyholder money, such as premium stabilization reserves or contingency reserves, which are held by the insurer and where the insurer is at risk under the contract to pay for unexpected losses. The termination risk charge should reflect any aspect of the group, its coverages, and its funding arrangements, which affect the likelihood and the size of possible deficits under the contract.

- *Pooling Charges.* While pooling charges are generally included in the development of the net premium figure, occasionally they are not. If not, they should appear as a separate retention item.

- *Profit Charge or Contribution to Free Reserves.* This is the profit that the insurer chooses to include in its pricing formula. Generally this charge does not include profit arising from the investment of assets. Nonprofit insurers call this "contributions to free reserves," while mutual insurance companies call it "contributions to surplus." While the size of the charge may vary between types of insurers, the nature of the charge does not. To the extent that all other retention items represent true expected costs, this figure, in combination with any margin built into investment income activities, represents true expected profit. Often, however, insurers build margins into any or all of the other assumptions used in deriving gross premiums, such that there may not be an explicit loading for profit in the retention calculation. This is a particularly helpful technique for nonprofit corporations. It is important that the pricing actuary understand the level and the effect of any such margins, and compare their effect with that of an explicit profit margin.

- *Investment Income.* Some insurers will provide for the crediting of investment income on reserves or other monies held and treat this income as an offset to other retention items. This should be kept in mind when comparing retention levels between insurers. If included at all, investment income is usually separated from other retention items in evaluating retention levels. The investment income credited will usually be net of investment management costs, and may be net of income taxes if such taxes are not included as an expense item. The investment credit may also be negative, actually creating an investment charge, if the policyholder has a negative fund balance. There may also be an investment charge due to the investment income lost on premiums that were paid to the insurer too late. In this case, it is common to use a higher interest rate on charges than the rate used for investment credits.

- *Explicit Margin.* Many times an insurer will include a specific margin in the retention calculation. This is essentially a comfort factor (a higher confidence interval) built into the rates. It will reduce the insurer's risk, since it will reduce the probability of a policyholder experiencing a deficit during the contract year. For this reason, there can be a reflection of this risk reduction in the termination risk charge.

Once all of the retention items have been identified, it is a relatively easy exercise to develop the rate per unit of exposure using standard techniques. At this point, the insurer may wish to limit the size of an implied rate increase to a particular percentage. It should be kept in mind that such limitations carry with them a reduction in expected profit which should be accounted for (to the extent possible) in the retention formula.

Under some coverages and situations, rate guarantees for periods longer than one year may occur. Where such a guarantee exists, the actuary should be sure to take into consideration the changes in the nature of the risk that occur because of the guarantee. These include the following.

- *Mis-estimation Risk.* Since the insurer is locked into rates for a longer period, the potential impact of mis-estimation of any of the costs under the contract (claim, expense, or risk) is relatively greater than it is for the standard one-year guarantee for any given group. This tends to argue for higher margin and/or higher risk charges.

- *Trend Risk.* One specific rating assumption, claims trend, is particularly risky for two reasons: (1) the effect of trend is magnified over time, as is the effect of mis-estimation of trend, and (2) the longer a trend must be estimated into the future, the more risk there is of inaccuracy due to changing conditions. This argues for extreme caution in the use of long-term rate guarantees for trend-sensitive coverages.

FINAL ADJUSTMENTS

There may be reasons why the insurer will wish to make a final adjustment in the rates which have nothing to do with premium adequacy. For example, the policy may be with a politically sensitive policyholder. Whatever the reason, such a decision should not be made without consideration and measurement of its financial impact on the corporation. It is therefore important that the pricing actuary be able to provide such measurements to senior management to provide a balanced response to such marketing or political pressures.

PLAN CHOICE CONSIDERATIONS

In medical or dental insurance, an employer may well provide its employees with the choice of a number of plans; perhaps a health maintenance organization (HMO), alongside a preferred provide arrangement (PPO). This is often called a "multi-option" program and is discussed in depth in the chapter titled "Managing Selection in a Multiple Choice Environment."

When a single insurer is not the source of all of the plan choices being provided, a comprehensive pricing strategy is not possible, and the insurer needs to be aware of the implications of the multi-choice situation.

In the U.S, starting in January, 2014, additional selection influences come from public exchanges as well as the employee cross-insurer selection in the increasingly common Private Exchange environment

It has been frequently observed that insureds choosing a plan with a higher level of managed care (such as an HMO) tend to have lower average costs than those choosing a plan with little or no managed care (typically an indemnity program). The indemnity insurer in such a situation needs to be aware of this and account for the higher average cost of those who are left behind by the HMO enrollees. There is an ongoing debate as to whether this difference in average cost is due only to different demographics, or whether the health status of those choosing an HMO tends to be better than those who remain with the indemnity program. This argues that the pricing actuary needs to consider this "going in" antiselection in the pricing of any plans involved in the multi-option situation.

The effect of antiselection on the experience of an indemnity program, assuming the above antiselection takes place, is that experience in the first year of a multi-option or exchange situation will be worse than would be otherwise expected, creating an artificial one-time increase in claim levels. The extent to which antiselection may continue in renewal years depends upon many factors, most of which involve various incentives to enrollees, and is beyond the scope of this chapter.

SMALL GROUP CONSIDERATIONS

The use of prospective experience rating for small groups presents another unique set of problems. The definition of "small" will depend on the coverage and the state. For medical coverage, this level is typically set under or at or under 50 employees until January 1, 2016, when Federal definition of the "small" group expands to include all employers with 100 or fewer employees. For life and accidental death coverages, the definition of small is usually set at under 500 lives.

Prior to January 1, 2014, in the small group medical market, successful companies have generally found it necessary to recognize a group's experience in some way in its prospective rating. The method used was either formula-based or based on case-by-case re-underwriting of the risk at renewal. Effective January 1, 2014, all "small" groups with fully insured medical coverage became subject to the community rating restrictions of the ACA, substantially eliminating application of experience rating in that market segment.

A typical formula-based method might work as follows. Seven rating categories are created, representing rates at 75%, 80%, 90%, 100%, 110%, 120%, and 125% of average. Each group is assigned to a rate category, based initially on the underwriting department's evaluation of the risk, and thereafter on its own experience. That assignment will be reexamined at each policy anniversary, and will be changed by one or more categories if the recent experience deviates by more than a specified amount from the level expected for the category. The number of years' experience used, the maximum number of rate categories of movement used, and the definition of the specified amount will depend on the coverage, the group's size, the number of years' experience available, and regulatory limitations. This method of rating is sometimes called band rating or tier rating. These rules implicitly apply credibility and pooling methods.

Formula-based methods in use today are generally not based on rigorous theory, but rather are shaped on market forces and the need to retain good risks in light of competitors' practices. Generally, when such formulas are applied, they are used only for groups larger than a certain size, such as six or ten lives.

The re-underwriting method involves examining the causes of an individual case's experience to determine prospective rates. For insurers with any significant volume of business, this is impractical unless used selectively, usually with those cases with the highest ratio of actual-to-expected loss ratios. For example, groups with 2-5 lives and actual-to-expected claims over 150% might be examined on a case-by-case basis, while groups of 25-49 lives might be examined at a ratio of 120% or higher. The cost-effectiveness of these activities is a significant question, however, and should be analyzed before investing any significant resources in implementing them.

As predictive models improve, and the predictive accuracy of rating formula increases, we can expect it is likely there will be less hands-on re-underwriting of groups and greater reliance on formulaic methods.

Some insurers have successfully combined band rating with the re-underwriting method. In such a scheme, the insurer will generally apply formula-based band rate changes up to a specified level. Beyond that level, the groups are re-underwritten, just as in the pure re-underwriting method.

RETROSPECTIVE EXPERIENCE RATING

THE RETROSPECTIVE PROCESS AND ITS CHARACTERISTICS

When insurers insure a group of substantial size, it has become a common practice to reflect the claim levels resulting from that group's own unique risk characteristics in rating for future years (prospective experience rating). It has also become common, at least for very large groups, to give the group the financial benefit of good experience, and hold them financially accountable for bad experience, in the year that such experience emerges from the insurance contract. This practice is called retrospective experience rating.

When experience turns out to be better than expected in the prospective rating assumptions, the excess can either be accumulated in an account held on behalf of that policyholder, or it can be refunded. If it is accumulated in an account, the account is generally called a premium stabilization reserve, a claim fluctuation reserve, or a contingency reserve. If it is refunded, it may be called either a dividend (by mutual insurance companies) or an experience rating refund (by everyone else), depending on the corporate structure of the insurer. In all cases, the calculation involves an evaluation of historical experience under the policy, in ways very similar to prospective rating methods.

TYPICAL EXPERIENCE REFUND FORMULA

If a refund formula applies to the policyholder, the amount of any refund will be the positive balance, if any, resulting from the formula. If a retrospective premium arrangement is in effect, the amount of additional premium due would be all or part of any negative formula balance.

Retrospective refund formulas are composed of some or all of the elements in the following generic formula:

Formula Balance = (Prior Formula Balance carried forward)
- + (Premiums)
- + (Investment earnings on money held)
- − (Claims charged)
- − (Expenses charged)
- − (Risk charge)
- − (Premium stabilization reserve addition)
- − (Profit).

The result of the retrospective rating formula, also called the formula balance, is often referred to as the policyholder account balance, representing the fund balance attributed to the individual policyholder, and which is refunded following its calculation. Each element of the formula balance will be examined individually.

PRIOR FORMULA BALANCE CARRIED FORWARD

If the prior years' formula balance has not been eliminated, the remaining balance is usually carried forward into the next year's formula.

A positive balance can be eliminated by either paying out the balance as a refund or a dividend, or by taking the balance out of the individual policyholder's account into the company's general surplus, or by a combination of the two.

A negative balance can be eliminated by a retrospective premium payment from the policyholder, if applicable, or by the company writing off the balance, thus funding it out of company surplus, or by a combination of both. However, if an insurer is going through the trouble of calculating such a balance, that balance generally is carried forward, hopefully to be offset by emerging future positive surplus.

Thus, the final balance in one year's calculation must be adjusted by such additions and subtractions to the policyholder account before being carried forward into the next year's formula calculation.

PREMIUMS

The premium amount in the formula will generally be just the premium paid by the policyholder for the contract year, possibly adjusted with interest charges or credits for the timing of premium payments.

INVESTMENT EARNINGS ON MONEY HELD

For large and sophisticated policyholders, if any significant balances are held by the insurer, such as claim reserves, then the crediting of investment income earned on those balances needs to be considered. On coverages with significant balances, such as claim reserves for long-term disability coverage, investment earnings can be a significant source of income to the policyholder's account. Generally, the larger and more sophisticated a policyholder is, the more pressure there is to credit investment income, which reflects the cash flow and amounts held for that policyholder.

The calculation of investment earnings involves the application of an investment rate of return to one or more average amounts on deposit. It is customary to credit the earnings on carried forward deposits linearly (or proportionately) over the course of the experience year. On the other hand, since premium deposits are generally under the control of the policyholder and may be subject to "timing the market," earnings credited on current year cash flows may take into account the actual timing of cash flows.

The rate of return will be either pre- or post-income tax, depending on whether the insurer paid income tax on the investment income. Taxation depends on the nature of the fund being held as well as the tax laws of the country having jurisdiction.

CLAIMS CHARGED

The development of this element of the formula involves several steps, as described in the following paragraphs.

Determining Historical Claim Experience

Just as in the case of prospective experience rating, it is necessary to be sure that the claim experience used for retrospective rating purposes is on an incurred basis. While paid basis approximations might be used for prospective rating, this is far more uncommon and dangerous in the retrospective situation. The danger arises from the fact that retrospective calculations are usually considered final accountings for the year, and any refunds paid out may not be recoverable if the paid basis approximation should prove to be erroneous. Since the retrospective calculation does not involve projections of future results, the financial calculation does not require measures of exposure for use as denominators. Also, the policyholder and the insurer are both primarily interested in the actual bottom line – the dollars of gain or loss that occurred. For these reasons, retrospective claim calculations are usually done on an aggregate basis, rather than on a per unit of exposure basis.

Managed care health coverages cause some unique considerations in the retrospective calculation. Quite often, deviations of actual utilization from expected is a risk that is taken by neither the policyholder nor the insurer. Rather, this risk is taken by the provider of services under a capitation agreement, perhaps with experience refunds (or withholds) payable to the provider after the close of his contract year as an incentive to keep utilization down. Frequently, such refunds represent some percentage of the savings due to utilization, with the remainder flowing to the insurer. To the extent that such refunds are made to providers, they obviously cannot be paid to policyholders. In addition, U.S. HMOs that are federally qualified currently cannot experience rate, although there has been some regulatory movement in that direction. For these reasons, HMO experience included in a retrospective premium calculation is rarely adjusted for deviations of actual from expected experience.

Just as in the prospective experience rating situation, incurred claims form the basis for the rating process, and the calculation of claim reserves is necessary to derive incurred claims. However, reserves for retrospective calculations generally include larger margins than for prospective calculations. This is true for the following reasons:

- Competitive pressure is far weaker with retrospective arrangements since the policyholder will eventually benefit if the pricing was too high.
- For continuing policyholders, any conservatism resulting in excess monies being held will likely be released in future retrospective calculations, so there may be less policyholder scrutiny of the reserve level.
- For terminating policyholders, conservatism translates into an added margin of comfort to the insurer that the policyholder's claims can be paid out of the policyholder's money.

Modifications to Claims Experience

Contractual guarantees made to the policyholder must be reflected and are generally treated as adjustments to incurred claims. These adjustments take the following forms:

- Specific stop-loss claims are removed from the experience. That is, the portion of individual claims in excess of the pooling level (whether a dollar amount, as for life and medical coverages, or a duration of claim, as for long-term disability) are subtracted from the incurred claims.

- Incurred claims in excess of the aggregate stop-loss pooling level are removed from incurred claims, following the specific stop-loss adjustment.

- The stop-loss pooling charge, representing the average expected cost of claims in excess of stop-loss limits, is often added back into incurred claims at this point, although it might just as easily be a separate charge in the retrospective rating formula. The theory underlying the stop-loss pooling charges is identical to that described earlier.

- Occasionally, alternative to the three bullets above, a company will replace a *percentage* of actual claims (the pooled portion of claims) with a *percentage* of expected claims (the pooling charge). This is one example of credibility pooling and is similar to the prospective version, except that the calculation is made according to the terms of the contract while in the prospective version, the parameters for credibility and pooling are unilaterally chosen.

- If the insurer provides conversion privileges to insureds leaving the group, the excess claim cost usually experienced in such situations is generally passed along to the policyholder. This is done by another adjustment to incurred claims. Typically in the U.S., conversion privileges exist on life and health coverages. In Canada, they typically exist only for life coverages.

- Charges to incurred claims for life coverage conversions are made on a per conversion basis. The charge is a function of the face amount of coverage converted, and sometimes the policyholder's age. Health conversion charges may be on a per conversion basis or based on an average charge made to all policyholders. Health per conversion charges are rarely based on employee age, although there is a theoretical basis to do so. In the U.S., since passage of COBRA continuation requirements, group medical conversions are far less frequent. Under the ACA and with the availability of coverage through Individual Public Exchanges, many states have eliminated the requirement that employers must offer medical conversion plans, since any member can purchase coverage through the exchange.

- Any other policy provisions or administrative practices which would affect how an employer will be held liable for the financial effects of incurred claims are reflected at this point.

The result of these adjustments is a figure referred to as charged claims or claims charged. This refers to the claims for which the policyholder will be charged in the retrospective calculations. Thus, a generic formula for charged claims is as follows:

$$\begin{aligned}
\text{Claims Charged} = &\ (\text{Claims paid}) \\
&+ (\text{Increase in claim reserves}) \\
&- (\text{Pooled claims}) \\
&+ (\text{Pooling charges}) \\
&+ (\text{Conversion charges}) \\
&+ (\text{Claim margins, if any}).
\end{aligned}$$

EXPENSES CHARGED

Here, again, the level of sophistication used in charging the expenses due to an individual policyholder depends upon the size and sophistication of the policyholder, as well as the abilities of the insurer.

Expenses for an insurance company are generally allocated to lines of business based upon corporate-wide expense studies. Each line of business then chooses unit expenses that are intended to closely reflect the costs attributable to those lines of business. These unit expenses may vary by coverage, size of policyholder, or other factors. They are usually expressed as some combination of percentage of premium, percentage of paid or incurred claims, per claim processed, per policy, or per certificate. Expenses related to investment income have generally already been deducted from the investment rate of return, and need not be included.

Expense charges may be broken out into various levels of detail, showing, for example, commissions and agency expenses, premium taxes or other assessments, conversion charges (if not already included in claims charged), corporate overhead, services to certificate holders, claim administration, risk charges, pooling charges (if not already included in claims charged), or others. There is normally a catchall grouping which is intended to summarize a number of expenses that are not large enough individually to justify a separate line of the experience report.

As in prospective experience rating, it is important to appropriately reflect the ACA-related taxes and fees in fully insured rating, including the insurer fee, and fees for reinsurance and Patient-Centered Outcomes Research Trust Fund.

Expenses attributed to an unbundled and thus optional insurer service such as a wellness program are typically separate so that they can be attributed only to those policyholders choosing the service.

Expenses in the first year or first few years may be higher than in renewal years due to initial acquisition costs. Acquisition costs are typically charged to policyholders using factors that vary by policy year. They can also be averaged by the use of factors that don't vary by duration, although this increases the termination risk to the insurer.

Certain types of groups will require special handling and the actuary should always be alert for such situations. Jumbo groups, for example, will often have dedicated administrative units where expenses can be charged directly and independently of the insurer's expenses due to supporting other business. As another example, multiple-employer "Taft-Hartley" trusts may require separate billing of individual employers, causing billing expenses to resemble a small group block of business instead of a single large group.

RISK CHARGE

This is a generic term that may be used to cover charges for a multitude of risks. Usually, however, it refers to the charge made by the insurer to cover the risk that the policyholder will leave the insurer in a loss position.

If the insurer's philosophy is to keep track of losses and attempt to recover them, the risk charge covers the risk that the insurer will cancel or non-renew the contract before the insurer has had a chance to recover any existing account deficits. In practice, the ability to recover past losses is quite limited, since policyholders regularly shop their coverage between insurers, and any risk charge must compete against other, eager insurers who have no deficit to recover.

If the insurer's philosophy is to let the whole portfolio stand on its own each year, the risk charge becomes a combination of (1) a margin used to achieve a more favorable confidence interval around the pricing target, and (2) a contribution to profit for doing business. It also becomes a way to make charges more equitable between policyholders and between lines of business.

While this charge may be based upon the judgment of the insurer, a theoretical development is necessary to know the appropriate rate. Risk charge development will take into consideration the expected statistical variance of a group based on the policyholder's size as well as perhaps the size of any existing deficits. It will generally also account for any monies on deposit with the insurer that can be used to offset losses, such as a contingency reserve, premium stabilization reserve, or claim fluctuation reserve, which serve to lower the probability of a deficit. Known margins in the rates have a similar effect.

PREMIUM STABILIZATION RESERVE ADDITION

Some insurers will try to reduce their risk of being in a deficit position by accumulating a portion of policyholder surplus in a reserve that can be used to offset experience fluctuations. The larger such a reserve becomes, the larger a policyholder's deficit could become before exhausting it; thus, the insurer's risk is reduced when this reserve is high. This relationship between the size of the reserve and the insurer's risk is generally reflected in the size of the risk charge. This relationship is generally well quantified for life and long-term disability insurance coverage, but less so for health coverages. This is due to the existence and relative importance of other risks in health lines, which are difficult to separate from the statistical risk.

Some insurers require that the policyholder surplus accumulate in such a reserve up to a particular limit before the surplus can be paid out as experience refunds to a policyholder. In some cases, there may be two such reserves for the policyholder – a mandatory one required by the insurer, and an optional one created at the request of the policyholder to reduce risk charges and premium fluctuations. If the group policy terminates, the reserve may or may not be payable to the policyholder.

When a policyholder's rate stabilization reserve is exhausted by adverse experience, substantial rate increases can result. This results from the need to rebuild the reserve while simultaneously adjusting rates to an adequate level.

PROFIT

Most insurers are reluctant to show an explicit profit charge on experience exhibits which are shown to policyholders. Rather, profit margins are often built into other assumptions, such as expenses, risk charges, or even claims charged.

Stock insurance companies are openly profit-making organizations. Mutual companies, theoretically owned by their policyholders, do not pay out earnings to stockholders, but nevertheless generally require a contribution to surplus by policyholders. Nonprofit corporations (mainly some Blue Cross / Blue Shield plans) are limited in the surplus they can accumulate, but will generally make charges to certain lines of business (such as the group line) to fulfill political, moral, or social obligations to subsidize other lines.

For coverages subject to increasing claim costs over time due to trend, contributions to surplus are required just to maintain their surplus and capital position. For example, if an insurer wants to maintain a surplus or free reserve level at 25% of premium, and if the increase in premium due to trend is 10% per year, then there must be a profit or contribution to surplus of $10\% \times 25\% = 2.5\%$ of premium just to maintain that 25% surplus position.

Regardless, then, of company's corporate structure, the group actuary needs to address the question of contributions to surplus.

APPLICABILITY

Retrospective experience rating formulas will not apply to all group policyholders. Their application will depend upon the following considerations:

- *Group Size.* A certain level of resources is needed to compile, analyze, and communicate the experience specific to a particular policyholder. This argues that there is a critical mass below which it is not cost effective for the insurer to apply such a formula. Further, a minimum size is needed to obtain some degree of statistical credibility in the first place. Otherwise, there is a risk of large swings in experience from year to year. While prospective experience rating is often used as a tool for management of a block of business, retrospective experience rating requires an insurer to take a risk based on the accuracy of its credibility formula. For these reasons, the minimum group size for retrospective formulas availability is generally much larger than the minimum size for prospective. For groups of 50 and fewer employees (or 100 and fewer after January 1, 2016) with medical coverage, both prospective and retrospective experience rating is limited to self-funded customers only.

- *Contract Provisions Regarding the Funding Arrangement.* As will be seen in the final section of this chapter, the choice of funding methods will have an impact on whether a retrospective formula will apply. A retrospective premium arrangement, for example, substantially changes the risks under an insurance contract and such an arrangement will replace the normal experience rating formula.

- *Company Policies and Practices.* Regardless of the theoretical reasoning, an insurer's policies and practices will be an overriding factor. Some insurers, such as some nonprofit corporations, will only provide for refunds in special circumstances. Others, such as mutuals, must generally have a contract clause providing for participation by almost every policyholder.

- *Company Financial Situation.* Unless a specified refund formula is guaranteed by the terms of the contract, the insurer's overall financial health is an overriding factor in any refund situation. This is a relatively small concern for insurers with substantial surplus, but for those with little surplus this can be a significant concern. Blue Cross plans in the U.S., for example, with their limitation on unallocated surplus (called free reserves), and further with their vulnerability to sudden inflationary increases in claim costs, generally keep such concerns foremost in their minds when determining refund policies.

Small groups, to whom the retrospective formula does not apply, must then live or die with their prospective rates, since they must be charged premiums in advance with no recourse by the insurer should they prove inadequate. The largest groups will generally have both prospective and retrospective formulas applied.

SPECIAL FUNDING ARRANGEMENTS

The term special funding arrangement (or alternative funding arrangement) is used to describe a special financial agreement outside the classical insurance arrangements described earlier. This can refer either to how and at what time cash will flow, or to the transfer of financial risk between the insurer and the policyholder.

RESERVELESS PLANS

Since roughly the 1960s, policyholders have been aware that claim reserves being held by insurers on an ongoing basis might be put to a better use by the policyholder until needed to actually fund claim payments at contract termination. In response to policyholder concerns, insurers began to find ways in which such monies could be returned to policyholders without creating undue risk to the insurer.

In a typical reserveless agreement, the insurer will forego premium payments up to a specified level – intended to equal part or all of the claim reserves – in return for a contractual promise by the policyholder that they will pay the needed amount as premium if and when the contract terminates. This final premium is called a "terminal" premium. This creates an added risk to the insurer that the policyholder will be unable to pay the premium when it comes due. For this reason, prudence suggests that the insurer financially underwrite the policyholder on an ongoing basis to ensure the ability to pay the terminal premium.

The reserveless agreement is sometimes structured to "lag" premium payments, meaning that each month's premium is effectively given a 90-day or 120-day grace period. At termination of the policy, all unpaid premiums would become immediately due. This financial structure of the reserveless plan is the source of many of its pseudonyms, such as "deferred premium" or "premium drag" plans.

If the policyholder does set up its own reserve on its own books for the terminal premium, the investment options available for those funds can be enhanced. Such investments will no longer be limited by insurance company investment limits, but rather by the rules governing welfare benefit plans. This is often perceived as a significant advantage by large employers, although actual investment results may not live up to expectations, as evidenced by a number of dramatic stock market drops over the years.

The insurer has a legal liability to pay insured claims, including those incurred but not yet paid at policy termination. Since the insurer must set up the financial liability regardless of the policyholder's promise to pay, there must be an offsetting financial asset to avoid funding this out of surplus. This is typically accomplished by structuring the contract to make the terminal premium due and unpaid on statement dates. As long as the premium is due within 90 days of the statement date, the U.S. National Association of Insurance Commissioners' (NAIC) statement blank allows it to be called an admitted asset. If it were not an admitted asset, the company would be forced to set aside assets that would otherwise be surplus, thus reducing the company's risk-based capital level. A similar 90-day rule exists in Canada.

Less sophisticated policyholders sometimes fail to understand that switching to a reserveless plan provides only a one-time premium reduction, and that renewal premiums in the second year of such a plan will most likely be substantially higher than those in the first year.

FULLY INSURED PLANS

In a fully insured plan, all cash paid out by the policyholder is paid to the insurer and treated as premium. Claims paid by the insurer are paid out of the insurer's accounts, with the insurer's money. Such a plan might be reserveless, or it might not.

Following are some of the considerations in using this type of arrangement:

- The insurer bears the immediate risk of adverse experience, as well as the potential profit of favorable experience.
- Insureds have the security of the insurer being claim guarantor.
- Premium tax will be payable on all money flowing to the insurer, thus increasing the cost of benefits.
- In the U.S., the contract will be subject to the insurance laws, rules, and regulations of the state of delivery of the contract. This will include all mandated coverages in that state. The Employee Retirement Income Security Act of 1974 (ERISA) rules generally apply to employers and their plans, while insurance laws apply to the insurers and the insurance contract, rather than to employers. Insurers will normally modify their contracts where necessary to meet employer needs but are not obligated to.
- In the U.S., there are rules in each state that govern whether a contract qualifies as a fully insured arrangement, and thus would be subject to benefit mandates, premium tax, and ACA taxes and fees (medical coverage). These rules are objective and are based upon how much risk is taken on by the insurer versus the policyholder, at least in terms of expected values. Because the ACA's fees have encouraged more small employers to move towards self-insured contracts, the NAIC is reviewing their recommendations to states for these insurance rules (as of 2012). Even in advance of the NAIC recommendation, many states have already adopted rules that are stricter than before, thus deterring smaller employers from moving from their fully insured contracts.

This is the traditional, classical funding arrangement of insurance coverage, and is therefore not strictly an alternate arrangement. It is the arrangement to which all the other methods are "alternates."

SELF-INSURED PLANS

Sometimes an employer will choose to create a self-insured plan and take on the role of primary risk-taker. The level of claim payments and all plan-related expenses become the responsibility of the employer, and benefit payments are not guaranteed by an insurance company.

The normal funding vehicle for such a plan is a trust, created for just this purpose. Employer and employee contributions are deposited to this fund, and benefits are paid out of it. The rules governing such plans generally arise out of ERISA (in the U.S., at least through 2013), employment regulations (Canada), or the applicable trust law.

With the advent of the ACA in the U.S., the federal government has defined minimum coverage standards as a part of the employer mandate. The employer mandate, effective with coverage periods beginning in January 1, 2015, states that applicable large employers with 50 or more full-time employees, including full-time equivalents (FTEs), may be subject to a penalty if they do not offer medical coverage to their full-time employees and eligible dependents. The coverage must provide minimum essential coverage, be affordable, and meet minimum value (MV) requirements. The mandate applies to both fully insured and self-insured customers, and applies whether the plan is grandfathered or non-grandfathered. It must also meet MV requirements, which means the plan must pay at least 60% or more of the plan's total allowed benefit costs anticipated for a standard population.

Although some very large employers may administer benefits themselves, most self-insured plans will contract with an insurance company or independent administrator to administer the plan. Services may include enrollment, eligibility, claim, and other administrative services, as well as sometimes consultation on plan design, actuarial and financial services, or others. Such a contract is often called an Administrative Services Only (ASO) agreement. Since the insurer bears no insurance risk, there will not be any risk charges in the charges for the ASO agreement. In a self-insured plan, any investment income earned by the fund on trust assets is earned directly, rather than on an insurer's portfolio of investments. Latitude in the choice of investments is increased significantly over the fully-insured case.

Since the employer will generally wish to provide conversion rights to plan members (at least for health and life benefits), the ASO agreement is often modified to provide for individually issued conversion contracts through the insurer, usually in exchange for a charge to the employer representing some or all of the excess mortality and morbidity expected under a conversion contract. This is quite common in medical coverages, and less so in life and LTD coverage (which are less commonly self-insured).

The employer may wish to insure against unusual claim fluctuations, and contract with an insurer (not necessarily the administrator) to do so. Just as in the experience rating situation, such insurance is referred to as stop-loss coverage, and it may cover excess claims on individuals (specific stop-loss), in the aggregate (aggregate stop-loss), or both. The premiums paid for such coverage are the self-insured equivalent to stop-loss pooling in an insured situation.

Employers must sort through several additional considerations in deciding whether to choose a self-insured plan. First, some taxes are avoided with self-insured plans, including state premium tax – since it is not channeled through an insurer and hence does not become premium – and the insurer fee component of the ACA. In addition, self-insured employers have more flexibility in determining their liability for the ACA reinsurance fee compared to fully insured employers.

Next, state or provincial mandates on insurance contracts will not apply, since there is no contract of insurance, only a contract for administrative services. Federal mandates, however, do apply.

Next, the employer's plan becomes the sole bearer of the insurance risk, unless there is stop-loss coverage or, in medical plans, capitation or similar agreements with providers. This argues that the plan sponsor should carefully evaluate its ability to absorb claim fluctuations in planning its funding mechanisms.

Finally, different coverages require varying degrees of expertise in specialized areas to successfully manage them. For this reason, the plan sponsor may wish to evaluate the advisability of self-funding, the details of the funding mechanism, and the choice of administrator or advisor separately by coverage. The cost-effectiveness of this will obviously depend on the size of the plan and is an important (but often overlooked) consideration.

MINIMUM PREMIUM CONTRACTS

A hybrid of insured and self-insured plans was developed in the 1960s, called a minimum premium plan (sometimes also called a split-funded plan). In this arrangement, a minimum premium rider is usually attached to a fully-insured contract, which modifies the funding mechanism to have most or all of the expected claims portion of the premium be used to fund claims directly without becoming premiums. This is accomplished by having the policyholder deposit funds directly to an account, from which the insurer (as administrator) can draw on as needed to pay claims. Sometimes the arrangement will be for funds to be transferred by wire to the account on a weekly basis upon notification by the insurer of the amount required. Claims are paid from this account by the insurer up to the amount in the fund. The insurer will generally pay the claims on drafts that draw on the fund directly and thus do not become premium. The premium amount then becomes the fully-insured premium minus the contributions paid into the fund and minus the premium tax on the self-insured portion. Not-for-profit insurers, who are generally exempt from premium tax, have not had to be as careful to keep the pre-attachment point dollars from flowing through accounts owned by them. In fact, there may be an advantage to have the dollars flow through the insurer's account if that allows the employer to enjoy the benefit of deeper negotiated provider discounts.

If claims exceed the expected amount, the insurer is liable for the excess amount, subject to any retrospective premium arrangements that might exist. The arrangement is thus very similar to stop-loss coverage, described later.

The original major advantage to this arrangement is that, in most jurisdictions, state premium tax is avoided on the contributions made to the fund. California is a notable exception to this rule. With the advent of stop-loss contracts, minimum premium plans have declined in popularity.

STOP-LOSS CONTRACTS

Stop-loss contracts, used with self-insured plans, provide for the insurance of claims in excess of particular levels, usually substantially in excess of the expected claim level. The chosen level beyond which claims are insured is generally called the attachment point.

Specific stop-loss insures the claims of individuals covered under the contract. Attachment points are usually stated as a round number, such as $50,000 or $100,000. The attachment point will generally be larger for larger plans, since a large plan will be able to absorb a given single large claim more easily than a small plan, everything else being equal. The equivalent of a specific stop-loss agreement is occasionally used for long-term disability plans, where the employer will self-insure disabilities for some period such as twelve months. Insured long-term disability coverage would then wrap around the self-insured coverage, and have an elimination period of twelve months.

Aggregate stop-loss attachment points are usually expressed in terms of a multiple of expected claims, such as 110% of expected claims. The net cost of this benefit is based upon the expected value and variance of the group's aggregate claims. Since the group is composed of (relatively) independent claims of individuals, large groups will have a smaller probability of aggregate claims exceeding a given attachment point. Another way of saying this is that larger groups will have more predictable and stable claims than smaller groups, so the theoretical cost of stop-loss insurance will be relatively less.

When specific stop-loss insurance is combined with aggregate stop-loss insurance, the specific coverage will apply first. When specific is applied first, this lowers the aggregate claims, and thus the cost of the aggregate insurance.

Stop-loss insurance can be purchased on either an incurred or paid basis. On an incurred basis, claims that are incurred during the contract period will be covered, regardless of when they are paid out. On a paid basis, the insurer will apply the attachment point to claims paid during the contract period. Suppose, for example, an insured is hospitalized for a long period, and reaches the attachment point prior to the end of the contract period. If the hospitalization continues into a new contract period, the employer's plan must once again begin paying, and must reach the attachment point again before the stop-loss insurance will pick up the claim.

A variant on the paid basis is the incurred-and-paid basis, where only claims that are both incurred and paid during the contract period will be covered, thus excluding payments on prior incurrals. One danger of stop loss on a paid basis is that should the self-insured policyholder go bankrupt, claims that are incurred during the contract term would be covered by the insurer if submitted before the end of the term, but identical claims would go unpaid if submitted after the end of the term. This would leave the patient at risk for the payment, and often the provider as well, since often the patient cannot afford to pay these type of high cost claims.

Some insurers and some jurisdictions consider stop-loss to insure the employer's liability to the plan, rather than the health benefits themselves. Under this logic, stop-loss insurance is a liability coverage rather than a health coverage and must follow the laws, rules, and regulations governing liability insurance. The safest way for an insurer to proceed is to determine the position of the jurisdictions in which it intends to do business.

An important element in the rating of stop-loss coverage (as well as stop-loss pooling, which is theoretically similar) involves the risk of bad estimation of expected claims. Suppose an aggregate attachment point is set at 105% of expected claims for a large group and the probability of the group's claims exceeding that limit is 10%. If the insurer has underestimated the expected claim level by that same 5%, the true expected claims are 105% of the presumed expected claims, and the true probability that claims will exceed the expected level is now 50%! This is a highly leveraged impact for such a small mis-estimation. Thus, in stop-loss rating, accurate projections and appropriate margins are far more important than in the normal insured situation.

The risk of mis-estimation of claims can be magnified if care is not taken to accurately estimate claim reserves in the experience period, even if the contract is on a paid basis.

Another unique danger to stop-loss coverage is the effect of leveraging on trends. The concept is similar to leveraging of trends by deductible, but the leveraging is amplified and is more critical in stop-loss situations. There is a useful, practical way of understanding the phenomenon of trend leveraging. The frequency histogram of the individual claim distributions as shown earlier in Figure 27.1 can be thought of as being elastic. Claim cost trends stretch that curve horizontally to the right, with the left endpoint of the curve being fixed at zero. If all the fixed values connected with the coverage, such as attachment points, stretch with the curve, then the claim cost under the curve will increase proportionately to the trend. Thus, a 10% higher attachment point on claims that have trended by 10% will result in a claim cost above the attachment point that is also 10% higher.

However, if the attachment point remains a fixed amount, as is usually the case in specific stop-loss, then the curve of claim costs will stretch while the attachment point does not, causing a higher proportion of the curve to exceed the attachment point. This causes the effective claim cost trend to be higher than the underlying cost trend. Aggregate stop-loss attachment points are usually expressed as a percentage of expected claims and therefore will stretch with the curve, eliminating the leveraging effect.

This leveraging effect argues for the importance of accurate and conservative trend assumptions for stop-loss coverage, even if the trend used in the associated total claim projection is not as conservative. A similar leveraging effect occurs if the initial estimated claims are inaccurate.

Specific changes in medical care and other environmental factors should also be kept in mind when pricing stop-loss coverage.

RETROSPECTIVE PREMIUM ARRANGEMENTS

In the retrospective premium arrangement, or "retro," the policyholder takes over some or all of the aggregate claim risk in exchange for reduced risk charges and often lower up-front premium payments.

For example, a policyholder and an insurer might agree that the policyholder would pay 90% of the otherwise applicable premium in the normal way. After the close of the experience year, if experience is worse than that anticipated in the rating, there would be an additional premium due (which might be payable in cash or out of the policyholder's premium stabilization reserve) up to an agreed-upon limiting amount. This limiting amount is conceptually similar to aggregate stop-loss, the major difference being the timing of premium payments and the risk of non-payment.

If experience is better than expected, there might be a refund payable to the policyholder or its rate stabilization reserve (under a modification of the experience rating formula), or the policyholder might just keep the initial 10% reduction.

The actuary should be careful in evaluating risk charges and premiums for a retro agreement, being sure that the premium charged for the retro itself is adequate to cover expected claims, taking leveraging into account. If refunds are made of claim amounts less than that used in the rating, this money will not be available to cover higher claim amounts on other groups.

The retro agreement usually takes the form of a rider attached to a standard group policy. It is used by some insurers as a back-door means of creating a reserveless plan, described earlier.

When a retro is in effect, it may be more difficult than otherwise for an insurer to accumulate a contingency reserve or premium stabilization reserve. This should be considered in setting retention levels for the retro rider.

FINAL CONSIDERATIONS

From all points of view, the choice of a funding mechanism depends on many things, including the following:

- The effect on retention items, including expenses (premium tax, claim administration, and others), risk charges, and profit charges;
- The insurer's ability to unbundle aspects of the financial and insuring agreement, and the policyholder's potential to shop around for services and coverages;
- The nature and size of the insurance risks assumed by each party; and
- Possible policyholder or insurer bias about particular funding methods.

As this chapter illustrates, the use of any alternate funding method suggests careful consideration of the risks involved and each party's ability to absorb them.

CONCLUSION

The interrelationship between prospective experience rating, retrospective experience rating, and various funding methods, becomes clearer the more they are studied. A comprehensive approach to ratemaking requires these relationships be recognized. It is critical that all three at least be considered when revising any one of them. Without this comprehensive view, unintended incentives will be created within the insurer's product line that will dilute the effectiveness of the insurer's marketing strategy. With it, the company can pursue its financial strategy in the most efficient way possible.

Understanding of the financial impact of these rating and funding matters is important to both parties of the insurance contract. There are often misunderstandings that could be easily avoided if appropriate education and explanation take place. For this reason, simplicity and ease of explanation become important aspects of successful financial arrangements.

28 GROUP INSURANCE RATE FILINGS AND CERTIFICATIONS

James T. O'Connor
Kristi M. Bohn
Margaret A. Chance

INTRODUCTION

In the early 1990s, the National Association of Insurance Commissioners (NAIC) and most states introduced regulatory reforms related to the underwriting, marketing, and rating of small employer group insurance. The extent of these early reforms varied somewhat by state, but most laws shared common elements. In 1996, the federal government enacted the Health Insurance Portability and Accountability Act (HIPAA), which set uniform requirements for small employer medical insurance carriers related to the underwriting and marketing of such insurance. In 2010, the federal government enacted the Affordable Care Act (ACA), which significantly restructured the rating and underwriting of small group products, most significantly beginning in 2014. The ACA requires that states and the federal government actively review the justification for rate increases being implemented by insurers in the small group market. While large employer group products were affected by the ACA in terms of loss ratios, eligibility, and plan design, very little was changed in terms of rating rules and underwriting allowances.

This chapter discusses these important laws and related regulations, as well as the required rate certifications. While the chapter focus is on small employer group plans due to the complexity of the requirements, the chapter provides an overview of other group insurance rate filings at the end.

NAIC MODEL LAWS AND REGULATION

In December, 1991, the NAIC adopted the "Small Employer Health Insurance Availability Model Act," which was adopted by many states. In March, 1993, the NAIC adopted the "Model Regulation to Implement the Small Employer Health Insurance Availability Model Act." Many states have included parts of the model regulation into their law. Later, the NAIC adopted the "Small Employer and Individual Health Insurance Availability Model Act," which governed rating and underwriting, but few states revised their small group laws to this last model.

Because the most common provisions of the states' small group rating laws are based on the 1991 NAIC model, this is the model law that this chapter will concentrate on in terms of grandfathered plan small group filing and certification considerations (the meaning of grandfathered plan is described further below). For non-grandfathered small group plans, the ACA now governs rate filings and certifications, though certain longstanding statutes, such as the 1991-type small group rating certification laws, continue to apply alongside the newer ACA requirements.

CONTINUED APPLICABILITY OF NAIC MODEL LAWS TO SMALL GROUP PLANS

This chapter begins with an overview of rate filing considerations under the 1991-type NAIC Model rating laws described above. While the applicable rating rules for non-grandfathered plans (often referred to as ACA-compliant plans) assure compliance with these older laws, compliance with these older laws must be considered while grandfathered plans remain in a carrier's small group portfolio.

To obtain and maintain grandfathered status, the plan must have existed on March 23, 2010, the insurer must have notified policyholders and enrollees that the plan is considered grandfathered, the insurer must have taken appropriate legal action to assert grandfathered status for the plan, and the insurer cannot make material changes to the plan.[1] Grandfathered plans are closed, in that the only new entrants allowed to each grandfathered plan are new family members of continuously enrolled employees of the employers who continuously offered the plan.[2]

Generally driven by carrier decisions in 2010 to not grandfather small employer group plans, some states do not have grandfathered small group plans. Businesses in those states will automatically meet the rating requirements of these NAIC Model type laws. In most states, these plans provide benefits to employers with 2-50 eligible employees, coinciding with the HIPAA definition of a small group to which all states and insurers needed to adhere in order to comply with the marketing and underwriting requirements. However, several state laws continued to define a small employer for rating purposes as having 2-25 eligible employees, or a range somewhat different than that of the HIPAA definition. A few states also extended the rating restriction down to a group of one employee (that is, sole proprietorships and self-employed).

It is also notable that CMS introduced a transitional policy for non-grandfathered coverage in the small group and individual health insurance markets that, with state approval, allows carriers to continue pre-ACA coverage for their inforce groups up until their annual renewal date on or after October 1, 2016. Under this rule, a group may possibly have their pre-ACA coverage up through September 30, 2017. Most states have opted for the maximum transition period allowed, although a number have either approved shorter periods or none at all. In regard to the small group rating and certifications discussed in this chapter, these "transition program groups" are treated the same as grandfathered groups. As such, when we refer to grandfathered groups throughout the chapter, the reference includes these transition program groups.

CLASSES OF BUSINESS

The NAIC Model type small group rating laws allow carriers to classify their small employer group business in up to nine classes. However, these classes can only reflect

---

[1] https://www.healthcare.gov/health-care-law-protections/grandfathered-plans/
[2] Technically, a grandfathered employer can switch its existing plan to a different insurance carrier, provided the new insurer's plan is essentially the same as the current plan of the employer. However, in practice, this is difficult to do since insurers have not kept their grandfathered plans open for new sales.

substantial differences in expected claim experience or administrative costs, and only if certain criteria are met. These criteria include business being sold through different distribution systems, acquiring a block of small group business from another carrier, or providing coverage to members of legitimate associations. States vary considerably in their adoption of class limits. Under the NAIC Model, the use of business classes can legitimately allow up to an additional 20% rating differential between blocks of small employer business. Starting in 2014, under the ACA, all non-grandfathered small group business is treated as one class or pool for rating purposes. Grandfathered business could use one or more additional classes. It is important to note that small group rate certification requirements apply to a carrier's entire portfolio of small group business, both grandfathered and non-grandfathered, and therefore the "between classes" limitation of 20%[3] should be considered when setting grandfathered and non-grandfathered rates.

ALLOWABLE CASE CHARACTERISTICS

Certain case characteristics are allowable rating factors under NAIC Model type laws and thus not subject to premium range limit tests. Case characteristics are demographic or other objective characteristics that are considered by the carrier in the determination of premium rates. As with the ACA, claim experience, health status, and duration of coverage are not allowable case characteristics. Generally, allowable case characteristics are age, gender (some states disallow), geographic area, family composition, and group size (some states disallow). Some states allow industry factors, generally with a maximum factor spread of 15%. Group size often has a maximum allowable factor spread of 20%, or in some states is limited to only allow for recognition of differences in administrative expenses. Some states allow tobacco use status as an allowable case characteristic, as does the ACA. There exists a lot of variation between states in their limits as to what may be used as an allowable case characteristic. The more case characteristics that can be justified for use as "allowable" will provide the carrier with more rating flexibility and a greater total spread of rates between groups. Due to rating system limits, compliance concerns, and market habits, most carriers have not employed all of the possible characteristics in their rating structures. Most state insurance departments require that the rating factors used for case and coverage characteristics be reasonable and based on actuarial analysis. Variance in both benefit parameters and coverage of the plan are allowable differences, that do not need to be included as part of the rate range variation that is limited by the law.

Non-grandfathered plans are subject to much more stringent rating requirements and are allowed fewer case characteristic variations under ACA regulations. Beginning in 2014, the ACA required non-grandfathered plans to use modified community rating, and limits rating characteristics to plan design, provider network, age (with a uniform set of factors required for use by all carriers), family composition,[4] geographic area (with area boundaries determined by each state rather than by the carrier), and tobacco use. Rates cannot vary based on any other characteristics.

---

[3] Varies by state.
[4] Some variation for family composition is technically allowed under the ACA. However, regulations restrict such variation to the summation of each family member's individual rates, except in states with pure community rating (such as New York).

THE INDEX RATE

For purposes of small group rate testing, an "index rate" is determined for each class of business for each period, which is the arithmetic average of the lowest and highest premium rate that *could* be charged within a given class of business. (Note, however, that this index rate is different than that referred to in ACA pricing, which is discussed later in this chapter). The index rate is calculated only after all the rates have been adjusted to account for all the allowable case characteristics and benefit design variations. Use of a unified rating manual for all plans sold within a class generally makes it easy to determine the index rate, provided that the carrier does not make exceptions to the manual. The highest possible rate can be 67% higher than the lowest possible rate (the 67% factor comes from a comparison of the highest to lowest rates allowed under the ± 25% rule). This is referred to as the first "within-class" rate test. Non-grandfathered business will always meet this test due to the ACA modified community rating requirements.

RATE INCREASE LIMITATIONS

The second within-class rate test of the NAIC Model Act limits rate increases applied to each group, to the sum of the following:

1. The percentage change in the new business rate;
2. 15% annually for the group's experience; and
3. Any adjustment due to change in coverage or case characteristics.

Non-grandfathered business will always meet this test since there is no rate differentiation allowed for a group's experience, and renewal groups get the same rate as new business groups.

RATING CONSISTENCY

The NAIC Model Law and many of the states' laws require that rating factors be consistently applied. This meant that rates for groups with similar allowable case characteristics and the same benefit plan would be identical, except for the risk factor applied to each group. Even the choice of risk factor should be objectively and consistently applied. One way to demonstrate such application is the use of a well-organized rate manual and objective application of an underwriting manual. Risk factors are not an allowed rating variation for non-grandfathered business.

One area of rating methodology that states have allowed under such requirements is the use of a composite (average per employee) rating approach for larger groups, while a person-by-person, or "list billed" rating is used for smaller sized groups. The use of different family composition rating structures (the rate tier structure), when a structure choice is given to the employer, is another example of inconsistent rating that is sometimes used by some carriers and allowed by many states. Technically, both situations might result in different rates for otherwise similarly situated groups. However, states have generally recognized the practical aspects of allowing both of these practices, provided that they are applied consistently. Nevertheless, composite rating and family composition methodologies are strictly limited for non-grandfathered business.

Another area of concern is the application of industry factors, in that it is possible that some employers are not coded in their correct industry, as this is sometimes difficult to ascertain, and further often a manual process. With a manual process, it is possible that the underwriter may inconsistently choose to not apply the appropriate industry factors when the experience of the small group is not in line with its industry. It would be difficult for the actuary to discover this inconsistency. The use of industry factors are not allowed for non-grandfathered business.

ANNUAL RATE CERTIFICATION

The NAIC Model Act requires each small employer carrier to file an annual actuarial certification with the commissioner, certifying that the carrier is in compliance with the Act. Most states require such a filing. The certification generally needs to be signed by a qualified Member of the American Academy of Actuaries. Professional standards require that it be in accordance with the Actuarial Standards Board's Actuarial Standard of Practice (ASOP) No. 26, "Compliance with Statutory and Regulatory Requirements for the Actuarial Certification of Small Employer Health Benefit Plans." The certification generally addresses the business over the past calendar year, but also may need to address the actuarial soundness of the rates both retrospectively and prospectively. While the laws generally presume that the opinions will be clean (without language which qualifies the opinion), the actuary needs to indicate in the certification whether or not there are any exceptions to compliance.

Applicability as to what the actuary certifies varies from state to state. Some states, like the NAIC Model Law, require that the certification address compliance with the requirements of the entire Act. This includes not only the premium rates charged, but also the underwriting and fair marketing provisions of the law. Included in the opinion regarding the premium rates is a certification concerning their actuarial soundness. On the other hand, many states simply require that the certification address only the premium rates, often without the need to address their actuarial soundness. Therefore, before issuing the certification, the actuary needs to be familiar with what each state requires, and qualify the opinion to the extent certain aspects have not been reviewed in the process of certification (such as underwriting or fair marketing procedures of the company). The ACA now also requires an annual filing of premium rates, even if there are no rate increases being implemented. This is in addition to the annual rate certifications filed with each state.

The NAIC Model Law also has a section on standards to assure fair marketing. Some key points that would need to be certified to, if required, are the following:

- Under HIPAA, any plan offered for sale by a carrier to a small employer (with certain exceptions primarily related to association plans) within a class must be available to all small employers within the same class. There are specified exceptions based on consistently applied employee participation and employer contribution rules, geographic location outside of the provider network area, provider network capacity limits, and carrier financial capacity. The last two require a cessation of marketing for 180 days.

- As part of its solicitation and sales materials, the carrier needs to make reasonable disclosure regarding four aspects of the rating and coverage:

- The extent to which premium rates are related to the health status of the employees and their dependents;
- The carrier's right to change premium rates and the factors that affect such changes;
- The provisions relating to any pre-existing condition provisions; and,
- The provisions relating to renewability of the policy and contracts.

* Commissions and other sales compensation cannot vary by the health status, claim experience, industry, occupation, or geographic location of the small employer within a state.

* Carriers may not make the terms of a producer's contract subject to the health status, claim experience, occupation, or geographic location of the small employer business the producer sells.

* No carrier or producer may encourage an employer to exclude an employee from coverage.

The ability of an actuary to certify adherence to these marketing requirements can be difficult, and is highly dependent on the quality of documentation maintained by the carrier. Most states recognize that verification of marketing compliance is not an actuarial function, and therefore do not require the actuary to certify to it. Where required, at a minimum the carrier should be able to present a log of all applications received, the underwriting action on each applicant, sales compensation contracts in effect, required disclosure statements in the sales materials, and evidence of the disclosure of the availability of the state mandated plans.

The small group carrier is required to maintain at its office a complete and detailed description of its rating practices and renewal underwriting practices. Included should be the documentation of the compliance testing of the certifying actuary.

RATE FILING REQUIREMENTS

For grandfathered small group plans, many states require filing of policy forms, certificates, applications, disclosure statements, and premium rates. Some require state insurance department approval before business can be sold in the state or new rates implemented. Others require informational filings and do not have approval authority over the rates. Some states will require filing of the rate manual documentation and/or an Actuarial Memorandum justifying the factors used for case characteristics as well as possibly the overall expected loss ratio and average rate increase. Some states require information on past loss ratios, past rate increases, and membership statistics. The amount and type of information required varies by state.

As of late 2010, the ACA requires that all non-grandfathered small group premium rates be filed with each state in which the insurer has affected business on an annual basis. If the rate increase is in excess of 10% (grandfathered or non-grandfathered), the carrier must also file additional information with the federal government and the state. As of 2014, this 10% test was conducted at the product level (that is, a group of plans that have the same HIOS product ID). However, as of the time of this writing, it is being considered to apply this threshold test for additional review for each benefit plan. The federal government does not have rate approval authority, but can influence the insurer and the governing states with regard to the implementation of the rate changes.

ACTUARIAL SOUNDNESS OF RATES

The NAIC Model Act and the laws of a number of states require the actuary to certify that the rates and rating methods of the small employer carrier are "actuarially sound." Certifying actuarial soundness of rates is perhaps the most controversial part of the certification process, for two reasons. First, the work involved to do a thorough review can be immense, especially if the certifying actuary has not done the pricing of the plans. Reliance on loss ratio reports and expected pricing targets is the most practical approach for testing for actuarial soundness. Second, many actuaries feel that, in at least some states, certain plans or benefit options, and especially for non-grandfathered plans, cannot be priced on an actuarially sound basis, due to the regulatory restrictions imposed on the rating and underwriting. ASOP No. 26 recognizes this problem and allows the opinion to be based on an expectation of the aggregate adequacy of all the small group plans.

NON-GRANDFATHERED SMALL GROUP PLANS

In addition to the NAIC Model type rating and certification requirements discussed above, the ACA introduced significant changes and limitations on rating of small employer groups. These changes will ultimately impact almost all employer groups once the transition program ends in 2017 and many grandfathered groups terminate their coverage.

RATE FILING REQUIREMENTS

As required by the Center for Medicare & Medicaid Services (CMS) for non-grandfathered plans, the core components of the rate filing are as follows:

- Part I – Unified Rate Review Template (URRT)

    The URRT is an Excel spreadsheet that the carrier must provide showing summary values pertaining to the rate increase request. Worksheet 1 of the URRT provides overall historical claims and premium experience for the most recently completed full calendar year (which is two years prior to the projection year). Worksheet 1 also provides summary manual rate data (if used), credibility information (that is, the percent reliance on past experience versus the manual rate), summary utilization and cost per service data, morbidity, trend, and other cost projection factors, the estimated projected index rate, the overall plan paid portion of projected allowed costs, average administrative costs, profits/risk margin, and the overall estimate for risk adjustment transfer payments or receipts. While Worksheet 1 focuses on aggregate data, Worksheet 2 provides this same information by product and benefit plan, and provides important data on each plan's ID, Name, Actuarial Metal Value, Pricing Actuarial Value,[5] membership projections, and the requested rate change. It is important to note that this is intended to be a rate *review* document and *not* necessarily a pricing template.

---

[5] As a technicality, this is a line item, but it is the factor that gets you from essentially the index rate to the premium rate, including expense variations by plan and non-EHB costs. The term "pricing actuarial value" is somewhat different from traditional meanings given to the term.

- Part II – Written Explanation of the Rate Increase

   For products with an average increase that equals or exceeds 10%, the carrier must provide a plain language narrative explaining the major reasons for the increase. This narrative is meant to provide the public with an understandable explanation of the major reasons for the increase, and is available on healthcare.gov, as well as state regulator and carriers' websites. While the 10% trigger is currently based on the average rate increase of all the plans that comprise a given product, this requirement may change in the future to be required at the plan level, as noted above.

- Part III – Actuarial Memorandum

   The Part III Actuarial Memorandum provides descriptive detail of the URRT components, the need for the requested rate change, and support for assumptions made. It must be signed and certified by a qualified actuary.

- Unique Plan Design Supporting Documentation and Justification

   As described later in this chapter, the cost sharing features of some plans are not fully handled by the Actuarial Value Calculator, which is used to assess compliance with the metal level corridors. If there are cases where the carrier's actuary needed to make a special actuarial adjustment to account for a unique plan design feature, the actuary must provide special documentation and certification.

While the above noted items focus on the core content of non-grandfathered small group rate filings, there is much more to the ACA filing process, including policy and application forms, service areas, provider network adequacy demonstrations, pharmacy content (formulary), and a review of Summary of Benefits and Coverages ("SBCs" provide consumers with a standard overview of major plan design and coverage elements). While not a topic of this textbook, much of the information provided in this section applies equally to the individual market's non-grandfathered filings' content and processes.

Chapter 18 provides an overview of the major aspects of the Affordable Care Act. This section focuses on those provisions as they relate to rate filing content and processes.

A helpful resource for preparing and reviewing small group rate filings is the most recent version of the Practice Note developed by the Academy of Actuaries.[6] Also, CMS provides regular website updates on regulations and guidance, which provides important tools and information, such as annual instructions on Parts I, II and III filing requirements and tools such as the Actuarial Value Calculator.[7]

APPLICABILITY

The laws described in this section apply to *non-grandfathered* health benefit plans that provide medical coverage to employees of small employers issued by health insurance carriers and HMOs. The ACA made massive changes to non-grandfathered small group plans. Non-grandfathered small group plans are basically all plans that did not obtain and

---

[6] At the time this text was written, the most recent version is an exposure draft for 2015 and beyond: http://www.actuary.org/files/RRPN_exposure_draft_092614.pdf

[7] CMS/CCIIO Regulations and Guidance: https://www.cms.gov/CCIIO/Resources/Regulations-and-Guidance/index.html

maintain grandfathered status. Transitional plans also exist in many states, which are a set of non-grandfathered plans that were allowed to temporarily delay many of the ACA's plan design and rating consequences described in this chapter.

The PACE Act passed in October of 2015, and significantly altered the initial ACA requirement that small groups become defined as employers sized up to 100 employees by January 1, 2016; the PACE Act retains the former 50 threshold, though allows states flexibility to use the 100 threshold.[8] Federal guidance counts full-time employees on the basis of working 30 hours per week. Determination as a small group is based on the number of full-time equivalent (FTE) employees.

CLASSES OF BUSINESS / SINGLE RISK POOL

Starting in 2014, under the ACA, all non-grandfathered small group businesses are treated as one class or pool for rating purposes. Rating classes no longer exist for non-grandfathered policies.

The ACA went one step further than removing classes of business. Starting in 2014, for purposes of setting premiums, health insurers must consider all enrollees in all health plans (other than grandfathered plans) offered by all insurers in the small group market to be members of a single statewide risk pool. This includes enrollees covered in plans both inside and outside the exchange. Some states have chosen to merge the individual and small group markets into one single risk pool.[9]

ALLOWABLE RATING CHARACTERISTICS

Beginning in 2014, the ACA requires non-grandfathered plans to use modified community rating, limiting rating characteristics to plan design,[10] age (with a uniform set of factors required for use by all carriers), family composition, geographic area (with area boundaries determined by each state), and tobacco use. Rates cannot vary based on any other characteristics.

Plan Design

All non-grandfathered plans sold inside and outside of the exchanges must fall into one of the following benefit categories:

Plan Type	Metal Target Actuarial Value
Platinum	90% of total allowed costs of benefits
Gold	80% of total allowed costs of benefits
Silver	70% of total allowed costs of benefits
Bronze	60% of total allowed costs of benefits

---

[8] Some states had already revised statute to the 100 definition prior to 2016, and states using the federal government to administer their exchange ("FFM states") had already been using the 100 threshold on the exchange, regardless of statute.

[9] As of October, 2015, Massachusetts, Vermont, and the District of Columbia merged the small group and individual risk pools.

[10] The plan design factor is driven by cost sharing, but could also reflect variations for items such as administrative costs, profit margin, and provider network.

Plans must be within ±2% of the target actuarial value in order to comply with the metal level requirements. The tool used to determine actuarial value is produced by CMS, standardized and currently used consistently across the U.S. and is commonly called the Actuarial Value Calculator.[11] Prior to creating plan design factors, carriers' actuaries must annually work with marketing departments to determine whether proposed plan designs meet these targets and corridors. The CMS tool is able to capture most elements of common plan design, but for material elements that the tool cannot handle, a special actuarial adjustment is required that must be certified either through a separate actuarial report or within the Part III Actuarial Memorandum. The actuary must make such adjustments in a manner as to be consistent with the data underlying the CMS tool. The certifying actuary must be a Member of the American Academy of Actuaries. A few states require that all of the Actuarial Value Calculator results be provided in the rate filing, which helps the regulator confirm that the carrier used the tool properly and that plans are compliant with metal level requirements.

After the plan design elements are determined to be allowed through using the Actuarial Value Calculator, the carriers' actuaries use their own actuarial value tools to determine plan factors. This is an important point: actuaries are not required to price plans based on the CMS tool. There are often important differences between the data and methodology underlying the CMS tool and the plan being priced, such as the expected population, leveraged cost variations, family composition mix, and the recognition of out-of-network benefits.

Carriers' actuaries who believe that their own data is not statistically credible enough from which to develop plan design factors often purchase tools from consulting firms, though some carriers base plan factors upon the free and publicly available federal Actuarial Value Calculator, with several adjustments. If using this tool, a common adjustment that the actuary considers is the effect of family coverage, since the Actuarial Value Calculator only reflects single coverage. Another common adjustment is for induced demand not fully reflected in the continuance tables by plan tier underlying the tool, since the Actuarial Value Calculator targets "plan share" rather than true actuarial value. Induced demand is the tendency for those with richer plans (low deductibles and copayments) to seek more services than those with less rich plans, irrespective of their health status; the ACA allows induced demand to be reflected in plan factors. However, the ACA does not allow recognition of enrollee antiselection to be reflected. Antiselection refers to the tendency for those who are less healthy to purchase richer plans. The spread of rates between metal level plans is a core concern of regulators, who are tasked with ensuring that selection based on health status does not play a role in rate setting, regardless of the source of data backing the plan factor development.

Provider Network

For carriers offering more than one provider network, network relativities are required. Due to federal guidance, the network relativity must be held constant throughout the state, even if in reality there is evidence that the network factor should vary by area. However, a carrier can create area-specific plans to reflect such differences. The Part III Actuarial Memorandum describes the network relativity factors, as well as the actuarial basis for those relativities.

---

[11] States could develop their own actuarial value tool, contingent upon CMS approval.

The overall product of the plan design factor (described above) and the provider network factor (as well as certain calibrations described later) is termed the "Pricing Actuarial Value" or "Pricing AV" and is shown on the Part I URRT Worksheet 2, as well as generally provided in a table in the Part III Actuarial Memorandum. The Pricing AV also includes non-EHB factors and expense/profit variations.

Age

Under the ACA, all carriers in a state use the same exact age curve. Most states use the standard age curve created by CMS,[12] though states are allowed to create their own age curve and submit to CMS for approval, which a few states have done.[13] This standardization makes it easy to compare rates, as one can focus on rates at one age and be able to know the rates at any age. In the Part III Actuarial Memorandum, the use of the age curve for the carrier's own projected enrollees is usually described, with an indication of the carrier's expected average age factor.

Family Composition

The standard method designated by the ACA for charging for family coverage is to add the premiums for each family member based on each family member's age factor, though a maximum of three children under age 21 can be charged. However, small employers often prefer composite rating (average per employee) and a tiered family composition rate structure (for example, single/family is a two tiered approach while single/couple/family is a three tiered approach). Under the ACA, state regulators can apply to federal regulators for approval of a standard composite rating/tiered methodology that carriers in that state must use if composite rating is allowed; many states have an approved composite method. For states without an approved composite method, there is a default approach that carriers must follow if a tiered family composite rate structure is used.[14]

In the rate filings of carriers, the Part III Actuarial Memorandum sometimes describes the upward rate effect on all premiums that was needed in order to calibrate for carriers not being able to charge for certain children. Further, the Part III Actuarial Memorandum might also describe whether and how family composite rating is used by the carrier, and how the use of (some) states' standard family composite tiers affected the calibration.

Geographic Area

Under the ACA, each state sets distinct boundaries (referred to as "regions" or "areas") that each carrier must use for rating purposes. Each carrier's premiums must be consistent throughout each distinct region. The boundaries were determined by state regulators, or by federal regulators when a state chose not to do so. Boundaries may change, but have not changed frequently thus far.

---

[12] The standard age curve used for 2014-2016, and perhaps beyond, can be found on Appendix I: https://www.cms.gov/CCIIO/Resources/Files/Downloads/market-reforms-guidance-2-25-2013.pdf

[13] State-specific age curves: https://www.cms.gov/CCIIO/Programs-and-Initiatives/Health-Insurance-Market-Reforms/Downloads/state-specific-age-curve-variations-08-09-2013.pdf

[14] § 147.102(c)(3), New guidance on family composite tiers was released by CMS on March 11, 2014

Each carrier determines its own area relativities, and provides the actuarial basis and resulting factors in the Part III Actuarial Memorandum. The actuarial basis considers past claims experience if available, which relies on relative area comparisons, though with claims that are risk-adjusted in order to not violate the ACA law that health risk differences should be uniformly shared throughout the state. The carriers' actuaries also consider variations by region in provider network arrangements that may not be able to be reflected in the statewide provider network factor (see above discussion), prospective changes to provider contracts, and projected enrollment in each area. When making changes to area factors, many carriers employ a moving weighted average approach, so that the changes are not abrupt and thus less disruptive. This approach also helps to add to the credibility of the data, which may be sparse in some areas; a moving average approach adds more "time" to the data and thus adds more statistical credibility.

A carrier does not need to sell in every area of the state, and does not need to sell everywhere within a given region. For example, an HMO's service area might not be able to meet the needs of a whole area. In this case, the carrier will fill in the service area template with some counties missing entirely, or possibly with some other counties listed as "partial" with further detail on zip codes where the carrier will sell. The service area template is required to be filed with the regulatory authority, and is very important in terms of communicating to the Exchange which products can be sold to specific people based on residence. The carrier proposes its service area and provides very detailed provider information in the network portion of the filing. Regulators scrutinize the network in terms of adequacy, and may require that the carrier reduce its service area if its network is not deemed accessible enough in certain counties or zip codes.

Tobacco Use

While the ACA allows for a tobacco use surcharge of up to 50%, many small group carriers do not assess the tobacco use surcharge in the small group market due to system constraints, administrative burden, competitive considerations, and/or because employers often do not desire this feature as it complicates enrollment, premium subsidization and financial planning. For those carriers that assess a tobacco surcharge, the plan also needs to offer wellness benefits including a smoking cessation program that allows the covered person to offset, at least in part, the tobacco surcharge for those that participate.[15] When used, it is common for tobacco use factors to be in the 10-30% range, based on external or internal actuarial studies that are typically documented in the Part III Actuarial Memorandum.

THE INDEX RATE

Prior to the ACA and still applicable to grandfathered plans, the index rate is defined as the arithmetic average of the lowest and highest premium rate that could be charged. The ACA entirely changed the meaning of the term index rate as applied to non-grandfathered plans. The index rate under the ACA is shown in the rate filing in the Part I URRT Worksheet 1, and is the estimated expected average allowed claims for essential health benefits (EHBs) for the carrier's single risk pool (that is, a carrier's entire book of non-grandfathered small group business in a given state). Allowed claims include both enrollee cost sharing such as deductibles, coinsurance and copayments, as well as amounts paid by the health plan. The Part III Actuarial Memorandum typically describes which benefits are not EHBs and the

---

[15] Federal Register Volume 78, page 13414; http://www.gpo.gov/fdsys/pkg/FR-2013-02-27/pdf/2013-04335.pdf,

actuarial basis for the split between EHBs and non-EHBs. This split is provided in the Part I URRT Worksheet 2.

RATING CONSISTENCY

Non-grandfathered plans achieve rating consistency in that very few allowable rating adjustments are allowed, and those that are allowed under the ACA are objective. Further, rates sold off of the exchange must be the same as rates sold on the exchange for similar plan designs, with very few exceptions.[16]

RATE JUSTIFICATION

Besides documenting the actuarial basis for the rating characteristics as described above, the Part III Actuarial Memorandum's major purpose is documenting the basis for the rate request. Note that rates must be filed on an annual basis, even if there is no rate change. Below are the major elements that the Actuarial Memorandum will include:

- Health Status and Non-Allowed Case Characteristic Changes

    The Part III Actuarial Memorandum provides a description for the financial effect of health status changes of both the carrier's projected enrollees as well as the statewide pool's projected enrollees. Aside from an overall rate change, the risk adjustment estimate also relates to the relative health risk difference between the carrier's pool and the statewide risk pool, though no risk adjustment method is perfect and some uncompensated health risk differences will continue to exist and may need reflection via the carrier's specific rate level. In the small group market, common reasons for changes in health status include items such as uncompensated age changes of the pool (meaning age changes that are not completely compensated through the age curve), changes in the characteristics of groups entering the pool (including groups sized 51-100 entering the small group market in some states), and changes in small groups leaving the pool (due to either groups terminating their sponsored plans, moving their employees to the individual marketplaces, as well as larger small groups leaving to self-insure their risk). Some of the morbidity change will be due to unexpected emerging experience that is now known since the prior year's rate filing, while some will be due to actuarial predictions for the upcoming year. The Actuarial Memorandum might provide two explanations on the change in morbidity (as well as other items described below), one to reconcile the two year roll-forward entries shown on the Part I URRT, and the other to reconcile the one year roll-forward from the immediately preceding year's rates.

- Plan Design and Coverages

    The Part III Actuarial Memorandum provides justification for any adjustments made to account for the effect of overall differences in benefit designs and different covered benefits. This impact includes anticipated changes in cost, given provider network arrangements associated with given benefit plans. The overall effect of induced demand is also generally documented in the Actuarial Memorandum.

---

[16] One allowable exception is pediatric dental benefits, which is typically provided off of the exchange but may be carved out on exchange, if standalone pediatric dental options exist. In this case, premiums for otherwise similar products might differ slightly.

- Trend

  The Part III Actuarial Memorandum provides justification for annual trend. Trend is typically broken down between unit cost per service inflationary trend and utilization trend, and sometimes case mix trend (that is, overall severity of services used). Trend is typically broken between inpatient, outpatient, physician services, and pharmacy, though many carriers evaluate trend at the medical versus pharmacy level.

  Leveraged trend is often documented, which is the effect of trend after taking member cost sharing differences into account (that is, leveraged trend is the insurer-paid trend). Because there does not exist a specific factor in the URRT to reflect a leveraged trend adjustment, the weighted average leveraged trend effect must be incorporated into the plan design pricing factor (that is, the paid-to-allowed factor).

- Administrative Costs, Taxes, and Fees

  The Actuarial Memorandum will document the actuarial basis for administrative costs, taxes, and fees. Administrative costs are usually projected based on recent past experience, with adjustments to take into account expected changes in salaries, commissions, materials, vendor fees, and overhead. State premium taxes, the health insurer fee, Patient-Centered Outcomes Research Institute (PCORI) assessments, exchange user fees, and risk adjustment fees[17] are projected as well, and the level is often dependent on the level of the elements described above. Exchange user fees are shared equally on the exchange and off the exchange.

- Profit and Risk Margins

  Carriers are typically able to include the profit and risk margin they deem warranted, though some state regulators may object if the value is deemed too high; the ACA's minimum MLR requirements effectively limit profits in hindsight. These are included under the "expenses" category of allowable adjustment factors, and, as such, can vary by plan where allowed by the state.

The carrier must justify the basis for the rate to be charged. Rate increases above 10% are subject to additional regulatory review, including that the carrier must also file additional information with the federal government via a system maintained by CMS called "HIOS" (Health Insurance Oversight System), which then makes data available to the public.[18] The federal government does not have rate approval authority, but can influence the insurer and the governing states with regard to rate changes.

ANNUAL RATE CERTIFICATION

Since state statutes regarding annual small group rate certifications may not have been repealed with the implementation of the ACA, some states continue to require an annual actuarial small group rate certification that retrospectively verifies compliance with the state's rating requirements. It is important to note that these certifications include both grandfathered and non-grandfathered business. Typically, they will be considered separate classes of business. Since the non-grandfathered business is subject to ACA modified

---

[17] The transitional reinsurance and risk corridor programs are not covered in this chapter due to the temporary nature of those programs. Information on those programs is provided in Chapter 18.

[18] https://ratereview.healthcare.gov/

community rating rules, if compliant, their rates will automatically meet the within-class tests required by the state's small group law, but the grandfathered plan rates will need to be checked to verify compliance with these two within-class tests (see the Index Rate and Rate Increase Limitations sections earlier in the discussion of grandfathered business).

Perhaps of greater concern is that the entire small group business portfolio of a carrier still needs to meet the between-classes test (see the discussion earlier on Classes of Business). Each class index rate (different from the index rate discussed above for the ACA URRT and Actuarial Memorandum) must be within 20%[19] of the index rate for every other class of business. Because this test is retrospective, it can be overlooked when setting rates for grandfathered and non-grandfathered business. Although the premium rates for the two types of business are generally independent from one another, they are still required to maintain this between-class index rate relationship. It is prudent for the actuary to proactively check compliance with this test when setting grandfathered rates.

OTHER SMALL GROUP RATE CERTIFICATIONS

Some states require a separate state version of the Actuarial Memorandum for the submission of small group rate changes, including an actuarial certification. The content tends to vary somewhat from the federal Part III Actuarial Memorandum template, although there is overlap. There may also be other state specific forms that are required as part of the rate filing with the state. It is advisable for the actuary to check state requirements when preparing the annual rate filing.

LARGE GROUP AND OTHER GROUP INSURANCE PLANS

For large group and other group insurance plans, many states require filing of policy forms, certificates, applications, disclosure statements, and premium rates. Some require state insurance department approval before business can be sold in the state. Others require informational filings and do not have approval authority over the rates. Some states require filing of the rate manual documentation, an Actuarial Memorandum justifying the factors used for case characteristics, overall expected loss ratio, the average rate increase, and/or data on past loss ratios, enrollment statistics, and past average rate increases. The amount and type of information required varies by state.

The ACA requires that if the large group health insurance rate increase is in excess of 10% (grandfathered or non-grandfathered), the carrier must also file additional information with the federal government and the state, as well as prominently display it on the carrier's website. This rate increase is viewed at the carrier's large group pool level, not at the specific employer/group level.

The ACA introduced a medical loss ratio (MLR) requirement starting in year 2011. This established a minimum MLR of 85% for large group business on an annual basis. The MLR calculation includes adjustments for health care improvement expenses, certain reserves, taxes, regulatory fees, assessments, and credibility based on the size of the carrier's block of business in the state. To the extent that the adjusted MLR for a carrier's combined block of

---

[19] This percentage can differ in some states.

large group business in a given state is less than 85% on a rolling three-year basis, the excess must be rebated.

PRICING CONSIDERATIONS AND STRATEGIES RELATED TO COMPLIANCE REQUIREMENTS

As discussed above, the ACA introduced a medical loss ratio (MLR) requirement starting in year 2014 in the individual, small group and large group markets. This established a minimum MLR of 80% for small group and individual business, and 85% in the large group market.[20] The MLR calculation includes adjustments for health care improvement expenses, certain reserves, taxes, regulatory fees, assessments, and credibility based on the size of the carrier's block of business in the state. To the extent that the adjusted MLR for a carrier's combined block of small group business in a given state is less than the minimum MLR, the excess must be rebated. This establishes a one-sided risk situation, in which good underwriting years can no longer offset poor underwriting years and effectively pushes up the expected long-term experience of the carrier to exceed the MLR thresholds. While the ACA MLR requirement is retrospective, many state regulators require that carriers demonstrate prospective actuarial compliance with the MLR thresholds.

Quite a few carriers decided to withdraw from the small group market prior to the ACA, feeling the underwriting and rating restrictions made other venues more attractive for use of the company's capital. Some expect that this exit of small group insurers will accelerate due to new restrictions imposed by the ACA, such as the inability to vary rates by a group's health status (effective in 2014), increased rate increase filing requirements (effective in 2010 and significantly so in 2014), and the MLR rebate requirements (effective in 2011).

---

[20] Publicly posted information on companies that fell below the minimum MLR can be found on the following website: https://companyprofiles.healthcare.gov/

29 MEDICARE-RELATED RATE FILINGS AND CERTIFICATIONS

Patrick J. Dunks
Eric P. Goetsch
updated by Bradley J. Piper

INTRODUCTION

Even prior to the passage of the Medicare Prescription Drug, Improvement, and Modernization Act of 2003 (MMA), employers had numerous options for providing Medicare-related coverage to Medicare-eligible retirees and Medicare-eligible dependents. However, prior to the MMA, most employers provided coverage through products that wrapped around Medicare's primary coverage. With the creation of Medicare's Part D prescription drug benefit, most employers providing coverage to Medicare-eligible retirees now also consider using different approaches involving federal subsidies to providing these retiree health benefits. However, regardless of how employers currently provide such coverage, the changes legislated by the Affordable Care Act (ACA) that decreased the funding for Medicare Advantage (MA), removed the tax advantages of the retiree drug subsidy (RDS), and altered the financial parameters of the Part D coverage gap may influence if and how employers will provide such coverage in the future.

EMPLOYER OPTIONS

Employers or unions can provide retiree medical benefits that add to traditional Medicare's Part A/B benefits by providing coverage that wraps around Medicare coverage, or they can replace Medicare's Part A/B and enhance its benefits through an MA Part C plan (Part C plans provide coverage for traditional Medicare Part A/B benefits plus provide additional benefits, as described later in this chapter). The latter approach, whether through a plan sponsored by an employer or union, or through one purchased from an MA organization, requires an actuarial certification of the MA Part C bid underlying the plan. The bid is a filing prepared for the Centers for Medicare & Medicaid Services (CMS), and it uses a standardized format that shows the development of the premium rate and various other key financial measures. Employers and unions are often interested in MA plans because they can be a lower cost coverage option and/or they can offer increased benefits without additional cost.

Employers or unions can provide prescription drug benefits to Medicare-eligible beneficiaries in various ways, by: (1) purchasing an employer group waiver plan (EGWP) from a third party (known as an 800 series EGWP), (2) providing primary coverage without a federal RDS, (3) providing primary coverage with a federal RDS, or (4) attaining a direct Prescription Drug Plan (PDP) contract with CMS and administering the plan directly (known as a Direct Contract EGWP). An EGWP can be either a stand-alone PDP or a Medicare Advantage plan with Part D (MA-PD). Pursuing the RDS requires an actuarial attestation which specifies that the plan passes both a gross and net actuarial equivalency benefit test. A direct PDP contract with CMS requires an actuarial certification regarding the plan design and its compliance with actuarial equivalency tests. All employer prescription drug coverage options for Medicare eligible retirees except providing primary coverage without a RDS provide financial value to employers by reducing net benefit costs via federal subsidies.

Federal support provided under MA and PDP/RDS may reduce employers' liabilities for post-retirement benefits, as recognized under various accounting standards, such as Financial Accounting Standard (FAS) 106 and SOP 92-6 for Taft-Hartley plans. However, Government Accounting Standards Board accounting rules (GASB 45) do not allow liabilities for future retiree benefits to be offset by expected future RDS subsidies.

INSURER APPEAL

MA organizations and PDPs tend to seek group enrollment because, in addition to the fundamental objective of growing their plan, marketing costs for group enrollment are substantially lower compared to those for a similar number of individual Medicare beneficiaries.

In the Medicare-related group market, many insurers and pharmacy benefit managers (PBMs) provide employers with administrative support to enable the employers to collect the RDS or support a non-RDS benefit offering (such as an EGWP with a wrap product). Insurers not providing such support risk losing commercial group accounts.

MEDICARE ADVANTAGE PLANS

MA group products are part of the MA program administered by CMS and described in the chapter "Government Health Care Plans in the United States." However, several CMS waivers for certain employer groups allow MA group products more flexibility than MA individual products.

EMPLOYER GROUP WAIVERS

In each service area, an MA organization must submit Part C and Part D bids for each MA-PD individual benefit plan, and Part C bids for each MA-only individual plan. For MA-PD group plans, the MA organization only needs to submit two Part C bids, one that can later be coupled with a calendar year Part D benefit design, and another that can later be coupled with a non-calendar year Part D benefit design. The Part C benefits are often the same across both Part C bids, but submitting the two Part C bids preserves the MA organization's option to enroll groups that prefer calendar year drug plans as well as non-calendar year drug plans. Most groups elect calendar year drug plans, as non-calendar year drug plans are not eligible for federal catastrophic reinsurance payments. For MA-only group plans, only one Part C bid needs to be submitted, as there is no reason to submit two bids; maintaining the calendar year/non calendar year drug plan options is not an issue for MA-only group plans. Whether filed for an MA-PD group or an MA-only group, the Part C bid allows the group to offer a calendar year medical benefit or a non-calendar year benefit – no distinction is required when the bid is submitted. MA organizations usually submit their employer group plan Part C bids with traditional Medicare benefits, reflecting the estimated cost of member out-of-pocket cost sharing limits. If CMS revenue exceeds the estimated net plan liability (including administrative costs and profit margin), the excess revenue is identified as funds to be used for additional employer group benefits (to be determined on a group-specific basis at a later date). CMS does not require (or accept) Part D employer group bids to be filed.

For each employer group, the MA organization may build a benefit plan tailored to that employer, as long as: (1) the benefit plan is, on average, at least as rich as traditional Medicare benefits and (2) the MA organization maintains an actuarial development in their files demonstrating how they spent the funds dedicated to providing additional benefits (contained in their Part C group bid) to benefit Medicare-eligible retirees. Such additional benefits often include reduced cost sharing as compared to traditional Medicare Part A/B levels, relaxed benefit limits, added benefits traditional Medicare does not cover, or reduced Part D premiums. MA organizations and employers negotiate employer-specific premiums, just as they do with other group coverage. However, CMS requires an MA organization's employer group waiver plan bid be, on average, consistent with the costs and revenues for the groups expected to enroll. Practically, this requirement limits flexibility because the negotiations must begin with the bid that was filed and adjust from that point, including maintaining similar profit margins. Further, Medicare-eligible retiree contributions are limited such that retirees are not disadvantaged relative to the premiums and benefits reflected in the bid. In other words, employees cannot be required to contribute more for additional benefits than what the employer is expected to pay for those benefits.

In general, MA organizations are allowed to expand their employer group product service areas (with CMS approval) to include all Medicare-eligible retirees residing in the designated state(s) for network products, as long as: (1) the majority of the employer's employees reside in the MA organization's individual plan service area and (2) the MA organization agrees to reimburse non-contracted providers at Medicare allowable fee levels. However, MA organizations without a national network may find that the residential restrictions to their plan service area hamper sales of the MA products to employers, as retirees moving outside of the plan service area cannot be enrolled in the employer's MA product (although stand-alone Part D Plans can be offered nationally, as discussed later in this chapter). Changes and further details about MA employer group waivers may be found at the CMS website.[1]

PART C EMPLOYER GROUP BIDS

As actuaries develop Part C bids for MA organizations, they estimate risk-adjusted benchmark CMS revenue. Benchmark CMS revenue amounts are published for each county and represent the maximum per member per month (PMPM) revenue amount CMS is willing to pay for each enrolled beneficiary by county. The ACA reduced the funding for these Part C benchmarks and, in turn, CMS revenue payments.

Benchmark CMS revenue is published on a 1.00 risk score basis, but the Part C bid process requires the MA organization to adjust that monthly rate higher or lower to reflect the estimated risk score of the enrolled population. Actuaries also develop medical and administrative cost estimates for traditional Medicare benefits and add a target profit load to the cost estimates. Finally, those cost estimates are subtracted from the benchmark CMS revenue estimate to project Part C savings, as defined by CMS. If cost estimates are greater than benchmark revenue, savings are, by regulation, zero. To maintain actuarial soundness and comply with CMS requirements, the revenue and cost estimates need to reflect the same underlying population characteristics. CMS requires the MA organization to provide additional benefits that, together with a relative administrative and profit load equal to that

---

[1] www.cms.hhs.gov

used for the traditional Medicare benefit bid, have value equal to or greater than Part C rebates. CMS defines Part C rebates as a percent of the Part C savings, where savings is defined in the prior paragraph (that is, the difference between the risk adjusted benchmark CMS revenue and the estimated cost of traditional Medicare benefits including an administrative and profit load). Part C rebates range from 50% to 70% of savings, where plans with higher quality rankings receive higher percentages. CMS retains the remaining savings. However, for employer group bids the MA organization can simply file a placeholder benefit rather than precisely defining the additional benefits, as required for individual MA bids.

When developing employer group Part C bids, actuaries consider available base period experience, other data sources, expected cost trends, anticipated population characteristics and associated risk scores, administrative costs, and target profit loads. Base period experience must be reported on the bid form.

For many MA organizations, employer group enrollment may be relatively low, so risk score and medical cost experience could be less than fully credible. In such cases, employer group bids are often based on manual rates developed from individual MA plan experience, with appropriate adjustments for group plan characteristics. The final bid is often a blend of the partially credible employer group experience and the manual rate developed from individual MA experience, using CMS credibility guidelines to determine the appropriate blending rate. If the MA organization does not have credible experience under the MA program, risk scores and cost estimates are often developed based on CMS projections, sample Medicare beneficiary experience under traditional Medicare, or other research. Even when experience is credible, risk scores and cost estimates from other sources are often used to test or validate experience data.

Adjustments applied to experience reflect recent emerging experience trends, expected provider reimbursement changes, changes resulting from care management modifications, expected traditional Medicare trends, and other factors. For organizations with MA provider contracts that mirror traditional Medicare reimbursement, expected provider reimbursement changes often mirror traditional Medicare trends.

Part C bids include estimated Part C risk scores for the expected enrollment, and these should be consistent with the underlying medical cost estimates, whether based on actual experience or manual rating approaches. The estimated risk scores should be adjusted for anticipated improvements in provider disease coding, the organization's capture of such coding, and any announced changes in the CMS-HCC risk adjustment mechanism.

The Part C bids should also reflect the plan's service area, any expected utilization changes due to benefit level changes, the impact of care management, expected administrative costs, and target profit levels.

CMS indicates that administrative cost targets should generally be consistent with the plan's most recent budgets and appropriate GAAP methodology to the extent this is consistent with the organization's standard accounting practices. CMS expects target profit levels to be consistent with the organization's other products.

CMS issues electronic bid forms, instructions, suggested actuarial certification language, and filing directions in early April each year. Part of the bid includes a certification by the actuary that the bid conforms to Actuarial Standards of Practice (ASOPs), as promulgated by the Actuarial Standards Board. The instructions ask the actuary to pay particular attention to ASOPs 5 (Incurred Health and Disability Claims), 8 (Regulatory Filings for Health Benefits), 23 (Data Quality), 25 (Credibility Procedures), and 41 (Actuarial Communications).

Bids and actuarial certifications are submitted on or before the first Monday of each June for the following calendar year. The first review, a "desk review" of the bid, looks at reasonableness and consistency, and focuses on that year's areas of emphasis as determined by CMS. CMS also performs bid audits, where the bids are put through a more detailed review and financial audits, where the experience data underlying the bid development is tested. CMS uses a combination of bid audits and financial audits to meet the requirement under current law to audit one-third of MA organizations every year.

MEDICARE SUPPLEMENT PLANS

Group Medicare Supplement health policy forms must be filed with state insurance departments. Employer group Medicare Supplement rates must be filed and approved in some states, while association group rates must be approved in all states. Typically, rate filings require actuarial memorandums or statements. Each state sets its own requirements for insurance products, so actuaries should research applicable statutes and rules for each state.

When developing Medicare Supplement rates, actuaries consider available experience, other data sources, expected cost trends, changes to Medicare Parts A and B coverage and cost sharing changes, anticipated population characteristics, administrative costs, target profit loads, loss ratio requirements, if any, and competitive issues.

For many Medicare Supplement insurers, employer group enrollment may be relatively low, so experience may not be fully credible. For this reason, group rates are sometimes developed based on individual Medicare Supplement plan experience, with appropriate adjustments for group characteristics (such as underwriting differences). If the Medicare Supplement insurer doesn't have credible experience, cost estimates are often developed based on rating manuals available for purchase, rate filings available for other carriers, or other sources. Even when experience is credible, alternate cost estimates are often used to test experience data. Adjustments applied to experience reflect recent experience trends, expected traditional Medicare trends, and other factors.

There are other employer group health products for Medicare-eligible retirees that are not technically Medicare Supplement policies, often called Medicare Wrap or Retiree Health plans. Depending on the state, fully insured versions of these plans may or may not be subject to rate approval authority, similar to most large group fully insured rates. Self-insured versions have no state regulatory oversight. In states where they are not subject to rate approval authority, the states may still require submission of the rates (and associated structures) for their records. Similar to large group fully insured products for the commercially insured population, employers and insurers negotiate rates for these types of plans.

PRESCRIPTION DRUG PLANS UNDER PART D

Prescription drug coverage provided through stand-alone PDP or MA-PD group products are part of the Part D program administered by CMS and described in Chapter 9, "Government Health Plans in the United States." However, similarly to the MA plans described earlier, numerous CMS employer group waivers have allowed group products with Part D coverage to be more flexible than similar individual products.

EMPLOYER GROUP WAIVERS

In each service area, a PDP or MA-PD organization must submit Part D bids for each benefit plan sold to individuals. For employer group plans, however, PDP and MA-PD organizations do not submit Part D bids.

For each employer group, the PDP or MA-PD organization may build a total prescription drug benefit plan tailored to that employer, as long as the benefit plan meets CMS' Part D equivalence requirements. Those requirements are that: (1) group-specific benefits must be, on average, at least as rich as standard Part D benefits, (2) the plan deductible must be no greater than the standard Part D deductible, (3) group-specific benefits in the coverage gap must be at least as rich as standard Part D benefits, and (4) catastrophic coverage must be at least as rich as standard Part D catastrophic coverage. Most employer group plans meet the first three requirements easily, but many plans must improve catastrophic coverage in order to satisfy all four requirements.

The ACA added the Coverage Gap Discount Program for Medicare Part D, whereby pharmaceutical manufacturers pay 50% of the ingredient cost for brand name drugs that fall in the coverage gap for non-low income beneficiaries. This additional source of funding has helped to generally make EGWPs financially advantageous relative to other coverage options. Starting on January 1, 2014, CMS mandated that the Medicare portion of an EGWP is a defined standard benefit.[2] All benefit enhancements above the defined standard benefit offered by EGWPs are considered other, non-Medicare health insurance (OHI) and are paid after the coverage gap discount is applied. This guidance facilitates the payments from pharmaceutical manufacturers, which would otherwise be greatly reduced if the plan was considered an enhanced PDP plan. The PBM or insurer must be licensed in the state in order to offer OHI. Some states require filings for these OHI products.

PDP and MA-PD organizations negotiate with employers over specific premiums for 800 series EGWPs. Large employers will typically self-insure in lieu of purchasing insured coverage. Direct Contract EGWPs are self-insured by the employer.

In general, PDPs are allowed to expand their group product service areas to include all Medicare-eligible retirees residing in the United States. CMS's website[3] should contain any modifications or further details. MA-PD group waivers are generally limited by MA requirements discussed earlier in this chapter.

---

[2] The defined standard benefit has a deductible, 75% coverage below the initial coverage limit, a coverage gap that is incrementally being reduced so that by the year 2020 it will provide 75% coverage, and catastrophic spending coverage. These spending bands are adjusted each year for inflation.
[3] www.cms.hhs.gov

All EGWP formularies must meet CMS requirements and provide coverage minimums. Modifications can be made to the basic filed formularies that enhance coverage, but changes cannot be made that remove drugs, increase cost sharing, or restrict access without prior CMS approval.

RETIREE DRUG SUBSIDY FOR PLAN SPONSORS UNDER PART D

To encourage employers and unions to maintain prescription drug coverage under their retiree health programs, the MMA provides for a subsidy to plan sponsors that meet certain requirements. The subsidy is 28% of each retiree's drug claim costs that fall within a corridor, defined by indexed thresholds that are updated annually by CMS. This federal subsidy was exempted from federal income tax through 2012; the ACA removed this tax exemption making the RDS option less attractive today compared to 2012 and prior. To receive the subsidy, a plan sponsor must provide prescription drug coverage that is at least actuarially equivalent to standard Part D coverage ("gross test"), must on average provide a net value (calculated by subtracting retiree premium from the gross value) that is at least equal to the net value of standard Part D coverage ("net test"), must apply in advance of each plan year, and must report actual drug claim costs to CMS after each plan year. The annual application requires an actuarial attestation that the plan meets the gross and net tests, as defined in CMS regulations. Additional details are available on CMS' website.[4]

The gross test examines whether the plan's prescription drug benefit provides coverage that is, on average, at least as rich as standard Part D coverage. The gross test must be performed separately for each benefit option within a group health plan. The gross test includes all Part D covered drugs. In other words, when performing the gross test, a benefit option's coverage of non-Part D drugs cannot contribute to the benefit value compared to standard Part D's benefit value. However, a benefit option's lack of coverage of mandated Part D covered drugs counts against it. The ACA enhanced the standard Part D benefit by gradually eliminating the coverage gap between the initial coverage limit (ICL) and the out of pocket maximum (OOP), starting in 2011 and continuing through 2020. However, the ACA also modifies the initial regulations provided in MMA to exclude the newly enhanced coverage when completing the gross value test; that is, the gross value is tested against the initially regulated standard Part D benefit, which had no coverage between the ICL and OOP.

The net test examines whether the portion of the group health plan benefit subsidy offered by the plan sponsor is at least as great as the value of the standard Part D subsidy made by CMS. The net test can be performed separately for each retiree group health plan offered by the plan sponsor, or can be combined across groups to pass the test in aggregate.

When performing the gross and net tests, actuaries consider available experience for the group, other data sources, expected cost trends, expected pharmacy rebates (if any, since the gross and net testing is to be performed net of rebates), formularies, the cost of drugs not covered by Part D, and anticipated population characteristics.

---

[4] www.cms.hhs.gov/EmployerRetireeDrugSubsid

As retirees tend to use many more prescriptions than their actively working counterparts, and many of those drugs are consistent over time, a plan sponsor's actuary is encouraged to use their retirees' experience to the extent reasonable. Possible adjustments to this experience include benefit design and premium changes, expected pharmacy or pharmacy benefit manager (PBM) reimbursement changes, expected drug cost trends, expected utilization trends, financial impact of drug rebates, expiration of patents on high cost drugs (leading to introduction of generic equivalents), expected utilization shifts from generic to new brand drugs, the release of new drugs, the impact of the experience's underlying benefit levels on utilization, formulary changes, drug utilization review modifications, medication therapy management modifications, and other factors. The unusual benefit design of the standard Part D benefit, which a plan sponsor is compared against, warrants consideration of the potentially different impact of the relevant factors on the employer's design plan. This includes design elements impacting different sizes of claims, as well as on overall cost. Many plan sponsors very readily demonstrate compliance with the gross test and the net test, such that many of these adjustments are immaterial in relation to the overall richness of the plan design and subsidization.

The gross and net tests are pass/fail tests. Given the lack of precision inherent in actuarial projections, test results that are initially close to the pass/fail line often warrant additional testing using alternate assumptions or methods. In the end, the actuary should be prepared to defend the selection of final assumptions supporting the attestation. The gross and net tests are prospective, so actual experience will not impact the results of the tests.

Actuarial Standards of Practice Nos. 5, 6, 8, 23, 25, 41, and 42 may provide guidance when performing RDS attestations. The American Academy of Actuaries issued a Health Practice Note that provides additional discussion concerning attestation issues.

The RDS application and attestation are administered entirely through CMS' website.[5] Data, reports, plan designs, and subsidies are reviewed by CMS' contracted actuaries to ensure that the actuaries making the plan sponsor's RDS eligibility determinations are using reasonable methods with appropriate data and adjustments.

PLAN SPONSOR CREDITABLE COVERAGE NOTICES

MMA requires plan sponsors to send creditable coverage notices to all Medicare-eligible covered individuals, whether actively employed or retired, by October 15 prior to the upcoming calendar year. Individuals maintaining creditable coverage (which applies to their pharmacy coverage specifically) will not be penalized if they join Part D late. Individuals without creditable coverage who do not elect Part D coverage upon initial eligibility, but enroll later, are permanently charged a late enrollment penalty of one percent of the nationwide average premium for each Medicare-eligible month they did not have creditable coverage.

Coverage is considered creditable if the benefit plan passes the gross test described earlier. In other words, the pharmacy coverage must, on average, be at least as rich as standard Part D coverage, though excluding the value of the enhanced coverage and pharmacy discounts created by the ACA. Unlike RDS, the net value test is not required for determining creditable coverage.

---

[5] www.cms.hhs.gov/EmployerRetireeDrugSubsid

CMS regulations offer safe harbors for plan sponsors to determine creditable coverage without the assistance of a qualified actuary. The previously footnoted CMS website contains details. If the creditable coverage determination does not fall under a safe harbor, a more rigorous application of the gross test described above is anticipated and an actuary's services are necessary.

MEDICARE SECONDARY PAYER (MSP)

The Medicare, Medicaid and SCHIP Extension Act of 2007 created a requirement that "Responsible Reporting Entities", generally plan sponsors through insurers, must file Social Security Numbers (SSNs) of every covered member over the age of 45 (initially 55) with CMS. This requirement allows CMS to check whether they are secondary on claims that have been submitted to them. If CMS determines that it paid a claim incorrectly (Medicare paid as primary when through SSN reference CMS believes itself to be secondary), a federal tax lien is assessed by the IRS and the plan sponsor must go through a lengthy appeals process if it feels CMS is in error.

In addition to the special rules that exist for insurers and plan sponsors of commercial health plans, MSP issues also affect MA organizations. MA organizations are reimbursed at a lower rate for members with other primary coverage, reflecting the estimated reduced costs these organizations will incur as the secondary provider. Bids for MA-PD group plans must account for the estimated percentage of membership that will have other primary coverage, reducing projected costs and revenues accordingly.

SECTION FIVE

UNDERWRITING AND MANAGING RISK

30 GROUP INSURANCE UNDERWRITING

James T. Lundberg
Ann Marie Wood
Gregory Fann
James Juillerat

INTRODUCTION

The purpose of large group underwriting is to segregate risks so that the insurer can achieve its strategic goals and financial objectives in the large case market. Underwriting methods include risk selection, thoughtful plan design, and numerous rating and analytic techniques. Large employers and their carriers have increasingly come to view their relationship as a partnership, and the role of the underwriter is often to devise risk and financial alternatives that satisfy mutual needs and goals. The Affordable Care Act (ACA), the continued evolution of managed care plan alternatives, and an array of employee choice models have dramatically increased the complexity of the large group underwriting process.

The majority of this chapters discusses the underwriting of various forms of group medical benefits. A separate discussion of underwriting group disability insurance and group life insurance is provided in the final two sections.

THE MARKET

The term "large group" can refer to as few as 50 or 100 employees, up to the largest health and welfare plan in the private or public sector. In the 1990s, most states passed small group reform laws that generally apply to groups with fewer than 51 employees. This leaves three larger group market segments:

- Pooled groups (typically 51 to 200 employees). The ACA requires this to move to 100 as the minimum starting in 2016.
- Experience-rated groups (200 to 1,000 employees).
- Large groups (1,000 or more employees).

This chapter uses the term "employees" broadly, even though the plan's members may not always be employees. Eligible groups are defined by law, and include single-employer plans, associations, labor unions, multiple-employer trusts, employer coalitions, and government plans. The most common coverages include life, disability, medical, and dental benefits. Plan designs are flexible and are often customized to meet the needs of larger groups. Employees may be able to choose from several coverage or benefit options, and they sometimes may even choose between competing insurers and provider networks.

The major focus of this chapter is underwriting of single-employer group medical plans in the U.S., with most of the emphasis being on groups with over 200 employees. We will highlight some unique challenges posed by "jumbo" groups (over 5,000 lives), and by a broad range of managed care options available to most large groups.

SOME BASIC PRINCIPLES

The underwriting of large groups involves risk selection and financial projections, based on aggregate data and historical trends, for a specific group plan or for a class of plans with similar characteristics. The very nature of group insurance offers some inherent risk and underwriting protection, because the employee risk pool consists largely of individuals who are sufficiently healthy to work full time.

Key risk factors include demographics, industry, financial outlook, workforce stability, work site location(s), insurer persistency, and levels of employee and dependent participation in the plan. For managed care plans, risk assessment includes an analysis of provider access (that is, how accessible will the provider network be to the employees) and projected in-network usage and cost savings.

Prior loss ratio or utilization data of a particular group is often considered in pricing. The degree of credibility given to prior experience data varies according to the size and nature of the group and type of coverage.

Fully insured experience rating is quite common for medical and dental plans with as few as 100 enrollees, usually with pooling of large medical claims. Retrospective experience rating is less common, but it can appeal to groups with 500 to 1,000 employees. Minimum size requirements are significantly higher for life and disability, where claim experience is more volatile due to lower frequencies of loss and varying amounts of coverage by employee. Credibility thresholds may be lower for products that have less volatility, such as group dental policies.

The prior claim experience of a large group has traditionally been the major factor used to project future costs, especially for health care. This is still true, but today's pricing models must also consider the dynamics of managed care plans, multiple-choice scenarios, relaxed rules for plan participation, defined contribution strategies, and the resulting implications for antiselection.

In many respects, the employer and carrier often have similar goals; for example, both want to see low claim costs, high quality, and satisfied employees. They may have somewhat different views on other aspects of the program, such as profit margins or funding methods. One of the underwriter's primary goals is to offer financial arrangements that enable both parties to accomplish their objectives.

SALES INTERACTION

It is important to involve the sales representative in the process of determining the best rate to be offered. One approach may be to structure a component of the incentive compensation program to encourage selling the value of the insurer rather than just price. Another is to reward the sales representative for selling rates at full margin, as determined by the underwriting and actuarial areas, instead of negotiating a lower rate just to increase the likelihood of closing the renewal or sale.

It is also important for the sales representative to appropriately qualify a prospect. This involves first determining the minimum information necessary for quoting experience rated business, and then communicating the purpose and value of obtaining the information to the prospective account. The effective date, current and requested benefits, prior carrier information, census, employees' ZIP codes, employer contribution, benefit design parameters, waiting periods, industry, sole insurer vs. multiple insurers, large claim data, specific provider use with billed or paid amounts, active and retiree information, current rates, and fees are often requested.

UNDERWRITING CYCLE

In the 1960s through 1990s, many insurers experienced a strong cycle of gains and losses, often manifesting as three years of gains followed by three years of losses. This phenomenon has been attributed to the timing lag of claims experience, the lag between premium quotes and actual implementation, and over-reliance on recent financial experience. Beginning in the 1990s, the underwriting cycle moderated significantly. This was likely due to increased computing power resulting in a shorter lag between experience and reporting, faster provider payments reducing the claims lag, and moderating medical cost trends.

Care should be given to not create an underwriting cycle by increasing premiums too much during periods of poor financial performance, while overly decreasing premiums when experience is better than expected. To reduce the underwriting cycle, it is important to recognize the underwriting cycle when setting premium rates, marketing goals, and management incentives.

EMERGING HEALTH CARE PROVIDER REIMBURSEMENT

New technology has introduced new ways that a health care provider may interact with patients. Telemedicine is emerging in many markets, allowing a patient to see a provider remotely instead of in-person. Examples include communication between provider and patient via telephone, e-mail, or video conference. The goal is to still have patient provider interaction but more efficiently and at lower cost. While this technology may produce savings, it is not common practice to prospectively reduce rates for telemedicine implementation. State regulations vary on practices that are allowed from a remote location. For example, some states allow a provider to prescribe certain drugs remotely while others do not.

Value-based payment initiatives are also affecting provider delivery and reimbursement. "Pay for value not volume" programs include pay for performance initiatives, shared savings, and bundled payments. It is incumbent on the underwriter to understand the nature of the changing claims data in the underwriting process.

ACA PROGRAM DESIGN CONSIDERATIONS

In the U.S., the ACA requires several items that large group underwriters should consider in reviewing the plan design for a particular customer. For example, groups with more than 50 FTEs (full-time equivalents) are subject to employer penalties if health benefit offerings do not meet certain criteria. The ACA specifies that plans offered by large employers must meet Minimum Value (MV). The following conditions must be met for a benefit plan to be MV:

- The actuarial value of the benefit must be at least 60%. Actuarial value is the proportion of health benefit dollars paid by the insurer as opposed to the member (computed as expected plan paid dollars divided by expected allowed dollars). The tool for testing the 60% threshold is standardized, and its production and release is managed by Health and Human Services (HHS).

- The ACA requires that certain classes of benefits be covered for a plan to meet MV (for example, inpatient, physician services, and pharmaceuticals). This guidance effectively eliminates "skinny" plans from qualifying as MV. Skinny plans are benefit plans that cover only limited benefits (for example, physician visits only), but cover these benefits at much greater level than 60% in order to compensate for other coverages that are entirely missing.

- Employer penalties would apply for those full-time employees whose benefits do not meet MV; the ACA defines full time as 30 hours or more per week. A 5% allowance is allowed for employees who fail to meet MV.

Benefit plans must allow the employee the option to cover dependents, though the ACA's definition of dependent does not include spouses. This leads to some market demand for premium tier structures that exclude spouses.

The ACA imposes maximum waiting periods before benefits must be offered to eligible new employees. The underwriter should consider the risk shorter waiting periods creates, especially for lower skilled jobs that could be sought solely for health benefits.

The plan must be affordable to avoid employer penalties, with affordable defined by the ACA at the individual employee level. Affordable plans cost the employee less than 9.5% of his or her income for employee-only (single) coverage. Employers must consider whether it is more beneficial to offer affordable coverage to all employees via more complex subsidization constructs that vary by employee income levels, or to simply risk paying penalties for certain employees. Typically, employer premium subsidization and income levels are such that penalties are not applicable, though there are circumstances where this is not the case. In reaction to these penalties, some employers have directed more premium subsidization towards single coverage, and away from dependent coverage to keep overall costs level. While the strategy regarding affordability is complex and determined by the employer, the insurer's underwriter should consider implications that changing employer subsidization policies have on the group's expected claims.

The ACA created penalties for those enrolled in particularly rich health benefit plans, which has become known as the Cadillac Tax. The ACA sets an upper limit each year for total premium. Starting in 2018 (assuming no repeal occurs), premiums in excess of the upper limit must be paid using post-income tax dollars for both employers and enrollees. Many employers are revising plan designs to have higher deductibles, member coinsurance, co-pays and out-of-pocket limits in reaction to this penalty.

PUBLIC EXCHANGES

The public exchanges created by the ACA were primarily designed for individuals and small employers, but they create an additional dynamic for the large group underwriter. From the employee perspective, the availability of exchange subsidies has changed the equation of comparing costs between individual plans and group plan options for employees and their dependents. This has led some employers to drop dependent coverage and transition non-Medicare retirees to public exchanges. Over time, the dynamics of the individual market rate levels and the subsidy calculation may allow older individuals to have an opportunity to retire early, creating a younger mix in the employer group market. Gravely ill employees may feel more inclined to leave their employer, or employer coverage, to seek out a specific treatment offered by the individual market, or simply to focus on getting well. COBRA enrollment will decline, particularly for those employers where health claims cost is high. Dependents from high income families are more likely to enroll in group policies than low income families for whom subsidies are available through the individual market. In other words, the underwriter should consider the changing demographics of groups due to the public exchange alternatives now available.

PRIVATE EXCHANGES

A recent development affecting large group health insurance is the advent of private exchanges. Spurred by the ACA, private exchanges serve a function similar to public exchanges by having insurers offer similar benefits and allowing choice between benefit plans, and often insurers, for employees. For example, an employer may decide to offer two benefit levels from three insurers and allow employees to make an individual choice inside this framework. This creates antiselection risk that the underwriter must consider. Often, private exchanges are established and administered by large employee benefit consulting groups.

NEW BUSINESS UNDERWRITING

CHARACTERISTICS OF THE GROUP

A number of criteria are used to screen, approve, and classify large group prospects. They vary by insurer, coverage, and size of group. This section will focus on seven key dimensions: (1) age and gender, (2) location or area, (3) type of industry, (4) financial strength, (5) ease of administration, (6) level of participation, and (7) prior persistency.

Age and Gender

Demographic composition is one of the most important risk characteristics of a group. Age is a highly correlating factor with future mortality and morbidity. Gender mix also impacts both life and health claim costs, and age-gender factors are good predictors for several specific medical conditions such as pregnancy and heart disease, though some states do not allow gender to be used as a rating factor in underwriting large groups. Average family size, and resulting adult/child mix, can be an important risk factor for medical plans. Plans with a high percentage of retirees will have higher claim costs for group life and medical (prior to Medicare offsets), and often require more intense administrative services. As predictive modeling becomes more prevalent in underwriting, care needs to be taken so that the predictive model does not overlap (double count) age and gender.

Location or Area

Geographic location(s) can also be a risk variable for most group coverage. There are significant regional and local differences in health care practices and prices. This can be attributed at least partially to the level of competition resulting from an over- or under-supply of providers. In many urban areas, costs are high due to cost shifting from Medicare, Medicaid, Health Maintenance Organizations (HMOs), and other preferential programs. However, rural providers often have a monopoly on patients, such that sometimes rural providers charge more per service than their urban and suburban counterparts.

Type of Industry

Industry is often a major factor in assessing new groups, and it is one of the primary considerations for disability insurance (where the defining benefit trigger relates directly the an insured's ability to perform the duties of his or her occupation). Some industries expose employees to health hazards or to high stress levels, while other industries have high costs because of benefit entitlement attitudes or close proximity and access to the health care system. More commonly, industry risk appears to be related to the age, gender, lifestyles, and socio-economic content of the insureds. When thinking about industry differences, it is important to identify what differences are already accounted for by other factors, and focus on accounting for the remaining unexplained risks caused by industry differences.

Some industries pose substandard risk and administrative challenges, due to unstable employment levels, workforce seasonality, low wages, or high turnover. This is compounded by requirements imposed by COBRA, HIPAA, and state regulations. Certain industries have a reputation for particularly rich or lean benefit plans or employer subsidization levels. Others tend to sponsor employee wellness programs. While there is little statistical evidence linking wellness programs to lower employee benefit costs, some underwriters view them favorably.

Financial Stability

Financial strength and credit rating are important risk criteria. Some important questions include: Does the group have a history of making timely payments? Is there a risk of insolvency? If there are alternate funding methods, who will bear the risk for claim runout liabilities? Who will hold the monies? Is the business cycle trending up or down? Does the employer plan an expansion or merger?

Business downturns often lead to reductions in staff. Since downsizing tends to be uneven among job classes, age groups, and locations, it can result in dramatic shifts in demographic factors. Also, actual or anticipated layoffs may produce a spike in disability claims and in utilization of elective medical and dental services. Due to employee antiselection and generous retrospective enrollment rules, the true average cost of COBRA is much higher than the 102% of unsubsidized active premium that employers are allowed to charge. Caveats are often included in quotes that reserve the right to reprice if the enrollment changes by 10% or more from the enrollment that the quote is based on. Life plans tend to see antiselection in the form of either premium waiver claims, requests for portable benefits, or applications for conversion policies.

Ease of Administration

Underlying administrative costs are a major consideration for the group underwriter and client. Larger groups offer the opportunity for higher productivity and economies of scale. On the other hand, this advantage can be offset by added complexity, such as when there are multiple sub-groups, plan designs, work sites, unions, vendors, procedures, dedicated customer service teams, numerous incoming enrollment reports, numerous outgoing analytical reports, or numerous points of contact.

The larger a group is, the greater the emphasis on administrative services and costs. Jumbo groups tend to have highly customized services requiring the underwriter to work closely with his or her administrative experts to assess cost. A major component of the case review is devoted to evaluating the customer's ability to provide accurate and timely data on employee enrollment, terminations, and status changes. Does the employer or carrier prepare and distribute benefit summaries, ID cards, claim forms, and other communication materials? If the employer has several affiliated companies or work sites, do they have uniform and adequate human resources and information technology resources? Very large groups may request carrier performance guarantees (discussed later in this chapter) that warrant pricing consideration.

Retiree sub-groups often require special administrative cost and pricing consideration, because coordination of benefits with Medicare is more common and complicates the claim adjudication process with many claims requiring special and burdensome oversight from the claims processing staff. Further, because of the older ages of these sub-groups, there are many more claims per person and more (and longer) customer service calls. Finally, retiree sub-groups typically have different geographic and travel network access needs than their at-work counterparts, which impacts administrative costs (positively or negatively) as compared to their at-work counterparts.

Level of Participation

In the past, insurers usually required that employers paid at least a minimum portion (such as 50%) of the premiums for each benefit plan. This requirement helped keep premiums attractive for healthier employees and dependents, and thus mitigated the risk to the insurer. The traditional minimum participation rule was 75%, but was often modified to consider all health plan options offered by the employer, as well as spouses' employers. However, the ACA now requires guarantee issue for major medical health insurance, even for large groups. Thus, many major medical insurers have added participation and contribution levels to their rating formulas. In the small group market, the ACA generally allows insurers to apply minimum participation and minimum contribution requirements. There are other considerations the underwriter must take into account. For example, if members choose a public exchange option, should they be counted towards participation? How should declining spouse participation be considered for employers that change spousal eligibility or subsidization?

Adequate plan participation is an important risk factor for a group, but can be difficult to assess in an environment of multiple options, dual-income families, and defined contribution packages. The large group underwriter should review the entire employee benefit program, including competitors' plans, and attempt to balance underwriting principles with market demands for consumer choice. To the extent that credible claim experience reflects the current participation levels, the underwriter has to anticipate future enrollment changes in developing prices or caveats.

Carrier Persistency

Installation and setup of a very large new group account can be extremely expensive, and competitive pricing pressures do not allow room to recoup these costs in the first or second contract year. Therefore, underwriters should carefully review a prospective client's track record of persistency with prior insurers. Groups that go to market every year, or every time a rate guarantee expires, may find fewer and fewer bidders. For requests for proposals (RFPs) for very large employers, it is common for bidders to offer administrative deals that decrease fees with increasing contract length.

Large employers must also consider the internal costs associated with implementing and communicating a new plan, and the potential disruption of patient-provider relationships due to changing managed care networks. Depending on the situation, these factors may result in a bias for the status quo, requests for multi-year contracts, or adding new insurer options to fill in geographic "gaps" or to foster employee choice.

Other Considerations

Larger employers often opt for self-funded Administration Services Only (ASO) contracts to obtain financial benefits, such as to avoid state premium taxes, insurers' risk margins, and state benefit mandates, as well as to more closely manage cash flows. Minimum premium plans are hybrids that offer most of the financial benefits of self-funding, along with risk protection that is similar to retrospective-rated insured plans. These funding alternatives are less common for HMOs, due in part to regulatory restrictions and complications of provider participation in risk when capitation arrangements are involved.

The underwriting of large groups has placed little emphasis on the health status of individuals, with the main exceptions being review of applications for large amounts of life insurance and pricing stop loss insurance.

HIPAA and related state regulations prohibit discrimination based on health status and promote health care access. HIPAA includes provisions that prohibit the use of evidence of insurability for late entrants and mandates that late entrants who experience a qualifying event be treated as on-time enrollees. HIPAA also includes Administrative Simplification and Privacy sections, designed to standardize the electronic exchange of health care data and protect the security and privacy of individual's health records. The portability protections of HIPAA have largely been made obsolete by the ACA's guarantee issue requirements in the individual market. HIPAA generally does not apply to group life and disability coverages.

The ACA attempts to further promote health care access and consumer choice, with a number of initiatives including: (1) expanding HIPAA protections through creating further prohibitions on pre-existing condition exclusions, (2) restricting the use of lifetime maximums, (3) prohibiting annual benefit maximums on essential health benefits, (4) requiring that most groups offer coverage to dependents up until age 26, and (5) most significantly, creating a health insurance exchange that is available on a guaranteed-issue basis without pre-existing condition exclusions. The ACA encourages groups to reconsider benefit design and premium subsidization, since low income employees that enroll in the insurance exchange create penalty risks and new administrative burdens for most groups.

Since most large employer groups allow for employee choice of plan, and employees are typically able to switch between plans during an annual open enrollment period without any underwriting or benefit restrictions, there is a high degree of employee antiselection. The cost of consumer choice varies, both within a group due to multiple benefit offerings, and from group to group.

Plan Design

Effective plan design can help to keep the total plan affordable for both employers and employees. The trend among larger employers has been to offer employees a broad menu of choices, with the employer making a fixed dollar maximum contribution toward the cost. Some larger employers are now scaling back the number of benefit plan and carrier choices, while many smaller employer groups are adding more plan options. Health care options often feature a dual choice scenario, where insurers compete at the individual employee level based on relative benefits, price, access, quality and other factors. Therefore, underwriters should review the design and features of their proposed plan(s) in relation to competing options, with a goal of optimizing enrollment and controlling antiselection.

Group term life insurance plan designs have become extremely flexible. Employees are often free to select an amount of insurance ranging from zero to several times annual earnings with few, if any, underwriting restrictions as long as they are actively at work, at least at the time of initial enrollment. Underwriting safeguards include a balanced spread of risk by age/gender, income, and plan option, as well as minimum participation rates, age reductions, and (at least short form) evidence of insurability for abnormally large amounts ($500,000 or more). Optional life plans often use attained age step rates. These issues are expanded on later in this chapter, as well as Chapter 11, "Group Life Insurance Benefits."

Plan design is an important factor in evaluating group short- or long-term disability benefit plans. Key elements include the length of the elimination period, the percentage of compensation to be replaced, benefit offsets for other sources of disability income (such as Social Security and Workers Compensation), the liberalness of the policy in regard to an "any" versus "own" occupation definition of disability, the use of limitations for certain types of disabilities such as psychiatric claims, and the maximum duration of benefit payments. The underwriter must look at features of a group disability plan in the context of overall economic conditions, the specific job skills of a particular industry, and the employment outlook for that job or geographic area, as well as the employer's commitment to assist and accommodate the return to work of rehabilitating employees. These issues are discussed later in this chapter, as well as in Chapter 12, "Group Disability Income Benefits."

Traditional fee-for-service health plans try to control costs through a combination of deductible and coinsurance features, contractual limitations and coverage exclusions, and by limits on negotiated provider fees, or similar plan design features. HMOs often have rich benefits for preventive and routine care by primary care providers in a network setting, with modest employee co-pays. More expensive specialty and facility care may be subject to pre-approval and higher employee out-of-pocket payments. Open access HMOs address consumer demand for self-referral by relaxing pre-authorization rules in exchange for higher employee co-pays or premiums. A Preferred Provider Plan or a Point-of-Service plan will usually allow a patient to use any provider, but the plan will pay a significantly lower proportion of benefits for non-network care, and employees may expose themselves to "balance billing" which is paying the difference between allowed cost and billed charges of a non-network provider.

The ACA requires that most medical plans provide 100% payment for in-network preventive benefits. Further, plans may no longer apply annual maximums lifetime maximums on essential health benefits. Plans exempted from the ACA's requirements include "retiree-only" plans, certain plans that sought and were granted exemption from the ACA, and those plans that sought and maintain "grandfathered" status (though these plans have limited relief from the ACA and must follow certain ACA provisions). For more information on the ACA rules and subsequent guidance, see the chapter titled "Health Care Policy" or visit the CMS website.[1]

Managed care plan design and network access must be viewed together. The underwriter has to project plan participation and in-network usage for all competing plans. This entails a geographic match of employee residences (or work sites) to network provider offices. For larger groups, it is also common to prepare a disruption analysis of the providers who participate in each network, to determine how a new insurer or new plan type would affect existing employee/physician relationships.

The variety and customized nature of large group insurance plans present a significant challenge to the underwriter, who must assess the relative value and effectiveness of all available plan designs, utilization controls, and health care delivery systems. Then, he or she must attempt to anticipate the impact of employee choice. This assessment will become even more complex now that health insurance exchanges have expanded employee choice, as well as providing employers a point of comparison of premium rates.

EVALUATING THE EXPERIENCE

The access to, and the use of, group-specific prior experience data is a unique feature of underwriting large groups. The larger the group, the more critical this information becomes. At the low end of the larger case market, an employer group with 100 employees might have manual or community rates. Through the mid-sized range, the underwriter will apply more and more credibility to prior experience data. For very large groups, it is common to apply full credibility to prior experience, especially for health benefits. Even at full credibility, large claims are often pooled across the block. As group size increases, the level for pooling large claims also increases. Intense competition for the most attractive groups may sometimes tempt the underwriter to use a credibility factor that may not be actuarially sound.

Prior experience reports come in many forms, formats, and degrees of accuracy. The underwriter is looking to answer two basic questions: (1) Can I identify meaningful past results and trends? and (2) How can I apply this information to projected costs for the proposed plan(s) and eligible group(s)?

The goal in evaluating prior experience data for new business is to know the risk as well as the existing insurer. While this is often impractical, there are many techniques to help determine if the information is valid, reliable, and useful. The underwriter might consider: Is the information current and complete? Is it accurate? Is it consistent over time? Is it based on the most appropriate plans and population? Does it reflect underlying business trends and cycles? Is claim data provided on a cash basis or incurred basis? Are there any fees included in the claim data? Do the reserve levels appear to be adequate? Are they redundant? Are claims reflective of enrollment for the given time period? Were there benefit changes during the given time period? Do claims include or exclude high dollar or catastrophic claims? The answer to any of these questions may provide a key piece in the underwriter's puzzle.

---

[1] http://www.hhs.gov/ociio/regulations/index.html

Various internal checks may be used to determine whether prior experience information is accurate and reliable. For example, reported premiums can be tested in relation to past premium rate and exposure data. Reserves for incurred but not reported claim liabilities may be compared to prior claim run-out data. Reviewing month-by-month data may reveal distortions due to unusual claim patterns or administrative problems. Using an independent source such as Equifax to obtain employer-related information is often helpful to the underwriter in verifying the accuracy of information.

Group Life

Group life claim experience tends to be relatively volatile, due to a low frequency of loss and often wide variation in amounts of coverage. Even for jumbo groups, many insurers try to smooth out the blips in claim experience by looking at several years of data or by using a blend of case-specific and book-of-business experience. Pooling of large claims is common, with the pooling point tending to increase with the size of the group. Claim experience is usually more stable for basic life plans due to employer contributions and uniform amounts of insurance coverage than for optional life plans, which tend to be employee-paid and offer more choices. Life evaluations are complicated by the fact that industry practices vary with respect to pooling, disability waiver of premium reserves, conversion charges, portability, report close-out dates, and interest payments to beneficiaries. The underwriter must know the competition to understand how these things will affect the experience.

Disability Income

Group disability income (especially long-term disability) experience also reflects low claim frequencies but large potential liabilities. As with life coverage, the underwriter will review multi-year data and will often use blending and pooling techniques to increase the statistical confidence of his or her projections. The underwriter must consider reporting lags, since many long-term disability plans have elimination periods of 90 or 180 days, meaning that claims may not be reported for many months after they are incurred and that a complete list of claims may not be available for recent reporting periods. Reserves for future benefit payments are critical, and industry methods vary such that the disability underwriter ideally will have sufficient information about each open claim (including age, duration, and diagnosis) to validate reserve levels. The experience data will also be reviewed to detect any abnormal patterns that may be due to business cycles or industry risks, because it is common to have more disability claims in times of economic downturn or in industries in decline.

Medical Plans

For a large, stable group, most carriers consider one year of medical claim experience to be an adequate sample to project future costs. For indemnity plans, the projection may involve simply adjusting incurred claims with expected large claims rather than actual large claims, and then inflating for trend. That is, projecting normal size claims from what has occurred is fairly typical, but normalization is still needed for large claims. The underwriter might also make adjustments to reflect differences in cost containment programs, claim controls, or provider discounts.

Managed care and multiple plan options can complicate the evaluation process. If the experience data reflect another insurer's managed care plan, it can be a challenge to understand the underlying price and utilization dynamics, and quantify the effects of replacing (or even more complex - coexisting with) that program. The underwriter must be able to build a model that compares the two offerings in terms of service area, size of network, access to providers, out-of-pocket differences, selection, antiselection, projected enrollment, in-network usage, provider payment/reimbursement contracts (by type of service or provider), and utilization management.

Service area and network size data are usually readily available. Ease of access can be measured by matching provider locations to a census of employees' home or work ZIP codes. Software tools can be used to determine the degree of access for urban, suburban, and rural areas. Another method is a disruption analysis, where prior claims or provider selections are matched to the bidder's contracted network. Enrollment and in-system usage for the proposed plan will depend on network area, size and access, and other factors such as employee out-of-pocket payments and competing HMO options. These estimates involve both art and science, but the tools have become quite sophisticated.

Provider contracts are usually proprietary, so determining the value of a competitor's provider reimbursement arrangement can be a difficult step in evaluating managed care experience data. It is desirable to maintain a database that precisely defines an insurer's own network contracts and corresponding provider discounts. When possible, the database should be used on an area-specific basis to compare discounts of the current insurer. This type of comparison takes on many forms, and is generally referred to as "re-pricing."

Large employer RFPs often provide experience reports that summarize billed charges, plan payments (after provider discounts and patient liability), utilization statistics, or other forms or combinations of claim experience. The data may be aggregated, or split by network area, type of service or provider, or benefit plan. Managed care claim experience often includes capitation payments, or various other forms of non-traditional provider compensation. The challenge for the underwriter is to identify the services that are included in these charges to project the corresponding cost of care under the proposed plans and compensation methods.

In addition to case-specific experience data, the underwriter may have access to plan-wide data for other insurers. Over time, an underwriter tends to develop a working knowledge of major competitors' provider arrangements and utilization results through experience and networking.

Beyond different prices per unit of care, utilization of services varies widely by type of health plan, network efficiency, and intensity of utilization management. The underwriter must try to quantify the value of health care management inherent in the prior claim experience and try to estimate the relative impact of tighter or looser controls for each proposed plan type. The looser end of the spectrum includes rich fee-for-service indemnity plans, with little financial incentive for either providers or patients to be concerned about third party payer costs. At the tighter end, an HMO plan might have restricted access, pre-authorization rules for most non-primary care, and provider compensation methods that reward low utilization rates for expensive services. Most modern health care plans fall between these extremes and feature varying degrees of compromise between optimal cost savings and consumer demand for access, choice, and minimal hassle.

The methods used to project claim costs under a new plan, using experience from a different plan, will depend on provider reimbursement arrangements. If both plans pay discounted charges for service, then one could merely adjust the current claim cost data for differentials in the plans' discounts, utilization management savings, and in-system usage, with appropriate consideration for trend. On the other hand, if the current plan pays on a discounted fee-for-service basis for care that would be capitated under the proposed plan, or vice versa, then the underwriter may have to use different pricing methods by type of service or provider.

In general, the first step is to look at each component of the prior experience data to identify the pieces that provide credible information about the utilization patterns of the employer group or sub-group. The next step is to identify which cost of care components under the proposed new plan should be adjusted to consider the prior experience data, and the amount of the adjustments. The cost for capitated services might be a fixed amount per head, or adjusted for age and gender, with little or no consideration given to prior claim data. On the other hand, the pricing of non-capitated services might be highly influenced by the prior experience data. So, the underwriter should have a good working knowledge of provider compensation methods and the types of providers and services for the old and new plan.

Today, evaluating and projecting managed care claim costs for large groups invariably requires dealing with multiple choice scenarios. The table below shows the type of format that might be seen in large group RFPs to illustrate the key assumptions made by the underwriter in projecting claim costs for multiple plan options. This example is of a large employer who currently offers one comprehensive major medical (CMM) plan for all employees, and will newly offer the three options shown in the illustration below – an HMO, a PPO, and a high deductible indemnity plan. Initial relative benefit values were determined as if all participants enrolled in each option. Provider discounts and utilization savings are relative to the base year claim data, which in this example reflects no discounts and minimal cost containment or utilization management. Selection and antiselection assumptions are based on the drivers discussed in Chapter 31, "Managing Selection in a Multiple-Choice Environment."

Weighting the selection and antiselection assumptions by enrollment produces a composite factor of 1.023, indicating that giving multiple plan choices to employees results in higher costs, an outcome which is often overlooked. However, despite this increase in cost, the projected annual cost of care is reduced from $10,350 to $8,514 per employee because of the effect of newly achieved provider savings and utilization discounts. Of course, the total cost for any of the proposed plans would also have to consider administrative expenses, risk charges, taxes, and other retention items.

The following illustration is simplistic in four major ways. First, it assumes that there is no existing managed care plan (and thus no average discount savings in the current plan), while most large employers are likely to offer one or more managed health care plans. If such a plan is reflected in the prior year claim experience, the factors to adjust for the changes in plan benefits, provider discounts, and utilization savings would change for each of the proposed plan options. For example, if the prior claim data reflected an average discount savings of 15%, then the relative adjustment factor for the proposed HMO plan would be about .88 (.75/.85). An alternative method is to add an extra step to build the estimated savings for existing managed care plans back into the prior claim data to approximate the cost of a pure indemnity plan and then proceed with the cost projections for all proposed plans using the full managed care adjustment factors as shown in our illustration.

Projecting Multiple Option Claim Costs					
			Proposed Flexible Options		
	CMM	HMO	Point-of-Service		High Deductible Indemnity
			In-Network	Out-of-Network	
Prior Year Claims per Employee	$9,000	$9,000	$9,000	$9,000	$9,000
Adjust for:					
Relative Benefit Value	× 1.00	× 1.15	× 1.05	× 0.95	× 0.65
Provider Discount Savings	× 1.00	× 0.75	× 0.82	× 1.00	× 1.00
Utilization Savings	× 1.00	× 0.91	× 0.96	× 1.00	× 1.00
Trend	× 1.15	× 1.11	× 1.12	× 1.15	× 1.17
Mix of Network Usage	N/A	N/A	80%/20%		N/A
"100% Enrollment" Claim Cost	$10,350	$7,841	$8,632		$6,845
Projected Enrollment	N/A	35%	60%		5%
Selection and Antiselection	1.00	0.92	1.11		0.70
Projected Claims per Employee	$10,350	$7,214	$9,582		$4,791

The second over-simplification is that the example does not contemplate the common scenario where an employer's plan offers competing dual choice plans. If we were to complicate the example by assuming two current insurers, with separate claim experience and demographic data available, then the underwriter might perform a separate claim cost projection for each of the two insurers' members, and then calculate composite costs for each proposed plan option based on a best estimate of any enrollment changes. If the new benefit program will include dual choice competition, then the factors to adjust for selection and antiselection should attempt to anticipate changes in the risk pool. In general, offering multiple benefit options to employees tends to increase the impact of antiselection and thus cost.

One key to projecting the selection impact on a plan is to understand the method used to calculate employee contributions, or conversely, the employer's premium subsidization. The third oversimplification in the example is the failure to include and consider this information in our analysis.

The final major over-simplification in the example is the use of a simple high deductible indemnity plan. With these plans, it is far more common to accompany them with an employee account that pays employee cost-sharing expenses. The antiselection analysis is more complex with plans tied to employee accounts. This is because the account offers unique tax benefits and changes the benefit design so that it attracts a mix of risks. Enrollment in these plans depends highly on the employer's communication of the benefit as well as the employees' comprehension of the option's overall value.

Medicare Part D

The Medicare Modernization Act created the biggest change in Medicare Programs since 1965. Beginning on January 1, 2006, Medicare beneficiaries can have a prescription drug benefit – Medicare Part D. The availability of this benefit has caused many employers to reconsider the health care options offered to their retirees, and has led insurers to reconsider the pricing of Medigap and Medicare carve-out contracts.

The ACA further made the Medicare Part D plan option attractive to employers who offer retiree healthcare coverage for a number of reasons. First, the Medicare Part D plan design is gradually becoming richer through 2020. Second, the federal government secured a 50% discount concession from manufacturers of brand name drugs offered on the Medicare Part D formulary, and such discounts make Part D pricing particularly attractive when compared to previous rates. Third, employers are newly discouraged from offering retirees commercial drug plans with the 28% rebate from the Retiree Drug Subsidy (RDS) alternative program, since RDS proceeds will no longer be exempt from federal tax income, starting in 2013. Not all employers or retirees will be best served by moving to Medicare Part D plans, because the commercial/RDS alternative can produce lower costs for those who offer a tighter generic-based formulary that avoids costly brand name drugs in the first place (avoided costs for both the employer and the retiree). Also, many employers who collect RDS do not pay income taxes.

Wellness Programs

Wellness programs are employer-sponsored activities and programs to improve employee wellness. Examples include on-site health screenings, self-assessment computer modules offered to employees, rebates for fitness club memberships, smoking cessation programs, on-site flu shot clinics, financial incentives for exercise and healthy eating, financial incentives for meeting certain biometric thresholds and participating in disease management educational programs. The impact of wellness programs on claim experience is difficult to measure. Most underwriters give little, if any, significant credit to premium rate projections for these programs on a prospective basis. Any impact is perceived to be reflected in claim experience further in the future than the time represented in a renewal projection. It is not uncommon to add the administrative expense for these programs to rates.

Dental and Vision Plans

Dental and vision plans carry an inherent risk of antiselection, since insureds often have discretion over the nature and timing of the services provided. Much of the care is elective, and the insured or provider may be able to select among plan options, schedule appointments, and select courses of treatment that will maximize benefit payments.

Most group dental plans have several features designed to reduce antiselection. Patients' out-of-pocket sharing is often low or non-existent for diagnostic and preventive procedures, moderate for basic restorative work, and substantial for expensive major services like crowns or orthodontia. Age or frequency limits are common for some procedures, such as X-rays. Most plans have "missing tooth" exclusions and restrictions on replacement work. See Chapter 6, "Dental Benefits in the US," for more information on dental plan design.

Traditional underwriting rules require strict minimum participation requirements for dental plans, or require that plans be packaged with group medical plans to limit antiselection.

However, market changes toward defined contributions and consumer choice are driving rapid growth in voluntary dental plans, where the employer contribution is small or zero. The underwriter's main defenses are higher premium rates, reduced benefits, and various types of contractual or underwriting protections. To keep premiums low, these plans usually have higher patient out-of-pocket costs, lower benefit maximums (such as $500 to $1,000 per year), and more restrictive contract provisions. A wide range of special protections includes an extended waiting period for most major services, and "lock-in" or "lock-out" provisions designed to prevent jumping into and out of the plan. See Chapter 22, "Estimating Dental Claim Costs," for more information on these strategies and tactics.

New business pricing methods for existing dental plans are similar to medical methods. Claim experience data is credible for stable groups with 200 or more employees, since dental claim experience is much less volatile than medical. With the growth of PPO and dental HMO plans, dental pricing must consider adjustments for different networks, dual choice options, and antiselection not unlike those required for medical plans. Groups with no prior dental plan require special underwriting care to offset accumulated neglect and a likely utilization blip in the first plan year.

Traditional group vision plans include frequency limits (such as one or two years between covered routine eye exams) and feature a closed list of covered benefits based on a fixed payment schedule. In the past, most such plans were packaged with medical plans, and the risk was predictable and stable. With new technology and wider choices in vision care, the trend is to replace traditional vision care plans with employer sponsored discount programs, HMO rider plans, or pre-tax health spending accounts.

DEVELOPING THE PROPOSAL

Basic Considerations

Large group RFPs are often correspondingly large with lengthy questionnaires and highly detailed financial exhibits. No matter how complex the task may be, the essence of the proposal process is to take all that has been learned about the group, plan design, and prior experience, and present a package that is both financially sound and attractive to the buyer.

Most large case RFPs include specifications for the proposed plan designs, which are frequently highly customized. The specifications for a jumbo group may include the option to carve out benefits or services to specialty vendors. Traditionally, large national employers place a high value on providing uniform benefits in all locations, which can be a challenge with varying state regulations (one reason many employers favor administrative services only arrangements). However, it is also common for the RFP to request bidders to propose alternate plans, if they believe this would improve their offer. Indeed, several of the Fortune 500 companies subscribe to "the best local plan" philosophy in purchasing managed care, especially for HMOs. Recently, Accountable Care Organizations (ACOs) are garnering much attention in the marketplace and are being placed as alternatives on many large employer RFPs. ACOs have similar aspirations as HMOs in terms of their focus on prevention, quality, and efficiency, but ACOs presently have less of a negative connotation than HMOs regarding limiting access to care and specialists. It remains to be seen whether ACOs will significantly contribute to curbing health care costs nationally; much of the financial responsibility is placed with providers themselves and their efforts will vary. Recent initial guidance from Centers for Medicare & Medicaid Services on their own ACO sponsorship for Medicare patients has been discouraging, because their proposed quality measures are numerous and unfocused, and the financial rewards for providers who achieve more efficient care are small with downside risk nearly as likely.

To complete the proposal exhibits that relate to claim risk, the underwriter must address plan design, funding arrangements, and enrollment patterns that may be unique. In theory, most rating and funding methods are similar (albeit with different risk charges) for groups with 1,000 or 50,000 employees. In practice, the larger the group, the more likely it is that the underwriter will encounter unanticipated risk issues that are not covered in his or her company's standard rate manuals.

Thoughtful underwriting requirements and caveats are equally as important as careful rate analysis. Where feasible, the major assumptions behind the claim projections should become stated conditions of the offer. Such caveats might address specified employer contributions, minimum participation (perhaps by plan option), stable demographics, major acquisitions or divestitures, restrictions on competing plans, and many other factors. Large employer groups are ever changing, so it is especially important to use caveats to cover contingencies that are beyond the insurer's control.

Comparing and validating competing insurers' likely projected claim costs for a managed care plan is a difficult task for employers and their consultants. Most of the larger broker or consulting firms send periodic surveys to health plans, and maintain extensive databases with cost and utilization figures by plan, location, and component of care. They also examine public data. Also, the RFP may include detailed questions and exhibits related to plan performance in managing health care costs. It is common to be asked to provide negotiated fees for sample procedures (or baskets of procedures, perhaps aimed at claims for those with chronic conditions) for several of their major worksite locations. An RFP for a self-funded plan may include an alternate request for insured premium rates, normally to keep the bidders honest. Conversely, an RFP for a fully insured plan may request a quote for a self-funded plan, to obtain more detailed information on the building blocks of the rates.

Another approach to keep a bidder transparent is to request a risk-sharing arrangement in an ASO RFP. Basically, each bidder is asked to project their annual (per contract) claim costs (the "target"). If actual claims exceed the target, then the administrator shares a percentage of the risk for excess claims up to a specified maximum, in the form of a year-end payment to the employer. Risk-sharing is typically based on incurred claims, often with deferred settlements to reduce the need to estimate Incurred But Not Reported (IBNR) liabilities.

A well-designed risk-sharing agreement should include a fair formula and reasonable caveats, such as:

- Adjustments for changes in demographics, or similar factors that are beyond the control of the administrator or network manager,
- A symmetric gain/loss sharing formula, or a risk charge,
- A risk-free corridor around the target claim cost (such as 3%), and
- Some form of pooling of experience, especially for non-jumbo groups.

In any event, the portion of risk shared for costs in excess of the upper end of the corridor cannot violate the self-insurance rules of the state. That is, too much risk taking on the administrator's part could cause the policy to be considered insured, and make the policy subject to benefit mandates and premium taxes.

Development of administrative expense charges might start with the administrator's standard expense allocation tables. These charges vary by product, and the tables usually group (at least direct) costs into major functional components, such as claim processing. The tabular charges are then modified to consider client-specific characteristics or services.

For jumbo groups, client-specific adjustments to expense charges may become more refined. If and where the administrator uses dedicated client service teams, the tabular expense charges for those functions might be replaced by the actual cost estimates. Cost accounting might also be used to determine the incremental expenses for extraordinary processes or services. Services provided by vendors or outsourcing firms may reduce the administrator's costs, but the savings may be offset by the cost of multiple interfaces. A thorough proposal should clearly define the type, scope, and intensity of services contemplated in the quoted price. It may be appropriate to remove charges for certain types of services from the base premiums or fees, and direct-bill based on actual emerging costs. Frequent direct-bill items include large (and hard to predict) printing and distribution jobs, and pass-through charges such as dedicated toll-free lines, wellness program charges, and costs relating to special reports and data to carve-out vendors and consultants.

Of course, expense charges should also include provisions for premium taxes, interest, risk charges, and profit. For managed care plans, there may be charges for network access from the prior administrator (where it may be unclear whether these charges are incorporated under administrative costs or collected through a load on claims) as well as the underwriter's own company, or there may be other payments to third parties. For larger groups, most of these charges tend to be customized to the group's own preferences, characteristics, and risk tolerance.

Very large groups often have less perceived need for insurance protection, so the quality and price of administrative services take on ever more importance as the size of the group increases. This has created the phenomenon of performance guarantees. This entails negotiating pre-set standards and metrics for customer service, and a schedule of premium or fee penalties (or far less often, rewards) if actual results deviate from the targets. Performance guarantees have been commonly used for ASO plans, but now arise in RFPs for all types of products and funding methods. Also, a bidder may proactively offer a performance guarantee to highlight a competitive strength and highlight their competitors' weakness.

Performance standards can cover the gamut of services and customer outcomes, but most often deal with the speed or accuracy of claim processing and customer service, including average call waiting times and issue resolution speed. Others might target specific concerns, such as prompt issue of employee ID cards, or responsiveness of the account manager. Managed care standards may encompass network size or access, distribution of provider directories, and member satisfaction surveys. Jumbo employers (with large fiduciary responsibilities) often request performance guarantees relating to quality of care, such as board certification, National Committee for Quality Assurance (NCQA) accreditation, and Healthcare Effectiveness Data and Information Set (HEDIS) clinical/utilization data. Trend guarantees may be categorized as a performance guarantee.

The underwriter should include a sensitivity analysis of the likelihood of performance guarantee settlements. One question to consider is whether, and to what extent, the existence of performance guarantees is likely to improve service results. This may depend on many factors, such as the degree to which services are centralized, whether the client has dedicated service teams, timeliness and management use of tracking reports, accountability for results within the company's claim, customer service, technology and care management leadership, and ability to influence the behavior of third parties (including providers).

Ideally, a performance guarantee should be set and monitored in a structured manner to encourage prompt identification and resolution of problems. This process should include notification of company leadership and care to alter operations as needed. This will minimize both the loss of administrative fees and the harming the company's reputation in the marketplace.

Funding Alternatives

Another major component in developing the proposal is to settle on the funding method(s) that will be offered. Funding methods requested in an RFP may or may not be a good fit with the bidder's risk tolerance, capabilities, and strategic goals. Sometimes, bidders may emphasize a funding option to give them a competitive advantage.

Another consideration is the extent to which the employer offers multiple choices among plans and vendors, and the employer's contribution strategy in relation to the cost of those options to employees. As discussed earlier, the amount that the employee pays out of pocket in premium, in combination with the benefits, drives their selection. High Deductible Health Plans (HDHPs) have been offered at an increasing rate, both as a sole offering or as an option with non-HDHPs. When offered as an option, the spread of rate relativities will introduce a material antiselection impact to consider.

HDHPs tied to accounts such as Health Reimbursement Accounts (HRA) and Health Savings Accounts (HSA) may also include contributions toward the deductibles by the employer, which again introduces significant antiselection considerations – even though those account values typically do not fall under the insurer's cost or risk. For some employees, an HDHP is a better option, but many will still elect the non-HDHP because of cash flow issues. For example, employee "A" may know he or she will spend out of pocket $3,000 a year in copays under a copay plan, but still elect against a $2,000 out-of-pocket HDHP because of the timing of cash. With the copay plan, the employee's cost is spread smoothly throughout the year versus the HDHP, which requires paying the entire $2,000 earlier in the year. Underwriters and employers should consider this issue when structuring HDHPs and employer contributions. A highly fragmented risk pool may render some funding methods less attractive for the insurer. If the employer is considering a wide range of plans and insurers, a bidder may invest in an offer of a specific option in order to mitigate their overall package's risk exposure.

Once the price has been determined, and the benefit, administrative, and funding options have been reviewed, then the challenge is to put together a package that produces the best synergy between the buyer's needs and objectives versus the carrier's strengths and strategic goals. This is where proposal underwriting becomes an art. The secret is to listen to the customer and read between the lines of the RFP. The RFP may have dozens of pages of questions, but in reality only a small subset of the answers will drive the sponsor's decision-making, with the underwriter's responses normally critical.

Depending on a group's size and the amount of financial risk they are willing to assume, there are a variety of funding alternatives available. Insurers assume all the risk in fully insured funding, and employers assume all the risk in self-funded arrangements. Employers may purchase reinsurance coverage on their self-funded programs to mitigate the impact of high dollar claims per participant (specific stop-loss) or overall higher claims than projected (aggregate stop-loss). The characteristics, basic features, and billing options will provide a range of advantages and disadvantages that can be used in determining which funding best meets the insurer and employer's needs.

As the market moves from managed care programs to consumer driven health plans (CDHPs), like HDHPs with HRAs and HSAs, underwriters will need to consider different criteria than in the past. HRAs and HSAs have different regulatory bases and may be offered as either full replacement programs or as options. Benefit design, employee cost, strength of competition, and the enrollment process are a few of the factors affecting the selection and pricing.

The cost of the HRA or HSA account portion of the CDHP is generally passed through to the employer at cost, and thus not quoted in an RFP. However, the underwriter must often include the account's separate administrative or technology fees.

RENEWAL UNDERWRITING

EVALUATING THE CASE

The first renewal elicits two common questions: "What happened here?" and "Why?" Other questions can be asked to help find the answers. Was the required participation level verified at time of issue? Did the enrollment rise, fall, or remain stable? Is there evidence of antiselection? At what point did paid claims attain a mature level? Were there any catastrophic claims? What is the required reserve for incurred but not reported claims? Were cost control measures effective? Are administrative procedures efficient? Are they expensive? What do I know now that I wish I had known a year ago?

The renewal evaluation focuses on the same types of risk characteristics and experience data used in the proposal process, but with access to more information. Claim data can be analyzed by age, gender, diagnosis, location, frequency, duration, network, and so forth. Reserve levels can be tested. Premiums can be reconciled to covered lives and volumes of insurance. Sources of data aberrations, such as claim backlogs, can be investigated.

Renewal data can be compared to assumptions regarding the intensity and cost of administrative services. At a minimum, the underwriter should be able to better predict the number of claims and other transactions. For a jumbo group, the actual costs for some functions or services may have been documented.

A common dilemma faced by the renewal underwriter is timing. In order to give the employer adequate notice of the new rates, claim data is often not on a mature basis, especially in the first plan year. Case-specific patterns that may impact IBNR calculations cannot be fully quantified in time to validate first-year reserves. Should you apply full credibility to your own data or also consider prior experience? What if the two are quite different? This can be an especially difficult question if there are any catastrophic claims early in the claim history.

DEVELOPING RENEWAL RECOMMENDATIONS

The usual first step in renewal discussions for insured plans is to present the new premium rates for the existing program. Hopefully, the employer has received periodic experience reports, so there are no major surprises. If the renewal premium is abnormally large, the underwriter must decide whether to remedy the situation all at once or over a period of two or more years. Sometimes introducing a funding alternative, such as a retrospective premium agreement, can help offset the need for higher rates.

Renewal recommendations may involve proposed plan design changes. This might be prompted by an analysis of utilization data, or by employer budget pressure. Approaches include increasing employee cost-sharing, adding a utilization review program, adopting a managed care plan, or finding ways to shift health care to more cost-effective models. Jumbo employers tend to have a high level of interest in issues relating to quality of care, to the point where quality and price are closely linked in renewal recommendations and negotiations.

Some large employers who have been in business for many years have a strong interest in reducing their liabilities for retiree benefits. This interest is spurred by an aging population and accounting rules. The renewal analyses of health plan benefits often include ways to reduce the cost of retiree plans, without undue cost-shifting to the retirees. One common strategy is to modify retired health plan benefits and contributions to try to encourage over-age-65 participants to enroll in Medicare Risk plans or Medicare Part D plans. Employers with early retirees may reevaluate their program structure in light of the insurance exchange, where rates are often attractive when compared to true cost.

For other types of plans and products, renewal recommendations often include an analysis of alternate rating and funding methods, including stabilization reserves, retrospective premiums, extended payment periods, and various forms of full or partial self-insurance.

In one sense, the renewal process is much like the proposal process, except that the underwriter should know a good deal more about the case, and about the customer.

REVISION UNDERWRITING

An interesting aspect of underwriting large groups, especially jumbo groups, is that their needs and benefits are constantly changing, and the underwriter may have frequent, even daily, involvement with the account. Revision underwriting includes developing cost estimates for any potential changes in plan design(s) or composition of the group. The latter might be required due to collective bargaining, enrollment shifts, acquisitions or divestitures, or downsizing.

RENEWAL MONITORING

The large group underwriter's role includes tracking of emerging claim experience and of other risk factors throughout the contract year. The underwriter might review premiums and claims each month, and do a more formal analysis of emerging trends, and re-projection of full year results, two to four times per year. Depending on the type of plan, the analysis might include a review of claims by diagnosis, type of provider, type of service, geographic area, business unit, demographic category, catastrophic claims, performance guarantees, and more. Often, the underwriter will review patterns of claim submission and processing, and will project incurred but unreported liabilities.

One purpose of renewal monitoring is for internal control and financial reporting requirements. Due to the size and varied funding methods used for large cases, accurate projection of experience is an important part of a company's financial reporting. It also enables the underwriting department to manage their book of business. Depending on the funding method, these reviews often include updating projections of insurer and employer settlements and liabilities. One example is projecting year-end returns or retrospective premiums under a participating contract. Other examples include projecting employer and insurer liabilities under a minimum premium plan, a self-funded plan with stop-loss coverage, or performance guarantees.

Renewal monitoring is also used to quickly identify emerging issues or problems, and to take corrective actions. The options often depend on the severity of the problem, the product and funding method, and the customer relationship. For example, one option may be to meet with the client to pre-sell a large upcoming renewal, or to propose benefit changes. If the funding method is such that the employer bears, or shares, the risk, the discussions may be more open-ended, with each party sharing ideas of how to address their mutual problem. The key is early communication of the issues, because customers are not fond of year-end surprises.

A new project for the group underwriter involves monitoring loss ratio rebates. The ACA requires a minimum loss ratio (MLR) of 85% for large groups in aggregate. However, certain expenses, such as ACA-related taxes and fees, expenses to improve quality of care, and expenses towards fraud and abuse reduction, do not count as administrative expenses against the 85% rule. The underwriter should watch for a pattern that would put the issuer at risk of dropping below the minimum MLR.

SPECIAL RISKS

ASSOCIATION PROGRAMS

Most states permit group insurance contracts to be issued to associations of specific types. These programs generally fall into two categories:

- An association of individuals, covering the bona fide members of an organization, such as a medical society or a bar association, that was formed to further some common interest or occupation.
- A multiple-employer trust (MET), where the policy is issued to the trustees of a fund established by two or more employers in the same industry and covers their employees.

Of the two, the association of individuals poses the greater risk of antiselection. In fact, there are few such plans being marketed today as group insurance (although there are many individual plans of coverage in effect). Most programs are limited to life or disability insurance coverage and rely heavily on medical evidence of insurability. The spread-of-risk safeguard normally inherent in group insurance programs is not found in these plans, where participation rarely exceeds 5% of the eligible members.

The second category, multiple-employer plans, offers many of the underwriting safeguards found in single-employer groups. Most such plans require substantial employer contributions and have minimum participation rules for each employer. The primary marketplace for multiple-employer groups is among small employer groups bound together in a strong trade association. Successful multiple-employer plans almost always display the following characteristics:

- The sponsoring association is a strong entity, with a high percentage of eligible firms participating as dues-paying members. These associations also provide many other services to their members.
- A large pool of eligible members.
- A relatively small average employer size. Member firms with more than 50 or so employees tend to find their coverage elsewhere.

In the past, as with any small employer group, successful underwriting of multiple employer programs includes preexisting condition exclusions, age rating, closely monitored premium collection, limited plan designs, and often limited evidence of insurability. Due to the ACA, pre-existing conditions and insurability analysis will not be possible. However, the exchange's existence offers many METs risk reduction, and may eliminate the need and desire for many association plans to offer health insurance.

Many multiple-employer plans are self-insured. These are referred to as Multiple Employer Welfare Associations (MEWAs). Several states have promulgated strict rules designed to protect the members of MEWAs from the risk of insolvency in response to a somewhat spotty financial history for these plans.

TAFT-HARTLEY GROUPS

In addition to the restrictions imposed by the Taft-Hartley Act, state laws differ widely with respect to eligibility rules, types of coverage permitted, minimum size requirements, and employee contributions. The underwriters must be satisfied that the trustees have established adequate facilities for administering the plan, and that the income of the fund is sufficient to cover the cost of administration as well as the cost of the insurance. Generally, successful programs have required that coverage be noncontributory, and 100% of the eligible employees of each contributing employer are insured at all times. Special care is needed to ensure coverage is limited to full-time employees, and the minimum number of hours worked requirement is high enough to exclude employees who will not earn enough employer contributions to cover the cost of their insurance. Termination and reinstatement of coverage present unique administrative problems, and thus cost concerns.

Purchasing Alliances

Purchasing alliances are formed when two or more non-affiliated large groups come together to solicit insurance bids via a common RFP. The groups may have secondary motives, such as to share the cost of hiring a consultant, to gain partners to lobby for a social issue, or to gain partners for a provider quality initiative, but the main purpose of such alliances is to enhance their purchasing power through economies of scale and added negotiating leverage.

These groups typically purchase fully insured plans in order to avoid issues of commingling employers' funds. Some of the first purchasing alliances were formed by political subdivisions, backed by enabling legislation. The individual groups might pay the same premium rates, or simply receive comparable size discounts off their separate rates.

A more recent form of purchasing alliance is a coalition of usually very large employers who combine forces to purchase managed care plans, sometimes directly from providers. This phenomenon has been largely localized, but there are a few national coalitions. The passage of federal Association Health Plan (AHP) legislation would likely increase the number of, and interest in, national coalitions.

Firms participating in coalitions usually have to agree to abide by ground rules that are set by the coalition in order to foster consistency and teamwork among the employee firms, and to elicit more attractive rates from bidding insurers. Examples of typical ground rules include common plan designs, restrictions on offering plans not sponsored by the coalition, a limited number of sponsored plans in any one area, and favored status for the best (or least expensive) local plan.

Large employer coalitions may focus on issues other than price, such as local provider quality, patient safety, and community prevention.

One of the side benefits that is most attractive to these sophisticated buyers is the added ability to monitor and influence quality of care issues. Again, the major objective is generally to negotiate lower rates. The incremental economies of scale may be quite small for these already jumbo buyers. The combined negotiating leverage of the coalition can be substantial, particularly in locations where the participating firms employ a high percentage of a plan's total membership. Some employers drop out of the coalition when they find that they do a better job negotiating fees on their own, or if they find that the non-financial issues that the coalition focuses on do not match their company's goals and values.

Some employer coalition RFPs mandate identical premium rates for all participating employers. This compounds the underwriter's biggest challenge with alliance plans: to help ensure that his or her plan attracts and retains a fair share of healthy enrollees, and a fair share of enrollees from the more desirable employer groups. The fact that contribution formulas usually favor low cost plans creates some delicate trade-offs.

UNDERWRITING GROUP DISABILITY INCOME

Group disability income provides benefits that require special underwriting consideration. Successful underwriting of group disability income starts with the recognition that disability claims are a subjective and volatile risk. The decision of whether to submit a claim for disability, or to stay on claim, often depends in part on the claimant's motivation, which is frequently related to his or her occupation, and is influenced by the amount of benefit being paid. Careful underwriting and claim management is necessary to control antiselection, as well as to properly classify the insurance health risk involved.

Long-term disability is more risky to the insurer than most other health insurance coverages, because it involves a low frequency of claims for large amounts, making financial results less stable and less predictable than for medical care.

Classification of groups for disability income rating purposes is generally by industry and occupation (for example, the industry may be "hospital", and the occupations within a specific hospital group may include physicians, nurses, office workers, and other staff). These two elements may be handled in combination or may be treated separately, depending on the company philosophy, the particular plan, and the characteristics of the group. Rates also vary by age and gender, and occasionally a plan is given rate credits for lower replacement ratios. Because of the very long-term nature of claims and the volatility that could be caused by a single claim, there tends to be a high degree of pooling. Experience rating is only used for very large groups, and case credibility factors are low. Groups of under 500 lives typically receive little or no credibility for long-term disability underwriting.

The underwriter must be careful in designing the plan limitations, exclusions, and benefit formula so as to avoid overinsurance. Overinsurance occurs when the benefit is so high as to create a moral hazard by influencing the insured's motivation to file a claim or return to work. One example of this principle is to fully offset (deduct from benefits otherwise payable) both primary and dependent Social Security benefits if the long-term disability gross benefit exceeds 50% of pre-disability earnings. A second way to avoid excessive replacement ratios is to step down, or have lower benefit percentages for higher amounts of coverage. The definition of "high" depends on many factors, including the industry, the size of the group, the extent of top-heaviness (since a high benefit on only one or two top executives is more questionable than high benefits for 25 or 50 executives), and whether the plan is contributory.

Liberal definitions of disability, such as own occupation to age 65, or use of a residual disability clause, are often restricted to white collar groups in otherwise select situations. Industries that are cyclical, seasonal, or subject to high turnover are typically ineligible for disability coverage. This is because layoffs can generate higher incidence rates, leading to possible misuse as unemployment insurance.

Growing firms are lower risk. Firms with a history of employment fluctuation are higher risk. A company that has reduced its work force recently is not necessarily a bad risk, but a company that is over-staffed in relation to recent orders and projected revenue can be a very poor risk.

A commercial rating report on the financial status of the employer should be ordered on large groups. Danger signs include a drop in revenues exceeding 25% in the past year, or excessive debt, or a history or prospect of financial instability. Again, the underwriter is concerned that the disability benefits might be used for unemployment benefits.

Single-employer groups, which may include hourly workers or union employees, can be insured for disability income with suitable loading in the rates for any extra risk. Disability plans covering the employees of a union-sponsored plan can be challenging, unless the union is interested in controlling claim costs and has a good record in administering welfare benefit plans. Collective bargaining agreements can also make it difficult to implement changes in plan provisions or premium rates in a timely fashion if experience deteriorates.

Groups with substantial proportions of commissioned salespeople can be insured, subject to careful determination of the amount of benefits and a well defined statement of eligibility for benefits. The disability benefits can be based on monthly earnings, which include commissions, using 1/12 of the earnings in the twelve month period prior to disablement. This is conservative for recently hired salespeople, and is designed to reduce the impact of a jumbo sale shortly after enrolling for long-term disability. Eligibility for commissioned salespeople is sometimes difficult to determine, because it is difficult to tell when they are actually losing money due to a disability, or even when they return to work.

Non-contributory plans, where employers pay the full amount of the premium, are especially desirable for long-term disability since individual selection is minimized, and a better spread of risk is assured.

Another consideration in underwriting long-term disability plans is the extent to which the employer actively supports disabled employees in returning to work. An employer that is committed to making workplace modifications, allowing flexible work schedules, or reassigning manual duties from one employee to another is an attractive prospect for long-term disability insurance, and will generally have lower claim costs than a similar employer with less interest in finding creative return to work solutions for disabled employees.

Insurers in the long-term disability market must be sure to accumulate adequate surplus when experience is good, in order to carry them through the down cycles. An underwriting response to a downturn can be perceived as more flexible than a rate increase. Underwriting can be quickly tightened in those industries and geographic regions which are most impacted by rising unemployment.

UNDERWRITING GROUP LIFE

Group term life underwriting risks share certain similarities with disability. Claim frequencies are low, and the amount at risk on any individual can be quite high. The potential for antiselection can be a concern with some plan designs, and allowing employee choice greatly increases the average cost per participant. A high percentage of plan participation is the best way to ensure a balanced spread of risk.

Fully insured experience rating is usually based on several years' experience, and applies low credibility to past experience, except for very large groups. Retrospective experience rating is usually reserved to basic life plans with significant employer contributions; optional life plans are usually non-participating (in part, to preclude the possibility of ERISA nondiscrimination problems that might cause the plan to be disqualified from income tax exemption, and cause resulting tax issues for the employees and their dependents).

Life coverage may be continued into retirement. It is standard within the industry to require reduction of benefits provisions and to limit maximum allowed retiree benefits, since they are often effectively guaranteed (continued until death). Special attention is given to certain concerns when evaluating retiree risk, including: (1) the financial stability of the group, (2) the historical and potential impact of lay-offs on the retiree liability, and (3) the anticipated aging of the retiree population. This last point is critical when either a multiple year rate guarantee or one rate for both actives and retirees is requested.

Alternate funding options may be limited to retrospective premium arrangements, and a few approaches to reduce insurer reserves. Self-insurance is not feasible, due to adverse tax implications for beneficiaries. Large employer group life plans also reflect the trend toward defined contribution and multiple choice (or cafeteria) plans. This results in employee-paid optional life plans with very large amounts of insurance. In many modern life plans, the concept of choice has been extended to include annual flex plan enrollments and qualifying life events. Underwriting safeguards include participation requirements, benefit formulas related to earnings, age based rating, evidence of insurability for very large amounts of insurance, and limits (such as an additional one times earnings) on open enrollment benefit increases.

Group life carriers have added new benefit features in recent years, in part to differentiate their products and to reduce the impact of intense price competition. These include living benefit provisions that allow for payment of a portion of the death benefit in the event of a terminal illness, and beneficiary financial counseling that offers investment and disbursement advice from an independent financial counselor. Group universal life plans also offer the combination of life insurance protection and tax-favored investment gains. Group variable universal life plans are also available and provide greater individual choice and control regarding the investment funds used. Universal life plans can also help to reduce the need for the employer to provide expensive retired life coverage on a group basis, a good fit with the defined contribution focus. Of course, new features can mean new risks.

Living benefit payments can represent added risk if a supposedly terminal claimant later recovers, which is more common than one might expect. The portability provision that is common to group universal plans, and is now being seen in some group term life plans, can result in antiselection, which can be especially intense if a large employer experiences a downsizing, since healthy downsized employees are more likely to lapse their coverage than unhealthy ones. Despite the challenges presented by intense competition and liberal plan provisions, a well-designed group life plan can still generate excellent underwriting and investment gains.

31 Managing Selection in a Multiple-Choice Environment

Clark E. Slipher
Catherine L. Knuth

Multiple-Choice Environment Defined

A multiple-choice environment is any situation in which individuals have a choice among insurance plans. This chapter will focus on the multiple-choice environment created when an employer allows its employees to choose among two or more medical insurance options (either multiple benefit plans offered by the same insurer, or plans offered by different insurers). One example is the use of a private exchange platform for offering employee benefits.

Favorable versus Unfavorable Selection

An informed and rational individual will usually choose the insurance plan that best meets his or her individual needs, so a multiple-choice environment usually leads to selection issues. The selection can be favorable or unfavorable to the insurer:

- *Favorable selection* (also known as positive selection) occurs when low-risk employees tend to choose the insurer or plan option. Low-risk employees are those that have a lower than average expected claim cost due to their age, gender, contract type (that is, single or family), or other aspect of their risk profile.

- *Unfavorable selection* (also known as antiselection, negative selection, or adverse selection) occurs when high-risk members tend to choose the insurer or option.

In a multiple-choice environment, if one or more options experience favorable selection, then one or more of the remaining options experiences unfavorable selection.

Why Offer Choice If It Costs More?

The overall combined cost in a multiple-choice environment is typically higher than the cost in a single-choice environment:

- Individuals use the opportunity to choose as a way to minimize their total out-of-pocket costs, at the expense of the insurer or employer (this is the cost of selection).

- There may be less economy of scale and less negotiating leverage with health care providers due to fragmentation of a group.

- Employee communications are generally more complex, and administrative expenses are greater.

Despite the additional cost and complexity, multiple-choice provides opportunities for an insurer or employer to offer insurance options that better fit customer or employee needs. The following situations illustrate how insurers and employers take advantage of a multiple-choice environment (even with the additional cost):

- *Introducing a new option.* Insurers and employers are often reluctant to totally replace a proven incumbent plan with an untested new product. Offering a new product as an option to the incumbent plan allows time for testing and transitioning to a new product.
- *Taking advantage of favorable selection.* Some insurers create plan features and pricing to attract low-cost risks. For example, healthy employees without strong ties to particular providers may be willing to choose a lower cost plan with a limited provider network. Active and fit employees may be drawn to plans that include wellness benefits. This may be particularly effective for one insurer offering a health plan option alongside other insurers' options.
- *Encouraging consumerism.* Offering a variety of health plan options is a natural extension of consumerism. Americans expect choice in other products they purchase, so why not in health care? Many insurers believe they can provide information and distinguishing plan features that can entice employees to choose their option, even at a higher price.
- *Implementing a defined contribution concept.* Some employers want to switch from providing a defined medical plan benefit to providing a defined monthly contribution toward the premium. Under the defined contribution concept, the employer lets each employee choose from a variety of health plan options. The employer's contribution to any plan's premium is a fixed dollar amount, regardless of the option the employee chooses. The employee must pay the difference between their option's total premium and the employer's fixed contribution. The defined contribution strategy allows employers to avoid having to decide between increasing monthly employee contributions or increasing employee cost sharing (deductibles and copays) each year. The employer can let each employee decide by offering a generous plan (with higher employee contributions) alongside a lower cost plan (with higher employee cost sharing).
- *Choice for the sake of choice.* Choice itself has intrinsic value. Offering choice distinguishes an insurer or employer as flexible, leading-edge, and sensitive to the needs of employees.

WHAT FACTORS INFLUENCE EMPLOYEE CHOICE?

In a multiple-choice environment, many factors influence an employee's choice of a health plan option, including:

- *Inertia.* Employees tend to stay with their existing plan selection, unless new information becomes available or something significant changes to compel them to consider other options. Often, a moderate premium increase is not enough to compel employees to consider another option because they are comfortable that they understand how their cost sharing works and that their providers are in the existing plan's network.

- *Plan provisions and costs*, such as covered services, employee cost sharing amounts, out-of-network benefit provisions, benefit exclusions, eligibility restrictions, waiting periods, and pre-existing condition exclusions.

- *Employee and dependent demographics*, such as age, gender, health status, family size, income, degree of risk aversion, and education.

- *Employer actions and attitudes*, such as employer contributions towards premiums, attitude toward the level of managed care, communications to employees, support for the enrollment process, and decisions on eligibility for retiree medical coverage (which may be limited to certain options, or may make certain options more advantageous prior to retirement).

- *Eligibility for other health insurance coverage.* An employee may also be eligible for coverage from the employer of his or her working spouse, or coverage from a governmental program such as Medicaid or Medicare. The alternative coverage may have much different benefit levels or level of subsidy from its sponsor.

- *Information available about options*, such as employee communications, advertising, and word-of-mouth. A key component of consumer-driven products is providing employees with additional information about the potential cost of their health care services and cost sharing. Many private exchange platforms include automated decision-support tools to help employees evaluate the benefits and costs of different plan options. Of course, increasing employee knowledge about their choices and health care treatment is good, but it also increases the potential of antiselection.

- *Provider network attributes*, such as provider availability, access restriction, reputation, fees, quality, and medical management restrictions such as specialist referral requirements.

- *Insurer and administration issues*, such as claim administration, customer service, availability of online tools, and reputation.

Employee choices are governed by a complex combination of the above factors and other considerations, which sometimes makes employee choices difficult to predict. For example, some employees will select a higher-premium plan with a broad provider network and lower cost sharing because they prioritize the security of known, low cost sharing for the provider of their choice over paying lower premiums and the possibility of higher cost sharing if they have a claim.

MULTIPLE-CHOICE SCENARIOS

The degree of choice an employer or insurer offers to employees in a multiple-choice environment can vary significantly. The following situations provide a few common scenarios:

- *Choice between medical coverage and no coverage.* An employee's most basic health plan decision is whether to be covered by the employer's plan. Large monthly employee contributions or high cost-sharing amounts (typically in the form of high deductibles) may deter an employee from enrolling in an employer's plan. An insurer should be aware that the choice between coverage and no coverage creates antiselection because an employee who waives the employer coverage often has lower expected health costs than an employee who takes the employer's coverage.

- *Choice between the employer's plan and other available coverage.* Employees in dual income families are often eligible for medical coverage provided by their own employer and by their spouse's employer (as a dependent). Some employers will pay cash (for example, $100 per month) to employees who waive the employer's coverage to take a plan offered by their spouse's employer. Some employers provide less premium subsidy where employees' spouses enroll in their plan when they are eligible for coverage under their own employers' plan. This practice is often called a "spousal surcharge".

- *Choice based on member cost sharing.* Options may differ by levels of deductible, coinsurance, copay, out-of-pocket limit, and other member cost-sharing features. Historically, employees could choose between two or three cost sharing levels for their entire family. However, an increased emphasis on consumerism and improved technology has prompted some plan sponsors to allow employees to customize their cost sharing levels using dozens of options. Plan sponsors may also provide computer selection models to help the employee optimize their plan choice. More options and better selection tools are useful for the employee, but increase the insurer and employer's antiselection risk.

- *Choice based on provider networks or medical management.* Choice between an open network product, such as a Preferred Provider Organization (PPO) which allows the use of non-network providers at higher cost sharing levels, and a restricted network product, such as a Health Maintenance Organization (HMO) which limits coverage to network providers, has existed for some time. Now, emerging provider fee, efficiency, and quality evaluation tools are causing insurers and employers to develop new provider network products. For example, new network products may use narrow provider networks, special provider fee schedules, additional medical management, or tiered benefit levels to distinguish themselves. The level of provider choice, the degree of medical management, and the presence of specific providers (a children's hospital, for example) may drive employee selection decisions.

- *Choice based on prescription drug formularies.* A plan's prescription drug formulary defines which drugs are covered and at what level of cost sharing (for example, high copay versus low copay). As the number of drugs available to treat the same condition increases, underlying drug prices change. As more expensive specialty medications become available, insurers closely manage their formularies in an effort to control plan costs for all insureds while providing effective coverage for all health conditions. Consumers, especially those with chronic condition prescription drug needs, are becoming increasingly aware of the differences between plans' drug formularies and this awareness can influence employee selection.

- *Choice among insurers.* Two or more insurers may offer health plan options to the same employee of one employer. For example, a large employer may offer employees a choice among a self-insured PPO option and two fully insured HMOs. The insurers compete for employees at multiple levels, such as price, cost sharing, provider network, covered services, customer service, insurer name recognition, and other features. Splitting the risk pool of employees among more than one insurer creates a dangerous antiselection situation because one insurer's losses caused by antiselection against one option are not offset by favorable selection gains achieved by another insurer.

- *Optional riders added to core coverage.* Some insurers or employers subsidize a core medical plan and allow employees to buy additional coverage (for example, vision, disability, and dental) at the employee's expense. The antiselection opportunity for these coverages varies by the predictability of the services they cover. For example, a vision care rider may be highly selected against by employees who know they need glasses. However, a rider that provides additional levels of accidental death coverage is less subject to antiselection.

- *Choice between consumer-driven plans and traditional plans.* Consumer-driven plans combine a high deductible health plan (HDHP) with a savings account (usually a healthcare reimbursement arrangement or a qualified health savings account) that can be used to pay for medical expenses below the high deductible. Unused account balances can roll over to the next year. Employers often allow employees to choose between an account-based plan and the employer's traditional medical plan, which may represent a dramatic difference in plan design (thus an opportunity for antiselection). Some critics of consumer-driven plans speculate that their savings are caused by favorable selection rather than changes in behavior. Initial results regarding the impact of selection have been mixed.

In practice, an employer or insurer often uses a combination of the above scenarios (or creates new types of choice) to create unique multiple-choice environments.

MEASURING SELECTION AND HEALTH STATUS

An underwriter pricing options in a multiple-choice environment must measure the current health status and/or estimate the future health status of employees expected to choose each option.

Traditionally, insurers estimated the impact of selection using employee age and gender. The age and gender mix of enrollees in each option, or the change in the mix over time, is one indicator of the selection bias of an option. Even small shifts in members from one plan to another can greatly influence the financial results of each plan. For example, the expected claim level for a 64-year-old male employee may be up to seven times that of a 23-year-old male employee. Age and gender analysis is still common because information on the age and gender of each employee is usually readily available.

More recently, insurers are supplementing traditional age and gender analysis with new risk and health status evaluation models, such as:

- *Health risk assessments*, which use questionnaires and employee self-reporting to identify health risk attributes of an employee. A health risk score is assigned to each employee based on risk attributes, such as smoking status, body mass index, exercise habits, seatbelt usage, and alcohol usage.

- *Risk adjusters*, which use a member's medical claim information (including diagnoses, medical services received, and prescription history) to statistically predict future claim costs. Many commercially-available and proprietary risk adjusters are available for premium rate development, experience analysis, and disease management applications. Statistical tests demonstrate that many risk adjusters have better ability to predict future health care costs than traditional demographic models, especially for larger groups of insureds. However, member claims experience is often not available when the insurer is newly quoting an employer group. Even if claims data is available, many employers do not have the amount of detail needed to run a risk adjuster.

Similar to the age and gender mix of members who select a particular plan option, the average health risk assessment score or risk adjuster score of those members can also provide a measure of selection.

SELECTION IMPACT OF EMPLOYEE CONTRIBUTIONS

The monthly employee contribution amount for each option in a multiple-choice environment has a significant impact on an employee's choice of plan. Employees are often willing to pay a higher monthly contribution if they expect the option will provide better benefits, lower cost sharing (deductible, copays), access to key providers, or some other value, especially when employees anticipate having a reasonably good chance of using the benefits.

Many employers use a defined contribution model in which the employer contributes a fixed dollar amount on behalf of each employee, regardless of which health plan option the employee selects. The employee's contribution is then calculated as the difference between the total premium rate for the selected plan option and the employer's fixed contribution.

This defined contribution model creates opportunity for employee selection that the insurer should contemplate when setting the premium rates. The following example illustrates the selection potential:

- An employer offers three health plans (A, B, and C) to employees. Plan A benefits are lean (20% less than Plan B); Plan B benefits are moderate; and Plan C benefits are rich (20% more than Plan B).
- The insurer sets the Year 1 premium rates for each plan based only on the expected benefit differences between the plans, with no adjustment for anticipated selection.
- The employer contributes a defined amount equal to $400 per month in Year 1. Employees contribute an amount (or receive a cash credit) equal to the difference between the premium rate for the plan they choose and the employer's fixed contribution.
- The employees have the following relative health status (or morbidity).

	Number of Employees	Relative Health Status (Morbidity)
Low Risk	50	50%
Average Risk	30	100%
High Risk	20	225%
Composite	100	100%

If we assume that the high risk employees always choose the richest plan (C), while the low risk employees always choose the leanest plan (A), then the Year 1 results are:

	Year 1 Premium Rates			
			Monthly Contributions	
Plan	Monthly Insurer Premium Rates	Number of Employees	Employer (Does not Vary by Plan)	Employee (Insurer Premium – Employer)
A	$400	50	$400	$ 0
B	500	30	400	100
C	600	20	400	200

If Plan A, B and C employees all had the same relative health status (i.e., 100%), the insurer's cost for the entire group would equal the premium collected for the group. However, because the average health status varies by plan, the insurer's total cost for all three plans is 11% greater than the premium collected, as shown in the following table.

	Year 1 Costs versus Premium		
Plan	Monthly Insurer Total Premiums	Monthly Insurer Total Actual Cost	Insurer Cost as a Percent of Premium
A	$20,000	$10,000	50%
B	$15,000	$15,000	100%
C	$12,000	$27,000	225%
	$47,000	$52,000	111%

Note: The actual insurer cost by plan is determined as follows (relative health status × insurer premium × employee count):

$$\text{Plan A: } \$10,000 = 50\% \times \$400 \times 50$$
$$\text{Plan B: } \$15,000 = 100\% \times \$500 \times 30$$
$$\text{Plan C: } \$27,000 = 225\% \times \$600 \times 20$$

This example suggests the antiselection risk is +11% ($52,000 / $47,000) because actual costs are 11% greater than the costs the insurer expected in the original premium rate development. The insurer would have needed to increase the Year 1 premium by at least another 11% in Year 1, in anticipation of the antiselection, in order to have any expectation of breaking even on this employer group.

In Year 2, assume the insurer increases premium rates by 20% (based on Year 1 loss of 11% plus expected annual health trend between Year 1 and Year 2), and the employer maintains its per-employee contribution of $400 per month. As a result, more younger and healthier employees move towards lower cost plans to avoid an increase in their respective contribution rates in Year 2. The less healthy employees in each plan stay in their current plan, while the healthier employees in each plan move to a lower-priced option.

Year 2 Premium Rates				
			Monthly Contribution	
Plan	Monthly Insurer Premium Rates	Number of Employees	Employer (Does not Vary by Plan)	Employee (Insurer Premium – Employer)
A	$480	60*	$400	$80
B	600	30*	400	200
C	720	10*	400	320

*Note: The Year 2 employee counts come from the following assumed movements among plans between Year 1 and Year 2:

    Plan A: 60 = 50 in Plan A in Year 1 plus 10 less healthy employees formerly in Plan B in Year 1 moving to Plan A in Year 2
    Plan B: 30 in Plan B in Year 1 minus 10 employees moving to Plan A plus 10 less healthy employees moving in from Plan C in Year 2
    Plan C: 20 in Plan C in Year 1 minus 10 employees moving out to Plan B in Year 2

Using the same methodology and assumptions discussed for Year 1, the insurer's total cost for all three plans is 8.3% greater than the premium collected, as shown in the following table.

Year 2 Costs versus Premium			
Plan	Monthly Insurer Total Premiums	Monthly Insurer Actual Total Cost	Insurer Cost as a Percent of Premium
A	$28,800	$16,800	58.3%
B	18,000	25,500	141.7%
C	7,200	16,200	225.0%
Total	$54,000	$58,500	108.3%

Note: The actual insurer cost by plan is determined as follows:

    Plan A: $16,800 = (50% x $480 x 50) + (100% x $480 x 10)
    Plan B: $25,500 = (100% x $600 x 20) + (225% x $600 x 10)
    Plan C: $16,200 = 225% x $720 x 10

Even with a 20% increase in Year 2 premiums (based on Year 1 observed experience), actual costs are once again greater than expected costs. The insurer would have needed to load the Year 2 premium by at least another 8.3% to break even. As a result, the employer can expect another large increase in premium rates in the next contract period, Year 3.

The example illustrates how an antiselection spiral can be encouraged, or even caused, by employer contribution methods and benefit plan design differences. To compensate for the antiselection cost, an insurer needs to anticipate the mix of subscribers choosing each respective plan option and include a selection load in the premium rate for each plan. The selection load can be spread as an even percentage load across all plans or the percentage load may vary by plan, with a greater load for the higher cost plans and lower load for the least costly plans. This tends to encourage subscribers to choose the lower cost plans and imposes a penalty on subscribers choosing the higher cost plans, but can exacerbate an antiselection spiral.

UNDERWRITING MULTIPLE-CHOICE SITUATIONS

An underwriter can use several techniques to assist in managing selection and its financial impact in a multiple-choice environment:

- *Additional premium margin.* The pricing example in the employee contribution discussion of this chapter shows a method of determining a selection load to be added to the premium to pay for the additional cost of selection. An insurer may also want to add an additional margin (1% to 3%) to the premium to account for the potential that the underwriting may not be able to perfectly predict the selection pattern and costs when determining prospective premium rates.
- *Employee Contribution or Plan Design Limits.* Reasonably limiting the cost and benefit differences between plans can help manage selection. For example:
  o Limit the spread in monthly employee contributions from the lowest cost option to the highest cost option (for example, maximum monthly spread of $50 for single coverage and $100 for family coverage). Options with very high employee contributions, relative to other options, tend to draw only a few, very unfavorable risks.
  o Limit the spread in benefits so that the value of the richest benefit option is not more than 20% to 30% greater than the value of the lowest option.
  o Mix favorable and unfavorable cost sharing or benefit provisions among options to avoid one option being labeled as the best plan for employees who expect high health costs. As an example, Plan A could have a lower deductible but higher member coinsurance than Plan B, restricting the overall difference between the plans' values.
  o Avoid options with specific selection potential (for example, only one option covers infertility benefits and others do not).
- *Participation requirements: One insurer offering multiple choices.* A single insurer can offset the antiselection in one option with the favorable selection in another option in a multiple-choice environment. Therefore, a standard minimum participation requirement that 75% of a large group's eligible employees enroll in one of the employer's options is often sufficient. The minimum participation percentage may increase as group size decreases for groups less than 100 employees (down to 100% for the smallest groups). Employees who waive the employer's coverage and opt for coverage in a spouse's plan are often excluded from the count of eligible employees in this calculation.
- *Participation requirements: Multiple insurers, each offering one or more choices.* When an employer's risk pool is split between multiple insurers, one insurer may attract an unexpected, unfavorable risk mix and not be able to offset the losses from another option's favorable risk mix since the other option is insured by someone else. Additional participation rules may be imposed to mitigate the antiselection risk inherent in these situations. For example:
  o An insurer requires that all insurers in the multiple-choice environment have consistent underwriting, eligibility, and/or pre-existing condition requirements. This rule ensures that another insurer does not dump unfavorable risks onto other insurers.
  o An insurer imposes an additional minimum participation requirement (for example, the insurer requires that 50% of all eligible employees must enroll in the insurer's plan

or plans) and reserves the right to withdraw or revise the premium quote if the additional participation requirement is not met.

- All insurers agree to a redistribution of income between the insurers based on the health status (measured by risk adjusters or age/gender analysis) of the employees who actually select each insurer option. Multi-employer purchasing pools sometimes use similar risk adjustment programs. Medicare Advantage plans as well as individual and small group non-grandfathered plans (starting January 1, 2014) use this approach.
- An insurer who expects a favorable risk mix may be willing to waive participation rules to take advantage of a situation.

PRICING STRATEGIES

A multiple-choice environment places additional pressure on the underwriting staff to anticipate selection between options and the resulting impact on insurer costs. Careful study of existing accounts may provide insights into selection dynamics. Once the selection can be predicted, actions can be initiated to influence future selection patterns.

The basic pricing strategy employed in multiple-choice situations is to determine the aggregate premium necessary to cover the aggregate cost of claims for all plan options. While each plan option should be priced on a somewhat independent basis, it is the aggregate result that should be the most important consideration.

Development of premium rates for each plan option normally follows the six steps described below. The tables included in this example are based on research for the situations described, and may or may not be applicable to a particular environment. The tables should be considered illustrative in nature and only used as a guide to the actuary developing selection tables for a specific purpose.

Step 1. *Determine the actuarial value[1] of each benefit option*, taking into consideration:
  (a) the expected cost of the benefits,
  (b) provider reimbursement arrangements,
  (c) medical management differences, and
  (d) administrative expense and margin requirements.

The actuarial value of each benefit option should be determined prior to considering any impact on the aggregate claims due to selection. These values reflect the required premium rates assuming every employee in the group participated in the option.

Step 2. *Estimate the enrollment mix by plan option.*

Employee contribution rates can serve as a basis for estimating the enrollment mix. Increasing contribution rates for specific options will tempt employees to choose other lower cost plan options. Each employee will decide if the option differences (benefits, network, managed care restrictions, and so forth) offset the employee contribution differences.

The following table presents a simple, illustrative model for estimating enrollment mix in a multiple-choice environment which consists of only two options: a plan with low cost

---

[1] The "actuarial value" referred to in this chapter is different from and should not be confused with actuarial value calculations required for plans compliant with the Affordable Care Act (ACA).

sharing and a broad provider network (Plan X) and a plan with higher cost sharing and a narrow provider network (Plan Y):

Contribution Differential (Per Employee per Month)**	Projected Enrollment Mix*	
	Plan X	Plan Y
Less than $50	85%	15%
$50 - $75	80	20
$76 - $100	70	30
$101 - $125	55	45
$126 - $150	45	55
More than $150	30	70

* Illustrative only
**Difference between Plan X and Plan Y, assuming Plan X is more expensive.

Step 3. *Estimate the relative health status factor for each option based on the expected enrollment mix from Step 2.*

The relative health status factor estimates the average expected costs for employees in each plan option relative to the overall cost of the group (100% is the overall health status/cost for the employer group) based on their age/gender and other health status or morbidity differences.

The relative health status factor can be estimated based on the expected enrollment mix between the two plan options. Generally, younger and other low-risk-factor employees are the first to venture to lean plans. As the lean plans become more familiar and their membership increases, their selection factor decreases. Eventually, the lean plan membership will gravitate toward the average characteristics of the total group membership. An illustrative table of relative health status factors follows:

Plan X Enrollment	Plan X Relative Health Status Factor	Plan Y Relative Health Status Factor	Overall Health Status Factor*
More than 79%	108%	24%	100%
60% - 79%	119%	56%	100%
50% - 59%	127%	67%	100%
40% - 49%	132%	74%	100%
20% - 39%	139%	83%	100%
Less than 20%	151%	94%	100%

* Weight based upon midpoint of the Plan X enrollment range

For example, if Plan X's expected enrollment is 70%, the employees selecting Plan X are expected to have costs equal to 119% of the overall group average and the other 30% of employees that select Plan Y are expected to have costs equal to 56% of the overall group average. The overall health status is 100% (by definition, but for checking purposes: $(70\% \times 119\%) + (30\% \times 56\%) = 100\%$).

Step 4. *Calculate the preliminary selection-adjusted rates for each option.*

The selection adjusted rates equal the Step 1 actuarial rates multiplied by the Step 3 relative health status factor for each option. The resulting selection-adjusted rates would be self-sustaining for each option if the expected mix of employees by option is exactly correct and does not change. However, static participation is unlikely if the employer uses the defined contribution model for setting employee contributions (described earlier in this chapter). The difference in employee contributions between Plans X and Y is likely to expand significantly using the Step 4 rates. This would cause further employee selection and an antiselection spiral, as illustrated earlier.

Step 5. *Calculate the average selection load.*

Calculate the average selection load as the ratio of the average of the Step 4 selection adjusted rates and the average of Step 1 actuarial rates.

Step 6. *Calculate blended-selection adjusted rates.*

Calculate the blended selection-adjusted rates by multiplying the Step 1 actuarial rates by the average selection load from Step 5. This step assumes that a single insurer insures both plan options. These Step 6 blended rates are appropriate for a single insurer environment because they are self-sustaining for the entire group, and they do not create the potential for additional selection. In a multi-insurer environment, the Step 4 preliminary selection-adjusted rates is more appropriate, because each option should be self-sustaining.

The following table illustrates the application of this six-step approach on a per member per month (PMPM) basis.

Option	(1) Actuarial Rates Before Selection	(2) Expected Enrollment	(3) Relative Health Status Factor	(4) = (1) x (3) Preliminary Selection-Adjusted Rates	(5) = (4) Avg. / (1) Avg. Average Selection Load	(6) = (1) x (5) Blended Selection-Adjusted Rates
Plan X	$600.00	70%	119%	$714.00	102.9%	$617.49
Plan Y	$480.00	30%	56%	$268.80	102.9%	$494.00
Average	$564.00	100%	100%	$580.44	102.9%	$580.44
Step 1: Plan Y is estimated to have a cost that is 80% of the Plan X cost before any selection bias is considered.						
Step 2: Estimated by underwriter, perhaps based on employee contribution differences.						
Step 3: Estimated by underwriter, perhaps based on expected enrollment %.						
Step 5: $580.44/564.00 = 1.029.						

Monitoring Results

Monitoring of experience for both specific employers and product lines is essential to effective product management in a multiple-choice environment. Effective management requires knowledge of selection preferences and the likely cost impact of these preferences. Key factors and statistics that an insurer should monitor are:

- Claim to premium loss ratios for various multiple option situations (for example, total replacement, consumer driven vs. traditional option). Loss ratios should be monitored for all options combined and on an option-by-option basis.
- Comparison of actual-to-expected selection patterns and health status indicators, segmented by anticipated selection variables (for example, employee contribution, cost sharing options available, network options).
- Comparison of changes in health status by employer group and by multiple-choice options over time.
- For an insurer whose plans are offered alongside other insurers' plans, a comparison of the demographic and health status characteristics of the employees and dependents selecting each insurer or plan.
- Monitoring of competitor and marketplace pricing and underwriting practices to the extent reliable public information is available. Also, comparisons of an insurer's health status versus industry or community benchmarks to help assess whether the insurer is receiving favorable or unfavorable selection relative to other insurers.
- Market research of current and potential insureds about what specific factors, preferences, and information influence their choices of health options.

Information learned from analysis of this information should be used to modify the insurer's multiple option pricing and underwriting strategy and models.

Summary and Conclusions

Today's group health marketplace is significantly more complicated than in the past. The health insurance companies who succeed will be those who understand the dynamics of the multiple-choice environment and act accordingly. Effective actuarial and underwriting analysis and the development of appropriate pricing strategies will be essential. A thorough understanding of the impact of selection on overall plan costs is important to the long-term financial success of any health insurer operating in this environment. Employers will continue to become more knowledgeable in this environment and will seek solutions to meet their specific cost and benefit coverage requirements.

32 CLAIM ADMINISTRATION AND MANAGEMENT

Jeffrey L. Smith
Sheila K. Shapiro

OBJECTIVES OF THE CLAIM ADMINISTRATION FUNCTION

The administration of claims is an integral part of the entire risk management process. It is also a central function in providing the product and service purchased by a group on behalf of its members. As such, the primary concern of claim management is to fulfill the intent of the insurance contract or administrative service contract. Claim management does not mean claim avoidance, nor is it merely a check-writing facility to compensate members for any and all financial losses. The objective is to provide precisely the payment prescribed by the contract, no more and no less.

It is with the contract that the claim management process begins. A clear, concise, and unambiguous contract is critical to an effective and efficient claim administration function. In actuality, no contract, despite the most careful drafting, can possibly include specific directions for every possible set of facts and circumstances encountered in the adjudication of claims. Clear contract language has become more of a challenge as definitions of eligible beneficiaries, as well as various types of services and providers, are modified by legislation, regulation or the judicial process. Still, the contract is the governing document. No actions in the claim adjudication process should contradict the provisions of the contract, unless by legislative, regulatory, or judicial mandate. Where the contract lacks specificity on a particular issue, the role of the claim management process is to produce a result consistent with the intent of the contract. This consistency will provide results that are likely to withstand audit scrutiny. Thus, a key element of the claim management process is the interpretation and application of a contract under varying circumstances and facts. In this context, the additional requirements of equity and consistency become important objectives of the claim adjudication process.

Knowledge of and adherence to regulatory requirements at the federal and state level is another key area of claim management. Claim audits examine timeliness, accuracy, and contract interpretation, and withstanding this scrutiny has become a critical component of the claim function. Additionally, performance guarantees for commercial customers, interest payments for providers (for claims that are not paid in timely fashion), and regulatory fines for non-compliance are commonplace. This oversight is intended to ensure that the insured or beneficiary receives the appropriate contracted benefit. Additionally, these audits are intended to ensure that the provider of service also receives the appropriate compensation in a timely fashion.

Effective management requires eligibility and claim payment data that satisfies diverse internal needs of the insurer.[1] Many of these needs are statistical and are used both to evaluate and monitor risk. Some of the necessary data, previously derived exclusively by the insurer, now comes from external sources. In tandem with clinical staff, claims management staff also measure and help determine effective use of premium dollars. The data acquisition process is as important to the organization as the accuracy of the claim payment itself.

INFORMATION REQUIREMENTS

Certain basic information is necessary for the proper handling of a claim. Although the specifics vary with the type of insurance coverage, the information needed generally falls into the following categories:

- Identification of the policyholder and claimant. This includes identifying the contracting group entity, the individual insured, and in the case of dependent coverage, the relationship of the claimant to the insured. This information is used to determine eligibility of the claimant under the contract.

- Proof of loss. That is, proof of death, disability, medical expense, and other loss triggers, consistent with the contract definition of an insured loss.

- Date(s) of loss. As the insurance contract is in force for only a specified period of time, the date of the incident or loss is necessary to determine whether the contract was in force on the date(s) of loss.

- Information to determine the amount of the contractual liability for the loss, if any. This information will vary greatly depending on the type of coverage.

- The individual or entity to which payment should be made. This would include identification of the beneficiary, for example, or an indication of assignment of medical benefits to a health care provider.

- Additional information regarding other coverage for coordination of benefits, required to ensure that the claim being paid is being processed at the correct rates.

As noted earlier, the primary use of information in the claim adjudication process is to assure that proper payment is made to the appropriate party. However, there are numerous purposes for the data compiled in the claim adjudication process, including such functions as financial and management reporting, pricing, establishing claim reserve liabilities, health care provider monitoring, predictive modeling of risk and behavior, health care utilization management (including incentive payments), and fraud and abuse control. Additionally, external reports may be used by self-insured clients and governmental agencies.

---

[1] The term "insurer" is used to describe any risk-taking entity. Many states have enacted uniform licensure laws that require any entity accepting risk to be licensed and regulated as, or similar to, an insurer. Other types of "insurer" entities include Health Maintenance Organizations (HMOs), Health Insuring Corporations (HICs), Accountable Care Organizations (ACOs), Consumer Operated and Oriented Programs (CO-OPs), Physician-Hospital Organizations (PHOs), etc.

LIFE AND ACCIDENTAL DEATH AND DISMEMBERMENT

In relative terms, the claim process for life and AD&D is a simple and objective determination of pertinent facts including verification of death, the eligibility of the deceased, and the date of death. Policy provisions may also require information regarding the circumstances of the death. That is, was the death accidental, from natural causes, or self-inflicted? Many policies have specific clauses specifying incontestable periods and exclusion of coverage for suicide.

Increasingly, group life insurers are being asked or required by customers and regulators to be proactive in identifying deceased certificate-holders. This can be done by reconciling employee data against databases such as the Social Security death master file.

The existence of disability provisions within a group life contract can add significantly to the complexity of the claim management process. This often involves obtaining evidence of disability and medical opinions as to the extent and probable duration of disability. Periodic follow-ups may be required to determine whether an insured remains totally disabled.

The process of assuring that payment is made to the appropriate party should be a straightforward procedure where a named beneficiary is present. The process can become quite complex, however, when no beneficiary has been named or when the named beneficiary is no longer living.

Policy provisions such as living benefits riders add an additional consideration to the claim management function. These policy provisions may specify circumstances under which a portion of the policy proceeds are to be disbursed prior to death, to pay for medical costs associated with terminal illness, or for long term care services, custodial or maintenance expenses.

DISABILITY

The management of a disability claim is a complex process that can potentially span a number of years. Historically, claim management techniques varied significantly between short-term disability insurance, which usually provides benefits for two years or less, and long-term disability insurance, which usually provides benefits to age 65 or beyond. Although some differences remain, plan sponsors and insurers sometimes see both as parts of the same disability claim management process.

The process begins with an initial determination of the potential liability. This process includes gathering data from the claimant and the employer (including a description of job duties), assessing the claimant's condition relative to the contractual definition of disability, reviewing the contractual provisions, and determining the amount potentially due the claimant as a result of these factors. This can vary from contract to contract and, in fact, may vary within a contract based on the duration of the disability. For example, it is not uncommon for the initial disability determination to be made on the basis of an individual's ability to perform the specific functions of his or her own occupation and, after an initial period of coverage, to have the definition shift to an "any occupation" type of standard.

The next step is the establishment of the disability status of the claimant. This process begins by obtaining an assessment from the claimant's own physician. The insurer's claim management staff, often including nurses and physicians, then reviews that assessment. For complicated or contentious situations, the insurer may require an independent medical examination. Occasionally, the process requires investigation and surveillance to be sure that the actual activities of the insured are consistent with the claim of disability, through "field investigations."

As a direct result of the investigation into the claimant's health status, the insurer will establish a plan for managing the disability. This plan may be as simple as an expected timeline for recovery, as in the case of a broken bone, or it may be a very complex program of vocational rehabilitation and workplace accommodation designed to hasten the claimant's return to work.

The determination of the appropriate level of periodic benefit payments usually begins with a determination of the claimant's pre-disability salary. Most benefits are calculated as a percentage of salary. This gross benefit will usually be offset against benefits available from other sources such as Social Security, Worker's Compensation or other employer-sponsored plans. The group contract will specify the specific offset provisions. Thus, the claim examiner must monitor and coordinate the payments with a number of external sources.

A key role of the claim examiner is to make sure that the claimant is taking advantage of all other benefit sources that will produce offsets to the insurer's payments. Some insurers provide direct assistance for their claimants in applying for social insurance benefits and appealing any negative decisions.

The ongoing nature of the disability claim also requires ongoing claim management, including periodic review and monitoring to assure that the claimant remains disabled.

Since the desired conclusion of any period of disability is the return of the claimant to full-time work, the management of disability claims often involves provisions and services designed to ease the transition from total disability back to active employment. If full recovery is not possible, consideration is made for partial recovery, the type of work that can be done, and the differential in work earnings. In this instance, partial benefits may be provided. Many large disability insurers also provide for rehabilitation services to actively support the insured's return to active employment. These services are usually coordinated with the plan sponsor, and can include such things as employee re-training for another activity, or work site accommodation for the physical needs of the employee. The company can be proactive in spending in this area, as a trade-off for lower continued disability payments.

There are several other considerations for disability claim managers dealing with long term claims. For example, it is typical for a group policy to provide for benefit limitations for certain types of disability. In such cases, it is important that these limitations be communicated with the employee, so that as the termination of benefits approaches, the employee can plan accordingly. In addition, some group disability contracts will also provide for indexing of benefits over time, or for cost of living adjustments. These are additional calculations to be managed by the claim adjustor.

If the disability will be present for the long term, the claim management process becomes less intensive; however, periodic updates need to occur to verify continued eligibility for benefits. If other solutions are not available, the company may wish to investigate alternatives to continued periodic benefit payments. If, for example, the disability is truly long term and not subject to significantly increased mortality, the company can consider alternatives such as a lump sum payment. This might give the employee the opportunity to pursue other options for either working or accommodating their modified lifestyle, while affording the company the ability to terminate the claim. Some claimants use lump sum payments to fund a new business or for re-education.

HEALTH INSURANCE

The cost of group health insurance is a significant and rapidly escalating expense for most employers. Thus, much attention is now focused on controlling health care claim costs. As with other coverages, the contract specifies the level and scope of coverage. Although there remain some indemnity plans paying a specified amount for a specific occurrence (such as a fixed amount per day in the hospital), most group health plans are reimbursement programs. These plans pay for the actual costs of providing necessary health care.

CLAIM ADJUDICATION PROCESS

The claim adjudication process generally consists of four steps, as described below. With the significance of changes brought about by managed care, notable exceptions to this general process exist. They will be described in detail in the next section. The claim adjudication process described below includes the considerations of the claims examiner in this process. This "claims examiner" is often the adjudication software used by the claim payment organization. It is not unusual for the vast majority of claims to be processed without the intervention of a human claim examiner. Human intervention is required for complex cases and claims where the payment amount is above a threshold that the insurer determines.

Step 1. *Benefit Eligibility and Proof of Loss.*

The basic step, in addition to the question of eligibility for benefits, is obtaining proof of loss resulting from a covered illness or accident. This step will normally include the compilation of itemized bills from hospitals, doctors and other health care institutions and professionals. In each instance, it will be necessary to have the dates on which each expense was incurred (when services were rendered), and what illness or accident generated the expense.

Individuals covered by group benefit plans may have a variety of benefit options. Today's systems must be flexible enough to determine eligibility and coverage selected at the patient level. Eligibility determination is the first step in the claim adjudication process. Health contracts vary greatly in the level and scope of coverage. Different benefit parameters often apply to different diagnoses within the same contract; however, this differentiation seems to be disappearing due to legislation enacted in response to the proponents of parity of payment for all types of illness or injury. While the insurance contract may be between the employer and the insurer, federal and state governments now are involved third parties and are instrumental in the determination of eligibility and claim payment. For example, eligibility of individuals whose (small) employer enrolled through a state or federal health exchange (the Small Business Health Options Program, or SHOP), created by the Affordable Care Act (ACA), is determined by the exchange and not the insurer. In some cases, the SHOP eligibility provisions differ from other group business.

The next step is a determination of which expenses are eligible for coverage. This step includes a review of the specific scope of the contract. For example, does the contract cover expenses related to diagnostic tests, prescription drugs, organ transplants, or bariatric surgery?

The scope and nature of benefits have been impacted by the ACA, with differences in definitions of benefits between types of plans: "grandfathered plans" existed prior to the enactment of the ACA and steps were taken to allow these plans to maintain many coverage and design features; "transitional" plans exist in many states and were granted special, temporary exemptions from some provisions of the ACA; "non-grandfathered" plans fully comply with the ACA, with a subset of "qualified plans" approved for sale through individual and small group exchanges. An additional consideration is benefit plans for large groups and/or self-funded plans governed by ERISA, which have more flexibility in coverage and plan design.

A claim examiner must often determine the individual's eligibility to receive benefits based on the presence of a pre-existing condition. This determination became more complex after the passage of the Health Insurance Portability and Accountability Act (HIPAA) and has further been changed by the ACA. The claim examiner needs to have information relative to the continuity of coverage from one employer to another, or from individual to group coverage. The specific group coverage may include a "no gain/no loss" rule governing the situation where coverage has been moved from one insurer to another. The ACA disallows major medical health plans from applying pre-existing condition exclusions, limitations and denials effective January 1, 2014, with earlier adoption for children.

Step 2. *Determine Eligible (Covered) and Allowable Charges.*

The next step in the basic health claim process is the determination of the amount of eligible charges. This process involves matching eligible benefits with the provider's master list of charges for the services provided. These are then edited to eliminate duplicate claims, non-covered benefits identified from the previous step, other party liability (discussed in more detail in Step 4 below), and other exclusions.

Allowable charges then are determined using the appropriate payment parameters. Most health care benefit plans contain reimbursement mechanisms that involve a contracted reduction from the eligible billed charges. The variety and complexity of these mechanisms make it imperative that the adjudication system access information that will determine whether the payment will be based on a schedule of discounted charges, grouping of charges (DRGs or OPGs for facility claims), bundled case rate reimbursements, RBRVS payment rates, a factor based on Medicare reimbursement, capitations, or some other special arrangement. Payment levels will differ based on the managed care philosophy that is exercised.

For the few group health plans that still have traditional indemnity insurance, allowed charges will simply be billed charges for institutional providers, and some form of usual, customary and reasonable (UCR) charge structure for professional charges. These UCR type structures generally reflect the prevailing charge levels in the community, based on a compilation of actual past charges. Most UCR schedules set payment at a percentile (such as 90th) of the actual distribution of charges for each specific procedure or diagnosis. Thus, it is critical to obtain the proper coding of claim charges by procedure. The most generally accepted source of UCR charges is the FAIR Health database.[2]

Step 3. *Determine Gross Benefit Level.*

Once the total allowable charges have been determined, it is possible to apply basic contract parameters to determine the gross benefit level. This includes the application of copayments, deductibles, coinsurance, out-of-pocket expense limitations, and any policy limitations. The ACA requires that coverage for Essential Health Benefits (EHBs)[3] does not contain any annual or lifetime benefit limits; however, some narrowly defined internal policy limits are still allowed, including visit/unit limits as well as allowable dollar limits on non-EHB coverages. The contract will specify the claim basis for these applications, gross charges, net allowances, or other mechanisms.

Another change brought about by the ACA is the requirement that all expenses accrue to a maximum out-of-pocket (MOOP) expense for all patient cost sharing. The primary impact of this change is that copayments (medical and pharmacy), which had previously not been included in the out-of-pocket (OOP) maximum, now accrue to an overall limit. Insurers who contract with an outside pharmacy benefit manager (PBM) for prescription drug coverage now have to interface with that PBM on a real-time basis to determine the member payment at the point of sale.

Some insurers have modified plan provisions to add another layer of patient payment maximum. What had previously been defined as the OOP has become a *coinsurance maximum*, and the MOOP is defined as the federal maximum limit (which includes member coinsurance and copayments). As an example, a comprehensive medical plan could have an annual deductible of $500, a coinsurance maximum of $2,500, and a MOOP of $6,850.[4]

Step 4. *Determine Net Payment Level.*

To arrive at a net payment level, the claim examiner must also consider the existence of other plan liability (OPL). While claims that are entirely the obligation of another party are eliminated in Step 2, claims that are the joint liability of two or more parties need further examination. The two major forms of OPL are coordination of benefits (COB) and subrogation (SUB).

COB provisions recognize the eligibility of family members who have benefits available from two health plans as a result of both adults in the family having family coverage. In the case of coverage for the adult, the group plan covering the adult as the employee is the primary plan, and the plan covering the other adult is the secondary plan. In the case of the dependent children, the predominant method (and the method contained in the NAIC model regulation) of determining primary plan eligibility is the "birthday rule." The plan maintained by the adult whose birthday falls earlier in the calendar year becomes the primary plan for the dependent children.

---

[2] FAIR Health, Inc. was established in October, 2009 as part of the settlement of an investigation by New York State into certain health insurance industry reimbursement practices which had been based on data compiled and controlled by a major insurer. http://www.fairhealth.org/, accessed February 17, 2016.

[3] While the EHB standards generally only apply to the individual and small group non-grandfathered marketplaces, the prohibition of annual and lifetime dollar limits on EHBs is applied more widely to all non-grandfathered major medical health insurance plans.

[4] Notice of Benefit and Payment Paramters for 2016, Final Rule. https://www.gpo.gov/fdsys/pkg/FR-2015-02-27/pdf/2015-03751.pdf, page 77

When benefits are paid under COB provisions, the primary plan first makes the benefit payment according to the terms of that contract. The secondary plan can use one of two common methods for determining benefit payment:

1. *Maintenance of Benefit.* Under this arrangement, the secondary plan pays the difference between the total eligible charges determined by the primary plan and the actual payment made by the primary plan. The only limitation, which is seldom reached, is that the payment made by the secondary plan does not exceed what the secondary plan would have paid if it were primary.

2. *Non-Duplication.* Under this arrangement, the secondary plan determines what it would have paid if it were primary and then subtracts what the primary plan paid. In this case, the patient would likely not receive payments totaling 100% of the eligible charges under the primary plan, unless the secondary plan was a 100% plan.

While the NAIC model regulation is silent with regard to these two methods, some states have written specific provisions in their administrative code identifying the approach to be used in that state. As is the case with most benefit provisions, self-funded plans administered under the provision of ERISA have much more flexibility in the administration of COB provisions. These plans can opt to follow the NAIC model regulation or adopt an alternative approach. The major issue in adopting a provision that differs from the NAIC model is coordinating with primary plans administered by insurers that use the NAIC model regulation. Differences in COB administration have the potential to create "loopholes," creating employee relations problems. Accordingly, most of these self-funded plans voluntarily follow the NAIC model regulation and adopt the Maintenance of Benefit approach.

There are other methods that have historically been used to administer COB provisions. These variations were designed to avoid plan liability and most of these methods have been defined by state insurance departments as "Unfair and Deceptive Practices."

While most plans recognize COB provisions, there are some that do not contain COB provisions, and that make benefit plan payments without consideration for COB. These plans typically provide limited benefits and include such plans as school accident plans, individual plans, some supplemental sickness and accident policies, fixed indemnity plans, and hospital indemnity plans that provide a limited indemnity payment per day of hospitalization.

Subrogation provisions generally are the result of integration of health insurance plans with automobile insurance policies containing a medical payments provision. Payment for claims that arise as a result of an automobile injury are commonly paid under the health insurance plan, and recoveries are then made against the auto insurer. It is common for health insurers to "pursue and pay" COB claims and "pay and pursue" subrogation recoveries.

To carry out the COB component of claim adjudication, the examiner first determines which coverage is primary and which is secondary or supplemental. If the coverage is primary, then the gross benefit determined above becomes the amount payable. If, however, the coverage is secondary, the examiner modifies the gross payment level according to the maintenance-of-benefits method or the non-duplication method identified above. The existence of grouping payment mechanisms (such as DRGs) has further complicated the coordination process, especially, as is most likely the case, when the two carriers use different reimbursement systems.

In actually making the benefit payment, the claim examiner must determine to whom payment is to be made. Often, especially in the case of high dollar amount claims, the benefits have been assigned to the institution or professional providing the medical care.

Managed Care and the Claim Adjudication Process

There are three basic items that tend to distinguish managed care plans in terms of claim adjudication. First, these plans include a network of providers under contract to the insurer or other risk assuming entity. Second, managed care plans use some degree of health care management, usually prospective to, or concurrent with, the delivery of health care services. Under typical managed care arrangements, claim payments are made directly to the network providers. Providers are responsible for collecting any patient liability, either at the time services are rendered or upon receiving a remittance advice from the health plan describing the amount that can be collected from the patient. Third, these plans may incorporate payment for services that relate to managing care of a population that may or may not contain a corresponding claim payment. In some cases, claims are created to document these payment transactions using either existing payment codes or codes created solely for this purpose.

Medical appropriateness and medical necessity are integral parts of the claim adjudication process for most managed care plans. Designed to review both the services provided and the most appropriate setting for those services, criteria of medical appropriateness are used to determine whether the payment of a claim is acceptable as submitted, requires some modification, or is denied.

Claim payment adjudication under managed care arrangements can take many forms, and is typically governed by contract agreements with network providers. As noted in Step 2 in the traditional claim payment process, discounts from billed charges, DRGs, per diems, and fee schedules are all reimbursement alternatives used by health plans in certain situations. But these payment arrangements have been supplemented by others as insurers, providers, and even governments have continued to influence payment rates to re-align provider and population incentives with health outcomes. In some cases, providers are paid a pre-determined amount per member per month (referred to as capitation) for the delivery of the services specified by the provider contract. In most cases, claims are still required to be submitted by these providers for services delivered under these contracts. These claims (typically referred to as encounters) are processed in the same fashion as noted above; however, there are no actual payments made to the providers. The claims are used for statistical and quality reporting purposes, payment of incentives, and for retrospective review of the cost, quality, and appropriateness of providers' service delivery.

In an attempt to create and maintain reasonable standards, most health plans have developed care protocols by diagnosis to establish acceptable and reimbursable treatment patterns. These protocols provide guidance to the claim examiner as to whether the medical care expenses are reasonable and appropriate, or whether further investigation is required. Given the additional complexity and ambiguity introduced by the inclusion of appropriateness and necessity concepts, it is common for a health plan to have a mechanism for claimants and providers to establish payment levels in advance of incurring the expense. To help patients plan for costs, some states recently legislated that health plans must be able to price a service in advance, at least upon request. Some states require specific appeal mechanisms, as well as health plans' commitment to follow the determination of a review by an outside organization. Already in place, the ACA added outside third party panel review of appeals as a new avenue for dissatisfied insured persons, though this option is only available after the internal appeals process has been followed through to completion.

Current managed care benefit programs (especially PPO and POS plans) commonly provide different payment levels for use of designated or preferred providers. This differentiation may also extend to referrals from preferred providers. The claim management process must routinely have data with respect to the status of providers, as well as the status and source of referrals, to properly adjudicate a claim in the managed care setting. In some instances, the financial responsibility for a referral may (based on the contract between the insurer and the provider) be that of the referring physician.

In extremely complex or expensive claim situations, the health plan may become directly involved in determining the plan of treatment, the place of treatment, and consideration of treatment alternatives. This case management function often involves identification of "centers of excellence" for certain treatments based on the volume of cases treated and quality outcomes as well as the authorization of payment for expenses outside the scope of the group contract, if the net result is quality care and cost effectiveness. For example, this could involve the use of specialized outside vendors for rehabilitation services, or could provide for installation of specialized medical equipment at the patient's home. The key is that effective case management should produce a better result for the claimant while lowering the overall cost of care.

Another issue that complicates the claim adjudication process is the continued trend toward specialization of service. These specialized arrangements (generally referred to as "carve-outs") have changed the claim adjudication process. Examples of these carve-outs are pharmacy benefits administered by a Pharmacy Benefit Manager (PBM) and services provided through behavioral healthcare provider networks, cardiology networks, chiropractic networks, and others. Some of these carve-out networks process and pay their own claims, while others rely on the health plan to process claims.

As noted earlier, the type of organizations taking on risk has expanded well beyond traditional insurance companies. The ACA has hastened many industry-wide changes. Generally, risk-taking provider organizations have very different business missions than the traditional commercial insurers. Many hospital and health systems now have insurance licenses and products in the market. Organizations which offered solely Medicaid and other government-specific (largely individual) products have expanded their product lines into group health products.

This shift in the market, combined with a general payment reform movement "from volume to value," is beginning to affect traditional claim payment practices. If reimbursement truly is driven by patient outcomes as opposed to fee-for-service procedures, the traditional claim processing function will lose value. Care management and predictive modeling will become much more valuable. The provider community, more centralized via consolidation and widespread employment of physicians, has adopted coordinated care models, like ACOs and patient-centered medical homes, which are structured to accept financial risk and provide more comprehensive and coordinated patient care. Grant funding, available at the federal and state levels, is boosting the pace of these changes. One noteworthy barrier remains. Despite the significant investment and promise of electronic health records, the ability to effectively share critical patient data may be hindered by regulation and lack of technological integration between providers. Organizations will likely have to shift resources to overcome this; the market and consumers will ultimately demand it.

Banking Arrangements for ASO and Minimum Premium Plans

With an Administrative Service Only (ASO) contract, plan sponsors can opt to have their claims processed by an administrator (often a health plan), and pay a fee for the services rendered. This fee covers the administrator's costs to administer the claim adjudication process, which may also include the fees for the use of the health plan's network or other services. Additional services might include the maintenance of eligibility records, actuarial support, and the administration of supplemental benefit plans.

For most ASO accounts, a separate banking account is set up and is funded directly by the plan sponsor to cover the actual benefit payments. A bill is usually sent from the administrator on a monthly basis for administrative fees.

In the case of a Minimum Premium Plan, a set rate is charged by the insurer each month to cover administration charges. A limit is also set each month on the amount of claims that can be charged against the bank account, which is funded directly by the plan sponsor. When claims exceed the limit on a cumulative basis for the contract period, the insurer/administrator pays claims using its own funds. There are many variations of minimum premium type arrangements and the administration can also vary significantly.

Ancillary Health Products

The claim adjudication process for most ancillary products (including dental and vision care plans) is very similar as that for medical plans. Issues of eligibility, determination of benefits to be paid, and identification of patient liability are much the same as that described for the medical plans, although differences created by the ACA generally do not apply to these types of free-standing benefit plans. Techniques used to manage or limit the insurer's liability for these plans include indemnity payment schedules and annual benefit maximums. Dental and vision care plans typically use a UCR fee schedule, but carry varying coinsurance payment levels by type of service, and have annual dollar benefit limits. Some expensive dental services, or services where the patient has a choice of materials to be used in the restoration process, are subject to a pre-determination of benefits in order to better manage the cost of those services.

The separation of the pharmacy benefit from the basic medical plan and the emergence of the PBM industry was largely a creation of HMOs that wanted a separate management and administrative system for this component of the benefit plan. Their objective was to make the plan more customer-friendly and be able to use different cost-sharing features than were available under the medical plan. Often, the most expensive drugs are subject to pre-authorization. In other cases, a mandatory generic substitution or mandatory mail order provision is included. Most of these plans offer electronic point-of-sale adjudication that transmits the prescription data on a real-time basis to the PBM. The PBM can electronically determine eligibility and transmit to the pharmacy any provisions that must be followed regarding coverage and payment for the drug prescribed. At that point, alternatives can be discussed with the patient, or corrections to the prescription can be made. These transactions have been made more complex with the advent of the ACA as described earlier.

Consumer-Driven Health Plans (CDHPs) and the Administration of Health Savings Accounts (HSAs)

The administration of CDHPs and HSAs presents additional challenges to the overall premium billing, enrollment, and claim adjudication processes. In the case of CDHPs, subscribers within an employer group are typically given three or more health plan options from which to choose, usually with varying levels of contribution requirements. With CDHPs, it is critical to accurately record the choices of each member on the enrollment and billing records. As long as this is done, the back end claim adjudication processes should follow standard procedures. There could, however, be some customer service issues as different members within the same employer group receive different levels of claim payments for their respective option of choice.

HSAs present the additional complication of dealing with a bank account as part of the overall administration process. While most services are still paid under the standard insurance arrangement, some benefit payments are paid directly from a member's Health Savings Account. This account functions much like checking/savings accounts. The member and/or employer will pre-fund the account with a set amount each year (usually paid monthly). Certain non-covered amounts (such as deductibles, copayments, member coinsurance amounts, and dental services) will be paid from the account. Balances can be carried forward from year to year, and used to pay for future services, including the cost of long term care programs.

In general, the claim adjudication process for a health plan functions the same for CDHPs and HSAs as it would for standard benefit programs. There are, as noted above, additional administrative complexities for these types of arrangements that increase the overall cost of administration. Many claim administrators interface electronically with financial institutions to manage the funds available, payment provisions and integration with the overall benefit program.

Other Issues in Claim Adjudication

Privacy and Security

The migration to electronic medical records makes data more readily available, speeds the treatment process, and creates portability as insured members' mobility and workplace locations continue to increase. Establishing standards for enrollment and eligibility information, medical records, and statistical data requires much more robust data security. The Health Insurance Portability and Accountability Act (HIPAA) has been the impetus for much change. The latest evolution is the HIPAA 5010 standards, which includes the EDI 834 transaction set. This is a benefit enrollment and maintenance document, which is used for enrollment activity (new enrollments/dis-enrollments or changes) but also contains benefits, plan, network, and employee demographic information. Claim payment systems need to accommodate this transaction set.

Claim History Database

An additional and important part of the claim function is the creation and maintenance of a claim history database. As medical bills are presented, this database is necessary to keep track of accumulation of deductibles, out-of-pocket expense limits, and benefit period maximums. It also provides a record for avoiding the payment of duplicate claims. Even under fully capitated programs, it has become important to track utilization of services in order to manage the contractual relationship with providers.

With increased competition in group health insurance, and increased regulatory intervention focused on the activities of health insurance underwriters, claim information is being used to a much greater extent in the risk assessment process. The claim information in these databases is being organized by diagnosis, by type of medical service (including the type of drugs prescribed), and by episode of care. The relationship between an individual's past claim history and future potential claims has been the subject of a great deal of research. Uses for this more refined claim data are numerous. These data are being used as a predictive modeling tool to supplement the traditional methods of assessing risk in the small group and individual markets. The ACA has abolished traditional underwriting in both the individual and small group markets, but the past claims information is valuable in assessing an insurer's risk and modeling its potential financial results and recoveries under various risk mitigation provisions. Medicare is using risk adjusters based on these data in setting premium rates for Medicare Advantage plans, and due to the ACA, risk adjusters are used to normalize financial results across insurers in the individual and small group markets. Predictive modeling, using information from the claim history database, has become an essential tool for risk assessment and mitigation.

Experimental Procedures

Continuing advances in medical technology are creating new issues in the claim management process. Medical advances are constantly creating new treatment approaches not contemplated by current insurance contracts. The most common problem for the claim administrator is in the area of experimental or investigational procedures. Some of these procedures may ultimately prove to be effective treatments, while others will prove to be ineffective or possibly even harmful. Coverage for these procedures has also been impacted by the ACA. Non-grandfathered benefit plans must now cover the costs of clinical trials. Additionally, "routine services" included in experimental and investigational procedures must also be covered; exclusions can only be for the experimental or investigational component of care. Individuals with a life threatening or serious illness, however, do not want to be denied the opportunity to receive any treatment that may provide a cure for their condition. Thus, the handling of these claims has become an increasingly difficult task. Many insurers look to national professional or governmental agencies to specify the safety or acceptability of specific procedures as non-experimental.

Upcoding and Unbundling

Another area requiring constant vigilance in claim management is the changing claim submission practices of physicians and other professionals. As insurers develop claim systems, screens, and edits to deal with these changes, providers continue to change the way they code claims, combining or unbundling services to maximize their reimbursement. Some insurers have now established sophisticated claim adjudication systems to capture and repackage unbundled services which produce a higher than intended reimbursement when billed as separate procedures.

Claim Processing Systems

Given the constant innovations in the areas of cost containment, managed care, medical technology, and benefit complexity, claim administration is becoming much more challenging.

Computer software has become central to the claim adjudication process. The newest systems have extensive on-line, interactive capabilities. Software has been developed with artificial intelligence to facilitate complex and detailed edits, and minimize intervention by the claim examiner. Getting all the necessary data into the system has also been a focus of improved technology. Most claim submissions now are received electronically directly from hospitals and physicians, or are submitted on machine-readable forms. Any remaining information received via hard copy is converted to an electronic image upon receipt. Accuracy challenges still exist that can impact the claim payment process, but they are likely to be overcome as data interchange capabilities are improved and system improvements are made.

New technologies are continuously incorporated into the operations of health plans and insurers. Most of these technologies allow for a high degree of automation, but some operations still require a high degree of human intervention and judgment.

The major components of the claim processing workflow are typically grouped as follows. Historically, many different vendors have provided these services, which were then integrated into one continuous process. With increased emphasis on standardization, security, and efficiency, current technology has allowed most insurers to have a self-contained process that includes all of these components:

1. Receipt processing - This consists of various systems which receive claims and the supporting documentation via a variety of sources. Claims can be received electronically or by facsimile from claim clearing houses, physician groups, and hospitals. In some cases, paper claims are still received, and in these cases organizations scan these documents, transferring them to an electronic medium. Once the claim is received, it is logged into a system and given a unique identifier.

2. OCR - Scanned paper claims and paper faxes also can be processed using Optical Character Recognition (OCR) technology. This allows for each document, once scanned, to be translated to data without the need for human intervention. It should be noted that not all scanned documents nor claims will process without human intervention, due to the aberrations and variations of documentation submitted.

3. Repair - Once claims are in an electronic format, they are processed into the health plan's "core processing" system. Here claims are either able to make a match on all of the necessary fields required to process a claim and then are auto-adjudicated (see #4), or they are rejected and manual intervention is necessary.

4. Auto-Adjudication – If all of the necessary fields are present on the claim, the system can adjudicate the claim and it is then ready for payment.

5. The payment process – Most payments made directly to providers, and even to individual claimants, are now made via electronic funds transfer. Payment by printed checks and remittance advices (the details of the payment of each claim associated with that check) occur in only a small number of cases.

These new systems have greatly enhanced the efficiency of the claim administration function, and have improved the timeliness of service to the claimant. The entire process will likely continue to improve in efficiency as new systems are developed and integrated with existing processing systems. The move toward a paperless environment has continued to evolve as systems become more interactive with internet access (via both members and providers).

The claim administration function has become increasingly reliant on the insurer's medical department, legal department and managed care specialists. Common databases and interactive systems have been created to manage the constant exchange of information between all of these areas as well as with medical care providers and group administrators.

Fraudulent Claims

There are several ways that an insurer can be the target of fraudulent claims. The two most visible have been: (1) fraud on the part of an employer or employee of an enrolled group, and (2) fraud on the part of an employee of the insurer. However, there are other types of fraud that may not, on the surface, be considered fraud but achieve the same result. That result is the payment by the insurer (or other health care organization) for claims for which it would otherwise not be responsible.

Fraudulent claims on the part of a person covered by a policy issued by the insurer, or the employer applying for group coverage, are generally the result of misleading or inaccurate information on the application for coverage, or inaccurate information supplied by the employer in order to obtain coverage for the employee.

There have been numerous examples of cases where a claim examiner authorized payment of a claim, and had a check or automatic deposit sent to an organization established by the claim examiner or a collaborator in the company who was authorized to set up company customer accounts.

Most state Medicaid agencies provide reporting to insurers on a periodic basis to validate the availability of private insurance coverage to avoid making erroneous or fraudulent payments. In some cases, these state agencies coordinate recovery of these payments with insurers.

Activities more transparent to the employer or covered employees and dependents, but equally egregious, are actions by providers that result in increased payments by insurers. Upcoding and unbundling (mentioned earlier in the chapter) could arguably be called fraudulent. Closer to the classic definition of fraud is the practice of billing for services that have not been provided. This could simply be the billing of more services than were provided, or billing for visits that did not occur. It could also include billing for services that the provider extends to the patient as "free," but results in a bill for a multitude of services to the insurer. It could also be interpreted to include those cases where a provider agrees to accept whatever the insurer will pay as payment in full, waiving co-pays and/or deductibles, implicitly inflating the amount charged to the insurer to cover the amount for which the patient would have ordinarily been responsible.

The relatively subjective nature of the determination of eligibility for some forms of disability presents additional sources of fraud. Cases of fraud include misrepresenting the employee's ability to work, not disclosing part-time work or earnings from other sources, and not disclosing benefits received from other sources (such as Social Security).

The improvements in technology associated with electronic transactions have improved the detection of fraudulent claims, making this crime more difficult to commit.

LONG-TERM CARE

An overview of claim administration concerns for long-term care insurance coverage is provided in Chapter 13, "Group Long-Term Care Insurance."

33 Health Risk Adjustment

Robert B. Cumming
P. Anthony Hammond
Syed M. Mehmud
Ross Winkelman

Introduction

Health risk adjustment can be defined as the process of adjusting measures of health care utilization or cost to reflect the health status of members. This chapter focuses on the use of risk adjustment for payment purposes. This chapter discusses applications under which the risk adjustment methodology is used to move money from organizations with lower than average risk to organizations with higher than average risk.

Health risk adjustment is commonly described as a two-step process. The first step involves risk assessment, which refers to the method used to assess the relative risk of each person in a group. The relative risk reflects the predicted medical claim dollars for each person relative to an average person. The second step is *payment adjustment,* which refers to the method used to adjust payments to reflect differences in risk, as measured by the risk assessment step. It is common to refer to a particular risk assessment method as a *risk adjuster.*

The use of health risk adjustment continues to grow, especially with methods based on medical diagnosis codes from claim data. The Affordable Care Act (ACA) introduced a diagnosis-based risk adjustment provision that transfers money among most health plans in the individual and small group markets. The federal government's Centers for Medicare and Medicaid Services (CMS) uses medical diagnosis codes to adjust payments to insurers that it contracts with to administer Medicare Advantage (Part C) and Medicare Part D. Many states use medical diagnosis codes to adjust payments to Medicaid managed care plans. The Actuarial Standards Board (ASB) has recognized the importance of risk adjustment and has issued a Risk Adjustment Actuarial Standard of Practice (ASOP).[1]

Employers use diagnosis-based health risk adjustment to analyze how employee contributions should vary by choice of health plan. Health insurers are increasingly using diagnosis or pharmacy-based methods of risk assessment for provider profiling, case management, provider payment, and rating/underwriting.

---

[1] Actuarial Standards of Practice, No. 45. *The Use of Health Status Based Risk Adjustment Methodologies*; http://www.actuarialstandardsboard.org/pdf/asop045_164.pdf

NEED FOR HEALTH RISK ADJUSTMENT

The use of health risk adjustment reflects the desire to provide equitable payments to health insurers and health care providers and make fair comparisons among insurers and providers. Risk adjustment is necessary, since the health status of enrollees can vary significantly across health insurers and health care providers. One major goal of risk adjustment is to induce health insurers and providers to compete on the basis of efficiency and quality, rather than selection of healthier risks. A second major goal is to preserve choice for consumers and have consumers pay an appropriate price for their choice of insurer or provider. The following discussion provides additional background about the major policy arguments for instituting health risk adjustment.

First, it is felt by many to be in the public's interest to have health insurers and administrators compete only on the basis of efficiency, and not compete on the basis of risk selection. One of the main policy goals for health risk adjustment is to remove incentives for risk selection. When employers and consumers compare premiums for health coverage offering similar benefits in today's market, they cannot distinguish an efficiently run plan from an inefficient one. Insurers and administrators that enroll a greater proportion of healthy individuals than their competitors will generally have lower premiums/costs. Thus, although some insurers may appear to be more efficient than others because of low premiums, they actually may not be managing the health care costs of their enrollees any better. In fact, they simply may be covering people who, on average, cost less. This distinction matters to purchasers of administrative services such as CMS, states, and self-insured employers, because these purchasers generally cannot control who they cover and want the administrator to manage the purchaser's spending as efficiently as possible. Even fully insured purchasers may want to understand this distinction, since inefficient claim cost management leads to surprisingly high renewal rate increases, and some purchasers would rather not change insurers frequently in search of the lowest price.

Second, there is the recognition that, under certain reforms including the ACA, insurers with a disproportionate share of high-risk enrollees may need to be compensated. For example, the ACA requires small group and individual insurers to issue coverage to all applicants (known as "guaranteed issue"). For the small group and individual market, the ACA limits the risk characteristics that can be used to adjust premiums to age, tobacco use, geography, and family status. In effect, a health risk adjuster reduces the premium for plans covering lower than average risks and increases the average premium for plans covering higher than average risks.

Whenever laws require insurers to guarantee issue, and to simultaneously limit the relative premiums they can charge insurance purchasers, the laws disassociate the premiums from the risks that the insurers assume. These limits on premiums become problematic when, intentionally or unintentionally, insurers enroll very different mixes of risks but are unable to vary their premium rates between the groups it covers to adequately reflect the variation in risk. The more rates are restricted, the greater the need for health risk adjustment.

Under the ACA, health insurers must set small group and individual premiums at an average risk, with variation for allowable adjustments. The insurers then receive supplemental payments, or pay supplemental charges, depending on whether their enrolled population is sicker or healthier than average. The intent of the ACA's risk adjustment program is to help stabilize premiums and reduce the incentive for insurers to seek low-risk individuals.

AVERAGE PREMIUM REFLECTS ENROLLEES' RELATIVE RISK

As noted earlier, in the absence of a health risk adjustment mechanism, an insurer's average claim cost (and premium) will reflect the relative risk of the population it insures, not just its relative efficiency.

Risk scores are generally constructed to be additive, in that an assumed risk weight for each of a person's conditions is added together to equal the total risk score for that person. The table below shows an example:

Risk Marker	Risk Weight
Male, Age 32	0.22
Diabetes with significant co-morbidities	1.32
Asthma/COPD	0.96
Low-cost dermatology	0.30
Total Risk Score	**2.80**

The following example shows the risk score development for an individual without any identifiable conditions. In many risk adjustment models, individuals without any claims, or with claims but without any identifiable conditions, receive a risk score greater than zero. This recognizes that in prospective models, which predict costs or morbidity for a future time period, individuals' medical costs regress towards the mean, implying higher costs for those with low historic costs and lower costs for those with high historic costs.

Risk Marker	Risk Weight
Male, Age 32	0.22
Total Risk Score	**0.22**

As an example of how this works, assume Insurer A and Insurer B each enroll 1,000 adults from one community, and that their risk profiles are as follows:

	Number of Enrolled Adults by Risk Category		
	Low Risk	**Average Risk**	**High Risk**
Insurer A	450	500	50
Insurer B	350	500	150

Assume that low-risk, average-risk, and high-risk adults in the community have average claim costs of $100, $200, and $600 per month, respectively. The average claim cost per enrollee for each insurer is the weighted average of these costs and the proportion of enrollees in each risk category.

Average Claim Cost for Each Plan		
	Calculation	**Weighted Average**
Insurer A	0.45(100) + 0.50(200) + 0.05(600)	$175
Insurer B	0.35(100) + 0.50(200) + 0.15(600)	$225

HEALTH RISK ASSESSMENT

There are many definitions of health risk, both technical and non-technical. People speak of themselves as being in good health or poor health, and actuaries speak matter-of-factly of good risks and bad risks. The example above delineates three categories of risk: low, average, and high. Of course, how such risk categories are defined can be very subjective. For purposes of risk classification, actuaries need to define health risk in objective, quantifiable terms. Thus, health risk is defined and measured in terms of the expected cost of medical care usage.

Risk assessment, the first step in health risk adjustment, is the process of determining the relative health risk of individuals in a particular risk class. Risk assessment involves risk classification, which is the traditional insurance practice of pooling individuals with similar risk characteristics, as well as risk measurement, which applies the statistical and actuarial methods for quantifying the level of risk of individuals within a risk class.

Health risk adjustment mechanisms present new challenges with respect to risk classification and risk measurement. Risk adjustment mechanisms ultimately involve monetary transfers, explicitly or implicitly, among insurers on the basis of the relative health risk of their enrollees. If the risk classification or risk measurement methods used do not accurately predict claim costs, the monetary transfers among insurers will be inadequate, and the goals of risk adjustment will not be fully met. Furthermore, to eliminate any financial incentive insurers may have for seeking the better risks in a market requiring them to "guarantee issue," the risk assessment method employed must be at least as predictive as any method an insurer might employ to select risks.

RISK ASSESSMENT METHODS[2]

To date, most research related to health risk adjustment has focused on the first step, risk assessment, and the risk classification schemes used for risk assessment. If a risk classification scheme is too broad, the claim cost of individuals in a risk class will vary significantly. Wide variation in claim cost of individuals in a risk class makes risk measurement for that class less accurate, and the entire risk adjustment mechanism becomes more susceptible to gaming.

Risk Classification Schemes

Risk classification schemes are generally based on one or more of the following criteria: demographics, prior utilization or claim expenditures, diagnosis and/or pharmacy information from administrative claim data, medical information or history, perceived health status, functional health status, and behavioral/lifestyle factors.

Demographics. Today's risk classification schemes based on demographics generally classify individuals by age, gender, family status, or geographic location. Demographic factors such as age and gender are often incorporated in diagnosis-based risk assessment methods, whereas geographic variation is typically recognized outside of a claim-based risk assessment model.

---

[2] Some of this summary of risk assessment methods was originally prepared as part of a draft discussion paper for the Health Insurance Association of America's Risk Adjustment Work Group. The research noted is cited in full in a bibliography at the end of this chapter.

Utilization Measures or Claim Expenditures. Utilization measures and/or claim expenditures are often used for risk assessment for rating purposes for employer groups. However, the use of claim expenditures or utilization measures is generally viewed as inappropriate for health risk adjustment, as defined earlier. For example, an inefficient insurer may be rewarded as higher historic costs would result in higher expected risk scores. For the purpose of health risk adjustment, the goal for risk assessment is to use only the impact of a person's health status on future expected costs. That is, in assigning a score to a person's health risk, the objective is to exclude the impact of factors such as provider fee levels, provider practice patterns, and health insurers' care management practices.

Diagnosis and Pharmacy Information. The use of diagnosis codes or pharmacy codes from administrative claim data for health risk assessment is very common. Some of the most common diagnosis and pharmacy-based methods are discussed in the following section.

Medicare, the individual and small group markets under the ACA, and many state Medicaid agencies use diagnosis-based methods. Large employers commonly use diagnosis-based methods to evaluate health insurers and administrators, and to adjust employee contribution levels when choice is offered. Health insurers are using diagnosis-based risk assessment methods for provider payment, provider profiling, case management, and rating/underwriting.

Medical Information or History. Risk classification schemes based on medical information or history classify risks on the basis of biomedical measurements or medical history questionnaires. Biomedical measurements that might be used include blood pressure, serum cholesterol level, height, weight, or similar medical information. Medical history questionnaires solicit information from individuals on general health statistics (height, weight) and prior medical conditions for which the individual has (or should have) sought medical attention. This approach is currently used by some insurers for underwriting determinations for life insurance. The ACA has eliminated the use of health underwriting in the individual and small group markets.

Perceived Health Status. Risk classification schemes may be based on the self-assessment of an individual's health status as determined by a questionnaire. One example of this is the 36-question health survey developed by Rand Health Sciences Program. Research on the survey's application for health risk adjustment has been conducted at Kaiser Permanente's Center for Health Research.

Functional Health Status. Risk classification schemes may be based on an individual's ability to perform various basic activities of daily living (such as bathing, dressing, transferring, toileting, continence, and feeding). This approach to risk assessment is frequently used to determine eligibility for long-term care benefits.

Lifestyle and Behavior Factors. Risk classification schemes may be based on certain behaviors or social habits such as smoking, fitness level, substance abuse, or diet. The results of one study[3] on health behaviors indicated significant differences in per capita claim cost between defined risk classifications. For example, current smokers were found to have 31% greater claim costs than individuals who do not currently smoke. Similarly, individuals with 'weight 20% or more above or below the midpoint of frame-adjusted desirable weight' range

---

[3] *Health Risks and Their Impact on Medical Costs,* a study by Milliman & Robertson, Inc, Staywell Health management Systems, Inc, in conjunction with the Chrysler Corporation and the UAW, 1995.

were shown to incur claims 37% higher than for individuals 'within 20% of the weight' range.

Multiple Classification Criteria. In practice, it is common to use one or more of the above criteria. For example, for health insurance payment purposes, most risk assessment schemes use both diagnosis and demographic information. In fact, almost all commercially available risk assessment tools use both diagnosis and demographic information in an integrated fashion to assign risk scores to each member. Risk assessment tools that have been designed for renewal rating purposes generally use even more information including diagnosis, pharmacy, demographic, claim expenditure, and claim utilization data.

Risk Measurement

Once a risk classification scheme is developed, it should be a relatively straightforward matter to calculate the average claim cost and relative risk of individuals in each risk class using classical methods. The average claim cost for all enrollees in a risk class is divided by the average claim cost of all enrollees to calculate the relative risk. The relative risk of individuals in a specific risk class may not be the same for each insurer, however. For instance, in the prior example, the relative risk factors for each insurer on its own would be as follows:

	Insurer A		Insurer B	
Risk Class	Average Claim Cost	Relative Risk Factor	Average Claim Cost	Relative Risk Factor
Low	$100	0.571	$100	0.444
Average	200	1.143	200	0.888
High	600	3.429	600	2.667
Total	$175	1.000	$225	1.000

When each insurer determines its relative risk factors and calculates its premium rates from its own risk factors, it will generate rates appropriate for the average costs in each of the risk classes. Neither of the insurers' relative risk factors would be appropriate for the risk adjustment mechanism, however, because the risk adjustment mechanism needs to reflect the relative risk factors for the entire market, that is, for all insurers combined.

When calculating relative risk factors for the entire market, the experience from all insurers must be combined. This process is complicated by data collection and timing issues. The data must be collected from all insurers on the same basis, which is difficult to do unless the risk classes are such that data can be collected easily. Further, there must be no room for discretion in determining whether an individual belongs in a specific risk class. For example, an individual's age is easily and unambiguously determined, but whether an individual is considered a cancer patient or diabetic may be more difficult – especially if the enrollee has both conditions. The risk classification scheme must clearly define in which category or categories an individual belongs.

Timing is also an issue, because the actuary must collect data from all insurers in the market. This is not always possible, so approximations may be made by using large employer data, for example, which might be reasonably predictive of claim costs until data from all insurers becomes available. For research purposes, that approximation probably is adequate for comparing one risk assessment method against another. For actual administration of a risk adjustment mechanism, such approximations may need to be adjusted as soon as credible data is received from all insurers in the risk pool, so that retrospective adjustments can be made to correct initial inaccuracies in the relativities.

Revisiting the prior example and assuming insurers A and B are the only two insurers in the market, the market-wide relative risk factors for the three risk classes and each insurer would be determined as follows:

	Proportion of Enrolled Adults by Risk Category		
	Low Risk	Average Risk	High Risk
Market Total	0.40	0.50	0.10

	Average Claim Cost for Market Total	
	Calculation	Weighted Average
Market Total	0.40(100) + 0.50(200) + 0.10(600)	$200

Using the weighted average cost for the market, the actuary can then calculate the relative risk factors for each insurer:

	Relative Risk Factors by Insurer	
	Weighted Average Claim Cost	Relative Risk Factor
Insurer A	$175	0.875
Insurer B	225	1.125
Market Total	$200	1.000

The risk assessment process has determined that Insurer A is 12.5% less risky than average, and Insurer B is 12.5% more risky than average. But how accurate was the risk assessment? The performance of risk assessments will be discussed later in this chapter.

DIAGNOSIS AND PHARMACY-BASED RISK ASSESSMENT

The following section describes common diagnosis and pharmacy-based risk assessment models, including:

- The HHS-HCC Risk Adjustment Model for Individual and Small Group Markets under the ACA
- CMS-HCC Risk Adjustment Model (Medicare)
- Adjusted Clinical Groups (ACGs)
- Chronic Illness and Disability Payment System (CDPS)
- Clinical Risk Groups (CRGs)
- Diagnostic Cost Groups (DCGs)
- Episode Risk Groups (ERGs)
- Impact Pro
- Medicaid Rx

- Milliman Advanced Risk Adjusters (MARA)
- Pharmacy Risk Groups (PRGs)
- RxGroups
- RxRisk
- Wakely Risk Assessment Model (WRA)

Model Considerations

Risk assessment models are revised and updated periodically. The models vary considerably in the details, but some common themes and major differences are discussed below.

Type of data used by a model. Most models use one or more of ICD-9-CM diagnosis codes from medical claim or encounter data (to be replaced by ICD-10-CM after October, 2015), National Drug Codes (NDCs) from pharmacy encounter data, or prior utilization and cost data. The type of data available for a given application limits the choice of risk assessment tools. It is increasingly common for model builders to include several data options for their models (for example, diagnosis only, or diagnosis and pharmacy combined).

Data elements used by a model. Most risk assessment models use very similar information. Reducing implementation burden is a key practical concern in risk adjustment, and therefore it is not surprising that there are a few data elements that are considered critical amongst most, if not all, modern risk assessment tools.

The eligibility of the insured is one critical element. The length of eligibility is used to assess credibility, and eligibility is also used to assess attribution to a plan or product, a concern when the insured switches such plan or product.

It is ideal if the data used to assess the risk is on the same basis as the data used to develop the risk adjuster.

Additive versus mutually exclusive categories. A common modeling framework used in developing risk assessment tools is linear regression. In such a model, an individual may be assigned to multiple condition categories. Each condition category has an associated risk weight, determined through regression. The risk score for the individual is then calculated by adding the indicated condition risk weights, plus the demographic category weights that are based on fitting the residual to age/gender based categories.

Another, less common, approach is to group each individual into a single cell, based on demographic and clinical characteristics. The cells are mutually exclusive; that is, an individual may not be grouped in more than one cell. Such an approach may have lower predictive accuracy compared to some regression based models, but it is simpler to implement and interpret.

Prospective or Concurrent. A prospective application of risk adjustment uses claim data from a given period of time to calculate expected member-level costs for a future period. A concurrent application is similar, but uses claim data from a given period to calculate expected member-level costs in that same period. It may seem odd at first to 'predict' costs for a period for which there are already actual costs. However, a risk assessment tool calculates expected amounts based on some representative population that is intended to reflect the *market norm,* and not any specific health insurer's actual cost-level information.

A prospective model emphasizes chronic conditions that result in a persistent level of cost, while a concurrent risk model places more emphasis on acute episodes with high costs that may or may not persist. For example, appendicitis may receive a low score in a prospective model, but may have a high score in a concurrent model.

In terms of statistical accuracy, a concurrent model is far more accurate than a prospective model, and produces larger money transfers among plans. However, concurrent models may be more exposed to improper coding, due to the larger payments than in prospective approaches. In addition, the timing of payments in concurrent models raises significant financial challenges as a health insurer may not know its final net costs until well after closing the books on a year.

A prospective approach is forward-looking and promotes the management of care for chronically ill patients. This is because risk adjustment payment transfers to an insurer caring for a chronically ill patient will be based on the average market cost. To the extent an insurer can manage the care more efficiently (and less costly), it will increase its profit margin.

A given risk assessment model may be prospective, concurrent, or include options for both. The decision to use one approach over another will depend upon the application and the sensitivity of stakeholders to issues around incentives, timing, and the magnitude transfer payments.

Hierarchical, Episodic, or Other Methods. Many condition groupings start with the grouping of diagnosis codes (ICD-9-CM or ICD-10-CM) into one of a number of clinically similar groups. Hierarchies are then imposed, which ensure that an individual is indicated as having a condition only for the most severe manifestation of a condition found in his or her claim data, and that the same condition is not counted more than once across the spectrum of severities.

Episodic groupers apply clinical and statistical algorithms to combine related services in a set timeframe into episodes, which are then mapped to episodic groups with associated risk weights. Other less commonly used methods include neural network and clustering methods.

Number of Groupings. Related to the above discussion, models vary greatly in terms of the specificity of their condition groupings. One model may have fifty different condition groupings indicated for an individual, while another may have over two hundred. A model with more specificity may not necessarily be better. The marginal increase in accuracy from additional conditions in a regression model decreases rather quickly, and the quality and accuracy of a model mainly depends on other important factors unrelated to the number of condition groupings (see the section below on the evaluation of risk adjusters).

Population. Populations differ greatly in the patterns of incident clinical conditions, prevalence of conditions and the expected costs for a given condition. Such differences can be seen across Medicare, Medicaid, and commercial populations. A given risk assessment tool will be calibrated to be used with a certain population, and may not produce usable results (due to poor accuracy or bias) when applied to a different population.

Cost, Support, and Usability. Models vary greatly in terms of cost, from free to several hundred thousand dollars a year (often depending upon the number of covered lives). Some models may be easier to implement within an insurer's existing database capabilities, while other models may require additional software to run. It is important to consider these differences when considering implementation challenges and timelines.

Commonly Used Models

The following provides a brief overview of some of the risk assessment models in use today.

HHS-HCC Risk Adjustment Model for Individual and Small Group Markets under the Affordable Care Act. The ACA's risk adjustment model is discussed in detail later in this chapter.

CMS-HCC Risk Adjustment Model (Medicare). The Medicare risk adjustment model is also discussed in detail later in this chapter.

Adjusted Clinical Groups (ACGs). The ACG model is a diagnosis-based risk assessment model developed by Jonathan Weiner and other researchers at Johns Hopkins University. This model was originally based on ambulatory diagnoses. Later versions use both inpatient and ambulatory diagnosis codes. The model groups diagnosis codes into Adjusted Diagnosis Groups (ADGs), and ADGs are then combined with age and gender to produce mutually exclusive Adjusted Clinical Groups (ACGs). ACGs differ from most other models in that the ACG categories are mutually exclusive; that is, a member is classified into only one ACG category. In general, this may make custom calibration by the end user easier. For example, adjusting one category does not impact other categories as it would in a regression model. However, one cannot recalibrate the model via linear regression since the categories are mutually exclusive. As mentioned earlier, mutually exclusive categorical models generally result in a decrease in the predictive performance, and lose some of the clinical granularity when compared to other methods.

Chronic Illness and Disability Payment System (CDPS). The CDPS is a diagnosis-based risk assessment model developed by Richard Kronick and other researchers at the University of California, San Diego. The CDPS is a free and open-source model. Although this model was originally developed for use with Medicaid populations, it can also be used with commercial populations, after appropriate recalibration. The CDPS model is an update and expansion of a prior model developed by Kronick and published in 1996 called the Disability Payment System (DPS). The DPS model was developed for the Medicaid disabled population.

The CDPS model assigns each member to one or more of over 60 medical condition categories based on diagnosis codes. Each member is also assigned to a demographic category based on age and gender. For each member, the model predicts total medical costs based on the medical condition categories and the age/gender category assigned. The model includes separate risk weights for adults and children, and for different Medicaid populations, such as the Temporary Assistance for Needy Families (TANF) and the Aged & Disabled populations.

CDPS and all other regression-based risk adjustment models use demographic information in addition to diagnosis and/or pharmacy codes. Age and gender are typically grouped into 10 to 30 categories, each with an associated risk score. The age cost curve looks similar to pure demographic factors, but is less steep. The reason for this is that higher costs at higher ages tend to be captured in the clinical portion of the model rather than the demographic portion, which essentially captures the residual, or the part of costs not explained by clinical groupings.

Clinical Risk Groups (CRGs). CRGs were developed by 3M Health Systems. CRGs use diagnoses and a selected set of procedure codes, considered non-discretionary, to calculate a risk score for each member. Similarly to the ACGs, the CRGs group an individual to a single, mutually exclusive risk group. The CRG version 1.4 (released 2006) contained over a thousand such groupings.

Milliman Advanced Risk Adjusters. Developed by Milliman Inc., this is a suite of tools with a broad set of uses, including budgeting, pricing, payment, stratifying risks, care management and reporting. The models can be used with diagnosis-only data, pharmacy-only, or in a combination model. The developers focused particularly on predictive accuracy of the models.

Diagnostic Cost Groups. The DCG model is a diagnosis-based risk assessment model originally developed by researchers including Randall Ellis and Arlene Ash at Boston University. The DCG models include a number of variations depending on the type of population being analyzed (commercial, Medicaid, Medicare), the source of the diagnosis data (inpatient only versus all encounters) and the purpose of the model (payment versus explanation).

The DCG model assigns each member to one or more medical condition categories called hierarchical condition categories (HCCs), based on diagnosis codes. Each member is also assigned to a demographic category based on age and gender. Based on these medical condition and age/gender categories, the model predicts the total medical costs for each member. Diagnosis codes are grouped into about 780 (version 2.1.1) clinically homogenous groups, which are then mapped into about 180 hierarchical condition groups. The model then predicts total medical cost for each patient based on the HCCs and age/gender categories. CMS uses a simplified version of this model for risk adjusting the payments to Medicare Advantage plans. The simplified model includes about 70 condition categories. More details of this model are included in a later section in this chapter on Medicare risk adjustment.

Episode Risk Groups (ERGs). ERGs were developed by Symmetry Health Data Systems, which is now part of Optum. ERGs are based on the Episode Treatment Groups (ETG) model also developed by Symmetry. The ETGs group claim expenditures based on an episode of care concept using clinically similar condition categories. The main purpose of the ETGs is to facilitate provider profiling. The ETGs allow users to compare the efficiency of physicians, clinics, and hospitals. For provider profiling and care management purposes, the ETGs provide more actionable information since the expenditures and utilization data is organized by episode, medical condition, and type of medical service, such as radiology use, emergency room use, and hospital inpatient use. This allows users to identify the drivers of potential excess utilization, since the tool allows one to drill down by physician, condition, and type of medical service. The tool can be used to identify where utilization and/or cost are outside of the norm and what is driving the variance.

The ERG model assigns each member to one or more medical condition categories, called episode risk groups. The medical condition categories assigned to a member depend primarily on that member's diagnosis codes and pharmacy data.

Impact Pro. Impact Pro is a tool specifically designed for underwriting and rating, and for identifying potential high cost members for case management. It is based on the ERGs, but includes other markers beyond diagnosis and demographic information that are predictive of high future medical expenditures, but would be inappropriate to include in a risk adjuster used for payment purposes.

Medicaid Rx. Medicaid Rx is a pharmacy-based risk assessment model developed by Todd Gilmer and other researchers at the University of California at San Diego. The model was originally designed and calibrated for a Medicaid population, but has been used for commercial populations. The model is an update and expansion of the Chronic Disease Score model developed by researchers at Group Health Cooperative of Puget Sound. The Medicaid Rx model assigns each member to one or more of about 45 medical condition categories based on the prescription drugs used by each member, and to one demographic category based on age/gender. Similar to CDPS, the model contains separate risk weights for adults and for children.

Pharmacy Risk Groups (PRGs). PRG is a pharmacy-based risk assessment tool developed and sold by Optum. The tool uses a mapping for National Drug Codes (NDCs) to about a hundred pharmacy risk groups (or PRGs). Using these PRGs and demographic categories, a score is computed for each member.

RxGroups. RxGroups is a pharmacy-based risk assessment model developed by DxCG Inc. in conjunction with Kaiser Permanente and clinicians from CareGroup and Harvard Medical School. This model uses a mapping of NDC codes into over a hundred and fifty mutually exclusive categories (called RxGroups) based on each drug's therapeutic indication.

RxRisk. RxRisk is a pharmacy-based risk assessment model developed by Paul Fishman at Group Health Cooperative of Puget Sound. RxRisk is a combination of the original Chronic Disease Score model, designed for adults, and the Pediatric Chronic Disease Score model. The RxRisk model assigns each member to one or more medical condition categories, and to one demographic category based on age/gender.

Wakely Risk Assessment Model (WRA). The WRA model was developed by Syed M. Mehmud at Wakely Consulting Group. This is an open-code model and is calibrated for a commercial population. The model incorporates cost changes due to benefit and coverage changes newly required under the ACA, and draws inspiration from the CMS-HCC and MedicaidRx models discussed earlier. The model can be used with diagnosis-only data, pharmacy-only, or in a combination model. One different aspect of this model is that it includes internal adjustments to correct for bias due to partial eligibility of risk scored members.

MEASURING PREDICTIVE PERFORMANCE

A 2007 Society of Actuaries study compared the performance of seven common diagnosis and pharmacy-based methods of health risk assessment ("A Comparative Analysis of Claims-Based Tools for Health Risk Assessment"). In this study, a variety of measures were used to compare the predictive accuracy of risk adjusters. In general, these measures compare actual claim dollars with predictions from the risk adjuster models. The comparison is performed on two levels: (1) by individual and (2) by group.

Measures of Predictive Accuracy – Individual Level

The individual measures of predictive accuracy include individual R-squared, and mean absolute prediction error.

Individual R-squared is described as the percentage of the variation in medical claim costs explained by the risk adjuster model (R-squared is also known as correlation). Variation refers to the difference in medical costs for a given individual compared to the average medical cost for all individuals. Individual R-squared is a standard statistical measure for assessing model results commonly used for measuring predictive accuracy of risk adjusters. It is a single summary measure on a standardized scale of 0 to 1, where 0 indicates that the model explains 0 percent of the variation in cost among the individuals and 1 indicates that the model explains 100 percent of the variation (that is, the model is 100 percent accurate in its predictions). The standardized scale helps with comparability between studies. The primary drawback of Individual R-squared is that it squares each prediction error, and therefore tends to be overly sensitive to the prediction error for individuals with large claims.

Mean absolute prediction error is calculated as follows. First, the prediction error for each individual is determined by calculating the difference between predicted medical costs and actual medical costs. Next, the absolute value of each of these prediction errors is calculated, and, finally, the mean of the absolute prediction error across all individuals is determined. This measure can be expressed as a percentage by dividing the result by the mean actual medical costs.

Measures of Predictive Accuracy – Group Level

A group level measure of predictive accuracy involves adding up the total predicted claims for a group of individuals and comparing that value to the actual claims for the same group. This comparison gives a *predictive ratio*. A predictive ratio that is closer to 1.0 indicates a better fit. The predictive ratio is the reciprocal of the common actual-to-expected (A to E) actuarial ratio.

The group level measures differ in terms of how the groups are determined. There are two general approaches: (1) *non-random groups* and (2) *random groups*. Non-random refers to grouping individuals based on selected criteria. The common criteria used for analyzing risk adjusters include groups based on medical condition or amount of claim dollars. Non-random groups can also be defined based on other criteria, such as being part of a particular employer group. This is sometimes referred to as using *real groups*. Random groups refer to groups created by selecting individuals at random from the study data set.

***R*-Squared and MAPE Results**

Table 30.1 shows a sample of the results from the 2007 SOA study. This table shows a summary of the R-squared and MAPE (%) measures for a prospective application of risk adjustment, which used diagnosis and pharmacy data from 2003 to predict 2004 medical expenditures, and truncated claims at $250,000. Results are shown using "offered" and "recalibrated" weights, where offered weights are the standard risk weights provided by the models and recalibrated weights are calculated based on the data set used for the study.

Table 33.1

Summary of R-Squared and MAPE Prospective Model: Claims Truncated at $250,000

Risk Adjuster	Type of Risk Adjuster	R-Squared		MAPE	
		Offered Weights	Recalibrated	Offered Weights	Recalibrated
ACG	Diag	19.2%	19.6%	89.9%	88.8%
CDPS	Diag	14.9%	17.7%	95.3%	91.9%
CRG	Diag	17.5%	N/A	90.9%	N/A
DxCG DCG	Diag	20.6%	21.3%	87.5%	87.0%
DxCG RxGroups	Rx	20.4%	20.5%	85.3%	85.3%
Ingenix PRG	Rx	20.5%	21.2%	85.8%	85.6%
Medicaid Rx	Rx	15.8%	17.7%	89.6%	88.4%
Impact PRO	Med+Rx+Use	24.4%	25.6%	81.8%	81.6%
ERG	Diag+Rx	19.7%	20.0%	86.4%	86.1%

Summary of Results

A few high-level conclusions can be drawn from the results from the 2007 SOA study. First, pharmacy-based models perform similar to the diagnosis-based models. Second, recalibration of the risk weights result in a significant increase in performance for some of the risk adjusters, such as CDPS and Medicaid Rx. Third, the predictive performance of the models has increased significantly since the prior SOA studies in 1995 and 2002. The models continue to significantly overestimate future cost for people who are currently low cost and underestimate future cost for people who are currently high cost.

Note that R-Squared values under 30% may not seem high to those who are not familiar with the limitations of predicting healthcare costs at an individual level. However, the accuracy is impressive when one considers the enormous variation of one person's health costs from year to year, and further considers that a very high proportion of the population (particularly a commercial population) incur no or low health care costs in any given year.

When a risk adjustment model is used on an individual basis, it is usually used to stratify the population and predict who will need case management, utilization management, or disease management interventions; or to predict special pricing (or eligibility or design) considerations for stop-loss insurance. In that framework, the models perform better than the above discussion suggests, because the segment of the population that is identified for interventions likely has a much higher correlation between actual and expected cost.

More importantly, risk adjustment models are often used for group-level decisions, such as pricing a group's insurance premiums, explaining why a group is different from an average cost benchmark or other groups, or exchanging payments between insurers. In those cases, the accuracy of all of the models increases dramatically, and results become highly credible and correlated. Rather than predicting just one person's cost, the models predict group aggregate cost, often relative to other groups.

When evaluating risk adjustment models, it is extremely important to consider the planned uses of risk adjusters. Further, analysis may show that all of the models do a sufficiently good job at a particular application, and that small accuracy differences might be immaterial, particularly in relation to cost differences, data requirement differences, and the staff resources that are needed to implement and maintain any particular risk adjuster.

The Society of Actuaries is in the process of updating the study, and is expected to release a new study in mid-2016. For a complete discussion of these results, see the Health Section page of the Society of Actuaries' website at www.soa.org.

EVALUATING RISK ADJUSTERS

The process of risk adjustment can be thought of as a combination of model and methodology. The prior section discussed the accuracy of a risk assessment model; however, implementation of methodology and practical constraints typically determine the preference for a particular risk adjustment approach. Following are a few key concepts to help evaluate risk adjusters.

Bias. Risk adjusters (including the transfer formula) should not be statistically biased. The bias-variance trade-off is well known to statisticians, and many feel that, for risk adjustment purposes, it is more important to be unbiased than it is to be accurate. Introducing factors that are not directly related to risk into the method will make it more difficult to determine how well the true risk adjustment is working. An example of potential bias would be a considerably higher required duration for eligibility by one insurer versus another. One insurer would then have a higher number of diagnoses, disease prevalence, and risk scores, all else being equal.

Transparency. Transparency refers to knowledge and availability of the exact methodology and algorithm that is used to calculate risk scores. Transparency helps parties understand *why* payment is being adjusted and increases awareness of how future payment accuracy can be improved. Greater transparency may avoid implementation confusion. However, the flip side of transparency is that a risk adjuster developer who invests capital and resources into a more accurate predictor of medical conditions will want to get economic benefit in return, which requires keeping a competitive advantage and thus the desire for some level of secrecy around the methods used to develop the risk adjuster. The cost of implementing a risk adjuster should not exceed its benefit to the insurer, nor to the market as a whole in terms of efficiency and savings.

Fairness & Gaming: A health risk adjuster needs to be accurate, practical, predictable, and not subject to gaming. Since risk adjustment monetary transfers depend on relative risk factors, any risk assessment method must be accurate and unbiased in order for the risk adjustment mechanism to be applied fairly. Any perception of unfairness by the marketplace may be highly contentious. If a risk adjuster can be gamed, the market will question whether it is equitable, and possibly raise legal challenges. Similarly, if the risk adjuster does not provide sufficient incentive for insurers to manage their costs, it will be perceived as unfair. Thus, risk adjustment transfers should be based on expected costs rather than on actual costs, to encourage efficiency.

Specific coding: The diagnosis grouping used for payment adjustment should encourage specific coding. For example, vague or unspecified diagnosis codes should not be a part of the risk adjustment approach. Along similar lines, a clinical grouping should not reward proliferation of codes. For example, multiple instances of the same diagnosis for a person, or several clinically similar diagnosis codes, should not result in a higher assessed risk (although some exceptions exist such as in cases where one instance may not be sufficient proof that a chronic condition exists and the system may require a confirmatory diagnosis on another claim).

Upcoding. Discretionary coding, or upcoding, should not be rewarded. Certain diagnoses or drugs are subject to high coding variation across providers due to their discretionary nature. Excluding these diagnosis and drugs from a risk assessment model decreases its sensitivity to coding variation, gaming, or upcoding. Risk assessment methods using diagnosis or pharmacy data are relatively objective, and such data can be readily collected and verified. For some uses of risk adjusters, it is important that the methodology only use diagnosis, pharmacy, and procedure codes that are not easily susceptible to discretionary use. Most models do not use procedure codes, due to concerns that physician practice patterns could have an impact on risk scores. However, some models (ERGs and CRGs) use a few procedure codes believed to be non-discretionary. Similarly, there is a concern that pharmacy-based models could be unduly influenced by physician practice patterns.

Data Quality & Credibility. Two important concerns in the application of risk adjustment are the type of available data and the quality of that data, including its timeliness and consistency. If diagnosis codes are not captured consistently across insurers, then risk adjustment may produce biased estimates based on differences in coding practices, rather than underlying morbidity risk of the populations.

Data Availability. Risk assessment methods based on medical information and treatment history may directly reflect broad classes of health status, such as high blood pressure. However, such data may be difficult to collect, as it is not routinely available for most health plans. It may also be very expensive to install a process for collecting this information uniformly on large populations.

Perceived health status and functional health status methods are necessarily subjective measures and can easily be gamed. This data is not typically collected by insurers, and would require surveys and other expensive data collection efforts. Since this data is subjective, its collection would need to be carefully designed and controlled to avoid gaming.

Behavioral and lifestyle factors can be obtained through either enrollment data or surveys, but this basis of risk assessment has some of the same problems as methods based on perceived health status. While some factors such as smoking and drinking have a direct impact on health care costs, the available data may be insufficient for risk assessment unless applied in combination with one or more other methods.

In practice, behavioral and lifestyle data is not commonly used or sought for group-level estimations, because the models already perform well at a group level. The slight addition to accuracy that would result generally does not warrant the expense, unless there is a low cost source of data available. However, in cases where risk adjusters have already been used to stratify individual level interventions, this type of data may be collected from willing individuals in order to personalize and prioritize a personalized health improvement plan.

Clinical Relevance. The grouping or categorization of individuals into risk classes in a risk adjuster should be clinically meaningful. This improves the credibility of a model, especially as perceived by clinicians and care providers. This also improves the understandability and interpretability of the risk adjustment process, including its utility for care management and monitoring quality of care.

Timing. Insurers are apt to prefer a health risk adjuster that allows them to determine, with reasonable certainty, what their payments will be at the time they set premiums. For example, in cases in which timing is critical, a prospective risk adjuster may be a better option than a concurrent approach. While a concurrent approach is more accurate, it involves waiting until after the period for which premiums had been set in order to use data for risk adjustment.

Implementation of a risk adjustment approach involves several decisions, many of which result in trade-offs. The evaluation of a model and methodology is determined by the specifics of a given application, including the nature of the application itself.

NEW RESEARCH INTO RISK ADJUSTERS

Risk assessment and adjustment has been a dynamic area of research over the last decade. Risk adjustment research continues to attract interest, perhaps because while risk assessment and adjustment models will never be perfect, they will continue to improve through further study.

A 2012 Society of Actuaries study titled "Uncertainty in Risk Adjustment" explores the risk score as a random variable with an underlying distribution. The research provides a theoretical foundation to calculate confidence intervals around a risk score estimate. The study shows how confidence intervals shrink considerably between member-level risk scores and group-level scores. The study also shows how accuracy in risk adjustment improves tremendously for groups of members given a small amount of correlation in terms of member morbidity. This confirms what has been anecdotally known in the industry for some time.

Health economists have published many studies on the association of morbidity and sociological factors (such as income and education). Another 2013 SOA research study titled "Nontraditional Variables in Healthcare Risk Adjustment" explores the quantitative association of socio-economic factors and health care morbidity. The study evaluates the impact of incorporating nontraditional variables such as income, education, and attitudes towards insurance into the risk assessment model. One of the major findings of the study is that nontraditional variables can be very important, but not for the reason one might first suspect. These variables often do not improve risk adjustment accuracy in a significant way; however, they address bias in predictions that may otherwise be open to potential selection. The paper develops a new measure, called *Loss Ratio Advantage (LRA)* that allows one to measure the importance of a nontraditional variable from this perspective in a consistent manner.

As mentioned previously, the SOA study on claims-based risk assessment is currently being updated, with an expected date of publication in mid-2016.

Risk Adjustment In The Affordable Care Act

The permanent ACA risk adjustment program is one of the most important risk mitigation mechanisms employed by the ACA, as it makes possible many of the other important reforms, including guaranteed issue and limits on rating variables.

The ACA requires health insurers to accept all individuals applying for coverage (as part of the guaranteed issue provision) in the small group and individual markets. The ACA also prohibits the use of health status of individuals and small groups when setting premium rates. Age can be used as a rating variable, but rates cannot vary by more than a ratio of three to one for the oldest to the youngest adults. Gender is not an allowable rating variable. These constraints create potential incentives for a health insurer to enroll a lower-cost portfolio of individuals, and therefore risk adjustment is an important tool to counteract this incentive, by mitigating antiselection and maintaining a competitive marketplace.

The ACA creates health insurance exchanges that are intended to increase competition. An exchange operates in parallel, and does not replace the current marketplace. One of the key characteristics of exchanges, relative to risk adjustment, is the requirement that low-income individuals who want to receive premium and cost sharing subsidies must enroll in coverage through an exchange. See Chapter 19, "Health Benefit Exchanges," for further discussion of exchanges.

In addition to risk adjustment, the ACA includes two other risk mitigation programs, reinsurance and risk corridors, and the three programs are commonly referred to as "The Three Rs". The risk adjustment program is the only permanent program; the other two are only in effect through 2016. The following tables summarize the markets to which each of the three programs applies, and the administrator of each program:

ACA Provision	Sold Within Exchange		Sold Outside Exchange		
	Individual	Small Group	Individual	Small Group	Grandfathered
Risk Adjustment	Yes	Yes	Yes	Yes	No
Reinsurance	Yes	No	Yes	No	No
Risk Corridor	Yes	Yes	No*	No*	No

ACA Provision	Who Administers	
	State Run Exchange	Federal Run Exchange
Risk Adjustment	State or HHS State can decide if HHS, all parameters will be Federal	HHS
Reinsurance	State or HHS (parameters may not be changed from Federal)	HHS
Risk Corridor	HHS	HHS

* Off exchange plans that are essentially similar to on exchange plans can attain qualified status and thus become eligible for the risk corridor program.

The risk adjustment program under the ACA is intended to mitigate antiselection among health insurers, and also between the markets inside and outside the Exchange. On an ongoing basis, the risk adjustment program will increase payments to issuers enrolling a high-morbidity population (such as those with chronic ailments), and correspondingly reduce payments to issuers enrolling a healthier population. The summary that follows categorizes aspects of the program into a) population, b) model, c) methodology, and d) process. The following is intended to communicate key and interesting elements of the ACA risk adjustment program, but many elements have necessarily been omitted from this summary.[4]

POPULATION

In any application of risk adjustment, it is important to be able to clearly define the population that will be risk-scored or risk-assessed. The population to be risk-scored under the ACA risk adjustment program consists of individual and small group plans that are ACA compliant, starting in 2014. Plans both inside and outside of the exchanges will be subject to risk adjustment. Only the diagnoses documented during an ACA compliant eligibility period will be allowable for risk adjustment. Members will be risk-scored regardless of the length of eligibility in an ACA-compliant plan. This is unique to the ACA risk adjustment program; in several other programs, such as Medicare, members must be eligible for a certain number of months to be included in the risk scoring process.

Defining the risk pool is equally as important as defining the population that is risk scored. The subtle distinction is that the risk pool describes who a particular member is compared against, whereas the population definition communicates who may be run through the program. The risk pools in the ACA risk adjustment program are by state and market, where market is defined as individual plans, small group plans, or catastrophic plans. For example, the risk score for a catastrophic health plan issuer in California will only be compared to other catastrophic health plan issuers in California.

MODEL

The terms "risk assessment" and "risk adjustment" tend to be used interchangeably in practice; however, they are separate and distinct concepts. Risk assessment is the process of risk-scoring members (model) and risk adjustment is the process of adjusting payments on the basis of those scores (methodology). The full description of a risk assessment model could be a book in its own right. The discussion in this subsection summarizes a few key characteristics of the ACA risk assessment *model*, and in the next subsection the risk adjustment *methodology* is discussed.

Calibration. One of the most important aspects of a risk assessment model is how the risk weights are defined. The ACA's model defines separate weights for adults (21+ years of age), children (2+ years of age) and infants. There are also separate weights for the ACA's metal tier plans (platinum, gold, silver, bronze, and catastrophic). Combined, there are 15 sets of risk weights in the model (three age groups and five plan groups).

The ACA model is calibrated using plan paid amounts (after member cost sharing) rather than allowed amounts; in other words, its intent is to estimate the *plan's* liability rather than

---

[4] The reader is encouraged to read source material from CMS' Center for Consumer Information & Insurance Oversight's (CCIIO's) Regulations and Guidance website: http://www.cms.gov/cciio/resources/Regulations-and-Guidance/index.html#Medical Loss Ratio

the total amount including the member's liability, which is the reason for the need for different sets of risk weights by metallic tiers. Platinum plans offer richer benefits (thus higher plan liabilities) and the calculated risk scores are correspondingly higher than for example the bronze plan and for the same underlying morbidity.

Groupings. At the core of a risk model is the definition of condition groupings. The ACA model uses a similar hierarchical condition grouping framework to the one used in the Medicare Advantage program, in which groupings are based on ICD-9 codes only. Each ICD-9 code maps to a condition category (CC). The condition categories in turn map to about 100 further aggregated hierarchical condition categories (HCCs). The hierarchical mechanism categorizes an individual into the most severe manifestation of a particular condition. For example, "cancer" falls under multiple HCCs, where one may indicate a less severe condition and another may indicate a more severe or metastasized form of the disease. If an individual is indicated for a more severe form, then the flag is removed for the less severe cancer indication, according to the hierarchy. This is done to avoid increasing the risk score for an individual for the same underlying condition, while capturing the appropriate severity. The grouping rules include additional complexity, including edits based on demographics, where certain HCCs may not be indicated for certain ages and/or gender, and associated conditions.

Data. As mentioned previously, the model uses only diagnosis data in order to assign members to certain conditions. The data elements required by the model are fairly standard, including member identifier, age, gender, enrollment information, and diagnosis codes.

It is crucial to understand which diagnoses are considered 'allowable' (or conversely, are not excluded), since allowable diagnoses can adversely affect the scores, or even the program, if they are not handled appropriately. Risk adjustment program methodologies typically include criteria for the types of diagnosis codes that are allowable for risk assessment, whereas other codes are excluded even before they are presented to the risk assessment model code. For example, in Medicare Advantage the diagnosis selection criteria are typically based on provider specialties. In the ACA model, the criteria vary depending on whether a code is on a professional claim, an inpatient claim, or an outpatient facility claim.

Diagnoses are generally limited in order to include those that are more reliable. For example, physicians may order laboratory profiles in order to test or rule out a particular condition, while noting the condition to be tested. A risk model may exclude diagnoses in such instances because an individual may not actually have the condition.

Adjustments. In addition to groupings and the weights, a model's weights may include adjustments. The ACA model adjusts final weights to account for whether a member is in a Cost Sharing Reduction (CSR) plan or has richer benefits, since a member may use more services in a plan that has reduced cost sharing, and the calculated risk score may not reflect that difference.

Risk Scoring Example. One of the best ways to understand a model is to work through an example. Assume a member who is an adult male, aged 35, has a platinum plan. Claim data reveals that the individual has ICD-9 code 51901 (infection of tracheostomy) and 7991 (respiratory arrest). Code 51901 maps to CC 125, whereas 7991 maps to CC 126. Since CC 125 takes precedence (higher severity), and both codes point to a similar underlying condition, the CC126 flag is ignored and the CC 125 flag is applied. Add the demographic based risk score (0.413) and the coefficient for HCC125 (40.054) to get the total risk score of 40.467 for the individual. Multiply this risk score with the appropriate factor for the CSR category. Since there is no cost-sharing reduction for this member, the final risk score is 40.467 x 1 = 40.467.

METHODOLOGY

Calculating the risk score is, of course, only a part of the overall process of risk adjustment. The details of the formula for calculating ACA risk adjustment transfers are somewhat complex, but the general principle is that the risk transfer is based on the difference in the relative risk scores (that is, relative to the risk pool) and the relative rating factors. An insurer will have already recognized differences in its premium revenue through the use of rating factors, and therefore the risk transfer should only reflect differences that are not included in the rating factors.

The formula for the ACA risk adjustment transfers is:

HHS Transfer formula:

$$T_i = \left[\frac{PLRS_i \times IDF_i \times GCF_i}{\sum_i (s_i \times PLRS_i \times IDF_i \times GCF_i)} - \frac{AV_i \times ARF_i \times IDF_i \times GCF_i}{\sum_i (s_i \times AV_i \times ARF_i \times IDF_i \times GCF_i)} \right] \overline{P_s}$$

Where:

T_i = Transfer for plan i.
$\overline{P_s}$ = State Average Premium.
$PLRS_i$ = Plan i's plan liability risk score.
IDF_i = Plan i's induced demand factor.
ARF_i = Plan i's allowable rating factor.
AV_i = Plan i's actuarial value.
GCF_i = Plan i's geographic cost factor.
s_i = Plan i's share of State enrollment, and the denominator is summed across all plans in the risk pool in the market in the state.

PROCESS

The model and the methodology are also part of the overall process of risk adjustment. The ACA risk adjustment process includes the timing window for data, which is based on calendar year incurred claims, paid through April 30th of the following year. The methodology is *concurrent*, so risk scores assessed using 2015 data affect risk adjustment transfers in 2015. The transfer calculations are completed around June of the year following the base period.

THE FIRST YEAR OF RISK ADJUSTMENT

Benefit year 2014 was the first year or risk adjustment. Summary results for the risk adjustment program were released on June 30, 2015. A number of interesting observations may be drawn from the results. First, despite significant technical challenges and an ambitious timeline, over 99.5% of issuers were able to submit the data necessary to calculate reinsurance and risk adjustment transfers. Successful calculation of these amounts does not imply accuracy of data, however, and a number of issuers experienced challenges in this regard.

Next, according to the CMS analysis, issuers that enrolled high-risk individuals received risk transfer payments as intended under the ACA risk adjustment program. These included issuers that enrolled a large share of HIV/AIDS patients, offered more comprehensive prescription drug plans, had important specialty facilities in their network (thus attracting individuals seeking specialized treatment), and had a history of serving members enrolled in the former state-run high risk pools. While this point serves to illustrate a key desired outcome from the ACA risk adjustment program – that issuers with higher risk populations receive a payment rather than making one – this outcome is a rather basic test of the program. It is much more difficult to establish whether the transfer of payments *adequately* compensated for that risk in the benefit year. More work will be done on this topic in the future.

Finally, the risk adjustment program is designed such that the sum of payments and charges net to zero within a state and within an ACA risk pool (that is, individual, small group, and catastrophic). In absolute terms, the totals were approximately $3.5 billion for the individual markets and approximately $1 billion for the small group markets. These figures serve to underline the importance of these transfers, and indeed of the risk adjustment program itself.

Another way to view this information is as a percent of premium by risk pool. The average transfers (either positive or negative) were approximately 10% of total annual premium for the individual risk pool, 6% for the small group risk pool, and 21% for the catastrophic risk pool. The percentages show that the risk transfers significantly exceeded profit margins, and thus will continue to be a very important pricing and financial item.

The 2014 results had a significant impact on many issuers. The average transfers as a percentage of premium, while considerable, mask the fact that for some issuers the transfers constituted almost half of their collected premium revenue. It is critical for issuers in these markets to understand the provisions and calculations of the permanent risk adjustment program. Health actuaries are expected to play a vital role in this regard.

RISK ADJUSTMENT IN MEDICARE

The Medicare program is certainly the most well known example of health risk adjustment using diagnosis information. The federal government uses diagnosis codes to measure health risk and adjust payments to Medicare Advantage and Medicare Part D insurers. For further details on the risk adjustment in Medicare, please refer to the chapters titled "Government Plans in the United States" and "Medicare-Related Rate Filings and Certifications."

The CMS Hierarchical Condition Category model, or CMS-HCC, was implemented in 2004 to adjust Medicare capitation payments that are made to Medicare Advantage (MA) and Medicare Part D (MA-PD) insurers. Nearly 30% of Medicare beneficiaries are enrolled in the privately insured MA and MA-PD market. Members vary in terms of their health care needs and expected costs, such that the financial viability of insurers enrolling high risk members would be threatened without the risk adjustment program. Therefore, the CMS-HCC model compensates insurers for enrolling high risk individuals and mitigates incentives to select risks.

The Medicare Advantage risk adjustment methodology has evolved over time. Prior to 2000, capitation payments varied based on factors that only explained about one percent of the variation in a members' cost (that is, the correlation R-squared was very low and not very predictive).

The Principal Inpatient Diagnostic Cost Groups (PIP-DCG) model was used from 2000 through 2003. This model explained about 5% to 6% of the variation in cost and was a significant improvement in terms of accuracy over the prior approach. A significant limitation of the model was that it used adjusted inpatient claim data and therefore only captured diagnoses for enrollees that had an inpatient admission, which would penalize an organization that managed and reduced inpatient admissions or re-admissions. This model was intended as a transition model towards an approach that used diagnosis codes from all service settings, overcoming the limitations of the PIP-DCG model.

The CMS-HCC model, which is currently in use, has an R-squared of about 12% to 13% as of 2011 (version 21, 2007 recalibration; 2009 clinical version). This model begins by classifying each of the 15,000 or so ICD-9-CM diagnosis codes into exactly one of about 800 diagnostic groups (or DXGs). These groups are then aggregated into 189 condition categories (CCs). The levels of aggregation are intended to capture conditions that are clinically similar and have similar expected costs.

Hierarchies are applied to the grouping, such that an individual is assigned to only the most severe manifestation of a condition. For example, if an individual is indicated both for Acute Myocardial Infarction and Coronary Atherosclerosis / Other Chronic Ischemic Heart Disease, then the former, more severe condition is recognized in the risk score. Hierarchies are intended to guard against double counting the risk from a condition, and appropriately capturing the severity of a condition. Using hierarchies, the CCs are collapsed to about 70 HCCs.

The CMS-HCC is an additive model; however, it includes some interaction terms for conditions where total costs are greater than the expected sum of the parts. For example, if an enrollee is indicated with both diabetes and congestive heart failure (CHF), then the expected cost is greater than the sum of the expected costs for diabetes and CHF. Therefore, the model includes some adjustments for pairs of co-morbid conditions where expected costs are not adequately represented by a linear additive formula.

CMS is continually conducting research to further refine the CMS-HCC model, in particular with regard to better predicting high-cost claimants.

REFERENCES

Anderson, Gerald F., et al., "Setting Payment Rates for Capitated Systems: A Comparison of Various Alternatives," *Inquiry*, 27: 225-233, Fall 1990.

Ash, Arlene, et al., "Adjusting Medicare Capitation Payments Using Prior Hospitalization Data," *Health Care Financing Review*, Vol. 10, No. 4, Summer 1989.

Brown, Robert, et al., "An Evaluation of Risk Assessment Methods," HIAA Internal Memorandum, August 1993.

Cumming, Robert B., et al, "A Comparative Analysis of Claims-based Methods of Health Risk Assessment for Commercial Populations," Society of Actuaries, May 2002.

Department of Health and Human Services, "Patient Protection and Affordable Care Act; HHS Notice of Benefit and Payment Parameters for 2014". 45 CFR Parts 153, 155, 156, 157 and 158

Epstein, Arnold M. and Edward J. Cumella, "Capitation Payment: Using Predictors of Medical Utilization to Adjust Rates," *Health Care Financing Review*, Vol. 10, No. 1, Fall 1988.

Hornbrook, M.C., et al., "Adjusting the AAPCC for Selectivity and Selection Bias Under Medicare Risk Contracts," *Advances in Health Economics and Health Services Research*, Vol. 10, pp. 111-149, 1989.

Mehmud, Syed, Rong Yi, "Uncertainty in Risk Adjustment", Society of Actuaries, 2012.

Mehmud, Syed, "Nontraditional Variables in Risk Adjustment", Society of Actuaries, 2013.

Robinson, James C., Harold S. Luft, et al., "A Method for Risk-Adjusting Employer Contributions to Competing Health Insurance Plans," *Inquiry*, 28: 107-116, Summer 1991.

Pope, Gregory C., et al., "Evaluation of the CMS-HCC Risk Adjustment Model," *The Centers for Medicare & Medicaid Services' Office of Research, Development, and Information*. Final Report, March 2011.

Robinson, James C., "A Payment Model for Health Insurance Purchasing Cooperatives," *Health Affairs*, Supplement 1993, pp. 65-75.

Weiner, Jonathan P., et al., "Development and Application of a Population-Oriented Measure of Ambulatory Care Case-Mix," *Medical Care*, Vol. 29, No. 5, pp. 452-472, May 1991.

Weiner, Jonathan P., "Johns Hopkins Ambulatory Care Groups (ACGs): A Case-Mix System for UR, QA, and Capitation Adjustment," *HMO Practice*, Vol. 6, No. 1, March 1992.

Ross Winkelman and Syed Mehmud, "A Comparative Analysis of Claims-Based Tools for Health Risk Assessment," Society of Actuaries Report, April 2007.

Society of Actuaries, "A Comparative Analysis of Claims-based Methods of Risk Assessment," 2007.

34 MEDICAL CLAIM COST TREND ANALYSIS

Joan Barrett

The measurement of periodic trends in health care costs is a key determinant of health insurer financial results, and prospective estimates of trend are a crucial element in pricing health insurance products. In insurance, the terms "trend rate" or "trend" generally refer to the rate of growth of incurred claim cost per member per month (PMPM), but can also refer to growth in sales, expenses, premium, or other factors. In this chapter, the emphasis is on medical claim cost trends, and the terms "trend rate" and "trend" are used interchangeably. Also, health care trend analyses are performed by many types of entities (insurance companies, self-insured employers, provider organizations, others) but this chapter will refer to all of them collectively as "insurers".

Trend analytics serve two major purposes. First, analyses of past trends may reveal important insights into an insurer's current benefit and rate structure and identify emerging areas of concern. Second, these same analyses assist in setting future premium rates and/or budgets. Trend analytics should not only review the insurer's actual experience, but also incorporate external information like economic trends and changes in clinical practice.

TYPES OF TREND

As noted above, the term "trend" refers to the growth in cost in general. Trend projections and analytics, however, happen at a very specific level. As result, it is important to clarify exactly which trends are being discussed at any point in time and to explain significant variances in reported results. One of the key determinants of trend methodology is the purpose for the trend, and three of the most common purposes are discussed in this section, with an emphasis on explaining key differences.

FINANCIAL REPORTING

The purpose of financial reporting is to determine an enterprise's financial performance during a given accounting period. Trend analysis for financial reporting should meet several criteria. First, reporting is done on a retrospective or look back basis, although most insurers also have a budgeting process that projects claims over the next few years. Second, although financial reporting is required at the enterprise level, it is often done at a local level, like a division or market, for internal management purposes. Finally, if the reporting is on a statutory basis, a margin or provision for adverse deviation is generally required. If reporting is on a generally accepted accounting principles (GAAP) basis, then the reporting is done on a best-estimate basis.

In keeping with standard accounting principles, in a financial reporting context, incurred claims are defined as follows:

> Net paid claims, paid during the accounting period,
> Plus claim reserves at the end of the period,
> Less claim reserves at the beginning of the period.

Net paid claims are any claims-related payment made to a claimant, provider or other payee and reflected in the general ledger during the accounting period.

Claim reserves represent an estimate of amounts for which an insurer is liable but that have not yet been reflected in the general ledger. In most cases, the insurer becomes liable for a claim on the date the service was received, such as the date the patient went to see the doctor or the date a surgery was performed. One major exception is inpatient hospital claims. Under most insurance contracts, the insurer becomes liable to pay all claims associated with a hospital stay on the day of admission. For example, suppose a patient is admitted to the hospital on December 30, 2015 and discharged on January 5, 2016, but switches insurers on January 1. In that case, the first insurer (pre-January 1) would be liable for the entire stay, including the costs associated with services received after January 1.

In most cases, the general ledger reporting system does not carry the level of detail needed to perform a trend study for financial reporting. In that case, one must rely on some type of electronic data warehouse (EDW) for data. In any given accounting period, the total net paid amount shown in the general ledger may or may not agree with the total shown in the EDW. There are two main reasons for this. First, the EDW likely only includes payments tied to a specific claim and, therefore would not include aggregated items like payments as a result of a lawsuit, year-end provider bonuses, etc. Depending on the type of analytics being done, it may or may not be important to include those amounts in the study. The other reason that the general ledger might not match the EDW has to do with processing times. In almost all cases, the relevant data will be loaded into the general ledger system by the last day or the last workday of the month. The cut-off date for loading data in the EDW may be different than the general ledger system, causing a timing difference.

PRICING

Pricing trend rates are used to project experience to a new time period for premium rate setting or for planning and budgeting purposes. Of course, considerable analysis is done on a detailed, retrospective basis in order to validate prior projections and to gain insights into how experience is emerging. Since detailed information is required, the analysis usually relies on data from an EDW, which, as noted above, may not include aggregated items like bonus payments and other amounts that could become important in the analytics.

Pricing trend rates may be calculated on an eligible, covered or net paid basis. First, eligible charges refer to billed charges before provider contracts or discounts are applied. A trend analysis using eligible charges is useful for looking at underlying patterns, without confounding the results with changes in provider contracting and cost-sharing patterns. Next, covered charges, also called allowed charges, refer to eligible claims after provider contracting provisions (e.g., discounts) have been applied, but before member cost sharing is applied. A trend analysis using covered charges provides information about underlying patterns, including changes in provider contracting, without confounding the results with changes in member cost sharing. Finally, net paid claims represent the bottom line, after provider contracts, member cost sharing and coordination of benefits savings. A trend analysis using net paid claims provides the overall net paid trend.

Pricing trends are very specific to a time period. For example, the pricing trend rate designed to project claims from calendar year 2015 to calendar year 2016 will probably be determined in the middle of 2015. As a result, the first step is to project the available data to a full calendar year basis. This is at least a two-part process as shown in Table 34.1.

Table 34.1

1.	Calendar Year 2015 PMPM incurred and paid through 6/30/2015	$119.00
2.	Incurred-but-not-paid completion factor	1.10
3.	Projected incurred claims through 6/30/2015 = 1. x 2.	131.00
4.	Seasonality adjustment	2.10
5.	Projected calendar year 2015 incurred claims = 3. x 4.	275.00
6.	Trend factor, 2015 to 2016	6.2%
7.	Projected calendar year 2016 claims = 5. x 6. + 5.	$292.00

The first step in Table 34.1 is to complete the available claims. In this example, the completion factor accounts for amounts that were incurred during the first six months of calendar year 2015, but not yet processed and reflected in the data as of the given paid through date.

The second step is to project claims in the first half of the year to the full calendar year. In this example, more claims are assumed to be incurred in the second half of the year than in the first half. This is a common phenomenon, especially if there is a high prevalence of high deductible plans. Consumers tend to use more services once their deductible and/or out-of-pocket maximum is satisfied and, of course, a higher percentage of covered dollars are paid after the deductible and out-of-pocket maximum is satisfied.

The formula for calculating incurred claims in this section is different from the formula for incurred claims in the financial reporting section. There are two reasons for this. First, the financial reporting definition applies only to retrospective claims whereas the pricing trend refers to some combination of retrospective and projected claims. Second, there is no need for an explicit correction factor in a pricing context, since the projections should always be based on the latest and greatest information.

EXPERIENCE ANALYSIS

As the name implies, an experience analysis is a look at how the experience for a specific block of business is changing over time. For example, one might want to look at which providers are driving trends in a market in preparation for contract negotiations.

An experience analysis is based on retrospective claims. Like financial reporting and pricing trends, the assumption for incurred claims must be completed in order to reflect information incurred but not included in the raw data. There are three main techniques to incorporate unreported claims into analytics based on reports produced by an EDW. The first is to use a standard set of completion factors that are stored in the EDW, as illustrated in Table 34.2. The advantage of this approach is that the factors can be updated as conditions change. The disadvantage is that maintenance and upkeep are required.

Table 34.2

	Incurred Period	Paid Through	Paid PMPM a.	Completion Factor b.	Completed PMPM c. = a. x b.
1.	Calendar Year 2014	3/31/2016	$247.50	1.01	$249.98
2.	Calendar Year 2015	3/31/2016	$264.50	1.04	$275.08
				Trend = 2c. / 1c. = 10.0%	

The second method is similar to the first method in that the EDW will show the claims incurred in a specified period and paid through a given date. In this method, no completion factor is applied within the EDW, but one is included later after an in-depth analysis of completion patterns. This method is common in financial reporting and pricing trend analytics.

A final approach is the equal runoff method illustrated in Table 34.3. In this approach, incomplete claims amounts are compared to similarly incomplete amounts in the prior period, and the implicit assumption is that the runoff amount and timing is similar in both periods. The advantage of this approach is that no EDW maintenance is required to update factors. This method works well for time periods with sufficient runoff so that the claims are not too volatile from period to period.

Table 34.3

	Incurred Period	Paid Through	PMPM
1.	Calendar Year 2014	3/31/2015	$242.00
2.	Calendar Year 2015	3/31/2016	$264.50
		Trend = 2. / 1. − 1 = 9.3%	

DEVELOPING PRICING TRENDS

Although there are many approaches to developing pricing trends, this chapter will concentrate on discussing one method in detail – the component method. The advantage of this approach is that it is straightforward to evaluate and explain specific trend impacts. The disadvantage is that it requires considerable resources to work through each component on a thoughtful basis. The actual method chosen by an insurer will depend on the materiality of the block of business in question and the availability of data and analytic resources, but the example shown here provides an overview of the key considerations in projecting a pricing trend. Table 34.4 provides a summary of the components to be discussed in this example.

Table 34.4

	Trend Component	Projected 2016 Trend as of 6/30/2015
1.	Core cost trends	5.2%
2.	Core utilization trends	1.8%
3.	One-time changes	-0.1%
4.	Population shifts	1.0%
5.	Structural changes	-3.8%
6.	Capitation trend impact	0.2%
7.	Best estimate trend	4.2%
8.	Expected impact of large claims	0.0%
9.	Other fluctuations	2.0%
10.	Total margin	2.0%
11.	Final Trend Projection	6.2%

The remainder of this section provides more detail on each of the components listed in Table 34.4. The underlying assumption in the remaining portion of this chapter is that the 2016 projected trend was calculated in July, 2015 with information available through 6/30/2015.

CORE COST TREND

The core cost trend refers to the rate of increase in the covered cost per service, before adjustments for specific factors such as aging or one-time changes that might skew results (such as an unusually high flu season). These changes are described in more detail below.

The core unit cost trend can be thought of in three parts. The first is the unit cost trend, which assumes a fixed basket of services that do not change year over year. It is similar to a Consumer Price Index (CPI) calculation, a common measure of inflation. In fact, medical CPI can be used to approximate unit cost trends for non-network providers. The calculation of this component of the core cost increase for network providers is illustrated in Table 34.5 and can also be thought of as the change due to contracting changes, all other things held equal. Table 34.5 represents the professional services component only. Most insurers calculate a unit cost trend for each component and then use a composite in the final estimate that is applied to overall costs. In this example, 2.3% (from professional services) is a component of the 5.2% shown in Table 34.4.

Table 34.5

Item	CPT-4 Code	Description	2015 Weight	2015 Fee Schedule	2016 Projected Fee Schedule
1.	99213	Office Visits - 15 minutes	50%	$50	$52
2.	99214	Office Visits - 25 minutes	20%	$75	$77
3.	59400	Routine Delivery (Surgical)	10%	$2,000	$2,050
4.	99396	Preventive Office Visits	5%	$150	$155
5.	88305	Surgical Pathology	10%	$100	$105
6.	01967	Routine Delivery (Anesthesia)	5%	$1,450	$1,460
		Market Weighted Average	100%	$330	$338
			Unit Cost Trend = $338/$330 - 1 = 2.3%		

In experience analysis, the actual contract amounts should be known and used in the calculation to the extent practical. In a projection, the expected contract changes for specific providers can be used to the extent they are known.

The second part of the core cost trend is severity. Severity refers to the increase in the intensity of treatment. Examples might include an overall shift away from 15- minute office visits to more 30-minute visits. Severity can be calculated using weighted classification systems such as Medicare's average Diagnosis Related Group (DRG) weight per admission, observed over time or on a service level. Table 34.6 shows an example of severity shift for a simplified set of professional services.

Table 34.6

Description	Projected Fee Schedule 2015 a.	Projected Utilization 2015 b.	Projected Utilization 2016 c.
Office Visits - 15 minutes	$50	50%	46%
Office Visits - 25 minutes	$75	20%	24%
Routine Delivery (Surgical)	$2,000	10%	10%
Preventive Office Visits	$150	5%	5%
Surgical Pathology	$100	10%	10%
Routine Delivery (Anesthesia)	$1,450	5%	5%
		100%	100%
Average Cost 2015 = Avg. of a. weighted by b.	$330		
Average Cost 2016 = Avg. of a. weighted by c.	$331		
Increase = $331/ $330 −	0.2%		

The third part of the core cost trend is the change due to mix of services. Mix may refer high-level changes such as the overall distribution between inpatient, outpatient and professional fees; or it may refer to something more specific like a change in the mix of providers, such as specialist care replacing primary care. Because of the complexity involved in analyzing all possible changes due to mix of service, it is often thought of a balancing item and determined by examining historical trends, as illustrated in Table 34.7.

In this example, the actual unit costs and severity numbers are calculated as described below. In the experience period the combined cost per service is a known quantity and so the severity is a balancing item calculated using the formula:

$$c. = \frac{(1+ d.)}{(1 + a.) \times (1 + b.)} - 1$$

During the projection period, however, the situation is reversed. It is usually easiest to project the severity and then calculate the combined cost trend using the formula:

$$d. = (1 + a.) \times (1 + b.) \times (1. + c.) - 1$$

Table 34.7

Quarter	Actual or Projected	Cost Increase Component as of 6/30/2015			
		Unit Cost Increase a.	Severity Increase b.	Mix Increase c.	Combined d.
1Q14	Actual	3.9%	0.5%	0.3%	4.7%
2Q14	Actual	4.3%	0.8%	0.4%	5.6%
3Q14	Actual	4.1%	0.3%	0.2%	4.6%
4Q14	Actual	3.8%	0.7%	0.3%	4.8%
1Q15	Actual	4.4%	0.4%	0.5%	5.3%
2Q15	Actual	4.0%	0.4%	0.7%	5.1%
3Q15	Projected	4.2%	0.5%	0.5%	5.2%
4Q15	Projected	3.8%	0.6%	0.5%	4.9%
1Q16	Projected	4.1%	0.5%	0.5%	5.2%
2Q16	Projected	4.3%	0.5%	0.6%	5.4%
3Q16	Projected	3.7%	0.5%	0.6%	4.9%
4Q16	Projected	4.0%	0.5%	0.7%	5.2%
Average 2016	Projected	4.0%	0.5%	0.6%	5.2%

Each of the components of the core unit cost trends as well as the combined trend should be tracked over time. This provides detail needed for future projections. It may also signal an inflection point in the overall trend curve.

The three components – unit cost, severity and mix – can each be customized or adjusted for various differences in market, product, or other characteristics. In practice, however, most insurers adjust unit cost trend estimates for product and area differences, but use overall book level data for severity and mix.

CORE UTILIZATION TREND

Core utilization represents ongoing changes in utilization due to external forces like the economy, workdays and changes in medical practice.

When the economy is stable, utilization changes can be predicted using econometric models based on leading indicators, such as the change in personal disposable income. In more turbulent economic periods, factors such as a fear of layoffs may disrupt historical patterns.

Utilization of services varies by weekday and the placement of holidays. For example, more people go to the doctor on a Monday than any other day of the week; fewer people are admitted to the hospital on a Friday than any other day of the week; and fewer prescriptions are filled on Wednesday than any other weekday.

Variations by weekday can impact trend by as much plus-or-minus 0.7% annually. Ideally, the weekday impact is calculated based on an analysis of seven years of data in order to capture all possible workday variations. In particular, the timing of the winter holidays can impact the overall utilization. If seven years are not available, then the impact can be estimated using other methods. One such method assumes weekdays have a weight of 1.0 and weekends and holidays have a weight of 0.5 as illustrated in Table 34.8.

Table 34.8

	2015	2016	Weights
Weekdays	262	262	1.00
Weekends and Holidays	103	104	0.50
Sum	365	366	
Weighted Sum	313.5	314.0	
Trend Impact = 314.0 / 313.5 - 1 = 0.2%			

Medical practice is constantly in changing. In some cases, changes come about because of a one-time event, like the introduction of a new drug or loss of patent protection of an existing drug. In other cases, the change may be more gradual, and these more gradual changes are included in the core utilization component of the trend calculation. In most cases, these gradual changes are either combined with changes to the economy or as a balancing item using techniques similar to the one shown in Table 34.7.

Core utilization trends are usually done on a book-of-business level and then used for all sub-groups. As with the core cost increases, utilization changes should be tracked over time.

ONE-TIME CHANGES

As noted above, core utilization represents the general tendency of people to use more or fewer services based on economic factors or market trends. By contrast, one-time changes represent a response to a specific, identifiable situation. The calculation of the impact of one-time changes depends on the nature of the situation.

One type of situation results when there is a significant increase or decrease in the claims level during one period, followed by a return to normal levels the following period. Examples include:

- <u>High flu incidence</u>. If the flu season shows abnormally high incidence or severity of flu cases, then claims will go up one year, but will most likely return to normal levels the next year. The CDC's surveillance data can be helpful in predicting flu season changes. It can be found at www.cdc.gov.
- <u>Weather events</u>. Utilization may decrease during extreme weather events like a hurricane. Once the event is over, claims tend to return to more normal levels, although there may be a slight temporary increase in utilization following the event due to catch-up impact.

Another common one-time change is a sustained change in claims level. Examples of sustained changes include:

- <u>Legislation</u>. Legislative changes, such as mandated benefits, often result in an on-going increase in costs. In some cases, legislative changes are included in the trend calculation and in other cases the changes are shown as a separate line item in a trend calculation.

- <u>Internal changes</u>. Most insurers are constantly reviewing their medical policies and claims processing procedures. These changes should be reviewed individually or collectively to see if there will a material impact on trends.

EXPECTED POPULATION SHIFTS

The underlying population for any block of business can be expected to shift year over year as members leave and enter the group. Geographic location is one measureable element of a population's cost that can be easily estimated. Sometimes trend projections will include a tacit assumption that the geographic mix will not change year over year. This is particularly true for analytics where most of the population is concentrated in one or two geographic areas. Alternatively, the impact of shifts in geographic mix can be estimated using a scale of area factors and the change in the distribution by area in each period. The area factors may be based on unit cost increases, as discussed above, or may reflect other factors such as utilization patterns. The scale should be updated on a regular basis to keep the relativities current.

Another measurable population element is the demographic or age-gender mix. Populations tend to age each year since remaining members of the group will be a year older than the prior year, and new entrants and terminations typically don't fully offset the impact of that aging. If the member turnover is relatively stable, the easiest way to estimate this impact is to look at the change in the distribution by age over time. If significant member turnover is expected, then other factors such as selection and changes in overall risk level of the group must be considered.

STRUCTURAL CHANGES

Each component of trend discussed so far has been based on the assumption that the underlying offering has not had structural changes, including (but not limited to) benefit changes, changes to clinical programs, or network changes.

If it is indeed the case that there are no structural changes, one trend impact remains: the impact of leveraging on net paid trends. The leveraging effect can be explained as follows. If covered charges are increasing but cost-sharing parameters, like the deductible or copay, stay the same, then the net amount paid by the plan grows at a rate higher than the covered charges, as illustrated in Table 34.9. The higher the deductible or other cost sharing parameter, the greater the leveraging effect.

Table 34.9

	Projected 2015	Projected 2016	Trend
Primary Care Office Visit:			
Average Covered Amount	$100	$105	5.0%
Copay	$25	$25	0.0%
Net Paid	$75	$80	6.7%

If there are structural changes, then the trend projection should reflect not only the change due to the leveraging effect, but also expected changes in insured behavior. First, if benefits are reduced, then utilization following the change may decrease due to price elasticity, which can also be explained as the tendency of insured members to use fewer benefits if they have to pay more for them. Similarly, if the cost of the benefit package increases, then healthier members may leave the group or switch to a lower cost plan within the package, with higher-risk members remaining. This type of selection can lead to higher overall costs.

Another type of behavioral change is the benefit "rush-hush-crush" cycle. In such a cycle, a benefit rush is triggered by any type of major change to a benefit plan that creates an air of uncertainty among the members. The two most common examples are the following:

- A full-replacement Consumer-Driven Health (CDH) Plan. CDH plans typically cover all services with coinsurance and only after a high deductible has been met. When an employer announces that they are replacing a copay-based plan with a full-replacement CDH plan, many members will opt to receive preference-sensitive services (such as discretionary knee and back surgeries) before the change.

- An insurer change. An employer's announcement regarding a change in insurer also creates an air of uncertainty, which may trigger a benefit rush.

An example of the costs associated with a "rush-hush-crush" cycle is illustrated in Figure 34.1.

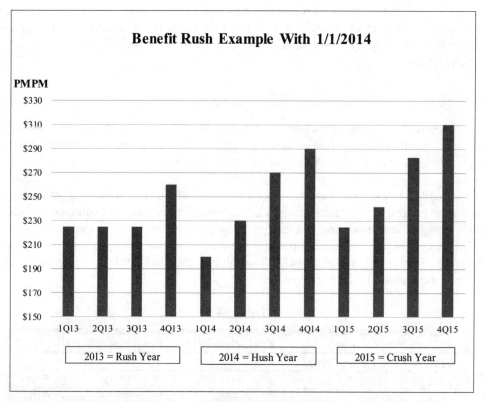

Figure 34.1

A benefit rush impacts trends over a 3-year period. The first year in the cycle, the year before the change becomes effective, results in an increase in claims and a corresponding increase in trends. In the example in Figure 34.1, the insurer announced in late 2013 that it would implement a full-replacement CDH effective 1/1/2014, resulting in the "rush" seen in the 4th quarter. In the second year there is typically a "hush", especially in the 1st quarter, also illustrated in the Figure. There are two reasons for the hush. First, some of the optional services received in the prior year will not be received in the second year. Also, members may hold off on receiving services until they know more about the new plan. In addition to these two one-time changes, the results for 2014 will reflect any realized savings resulting from the plan change and a new seasonality pattern caused by the introduction of the higher deductible. In the third year, utilization returns to normal levels, but trends are higher because they are trending from the basis of a low second year.

The counterpart to a benefit rush is a benefit delay. A benefit delay is often caused by an announcement of an increase in benefits, such as increase in the allowed amount for hearing aids. In that case, members may wait until the benefit goes into effect to get a new device.

CAPITATION

Many providers are paid a capitation rate, or a monthly PMPM cost in exchange for performing a package of services for a designated patient. For example, Dr. Jones may be paid $50.00 per month for each member of a given population for performing all office visits and related lab and radiology services. In addition to the monthly capitation fee, Dr. Jones may be paid an annual bonus if certain quality and efficiency criteria are met.

Capitation can have a material impact on trend if the average capitation fee increases or decreases materially; if the percentage of patients in a capitation arrangement increases or decreases; or if there is a material increase or decrease in the annual bonus payout.

FINAL TREND RATES

In many cases, the component method described above provides a sound foundation for making a business decision regarding which trend rate to actually use in determining a premium rate or final budget. In addition, an insurer may want to add a margin to the trend rate in order to minimize the chances of a loss in an insured block or of not meeting a budget. One approach to adding margin is to use a constant factor, say 2%, year over year. The advantage of this approach is that it is relatively simple to explain. However, the certainty in trend projections can change from period to period, driving a change in the trend rates that may be too much in some periods and not enough in others. As an alternative to the constant margin factor, the insurer may want to vary the margin each year based on the level of confidence in the underlying best estimate trend.

In other cases, the insurer may want to use trend rates below the best estimate rates in order to remain competitive in a given market. If that approach is used, then the insurer may want to test the level of risk associated with the low trend rates under various sales and actual trend rates.

If there is some type of pooling or stop-loss arrangement in place, then there will be fewer low frequency and high cost claims and the overall variability in the trend results will be dampened. In addition, the trend for the portion of net paid claims over the stop-loss limit will be higher than the overall rate due to leveraging (as described earlier in the subsection on structural changes). As a result, the trend for the portion of the claims below the stop-loss limit will be lower than the overall rate.

MONITORING AND ANALYZING TRENDS

Most insurers produce historical and projected financial and pricing trends on either a quarterly or monthly basis. Some of the key questions that are asked during this process include:

- How accurate were the original projected trend and PMPM estimates?
- Which assumptions were driving any variation from the actual to expected trend estimate?
- How can the process be modified to achieve greater accuracy in projections?
- What other factors, expected or unexpected, drove the trends?

This section examines several techniques for analyzing trends. Except as noted in each example, the projected trends described in the previous section are analyzed using data through 3/31/2017. The data has been completed.

VALIDATING PRIOR PRICING TREND ESTIMATES

The first step in analyzing a prior trend estimate is to determine the difference in the original estimate and the current estimate of the trend. If the component-by-component approach was used to develop the original estimates, then each component should be recast with actual experience. Often the easiest way to do this recast is to repeat the original analysis substituting actual experience for projected experience. This serves two purposes. First, it provides updates to the historical data that will be used in the next projection. Second, as illustrated in Table 34.10, the recast can provide helpful information about which areas need further analysis.

Table 34.10

		2016 Projected Trend as of 6/30/2015	Actual 2016 Trend as of 3/31/2017	Difference
1.	Core cost trends	5.2%	7.7%	2.5%
2.	Core utilization trends	1.8%	1.7%	-0.1%
3.	One-time changes	-0.1%	1.0%	1.1%
4.	Structural changes	-3.8%	-2.0%	1.8%
5.	Population shifts	1.0%	0.5%	-0.5%
6.	Capitation trend impact	0.2%	0.1%	-0.1%
7.	Best estimate trend	4.2%	9.0%	4.7%
8.	Expected impact of large claims	0.0%	-3.0%	-3.0%
9.	Other fluctuations	2.0%	0.0%	-2.0%
10.	Total margin	2.0%	-3.0%	-5.0%
11.	Final Trend	6.2%	6.0%	-0.2%

In this example, the actual trend and the projected trend are very close in total. A closer look, however, shows that several assumptions were understated, especially the core cost trends. The understated assumptions were offset by the margin and a decrease in high-cost claims.

There are several reasons why the core costs trends may have been understated. First, there may have been a one-time, unforeseen contract negotiation that resulted in an increase in the unit cost trends. Alternately, there may have been a systematic understatement of the core cost trends. From the data shown below in Figure 34.2, it appears that the unit cost trend was understated when that number was originally projected as of 6/30/2015. As more information became available, the trend was recast upwards almost every quarter. If this pattern repeats itself for other projection periods, then, chances are, there is a systematic issue that needs to be addressed.

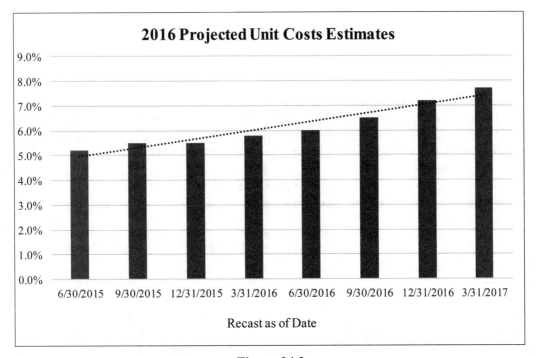

Figure 34.2

In addition to using recast techniques, it may be helpful to use basic statistical techniques like hypothesis testing and confidence intervals to validate the original assumptions. In setting the final rates, the insurer may want to make smaller, more gradual changes to the assumptions.

ANALYZING RESULTS

One of the more important aspects of trend analysis is to go beyond population shifts and one-time changes to determine the key drivers of costs and trends. One of the most common ways to determine these drivers is to analyze trends by service type, as shown in Table 34.11.

Table 34.11

	2015 PMPM	2016 PMPM	Trend
Inpatient	$58.00	$64.00	10.3%
Outpatient	$120.00	$128.00	6.7%
Professional	$85.00	$86.00	1.2%
Mental Health/Substance Abuse	$12.00	$13.50	12.5%
Total	$275.00	$291.50	6.0%

This same type of analysis can be used to look at costs and trends by diagnostic category, geographic area and/or product.

If this were the only information available, one might conclude that the major trend drivers were inpatient and mental health and substance abuse (MHSA). However, if we look at trends over a two-year period as shown in Table 34.12, it is clear that the inpatient trends are lower than the overall trends. Instead, it appears that the high inpatient trend in 2016 was an unusual event. The high trends may be due to the fact that inpatient trends are increasing or in could be a one-time fluctuation. This will become more clear as 2017 experience emerges. In addition, observing MHSA in isolation shows a high trend, but because MHSA is a small portion of the total, it is probably not a significant driver of the overall trend.

Table 34.12

	2014 PMPM	2015 PMPM	2016 PMPM	2015 Trend	2016 Trend	Average Annual Trend
Inpatient	$57.00	$58.00	$64.00	1.8%	10.3%	6.0%
Outpatient	$100.00	$120.00	$128.00	20.0%	6.7%	13.1%
Professional	$80.00	$85.00	$86.00	6.3%	1.2%	3.7%
Mental Health/Substance Abuse	$13.00	$12.00	$13.50	-7.7%	12.5%	1.9%
Total	$250.00	$275.00	$291.50	10.0%	6.0%	8.0%

A contribution analysis like the one shown in Table 34.13, confirms that MHSA is not a trend driver. Based on this information, outpatient looks like the major driver and, perhaps, the priority for further analysis.

Table 34.13

	2015 PMPM	2016 PMPM	Change in PMPM	Contribution to Trend
Inpatient	$58.00	$64.00	$6.00	36.4%
Outpatient	$120.00	$128.00	$8.00	48.5%
Professional	$85.00	$86.00	$1.00	6.1%
Mental Health/Substance Abuse	$12.00	$13.50	$1.50	9.1%
Total	$275.00	$291.50	$16.50	100.0%

TAKING A BROADER AND LONGER VIEW

As discussed in the introduction, external factors, such as changes in clinical practices and the economy, frequently have a significant impact on trends. Although an understanding of external factors can greatly enhance an insurer's understanding of its results and improve the accuracy of its projections, the actual impact will vary from insurer to insurer depending on the specific circumstances of each insurer.

LOOKING BACK

One of the best examples of the benefits of a broader view is the volatile trends seen in the 1990s as illustrated in Figure 34.3.[1]

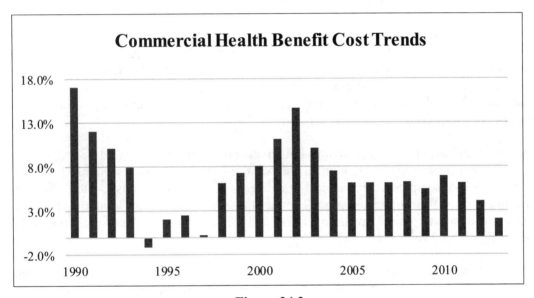

Figure 34.3

Although there were several reasons for this volatility, one of the key factors was the rapid rise of network plans. In 1988, 73% of all enrollees in employee-sponsored health plans were enrolled in traditional, or indemnity, plans. Providers under these plans were paid at billed charges, perhaps subject to reasonable and customary restrictions. The remaining 27% of enrollees were covered under network plans which offered richer benefits for services received by network providers. In exchange for this steerage, the network provider's covered charges were less than the billed charges. In most cases, richer benefits were more than offset by the lower covered charges, resulting in substantial savings. In 1996, only 27% of enrollees were covered by a traditional plan. This dramatic drop accounts for much of the reduction in trends during the first half of the 1990s.

Although these national averages are interesting, the trend impact varied considerably from insurer to insurer depending on their mix of business at any point in time. Similarly, the ability to prospectively estimate the relative cost of a network plan relative to conventional

---

[1] Source: Mercer: http://www.mercer.com/content/mercer/global/all/en/newsroom/survey-predicts-health-benefit-cost-increases-will-edge-up-in-2015-spurring-employers-to-take-action.html

plans varied considerably depending on the availability of reliable data and analytical resources.

In the late 1990s trend increased rapidly. In part, this was just the result of the fact that much of the savings from the rise of network plans were already reflected in the claims costs. For the most part, these savings stayed in place, but trend rates accelerated.

LOOKING FORWARD

In 2014 trends were at the lowest level in almost 20 years. It is unclear whether they will stay at that level or climb to levels higher than the past. Although there is much speculation about which factors may influence future trends, three likely causes are the impact of exchanges, the evaluation of cost savings initiatives, and the economy.

First, if public and private exchanges continue to grow as many expect, then enrollees can be expected to change health plans more frequently than in the past, perhaps even annually. This may or may not make health care more affordable overall, but for an individual insurer this will require a more in-depth understanding of the impact of the population shift component of trends. This in-depth understanding will require an analysis of risk adjustment and selection impacts.

Second, there are many cost-saving initiatives being discussed right now, including accountable care organizations, clinical interventions, and wellness programs. For many insurers, the standard measure of cost-effectiveness is a single statistic—the return on investment or ROI. In order to properly reflect these impacts in trend analytics, however, insurers will have to project savings over time and then test not only the overall savings, but the timing of the savings.

Third, many insurers have traditionally relied on leading indicators, such as personal disposable income, to determine if trends are expected to increase or decrease in the near future. Now that health reform has expanded past the traditional base and the economy appears to be stabilizing, other economic factors may provide better estimates to predict health care trends.

As mentioned earlier, the three examples above provide some guidance on how to approach specific situations impacting trend. Clearly, these examples and potential approaches are not exhaustive. As each new situation arises, one of the major challenges will be to find data appropriate to the circumstances. Regardless of whether the insurer uses internal or external data, an important part of trend analytics will be a clear understanding of the data and how it applies to the situation at hand.

Section Six

Group Insurance Financial Reporting

35 Group Insurance Financial Reporting

Tim Harris and Sherri Daniel

This chapter discusses actuarial aspects of group insurance financial reporting from the point of view of a commercial insurance company. Specific topics include the various types of group insurance financial reporting, group-specific considerations involved in preparing financial reports, the specifics of annual statement financial reporting for group coverages, and recent developments affecting group financial reporting. Most of the concepts presented for commercial group insurers are also applicable to other risk-taking organizations, such as HMOs, Blue Cross and Blue Shield health service corporations, and provider-sponsored organizations.

This chapter provides both a U.S. and a Canadian perspective. The Canadian view is that of a domestic, federally licensed life insurance company, since other group carriers will have similar reporting requirements. The major considerations in financial reporting for group insurance in Canada are similar to those in the U.S. However, there are significant differences in the regulatory environment.

In both the U.S. and Canada, regulatory financial reporting continues to evolve as both countries contemplate and implement changing accounting standards to align more closely with International Financial Reporting Standards (IFRS). In general, IFRS relies heavily upon the professional's judgment and overall guiding principles rather than upon prescriptive rules forcing how each risk must be accounted.

In the U.S., the historical use of such prescriptive rules has instructed, clarified and standardized accounting and given practitioners a level of comfort that their assumptions and methods were reasonable. Contemplation of IFRS in the U.S. has been gradual; not only must the governing accounting bodies determine whether revising standards is a worthwhile effort, but they must also offer guidance on transition accounting from one standard to the next. As such, the adoption of new accounting practices has been rolled out in phases in the U.S. For example, contemplation of accounting and reporting changes for certain liabilities, such as short-term disability and health insurance, has been particularly slow. This is primarily because these liabilities resolve quickly enough so that the changes that would be contemplated are not as critical as when compared to disclosing and measuring the emerging experience of longer term liabilities, such as life insurance and annuities.

Actuarial principles in Canada currently rely heavily on the judgment of the actuary, and Canadian accounting is much further along than the U.S. in terms of moving to a principle-based approach. Canadian GAAP transitioned to IFRS for most entities on January 1, 2011, except for the calculation of the actuarial reserves, for which there is not currently an IFRS standard.

TYPES OF GROUP INSURANCE FINANCIAL REPORTING

The major types of group insurance financial reporting include the following:

- Group insurer financial reporting
  - Statutory
  - GAAP (generally accepted accounting principles)
  - Tax
  - Managerial
- Policyholder financial reporting
- Provider reporting

Each type of reporting is discussed in the following sections.

STATUTORY

United States

Statutory financial reporting refers to the accounting conventions required to be used by all life and health insurance companies to complete the NAIC annual statement blank. These annual statements are required to be filed with the state insurance departments of every state in which the insurer does business. Life insurance companies, HMOs, health service corporations (Blue Cross and Blue Shield), and property-casualty companies write health insurance in the United States. Each company must report financial results on the life, the health, or the property-casualty annual statement blank. The domiciliary state has the discretion to decide which annual statement blank a company must file. If a life insurance or property-casualty company writes predominantly health lines of business, that company should file a health blank. According to the annual statement instructions, the state is guided by the Health Statement Test to determine if a company should file the health blank. This chapter discusses reporting from both the life blank and the health blank point of view.

The focus of U.S. statutory reporting is to demonstrate the solvency of the insurer. As such, these financial reports have a balance sheet orientation and require conservative standards for asset and liability valuation. Examples of conservatism in statutory accounting for health insurers' assets include the following.

- Certain assets are non-admitted in the determination of statutory solvency. Non-admitted assets include agents' balances (amounts which are owed the insurer by agents), furniture and equipment, and properties used in business.
- The NAIC prescribes asset values, rather than allowing flexibility.
- Deferred acquisition costs, which GAAP accounting allows as an offset to reserve liabilities, are not allowed.

There are a number of examples of conservatism on the liability side of the balance sheet, as well.

- The Commissioner's Reserve Valuation Method limits the recognition of expense allowances in life insurance and annuity reserves.
- Lapses may be assumed in policy reserve calculations only in specific circumstances,

including certain health policy reserves. This is of limited relevance to group insurance, since most group insurance doesn't generate policy reserves. Exceptions include group permanent life insurance and long term care benefits.

- Minimum morbidity and mortality tables, which generally include material conservatism, are required when determining reserves for many lines of coverage.

- Maximum interest rates are usually specified in setting reserves.

- Asset Valuation Reserve (AVR) and Interest Maintenance Reserve (IMR) are required reserves intended to provide a cushion against investment losses and interest rate fluctuations. Not all entities providing health insurance are required to hold these reserves.

Historically, group insurance actuaries were more concerned with the liability side of statutory financial reporting. An actuarial opinion as to the adequacy of actuarial items is required to be filed with the annual statement. Generally, the items on which the opinion is based are included in Exhibit 5 (life insurance and annuity reserves), Exhibit 6 (health insurance reserves), Exhibit 7 (deposit-type contract reserves), Exhibit 8 (claim liabilities), and Page 3 (total liabilities and surplus) of the annual statement. This perspective has changed with the advent of asset adequacy analysis requirements required by the current NAIC Standard Valuation Law (SVL) and the Actuarial Opinion and Memorandum Regulation (AOMR).

The major actuarial assumptions and methods of statutory financial reporting are specified in the SVL. In the past, these assumptions and methods have been viewed as a "recipe" for the actuary to follow that would allow him or her to opine that the reserves are adequate. More recent regulation, including the focus on asset adequacy analysis, has encouraged a departure from this "cookbook" approach toward more responsibility and freedom for the actuary, in order to ensure that the reserves are adequate rather than merely compliant with specific rules.

In a long-awaited change to the model SVL, the NAIC voted in September, 2009 to move the industry towards a principle-based approach to better reflect the risks of different products. These changes moved the actuary from calculating reserves based upon a formulaic approach toward more accurate reflection of product features. While the initial guidance is biased largely towards life insurance application, the Valuation Manual will evolve to include other products. States are adopting the model SVL language into law more quickly for life insurance products than any other product, particularly since the initial NAIC SVL analysis and the Valuation Manual were much further down the road for life insurance. For this reason, some states' commissioners do not yet support changing state law for other product lines.

In addition to state law, there are a number of Actuarial Standards of Practice (ASOPs) that directly relate to actuarial opinions for group insurance.

ASOP No. 7, "Analysis of Life, Health, or Property/Casualty Insurer Cash Flows"

The scope of this ASOP is much broader than the AOMR; it also applies to product development, financial forecasts, evaluation of investment strategies and much more. It applies to life, health, and property-casualty insurers. The ASOP describes the items that an actuary should consider on both the liability and the asset side of the tested scenarios. The

ASOP describes the need for the actuary "to determine whether the tested scenarios reflect a range of conditions consistent with the purpose of the cash flows" within scenario testing and the actuary's need "to determine whether the actuarial assumptions within each scenario are consistent where appropriate..." Material inconsistencies must be disclosed.

ASOP No. 22, "Statements of Opinion Based on Asset Adequacy Analysis by Actuaries for Life or Health Insurers"

This ASOP mentions cash flow testing under moderately adverse scenarios as the most common method for forming an actuarial opinion on asset adequacy, but it also describes scenarios where an actuary might form an opinion using a different method. In states that do not require asset adequacy analysis as the basis for an actuarial opinion, this ASOP does not require the actuary to perform such an analysis. If state law departs from this ASOP, the actuary should follow state law but disclose this conflict in both the opinion and supporting memorandum.

ASOP No. 28, "Statements of Actuarial Opinion Regarding Health Insurance Liabilities and Assets"

Actuarial opinions related to liabilities and assets under statutory, GAAP, and IFRS rules are subject to this ASOP in addition to the standards described above. The ASOP states that "the actuary should consider the amount to be reasonable if it is within a range of estimates that could be produced by an appropriate analysis that is, in the actuary's professional judgment, consistent with either ASOP No. 5, Incurred Health and Disability Claims, or ASOP No. 42, Determining Health and Disability Liabilities Other than for Incurred Claims." The ASOP instructs the actuary to take into consideration the specific policy and contract provisions affecting liabilities and assets, and also instructs the actuary to make sufficient provision for adverse deviation from reasonable assumptions, where the provision would cover moderately adverse conditions. The ASOP also instructs the actuary to properly disclose which portion of liabilities the opinion covers, and whether the opinion applies in aggregate or individually.

This ASOP was significantly revised in June, 2011 (effective on or after December 31, 2011) in order to encompass opinions on assets, which aligns with the changes that were made for the 2010 update of the NAIC Health Annual Statement Instructions. Further, changes were made to make it clear which type of actuarial opinions are not subject to the ASOP, including property-casualty reserves (where ASOP No. 36 applies) and retiree group benefit obligations (where ASOP No. 6 applies).

Canada

Statutory financial reporting refers to the accounting policies used to complete the Life-1 annual statement. A life company is required to file this completed statement with the Office of the Superintendent of Financial Institutions (OSFI) of Canada. Unlike U.S. insurers, who may publish statutory and GAAP financial statements, Canadian insurers may only publish financial statements that are based on statutory accounting.

As of January 1, 2011, all publicly listed companies and certain publicly accountable profit-oriented enterprises were required to report under IFRS. This move was made in order to increase transparency and consistency, but at the same time, it increased the role of accounting and actuarial professional judgment. This change affects nearly every type of business – not just insurance – but there are many specific areas that affect group insurance statutory reporting.

Under IFRS 1, *First Time Adoption of International Accounting Standards*, retrospective application of the international standards is required, with just a few exceptions on certain items that were too burdensome to determine. This means that most enterprises must review and restate prior years' financial reports and recreate what the income statement and balance sheets would have looked like had IFRS been in effect at the implementation date. This transition also requires special additional disclosures in the years leading up to the change.

IFRS accounting standards are codified in a series of numbered standards. Standards issued prior to 2001 are referred to as International Accounting Standards, or IAS standards), whereas standards issued after that date are referred to as IFRS standards. IAS standards have been replaced in some cases by IFRS standards.

One accounting difference in more recent accounting standards is how impaired assets are recognized. With IAS 36, *Impairment of Assets*, impairments must be recognized immediately if the recoverable value is less than the value that is carried, though the recoverable value is the higher of the fair value (reduced by the cost to sell the asset) and the discounted value of the expected cash flows. If this estimate changes later, a full or partial reversal of the impairment entry is allowed (though reversals based on goodwill are not allowed). Prior to this, the recoverable value was the undiscounted value of expected cash flows (there was no fair value reference), and reversals of asset impairments were prohibited.

IFRS 7, *Financial Instruments – Disclosure*, requires that the entity disclose enough information to enable users to evaluate the importance of financial instruments to the entity's financial position and performance, as well as the nature and extent of risks and how the entity manages those risks. Disclosure of risks must be based on the same information shared internally with key management personnel.

Under IFRS, goodwill must be reviewed for impairment separately for each independent grouping of assets and cash flows within a larger business. Further, many entities had to change their asset valuation model for occupied properties, investment properties, equipment, private debt instruments, private equities, joint ventures and limited partnerships, particularly where an assessment of market price was achievable. Canadian GAAP allowed reinsurance assets to reduce the actuarial value of liabilities. This is not allowed in IFRS, and the new presentation is in line with U.S. GAAP where the reinsurance recoverables are treated as assets.

IFRS has different reporting rules for different types of contracts. IFRS 4 relates to insurance contracts, IAS 18 is for service contracts, and IAS 32 and 39 are for investment contracts. The first step in classifying a contract is to determine if there are components in the contract, which can be unbundled with possibly different reporting standards applying to each. IFRS 4 defines an insurance contract as a contract under which one party (the insurer) accepts significant insurance risk from another party (the policyholder) by agreeing to compensate the policyholder if a specified future event (the insured event) adversely affects the policyholder. Insurance risk is risk, other than financial risk, transferred from the contract holder to the contract issuer. Significant insurance risk exists if an insured event could cause an insurer to pay significant additional benefits in any scenario, excluding scenarios that lack commercial substance. Classification is done on a contract by contract basis. IAS 31 provides guidance for determining whether a contract is a financial instrument, and IAS 39 is the financial reporting standard for financial instruments other than insurance contracts. It includes requirements for separate reporting of embedded derivatives at fair value and for unbundling of service contracts that are subject to IAS 18.

Useful guidance on the classification of insurance contracts is available in the International Actuarial Standard of Practice Guideline 3 (IASP 3), published by the International Actuarial Association. Group insurance contracts are particularly susceptible to unbundling and care must be taken in the classification of the different elements.

The portion IFRS 4, *Insurance Contracts*, relating to valuation is an interim standard, and allows for wide use of professional judgment in terms of insurance liability measurement, and therefore allows Canadian GAAP standards to continue; the Canadian Asset Liability Method (CALM) is mandatory until IFRS 4 phase 2 becomes final and other phases of the standard are adopted. Current Canadian GAAP rules are discussed below, since the concepts below still hold true under IFRS.

The CALM method defines reserves to be the amount equal to the carrying value of the insurance enterprise's assets that, taking into account the other pertinent items on the balance sheet, will be sufficient without being excessive to discharge the enterprise's obligations over the term of the liabilities for its insurance policies (including annuity contracts), and to pay expenses related to the administration of those policies. Most insurance companies are classifying assets that back liabilities as "Held for Trading" or HFT.

All elements that can impact the financial results should be included in the valuation. The general principles that should be adhered to are as follows.

- Liabilities should be computed on a going-concern basis.
- The actuary should use expected experience in the valuation, but with a separate provision for adverse deviation (PFAD) whenever an assumption about the future is required. The PFAD should be limited and reasonable. This is quite different from U.S. statutory reporting in that there are no mandated bases for reserve calculations.
- All acquisition costs, without arbitrary limits, should be incorporated in the computation of actuarial liabilities.
- Most costs should be included, except for income taxes, marketing overhead, and shareholder transfer.
- Surrender privileges and policy lapsation should be considered.

These principles have been accepted by regulatory authorities, but with strengthened solvency safeguards. The federal law requires that an insurer's board of directors appoint an actuary who must be a Fellow of the Canadian Institute of Actuaries (the "appointed actuary"). The appointed actuary must value the actuarial and other policy liabilities of the company, as well as any other matter specified by the Superintendent. The actuary's valuation must be done in accordance with generally accepted actuarial practice, with such changes as may be specified by the Superintendent.

Until international standards become final, generally accepted actuarial practice is the responsibility of the Canadian Institute of Actuaries (CIA), and current practice is to be found in the Standards of Practice. The General Standards (Section 1000) puts forth that the standards are the only explicit articulation of accepted actuarial practice. Explanations, examples, and other useful guidance may be found in educational notes, historical standards, and other actuarial literature. The Practice-Specific Standards for Insurers, Section 2300, Life and Health Insurance, articulate the standards that apply to insurers, including group insurance. These standards require reserves to be calculated using scenario projections of asset and liability cash flows, including margins for adverse deviation, rather than the discounting of expected benefits at predetermined interest rates. The reserve is equal to the carrying value of a group of assets necessary to provide sufficient cash flow to meet the total liability cash flows as they become due.

There are no specific articles related to group insurance. The concepts and methods are considered to be universal in their application. There are examples of how concepts should be applied in specific types of group contracts. A significant concept in the standard is the term of liabilities. For group policies with no rate increase constraints, the term of the liabilities is the first renewal after the valuation date.

There are a number of other solvency safeguards contained in the legislation, especially Sections 368 and 369 of the Canadian Insurance Companies Act (ICA). These include the following:

- The actuary is required to examine the current and future solvency position of the company.
- The actuary is required to report to the chief executive officer and the chief financial officer any matters that have come to the actuary's attention in the course of carrying out the actuary's duties and in the actuary's opinion have material adverse effects on the financial position of the company and require rectification.
- A copy of the report referred to above is to be provided to the directors.
- If, in the opinion of the actuary, suitable action is not being taken to rectify the matter, the actuary is required to send a copy of the report to the Superintendent.

GAAP

United States

Group GAAP financial reporting refers to the accounting conventions adopted by the Financial Accounting Standards Board (FASB) in its Statement of Financial Accounting Standards (SFAS) No. 60: Accounting and Reporting by Insurance Enterprises. Additionally, SFAS No. 97 details GAAP for universal life type policies.[1] Life and health insurers whose stock is publicly traded are required by the Securities and Exchange Commission (SEC) to prepare financial reports on a GAAP basis. Mutual companies have been required by the American Institute of Certified Public Accountants (AICPA) to use GAAP for statements

---

[1] As part of the codification process for GAAP reporting, these two standards have been incorporated into ASC 944 but the underlying requirements are unchanged.

ending December 15, 1997 and later, or risk having their audit opinion qualified as not conforming to GAAP.

GAAP financial reporting standards provide a consistent framework for comparing the financial results of different entities and attempt to more accurately reflect the earnings during a reporting period. The focus of GAAP is on the income statement. Accurate reporting of income by year and the trend in these numbers are important, since they are often used in securities valuations.

Statutory financial reporting in the U.S. emphasizes solvency and produces a conservative valuation of both assets and liabilities. As such, it can distort both the current level of earnings and the historical trend in earnings. The major modifications to statutory reporting necessary to produce GAAP financial results are as follows:

- Removal of some of the conservatism in reserving assumptions (GAAP reserves still include some conservatism, referred to as "provision for adverse deviation");
- Full recognition of deferred taxes;
- Recognition of the market value of most assets;
- Recognition of lapses in reserves;
- Capitalization of deferred acquisition costs;
- Recognition of all receivables and allowances; and
- Removal of the AVR and IMR.

Conceptually, GAAP financial reporting attempts to match the incidence of revenues and expenses, while statutory financial reporting tends to accelerate expense recognition and delay revenue recognition (or at least offset revenue recognition with corresponding liabilities, producing the same effect).

Statutory financial reporting attempts to determine the value of the insurer if it were forced to liquidate; GAAP financial reporting attempts to determine the value of the insurer on a going-concern basis. In addition, the conservative assumptions required in many statutory reserve items can be replaced by a much less conservative GAAP margin for adverse deviation.

Canada

As mentioned earlier, in Canada statutory reporting is done using IFRS and Canadian GAAP for reserves (at least until international standards for insurance contracts become final). Companies are required to file quarterly and annual financial reports with OSFI. The quarterly return is an abbreviated version of the Life-1 annual statement.

The actuary is required to file a report with the Life-1 annual statement which provides the regulatory authorities with the following:

- A description of all the assumptions used, and a full and complete justification for each assumption.
- A description of any approximations used.
- Any changes in the assumptions and the effect thereof.

- A signed statement which affirms compliance with the Standards of Practice of the Canadian Institute of Actuaries.
- A description of how the actuary is compensated and a signed statement to the effect that the actuary has performed his duties without regard to personal considerations.
- A signed copy of the opinion of the actuary.
- Any other information that the Superintendent may require.

The instructions for completing the actuary's report exceed 50 pages and the report itself will often run to hundreds of pages.

The company must also prepare the Minimum Continuing Capital and Surplus Requirement (MCCSR) form and the completed form must be signed by the appointed actuary and a senior company officer. The MCCSR is the amount of capital that the supervisory authorities require. This is similar to risk-based capital calculations as they now exist in U.S. financial reporting. In addition, the actuary must file a signed report on the manner in which the MCCSR elements were calculated, with descriptions of all areas where judgment was used. OSFI annually revises the MCCSR guidelines.[2] The revisions are made to refine and improve the capital adequacy calculation. Significant changes are expected in the next few years as the calculation will move towards the concepts embodied in Solvency II currently being proposed for European insurance companies. The changes will mostly impact policies with long term guarantees. Group business, which generally does not provide such guarantees, will be less affected. The amount of capital required in Canada is further described in the next chapter of this text.

Although Dynamic Capital Adequacy Testing (DCAT, from Section 368 of the ICA) has been mandatory in Canada for a number of years, OSFI issued a new guideline in 2009 on stress testing for financial institutions. DCAT is one example of this stress testing. DCAT testing is required on an annual basis by regulatory authorities. It is meant to measure the state of a company's financial health and its ability to continue in business, and is therefore dynamic and forward-looking. The company's financial position is "tested" over a five-year projection period, under various "stress" conditions from plausible adverse scenarios:

- External environment (economic, government actions, legal),
- Business experience (claims, productivity, sales, surrenders), and
- Business planning (investment, products, bonus, capital).

The scenarios are chosen to be basic risks that are relevant to insurers (such as mortality and morbidity), as well as ripple effects (such as a change in economic scenario that may trigger changes in disability rates). Expense rates and investment income are integrated into these scenarios. Combinations of various risks are simulated. From time to time, OSFI requires companies to test prescribed scenarios which are generally based on severe events. The stress testing is often conducted on a stochastic basis with randomly generated scenarios derived from known distribution.

---

[2] www.osfi-bsif.gc.ca/app/DocRepository/1/eng/guidelines/capital/guidelines/mccsr2012_e.pdf

The DCAT is presented to the Board of Directors and Senior Management. This presentation includes:

- An analysis of the projections made under these various stress conditions,
- A history of the company's progress in capital ratios for recent years,
- A discussion of the company's condition,
- A test of management reaction under significant scenarios, and
- Recommendations and progresses on past recommendations.

The actuary must also conform to the Standard of Practice on Dynamic Capital Adequacy Testing promulgated by the Canadian Institute of Actuaries.

A company's group insurance portfolio must be included in the investigation of capital adequacy. To the extent that there are future guarantees as to mortality, morbidity, expenses or other risk factors, the actuary must assess the company's position with respect to those guarantees and the impact they may have on the capital position in the event of possible deterioration. The Superintendent of Insurance requires that the Dynamic Capital Adequacy Report be filed with the regulatory authorities.

Assuris Reporting

The life insurance industry in Canada established a consumer protection plan in 1990 known as Assuris, which indemnifies (within certain limits) the policyholders of an insurance company in the event of the insolvency of the company. Assuris is a not-for-profit organization funded by the entire life insurance industry in Canada. All direct writing companies are obligated to belong to the plan and are required to file the statutory calculation of minimum surplus with the industry organization that administers the plan. The minimum surplus standard is based on risk factors applied to the actual asset mix and liabilities of the company.

TAX

United States

Tax financial reporting refers to the accounting conventions required by the various taxing authorities in the determination of the tax liability of life and health insurance companies. The discussion that follows focuses mainly on the impact on actuarial items of U.S. federal income tax requirements. State premium taxes and assessments will not be discussed. State income taxation exists in a minority of states, but is often offset by premium taxes.

In general, statutory financial reports are the starting point for tax reporting, with certain adjustments of reserve items. The most obvious example of these adjustments is the required use of minimum interest rates for tax reserves. These rates often exceed the statutory maximum interest rates, and thus lower the recognized tax reserve and increase taxable income relative to statutory values.

A related item that affects the taxable income of life and health insurers is the proxy deferred acquisition cost tax (DAC tax). The DAC tax requires insurers to delay the recognition of certain expenses when calculating current taxable income. The expense deferred is not related to any real expense related to sales efforts or results, but is merely a specified percentage of inforce premium. The justification for the deferral is that the expense approximates the actual acquisition expenses that should have been deferred (in order to better match revenues and expenses). This provision has been compared to an interest free loan to the federal government, since the capitalized costs are recouped over a ten-year period. The DAC tax rate varies by product and applies to group life insurance, group annuities, and those group products that are treated as guaranteed renewable or noncancelable accident and health policies for tax purposes. It does not apply to most forms of group health insurance, but group long-term care contracts are often subject to this tax.

For tax basis calculations, group carriers must also reduce their provisions for refunds and unearned premiums by 20% for the purpose of determining their taxable income. Again, the intent of this provision is more relevant to insurance coverages with high acquisition expenses, but is applied to group business as well.

Canada

An insurance company is subject to a variety of taxes such as federal income tax, investment income tax, provincial income tax, taxes on capital (federal and provincial), other general business taxes, and premium tax. Of these taxes, only federal income tax and investment income tax are discussed here. Provincial income tax is usually based on the federal calculation, and the other taxes are calculated in a straightforward manner.

Federal income tax starts with the income based on statutory accounting, and is then adjusted by modifying a number of income and expense items. For group insurance, the four most important items are: (1) changes in actuarial reserves, (2) reserves for incurred but unreported claims, (3) provisions for deferred policy acquisition costs and (4) provisions for experience rating refunds. Various sections of the income tax act ensure that the deductions for the increases in these items are reasonable, justified, and not more than the corresponding statutory expense. For group term insurance that provides coverage for a period not exceeding 12 months, the actuarial reserve is limited to an unearned gross premium reserve determined by apportioning the premium paid equally over the policy period. Tax reserves for amounts due after the valuation date on known claims incurred prior to that date are generally limited to 95% of the statutory reserves. The reserve for incurred but unreported claims is limited to 95% of the statutory reserve. Expenses incurred on account of the acquisition of an insurance policy (other than a noncancelable or guaranteed renewable accident and sickness policy or life policies except group term life with a coverage period of 12 months or less) must be capitalized and amortized over the term of the policy where the term extends beyond the end of the taxation year. The provision for experience rating refunds is limited to amounts that will ultimately be paid or unconditionally credited to the policyholder, but not greater than 25% of the annual premium, a reasonable amount, or the amount of the statutory reserve. Investment income tax, at the rate of 15%, is paid by life insurers on investment income earned on assets supporting the following liabilities:

- Group life insurance contract rate stabilization reserves,
- Group life active life reserves (paid-up, level premium, conversions), and
- Experience rating refund liabilities that are not due within twelve months.

MANAGERIAL

Managerial financial reporting can be described as modifications of other financial reporting methods to provide a more accurate picture of the impact of management decisions on the value of the insurer. The considerations described below apply to both U.S. and Canadian management reporting.

Generally, managerial financial reporting starts from a GAAP basis, making adjustments to address GAAP's limitations. Examples of these limitations are the artificial limit on the deferrable acquisition costs, the use of reasonable and conservative reserve valuation assumptions rather than best estimates, and the lock-in of assumptions.

Following are several possible reasons to produce managerial financial reports:

- To measure financial results in alternate ways, such as by product, by cost center, or by strategic business unit;
- To relate financial results to pricing methods;
- To improve communication of results to management; and
- To include projections of future experience, in order to determine the true value added by management during a reporting period.

Management reporting is discussed further in Chapter 41, "Analysis of Financial and Operational Performance."

POLICYHOLDER

United States

Policyholder financial reporting generally provides information for three purposes: assessing the results of risk-sharing arrangements, fulfilling government reporting requirements, and enabling policyholders to complete their own financial reports.

Reporting of the financial consequences of risk-sharing arrangements provides the policyholder with documentation of the flow of funds involved in the insurance arrangement. The form and content of these reports depends upon the nature of the risk-sharing arrangement and are discussed later in this chapter.

Government reporting requirements include reporting for ERISA (the federal law governing employer-sponsored plans) and Internal Revenue Service (IRS) reporting for Voluntary Employee Benefit Associations (VEBAs), also known as 501(c)(9) trusts. ERISA plans are generally required to complete Form 5500 annually, to be filed with the Department of Labor (DOL) and the IRS. VEBAs are required to file IRS Form 990, which is essentially a tax return for non-profit organizations. A VEBA may be subject to tax on non-exempt function income. Interest income on excess actuarial reserves may be considered non-exempt function income, but safe harbors are provided within the regulations.

Policyholders often need certain information in order to complete their own financial reports. Actuarial reserves for self-funded policies and reserveless policies (where reserves are held by the policyholder rather than by the insurer) are an example. Some policyholders may also desire estimates of retrospective premium liabilities or refunds payable. The proliferation of self-funding arrangements and the rapid increase in medical costs have led to a greater need for regular re-determination of actuarial reserves. Claims experience and enrollment reports that assist policyholders with determining their liabilities arising from post-retirement benefits and from post-employment benefits are further examples of policyholder reporting.

Canada

Policyholder financial reporting in Canada is similar to the U.S., with the exception of governmental reporting requirements. In Canada, the insurer must issue to the policyholder income tax forms (T-4) for taxable disability income benefits and interest earnings forms (T-5) for death-related benefits, including lump sum and survivor income benefits. In addition, an insurer must issue T-5 for any interest earned on rate stabilization reserves if such reserves exceed 25% of the policyholder's annual premium. Finally, interest credited to refund deposit accounts is to be reported to tax authorities, as it represents income taxable in the hands of the policyholder.

PROVIDER

United States

Provider reporting generally provides information for two purposes: provider risk-sharing arrangements and medical management reporting.

Provider risk sharing refers to the practice of making a portion of the provider's reimbursement contingent upon the occurrence of certain events. It is a concept that is central to the operation of many Health Maintenance Organizations (HMOs). For example, the provider might enter into a contract with the HMO, trading fee-for-service reimbursement for capitation with a risk-sharing payment. The risk-sharing payment might be partly funded through a withhold, and partly out of current profits. These arrangements are becoming more common, even outside of HMO contracts.

The risk-sharing payment is often linked to the level of utilization or the average cost per member of services over which the provider is felt to exercise some degree of control. Often, stop-loss mechanisms are used to reduce the impact of large claims on the provider's risk-sharing payment.

The retrospective settlement of the risk-sharing payment and the financial implications to both the provider and the HMO create a need for reporting capabilities which support the settlement. In addition, providers who assume the risk associated with providing services may need to establish reserves in their own financial statements. Often, data for specific insureds or facilities must be tracked separately, in order to administer the settlement.

In addition to provider risk-sharing, medical management reporting has increased in importance. Medical management reports may include reporting to regulatory entities, reporting to industry groups, and reporting to providers. Such reports are starting to contain increasing clinical information, including outcomes and other quality measures.

Several states have started requiring financial information related to health care in addition to the information found in the NAIC annual statement blank. With the concern over the impact of cost reduction on the quality of care, financial reporting to industry groups has increased. Finally, as health care payers become more aware of the impact of medical management on utilization, costs, and quality of care, reporting will increase.

Canada

In Canada there is no reporting requirement to providers, as they do not take any insurance risk or share in any insurance profit.

SPECIFIC CONSIDERATIONS FOR GROUP INSURANCE

There are many areas in which the financial reporting of group insurance differs from the reporting for individual insurance:

- Alternative funding methods,
- Policyholder accounting,
- Administrative arrangements,
- Excess coverages,
- Regulatory requirements, and
- Other liabilities.

ALTERNATIVE FUNDING METHODS

The introduction of alternative funding methods for group insurance (discussed in Chapter 27) complicates the various types of financial reporting previously discussed. In a pure insurance arrangement, the policyholder remits a fixed premium as consideration for complete indemnification of the covered benefits under the policy. From the insurer's standpoint, the financial results of all policies written this way can be aggregated. Thus, many of the actuarial items can be determined in the aggregate, or for groupings of policies with substantially similar characteristics. This means, for example, that the actuary may only need to determine one reserve to cover the incurred but unpaid claims for an entire block of business. By using a large volume of data, the reserve can be more credible and require less margin for adverse deviation.

With some alternative funding methods, claim reserves must be determined at the policy level in order to determine the premium refund reserve associated with the policy. By segmenting claims data to the policy level, some credibility is lost. However, any increase in the margin in the claim reserves included in the refund calculation may simultaneously understate the refund reserve. (Some carriers avoid this problem by creating an explicit margin to claim reserves that is not included in the refund calculation.) Also, an inaccurate estimate of the claim reserve can have a major adverse impact if the insurer refunds or releases funds to the policyholder that are eventually required to pay higher than anticipated claims runout.

Alternative funding methods span the risk transfer continuum from the fully insured contract to a self-insured contract. In looking at financial reporting of alternative funding arrangements, administrative service fee income becomes a material element of reporting.

Where there is a retrospective premium rider, retrospective premiums create due and unpaid premiums on the financial statement. Under this type of contract, a group policyholder agrees to remit additional premiums (up to a cap) after a policy year is over, based on a retrospective look at the group's financial results. Generally, a due and unpaid premium asset is calculated as of the valuation date, based on interim estimates of financial results. These financial results require estimates for claim reserves and expenses charged to the policyholder. Misestimation of these items can cause positive or negative financial results to emerge, once the final policyholder accounting is issued.

Retrospective experience rating refunds (or dividends, if the insurer is a mutual company) require calculation of an additional liability, generally called a refund reserve, dividend liability, or a rate credit reserve. An insurer may agree to let the policyholder share in any positive results generated by the policy (much like a dividend in individual participating life insurance). Similar to retrospective due and unpaid premiums, interim estimates of financial results are required to estimate the amount of any refund, and the current estimate is held as a liability on the financial statement.

Experience combinations refer to the practice of combining several policies of one policyholder prior to the determination of the financial results, allowing surplus under one policy to offset deficits on another. This can be accommodated on the financial statement by creation of category of assets and liabilities referred to as transfers.

Reserveless agreements refer to the situation where the policyholder holds the actuarial reserves for a policy. While the insurer must still set up claim reserves to cover this liability (because it is their contractual obligation to pay those claims), the policyholder promises to pay for those claims if the policy ever cancels. The policyholder may present a letter of credit to the insurer to secure this obligation. These agreements are often called terminal premiums, as they only become due and payable if the policy terminates. These terminal premiums are accounted for as offsets to the actuarial reserves, either as an asset or a negative liability. Terminal premiums can be used with nearly all forms of alternative funding methods. If used with refund arrangements, due and unpaid premiums or refund reserves can be affected. Unsecured terminal premiums can create some financial reporting problems. The valuation actuary needs to determine the level of security needed to allow terminal premiums to offset actuarial reserves for financial reporting. One possible approach would be to discount the value of the terminal reserve to reflect the probability of being able to collect it upon termination of the policy. This treatment requires ongoing evaluation of the financial risk of the policyholder.

In a minimum premium plan, the policyholder funds the claims portion of the policy with funds held in its own bank account, or reimburses the insurer for claims paid on the insurer's bank account. In most jurisdictions, the policyholder can avoid premium taxes on the claims portion of the premium by doing so. The self-funded portion of claims is often referred to as the premium equivalent. The NAIC annual statement does not require the reporting of premium equivalents within the income statement. This is important to remember when comparing the annual statements of different group insurers. Minimum premium plans can be used in conjunction with other alternative funding methods (often retrospective refunds). The accounting for these plans is similar to that of the reserveless arrangements—claims are charged against the policyholder's funds first, and excess claims are then charged to the insurer.

Fee income can arise in a number of ways. Insurers may unbundle certain expense charges, and charge the policyholder for these on an "as used" basis. Examples would be fees charged for utilization review or preferred provider organization (PPO) access fees. Some policyholders use third party administrators to perform administrative duties for the insurer. In these instances, the insurer collects premiums paid by the policyholder and remits service fees to the third party administrator. A third type of fee income arises when the policyholder contracts with the insurer on an administrative services only (ASO) basis.

Accounting for fee income is similar to premium accounting. The main difference is that the fee income is often not immediately determinable. Fees are often charged in relation to the expense involved in the tasks performed. An example would be a claim administration expense, charged on a per draft basis. Such a charge would require knowledge of the number of drafts issued during an accounting period. For these reasons, estimates of fee income may be used in financial reports. ASO fees are reported as part of Exhibit 2 (General Expenses) for companies filing the NAIC annual statement blank for life and accident and health companies. (The net effect of ASO fee income and expenses associated with the administration of these contracts is typically disclosed in the Notes to Financial Statements section.)

POLICYHOLDER ACCOUNTING

In many alternative funding methods, the policyholder participates in the insurance risk to some degree. This creates the need for financial reporting to the policyholder. It also requires special calculations whenever the insurer prepares its own financial reports.

As discussed previously, alternative funding arrangements generally require the estimation of policy level financial results on the valuation date, in order to determine the financial impact on the insurer. A simplified calculation of such policy level financial results might resemble the following format:

> Gain = (Collected Premium, less Pooled Premium)
> less (Paid Claims, less Pooled Claims)
> less (Ending Claim Reserve, less Beginning Claim Reserve)
> less (Expenses, Risk and Profit Charged)
> plus (Interest Credited)

When the bottom line is a loss, the insurer will determine if other funds are available to use as premium, which will depend on the funding arrangement. For example, if the policyholder agreed to provide an additional 5% of billed premium as a retrospective premium, the insurer would set up a due and unpaid premium reserve to cover the loss up to that 5% amount. This increases the amount of reported earned premiums. When the bottom line is a gain, the insurer will determine if the policyholder is eligible for a refund. The amount of the anticipated refund is a liability to the insurer, and it is held as a refund reserve.

The refund reserve lowers the reported earned premiums. (In the U.S., this reserve is often reported in Exhibit 6 of the NAIC annual statement under "reserve for rate credits.")

Since the policyholder is sharing in the risk of the policy, a financial report must be prepared detailing the results of the policy period. Typically, these reports are produced within two or three months after the end of the policy period. If the policy cancels, many insurers retain the right to wait up to 15 months before issuing the final accounting. This reduces the risk of misestimation of any remaining claim reserves.

Producing policyholder reports soon after the policy period closes makes it necessary to estimate reserves for incurred but unpaid claims. These estimates are generally not the same as estimates used in the insurer's financial statements, since the insurer has the benefit of greater hindsight regarding the claim runout. Since these estimates differ from the ones used in the insurer's financials, a gain or loss in the insurer's own financial reports may be recognized at the point the policyholder statement is issued.

Another consideration arises because of the insurer's distribution of policies by renewal date, which is often skewed toward the beginning of the year. This happens because many policyholders prefer January 1 as their renewal date. In the first quarter, the insurer may have a higher than normal amount of policyholder accounting statements issued. This can create a reported gain or loss in the first quarter, which probably was attributable to the prior calendar year and ideally should have been reported on the prior year's annual statement.

For certain funding arrangements in a positive financial position, increasing the claim reserve within certain limits will merely decrease the refund reserve, and vice versa. This phenomenon provides an automatic source of margin in setting claim reserves, at least until issuance of the policyholder's statement. However, once a refund is paid, a loss may not be recoverable, at least until the next policy period.

ADMINISTRATIVE SERVICE AGREEMENTS

In addition to alternative funding methods, policyholders may enter into administrative service agreements with an insurer. Some of these arrangements were discussed under the heading of fee income. The main types of administrative arrangements are the following:

- Self-administration
- Third-party administration
- Funds held by the insurer
- Funds held by the policyholder
- Premium billing

Self-administration refers to the transfer of responsibilities normally performed by the insurer (such as premium billing or eligibility functions) to the policyholder. Transferring these responsibilities to the policyholder may make it more difficult to estimate assets and liabilities for the financial statements. For example, if the policyholder is responsible for determining the amount of premium owed to the insurer, the insurer may not be able to accurately estimate the amount of any due and unpaid premium. Claim reserves may be similarly affected by policyholders that pay their own claims or determine eligibility for claim payments.

Third-party administration refers to the transfer of responsibilities normally performed by the insurer (usually claims payment, but sometimes also premium billing or eligibility functions) to a third party. The same financial reporting concerns as with self-administration apply. In addition, the introduction of a third party into the chain of correspondence may lengthen the period from the point that a claim is incurred until it is eventually paid. Thus, the claim reserve estimate may need to be adjusted. The actuary should be aware of differences in the method of processing claims, the definition of incurred dates, and differences in claim adjudication, and how these impact the financial statements.

In both self-administration and third-party administration, the insurer generally reserves the right to audit the functions performed. This provides some protection against inappropriate practices that may adversely affect the financial results of the insurer.

"Funds held by the insurer" refers to policyholder money left on deposit in an account with the insurer. These accounts usually take the form of premium stabilization reserves or funds (PSRs or PSFs), also called Rate Stabilization Reserves, or straight deposits. An insurer may require a PSR as a margin against adverse experience, before agreeing to certain funding arrangements. Generally, PSRs are considered in the calculation of refund reserve. Straight deposits are usually not available to the insurer, and are not considered in the refund reserve calculation.

Deposits will also impact financial reporting when interest is credited to the policyholder. The insurer will recognize a gain or a loss depending on the difference between net investment income earned on these funds and the interest credited.

"Funds held by the policyholder" refers to reserves, self-funded claims, or other items held by the policyholder but subject to the insurance contract. The policyholder may establish a line of credit to ensure payment of retrospective premiums or terminal premiums. These items are accounted for as if the insurer had possession of the funds.

Premium billing methods can affect the calculation of due and unpaid premiums or refund reserves. Examples are non-monthly premiums and delayed premiums (premium drags). Non-monthly premiums create administrative difficulties, but otherwise do not pose a problem. Delayed premiums can introduce the risk of non-payment and so the financial solvency of the policyholder should by underwritten at issue and at renewal.

Stop-loss coverages (specific or aggregate) are generally written to limit the policyholder's exposure to losses on an underlying policy administered by the insurer, the policyholder or a third party. If the coverage is sold with level premiums, the durational nature of the claim liabilities (heavily increasing as the duration increases) suggests an unearned premium or policy reserve may be appropriate, in addition to normal reserves.

REGULATORY REQUIREMENTS

Certain regulatory requirements can impact the liabilities of group insurers. In the U.S., the valuation laws of each state specify reserve assumptions and methodologies. In the past, it was generally sufficient to satisfy the requirements of the state of domicile of the insurer.

More and more, states are revising their requirements to cover any insurer doing business in their state. To the extent these laws differ, an insurer might be required to use the most conservative state's law as the basis of its statutory financial reporting.

The Actuarial Opinion and Memorandum Regulation sets forth the requirements for an actuary who signs a statement of opinion as to the adequacy of annual statement reserves in light of the underlying assets. It also provides sample wording for the actuarial opinion. The regulation also specifies when asset adequacy analysis is required for insurance companies.

Asset adequacy analysis has been an annual statement requirement since 1992. Basically, the actuarial opinion must include a statement as to whether or not asset adequacy analysis was done as part of the determination of the adequacy of the reserves. Companies may need to set aside aggregate reserves beyond the statutory based minimum reserves, based on their asset adequacy analysis. The valuation actuary will typically disclose the type of asset adequacy analysis that was done as part of the actuarial opinion on reserves, which accompanies the annual statement.

State specific health care reform initiatives may also create new financial reporting requirements for insurers. Some states use assessments to fund risk pools and to subsidize payors using community rating techniques. Financial reporting is typically required to determine both the total assessment and the amount to be allocated to each payor.

Under the Affordable Care Act, new reporting requirements will be required. This will help comparative effectiveness research, as well as helping to administer penalty taxes for coverage that is either not generous enough or too generous. More on this topic can be found in Chapter 18, "The Affordable Care Act."

PROVIDER INCENTIVE ARRANGEMENTS

In the U.S., provider incentive arrangements are most common in HMOs, but have also been used with PPOs and other managed care products. Generally, these arrangements involve financial rewards for providers tied to specific performance objectives. These arrangements require estimates of their value on the valuation date, to measure their impact on the financial results of the insurer. A liability must be shown to reflect the amounts that may eventually be paid to providers under the terms of the incentive arrangement.

Another complicating factor is in the way provider incentives are administered. The incentives are generally calculated based on the specific individuals a provider treats, rather than at a group level. This requires a mechanism to allocate the provider's incentive payment to each of the insurer's groups. This is a particular problem with policyholder accounting for alternative funding contracts.

CAPITATED PROVIDER CONTRACTS

Capitated provider contracts are quite common in HMOs and may require unique treatment in the HMO financial statement. Under a capitation contract, the insurance risk is transferred from the HMO to the provider, which would generally eliminate the HMO's liability for the capitated services. However, in some situations the capitated entity may not have the financial strength to assume the capitated risk, and the HMO may end up assuming some of the capitated risk. Therefore, a reserve may need to be established, even though the HMO has capitated a provider.

UNCOVERED EXPENDITURES

Uncovered expenditures are costs to an HMO or managed health care plan that are the obligation of the HMO, for which the HMO enrollee may also be liable in the event of the HMO's insolvency. Statutory requirements for HMOs generally require that the HMO allocate its liabilities between uncovered and covered expenditures.

DEFICIT CARRYFORWARDS

Deficit carryforwards arise from alternative funded groups that incur a deficit and renew their policies for another period. If these are recognized on the financial statement, they can be a significant source of gain in future periods. An important issue is whether to anticipate recoveries of these deficits in determining financial results. GAAP accounting principles seem to imply that these deficits be carried as assets at their realizable value. Statutory financial reporting practice is to ignore these deficit carryforwards, unless there is a contractual agreement between the insurer and an employer that requires the employer to pay deficit carryforwards in case of termination of coverage.

INTEREST ON POLICY FUNDS

Interest on policy funds held by the insurer on behalf of the policyholder creates a liability to the insurer, to the extent that these funds must ultimately be credited to the policyholder. Interest earned in excess of that credited to the policyholder will be a gain to the insurer. In alternative funding contracts, interest on policy funds may be accounted for as a separate item to policyholders, or it may be used as an offset to expenses.

POLICY YEAR ACCOUNTING

This will often differ from the statutory accounting period (calendar year) or the fiscal accounting period. The timing of the issuance of the policyholder accounting may impact the financial results where policyholder accounting items differ from the estimates included in the statutory or GAAP financial reports.

RETENTION FORMULAS

Retention represents charges made to a policyholder by an insurer for all items other than claims themselves, such as risk, taxes, and expenses. Retention may be determined using factors or formulas, or based on an actual accounting. Retention charges are an important part of the accounting for alternative funding methods. Retention may be difficult or impossible to determine for certain insurers, such as staff model HMOs, where the line between claims and expenses is hazy.

In order to determine whether a policy is generating a gain or a loss for the period, each element of gain or loss, including expenses, must be estimated. Interim estimates of expenses may differ from what actually gets charged to the policyholder in policyholder accounting. These differences will be gains or losses in the insurer's financial reports in the period in which accounting is finalized.

POST-RETIREMENT AND POST-EMPLOYMENT BENEFITS

SFAS No. 132, No. 106, No. 88[3] and No. 35[4] are FASB's statements on accounting for post-retirement benefits other than pensions. GASB No. 43 and No. 45 (soon to replaced by GASB No. 74 and 75) are similar, but are the government accounting standards that apply to states, cities, counties, schools and municipalities' retiree benefits. The rapid increase in health care costs and promises to provide retirees medical care for life have combined to create very large unfunded liabilities for many employers. While these benefits are traditionally funded on a pay-as-you-go basis, they are accounted for on an accrual basis over the working years of each potential retiree.

SFAS No. 112[5] is FASB's statement on accounting for post-employment benefits. Post-employment benefits include severance pay, continuation of life and health insurance upon severance (as opposed to retirement), outplacement assistance, certain disability liabilities, and more. The post-employment benefits covered by SFAS No. 112 do *not* include pensions or other postretirement benefits such as retiree life insurance and retiree health care benefits. Like retiree benefits, employers must accrue costs annually over time if the benefits meet certain conditions.

These accounting standards affect the financial statements of insurers' clients, and also the insurers themselves as employers. International accounting standards may be adopted for both types of benefits soon.

RATING AGENCIES

Financial reporting can be impacted by the desire of insurers to gain the highest possible rating from the various rating agencies. Risk-based capital and assigned surplus formulas are often used to determine the appropriate level of surplus that should be maintained.

CODIFICATION (STATUTORY ACCOUNTING PRINCIPLES)

The NAIC codified Statutory Accounting Principles effective January 1, 2001. The codification is contained in the "Accounting Practices and Procedures Manual." As of each March, the Manual is updated for that year. The text is a wealth of information for accountants and actuaries.

Of particular interest to actuaries are SSAP No. 51, "Life Contracts," SSAP No. 54, "Individual and Group Accident and Health Contracts," and SSAP No. 55, "Unpaid Claims, Losses and Loss Adjustment Expenses." In addition, "Appendix C – Actuarial Guidelines," provides a single reference source for the NAIC's guidance to actuaries.

---

[3] SFAS 132, 106, and 88 are now incorporated into ASC 715 as part of the codification of U.S. GAAP reporting.
[4] ASC 960
[5] ASC 712.

REINSURANCE

Many insurers reinsure a portion of their group business with professional reinsurers. Normally, reinsurance treaties renew annually and reinsurers require the ceding insurer to report certain information on a periodic basis:

- Administration of the treaty (including number of lives, amounts reinsured, census movements by age, group and gender);
- Premium billing and collection data;
- Validation of the exposure to certain unusual types of risks, such as risk concentration in certain areas or high cost diseases;
- Identification of exposure to large amounts of risks, and to risk concentration;
- Copies of annual reports made to authorities;
- Pricing assumptions, including evaluating reinsurance renewal terms; and
- Reserve setting assumptions and amounts.

The reinsurer normally requires information to be sent on an annual basis, usually 120-150 days prior to the treaty renewal date.

NON-INSURANCE COMPLIANCE REQUIREMENTS

In recent years, following financial turmoil, illegal activities, privacy leaks and a trend toward outsourcing, supervisory and regulatory authorities have strengthened some of the compliance requirements on insurers for non-insurance reasons such as, but not limited to outsourcing of certain business activities, transportation of medical information, privacy, terrorism financing, and money laundering.

SUMMARY AND CONCLUSIONS

There are special considerations to financial reporting for group insurance, primarily due to the flexibility offered to groups in financing their benefit. The group market has continued to evolve with new funding arrangements and products, and the accounting standards have been rapidly changing and will continue to change to advance transparency, comparability, and principle-based measurement. Anyone performing financial reporting for group insurance should understand the current environment and keep up with the changes taking place.

36. GROUP INSURANCE RESERVES

Daniel D. Skwire

INTRODUCTION TO GROUP INSURANCE RESERVES

Insurance products pose unique accounting challenges because their cash flows are spread out over time. Premiums for a given year of coverage, for example, may be paid in full on the first day of the year, in equal installments each month, or in a manner that allows for retrospective adjustments based on the year's claim experience. Likewise, the payments made by an insurance company for a covered loss may occur in a single lump sum, in multiple disbursements over time, or in a series of regularly scheduled payments that continue for many years. Similar situations can occur with administrative expenses, commissions, and other items.

Reserves are a timing mechanism used to smooth the emergence of profits for insurance products. Reserves have no impact on the profitability of a product over its entire lifetime, but they do affect the profitability in a given reporting period.

As a simple example, suppose a group life insurer sells a policy that provides one month of coverage to an employer. The insurer collects $1 million of premium in December as an advance payment for the coverage that becomes effective January 1. An employee dies at the end of January, and the insurance company makes a benefit payment of $800,000 in early February. If no reserves were used, then the insurer's profits and losses, ignoring expenses and other items for simplicity, would emerge as follows:

Table 36.1

Profits and Losses with No Reserves		
Month	Cash flow	Total Profit
December	$1,000,000	$1,000,000
January	$0	$0
February	($800,000)	($800,000)

Two types of reserves can be used, however, to present a more reasonable pattern of profits on the company's financial statement. The first, a premium reserve, adjusts the timing of the premium so that it is reported in January, when coverage is actually in force. The second, a benefit reserve, adjusts the timing of claims so that the *expected* losses are also reported in January, at the same time as the corresponding premium. The following table shows the emergence of profits if the expected losses are the same as the actual losses:

Table 36.2

	Profits and Losses Including Reserves (Actual Experience Equals Expected Experience)			
	(A)	(B) Less Change in Premium Reserve	(C) Less Change in Benefit Reserve	(D)=(A) - (B) - (C) Total Profit
Month	Cash Flow			
December	$1,000,000	$1,000,000		$0
January	$0	($1,000,000)	$800,000	$200,000
February	($800,000)		($800,000)	$0

The total profit over the life of the product is still $200,000, but due to the use of reserves, the pattern of profits now emerges more smoothly and appears in the period when the insurance coverage was in force. From an accounting perspective, an increase in reserves reduces profits, while a decrease in reserves increases profits.

It is not always the case, of course, that the insurance company's estimate of losses used to set up a benefit reserve will exactly match the actual losses paid in a future period. In that case, the difference between the estimated and actual losses will appear as a gain or a loss once the actual payments are made. The following table illustrates how this would occur if the insurance carrier originally estimated that the claims would be $900,000 instead of $800,000:

Table 36.3

	Profits and Losses Including Reserves (Actual Experience Doesn't Equal Expected Experience)			
	(A)	(B) Less Change in Premium Reserve	(C) Less Change in Benefit Reserve	(D) = (A) – (B) – (C) Total Profit
Month	Cash Flow			
December	$1,000,000	$1,000,000		$0
January	$0	($1,000,000)	$900,000	$100,000
February	($800,000)		($900,000)	$100,000

In this case, the insurer's higher estimate of expected claims results in a smaller profit reported in January, with the impact of the favorable experience reflected in February. Once again, however, the total profit over the life of the policy is $200,000.

This chapter describes the primary types of reserves used in financial reporting for group insurance products. It is written from the perspective of an insurance company, although similar principles would apply for other risk-bearing organizations. Although there are important differences in the specific requirements of different accounting methods and different countries, the focus of this chapter is on the underlying principles of the reserves rather than the detailed requirements.

BENEFIT RESERVES

The most important and complex category of reserves for group insurance consists of benefit reserves, which relate to the expected amount and timing of benefit payments made under group insurance policies. The major categories of benefit reserves are discussed below.

CLAIM RESERVES

Claim reserves represent the present value of future benefit payments for claims that have already been incurred, meaning that the insured member covered by the group policy has already sought medical treatment, become disabled, or died. Chapter 37 of this text deals with the calculation of claims reserves for short-term benefits, such as medical and dental insurance, where claim payments are typically made over a period of a year or less. For these types of coverage, insurers rely heavily on their own recent experience to estimate the claim reserves that should be held.

Chapter 38 of this text deals with the calculation of claim reserves for long-term benefits, such as long-term disability and long-term care, where claim payments are typically made over a period of many years. For these coverages, insurers use published tables (often adjusted for their own experience, where credible) to help them estimate the likelihood that a given claim will remain eligible for future benefits.

INCURRED BUT NOT REPORTED (IBNR) RESERVES

IBNR reserves are a special subset of claims reserves, for which the claims have not yet been reported to the insurance company, even though the employee has already sought treatment, died, or become disabled. For short-term benefits, IBNR reserves are usually computed as part of the claim reserve described above since that calculation is done in aggregate for an entire block of business. For long-term benefits, however, where the claim reserve is computed specifically for each known claim, a separate estimate must be made for the cost of IBNR claims. This calculation is described in Chapter 38.

ACTIVE LIFE RESERVES

Most group insurance policies charge a premium for each year that is closely related to the amount of expected incurred claims for that year for the group as a whole, using the current demographics of the group as a guide. In some situations, however, group insurance policies may be priced using an issue-age premium rate, more commonly seen for individual insurance. This is typically the case for group long-term care coverage, for example, and may also occur with certain types of disability or ancillary health products. Here the premium rate is based on the age at which the employee first became eligible for coverage, and the premium rate does not change over time as the employee grows older or the demographics of the group itself change.

Group insurance claim costs tend to increase by age, since the likelihood of needing medical treatment or of becoming disabled also goes up with age. When insurance is provided using a level, issue-age premium, then that premium effectively pre-funds higher claims in later years by charging a little extra in earlier years when expected claims are lower. The active life reserve ensures that policies sold with a level premium do not appear to be highly profitable in early years when expected claims are low relative to the premiums charged, and then appear to be unprofitable in later years when expected claims are higher than in early years.

Active life reserves are held over the time period for which premiums are paid for a given coverage. The active life reserve equals zero when a policy is issued, as well as when premiums end. While the policy is in force, the active life reserve is computed as the present value of future benefits less the present value of future premiums. Each accounting system has numerous rules on exactly how future premiums and claims are estimated for this purpose, and the calculation can be quite complex. It may rely on company experience, pricing assumptions, or published tables, for example, and—depending on the accounting framework—it may or may not include assumptions around policyholder persistency.

A detailed discussion of the calculation of active life reserves is beyond the scope of this text, but it is important to recognize that active life reserves are required in situations where there is a mismatch between in the pattern of premiums and expected claims for a given employee over time (for example, a level premium but an increasing pattern of expected claim costs) and that the need for active life reserves does not depend on whether a policy is written on a group or an individual platform.

DISPUTED OR LITIGATED CLAIM RESERVES

In some situations, an insurer may determine that no payments are due for a certain claim, but the claimant may dispute that decision and file an appeal or a lawsuit. In these situations the insurer may decide to hold a reserve for the disputed claims. The most conservative course is to hold a reserve equal to the full amount of past payments that were not made, plus the full amount of the claim reserve that would be held for future payments if the claim were not disputed. In some situations, however, the insurer may hold a smaller reserve, based on its estimate of the likelihood that the appeal or lawsuit will succeed, or even hold no reserve at all if it is highly confident of its decision.

PREMIUM RESERVES

Premium reserves adjust for the timing of premium relative to the timing of coverage provided. There are two basic types of premium reserves that are used to accomplish this purpose: unearned premium reserves and premiums due.

UNEARNED PREMIUM RESERVES

Unearned premium reserves are used when a premium is paid in advance of a coverage period. For example, if a policyholder pays a full year's premium of $1.2 million in January, then an unearned premium reserve would be used to spread the premium evenly over the 12 months of the year. For the month of January, the premium cash flow would be $1.2 million and the insurer would set up an unearned premium reserve of $1.1 million, resulting in $0.1 million of earned premium appearing on the income statement ($1.2 million, minus the increase in reserves of $1.1 million). In each subsequent month, the premium cash flow would be zero, but the insurer would reduce its unearned premium reserve by $0.1 million, producing $0.1 million of earned premium on the income statement each month from the decrease in reserves.

PREMIUM DUE

Premium due is a negative reserve (technically, an asset) for the insurer and it reflects premium that is due from the policyholder to the insurer for a coverage period that has already gone by. This situation arises when premiums are paid in arrears, as is sometimes the case for certain types of coverage paid through payroll deduction, due to the time lag necessary to set up the administrative procedures to process the deductions.

EXPENSE RESERVES

There are two primary types of expense reserves that are used for group insurance: claim expense reserves (also known as loss adjustment expense reserves) and deferred acquisition costs (DAC).

CLAIM EXPENSE RESERVES

Claim expense reserves represent the present value of future expenses directly related to making claim payments. These expenses include claim investigation costs as well as the administrative cost of disbursing the payments. Claim expense reserves can be calculated using detailed unit expense assumptions, but they are also sometimes estimated as a percentage of the claim reserve and IBNR reserve. Claim expense reserves tend to be highest, as a proportion of total liabilities, for those coverages like disability and long-term care that involve complex claim investigations and adjudication, including requirements for ongoing proof of loss.

DEFERRED ACQUISITION COSTS

Deferred Acquisition Costs are a type of negative reserve used to spread out the costs of acquiring business over the lifetime of the policy. These costs may include first-year commissions that are higher than renewal commissions, underwriting expenses, and volume-based compensation paid to sales staff. In the United States, DAC is held for GAAP accounting but not for statutory accounting, and the expenses that are deferred for GAAP purposes include only those that vary with, and are directly related to, the production of new business. The calculation methods used to compute DAC are similar in concept to the methods used to compute active life reserves.

OTHER RESERVES

There are a number of other types of reserves that may be held for group insurance, and that do not fit conveniently into the categories of benefit, premium, or expense reserves.

ASSET ADEQUACY RESERVES

Statutory accounting in the United States requires that each insurance company provide a formal opinion from an appointed actuary that the company's reserves, in light of the assets supporting them, make adequate provision for future benefits and expenses. The analysis performed by the actuary to support this opinion is called asset adequacy analysis, and it often considers the amount and timing of asset, as well as liability, cash flows. This analysis is particularly important for products such as long-term care and long-term disability, which build up significant assets and rely heavily on the investment income earned by those assets to make future benefit payments. For these products, multi-scenario cashflow testing is the preferred approach for performing asset adequacy analysis. For short-term products with immaterial asset risk, simpler methods such as an analysis of reserve margins may suffice. Similar analysis is required in other accounting and regulatory systems.

To the extent that an appointed actuary's asset adequacy analysis reveals that the assets backing reserves may not be sufficient to fund future benefits and expenses under "moderately adverse" assumptions, the company may be required to hold an additional asset adequacy reserve to make up the shortfall. This situation arises when a company has imperfect matching of its assets and liabilities. An example might be if its assets are invested for a shorter duration than its liabilities and interest rates fall, meaning that the cash flows from maturing assets must be reinvested at lower interest rates than were anticipated when the product was priced and the claims were incurred. Asset adequacy reserves can also become necessary if a company's asset portfolio has become impaired due to credit quality issues.

PREMIUM DEFICIENCY RESERVES

Premium deficiency reserves are required when it appears that the future premiums to be paid for a policy will not be sufficient to fund future claims and expenses. The need for premium deficiency reserves arises when the emerging experience on a policy form is less favorable that the assumptions used to price the policy. It is a separate consideration from the need for active life reserves, which is based on the underlying pattern of premiums and expected claims, rather than on the emerging experience.

Statutory accounting in the United States lays out certain considerations for the development of premium deficiency reserves. For example, policy forms may be broadly grouped into similar categories, rather than evaluating each policy form completely on its own, and the need for deficiency reserves should be assessed over the remaining contract period (often the end of the premium or coverage guarantee period for group insurance). The insurer can ignore sales-related expenses, since those have already occurred, and model only future benefits and expenses related to the policies being studied. And, to the extent that there is a reasonable expectation that future rate increases can be achieved (for example, they have been approved by regulators but not yet implemented), then the expected amount of those rate increases can offset some or all of the need for deficiency reserves.

PROVIDER-RELATED LIABILITIES

Provider-related liabilities are established to cover future non-claim payments that may arise from risk-sharing agreements between risk-assuming entities (typically insurance carriers or health plans) and providers. Examples include capitation arrangements, case rate arrangements, stop-loss provisions, and incentive payments to providers. In computing provider-related liabilities, the actuary should study the details of any such agreements with providers in order to estimate the amount and probabilities of future payments. Another consideration is the financial strength of the provider and whether any contingent liability exists for the risk-assuming entity in the event that a provider fails or leaves the organization's network.

EXPERIENCE REFUND RESERVES

As described in Chapter 27, "Experience Rating and Funding Methods," some group coverages are written with experience rating provisions that provide for payments to be made from the insurer to a policyholder if the experience on a policy form is favorable. In situations where it appears that experience has, in fact, been favorable, and that a payment is likely to be made to the customer, then the insurer must hold an experience refund reserve using an estimate of the amount of the payment.

FURTHER GUIDANCE

The process of establishing and testing reserves for insurance products is one of the primary functions that actuaries perform. There is a wealth of guidance available to practicing actuaries, ranging from high-level standards of practice to very detailed technical requirements for specific accounting systems. Some of the most important are discussed briefly below.

ACTUARIAL STANDARDS OF PRACTICE

A dozen or more actuarial standards of practice address varying aspects of the reserving process, from the calculation of claim reserves and active life reserves, to performing asset adequacy analysis, to drafting statutory reserve opinions. Of particular interest are ASOP No. 5 ("Incurred Health and Disability Claims"), ASOP No. 18 ("Long-Term Care Insurance"), and ASOP No. 42 ("Determining Health and Disability Liabilities Other Than Liabilities for Incurred Claims"). The complete, current list of actuarial standards of practice can be found at www.actuarialstandardsboard.org.

ACCOUNTING GUIDANCE

Statutory accounting rules for the United States are found in the NAIC's Accounting Practices and Procedures Manual (www.naic.org). U.S. GAAP accounting rules are contained in the FASB Accounting Standards Codification (www.fasb.org). Information on International Financial Reporting Standards can be found at www.ifrs.org.

ACTUARIAL PRACTICE NOTES

The American Academy of Actuaries publishes practice notes on a wide range of topics, including reserving issues. These publications document current industry practices on items such as reserve calculation and asset adequacy testing. While they do not establish required rules, they are a useful source to understand how other practicing actuaries interpret and apply accounting rules and standards of practice. They are available at www.actuary.org.

37 Claim Reserves for Short-Term Benefits

Doug Fearrington
Mark E. Litow
Hans K. Leida & Doug Norris

This chapter presents basic principles, considerations, and methods for developing claim reserves for short-term group benefits. Appropriate estimation of claim reserves is extremely important in establishing profitability or solvency of companies, as well as in estimating earnings and determining appropriate rating strategies. Poor methodology in determining claim reserves, in conjunction with a lack of understanding of principles, is a major reason why some companies have been unable to recognize poor or deteriorating experience, and have subsequently suffered high losses.

This chapter is divided into the following sections:

- Definitions of claim reserves and component parts,
- Considerations in establishing claim reserves,
- Reserve methods,
- Stochastic approaches, and
- Standards of Practice.

Definitions of Claim Reserves and Component Parts

In defining claim reserves, a number of terms must be understood:

- *Valuation Date.* This is the date at which reserves are estimated.

- *Incurral or Loss Date.* This is the date the event that establishes a reserve or liability occurs. This can be the date of death, disability, hospitalization, or other insured event (in some cases, the incurred date for a maternity claim may be the date of conception). Any claim incurred on or before a valuation date represents an item that must be reserved for if benefits have not already been paid for such a claim.

- *Service Date.* This is the date that a service is actually rendered or performed, and each service date must be assigned an incurral date. However, many different methods exist for assigning incurral dates to a service date, and this can have a significant impact on claim reserves.

- *Reporting Date.* This is the date at which the claim is reported. Claims unreported as of the valuation date are referred to hereafter as unreported claims, while known claims are labeled reported claims.

- *Payment Date.* This is the date at which payment is made on a claim. Payment of a claim necessarily moves the amount paid from reserve status to paid status.

- *Lag.* This is the period of time between two dates. Typical lags include the following:

  - Reporting lag (between the incurral date and reporting date)
  - Service lag (between the incurral date and service date)
  - Payment lag (between the incurral date and payment date)
  - Accrual lag (between the service date and payment date)

Each of these various lags can be used to help establish claim reserves, particularly through development type methods, as discussed later.

A claim reserve can be defined as an estimate of the amount remaining to be paid on a claim for an event that been incurred before the specified valuation date. The term "claim reserve," as used in this chapter, includes both claim reserves and claim liabilities. Based on statutory accounting definitions, a claim *reserve* is an amount set aside to pay for a service that will be rendered in the future, and which is related to a loss event that has already occurred. In contrast, a claim *liability* is an amount set aside to pay for a service that has already been rendered. Such unpaid claims include the following:

- Due and unpaid, meaning that a claim is reported and a dollar amount has been assigned to it by the company, but no payment has been made;

- In course of settlement, meaning that a claim has been reported but is still under investigation and no dollar amount has been assigned;

- Incurred and reported, meaning that a claim has been submitted, but has not been paid. The incurred and reported amount consists of the amount in course of settlement plus the amount due and unpaid;

- Incurred but unreported, meaning that the claim has a loss date on or before the valuation date but is unknown to the company as of the valuation date;

- Unaccrued, which means that the actual services are after the valuation date, but are still tied or related to a loss date on or before the valuation date. (Such unaccrued losses can be for a reported or unreported claim. Long-term disability and long-term care typically have a high proportion of the claim reserve in this category);

- Deferred maternity or other extended benefits, which are losses in which a loss date is triggered on or before the valuation date, but benefits tied to that loss date are deferred into the future by contractual provisions; and

- Other special reserves such as disability claims under group life insurance, where premium is waived in the future due to a disability occurring on or before the valuation date.

The consistent use of the principles underlying claim reserves and other factors involved in the development of premiums should be maintained to the extent possible. In other words, if incurral dates or other definitions underlying claim reserves are used in developing company reserves and liabilities, the same principles should be used in developing premiums. Otherwise, financial results will show inconsistent revenues and disbursements as of the valuation date which will then produce a misleading financial picture.

CONSIDERATIONS IN ESTABLISHING CLAIM RESERVES

The level of established claim reserves is highly dependent on the incurral dating methods used, the basis of the reserve calculations, and many other influences. The important consideration is that once the company becomes responsible for payment, as determined by the contract, the liability or reserve must be established. Differences due to incurral dating methods occur because some methods reserve for services only as they occur (pay as you go), while other methods establish reserves for services in the future.

Reserves can also vary depending on whether calculations are performed on a statutory, GAAP, tax, or other basis. These reserve bases may differ in terms of the required or commonly used margins, interest rates, morbidity tables, and methodologies.

In particular, regulatory and professional standards require that statutory claim reserves include some margin for unforeseen fluctuation or adverse experience. Because of this, medical claim reserves often include a small percentage margin in addition to a best estimate. For example, for statutory medical claim reserves, this margin is often 5% to 15% of the best estimate amount. Periodic tests of the liabilities will help determine how much of a margin is needed to cover unexpected results. Statistical methods may also be used to set margin levels based on a confidence interval approach.

On reserves where the payout may take longer than six months to a year, a discount factor can be used, either as prescribed by regulation or determined by interest earned by the company. On reserves where the payout is typically much quicker, such as major medical, usually no discount is applied. This effectively adds a very small degree of conservatism to these reserve estimates.

These considerations are important. When they apply, they should be recognized in the method chosen, as described in the next section on reserve methods. Omission of these considerations can, in some cases, lead to estimates that are inaccurate, even when all other parts of the method are applied properly. Additional items that may affect claim reserve values are discussed in the following paragraphs.

CONTROLS AND RECONCILIATION

It is important for the actuarial department to communicate closely with the accounting department, to ensure that the data being used by the actuary reconciles and is consistent with the data and reporting practices used by the accounting department. Inventory counts, reported hospital admissions, and other information relied upon should also periodically be tested for accuracy. Care must also be taken to consistently and appropriately account for recoveries through coordination of benefits or subrogation payments, pharmacy rebates, and other such items. Another common source of discrepancies is the difference in the way dates are defined for different data elements.

INTERNAL COMPANY PRACTICES

Many organizations have their own internal practices, which may cause lags to be faster or slower than normal. Also, fluctuating payment patterns can be caused by staffing practices and staffing events (such as vacations and layoffs, or unusual weather such as snow storms or floods), changes in computer systems, and other company specific practices. The impact of these factors, where significant, should be examined by analyzing the various lags, as applicable.

The impact of such fluctuations can be significant. For example, a change in computer systems may be preceded by a speed up in claim processing time as the processing area cleans up its inventory of unpaid claims in anticipation of the computer change. During the system change itself, unanticipated bugs or errors may emerge that slow processing time and create claim backlogs. This fluctuation in payment patterns will create experience data that is not as reliable in estimating incurred claims as data from a stable payment situation.

Many companies keep inventory logs where claims are tracked that have been received but are unpaid. Claims that are "pended" for more information may also be tracked. The available claim inventory information should be reviewed over time, and appropriate adjustments made if claim inventories have changed significantly. Most companies have processes where providers file claims electronically. As remaining providers gain this capability, the reporting lag can shrink dramatically. These are examples of why it is important to know if and when payment processes change.

Also, practices can differ dramatically for different companies. For example, different companies use different claim dating practices, which can significantly affect lag patterns and claim reserves. Some organizations also attempt to explicitly adjust for specific fluctuations, such as the number of workdays available to pay claims in each month

EXTERNAL INFLUENCES

Company lags can also be affected significantly by environmental influences, such as epidemics, governmental mandates, or new laws. For instance, a government-induced slowdown of payments for Medicare at the end of 1989 and 1990 caused many companies to experience slowdowns in Medicare payments. This was later followed by a flood of claims once the artificial slowdown was lifted. Also, some medical care providers will file claims more quickly at the end of their fiscal year, in preparation for tax reporting.

POLICY PROVISIONS

The types of benefits, utilization incentives or disincentives, claim sizes in general, and other policy provisions, can dramatically affect the pattern of claim payments. For instance, major medical policies with high deductibles can experience significant seasonal payment patterns as policyholders do not trigger carrier payments immediately.

In evaluating such factors, one must consider the frequency of claim payment, as well as the severity of claims. For instance, disability claims will have a long runout due to the month by month payment pattern and general duration of disabilities; these claims represent a continuing contingent benefit where each payment is made only if the individual is still disabled. (The reserving of long-term disability claims is discussed in Chapter 38). On the other hand, major medical claims will have a faster runout, since most of the services will occur closer to the date of accident or illness. For life insurance, claims are typically paid within a few months of death, thus producing an even more predictable runout than for health claims.

INSURANCE CHARACTERISTICS

Claim reserves will also vary depending on the type of risk covered. In general, new plans will typically have long lags initially, because of (1) the insureds' lack of familiarity with plan benefits and claim filing procedures, (2) the impact of any pre-existing condition provisions, and (3) the company's lack of familiarity with a new type of benefit (resulting in longer investigation times). However, once this initial period after issue has passed, lags will typically become shorter, meaning that reserves will become a lower portion of incurred claims for a while.

Still later, lags may eventually increase over time, due to the severity of claims increasing over time. This phenomenon is particularly noticeable on major medical or other A&H types of coverage where underwriting has a strong effect. Such a result occurs because larger claims generally take longer to process and investigate, are more likely to be appealed, and also take longer periods of time before they are paid off. In fact, some companies will identify and reserve for large claims separately.

RESERVE CELLS

Typically, separate reserves are estimated for each homogenous category of business, and sometimes for each type of claim. This reflects that different types of claims may exhibit different claim lags and trends.

For medical benefits, reserves for hospital benefits may be estimated separately from those for physician benefits due to different trends as well as the claim lag. The vast majority of facility, professional and pharmacy claims are submitted electronically now, but the time it takes to adjudicate and process claims can still vary significantly across service types. Typically, hospital claims are more complex (and may be for larger amounts), and will tend to have a longer lag than professional claims. Compared with hospital or physician lags, drug claims have very short claim lags as they are nearly always processed real-time, and may be processed by an outside vendor.

In addition, since the data and information used for reserving may also be used to help analyze changes in underlying claim costs, many companies reserve in detail to stay apprised of emerging changes in claim levels. Similarly, some companies reserve at the same level of detail that is used to analyze profitability and rate levels. For example, reserve cells can be set up by group size (individual, small group, large group), by medically underwritten versus guaranteed issue, by over 65 versus under 65, by deductible size, by network, or by region. Insurers also reserve for Medicare vs. non-Medicare members.

The drawback of increasing the number of reserve cells is that the estimation error may be increased for cells that are too small. In addition, there is the practical consideration of the level of detail of the data, and the time and resources involved in estimating numerous reserve cells. Understanding the nature of the benefits and the business will help decide what reserving cells make sense.

MANAGED CARE

Use of managed care initiatives or discounts in providing health care may also alter the level of claim reserves. If managed care results in changes in utilization levels, particularly relating to large claims that have longer lags, the underlying lag factors may change. Changes in an organization's discount levels over time may further affect reserve calculations, for the simple reason that, as charge levels move, the claim cost level will change, and with it the level of necessary claim reserves. Moreover, many reimbursement contracts with hospitals include outlier provisions, governing the treatment of large claims. It is important to understand these provisions, and how they are changing over time, when setting reserves. They may include fixed dollar amounts (for instance, in the definition of an outlier) that leverage over time as claim costs rise. Sometimes the provisions cause an outlier's payment basis to revert retroactively to a different payment basis starting with the first dollar of claim.

Managed care programs, such as large case management and pre-admission certification, may provide an early warning of unreported large claims. Information such as the number of approved hospital days or admissions can be used in setting claim reserves and is generally available prior to claim payment information.

Managed care programs often involve provider risk sharing arrangements such as withholds, capitated services, settlements, or bonus or incentive payments. When estimating claim reserves, the type and scope of these arrangements should be reflected in the reserves. In some cases, the organization financially responsible for a claim may not be the same as the organization responsible for processing the claim.

These risk-sharing arrangements often depend on the number of services or their dollar value, and sometimes in very complex, multi-layered ways. Because of this, the level of claims and claim reserves can affect estimates of payouts and recoveries related to provider risk-sharing arrangements. Further reserves may be needed to recognize payout of provider risk-sharing amounts. Also, it is critical to understand what risk arrangement amounts are (and are not) included in the claim data used to estimate claim reserves.

Risk sharing arrangements between providers and insurers are becoming more common. This is both a result of provider groups consolidating into larger, more sophisticated entities that can tolerate more risk, and the increased acceptance of risk adjustment practices; and is also a result of the emphasis on risk sharing under "accountable care organizations" under the ACA.

TRENDS

Trends refer to the changes in the cost of claims over time. This influence is generally a factor only in medical care reimbursement plans, and can have a significant impact on experience. However, trends will not often have a dramatic impact on lag factors unless the trends change dramatically over a short period of time, so that they affect lags differently from one period to the next. Some reserve calculation methods are better able to cope with these accelerations and decelerations than others. More importantly, the trends resulting from the reserve calculation will be used to test the reasonableness of the results, and will be of interest in and of themselves. Chapter 34 of this text is dedicated to the subject of trend.

SEASONALITY

Claims may increase or decrease significantly at various times of the year. If this is the case, lags should be studied by seasonal and not calendar-year periods. Examples of benefits that may produce strong seasonal patterns are prescription drug plans, calendar year plans with high deductibles or out-of-pocket limits, and plans where incurral dating is based on assigning loss dates to the earliest date or time period within a calendar year. In particular, prescription drug plans under Medicare Part D can exhibit complex seasonal patterns due to the multiple benefit coverage phases a member moves through as they incur claim costs during the year. Major medical plans can also experience seasonal claim patterns as a result of seasonal-based conditions, such as influenza.

ECONOMIC CONDITIONS

Recessions will affect claims for elective treatments, such as dental and cosmetic surgery, but cause an increase in incidences and durations of claim where people fear the loss of coverage. After a recession, there may be a surge of pent-up demand for elective treatments.

CLAIM ADMINISTRATIVE EXPENSES

Accounting standards require recognition of a liability for the administrative expenses related to the incurred but not paid claims. It is common to determine this liability as a percentage of the claim reserve.

RESERVE METHODS

This section describes the methods typically used to develop claim reserves for group insurance products, including data requirements and recognized tables applicable for each method.

In using various claim reserve methods, the differences between types of business and runout patterns must necessarily be recognized. Long-term disability claims will not have the same type of runout as major medical claims, and neither will have the same type of runout as group life insurance claims. Thus, some of the methods noted below are appropriate for certain types of business, but not for others.

Software implementations of many of these methods are commercially available. In implementing, it is important to think about how reserve amounts will be tracked in data warehouses, so that they will be readily available for further analysis. This may also involve determining appropriate allocations of reserves to subsets of each reserve cell.

FACTOR METHOD

This method is generally used for reserves that are easily estimated due to a short lag or run off period. An example would include group life insurance, where reserves are often established as a percentage of premium (a typical percentage for group life insurance might be 8% to 12% of annual premium in force on a valuation date). The percentage used under this method is usually based on an analysis of reserves from past valuation dates, comparing the annual premium in force at those dates with claims paid after the valuation date on claims incurred on or before the valuation date. For example, if a company had $10,000,000 of annual premium in force on December 31, and paid death claims of $900,000 after December 31 on claims incurred on or before December 31, a reasonable estimate of the claim reserve for next year might be 9% of current in force premium. Thus, if annual premium in force is $15,000,000 at any year end, the corresponding claim reserve established might be $1,350,000.

An obvious drawback of this method is that it assumes that claim lags remain stable over time. For coverages where that is not the case, this method generally will not produce accurate results. An advantage of the method is that it is simple and requires relatively little data.

LAG (OR DEVELOPMENT) METHOD

The data necessary to utilize a development method are typically (a) claim payments split by both period of incurral and period of payment, and (b) earned premiums or exposed lives, for the same incurral periods. The incurred periods should preferably be of small duration, such as monthly or quarterly, especially for products vulnerable to significant fluctuation in experience because of inflation, seasonality, or other influences.

The underlying principle of a development method is that contingencies affecting the progression of claim payments for a particular claim are inherently and properly modeled by an assumed runoff pattern; this includes probabilities of claim termination estimated from past experience, and adjusted to properly reflect the current environment and administrative practices of a company.

The minimum volume of claim payments normally needed to use this method will vary depending on the benefits covered, duration since plan inception, and the growth rate of business. Major medical plans, whether indemnity, managed care or some blend, may require roughly $1,000,000 or more of claim payments in each cell per year to obtain credible results. Various types of policy forms should be combined for analysis only if the runoff pattern of claims is expected to be similar and the relative distribution of plans included remains unchanged.

The following steps describe the general lag or development method. Unless otherwise noted, "lag" as used here refers to the payment lag or lag between incurral month and payment month. Many modifications exist to this approach, but the underlying principles are the same.

Step 1. Develop paid claims by period of incurral and payment. Table 37.1 below shows a portion of a month by month runoff for a period of one year. In practice, Table 37.1 would be maintained for a number of years (up to four or five) of incurred and paid claims, in order to be able to examine any changes in the payment pattern for this block of business. This tabulation of claims is often referred to as a "claim triangle" or "lag triangle."

Table 37.1

CLAIMS BY PAYMENT MONTH (in thousands)													
Month of Incurral	Jan	Feb	Mar	Apr	May	Jun	Jul	Aug	Sep	Oct	Nov	Dec	Total
January	50	200	200	100	50	25	0	0	0	0	0	0	625
February	N/A	60	250	200	150	75	30	0	0	0	0	0	765
March	N/A	N/A	50	220	300	130	80	10	0	0	0	0	790
April	N/A	N/A	N/A	50	200	200	100	100	50	10	0	0	710
...	...	...	...	...	...	...	...	...	...	...	...	...	...
November	N/A	N/A	N/A	N/A	N/A	N/A	N/A	N/A	N/A	N/A	70	230	300
December	N/A	N/A	N/A	N/A	N/A	N/A	N/A	N/A	N/A	N/A	N/A	75	75

Step 2. Develop a claim runout or lag chart, for which several similar methods exist. One method involves calculating, for each given incurral month, the percentage of ultimate claims that are paid after one month, two months, and so on. This process is used to develop completion percentages and corresponding incurred claims, where incurred claims are determined from payments to date (in Step 1), divided by the appropriate completion percentage. Starting with the data in Table 37.1, these calculations produce the results shown in Table 37.2.

Table 37.2

CLAIM COMPLETION PERCENTAGES (Proportion of ultimate total paid through month of payment)											
Month of Incurral	Jan	Feb	Mar	Apr	May	Jun	Jul	Aug	Sep	Oct	Nov	Dec
January	0.080	0.400	0.720	0.880	0.960	1.000	1.000	1.000	1.000	1.000	1.000	1.000
February	N/A	0.078	0.405	0.667	0.863	0.961	1.000	1.000	1.000	1.000	1.000	1.000
March	N/A	N/A	0.063	0.342	0.722	0.886	0.987	1.000	1.000	1.000	1.000	1.000
April	N/A	N/A	N/A	0.070	0.352	0.634	0.775	0.916	0.986	1.000	1.000	1.000
...	...	...	...	...	...	...	...	...	...	...	...	...
November*	N/A	N/A	N/A	N/A	N/A	N/A	N/A	N/A	N/A	N/A	0.088	0.375
December**	N/A	N/A	N/A	N/A	N/A	N/A	N/A	N/A	N/A	N/A	N/A	0.088

* Consistent with incurred claims of $800. ** Consistent with incurred claims of $850.

Table 37.2 shows that payments for November and December incurrals are still very incomplete. However, patterns established from earlier months, such as January through April, can be used to estimate what total incurred claims for these months of incurral could be. For instance, November has $300 of claim payments through December, and months January through April of incurral suggest a completion factor of around 35-40% (the ratio of paid to estimated incurred claims at any valuation date). Thus, November incurrals might be estimated at $750 to $800 (the example uses $800, resulting in a reserve of $500). For December, incurred claims of $850 have been estimated, based on the following factors:

- December payments are a little higher than previous months.
- The estimated level of incurrals for earlier months.
- The completion percentages attained for each incurred month, in the first month of payment, have always been less than 9%.

Months with completion factors lower than a chosen percentage are generally deemed to produce non-credible estimates of claim reserves for those periods. That percentage may vary by benefit type, and is somewhat subjective[1]. Typically, the percentage will be in the 35%-70% range. In that case, claim reserves are often based on an alternative estimate of the average incurred claim cost per contract or member. Two common methods of developing the alternative estimates are (1) an estimate based on the trend in claim cost (claim dollars per unit of exposure, such as PMPM), or (2) an estimate based on applying an assumed loss ratio (ratio of incurred claims to earned premium) to earned premium. The known claim payments are subtracted from these estimates to determine the claim reserve. In estimating the average cost per member, it is important to consider changes in demographics, benefits, provider contracts (fee levels and what services are being capitated), seasonal factors, and care management programs over time.

When using development methods, many of the considerations discussed in the previous section can cause dramatic changes in completion factors over time. For that reason, other methods are necessary to confirm results from the lag method. Further, where strong seasonal influences affect a block of business, completion factors should be analyzed for corresponding time periods in earlier calendar years. Thus, where loss ratios differ significantly by calendar quarter, completion factors should be analyzed separately as they relate to each calendar quarter.

Another approach using a development type method is the development of paid loss ratios by incurral period. For instance, for any incurral quarter, paid loss ratios can be tracked relative to incurral quarter. Table 37.3 below illustrates this for quarters of incurral during calendar years Z and $Z+1$. (This example is unrelated to the earlier examples).

Projecting from the pattern in Table 37.3, the ultimate loss ratio for the third quarter of $Z+1$ would be based on the current value of 0.22 divided by the relative completeness of earlier quarters at the same point in time. For quarter $1/Z$ the completeness and completion factor (CF) is $0.20 \div 0.50 = 0.400$; for $2/Z$ the CF is $0.22 \div 0.48 = 0.458$; for $3/Z$ the CF is $0.23 \div 0.53 = 0.434$; The average of these ratios is 0.43, producing a final loss ratio for $3/Z+1$ of 0.52, or $0.22 \div 0.43$,. This calculation assumes that each of the first three quarters of year Z is fully complete by the end of year $Z+1$.

Development methods can also estimate claim reserves by component, analyzing each of the various lags noted earlier in this chapter. The techniques are generally the same, but the detail is greater, and each component part must be accounted for in producing the aggregate claim reserve.

---

[1] However, stochastic methods may be used to help determine this percentage based on a desired confidence level.

Table 37.3

Loss Ratios Paid To Date Through Each Quarter								
Quarter of Incurral	$1/Z$	$2/Z$	$3/Z$	$4/Z$	$1/Z+1$	$2/Z+1$	$3/Z+1$	$4/Z+1$
$1/Z$	0.04	0.20	0.35	0.43	0.48	0.50	0.50	0.50
$2/Z$	—	0.08	0.22	0.35	0.42	0.47	0.48	0.48
$3/Z$	—	—	0.09	0.23	0.40	0.48	0.53	0.53
$4/Z$	—	—	—	0.07	0.26	0.45	0.55	0.58
$1/Z+1$	—	—	—	—	0.10	0.27	0.48	0.60
$2/Z+1$	—	—	—	—	—	0.09	0.25	0.45
$3/Z+1$	—	—	—	—	—	—	0.07	0.22
$4/Z+1$	—	—	—	—	—	—	—	0.08

The development method presents problems where claim payment patterns involve a long payout period with considerable fluctuations, such as long-term disability insurance. An uneven payment pattern, such as sporadic large settlements, could make the development method unreliable. Where occasional large payments could distort the lag triangle, one option is to remove these outlier payments and consider them separately.

Another vulnerability of the development method involves mix changes within lag cells. In such cases, other methods are used, such as the tabular or average size claim methods discussed below.

TABULAR METHOD

For products such as group long term disability (LTD) insurance, where benefits can be paid for many years on a single claim, industry practice and regulatory standards require the use of a tabular method to compute reserves. Under this method, a reserve is computed for each claim (rather than for the block as a whole), using a table of expected recovery and mortality rates. The actuary projects future benefits expected to be paid to the claimant, and then determines the present value of those benefits, discounting for recovery and mortality (using the tabular rates) as well as for interest. Minimum statutory reserve standards for LTD are set by each state. In April, 2014 the NAIC adopted the 2012 Group Long-Term Disability (GLTD) Valuation Table as the statutory standard in its model regulation regarding health insurance reserves. LTD claim reserves typically vary by age at disability, duration of claim, elimination period, gender, and other factors. Further information on reserving practices for LTD and other long-term health products is contained in Chapter 38.

AVERAGE SIZE CLAIM METHOD

Under this method, the claim reserve for reported claims is estimated by reviewing claim sizes for previously closed claims. The total reported reserve is then calculated as the estimated average size multiplied by the number of reported claims, less any payments made on these claims prior to the valuation date. This method works well if closed claims to date accurately represent a fully developed block of business. If a block of business is new, and the data does not yet represent a credible estimate of the average size claim, this method should not be used.

With this method, a reserve is also needed for unreported claims – the incurred but not reported (IBNR) reserve. In this case, the IBNR reserve might be based on loss ratio estimates or the average number of IBNR claims incurred but not reported as of prior valuation dates, adjusted for exposure differences.

LOSS RATIO METHOD

Consistent with reserves for unreported claims, the reserve under this method is based on earned premium times an estimated loss ratio minus paid claims. Often, the estimated loss ratio is based on initial pricing assumptions. This method is generally used only where sufficient information is not available to use other methods, such as for new blocks of business or periods of time when experience is not credible (for example, the recent period described in the lag method above). This method is also useful for confirming estimates made under other methods. Similarly, an estimate of the claim cost per month or per year of exposed life can be substituted for a loss ratio estimate by using exposure instead of earned premium.

EXAMINER'S METHOD

Under this method, claim department or other qualified personnel are asked to estimate the remaining claim payments expected on known claims, based on the characteristics of each claim. In some contexts, particularly companies with casualty insurance histories, the result of this method is called "case reserves," referring to the reserves being set for each case (claim).

Generally, these estimates are based on doctors' statements and past history for such claims. This method is often used to estimate the liability arising from claims subject to lawsuits. In that case, the legal department should be involved in the process.

As with the average claim size method, this method produces a reserve only for reported claims, and a separate reserve (the IBNR) must be set aside for unreported claims. For coverages with large numbers of frequent claims, such as major medical, this approach is generally not practical unless it is restricted to a small subset of large claims.

STOCHASTIC APPROACHES

Almost any of the deterministic methods outlined above can be given a stochastic treatment, with varying degrees of rigor and sophistication. As a general definition in this context, a stochastic method simply refers to any approach that makes probabilistic statements about the level and adequacy of the reserve amount. In practice, most stochastic methods explicitly treat some component of the reserve as a random variable, and then model these components, as opposed to directly adopting an overall distributional form (typically parametric) for the total reserve. The reserve is then calculated as a function of these random components, and the variability of the reserve becomes a reflection of the variability of the components.

There are several benefits of adopting a stochastic approach. First, it provides explicit guidance for establishing provision for adverse deviation in statutory filings. It also provides explicit guidance to management on potential variability in reported earnings and reserve levels. It allows for quantification of variability in internal processes, such as payment systems, and external processes, such as seasonality and claim trend.

Further, a stochastic approach allows for improved evaluation of separate reserve estimates for alternate lines of business. While both reserves may represent "best estimates," the uncertainty associated with one may greatly exceed that of the other. (In other words, not all best estimates are created equally.)

In short, stochastic methods provide a means to quantify uncertainty around reserve estimates. Notably, a reserve that is developed and booked from a stochastic method does not necessarily provide any more accuracy than a reserve developed and booked from a deterministic method; after all, under both approaches, only a single number is recorded. Instead, an appropriately developed stochastic method provides up-front guidance as to the nature and size of the statistical error associated with the financial entry. Of course, to the extent that not all business risks are modeled, it is important to remember that statistical error is only one source of error in financial entries.

There are drawbacks and complicating issues to consider when adopting a stochastic methodology. To start with, it is important to consider the sophistication of the audience. An advanced statistical method, producing what we deem to be a rigorous prediction interval, may instill a false sense of confidence in an audience unfamiliar with such approaches. What's more, there is the potential for surprise and confusion when future adjustments are made to past reserves. For example, the statement "The reserve level which last month represented an 80th percentile, now only has a 20% chance of being adequate" is not necessarily inconsistent, but is likely to be frustrating.

The complexity of the methodology may also be an issue. Pursuit of rigor must be balanced with time constraints and logistical feasibility. Furthermore, a methodology that only one or two people on staff can fully understand might create problems in training, communication, and interaction with other actuarial functions such as financial forecasting or renewal pricing.

It is important to understand the limits of any stochastic approach. Not every stochastic model can be applied to every set of data or line of business, and not every process can be modeled rigorously. It is important for the analyst to know when to say, "Here is an estimate for which I can, at best, provide only a subjective range."

STOCHASTIC MODELING TECHNIQUES

This section outlines some general modeling techniques that are useful when adopting a stochastic approach.

As mentioned earlier, most stochastic approaches for estimating short term reserves involve actually modeling *components* of the reserve, and then *combining* the individual model results in some fashion. As an example, consider a loss ratio method that projects an estimated loss ratio for each reporting month. One possible stochastic approach would be to:

1. Specify each monthly loss ratio as an independent normal random variable, each with its own mean and variance. In this approach, the monthly loss ratios are the "components."

2. From each of the monthly loss ratio distributions, take a large number of samples. With each sample selected, calculate the product of the loss ratio and the matching monthly premium.

3. For each sample realization, sum this product across all months and subtract any payments made to date. (This is the "combining" step, producing an estimated reserve from each set of samples.)

4. After sampling is completed, compute statistics about the set of all realized reserve sample estimates.

This example leads to a more detailed discussion of the potential techniques available for building stochastic models. No techniques are meant to be viewed only in isolation, and employing a combination of methods is more likely to be of value than rigidly adhering to only one approach.

Parametric Distribution-Fitting: Much like the example above, this technique involves fitting a parametric distribution directly to data, or, when there is no data to work with, specifying a distributional form based on professional judgment. The technique works best when the process being modeled is stationary over time.

For example, consider a claim reserve calculation using the development method, where we might be attempting to fit a lognormal distribution to the run-out pattern from the claim triangle. If the same parameter estimates (the mean and variance of the lognormal form) fit well for each incurred month being analyzed, and we expect the fit to be valid going forward, we may have success with this technique. However, if trends or cyclical patterns are present in the data, indicating that the mean or variance may not be constant from month to month, an alternate technique that addresses these patterns may be preferable.

Ordinary Least Squares Regression: Multivariate regression models represent a straightforward approach to handling situations where we want to investigate the effects of specific explanatory variables, such as a time trend or seasonality. For instance, as a continuation of the example above, suppose that we believe the mean of the lognormal distribution is subject to a linear time trend with a significant seasonal effect occurring in January of each year. Then, we could model the mean of the distribution with

$$\mu_t = A \times t + B_t \times (\text{January indicator}) + C + e,$$

where t represents time and e represents the error term.

Alternately, linear regression models can be used as simple forecasting models for future values of loss ratios, development factors, incremental payments in a claim triangle, or other factors.

One prominent drawback of regression models is their underlying assumptions of normality and constant variance.

Generalized Linear Models: True to their name, general linear models represent a more generalized form of multivariate linear regression. Specifically, these models allow for occasions where the dependent variable being modeled is either bounded (for example, required to be strictly greater than zero) or not normally distributed (as would be the case if the variable were bounded). A detailed description of these types of models is beyond the scope of this chapter, but references included in the bibliography illustrate their application to actuarial reserve estimation.

Stochastic Time Series Models: Time series models are useful for handling situations where values are correlated across time. For example, suppose that we had hoped to use the above linear regression model, but had noticed that the residuals from fitting such a model seemed to have a cyclical pattern present. In that case, an ARIMA (auto-regressive moving average) model fit to the residuals may be of value. The form of the model would then be:

$$\mu_t = A \times t + B_t \times (\text{January indicator}) + ARMA(p,q) + C + e$$

Monte Carlo Sampling and Simulation: Monte Carlo sampling techniques are of significant practical value when attempting to combine results from any of the techniques described above. While certain model forms lend themselves to analytical solutions, in practice it can be much more efficient to combine results through sampling techniques. Many commercial packages are available, as well as free software such as the R statistical programming and software environment and the OpenBUGS software platform.

STOCHASTIC MODELING CONSIDERATIONS

There are some preliminary considerations to be made when developing a stochastic approach to reserve estimation. In general, these issues will play a significant role in determining the set of feasible stochastic techniques, the degree of sophistication possible, and the amount of actuarial judgment involved in interpreting results.

Availability of data: The amount of available data will affect the extent of historical validation that can be performed, and the degree to which any model assumptions can be tested or confirmed. This will directly affect the validity of model results and the degree of care that is needed in communicating results.

Appropriateness of data: Consideration should be given to whether the processes reflected in the historical data are likely to be representative of the processes being modeled going forward. This involves looking at the maturity of the block of business being modeled, as significant changes in size may limit the range of stochastic techniques available. Also, any changes in the payment processes, whether one-time or permanent, are an important element to be examined.

Access to statistical software: In general, it is advisable not to re-invent the wheel when it comes to implementing more advanced models. Obviously, lack of access to modeling software, or a lack of understanding of its application will limit the choices available. Now that high quality statistical software (such as R) is freely available, the limiting factor is most often personnel with the expertise to use and understand the software.

In addition to these considerations, there are advanced issues that should be addressed. First, it bears repeating that specifying an *appropriate* model for the data at hand is one of the most important parts of the modeling process. It can be tempting to blindly apply a technique developed in a paper or publication without considering the appropriateness of the technique. Furthermore, when implementing stochastic approaches, validation is all the more necessary since the results are predicated directly on the assumptions used. Common techniques in such validation include goodness-of-fit testing, residual analysis, and hold-out sample evaluation.

Another important issue is that, to the extent that a reserve estimate is broken down into "component" model estimates, covariance between those components becomes a primary modeling concern. While it can be tempting simply to assume independence, potential covariance should be evaluated both within a component model and across models.

To illustrate the covariance issue, suppose that we are projecting incremental payments to be made within a claim triangle using time series models (a variation of a development method). The diagram below illustrates the potential covariance that may need to be addressed.

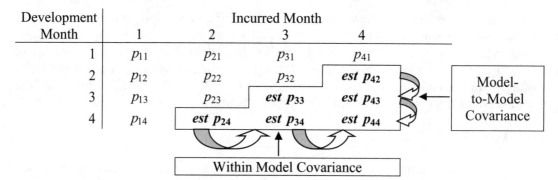

Est p_{42} produced from Model 1
Est p_{33} and p_{43} produced from Model 2
Est p_{24}, p_{34}, p_{44} produced from Model 3

Within Model Covariance:
    Covariance of est p_{33}, p_{43} in Model 2
    Covariance of est p_{24}, p_{34}, p_{44} in Model 2

Model-to-Model Covariance:
    Model 1 to Model 2
    Model 1 to Model 3
    Model 2 to Model 3

The reserve estimates produced by stochastic approaches are just estimates, and it is also important to remember that, for many techniques, the parameters specified are estimates themselves. It may be necessary to reflect associated uncertainty of any parameters in producing prediction intervals for reserves. This additional uncertainty will typically widen the interval. Finally, when communicating results to non-technical audiences, it is important to emphasize that there are additional sources of uncertainty beyond the statistical uncertainties in the model. Two major examples are (1) external business risks, and (2) the risk of human error in producing models and assumptions.

FINAL COMMENTS

As with any modeling exercise, continual monitoring and evaluation are advisable. Despite best efforts at historical validation of a technique, the true test of the reliability of the ranges produced falls to subsequent monitoring as future values are realized.

Given the wide variety of techniques available for setting reserves, it may be difficult to choose a method for a given coverage and situation. In such cases, it can be useful to retrospectively apply many methods to past experience (where the actual incurred claims are now known with near certainty), in order to evaluate which methods produce the most accurate results over time. The Society of Actuaries also commissioned a study (see references below) in 2009 to evaluate many common methods on a variety of health coverages.

STANDARDS OF PRACTICE

Many guidelines and standards of practice now exist and apply to the calculation of claim reserves. These guides and standards provide discussion of definitions, methods, and considerations in calculating claim reserves, and include the following:

- The Code of Professional Conduct of the American Academy of Actuaries, as it relates to methodology and assumptions;
- The Actuarial Standards Board's Actuarial Standards of Practice (ASOPs):

    No. 5, "Incurred Health and Disability Claims,"

    No. 11, "Financial Statement Treatment of Reinsurance Transactions Involving Life or Health Insurance,"

    No. 18, "Long-Term Care Insurance,"

    No. 21, Responding to or Assisting Auditors or Examiners in Connection with Financial Statements for All Practice Areas,"

    No. 22 "Statements of Opinion Based on Asset Adequacy Analysis by Actuaries for Life or Health Insurers,"

    No. 25 "Credibility Procedures,"

    No. 28 "Statements of Actuarial Opinion Regarding Health Insurance Liabilities and Assets," and

    No. 42 "Determining Health and Disability Liabilities Other Than Liabilities for Incurred Claims."

- Actuarial Compliance Guideline #4, "Statutory Statements of Opinion Not Including An Asset Adequacy Analysis By Appointed Actuaries for Life or Health Insurers."
- NAIC guidelines and model regulations relative to reserve standards and opinions, in particular, The NAIC Health Reserves Guidance Manual. The end of this manual includes a comprehensive list of reference documents.
- Statement of Statutory Accounting Principles (SSAP) No. 54, "Individual and Group Accident and Health Contracts," National Association of Insurance Commissioners, and No. 55 – "Unpaid Claims, Losses and Loss Adjustment Expenses," effective January 1, 2001.
- Literature published in textbooks and by the actuarial profession.

ASOP No. 5 directly discusses the calculation of incurred claims for health and disability claims, and this chapter is intended to be consistent with it. This ASOP discusses the considerations and analysis that are done to develop an incurred claim estimate, as well as the methods used in estimating incurred claims. The standard also includes a reference to ASOP No. 23, "Data Quality", which suggests that data used to estimate incurred claims must be reviewed for accuracy and completeness. ASOP No. 41, "Actuarial Communications" should also be adhered to in all actuarial work.

ASOP No. 42 discusses liabilities other than claim reserves such as contract reserves, premium deficiency reserves, claim settlement expense reserves, and various reserves related to provider contracts. Some of these are short term reserves that must be established when appropriate.

While this chapter only briefly mentions claim expense reserves, these reserves do need to be established. Expense reserves can be calculated as part of the claim reserve (as described herein), but are often calculated separately from claim reserves (consistent with experience or pricing assumptions as appropriate).

REFERENCES

Chadick, C. et al. 2009. "Comparison of incurred but not reported (IBNR) methods." Society of Actuaries sponsored study.

Litow, M.E. 1989. "A Modified Development Method for Deriving Health Claim Reserves." *TSA* 41:89.

38 CLAIM RESERVES FOR LONG-TERM BENEFITS

Daniel D. Skwire

The two primary forms of long-term health benefits are long-term disability (LTD) insurance and long-term care (LTC) insurance. Detailed discussions of these benefits are provided in Chapters 12 and 13 of this text, respectively. Although LTD and LTC plans insure different risks, their similar structure and long-term nature mean that they share many of the same considerations in the calculation of claim reserves.

There are several aspects of LTD and LTC contracts that are particularly important with respect to claim reserves:

- *Periodic Benefits*: Unlike most short-term health products, LTD and LTC plans typically have a benefit equal to a specified monthly or daily amount. LTD plans generally specify a monthly indemnity amount, often as a percentage of covered salary. LTC plans generally reimburse actual expenses up to a specified daily benefit amount.

- *Long-Term Benefit Periods*: LTD and LTC plans have maximum benefit periods that are quite long relative to other health benefits. The maximum benefit period for LTD is often to age 65 or to the Social Security normal retirement age. LTC plans often specify a lifetime dollar maximum benefit, which determines the maximum length of time for which benefits may be paid.

- *Elimination Periods*: The elimination period is the period of time after someone experiences the insured event under the policy, but before benefits begin to accrue. LTD and LTC plans offer a variety of elimination periods, often 90 days or more.

- *Optional Benefits*: Both LTD and LTC plans offer a variety of optional benefits that may affect the timing or the amount of monthly payments. Examples of optional benefits include partial disability benefits (which pay an amount less than the monthly benefit if the person is able to work part-time while disabled) and cost of living adjustments (which increase a benefit by an inflation factor while a person is disabled).

- *Integration of Benefits*: LTD plans often contain provisions that reduce the amount of benefits paid to reflect social insurance benefits received while disabled (such as Social Security or Worker's Compensation). LTC plans typically integrate with Medicare long-term care benefits.

- *Limitations and Exclusions*: Certain types of claims, such as intentionally self-inflicted injuries, are excluded from coverage altogether, and need not be considered in claim reserves. Other types of claims may be subject to limited pay periods, which should be reflected in the reserving process. One common example consists of mental illness claims, which are often limited to a payment period of two years over the lifetime of the claimant for LTD policies.

The product features discussed above affect the beginning date, the ending date, or the amount of benefits paid under LTD and LTC plans. They therefore have a significant impact on the value of the benefits, and they must be explicitly considered in the calculation of claim reserves.

COMPONENTS OF LONG-TERM CLAIM RESERVES

Long-term claims may be divided into three primary categories, each of which is treated separately for the purpose of claim reserve calculations:

- *Open Claims*: These are claims that have benefits currently being paid. These benefits will be paid no longer than the benefit period (BP).

- *Pending Claims*: These are claims that have been reported to the company but have not yet begun receiving payments. Payments may be held up waiting for approval from a claim manager, or they may still be within the elimination period (EP).

- *Incurred but not Reported (IBNR) Claims*: These are claims for which the loss has already occurred (the person has become disabled or satisfied the LTC benefit requirements), but which have not yet been reported to the company.

The three categories of claims can be illustrated by a timeline. For claims that are reported during the elimination period, the timeline typically looks like the following:

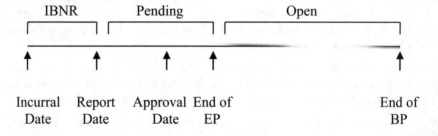

For claims that are reported after the completion of the elimination period, the timeline looks like the following:

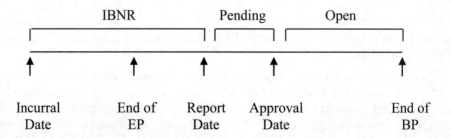

A separate reserve calculation is performed for each of the three claim categories. The type of calculation for each category reflects the amount of information that is available. Open claims have the most detailed information, so the most precise calculation can be used. For pending claims and IBNR claims, less information is available, so there is a greater need for estimation. The following sections describe the reserving methodology for each category of claims.

RESERVE METHODOLOGY FOR OPEN CLAIMS

Reserves for open claims are the largest component of claim reserves for LTD and LTC plans. They are often called "tabular reserves," because the calculation method involves using tables of expected claim termination rates. The formula for a tabular claim reserve at claim duration n may be written in simplified fashion as follows:

$$V_n = \sum_{t=n}^{BP} Benefit_t \cdot Continuance_t \cdot InterestDiscount_t$$

This formula expresses the tabular claim reserve as the sum, for each month from the current claim duration until the end of the benefit period, of the product of three items:

- *Benefit*: The monthly benefit, which may vary from month to month based on the product provisions.
- *Continuance*: The probability of a claim continuing to receive payments in a future time period (the probability that the individual will not recover or die).
- *Interest Discount*: The time value of money, reflecting the fact that the payment will not be made until sometime in the future.

The calculation of the benefit term in the claim reserve formula may be quite simple or quite complex, depending on the product provisions. Some plans may pay a flat amount each month, while others may increase or decrease for a variety of reasons, including optional benefits, benefit integration, or cost of living adjustments. Any expected increases or decreases in the benefit amount should be considered as part of the claim reserve calculation.

The calculation of the continuance factor is generally performed by using data contained in a continuance table, which may be based on either industry experience or company-specific experience. A sample continuance table is shown below:

Table 38.1

Sample Continuance Table			
Claim Duration (months)	Age At Claim		
	35	45	55
0	1000	1000	1000
1	975	950	900
2	950	900	800
3	925	850	700
4	900	800	600
5	875	750	500
6	850	700	400
7	825	650	300

This sample continuance table, which is designed for illustrative purposes only, allows the calculation of continuance factors for the first seven months of claim for people who become disabled at ages 35, 45, or 55. The number at the top of each column, for claim duration 0, is the radix, or the initial number of disabled individuals. The chance that an individual who becomes disabled at a certain age will remain disabled for a certain number of months can be computed as the ratio of the value in the table for that month, divided by the radix. So the chance that a 35-year-old who has just become disabled (at time 0) will remain disabled until the end of 3 months can be computed as 0.925, or (925/1000). Similarly, the chance that a person who became disabled at age 55 and has already been disabled for two months will remain disabled for an additional two months, may be computed as 0.75, or (600/800).

In order to perform a sample claim reserve calculation, the simple formula for tabular claim reserves provided above may be restated in actuarial notation as follows:

$$V_n = \sum_{t=n}^{BP-1} Benefit_{t+1} \cdot \frac{l_{t+0.5}}{l_n} \cdot (1+i)^{-(t-n+0.5)/12}$$

Where:

n = Claim duration at the valuation date, in months (the claim reserve is computed as of the end of duration n)

$Benefit$ = Benefit paid in month t. The first benefit occurs in the month immediately following the valuation date.

t = Claim duration, in months from claim incurral date

BP = Final claim duration in which benefits may be paid

l_x = Value from continuance table at claim duration x for the appropriate age at disability

i = Annual interest rate

This formula assumes that claim payments are made in the middle of a month, so the continuance and interest discount terms reflect a mid-month assumption. Continuance table values for the middle of a month are computed through averaging:

$$l_{x+.50} = \frac{l_x + l_{x+1}}{2}$$

EXAMPLE:

Using the continuance table above, and an interest rate of 5%, compute the tabular claim reserves at the end of months 3, 4, and 5 for a 45-year-old claimant who has a policy with a 3-month elimination period, a 3-month benefit period, and a flat monthly benefit of $1000.

End of Month 3:

$$V_3 = 1000 \cdot \frac{825}{850}(1.05)^{\frac{-1}{24}} + 1000 \cdot \frac{775}{850}(1.05)^{\frac{-3}{24}} + 1000 \cdot \frac{725}{850}(1.05)^{\frac{-5}{24}}$$

$$V_3 = 968.62 + 906.22 + 844.32 = 2719.16$$

End of Month 4:

$$V_4 = 1000 \cdot \frac{775}{800}(1.05)^{\frac{-1}{24}} + 1000 \cdot \frac{725}{800}(1.05)^{\frac{-3}{24}}$$

$$V_4 = 966.78 + 900.74 = 1867.52$$

End of Month 5:

$$V_5 = 1000 \cdot \frac{725}{750}(1.05)^{\frac{-1}{24}}$$

$$V_5 = 964.70$$

RESERVE METHODOLOGY FOR PENDING CLAIMS

The reserve calculation for a pending long-term claim is similar to the calculation for an open long-term claim, but it involves an additional factor reflecting the likelihood that the claim will eventually receive a payment. This factor, called the pending factor, includes the probabilities that a claim will remain disabled through the elimination period and that it will be approved for payment, as well as including any necessary interest discounting.

For pending claims that are still in the elimination period, the claim reserve may be computed as the product of the pending factor and the tabular claim reserve at the end of the elimination period. (Discounting for interest between the valuation date and the end of the elimination period might be conservatively ignored.)

For pending claims that have completed the elimination period, the claim reserve may be computed as the product of the pending factor and the sum of (a) the tabular reserve at the current claim duration, and (b) the accumulated value of past claim payments that have not yet been made since the claim is not yet approved.

The pending factor is developed by each company based on its own experience. Theoretically, a different pending factor could be used for claims within the elimination period than for claims that have completed the elimination period. In practice, however, most companies use a single pending factor that reflects the combined probability of a claim completing the elimination period and being approved for payment, along with any margin for conservatism that the actuary feels is appropriate. Pending factors often range from 60-80%, although the values can vary significantly for different companies. As discussed in the section on IBNR claim reserves, some companies may combine the pending claims with IBNR claims in the development of an IBNR reserve.

EXAMPLE:

- Monthly Benefit of $1000, paid at the end of each month of disability.
- Elimination Period of 3 months
- Interest Rate of 5%
- Tabular Reserves of $25,000, $28,000, and $32,000 at the end of months 3, 4, and 5, respectively.
- Pending factor of 75% for all claims.

Compute the pending reserve, assuming the claim is reported at the end of month 2.

$$V_2 = 75\% \cdot \$25,000 = \$18,750$$

Compute the pending reserve, assuming the claim is reported at the end of month 5.

$$V_5 = 75\% \cdot \left[\$32,000 + \$1,000 + \$1,000 \cdot (1.05)^{1/12}\right] = \$25,503$$

Note that this second reserve calculation includes the payment from month 5 (which is due at the end of month 5 and therefore has no accumulated interest) and the payment from month 4 (which was due at the end of month 4 and has one month of accumulated interest). No payments are included from months 1 through 3, since the policy has an elimination period of 3 months.

RESERVE METHODOLOGY FOR IBNR CLAIMS

Because IBNR claims are not known at the time of valuation, the reserve calculation typically involves an estimation process based on historical experience trends and the size of the current block of business. The most common methods used for computing IBNR claim reserves for long-term benefits are the percentage of premium method, the lag method, the loss ratio method, or some combination of these methods. The choice of which method to use depends on the design of the benefits and the amount of credible historical data that is available.

THE PERCENTAGE OF PREMIUM METHOD

A company that wishes to use the percentage of premium method to compute an IBNR reserve as of 12/31/2014 would conduct a study to determine how many claims were incurred but not reported at a previous valuation date. Suppose the company decides to study the valuation date of 12/31/2012, which is two years prior to the current valuation date, so that it can be reasonably certain that any claims which were incurred but not reported at that time have since been reported.

To conduct the study, the company creates a list of all claims that were incurred *prior to* 12/31/2012, and that were reported to the company *after* 12/31/2012. These are the IBNR claims as of 12/31/2012. It then computes a tabular reserve for each of these claims *as of* 12/31/2012. The total of the tabular reserves for each of these claims equals the claim reserve that the company would have held for its IBNR claims on 12/31/2012 had those claims been reported. This amount is then expressed as a percentage of the earned premium for the business during the year 2012, assuming the volume of business didn't grow or shrink significantly during the year. This percentage is the IBNR reserve factor. To compute the IBNR reserve as of 12/31/2014, the company simply multiplies the 2014 earned premium by the IBNR reserve factor.

IBNR reserves are typically expressed as percentage of premium because the premium reflects the size of the block and is not distorted by the amount of reported claims in a particular year. If the IBNR reserve factor were expressed as a percentage of tabular reserves, a company might find itself in the counter-intuitive position of setting up a larger IBNR reserve in years when more claims were reported, and a smaller IBNR reserve in years when fewer claims were reported. The IBNR reserve factor should be reviewed and updated on a regular basis to ensure that it reflects recent trends in claim lags.

THE LAG METHOD

Where credible historical data is available, the lag method is preferable for computing IBNR reserves, because it reflects a company's actual claim development patterns as accurately as possible. For the purpose of this calculation, "lag" refers to the time period between the incurral date of a claim and the date that the claim is reported to the company. When computing IBNR reserves based on a lag method, however, some companies elect to include pending claims by defining the lag as the time period from claim incurral to the first claim payment, as opposed to the reporting date. This methodology, which is more common for LTC claims than for LTD claims, eliminates the need for a separate pending claim reserve.

Due to their long elimination periods, which may exceed 12 months in some cases, LTD benefits often have very long reporting lags, and it may sometimes take two years or more past the incurral date for a claim to be reported to the company. LTC benefits typically have somewhat shorter reporting lags, since their elimination periods are 12 months or less, and since a plan of care is generally established shortly after the commencement of a claim.

Suppose a company is interested in using the lag method to determine an IBNR reserve factor for use in computing an IBNR reserve at the end of 2014. It begins by developing tables of completion factors based on recent historical experience on the time lag between claim incurral dates and claim reporting dates. For a given incurral period, these completion factors reflect the percentage of incurred claims that have been reported to the company after a certain number of months. The completion factors are typically quite low during the early months of claim while the claim is still in its elimination period, and they then increase rapidly once the elimination period has been satisfied.

A table of IBNR completion factors for an LTD or LTC policy might look like the following:

Table 38.2

IBNR Completion Factors		
Months from Incurral	90 Day EP	180 Day EP
1	10%	5%
2	40%	10%
3	60%	20%
4	80%	40%
5	85%	60%
6	90%	80%
9	95%	90%
12	98%	95%
24	100%	100%

Once the completion factors have been developed, the IBNR reserve for a given valuation date can be computed by looking back at the reported claims for the prior 24 months and applying the completion factors to estimate the amount of unreported claims, which then becomes the IBNR reserve. The example below computes an IBNR reserve for a policy form where experience has shown that all claims are reported within 6 months. For each month, the IBNR reserve equals reported claims divided by the completion factor, less the reported claims.

Table 38.3

IBNR Reserve Using Lag Method as of December, 2014			
Month	Reported Claims	Completion Factor	IBNR Reserve
12/2014	50,000	10%	450,000
11/2014	150,000	20%	600,000
10/2014	250,000	30%	583,333
9/2014	550,000	50%	550,000
8/2014	800,000	75%	266,667
7/2014	1,000,000	100%	-
Total IBNR Reserve			$2,450,000

THE LOSS RATIO METHOD

The lag method depends heavily on historical data, and in some cases historical data is either unavailable or is not credible. This is often the case with a new policy form, or for early claim durations where completion factors are very low because so few claims have been reported. In these situations, the loss ratio method may be used to compute the IBNR reserve.

Under the loss ratio method, the company computes its IBNR reserve at the end of a year by assuming that the incurred loss ratio for that year will be a target amount, generally tied to pricing assumptions or recent experience. It then computes its IBNR reserve by multiplying earned premium for the past year (or other time period) by the assumed loss ratio and subtracting the amount of reported claims for that time period.

Under this method, the company's experience for the year will equal the target loss ratio, unless the actual loss ratio exceeds the target loss ratio. In that case, some IBNR reserve should still be established since there are very likely to be some unreported claims. One drawback to the loss ratio method is that the company's financial statements may not accurately reflect underlying changes in experience. For this reason, the loss ratio method should be used cautiously, and only when the lag method is impractical.

COMBINATION METHODS

Many companies use combinations of the IBNR methods described above to take advantage of historical experience where it is meaningful, but to avoid distorting results when the experience is less credible. One example of a combination approach is to use the loss ratio method for estimating IBNR for recent months (since a high proportion of claims incurred in those time periods are still in their elimination periods and the completion factors are low) and to use the lag method for earlier periods. An example of this type of calculation is shown below. It begins with the lag method shown above for older claims but uses an assumed loss ratio for the most recent three months:

Table 38.4

IBNR Reserve Using Combination Method as of 12/31/2014					
Month	Premium	Reported Claims	Loss Ratio	Completion Factor	IBNR Reserve
12/2014	$1,250,000	50,000	80%		950,000
11/2014	$1,250,000	150,000	80%		850,000
10/2014	$1,250,000	250,000	80%		750,000
9/2014	$1,250,000	550,000		50%	550,000
8/2014	$1,250,000	800,000		75%	266,667
7/2014	$1,250,000	1,000,000		100%	-
Total IBNR Reserve					3,366,667

CONSIDERATIONS IN CALCULATING CLAIM RESERVES

MORBIDITY ASSUMPTIONS

The selection of an appropriate morbidity basis (continuance table) is essential in computing claim reserves for long-term health benefits. The determination of the appropriate basis depends on the type of benefit being reserved, and on the purpose for which the reserves are being computed. Different tables are needed for LTD plans than for LTC plans. In many cases, it is also necessary to use different tables for reserves that are computed for statutory, GAAP, and tax financial reporting, as well as for experience analysis and management reporting.

Continuance tables for LTD benefits commonly vary by gender, elimination period, age at disability, and claim duration. Some of the more recent tables for LTD insurance also vary by the cause of disability and by the definition of disability. LTC tables may also vary by benefit period, with lower termination (of morbidity) rates for lifetime benefits.

For LTD claims incurred prior to October, 2014, the statutory minimum reserve basis specifies the 1987 Commissioner's Group Disability Table (1987 CGDT). Companies are allowed to modify the claim termination rates contained in this table for the first two years of disability "based on the insurer's experience, if the experience is considered credible, or upon other assumptions designed to place a sound value on the liabilities." Further, they may modify the claim termination rates contained in this table for the following three years of disability "based on the insurer's experience if such experience is considered credible and for which the insurer maintains underwriting and claim administration control." The 1987 CGDT is based on industry experience from the early 1980s, and is generally felt to be conservative (that is, it results in higher-than-needed reserves) for early claim durations.

The NAIC has recently adopted a new statutory morbidity basis for group LTD claims, known as the 2012 Group Long-Term Disability Table (2012 GLTD). This table is the required statutory minimum valuation basis for LTD claims incurred on or after 1/1/2017, but it may be used at the company's option for claims incurred 10/1/2014 or later. This table has several important differences from the 1987 CGDT:

1. It is based on a much larger volume of experience and on much more recent experience.

2. It separates claim termination rates into deaths and recoveries, while the 1987 CGDT provided only a total claim termination rate that combined deaths and recoveries.

3. Claim termination rates vary by claim diagnosis, definition of disability, and indexed gross benefit amount.

4. Companies are required to modify the table for their own experience using specified methods for assessing credibility and determining the amount of the adjustment. These methods are specified in Actuarial Guideline XLVII, "The Application of Company Experience in the Calculation of Claim Reserves Under the 2012 Group Long-Term Disability Valuation Table".

LTC continuance tables are similar in structure to LTD tables, and they may also be based on published industry data. Continuance tables for nursing home care were created by the Society of Actuaries (SOA) from the 1985 National Nursing Home Survey (NNHS), and published in the Transactions of the Society of Actuaries. These tables are commonly referred to as the "Wilkins Tables." The NNHS is conducted by the National Center for Health Statistics, and is periodically updated, but is based on population, not insured data. The SOA Long-Term Care Experience Committee publishes periodic reports of LTC experience on lives insured under private LTC plans in the United States. The most recent report was released in early 2015.

LTC experience for specific companies has been shown to vary widely from the morbidity rates contained in population studies, and from the composite data from the experience committee, and the NAIC has not specified a table for use in computing statutory reserves for LTC benefits. In addition, claim termination rates for most companies have been observed to decline over time. Therefore, most LTC insurers compute claim reserves based on their own experience, if it is credible, or on a morbidity basis that is consistent with the pricing basis for the policy, though often with an added margin for conservatism. The selection of the appropriate morbidity basis for reserving LTC claims is a complex question that should be carefully considered by the actuary responsible for computing reserves.

For both LTD and LTC claim reserves, it is essential for companies to regularly compare their actual morbidity experience to the assumptions used in claim reserves (see the section on "Evaluating Claim Reserve Adequacy" later in this chapter).

INTEREST RATES

Interest rates for statutory reserves are generally specified by law. For LTD in most states, the statutory interest rate is the maximum interest rate permitted for the valuation of single premium immediate annuities, less 100 basis points. For LTC, the statutory interest rate in most states is the maximum interest rate permitted for the valuation of whole life insurance contracts. Interest rates for tax reserves are specified by the Internal Revenue Service. Interest rates for GAAP reserves are generally equal to a company's expected investment income rate on the assets backing its claim reserves, less a margin for conservatism. The GAAP interest rate may be a single assumption for all claim incurral years, or it may vary by year of disability.

POLICY PROVISIONS

Claim reserve calculations must make explicit allowance for many policy provisions. In some cases, such as the own occupation period for LTD, or the period allowed for home care benefits for LTC, the impact of these provisions is seen in the choice of a morbidity basis. In other cases, however, these policy provisions affect the amount and the timing of benefit payments.

Common policy provisions that should be considered in claim reserving include the following:

- *Cost of Living Adjustments (COLA)*: COLA benefits increase the amount of claim payments for inflation. The increasing pattern of benefits must be explicitly reflected in the calculation of reserves.

- *Partial and Residual Benefits*: Partial and residual benefits are common on LTD policies. These benefits take many different forms, but typically pay an amount less than 100% of the monthly benefit if the claimant is able to work part-time during a period of disability. The fractional portion of the benefit that is paid should be reflected in the reserve calculation.

- *Survivor Benefits*: Survivor benefits may pay a death benefit equal to a few months of payments to a designated beneficiary if a claimant dies while receiving benefits. The expected cost of this benefit, while often small, should be reflected in the claim reserve calculation.

- *Benefit Integration*: Many LTD and LTC plans are integrated with benefits for social insurance, meaning that the benefit must be reduced for amounts received from these other sources. This reduction must be reflected in the reserve calculation. Many companies also estimate the impact of future offsets for social insurance benefits not yet being received by the claimant.

- *Benefit Limitations*: Many LTD benefits have a limited benefit period, such as two years, for some specified conditions. This limited benefit period must be reflected in the reserve calculation. Consideration should be given to the fact that benefit limitations are not always fully effective, since a claimant may be disabled from more than one condition, or the primary cause of disability may change over time.

- *Waiver of Premium*: Some LTD and LTC benefits contain a provision that waives premiums if the insured is on claim, or (in the case of survivor waiver benefits on LTC), if a person's spouse has passed away. For LTD claim reserves, it is usually not necessary to hold an additional reserve for waiver benefits, due to the term structure of the premiums. On the other hand, for LTC claim reserves, waived premiums are most often treated as an additional monthly benefit, since LTC policies have level issue-age premiums and the coverage is usually guaranteed renewable.

- *Non-Level Daily Benefits*: Many LTC claimants do not receive a level benefit from day to day, because they receive different levels of care on different days of the week. This means that they are eligible for different levels of reimbursement on a day-by-day basis. The pattern of daily benefits can affect both the amount that is paid each day and the length of time for which benefits may be paid, under policies that have specified lifetime dollar maximum benefits. In computing reserves for policies with non-level daily benefits, it is necessary to reflect the actual payment patterns, through specific calculations or averaging techniques.

CLAIM EXPENSES

In reserving for long-term health benefits, insurers must also make provision for the expenses that are related to the management and payment of these claims. Claim expenses are often expressed as a percentage of claim payments, such as 3-7% of paid claims. Therefore, the claim expense reserve is equal to that percentage times the tabular claim reserve.

The NAIC requires companies to hold claim expense reserves for statutory purposes, and these reserves are computed for GAAP purposes as well. The IRS does not permit the deduction of claim expense reserves, however, so no such reserve is computed for tax purposes.

LTC CASE RESERVES

Some LTC companies who have small claim blocks may elect to compute "case reserves" for some claims, meaning that their reserves are based on an evaluation of a specific claimant's medical condition and plan of care, rather than on aggregate morbidity assumptions contained in a published table. This approach is very labor intensive, and is most often used on blocks of claims that either do not have sufficient size to develop credible morbidity assumptions, or have a large enough reserve amount involved to justify it.

DATA INTEGRITY

Unlike the aggregate reserves computed for short-term health benefits, tabular reserves for long-term benefits are heavily dependent on the underlying seriatim claim data. Seemingly small errors in a claim data file can have an enormous impact on the tabular reserve that is computed for a particular claim. The failure to recognize a two-year benefit limitation on a specific claim, for example, may result in a reserve that is too high by several hundred percent.

Common errors in claim data include the following:

- Missing data,
- Misstated age or gender,
- Inaccurate elimination periods or benefit periods,
- Incomplete or inaccurate information on benefit integration,
- Inaccurate or inconsistent determination of the incurral date,
- Inaccurate information on cause of disability, and
- Incorrect coding of claim status (open, closed, or pending).

Companies should conduct regular audits to ensure that their claim data is being captured accurately and interpreted properly in reserve calculations.

EVALUATING CLAIM RESERVE ADEQUACY

RUNOFF STUDIES

Frequent testing of claim reserves is necessary to ensure the adequacy of the reserves. One method to test reserve adequacy is a claim runoff study, in which previous reserve balances are compared to subsequent claim payments and reserve balances, with appropriate adjustments for interest. The object is to determine whether the previous reserve balance was adequate to cover the subsequent payments and reserves.

The following table contains an example of a runoff study to test the tabular reserves computed at 12/31/2013, relative to payments and reserve balances for the year 2014:

Table 38.5

\multicolumn{6}{c}{Claim Runoff Study}
Incurral Year	12/31/2013 Reserve	2014 Payments	12/31/2014 Reserve	12/31/2013 Runoff	12/31/2013 Margin
2011	900,000	100,000	800,000	859,495	40,505
2012	800,000	75,000	750,000	787,478	12,522
2013	700,000	80,000	700,000	744,739	(44,739)

In Table 38.5, the 12/31/2013 runoff is computed as the present value (at 5% interest as of 12/31/2013) of the 2014 payments, plus the present value of the 12/31/2014 reserve. The 2014 payments are assumed to occur in the middle of 2014. The 12/31/2013 margin is computed as the 12/31/2013 reserve less the 12/31/2013 runoff.

Table 38.5 presents runoff experience by claim incurral years, which is a common reporting approach used for long-term health benefits. Companies can use the results of this type of runoff study to identify areas where their claim reserve basis appears to be weak or strong. For example, the results in Table 38.5 show a negative margin for claims incurred in 2013, which were in their first duration as of 12/31/2013. This suggests that the morbidity basis used to compute claim reserves may be weak in the first duration. Table 38.5 also shows a positive margin for claims incurred in 2012 and 2011, suggesting that the morbidity basis is adequate in the second and third claim durations.

A/E CLAIM TERMINATION RATE STUDIES

Claim runoff studies provide a high-level indication of the adequacy of claim reserves, with detail by claim duration. The results of runoff studies can be somewhat difficult to interpret, however. For example, a basis that produces reserves of increasing weakness by claim duration may appear to generate positive margins, because the runoff is significantly understated.

For companies that have sufficient data, further information on reserve adequacy may be obtained through the development of an actual to expected (A/E) claim termination rate study. This type of study uses a company's actual claims as an exposure base and then compares the actual claim terminations experienced by the company to the expected claim terminations based on the table used for reserving. A/E ratios of greater than 1.00 indicate that more claims are terminating than assumed in the reserve basis, suggesting that the reserve basis is adequate. A/E ratios of less than 1.00 indicate that fewer claims are terminating than assumed in the reserve basis, suggesting that the reserve basis is inadequate.

The following table contains an example of an A/E claim termination rate study:

Table 38.6

Claim Termination Rate Study			
Claim Duration	Actual Terminations	Expected Terminations	A/E Ratio
1	80	120	0.67
2	120	130	0.92
3	100	75	1.33
4+	250	200	1.25
Total	550	525	1.05

Claim termination rates vary significantly by claim duration, so it is essential to look at results by claim duration when conducting a claim termination rate study. The study in Table 38.6 shows overall claim termination rates that are 105% of expected, but also reveals lower-than-expected claim terminations in durations 1 and 2, and higher-than-expected claim terminations in durations 3 and higher. Even though the overall claim termination rates may appear adequate, a company might wish to use the information in Table 38.6 to determine adjustments to its morbidity basis that would result in more accurate reserving by claim duration.

There are several important considerations in preparing a claim termination rate study:

- *Credibility*: It is important to ensure that there is sufficient data in the study before drawing conclusions about the experience.
- *Types of terminations included*: Generally speaking, only those terminations due to recovery and death should be included since most morbidity tables reflect only these types of terminations. Claims that terminate due to the end of the benefit period or the presence of a benefit limitation should not be counted as terminations.

- *Exposure characteristics*: A company should be aware of any characteristics of its claim exposure that may not be reflected in the morbidity basis used to determine expected claims. For example, if a company's expected morbidity basis did not vary by type of disability, and if its exposure had a large number of claims for short-term causes of disability such as maternity, it might expect to see very high A/E termination rates. In this case, rather than adjust its overall morbidity basis, it might want to consider performing separate studies for maternity claims and all other claims, and developing two separate A/E results.

- *Voluntary Claim Settlements*: Some insurers occasionally offer claimants the opportunity to receive a single lump sum claim payment (a "settlement") in lieu of continued monthly payments. In exchange for this payment, the claim is terminated with no possibility of reopening. When performing a claim termination study, however, it is common to exclude settlements from claim terminations, or to count them only as partial terminations, since settlements are usually offered only to claims that have a low probability of death or recovery and are expected to continue receiving payments in the absence of a settlement. Counting settlements as claim terminations may result in an overstatement of A/E claim termination rates.

A/E claim termination studies can be used in combination with claim runoff studies to modify the claim reserve morbidity basis. For example, a company may identify deficiencies in its reserve basis through a runoff study. It may then perform an A/E claim termination rate study to determine specific adjustments to its morbidity basis by claim duration. The adjusted morbidity basis can then be used to compute a new set of claim reserves, which can be tested against recent payment experience by repeating the claim runoff study. In this manner, a company can demonstrate that a proposed new claim reserve morbidity basis will produce reserves with an adequate runoff.

CONSIDERATIONS FOR SELF-INSURED PLANS

Some employers may offer LTD benefits to their employees on a self-insured basis (this is quite rare for LTC). In this case, the claim reserve liability must be computed and held by the employer, rather than by an insurance company. The considerations in calculating claim reserves for a self-insured plan are generally the same as for an insured plan. However, there are certain accounting guidelines related to the reporting of these liabilities that must be considered by employers. Private sector employer who report under GAAP accounting are subject to ASC 712 which requires them to compute a GAAP liability similar to what an insurance carrier would hold if the plan were insured.

Public sector employers, depending on the structure of their self-insured plans, may be subject to special accounting standards developed by the Government Accounting Standards Board (GASB) that apply to post-employment benefits other than pensions, a category that includes long-term disability benefits. The standards require employee benefit plans and employers, to make certain disclosures about the financial status of the plan, including current funding levels. They also require the use of certain pension accounting methods in the creation of the required reports. The original standards, GASB 43 and 45, have recently been replaced with GASB 74 and 75. The new, stricter standards require public employers to recognize the liability for their self-insured plans on their balance sheets, rather than only to disclose the amount in a note to the financial statements. They also provide a more limited set of options for the actuarial cost methods to be used in valuing the liability.

FURTHER INFORMATION AND RESOURCES

Many guidelines and standards of practice now exist and apply to the calculation of claim reserves for LTD and LTC benefits. These guidelines and standards include the following:

- The Guides to Professional Conduct of the American Academy of Actuaries, as they relate to calculation and assumptions.
- Actuarial Standards of Practice (ASOPs) developed by the Actuarial Standards Board including ASOP No. 5, "Incurred Health and Disability Claims"; ASOP No. 18, "Long-Term Care Insurance," and ASOP No. 42, "Determining Health and Disability Liabilities Other Than Liabilities for Incurred Claims."
- Health practice notes issued by the American Academy of Actuaries.
- NAIC guidelines and model regulations relative to reserve standards and opinions
- NAIC Accounting Practices and Procedures Manual
- GAAP accounting standards, including SFAS 60 and ASC 712 (insurers and private employers), and GASB 74 and GASB 75 (public employers)
- Canadian Office of the Superintendent of Financial Insurance (OSFI) and the Canadian Institute of Actuaries publications and papers
- Literature published in textbooks and by the actuarial profession.

These guidelines require appropriate review, methods, and assumptions, and suggest that mere mechanical calculations performed without actuarial judgment and analyses are not appropriate. It is not generally accepted actuarial practice to use factors and values directly from published tables or computer programs (such as those supplied by the Society of Actuaries or commercial vendors) without performing the proper analysis to determine whether the reserves developed in this manner are reasonable and adequate.

39 Risk-Based Capital Formulas

Rowen B. Bell
Robert B. Cumming
Constance Peterson

This chapter describes risk-based capital formulas, including their structure, development, and use. Risk-Based Capital (RBC) is a method of measuring the minimum amount of capital appropriate for an insurer to support its overall business operations, taking into consideration the insurer's size and risk profile. Capital provides a cushion to protect against insolvency, and RBC limits the amount of risk an insurer can take by requiring those with a higher amount of risk to hold a higher amount of capital. RBC is intended to provide a measure for a minimum regulatory capital standard, and it is not necessarily the full amount of capital an insurer would want to hold to meet its safety, growth and competitive objectives. In addition, RBC is not designed to be used as a stand-alone tool in determining financial solvency of an insurance company; rather, it is one of the tools that give regulators legal authority to take control of an insurer.

Risk-based capital formulas are important tools in the financial assessment and management of insurers. Under a broad definition, risk-based capital formulas would include any formula that calculates a target capital based on factors that reflect the level of financial risk for an organization. However, in more common usage, risk-based capital refers specifically to the formulas used by state regulators in the U.S. to set minimum capital requirements for insurers and to determine when to take regulatory action.

This chapter focuses on the Health RBC formula. The Life RBC formula, which applies to life insurers with a limited volume of health insurance, is similar in nature and has been in existence much longer than the Health RBC formula. The Life RBC formula has different parameters, and it focuses more on long-term risks and asset-based risks than the Health RBC formula.

This chapter does not cover the Life RBC formula in depth because its goal is to highlight the most important concepts and give the reader an introductory understanding of the topic. Those who would like more information on either RBC formula are encouraged to seek out current information through the American Academy of Actuaries' (AAA) and the National Association of Insurance Commissioners' (NAIC) websites. The chapter titled "Group Insurance Financial Reporting" provides an overview of how Canada approaches risk-based capital formulas.

History of RBC Formulas

Before RBC was created, regulators used fixed capital standards as a primary tool for monitoring the financial solvency of insurers. Under fixed capital standards, insurers are required to maintain the same minimum amount of capital, regardless of the financial condition of the company. The requirements required by the states ranged from $500,000 to $6 million, and was dependent upon the state and the lines of business that an insurer wrote. Insurers had to meet these minimum capital and surplus requirements in order to be licensed and write business in the state. As insurers changed and grew, it became clear that the fixed capital standards were no longer effective in providing a sufficient cushion for many insurers.

The NAIC's RBC regime began in the early 1990s as an early warning system for U.S. insurance regulators. The NAIC established a working group to look at the feasibility of developing a statutory risk-based capital requirement for insurers. The RBC regime was created to provide a capital adequacy standard that is related to risk, raises a safety net for insurers, is uniform among the states, and provides regulatory authority for timely action.

The adoption of the U.S. RBC regime was driven by a string of large-company insolvencies that occurred in late 1980s and early 1990s. The NAIC adopted separate risk-based capital formulas for property & casualty (P&C) versus life insurers in the early 1990s. Prior to that time, various states, including New York, Minnesota and Wisconsin, had experimented with risk-based capital formulas and requirements, but most states were using a months-in-reserve basis to assess the adequacy of insurers' reserves.

Some insurers whose business included significant amounts of group health insurance were, for historical reasons, organized as either life or P&C insurers. However, many other group health insurers were organized under other portions of state insurance codes, such as HMO statutes. By the mid-1990s, some issuers of health insurance were calculating RBC, while others were not.

To rectify this, the NAIC adopted a risk-based capital formula for health organizations. Beginning with the 1998 annual statement, health entities were required to calculate and report an estimated level of capital needed for financial stability, depending upon the health entity's risk profile, known as Risk Based Capital (RBC).

By 2001, some frustration had emerged among regulators over the fact that two identical health insurers could have different risk-based capital results, due solely to the fact that one company filed the Blue blank, and hence used the Life RBC formula, while the other filed the Orange blank and used the Health RBC formula. To rectify this, the NAIC adopted rules by which health insurers who had traditionally filed the Blue blank or Yellow blank (P&C) were encouraged to migrate to the Orange blank, implying that these insurers would file the Health RBC Report going forward.

Consequently, by 2006 the vast majority of insurers specializing in group medical insurance filed the Orange blank and used the Health RBC formula. However, most of the insurers that primarily write disability income, long-term care, or group life continue to file the Blue blank and the Life RBC formula, as these products have characteristics that would make the Life RBC formula more appropriate.

A "Health Blank Test" that determines which blank is appropriate for an insurer to file was added in 2003. In this test, health insurance premiums and reserves for specified health products are compared to total premiums and reserves. Health premiums included in this test consist of Medical, Medicare Supplement, Dental and Vision; disability income, Long-Term Care, AD&D, Credit Insurance, and Workers' Compensation Carve-out are excluded. If the ratio of Health Premiums and Reserves are greater than 95% for both the current and prior year, an insurer must file the Health blank and be subject to the Health RBC formula.

NAIC RBC MODEL ACTS

The NAIC has developed model laws for states to use in implementing risk-based capital requirements for insurance companies. In 1998, the NAIC developed and adopted the "Risk-Based Capital (RBC) for Health Organizations Model Act." This model act is very similar to the life and P&C model act, which was adopted by the NAIC in 1993. The life and P&C model act has now been adopted in nearly all states. As of 2015, 46 states have adopted a health RBC statute.

The RBC model act specifies the regulatory actions available to, or required of, the Insurance Commissioner. The level of action depends on the ratio of the insurer's actual capital to the required capital based on the risk-based capital formula. However, the model act does *not* specify the actual RBC formula, other than stating that it should depend on the insurer's assets, credit risk, underwriting risk, and other business risks. The actual formula is specified by the NAIC. This allows the NAIC to modify and refine the formula over time without requiring each state to take legislative or regulatory action to adopt the changes.

According to the model act, each insurance company compares their Total Adjusted Capital (TAC) to their authorized control level (ACL) capital requirement, calculated according to the risk-based capital formula. TAC includes statutory capital and surplus, plus certain adjustments for life and P&C subsidiaries. If the ratio of TAC to ACL RBC falls below 200%, then varying degrees of regulatory action are available to, or required of, the Commissioner, as summarized in Table 39.1 below. In setting their own capital goals, insurers typically benchmark their TAC against the formula, relative either to the ACL or to the Company Action Level (CAL).

Table 39.1

Regulatory Actions	
TAC-to-ACL Ratio	Regulatory Action
≥200%	None
150% to 200%	Company Action Level Event
100% to 150%	Regulatory Action Level Event
70% to 100%	Authorized Control Level Event
≤70%	Mandatory Control Level Event

Each of these regulatory actions is further described below:

Company Action:
Company must submit a correction action plan to the Commissioner.

Regulatory Action:
Company must submit a corrective action plan, and the Commissioner may examine the company and issue an order specifying correction actions.

Authorized Control:
Commissioner may take the actions identified above, or may place the company under regulatory control, if deemed to be in the best interests of the policyholders and creditors of the company.

Mandatory Control:
Commissioner must take regulatory control of the company.

In 2009, the NAIC added a "Trend Test" for health insurers filing the Orange blank. Insurers whose ratio of TAC-to-ACL is between 200% and 300% and have a combined ratio greater than 105% could trigger a "Company Action Level Event" per the Trend Test. This calculation is considered to be only informational until state statutes are implemented. However, this modification to the Model Law for Health Organizations has become an accreditation standard,[1] effective January 1, 2016.

Formally, this schedule of regulatory actions applies only in states that have adopted the RBC model act. As noted above, the Health RBC model act (in some form) has been adopted in 46 states to date. Even when not adopted, the influence of Health RBC is persuasive. First, all insurers filing the Orange blank are required to calculate Health RBC and disclose the results of the calculation in the "Five Year Historical Exhibit" of the annual statement, even if their domiciliary state has not adopted the Health RBC model act. Due to this requirement, every health insurer's RBC position is a matter of public record. Second, regulators are very familiar with the RBC concept and are likely to express formal concern over health insurers whose ratios of TAC to ACL fall below 200%. Third, the concept of Health RBC has been embraced by organizations with quasi-regulatory functions, such as various rating agencies and the Blue Cross and Blue Shield Association, which requires plans to maintain a certain TAC to ACL ratio in order to retain the ability to use the Association's trademarks. Other insurers' own capital targets typically are a higher ratio than the regulatory one, as well, often on the order of 500% or more of ACL.

---

[1] An accreditation standard is a standard that a state must substantially have in place in order to meet regulatory standards that allow a non-domicile state to rely on the state's regulatory oversight.

HEALTH RBC FORMULA

The Health RBC formula defines a capital requirement based on the key factors that affect the level of uncertainty in a company's future financial results. These key factors include the amounts and types of insurance products sold by the company, the health plans' performance and loss ratios, the methods used to reimburse health care providers, and the types of assets held by the insurer.

In developing an understanding of the Health RBC formula, one should keep two items in mind.

First, Health RBC is an example of a "standardized approach" to a capital formula, in that the capital requirement is determined by applying fixed factors to information available from an insurer's annual NAIC filing pages or internal records. The factors used in the formula are intended to represent an aggregate perspective on risk that can be applied across insurers and time periods. Recently, the regulatory community has been interested in capital formulas that are company-specific internal models – often referred to as the "advanced approach" to capital formulas. Such formulas should better reflect the risk factors pertaining to a company at a point in time. As of this writing, while certain aspects of the NAIC Life RBC formula (for example, C-3 Phase II) reflect an advanced approach, the Health RBC remains a standardized approach.

Second, Health RBC was designed to identify financially weak insurers, rather than a barometer by which to assess financial strength. It is generally acknowledged that a company having a TAC-to-ACL ratio of 100% is at greater risk of financial distress than a company having a TAC-to-ACL ratio of 150%. However, it does not follow from this that an insurer having a TAC-to-ACL ratio of 400% is less financially sound than one having a TAC-to-ACL ratio of 600%. If one were building a formula to measure financial strength, the result would look different than the NAIC RBC formula.

RBC ratios have become a focus of legislators and industry observers. An RBC ratio that is "too high," ironically, has a negative connotation as the company may be perceived as "hoarding" its capital and perhaps charging prices that are too high. There is no consensus on the "best" number or range for reasonable reserve levels. It is a decision to be made by the company's directors and management.

In light of these items, while it is important for every insurer to understand its NAIC Health RBC in light of possible regulatory consequences, the insurer may want to develop its own internal risk-based capital formula, reflecting company-specific risks, for use as a management tool.

The NAIC's RBC formulas have been refined over time. The formula structure and parameters described below are applicable for 2015.

CALCULATION OF RBC AFTER COVARIANCE

In the Health RBC formula, the RBC after covariance (RBCAC) is defined as:

$$RBCAC = H_0 + \{H_1^2 + H_2^2 + H_3^2 + H_4^2\}^{1/2}$$

where:

H_0 is the Asset Risk for Affiliates
H_1 is the Asset Risk for Other Assets
H_2 is the Underwriting Risk
H_3 is the Credit Risk
H_4 is the Business Risk

The authorized control level (ACL), referenced earlier, is defined as one-half of the RBC after covariance.

The covariance adjustment refers to the square root of the sum of the squares, as opposed to simply adding the pieces together. The covariance adjustment is made due to the fact that largely independent, deleterious swings in multiple categories are unlikely to occur simultaneously. Accordingly, the covariance adjustment lowers the level of capital required.

In practice, the covariance adjustment has a profound impact on how one should view the Health RBC formula, due to the distribution of a health insurer's risks by major risk category. The figures in Table 39.2 below are derived from one author's study of the aggregate risk profile of all Blue Cross/Blue Shield plans as of year-end 2001:

Table 39.2

Risk Category	Relative Risk (indexed to $H_2 = 100$)	Marginal Impact of RBCAC of $1,000 Increase in Risk
H_1	34.9	$325
H_2	100.0	$931
H_3	8.6	$80
H_4	15.9	$148

The "relative risk" column indicates, for example, that for every dollar of H_2 risk, the typical BC/BS plan had 34.9 cents of H_1 risk.

The implication of Table 39.2 is that, for most companies filing the Health RBC formula, the H_2 category will dominate the output of the formula, and the H_1, H_3, and H_4 risk categories are of lesser importance. In light of this observation, this discussion of the RBC formula focuses on the H_2 (underwriting) risk category, with lesser coverage of the other categories.

For complete details on the Heath RBC formula, the reader should review the *NAIC Health Risk-Based Capital Report Including Overview and Instructions for Companies*, which is published by the NAIC and updated on an annual basis.

Underwriting Risk (H₂)

This reflects the risk of underestimating the cost of insurance or having inadequate premium rates in the future. As discussed above, this factor dominates the RBC requirement for most health insurers.

In general, underwriting risk is calculated separately for each health insurance product by applying a risk factor against some measure of the insurer's exposure. The exposure measure is usually either earned premium or incurred claims, measured on an annual basis and net of any ceded reinsurance.

As noted earlier, generally the risk factors for each product are common across all companies, rather than being fine-tuned to reflect company-specific circumstances. There are two exceptions to this. First, in some cases the factors are tiered by size, implying that a large company achieves a lower average risk per exposure unit than a small company. Second, some risk factors are adjusted in order to reflect the nature of the insurer's provider reimbursement contracts.

The RBC formula subdivides underwriting risk into Claim Experience Fluctuation Risk versus Other Underwriting Risk. Each of these components is described in detail below.

Claim Experience Fluctuation Risk

The Claim Experience Fluctuation Risk portion of the formula covers medical insurance and similar products, with some exceptions. As of 2014, there are five product groupings:

- *Comprehensive Medical and Hospital.* This covers all group and individual medical products, excluding the Federal Employees Health Benefits (FEHB) and TRICARE programs.[2] Also excluded are administrative-service only coverages. Medicaid risk and Medicare Advantage products are included in this category, but are reported separately from commercial products.
- *Medicare Supplement*
- *Dental and Vision*
- *Medicare Part D only plans*
- *Other.* This catch-all category includes non-Medicare standalone drug products and other coverage not specifically addressed in the other categories.

Within each product grouping, the risk charge is calculated as (Premium) times (the ratio of Incurred Claims to Premium), times (the Risk Factor), times (Managed Care Risk Adjustment Factor). However, there is a floor on the risk charge; this floor is referred to as the "alternative risk charge," and reflects the risk that exists from catastrophic claims on individual members regardless of how few members the company insures. In practice, the alternative risk charge is only relevant for small insurers or for insurers writing a very small amount of business in one of the product groupings.

---

[2] TRICARE is the health care program for almost 9.5 million people worldwide including active duty service members, National Guard and Reserve members, retirees, dependents, and others registered in the Defense Enrollment Eligibility Reporting System.

As mentioned above, the Risk Factor varies based on the type of coverage and the amount of Underwriting Revenue. Table 39.3 shows the risk factors. A weighted average Risk Factor is calculated based on the amount of underwriting revenue (annual earned premium) in each tier. For example, an insurer having $250 million of premium in the Comprehensive Medical grouping would have a weighted average risk factor of 9.6% for that grouping (15% x $25M/$250M + 9% x $225M/$250M).

Table 39.3

	Underwriting Risk Factors by Underwriting Revenue Tier		
Coverage	$0-$3 Million	$3-25 Million	$25+ Million
Comprehensive	15.0%	15.0%	9.0%
Medicare Supp.	10.5%	6.7%	6.7%
Dental & Vision	12.0%	7.6%	7.6%
Medicare Part D	25.1%	25.1%	15.1%
Other	13.0%	13.0%	13.0%

The relative level of factors by product grouping is intended to reflect differences in the relative volatility of experience. For example, the risk from catastrophic claims is clearly less for dental and vision insurance than for medical. Therefore, it is logical that dental and vision should have a lower capital requirement per dollar of premium than medical.

The purpose of the Managed Care Risk Adjustment Factor is to reflect the fact that certain contractual reimbursement arrangements with providers lead to greater predictability of future claim levels, thus reducing the need for capita to support fluctuations in experience.

In order to calculate this factor, the insurer takes all of the claims paid over the previous twelve months, and assigns those claims to one of five managed care categories. The formula uses paid claims rather than incurred claims, in order to eliminate the risk of misestimated claim reserves, as well as due to the difficulty of estimating claim reserves by category. The five categories are the following:

Category 0: This is the default category and includes payments made on a fee-for-service basis (with or without a percentage discount from charges), or according to a UCR (usual, customary and reasonable) schedule. It also includes payments made to capitated providers under contractual stop-loss provisions.

Category 1: This category includes payments made based on such contractual arrangements as provider fee schedules, hospital per diems or case rates, and non-adjustable professional case and global rates. The common element here is that there are contractual protections to the insurer regarding the level of allowed charges.

Category 2: This category includes payments that would normally fall under Category 0 or Category 1, but that also fall under the scope of a withhold or bonus arrangement with the provider. Category 2 is divided between providers reimbursed under a UCR schedule (Category 2a) and those reimbursed on a provider fee schedule (Category 2b).

Category 3: This category includes capitation payments, so long as those payments are contractually fixed (either as a percentage of premium or as a dollar amount per member) for a period of at least 12 months. Arrangements that include a provision for prospective revision within 12 months or for retroactive revisions do not qualify and are classified as Category 1 or 0, respectively. Also, capitated payments to intermediaries that are not subject to state regulation and do not file the Health RBC with the state are subject to special limitation: if payments by the intermediary exceed 5% of total payments, then the excess is reported as Category 0 instead of Category 3.

Category 4: This category applies primarily to a staff model HMO, and includes non-contingent salaries to persons directly providing care and facility-related medical expenses generated within a health facility that is owned and operated by the health plan. Since staff model HMOs have the most alignment between the practicing provider and the risk-taking party, and a natural dampening of financial risk due to salary arrangements, Category 4 has the highest discount factor.

Table 39.4 below shows the risk adjustment discount factor associated with each of these managed care categories.

Table 39.4

Managed Care Risk Adjustment Discount Factor		
Category	**Description**	**Discount Factor**
0	Arrangements not included below	0%
1	Contractual fee payments	15%
2	Bonus/withhold arrangements	Variable 0.08% to 15%
3	Capitation	60%
4	Non-contingent expenses	75%

The overall Managed Care Risk Adjustment Factor is calculated as a weighted average of the factors for each category, where the weights are the proportions of total claim payments by category. The overall factor is then applied to all product groupings, except Medicare Part D and Other. For Medicare Part D, there is a risk adjustment factor component to the RBC calculation, but it is not related to managed care techniques; instead, it relates to risk-mitigating catastrophic reinsurance provisions that exist in the Part D contract between the insurer and the federal government.

Other Underwriting Risk

This portion of the formula includes health insurance coverages not included in the Claim Experience Fluctuation Risk portion, as well as some additional adjustments.

Disability Income: Table 39.5 shows the Health RBC tiered factors for disability income coverages, which are applied against earned premium. The factors vary by group vs. individual coverage, and by amount of premium. Within group, the factors also vary by long-term vs. short-term; within individual, the factors also vary by renewability provision. There are also factors for three distinct types of credit disability coverages, which are not shown in the table below.

Table 39.5

RBC Factors for DI by Earned Premium Tier		
Coverage	$0-50 Million	$50+ Million
Non-Cancelable Individual	35%	15%
Other Individual	25%	7%
Group Long-Term	15%	3%
Group Short-Term	5%	3%

For purposes of applying the earned premium tiers, all individual products are combined, and all group products are combined, but the individual and group products are not combined with one another, and the ordering of products is RBC-maximizing. For example, if an insurer has $40 million of LTD premium and $40 million of STD premium, then the entire LTD premium receives the 15% factor, while the STD premium receives an average factor of 3.5% ($10 million at 5%, making $50 million in total group premium at the higher factors, and then $30 million at 3%). If this insurer also has $40 million of non-cancelable individual DI premium, then that entire premium receives the 35% factor.

There is an additional factor for disability coverages equal to 5% of claim reserves.

Long-Term Care: Historically, the Health RBC approach for LTC insurance was very similar to that used for disability income insurance. More recently, the approach has been thoroughly revised and now includes three components: one based on premium, one on incurred claims (adjusted for two-year rolling average loss ratio), and one on claim reserves.

In the premium component, a factor of 10% is applied to the first $50 million of earned premium, with a factor of 3% applied to the excess. An additional 10% factor applies to non-cancelable premiums.

In the incurred claim component, one factor is applied to the first $35 million of claims, and a lesser factor is applied to the excess. As long as earned premiums are positive, the factors are 25% and 8%. Otherwise, higher factors of 37% and 12% are used, in order to compensate for the absence of a premium component.

The final component is equal to 5% of the LTC claim reserves.

Other coverages: Table 39.6 summarizes the RBC factors for other miscellaneous types of accident and health insurance.

Table 39.6

RBC Requirements for Miscellaneous Coverage Types	
Coverage	RBC Requirement
FEHB and TRICARE	2% of incurred claims
Stop Loss and Minimum Premium	25% of premium
Supplemental Benefits within Stand-Alone Medicare Part D Coverage	25% of claims
Hospital Indemnity and Specified Disease	3.5% of premium + $50,000
Accidental Death and Disability	5.5% of premium less than $10 million plus 1.5% of premium in excess of $10 million plus Maximum of [3 times the maximum retained risk or $300,000]
Other Accident	5% of premium

The factor for FEHB and TRICARE is lower than for other medical business due to the financial safeguards that are built into these federal programs; these contracts are essentially cost-plus administration arrangements, and thus have about the same risk profile as an ASO (administrative services only) employer. The risk factor used for stop loss reflects the higher claims variability of this coverage.

Rate Guarantees: When a health insurer guarantees premium rates for future periods on a product whose claim costs increase with healthcare inflation, the risk of future underwriting losses is increased. In recognition of this risk, Health RBC includes additional charges on the earned premium from such policies where the rate guarantee exceeds 15 months. The factor is 2.4% for guarantees of 15 to 36 months, and 6.4% for longer guarantees.

Premium Stabilization Reserves: These reserves usually consist of accumulated experience rating refunds that can be drawn on in the event of poor future experience, thus helping to reduce the insurer's risk. No credit is provided for premium stabilization reserves for FEHB premium, since the impact of such reserves is already reflected in the lower RBC factor for this business. For other premium stabilization reserves, the insurer's underwriting risk is reduced by 50% of the amount of the reserves held.

ASSET RISK – AFFILIATES (H_0)

This reflects the risk that an investment in the stock of an affiliated company may lose some or all of its value. Separate approaches are used for affiliates that are subject to RBC versus those that are not.

For investments in affiliates that are subject to risk-based capital, such as directly or indirectly owned insurance subsidiaries, the RBC is calculated on a "see-through" basis. That is, the RBC requirement for a stock investment in such affiliates is based on the RBC after covariance for the subsidiary, prorated for the percentage ownership of that subsidiary. There are limits and adjustments based on how the affiliate's RBC compares to the affiliate's surplus and the book value of the affiliate. The see-through approach, combined with the fact that H_0 risk is not subject to the covariance adjustment, tends to imply that in situations where one insurer owns another, the RBC after covariance of the parent will be similar to what it would be if the two insurers were merged.

For other investments in affiliates, the RVC requirement is calculated as a factor times the book value of the stock of those affiliates. The factor is 30%, except for non-U.S. insurance subsidiaries where the factor is 100%.

The H_0 risk category also includes a provision for certain off-balance sheet items, including contingent liabilities, non-controlled assets, assets pledged as collateral, and guarantees to fulfill obligations of affiliates to external entities (should affiliates become unable to meet obligations). The RBC requirement is calculated as 1% of the reported value of these items.

ASSET RISK – OTHER (H_1)

Asset risk reflects the risk that investments may default or decrease in value. In general, the risk-based capital requirement for an asset is calculated as the book value of the asset times a factor. The factor varies depending on the type of asset, ranging from 0% to 30%. In addition, the factor is doubled (but capped at 30%) for certain assets held in the 10 largest securities issuers, reflecting the additional risk to the company of having a high concentration of assets from a single security issuer. For example, if an insurer holds the vast majority of its equity and debt securities portfolio in ABC Energy Company and XYZ Widget Corp, the factor applied to stock or bonds of those companies is double the factor applied to other securities. This is intended to reflect the risk that, if one of those "high concentration" companies defaulted or declined in value, the impact to the insurer would be disproportionately significant.

Not all of the assets on an insurer's balance sheet are covered within the H_0 or H_1 risk categories. As discussed later, some assets, such as reinsurance receivables, are handled in the credit risk (H_3) portion of the formula; others, such as due and unpaid premium, are not contemplated within the RBC formula.

As discussed earlier, the importance of asset risk within Health RBC is somewhat diminished by covariance. What follows is a brief discussion of asset risk factors for those asset classes most commonly held by health insurers. There are risk factors for other classes of invested assets besides those discussed below (for example, preferred stock).

Cash and bonds: U.S. government bonds are considered to be risk-free and hence have a risk factor of 0%. Cash, money market mutual funds, and corporate bonds that are designated as Class 1 by the NAIC's Securities Valuation Office (SVO) receive a risk factor of 0.3%, reflecting the minimal default risk of these assets. Other bonds have risk factors based on their SVO designation, from 1% for Class 2 (investment grade) up to 30% for Class 6 (in default).

Common stock: Investments in unaffiliated common stock, including most mutual funds, receive a risk factor of 15%, with the exception of Federal Home Loan Bank stock, which has a risk factor of 2.3%.

On the surface, it seems that the risk charge for an investment in the stock of a non-affiliate is one-half of that for a comparable investment in the stock of an affiliate, where the risk factor is 30%, as discussed above. However, that analysis ignores the impact of covariance. Since affiliated stock lies outside the covariance adjustment, while unaffiliated stock lies within, in reality the effective risk charge per dollar invested is considerably smaller for unaffiliated common stock than for affiliated common stock.

Property and Equipment: All property and equipment owned by the insurer, including health care delivery assets, receives a 10% factor. However, this factor is applied against the admitted asset balance only, and statutory accounting places considerable restrictions on the admissibility of these types of assets.

CREDIT RISK (H_3)

Credit risk reflects the risk that amounts owed to the health insurer will not be recovered. This risk is common to all types of businesses, although some receivables are unique to health insurers, such as pharmacy rebate receivables. Also, the calculation of H_3 contemplates the possibility that capitated providers will not fulfill their obligations.

As discussed earlier, for most health insurers, the impact of the H_3 risk category is marginalized by covariance. However, for an insurer that makes heavy use of capitation arrangements, it is possible that the H_2 and H_3 categories will be in closer balance, implying that both would play a significant role in determining RBC after covariance.

The credit risk for capitation reflects the risk that capitated providers may not provide the promised services and the health insurer will incur additional expenses in arranging for alternative coverage. The RBC requirement of 2% of the annual capitations paid directly to providers, which is approximately one week of paid capitations, and 4% of the annual capitations paid to intermediaries. If the health insurer receives acceptable letters of credit or has withheld funds for a particular provider, then the capitations for that provider are exempted.

For other types of credit risk, the current RBC requirements are 0.5% of reinsurance receivables from non-affiliates, 1% of investment income receivable, 5% of health care receivables, 5% of amounts due from affiliates, and 5% of receivables related to ASC and ASO plans. Health care receivables include pharmacy rebates, claim overpayments, loans and advances to providers, and provider risk sharing arrangements.

BUSINESS RISK (H_4)

The business risk category of the Health RBC formula includes several miscellaneous types of general business risks not included elsewhere, each of which is discussed below. The practical importance of these risk categories, however, is severely limited due to the impact of covariance.

Administrative Expense Risk: Administrative expenses for health insurance are subject to mis-estimation, just like claim expenses. Assumptions regarding both claims and administrative expenses drive premium rates and thus impact plan performance, but the degree of misestimation for administrative expenses should be somewhat less. Thus, the risk factors applied to administrative expenses are somewhat less than the factors applied to claims. The weighted average risk factor varies between 4% and 7% of annual administrative expenses, dependent on premium volume. ASC and ASO revenues, expenses, and commissions are excluded from the administrative expense risk and are discussed below.

Risks from ASC/ASO Business: Administrative services contract (ASC) and administrative services only (ASO) are both contracts where the health insurer agrees to provide administrative services for a third party, typically a large employer, that is at risk for medical expenses. The NAIC defines the distinction between the two as follows: under an ASC contract, benefits are paid from the health insurer's bank account and the health insurer receives reimbursement from the third party, while under an ASO contract, benefits are paid from a bank account owned or funded by the third party. Alternatively, benefits under an ASO contract could be paid from the health insurer's bank account, but only after the health insurer has received funds from the third party to cover the benefit payments. Under both types of contracts, there is a risk that the insurer may misestimate the amount that it charges the customer for administrative services. For this reason, a risk factor of 2% is applied against the annual administrative expenses for ASC/ASO contracts. Under an ASC contract only, there is some additional risk since the insurer is fronting the cash for the benefit payments. If the third party goes bankrupt, the health insurer might not be able to collect these amounts. Accordingly, there is a 1% additional risk factor applied to annual benefit payments administered under ASC contracts.

Guaranty Fund Assessment Risk: A 0.5% risk factor is applied against premiums that are subject to guaranty fund assessments, reflecting the risk that future assessments will be higher than expected.

Excessive Growth Risk: The RBC requirement for excessive growth only applies if a health insurer's underwriting RBC increases from one year to the next by more than the "safe harbor" level. The safe harbor level is calculated as the current year underwriting revenue, divided by the prior year underwriting revenue, plus 10%. The excessive growth RBC requirement is 50% of growth in underwriting RBC beyond this safe harbor amount. Since the safe harbor includes the growth in revenue, this is really not just an adjustment for excessive growth in the amount of business a health insurer has, as the adjustment would apply if a health insurer changes to a significantly more risky mix of business or provider reimbursement arrangements.

RESERVING RISK

Theoretically, a capital provision for reserving risk would be appropriate to reflect the possibility that the insurer's future surplus will be impaired due to unfavorable development in the claim liabilities and reserves established as of the valuation date.

However, the Health RBC formula does not contain such a provision, except for long-term care and disability. Instead, the formula implicitly assumes that the insurer's claim liabilities are accurately stated. This reflects that the actuarial opinion accompanying the Orange blank includes a statement by the opining actuary that the recorded reserves make "good and sufficient provision" for the company's liability.

The absence of reserving risk from the Health RBC formula has two interesting implications. First, it implies that an insurer's capital level is disconnected from the level of conservatism in its actuarial reserves. This is a counter-intuitive result. If two insurers bear the same risk profile, but Company A holds more conservative reserves for those risks than Company B, then in theory Company A needs less capital than Company B, since the additional conservatism in the reserves is functioning as capital. However, under Health RBC, the two companies would have the same capital requirement.

The second implication is related but is somewhat subtler. Recently, the phrase "Total Asset Requirement" (TAR) has been introduced into actuarial jargon as a synonym for the sum of an insurer's statutory reserves and required capital. Conceptually, one might want the insurer's TAR to be adequate with high probability, say 95%. In this case, since the required capital (that is, Health RBC) contains no provision for reserving risk, it would be necessary for the statutory reserves to be set at such a level so that the reserves themselves would be adequate 95% of the time. This argument has been used by some actuaries to justify the level of conservatism normally found in group medical claim liabilities. If, instead, there were a capital requirement for reserves, then the desired level of confidence on the insurer's TAR could be achieved without needing the reserves themselves to be set at a 95% confidence level. Indeed, from a theoretical perspective, one might argue that medical claim liabilities should be set at a 50% confidence level, and that a significant capital requirement should be imposed on the liabilities in order to achieve the desired high level of confidence (such as 95%) from a TAR perspective.

DEVELOPMENT OF THE HEALTH RBC FORMULA

The initial work on the current Health RBC formula started in 1993, when the NAIC sent a request to the American Academy of Actuaries for assistance in developing a RBC formula for health insurers. The Academy set up a work group that prepared a set of recommendations for the NAIC. The group's work focused on the structure and parameters for the calculation of the underwriting risk, since this component tends to dominate the RBC requirement for health insurers, and since this was an area where the treatment of health insurance in the existing Life and P&C formulas was overly simplistic.

RUIN THEORY MODEL

To develop risk parameters for underwriting risk, the work group developed a stochastic "ruin theory" model. This model was used to determine the level of capital needed to give a 95% probability that an insurance company would not become insolvent over a five-year time horizon. The model projected financial gains and losses on a year by year basis. This model was used to determine how capital requirements should vary for different volumes of business and for different types of coverage.

The key factors that impacted the risk for a given scenario included the following:

- The risk of catastrophic claims and other statistical fluctuations in claim levels
- The risk of misestimating trends or other pricing errors
- The length of time needed to recognize a pricing error, implement an adjustment, and have the adjustments become effective

To model the risk of statistical fluctuations in claim levels, a claim probability distribution for an individual person was developed for each type of coverage. A Monte Carlo method was then used to develop a distribution of total claims for a portfolio of business.

To model the risk of misestimating trends and other pricing errors, the work group studied the fluctuation in loss ratios over time for different types of coverage. This information was used to develop a probability distribution for pricing errors. This distribution, along with the individual claim distribution, became the basis for the model's stochastic simulation.

LIFE RBC FORMULA

As discussed earlier, today most companies whose primary business is group medical insurance file the Orange blank and therefore use the Health RBC formula. However, most companies writing disability income, long-term care, or group life insurance file the Blue blank, and therefore use the NAIC's Life RBC formula.

The Life RBC formula is significantly more complex than the Health RBC formula, and its level of complexity has increased in recent years. Because of this, we will not attempt to provide a comprehensive review of the Life RBC formula, but will instead discuss some highlights relevant to group insurance. For a full description, the reader is referred to the *NAIC Life Risk-Based Capital Report Including Overview and Instructions for companies.*

As of 2015, the Life RBC formula for RBC after covariance is:

$$RBCAC = C_0 + C_{4a} + \{(C_{1o} + C_{3a})^2 + (C_{1cs} + C_{3c})^2 + C_2^2 + C_{3b}^2 + C_{4b}^2\}^{1/2}$$

where;

$C_0 =$ Asset Risk for Affiliates
$C_{1cs} =$ Asset Risk for unaffiliated common stock and affiliated non-insurance stock
$C_{1o} =$ Asset risk – All other
$C_2 =$ Insurance risk
$C_{3a} =$ Interest rate risk
$C_{3b} =$ Health credit risk
$C_{3c} =$ Market risk
$C_{4a} =$ Business risk
$C_{4b} =$ Health administrative expense component of business risk

We noted previously that, for a typical health insurer, the underwriting risk component (here called "insurance risk") tends to dominate RBC after covariance. For a typical life insurer this is not the case. Other risk categories, such as asset risk and interest rate risk, tend to be more important for a life insurer than insurance risk. This implies that life insurers who also write health insurance may enjoy a lower effective capital requirement for health insurance than monoline health insurers, thanks to the so-called "diversification benefit" provided by the covariance adjustment.

INSURANCE RISK FACTORS

In general, the approach to the C_2 component of the Life RBC formula is heavily based on the Health RBC treatment of the H_2 component, as discussed above. The following summarizes some of the key differences in insurance risk factors between the Life and Health RBC formulas:

- *Individual Medical:* The Life formula applies a 20% load to the RBC requirement for individual comprehensive medical coverage, in recognition of the risk arising from the additional time needed to get premium rate increases filed and approved for individual products.

- *Claim Reserves:* The Life formula applies a 5% charge against all health claim reserves reported in Exhibit 6 of the Life and A&H annual statement (reserves for unaccrued benefits, as opposed to liabilities for unpaid claims), whereas the Health formula does this only for long-term care and disability reserves. This charge does not resolve the issues discussed above regarding reserving risk for health products that have claim liabilities rather than claim reserves, such as medical insurance.

- *Disability Income and Long-Term Care:* Superficially, the risk factors in the Life RBC formula for disability income and long-term care insurance appear to be materially higher than those found in the Health formula. This reflects a complex series of tax adjustments that have been implemented in certain portions of the Life formula. Once tax effects are netted out, the treatments of these products are consistent between the two formulas.

- *Group Life:* The Life formula includes a provision for group life insurance. The RBC requirement is based on a factor times the net amount at risk. The factor is tiered based on volume. For example, the factor is 0.18% for the first $500 million and grades down to 0.08% for amounts over $25 billion. The net amount at risk is based on life insurance face amount in force, less reserves.

- *Workers' Compensation Carve-Out:* During the late 1990s, it was common practice among P&C insurers to carve out the portions of workers' compensation risk that represented health and disability risk, rather than compensation liability risk, and cede it to life insurers. At the time, the RBC requirement in the Life formula for such risks was considerably less than that found in the NAIC P&C RBC formula. Thus, the assumptions of W/C carve-out risk by life insurers may be partly attributable to the desire to minimize capital requirements. The Life formula was modified to include special factors for this type of risk that are more consistent with the treatment in the P&C formula.

Comparison of the Life, P&C and Health RBC Formulas

Description of RBC components

Life RBC:
C_0 Insurance affiliate investment and (non-derivative) off-balance sheet risk
C_{1cs} Invested common stock asset risk
C_{1o} Invested asset risk, plus reinsurance credit risk except for assets in C1cs
C_2 Insurance risk
C_{3a} Interest rate risk
C_{3b} Health provider credit risk
C_{3c} Market risk
C_{4a} Business risk - guaranty fund assessment and separate account risks
C_{4b} Business risk - health administrative expense risk

> Company action level RBC =
> $C_0 + C_{4a} + \{(C_{1o} + C_{3a})^2 + (C_{1cs} + C_{3c})^2 + C_2^2 + C_{3b}^2 + C_{4b}^2\}^{1/2}$

P&C RBC:
R_0 Insurance affiliate investment and (non-derivative) off-balance sheet risk
R_1 Invested asset risk - fixed income investments
R_2 Invested asset risk - equity investments
R_3 Credit risk (non-reinsurance plus one half reinsurance credit risk)
R_4 Loss reserve risk, one half reinsurance credit risk, growth risk
R_5 Premium risk, growth risk

> Company action level RBC =
> $R_0 + [(R_1)^2 + (R_2)^2 + (R_3)^2 + (R_4)^2 + (R_5)^2]^{1/2}$

Health RBC:
H_0 Insurance affiliate investment and (non-derivative) off-balance sheet risk
H_1 Invested asset risk
H_2 Insurance risk
H_3 Credit risk (health provider, reinsurance, misc. receivables)
H_4 Business risk (health administrative expense risk, guaranty fund assessment risk, excessive growth)

> Company action level RBC =
> $H_0 + [(H_1)2 + (H_2)2 + (H_3)2 + (H_4)2]^{1/2}$

Developments of Health RBC

In June, 2008, the NAIC began its Solvency Modernization Initiative (SMI), which was generally completed in 2012. The SMI is a critical self-examination of the United States' insurance solvency regulation framework, and includes a review of international developments regarding insurance supervision, banking supervision, and international accounting standards and their potential use in U.S. insurance regulation. While the U.S.

insurance solvency regulation is updated on a continuous basis, the SMI focuses on five key solvency areas: capital requirements, international accounting, insurance valuation, reinsurance, and group regulatory issues.

As part of the SMI, the NAIC solicited the opinion of the American Academy of Actuaries, which sent a letter summarizing its findings in January, 2011. This letter summarized risks that have not yet been addressed by each of the current RBC formulas, and points out that all three RBC formulas are missing an explicit safety level for aggregate RBC. That is, each material risk has been studied and calibrated individually without a study of the overall risk profile. Although the SMI project was completed in 2012, the NAIC continues to review recommendations for implementation.

The workgroup identified missing risk considerations that are important to Health RBC, including pandemics, biologic terrorism, increased compliance costs and regulatory oversight (particularly in light of the Affordable Care Act), financial and reputational risks caused by privacy breaches, longer-duration products that have newly emerged and are not properly addressed by the Health RBC formulas, and a number of financial risks caused by the Minimum Loss Ratio, rate review, guaranteed issue, and risk adjustment provisions of the Affordable Care Act. Consideration of how to address these risks within the RBC formula continues to be discussed at the NAIC. For example, Interrogatories on Pandemic & Biological Risk were developed. In 2014, it was found that only eight of the 858 companies completing the pandemic risk page said they allocate a component of surplus for pandemic and biological risks. As a result of analyzing this information, the page was deleted for the 2015 reporting year.

The continuous review process that is implicit in the development and evolution of the Health RBC formula is intended to ensure that updates to the formula to address emerging risks are considered and implemented as appropriate.

Section Seven

Financial and Actuarial Analysis

40 APPLIED STATISTICS

Robert B. Cumming
Stuart A. Klugman
Hans K. Leida
Doug Norris

This chapter provides a brief summary of applied statistics for the practicing actuary. The exposition relies on a number of real-world examples. The intent is to show actuaries a sampling of possible statistics applications and to introduce some basic concepts and considerations. Given the focus and space limitations, this chapter is not a how-to document, nor does it provide in-depth theoretical background. There is a bibliography at the end of this chapter for further, more detailed information on theory and methods.

This chapter is organized into key topics for actuaries, including group insurance data, stochastic simulation, regression, parametric modeling, credibility theory, confidence intervals and the Central Limit Theorem.

GROUP INSURANCE DATA

Group insurance data, especially group health data, exhibits the behavior of a two-year old child. It can be easy to deal with and understand, then become inconsistent and uncooperative in the blink of an eye. Group insurance data violates many of the standard assumptions that make statistical methods so powerful. For example, group insurance data is neither necessarily independent nor identically distributed. Claim cost probability distributions are typically skewed, and the amount of skewness varies depending on group size, among other factors. Also, many times there is only one observation available per event, so a random sample, for use in developing distributions or estimators, is never available. Even time series techniques can be difficult due to the level of correlation. Finally, this type of data can be subject to varying levels of trend.

Most actuaries opt to use actual claim data instead of trying to develop parametric models. There are two reasons for this. First, overcoming the data issues mentioned above is time consuming, and may not provide additional precision. Second, the data already contains many important factors, so instead of developing complicated models that take these factors into account, the data is used directly.

These characteristics of the data help explain why many of the models used by group actuaries have not been very sophisticated. Using significant analytical horsepower on messy data merely gives the illusion of better estimates.

However, the complicated nature of the health insurance business calls for better analytical tools. More computing power and inexpensive statistical software make these methods more accessible to the practicing actuary. "Big data" techniques have gained popularity among actuaries, and the amount of data currently available presents both opportunities and challenges. As mentioned above, it is important to know what the underlying assumptions are for a given technique, how the data complies with these assumptions, and what happens when some of the assumptions are not met.

STOCHASTIC SIMULATION

Stochastic simulation is a useful technique for modeling a wide variety of complex insurance systems. Stochastic simulation, also known as Monte Carlo simulation, has been used to model many actuarial applications, including financial and utilization projections for continuing care retirement communities, capital requirements for risk based capital models, aggregate claim distributions, stop loss pricing, reserve distributions, and investment and asset allocation strategies. Before a discussion about stochastic simulation, it is useful to review background on the differences between *stochastic* and *deterministic* models.

STOCHASTIC VERSUS DETERMINISTIC MODELS

Generally speaking, deterministic models provide information regarding the *expected or average value* of a random variable. In contrast, stochastic models are used to provide information regarding the *statistical distribution* of a random variable. The random variable might be the surplus of an insurance company, the number of people in a nursing facility, or the aggregate medical claims for a group of 1,000 people. For example, a deterministic model can be used to estimate the expected surplus of an insurance company after five years. However, the model does not provide an estimate of the likelihood of that expected surplus value, nor of other possible values. In particular, it doesn't provide an estimate of the likelihood of negative surplus, which constitutes insolvency of the company. To investigate the likelihood of insolvency, a stochastic model is needed.

Before performing a simulation, the first step is to construct a stochastic model for the insurance system. In general, a stochastic model differs from a deterministic model in that some of the inputs are probability distributions rather than point estimates. For example, medical trend might be modeled with a probability distribution rather than a single point estimate. Usually, the most difficult part of constructing a stochastic model is developing probability distributions for the various input parameters. After the stochastic model is constructed, simulations can be performed. Two other important areas of study in performing stochastic simulation include the number of simulations necessary to accurately estimate results and the computer generation of random numbers. These topics are discussed in some of the references listed at the end of this chapter.

SIMULATION IN ACTION

Real-world insurance systems are often so complex that it is practically impossible to determine exact deterministic model solutions. In such situations, stochastic simulation becomes the only practical approach to obtain results.

The major advantage of simulation is that there is virtually no restriction on the setting to which it can be applied. In particular, it is not necessary that the random variables be identical or independent, so long as the nature of the departure is known. Also, there is no limit on how accurate the results can be, other than the aforementioned difficulty in determining appropriate probability distributions for the inputs. If the underlying random variables are modeled appropriately, then the introduction of additional trials will improve the accuracy of the overall simulation. The disadvantage of simulation is that it can be slow.

A stochastic simulation is composed of many "runs" or "trials." For each trial, a random number is generated each time a random variable is encountered in the stochastic model. This random number is used to determine the outcome for that random variable. For example, the random variable might be the level of medical claims for an individual or group. For each trial, the financial, population, or other quantities of interest are calculated, and with the results of many trials, a probability distribution for those quantities can be developed.

The following examples illustrate the stochastic simulation process.

SIMPLE EXAMPLE

This example illustrates the general process of performing a stochastic simulation. Consider the following insurance system:

- Number of people insured at start of period = 5
- For each insured person at the start of the period, the probability of lapse is 20% and the probability of death is 20% during the period.

Deterministic Model: The deterministic model for this insurance system would give us the following results:

Time	Number Lapsed	Number Dead	Number Alive	Total
Start	0	0	5	5
End	1	1	3	5

In the deterministic model, we calculate the expected value for the number of people lapsing and dying. The expected value is calculated as the number of people (5) times the probability of lapse (20%) or death (20%). This model doesn't tell us anything about the likelihood of different outcomes. For example, what is the likelihood that two people die, or that everyone is still alive, at the end of the period? To answer these questions we must construct a stochastic model.

Stochastic Model: The key input in our stochastic model is a probability distribution for the status of each person at the end of the period. Given the above information, the probability distribution for the status of a person at the end of the period is as follows:

Status at End of Period (x)	Probability [$f(x)$]
Lapsed	0.2
Dead	0.2
Alive	0.6

Stochastic Simulation: The stochastic simulation process involves the following steps: (1) determine the cumulative probability distribution (CPD) for each random variable in our model, (2) for each trial, generate a random number for each random variable, (3) based on the random numbers, determine the value for each random variable, and (4) calculate quantities of interest and summarize results of the trials.

Step 1: The cumulative probability distribution is:

Status at End of Period	CPD
Lapsed	0.2
Dead	0.4
Alive	1.0

Step 2: Generate random numbers using a $U(0,1)$ distribution:

The following shows the random numbers for two trials. For each trial, we generate a random number for each of the five people.

Trial	Person				
	1	2	3	4	5
1	0.783	0.280	0.561	0.467	0.989
2	0.506	0.392	0.101	0.875	0.370

Step 3: Based on the generated random numbers, determine values for random variables in the stochastic model:

Each random number in the table above corresponds to a particular status at the end of the period for that person. We compare the random number against the cumulative probability distribution in Step 1 to determine the status. If the random number is between 0.0 and 0.2, then that person lapses. If the random number is between 0.2 and 0.4, then that person dies. If the random number is between 0.4 and 1.0, then that person stays alive. Given this relationship, the following table shows the status of each person for each trial:

Trial	Person				
	1	2	3	4	5
1	alive	dead	alive	alive	alive
2	alive	dead	lapsed	alive	dead

Step 4: Calculate quantities of interest and summarize results:

For each trial, the following table summarizes the number of people who lapse, die, and remain alive.

Trial	No. Lapsed	No. Dead	No. Alive	Total
1	0	1	4	5
2	1	2	2	5

If we count up the number of trials where a particular outcome occurs, and divide this by the total number of trials, the resulting proportion tells us the estimated probability outcome. For example, the following table shows the probability distribution for the number of people who die based on a 1,000 trial simulation.

Number of Deaths	Probability based on 1,000 Trial Simulation	Actual Probability (based on binomial)
0	0.334	0.3277
1	0.423	0.4096
2	0.192	0.2048
3	0.045	0.0512
4	0.006	0.0064
5	0.000	0.0003
Average # Deaths	**0.966**	**1.0000**

For this simple model, we can analytically determine the exact answer using a binomial distribution. The actual probabilities are shown in the last column in the table given above.

The above table shows results for a 1,000 trial simulation. In real applications, we typically perform far more trials. As we increase the number of trials, the results from the stochastic simulation should become closer and closer to the expected outcome.

By monitoring the variation in results as the number of trials is increased, it is possible to get a sense of whether results appear to be stable or not. This can help inform the decision of the number of trials needed for a given simulation. Depending upon how simple the underlying distributions are, one could determine a confidence interval for the expected outcome, given the number of trials performed.

REGRESSION

This section discusses regression analysis and the method of least squares. Regression analysis is used to study the relationship between two or more variables. One common situation is to use regression to fit a line to actual data points. The fitted line might then be used to predict the outcome for the dependent variable given values for the independent variables. It might also be used to determine a parameter of interest, such as the average trend in medical costs. The method of least squares is a commonly used technique to determine the best fitting line for a collection of data points.

SIMPLE LINEAR REGRESSION

Given two random variables, X and Y, the basic purpose of regression analysis is to estimate the expected value of Y given a particular value of X. The regression is linear if the expected value of Y given $X = x$ can be expressed as

$$E[Y|x] = a + bx.$$

The constants a and b are referred to as regression coefficients. The regression equation shown above is referred to as simple or bivariate since there is only one independent variable. If there is more than one independent variable, the regression is referred to as multiple or multivariate.

If the regression of Y on X is linear, then

$$E[Y|X] = E[Y] + (x - E[X]) \times \frac{Cov(X,Y)}{Var(X)}.$$

If $Cov(X,Y) = 0$, then X and Y are said to be uncorrelated. Note that if two random variables are independent, they are also uncorrelated. However, two random variables that are uncorrelated are not necessarily independent.

METHOD OF LEAST SQUARES

Least squares is a method of curve-fitting that can be used to estimate the a and b coefficients in the linear regression equation shown above. Given a set of paired data (x_i, y_i), for $i = 1, 2, \ldots, n$. each y_i can be expressed as

$$y_i = a + bx_i + e_i.$$

The e_i variable is called the "error" term. The e_i term represents the error between the actual value (y_i) and the fitted value $(\hat{y}_i = a + bx_i)$. One way to measure how well a particular line fits the data is to calculate the sum of the squared error terms. The lower this sum, the lower the cumulative error, and the better the fit. The method of least squares gives the values of a and b that minimize the sum of the squared errors.[1] That is, the a and b least squares coefficients result in the lowest possible value for the quantity $\sum_i e_i^2$.

---

[1] While least squares estimation has many desirable statistical properties, it can also tend to give too much weight to outliers, since it minimizes *squared* error rather than *absolute* error. In practice, the effect of a deviation on a company's balance sheet is typically more consistent with absolute error. Robust regression techniques can be used to try to compensate for this limitation of least squares estimation.

The least squares coefficients can be calculated as

$$b = \frac{\sum_i [(x_i - \bar{x}) y_i]}{\sum_i (x_i - \bar{x})^2}$$

$$a = \bar{y} - b\bar{x}.$$

The sum of the squared errors can also be written as

$$\sum_i (y_i - \bar{y})^2 = \sum_i (\hat{y}_i - \bar{y})^2 + \sum_i (y_i - \hat{y}_i)^2$$

(Total Variation) = (Explained Variation) + (Residual Variation)

Therefore, the total variability of y can be separated into the portion explained by movement of y with x (the explained variation) and the portion that is not due to the movement of y with x (the unexplained or residual variation). The fraction of the total variation that is explained by the linear relationship of y and x is called the coefficient of determination and is often denoted as R^2.

TRANSFORMATIONS

The use of least squares methods is not limited to situations where there is a linear relationship between two variables. In situations where the hypothesized relationship is non-linear, it is often possible to transform the relationship into a linear form. This allows use of the standard formulas given above for calculating the regression coefficients. The most common transformations involve taking the logarithm, reciprocal, or square root of both sides of the mathematical relationship between the dependent and independent variables.

For example, suppose that $Z = c \cdot W^d$. With natural logarithms, this relationship can be transformed into the form $\ln(Z) = \ln(c) + d \cdot \ln(W)$. This is the standard linear equation with $Y = \ln(Z)$, $a = \ln(c)$, $b = d$, and $X = \ln(W)$.

WEIGHTED LEAST SQUARES

The least squares approach described above minimizes the sum of the squared errors placing *equal weight* on each error term. In situations where the data points do not have equal levels of credibility, it may be desirable to weight the error terms differently. For example, suppose loss ratios (LR_t) are tracked by policy duration (t) for a block of health insurance business. This gives a series of data points (LR_t, t) for $t = 1, 2, \ldots, n$. In such situations, premium volume or exposure will be much higher for the early durations than for the later durations, and more weight or credibility would be placed on the early duration data points.

For weighted least squares, a and b would be selected so as to minimize the quantity

$$\text{Weighted Error} = \sum_i w_i[y_i - (a+bx_i)]^2$$

where w_i is the weight or credibility placed on the ith data point.

EXAMPLE: Selection Factors

This example illustrates the use of least squares to fit a curve to a series of data points. In this example, we use a transformation to convert the underlying relationship into a linear form. Also, due to different levels of credibility for different data points, we use the weighted least squares approach.

We have summarized the experience for a block of individual major medical coverage by policy duration. Policy duration is measured in calendar quarters since time of issue. Before summarizing the data by duration, we (1) removed the effects of inflation by trending all the claims to the same point in time; and (2) adjusted the earned premium to a common rate basis. The durational experience is shown in Table 40.1.

Table 40.1

Quarterly Policy Duration (t)	Trend Adjusted Claims	Earned Premium (EP)	Loss Ratio (LR)
1	1,427,208	6,105,064	23.4%
2	2,460,583	8,313,219	29.6
3	3,127,488	7,390,382	42.3
4	3,180,396	6,668,387	47.7
5	2,622,893	6,045,283	43.4
6	3,008,615	5,491,767	54.8
7	2,745,605	5,065,495	54.2
8	3,028,875	4,579,158	66.1
9	2,291,655	4,226,507	54.2
10	2,429,329	3,911,945	62.1
11	2,127,282	3,451,455	61.6
12	1,893,402	2,475,416	76.5
13	1,091,865	1,724,905	63.3
14	641,909	1,218,075	52.7
15	662,507	919,120	72.1
16	495,989	581,130	85.3
17	280,048	312,557	89.6
18	131,357	134,925	97.4
19	1,312	25,651	5.1
Total	33,648,318	68,640,441	49.0

The loss ratios (LR_t) by duration (t) represent a set of (x,y) data points where $y = LR_t$ and $x = t$. We used the method of least squares to fit a curve to these data points. The wear-off of initial underwriting[2] causes the loss ratios by duration to rise steeply at first. Cumulative antiselection at the later durations can cause the loss ratios to continue to rise, but generally at a slower rate than during the early durations. This means that the selection factors by duration tend to have a concave down shape rather than the straight line of a linear relationship. This non-linear shape is the reason we assumed that $LR_t = \ln(a+bt)$. Consequently, we exponentiate each side to transform to $\exp(LR_t) = a+bt$, a linear form.

As can be seen in the table above, the amount of exposure or earned premium varies significantly by policy duration. For example, the amount of earned premium for duration quarter two is over 300 times as great as the earned premium for duration quarter 19. Due to the limited amount of premium for the later durations, we certainly would not want to put as much credibility on the later durations as on the early durations. Therefore, we decided to use the method of *weighted* least squares, using earned premium by duration as weights.

Using the method of weighted least squares, we get the fitted loss ratios shown in the following table.

Table 40.2

Quarterly Policy Duration (t)	Fitted Loss Ratio	Actual Loss Ratio
1	30.7%	23.4%
2	34.8	29.6
3	38.7	42.3
4	42.5	47.7
5	46.1	43.4
6	49.6	54.8
7	53.0	54.2
8	56.2	66.1
9	59.4	54.2
10	62.5	62.1
11	65.5	61.6
12	68.4	76.5
13	71.2	63.3
14	73.9	52.7
15	76.6	72.1
16	79.2	85.3
17	81.7	89.6
18	84.2	97.4
19	86.6	5.1

---

[2] The Affordable Care Act prohibits medical underwriting for non-grandfathered, non-transitional individual major medical policies with coverage beginning in 2014 or later. The durational effects in the example are reflective of the pre-ACA environment, where underwriting was permitted in most states. The durational effects in the example are still relevant for blocks of grandfathered or transitional policies that were issued prior to 2014 and were subject to underwriting.

The fitted loss ratio is calculated using the equation:

$$\text{Fitted loss ratio} = \ln(a+bt)$$

where $a = 1.302796$ and $b = 0.05652$. The equations for calculating the a and b coefficients are shown below:

$$b = \frac{\sum_t EP_t \cdot \sum_t EP_t \cdot t \cdot \exp(LR_t) - \sum_t EP_t \cdot t \sum_t EP_t \cdot t \cdot \exp(LR_t)}{\sum_t EP_t \cdot \sum_t EP_t \cdot t^2 \left(\sum_t EP_t \cdot t \right)^2}$$

$$a = \frac{\sum_t EP_t \cdot \exp(LR_t) - b \cdot \sum_t EP_t \cdot t}{\sum_t EP_t}$$

Figure 40.1 shows a plot of the actual and fitted loss ratios by policy duration.

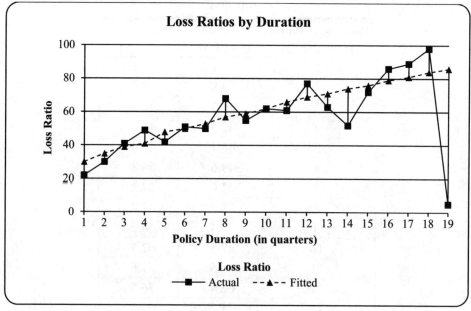

Figure 40.1

ADVANCED REGRESSION TECHNIQUES

There are a wide variety of more advanced regression techniques. These include the use of more than one independent variable (multiple regression), stepwise regression, logistic regression, and neural networks, to name just a few.

MULTIPLE REGRESSION

Multiple regression is useful when there are a number of variables that impact the quantity in which we are interested. One example of this comes from diagnosis-based risk adjustment models, such as the HHS-HCC models used to calculate the Affordable Care Act (ACA) risk adjustment transfer payments between carriers. These models are designed with many independent variables (commonly 100 or more). In these models, each independent variable represents the presence or absence of a particular medical condition, such as diabetes, skin cancer, or hypertension. For each variable, there is a parameter or coefficient that represents the marginal cost of having that medical condition. Multiple regression techniques are used to determine an appropriate set of parameters based on actual claim data for a large set of members.

Risk adjustment models have become more sophisticated over time, and many now use other data elements beyond diagnosis codes, such as prescription drug codes or even lifestyle data available through marketing databases. Besides having a variety of uses in health plans on commercial populations, such as to normalize risk between commercial ACA carriers, risk adjuster models are also used in many managed Medicaid programs, as well as in Medicare Advantage and Medicare Part D plans. More information can be found in research sponsored by the Society of Actuaries.[3]

OVERFITTING AND REGULARIZED REGRESSION

One limitation of regression methods relates to the problem of *overfitting*, which occurs when a regression model misinterprets random data qualities as representative of a predictive relationship between variables. This often occurs when the number of parameters is high relative to the number of observed data points. As an example, one can always perfectly fit an *(n-1)* degree polynomial through any collection of *n* data points; however, the calculated polynomial may not have the ability to reasonably estimate any data points not used in its construction. The performance of regression models should be judged based on their accuracy with data not used to develop the model. For this reason, it is common to set aside a portion of the available data prior to fitting the model in order to create a validation data set.

Regularization techniques are often used in regression model construction in order to combat potential overfitting. These techniques introduce a penalty function to the overall error function being minimized. For linear regression, some of the more common regularization techniques are ridge (or Tikhonov) regularization, LASSO regularization, and elastic net regularization. Implementations of these methods can be readily found for the SAS and R programming languages,[4] among others.

STEPWISE REGRESSION

The process of stepwise regression is to begin with a set of independent variables and pare them down to include only those that make a significant contribution to the regression model.[5] This can be done in a variety of ways, such as starting with the entire set of independent variables

---

[3] See "A Comparative Analysis of Claims Based Methods of Health Risk Assessment for Commercial Populations" by Ross Winkelman and Syed Mehmud (Society of Actuaries, 2007).

[4] In addition, the open-source statistical software R includes the ability to perform the majority of the other statistical techniques discussed in this chapter, so might be a good choice for students interested in trying these methods out. As of this writing, *R* is freely available at www.r-project.org for a variety of computer platforms.

[5] The general principle of *parsimony* says that simpler models should be preferred over more complex ones, all else being equal. Stepwise regression is one way to find a more parsimonious model.

and discarding those that are not statistically significant. Alternatively, an analysis can start with the individual variable that makes the greatest contribution and then add additional variables to the set. There are many ways to set the criteria for including independent variables in the model. This methodology is covered in most textbooks on regression.

An application of this technique is in forecasting incurred fee-for-service non-drug health claims. This can be a very difficult task, especially if the forecast is for more than one or two months. The level of claims depend on a variety of factors such as claim inventories, the level of paid claims for the current and prior months, and drug claims. Other factors might also include the severity of the flu season or changes in a therapeutic regimen. Assuming a credible dataset is available, all of these factors can be fed into a stepwise regression analysis. One of the benefits of this technique is that there are confidence intervals for each estimate. The SAS and R software packages mentioned earlier include an option to do stepwise regression, as do most other common statistical software packages.

LOGISTIC REGRESSION

Suppose an estimate is needed, of the probability p that one of two alternatives occurs, given the explanatory variables $x_1, x_2, \ldots, x_n$. For example, the probability that an individual will have an inpatient stay in a given year, using the individual's observed medical and prescription drug data for the prior year as predictive variables, is desired for a projection.

Based on the prior sections, a multiple linear regression model might appear to be an appropriate fit for the data. However, this is problematic, because the multiple regression model assumes the dependent variable is continuous. If the data is coded so that members observed to have an inpatient stay are flagged with a one, and that members without an inpatient stay are flagged with a zero, then the multiple regression model might predict that someone has flags other than 0 or 1, such as −2.2 or +5. It is unclear how to interpret such results.

Logistic regression is designed to avoid this issue by using the logit function.[6] The *logit* function is

$$\text{logit}(p) = \ln\left(\frac{p}{1-p}\right).$$

This function has the key property of translating a probability p defined on the closed interval [0, 1] to a range spanning the entire real line, which is the range of output we get from a linear model.

More precisely, the form of the logistic model is as follows:

$$\text{logit}(p) = \ln(o) = \ln\left(\frac{p}{1-p}\right) = \beta_0 + \beta_1 x_1 + \beta_2 x_2 + \cdots + \beta_n x_n,$$

---

[6] The logit function is the inverse of the *logistic* function $f(x) = \dfrac{1}{1+e^{-x}}$, from which the model gets its name. Logistic regression is an example of a *generalized linear model*, a wide class of models generalizing linear regression.

where o is the *odds ratio* $p/(1-p)$ and β_0 through β_n are coefficients to be estimated. Each coefficient explains how the "log-odds" change for a given change in the corresponding explanatory variable.

Exponentiating both sides of the equation above, gives

$$o = e^{\beta_0} e^{\beta_1 x_1} e^{\beta_2 x_2} \cdots e^{\beta_n x_n}.$$

A simplified example should help to clarify. Suppose we only have one explanatory variable x_1, a flag that is equal to one if a member has been diagnosed with cancer in the base year and zero otherwise. Suppose also that the coefficient β_1 is estimated as 0.693. Then when $x_1 = 1$, the odds are increased by a factor of $e^{0.693} \approx 2.0$, and when $x_1 = 0$, the odds are unchanged. In other words, this fictitious model says that observing a cancer diagnosis doubles the odds of having an inpatient stay in the following year.

Coefficients for logistic models are typically estimated numerically using maximum likelihood estimation. Many inexpensive or free statistical software packages are available to perform these calculations.

The logistic regression model has many cousins that are useful in other situations, such as when the dependent variable is discrete, but not binary. These are covered in many statistics textbooks.

EXAMPLE: Small Group Lapse Rates

For a more realistic example, we turn to lapse rates in an actual portfolio of small group major medical policies. In this example, "lapse rate" will reflect the probability that a group terminates its contract with the insurer (voluntarily or otherwise), and not the turnover of individual members within each group.

One factor that influences lapse rates among small groups is the change in each group's premium rates from one year to the next. This example is based on a study of approximately 24,000 small group renewals at an insurer. For each renewal, the percentage change in premium rates (prior to any benefit changes) was recorded, along with whether or not the group terminated at renewal.

In the study, the average rate change was an increase of 7.6%, and 8.8% of groups lapsed overall. For forecasting purposes, we would like to predict how many groups will lapse at future renewals. One option would be to predict that 8.8% of groups will lapse uniformly across the portfolio. However, a better prediction would take into account the rate increase received by each group, as larger increases typically increase the lapsation probability dramatically.

To model this relationship, we can fit a logistic regression model to the observed data. The regression equation takes the form

$$\text{logit}(p) = \beta_0 + \beta_1 x_1,$$

where p is the probability of lapsation and x_1 is the rate change offered to the group (for example, +10%).

On this data, the coefficients were estimated as $\beta_0 = -3.00$ and $\beta_1 = 6.15$. In other words, for every percentage point of rate increase, the odds of lapsing increase by a factor of $e^{6.15 \times 0.01} \approx 1.063$.

We can predict the probability of lapsing for a particular group as well. For example, suppose a group is going to receive a 20% rate increase. Then the odds of lapsing are given by

$$o = \frac{p}{1-p} = e^{\beta_0} e^{\beta_1 x_1} = e^{-3.00} e^{6.15 \times 0.20} \approx 0.17.$$

Solving the equation above for p gives an estimated a probability of lapsing of approximately 15% for this group. Figure 40.2 below compares the modeled probability to the observed lapsation for the renewals in the study.

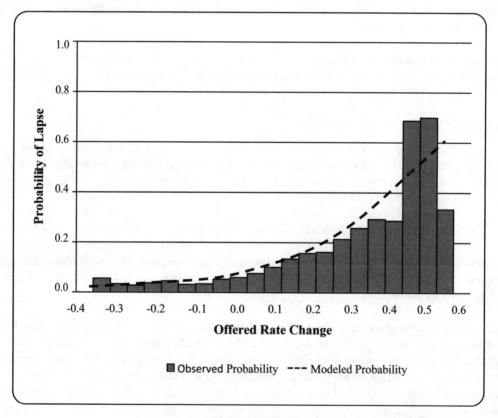

Figure 40.2

This logistic model could be improved by including other group characteristics that might influence lapse rates as additional explanatory variables, such as the size and duration of each group. The model might also take into account environmental factors such as the economic climate and competitiveness of the insurer's rates in the marketplace over time.

NEURAL NETWORKS AND COMPLEXITY THEORY

Neural networks are mentioned here because they are a nonlinear extension of linear regression. This tool takes inputs like those mentioned in the discussion of stepwise regression and constructs a predictive model. There are advantages and disadvantages to the use of neural networks. The main advantage is that a model does not need to be specified. The program uses the data to construct the appropriate model. This is also one of the greatest drawbacks to the methodology, since there is no straightforward way to determine how the independent variables flow through the calculations. This makes it difficult to explain the results.

Neural networks, agent-based models, and related complexity science techniques are beginning to be used by practicing actuaries. Given the increasing availability of large data sets and powerful computing resources, it seems likely that their use will become more prevalent in the future. There are many good books on this topic and there are some inexpensive (even free) software packages that will enable the actuary to experiment with these methodologies. For a comprehensive survey of complexity techniques, the reader may refer to the 2010 SOA study "Complexity Science—an introduction (and invitation) for actuaries" by Alan Mills.

PARAMETRIC MODELING

Parametric methods are not typically used in modeling group insurance. When statistical distributions are needed, actuaries will most often rely on stochastic simulations based on empirical data (simulations address many of the drawbacks regarding empirical methods, such as the desire to test different hypotheses related to the distribution, or the sometimes rough nature of the underlying data.) However, parametric techniques have some desirable properties and should be part of any practicing actuary's arsenal.

The material in this section is a brief summary of some of the considerations involved when using parametric models. This information is taken from the text *Loss Models: From Data to Decisions*, 2nd Edition by Klugman, Panjer, and Willmot [2004].

THE EMPIRICAL APPROACH

Given a sample of size n from a population, the empirical distribution is a model that assigns probability $1/n$ to each observed value. The next step is to pretend that the model accurately describes the population and then to compute quantities of interest from the model. The following example illustrates this process.

Example: Individual Dental Claims[7]

Basic dental coverage claims were recorded for a period of time. The policy has a deductible of $25, no limit, and no coinsurance. In a one week period, there were 10 claims, which resulted in the following 10 payments (post-deductible, arranged in increasing order):

$$\$14 \quad \$63 \quad \$88 \quad \$101 \quad \$104 \quad \$150 \quad \$178 \quad \$248 \quad \$259 \quad \$292$$

The following questions are of interest:

- What is the expected payment?
- What would the expected payment be if the deductible is removed and how many extra payments will there be?
- If the deductible is increased to $50, what will be the expected payment, and how many fewer payments will there be?
- How will the answers to these questions change if there is 10% inflation?

The empirical model assigns probability 0.1 to each of the ten numbers. The mean is computed by multiplying each payment by 0.1 to yield an expected claim payment of $149.70.

If the deductible is removed, $25 must be added to each claim payment. The empirical estimate of the mean is $174.70, but removing the deductible will introduce additional payments in the $0 to $25 range. Normally, insurance companies have data on payments below the deductible in order to determine when the deductible is reached. As a result, adjustments can be made to the empirical distribution for claims below the deductible. On the other hand, if the deductible is raised to $50, the ten payments become nine (the covered expense of $39 does not produce a payment):

$$\$38 \quad \$63 \quad \$76 \quad \$79 \quad \$125 \quad \$153 \quad \$223 \quad \$234 \quad \$267$$

Thus, if the deductible is raised to $50, the empirical estimate of the expected payment is the sample mean of $139.78, and the empirical estimate of payment frequency is that 10% of the payments will be eliminated. Note that if the deductible is raised to $60, the empirical estimate of the expected payment will be reduced by $10, and the estimated reduction in the number of payments remains at 10% (one of the ten original claims does not meet the higher deductible). This lack of continuity is a drawback of the empirical approach.

USING PARAMETRIC MODELS

Construction of a *parametric model* follows three steps. The first is to postulate a model. This typically consists of choosing from a named distribution family such as gamma or Weibull. Such families consist of the probability density function (*pdf*) of the random variable that defines the distribution of claims in the population. The function has one or more unspecified quantities, called *parameters*. By changing the value(s) of the parameter(s), various distributional shapes are obtained that are somewhat similar, in the

---

[7] All the numerical values used in the remainder of this chapter are artificial. Context is provided to make them more readable, but no conclusions regarding appropriate models for actuarial practice should be drawn.

sense that a family has certain general characteristics, but that allow some flexibility to provide a match to the data.

The second step is to use the data to estimate the value of the parameter(s). While many methods are available, in the absence of a compelling reason to do otherwise, maximum likelihood estimation is the preferred method.

The third step is to validate the choice of model by verifying that it adequately represents the data. This is often done with the chi-square goodness-of-fit test.

EXAMPLE: Basic Dental Coverage (Continued)

If we choose the covered expense for our random variable x, rather than the claim payment post-deductible, the resulting model will represent covered expenses. We are concerned with the probability (or probability density function) of observing a particular claim value, given the parametric model. With a continuous model and a deductible of $25, the contribution of an observation of x is $f(x)/[1-F(25)]$.

Suppose we have already found that a Weibull model is an appropriate choice for these claims. That is,

$$f(x) = \tau\theta^{-\tau}x^{\tau-1}e^{-(x/\theta)^\tau}, \quad F(x) = 1 - e^{-(x/\theta)^\tau}, \quad x, \ \theta > 0.$$

Also suppose that the likelihood function is maximized at $\tau = 2.11526$ and $\theta = 197.566$.

When using parametric models, once the model is determined, the data is discarded and all future calculations are done under the assumption that the population of claims follows the estimated parametric distribution. One drawback of the parametric method is that, to the extent the chosen model is not a perfect fit for the data, there is some information being lost.

When the deductible is removed, the expected claim payment value is the mean of the Weibull distribution, $174.98. The probability of a claim being below $25 is 0.0125 and so the number of payments could be expected to increase by $1/0.9875 - 1$ or 1.3%. Similarly, the probability of a claim being below $50 is 0.0532, and so raising the deductible will eliminate $1 - 0.9468/0.9875$ or 4.1% of the payments.

Each of the above numbers can be calculated directly, either from the distribution itself, or from known characteristics of the Weibull distribution. It is possible to answer many other questions, but that will not be done here.

PARAMETRIC VS. EMPIRICAL MODELS

Parametric models are more tractable mathematically. However, the ability to manipulate data with today's computers mitigates this advantage somewhat. Empirical models do not have the nice mathematical properties of parametric models, but they reflect the actual experience of a population covered by a specific set of benefits.

One important byproduct of parametric models is the ability to construct confidence intervals.

Both methods are capable of reflecting inflation. This involves adjusting the empirical distribution for claims under the deductible as mentioned above.

As claim data changes due to trend, mandated benefits, and a variety of other influences, there is no guarantee that a parametric distribution that fits the data one year will be adequate the next, even if adjusted for these external influences. As a result, there could be discontinuities in premium rates, capitation rates, and reserves. Also, inferences drawn from one distribution may not be true under another distribution. As a result, it is sometimes necessary to use actual data. For example, it is easier to convince corporate management, regulators, and customers, that reserves or premium rates are appropriate if the actuary uses actual experience data. Also, there are times when actuaries are required to use actual claim data in their calculations.

Choosing a parametric model, and comparing the results with original empirical data, produces two sets of answers to the same problem. Aside from the smoothness provided by the parametric solution, there is no reason to believe that the parametric answers are more accurate. The true values can never be known (otherwise these statistical approaches would not be needed), and so the best that can be done is to ask which procedure, over the long run, tends to produce better answers.

There are two quantities of interest when evaluating an estimation procedure. *Bias* refers to the extent by which, on average, the process over- or under-estimates the true value. In particular, an *unbiased* estimation method has errors that cancel out over the long run, yielding an average error of zero. *Variance* refers to the degree to which the estimation method produces values that vary from its long-run average. This is the usual variance measure, and is often called sampling error or sampling variation. The ideal situation is to have a method that is unbiased, and has the smallest variance among unbiased methods. For large samples, maximum likelihood estimators will be unbiased and have the smallest variance.[8]

Another advantage of the parametric method is that, via the likelihood ratio test (available in most mathematical statistics texts), various statements about the population can be tested. One example would be to see if the deductible affects the distribution.

An additional benefit of a parametric model is the ability to smooth grouped observations, which is demonstrated in the next example.

EXAMPLE: Grouped Dental Expenses

Covered expenses on dental coverage were recorded and grouped. The coverage had a deductible of $50. The results were 57 claims between $50 and $100, 42 between $100 and $150, 65 between $150 and $250, 84 between $250 and $500, 45 between $500 and $1,000, 10 between $1,000 and $1,500, and 14 above $1,500.

A histogram describing the claims up to $1,500 appears in Figure 40.3. When constructing a histogram from grouped data, the height of each bar is the number of claims in the interval

---

[8] Maximum likelihood estimators are described in most undergraduate statistics textbooks. Much is known about the maximum likelihood estimators for many well-known parametric families, which allows for computational ease in choosing parameters

divided by both the sample size and the width of the interval. The first bar has a height of $\frac{57}{(317)(50)} = 0.003596$. Empirical estimates can be obtained by treating the histogram as a probability density function. Parameters can be estimated by maximum likelihood.

Assuming a lognormal distribution, where $F(x) = \Phi[(\ln x - \mu)/\sigma]$ and $\Phi(x)$ is the standard normal cumulative density function, we can calculate the values of μ and σ that will give us a maximum likelihood function. The texts referenced at the end of this chapter provide additional and related formulas.

In this case, we find that the likelihood function is maximized at $\mu = 5.32037$ and $\sigma = 1.09285$. These parameters allow us to define our model for dental claim costs. Now that we have a model, questions about inflation or deductible changes can be answered. The quality of the model can be checked by comparing the density function of the lognormal model to the histogram. Figure 40.3 demonstrates that the model provides an excellent fit.

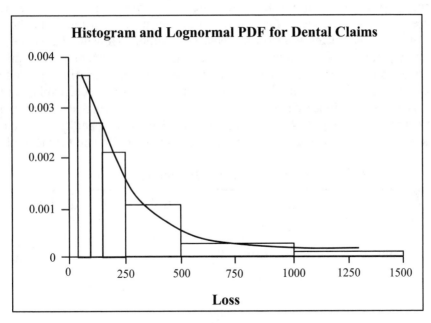

Figure 40.3

DETERMINING AN ACCEPTABLE PARAMETRIC MODEL

Once it has been decided to use a parametric model, the search begins for the right model There are a large number of parametric families. Motivation for many of these in an actuarial context is given in Venter [1984]. One feature of many of these families is that they are special or limiting cases of others. For example, when one of the parameters of the Burr distribution is set equal to one, a Pareto distribution is obtained. Because few of the models have a direct physical motivation, it is usually not possible to postulate a model in advance. If time and computational resources allow, it may be reasonable to simply try a wide variety of models and see which performs the best.

For each model, the chi-square goodness-of-fit test can be constructed. As a hypothesis test, it can be used to determine which models are acceptable. The *p*-value from the hypothesis test can also be used to rank the models from best (highest *p*-value) to worst. Another way to rank models is by the value of the likelihood function at its maximum. The model that maximizes the likelihood function at the highest value would seem to be the best.

Adding an extra parameter guarantees a higher likelihood value, but also makes the model more complicated. Therefore, when selecting an appropriate model, one must balance the need for a high degree of fit with the need for simplicity. The *principle of parsimony* suggests that, given two models of comparable quality, the simpler or more elegant model should be chosen. It is easier to interpret and explain simpler models, and it is also easier to gather necessary data for a simpler model. The likelihood ratio test suggests that to justify an additional parameter, the natural logarithm of the likelihood function should increase by at least 1.92 (representing a 5% significance level for the Chi-squared distribution).[9]

EXAMPLE: Grouped Dental Claims (Continued)

In the following table, results from fitting ten models by maximum likelihood are presented. All pass the goodness-of-fit test. The best (smallest negative logarithm) likelihood value belongs to the four parameter transformed beta distribution. However, it is only 0.6136 below the three-parameter Burr value, and so the extra parameter cannot be justified. The same holds when comparing Burr to the two-parameter paralogistic distribution. With regard to *p*-values, the transformed beta scores best, but the clearly acceptable paralogistic distribution is a much simpler choice. Also, because the lognormal distribution is well-known, the comparison in Figure 40.5 looks good, and its likelihood and chi-square numbers are very good, a case could be made for using the lognormal distribution for the model.

Results of Fitting 15 Models

Model*	$-\ln L$**	Chi-square	df	p-value
Paralogistic(2)	564.1091	1.50	4	0.8271
Loglogistic(2)	564.5449	2.38	4	0.6667
Pareto(2)	564.6012	2.44	4	0.6555
Lognormal(2)	564.6048	2.44	4	0.6555
Inv. Paralogistic(2)	565.2276	3.72	4	0.4448
Inv. Gaussian(2)	565.4414	4.02	4	0.4031
Weibull(2)	566.7777	6.72	4	0.1512
Burr(3)	564.0751	1.43	3	0.6996
Generalized Pareto(3)	564.2134	1.69	3	0.6395
Transformed beta(4)	563.4615	0.24	2	0.8879

* Number of parameters is in parentheses.
** Negative of the logarithm of the likelihood function.

---

[9] This is because twice the log of the likelihood ratio is approximately χ^2-distributed when the sample size is large, due to Wilk's Theorem, with the degree of freedom equal to the difference in the number of parameters in the numerator and denominator. The 95% confidence level for a χ^2 distribution with one degree of freedom is approximately 3.84, which when divided by two is 1.92. For more on this, see the "Loss Models: From Data to Decisions" reference at the end of the chapter.

FREQUENCY MODELS

The discussion so far has involved continuous models for the amount of a claim or payment. Another random variable of interest in insurance modeling is the number of claims in a given period for a given block of business (which again may be a single policy, a single group, a line of business, or an entire company). The only difference is that the model should place probability only on non-negative whole numbers. The methods of analysis (maximum likelihood estimation, likelihood ratio test, chi-square goodness-of-fit test) are the same, but there are a few differences.

A collection of frequency models can be found in Panjer and Willmot [1992] and in Klugman, Panjer, and Willmot [2004]. The three best known models are the Poisson, binomial, and negative binomial distributions. Unlike loss distributions, selection of frequency models might be motivated by requiring the physical process to have certain attributes. These models can be generalized by allowing the probability of zero claims to be an arbitrary number and then multiplying the remaining probabilities by a constant so that all of the probabilities sum to 1. These are called zero-modified models.

Frequency distribution analysis is helpful for casualty coverages, where there may be relatively few, large claims. Since most group coverages involve many, relatively small, claims, it is unusual for group actuaries to separately model the frequency of claims. Rather, they tend to work with compound distributions, which are claim distributions that include the probability of a zero claim. Unfortunately, the use of parametric methods for compound distributions is much more difficult than in the cases above. The actuarial profession continues to progress toward finding applications for these models.

CREDIBILITY THEORY

Credibility theory has a number of practical applications in group insurance, including experience rating and ratemaking. This section provides some background on credibility theory and suggests some further reading for those interested in group insurance applications.

BÜHLMANN'S CREDIBILITY MODEL

Bühlmann's credibility model is commonly expressed as

$$C = ZA + (1-Z)E,$$

where Z is the credibility factor, A represents the actual outcome (for example, the actual incurred claims for a particular employer group), E represents an estimate of the outcome (for example, an estimate of incurred claims based on the experience of other employer groups), and C is the compromise estimate. In Bühlmann's model, the credibility factor is defined as

$$Z = \frac{n}{n+k}.$$

In this equation, n is the number of trials or exposure units, and

$$k = \frac{\text{expected value of the process variance}}{\text{variance of the hypothetical means}}$$

If we are considering group health insurance, the *expected value of the process variance* would be the variance in incurred claims for a typical or average employer group. The *variance of the hypothetical means* would be the variance of the expected level of incurred claims among the employer groups.

APPLICATIONS OF CREDIBILITY THEORY

Fuhrer [1989] develops and applies credibility formulas specifically designed for group health insurance. The formula development recognizes the group health insurance dynamics of varying group size, group member turnover, large claims, high deductible plans, competitive requirements, and varying experience periods by modifying the credibility factor or other elements of the basic credibility formula.

For large claims, there is an approach suggested to limit the impact that one insured's large claim has on the A in the formula above. In general, these large claims are removed, or pooled, from the actual experience and replaced with an expected amount. Fuhrer suggests that the credibility formula can be used to determine the optimum pooling level.

The selection of Z, the credibility factor, should be sensitive to the underlying experience data. Fuhrer develops some approaches to determining Z that are sensitive to the size of the group and the coverage, as well as the degree of turnover within the group.

CONFIDENCE INTERVALS

Confidence intervals are used to communicate information regarding the range of possible outcomes, as opposed to just the average or expected outcome. For example, if the 80% confidence interval for actual claim runout is plus or minus 10% from the best estimate of the claim liability, this means that, on average, four out of five times the actual claim runout will be within 10% of the estimate. The 80% probability is referred to as the degree of confidence for this confidence interval.

The endpoints of the confidence interval are referred to as confidence limits. There may be confidence limits on both sides of the estimate, as in the above example, or on just one side of the estimate. This will depend on the purpose of the confidence interval. For example, a one-sided evaluation is more common when analyzing the adequacy of a statutory claim reserve estimate, since the key issue is the degree of confidence that the reserve estimate plus margin will exceed the actual runout. Conditional tail expectation (CTE) represents one example of a one-sided confidence interval application.

EXAMPLE: Claim Liability Margin

Suppose a medical insurance company wishes to determine an appropriate margin to use with its statutory claim liability. In particular, the company wishes to add an explicit margin to the best estimate of the claim liability so that there is a 75% to 95% probability that the resulting claim liability will be sufficient to cover the actual claim runout. This company has been using a substantially unchanged process during the last four years to determine its best estimate of the claim liability (the margin will be added to the best estimate to produce a more conservative estimate for statutory purposes—the point of this example is to estimate the appropriate margin to achieve a specified level of confidence).

For each month-end, we have compared the actual claim runout with the original claim liability estimate. Table 40.3 summarizes the percentage difference between the actual claim runout and the original best estimate claim liability based on results for 43 month-ends. The percentage difference is referred to as the "required margin" and is ranked from low to high in the table. Table 40.3 also shows the sample mean and sample standard deviation for this set of data points.

Table 40.3

Ranking of Required Margin		
Rank	Required Margin	Cumulative Probability*
1	−18.18%	1.2%
2	−15.78%	3.5%
3	−10.45%	5.8%
4	−10.23%	8.1%
5	−9.25%	10.5%
6	−9.18%	12.8%
7	−8.48%	15.1%
⋮	⋮	⋮
37	9.68%	84.9%
38	10.00%	87.2%
39	12.13%	89.5%
40	19.91%	91.9%
41	21.02%	94.2%
42	21.95%	96.5%
43	27.55%	98.8%
Sample Mean	0.50%	
Sample Standard Deviation	9.89%	

* Probability = (rank −.50) / 43.

Using the data in Table 40.3 we determine confidence intervals using two approaches. The first approach uses the raw data shown in the table. The second approach uses a normal distribution fitted to this data. The benefit of using the raw data is that we don't need to make an assumption regarding the underlying distribution. Such an assumption may introduce a bias or error if it is incorrect. The benefit of using a normal (or other parametric) distribution is that it tends to smooth out the results. Table 40.5 on the following page summarizes the results, showing the margin needed in order to have a given confidence level that the reserve estimate plus margin will exceed the actual claim runout. The required margin levels based on the normal distribution are determined using the following one-sided confidence intervals:

Upper Confidence Limit = *Sample Mean*
$+ X \times$ *Sample Standard Deviation,*

where X depends on the desired confidence level and is shown in the following table.

Table 40.4

One-Sided Confidence Level	X = Number of Standard Deviations
50%	0.00
75%	0.68
80%	0.84
85%	1.04
90%	1.28
95%	1.64

For example, there is an 85% probability that the value of a normally distributed random variable will be less than the mean plus 1.04 times the standard deviation.

Note that this analysis assumes that the distribution of the required margin has not changed significantly over time and that the required margin at each point in time is independent. If there has been a trend over time in the level of required margin or if there is some correlation between the level of required margin over time, it may be possible to develop a more accurate confidence interval by taking these factors into account.

Table 40.5

Probability of Claim Reserve Plus Margin Being More than Actual Runout	Required Margin Level (Based on Actual Experience)	Required Margin Level (Based on Normal Curve Using Historical Standard Deviation)
75%	6.17%	7.23%
80%	8.91%	8.81%
85%	9.70%	10.79%
90%	13.69%	13.17%
95%	21.34%	16.73%

CENTRAL LIMIT THEOREM

A discussion of applied statistics would not be complete without covering the central limit theorem. The central limit theorem can be stated as follows:

If $x_1, x_2, \ldots, x_n$ constitute a random sample from an infinite population having mean μ and variance σ^2, then the limiting distribution of

$$z = \frac{\sum_i \frac{x_i}{n} - \mu}{\frac{\sigma}{\sqrt{n}}}$$

as n approaches infinity, is the standard normal distribution.

This theorem is sometimes misunderstood when analyzing the level of risk associated with populations of different sizes, which is illustrated in the example of the next section.

EXAMPLE: Orthopedic Capitation

Suppose a group of orthopedic surgeons is evaluating a specialty capitation reimbursement arrangement and want to know how risky it is. They might want to know the minimum number of members that should be covered under the arrangement so as to reasonably limit their risk. The orthopedic surgeons believe that as the number of covered lives increases, the risk decreases. For this situation, we define the orthopedic surgeons' gain/loss on this reimbursement arrangement as follows:

(Gain/loss) = *(Total capitation revenue for the covered members for a given period of time)*
less
(The value of the services actually provided to the covered members valued using a discounted fee schedule)

To evaluate statistical risk levels, it is useful to distinguish between relative risk and absolute risk (of course, there are other risks besides statistical risk, such as misestimation or pricing errors.) For this situation, absolute risk can be viewed as the probability that the orthopedic surgeon group will lose $10,000 or more for a given period of time. Relative risk can be viewed as the probability that the orthopedic surgeon group will have claims equal to 100% or more of the capitation revenue.

Based on the central limit theorem, the relative risk decreases as the number of covered members increases. However, the absolute risk still increases as the number of lives increases. That is, the greater the number of covered lives, the greater the probability that the orthopedic surgeon group will lose a given amount of money.[10]

---

[10] Of course, if the capitation covers only professional services and the orthopedic surgeon group has excess capacity, the "risk" is not necessarily a financial risk but more of a time risk. That is, the orthopedic surgeon's revenue stream is fixed, but the amount of time that will be spent providing services to this group is uncertain (and additional time spent here is time that could be spent on other patients, if they can be found).

Figures 40.4 and 40.5 illustrate the dispersion of the resulting gain/loss. Figure 40.4 shows the dispersion expressed in absolute dollar terms. Figure 40.5 shows the dispersion expressed as a percentage deviation from expected.

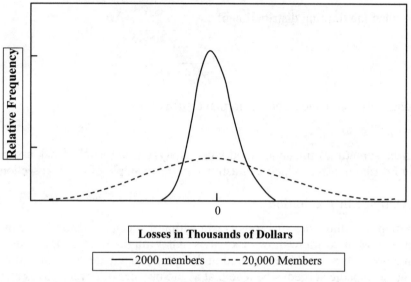

Figure 40.4

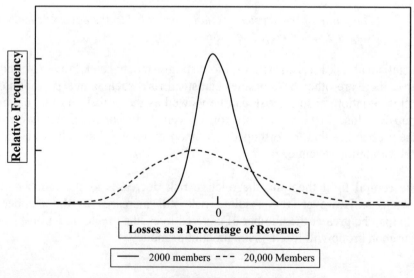

Figure 40.5

This type of information can be used to help evaluate the level of statistical risk associated with different capitation arrangements (of course, there are other risks besides the statistical risk, as noted above.) In generating the above results, we assumed no specific stop-loss. In practice, most arrangements have a stop-loss built in, or the physician group will purchase stop-loss from a third party.

REFERENCES

Bowers, N., H. Gerber, J. Hickman, D. Jones, and C. Nesbitt, *Actuarial Mathematics*, 2nd Edition, Chicago: Society of Actuaries, 1997.

Bühlmann, H., "Experience Rating and Credibility," *The ASTIN Bulletin* 4 (1967), 119-207.

Cunningham, R., T.N. Herzog, and R.L. London, *Models for Quantifying Risk*, 4th Edition, Winsted: ACTEX Publications, 2011.

Daykin, C., T. Pentikäinen, and M. Pesonen, *Practical Risk Theory for Actuaries*. London: Chapman and Hall, 1994.

Fuhrer, C., "Some Applications of Credibility Theory to Group Insurance," *Transactions of the Society of Actuaries*, XL (1988), 387-404.

Granger, C.W.J., *Forecasting in Business and Economics*. San Diego: Academic Press, 1980.

Heckman, P. and G. Meyers, "The Calculation of Aggregate Loss Distributions from Claim Severity and Claim Count Distributions," *Proceedings of the Casualty Actuarial Society*, 70 (1983), 22-61.

Herzog, T.N., *An Introduction to Stochastic Simulation* (Course 130 Study Note). Chicago: Society of Actuaries, 1983.

Herzog, T.N. with Lord, G., *Applications of Monte Carlo Methods to Finance and Insurance*. Winsted: ACTEX Publications, 2003.
Hogg, R. and S. Klugman, *Loss Distributions*. New York: John Wiley and Sons, 1984.

Hosler, V.R., "The Application of Fuzzy Sets to Group Health Underwriting," *Actuarial Research Clearing House*, 1992.2 (1992), 1-63.

Hossack, I., J. Pollard, and B. Zehnwirth, *Introductory Statistics with Applications in General Insurance*. Cambridge: Cambridge University Press, 1983.

Kellison, S.G., and R.L. London, *Risk Models and Their Estimation*, Winsted: ACTEX Publications, 2011.

Klugman, S., H. Panjer, and G. Willmot, *Loss Models: From Data to Decisions*, 2nd Edition: John Wiley & Sons, 2004.

Longley-Cook, L.H., "An Introduction to Credibility Theory," *Proceedings of the Casualty Actuarial Society*, 49 (1962) 194-221.

Miller, R.B. and D. Wichern, *Intermediate Business Statistics*. New York: Holt, Reinhart and Winston, 1977.

Mills, A. "Complexity Science—an introduction (and invitation) for actuaries." Society of Actuaries research study, June 2010.

Ostaszewski, K., *Fuzzy Set Methods in Actuarial Science*. Chicago: Society of Actuaries, 1993.

Panjer, H., "The Aggregate Claims Distribution and Stop-Loss Reinsurance," *Transactions of the Society of Actuaries*, XXXII (1981), 523-535.

Panjer, H. and G. Willmot, *Insurance Risk Models*. Chicago: Society of Actuaries, 1992.

Rao, C., *Linear Statistical Inference and Its Applications*. New York: John Wiley and Sons, 1965.

Robertson, J., "The Computation of Aggregate Loss Distributions," *Proceedings of the Casualty Actuarial Society*, 79 (1993), 57-133.

Society of Actuaries Committee on Actuarial Principles, "Principles of Actuarial Science," *Transactions of the Society of Actuaries*, XLIV (1992), 565-628.

Venter. G., "Transformed Beta and Gamma Distributions and Aggregate Losses," *Proceedings of the Casualty Actuarial Society*, 71 (1984), 156-193.

41 ANALYSIS OF FINANCIAL AND OPERATIONAL PERFORMANCE

Douglas B. Sherlock

"Life must be lived forward, but it can only be understood backward."
Søren Kierkegaard

This chapter concerns the evaluation of financial and operational performance of health plans, through analysis of their annual statements. An organizing, and admittedly simplifying, principle in this discussion is that the responsibility of the insurance enterprise is to maximize its owners' value, even in the case of non-profit or mutual plans. Earnings and earnings growth are the drivers of value, and the factors influencing them provide a systematic framework for the analysis of a health plan.

MAXIMIZATION FRAMEWORK

All enterprises, including health plans, can be analyzed based on their effectiveness at maximizing their owner's value. While some health plans do not have public shareholders, the objectives of a publicly held stock company corporate model is also a convenient paradigm for understanding not-for-profit enterprises, whose primary obligation is to benefit the public, and for mutuals, whose obligation is to their policyholders. This is the case even though the accounting conventions for reporting the realization of such value may differ between these organizational forms.

Investors gauge a publicly held stock company's success in maximizing value based on the stock price of the underlying enterprise. However, stock price generally is only indirectly affected by the actions of the management team. Moreover, the enterprise may be privately held, and therefore not have a public market for its stock, or it may be non-profit or mutual.

Management endeavors to maximize shareholder value by achieving superior performance of the underlying enterprise, which they hope is recognized and rewarded by investors through share price improvement. To connect the value of ownership with corporate performance, investors employ models that express corporate performance in terms of valuation. Unlike stock prices, such models are designed to directly reflect management performance, being based on the company's financial statements. To the degree that these models arrive at different values than the actual stock price, investors may interpret the difference as a reason to buy or sell the stock. Thus, reporting in accordance with generally accepted accounting principles (GAAP) is designed to inform the owners of an enterprise of management's progress in achieving this maximization objective.

The classic model to estimate value (or valuation analysis) is the discounted future cash flow model. This model is based on the notion that the value of the enterprise is determined by the amount and timing of the cash available for distribution to its owners. Cash distributed to shareholders is most often in the form of dividends, although the actual cash flow available to owners may also be realized in other ways.

Thus, value can be affected by management actions relative to the dividends and other cash flows distributed to investors, and these distributions' long-term growth rate. Value is also affected by something on which management has limited influence – the discount rate used in the valuation, chiefly reflecting the riskiness of the business activities conducted by the enterprise. Evidence that this hypothesized link between value and the growth of free cash flows is broadly accepted by investors includes the Price/Earnings multiples for stocks and in the commonly used PEG ratio. (A PEG ratio is a stock's P/E ratio divided by the annual growth rate of the underlying company's earnings).

The link between value and growth in free cash flow can be seen mathematically, as well. The Gordon Constant Growth Model is a simplified discounted future cash flow model that assumes that dividends grow in perpetuity at a constant rate. (We have made the simplifying assumption in substituting earnings for dividends.)

$$P = \frac{D}{k-G},$$

where

P = Price per share
D = Expected dividend per share one year from now
k = Required rate of return for equity investor
G = Growth rate in dividends (in perpetuity)

Dividing by D, then

$$\frac{P}{D} = \frac{1}{k-G}$$

The Gordon Constant Growth Model, rearranged, highlights that the P/E ratio relates to the discount rate and the growth of earnings. So, if we hold constant a discount rate of 13.0%, an enterprise with a growth rate of 3.0% merits a P/E of 10.0 times while an enterprise with growth of 6.0% merits a P/E of 14.3 times. In short, maximizing value means maximizing earnings growth.

Financial statements can provide users with insights on a company's level of free cash flow, dividends, and earnings. Financial statements prepared in accordance with GAAP are relied on by shareholders to measure how enterprises are maximizing their value. In other words, these financial statements are designed for external users, mainly owners, and they reflect that equity shareholders are paid only after creditors' claims are satisfied. By contrast, other financial statement presentations, such as those using statutory accounting, are designed to measure solvency for an audience of creditors (or their advocates) and regulators. So the significance of GAAP financial statements is that they capture the overall performance of the enterprise, which can, if owners choose, be translated through valuation models that measure how well management is honoring its obligation to maximize shareholder value.

While investors often use valuation models, generally at any point in time there are few health plans contemplating business changes for which valuation models would be necessary. However, valuation models provide a starting point for a systematic look at performance metrics, by measuring a variety of factors that contribute to value maximization.

GROWTH AND RETURN ON EQUITY

Given the essential role of earnings growth in shareholder value, what then do reported financials tell users about earnings growth? Return on equity (ROE) is a key metric of growth from an owner's perspective. It can be thought of as measuring how fast the enterprise's net worth grows, assuming reinvestment of all earnings. It also reflects the limits of such growth, absent any external capital sources. In other words, return on equity is the same thing as sustainable growth rate for enterprises that pay no dividends. The sustainable growth rate is calculated as the product of the Earnings Retention Rate (or 1 - Dividends/Earnings) and ROE.

By definition, return on equity is calculated as Net Income divided by Shareholders' Equity, as shown below.

$$\text{ROE} = \frac{\text{Net Income}}{\text{Shareholder Equity}}$$

As an example, suppose an enterprise begins year 1 with $100 in equity. It then earns $15 during that year, for a 15% ROE. Further suppose that it reinvests those earnings into the enterprise, so that equity is $115 by year end. Thus, the enterprise's growth in equity equals its ROE, 15%.

Suppose that in year 2, this enterprise earns a 15% return on equity, the same as in year 1. A 15% ROE on beginning equity of $115 would equate to net earnings of $17.25, since the 15% must be earned on a higher equity ($115) than the prior year. Earnings of $17.25 is a 15% increase from year 1's net earnings. Thus, ROE is the same as growth rate if no dividends are paid and no external equity sources are added (which can only happen if the ROE is sustainable.)

By the same token, ROE measures the internal *limits* on the enterprise's growth. The amount of equity required by an enterprise stems from the technical requirements of its business model. For instance, a health plan must have a certain level of investment in real estate and information systems to serve its customers.

The type of capital used to fund those assets differs. For instance, real estate can sustain higher levels of debt than information systems. Since the capital mix must include some equity, the available equity constrains that total investment and the number of customers served. So, for the health plan to grow faster than the ROE, it would need to access external equity. External equity diminishes the percent of the company owned by existing shareholders.

FACTORS OF GROWTH

The analyst's venerable warhorse, the DuPont Formula, analyzes ROE into the factors of an enterprise that contribute to its growth. In other words, as shown in the following schedules, return on equity is the product of business model characteristics that are quantified in its component metrics.

The first part of the DuPont Formula analyzes the return on assets, sometimes called the return on investment, as the product of margin and turnover ratios. (A turnover ratio is the ratio of revenue generated by assets to those assets.) These are metrics of assets required to serve customers and the level of earnings that each customer generates.

$$(\text{Total Asset Turnover}) \times (\text{Net Profit Margin}) = (\text{Return on Assets})$$

The formulas for these ratios are, respectively, as follows:

$$\left(\frac{\text{Revenues}}{\text{Total Assets}}\right) \times \left(\frac{\text{Net Income}}{\text{Revenue}}\right) = \left(\frac{\text{Net Income}}{\text{Total Assets}}\right)$$

The second part of the DuPont Formula analyzes how financial leverage amplifies return on assets into return on equity. This is done with the total leverage ratio, which is a metric of how much the total assets are, relative to the equity (as opposed to debt) that is used to finance those assets.

$$(\text{Return on Assets}) \times (\text{Total Leverage Ratio}) = (\text{Return on Equity})$$

The formulas for these ratios are, in turn:

$$\left(\frac{\text{Net Income}}{\text{Total Assets}}\right) \times \left(\frac{\text{Total Assets}}{\text{Shareholder Equity}}\right) = \left(\frac{\text{Net Income}}{\text{Shareholder Equity}}\right)$$

The factors building to ROE can thus be thought of as the answers to a series of questions summarizing the characteristics of the enterprise, as follows:

Total Asset Turnover: This ratio is the net sales of the enterprise, divided by the assets used to support it. In other words, how much *total* investment (such as real estate, information systems, and perhaps medical equipment, funded by equity and debt), is needed to meet the requirements of this business?

Profit Margin: How profitable is each customer? In other words, for every dollar of sales, what percent does this enterprise earn as profits?

Return on Assets: What is the level of profits, expressed as a percent, that can be earned on the assets of the enterprise as a whole?

Total Leverage Ratio: To what degree can the enterprise be operated using other peoples' money? That is, by how much can trade and other creditors' money be employed to magnify Return on Assets for the benefit of shareholders?

Decomposing ROE is important in understanding business models and strategies, which can be radically different from company to company, even in the same industry, and even if ROE is the same. For instance, a health plan with a low profit margin can have high ROE and high growth, if it also has a high total asset turnover or a high total leverage ratio.

Tables 41.1 – 41.4 represent three prototypical health plans. The staff and IPA plans (meant to exemplify most commercial and Blue Cross/Blue Shield insurers, as well as IPA model HMOs) are loosely based on actual enterprises. Table 41.1 contains the income statements; Table 41.2 contains the related balance sheets; Table 41.3 provides certain key ratios; and Table 41.4 provides a DuPont Formula analysis for these enterprises.

As shown in Table 41.4, all the health plans have the same ROE, but they achieve it in quite different ways. The staff model plan has a higher profit margin than the IPA, which is necessary since it has a lower total asset turnover. Moreover, financial leverage, measured by the total leverage ratio, is employed to achieve the benchmark ROE.

The Administrative Services Only (ASO) business has the highest profit margins, on much lower total asset turnover. Its ROE is somewhat magnified by financial leverage.

The following sections provide further discussion on this summary of the DuPont Formula factors of growth.

Table 41.1

Financial and Operational Performance and Analysis

Income Statements

	Staff	IPA	ASO
Insured			
Insured Member Months	9,500,000	5,600,000	
Insured Revenues PMPM	$ 209	$208	
ASO			
ASO Member Months	2,600,000	200,000	5,800,000
ASO Revenues PMPM	$ 20	20	$ 20
Total Member Months	12,100,000	5,800,000	5,800,000
Revenues			
Premium Revenues	$1,987,000,000	$1,167,000,000	$ —
Other Revenues	52,000,000	4,000,000	116,000,000
Total Revenues	$2,039,000,000	$1,171,000,000	$ 116,000,000
Expenses			
Health Benefit Expenses	$1,672,000,000	$ 985,000,000	$ —
Administrative Expenses	267,000,000	103,000,000	103,000,000
Total Expenses	1,939,000,000	$1,088,000,000	$ 103,000,000
Operating Profits	100,000,000	$ 83,000,000	$ 13,000,000
Non-Operating			
Investment Income	$11,000,000	$ 5,000,000	$ —
Interest Expense	5,000,000	1,000,000	1,000,000
Total Non-Operating	$6,000,000	$ 4,000,000	$ (1,000,000)
Pretax Income	$106,000,000	$ 87,000,000	$ 12,000,000
Income Taxes		32,000,000	4,000,000
Net Income	$106,000,000	$ 55,000,000	$8,000,000

Table 41.2

Financial and Operational Performance and Analysis

Balance Sheet

	Staff	IPA	ASO
Assets			
Current Assets			
Cash and Equivalents	$ 511,000,000	$ 327,000,000	24,000,000
Accounts Receivable	69,000,000	65,000,000	10,000,000
Inventories	23,000,000	—	
Prepaid Expenses	11,000,000	8,000,000	
Other Current Assets	—	4,000,000	
Total Current Assets	$ 614,000,000	$ 404,000,000	$ 34,000,000
Fixed Assets	$ 316,000,000	$ 26,000,000	$ 26,000,000
Other Assets	65,000,000	19,000,000	19,000,000
Total Assets	$ 995,000,000	$ 449,000,000	$ 79,000,000
Liabilities			
Current Liabilities			
Claims Payable	$ 122,000,000	$ 160,000,000	$ —
Other Accounts Payable	135,000,000	23,000,000	23,000,000
Prepaid Premiums	11,000,000	—	
Other Current Liabilities	—	9,000,000	9,000,000
Total Current Liabilities	$ 268,000,000	$ 192,000,000	$ 32,000,000
Long-Term Debt	116,000,000	2,000,000	2,000,000
Other Liabilities	137,000,000	9,000,000	9,000,000
Equity or Fund Balance	474,000,000	246,000,000	36,000,000
Total Liabilities and Net Worth	$ 995,000,000	$ 449,000,000	$ 79,000,000

Table 41.3

Financial and Operational Performance and Analysis

Key Ratios

	Staff	IPA	ASO
Fixed Asset Turnover	6.45	45.04	4.46
Fixed Assets Per Member	$ 26.12	$ 4.48	$ 4.48
Long-term Debt to Fixed Assets	36.7%	7.7%	7.7%
Long-term Debt to Total Capital	19.7%	0.8%	5.3%
Days of Accounts Receivable	12.4	20.3	31.5
Days of Claims Payable	26.6	59.3	NM
Health Benefits Ratio (Unadjusted)	84.1%	84.4%	NM
Administration to Revenues (Unadjusted)	13.1%	8.8%	88.8%
Operating Profit Margin	4.9%	7.1%	11.2%

Table 41.4

Financial and Operational Performance and Analysis

DuPont Formula

	Staff	IPA	ASO
Return on Equity	22.4%	22.4%	22.4%
=			
Total Leverage Ratio	2.10	1.83	2.19
×			
Return on Assets	10.7%	12.2%	10.1%
=			
Net Profit Margin	5.2%	4.7%	6.9%
×			
Total Asset Turnover	2.05	2.61	1.47

TOTAL ASSET TURNOVER

"Total asset turnover" is the net sales of the enterprise, divided by its total assets. This ratio is one of the more illuminating indicators of health plan model designs. Changes in this ratio tend either to (1) take a long time to implement, or (2) require a major acquisition or divestiture.

Assets recorded in the financial statements of health plans reflect the tools necessary to perform the various activities required by its membership. These assets include office space and information systems, but may also include health care delivery assets, as well as intangible assets that result from the health plan making an acquisition of another company.

As shown in Table 41.2, the size and nature of assets vary by model design. Since staff model health plans deliver health care, they must make substantial investments in health care delivery capabilities. They often have greater total assets, leading to lower total asset turnover. Assets of staff model plans emphasize fixed assets, as opposed to current assets. Examples of such fixed assets may include clinics, pharmacies, and, in some cases, hospitals.

Accordingly, staff model plans have a relatively high amount of fixed assets per member and much lower fixed asset turnover compared with IPA model plans, as shown in Table 41.3. Over the past several decades, there has been a trend away from staff model plans. For the health plan industry as a whole, there has been a significant change in the character of the assets, in favor of cash and financial assets, and away from fixed assets.

On the other hand, unlike IPA models, staff models are less likely to require investments in liquid assets to pay for care that they have incurred but for which they have not yet paid (IBNP or IBNR reserves) than IPA models, since they are providing this care internally. Table 41.3 shows that the "days of claims" in reserve is substantially lower for the staff model plan. This lower ratio does not necessarily mean that the staff model is paying claims faster, or that its reserve policies differ from the IPA. Rather, since it is providing care directly, it has less need to reserve for obligations to external providers.

By contrast, enterprises focused on ASO services, including third-party administrators, have neither any health care delivery investment requirements, nor must they retain substantial cash equivalents to satisfy the payment of claims. Their revenues per member are low, since medical costs are paid for by the benefit plan sponsor, as shown in Table 41.1. Thus their total asset turnover tends to be very low.

Health plans' current assets include accounts receivable from their customers. This typically equates to a few weeks of the health plan's revenue, as shown in Table 41.3. Prepaid expenses are also common, including insurance purchased by the health plan. Staff model plans are more likely to have in-house pharmacies. Accordingly, they are more likely to report inventories of medicines among current assets, as shown in Table 41.2.

In addition, cash and other liquid investments are held by the health plan to pay for health services rendered by external providers. Highly liquid assets are considered by state health insurance departments to have the greatest value protecting health care providers and members from the risk of financial losses if the health plan fails.

The size and nature of liquid assets tend to vary with the organizational structure. Non-profit Blue Cross Blue Shield Plans often possess higher levels of investment assets and a heavier concentration in equity securities than do publicly traded enterprises. The greater capital may stem from the need to meet Blue Cross Blue Shield Association licensure requirements (normally higher than state requirements), as well as, for the most part, their lack of access to the public equity markets. Their willingness to employ a riskier mix of assets may result from their portfolios' excess over state capital requirements.

A complication in quantifying the capital intensity of health plans is that some plans "rent" information systems or provider capacity, so they do not have to own them. In effect, both the liabilities and assets are kept off balance sheet, with the cost reflected in higher operating expenses.

PROFIT MARGINS

Profit margins and their variants are probably the most familiar metrics employed by financial analysts. Interpretation of profit margins is most meaningful in short term periods, when one can assume stable levels of assets and leverage. Within that period, profit margins capture the relationships between a health plan and its customers and its internal and external suppliers. Analysis of profit margins can be thought of as part of a family of income statement-based performance metrics.

THE MARGINS THEMSELVES

Profit margins are earnings expressed as a percent of total revenues. Revenues are most illuminating if they include premiums and ASO fee income, but exclude investment income. Insurers often refer to profit margins as "underwriting income" or "operating income." The investment income exclusion is preferred, because investment income relates to a plan's investment portfolio, while premium and ASO fees each derive from the relationships between the plan and its customers.

The two most common margin ratios employed by financial analysts are 'operating profit margin' and 'net margin', shown in Tables 41.3 and 41.4, respectively. Operating margin is operating profits divided by revenues, and net margin is net income divided by revenues. Operating income consists of revenues less health benefit and administrative expenses. Net income is operating income less net interest expense and income taxes.

The profit margins for insured businesses are overstated, since they imply a level of cash flow available to owners that excludes the impact of any additional statutory reserve requirements. For example, a presentation more reflective of health insurers' free cash flows would increase expenses by the increase in required reserves in the measurement period.

RELATED RATIOS

The most common income statement ratios are the health benefit ratio and the administrative expense ratio, shown in Table 41.3. In a health plan whose only product is insurance, these ratios relate directly to the profit margin, since 100% minus the health benefit ratio, minus the administrative expense ratio, equals the operating profit margin. As discussed below, there is nuance in application and interpretation of these related ratios.

Administrative Expense Ratio

The administrative expense ratio is administrative expenses divided by revenues. The intent of this metric is to quantify the proportion of revenues attributable to such activities as claims processing, customer service, medical management, sales, and so forth.

Care should be taken to properly treat non-premium revenues and associated expenses, so that the resulting ratio is not misleading. Table 41.3 illustrates the problem. The unadjusted administrative expense to revenue ratio is higher for the staff model plan than for the IPA. Unlike the IPA plan, the staff model plan's revenues include ASO fees. There is an upward distortion in its ratio for precisely the same reason that the ASO also has a very high administrative expense ratio. In both cases, comparisons can be misleading because the revenue denominator includes fees for which no health care is associated, while only in the IPA case does the denominator reflect health plan revenues needed to cover health care costs.

To eliminate this distortion, the administrative costs need to be allocated between insured and ASO products. This is difficult for an external analyst, since cost drivers are normally not disclosed. There are two approaches that improve upon the calculation used in Table 41.3. First, one may assume that the ASO product operates at breakeven. Second, one may assume that both ASO and insured products have similar cost structures. These methods are shown in Tables 41.7 and 41.8 later in this chapter.

The first allocation approach assumes that the ASO operates at breakeven. This is shown in the second and third columns of Tables 41.7 and 41.8. ASO fees are subtracted from the organization's total administrative costs. The difference provides an administrative expense estimate for the insured business. As shown in Table 41.8, ASO administrative expense is estimated to be 100% of revenues, and the insured administrative expense ratio is well below the "Total" ratio in the first column.

The second approach, allocating costs by product, assumes that their PMPM costs are exactly the same. The fourth and fifth columns of Tables 41.7 and 41.8 show the application of this assumption. The claim costs are shown in Table 41.7. Note that the administrative costs PMPM are the same as for each of the products. As with the break-even approach, in Table 41.8, the ratio of administrative expense to premium in the insured line is lower than the combined total. However, for the ASO business, administrative costs are greater than 100% of revenues.

While both allocation methods are more reasonable estimates of administration as a percent of total revenues, they are naïve. Comparing these allocation approaches to the actual administrative costs of Medicare Advantage illuminates their weaknesses: Medicare Advantage administrative cost PMPM is typically more than twice as high as its commercial equivalent, and sometimes two percentage points lower relative to premiums. A more effective method would rely upon actual metrics of key activities in each function to drive estimates of the costs of those functions in each product. However, these are rarely available to external users of financial statements and, notwithstanding their value, may be difficult to access and employ even for internal users.

Health Benefit Ratio

The "health benefit ratio" is often called the medical loss ratio, or "MLR." However, the acronym MLR is more often used to refer to the "minimum loss ratio" required under rate regulation. To avoid ambiguity, we will not refer to the medical loss ratio.

The health benefit ratio is the proportion of premiums represented by health benefit expenses. It should be calculated as claims (health benefit expenses) as a percent of their associated premiums, not total revenues, in order to match insurance expenses with insurance revenues. In Table 41.8, the second column, based on premium revenues, is a more realistic and actionable calculation than is the first column, based on total revenues.

When booking claims, companies may vary which expenses they include with health benefits, affecting the ratios.

Health plans vary in whether they consider medical management costs to be health benefit or administrative expenses. Considering them to be administrative expenses might highlight the potential benefits to health care costs of these expenses. The exclusion of medical management costs from health benefits is also in accordance with the requirements of the National Association of Insurance Commissioners (NAIC) for most purposes.

Health care expenses paid to providers under capitation can affect the ratios, and must be accounted for carefully. Capitation is the payment of a fixed per capita amount to a health care provider, in exchange for an agreed upon set of services. The scope of capitation can range from certain specialty services to substantially all care required by the membership. A capitated provider is a subcontractor to the health plan, and the recognition of capitation as an expense implies that the plan has satisfied its requirements to its members served by the capitated provider. However, if the capitated provider loses money on the relationship, there is a risk that the provider's resulting insolvency would require the plan to cover its losses. When such circumstances appear possible, it may be appropriate for the plan to consolidate the economics of the capitated entity for analytical purposes. This can be difficult if the entity is unwilling to provide financials, or if the entity also is the subcontractor to other health plans.

QUIRKS IN ADMINISTRATION AND HEALTH BENEFIT RATIOS DUE TO CAPITATION

Capitation of health services can affect comparability of financial statements between otherwise similar health plans, especially respecting the segmentation of expenses into administrative and health benefit components. For instance, all things being equal, a health plan with a capitated arrangement with providers will have a higher health benefit ratio and a lower administrative ratio than one without. This may be solely due to administrative expenses delegated to the capitated entity being included with the capitation, thus excluded from the health plan's administrative costs. The greater the proportion of health benefits that are capitated, the greater the potential for distortion and loss of comparability.

For this reason, certain adjustments may improve comparability. Three alternative approaches are apparent. First, it can be helpful to remove such capitated services from both administrative expense and from health benefits. This may be especially appropriate for specialty health services of limited scope, such as mental health and pharmaceutical benefits.

A second approach is to consolidate the economics of the capitated entity. This may be most appropriate in cases of global capitation in which substantially all of the health care benefits are capitated. A third situation is when a subset of the members is subject to global capitation. In that case, one might perform the administrative and health benefit ratios only for the members not subject to capitation.

THE SAME-SIZE-INCOME STATEMENT

Because profit margins are expressed as a percent of revenues, they can also be viewed as a component of a financial analysis exercise called a "same size" income statement. In this analysis, all relevant income statement items are expressed as percentages of revenue. In this way, profit margins can be divided into component parts, all of which are expressed independently of the size of the enterprise.

The same-size-income statement permits comparisons among health plans and year-over-year comparisons of the same enterprise. This is shown in Table 41.5; only the operating items in the Table 41.1 income statement have been included for brevity and relevance. This approach can be more useful than raw income statement information. Differences from values for similarly situated peers, and changes in a single plan's results can be immediately understood in terms of their impact on profit margins.

Table 41.5

Financial and Operational Performance and Analysis

Same Size Income Statement, Unadjusted

	Staff	IPA	ASO
Revenues			
Premium Revenues	97.4%	99.7%	0.0%
Other Revenues	2.6%	0.3%	100.0%
Total Revenues	100.0%	100.0%	100.0%
Expenses			
Health Benefit Expenses	82.0%	84.1%	0.0%
Administrative Expenses	13.1%	8.8%	88.8%
Total Expenses	95.1%	92.9%	88.8%
Operating Profits	4.9%	7.1%	11.2%

ADJUSTMENTS FOR REVENUE REPORTING DIFFERENCES

The same-size-income statement eases comparability by standardizing financial statements and is simple and quick to do. But this approach has some significant limitations. However, there are solutions that should be considered by the analyst to make the best use of this analytical tool. Treatments of revenue that may be unique to the enterprise include classifications of reinsurance, commissions, investments, and ASO revenue.

Reinsurance. Some enterprises include reinsurance recoveries as a revenue item. It is more useful to consider reinsurance recoveries as offsets to health care costs. This is particularly helpful when including very large health plans in the comparisons, in that they often do not purchase reinsurance.

Commissions. Payments to brokers that distribute a health plan's products are sometimes excluded from premiums. Unless the broker is acting as a fiduciary to the customer, and the health plan's role is limited to collecting fees authorized by the customer, commissions are expenses of the health plan. They should be considered an administrative expense, and revenues should include such commissions.

Investment Income. Health plans temporarily retain a financial "float," stemming from premiums received in advance claim payments. Plans may earn investment income on this float. Sometimes, investment income is included in operating revenue. However, there are reasons why excluding investment income from revenues is more useful analytically. First, the investment returns themselves are subject to only limited managerial influence, since external short-term capital markets establish rates of return. Second, investible float is not the only source of investment income. Many health plans are also active in capital markets, and the proceeds of capital formation are invested in financial instruments pending deployment for operational purposes or acquisitions. Exacerbating this problem is that health plans using the credit markets incur interest expense, a non-operating expense, while generating investment income. In short, since it is difficult to separate float-based investment returns from capital market activity, it is more illuminating to group investment returns with capital costs as non-operating income.

Administrative Services Only Products. Increasingly, health plans offer products in which health benefit plan sponsors, as opposed to the health plans themselves, absorb variances in health care costs. In that case, the only revenue booked by the health plan consists of payments for a package of administrative services, such as claim processing and customer service inquiries.

If one calculates administrative expenses relative to revenues, the ratio seems high compared with insured ratios, since the denominator (revenue) does not include the cost of health care cost risk. Recall that health care costs are typically 80-90% of premium revenue.

One way of overcoming this dissonance is to express administrative costs as a percent of "premium equivalents." That is, the analyst estimates what the premiums would have been had the health plan actually bore health care cost variance risk by adding health benefits to the fee revenue. While inappropriate in the GAAP or statutory financial statements, this approach may have intuitive appeal to a generalist reader. ASO products may incur significantly lower costs in some administrative functions.

To get a better understanding of the enterprises that offer such products, it is helpful to analyze ASO products separately from insured products. We earlier provided a discussion of how this segmentation may be done, given the limited information sometimes available to the external analyst.

Table 41.6

PMPM Income Statement, Unadjusted

Financial and Operational Performance and Analysis

	Staff	IPA	ASO
Revenues			
Premium Revenues	$ 164.21	$ 201.21	$ –
Other Revenues	$ 4.30	$ 0.69	$ 20.00
Total Revenues	$ 168.51	$ 201.90	$ 20.00
Expenses			
Health Benefit Expenses	$ 138.18	$ 169.83	$ –
Administrative Expenses	$ 22.07	$ 17.76	$ 17.76
Total Expenses	$ 160.25	$ 187.59	$ 17.76
Operating Profits	$ 8.26	$ 14.31	$ 2.24

PMPM ANALYSIS

Besides the revenue reporting issues discussed above, another limitation on the usefulness of the same-size-income statement is that it confounds two somewhat independent relationships; the competitive pressures on health plan pricing and the challenges of actually managing the operations themselves. In other words, on a day-to-day basis, companies must manage operations independently of the pricing pressures faced by the health plan in the market. The traditional solution for analysts is to divide each of the expense items by the membership to which the expenses apply, rather than by the revenues. Corresponding with how health plans bill for insurance, the cost attributes are standardized in units of "Per Member Per Month" (PMPM), as shown in Table 41.6 above.

Table 41.7

Adjusted Same Size Income Statement, Staff Model

Financial and Operational Performance and Analysis

	ASO Breakeven Assumption			Similar Administrative Cost Assumption	
	Total	Insured	ASO	Insured	ASO
Revenues					
Premium Revenues	97.4%	100.0%		100.0%	0.0%
Other Revenues	2.6%		100.0%	0.0%	100.0%
Total Revenues	100.0%	100.0%	100.0%	100.0%	100.0%
Expenses					
Health Benefit Expenses	82.0%	84.1%		84.1%	0.0%
Administrative Expenses	13.1%	10.8%	100.0%	10.5%	110.3%
Total Expenses	95.1%	95.0%	100.0%	94.7%	110.3%
Operating Profits	4.9%	5.0%	0.0%	5.3%	–10.3%

By isolating costs in this standardized form, the PMPM approach has the advantage of providing more actionable information. For example, a change in administrative costs, when reported in a same-size-income statement, can be obscured by changes in revenues. The PMPM approach clearly isolates administrative cost changes.

One drawback to the PMPM approach is in communications with generalists, including board members or other external audiences. Since ratios similar to those from the same-size-income statement are more familiar, this approach is sometimes disorienting to some users of financial statement analyses.

The use of PMPM values still requires that the issues of reinsurance, commissions, investment income, medical management, and capitation be addressed. As previously stated, it is advisable to segment ASO products, ideally with high quality segment cost breakouts.

Table 41.8

Adjusted PMPM Income Statement, Staff Model

Financial and Operational Performance and Analysis

		ASO Breakeven Assumption			Similar Administrative Cost Assumption	
	Total	Insured	ASO		Insured	ASO
Insured						
Insured Member Months	9,500,000	9,500,000			9,500,000	
Insured Revenues PMPM	209					
ASO	–					
ASO Member Months	2,600,000		2,600,000			2,600,000
ASO Revenues PMPM	20					
Total Member Months	12,100,000	9,500,000	2,600,000		9,500,000	2,600,000
Revenues						
Premium Revenues	$ 164.21	$ 209.16	$ –		$ 209.16	$ –
Other Revenues	4.30		20.00			20.00
Total Revenues	$ 168.51	$ 209.16	20.00		$ 209.16	$ 20.00
Expenses						
Health Benefit Expenses	$138.18	$ 176.00			$ 76.00	
Administrative Expenses	22.07	22.63	20.00		22.07	22.07
Total Expenses	$160.25	$ 198.63	20.00		$ 198.07	$ 22.07
Operating Profits	$ 8.26	$ 10.53	$ –		$ 11.09	$ (2.07)

DECOMPOSING PMPM COSTS

PMPM costs can be made more actionable if they are segmented into aspects of the business that can be managed. For this, it is helpful to break expenses into functional areas. Table 41.9 is a sample list of such functions. This segmentation is more useful than natural accounting categories, like depreciation and salary, since functions (not resources) are the focus of managerial actions.

Table 41.9

Administrative Functional Areas of Health Plans

Financial and Operational Performance and Analysis
- Rating and Underwriting
- Product Development / Market Research
- Sales and Marketing (Except Advertising and Promotion)
- Commissions (External)
- Advertising and Promotion
- Enrollment / Membership / Billing
- Customer Services
- Provider Network Management and Services
- Medical Mgmt. / Quality Assurance / Wellness
- Claim and Encounter Capture and Adjudication
- Total Information System Expenditures (As Expensed)
- HIPAA
- Finance and Accounting
- Actuarial
- Corporate Services (HR, Facilities, Legal, Regulatory)
- Corporate Executive / Governance
- Association Dues and License/Filing Fees

The PMPM values can be made more operationally actionable through further analysis. Per member per month values, in total or by function, may be expressed as the product of the health plan's staffing ratio and total costs per FTE. The total costs per FTE can, in turn, be expressed as the sum of the per-FTE staffing costs and non-labor costs.

This analysis is most powerful when it is compared with other health plans, or other measurement periods for the same health plan. Thus, if PMPM customer service costs are high, the source of variance can be pinpointed to either high levels of staff, high compensation or high costs other than compensation.

While this analysis of PMPM costs can be performed for each function of a health plan, additional metrics are available for functions that have an identifiable unit of output. Examples of such outputs include claims processed, customer service inquiries or enrollment transactions. Accordingly, variances in the customer service costs per FTE can be analyzed as the product of cost per inquiry and inquiries per FTE per year. These two metrics are, respectively, a unit cost measure and a productivity measure. Inquiries per FTE per year can be further analyzed into members per FTE and inquiries per member. The latter ratio can be thought of as a metric of primary demand.

RETURN ON ASSETS

In the context of the DuPont Formula, return on assets is the product of total asset turnover and the net profit margin. Recall from previous sections that the total asset turnover describes the technical parameters of how a health plan serves its customers, making this ratio one of the better indicators of health plan model designs. By contrast, the family of profit margin ratios, of which the net profit margin is the broadest, captures the relationships between a health plan and its customers and its internal and external suppliers.

Taken on its own, return on assets (ROA) is defined as net income divided by total assets. Sometimes called return on investment (ROI), it is a measure of how profitable a business is relative to the capital deployed, regardless of whether that capital is equity or debt. Debt, in this instance, includes not just traditional long-term debt but other "trade" obligations including claims payable and obligations to employees.

As shown in Table 41.2, the investments (or assets) of the plan normally include facilities and information systems, but may also include health facilities and goodwill accumulated through business combinations depending upon the plans' model design and growth strategies.

For instance, the staff model plan has much higher fixed assets than its IPA and ASO counterparts. As shown in Table 41.3, fixed assets per member (fixed assets divided by average members) is more than three times higher. The fixed asset turnover (revenues divided by fixed assets) is higher for the IPA compared with the staff model plan. The fixed asset turnover for the ASO is lower than for the other two plans, but that is because the revenue per member is so much less. An indirect effect of the higher claim reserve levels required for IPA plans is that their levels of cash and equivalents must also be higher.

Accounts receivable are nearly always an important asset of health plans. As shown in Table 41.3, they are similar across model designs. The days of accounts receivable (accounts receivable, divided by annual revenues, times 365 days) typically amounts to two weeks of revenues. This is a ratio that can vary by type of customer and the interaction between its terms of trade and the calendar. For example, some customers pay health premiums on the first of the month, except if it falls on a weekend, in which case it will pay on the Friday before. This also affects the liability "prepaid premiums," as discussed below.

In addition to the purely technical requirements of model design, there are environmental conditions faced by health plans that affect the size of assets, but are not separately reported in health plan financial statements. These include statutory requirements and the ability of the health plan to access the capital markets.

Statutory requirements typically increase capital needs above and beyond what the enterprise's owners may consider necessary for the solvency of the health plan. State insurance departments' interest in such capital levels are intended to protect health care providers and customers from the risks of insolvency. Thus, certain types of assets, such as information systems, are not accorded value commensurate with their cost. For this reason, this additional required capital tends to be in the form of highly liquid assets, since they are less likely to be discounted by regulators. Accordingly, to achieve the same ROA as without such requirements, profit margins must be higher.

The availability of external sources of capital may also affect capital levels. It appears that publicly-traded companies, which have greater access to equity than other enterprises, tend to operate with thinner capital structures. This may reflect both the availability of external sources of capital and the ongoing discipline of these plans' capital markets. Finally, management preferences can also lead to more capital being retained on the plan's balance sheet. Such a decision may not be optimal from the standpoint of capital efficiency, but it may preserve scarce management time from the need to regularly consult with insurance regulators or to continuously seek external sources of capital.

TOTAL LEVERAGE RATIO

The total leverage ratio is total assets divided by equity. The difference between assets (which equal total liabilities plus equity) and equity is debt and other liabilities (including health claim reserves), both short and long term.

Leverage amplifies the return on assets as shown in Table 41.4. It can take a relatively modest return on assets, in the cases of the Staff and IPA model plans, and sharply increase the return on equity to double-digit levels. This is especially the case if the debt is trade-related, in which capital costs may not be displayed on the income statement. A more familiar illustration of this amplification may be as follows: if the expected appreciation on one's home is merely 5% but 75% of its value is debt, then the return on one's equity is a more exciting 20%.

Like the asset side of the balance sheet, the liability side's characteristics relate to model design, as shown in Table 41.2. Long-term debt is relatively unusual for health plans, and when it exists, tends to be related to, or even collateralized by, fixed assets. The ratio of long-term debt to fixed assets, and of long-term debt to total capital, seen in Table 41.3, are both high in the staff model plan because it has fixed assets such as facilities. Long-term debt is commonly employed by vertically integrated plans with provider-related assets, such as hospitals or clinics. A complete discussion of the cost of debt, and associated ratios such as debt-to-equity, fixed charge coverage and debt-to-EBITDA is not presented here, since traditional long-term debt is relatively unusual. When it does exist, it typically represents a small proportion of a health plan's total capitalization.

IPA model plans have greatest exposure to liabilities other than long-term. As shown in Table 41.2, often the largest liabilities are current (due within a year) and relate to the terms of trade with providers. The most important current liability is claims payable, a liability resulting from the need to match expenses (mainly estimated) with revenues (more concrete). Claims payable is sometimes called the incurred but not paid reserve (IBNP). It is comprised of actual known claims to be paid, plus an estimate of unknown claims on the date of the financial statement. The administrative cost of processing IBNP claims is also typically included as a liability. The actuarial process used to derive these estimates is described elsewhere in this text.

The days of claims payable is a measure of this important source of financial leverage. It is calculated as claims payable (IBNP) divided by annual claims, all multiplied by 365. For an IPA model, it is a measure of the length of time between when the claim is incurred and when it is finally paid. The time required for the provider to submit the claim and for the plan to process and mail the claim impact the actual time to process the claims. This can accumulate to months of time. Typical values for the various plans are shown in Table 41.3.

The IPA has days of claims payable that are typical for third party payers; one to two months. By contrast, the value is much lower in the staff model plan. In the case of a staff model plan, some health care provided to members is provided internally, and hence incurs no claim. The apparently lower days of claims payable actually reflects a model design that entails the direct provision of care. A similar calculation quirk can be found in capitated arrangements. To the extent that costs are delegated, they are not normally reserved for at the health plan level. To better estimate the length of time between when claims are incurred to when they are paid, both numerator and denominator should reflect only the dollars of claims submitted for reimbursement.

Prepaid premiums are common in plans that serve Medicare Advantage members, in cases in which month's end occurs on weekends – payments in this case are made on the Friday prior. None of the illustrative insurers actually had this liability, as shown in Table 41.2. Accounts payable and compensation payable resemble the values found in other industries.

KEY QUALIFICATIONS TO THE ANALYSIS

For a financial analysis, it is often necessary to make adjustments in reported financials to eliminate the effects of unusual or non-recurring items. This is called normalization. Such items may include: (1) those that qualify as extraordinary for accounting purposes, (2) disputed items resolved after the fact, and so reported in a later period, (3) expenses discovered after the fact, (4) significant IBNR adjustments, and (5) other items of the analyst's judgment. For instance, depending on the purpose for which the analysis is used, these others may also include legal settlements and start-up costs for new products.

OTHER FINANCIAL ANALYSES AND APPLICATIONS

We began this chapter with a framework for discussing financial ratios. This section briefly touches on common applications of those ratios. These include year-over-year analyses, comparisons with other enterprises, and financial planning and analysis.

Year-over-Year. This analysis looks at financial ratios over different twelve-month periods. Year-over-year variances can be identified and remedied, especially using same size income statements. This approach has near perfect comparability.

Comparing similar twelve month periods has the virtue of eliminating the effects of seasonal patterns. Marketing is especially heavy late in the year, and the medical costs that drive medical management also exhibit seasonal patterns. Accordingly, twelve month comparisons are often more useful than successive quarter comparisons.

It is often helpful to decompose the sources of change in revenues and expenses. So, for instance, revenue growth can be separated into membership growth and premium rate growth. Such parsing of growth rates should be interpreted in light of any changes in the nature of the product, such as the increasing acceptance of low premium, high deductible products.

A drawback of an enterprise's use of longitudinal comparisons is that the historical results can cause the performance bar to be set too high or too low.

Comparisons with Other, Similar Enterprises. By comparing with similar insurers, a health plan can identify whether it operates at best practice and set best practice goals if it does not.

Ideally, the insurers being compared should have similar business models, offer similar products, and perhaps also have similar operational philosophies. Having similar geographic focus and capital cost conditions is also helpful. While economies of scale are generally limited to a few functions and a modest impact, achieving similarity in size may enhance comparability.

To do such comparisons, data must be gathered from a universe of peer companies. Free data is available on publicly traded insurers from the Securities and Exchange Commission's website. Data on local competitors is available through the National Association of Insurance Commissioner's website or through state insurance departments, usually at modest cost.

It is important to be mindful of the reliability of the data, especially in the case of subsidiaries. Many health plans that report to state regulators are subsidiaries of large multi-state plans. Their income statement information may reflect intersegment charges whose purpose is repatriation of cash, rather than actual costs.

Other drawbacks to publicly available information are that cost segmentation by product may not be available in a useful form, and cost definitions may vary from insurer to insurer. For instance, the medical management costs of publicly traded companies are variously reported as administrative costs or health care costs, depending on the reporting company.

More precise cost information and product segmentation is available for a fee through commercial sources. These can be accessed through participation in a benchmarking study with other similar organizations, or by licensing the resulting materials. The drawback of these sources is that, for competitive reasons, the identities and values of the insurers contributing to the data set may not be known to the user. Instead, comparisons are made between the health plan and, de-identified quartile, median, or similar values.

Financial Planning and Analysis. Financial planning and analysis involves establishing goals and measuring performance relative to those goals. There are analytical advantages to selecting a single metric to maximize, say return on equity and growth, and employing the financial ratios to support this analysis.

The process of financial planning and analysis occurs prospectively, in an annual or long-term budget, and then retrospectively, through a review of how performance compares to these objectives. In this way, financial planning complements financial analysis.

If one of the tasks in planning is determining the attractiveness of specific potential endeavors, then a discount rate should be applied reflecting the riskiness of that business. The time horizons should reflect the needs of the planning process. Some believe that the horizons for such projections should be limited by the ability to have confidence in their reliability. Three to five years is a common time horizon.[1]

---

[1] Editor's note: There is some controversy over this. Some feel that failure to complete any projection is equivalent to saying there will be zero impact from such future activity. In that case, we may be better off with a

In addition to estimating membership, prices, and costs, it is beneficial to estimate the effect on Risk Based Capital (RBC) requirements. For instance, when modeling the effect of a sale of an insured business line, considerations should include not only the proceeds of the sale, but the effect on shareholder value as a result of reducing RBC requirements.

Interim results can be measured against long-term projections. Similarly, performance can be compared with peers, through statutory statements, SEC documents, or commercial services, as discussed above.

External Manifestations of Shareholder Value

Maximization of owners' value is a useful paradigm for financial analysis of health plans, regardless of organizational form. However, there can be major differences between this objective and its recognition by the stock market. This concern is only relevant to publicly-traded insurers; there is never stock market recognition for any of the companies that are not publicly traded, and health plans that are not publicly traded serve one-half of all insured Americans.

Even for publicly-traded insurers, the efficient market hypothesis notwithstanding, stock prices can be an imperfect metric. For example, stock prices sometimes reflect short-term phenomena, investment analysts may not understand the market realities, and it may be impossible to clearly communicate detailed or confidential aspects of strategies to them. While in theory, the risk of an unfriendly takeover should force the link between stock price and managerial actions, actually there are few, if any, examples of hostile takeovers. This may change if the health plan industry becomes more of a transaction-oriented business.

Regardless of the stock price performance, planning should be for the long term. Stock prices, over the long term, should reflect performance of the plan. To focus on share price rather than health plan performance may lead to decisions that harm, rather than enhance, long term shareholder value.

The market valuation of a company has an element that is partly external and partly manageable by the company. We began this chapter highlighting the implications of the Gordon Constant Growth Model. The required rate of return for an equity investor is largely beyond the scope of this discussion. In brief, that required rate of return reflects the assessment of the market of the riskiness of the investment in the company. While some of that required rate of return relates to the riskiness of the industry and the economy as a whole, it may also reflect the uncertainty of either the market's assessment of management, or the transparency of information that it provides to shareholders. Thus, external manifestations of shareholder value through share price can be best achieved through shrewd management of earnings and growth, combined with maximum feasible transparency.

---

not-so-great best estimate than an even worse estimate of zero. Some actuaries segregate this element of their projection, so users can do with it as they please.

CONCLUSION

This discussion of financial and operational performance began with the simplifying organizing principle that successful health plans operate to maximize their value over the long term, regardless of their ownership structure. The Gordon Constant Growth Model highlights the importance of growth in earnings, as a driver of value.

In turn, earnings growth is both predicted by, and limited by, return on equity. Return on equity, as the DuPont Formula shows, is achieved through efficient capital deployment, high long-term profitability, and prudent use of financial leverage. Many other ratios used in the analysis of financial and operational performance support and refine the profit margin, total asset turnover, and total leverage ratio components of return on equity.

This analysis may also be deployed in numerous applications including year-over-year analyses, comparisons with other enterprises, and financial planning and analysis. The suggested framework assures that the analysis is exhaustive and oriented to the health plan's goals.

42 ENTERPRISE RISK MANAGEMENT FOR GROUP HEALTH INSURERS

Thomas Nightingale

"[T]here are known knowns; there are things we know we know. We also know there are known unknowns; that is to say we know there are some things we do not know. But there are also unknown unknowns – the ones we don't know we don't know."

Secretary of Defense Donald Rumsfeld, February 2002

INTRODUCTION

The benefit Enterprise Risk Management (ERM) brings to an organization had previously not been widely accepted by group health insurers. In part, this is because ERM was initially developed within the banking and investment industry, with an emphasis on risks important to them, such as market or credit risk and asset-liability mismatch. The weaknesses brought to light by the 2008 financial crisis justify a focus on market risk and credit risk for these types of institutions. But most group health insurers do not have the same degree of exposure to this type of risk due to the short-term nature of their liabilities, so they have been skeptical of ERM's benefits.

Group health insurers are primarily exposed to underwriting risk or rate inadequacy – the inability of premium to cover claims and other expenses. On its face, rate inadequacy is at least a clearly defined problem, if not a simple one. If claim trend can be projected accurately, and if premium rates are high enough while claims and expenses are low enough, then the problem disappears. ERM would seem to be, as some have put it, "a solution looking for a problem."

However, reasons for rate inadequacy are not limited to morbidity or actuarial risk. Inadequate rates are not simply a problem of incorrectly projecting claim trend. Required premium may be correctly estimated, yet rate increases may be denied or delayed by the state insurance department. Further, management's opinion of the importance of margin versus membership tends to be cyclical, and required rates may not be close to what is agreed upon between underwriters and salespeople for long stretches of time.

Since the passage of the Affordable Care Act (ACA) in March, 2010, regulatory risk has increased considerably. In addition to greater scrutiny of rate filings, minimum loss ratio requirements mandated by the ACA may place a maximum on the level of increase that can be requested, regardless of whether the resulting rates will cover claims and other expenses. Other circumstances may not directly affect premium level or claim experience, but may still result in rate inadequacy. For example, declining enrollment, perhaps caused by increased competition, could ultimately result in an inability to cover administrative overhead.

Group health insurers operate in an environment of competing and potentially harmful forces. Complexity often means that there is a lack of understanding of root causes, interactions between parts, and feedback loops. Insurance pools can occasionally undergo an antiselection spiral, a classic example of a feedback loop. Emerging risk hides within this complexity, and in the gaps between silos of knowledge. Premium rates may be inadequate, not because trend was underestimated, but because of math or logic errors in a complex projection model.

However, risk for a group insurer is more than just not being able to connect the dots of people and processes within a complex infrastructure. Even with good knowledge of the organization and the outside environment, interpreting that information and determining the correct course to follow in an uncertain future is not always clear. Poor leadership or judgment by senior management may result in making wrong strategic choices, which compromise the company's ability to effectively compete in a changing market.

Organizations that failed during the 2008 financial crisis were vulnerable to market and credit risk because of deeper underlying problems. These problems included poor understanding of the business complexities and misaligned management incentives. Similarly, a multitude of circumstances and events may ultimately lead to inadequate premium rates; and each of those circumstances and events are multifaceted, often with subtle underlying causes. The ERM process is structured to manage the underlying causes, as well as the symptomatic reasons for failure.

Recognition of ERM's value has, over time, become more firmly established. Credit rating agencies are now asking group health insurers about their ERM practices and, increasingly, Boards of Directors are insisting that management develop and implement an ERM program. A significant step forward occurred in 2011 when, as part of the Solvency Modernization Initiative, the National Association of Insurance Commissioners (NAIC) voted to adopt a new insurance regulation: the Own Risk and Solvency Assessment (ORSA), through which insurers will be expected to regularly assess their enterprise-wide risk management process and the adequacy of their capital under both normal and stressed environments.

In addition to a new model act, the NAIC subsequently issued a Guidance Manual[1] providing expectations regarding the scope of ORSA and the information to be included in the ORSA Summary Report. The American Academy of Actuaries has also provided guidance on ERM. In 2012, the Actuarial Standards Board released two Actuarial Standards of Practice (ASOPs) addressing risk evaluation systems[2] (including risk models, economic capital, stress testing and emerging risk) and risk treatment[3] (including risk appetite, risk tolerance, and mitigation activities).

TRADITIONAL RISK MANAGEMENT

Every organization, regardless of size or industry, exists and functions in an environment with inherent risks. The organization's ability to complete its intended mission and achieve corporate goals is constantly being challenged by potentially harmful circumstances and events that can arise from both internal and external sources. In response to this situation, organizations take a variety of actions intended to counteract or avoid either the possibility of harm occurring or to limit the financial effect of the harmful event.

---

[1] NAIC Own Risk and Solvency Assessment Guidance Manual, July 2014.
[2] ASOP #46, Risk Evaluation in Enterprise Risk Management, September 2012.
[3] ASOP #47, Risk Treatment in Enterprise Risk Management, December 2012.

Every organization manages risk, but that is where the similarity ends. The universe of potentially harmful conditions is unique to every organization; hence, the response taken is unique. Of course there is overlap of risks from one company to another. External forces such as inflation, regulation, or technological innovation are often felt by all within an industry. But internal forces and the approach taken by management to meet these and other market conditions will be different for every organization, thus generating unique risks.

Within industries, various risk management techniques have been developed to address mutual concerns. Options, futures, and other financial risk management techniques, such as durational matching and cash flow testing are used to manage credit and market risk within the banking and investment industry. In manufacturing, root cause analysis and continuous quality improvement are used to minimize production errors. Insurance risk is addressed through actuarial science. SWOT (strengths-weaknesses-opportunities-threats) analysis is a management technique used in many industries to set corporate strategy in response to competitive risk.

All of these risk management methods address important concerns, but each of them is focused on only a limited portion of the overall risk profile. Further, day-to-day decisions made by management and by employees cause a company's risk profile to be dynamic as well as unique. Organizational performance is the result of complex interactions among multiple factors and human decisions. This behavior cannot be determined by studying the components in isolation, and the entire risk profile cannot be managed in silos. Since traditional risk management approaches are focused on particular risks or types of risk, they lack the necessary integration and coordination required to manage the entire threat universe. ERM arose in order to fill this vacuum.

ENTERPRISE RISK MANAGEMENT

The concept of ERM and the need for a new approach to risk management developed as organizations and their environment became increasingly complex. As the organizational flow-chart of even a relatively small company will demonstrate, the delivery of a product or service in today's high-tech world requires a diversity of specialized functions and people, each of which provide inputs that must be combined into a whole. It is management's responsibility to coordinate the process of combining the parts into the whole, but this does not mean that management understands each of the parts, or even completely understands the process of combining the parts.

Unfortunately, threats to the organization develop and hide in these gaps of knowledge and understanding. A goal of ERM, therefore, is to help management better comprehend the organization's complex interactions and, in doing so, identify and mitigate any risks hiding in these gaps. ERM differs from traditional risk management in this respect. While traditional risk management focuses on specific known threats to the organization, ERM attempts to identify and mitigate risk created by interaction among the parts, or risk that is not apparent due to corporate and environmental complexity – "unknown unknowns."

Features of ERM that distinguish it from traditional risk management include the following:
1. Instead of focusing only on risk mitigation or avoidance, ERM works to create organizational resilience in achieving corporate goals.
2. ERM views the organization holistically, rather than in silos.
3. ERM is embedded within the management framework; it is the responsibility of all, rather than that of just a single risk manager or department.
4. ERM helps provide a common language to discuss risks and opportunities across the organization.
5. ERM provides a framework for identification and evaluation of potentially harmful conditions and events.
6. ERM helps ensure the organization assumes no more risk than necessary in order to achieve its goals.

As the last two attributes indicate, ERM focuses on identification and control of threats to the organization and, as required, ERM will make use of traditional risk management techniques. But managing risk is a means to an end, not an end in itself. As identified in the very first attribute, the primary function of ERM is to help ensure that corporate goals are achieved. ERM is a method to improve organizational performance and resilience using risk management as a tool.

Since managers are tasked with meeting goals and improving performance, it should not be surprising that the basic components of ERM are performed, perhaps informally, in many if not most organizations today. Managers try to view the organization holistically. They try to assess and mitigate risk to the organization. But they don't call it ERM; they call it doing their job – managing the organization. The difference between what managers are currently doing and what ERM would ask of them is to be more rigorous in the application of the ERM concepts.

There is a cost to be paid for the additional rigor, however, particularly in management and staff time. Given limited resources, the necessary effort is unlikely to occur if the resulting benefit cannot be clearly communicated. Managers tasked with implementing ERM should emphasize ERM's focus on performance improvement when discussing the program. If corporate goals are constantly used as a benchmark for determining effort and program design, then its value is more clearly understood. Also, by emphasizing and focusing on corporate goals, ERM can be seen as more than just another off-the-shelf program. It is a process that is scalable to any organization and can be adapted to meet unique needs and circumstances.

ERM Conceptual Framework

The typical risk management approach, often referred to as the control cycle, includes a process of identifying risk, evaluating risk and mitigating risk. First, identify circumstances and events that may cause operational or financial harm to the organization. Next, determine the likelihood and severity of these potentially harmful events. Then, decide on methods for reducing the possibility these events will happen, or ways to mitigate their financial impact when they do happen. Of these three components – identification, evaluation, and mitigation – the process of identifying risk and compiling a complete picture of the corporate risk profile is where most risk management programs fall short of what ERM intends to accomplish. If the risk management process limits its focus to harmful situations that are apparent and known, then it is likely missing other risky conditions.

The perceived risk profile, which includes known risks, and the true risk profile, which includes unknown risks, will always differ to some degree. A goal of ERM is to expand the awareness of risk, so that what is perceived more closely aligns with actual risk to the organization.

FACTORS THAT OBSCURE EMERGING RISK

The perceived risk profile is, in effect, a hypothesis about the various risky conditions affecting the organization. If a potentially harmful condition is not perceived, it is a type 2 error in the risk hypothesis – a false-negative indication that no potentially harmful condition exists when in fact it does. Some type 2 errors, what could be called "risk blindness," are the result of an uncertain and chaotic environment. Risk blindness can also be self-induced; perhaps the result of poor leadership. Organizations that fail to see emerging risk, and then fail to react appropriately, may not have established appropriate risk indicators, or do not perform analysis to fully understand the business system and the environment.

The specific chain of events that lead to a harmful event are often unique, but there tends to be considerable consistency in the underlying reasons why the crisis was not detected in a developmental stage; that is, why a type 2 error occurred in the risk hypothesis. These reasons include (1) an uncertain future; (2) poor information about current conditions in the organization and the environment; (3) poor understanding of organizational complexity; (4) poor judgment in deciding how to respond to organizational challenges; and (5) financial incentives given to management that do not align with other stakeholders.

UNCERTAIN FUTURE

As Yogi Berra said, "the future isn't what it used to be." His quip states succinctly that the future is likely to be different than expected. The time factor is what most often comes to mind when considering risk. Claim trend must be projected when setting rates, but actual claim experience may differ. In spite of that, it is the rare organization that tests alternate scenarios of the future or develops contingency plans based on those scenarios. Financial projections and business plans are often based on a single view of what the future will look like, ignoring that there are many possible views that could occur.

POOR INFORMATION

The present isn't what it used to be either, one might add. Expectations for the future are anchored in the present, relying on knowledge about current conditions in the company and in the outside environment. To the extent current knowledge is limited or inaccurate, expectations for the future may be flawed. The information factor is a second, but still important, reason for risk blindness. Emerging risk can only be managed if complete, accurate, relevant, and timely information about current company conditions gets to the appropriate decision-makers. Often, needed data is not available or there may be too much information, making it difficult to identify what is relevant and important for communication to management.

POOR UNDERSTANDING

Even when the right information gets to the right person, it may not always be possible to understand its meaning. The conceptual factor is the next barrier faced when trying to make sense of complex organizations operating in a complex world. The information presented may be ambiguous or may conflict with other information. The interaction between parts may not be obvious and conditions harmful to the company may only occur after a long sequence of seemingly innocuous events. The world is chaotic and managers often have limited ability to see meaning through the chaos.

POOR JUDGMENT

Corporate managers are not simply machines that absorb knowledge. Managing a corporation means taking action – directing, coordinating, planning, implementing – and taking action requires the ability to judge what the right actions should be and the likely consequences of those actions. The judgment or leadership factor may be the most difficult barrier to overcome in addressing emerging risk, since the actions taken may precipitate the very risks one seeks to avoid. Judgment errors may occur when the organization lacks a culture of dissent, or when there is little diversity of opinion. Judgment is also affected by the normal human tendency to fixate on current conditions and assume the future will look like the present. Corporate leaders need to anticipate changing conditions if they want to stay ahead of the competition.

MANAGEMENT INCENTIVES

An important subset of the last factor is the effect financial incentives have on management's judgment and leadership. As the 2008 financial crisis demonstrated, management may expose an organization to greater risk in an effort to generate high corporate earnings. Financial rewards given to corporate executives often have significant upside potential when the company does well, but limited downside risk to the executives when the company does poorly. This incentive arrangement may encourage corporate managers to be overly aggressive in pursuing business opportunities, ignoring the organization's ability to sustain future adverse conditions. In this situation, the interest of management and the interest of shareholders or other stakeholders are no longer aligned.

ERM IMPROVES PERCEPTION OF EMERGING RISK

Due to the above risk blindness factors, emerging risk is an ongoing challenge for every organization, including group health insurers. Every complex situation has the potential for unseen risk. In addition, areas of emerging risk are often connected to areas of poor performance within the organization, or in how the organization relates to its external environment. Fortunately, ERM provides a way to address these issues. The six attributes of ERM described in the introduction are designed to reduce type 2 error, by improving detection of emerging risk and then to appropriately manage risk consistent with corporate goals.

By providing a framework for identifying and evaluating risk under a variety of scenarios, ERM improves organizational resilience to future adverse conditions. By focusing on corporate goals, ERM helps determine what information is relevant to decision-making. By providing a common language for discussing risk and by taking a holistic approach to analyzing risk, ERM helps make sense of a complex environment. Because ERM is embedded in the management structure and is the responsibility of all, it supports conditions necessary for good judgment and decision-making. And, by defining risk appetite consistent with corporate goals and risk capital, ERM better aligns management interests with shareholder and stakeholder interests.

The ERM process decomposes organizational complexity into more tractable parts, while still retaining a holistic view. In doing so, type 2 error is reduced and opportunities are identified for improved organizational performance.

THE PROCESS OF MANAGING ENTERPRISE-WIDE RISK

The basic components of risk management are the same – identify risk, evaluate risk, and mitigate risk. ERM differs from traditional risk management in how this process is approached. Expanding the risk profile by searching for unknown risk is a core difference between ERM and traditional risk management. Once the risk profile is established, ERM passes the baton to more traditional risk management methods of evaluating and mitigating known risk. ERM completes the process by ensuring a holistic, integrated approach to risk management, and by determining appropriate risk capital. It then follows up with monitoring and oversight.

EXPANDING THE PERCEIVED RISK PROFILE

The perceived risk profile is the organization's hypothesis of potentially harmful conditions. Based on this hypothesis, risk mitigation steps are taken, and risk capital is maintained for harmful events that are not controlled by other means. While the intent of ERM is to improve the accuracy of the risk hypothesis, complete accuracy is not possible in a chaotic and uncertain world. The effect of the ERM process, then, is that increased sensitivity to risk will predominate over improved accuracy. The risk profile will be expanded by reducing type 2 error or "unknown unknowns." But the risk profile might also be expanded to include more type 1 error – a false-positive indication that a potentially harmful condition exists, when in fact it does not.

Expanding the perceived risk profile to align more closely with the true risk profile has two steps: (1) develop a detailed description of the business system; and (2) construct a risk hypothesis for the organization, by determining areas of uncertainty and risk of harm within the system.

DESCRIBING THE BUSINESS SYSTEM

In order to optimize business performance, it is necessary to manage uncertainty; both internally and externally, now and in the future. Managing uncertainty requires knowing where the potential for failure resides in the system, which is identifiable only with a clear understanding of how the business works, how it relates to other players in the system, and how this relationship can change over time.

Describing the business system and its environment is the most challenging part of the ERM process. If not constrained, it could easily become unmanageable and costly. This should not be a quixotic search for every unknown risky condition, regardless of its potential for causing harm. Further, as noted above, risk detection and analysis methods are never perfect. Increasing sensitivity to risk will result in fewer false-negatives in the risk hypothesis, but it may also increase false-positives with a consequent, and possibly unnecessary, expenditure of resources.

Because the consequences of type 2 error can be catastrophic to the organization, the ERM process emphasizes increased sensitivity to risk, accepting the potential for additional cost from excess type 1 errors (for example, cost from risk mitigation strategies, or additional reserves). But balance needs to be maintained. Too many false-positive indications from overly sensitive monitoring will overwhelm the ERM process and may discredit the effectiveness of the program.

In order to control type 1 error and its associated cost, the system description should be directed and constrained by focusing primarily on reasons for type 2 error, and by considering factors that are most important for improving business performance and achieving corporate goals. Risk identification should be focused on risks that are both material to the size and capital position of the insurer and relevant to its business plan.

The following are examples of typical questions that might help describe the business system. This illustration is not intended to be an exhaustive list. Each organization should consider for itself what questions are most important, within their business plan and operating system.

Uncertain Future

Normal and stressed environments: Describe possible future conditions with a focus on situations that will cause stress to the organization. How will those situations affect the organization's balance sheet, income statement, and cash flow?

Primary objectives: Business plans are all based on various assumptions about what will happen in the future. What are those assumptions? What are the key variables? What needs to happen in the short term and long term for corporate goals to be met? What else can happen in the future and what would the consequences be for the organization?

Strengths and weaknesses: What are the organization's current core competencies in terms of people, process, and technology, and what will be required over the next ten years? How does the organization compare to its main insurance competitors? Or to other non-insurance vendors in the market space (for example, third-party administration, data and health risk analytics)?

Pricing Assumptions: What are the primary assumptions by line of business and how can they vary? Is price competition increasing, declining or remaining stable? What lines of business are the primary sources of profitability for the organization? If future enrollment in the lines of business changes size relative to each other, what is the effect on aggregate profits?

Major initiatives: Describe major business initiatives and the critical factors required for success. Identify important milestones and timeline. Is a strong project management process in place for each initiative?

Investments: What is the effect on cash flow and investments of a market downturn or rising interest rates, combined with a claim trend significantly greater than expected?

Poor Information

Standard Reporting: What information is needed to properly monitor and manage the business system? Does current reporting include this information? Will the information collected indicate if the system is reaching critical stress points? If not, what information should be collected for this purpose?

Data Analytics: Is there a centralized data warehouse? Describe its capabilities and limitations. What analytic capabilities are available for monitoring key utilization and cost measures, claim trend, and financial performance? What information and analytics are required by patients, group accounts, and health service providers?

Performance Indicators: What are important performance measures that indicate whether milestones and goals are being achieved? Are the indicators routinely monitored? Is there an effective process for communicating important information to key decision-makers? What is that process?

Competitive information and analysis: Is competitive data being collected and analyzed? What information about the competitive environment *should be* collected and analyzed?

Communication: How is critical information communicated to management?

Poor Understanding

Operations: How is operational performance measured and monitored? Where in the system is management's understanding of process superficial? Where do internal and external business units interact? What feedback loops exist in the system? Are there correlations among business units? Are these interactions important to performance and goal achievement? How do the interactions change over time? How will each operational unit perform under stressed conditions?

Environment: What market and economic forces are driving changes in the industry? Identify environmental stress points. How will this impact the organization? What technological forces are driving changes in the industry and how does this relate to the organization's core competencies?

Subsidiaries: Describe the services provided by any subsidiaries or divisions that operate autonomously. What is the organization's visibility to subsidiaries' operations? Are subsidiaries or autonomous divisions geographically separated from the parent organization? Are internal controls and limits of authority in place and followed at subsidiaries?

Pricing and forecasting models: Are the forecast and risk measurement models (for example actuarial models) relied upon for making decisions? Are the forecasts of future performance clearly understood? Describe the primary formulas and key assumptions. Have complex models been peer reviewed and tested? Are models updated to reflect emerging experience and current knowledge of the environment?

Compliance: Who has oversight over compliance with state and federal insurance laws and regulations? Describe the process of monitoring and ensuring the organization complies with new regulations. How will regulatory change affect the organization?

Major change initiatives: How does the organization manage complex corporate change? Describe the reasons for success or failure of prior initiatives.

Poor Judgment

Forward Thinking/Strategic Planning: Describe the strategic planning process. What are the major challenges facing the organization over the next five years? How does the organization need to change to meet these challenges? What contingency plans are in place if the strategic environment changes?

Decision-making: Describe the decision-making process for major initiatives. What are the limits of authority for committing the organization to a business plan? Is there effective Board oversight? What conditions might cause management to bypass the normal decision-making process?

Evaluation of alternatives: Are alternatives routinely evaluated prior to major corporate decisions? What is the process for evaluating alternatives?

Dissent: Is there an open culture for dissent and discussion of risk? Are there past examples of poor results from major decisions? How was that decision process similar or different from normal?

Management Incentives

Incentives: Describe the management incentives formula. What is the expected effect of management incentives on the decision-making process? Are management incentives aligned with corporate mission and goals, and with other stakeholders? What conditions might change the effect management incentives have on the decision-making process? Is the management incentive program routinely reviewed and updated by the Board?

Risk appetite and tolerance: Is there a clear definition of risk appetite and risk tolerance consistent with company goals and available capital? Are these limits adhered to?

Ethics: Is there a stated code of ethical conduct for the organization? Are there consistent, meaningful, and enforceable penalties for violating the ethical code? What situations might put pressure on ethical conduct?

Responding to these and other relevant questions will often require development of abstract models of the system. Such models can be used to test the sensitivity to underlying assumptions and variability. This will help build a description of the organization that focuses on system components and connections that matter to corporate mission and goals. Various techniques are available to develop responses and build a description of the business system.

Operational and conceptual flow charts of the business system can be developed, with varying levels of detail depending on the need. Critical dependencies, both internal and external, should be examined. Interactions and correlations between components and feedback loops should be identified.

Financial modeling and projections, with scenario testing of key variables, will help identify areas of uncertainty and critical assumptions in business plans. The speed of company response to changes in the environment should be considered in these models. For example, there is typically a lag time between when claim trend changes and when the change is sensed by the organization. There is additional lag time for the organization to be able to file and implement a resulting rate change.

Other approaches to understanding complex processes include the following:

- Game theory can help evaluate possible responses to initiatives from competitors, brokers, and customers. Game theory can also be used to evaluate the potential effect of management incentives on decision-making.
- Decision analysis training, and adhering to a decision-making framework that acknowledges risk appetite and risk tolerance, will help management evaluate the adequacy of their decisions.
- Root cause analysis can be used to understand prior failures and how to improve future performance, by eliminating underlying causes. It can also be used to analyze successes, to determine whether they might be repeated in the future.
- Benchmarking key system variables to "best practices," and understanding any reasons for their variance from that high level of performance, will help identify areas of low performance.
- Cultural assessments can help to identify underlying constraints to an open decision-making process within the organization.

THE RISK HYPOTHESIS

The business system description is used to develop a list of potential events that may cause business plan outcomes to vary from expected. This forms the organization's risk hypothesis. It is a structured understanding of the risk profile, affecting the organization and its ability to achieve corporate goals, under both normal and stressed conditions. The risk hypothesis feeds the risk management process, and a risk "dashboard" is developed. The risk dashboard is a high-level overview of risk characteristics, such as likelihood and severity of harm. It also includes a description of risk mitigation strategies and the status of their implementation.

Prior to taking the time and effort to describe the system, the organization was likely aware of many major risks. This would include the risk of rate inadequacy caused by actual claim trend exceeding expected trend. Other "known knowns" might include operational hazards, such as fire or earthquake, or legal risk due to an inadvertent release of protected health information. However, the effort to develop a detailed description of the system is undertaken to help identify previously *unknown* risk.

Unknown risks are embedded in the complexity of the system and tend to be more subtle, the result of unstated assumptions the organization is making about current conditions or about the future. The interrogatory approach used above for describing the system is intended to assist the search by focusing on areas most likely to include unstated assumptions that could affect the company's ability to achieve its goals. Poor data and "black-box" models are examples of unstated assumptions. It is *assumed* that current information is providing the correct indications. It is *assumed* that the models are operating as intended. However, the organization cannot be sure that these assumptions are true given the current state of analytics and understanding. Deficiencies identified in the decision-making process and misaligned management incentives also create the potential for future results to vary from expected.

The process of identifying areas of uncertainty and risk will likely place a spotlight on low business performance and, conversely, areas of low performance should be scrutinized since they are a breeding ground for emerging risk. Possible indicators of emerging risk due to low performance include the following:

- High employee turnover,
- Frequent reassignment or replacement of project managers for major initiatives,
- Frequent downtime of computer systems,
- Frequent manual overrides or intervention required,
- Numerous manual processes,
- Frequent complaints from internal or external customers,
- Significant variance of key indicators from normal or best practice, and
- Reactive approach to problem-solving instead of being proactive.

Another indicator of low performance, and possibly a useful measure of the magnitude of type 2 error in the risk hypothesis, is the frequency of surprises. How often is the organization confronted with the unexpected? How often are big expenses an unknown to management and the actuarial and finance departments? How many write-offs are there? What are they for? How close were budgeted costs to actual costs? Which departments have wide variances? How often is management presented with new information that should have been known previously and may have affected prior decisions? Surprises do not need to be full-blown crises. Even small unexpected events, if they occur often, could indicate that the set of unknown risk is material.

Each of these indicators provides input to the risk hypothesis. In addition, the organization should take advantage of the work done by the Academy and the NAIC to develop the statutory Risk-Based Capital (RBC) formula. The components and subcomponents of the formula reflect risks typical for health insurance companies, so they should not be overlooked in the development of a risk hypothesis or risk profile.

RISK MANAGEMENT

Once the risk profile has been developed and expanded, traditional risk management techniques are used for (1) evaluating the likelihood and magnitude of potential harm from the risky conditions in the profile, and (2) developing risk mitigation strategies. The risk management process should continue to focus on company goals, and a holistic view of the organization should be maintained. Prior to implementing a risk mitigation strategy, its effect on the entire company should be evaluated. Strategies directed at a specific risk may have unintended consequences elsewhere in the organization.

RISK EVALUATION

The evaluation process is not an exact science. Probability values are difficult to determine in many cases. If the harmful event were to occur, the magnitude of the loss is often speculative. However, the tools developed for use in describing the system, such as financial models and scenario testing, can often be used as an aid in estimating how often an event is likely to occur, and what the ramifications might be. General ranges of likelihood and severity can be developed with the help of subject matter experts, and can be augmented with internal or industry data.

Here again, the work of the Academy and the NAIC to develop the statutory RBC formula may provide useful insights into the characteristics of risk typically faced by health insurers. Care should be taken, however, since each organization is unique. There may be more or less vulnerability to various risks than that of the average health insurer contemplated when the Academy and NAIC jointly developed the RBC formula. Given ERM's goal of increasing organizational resilience, having an effective ERM program in place will presumably *reduce vulnerability to risk,* compared to the average health insurer.

For each risk in the organization's hypothesis, it is helpful to categorize the probability of occurrence into low, medium, and high likelihood ranges. Severity of harm can be categorized by various levels of significance such as minimal, moderate, high, and catastrophic. The category an event is placed into can be determined by its potential effect on total company surplus, or can be based upon the time required to resume normal operations. Risk evaluation data should be collected in a risk register to record scenarios and risky events that have been considered, along with an evaluation of their likelihood and severity. The degree of detail in the risk register will vary depending upon the complexity of the business system and the risk being evaluated. Typical information contained in the register will include the following items:

- Description of the risk scenario,
- Details of how and when the scenario was identified,
- Which corporate objectives/goals the scenario affects,
- Description of the method used to quantify risk exposure and the time horizon for modeling,
- The range of outcomes considered,

- Outcome of a reverse stress test[4],
- Assessment of likelihood, speed of onset, and impact prior to mitigation under both normal and stressed environments,
- Description of mitigation strategies and assessment of their effectiveness, cost, and speed of response,
- Assessment of likelihood and impact after mitigation under both normal and stressed environments, including an assessment of the effect on the organization's balance sheet, income statement, and cash flows,
- Assignment of responsibility for monitoring the risk scenario, and
- Details regarding action plans to contain scenario impact within the organization's risk tolerance.

The ORSA Guidance Manual recognizes that quantifying exposure may be difficult for some risks, so qualitative measures may be appropriate. However, for each risk, an attempt should be made to evaluate a range of possible outcomes, particularly under stressed conditions, and the effect of those outcomes on capital.

RISK MITIGATION

The final step in the risk management process is deciding what to do about the various potentially harmful conditions that have been identified and evaluated. Risk mitigation can take any number of forms, depending upon the type of risk and its potential for damage to the organization.

First, *risk avoidance* is the most extreme method of managing risk and has limited use for the core business. Some risk will always exist, unless the organization simply chooses to dissolve itself, which is an unlikely occurrence and certainly not in line with achieving corporate goals. Core business risk must be managed using one of the other methods; it cannot be avoided. However, future business plans may include options to expand or diversify into new areas. Such risks can be avoided by declining to exercise those options.

The next method of risk mitigation is *risk transfer*. While most risks cannot be completely avoided, the financial harm that may occur can occasionally be transferred to another party. The most common method of risk transfer, of course, is insurance. Fire and hazard insurance, liability insurance, and workers compensation insurance are common for most businesses. For group health insurers, large claim risk may be ceded to a reinsurer. Utilization or claim cost risk is often transferred to health care providers via capitation arrangements or other reimbursement methods such as case rate pricing.

Next, controlling risk through performance improvement is the only option available for most core business risk, which cannot be avoided or transferred without closing the doors. *Risk control* methods vary depending upon the type of risk. Strategic risk can be addressed through strategic planning, business initiatives, and developing contingency plans. Operational risk is mitigated through internal controls, business continuity plans, project change management, ethics and compliance, monitoring, and communication. Actuarial and underwriting risk is controlled through best practice methodology and internal policies,

---

[4] A reverse stress test identifies the conditions that would cause risk capital to be exceeded.

which are in turn supported by a high performing infrastructure (including the data warehouse and analytic support).

In order to evaluate the best approach for mitigating or controlling risk, it is helpful to clearly define the type and amount of risk the organization is willing to assume – its risk appetite. This will likely have a direct relationship to the organization's business plan. In addition to risk appetite, risk tolerances and limits should be identified for each risk and for the risk portfolio as a whole. Risk tolerance indicates the risk bearing capacity of the organization in terms of available capital.

Not all risk control methods are directed by the organization itself. Society has an interest in maintaining the stability and viability of insurance companies. If they become bankrupt, any claims against the organization will revert back to the insured customers. Therefore, states establish monitoring mechanisms and require that insurers maintain minimum surplus, or risk-based capital, levels. If surplus falls below these minimums, insurance department intervention may occur. For more information on this subject, see Chapter 39.

RISK DASHBOARD

The risk dashboard provides a high-level overview of the organization's exposure to risk under both normal and stressed conditions. It summarizes detailed information from the risk hypothesis and the risk register. This includes estimates of risk likelihood, severity, and mitigation approaches. The organization's risk tolerance is also identified and compared to likely outcomes under stressed conditions. The following characteristics should be entered into the dashboard for each identified risk:

- Brief description of the risk,
- Line of business affected,
- Gross likelihood – prior to mitigation, the expected frequency of occurrence under normal and stressed conditions,
- Gross impact or severity – prior to any mitigation, the potential magnitude of loss under normal and stressed conditions,
- Gross risk rating - the combination of likelihood and severity,
- Control effectiveness – ability of mitigation strategies to reduce likelihood or severity,
- Net likelihood – expected frequency after mitigation strategies,
- Net impact or severity – potential magnitude after mitigation strategies,
- Net risk rating – combination of likelihood and severity after mitigation under normal and stressed conditions, including the effect on capital,
- Tolerance – willingness to accept residual risk after mitigation; capital available to support risk,
- Net risk rating vs. tolerance, and
- Action plan status – implementation status of mitigation strategies.

The risk dashboard should be continuously monitored and updated. Staff responsible for implementing mitigation strategies and process improvement should be identified and held accountable. To the extent that risk exceeds tolerance, additional mitigation strategies should be identified, or other actions such as risk avoidance or transfer should be taken. Within the organization's tolerance, any remaining risk is retained and must be supported by corporate risk capital.

RISK CAPITAL

Insurance organizations are perceived and treated differently by society than other corporations. When a consumer products company or a retail service organization goes out of business, customer losses are limited and will likely not have a life changing impact. When an insurance organization goes out of business, however, policyholders are potentially left with financial expenses well beyond their means. In the case of health insurance, a policyholder or a family member may be unable to receive needed medical treatment. Ultimately, the financial cost of an insurer default could fall back on society through welfare payments, Medicaid expenses, and lost productivity. For these reasons, states have an interest in maintaining strong, well-capitalized insurance companies and have mandated minimum levels of risk capital.

STATUTORY RISK-BASED CAPITAL

Statutory RBC is based on a generic formula that varies by type of insurance organization (life, casualty, or health), reflecting the risk characteristics typical for each type of insurer. The formula uses information from the statutory financial statement, such as asset mix and premium revenue by line of business. These and other values are multiplied by factors that reflect the risk inherent in the business. For example, the risk factor applied to net premium for comprehensive medical insurance is larger than the factor applied to Medicare supplement net premium. The lower factor for Medicare supplement reflects the lower potential variability of claim experience in that line of business. For asset default risk, United States government bonds use a factor of zero, indicating no risk of default, but a higher factor is applied to the value of other securities.

For health insurers, underwriting risk (H2) is the largest contributor to the risk-based capital charge. Other major components of the formula include asset risk (H1), including that from affiliates (H0), credit risk (H3) and general business risk (H4). The RBC amount is based on a covariance formula that combines each of the components. Essentially, the formula assumes H1, H2, H3, and H4 are independent and uncorrelated, but risk from subsidiaries (H0) is highly correlated with the parent.[5] The base RBC amount, after covariance, is then multiplied by 50%, resulting in the Authorized Control Level (ACL) RBC. If total capital declines to the ACL, the insurance department may assume control of the insurer.

Prior to reaching the ACL RBC, however, various other actions may occur at defined trigger points. Company Action Level RBC is 200% of ACL RBC; a point at which the insurer must develop a corrective action plan and submit it to the insurance department. Regulatory Action Level RBC is 150% of ACL RBC, at which point the insurance department will issue corrective orders to the insurer. Mandatory insurance department control of the insurer occurs if total capital declines to 70% of ACL RBC.

---

[5] 2013 NAIC Health RBC Report – Overview and Instructions for Companies

CORPORATE RISK CAPITAL AND PROSPECTIVE SOLVENCY

While the statutory RBC requirements provide the state and society with protection, they do not necessarily correspond to an appropriate level of risk capital from the insurer's perspective. Insurance companies want to avoid insurance department intervention, so they will likely treat the highest statutory trigger point as an effective default on company obligations, for purposes of managing the organization. Therefore, the appropriate risk capital level from the insurer perspective might be an amount equal to the highest statutory trigger point (200% of ACL RBC) *plus an additional amount of surplus* capital that reduces the likelihood of default and state intervention to an acceptably low level.

Determining the value of the additional surplus or risk capital is not straightforward, however. The risk dashboard contains a list of harmful conditions and events with potential severity levels and likelihoods, but it does not provide a true aggregate loss distribution for the organization as a whole. For many of the risks, probability of occurrence and magnitude of loss are broadly estimated. Further, degree of correlation or independence of the various risks is often speculative. Choosing the single highest severity of the dashboard risks would be inadequate for risk capital, since multiple events may happen simultaneously with more than minimal probability. On the other hand, adding the severity of all dashboard risks is probably excessive since they will not all occur at once. As reflected in the statutory RBC covariance formula, many of the risks are independent.

Because of the difficulties in calculating a company-specific target for risk capital, many group health insurers use "rule-of-thumb" methods, such as the number of months of claims and expenses that could be supported by existing surplus. Given the large contribution to a health insurer's aggregate risk profile from underwriting risk, this approach is not unreasonable. Alternatively, an organization could target a risk capital level that is at least twice the highest statutory trigger point, or 400% of ACL RBC. This would provide to the insurer the same protection from insurance department intervention that the insurance department requires to protect the state from insurer bankruptcy.

While the statutory RBC formula is generic, it was developed with the benefit of knowledge gained from struggling health insurers in the past. The formula and its component factors reflect risks typical of health insurers, so it provides an extremely useful starting point for corporate risk capital. But it is generic and, therefore, does not have the ability to make provision for conditions unique to an organization.

In spite of the limitations, risk modeling based on the comprehensive risk profile contained in the dashboard, even at a high level, will provide more current, company-specific results compared to statutory RBC, and will likely be superior to rule-of-thumb methods. The ORSA Guidance Manual supports this approach. The impact on capital of various scenarios and combinations of events in the risk profile could be modeled with many of the same tools used for describing the system. This process can be focused on important scenarios by using reverse stress tests to identifying conditions that would result in capital being exceeded. By varying the occurrence of harmful events or combinations of events along with varying levels of severity, a reasonable approximation of the aggregate risk profile can be achieved. The desired risk capital level can then be established to support the vast majority of these scenarios.

One outcome from the above process might be an estimate of economic capital, which is the amount of capital required to support the organization's business plan over a defined period of time, given the estimated risk profile, and based on the likelihood of the capital being sufficient. Likelihood for economic capital is determined using a measurement method such as value-at-risk (VAR)[6] or conditional tail expectation (CTE)[7]. This implies a fairly sophisticated aggregate loss distribution has been created, which may not always be possible. Regardless, it is important that some estimate of corporate-wide risk capital be developed, even if less robust approximations are used.

Once total corporate risk capital or economic capital is determined, it should be compared to the organization's aggregate risk tolerance to determine if enough capital is available for the proposed business plan. To the extent this test of prospective solvency indicates a potential capital deficiency, the business plan may need to be modified or additional risk mitigation activities should be considered.

Corporate risk capital can also be attributed to the various lines of business based on risk. This can be used as a measure for establishing target profitability by line of business. Higher risk lines are allocated more risk capital, requiring greater profit from those lines, in order to achieve the return on capital demanded by corporate management and by shareholders. To facilitate this, line-of-business should be a characteristic identified in the risk dashboard. If a line of business is unable to generate the required risked-adjusted return on capital (ROC), the organization will need to reevaluate risk mitigation strategies or decide if the required ROC for that line is appropriate. If the difference between the achieved and desired ROC cannot be narrowed sufficiently, exiting that line of business should be considered.

UNKNOWN RISK

In spite of the effort used to describe the business system and identify unknown risks, type 2 error in the risk hypothesis cannot be completely eliminated. Therefore, risk capital that is based on the known risks in the dashboard will, by definition, never be 100% adequate. The existence and magnitude of any deficiency will depend on several factors. Conservatism in the risk modeling could offset some or all of the deficiency from type 2 error. However, the degree of offset cannot be determined since type 2 error is, by definition, unknown risk.

In light of this, the adequacy of risk capital can only be assumed, taking into account the quality of the search for unknown risks and the subsequent risk modeling process. If a rigorous search for type 2 error has been conducted, and appropriate modeling performed, then it might be assumed that any remaining unknown risk is not material, relative to the size of the organization and the overall level of risk capital. On the other hand, if no search for unknown risk has occurred, or the search and subsequent modeling were superficial, then no such assumption can be made. One possible conclusion from this is that risk capital is *presumed to be inadequate* in the absence of an effective ERM process. This appears to be the direction in which the NAIC, credit rating agencies, and company boards are going. Effective ERM is considered a prerequisite to an organization's long-term viability.

---

[6] VAR quantifies the capital needed to withstand a loss at a certain probability and time horizon.
[7] CTE quantifies the capital needed to withstand the expected loss given the loss has exceeded the loss at a certain probability and time horizon.

OVERSIGHT AND MONITORING: ERM GOVERNANCE

ERM is a process, not a program. But to be effective, the process, particularly that of expanding the perceived risk profile, must be rigorously implemented and company resources will be expended. Management and staff time, investment in new technologies, consulting services, or training programs are a few examples. As with any process improvement implementation, initiating effective ERM will likely be disruptive to the organization.

Given the normal tendency of organizations to resist change, effective implementation of ERM is unlikely to occur without Board oversight and support from senior management. In addition, the process will require guidance, facilitation, and monitoring. A risk management oversight committee, perhaps headed by a Chief Risk Officer, can support this need. For a large and diverse organization, dedicated staff to assist in describing the business system and evaluating risk may be necessary. The roles played by each of these parties are critical.

The role played by the insurer's Board of Directors starts with ensuring senior management support of the ERM process. They can help management determine risk appetite and limits, evaluate and guide management's decision-making process, and align management incentives with stakeholders and company goals.

Senior management oversees the implementation of ERM, starting with communicating their support of the ERM process to the rest of the company. They can maintain a culture of performance improvement and learning from both successes and failures, and allow for open discussion of risk. Risk-aware decision making at all levels of the organization should be encouraged. Senior management provides direction to the risk management oversight committee and the Chief Risk Officer, determine risk appetite and limits, and establish limits of authority for risk assumption.

The risk management oversight committee defines risk management roles and responsibilities and oversees the ERM process. The committee provides direction and consultation to the Chief Risk Officer and assists in prioritizing risk and communicating the ERM process to senior management and the Board. The committee also helps evaluate and guide organizational awareness of risk through communication.

The Chief Risk Officer (CRO) is the primary champion of the ERM process. The CRO leads the risk management oversight committee, directs the ERM process, and provides guidance to business units in prioritizing, evaluating, and mitigating risk. The CRO guides collecting and dispersing risk information, monitoring operational performance and environmental factors, and evaluating business performance. In addition, the CRO should also direct the evaluation of required risk capital and prospective solvency. The CRO tests the perceived risk profile using a system of measurable indicators, and modifies the risk profile and risk models using emerging experience and knowledge. In performing these functions, it is important that the CRO consider the organization holistically, not in silos, and documents the entire ERM process.

A primary responsibility of the CRO is to ensure that the organization continues to learn lessons from emerging experience and that the risk profile is continuously updated. ERM is not a one-time effort. It is an iterative process of continuous improvement.

OWN RISK AND SOLVENCY ASSESSMENT

Once enacted in an insurer's state of domicile, the ORSA regulation requires that "an insurer shall maintain a risk management framework to assist the insurer with identifying, assessing, monitoring, managing and reporting on its material and relevant risks."[8] The insurer is required to conduct an ORSA review at least annually, but more often if there is a material change in the risk profile. Also, an ORSA Summary Report is to be provided to the commissioner once a year.

The ORSA process and the information to be included in the Summary Report are described in the ORSA Guidance Manual. The Guidance Manual notes that ORSA has two primary goals: "to foster an effective level of ERM at all insurers" and "to provide a group-level perspective on risk and capital." As such, the ORSA and the ORSA Summary Report provide a link between the insurer's risk management process, capital management and its multi-year business plan.

It is noted in the Guidance Manual that, while the format, structure and level of detail of the ORSA Summary Report may be tailored for the regulator, the content should be consistent with the ERM information provided to senior management and the board of directors. In other words, ORSA is to be embedded in the ERM framework and the Summary Report provides documentation of the ERM process actually occurring within the organization. ORSA is not intended to be a separate process. However, organizations with informal or rudimentary ERM programs will find that complying with the ORSA regulation will require, at a minimum, greater structure and more documentation.

The foregoing description of the ERM conceptual framework, the process of managing enterprise-wide risk, analysis of risk capital, along with ERM process oversight and monitoring align well with the three sections of the ORSA Summary Report and provide the underlying basis for an ORSA. When performing the ORSA and developing the Summary Report, Actuarial Standards of Practice related to ERM (#46 and #47) should be reviewed, along with other relevant standards[9].

Section 1 of the report is a high-level description of the insurer's risk management framework. The Guidance Manual states that an effective ERM framework should include five key principles, each of which should be addressed in the Summary Report.

1. Risk Culture and Governance – The insurer should provide a clear definition of roles, responsibilities and accountabilities for the board of directors, management, the ERM oversight committee and the Chief Risk Officer. Risk culture is demonstrated by a consistent use of risk-based decision making throughout the organization.

---

[8] Risk Management and Own Risk and Solvency Assessment Model Act, adopted 9/6/2012.
[9] Including ASOP #23, Data Quality; and ASOP #41, Actuarial Communications.

2. Risk Identification and Prioritization – While risk identification is the responsibility of everyone, the ERM oversight committee is primarily accountable for ensuring the process is working as intended across the organization. The oversight committee also needs to work with management to prioritize risks for purposes of assessment, mitigation, and monitoring.

3. Risk Appetite, Tolerances, and Limits – Formally stating risk appetite and tolerance provides a benchmark against which decision makers can evaluate new initiatives and new risks as they arise. Without these formal statements, risk-based decision making will likely be ad hoc and inconsistent. Risk appetite should be aligned with the company's business plan; while risk tolerance, and associated limits, should be directly related to risk capital.

4. Risk Management and Controls – This is the process of assessing, mitigating and monitoring any identified risks. While the ERM oversight committee is responsible for ensuring the process is working, mitigation and monitoring activities will occur across the organization. The company's internal audit function should be involved in establishing appropriate controls to ensure key risk owners are engaged in the process and that results can be relied upon.

5. Risk Reporting and Communication – Heat maps and the risk dashboard will likely form the core of any ERM status reporting to senior management, the board of directors and throughout the organization. However, it is important that everyone be aware of their accountability for risk identification and for incorporating risk-awareness into their day-to-day functions. This will only occur if there is transparency into the process and everyone understands their role.

Section 2 of the Summary Report is an assessment of the insurer's risk exposure. This should describe and demonstrate the process of assessing risk both qualitatively and, if possible, quantitatively. Each material and relevant risk should be considered under normal and stressed conditions, considering a range of potential outcomes, and the effect that has on the balance sheet, income statement and future cash flows. The impact on risk capital and available capital should be considered.

The Summary Report should provide descriptions and explanations of assessment methods, key assumptions, mitigation activities, and the outcomes of any plausible scenarios. Single risk and multiple risk scenarios should be considered, particularly where interactions are possible.

Section 3 of the Summary Report is an assessment of risk capital and prospective solvency at the enterprise-wide, or group level. This should provide a comparison of risk capital needs, given the insurer's portfolio of risk and its stated risk appetite, to available capital. This is not a minimum capital test; it is a determination of the amount of capital necessary to achieve company goals and objectives. Methods and assumptions used to quantify risk capital should be clearly defined. This should include the measurement method used to determine aggregate risk capital, such as VAR or CTE, and the target level used, such as X% VAR or Y% CTE. Finally, the method used to aggregate risks and to account for any diversification benefits should be described.

Prospective solvency considers the resources needed to support the organization's business plan over several years. This implies the need for a capital forecasting model that can reflect different risk scenarios and changes to internal operations and external environments under both normal and stressed conditions. Future changes to existing risks and new emerging risks should be considered. The ORSA Guidance Manual notes that the prospective solvency assessment should be a feedback loop. To the extent the assessment raises concerns about capital adequacy, additional risk mitigation steps might be taken or the business plan may need to be altered. The report should describe how the insurer intends to meet its current and projected capital needs.

GROUP HEALTH INSURANCE AND ERM

To summarize, ERM is a rigorous and holistic process for proactively managing uncertainty with the primary goal of improving business performance. Since all organizations, presumably, want to optimize performance, the ERM process will provide value regardless of size or industry. ERM is not just for banks and investment companies.

As noted in the introduction, ERM is a relatively new concept, particularly to group health insurers. Prior to the mid-2000s, for most group health insurers, enterprise-level risk management was an informal process primarily relying upon open communication and informed decision-making. At that time, internal audit departments performed much of the company-wide risk management function; however, this effort focused on internal controls and compliance issues.

Since then, at the behest of the Board of Directors, and in response to pressure from rating agencies, health insurers have begun to implement more formal risk management programs, including identification of major known risks, assignment of responsibility for risk mitigation, and development of risk avoidance or mitigation methods.

These programs tend to focus on operational or actuarial risk, occasionally utilizing risk modeling or scenario testing. In practice, however, the programs tend to be limited in scope and may ignore potentially important variables. Strategic risk management is still informal and efforts to close gaps in knowledge are often superficial.

Without doubt, these programs represent an improvement in the risk management approach, but they do not include many of the key features that distinguish ERM from typical risk management. They still tend to address risk in departmental silos and, importantly, they do not focus on developing organizational resilience. For many health insurers, determination of corporate risk capital is based on high-level rules of thumb and little effort is made to attribute risk capital to lines of business or perform prospective solvency testing.

The cost-benefit equation for a rigorous ERM program is still being debated at many group health insurance organizations. As noted above, relating the cost of risk management to the benefit of achieving corporate goals may help resolve this debate. ERM also provides additional value, in many ways.

Credit rating agencies now include ERM in their review of companies. Demonstration of an effective ERM program therefore lowers borrowing cost. Also, the ORSA Guidance Manual indicates that insurers with a robust ERM framework may not require the same scope or depth of regulatory review as those insurers with less robust ERM programs

By implementing an effective ERM program, management will likely be allowed more flexibility by the Board of Directors in managing the company. The ERM process also provides management with relevant, goal-oriented information, and a better understanding of the business system. This improves the likelihood that their business decisions – judgments – will have the results they expect. Further, in the absence of an effective ERM program, corporate risk capital is necessarily greater than it would otherwise need to be, thereby limiting capital available for new investment.

Other benefits are more difficult to demonstrate. The most obvious harmful events are likely known by management, even without having an ERM program in place to expand the perceived risk profile. These significant events are, perhaps, already managed or mitigated. And by definition, management is unaware of unknown risk; so it cannot be used, before the fact, as justification for investment in a rigorous ERM effort.

The problem of type 2 error in the risk hypothesis is not easy to overcome. Unless some method for estimating unknown risk is developed, it may continue to be ignored. One method, previously mentioned, might be to track "surprises." Frequent surprises or low level crises might provide enough validation of material type 2 error to initiate a more comprehensive search for unknown risk. Root cause analysis of successes, as well as failures, may also provide useful information. Success does not always occur for the most likely or obvious reasons. If the organization will not commit necessary resources for identifying unknown risk, ERM may need to piggy-back on other process improvement initiatives and make the best possible use of available management information and existing operational monitoring systems.

Since the Affordable Care Act was passed, uncertainty and risk to health insurance companies has increased significantly. Given the complexity of the ACA, this uncertainty is unlikely to abate any time soon. The type of analysis recommended and used in an ERM process is also the type of analysis that will be useful for managing organizational change required by the ACA. In this time of high uncertainty, moving ERM from a management presentation into action will provide enormous benefit in securing a viable future for many group health insurers.

43. Management of Provider Networks

Robert B. Cumming

This chapter provides an introduction to the management of health care provider networks from the perspective of a health care insurer. Provider networks are an integral part of many health insurance products, and significant efforts are expended in contracting with and managing provider networks. Actuaries, in particular, often play a key role in analyzing various financial aspects of provider networks.

This chapter first describes various dimensions of network performance, including techniques and strategies employed to maximize performance. It then presents various considerations when establishing a provider network, including the impact of the Affordable Care Act (ACA) on provider networks.

The frame of reference for most of the discussion in this chapter is in terms of U.S. practices for providers of medical services. Many of the general concepts and management techniques discussed also apply to dental providers. A short section at the end of this chapter discusses the environment in Canada.

Provider Networks

A provider network is a collection of health care providers that have some common attributes. Specifically, providers in a given network have satisfied a set of selection criteria and have signed a contract agreeing to various financial and operational requirements. The major financial and operational requirements may include reimbursement levels, accessibility requirements, quality standards, and patient satisfaction.

Goals of Provider Networks

Provider networks may be established by health insurers, non-insurance organizations such as third party administrators (TPAs), or by health care providers themselves. Health insurers and TPAs establish provider networks to help achieve particular goals, such as the following:

- Improve the affordability of health care,
- Improve the quality of health care, and
- Improve member satisfaction.

Each of these goals can be viewed as one dimension of network performance. In developing a network, the overall objective is to maximize these performance measures while keeping the network as broad (marketable) as possible.

Networks established by health care providers may be organized with other goals in mind, such as to preserve market share or to provide negotiation leverage through size and a united front. However, provider-based networks are subject to anti-trust claims if they are not structured to achieve significant efficiencies for end consumers. The Federal Trade Commission (FTC) typically looks at the level of financial risk sharing and clinical integration among the providers in making this determination.

MEASURING NETWORK PERFORMANCE

In order to judge the performance level of a network, it is necessary to define and measure cost, quality, and member satisfaction. Of these three measures, cost is often the primary focus in evaluating performance. Cost performance is objective and is relatively easy to measure.

Measuring Cost Performance

Cost performance is intended to measure the level of financial savings generated by a particular network. Savings may be generated in three ways: (1) negotiating lower per unit prices for health care services, (2) reducing the number of health care services performed, or (3) substituting less expensive services for more expensive services. The combined effect of these three factors gives the overall level of savings for the network.

Commonly used measures of cost performance include the following:

- *Price Level Measures.* These include a percentage discount from billed charges, price levels expressed on a standard scale (such as physician fee levels expressed as a conversion factor using RBRVS relative values), or the average fee for a category of medical services (such as average charge per hospital inpatient day, admission or Diagnosis Related Group).

- *Utilization Measures.* These include utilization rates per 1,000 covered members per year (such as hospital inpatient admits and days, office visits, prescriptions, emergency room visits), utilization rates per patient (such as the percentage of patients referred to a specialist, or the number of diagnostic tests per office visit), hospital inpatient average lengths of stay, or estimates of the percentage of hospital days and admissions that are unnecessary based on clinical chart reviews.

- *Claim Cost Measures.* This includes claim cost per member per month or claim cost per episode of care.

When comparing providers and networks, utilization and cost measures should be adjusted, to the extent possible, for demographic factors and health status.

When evaluating the overall performance of one network versus another, it is common to use measures such as the risk-adjusted claim cost per member per month. In this approach, the risk adjustment is commonly performed using diagnosis-based health risk assessment tools, such as the Diagnostic Cost Grouper (DCG) or Milliman's Advanced Risk Adjustor (MARA). These tools provide an overall risk score for the population covered under each network.

When evaluating the performance of specific health care providers (for example, orthopedic group A versus orthopedic group B) it is common to use claim cost per episode of care. The episode-based approach allows the measure to be based on the specific types of services delivered by each health care provider. Also, given the growth of open access products, it is less common to have membership assigned to specific health care providers. Without assigned membership, it is not possible to use a population-based health risk assessment tool. It is possible to attribute members in open access products to different health care providers. However, member attribution tends to be more complex and less objective than using upfront member assignment where available.

In order to monitor performance, utilization and claim cost measures may be compared to various benchmarks. Typical benchmarks include prior performance, the performance level of competitors in the same geographic area, and optimal performance. Optimal performance reflects utilization levels consistent with the best observed health care management practices and results.

In judging the cost performance of a network, it is important to look at utilization as well as price levels. In networks where it is not carefully monitored, utilization may increase as providers seek to recover revenue lost due to price discounts.

Measuring Quality

There has been an increased emphasis on measuring quality and comparing quality across provider networks. This emphasis tends to be driven by the desires and requirements of influential payers such as government entities, large employers, and employer coalitions. Financial incentives for providers to reduce services have heightened concern about maintaining quality and have resulted in efforts to better measure it. However, there are still many issues related to defining meaningful and objective measures of quality.

Classical quality assessment looks at three dimensions of health care delivery: structure, process, and outcome. Structural measures of quality focus on various attributes of the care delivery system, such as the qualifications of the physicians and hospital. Process measures focus on the administration of care and often involve measuring conformity to standard protocols through case audits and peer review. Outcome measures focus on the end effects of the care that was delivered. An example of an outcome measure is mortality levels. Although each dimension of quality is important, relevance increases as one progresses from structure to process to outcome. However, so does the difficulty of measurement.

One may divide the measurement of outcomes into two categories: administrative and clinical. Examples of administrative measures are access to services, member satisfaction, and member disenrollment rates. Clinical outcome measures tend to be more complex to deal with. There are a variety of outcomes that might be measured, including mortality, morbidity, disability, discomfort, and a sense of well-being. Furthermore, there may be trade-offs between different types of outcomes when evaluating the efficacy of a procedure. For example, operating on an arthritic knee can greatly improve long-term disability. However, short-term disability may be worsened, and there is a small risk of surgical mortality.

In assessing the quality of particular providers, it is possible to build on the requirements of other payers. For example, the Centers for Medicare and Medicaid Services and most state agencies rely heavily on accreditation of hospitals by the Joint Commission. The Joint Commission is a private body that accredits hospitals and other institutional providers. The measures used by the Joint Commission tend to focus on structure and process.

The National Committee for Quality Assurance (NCQA) helps employers and consumers distinguish between health plans by publishing quality and value measures. The NCQA operates an accreditation program, and publishes a report card that ranks health plans into five categories: Excellent, Commendable, Accredited, Provisional, and Denied. The ranking is based on: (a) NCQA's own requirements, (b) Healthcare Effectiveness Data and Information Set (HEDIS) measures, and (c) Consumer Assessment of Healthcare Providers and Systems (CAHPS) measures. NCQA evaluates core systems, processes, and actual results as part of the accreditation. The NCQA also has an accreditation program for Accountable Care Organizations (ACOs).

HEDIS is a highly publicized effort directed at standardizing quality of care measures. HEDIS uses a variety of process and outcome measures to assess quality of care and provides various benchmarks for the measures.

Measuring Member Satisfaction

Regardless of quality assurance programs and clinical outcome studies, managed care organizations need to attract and retain members to be viable. Thus, member satisfaction is an important aspect of quality for health plans and successful providers.

There are two types of measures of member satisfaction. The first type focuses on how members feel about various aspects of the medical care they receive, such as access, friendliness, continuity of care, communication, and perceived quality. It also includes how members feel about the health plan itself. The second type focuses on behavioral indicators of satisfaction, such as disenrollment rates and use of out-of-network providers.

Closely related to member satisfaction are direct measures of member access to care. This includes measures such as average waiting time for non-urgent office visits, average waiting time in the doctor's office, average waiting time for telephone access to a nurse or physician, and percentage of members who have visited a primary care physician within the past three years.

The Consumer Assessment of Healthcare Providers and Systems (CAHPS) assesses the experiences of health care consumers in various ambulatory settings, including health plans, dental plans, medical groups, and physician offices. The CAHPS survey focuses on member satisfaction and asks enrollees about their recent experiences with health plans, the physicians in the health plans' network, and their services.

NETWORK EVALUATION

When deciding which health plan network or networks to use, large self-insured employers often perform a network evaluation. In practice, these network evaluations tend to focus on access, disruption, and provider payment levels. Evaluation of access tends to be a minimum requirement, with disruption and cost driving the final decision.

Access

Reasonable geographic access to a range of health care providers is typically considered a minimum requirement. The acceptable standards often vary between rural and urban areas. For example, in urban areas, the measurement standard might be two primary care providers and one hospital within 15 miles.

Disruption

Disruption occurs when a provider is in-network for the current network but is out-of-network for the new network. This can lead to two types of disruption: (1) provider disruption – this occurs when members change providers in order to maintain in-network benefit levels or (2) benefit disruption - this occurs when members accept out-of-network benefit levels in order to continue to use their current providers.

Disruption is typically measured by estimating the proportion of claim dollars that will be in-network. The measure is typically calculated using the current mix of claim dollars by health care provider for the particular employer doing the evaluation; that is, assuming no change in the mix of health care providers. In reality, when a new network is implemented there will likely be some shift in provider mix in order for employees to maintain in-network benefit levels.

Provider Payment Levels

There are a variety of approaches used to evaluate provider payment levels. The approaches vary in terms of increasing complexity and potential accuracy, roughly as follows:

- *Average provider discount based on employees or members by zip code.* This analysis is often based on standardized data sets that are sent from health plans to consultants on a regular basis. This approach does not capture the employer's actual mix of health care providers or the mix of health care services within a particular zip code area.
- *Average provider discount based on employer's mix of claim dollars by health care provider tax ID.* This approach captures the mix of health care providers for a specific employer but does not capture the specific mix of services or case mix for the employer.
- *Average fee schedule or payment rates based on employer specific mix of health care providers and service mix.* This approach can capture both provider mix and service mix but can get fairly complicated and time consuming. In theory, this approach gives the same result as a detailed repricing of the employer's claims.
- *Risk-adjusted total cost of care.* This approach is generally considered the gold standard in terms of measuring network and health plan performance. This approach captures not only the value of the network but also the value of the care and disease management programs that are commonly packaged together with the network by the health plan. This approach requires the use of a risk assessment tool, and requires access to detailed, accurate claim data.

TO BUILD OR NOT TO BUILD?

A health plan may have the option of building its own network or renting an existing network. This decision often needs to be evaluated market by market. Building a network involves greater upfront costs but lower ongoing costs as compared with renting. Also, building often involves a longer lead time but provides more control over the network than renting.

Key factors which affect the decision of whether to build or rent include the number of members in the market (this impacts the health plan's ability to spread the fixed costs of developing a network), the percentage market share (this impacts the health plan's ability to negotiate competitive discounts), and access to competitive rental networks for a reasonable access fee. The decision to build or rent may also vary by type of service or provider. For example, most large health plans have their own physician and hospital networks but often rent networks for pharmacy or certain specialty care services (such as mental health and chiropractic).

A patchwork approach might also be used. Many health plans directly own and contract a provider network in their home geography or selected geographies but will rent networks outside of their core service area. This approach allows such health plans to be able to offer a nationwide network to employers that often have worksites and employees spread across the country. Even employers not considered national brands often have employees located in other states (such as the sales force or a specific factory). In order to be considered by the employer group, the health plan will need a strong national provider network. This consideration became more critical when employers shifted their preference to a single, consistent plan administrator across the country. The pendulum has recently started to swing back; more national employers are considering a "best in region" contracting approach for health plan services and are willing to work with and manage multiple health plan partners.

IMPACT OF THE ACA ON PROVIDERS AND NETWORKS

The passage of the ACA has had a number of impacts on health care providers and provider network strategy. These include (1) general market changes, including increased demand for health care services, increased access concerns, less bad debt, and more business at lower fee levels; and (2) narrow networks, including renewed focus on narrow, high performing networks.

Of course, some of these changes are still playing out and the full impact of the ACA is yet to be seen.

General Market Changes

The ACA affected a number of broad-based market factors. One of the core goals of the ACA was to ensure affordable access to health insurance and therefore health care services. To the extent that people have health insurance coverage, they are more likely to seek and use health care services, especially preventive care, primary care, and more discretionary care treatments. Expanded access to insurance likely causes an increased demand for such services, which increases concerns regarding scarcity of primary care services. Although primary care access was a significant concern before the implementation of the ACA, there has yet to be a significant outcry regarding increased access problems. Perhaps, the generally low utilization trends in the past few years provided enough capacity in the system to handle the influx of newly covered members and patients. At the same time, increased access to preventive and primary care services might decrease the need for specialty and hospital services over the longer term. This might result in an oversupply of some such providers.

The ACA is expected to result in less bad debt for health care providers. As there are fewer people without health insurance, there should also be a commensurate decrease in bad debt for health care providers. To the extent health care providers have less bad debt, they might be willing to contract for lower year-over-year fee increases. However, the increased popularity of high deductible benefit plans has correspondingly increased the pressure on bad debt and collections. This increased bad debt is more significant for physician services than for hospital inpatient services, as inpatient costs tend to be so expensive that much of the cost is mainly covered by the insurance plan.

Another pressure point is the increase in the Medicaid covered population. Many of the newly insured are covered under state Medicaid or Medicaid-like programs. These programs often pay health care providers at a much lower fee level than commercial plans, and thus might result in increased financial burdens for care systems that treat a large share of such patients.

Resurgence of Narrow Networks

Perhaps the biggest impact of the ACA on provider networks is the resurgence of narrow networks. Since the ACA requires guaranteed issue and community rating in the individual and small group markets, health plans can no longer use underwriting to manage risk selection, costs, and premium rates. Thus, many health plans have implemented products based on narrow, high value networks in order to manage costs or gain a competitive advantage.

Although narrow networks have been around for many years, the new focus on the individual marketplace makes such networks a more workable proposition. In the group marketplace, it was often necessary to have a very broad network in order to compete, as provider disruption would often trump savings. This is less true in the individual marketplace, as the network only has to meet the needs of one person or family at a time rather than the needs of everyone that happens to work at a particular employer. If a narrow network does meet an individual's needs, that person simply selects a broader network typically at a higher price point, or a different narrow network with their desired providers.

Narrow, high performing networks can result in a more competitively priced product through the following possible mechanisms:

- Reducing the number of providers in the network by selecting the more cost efficient care systems or providers.

- Negotiating an additional fee discount in return for featuring a particular care system or provider in the narrow network. Providers might offer an additional discount to reflect the additional patient volume or to assure existing volume.

- Shifting the risk to care systems that believe that they can become more cost efficient or have adopted a strategy to focus on cost efficiency. Many care systems have adopted such a strategy since they believe it is critical to long term survival and competitiveness. Once they adopt such a strategy, they generally want to quickly add patient volume so that any investments made to increase their own cost efficiency have a quicker payback.

Besides lower cost for consumers, narrow networks have other positive market impacts. In particular, narrow networks help to create competition among care systems in terms of cost efficiency and value. This is especially true if there are a number of options offered in a given market, with each option built around a particular care system. Care system competition and accountability may be necessary for an efficient private marketplace for health care services.

The significant narrowing of provider networks has already resulted in a media backlash. The press has reported that many new narrow networks exclude some high-cost specialty providers, national brand care systems, and academic medical centers. The press has also noted in numerous articles that the provider networks available to individuals on the exchange are often substantially less broad than the typical network offered to employer groups in that geographic region. The press has generally failed to mention that individuals typically have a choice between broad and narrow network products, and that such choices are typically not available to group members.

The issue of narrow networks will likely continue to be a highly charged political topic for the foreseeable future.

CONSIDERATIONS IN ESTABLISHING A PROVIDER NETWORK

There are a variety of factors that should be considered when establishing a provider network. These factors include the following:

- Population to be served,
- Type of product,
- Accessibility of providers,
- Trade-off between size of network and level of discounts,
- Network tiering,
- Trade-off between size of network and level of medical efficiency,
- Entities with which to contract,
- Target reimbursement levels and methodology,
- Current referral patterns, and
- Specialty networks.

Each of these considerations is discussed below.

Population To Be Served

Insurers often form unique networks for different populations or markets. For example, a Blue Cross / Blue Shield plan may establish different provider networks for its commercial business, Medicare Risk business, and managed Medicaid business. Each network should be designed to match the population to be served. The networks may differ in terms of the proportion of providers who participate, the type and specialty mix of the providers, the geographic location of the providers, and the reimbursement methodology and level.

Networks designed for Medicare and Medicaid populations often have fewer providers participating than a network designed for a commercial population. This may be due to a variety of reasons. One reason is that broad access to providers in general may be more important for marketing a commercial product to employers than to individuals covered under Medicare and Medicaid. Also, reimbursement rates may be lower, particularly for Medicaid, and therefore acceptable to fewer providers. In addition, Medicare contracts often involve greater provider risk sharing, which may be acceptable to fewer providers.

The mix of provider specialty types in a network should be tailored to the population to be served. For example, Medicaid Aid for Families with Dependent Children (AFDC) medical populations require significant access to maternity and child care, and Medicare networks require more specialty services.

The location of the providers that participate in a network may depend on the population to be served. For example, Medicaid populations are often concentrated in inner city areas and have limited means of transportation. In order to have accessible providers, it is critical to include hospitals and physicians located in the inner city that serve these populations.

Type of Product: Primary Care vs. Open Access

The type of product will affect various aspects of provider contracts, which will impact provider selection and decisions regarding participation. For example, is the network being designed for a primary care or open access product? A primary care product involves member selection of a primary care provider and typically has some level of referral requirements. In an open access product, a member can go to any in-network provider without a referral and does not need to select a primary care provider.

Some medical groups prefer primary care products, since they have more influence over where members go for care, and members tend to be stickier, meaning they do not change primary care providers as often as members in open access products. As a result, some medical groups are more likely to provide deeper discounts and are more likely to take risk for a primary care product. On the other hand, a primary care product often requires some level of referral authorization that results in additional administrative and care management responsibilities for the primary care providers.

Accessibility of Providers

The geographic accessibility of providers is often measured in terms of the distance between a covered member's home or place of work and the providers' locations . Networks should have as wide a geographic spread as possible to maximize the proportion of the population that can readily access a provider within a short distance. Accessibility also depends on the providers' ability to take on new patients and on their office hours. Increased accessibility will increase the marketability of the product and will increase the reimbursement savings generated on point-of-service and PPO products.

Trade-Off between Network Size and Discounts

In developing a provider network, there is typically a trade-off between the size of the network and the level of discounts that can be negotiated. Generally speaking, an insurer can achieve lower negotiated fee levels if they are willing to accept fewer providers participating in the network. A smaller network is more likely to result in an increase in business for a provider and the provider may be willing to accept a larger discount. In addition, if an insurer is willing to exclude some providers, it may have greater negotiation leverage with the remaining providers.

Some insurers develop an array of networks that vary in terms of size, level of provider discounts, and therefore premiums. For example, some larger plans may have three or more networks in order to meet the diverse needs and desires of their commercial customers. This might include a "par" or participating network, including nearly all the providers in the service area, a PPO network including a subset of the par providers, and an HMO network including an even smaller subset of the PPO providers.

Network Tiering

More and more carriers are offering networks with multiple tiers of providers. In these networks, providers are slotted in two or more tiers, as opposed to either being in or out of the network. In tiered networks, the member benefit level (including cost sharing) will vary based on the provider or provider system selected by the member. For example, hospitals may be slotted into three tiers: (1) Tier 1: no-copayments, (2) Tier 2: $500 copay per admission, and (3) Tier 3: $1,000 copay per admission. Some health plans have even designed products where the employee premium varies directly based on the network tier or care system selected. In such products, a unique premium level is attached to each major care system based on that care system's relative total cost of care. This type of product helps facilitate the movement of employers to a defined contribution funding approach, as any care system that costs more than the defined contribution can be a buy-up option for the employee. This type of product promotes provider competition without limiting provider access, as all care systems are made available, even if some are more expensive than others.

The advantages of a multi-tier network are that nearly all providers can be included, as long as there are enough tier levels and enough variation among the tier levels; and that there are more member/employee choices. The major disadvantage is that multi-tier networks are more complicated. Other challenges include assuring adequate Tier 1 access across all specialties and aligning Tier 1 physicians with Tier 1 hospitals.

Tier placement of providers is typically based on either cost measures alone or on combined cost and quality measures. Tiering based only on cost is simpler, and allows members to make their own decisions regarding the cost and quality trade-off (assuming members have access to relevant quality data). However, using only cost might inadvertently channel members to low quality providers if members are not cognizant of differences in quality levels across providers.

Trade-Off between Network Size and Medical Efficiency

A smaller network allows an insurer to be more selective with respect providers who demonstrate efficient practice patterns. This can generate significant savings through lower utilization if medical efficiency criteria are used in the selection or building process

Medical efficiency can be evaluated using either clinical reviews or analytical methods. Clinical reviews involve health care professionals, such as physicians or nurses, reviewing the treatment decisions and care provided to individual patients as documented in the hospital or clinic patient charts. These types of reviews can be expensive, time consuming, and—some argue—subjective. Due to the drawbacks of clinical reviews, most carriers use analytical methods. A key issue when trying to compare the medical efficiency levels of different providers is the need to adjust for differences in health status or severity in the patients they treat. Analytical methods often involve the use of risk assessment models or episode grouping software. diagnosis-based risk assessment models, such as the Diagnostic Cost Grouper (DCG), Adjusted Clinical Groups (ACGs), or Milliman's Advanced Risk Adjuster (MARA) adjust for differences in the health status of the members. These models are discussed in more detail in the chapter on health risk adjustment. Episode grouping software groups together all the care provided to a patient that relates to a particular episode of treatment. These models then classify the episodes into clinically distinct groups.

Contracting Entities

Health care providers have formed various types of organizations for the purpose of sharing risk and contracting with insurers. Insurers are often faced with decisions regarding whether they should contract through such an organization or contract and negotiate directly with the individual providers.

These organizations may bring together providers based on various characteristics, such as type of provider, physician specialty, level of care, and geographic area. They may include only hospitals, only physicians, or both hospitals and physicians. For example, an independent practice association (IPA) brings together independent physicians for the purpose of contracting with managed care plans. IPAs typically include all specialties, but can also be comprised solely of primary care or a single specialty. Similarly, a physician-hospital organization (PHO) brings together one or more independent hospitals with many physicians, oftentimes both hospital-employed physicians and community-based physicians. An Accountable Care Organization (ACO) is similar to a PHO but, by definition, takes accountability for the triple aim goals of improving affordability, quality, and patient satisfaction related to health care. There is a significant increase in interest in ACOs due to federal reform and the desire by Medicare, some Medicaid states, and private commercial payers to contract with ACOs under shared savings or shared risk models.

There are advantages and disadvantages in contracting with such provider organizations. Advantages include the ability to sign up a large number of providers with a single contract; a ready-made set of providers that are coordinated geographically or by type of service; greater ability to shift risk if the provider organization is set up to accept and share risk; and better coordination of care.

Disadvantages include less negotiation leverage (with lower discounts) since it is a larger organization; the possible need to pay an access fee for use of a ready-made network; and the inability to sub-select only the most efficient and high quality providers. Furthermore, the provider organization may have limitations on its ability to negotiate on behalf of its constituent providers, and it may be difficult for the provider organization to reach a decision due to the diverse interests of their members. If thinly capitalized, the provider organization may have solvency problems if it accepts risk without passing it on to the actual entities that provide the care, such as the hospital. Also, in the future, the provider organization could switch to a different insurer or may form its own insurance company, taking the membership with them. Frequently, such provider organizations rely on the health plan to perform special reporting and analysis in order for the provider organization to perform its own provider reimbursement and analysis.

Provider organizations vary dramatically in terms of their level of integration and their cohesiveness. The degree of financial, operational, and legal integration may affect whether an insurer decides to negotiate with the provider organization or with each individual provider separately. For example, a hospital that owns a series of primary care clinics may be much easier to negotiate with than a physician-hospital organization (PHO) where the physicians own their own practices and the only thing that binds them together is a relatively modest capital investment in the PHO. Similarly, a physician group practice is typically much more cohesive than a network of independent physicians.

Target Reimbursement Levels

An insurer should have a clear idea of its target reimbursement levels when setting up a network. Two opposing factors affect the choice of the target reimbursement levels. First, higher reimbursement levels may endanger competitive premium rates. Second, there is a need to pay a competitive reimbursement level to providers, in order to have a reasonable portion of the providers sign-up for the network.

Two types of analyses are typically done in setting the target reimbursement levels. The first analysis is a study of existing regional managed care reimbursement levels in the particular geographic area. The source data for this may come from provider fee surveys, regulatory filings, consultants, experience reports for employers used in underwriting new groups, and brokers. The second analysis is a projection of premium rates, and the resulting enrollment, based on various scenarios for reimbursement levels. The relationship of the projected premium rates to those of the competitors will affect the marketability of the product and the expected enrollment.

Current Referral Patterns

Health care providers have existing relationships, formal and informal, with other providers. These determine where they send their patients for care that they cannot provide directly. For example, physicians may have admitting privileges at one or more hospitals, which essentially limits the hospitals to which they can admit their patients. Also, many primary care physicians may have established informal referral patterns, recommending particular specialists for their patients.

It is advantageous for a network to incorporate or build on existing referral and admission patterns. The advantages include fewer operational barriers, a higher proportion of in-network utilization, and greater physician satisfaction with the health plan and its operation. This must be counterbalanced by the need to limit the number of hospitals and specialists that are in the network in order to assist negotiating competitive reimbursement levels.

Specialty Networks

The development of networks for specialty providers is similar in concept and involves similar considerations. However, there are some unique considerations that depend on the type of provider. The factors that drive this variation include local supply and demand, as well as the amount of variability in treatment protocols.

The impact of local supply and demand can vary significantly by type of provider. For example, in many locations, the supply of dentists is considered to be low relative to demand. This makes it more difficult to develop dental networks with significant fee discounts. This can differ significantly from the dynamics for some types of physicians and hospitals, where the supply might exceed demand. Due to difficulty in negotiating significant discounts for dental services, a dental network often does not add as much relative value as a physician network.

Some specialty providers are involved in providing care that, in the opinion of some, involves more discretion, more variability in practice patterns, and more difficulty in assessing the value of the care provided. Due to these considerations, as part of the network development, it can be worthwhile to put more effort into the selection and profiling of these providers.

Specialty networks are commonly used for ancillary providers or for highly complex procedures. For example, specialty networks might be used for chiropractic services, mental health, dental, lab, etc. In addition, it is also common to establish special networks, often referred to as centers of excellence, for highly complex or highly variable services such as transplants, bariatric surgery, spine surgery, etc.

MANAGING NETWORK PERFORMANCE

The three dimensions of network performance are cost, quality, and member satisfaction. Managed care plans use various techniques to try to maximize these performance measures. The techniques include selection and retention of providers, negotiated reimbursement levels and structure, and care and disease management.

The first two techniques are described below. Care and disease management programs are discussed in more detail in Chapter 44.

SELECTION AND RETENTION OF PROVIDERS

Health plans seek to select and retain high quality, efficient providers. Most health plans consider physician selection and retention as a critical factor in the success of the health plan. This section outlines some criteria used by health plans in selecting providers, information used to decide which providers should be renewed, and strategies for selecting a network. Of course, the selection and retention of providers should also reflect the various overall considerations listed earlier under the section on "Considerations in Establishing a Network."

Selection Criteria

In selecting physicians, health plans review a variety of qualitative and quantitative information. The review process may include credentialing, office evaluation, medical record review, and analysis of utilization or cost data. These steps are described below as they are applied in the selection of physicians. Similar steps and processes are used in selecting other health care professionals and in selecting hospitals.

Credentialing involves reviewing and verifying the credentials of the physician, such as their training, licensure, specialty certification, hospital privileges, and malpractice insurance history. Nearly all health plans perform basic credentialing which includes verifying that the physician is licensed and has the appropriate credentials to practice. Many health plans also check for disciplinary actions or substance abuse problems.

An *office evaluation* typically involves a visit to the physician's office to evaluate the ambience of the office, accessibility for patients, and in-office service capabilities. This might include looking at office hours and the appointment book to check the capacity to take on more patients and ability to provide timely appointments. An office evaluation tends to be more commonly used by HMOs than PPOs.

Some health plans review a sampling of *medical records*. This might be done by the medical director or by an outside clinical consultant. The purpose of the review is to analyze the physician's practice pattern with respect to quality and cost efficiency. Issues concerning confidentiality must be clarified before examining patient records.

Some health plans *review utilization or cost data* in selecting physicians for a network. However, this approach is limited in that many health plans do not have access to a credible volume of data for a given provider. Also, there is some controversy regarding such "economic credentialing" due to its limitations and the potentially negative impact on quality of care. Due to these factors, most health plans put a minor importance on utilization and cost data during the *initial* selection process. Health plans tend to put more emphasis on subjective, qualitative information in judging practice patterns and focus on selecting physicians who are flexible and receptive to managed care principles.

Also, if the appropriate data is available, health plans may review what portion of their inforce members currently are using the provider.

Renewal of Contracts

Health plans use a variety of information in deciding whether to renew contracts with providers. For physicians, the renewal process typically involves re-credentialing and a review of performance information. The sources for the performance information include quality review, consumer complaints, profiling, and consumer surveys.

Health plans prefer to keep physician turnover as low as possible. Large employers often look at physician turnover rates in judging the performance of a health plan. High rates of turnover tend to indicate that physicians are unhappy with the plan or that the plan did not do a very good job in selecting physicians in the first place. High rates of turnover also result in problems with member relations, since most members do not like to change physicians.

Strategies for Selecting a Network

There are a variety of strategies employed in constructing provider networks. The strategies may be referred to as "careful selection," "prune later," and "broad as feasible." For non-tiered commercial networks, it is more common to focus on the breadth of network. For Medicaid and Medicare networks, it is more common to focus on careful selection, due to the tighter financial requirements.

Careful selection of physicians from the outset provides a more cohesive and reasonably small network, with which the health plan can work efficiently. Also, it tends to be more difficult to non-renew a provider than to not select that provider in the first place. The prune later approach is typically coupled with a broad initial selection. This strategy reflects that careful selection at the outset can be very time consuming and useful data is very limited. A broad network initially will also help encourage rapid enrollment growth. However, if a significant number of physicians are pruned later, there may be significant member and customer dissatisfaction. Furthermore, providers may be litigious when involuntarily removed from a network.

Health plans may employ different strategies for physicians versus hospitals, or by type of physician specialty. For example, a health plan may use the broad as feasible approach for selecting primary care physicians due to their marketing value and a careful selection approach in setting up an oncology or cardiac care network, due to efficiency and quality concerns.

NEGOTIATED REIMBURSEMENT

Health plans use negotiated reimbursement arrangements to help control costs and to improve quality and member satisfaction. Cost control comes through negotiating discounts from current payment levels and through financial incentives to deliver cost-effective care. Increasingly, quality and member satisfaction measures are also being emphasized with financial incentives for providers.

Cost Control

Provider networks typically involve negotiated fee arrangements, including the following types of arrangements:

- Discounted fee-for-service,
- Fee schedule,
- Bonuses (including gain share arrangements) and withholds (including loss and gain share arrangements),
- Per diem,
- Per case (per admission or per visit to emergency room, for example),
- Global rates (incorporate hospital and physician charges in one rate, also known as bundled payments),
- Case rate per episode of care (sometimes called "encounter capitation"), and
- Capitation.

Some of these fee arrangements are described in more detail elsewhere in this text.

In designing the reimbursement approach for a network, there are a number of important factors that should be considered, including the overall impact and interplay of the financial incentives, the need for risk adjustment, and acceptable levels of risk for providers.

It is important that the financial incentives be coordinated and monitored to avoid cost shifting and other perverse incentives which don't encourage lower *overall* costs and which may impair quality.

As providers assume greater risk, there is need for risk adjustment that goes beyond age and gender. Most health plans use risk adjustment that recognizes the health status of patients.

Provider entities that are capitated but do not provide all the required services themselves may have significant solvency risk.

Traditionally, capitation and similar risk sharing approaches were limited to systems where the member chose a primary care physician (PCP) or clinic. With the growth of open access products, there is the need to attribute members to health care providers, since there is no upfront assignment or choice. There are a variety of methods to attribute members. The methods focus on which provider or care system provided the majority or plurality of care during a specific time period. Attribution of members facilitates performance analysis and provider risk sharing.

In the current marketplace, there is significant growth in the use of risk-sharing arrangements with providers based on a "risk adjusted total cost of care." These arrangements can be structured as gain share only (also referred to as "shared savings"), or as gain and loss share. The gain or loss is determined by comparing actual claim costs to a target. The target is often based on prior year cost levels for that health care provider, adjusted for changes in health status and trend (often using something near the general Consumer Price Index for the trend). Adjustments are typically made for large claims.

Negotiation Strategies

Health plans achieve leverage in their negotiations through their willingness to leave some providers out of the network and through their ability to direct members to particular providers for care. Providers accept discounted fee levels in order to maintain their market share or to gain market share by being part of the network. Providers accept risk because they perceive themselves to be more efficient than the average provider and, therefore, able to increase their reimbursement by accepting risk.

Health plans use a variety of contracting approaches. Depending on the type of provider or size of the provider, these may include reimbursement offers made on an accept-or-reject basis, negotiated reimbursement levels, and requested bids from providers. Generally speaking, when dealing with individual physicians or small groups, the approach is often accept-or-reject. When dealing with large medical groups, hospitals, or certain key providers, the health plan often must negotiate or request proposals. In these negotiations, it is often times helpful for the health plan to have a larger market share or the support of a large employer.

MANAGEMENT OF PROVIDERS IN CANADA

In Canada, the government provides and finances universal health insurance for all citizens. Each province has its own health insurance program; however, the provincial programs must include some standard features in order to receive the federal subsidy. The process of negotiating hospital and physician reimbursement tends to be very different in Canada than in the U.S. since the provinces are the sole payers. As a result, there is no competitive marketplace with multiple payers, each independently negotiating with health care providers. In general, the health care providers must accept whatever the provincial governments are willing to pay.

The provinces use a variety of techniques to manage providers and health care costs, including the following:

- Global hospital budgets,
- Physician fee schedules,
- Physician utilization controls, and
- Control of physician supply.

Each of these techniques is briefly discussed below.

Global hospital budgets are negotiated each year between the provincial governments and each individual hospital. These budgets cover the operating expenses of the hospital, which are kept separate from capital expenditures. Since the government must approve the funds required to operate any new facility or equipment, the government also controls capital expenditures by hospitals. As a result, highly advanced equipment is much less prevalent and tends to be concentrated in selected hospitals, such as university hospitals. Operating under a fixed budget is similar to being capitated. However, due to the global nature of the budgets, Canadian hospitals have had to face other economic consequences. For example, a hospital may budget for a certain number of elective surgeries. If more than a predetermined number of patients need the procedure, queues result and patients are ranked according to need. Some policymakers and providers are concerned about adequate capital replenishment.

Physician fee schedules are negotiated between the provincial governments and the provincial medical associations. Physicians are then paid on a fee-for-service basis using the negotiated schedule. Since the government is the only payer, a monopsony[1] exists and the negotiations are somewhat one-sided. If medical associations feel the fee levels are inadequate, they have the option of striking. Due to the use of a fee-for-service payment mechanism, utilization controls are important in controlling overall health care costs.

Utilization controls on physician services are employed by some of the provinces. The most common approach involves setting utilization targets and then adjusting fee levels downward if the utilization targets are exceeded. While this mechanism does not control utilization itself, it does control the impact of higher utilization on overall claim costs. Quebec uses a unique approach to control utilization by setting billing caps for physicians. If the physician exceeds the cap in a particular quarter, the physician's fees are reduced by 75% for the remainder of the quarter. Such low fee levels financially discourage providing more services than necessary to reach the cap.

The *physician supply* is controlled by provinces through their control over the funding of medical schools. Also, the provinces have emphasized primary care educational programs rather than specialty training.

---

[1] A market with only one buyer for the services of multiple providers.

44. MEDICAL CARE MANAGEMENT

Alison Johnson

INTRODUCTION

The medical management of health care has been an important part of insurer functions since the advent of health maintenance Organizations. There are a variety of opinions about the effectiveness and even the appropriateness of this kind of care management by insurers. An understanding of medical management methods and their likely impacts can help actuaries as they analyze and model aspects of health care cost and utilization.

This chapter begins by describing the history of medical management practices, including the impact of the Affordable Care Act (ACA) passed in March, 2010. Descriptions of medical management practices such as utilization and case management are next, including check lists of key parts of various programs.

A discussion of current topics and trends completes the chapter.

HISTORY OF MEDICAL MANAGEMENT

Medical management of patient care is rooted in early arrangements, which combined insurance financial risk and medical care delivery. In the 1930s, physicians offered prepaid medical care to groups of people, primarily construction, mining, railroad and utility workers and their families.

Eventually unions, granges, cooperatives, and benevolent societies took over the organizing function from physicians. They collected dues from members and assumed the administrative functions of membership management, such as establishing eligibility and tracking enrollment. These organizations also began to formalize relationships with doctors and hospitals through contracts.

Insurers began hiring nurses in the 1970s to review claims. Their charge was to review claims for correct billing and for the medical necessity of tests and procedures. This function has evolved to include assisting insurer members manage their health issues—both acute and chronic—and promoting healthy lifestyle choices.

Studies are currently underway to accurately measure the clinical and financial impact of medical management activities. Measuring return on investment (ROI) has become increasingly important as health care costs continue to rise. Many attempts have been made to calculate the cost savings due to medical management programs. These studies are hampered by several issues:

- Timeframes: Medical management programs often target chronic illnesses that evolve over many years. Demonstrating cost saving over decades is challenging.
- Confounding Variables: Many variables, such as the normal aging process, changing financial situations, other disease processes and multiple interventions make it difficult to measure the impact of a single intervention such as utilization management.
- Lack of Methodological Rigor: Simplified statistical measures have led to erroneous conclusions, such as not considering regression to the mean among people with chronic illness.

At least one recent textbook exists on the subject of measurement of medical management and other health care intervention programs.[1] In addition, the Society of Actuaries offers many papers and perspectives on cost savings that can (or cannot) be attributed to medical management programs.

Of course, the cost picture is incomplete unless other impacts are considered: impact on the patient's overall health and ability to work and be productive, impact on society, and impact on an individual's wellbeing.

Medicaid programs in the U.S. offer medical management services through a variety of state initiatives. Managed care is now the dominant delivery system in Medicaid, offered in 70% of state Medicaid plans. In addition, Medicare has offered managed care programs for many years. These managed care programs continue to evolve.

The ACA has enabled millions of previously uninsured Americans to access health insurance, and many of these are experiencing medical management, requiring new strategies and a steep learning curve, with the potential to affect access to care.

Medical management programs have traditionally been performed by insurers, but with health care reimbursement shifting toward more value-based reimbursement of providers, and with the shift of risk toward providers and Accountable Care Organizations (also known as ACOs, and described at the end of this chapter), some or all components of medical management are being performed by the provider or ACO. In this chapter, the term "insurer" is used to refer to whatever entity is taking the risk, which is generally the entity that is administering the medical management programs.

MEDICAL MANAGEMENT

Medical management is comprised of a set of activities and programs that the insurer or provider delivers or administers to control costs and ensure that members receive quality health care. Some typical programs are utilization management, case management, disease management, wellness programs, care navigation and patient-centered medical homes.

The first medical management programs were developed to contain rising medical costs. These programs were labeled "Utilization Management" or "Utilization Review." These programs include precertification, admission notification, concurrent review, referral management, and

---

[1] Duncan, Ian. *Managing and Evaluating Healthcare Intervention Programs, Second Edition,* Actex Publications.

retrospective review. They were helpful in standardizing care and expectations among the provider and member communities.

The next wave of medical management programs included case management (CM). These programs paired a registered nurse (RN) with a high cost member to help the member make health care choices and stay healthy. Programs include catastrophic CM, maternity management and transitional CM. Disease management programs are another form of case management, concentrating on the care of people with chronic illness such as cardiac disease, diabetes and end stage renal disease.

Prevention programs, such as immunization drives, healthy diet programs, and cancer screening focus on preventing illness or promoting early detection of disease. Demand management programs provide immediate services to members when they need them. Nurse phone lines are the most familiar form of demand management programs. Wellness programs identify health risk factors such as smoking and obesity and work directly with members to reduce these risks factors before disease and illness develop. Care navigation assists patients, especially those with complex medical needs, in finding appropriate benefits and care for their condition. Finally, patient-centered medical homes provide a primary care infrastructure to coordinate all care of patients, especially those with complex medical and behavioral health needs, and to accept financial responsibility for those patients.

UTILIZATION MANAGEMENT

Utilization Management (UM) and Utilization Review (UR) are the best known types of medical management programs and have the longest history. Two trends fueled the move to utilization review:

- Observable differences in utilization patterns across physicians and across hospitals
- Insurer certificates of coverage that included 'medical necessity' as requirement for coverage.

Physicians and hospitals are required to inform the UM program administrator prior to a member receiving certain high cost services to ensure that the services are medically necessary and are included in insurance coverage. The program administrator ensures the member is currently enrolled, checks available benefits and, if warranted, establishes the medical necessity for the procedure. Typical areas for utilization review include the following:

- Hospital admissions,
- Referral to a specialist physician,
- Expensive durable medical equipment (DME),
- Expensive scanning and radiology technology (PET and MRI),
- Cosmetic surgery, and
- Alternative therapies.

PRECERTIFICATION

Precertification Programs require providers (hospitals, physicians and others) to obtain approval for services from the insurer before those services are provided to members. Some common forms of precertification include referral to a specialist physician, elective surgery, and expensive DME.

SPECIALTY REFERRALS

Treatment by a physician who specializes in one area of medicine is generally more expensive than treatment by a primary care physician. Specialists are able to contract with insurers for higher rates. There may also be additional expenses associated with the transfer of medical records and redundancy if tests needed for diagnosis are repeated at the specialist's office. For these reasons, insurers may require authorization before a member may see a specialist.

For example, a physician may notify the insurer of his or her intention to refer a patient to a dermatologist for treatment of a persistent rash. It is rare for insurers to deny payment for specialty visits. However, they may note how often primary care doctors make referrals and encourage them to obtain training and provide more services in their own office.

ELECTIVE SURGERY

If a hospital admission is pre-planned, such as elective surgery, the physician's office will coordinate with the insurer or other risk-bearing entity for approval of the surgery. This can be a few simple questions on the telephone or an extensive review of the patient medical records. For example, a physician's office may call the insurer because to schedule a patient for breast reduction surgery. This type of surgery can be performed for medical reasons, such as back and shoulder pain, or for cosmetic reasons only. The insurer then requests and reviews the patient's medical records, approving the surgery if it meets the insurer's guidelines, or prompting discussion between the insurer's medical director and the surgeon.

DURABLE MEDICAL EQUIPMENT (DME)

DME includes medical equipment intended for use more than once or twice. Items for home use such as wheel chairs, scooters, crutches, hospital beds and artificial limbs are considered durable. Bandages, syringes and colostomy supplies are non-durable medical equipment because they are used once. Issues in utilization management for DME include the following:

- Rent vs. Purchase: The insurer may need to decide whether it is best to rent or lease equipment or to purchase it for members. Some items, such as hospital beds, are typically used for a short time and therefore rented or leased. Other items, such as artificial limbs, are used for a very long time and are purchased.
- Review List: Some DME items are of such low cost that it does not make sense from a business perspective to review these items. Most companies establish a minimum dollar threshold and do not review equipment purchases below that amount.
- Timing: This controversial issue deals with when items are purchased. Insurers are reluctant to purchase or lease equipment in anticipation of member needs, as those needs

may change, the member may change insurance plans, or the member may die. Some typical items for DME review are wheel chairs, electric scooters, oxygen equipment, hospital beds, insulin pumps, and some orthotics.

RADIOLOGY MANAGEMENT

A variety of less invasive but very expensive scanning technologies have become available in recent years. All of these technologies allow physicians to obtain a detailed look at the inside of the human body without a surgical incision, an important advance in diagnosing diseases and disorders without the need for exploratory surgery.

X-ray-based computerized tomography (CT) scans were the first of this type of imaging to be introduced in the early 1970s. Magnetic resonance imaging (MRI) became widely available in the late 1980s and 1990s. The newest technology is Positron Emission Tomography (PET) scans. They have been available as a diagnostic tool since the late 1990s.

These scans are expensive, and insurers frequently add the most recent (and most expensive) technology to their utilization review lists. They may require prior authorization of the use of these procedures or may review and discuss overuse with individual physicians. MRIs are about twice the cost of CT scans, and PET scans can be two or three times more expensive than MRIs.

In recent years, radiology management companies have begun to proliferate. These organizations profile ordering physicians and offer education from a radiologist to help ordering physicians understand the most effective use of radiology services. They pre-authorize radiology services at the time of ordering, including immediate consultation with a radiologist, to assist practitioners with selecting the appropriate exam. The organizations typically also accumulate information about exams, reducing duplication of future services.

ADMISSION NOTIFICATION

Admission notification systems require that the hospital or member notify the insurer when the member is unexpectedly hospitalized. Since most hospitalizations are not pre-planned, these programs are an important source of information for the insurer. Typically, a clerk at the hospital notifies the insurer's UM department of all members who have been hospitalized each day, including Saturday and Sunday. UM nurses can then work with the hospital to assure that members receive efficient care and help arrange for any needed medical services after discharge.

ADMISSION AVOIDANCE

Admission avoidance programs focus on preventing the need for hospital admissions among insured members. Typically, the first step in developing such a program is analysis of admission rates per 1,000, and comparison of those actual rates to expected rates. This analysis is used to identify diagnoses that are suitable targets for admission avoidance. The types of diagnoses identified direct the strategies the insurer chooses. Some examples include the following:

- Surgical Diagnoses: Analysis may indicate that many more hysterectomies are performed than would be expected for the population. The insurer can review evidence based literature about indication for surgery and share this information with physicians. Pre-certification programs for selected elective surgeries reinforce the need to assure that members have met surgical need criteria before surgery is scheduled.
- Chronic Conditions: Some chronic conditions, such as diabetes and congestive heart failure, may result in frequent visits to the emergency department and hospital admissions. Better outpatient support by nurse call lines, patient education, and other clinic based programs help patients achieve control over their disease and avoid hospital admissions.
- Social Admissions: Patients are sometimes admitted to the hospital because a relatively minor health issue cannot be safely handled due to special social circumstances, such as homelessness or mental illness. Strengthening the emergency department's ability to assist with social issues can also avoid hospital admissions.

READMISSION AVOIDANCE

Patients readmitted to the hospital within 30 days for the same or similar diagnosis are considered potentially avoidable readmissions. Outreach programs deployed by hospitals and insurers have successfully reduced these repeat hospital admissions with programs that call patients after discharge to assure that they understand their post-hospitalization medication regime and have arranged for follow-up outpatient care. Medicare no longer pays hospitals for certain admissions that occur within 30 days and are related to the original admission.

CONCURRENT REVIEW

Nurses who perform concurrent review follow a patient's care while the patient is in the hospital. They review the care the patient is receiving, compare that care to clinical guidelines, and work with hospital discharge planners to attain efficient care and timely discharges. This is perhaps the most controversial of all utilization management activities. Table 44.1 summarizes some of the issues in concurrent review programs.

Many hospitals employ hospitalists, physicians, and other providers who specialize in the care of inpatients. They provide comprehensive management of patients during their hospital stay and communicate with outpatient providers at the point of hospital discharge. This model generally provides very efficient care during hospitalization.

These competing interests can cause friction between insurers, hospital administrators, and doctors. In the best situations, all three groups work together to assure that patients receive safe and efficient care. A recent trend in medical management, spurred at least in part by the ACA, is a model that puts the provider organization at risk for poor financial outcomes. This is discussed later in this chapter in the section on patient-centered medical homes.

Table 44.1

	Issues in Concurrent Review of Hospital Stays
Insurer Perspective	• Services – Hospital care may duplicate diagnostic testing or other services that the member has already received as an outpatient.
	• Efficiency – Services to members may be delayed due to hospital scheduling choices. For example, non-emergent surgery may not be available as the hospital is reluctant to incur overtime costs for bringing in a surgical crew after hours.
Hospital Perspective	• Services – It can be difficult or impossible to obtain timely information from doctor's office and labs that are not open after hours or on weekends. Many hospitals deliver most of the diagnostics tests in their area. Labs and clinics should be coordinating with them.
	• Efficiency – Overall hospital efficiency is more important than efficient case by case management.
	• Discharges – Timely patient discharge may depend on factors outside the hospital's control, such as the availability of nursing home beds or home health care.
Physician	• Services – Hospital services are provided according to the physician's orders. Typically, however, the physician has no financial interest or liability for those services.
	• Efficiency – The physician's personal efficiency is more important than hospital efficiency, or the efficient delivery of care for just one case. The physician delivers most care in the clinic, visiting the hospital patients once or twice each day. The hospitalist approach to inpatient care is an exception to this model and one that is growing in popularity.
	• Coordination of Care – The physician typically cares for the patient across all settings (clinic, hospital, nursing home).

EXAMPLE OF A CONCURRENT REVIEW PROCESS

A hospital faxes a list to the insurer of all members admitted to their hospital in the past 24 hours. The insurer nurse reviews the list and calls the utilization review nurse at the hospital, asking for an update on the clinical status of all patients. The nurses discuss the cases, reviewing any barriers to safe and efficient care, and they make plans for care delivery, communication with the patient and family, and coordination of the next phase of care. Clinical guidelines often form the basis for this conversation.

The insurer's nurse checks the member's benefits and may suggest referral to special case management or disease management services offered by the plan. If needed, the insurer's nurse will advise the hospital nurse of providers such as home care agencies and nursing homes that are in the insurer network. The hospital nurse then handles communication with the physician, patient, and family.

Retrospective Review

Retrospective review is a review of medical records after services have been delivered to the patient. Insurers and government agencies such as Medicare and Medicaid perform these reviews to search for quality of care issues, billing errors or unnecessary services. Retrospective reviews are often a cornerstone of fraud and abuse detection. Computer analyses of billing and claims patterns may be used to select charts for retrospective review. The provider may be required to copy the medical record and send it to the reviewing agency, or the provider may be required to provide space for an on site review of records.

Case Management

Case management programs help members manage their own heath and navigate the health care system. Case management can be an informal system, as when a clinic RN helps members with complex problems, or a very formal system implemented by an organ transplant program.

Case management means delivering a set of personalized services to improve a person's health. It's not a random event, delivered only when a patient is in trouble, but a planned approach to finding and helping people that would fall through the cracks without special attention.

There are four steps in case management:

1. Screen for people appropriate for the program.
2. Plan and deliver care, using standard approaches.
3. Evaluate the plan's effectiveness for each person, and rework it as necessary.
4. Evaluate the overall program effectiveness, and make necessary changes.

Screening

The purpose of screening is to find the people who will benefit from the case management program.

A common issue with screening programs is that they identify people who will benefit only marginally from case management, or they identify people too late, after a preventable hospitalization or other serious medical event.

A screening program must be easy to administer, and should identify 1% to 5% of the population for case management. Some screening programs rely on a questionnaire, completed after enrollment or at the first doctor's visit. Other screening programs review claims data, searching for specific diagnosis or utilization patterns.

Plan and Deliver Care

The case manager does not deliver care directly, but assures that the patient is receiving efficient and effective care. One key tool is a standard set of guidelines that help the case manager determine the ideal treatment for each patient. Another tool is detailed knowledge of community and insurer resources. Telephone assessment skills are also essential.

EVALUATE THE PLAN'S EFFECTIVENESS

An effective CM plan balances outcomes in four areas:

- Cost and utilization
- Clinical outcomes
- Functional outcomes
- Customer satisfaction

These four areas should be balanced to achieve optimal outcomes for the patient. Many patients chose to trade off clinical outcomes for better functional outcomes. The case manager is usually the one who keeps an eye on the finances, communicating with the member's insurer about covered benefits. Many case managers consider the total financial picture, helping members view their personal finances, insurer benefits, and community resources together.

A Return on Investment (ROI) analysis is frequently performed during program evaluation. The use of the term ROI in this context is different from the ROI typically used by actuaries in profitability analysis. In this context, the total cost of the program (mostly nurses' salaries) is compared to the program's savings. It is difficult to measure the financial return of case management, because changes in health care costs over time cannot be assumed to be the result of only the case manager's intervention. Consequently, there is no standard, accepted method for calculating the savings from case management. Typically, the case management department manager and the finance department will develop an agreed-upon method for counting savings that includes assumptions about the case manager's impact on the members' use of emergency department, hospital inpatient, and other medical services.

EVALUATE THE PROGRAM'S OVERALL EFFECTIVENESS

This last step is an annual event, meant to examine the case management steps together, for all patients managed by the program. The program manager assesses the outcomes to answer the following questions:

- Is your screening program finding people appropriate for your program?
- What has been learned from planning and delivering care? What kind of aggregate patient results are being produced?

Program evaluation is followed by planned program changes in a continuous improvement cycle.

Case managers are usually registered nurses, but may also be social workers or occupational health professionals. Case managers can become certified in case management as a specialty by passing a certification exam. Case managers may work for a health insurer, a hospital, a clinic, or an employer.

Insurer case managers generally focus on coordinating a variety of services for members, and are frequently charged with managing the member's benefits in a manner that conserves the insurer's dollars and assures that members receive the care they need. Insurer case managers typically perform the following duties:

- Check benefit coverage levels;
- Negotiate special rates with non-contracted providers, if possible;
- Recommend exceptions to current coverage in lieu of more expensive services;
- Coordinate referrals to specialty care so that all or most care is delivered within the insurer's network;
- Suggest and arrange for special services;
- Coordinate insured care with community services; and
- Coordinate payment with other payers, such as Medicaid or other insurers.

Hospital and clinic case managers coordinate services for people while they are seeking services at the clinic or hospital. Hospital case managers typically perform the following duties:

- Check coverage with the insurer to assure appropriate payment for the clinic or hospital;
- Coordinate the services needed immediately to effect a safe hospital discharge or return home from the clinic;
- Educate patients about their medical conditions and how best to care for themselves;
- Make follow-up telephone calls after patients have received services at their hospital or clinic; and
- Closely coordinate services among various providers, as care is being delivered.

Employer-based case managers are present when large groups of people work together and services can be delivered on site. The focus of their work is to promote health among the worker, reducing work absences. Clinic and industrial health nurses may also work at the site of employment, providing basic medical services to ill or injured workers. The employer-based case manager typically performs the following duties:

- Monitor reasons for employee work absences;
- Follow up with workers after health related work absences;
- Deliver education programs for groups and individuals;
- Provide one-on-one assistance for people with chronic illnesses or special conditions; and
- Administer worksite wellness programs.

CATASTROPHIC CASE MANAGEMENT

Catastrophic case management programs focus on people who have experienced catastrophic health care events, or whose claims expense have reached stop loss thresholds. Many times both of these events have happened. Typical catastrophic diseases include end stage renal disease (ESRD), conditions that require organ transplantation, some cardiac conditions, some cancer treatments, and many terminal illnesses.

During this time, a person may be very ill, confused by the treatment choices, overwhelmed by the possible consequences, and forced to travel long distances to receive specialty care.

Catastrophic case managers can help people make choices, receive emotional support, conserve resources, and return to independence. These case managers generally work closely with family members, as catastrophically ill people may be unable to participate fully in all of these activities.

MATERNITY CASE MANAGEMENT PROGRAMS

These programs are generally aimed at providing prenatal care to pregnant women early in their pregnancy as possible. They especially focus on women at risk for poor pregnancy outcomes.

The case manager's role in maternity case management includes the following tasks:

- Identify pregnant women early, generally through reporting from physician offices and member outreach;
- Call women to ask questions that may identify a high risk pregnancy;
- Make periodic calls to encourage medical care, smoking cessation, good nutrition and attendance at prenatal classes; and
- Facilitate follow-up and physician visits for women with high risk pregnancies.

Table 44.2 summarizes some key points about maternity case management.

Table 44.2

Key Points about Maternity Case Management
• Better birth outcomes are generally defined as less prematurity, less neonatal mortality, fewer neurologic and developmental problems, and fewer cognitive capacity problems (adaptive skills and scholastic performance).
• Low birth weights are closely linked to negative birth outcomes.
• The effectiveness of standard prenatal care in preventing poor birth outcomes is not entirely clear from prior research, but some studies do show a strong positive link.
• The quality of prenatal care (medical tests, type and amount of education, continuity of care) may be more important than the quantity (number and timing of visits).
• The main risk factors for low birth weight babies are previous late term abortion, previous live birth that died, and current unwanted pregnancy.
• Women at higher risk for poor birth outcomes are typically high utilizers of medical care both for their pregnancy and for other medical conditions.

TRANSITIONAL CASE MANAGEMENT

Transitional case managers specialize in helping people navigate specific cross roads in health. They generally operate in two types of programs:

- Disease-focused; or
- Nursing home or extended care placements.

Disease-focused case managers support people newly diagnosed with a disease that will require life style modifications, such as diabetes or arthritis. They assist people by providing intense support and education so that people can once again become self sufficient in caring for themselves.

Transitional case managers can also step in when there is a need for a person to be temporarily or permanently placed in a rehabilitation or nursing facility. They can help the patient and family select a facility and make all necessary arrangements. They can also set realistic expectations about if and when a person may be able to return to his or her former living arrangement.

DISEASE MANAGEMENT

Disease management, also called condition management, is a newer offering in the managed health care industry. People with some chronic illnesses incur greater health care expenses for diagnostic and monitoring tests, medication and other treatment, and emergency care when their chronic illness is not well controlled. Disease management is frequently used in chronic disease situations, particularly diabetes, asthma and heart disease.

As a financial risk management tool, health care managers have been seeking ways to reduce the costs and to improve the health status of this group. Disease management varies from handing out a pamphlet to aggressive individual patient management. Table 44.3 summarizes some important aspects for a successful disease management program.

Table 44.3

Important Aspects of Disease Management Programs
• Population identification process
• Evidence-based practice guidelines
• Collaborative practice model to include physician and support service
• Risk identification and matching of interventions with need
• Patient self-management education (may include primary prevention, modification programs, and compliance/surveillance)
• Process and outcomes measurement, evaluation, and management
• Routine reporting/feedback loop (may include communication with patient insurer and ancillary providers, as well as practice profiling)
• Appropriate use of information technology (may include specialized registries, automated decision support tools, and call-back systems)

Most disease management programs involve more than simply mailing brochures to patients. They include continued coordination and follow up with the primary physician and patient. They may coordinate communication between the disease manager, the patient and physician. For most patients with chronic conditions, there is behavior coaching to help improve medication adherence, diet, risk avoidance such as smoking cessation, and exercise.

Many insurers contract with vendors to provide disease management services to their members. Other companies develop their own programs. Below are some of the key aspects of disease management programs.

Population Identification Process

Programs may use a combination of health risk appraisals, claims information, predictive models, member questionnaires and phone calls, referrals from case managers and physicians and other methods for identifying patients for inclusion.

Process for Enrolling and Risk-Stratifying Members in the Program

This includes sorting members by severity, age or geographic region, and obtaining member agreement to participate. Enrollment may be annual or continuous, and members may need to be re-assessed and moved between severity groups. If members are likely to recover, a disenrollment process will be necessary.

Clinical Information Sources

Information is needed to manage cases. This may include clinical practice guidelines, reference material, access to disease experts, and other clinical information sources. A Disease Management program will also have tools to measure functional status, change readiness, quality of life, compliance, or other clinical aspects of care.

Care Delivery Model

Components of the model may include phone calls, visits, telemonitoring, educational materials, and other methods for working with enrolled members. Days and hours of service must be established, as well as staff qualifications and case loads. Interventions should be matched with member risk levels, and the program must have a process for managing co-morbid conditions and for managing primary and secondary risk factors.

Collaborative Practice Model to Include Physician and Support Service

The program must have methods for interaction and involvement with community primary care physicians and specialists. This may include physician educational efforts, and physician satisfaction or complaint data. The program may also have relationships with physicians, hospitals, home care agencies and other providers.

Patient Self-Management Education

This will consist of primary prevention, modification programs, compliance or surveillance processes, and automated reminder systems.

Process and Outcomes Measurement, Evaluation, and Management

The program should measure cost and utilization outcomes, member and provider satisfaction, and functional status and quality of life measures. Programs typically include some type of quality assurance and quality improvement process, and may be URAC or NCQA accredited. Internal audit processes are common.

Disease management programs do improve the clinical outcomes of care, but the financial ROI for disease management is difficult to measure. As with case management, it may not be possible to separate the impact of the disease management program from other factors.

Information Technology

An advanced information technology base is required for disease management programs, including specialized registries, automated decision support tools, and call-back systems.

Privacy and Confidentiality

Programs must maintain member and provider confidentiality.

WELLNESS

Wellness programs (sometimes called prevention programs) identify members or employees with higher than average risk factors for the eventual development of illness or disease. Those people are then encouraged, coached, and counseled to adopt healthier life styles. Employers and insurers hope that the reduction of risk factors will result in lower health care costs, less missed work time and greater productivity. Modifiable risk factors include lack of regular exercise, smoking, high cholesterol, obesity, high blood pressure, and high alcohol use. The medical costs of people with risk factors can be as much as a third higher than the general population.

It can take many years for wellness programs to produce medical cost savings to the insurer. Some believe that employers can realize earlier cost savings from worker absenteeism decreases and productivity increases.

CARE NAVIGATION

Care navigation provides assistance to people for selection of insurance benefits or for coordination of complex care needs. Assistance with navigating insurance coverage means selecting a coverage plan that provides meaningful benefits to the individual at an affordable cost. This type of care navigation is prominent among Medicare recipients, as they select from an array of add-on benefits to the standard package of benefits provided by the Federal government. Selection of prescription coverage is particularly confusing for many.

The second type of care navigation provides assistance with coordinating medical care that is received in a variety of settings and from a variety of providers. Ill people who are in need of medical services that may include office visits, radiation, surgery and chemotherapy visits, medication and transportation may be offered care management services by their insurers to assist with scheduling and coordination among providers. Care navigation services can be purchased independently, often to help in managing the care for an ill or elderly person unable to make arrangements for care independently.

PATIENT-CENTERED MEDICAL HOMES

Patient centered medical homes (PCMHs), also called health care homes, are a formal model of care that emphasizes a personalized relationship with a qualified medical provider, generally a primary care physician or nurse practitioner, working with a team of health care workers to provide and coordinate care for each individual. The hallmarks of this model include the following:

- Acceptance of financial responsibility by the care team;
- Comprehensive coordination of all services, including medical, specialty, substance abuse, and mental health;
- Improved accessibility of in-person appointments and phone and email access to the care team; and
- Commitment to quality and safety, often measured by insurers and accreditation bodies.

Medical or health care homes require engagement and commitment from providers and patients to achieve efficiency and effectiveness. This has been a significant challenge for these models. Responsible provider systems, accustomed to treating those who seek care, are required to provide outreach to their patients and coordinate multiple streams of information. Patients, accustomed to open access to care and little emphasis from the medical field on prevention, must now engage with providers and steadily work towards improved health.

Information systems that collect and use information to spot gaps in care and provide best practice guidance have become necessary for provider systems. The emphasis on cost containment and activating patients to engage in their care has shifted from insurers to provider systems with this model.

RECENT DEVELOPMENTS AND TRENDS

Several topics have emerged as hot topics in medical management recently. These are areas likely to shape the delivery and financing of care in the near future.

CHRONIC ILLNESS AND THE AGING POPULATION

As the baby boomer population ages, their needs and desires influence care delivery and management. Chronic illnesses such as arthritis and diabetes now affect a larger portion of the overall population. New methods to treat and control these chronic illnesses are being developed. This trend is most apparent in the development of drugs and medical devices for chronic ailments.

Many new medications have been developed to treat cardiac conditions and to treat precursors to heart disease, such as elevated lipid (fat) levels in the blood or high blood pressure. People may be on these medications for decades. Medical devices such as insulin pumps for diabetics and implantable defibrillators for certain cardiac patients add to the cost and complexity of medical care. Chronic illness among the baby boomer generation is expected to continue to fuel the development and marketing of new drugs and medical devices, and the consumer movement in health care that demands more convenient and personalized care.

MEDICAL ERRORS

Errors by medical professionals (primarily doctors and nurses) were highlighted in a report "To Err is Human" by the Institute of Medicine, published in 1999, and their follow-up report "Crossing the Quality Chasm", published in 2001. The first report found that medical errors were a leading cause of death and injury. Projections from two large-scale studies estimate that between 44,000 and 98,000 people die in American hospitals as a result of medical errors each year.

These reports have been picked up by the media and widely reported, causing concern by regulatory bodies, consumer groups and the medical profession. The Quality Chasm report offers pointed advice for improving the safety of care, including 10 simple rules for care delivery professionals and a list of obstacles and policy remedies. Accreditation bodies such as the Joint Commission on Accreditation of Healthcare Organization (JCAHO) and the National Committee for Quality Assurance (NCQA) are concerned about these issues, as are Hospitals and Integrated Delivery System and doctors and nurses. Many new initiatives have been started, as results of the findings are recommendations of the Institute of Medicine.

MEASURING RETURN ON INVESTMENT (ROI)

Medical management activities have come under increased financial scrutiny as the overall cost of medical services and the concomitant cost of health insurance have increased. Actuaries have been called on to help with the measurement of cost savings. The program cost side of the equation is relatively easy to calculate. This is typically done by combining the nursing costs with department and overhead expenses. The program savings side of the equation, however, is challenging.

Two general methods are used to measure the cost savings due to medical management programs and activities. Control group methods divide a population into a group that is managed and a group that is not. The financial results of the two groups are compared. A second method is the pre/post method. In this method costs for medical care are compared before and after management.

Both methods have strengths and weaknesses. The pre/post method is more popular. This is because populations in need of management are much smaller than the general population. The pre/post method provides a larger group for analysis, as the entire group is compared in two time frames. The other reason is that clinicians and insurers, who are aware that some medical management activities, such as disease management, improve the clinical health of members, and they do not want to withhold these services from people in the control group.

Measurement issues with disease management include regression to the mean, selection bias, statistical validity of the population size, and technological advances or benefit design changes over time. Disease members may be identified and enrolled in management programs when medical expenses are high. Chronic illness follows a natural course of exacerbation and recovery. Costs are higher during an illness exacerbation. This natural cycle of fluctuating costs can result in the overstatement of savings attributable to the program, if members are identified at the high point of utilization, and recovery would have occurred even without the program.

Diseased people who elect to join a disease management program may have a significantly different utilization pattern than people with the same disease who do not join. If the program's impact is measured by comparing the enrollees to non-enrollees, results may reflect this selection bias. Also, only a small portion of the general population has a chronic illness. If the overall population is small, there may not be enough people in the disease management program to allow for a statistically valid analysis.

As costs continue to climb, methods to measure the impact of medical management programs will continue to be examined, and it is reasonable to expect that standardized methods for financial measurement will emerge.

BEHAVIORAL HEALTH ISSUES

Behavioral health problems include mental illness and alcohol and drug abuse problems. There are several issues developing in the behavioral health area:

Treatment for these conditions has not always been covered at the same level as coverage for medical conditions. This, in part, has led the U.S. Congress to pass mental health parity legislation that assures the same coverage for behavioral health treatment as is available for medical treatment.

The medical community has long recognized that medical and behavioral health are related. Treatment for behavioral health conditions is frequently carved out and managed by a separate company and provider group. Sensitivity to the need for confidentiality can mean that the provider groups are not sharing information about the patient and coordinating care. Lack of treatment for behavioral health conditions, such as substance abuse, can result in serious and expensive medical conditions such as liver failure. In addition, certain behavioral health diagnoses have increased, including attention deficit disorder, bipolar (manic depressive) illness, depression, and autism. It is unclear whether the increase in diagnoses is a result of an actual rise in the incidence of illness or of better diagnosing on the part of physicians.

A variety of new behavioral health treatments have become available, including new medications, residential treatment facilities and many intensive and lengthy treatments, sometimes lasting many hours several days per week. The expectation is that costs for behavioral health problems will increase as a result of these many factors.

NURSING

Nursing is the largest profession in health care. Dire predictions have been made about the shortage of nurses expected in the next decade. The Institute of Medicine (IOM) released a two year study on the nursing profession in 2010. It has become one of the most frequently downloaded reports ever produced, and is shaping policy making and education in nursing. The report include the following conclusions.

- Nurses should practice to the full extent of their education and training. This recommendation includes the emerging field of nurse practitioners and other advance practice nurses.

- Nurses should achieve higher levels of education and training through an improved education system that promotes seamless academic progression. The baccalaureate degree is identified as the necessary undergraduate education.

- Nurses should be full partners, with physicians and other health care professionals, in redesigning health care in the United States. The nursing perspective is recognized as uniquely different than that of physicians.

- Effective workforce planning and policy making require better data collection and information infrastructure.

ACCOUNTABLE CARE ORGANIZATIONS (ACOs)

Many new insurance products shift the risk to providers by paying them a set rate for the members under their care. A clinic or group of providers, and the hospital and ancillary services they work with, will accept total financial risk for a defined group of people. These new arrangements press providers to keep their members healthy so that they do not require expensive interventional services. As a result, organizations and individuals who care for members have become very interested in deploying medical management strategies.

Prior to the developed of these risk transferring arrangements, the motivation to contain costs rested with who wanted to keep more of the premium dollar. Now providers have the financial motivation, and the means to pay for medical management services. Medicare has been the primary driver of these new arrangements, with experiments currently underway.

Some of the system changes ACOs are pushing forward include the following:

- Broader practice scopes for primary care;
- Better collaboration between primary care and specialist;
- Closer provider coordination across care site such as hospital, nursing home and clinic;
- Shared electronic medical records among providers and institutions; and
- Better data collection about care outcomes and the establishment of outcome targets by providers

REFERENCES

Tufts Managed Care Institute. *A Brief History of Managed Care.*

Medicare Accountable Care Organizations. http://www.cms.gov/Medicare/Medicare-Fee-for-Service-Payment/ACO/index.html?redirect=/ACO/. Accessed November 6, 2014

Altman, Drew E. and Larry Levitt, "The Sad History of Health Care Cost Containment As Told In One Chart," *Health Affairs*, January 23, 2002.

Berwick, Donald M., "A User's Manual for the IOM's 'Quality Chasm' Report," *Health Affairs*, Vol. 21, No. 3, May/June 2002.

National Academy Press. *Crossing the Quality Chasm: A New Health System for the 21st Century*, 2001.

NCQA. *Disease Management Accreditation and Certification.* 2001.

Johnson, Alison, M. Brovcik and A. Wobbema, "Making the Case for Wellness in the Workplace," Benefit Perspectives, Fall 2005.

Peeno, Linda, MD. *Presentation to the Romanow Commission on the Future of Health Care in Canada.* Louisville, KY, May 31, 2002.

Reeder, Linda, RN, CM, CNA, MBA. *Anatomy of a Disease Management Program.* Nursing Management, April 1999. www.nursingmanagement.com

The Affordable Care Act. http://www.hhs.gov/healthcare/rights/ Accessed November 6, 2014.

The Future of Nursing: Leading Change, Advancing Health, Washington, D.C.: National Academies Press, 2010.

To Err Is Human: Building a Safer Health System. Washington, D.C.: National Academies Press, 2000.

American Academy of Actuaries Issue Brief. "Disease Management Programs: What's the Cost?" April 2005.

Accreditation Association for Ambulatory Health Care, Inc. "The Medical Home – Avoiding the Rush to Judgment", 2014.

About the Editors

Principal Editor

Daniel D. Skwire, FSA, MAAA

Dan is a Principal and Consulting Actuary with Milliman, Inc. in Portland, Maine. He joined the firm in 1998 and has 25 years of experience in the actuarial profession, with a specialty in disability insurance and group life insurance. His clients include insurers, reinsurers, employers, and distribution groups. He has assisted these organizations with projects including product design, pricing, valuation, reinsurance, and mergers and acquisitions. Prior to joining Milliman, Dan was responsible for pricing disability products at Unum.

Dan is a Fellow of the Society of Actuaries and a Member of the American Academy of Actuaries, as well as a member of the National Academy of Social Insurance. He has served on the SOA Health Section Council and the International Actuarial Association Health Section Council, and he is currently the Chair of the SOA Disability Special Interest Group and of the International Actuarial Association's Income Protection Topic Team. He is a regular speaker at industry meetings, and he has published articles in a variety of professional publications, including the *North American Actuarial Journal*, *Contingencies*, and *Best's Review*. He has written extensively on the connections between insurance and literature, including essays on the insurance careers of Wallace Stevens and Franz Kafka, and on the role of finance and insurance in the works of Jane Austen and Charles Dickens. Dan is a graduate of Williams College with a degree in mathematics and history.

Associate Editors

Kristi M. Bohn, FSA, MAAA, EA

Kristi has worked at the State of Minnesota Commerce Department since March of 2014, where she reviews major medical, Medicare supplement, disability, vision, dental, long term care and fixed indemnity rate filings, as well as participates in overseeing insurer solvency. Prior to working at Commerce, she was the Staff Health Fellow for the Society of Actuaries where she helped plan the content for continuing education events, assisted in oversight groups for actuarial studies, and reviewed actuarial health publications. From 2004-2012, Kristi worked at Blue Cross Blue Shield of Minnesota, where she held several positions including the director of the group actuarial division and a role as a benefit consultant within sales. She also worked in the retirement business at Towers Perrin from 1994-2004, where she led pension and retiree welfare valuation work, managed staff, and helped her clients administer their plans. She is a long-term volunteer for the actuarial exam program. Kristi graduated from Cornell University in 1994 with a B.S. in Statistics and Biometry.

MARGARET DONAVAN CORMIER, FSA, MAAA

Maggie is a Senior Director and Assistant Actuary with The Standard in Portland, Oregon. She joined The Standard in 2014 and has nearly 20 years of actuarial experience. At The Standard, she is responsible for individual disability pricing and product development. Prior to working at The Standard, she worked for Guardian Life and Unum, where her work focused on disability pricing. She began her actuarial career with Blue Cross Blue Shield of Vermont.

Maggie is a Fellow of the Society of Actuaries and a Member of the American Academy of Actuaries. She has volunteered with the Society of Actuaries to organize disability sessions and has presented at Society of Actuaries meetings. Maggie has a Bachelor of Arts in Mathematics from Williams College and a Masters of Science in Applied Mathematics from University of Washington.

STEPHEN J. KACZMAREK, FSA, MAAA

Steve is a Principal and Consulting Actuary with Milliman, Inc. in Hartford, Connecticut. He has 23 years of professional actuarial experience, primarily in the group insurance and employee benefits field. His consulting work focuses on Medicare Part D and other pharmacy benefits, health care reform and competing on state health exchanges, and health care product strategies. Prior to joining Milliman, Steve worked for CIGNA HealthCare where he served in a variety of health care positions and was awarded two consecutive Pinnacle awards for his contributions to the company's financial success. He began his actuarial career at the Travelers Managed Care and Employee Benefits division as a pricing actuary.

Steve is a Fellow of the Society of Actuaries and a Member of the American Academy of Actuaries. He graduated in 1986 from the United States Military Academy at West Point with a Bachelor of Science Degree in Quantitative Economics. He served in the United States Army for seven years with tours of duty with the 82nd Airborne Division and with VII Corps in Germany and the Middle East.

Steve is a frequent speaker at national employee benefits conferences and actuarial meetings. He has authored numerous articles in the last decade in a variety of publications.

SARA C. TEPPEMA, FSA, MAAA

Sara is Director of Actuarial Services for Valence Health, where she leads a team providing actuarial and financial modeling solutions to provider-owned health plans, accountable care networks and other provider organizations. She has over 25 years of experience providing a wide range of consulting services to a variety of clients, including employers, payers, providers and government entities. Prior to joining Valence, she worked for the Society of Actuaries, where she was most recently Senior Fellow for Practice Research. Prior to the SOA, Sara worked for Aon Hewitt where she consulted with employer clients and managed Aon Hewitt's internal health care solutions development function.

Sara is an active professional volunteer, serving on the SOA's Research Executive Committee, as well as several other committees of the SOA, the American Academy of Actuaries and the American Public Health Association. She is a frequent speaker at actuarial meetings. She is a Fellow of the Society of Actuaries, a member of the American Academy of Actuaries and she has a degree in mathematics from the University of Illinois at Urbana-Champaign. She lives outside of Chicago with her husband and three daughters, and when she is not working and editing textbooks, she is playing her piano or listening to her musical family.

FOUNDING EDITOR

WILLIAM F. BLUHM

The founding editor of *Group Insurance*, Bill Bluhm is a retired principal and consulting actuary with Milliman, Inc. While at Milliman, he worked with health care providers, insurers, governments, and others on matters relating to individual and group health insurance. In addition to the first six editions of this text, Bill's prior publications include another textbook, *Individual Health Insurance*, and two award-winning papers: "Cumulative Antiselection Theory" and "The Minnesota Antiselection Model."

Bill has served as president of the Conference of Consulting Actuaries and the American Academy of Actuaries. In his retirement, he is the owner of the Dancing Dragonfly winery in St. Croix Falls, Wisconsin.

ABOUT THE AUTHORS

The following authors contributed directly to the production of the seventh edition of Group Insurance.

MICHELLE N. ANGELONI, FSA, MAAA

Michelle is an Actuary with the Hartford, Connecticut office of Milliman. She joined the firm in 2010. Michelle's clients include insurers, health benefit plan sponsors, pharmacy benefit managers, and Medicare Part D prescription drug plan (PDP) sponsors. Her expertise includes pricing medical and pharmacy benefits, development of actuarial reserves, and performing experience analyses. She has worked for both private and public sector plan sponsors. Michelle has significant experience working with PDP sponsors including bid development, formulary design, and other support related to analysis of ongoing performance. She also assists employers and pharmacy benefit managers with group prescription drug services, including creditable coverage testing and Retiree Drug Subsidy attestations.

Michelle is a current member of the Society of Actuaries' Probability Exam Committee and has served as an adjunct professor to the University of Connecticut's Actuarial Science Program. Michelle is a Fellow of the Society of Actuaries and a Member of the American Academy of Actuaries. She earned her Bachelor of Science Degree in Mathematics and Actuarial Science from the University of Connecticut.

JOAN BARRETT, FSA, MAAA

Joan recently joined Axene Health Partners as a consulting actuary. Prior to that, Joan was Vice President at United Healthcare, responsible for the National Accounts Actuarial department supporting Fortune 500 customers in understanding the driving forces behind their health care costs and developing solutions, such as plan design strategy, incentives and communications to contain the cost and improve member health. She was also responsible for consumer research, including analysis of consumer-driven health plans and the role of consumer decision-making on health care cost and quality in general.

Joan is one of the primary authors of the Consumer Activation Index, a systematic approach to track and measure consumer decision making. She is a Vice President of the Board of Directors for the Society of Actuaries and is passionate about the need for actuaries to advance in the area of analytics, and is also passionate about the basic and continuing education of actuaries. She is a Fellow of the Society of Actuaries and a Member of the American Academy of Actuaries and speaks regularly at industry meetings. She is a graduate of Frederick College and holds a Master's Degree from Miami University.

JOHN W. BAUERLEIN, FSA, MAAA

John is a Principal and Consulting Actuary with Milliman, Inc. in Atlanta, GA. He has 20 years of professional actuarial experience, primarily in the group insurance and employee benefits field. His consulting work focuses on health plan profitability, product strategies, and provider network evaluation. Prior to joining Milliman, John served as the Director of Actuarial Services for PacifiCare Health Systems. Earlier in his career, he worked for a group insurance carrier and a national employee benefits consulting firm. He graduated in 1983 from the University of California at Los Angeles with a Bachelor of Arts Degree in Applied Mathematics. John earned his FSA designation in 1986.

John has a broad range of group insurance actuarial expertise, specifically in health care. He consults regularly with health insurers, HMOs, hospitals, and physician organizations. John also consults to large employers on their health and welfare benefit programs. His recent work has focused on benchmarking provider reimbursement, and communicating network performance to current and potential purchasers of health plan services and products. John is a frequent speaker on these and other related actuarial topics.

ROWEN B. BELL, FSA, MAAA

Rowen is an Actuarial Advisor in the Chicago office of Ernst & Young LLP's Insurance and Actuarial Advisory Services practice. His professional interests center around health insurance financial reporting and solvency management issues. Prior to joining Ernst & Young, Rowen served as Director of Financial Regulatory Services for the Blue Cross Blue Shield Association, and as an officer in the Corporate Actuarial department at Trustmark Insurance.

Rowen has been very active in the activities of the American Academy of Actuaries and currently sits on the Academy's Board of Directors. He has represented the Academy on multiple occasions in discussions with the NAIC, FASB, and AICPA on financial reporting and solvency issues. He is a former Chair of the Academy's Health Practice Financial Reporting Committee and a former Vice-Chair of the Academy's Health RBC Task Force.

Rowen has an MBA in Finance and Accounting from the University of Chicago's Graduate School of Business. He also has a master's degree in mathematics from the University of Chicago, and a bachelor's degree in mathematics from Queen's University in his native Canada.

GERALD R. BERNSTEIN, FSA, MAAA

Gerry is a Principal with the Milwaukee office of Milliman and has been with the firm since 1981. His area of expertise is group health care programs, with emphasis on all forms of managed care. He has assisted clients with plan design, pricing, provider reimbursement, experience analysis, financial projections, liability estimation, retiree medical projections, retiree drug subsidy applications, and Medicare/Medicaid contracting. Gerry has advised HMOs, PPOs, provider groups, state and local governments, school districts and insurance companies.

He has assisted Medicare Advantage plans with their bid preparation and strategic issues and has assisted PACE (Programs for All-inclusive Care for the Elderly) organizations across the country with the development of their Part D bids and other issues.

Gerry is a Fellow of the Society of Actuaries and a Member of the American Academy of Actuaries. He earned a bachelor's degree in actuarial science from the University of Wisconsin - Madison.

SHELLY S. BRANDEL, FSA, MAAA

Shelly is a Consulting Actuary with the Milwaukee office of Milliman. She has over 15 years of actuarial health care consulting experience. Her area of expertise is managed health care programs. She has assisted various entities including health plans, employers, insurance companies, and Medicare/Medicaid programs. She has helped clients with product development and pricing, Medicare and Medicaid bid development, experience analysis, valuation of reserves, and strategic analysis.

Shelly is a Fellow of the Society of Actuaries and a Member of the American Academy of Actuaries. She earned her Bachelor's degree in Mathematics & Statistics from the Miami University (Ohio).

JACK P. BURKE, FSA, MAAA

Jack is a principal and consulting actuary with Milliman in the Philadelphia office having joined the firm in 1999. He has extensive experience in all aspects of the small employer managed care market including operations, systems, product design and development, legislation, underwriting, pricing, management of distribution systems, and overall business strategy.

Since joining Milliman, Jack has been involved in a variety of projects involving small and large group commercial products, Medicaid and Medicare. He has also developed expertise in consumer-driven products, including HSAs.

Prior to joining Milliman, Jack worked at Aetna and United Healthcare. While at United Healthcare, he was vice president in charge of product management of health plan products. Prior to that, Jack was vice president of small group, responsible for growing United Healthcare's share of the small-employer market. Prior to that, Jack spent 13 years at Aetna, where he gained broad management experience, including running a 180-person production unit and managing a large HMO system development project. At Aetna Health Plans, Jack was the CFO for, and ultimately head of, a 600-person, $1.6 billion strategic business unit selling group insurance and managed care to small employers. Jack graduated with a BS in Mathematics in 1983 from the University of Notre Dame.

STEPHEN T. CARTER, FSA, MAAA, EA, FLMI

Stephen is Vice President of Actuarial Services for Companion Life Insurance Company, a subsidiary of Blue Cross and Blue Shield of South Carolina. He was previously Vice President of Product Management for Provident Life and Accident Company. He has been Chairman of the Committee on Health and Group Insurance for the Society of Actuaries, Vice President of the Health Section Council, and President of the Southeastern Actuaries Club.

He holds the degrees of Bachelor of Industrial Engineering from Georgia Institute of Technology and Master of Actuarial Science from Georgia State University.

FRANK CASSANDRA, FSA, MAAA

Frank is a Senior Vice President with the Metropolitan Life Insurance Company. He currently heads the Corporate Risk Management Department at MetLife. In this position, he is responsible for providing an enterprise-wide, independent, and comprehensive framework to appropriately identify, aggregate, measure, manage and report risks across the organization.

Frank joined MetLife in 1986 as an Actuarial Assistant in the Group Insurance Department. Prior to his current role, Frank has served as the Chief Financial Officer for MetLife's Institutional Business and also for MetLife's U.S. Insurance Products. In 1996, Frank was awarded MetLife's Alexander J. Bailie Award for actuarial professionalism and dedication.

Frank received his B.S. degree in Applied Mathematics (summa cum laude) from Polytechnic University, Brooklyn, New York in 1986. He currently resides in Staten Island, New York and Tuckerton, New Jersey.

MARGARET A. CHANCE, FSA, MAAA

Margaret is a Principal and Consulting Actuary with the Chicago-Milwaukee Health Practice of Milliman. She has 19 years of actuarial experience, primarily working with individual and small group health insurance products. Margaret has assisted a variety of clients with product development and pricing, strategic planning, experience analysis, financial modeling, and state insurance department rate filings. She has assisted a variety of clients in recent years with the evaluation and implementation of various components of health care reform, particularly around strategic planning, product development, and pricing.

MALCOLM A. CHEUNG, FSA, MAAA, LTCP

Malcolm recently retired as Vice President of LTC for the Prudential Insurance Company of America in Roseland, NJ, and is currently an independent consultant. Until 2013, he had overall operational and bottom-line responsibility for Prudential's group and individual long term care insurance products. In this role, Malcolm led the LTC organization to industry leading growth in sales and inforce. With Prudential's strategic decision to discontinue LTC sales in 2012, his focus then shifted to overseeing the experience analysis and re-pricing efforts associated with the management of the closed block. Prior to joining Prudential in 1999, Malcolm worked for John Hancock Mutual Life Insurance Company, where he had more than eight years of experience in their Group Long Term Care division, first as their senior actuary, and then as the vice president of the division

Malcolm received a BA degree in statistics from Princeton University and an MS in statistics from Stanford University. He is a Fellow of the Society of Actuaries, where he is a past Chairman of the LTC Insurance Section Council, and is a member of the American Academy of Actuaries, where he serves on the Long Term Care Reform Subcommittee. Malcolm is also a past Chairman of the ACLI's LTC Policy Committee and a past member of AHIP's LTC Policy Committee and Product Leadership Council. He has been a frequent public speaker on long term care insurance issues and has more than 35 years of insurance and employee benefits consulting experience.

KARA L. CLARK, FSA, MAAA

Kara is Vice President, Health Analytics, Research & Reporting, within Walgreen's Clinical Office. In this role, she leads a multidisciplinary team that provides health outcomes research, actuarial analytics, and client reporting for Walgreen's clinical programs and services.

Ms. Clark has over 25 years of experience in the health care industry, working for corporate, consulting and professional association organizations, including Ernst & Young LLP, Hewitt Associates, and the American Hospital Association. She also served the Society of Actuaries for nearly nine years as the Health Staff Fellow and Managing Director of Strategy. Ms. Clark has a degree in economics from the University of Illinois at Urbana-Champaign and a Master of Business Administration from the Kellogg School of Management Northwestern University.

JOHN P. COOKSON, JR. FSA, MAAA

John is a principal with the Philadelphia office of Milliman. He joined the firm in 1973. His areas of expertise include all aspects of group health insurance and statistical methods for solving actuarial problems. He has substantial experience in trend analysis and forecasting, dental insurance, stop loss, and risk analysis. He was the founder and publisher of the Milliman Health Cost Index™ – a proprietary index of medical cost trends. He has been involved in the transition of the Milliman Health Cost Index to the S&P Medical Trend Indices, and in the continued monitoring and development of S&P's Indices. He developed the Hospital Efficiency Index™ – a method for evaluating the efficiency of hospital utilization, and was responsible for the initial development of Milliman's Dental Cost Guidelines and Aggregate Stop Loss Net Claim Cost Guidelines.

John was a member of the 2010-2012 Medicare Trustees' Technical Review Panel, which periodically reviews the assumptions and methods underlying the Medicare trustee's short- and long-term projections of the Medicare program.

More recently, John has been involved in the development of simulation models used in the successful placement of a series of insurance linked securities tied to health insurance loss ratios ("cat bonds"). These models and the Health Cost Index also serve as a basis for Milliman's work in risk-based capital models.

John has published numerous articles and is a frequent speaker on a broad range of insurance topics. This included a quarterly Commentary in the Health Cost Index™ Report on health cost trends. John is the author and co-author of two chapters of early editions of Group Insurance: Underwriting Gain and Loss Cycles, and Medical Claim Cost Trend Analysis.

John is a past chairman of the Health Section Council and a former member of the Health Benefits Systems Practice Advancement Committee of the Society of Actuaries, and former Chair of Health Section Research.

PAUL L. CORREIA, FSA, MAAA

Paul is a consulting actuary at Milliman who specializes in disability and group life insurance. He is a member of the American Academy of Actuaries and a Fellow of the Society of Actuaries. He has a Master's degree in mathematics from the University of Maine and a Bachelor's degree in mathematics from the University of Vermont. Paul has experience in pricing, product development, underwriting, and valuation for a variety of disability and group life insurance programs. He was recently retained by the Society of Actuaries to research credibility methods for group disability insurance.

ELAINE CORROUGH, FSA, MAAA, FCA

Elaine is a Partner and Consulting Actuary with Axene Health Partners in Portland, OR. She has over 20 years of health actuarial experience working with health plans, hospital systems, physician groups, and employers. Her recent work has focused on innovative payment models and risk arrangements for Medicaid and Medicare Advantage contracting as well as more traditional ACA rate filings and actuarial certifications. She particularly enjoys assignments requiring assimilation and documentation of new regulations, technologies, and data sources into existing actuarial processes and methods.

Elaine is a Fellow of the Society of Actuaries, a Fellow of the Conference of Consulting Actuaries, and a Member of the American Academy of Actuaries. She is currently chair of the SOA's Health Section Council. In addition to the Health Section Council and other committees of the SOA, AAA and CCA, she has contributed to the Society of Actuaries' Basic Education curriculum for aspiring health actuaries, including original writing, syllabus review, and testing input. Elaine earned a Bachelor of Arts degree in Classics (with an emphasis on languages) from Washington University in St. Louis in 1992.

ROBERT B. CUMMING, FSA, MAAA

Bob is Senior Vice President, Actuarial & Underwriting at HealthPartners and President of HealthPartners Insurance Company and HealthPartners Administrators Inc. HealthPartners is an integrated health plan with both medical and dental clinics and a hospital. HealthPartners has about 20,000 employees, 1.5 million members and $5 billion in annual revenue. Bob focuses on market and product strategy, process improvement, and sales efforts.

Prior to joining HealthPartners, Bob was a Principal at Milliman, Inc. His area of expertise is managed health care programs. He assisted clients in the areas of risk analysis and predictive modeling, underwriting process improvement, Medicaid rate setting, product development and network evaluation, and regulatory filings. Bob has advised Blue Cross/Blue Shield plans, HMOs, health care providers, governmental agencies, insurance companies, and employers.

Bob is a graduate of the University of Minnesota, a Fellow of the Society of Actuaries and a Member of the American Academy of Actuaries.

SHERRI DANIEL

Sherri was an Actuarial Assistant in the St. Louis office of Milliman, Inc. from 1995 to 2015 where she provided support to insurers in their financial reporting as well as to state departments of insurance in their financial examinations. Prior to joining Milliman, Sherri worked for a couple of insurance companies focusing on financial reporting and modeling. She has worked extensively in the projection of financial operations for health insurance risk-bearers. Sherri holds a BA in Mathematics from the University of Missouri – Columbia.

PATRICK J. DUNKS, FSA, MAAA

Pat is a Principal with the Milwaukee office of Milliman, Inc., joining the firm in 1985. His area of expertise is managed health care programs with emphasis on managed Medicare products. He has assisted clients with Medicare contracting, liability estimation, risk adjustment, medical cost estimates and projections, provider reimbursement strategies, product development, risk-sharing arrangements, provider negotiations, experience analysis, trend analysis, Medicaid contracting, e-health product development, mergers and acquisitions, and managed workers' compensation programs. Pat has advised HMOs, PPOs, hospitals, medical groups, PHOs, Blue Cross / Blue Shield plans, and insurance companies. He is a frequent speaker at managed care industry meetings.

Pat has assisted many managed care organizations with their managed Medicare products. His assistance has ranged from the initial stages of development through successfully managing the products. His extensive Medicare product experience includes assisting many HMOs and provider organizations with Medicare Advantage start-up issues and in understanding and adjusting to CMS' risk-adjusted payments. Pat has also provided input to CMS regarding managed Medicare product issues. His experience includes an actuarial review of the health status risk adjustor methodology for Medicare Advantage organizations as an active participant on an American Academy of Actuaries task force.

After completing undergraduate work at Saint Norbert College in DePere, Wisconsin, Pat earned a master's degree in mathematics from Purdue University.

JOHN W. ELLIOT

John is a Vice President of Sales for a major health insurance organization. Over his twenty year career, he has held a variety of roles in the large group insurance market including underwriting, data analysis, consulting, and account management.

John has a Masters in Economics from DePaul University and a Bachelor's degree in Finance from Valparaiso University. He lives in Chicagoland area with his wife Beth and seven dogs.

GREGORY G. FANN, FSA, MAAA

Greg is a Consulting Actuary in the Murrieta, CA office of Axene Health Partners. He has broad expertise in group, individual, and government health care products. Greg has provided consulting services to health plans related to strategic initiatives, navigating the Affordable Care Act, rate development, Medicare Advantage bids, valuation of liabilities, feasibility studies, Federal Employee rates, litigation support and competitive Medicaid bids. He has assisted states with rate review and PACE (Programs for All-inclusive Care for the Elderly) rate development and helped providers evaluate Accountable Care Organization savings. He has also assisted the federal government with Medicare bid audits and regulation implementation.

Greg is a frequent contributor to actuarial publications and speaks regularly at industry meetings. He is a thought leader on the market implications of the Patient Protection and Affordable Care Act and his 2014 Health Watch article was cited by *Forbes* and *Newsmax*.

He is an elected member of the Health Section Council of the Society of Actuaries where he has a leadership role in driving strategic initiatives and planning the health sessions for the Society of Actuaries Annual Meeting. Greg enjoys volunteering and networking and is passionate about connecting actuaries to opportunities. He also chairs the Society of Actuaries Group Managed Care Specialty Examination and was an American Academy of Actuaries Task Force member on ASOP #50 "Actuarial Value/Minimum Value under the Affordable Care Act."

Greg is a Fellow of the Society of Actuaries and a Member of the American Academy of Actuaries. He is a graduate of Furman University and holds a Master's Degree in Actuarial Science from Georgia State University.

JOANNE E. FONTANA, FSA, MAAA

Joanne is a Consulting Actuary with the Hartford office of Milliman, Inc. She joined the firm in 2006. Her clients include insurance companies, employers, and government entities, with particular emphasis on the dental industry. Joanne's focus has been largely on managed care and dental, with experience in premium rate development, reserving, and provider contract analysis, as well as valuation of post-retirement health and non-pension benefits. Over the past few years she has worked closely with several dental industry organizations to assess the impact of health care reform on the dental industry. Joanne also serves as co-chair of the Society of Actuaries dental subgroup within the Health Section. Prior to joining Milliman, Joanne spent more than ten years with Cigna, where she held various actuarial leadership roles in health care. She also served for two years as the human resources director of Cigna's actuarial student program.

Joanne earned her Bachelor of Arts degree in Mathematics and Economics from Cornell University.

CHRISTOPHER S. GIROD, FSA, MAAA

Chris is a principal and consulting actuary in the San Diego office of Milliman. He joined the firm in 1994 after working for six years at Pacific Heritage Assurance Company in Portland, Oregon.

Chris specializes in helping clients project and understand the risks and financial implications associated with their health care products, reimbursement systems, and risk-sharing arrangements. He has worked with insurance companies, HMOs, PPOs, Blue Cross Blue Shield plans, provider organizations, employers, medical device manufacturers, and government agencies to help them assess risks associated with commercial, Medicare, Medicaid, and CHAMPUS populations.

Chris graduated from Linfield College in McMinnville, Oregon with a BS in mathematics in 1988.

ERIC P. GOETSCH, FSA, MAAA

Eric is a Principal and Consulting Actuary with the Milwaukee office of Milliman. He joined the firm in 1994. Eric's area of expertise is managed health care programs with an emphasis on Medicare Advantage. He has assisted clients in the areas of strategic analysis, premium and capitation rate development, experience analysis, evaluation of provider reimbursement and risk sharing arrangements, liability estimation, and other actuarial projections. He has worked with managed care organizations, state government agencies, insurance companies, employers, and other organizations.

Eric is a Fellow of the Society of Actuaries and a Member of the American Academy of Actuaries. He earned his Bachelors degree in Mathematics from Marquette University and his Masters degree in Actuarial Science from the University of Wisconsin-Madison.

P. ANTHONY HAMMOND, ASA, MAAA

Tony is Market Vice President at Humana. Prior to joining Humana, Tony was Principal and Senior Actuary with Greenwood Consultants, an independent actuarial consulting firm. Tony has also held positions as Vice President or Chief Actuary of several health plans throughout his career.

Tony has been very involved in health insurance policy issues over the years, working extensively with the American Academy of Actuaries, the Health Insurance Association of America, the Institute for Health Policy Solutions and as a private consultant. In that regard, he has testified, analyzed and commented on a range of health insurance issues, especially Medicare products and prescription drug costs, health risk adjusters and the impact of health policy alternatives on employer-sponsored group, individual and child health insurance coverages. Tony has authored various papers on health policy issues.

Tony is an Associate of the Society of Actuaries and a Member of the American Academy of Actuaries. He has served on numerous Society and Academy health insurance committees and work groups.

TIMOTHY HARRIS, FSA, MAAA

Tim is a consultant with Actuarys, LLC, a Veteran Owned Small Business, and has over 40 years of experience in the Actuarial field. Consulting projects include assignments for state and federal government agencies, HMOs, health care providers, employers, and insurance companies.

Tim is a Fellow of the Society of Actuaries and a Member of the American Academy of Actuaries. He has served on many professional committees. Tim has served on the Society of Actuaries' Board of Governors. He is a past member of the Life Committee of the Actuarial Standards Board. He has also been a member of the Medicare Cost Containment Work Group and the Medicaid Work Group of the Academy of Actuaries.

Tim has spoken at meetings of the Society of Actuaries and other insurance organizations. He has written numerous articles and papers. He wrote a book entitled *Living to 100 and Beyond* on the increasing longevity of humans and its impact, highlighting increased longevity of humans and the implications for individuals, social insurance programs, and insurance companies. He co-authored for Actex the textbook *Actuarial Aspects of Life Insurance and Annuities* and has recently written another book for Actex, *Health Care Coverage and Financing in the United States*. In addition, Tim developed and annually updates a manual summarizing life and health insurance valuation laws, regulations, and their interpretations for the American Academy of Actuaries.

Tim holds Bachelor of Science degrees in Physics and Mathematics from Purdue University.

ALISON JOHNSON, RN, MBA, DNP

Alison is a psychiatric nurse practitioner and a registered poetry therapist at Abbott Northwestern Hospital in Minneapolis, MN. She is a former Principal with Nilan Johnson Lewis, a Minneapolis law firm, joining the firm after seven years as a Health Care Management Consultant with Milliman. Her experience includes working with government agencies, health plans, and large employers, particularly in the automotive industry. She serves as a surveyor for the National Committee for Quality Assurance.

Alison specializes in behavioral health care, providing direct service to medically and psychiatrically complex people. As a consultant, she specialized in disease and case management, assisting clients with the development, implementation, and evaluation of these and other care management programs, evolving them to care management program that boost quality and contain medical costs.

She began her nursing career at the University of Washington Hospital system and has held positions in Washington (Group Health Cooperative of Puget Sound), Alaska (Kodiak Island Hospital), Oregon (Bay Area Hospital) and Minnesota (Regions Hospital, Abbott Northwestern Hospital, Fairview Medical Center).

Alison's nursing, financial, and consulting career spans more than 30 years, including 16 years of hospital nursing and administrative work, 14 years of finance and consulting experience, and three years as a mental health provider.

JAMES A. JUILLERAT, ASA, MAAA

James is Vice President and Chief Actuary with Optima Health in Virginia. Optima Health is an integrated health plan with both physician, and hospital systems. James has 20 years of experience in all aspects of small group, large group, individual, and state Medicaid managed care programs. James has overseen functions including health valuation and more recently estimating the 3R's payable/receivables. James also has developed and settled provider profit sharing arrangements and has served as Appointed Actuary.

James is an Associate of the Society of Actuaries and a Member of the American Academy of Actuaries. He earned his Bachelor's degree in Mathematics with a minor in Physics from Missouri State University

STUART A. KLUGMAN, FSA, CERA, PHD

Stuart is an SOA Staff Fellow. He taught actuarial science for 35 years at two universities and has worked with hundreds of potential actuaries. Stuart has also worked for many years within the SOA's Education system. He has been involved as author or editor of three books used on SOA exams, has served on the SOA Board as member and as Vice-President, and is a two-time recipient of the SOA Presidential Award.

DARRELL D. KNAPP, FSA, MAAA, CPA

Darrell is Executive Director in the Kansas City office of Ernst & Young LLP. He specializes in managed care consulting including provider capitation analysis, product development, and financial reporting. He has also been head of the financial area of a major insurer's group insurance division.

Darrell received his Bachelor of Science Degree in Business Administration, majoring in Actuarial Science and Accounting, from Drake University in 1981. He coauthored the paper "A Model for Evaluating a Multiple Option Plan Package" and has spoken at numerous industry meetings.

He is a Member of the American Academy of Actuaries State Health Committee, and chaired the Health Practice Financial Reporting Committee and has served on the American Academy of Actuaries Board of Directors. He also served many roles in the Society of Actuaries Education and Examination Committee including General Chairperson.

CATHERINE L. KNUTH, FSA, MAAA

Catherine is a Principal and consulting actuary with the Milwaukee office of Milliman, Inc. She joined the firm in 2007. Prior to joining Milliman, Catherine spent ten years consulting with employers, providers, and health plans in the areas of plan design, pricing, liability estimation, experience analysis, and actuarial projections and eight years as a director of small-group actuarial services for a national publicly traded health insurance corporation.

Catherine provides Medicare Part D bid development and related assistance to Programs for All-Inclusive Care of the Elderly (PACE) and assists employer and health care plan clients with benefit/product strategy, plan design, pricing, post-retirement medical valuations, and liability estimation.

Catherine is a Fellow of the Society of Actuaries and a Member of the American Academy of Actuaries. She earned a bachelor's degree in mathematics from Marquette University.

HANS K. LEIDA, PHD, FSA, MAAA

Hans is a Principal and Consulting Actuary in the Minneapolis office of Milliman. He joined the firm in 2006. He has consulted to insurance companies, Blue Cross Blue Shield plans, HMOs, government health programs, and employers. Recently, he has been working on individual and small group health insurance pricing under the Affordable Care Act's health care reforms. Hans has been quoted in the media on health care reform in publications such as *The Wall Street Journal*, *Reuters*, *Bloomberg Businessweek*, and *Modern Healthcare*.

Hans has completed many projects involving individual and group health strategy, pricing, and rate filings. In 2007, he co-authored a paper for America's Health Insurance Plans (AHIP) on the impact of guaranteed issue and community rating laws adopted by certain states in the 1990s. That paper (which was updated in 2012) has been widely cited with the advent of federal health care reform, most notably by the Chief Justice of the U.S. Supreme Court (King v.

Burwell). More recently, Hans co-authored the second edition of *Individual Health Insurance*, which has been on the Society of Actuaries' exam syllabus for many years.

Hans also has significant experience with risk adjustment and predictive modeling of health care costs. He was the lead developer of the prescription-drug-based risk adjuster included in the Milliman Advanced Risk Adjusters (MARA) software product.

Hans received his BA in Mathematics and English at the University of St. Thomas and his PhD in Mathematics (Algebraic Topology) at the University of Wisconsin–Madison.

DAVID M. LINER, FSA, CERA, MAAA

Dave is a Principal and Consulting Actuary with the health care consulting practice in Milliman's Hartford, Connecticut office. He joined the firm in 2008. Dave advises a wide spectrum of clients across the U.S. health care sector. He specializes in commercial health insurance, employee benefits consulting, Medicare Part D, pharmacy benefit management, and stop-loss reinsurance markets. Since the passage of the Affordable Care Act in 2010, Dave has provided strategic and actuarial consulting services to help many clients navigate a dynamic regulatory environment. He has helped new entities achieve business objectives ranging from initial formation to operational commencement. For established entities, Dave has evaluated the effect of emerging regulations and complex market forces on current and potential lines of business.

Dave is a Fellow of the Society of Actuaries, a Chartered Enterprise Risk Analyst, and a Member of the American Academy of Actuaries. He earned a Bachelor of Arts in Mathematics and Actuarial Science from the University of Connecticut.

JAMES T. LUNDBERG

Jim is group Dental Underwriting Head for Aetna, Inc. working out of Blue Bell, PA. He has 30 years' experience in various underwriting and financial roles. His most recent prior assignments involved underwriting group health plans for national accounts with Aetna and Prudential Health Care. His career path included a stint as a Senior Account Manager in an employee benefits consulting firm.

Jim has a B.S. degree in Psychology from North Park College. His leisure activities include golf, tennis, and kayaking. He lives in Newtown, PA, with his wife, Mary Anne, and their two children.

TRACY A. MARGIOTT, FSA, MAAA

Tracy is an Actuary with the Hartford, Connecticut office of Milliman. She joined the firm in 2012. Tracy provides health benefit consulting services to both public and private sector clients, including insurance companies, employers, pharmacy benefit managers, Medicare plan sponsors, and government entities. Tracy leads a variety of projects involving analysis of medical and prescription drug benefit plans. Her experience includes pricing health benefits, estimating claim reserves, evaluating plan performance, and projecting medical stop-loss claims using stochastic methods. Tracy has significant experience with both the individual and group Medicare Part D markets. She supports Medicare Part D plan sponsors with plan design, formulary design, and pricing of prescription drug plans. She also advises employers and pharmacy benefit managers on the design and pricing of Employer Group Waiver Plans (EGWPs).

Tracy is a Fellow of the Society of Actuaries and a Member of the American Academy of Actuaries. She earned her Bachelor of Science Degree in Mathematics and Actuarial Science from the University of Connecticut.

BRIAN MARSELLA

Brian is Vice President, Large Case Sales and Producer Relations at Aetna. In this role, he collaborates with local markets to drive the strategic development of large case initiatives, including new products, product enhancements, and market development strategies. Prior to joining Aetna in 2004, Brian served in a variety of underwriting and sales roles at Cigna. He has an undergraduate degree in economics and political science from the College of the Holy Cross and an MBA in Marketing and International Business from Northwestern University Kellogg School of Management.

SYED MEHMUD, ASA, MAAA, FCA

Syed is a senior consulting actuary with Wakely Consulting Group in Denver, CO. Prior to joining Wakely he was a consultant with Milliman for several years. Syed's work has involved data analytics, reserving, pricing, forecasting, and other traditional actuarial duties in health care. He is helping multiple states with analysis and strategy related to health care reform.

He specializes in applications of predictive modeling and is the author of an upcoming ebook: *Predictive Modeling–Principles & Practice*. Mehmud has worked on actuarial pricing and developing risk adjusted capitation rates in several states, primarily in Medicaid and commercial markets. This year he is co-leading a national risk adjustment effort that aims to provide plans with information needed for actuarial pricing in 2014 and onwards. A primary area of interest is health care claim-based risk adjusters. Mehmud was co-author of a Society of Actuaries' (SOA) report, "A Comparative Analysis of Claim-Based Tools for Health Risk Assessment" (2007). He is also the principal investigator in two SOA research studies, one dealing with the quantification of uncertainty in risk adjustment, and another regarding the identification and impact of nontraditional variables beyond traditional risk adjustment.

Syed is a graduate from Franklin & Marshall College with a B.A. in mathematics and Physics.

STELLA-ANN MÉNARD, FSA, FCIA

Stella-Ann Ménard is Manager, Group Insurance Pricing and Financial Analysis at ManuLife/Standard Life. A specialist in the area of group insurance risk management, her specific areas of expertise include line of business strategy, financial projections, profitability analysis, rate development, group underwriting, reinsurance, and valuation. Prior to joining Standard Life in 2002, she worked in actuarial roles at several other insurance and reinsurance companies. She has a degree in actuarial science from Université Laval.

COURTNEY MORIN, FSA, MAAA

Courtney is Director at Northeast Delta Dental in Concord, New Hampshire, and their appointed actuary. Her responsibilities include rate development and management, pricing, product design, reserving, regulatory compliance and financial monitoring for group dental and vision products, as well as individual dental products.

Courtney is a Fellow of the Society of Actuaries and a Member of the American Academy of Actuaries. She started at Northeast Delta Dental immediately after earning her bachelor's degree in mathematics from Clark University in 2004. Courtney and her husband, Jason, currently reside in southern New Hampshire and are the proud parents of three young children. As a family, they enjoy skiing, hiking and camping in the White Mountains of New Hampshire.

THOMAS E. NIGHTINGALE, FSA, CERA, MAAA

Tom is Vice President and Chief Actuary at Blue Cross Blue Shield of Kansas City. He manages the Finance, Actuarial, and Corporate Forecasting departments at Blue KC. His responsibilities currently include pricing, valuation, accounting, budgeting, purchasing, financial reporting, and forecasting. As a member of the company's Enterprise Risk Management Council, Tom provides leadership and direction regarding the organization's risk management activities. Prior to joining Blue KC, he was a Consulting Actuary with Milliman. Tom is a Fellow of the Society of Actuaries and a Chartered Enterprise Risk Analyst.

DOUGLAS T. NORRIS, FSA, MAAA, PHD

Doug is a Principal and Consulting Actuary with Milliman in Denver, Colorado, focusing on commercial health care products. Doug specializes in Affordable Care Act implementation for commercial health carriers, including strategy and tactics, legislation (such as the "3R" risk mitigation programs) impact modeling, contract negotiations, risk adjustment considerations, and plan pricing. He also has expertise in commercial major medical large group pricing and strategy, predictive modeling and risk adjustment, CMS Innovation program payment and delivery modeling analyses, TRICARE and USFHP contract negotiations, behavioral health integration, drug and therapy efficacy modeling, and health underwriting implementation. He is a past chair of the Society of Actuaries' Predictive Modeling and Futurism section, and is always looking to collaborate on articles exploring new actuarial techniques.

Doug is a Fellow in the Society of Actuaries and a Member of the American Academy of Actuaries. He earned his bachelor's degree in mathematics at Western Washington University, and his doctorate in mathematics (optimization theory) at the University of Colorado – Boulder. In his spare time, he is a hockey goaltender, high-altitude hiker, nature photographer, and hockey historian.

JAMES T. O'CONNOR, FSA, MAAA

Jim is a principal and consulting actuary with the Chicago-Milwaukee Health Practice of Milliman. He joined the firm in 1987 after working nine years for a health insurer. He has specialized in the individual health and small group insurance markets. Jim has been very involved in assisting clients and others regarding the requirements, potential impact, product development and pricing, reserving, and implementation of health care reform. He has written a number of papers related to the Affordable Care Act (ACA) and its impact on health plans. He and the results of his ACA studies have often been referred to in various national and local publications. His clients include health insurance companies, other health plans, employers, and health care providers, as well as industry associations and policy groups.

Jim has been active in the American Academy of Actuaries and the Society of Actuaries, serving on subcommittees and work groups and frequently speaking on issues related to small group and individual insurance. He has been a Fellow of the Society and a Member of the Academy since 1982.

AMY PAHL, FSA, MAAA

Amy is a Principal and Consulting Actuary in the Minneapolis office of Milliman. She has been with the firm since 2001. Amy was previously employed by LifeCare Assurance Company and Allianz Life Insurance Company of North America. She specializes in long term care insurance products with experience in plan design and pricing, state insurance department filings, inforce management, valuation, and financial reporting.

Amy is a Fellow of the Society of Actuaries and a Member of the American Academy of Actuaries. She speaks regularly at industry meetings and has authored several articles on long term care insurance.

Amy is a graduate of Macalester College with a B.A. degree in Mathematics and Economics.

DORINA A. PARITSKY, ASA, MAAA

Dorina is a Vice President of Actuarial Pricing at United Healthcare, currently responsible for pricing support of Stop Loss and Self-Funded product lines. Dorina has focused on health care pricing for over 20 years, and has extensive expertise in providing support to both fully insured and self-funded customers. Prior to United Healthcare, Dorina held actuarial management and leadership roles at Oxford Health Plans and The Guardian Life Insurance Company of America. Dorina graduated from Kharkov State University, is an Associate of the Society of Actuaries since 1993, Member of the American Academy of Actuaries since 1999, and a proud mother of 3 children.

NICOLA PARKER-SMITH, FSA, FCIA

Nicola is Assistant Vice-President, Group Underwriting, at Sun Life Assurance Company of Canada. She is accountable for the financial underwriting of Sun Life's Group Benefit business. Before joining the underwriting team, Nicola was AVP, Group Creditor Business where she was accountable for Sun Life's creditor insurance business. Prior to Sun Life's acquisition of the Clarica Life Insurance Company of Canada, Nicola was Actuary, Group Insurance Pricing at Clarica. She joined Mutual Life (now Clarica) in 1986 and has experienced various work assignments in actuarial valuation and pricing in Group Benefits, Group Pensions and Individual Insurance.

Nicola became a fellow of the Society of Actuaries and a fellow of the Canadian Institute of Actuaries in 1992. She received a bachelor's degree in mathematics from Queens University in Kingston, Ontario.

ERIC J. PATEL, PAHM

Eric is a Health Care Consultant with the Hartford office of Milliman, Inc. He joined the firm in 2005. His area of expertise is data analytics with a focus on medical and pharmacy benefit claims analysis. His clients include pharmacy benefit managers, insurers, and employers. Eric has been actively involved in Medicare Part D since inception and has helped clients with pricing, data auditing, strategic formulary design, and risk score optimization. He also has experience with GASB 45, reserving, and the use of alternative risk transfer mechanisms for employer benefits.

Eric is a Professional of the Academy of Healthcare Management. He earned his Bachelor of Arts Degree in Mathematics with concentration in Statistics from Wake Forest University.

CONSTANCE PETERSON, B.S., M.ED.

Constance is a Senior Analyst with the Minnesota Department of Commerce. Since 1991, she has performed both routine and complex financial and statutory compliance and analyses on life, health and property and casualty insurers operating in Minnesota. She also reviews and recommends actions regarding major transactions by insurers, including licensure, mergers, acquisitions, and complex reinsurance programs including the formation of life reinsurance captives. She has taught classes for the NAIC on Regulating for *Solvency* and *Introduction to Financial Regulation*. Her previous experience includes five years of examining Minnesota state chartered banks and teaching junior high mathematics.

After completing undergraduate work in mathematics at the University of Minnesota, Minneapolis, Constance also earned a Masters of Education from the College of Education, as well as three years of advanced studies in statistics and research methodology/experimental design.

JULIA T. PHILIPS, FSA, MAAA

Julia has been a Life and Health Actuary with the Minnesota Department of Commerce since 1995. She reviews insurance rates and forms for compliance with state law, reviews reserve levels and financial stability of life and health insurance companies, reviews actuarial statements for compliance with actuarial standards, provides technical advice to state policy-makers on insurance reform proposals, and participates in model law and regulatory guidance development for the National Association of Insurance Commissioners.

Julia is a Fellow of the Society of Actuaries, a Member of the American Academy of Actuaries, and a graduate of UCLA. She also received a Master of Arts degree from the University of Minnesota in Mathematics. She previously chaired the Editorial Advisory Board of *Contingencies* magazine, served on the Board of Governors of the Society of Actuaries, and served on the Actuarial Board for Counseling and Discipline.

BRAD PIPER, FSA, MAAA

Brad is a Principal and Consulting Actuary with the Chicago-Milwaukee office of Milliman, joining the firm in 2000. His area of expertise is managed health care programs with an emphasis on Medicare Advantage products. He has worked with Medicare Advantage organizations since the program's inception in 2006. He assists Medicare Advantage organizations with strategic planning, bid preparation, RDS attestation, contracting and risk sharing arrangements, feasibility analysis, the impact of health care reform, and other issues related to Medicare. He works with a broad range of organizations from start-ups to well-established health plans.

Brad is a Fellow of the Society of Actuaries and a Member of the American Academy of Actuaries. He earned a bachelor's degree in mathematics from Marquette University.

EDWARD P. POTANKA, JD

Edward is Vice-President and Assistant Chief Counsel in the Legal Department of Cigna Corporation. He has been an attorney in a variety of roles with Cigna and its predecessor, Connecticut General Life Insurance Company, for forty-two years. In his current position, Mr. Potanka is responsible for counseling Cigna's group health insurance, managed care, provider contracting and third party administration operations. He has written and spoken extensively on the legal and regulatory aspects of group health insurance and managed care. Mr. Potanka is an honors graduate of Amherst College and the Cornell Law School, and is a member of the Connecticut Bar Association.

HERSCHEL REICH, FSA, MAAA

Herschel is Senior Consultant for Reden & Anders and manages their New York Office. In this capacity, he works with his clients on strategic pricing, underwriting, marketing, acquisition, and product positioning strategies. He has worked extensively in the actuarial health care and managed care arena for over 20 years. Prior to joining Reden & Anders, Herschel held actuarial and executive leadership roles in group health care, dental and vision for The Guardian Life Insurance Company of America. He is a frequent speaker at both actuarial and health care industry meetings. Herschel received a Bachelor of Arts degree in mathematics from the Bernard M. Baruch College and is a Fellow of the Society of Actuaries since 1989 and a Member of the American Academy of Actuaries since 1987.

BRUCE D. SCHOBEL, FSA, MAAA, FCA

Bruce retired in 2012 after 22 years as Vice President and Actuary of New York Life Insurance Co. Before joining New York Life, he was a principal with William M. Mercer, Inc. During 1979-88, Mr. Schobel held various actuarial and policy-related positions with the Social Security Administration.

A graduate of Massachusetts Institute of Technology, he is a Fellow of the Society of Actuaries and the Conference of Consulting Actuaries, a Member of the American Academy of Actuaries, a Chartered Life Underwriter, a Certified Employee Benefit Specialist and a Founding Member of the National Academy of Social Insurance. He has served on the Boards of the AAA, CCA and SOA, and was president of the Society of Actuaries during 2007-08. Mr. Schobel is a frequent speaker on social insurance topics, and his papers and articles have appeared in a number of actuarial and non-actuarial publications.

SHEILA SHAPIRO

Sheila is a Senior Vice President and the Chief Operations Officer at Blue Cross Blue Shield of Montana. She has also served in similar capacities at Premera Blue Cross in Seattle and Molina Healthcare, Inc. in Long Beach, California. She has over 20 years of experience in managing diverse operations for health insurance plans and HMOs.

Sheila has a BS in Business Administration from Arizona State University and an MA in Management from the University of Phoenix.

ANDREA B. SHELDON, FSA, MAAA

Andrea is a Principal and Consulting Actuary with the Hartford office of Milliman, Inc. She joined the firm in 2004.

Andrea specializes in understanding the risks and financial drivers of health care benefits. She advises insurers, pharmacy benefit managers, employers, government entities, and religious organizations on medical, pharmacy and dental benefits.

Andrea focuses on health care benefit pricing, valuation, experience analysis, and claim projections. She performs quantitative analyses of financial drivers as well as provides product development consulting on health care benefits programs.

Andrea has been actively involved in Medicare Part D since its inception. She supports Medicare Part D plan sponsors with strategic planning, benefit design, formulary design, pricing and bid submission of prescription drug products. She assists employers and pharmacy benefit managers with the design and pricing of Employer Group Waiver Plans (EGWPs), creditable coverage modeling, as well as Retiree Drug Subsidy attestations.

Andrea is a Fellow of the Society of Actuaries and a Member of the American Academy of Actuaries. She earned her Bachelor of Science Degree in Mathematics and Quantitative Economics from Tufts University.

DOUGLAS B. SHERLOCK, CFA

Douglas is President of Sherlock Company, which assists health plans, their business partners and their investors in the treasury, strategic and control functions of finance. Now in its twenty-ninth year, Sherlock Company provides benchmarking data and analysis for the management of health plan administrative activities, performs valuation and due diligence for business combinations and other capital transactions and offers research publications concerning the financial affairs of health plans.

Prior to founding Sherlock Company, Sherlock was Vice President of Financial Analysis of U.S. Healthcare, Inc., a predecessor to Aetna Inc., where he directed the company's merger and joint venture activity, its investor relations program and its Medicare Advantage business. Previously, Sherlock was a Vice President of Salomon Brothers, Inc. where he specialized in the financial research concerning publicly traded health plans and hospital systems for institutional investors.

Sherlock is a Chartered Financial Analyst and holds an M.B.A. in finance from Loyola University Maryland. He received his bachelor's degree in economics from Franklin and Marshall College, Lancaster Pennsylvania.

JEFFREY L. SMITH, MAAA, MCA

Jeff is President and Consulting Actuary with the Diamond Consulting Group, Inc. Jeff has over 40 years of health actuarial experience. His experience includes work with insurance companies, managed care organizations, regulators, providers and employers. Jeff formed the Diamond Consulting Group firm initially in 1997 and re-activated the company in 2012 after spending 13 years with Milliman, Inc. Jeff previously served as Vice President with United HealthCare Corporation, where he was named its first Actuarial Officer. Jeff also served as Vice President of finance and administration for United HealthCare of Ohio. He spent 19 years with Blue Cross and Blue Shield Plans in Ohio, serving as Vice President and Chief Actuary, as well as Chief Financial Officer.

Jeff is a Member of the American Academy of Actuaries and a Fellow in the Conference of Consulting Actuaries. He received a BS in Mathematics from Ohio State University and an MBA from the University of Dayton.

MICHAEL J. THOMPSON, FSA, MAAA

Michael is a Principal with PricewaterhouseCoopers. He has over 25 years of experience in health care and employee benefits strategy development and implementation, design, financing, pricing, operations and analysis. Mike consults with major employers and health plans on integrated health, wellness and consumerism, defined contribution retiree health, vendor performance management, human capital effectiveness and health care supply chain management strategies.

Mike serves as one of PwC's national thought leaders for health care consumerism strategies for the health industries practice, participates on the steering board of the World

Economic Forum "Working for Wellness" initiative as well as a delegate to the Montage Group focused on cross-sector collaborative solutions, and is a frequent speaker on next generation health strategies. In the past few years, Mike has served as a leader promoting health industry efforts based on the principals of Six Sigma.

Mike is a Fellow of the Society of Actuaries (SOA) and serves on the Federal Health Committee, Disease Management Committee, Medicare Committee, as well as chairman of the Quality Initiatives Subcommittee of the American Academy of Actuaries (AAA). Mike also serves on boards of the New York chapter of the National Alliance on Mental Illness and the New York Business Group on Health.

Mike is a primary author of multiple articles and publications including "Employer Driven Consumerism–Integrating Health into the Business Model" (Employee Benefits Quarterly), "The Factors Fueling Rising Healthcare Costs 2006" (AHIP Publication), "Pay for Performance–Rewarding Improvements in Quality of Healthcare" (AAA Issue Brief), "Healthcare Transformation, Leadership and the Evolution of Consumerism" (WELCOA), and "The Healthcare Balancing Act: Aligning Objectives, Intentions and Incentives" (View).

WILLIAM J. THOMPSON, FSA, MAAA

Bill is a Principal and Consulting Actuary in the Hartford office of Milliman, Inc. He established the Hartford office when he joined the firm in 1988. His clients include insurance companies, health care CO-OPs established under the Affordable Care Act, Plan Sponsors, and employers. Prior to joining Milliman, Bill held several actuarial positions at John Hancock and at Aetna. In total, he has over 45 years of actuarial experience, virtually all of it in health care.

Bill has served on several Milliman and Society of Actuaries committees. He is past chair of the Actuary of the Future (Stuart A. Robertson) Scholarship Fund administered by the Actuarial Foundation. He serves as a facilitator for the Society of Actuaries Fellowship Admissions Course and Associateship Professionalism Course. He is also a member of the faculty of the American Academy of Actuaries Life & Health Qualifications Seminar.

LEIGH M. WACHENHEIM, FSA, MAAA

Leigh is a Principal and Consulting Actuary with Milliman in Minneapolis. She joined the firm in 1994. Her project work has focused on the development and effective management of health insurance plans, including: product design, rate development and management, regulatory compliance, financial forecasting and experience monitoring, and financial reporting. She has worked with insurance companies, Blues plans, HMOs, government agencies, and trade groups. Other work has included the evaluation of blocks of business for potential sale or acquisition, financial modeling to evaluate the impact of proposed legislation, development of benchmarks for experience evaluation and resource allocation, and litigation support.

Leigh has also been active with the American Academy of Actuaries and the Society of Actuaries. She currently chairs the Medicaid Work Group of the Academy and formerly chaired the Health Section Council and the Seminars Committee of the Health Benefit Systems Practice Advancement Committee. She has also authored articles that appear on the Society exam syllabus and has been a frequent speaker at Society and other industry meetings.

LAURENCE R. WEISSBROT

Laurence retired from Northeast Delta Dental in Concord, New Hampshire, where he was a Vice President and their appointed actuary. He managed the Actuarial Research and Underwriting department within the Finance Division. His responsibilities included pricing, reserving and product development, as well as general company management duties. He joined NEDD in September of 1998 and retired at the end of 2013.

Laurie had over 44 years' experience as an actuary, most of it in group (medical, dental, life, AD&D, vision, short- and long-term disability). He worked both as an insurance company actuary (The Hartford, Mass Mutual, State Mutual, The Travelers, Allmerica) and as a consulting actuary (Johnson & Higgins, Tillinghast, USI Consulting). A member of the Society of Actuaries from 1977 to 2014 and the Academy of Actuaries from 1978 to 2014, he received his Bachelor's degree in Mathematics from City College of the City University of New York in 1969.

With Laurie's keen eye for detail, he has edited several books, including Ian Duncan's textbook on *Healthcare Risk Adjustment and Predictive Modeling*, and is still available for the occasional editing assignment. In retirement, he gets to devote more time to his passion, singing light opera; he has appeared in dozens of amateur Gilbert & Sullivan productions, both in the U.S. and in Europe. He lives in Concord, New Hampshire with his wife, Charlotte.

ROSS WINKELMAN, FSA, MAAA

Ross, Director at Wakely Consulting Group, has experience in health care financial analysis, valuation, pricing, and product development within most types of health products, including individual, small group, large group, Medicare Supplement, Medicare Advantage, Medicaid, vision, dental, LTC and disability. He recently focused on the use of risk adjusters for various applications and has led efforts to identify optimal rating and underwriting methods. He has written and advised on important research projects for the Society of Actuaries (SOA), many of these projects relating to risk adjustment. Ross has been an elected council member of the SOA's Health Section and a member of its research committee, the vice-chair of the SOA's Communications and Publications sub-committee, and a member of the SOA's managed care exam committee.

Ross was a contributing author for the book *True Group Long Term Care*, and his SOA publications include "A Comparative Analysis of Claims Based Tools for Health Risk Assessment" (2007), "Health Plan Provider Network Risk" (2006), "Optimal Renewal Guidelines for Small Group Rating" (2005), "Coverage of Spring SOA Meeting in New Orleans" (2005).

Ross is a Fellow of the Society of Actuaries and a Member of the American Academy of Actuaries and speaks regularly at industry meetings. He is a graduate of Purdue University with a B.A. degree in Mathematics and Statistics.

DALE H. YAMAMOTO, FCA, MAAA, EA

Dale is the founder and President of Red Quill Consulting, Inc. He has over 30 years of professional actuarial and consulting experience and has been the national health actuarial resource for two major consulting firms (Hewitt Associates and Towers Perrin). Dale has also held positions as the corporate actuary for a Fortune 50 company and as an actuary for two major insurance companies.

He chaired the 2000 Technical Review Panel of three actuaries and three economists appointed by the Medicare Board of Trustees to review the financial methods and assumptions of the Medicare program. Dale has testified before Congress on the topic of health care and Medicare reform. Dale was one of four senior health actuaries who reviewed the Administration's pricing of the Health Security Act premium estimates for the American Academy of Actuaries. He served on the Board of Governors of the Society of Actuaries

(2000-2005) and the Board of Directors of the Conference of Consulting Actuaries (1999-2005 and 2006-present). Dale has also published several articles on the subject of group benefits, including a textbook (*Fundamentals of Retiree Group Benefits*), and has delivered speeches at a number of professional actuarial and industry meetings.

Dale is a Fellow of the Conference of Consulting Actuaries, a Member of the American Academy of Actuaries, a Member of the National Academy of Social Insurance and an Enrolled Actuary under ERISA. He was a Fellow of the Society of Actuaries until 2012 after completing all of the qualification requirements to be a fully credentialed actuary in 1980. He holds a B.S. degree in mathematics from the University of Nebraska.

INDEX

A

Accelerated benefits provision 174
Accidental Death and Dismemberment 171, 179, 416, 557
Accounting Practices and Procedures Manual 633, 641, 676
Activities of daily living (ADL) 199, 204-206, 442
Actuarial certification 438, 489, 499, 501
Actuarial practice notes 642
Actuarial soundness 489, 491
Actuarial standards of practice 304, 339, 505, 508, 641, 659, 752, 770
AD&D 171, 179, 416, 557
Adequacy of reserves 673-675
Adjusted clinical groups 577, 580, 784
Administrative service agreements 629
Advertising 92, 239
Affordable Care Act 6, 17, 40, 56, 88, 132-134, 140, 237, 268, 291-305, 307, 309, 381, 571, 588, 775, 793
Agent 20
Alternative funding methods 455, 626-632
American Academy of Actuaries 230, 304, 489, 642
American Marketing Association 15
Americans with Disabilities Act 265, 426
Analysis of trend 595-610
Antiselection 77, 317-318
Antitrust Laws 250
Any willing provider 255
Appointed actuary 618
ASO contracts 10, 520
Asset shares 447
Associations 8, 535, 624
Assuris 286, 622
Average Wholesale Price (AWP) 95, 392, 396

B

Bed reservation benefit 210
Behavioral health issues 809
Benefit amounts
   LTD 191
   OASDI 145-148
   offsets (LTD) 192
Benefit triggers 204, 451
Biosimilars 100-101, 304
Blue Cross / Blue Shield 11
Bonus pools 65
Broker 20, 445
Brokerages 20
Bühlmann's credibility model 719

C

Cafeteria plans 224, 273
CALM 618
Canada Health Act 151-153
Canada/Québec Pension Plans 282
Canadian Institute of Actuaries 276
Canadian integration 423
Canadian private medical plans 160
Capital requirements 233
Capitated provider contracts 631
Capitation 65-66, 169, 376-378, 605, 738
Care management 213, 373, 377
Case management 451, 800, 802-804
Catastrophic claim pooling 460-461
Central Limit theorem 723
Certificate of Authority 252
Child care leave of absence 252-253
Chronic illness and disability payment system 580
Civil Rights Act 264
Claim cost estimation
   dental benefits 367-386
   disability benefits 419-434
   life benefits 403-418
   long-term care 449
   medical benefits 337-366
Claim cost trend analysis 595-612
Claim probability distributions 350, 396

Claim reserves 637, 643-660, 661-676
Claims adjudication 559
Claims administration 555-570
  AD&D 557
  dental 369
  disability 557
  health 559
  life 557
  long term care 199-216
  managed care 563-565
Clinical risk groups 580
COBRA 68, 263-264, 268
Codification 633, 641
Cognitive impairment 205, 212
Coinsurance 79, 161, 370, 377, 394-395
Commissions 20, 329, 490, 740
Compcorp 286
Competitive environment 31, 759
Compliance testing 32, 36, 490
Confidence intervals 457, 720
Consultants 20
Consumer-driven health plans (CDHPs) 532, 566,
Consumer protection 235, 249
Continuation of coverage 66, 68, 263-264, 277, 633
Contract provisions 242
Contract reserves 234, 441-442
Conversion privilege 185, 277, 474
Coordination of benefits 86, 245
Copays 61-62, 397
Corporate practice of medicine 250, 254-255
Cost of Living Adjustment 147, 194, 277, 426, 671
Cost-sharing provisions 60, 103-104, 369-370
Coverage
  dental 369
  LTC 204-206
  maximums 64
Covered facilities 56
Covered professional services 55, 58
Credibility theory 719-720
Credibility weighting 464-465
Credit insurance 223, 433, 679
Creditable coverage 508
Creditor groups 9
Critical Illness Benefits 217, 418

$\mathcal{D}$

Data 328-329, 338-347, 420-422, 369-370, 627-628
Death benefit (group LTC) 209
Deductible 61, 161, 168

Deferral periods 79
Deferred acquisition costs 639
Deficiency reserves 640
Deficit carryforwards 632
Deficit Reduction Act 442
Defined contribution programs 542
Definition of disability 189, 195
Demographics 79, 201, 393, 574
Dental
  claim costs 367-385
  HMO 72
  plans 80-84
Dependent life 416
Diagnostic cost groups 581
Disability income benefits 189-198
Disability provisions 173-174
Disclosure 235-236, 260-261, 437, 617
Discretionary groups 10
Disease management 46, 60, 794-799, 804-809
Dispense as written 107
Dispensing fees 393-394
Distribution Models 21-23
Dowry provision 182
Dynamic capital adequacy testing 621-622

$\mathcal{E}$

Eligibility
  dental 77
  dependent group life 181
  LTC 212
  group term life provisions 172
  Medicaid 141
  OASDI 145-146
Elimination period 190, 196, 424, 661
Employee contribution 428, 546
Employer contributions 359
Employment insurance 280-281
Employment Standards Act 279
Enterprise risk management 751-773
Episode risk groups 581
ERISA 260-263
Exclusions 55, 66, 76, 165, 168, 193, 211, 661
Exclusive provider organizations (EPO) 69, 247
Experience rating 384-385, 445, 455-484
Experience refund formula 471
External data sources 339

$\mathcal{F}$

Fair marketing requirements 489
Fairness 236, 585
Family Medical Leave Act 197, 267

Fee schedules 64, 374-375
FEGLI 9
FEHB 9
Field force 21-22
Filing regulations 238, 252, 438, 485-500, 501-509
Financial reporting
  Canadian 616-619, 623, 625, 626
  GAAP 614
  managerial 624
  policyholder 624
  provider 625
  statutory 614-619
  tax 622-623
  U.S. 614-626
Financing
  Health care 48-50
  Medicaid 142-143
  Medicare 116-117
Flat dollar plans 171
Flexible Spending Accounts (FSA) 70, 273-274
Forecasting 710-711, 760, 772
Formularies 105-109, 399-401, 544
Fraudulent claims 569
Frequency models 719
Fully insured plans 479, 536

G

GAAP financial reporting 619-620
Generic Product Identifier (GPI) 391
Generics 105, 107
Geographic area 344, 360, 379, 495
Goods and services tax 286
Government employee groups 9
Grievance procedures 84, 252
Gross Domestic Product (GDP) 46-47, 113, 132
Group definitions 242
Group field force 21-22
Group legal coverage 220
Group transfer 446
Group universal life 184-187, 417
Group variable universal life 187-188
Growth measurement 729-734
Guaranty associations 234, 241
Guaranty funds 234

H

Health benefit exchanges 307-321
Health care policy 39-50
Health care providers 775-776

Health Insurance Portability
  and Accountability Act (HIPAA) 202, 213, 265, 356, 441, 485, 560, 566
Health Maintenance Organizations (HMO) 11-12, 69, 251-258, 544
Health policy principles 40-41
Health reimbursement accounts 270-271, 531-532
Health reserves guidance manual 234
Health risk assessment 574-587
Health savings accounts 54, 271, 531, 566
Hearing benefits 219-220
HEDIS 41, 366, 778
High risk pools 309
Hospital Indemnity Protection (HIP) 222
Hospital Insurance (Medicare) 116-117
Human rights legislation 278

I

Idea screening 16, 27, 30
Impact Pro 581
Incentive coinsurance 79
Incurral date 54-55
Indemnity benefits 53, 219
Indemnity plans 523-524
Index rate 488, 491, 496, 499
Individual mandate 298, 310-311, 318
Individual medical assessment 445-447
Individual multi-life 164
Inflation protection 207-208
Insolvency protection 252
Insured status (Social Security) 146-147
Integrated delivery system 66, 808
Intermediaries 20-21
Internal data sources 340-341
International Financial Reporting Standards (IFRS) 613-622
Internet marketing 24-25
Investment income 325, 468
IRIS 242

L

Labor unions 8
Last survivor provision 183
Least expensive alternate treatment (LEAT) 76, 83, 86
Least squares 704-708
Leverage ratio 745-746
Licensing 23, 231, 238, 239
Life insurance 171-181
  credit 223-224
  dependent 179-182

permanent 183-184
supplemental 177-179
term 171-176
universal life 184-187
variable universal life 187-188
Limitations 76, 107, 193, 488, 672
Linear regression 704, 713
Liquidation 241
Living benefits 418
Long-term benefit reserves 661-676
Long-term care insurance (LTC) 199-216, 435-454
Long-term disability 189-197, 419-431, 523, 537-538, 557, 661, 669-670
Loss Ratio Study 420

M

Mail order programs 102
Managed care 69-70, 144-145, 648-649, 778-779
Managerial reporting 624
Mandated benefits 67-68, 210-211, 197, 244-245
Manual claim tables 405-406
  adjustment 412-415
  development 406-411
Manual premium tables 404-405
Manual rates 332-335, 341-343, 349-354
Market assessment 31-32
Market-driven process 17
Marketing 15-18, 200-202
Market segmentation 18-19,
Mass marketing 23
Maximum allowable charge 86-87
Maximum limits (dental) 370
Medicaid 13, 141
Medicaid Rx 581
Medical benefits 53-70
Medical care management 793-811
Medical claim systems data 340
Medical CPI/PPI 336, 599
Medical errors 808
Medical savings account (MSA) 213
Medicare
  Affordable Care Act 299-305
  Canada 153-160
  health plans 115-116
  integration 118-123
  Modernization Act 139
  Part C 13, 118, 300
  Part D 506, 527, 533, 571
  provider reimbursement 137-138
  risk adjustment 580-581
  supplement 13, 118, 134, 246, 505

trend 504-505
U.S. 12-13, 132-141
Medicare Advantage 502-505
Medicare+Choice 139
Mental Health Parity Act 267
Mid-market groups 19
Milliman Advanced Risk Adjusters 581
Minimum Continuing Capital Requirements (MCCSR) 275, 621
Minimum premium contracts 481
Mortality studies 448-449
Multi-option settings 383
Multiple-choice environment 541-553
Multiple-employer trusts 242, 403, 513, 534
Multiple of earnings plans 171

N

NAIC 7, 20, 56, 186, 233-234, 239, 436, 485,
  annual statement instructions 614-616
  model regulation 186, 246, 251, 436, 485-491
  rate filing regulations 238-239, 485-500
  RBC model acts 679-680
National Drug Code (NDC) 100, 388, 389
National health expenditures 49, 155
Net Plan Liability 390-397, 399-401
Network performance 775-791
New business underwriting 517-532
Newborns' and Mothers' Health Protection Act 266
1985 CIDA Table 432-433
1987 CGD Table 421-428, 670
Nonforfeiture benefits (GLTC) 208-209

O

Open pharmacy laws 256-257
Out-of-Canada coverage 165

P

P&T Committees 108
Parametric modeling 713
Participation 78-79, 143-144, 201-202, 380, 428
Patient Protection and Affordable Care Act (see Affordable Care Act)
Per diem contracts 64
Permanent life 183-184
Pharmacy Benefit Manager (PBM) 94, 98, 340, 387, 564
Pharmacy networks 109-110
Pharmacy risk groups 582

Physician Hospital Organizations (PHO) 11, 785-786
Plan variation adjustments 424-427
Point-of-Service (POS) 69, 254, 257
Policyholder accounting 628
Pooling methods 460-471
Portability (of GLTC) 212
Position plans 172
Predictive modeling 517, 556
Predictive performance measurement 582-587
Pre-existing conditions 76, 211, 245-246, 293, 346, 535
Preferred Provider Organization (PPO) 69-70, 80-81, 247, 374
Premium taxes 285, 330
Premiums
   deficiency reserves 234, 640-641, 660
   GLTC 203-204
   gross premium development 325-332
   long-term disability 422-423
   rate certifications 489, 498-499
   subsidies 297
Prescription drug plans under Medicare 506
Prescription drugs 162-163, 91-112
   Industry pooling reporting 159-160
Price protection 400-401
Pricing assumptions 325-332
Pricing models 447-453
Pricing strategies 550-552
Prior coverage 359, 380
Product development 16-17, 27-37
   assess 34
   build 33
   cycle 27-28
   design 32
   revise 35
   sell 34
   teams 35-36
Profit charges 330-331
Profit criteria 453
Profit measurement 476-477, 736-738
Prompt pay legislation 240
Property and casualty 221
Prospective experience rating 458-471
Provider incentive arrangements 631
Provider liabilities 234
Provider networks 775-791
Provider-owned organizations 11
Provider reimbursement arrangements 137, 347, 373, 515
Provincial medicare plans 153-160
Purchasing alliances 536

Q

Quality of care 41-47, 303, 252
Quebec Pension Plan 282-283, 287
Quebec Prescription Drug Act 159

R

R-squared 582-584, 593
Rate certification 489-491, 498-499
Rate manual 337-338, 488-491
Rate regulation 238, 253
Rate stabilization reserve 476
Rating
   agencies 633
   consistency 488, 497
   factors 393-395, 591
   parameters 77-80, 360-361
   structures 332, 487-488
Reasonableness 235-236
Rebates 110-111
Receivership 233
Regression 704, 708-713
Regulation
   advertising 239
   Canadian 275-290
   consumer protection 235-236, 249
   enforcement 231-234
   federal 176, 258-274, 275-276
   financial reporting 313-634
   GLTC 246-247, 436-443
   goals 230
   HMO 251-258, 258-260
   legal basis 230-231
   long-term care insurance 246-247
   Medicare supplement 246
   preferred provider arrangements 247-251
   principles of 229-236
   solvency 240-242
   state/provincial 237-258, 276-278, 436-441
Reinsurance 297, 441, 634, 740
Remarriage provision 182
Renewal underwriting 532-534
Replacements 245-246, 439
Reserveless plans 478-479
Reserve assumptions
   expenses 672
   interest rates 671-672
   morbidity 699-670
   policy provisions 671-672
Reserve components 662

Reserve methods 649-654, 661-676
  average claim size 653
  CALM 618
  examiner's 654
  factor 650
  IBNR claims 666-669
  lag 650-653, 667-668
  loss ratio 654, 668-669
  tabular 653
Reserves 635-642, 643-660, 661-676
  active life 637-638
  asset adequacy 640
  claim 637, 643
  claim expense 639, 672
  contract 234
  expense 639
  experience refund 641
  incurred but not reported (IBNR) 637
  litigated claim 638
  long-term 661-676
  premium deficiency 234, 640, 660
  rate stabilization 476
  short-term 643-660
  unearned premium 638-639
Retiree group benefits 113-129
Retrospective experience rating 471-478
Retrospective premium arrangements 483-484
Return on assets 744-745
Return on equity 729-734
Revision underwriting 533
Risk adjustment 140, 296-297, 317-318, 347, 361-362, 571-594, 683-685, 708-709, 789
Risk assessment methods 574-588
Risk-based capital 677-695
  covariance 682, 687-692
  health 694-695
  history 678-679
  life 692, 694
  NAIC model acts 679-680
Risk charges 330-331, 475-476
Risk management 751-773
Risk measurement 576-577
Risk pooling 460-471
Risk selection 403-404
Risk transfer 591-592, 764-765
Ruin Theory Model 691-692
RxGroups 582, 584
RxNorm Concept Unique Identifier (RxCUI) 390
RxRisk 582
Runoff studies 673-675

S

Salary bracket plans 172
Sales tax 170, 285-286, 390
Sampling 369, 656-657, 699, 716
Seasonality 649
Self-insured plans 7, 12, 479, 675
Service benefits 53
Service indemnity models 202, 205
Service reimbursement models 202
Shareholder value 727-749
Short-term disability 195-197, 431-434
Short-term reserves 643-660
Simulation 460, 657, 700-703
Small group reform 246
Social Insurance 9
Social Security (OASDI)
  benefits 145-148
  offset 183, 422-424
Society of Actuaries studies 407
Solvency 240-242
Spousal rider 210
Standards of Practice 304, 339, 641, 659-660
State insurance departments 238
Statutory financial reporting 614-619
Stochastic simulation 700-703
Stochastic time series 657
Stop-loss contracts 481-483
Strategic analysis 28-29, 760
Student medical plans 222-223
Subrogation 68
Supplemental life 177-179
Supplementary medical insurance (Medicare) 116, 133
Survivor income benefits 182-183, 416

T

Taft-Hartley groups 535
Tax treatment
  health insurance 302, 269-274
  life insurance 174-176, 178-179, 181-182, 184, 186, 272
  survivor income 183
Taxation
  Affordable Care Act 302
  cafeteria plans 224-225
  Canada 170-171, 284-286, 290
  disability 272
  federal 174-176, 178, 181-182, 183, 186-187, 269-274
  GLTC (long term care) 213-214, 224
  group insurance 269-274

health 269-272
  prefunding 274
  premium 285-286, 330
Termination (of GLTC) 212
Term life insurance 171-176
Terrorism risks 431
Travel accident insurance 221-222
Trend analysis 595-610, 648-649, 807-810
Turnover 730-736, 744

U

UB-92 claim form 340
UCR provisions 86-87
Underwriting
  characteristics of group 517-522
  dental 77-80
  disability income 523, 537-538
  GLTC 203
  group life 538-539
  large groups 513-539
  medical plans 523-526
  multiple-choice situations 549-550
  renewal 532-534
  special risks 434-436
Unitary drug pricing laws 256-257
Universal life 184-188, 417-418
Upcoding and unbundling 567, 569, 586
Utilization management programs 83, 256, 326, 346-347, 524-525, 794-798

V

Valuation actuary 627, 631
Variable universal life 187-188
Vision plans
  Canada 165
  U.S. 219-220
Voluntary plans 78, 87, 178, 179, 195, 217-218, 382-383, 428

W

Waiting period 79, 205, 371, 516
Wakely Risk Assessment Model 582
Wellness 46, 59, 293, 301, 527, 806
Wholesale Acquisition Cost (WAC) 95, 388
Worker's compensation 281-282, 289
Worksite marketing 24